P9-DGK-261

IUPUI
UNIVERSITY LIBRARIES
COLUMBUS CENTER
COLUMBUS, IN 47201

CONTEMPORARY POPULAR WRITERS

Contemporary Writers Series

Contemporary Dramatists
Contemporary Literary Critics
Contemporary Novelists
(including short story writers)
Contemporary Poets
Contemporary World Writers

CONTEMPORARY POPULAR WRITERS

Editor
DAVE MOTE

With a Preface by
JEROME KLINKOWITZ
and
JULIE HUFFMAN-KLINKOWITZ

ST. JAMES PRESS
AN IMPRINT OF GALE

DETROIT • NEW YORK • TORONTO • LONDON

Dave Mote, *Editor*

ST. JAMES PRESS STAFF

Joann Cerrito, *Project Coordinator*
Laura Standley Berger, Peg Bessette, Nicolet V. Elert, Miranda H. Ferrara,
Janice Jorgensen, Margaret Mazurkiewicz, Michael J. Tyrkus, *Contributing Editors*
Peter M. Gareffa, *Managing Editor, St. James Press*

Mary Beth Trimper, *Production Director*
Shanna Heilveil, *Production Assistant*

Cynthia Baldwin, *Art Director*
Mary Krzewinski, *Senior Art Director*

Victoria B. Cariappa, *Research Manager*
Jennifer Lund, *Research Specialist*
Michele P. Pica, Tracie A. Richardson, Cheryl L. Warnock, *Research Associates*

While every effort has been made to ensure the reliability of the information presented in this publication, St. James Press does not guarantee the accuracy of the data contained herein. St. James Press accepts no payment for listing; and inclusion of any organization, agency, institution, publication, service, or individual does not imply endorsement of the editors or publisher.

Errors brought to the attention of the publisher and verified to the satisfaction of the publisher will be corrected in future editions.

∞™ The paper used in this publication meets the minimum requirements of American National Standard for Information Sciences—Permanence Paper for Printed Library Materials, ANSI Z39.48-1984.

This publication is a creative work fully protected by all applicable copyright laws, as well as by misappropriation, trade secret, unfair competition, and other applicable laws. The authors and editors of this work have added value to the underlying factual material herein through one or more of the following: unique and original selection, coordination, expression, arrangement, and classification of the information.

All rights to this publication will be vigorously defended.

Copyright © 1997
St. James Press
835 Penobscot Building
Detroit, MI 48226

All rights reserved including the right of reproduction in whole or in part in any form.

Library of Congress Cataloging-in-Publication Data

Contemporary popular writers / editor, Dave Mote.—1st ed.
p. cm.
Includes indexes.
ISBN 1-55862-216-0
1. English literature—20th century—Dictionaries 2. English literature—20th century—Bio-bibliography—Dictionaries. 3. American literature—20th century—Bio-bibliography—Dictionaries 4. Popular literature—Great Britain—Bio-bibliography—Dictionaries. 5. Popular literature—United States—Bio-bibliography—Dictionaries. 6. Authors, American—20th century—Biography—Dictionaries. 7. Authors, English—20th century—Biography—Dictionaries. 8. American literature—20th century—Dictionaries. 9. Popular literature—Dictionaries.
I. Mote, Dave
PR478.P66C66 1996
820.9'00914—dc20 96-20634
[B] CIP

Printed in the United States of America
Published simultaneously in the United Kingdom

St. James Press is an imprint of Gale

10 9 8 7 6 5 4 3

CONTENTS

PREFACE

Once upon a time, popular writing was conceived as something that inhibited a people's artistic expression. And that time was not so very long ago. One need only look back to the 1950s—and all those Irving Stone novels like *The President's Lady* and *Lust for Life,* and Walt Disney films such as *Bambi* and *Lady and the Tramp*—to see that the phrase "popular culture" could be taken as a contradiction in terms. If *culture* indicates a shared body of practices, values, and beliefs that distinguish a people, then much of what constituted popular culture during the Eisenhower era tended to reinforce stereotypes and impose a very limited sense of order—just the opposite of what a socially visible culture is. And how popular is a theme or a form when it emerges not from a people themselves but from an institution that seeks to impose a hygienic, even prophylactic, vision of life on the expressive desires of the people it professes to serve?

Much has been written about the breakout from 1950s conformity that began in the 1960s and has continued in quieter but equally persistent ways through the present age. Some see it as a sexual revolution against the repressions of religion. In the United States, John Updike began writing stories that struggled against what he saw as a narrowly confining Calvinism, while in England David Lodge launched a series of novels about his own love-hate relationship with practical Catholicism. Others have identified the culprit as Cold War politics or repression of racial diversity, two topics on which Norman Mailer has been more than eloquent. But in all cases the cultural transformation parallels an important change in the way popular writing is regarded. Beginning with the 1960s, such work is no longer just entertaining and pleasantly diverting. Instead, it becomes at the same time serious and important even as it continues to please readers on a mass scale. When Kurt Vonnegut's *Slaughterhouse-Five,* let alone Thomas Pynchon's *Gravity's Rainbow,* elbows its way onto a bestseller list previously reserved for what the publishing industry itself calls "manufactured fiction," and when a subsequent generation would rather read about the intricacies of John Grisham's law firms than turn more pages of Hollywood jet-set glitz, it becomes apparent that narrow definitions of popular culture are no longer in control.

Forty years, even in the context of today's rapid changes, is not a very long time—just half a lifetime, according to the latest charts. And for popular culture, many figures span the eras of conformity and rebellion. In *The Right Stuff,* ostensibly a book about the early astronauts' role in America's space program, Tom Wolfe chose to anchor his narrative on the story of the country's most famous flyer who did not become an astronaut: Chuck Yeager. This was a wise decision, because Yeager could be written about in terms of not just two eras but three—not only the immediate pre-space and post-space contexts but in full consideration of the World War II experience that motivated much of what happened in Western popular culture for half a century afterwards. The student of popular writing also shares Wolfe's advantage, for flanking *The Right Stuff* (1979) are William R. Lundgren's *Across the High Frontier—The Story of a Test Pilot—Major Charles E. Yeager, USAF* (1955) and the subject's own 1985 memoir, *Yeager: An Autobiography.* Lundgren's book only tells the first half of Yeager's story, but the author locates that story squarely within the era's traditions of social order and teamwork. In Wolfe's hands 24 years later, Chuck Yeager is a maverick, such an unfettered individualist that he resists what others see as the obvious, inevitable future. Yet when Yeager himself writes in 1985, his becomes a truly postmodern work, written in awareness of not only the full course of events but of Lundgren's and Wolfe's interpretations—and in the process he is able to take apart and expose for their conventionality each of the previous authors' unstated assumptions.

Chuck Yeager may be the best known for doing it, but many other popular writers show great genius in reinventing history according to the new perspectives that liberation from conformity allow. From a post-imperialist England, Bruce Chatwin writes novels that reconstrue the world order—or disorder, for that matter. In *Utz* he takes on not just Eastern Europe, a region British novelists from Evelyn Waugh to Malcolm Bradbury have found ridiculously comic, but the whole notion of economic, artistic, and moral standards as they influence our understanding of human value. From the American Southwest Leslie Marmon Silko does the same for Native American culture; her *Ceremony,* together with High Plains stories by Louise Erdrich and novels by James Welch, not only recaptures certain tribal essences but redefines the interface between red and white societies.

Even such common and supposedly unpolitical matters as those of sport change in popular hands, from football in Don DeLillo's *End Zone* to baseball in W. P. Kinsella's *Shoeless Joe.* This last work, filmed as *Field of Dreams,* indicates the distance popular writing has come in transcending the force of collectivism that constrained similar novels of the 1950s. As a thematic device, having a farmer take precious acres out of corn production and landscape them as a baseball field is quirky, preposterous, and imaginatively liberating all at the same time. As such, it could be seen as simply a knee-jerk liberal response to confining conservativism. Yet beyond this response is Kinsella's structural brilliance in using the field of dreams not just to show off his farmer's fantasy but also to structure a rehabilitation of two failed ideals: that of Shoeless Joe Jackson, an athletically gifted but naive player consumed (most have said unfairly) in the complex gambling scandal of the 1919 World Series, and novelist J. D. Salinger, who was banned in the 1950s, misunderstood in the 1960s, and who consequently removed himself (some say because of madness) from public view for a generation afterwards. It was narrowly defined, even totalitarian popular culture that did Jackson and Salinger in, Kinsella implies. Now, as a 1980s novel and 1990 film—as the most widely rented and purchased video cassette, in fact, and as a historical site in Dyersville, Iowa, where the movie setting has been privately maintained—this popular writer's vision restores the value of athlete and novelist alike in people's eyes.

It is with the mystery novel—that most typical of all popular forms of writing—that a change in attitude is obvious. An anthropologically sound understanding of the Navajo people, for example, motivates Tony Hillerman's work. He has a deep and abiding respect for their culture and an archaeologist's gift for discovering the roots of values and behavior. Such abilities, combined with a serious novelist's talent for characterization and plotting, produce works that make a pleasurable learning experience almost inevitable. A similar response underlies Carl Hiaasen's success. Although his novels explore the sometimes seedier aspects of crime and the less savory aspects of lowlife characters, he never writes down to his readership. Instead, much like Carl Sagan's popular treatments of astronomy and Stephen Jay Gould's fascinating syntheses among the natural and social sciences, Hiaasen assumes a level of intelligence in his readers—a level of intelligence that makes both science and criminology an art from in the hands of capable writers. In a Carl Hiaasen novel one encounters not just hoodlums but corporate exploiters, not just a tenderloin of honky-tonk nightlife but a subtle understanding of his region's natural ecology as well. Moreover, he approaches such issues in a humorous way, engaging the reader's imagination in a way that is immensely entertaining as well as instructive.

Traditionally, the British mystery has been a staple of popular writing, and the continued popularity of Agatha Christie's work reaffirms this principle in our own age. Yet newer writers look back to specific features of Christie's art for their inspiration; not just her facility with plot and nuances of characterization but her knowledge of the socio-anthropological as well. To make their cases evident two of Christie's prime successors, Anne Perry and Ellis Peters, locate their work in other time periods. Perry's Victorian era and Peters's late middle ages have been used for narratives before, so much so that ready markets are available for popular historical treatments. But Perry's 19th-century London and Peters's 12th-century Shrewsbury are nothing like readers would have encountered in novels written a generation or two before. Just as Tony Hillerman forsakes stage Indians in favor of fully developed Native American characters, Anne Perry moves well beyond the common stereotypes of Victorian behavior in order to draw on complexities equal to our own. Her Inspector Pitt may be a ratiocinative genius, but he also comprehends social forces—specifically the economic and sexual politics that underlie the lives of what critic Stephen Marcus called the "other" Victorians, those whose experiences fail to conform with the projected image of taste and decorum.

Ellis Peters makes even richer use of cultural dynamics by setting her novels on the borderline between the ancient and the modern, where she can exploit the rich contrasts between the religious and the secular. Her Brother Cadfael brings a unique perspective to mystery writing, that of the medieval cloister. From this seat of quiet contemplation he does what the mystery writer herself does: probe and examine, weigh and consider. The difference is that from his secure and stable position he is able to accord much deeper sympathy to the other. Indeed, for Brother Cadfael the other is comprehended with the same appreciation given to one's own values. Both Perry and Peters avoid simplifications of the past and refuse to recolor it with contemporary attitudes. Instead, they strive for full imaginative participation in the era's life. And as with Tony Hillerman's and Carl Hiaasen's work, the reader will not just be entertained but will learn something.

The act of learning demands full participation in engaging other viewpoints, other values, and other beliefs. As an historical novelist, Edith Pargeter drops her pseudonym of Ellis Peters to write in her own name of the Welsh-English conflicts that characterize, even to this day, the border country of Brother Cadfael's Shrewsbury. As a white American Southerner, William Styron takes on the challenge of not just confronting but artistically assuming the controversies that characterize his identity as a literary artist. *The Confessions of Nat Turner,* formally a novel written by Styron in the politically volatile 1960s, is cast as a memoir drafted by the African-American leader of a slave rebellion in 1831. The challenges in undertaking such a task are enormous, and have generated a critical response almost equalling the book's importance by itself. At stake is the matter of trying to encompass the diverse, of seeking to comprehend an otherwise alien history from the inside rather than from without. A similar task is faced by Toni Morrison, who must create an internal African-American history where no recorded antecedents exist.

Fully embracing the other is what critic Alan Nadel claims popular writing of the late 1940s and 1950s failed to do. What served instead was a "containment culture" that restricted choices to those that served a narrowly defined national interest of restraining socialist ideology abroad and minority interests at home. A civil rights and feminist movement initiated major changes on the domestic side, and the controversial nature of the Vietnam War led to transformations in attitudes (if not policies) abroad. It is rewarding to see the emergence of truly serious popular writing during this same era of change—and to realize that it was serious not because such works had lost any of their entertainment value or pleasure, but because expressions of popular feeling were now being taken seriously by cultural arbiters formerly more concerned with maintaining officially sanctioned order. Not that every popular writer these days presents readers with issues of millennial importance—good reads by Judith Krantz and Barbara Cartland will have their space reserved in beach bags of vacationers and briefcases of frequent flyers, and for every Grace Paley and Bruce Chatwin striving to probe to the core of women's and men's interest there is an Erica Jong or Robert James Waller to dress out the topic in the clothing of shameless mimicry. But from Salman Rushdie's children born at the zero hour of postimperialism to Amy Tan's fellow members of the multicultural club that post-1950s America has become, popular writing promises rewards well beyond the distraction from matters of importance that characterized the field not so very long ago.

Jerome Klinkowitz and Julie Huffman-Klinkowitz

EDITOR'S NOTE

This first edition of *Contemporary Popular Writers* provides information about nearly 300 authors and their works. Included are authors, both living and dead, who were active in the early 1960s or later and remain popular in the mid-1990s. *Contemporary Popular Writers* will be of great use to young adults and adults interested in learning more about their favorite writers, and to scholars seeking information about popular literature.

The intent of this book is not to profile the top-selling authors; the result would be an inventory of romance, mystery, and suspense novelists, sprinkled with a few authors from other genres. Instead, this book represents the most popular writers in several fiction and nonfiction categories, including some poets, short-story writers, biographers, and other niche authors. The number of authors from each genre is only roughly proportional to the size of that segment in the popular literature marketplace. Entrants were selected with the help of advisers in Australia, Canada, New Zealand, the United Kingdom, and the United States.

Entries in *Contemporary Popular Writers* are organized into the following sections, with boldfaced rubrics to help users find information quickly and easily:

- *Biographical data,* listing, if known, the entrant's nationality, date and place of birth, educational institutions attended, spouse's name, date of marriage, number of children, career information, awards received, memberships, agent, and address.

- *Bibliography of the author's works,* listing, title, publisher, and publication date of all the entrant's works, as well as locations of manuscript collections. Some entries also provide information on media adaptations, theatrical activities, and critical studies about the entrant.

- *A signed critical essay,* discussing the entrant's work. The views expressed in the essays are wholly those of the writer and should not be construed as those of St. James Press or the editor.

I would like to thank Joann Cerrito of St. James Press, who supplied biographical and bibliographical information and made sure that this volume found its way to the printer.

Contemporary Popular Writers is humbly dedicated to my prize and inspiration, Sarah, and our honeymoon gift, Mattie-Catherine, born shortly before this book went to press.

Dave Mote
Editor

ADVISERS

Kristine Anderson
Laurie Clancy
Anne French
Fran Majusky
Kirby Mills
Sheila Pepper
Jean Varty

CONTRIBUTORS

John C. Ball
Samantha Barber
Karin Beeler
Stan Beeler
Christopher Michael Bell
Ian A. Bell
Samuel I. Bellman
Bennis Blue
Paul Bodine
Anne Boyd
Tammy J. Bronson
Jackie Buxton
Victoria Carchidi
Sean Carney
Bruce Guy Chabot
Laurie Clancy
Daniel A. Clark
Tracy Clark
Samuel Coale
Jennifer Coman
Jane Conkright
Paul A. Doyle
Doug Dupler
Carolyn Eckstein-Soule
Amy Eldridge
Melissa L. Evans
Amy Faulkenberry
Diana Pharaoh Francis
Jill Franks
Chris Godat
George Grella
June Harris
Aimee Houser
Nicola King
Jerome Klinkowitz
Judith C. Kohl
Michael R. Little
Andrew Macdonald
Gina Macdonald
Colin Maiorano
John McLeod
D. Quentin Miller
P. Andrew Miller
Robert A. Morace
Elizabeth Mulligan
Maril Nowak
Malcom Page
Eric Patterson
Susan Rowland
Geoff Sadler
Jack Shreve
Maggi Sullivan
Fraser Sutherland
Christopher C. Swann
Christina Sylka
C. W. Truesdale
Christopher Wigginton
Bill Witherup
Tim Woods

CONTEMPORARY POPULAR WRITERS

LIST OF ENTRANTS

Douglas Adams
Cleveland Amory
V. C. Andrews
Maya Angelou
Piers Anthony
Jeffrey Archer
Isaac Asimov
Margaret Atwood
Jean Auel

Richard Bach
Nicholson Baker
James Baldwin
Amiri Baraka
Clive Barker
Dave Barry
Charles Baxter
Ann Beattie
Peter Benchley
Pierre Berton
Maeve Binchy
Lawrence Block
Judy Blume
Erma Bombeck
T. Coraghessan Boyle
Ray Bradbury
Barbara Taylor Bradford
Marion Zimmer Bradley
Jacqueline Briskin
Anita Brookner
Terry Brooks
Dee Brown
Rita Mae Brown
Sandra Brown
John Brunner
William F. Buckley, Jr.
Jimmy Buffett
Charles Bukowski
William S. Burroughs
Leo Buscaglia
Octavia E. Butler
W. E. Butterworth
A. S. Byatt

Truman Capote
Orson Scott Card
Barbara Cartland
Raymond Carver
Bruce Chatwin
John Cheever
Deepak Chopra
Agatha Christie
Tom Clancy
Mary Higgins Clark
Arthur C. Clarke
James Clavell
Jon Cleary
Jackie Collins

Pat Conroy
Robin Cook
Catherine Cookson
Stephen Coonts
Bernard Cornwell
Patricia Cornwell
Douglas Coupland
Bryce Courtenay
Michael Crichton
Amanda Cross
Clive Cussler

Roald Dahl
Janet Dailey
Robertson Davies
Len Deighton
Don DeLillo
Nelson DeMille
Colin Dexter
Pete Dexter
Philip K. Dick
James Dickey
E. L. Doctorow
Stephen R. Donaldson
Margaret Drabble
Daphne du Maurier
Dominick Dunne

Umberto Eco
David Eddings
Stanley Elkin
Bret Easton Ellis
Harlan Ellison
Louise Erdrich
Loren D. Estleman

Howard Fast
Harvey Fierstein
Carrie Fisher
Fannie Flagg
Ian Fleming
Ken Follett
Shelby Foote
Frederick Forsyth
Alan Dean Foster
Marilyn French
Robert Fulghum

Gabriel Garcia Marquez
John C. Gardner, Jr.
John E.Gardner
Alan Garner
Elizabeth George
William Gibson
Ellen Gilchrist
Gail Godwin
Eileen Goudge
Stephen Jay Gould

Sue Grafton
Spalding Gray
Andrew M. Greeley
Martha Grimes
John Grisham
Lewis M. Grizzard, Jr.
Allan Gurganus

Arthur Hailey
Alex Haley
Thomas Harris
Josephine Hart
Stephen W. Hawking
Robert A. Heinlein
Joseph Heller
Mark Helprin
Frank Herbert
James Herriot
John Hersey
Georgette Heyer
Carl Hiaasen
Jack Higgins
Patricia Highsmith
Oscar Hijuelos
Tony Hillerman
S. E. Hinton
Shere Hite
Alice Hoffman
Victoria Holt
Susan Howatch
L. Ron Hubbard

John Irving
Susan Isaacs

John Jakes
Clive James
P. D. James
Tama Janowitz
Erica Jong

Garrison Keillor
Jonathan Kellerman
Thomas Keneally
Jack Kerouac
Ken Kesey
Stephen King
Barbara Kingsolver
W. P. Kinsella
Dean R. Koontz
Michael Korda
Judith Krantz

Louis L'Amour
David Leavitt
John le Carré
Laurie Lee
Ursula K. Le Guin
Madeleine L'Engle
Elmore Leonard
Ira Levin
Rush Limbaugh III

Johanna Lindsey
David Lodge
Robert Ludlum

John D. MacDonald
Ross Macdonald
Helen MacInnes
Alistair MacLean
Norman Maclean
Norman Mailer
Bernard Malamud
William Manchester
Ngaio Marsh
Armistead Maupin
Ed McBain
Anne McCaffrey
Cormac McCarthy
Colleen McCullough
Joe McGinniss
Jay McInerney
Terry McMillan
Larry McMurtry
John McPhee
Barbara Mertz
Judith Michael
James A. Michener
N. Scott Momaday
Toni Morrison
John Mortimer
Walter Mosley
Farley Mowat

Gloria Naylor
Larry Niven

Joyce Carol Oates
Patrick O'Brian
Tim O'Brien
Sharon Olds
P. J. O'Rourke
Cynthia Ozick

Camille Paglia
Grace Paley
Michael Palmer
Sara Paretsky
Robert B. Parker
M. Scott Peck
Walker Percy
Anne Perry
Rosamunde Pilcher
Robert M. Pirsig
Belva Plain
Faith Popcorn
Terry Pratchett
Eugenia Price
E. Annie Proulx
Mario Puzo
Thomas Pynchon

Ayn Rand
Ruth Rendell

Anne Rice
Tom Robbins
Rosemary Rogers
Leon Rooke
Philip Roth
Mike Royko
Ann Rule
Salman Rushdie

Oliver Sacks
Carl Sagan
J. D. Salinger
Lawrence Sanders
John Saul
Erich Segal
Irwin Shaw
Gail Sheehy
Sidney Sheldon
Carol Shields
Anne Rivers Siddons
Leslie Marmon Silko
Robert Silverberg
Dan Simmons
Jane Smiley
Martin Cruz Smith
Wilbur Smith
Susan Sontag
LaVyrle Spencer
Danielle Steel
Mary Stewart
R. L. Stine
Irving Stone
Peter Straub
William Styron
Rosemary Sutcliff

Amy Tan
Paul Theroux
Hunter S. Thompson
Jim Thompson
Alvin Toffler

J. R. R. Tolkien
Sue Townsend
William Trogdon
Joanna Trollope
Margaret Truman
Thomas Tryon
Barbara Tuchman
Scott Turow
Anne Tyler

John Updike
Leon Uris

Eric Van Lustbader
Gore Vidal
Judith Viorst
William T. Vollmann
Kurt Vonnegut

Alice Walker
Irving Wallace
Robert James Waller
Joseph Wambaugh
James Welch
Fay Weldon
Morris West
Donald E. Westlake
E. B. White
Jude Gilliam White
Phyllis A. Whitney
George F. Will
Walter Jon Williams
Jeanette Winterson
P. G. Wodehouse
Gene Wolfe
Tom Wolfe
Stuart Woods
Herman Wouk

Timothy Zahn

A

ADAMS, Douglas (Noel)

Nationality: British. **Born:** Cambridge, 11 March 1952. **Education:** St. John's College, Cambridge, B.A. in English literature, 1974. **Family:** Married Jane Belson in 1991; one daughter. **Career:** Freelance writer; script editor, *Doctor Who* series, BBC TV, 1978-80; non-executive director, The Digital Village; chairman, Completely Unexpected Productions Ltd. **Agent:** Ed Victor Ltd., 6 Bayley Street, Bedford Square, London WC1B 3HB, England.

Publications

Novels

The Hitch-Hiker's Guide to the Galaxy:
- *The Hitch-Hiker's Guide to the Galaxy.* London, Pan, 1979; New York, Harmony, 1980.
- *The Restaurant at the End of the Universe.* London, Pan, 1980; New York, Harmony, 1982.
- *Life, the Universe, and Everything.* London, Pan, and New York, Harmony, 1982.
- *The Hitch-Hiker's Trilogy.* New York, Harmony, 1983.
- *So Long, and Thanks for All the Fish.* London, Pan, and New York, Harmony, 1984.
- *The Hitch-Hiker's Guide to the Galaxy: A Trilogy in Four Parts.* London, Heinemann, 1986; as *The Hitch-Hiker's Quartet,* New York, Harmony, 1986; as *The Illustrated Hitch-Hiker's Guide to the Galaxy,* London, Weidenfeld and Nicolson, 1994.
- *The More Than Complete Hitch-Hiker's Guide: Five Stories.* New York, Longmeadow Press, 1987.
- *Mostly Harmless.* London, Heinemann, and New York, Harmony, 1992.

Dirk Gently:
- *Dirk Gently's Holistic Detective Agency.* New York, Simon and Schuster, and London, Heinemann, 1987.
- *The Long Dark Tea-Time of the Soul.* London, Heinemann, and New York, Simon and Schuster, 1988.
- *Dirk Gently's Holistic Detective Agency; and, The Long Dark Tea-Time of the Soul.* London, Pan, and New York, Harmony, 1985; as *Two Complete Novels,* New York, Wings, 1994.

Plays

The Hitch-Hiker's Guide to the Galaxy (broadcast, 1978; produced, 1979).

The Original Hitch-Hiker Radio Scripts. London, Pan, and New York, Harmony, 1985.

Radio Play: *The Hitch-Hiker's Guide to the Galaxy,* 1978.

Television Plays: For *Doctor Who* series.

Other

The Meaning of Liff, with John Lloyd. London, Pan, 1983; New York, Harmony, 1984.

Last Chance to See, with Mark Carwardine. London, Heinemann, 1990; New York, Harmony, 1991.

The Deeper Meaning of Liff, with John Lloyd. London, Pan, 1990.

Editor, with Peter Fincham, *The Utterly Utterly Merry Comic Relief Christmas Book.* London, Collins, 1986.

*

Critical Studies: *Don't Panic* by Neil Gaiman, London, Titan Books, 1987, 2nd ed., 1993; "Douglas Adams's "Hitch-Hiker" novels as Mock Science Fiction," by Carl R. Kroph, in *Science Fiction Studies,* March 1988.

* * *

Douglas Adams is best known for his first novel, *The Hitch-Hiker's Guide to the Galaxy* (1979), a blend of satire, deadpan humor, and absurdity. But he has been writing comedy for over two decades, proving immensely popular in both his native England and America. What has brought him the most fame has been his use of, and irreverence for, science fiction. By using the conventional devices of the genre to spoof humanity, he has created a fresh vision in this typically serious field of literature and has prompted comparisons to Lewis Carroll, Jonathan Swift, and Kurt Vonnegut.

A former writer for the British comedic troupe Monty Python, Adams wrote scripts for radio and television after receiving his degree in English Literature with honors from Cambridge University in 1974. Drawing on his experience in comedy, he wrote *The Hitch-Hiker's Guide to the Galaxy* and immediately earned a following among college students. The novel deals with the adventures of Englishman Arthur Dent, the only survivor of Earth after the planet is destroyed to make room for a new intergalactic highway. Rescued by Ford Prefect, a traveling researcher and interstellar hitch-hiker, Dent encounters a number of bizarre creatures, including the alien Vogons (who torture Dent and Prefect by reading terrible poetry aloud to them), the Galactic President Zaphod Beeblebrox, the depressed robot Marvin, and the creator of Earth, Slartibartfast, who is working on Earth Mark Two. As Lisa Tuttle wrote in the *Washington Post,* "There's nothing dull about the *Guide,* which is inspired lunacy that leaves hardly a science fiction cliché alive."

Adams continued to chronicle the absurd adventures of Dent in subsequent books. *The Restaurant at the End of the Universe* (1980) describes the fabled Milliways, a restaurant where patrons can witness the final moments of the cosmos. *Life, the Universe, and Everything* (1982) features the supercomputer Deep Thought, which determines that the answer to the mystery of the universe is 42. The time-traveling Dent also confronts an enraged being whom Dent has mistakenly killed in each of the being's reincarnations, including a fly, a rabbit, and a bowl of petunias. *So Long, and Thanks for All the Fish* (1984) returns Dent to Earth, where the only clue the inhabitants have that the earth was destroyed is the beautiful Fenchurch, who is dismissed as delusional and with whom Dent falls madly in love. All of the books continue Adams' use of absurd humor to poke fun at trendy preoccupations such as car worship, jogging, religious enthusiasm, and science fiction itself. While some critics fault Adams for uneven writing and too many departures into silliness, he is heralded as an original and offbeat voice. And despite Adams' insistence that he is a writer of comedy, critics such as Mat Coward describe Adams as "a genuine [science fiction] writer, despite his irreverence for the genre."

Departing from Arthur Dent and the other characters in the *Hitch-Hiker* novels, Adams wrote *Dirk Gently's Holistic Detective Agency* (1987). As in his *Hitch-Hiker* novels, Adams writes tongue-in-cheek about the human race being saved from extinction. But the characters are new, including Richard MacDuff, a computer software genius; Reg, a time-traveling Cambridge professor who is so old he cannot remember who he is; and Gently, a private detective with psychic abilities. Adams not only spoofs science fiction but takes a swing at the detective story, reversing Sherlock Holmes' famous statement that once the impossible is ruled out, whatever remains, however improbable, must be the truth.

The Long Dark Tea-Time of the Soul (1988) continues with Dirk Gently but throws in the Norse gods. They include Odin (as a one-eyed old man resting comfortably in a nursing home) and Thor, the god of thunder, who is frustrated and angry with both Odin and humans, particularly a check-in clerk at an airport ticket counter whom he crisps in a sudden fireball. The snappy lines and humor continue, along with some examination of religion and God. Yet Adams' absurdities and focus on perverse trivialities begin to wear thin. Nevertheless, his skewed vision appeals to readers tired of self-righteous, serious science fiction and preserves the tradition of oddball, Monty Python-esque humor.

—Christopher Swann

ALLAN, John B. *See* **WESTLAKE, Donald E.**

AMORY, Cleveland

Nationality: American. **Born:** Nahant, Massachusetts, 2 September 1917. **Education:** Harvard University, B.A., 1939. **Family:** Married 1) Cora Fields Craddock, 1941 (divorced, 1947); 2) Martha Hodge, 1953 (deceased); children: Gaea McCormick. **Career:** Newspaper reporter for the Nashua (New Hampshire) *Telegraph* and for the *Arizona Daily Star;* managing editor, Prescott (Arizona) *Evening Courier;* associate editor, *Saturday Evening Post,* 1939-41. Free-lance writer since 1943. Has also worked as a radio commentator and as the editor of *Parade.* Founder and president of The Fund for Animals; President of the New England Anti-Vivisection Society. **Awards:** L.H.D., New England College and Mercy College. **Address:** 200 W. 57th St., New York, New York 10019-3211, U.S.A.

Publications

Novels

Home Town. Harper, 1950.
The Trouble With Nowadays: A Curmudgeon Strikes Back. Arbor House, 1979.

Other

The Proper Bostonians. Dutton, 1947. Reprinted by Parnassus Imprints, 1984.
The Last Resorts. Harper, 1952.
Who Killed Society? Harper, 1960.
Man Kind?: Our Incredible War on Wildlife. Harper, 1974.
Animail. Windmill Books, 1976.
The Cat Who Came for Christmas. Little, Brown, 1987.
The Cat and the Curmudgeon. Little, Brown, 1990.
The Best Cat Ever. Little, Brown, 1993.

Editor, with Earl Blackwell, *Celebrity Register,* Harper, 1959.
Editor, with Frederic Bradlee, *Vanity Fair: Selections from America's Most Memorable Magazine; A Cavalcade of the 1920s and 1930s,* Viking, 1960.

* * *

Cleveland Amory is a self-styled "curmudgeon at large," popular writer, media figure, and animal rights advocate. His long and prolific writing career has demonstrated his ability to explore social and historical issues with a cranky, richly satirical style that blends serious, even high moral purpose with bristling wit and humor.

In his first work, *The Proper Bostonians* (1947), Amory offered a deeply researched but entertaining history of Boston's elite "first families," using family documents, legends, and interviews. Reviews were respectful if not uncritical. The *Christian Science Monitor* praised the study as a "solid and authoritative book," and *Commonweal* found it "deliberately outrageous." But a number of reviewers noted that its value lay more in its colorful anecdotes than in the reliability of its historical research.

In his first novel, *Home Town* (1950), Amory presented a satire of the publishing business in the tale of Arizona journalist Mitch Hickok, who encounters the odd rituals and machinations of New York publishers while promoting a new novel. *Home Town* was largely dismissed as lightweight, dull, and unworthy of the author of *The Proper Bostonians.* Amory returned to nonfiction with *Last Resorts* (1952), an examination of the resorts and recreational getaways of the rich and famous, from Palm Beach and Palm Springs to the Berkshires and Long Island. Reviewers universally lauded Amory's humorous glimpses of the well-heeled at play as well as the satirical bite of his prose.

In *Who Killed Society?* (1960), Amory chronicled the emergence of American high society and its current "top 400" families through historical sketches, profiles of individuals, and amusing anecdotes. Amory's theme was that American high-society was "killed," or at least radically transformed, by publicity, which robbed the rich of the anonymity needed to cultivate their good taste. Although some critics viewed it as merely an extended exercise in name dropping, *Atlantic* magazine found it "consistently entertaining," the *Chicago Tribune* called it a "seriously researched history of American manners and morals." Similarly, *Saturday Review* described it as "lively and entertaining."

With *Man Kind? Our Incredible War on Wildlife* (1974), Amory abandoned humorous dissections of the rich and famous for a scathing jeremiad against the animal industry—the trappers, hunters, and government agencies in the business of killing animals for sport, profit, or agricultural development. Unapologetically unobjective in his point of view, Amory proposed specific policies to change trapping and fishing practices and encouraged humane societies' efforts to curtail the use of animal fur for coats. The *Washington Post* called *Man Kind?* "eloquent and hard-hitting"; the *New York Times* described it as "highly readable . . . and vivid"; and *National Review* praised Amory for making his case "brilliantly, with wit and passion."

In 1976, selections from Amory's syndicated column "Animail" were published under the same name, combining some of Amory's more memorable answers to such questions as "What does the expression white elephant come from?" with animal-related anecdotes, poems, and stories.

Amory returned to fiction with *The Trouble with Nowadays: A Curmudgeon Strikes Back* (1979), in which, in the guise of an old crank in a men's club, he examines disturbing trends such as the liberation of women, undisciplined children, modern literature, and "the servant problem." *Publishers Weekly* praised Amory for getting the "Old Curmudgeon's" crusty manner "just right," while *Best Sellers* labeled *Trouble* "the grandest, funniest" satire of Amory's career. The *New York Times* called Amory a "rare" writer capable of morally informing while amusing his readers.

Amory's next three books all stemmed from his real-life rescue of a down-on-his-luck cat in a New York alley on a Christmas Eve in the 1970s. The *Cat Who Came for Christmas* (1987) recounted the rescue and ensuing friendship when Amory and "Polar Bear" gradually adopt each other. Interwoven in Amory's celebration of feline companionship is an affecting depiction of conditions in animal shelters and a fresh take on the history and mystery of the domestic cat. The book was warmly received and sold more than a million copies in its first year. Amory followed it with *The Cat and the Curmudgeon* (1990), which might well have been subtitled "The Further Adventures of Polar Bear and His Human." To his amusing narrative of Polar Bear's reluctant brush with celebrity and his gradual realization that his pet is every bit as curmudgeonly as its owner, Amory added a serious chapter on animal cruelty issues.

In the final installment of the trilogy, *The Best Cat Ever* (1993), Amory chronicled Polar Bear's failing health and eventual death, interspersing the narrative with autobiographical sketches of his own life, from his privileged Boston childhood to his experiences in the publishing and animal protection fields. Although many reviewers viewed Amory's cat books as appealing primarily to young adult readers or pet lovers, his occasional reflections on his animal rights activities and his own life were generally well received.

—Paul S. Bodine

ANDRESS, Lesley. *See* **SANDERS, Lawrence.**

ANDREWS, V(irginia) C(leo)

Nationality: American. **Born:** c. 1936, in Portsmouth, Virginia. **Education:** Attended schools in Portsmouth, Virginia. **Career:** Writer. Formerly worked as a fashion illustrator, commercial artist, portrait artist, and gallery exhibitor. **Died:** 19 December 1986 of cancer in Virginia Beach, Virginia.

Publications

Novels

Flowers in the Attic. Simon & Schuster, 1979.
Petals on the Wind. Simon & Schuster, 1980.
If There Be Thorns. Simon & Schuster, 1981.
My Sweet Audrina. Poseidon Press, 1982.
Seeds of Yesterday. Poseidon Press, 1984.
Heaven. Poseidon Press, 1985.
Dark Angel. Poseidon Press, 1986.
Garden of Shadows. Pocket Books, 1987.
Fallen Hearts. Pocket Books, 1988.
Gates of Paradise. Pocket Books, 1989.

* * *

The Southern gothic sagas of V.C. Andrews have an enormous following, especially among teenage girls. Her first novel, *Flowers in the Attic* (1979), is surprisingly about incest. Chris, Cathy, and their two younger siblings are locked in their grandparents' attic for over three years. What is hinted at is that their mother will lose her inheritance if the grandfather knows of the children's existence. Chris and Cathy reach puberty while still locked in the attic, become mutually attracted to each other, and eventually consummate the relationship. Of course, after making love the tension only increases and sets the stage for further corruption in succeeding novels. The novel is overwritten, overlong, and unbelievable. To make matters worse, there is not much action. What is the appeal here? According to Roger Sutton, the draw of these books lies in "the mystery, secrecy, and frustrated passion surrounding sex, particularly the emerging sexuality of the adolescent."

The saga continues in *Petals on the Wind* (1980), which focuses on revenge against the grandmother. In the third installment, *If There Be Thorns* (1981), Chris and Cathy are grown up and raising sons Jory and Bart from Cathy's previous marriages. The tension rises as nine-year old Bart is coddled by a strange woman living nearby who wants to be called "grandmother." Her creepy butler hovers on the fringe, whispering disgusting secrets to him about his mother and father.

Seeds of Yesterday (1984) concludes the saga with son Bart moving back to Foxworth Hall where it all began. The scattered family gathers together with the addition of mysterious Uncle Joel, back from spending years in a monastery. All of the characters wander around acting creepy, hiding guilty secrets or illicit desires. After lessons on the corrupting nature of wealth, Andrews finally ends the saga happily with true love conquering all.

In her next saga, Andrews introduces a poor rural family, the Casteels of West Virginia. Yet again she spins a gothic melodrama of children subjected to all kinds of evil and abuse. In *Heaven*

(1985), the eponymous protagonist, Heaven Leigh, wonders why her father and "mother" hate her. She finally learns that her real mother was a wealthy Boston woman who died in childbirth, leaving Luke bitter and abusive. After the second wife leaves Luke, he sells Heaven and her siblings for $500 each. The novel is crudely plotted and clumsily written, yet the combination of seething sexuality and strange events holds the attention of a vast readership.

The second installment of the Casteel series, *Dark Angel* (1986), finds Heaven Leigh arriving at the New England home of the wealthy grandmother she had never met. She hopes to get a college education, return to West Virginia, and reunite her brothers and sisters. But her grandmother has no interest in her whatsoever and pawns her off on her second husband, Tony. After quarreling with old boyfriend Logan, Heaven falls for Tony's son Troy. She then learns the horrible secret of her lineage. Heaven's world is shattered. She picks up the pieces in *Fallen Hearts* (1988) by returning to her roots in West Virginia and marrying her high school sweetheart, Logan.

With all of her works, Andrews gives the reader accounts of rape, incest, child abuse, death, and neglect, creating in the process twisted Southern fairy tales which will, after unbelievable amounts of tragedy, end up happily.

—Jennifer G. Coman

ANGELOU, Maya

Nationality: American. **Born:** Marguerita Johnson, St. Louis, Missouri, 4 April 1928. **Education:** Attended schools in Arkansas and California; studied music privately, dance with Martha Graham, Pearl Primus, and Ann Halprin, and drama with Frank Silvera and Gene Frankel. **Family:** Married Tosh Angelos (divorced); 2) Married Paul de Feu in 1973 (divorced); one son. **Career:** Actress and singer; associate editor, *Arab Observer,* Cairo, 1961-62; assistant administrator, School of Music and Drama, University of Ghana Institute of African Studies, Legon and Accra, 1963-66; freelance writer for *Ghanaian Times* and Ghanaian Broadcasting Corporation, both Accra, 1963-65; feature editor, *African Review,* Accra, 1964-66; lecturer, University of California, Los Angeles, 1966; writer-in-residence or visiting professor, University of Kansas, Lawrence, 1970, Wake Forest University, Winston-Salem, North Carolina, 1974, Wichita State University, Kansas, 1974, and California State University, Sacramento, 1974. Since 1981 Reynolds Professor, Wake Forest University. Northern coordinator, Southern Christian Leadership Conference, 1959-60. Also composer, television host and interviewer, and writer for Oprah Winfrey television series *Brewster Place.* **Awards:** Yale University fellowship, 1970; Rockefeller grant, 1975; *Ladies Home Journal* award, 1976. Also the recipient of numerous other awards and honors, including the North Carolina Award in Literature, 1987; Langston Hughes award, City College of New York, 1991; Innaugural poet for President Bill Clinton, 1993; Grammy, for Best Spoken Word Album, 1994. Honorary degrees: Smith College, Northampton, Massachusetts, 1975; Mills College, Oakland, California, 1975; Lawrence University, Appleton, Wisconsin, 1976. **Member:** American Revolution Bicentennial Council, 1975-76; board of trustees, American Film Institute, 1975; advisory board, Women's Prison Association; Harlem Writer's Guild; National Commission on the Observance of International Women's Year; **Agent:** Lordly and Dame Inc., 51 Church Street, Boston, Massachusetts 02116-5493, U.S.A.

PUBLICATIONS

Poetry

Just Give Me a Cool Drink of Water 'fore I Diiie. New York, Random House, 1971; London, Virago Press, 1988.
Oh Pray My Wings Are Gonna Fit Me Well. New York, Random House, 1975.
Poems. New York, Bantam, 1981.
Shaker, Why Don't You Sing? New York, Random House, 1983.
Now Sheba Sings the Song. New York, Dial Press, and London, Virago Press, 1987.
I Shall Not Be Moved. New York, Bantam Books, 1991.
A Brave & Startling Truth. New York, Random House, 1995.
Phenomenal Woman. New York, Random House, 1995.

Recordings: *Miss Calypso,* Liberty, 1957; *The Poetry of Maya Angelou,* GWP, 1969; *Women in Business,* University of Wisconsin, 1981.

Plays

Cabaret for Freedom (revue), with Godfrey Cambridge (produced New York, 1960).
The Least of These (produced Los Angeles, 1966).
Ajax, from the play by Sophocles (produced Los Angeles, 1974).
And Still I Rise (also director: produced Oakland, California, 1976). New York, Random House, 1978; London, Virago Press, 1986.
King (lyrics only, with Alistair Beaton), book by Lonne Elder III, music by Richard Blackford (produced London, 1990).

Screenplays: *Georgia, Georgia,* 1972; *All Day Long,* 1974.

Television Plays: *Sisters, Sisters,* with John Berry, 1982.

Television Documentaries: *Black, Blues, Black,* 1968; *Assignment America,* 1975; *The Legacy,* 1976; *The Inheritors,* 1976; *Trying to Make It Home (Byline* series), 1988; *Maya Angelou's America: A Journey of the Heart* (also host); *Who Cares About Kids, Kindred Spirits, Maya Angelou: Rainbow in the Clouds,* and *To the Contrary* (all Public Broadcasting Service productions).

Other

I Know Why the Caged Bird Sings. New York, Random House, 1970; London, Virago Press, 1984.
Gather Together in My Name. New York, Random House, 1974; London, Virago Press, 1985.
Singin' and Swingin' and Gettin' Merry Like Christmas. New York, Random House, 1976; London, Virago Press, 1985.
The Heart of a Woman. New York, Random House, 1981; London, Virago Press, 1986.
All God's Children Need Traveling Shoes. New York, Random House, 1986; London, Virago Press, 1987.
Mrs. Flowers: A Moment of Friendship (for children). Minneapolis, Redpath Press, 1986.

Conversations with Maya Angelou, edited by Jeffrey M. Elliot. University, University of Mississippi, and London, Virago Press, 1989.

Wouldn't Take Nothing for My Journey Now. New York, Random House, 1993.

*

Manuscript Collection: Wake Forest University, Winston-Salem, North Carolina.

Theatrical Activities: Director: **Plays**—*And Still I Rise,* Oakland, California, 1976; *Moon on a Rainbow Shawl* by Errol John, London, 1988; **Film**—*All Day Long,* 1974. Actress: **Plays**—in *Porgy and Bess* by George Gershwin, tour, 1954-55; *Calypso Heatwave,* New York, 1957; *The Blacks* by Jean Genet, New York, 1960; *Cabaret for Freedom,* New York, 1960; *Mother Courage* by Berthold Brecht, Accra, Ghana, 1964; *Medea,* Hollywood, 1966; *Look Away,* New York, 1973; **Film**—*Roots,* 1977.

* * *

Author of five autobiographies and four volumes of poetry, as well as plays and screenplays, Maya Angelou is prolific and immensely popular. Her work in the fictional genre of creative autobiography is as engaging as her poetry, and is as truthful as autobiographies can ever hope to be. Her selection of scenes is based on their emotional weight; she does not try to capture all the weeks and months and years, as a diary might, but only those that hold the most growth and meaning. The first and fourth books, *I Know Why the Caged Bird Sings* (1970) and *The Heart of a Woman* (1981), have received the most critical acclaim. But all of the works are exciting because of Angelou's honest, funny voice, her indomitable spirit, and her rich life of moves, travels, lovers, friends, mothering, and jobs.

I Know Why the Caged Bird Sings is written from the child's point of view and covers up to age 16 of Angelou's life. Its climax is the narrator's rape by her mother's boyfriend at age eight. The next eight years deal with the girl's attempt to heal the wound left by this violation. Critics have praised the book for its sense of affirmation in the face of trauma and hardship. Myra McMurry wrote that "*Caged Bird* is Angelou's answer to the question of how a Black girl can grow up in a repressive system without being maimed by it." Young Maya's answer is to become mute. When she is transferred back to Stamps, Arkansas, Maya reblossoms under the tutelage of Mrs. Bertha Flowers. Marguerite (Angelou's given name) also finds solace in the love of her mother and grandmother, both of them women of great power, resourcefulness, and faith.

The next two volumes in the series of autobiographies, *Gather Together in My Name* (1974) and *Singin' and Swingin' and Gettin' Merry Like Christmas* (1976), were more guardedly praised. Lynn Sukenick, for instance, believed that Angelou's tone of self-mockery was a defense mechanism that prevented her from honestly analyzing her teenage self, who was involved in prostitution and drugs. Others, such as Anne Gottlieb, praise the same works for their honesty, adding that Angelou has a "lilting rhythm completely her own" based on "black church singing and preaching, soft mother talk, and salty street talk."

The Heart of a Woman was well received for several reasons. Its scope was larger than that of the previous two books: it covered the period of Angelou's involvement in the Civil Rights movement, her relationship with African activist Vusumzi Make, and her meetings with James Baldwin, Malcolm X, Martin Luther King, Jr., Rosa Guy, Paule Marshall, and Max Roach. Committed to writing and civil rights, Angelou moved to New York City in the early 1960s, enabling her to meet these influential friends and mentors. This book has an emotional depth and psychological realism that compare favorably to her first book. In *The Heart of a Woman* (1981) Angelou writes honestly of her affair of the heart with Make, which ended when she learned that, living in Africa, she was expected to live like an African wife—submissive to men, stay-at-home, and unconcerned about her husband's infidelities. From Egypt Angelou moves to Ghana, where she enrolls her son Guy at the University of Ghana.

All God's Children Need Traveling Shoes (1986) begins with an important life-landmark: the separation of mother and son as Guy goes off to school. His words "Maybe now you'll have a chance to grow up" ring true, as he had been the center of her life since she was 16. She takes an administrative post at the University and shares a home with other African American women who, like herself, have come to Ghana to trace their roots, understand their culture, and find their identity. Also, they are powerfully attracted by Ghana's leader Kwame Nkrumah, who openly welcomed African Americans engaged in quests for their ethnic and racial identities.

Angelou's quest is to help African Americans and all people to "endure, dream, and survive," according to her. It is the pursuit of that quest that makes her life "a poetic adventure." Highlights of Angelou's quest are presented in her *Conversations with Maya Angelou* (1989) and *Wouldn't Take Nothing for My Journey Now* (1993).

—Jill Franks

ANTHONY, Piers

Nationality: American. **Born:** Piers Anthony Dillingham Jacob, Oxford, England, 6 August 1934; became United States citizen, 1958. **Education:** Goddard College, Plainfield, Vermont, B.A. 1956; University of South Florida, Tampa, teaching certificate 1964. **Military Service:** Served in the United States Army, 1957-59. **Family:** Married Carol Marble in 1956; one daughter. **Career:** Technical writer, Electronic Communications Inc., St. Petersburg, Florida, 1959-62; English teacher, Admiral Farragut Academy, St. Petersburg, 1965-66. Since 1966 freelance writer. **Awards:** Pyramid *Fantasy and Science Fiction* award, 1967; August Derleth award, 1977. **Address:** c/o Xanth Trading Company, P.O. Box 1568, Clayton, Georgia 30525, U.S.A.

Publications

Novels (series: Apprentice Adept; Aton; Battle Circle; Bio of a Space Tyrant; Cluster; Geodyssey; Incarnations of Immortality; Jason Striker; Kelvin of Rud; Mode; Tarot; Xanth)

Chthon (Aton). New York, Ballantine, 1967; London, Macdonald, 1970.

Of Man and Mantra: A Trilogy. London, Corgi, 1968.
Omnivore. New York, Ballantine, 1968; London, Faber, 1969.
Orn. Garden City, New York, Doubleday, 1971; London, Corgi, 1977.
Ox. Garden City, New York, Doubleday, 1976; London, Corgi, 1977.
The Ring, with Robert E. Margroff. New York, Ace, 1968; London, Macdonald, 1969.
Macroscope. New York, Avon, 1969; London, Sphere, 1972.
The E.S.P. Worm, with Robert E. Margroff. New York, Paperback Library, 1970.
Race Against Time (for children). New York, Hawthorn, 1973.
Rings of Ice. New York, Avon, 1974; London, Millington, 1975.
Triple Détente. New York, DAW, 1974; London, Sphere, 1975.
Phthor (Aton). New York, Berkley, 1975; London, Panther, 1978.
But What of Earth?, with Robert Coulson. Toronto, Laser, 1976; original version by Anthony published as *But What of Earth?: A Novel Rendered into a Bad Example,* New York, Tor, 1989.
Steppe. London, Millington, 1976; New York, Tor, 1985.
Cluster. New York, Avon, 1977; as *Vicinity Cluster,* London, Millington, 1978.
Piers Anthony's Hasan. San Bernardino, California, Borgo Press, 1977; as *Hasan,* New York, Del, 1979.
A Spell for Chameleon (Xanth). New York, Ballantine, 1977; London, Macdonald, 1984.
Chaining the Lady (Cluster). New York, Avon, and London, Millington, 1978.
Kirlian Quest (Cluster). New York, Avon, and London, Millington, 1978.
Battle Circle: A Trilogy. New York, Avon, 1978; London, Corgi, 1984.
  Sos, the Rope. New York, Pyramid, 1968; London, Faber, 1970.
  Var, the Stick. London, Faber, 1972; New York, Bantam, 1973.
  Neq, the Sword. London, Corgi, 1975.
Pretender: Science Fiction, with Frances Hall. San Bernardino, California, Borgo Press, 1979.
The Source of Magic (Xanth). New York, Ballantine, 1979; London, Macdonald, 1984.
Castle Roogna (Xanth). New York, Ballantine, 1979; London, Macdonald, 1984.
God of Tarot. New York, Jove, 1979.
Vision of Tarot. New York, Berkley, 1980.
Thousandstar (Cluster). New York, Avon, 1980; London, Panther, 1984.
Faith of Tarot. New York, Berkley, 1980.
Split Infinity (Apprentice Adept). New York, Ballantine, 1980; London, Granada, 1983.
Blue Adept (Apprentice Adept). New York, Ballantine, 1981; London, Granada, 1983.
Mute. New York, Avon, 1981; London, New English Library, 1984.
The Magic of Xanth (includes *A Spell for Chameleon, The Source of Magic,* and *Castle Roogna*). Garden City, New York, Doubleday, 1981; as *Three Complete Xanth Novels,* New York, Wings Books, 1994.
Centaur Aisle (Xanth). New York, Ballantine, 1982; London, Macdonald, 1984.
Ogre, Ogre (Xanth). New York, Ballantine, 1982; London, Orbit, 1984.
Juxtaposition (Apprentice Adept). New York, Ballantine, 1982; London, Grafton, 1986.
Viscous Circle (Cluster). New York, Avon, 1982; London, Panther, 1984.
Double Exposure (includes *Split Infinity, Blue Adept,* and *Juxtaposition*). Garden City, New York, Doubleday, 1982.
Dragon on a Pedestal (Xanth). New York, Ballantine, 1983; London, Orbit, 1984.
Night Mare (Xanth). New York, Ballantine, 1983; London, Orbit, 1984.
Refugee (Space Tyrant). New York, Avon, 1983; London, Grafton, 1986.
On a Pale Horse (Immortality). New York, Ballantine, 1983; London, Panther, 1985.
Mercenary (Space Tyrant). New York, Avon, 1984; London, Grafton, 1986.
Bearing an Hourglass (Immortality). New York, Ballantine, 1984; London, Severn House, 1986.
Crewel Lye: A Caustic Yarn (Xanth). New York, Ballantine, 1985; London, Macdonald, 1986; London, New English Library, 1990.
Total Recall (novelization of screenplay). New York, Morrow, 1989; London, Legend, 1990.
Man from Mundania (Xanth). New York, Avon, 1989; London, New English Library, 1990.
Through the Ice (completion of work by Robert Kornwise). Novato, California, and Lancaster, Pennsylvania, Underwood-Miller, 1989.
Chimaera's Copper, with Robert E. Margroff (Kelvin). New York, Tor, 1990; London, Grafton, 1992.
Balook. Novato, California, and Lancaster, Pennsylvania, Underwood-Miller, 1990.
Orc's Opal, with Robert E. Margroff. New York, Tor, 1990; London, HarperCollins, 1993.
And Eternity (Immortality). New York, Morrow, and London, Severn House, 1990.
Firefly. New York, Morrow, 1990.
Dead Morn. Houston, Tafford, 1990.
Isle of View (Xanth). New York, Morrow, 1990; London, New English Library, 1991.
Phaze Doubt (Apprentice Adept). New York, Putnam, 1990; London, New English Library, 1991.
Tatham Mound. New York, Morrow, 1991.
Virtual Mode (Mode). New York, Putnam, 1991; London, HarperCollins, 1991.
Question Quest (Xanth). New York, Morrow, 1991; London, New English Library, 1992.
Mer-Cycle. Houston, Tafford, 1991; as *Mercycle,* New York, Ace, 1992; London, Grafton, 1993.
Fractal Mode (Mode). New York, Ace, and London, HarperCollins, 1992.
Mouvar's Magic, with Robert E. Margroff. New York, Tor, 1992; London, HarperCollins, 1994.
The Color of Her Panties (Xanth). New York, Morrow, 1992; London, New English Library, 1992.
The Caterpillar's Question, with Philip José Farmer. New York, Ace, 1992.
Across the Frames, with Robert E. Margroff (includes *Dragon's Gold, Serpent's Silver,* and *Chimaera's Copper*). New York, Guild America Books, 1992; as *Three Complete Novels,* New York, Wings Books, 1994.
Final Magic, with Robert E. Margroff (includes *Orc's Opal* and *Mouvar's Magic*). New York, Guild America books, 1992.
Killobyte. New York, Ace, 1993.
Demons Don't Dream (Xanth). New York, Tor, and London, New English Library, 1993.

If I Pay Thee Not in Gold, with Mercedes R. Lackey. Riverdale, New York, Baen, 1993.
Isle of Women (Geodyssey). New York, Tor, 1993.
Harpy Thyme (Xanth). London, New English Library, 1993; New York, Tor, 1994.
Chaos Mode (Mode). New York, Ace, and London, HarperCollins, 1994.
Shame of Man (Geodyssey). New York, Tor, 1994.
Geis of the Gargoyle (Xanth). New York, Tor, 1995.
Roc and a Hard Place. New York, Tor, 1995.

Novels with Roberto Fuentes (series: Jason Striker in all titles)

Kiai! New York, Berkley, 1974.
Mistress of Death. New York, Berkley, 1974.
Bamboo Bloodbath. New York, Berkley, 1975.
Ninja's Revenge. New York, Berkley, 1975.
Amazon Slaughter. New York, Berkley, 1976.

Short Stories

Prostho Plus. London, Gollancz, 1971; New York, Bantam, 1973.
Anthonology. New York, Tor, 1985; London, Grafton, 1986.
Hard Sell. Houston, Tafford, 1990.
Alien Plot. New York, Tor, 1992.

Other

Bio of an Ogre: The Autobiography of Piers Anthony. New York, Ace, 1988.
Piers Anthony's Visual Guide to Xanth, with Jody Lynn Nye, illustrated by Todd Cameron Hamilton and James Clouse. New York, Avon, 1989.
Letters to Jenny, edited by Alan Riggs. New York, Tor, 1993.

Editor, with Barry N. Malzberg, Martin H. Greenberg, and Charles G. Waugh, *Uncollected Stars.* New York, Avon, 1986.
Editor, with Robert Gilliam, *Tales from the Great Turtle.* New York, Tor, 1994.

*

Manuscript Collection: Syracuse University, New York.

Critical Study: *Piers Anthony* by Michael R. Collings, Mercer Island, Washington, Starmont House, 1983.

* * *

Piers Anthony's writing career has been marked with both stupendous bestsellers and comatose flops. His prolific writings include both fantasy and science fiction, a series of martial arts novels, and a less-than-successful foray into horror with *Firefly.*

Anthony's first novel, *Chthon* (1967), was nominated for both a Hugo and a Nebula award. It and its sequel, *Pthor* (1975), helped to define his recurring character types, themes, and motifs. Of these motifs, most often incorporated into his novels are issues of maturity and immaturity, social order, and sexuality. He explores the causes and effects of cataclysmic change and often draws on music as an image and metaphor. He is interested in the roles of myth and symbol in culture and often uses extravagant humor to point out ironies in our beliefs and assumptions about life.

Chthon is the story of Aton Five, a prisoner attempting to escape the garnet mines on Chthon. Eventually he makes contact with the sentient planet and comes to terms with it. In *Pthor,* Aton's son allies with and then opposes the cavern-deity Chthon. The final confrontation becomes a future Ragnarok, with the survival of the universe at stake. In these two novels, Anthony weaves a web of myth and legend drawn from classical antiquity, Norse and Christian mythology, folktales, and other literature. He also demonstrates his trademark use of language with cunning wordplay and intricate worldbuilding.

Anthony's *Battle Circle* trilogy (1968-1975) and *Bio of a Space Tyrant* series (1983-1986) addressed issues of social order, power, and control. In the *Battle Circle* books, Anthony outlines the rise and fall of the Battle society, a construct imposed on a post-holocaust America as a means of providing safety outlets for violence and aggression while preventing the imperial urge. The *Bio of a Space Tyrant* follows Hope Hubris through a life based on the experiences of the Vietnamese and Cuban boat-people—refugees without a home, without succor. While some of these novels are violent, graphic, and often disturbing, they represent Anthony's social commentary on the trends and problems within today's society. He examines the need for order, and yet questions the nature of that order.

Perhaps most popular of all his works is the *Magic of Xanth* series (1977-1996). These are light-hearted fantasies which showcase Anthony's wordplay, especially puns. Xanth is a magical peninsula bordering Mundania (a.k.a. the real world). The land is populated with every variety of magical creature including centaurs, dragons, ogres, and zombies, as well as a variety of creatures such as shoe-trees that grow shoes and butterflies that drip butter. The country is as much a focus as are the various questing figures in each of the novels.

One of the criticisms that Anthony has faced with the *Magic of Xanth* series, and later in his *Apprentic Adept* (1980-1990) series and *Incarnations of Immortality* series (1983-1990), is that after the first few novels he begins to hack out books as fast as he can. His stories lose their sense of wonder; what begins as ingenious and imaginative grows cliched, much like the child who, convinced of his own creative genius, repeats a trick.

Most critics agree that the first few novels in these series are quite good, with the exception of the *Blue Adept* (1981), which has been charged with flat narration and boring characterization. But his *Magic of Xanth* series loses some of its charm after six or eight books of puns and rehashed plots, while the suspense and unique worldbuilding details of the first three *Incarnations of Immortality* begin to pall and grow boring after the fifth book.

On a Pale Horse (1983), the first of the *Incarnations of Immortality,* may be the best of Anthony's fantasy novels. It is set in a world where God, Satan, Nature, War, and Time are all offices to be filled by various mortal individuals. In this first novel, the new Death (who is given the office based on the fact that he killed the previous Death) finds himself in a nearly incomprehensible role, attempting to figure out just what he must do to negotiate the politics of his new office. Here he falls in love, is tempted by the Devil, is advised by various powerful office-holders with agendas of their own, and finds himself walking a narrow tightrope between good and evil. The characterization and dramatization are superbly handled and engage the reader. Besides clever social commentary, it provides a good read.

—Diana Pharaoh Francis

ARCHER, Jeffrey (Howard)

Nationality: English. **Born:** 15 April 1940, in Weston-Super-Mare, England. **Education:** Attended Brasenose College, Oxford, 1963-66. **Family:** Married Mary Weeden, 1966; children: two sons. **Career:** Writer. Arrow Enterprises Ltd., London, chairperson of the board, beginning 1968; Conservative member of the British Parliament, 1969-74; deputy chairperson, British Conservative Party, 1985-86. Chairperson, Nigeria Consultants, Inc.; member, Greater London Council for Havering, 1966-70; executive, British Theatre Museum. **Member:** Royal Society of the Arts (fellow). **Address:** 93 Albert Embankment, London SE1, England; The Old Vicarage, Grantchester, England.

Publications

Novels

Not a Penny More, Not a Penny Less. Doubleday, 1976.
Shall We Tell the President? Viking, 1977.
Kane & Abel. Simon & Schuster, 1980, HarperCollins, 1993.
The Prodigal Daughter. Linden Press, 1982, HarperCollins, 1993.
First among Equals. Linden Press, 1984, HarperCollins, 1993.
A Matter of Honor. Linden Press, 1986, HarperCollins, 1993.
As the Crow Flies. HarperCollins, 1991.
Honor among Thieves: A Novel. HarperCollins, 1993.
Twelve Red Herrings. HarperCollins, 1994.

Short Stories

A Quiver Full of Arrows. Linden Press, 1982, HarperCollins, 1993.
A Twist in the Tale. Simon & Schuster, 1989, HarperCollins, 1994.

Fiction for Children

By Royal Appointment. Octopus, 1980.
Willy Visits the Square World. Octopus, 1980.
Willy and the Killer Kipper. Hodder & Stoughton Children's Books, 1981.

*

Media Adaptations: *Not a Penny More, Not a Penny Less* was adapted for British television and serialized on British radio; *Kane & Abel* was made into a mini-series for CBS-TV, fall 1985.

* * *

On the verge of bankruptcy, Jeffery Archer became interested in writing to make money. *Not A Penny More, Not A Penny Less* (1976) is Archer's first novel and personal financial savior. The plot of the book mimics the circumstances that brought him to the place in his life where he quit his elected position to the House of Commons; Archer, feeling the financial woes of his misfortune, became inspired and created an instant bestseller in the United States. Several failed attempts were made to get his first novel published in England, although it was eventually adapted for television and as a radio series in that country.

Archer credits his success partially to his publisher, Joni Evans at Simon & Schuster. She accepted his third novel, *Kane & Abel* (1980), which sealed his fame. The idea for the book came from Archer's introduction to two businessmen who were friends in New York City fifteen years before Archer wrote the novel. Each man told of his climb up the ladder of success, and Archer thought the story of their relationship would be more interesting if they were enemies. He was right. *Kane & Abel* had sold over 250,000 copies in hardback and more than 4 million in softcover by the mid-1990s, and the novel was made into a mini-series for the Columbia Broadcasting System in 1985.

Archer published some children's fiction in the early 1980s before returning to novel writing. Stemming from *Kane & Abel* was Archer's fourth novel, *The Prodigal Daughter* (1982). Not believing that Archer's fans would accept the idea of a woman president in the United States, critics ridiculed him. He followed *Prodigal* with *First Among Equals* (1984) and *A Matter of Honor* (1986). The latter was purchased by Stephen Spielberg within hours after he read the book. The publishers of the novel placed a preorder of 250,000 copies, but after reading it boosted the order to 400,000. Archer said at the time that he believed that *A Matter of Honor* was his best work.

Archer's output slowed in the late 1980s. Then he released a succession of novels in the early and mid-1990s; *As the Crow Flies* (1991), *Honor among Thieves: A Novel* (1993), and *Twelve Red Herrings* (1994). The books received mixed critical response and generally failed to achieve the same level of praise as *A Matter of Honor,* but sold relatively well.

Archer is practical and humble regarding his talent. He credits his success to some native talent and a great deal of energy. A simple belief he lives by is that if you have one gift plus energy you will be a king, if you have no gift and energy a prince, and if you have no gift and no energy you will be a pauper. Archer is motivated by a strong desire to write the best novel he can. He says that he really wants to write a book that is impossible to put down, but he admits he is not the greatest of writers. He longs for the plot twister that keeps himself and his readers excited about turning the page, even as he is writing—if he doesn't know what is going to happen next as he writes, neither will his readers, he believes.

—Tammy J. Bronson

ARD, William. *See* **JAKES, John.**

ASIMOV, Isaac

Pseudonyms: Dr. A.; Paul French. **Nationality:** American. **Born:** Petrovichi, U.S.S.R., 2 January 1920; emigrated to the United States in 1923; naturalized, 1928. **Education:** Columbia University, New York, B.S. 1939, M.A. 1941, Ph.D. in chemistry 1948. **Military Service:** Served in the United States Army, 1945-46. **Family:** Married 1) Gertrude Blugerman in 1948 (divorced 1973), one son and one daughter; 2) Janet Opal Jeppson in 1973. **Career:** Instructor in Biochemistry, 1949-51, assistant professor, 1951-55, associate professor, 1955-79, and from 1979, professor, Boston University School of Medicine. **Awards:** Edison Foundation National Mass Media award, 1958; Blakeslee award, for nonfiction, 1960; World Science Fiction Convention Citation, 1963; Hugo award, 1963, 1966, 1973, 1977, 1983; American Chemical Society James T. Grady award, 1965; American Association for the Advancement of Science-Westinghouse Science Writing award, 1967; Nebula award, 1972, 1976; *Locus* award, for nonfiction, 1981, for fiction, 1983. Guest of Honor, World Science Fiction Convention, 1955. **Died:** 6 April 1992.

Publications

Novels (series: Foundation; Norby; Robots; Trantorian Empire)

Triangle: (Empire). Garden City, New York, Doubleday, 1961; as *An Isaac Asimov Second Omnibus,* London, Sidgwick and Jackson, 1969.

Pebble in the Sky. Garden City, New York, Doubleday, 1950; London, Corgi, 1958.

The Stars, Like Dust. Garden City, New York, Doubleday, 1951; London, Panther, 1958; abridged edition, as *The Rebellious Stars,* New York, Ace, 1954.

The Currents of Space. Garden City, New York, Doubleday, 1952; London, Boardman, 1955.

The Foundation Trilogy. Garden City, New York, Doubleday, 1963; as *An Isaac Asimov Omnibus,* London, Sidgwick and Jackson, 1966.

Foundation. New York, Gnome Press, 1951; London, Weidenfeld and Nicolson, 1953; abridged edition, as *The 1,000-Year Plan,* New York, Ace, 1955.

Foundation and Empire. New York, Gnome Press, 1952; London, Panther, 1962; as *The Man Who Upset the Universe,* New York, Ace, 1955.

Second Foundation. New York, Gnome Press, 1953; as *2nd Foundation: Galactic Empire,* New York, Avon, 1958.

The Caves of Steel (Robots). Garden City, New York, Doubleday, and London, Boardman, 1954.

The End of Eternity. Garden City, New York, Doubleday, 1955; London, Panther, 1958.

The Death Dealers. New York, Avon, 1958; as *A Whiff of Death,* New York, Walker, and London, Gollancz, 1968.

The Naked Sun (Robots). Garden City, New York, Doubleday, 1957; London, Joseph, 1958.

Fantastic Voyage (novelization of screenplay). Boston, Houghton Mifflin, and London, Dobson, 1966.

The Best New Thing (for children). Cleveland, World, 1971.

The Robot Novels (includes *The Caves of Steel* and *The Naked Sun*). Garden City, New York, Doubleday, 1972; with *The Robots of Dawn,* New York, Ballantine, 1988.

The Gods Themselves. Garden City, New York, Doubleday, and London, Gollancz, 1972.

Murder at the ABA. Garden City, New York, Doubleday, 1976; as *Authorized Murder,* London, Gollancz, 1976.

The Far Ends of Time (omnibus). Garden City, New York, Doubleday, 1979.

Prisoners of the Stars (omnibus). Garden City, New York, Doubleday, 1979.

Foundation's Edge. Garden City, New York, Doubleday, 1982; London, Granada, 1983.

The Robots of Dawn (Robots). Huntington Woods, Michigan, Phantasia Press, 1983; London, Granada, 1984.

Norby, the Mixed-Up Robot (for children), with Janet Asimov. New York, Walker, 1983; London, Methuen, 1984.

Norby's Other Secret (for children), with Janet Asimov. New York, Walker, 1984; London, Methuen, 1985.

Norby and the Lost Princess (for children), with Janet Asimov. New York, Walker, 1985.

Robots and Empire. Huntington Woods, Michigan, Phantasia Press, 1985.

Norby and the Invaders (for children), with Janet Asimov. New York, Walker, 1985.

Norby and the Queen's Necklace (for children), with Janet Asimov. New York, Walker, 1986.

Foundation and Earth. Garden City, New York, Doubleday, and London, Grafton, 1986.

The Norby Chronicles (omnibus; for children), with Janet Asimov. New York, Ace, 1986.

Fantastic Voyage II: Destination Brain. Garden City, New York, Doubleday, and London, Grafton, 1987.

Norby, Robot for Hire (omnibus; for children), with Janet Asimov. New York, Ace, 1987.

Norby Finds a Villain (for children), with Janet Asimov. New York, Walker, 1987.

Prelude to Foundation. New York, Doubleday, and London, Grafton, 1988.

Norby Through Space and Time (omnibus). New York, Ace, 1988.

Nemesis. New York and London, Doubleday, 1989.

Norby Down to Earth (for children), with Janet Asimov. New York, Walker, 1989.

Norby and Yobo's Great Adventure (for children), with Janet Asimov. New York, Walker, 1989.

Nightfall, with Robert Silverberg. London, Gollancz, and New York, Doubleday, 1990.

Norby and the Oldest Dragon (for children), with Janet Asimov. New York, Walker, 1990.

Norby and the Court Jester (for children), with Janet Asimov. New York, Walker, 1991.

The Child of Time, with Robert Silverberg. London, Gollancz, 1991; as *The Ugly Little Boy,* bound with *The [Widget], the [Wadget], and Boff,* by Theodore Sturgeon, New Yor, Tor, 1989.

The Positronic Man, with Robert Silverberg. London, Gollancz, 1992; New York, Doubleday, 1993.

Novels as Paul French (for children; series: Lucky Starr in all titles)

The Adventures [Further Adventures] of Lucky Starr. Garden City, New York, Doubleday, 2 vols., 1985.

David Starr, Space Ranger. Garden City, New York, Doubleday, 1952; Kingswood, Surrey, World's Work, 1953; as *Space Ranger* (as Isaac Asimov), London, New English Library, 1973.

Lucky Starr and the Pirates of the Asteroids. Garden City, New York, Doubleday, 1953; Kingswood, Surrey, World's Work, 1954; as *Pirates of the Asteroids* (as Isaac Asimov), London, New English Library, 1973.

Lucky Starr and the Oceans of Venus. Garden City, New York, Doubleday, 1954; as *The Oceans of Venus* (as Isaac Asimov), London, New English Library, 1974.
Lucky Starr and the Big Sun of Mercury. Garden City, New York, Doubleday, 1956; as *The Big Sun of Mercury* (as Isaac Asimov), London, New English Library, 1974.
Lucky Starr and the Moons of Jupiter. Garden City, New York, Doubleday, 1957; as *The Moons of Jupiter* (as Isaac Asimov), London, New English Library, 1974.
Lucky Starr and the Rings of Saturn. Garden City, New York, Doubleday, 1958; as *The Rings of Saturn* (as Isaac Asimov), London, New English Library, 1974.

Short Stories (series: Black Widowers)

I, Robot. New York, Gnome Press, 1950; London, Grayson, 1952.
The Martian Way and Other Stories. Garden City, New York, Doubleday, 1955; London, Dobson, 1964.
Earth Is Room Enough. Garden City, New York, Doubleday, 1957; London, Panther, 1960.
Nine Tomorrows: Tales of the Near Future. Garden City, New York, Doubleday, 1959; London, Dobson, 1963.
The Rest of the Robots. Garden City, New York, Doubleday, 1964; London, Dobson, 1967; abridged as *Eight Stories from The Rest of the Robot,* New York, Pyramid, 1966.
Through a Glass, Clearly. London, Four Square, 1967.
Asimov's Mysteries. Garden City, New York, Doubleday, and London, Rapp and Whiting, 1968.
Nightfall and Other Stories. Garden City, New York, Doubleday, 1969; London, Rapp and Whiting, 1970.
The Early Asimov; or, Eleven Years of Trying. Garden City, New York, Doubleday, 1972; London, Gollancz, 1973.
The Best of Isaac Asimov. London, Sidgwick and Jackson, 1973; Garden City, New York, Doubleday, 1974.
Have You Seen These? Cambridge, Massachusetts, NESFA Press, 1974.
Tales of the Black Widowers. Garden City, New York, Doubleday, 1974; London, Gollancz, 1975.
The Heavenly Host (for children). New York, Walker, 1975; London, Penguin, 1978.
Buy Jupiter and Other Stories. Garden City, New York, Doubleday, 1975; London, Gollancz, 1976.
The Dream, Benjamin's Dream, Benjamin's Bicentennial Blast: Three Short Stories. New York, privately printed, 1976.
The Bicentennial Man and Other Stories. Garden City, New York, Doubleday, 1976; London, Gollancz, 1977.
Good Taste. Topeka, Kansas, Apocalypse Press, 1976.
The Key Word and Other Mysteries (for children). New York, Walker, 1977.
More Tales of the Black Widowers. Garden City, New York, Doubleday, 1976; London, Gollancz, 1977.
Liar! Cambridge, Cambridge University Press, 1977.
Little Lost Robot. Cambridge, Cambridge University Press, 1977.
Casebook of the Black Widowers. Garden City, New York, Doubleday, and London, Gollancz, 1980.
The Complete Robot. Garden City, New York, Doubleday, and London, Granada, 1982.
The Union Club Mysteries. Garden City, New York, Doubleday, 1983; London, Granada, 1984.
The Winds of Change and Other Stories. Garden City, New York, Doubleday, and London, Granada, 1983.
Banquets of the Black Widowers. Garden City, New York, Doubleday, 1984; London, Grafton, 1986.
The Disappearing Man and Other Mysteries (for young adults). London, Walker, 1985.
The Edge of Tomorrow. New York, Tor, 1985; London, Harrap, 1986.
The Alternate Asimovs. Garden City, New York, Doubleday, 1986; London, Grafton, 1987.
Robot Dreams. New York, Berkley, 1986; London, Gollancz, 1987.
Other Worlds of Isaac Asimov, edited by Martin H. Greenberg. New York, Avenel, 1987.
The Best Mysteries of Isaac Asimov. Garden City, New York, Doubleday, 1986; London, Grafton, 1987.
The Best Science Fiction of Isaac Asimov. Garden City, New York, Doubleday, 1986; London, Grafton, 1987.
Azazel. New York, Doubleday, 1988; London, Doubleday, 1989.
The Asimov Chronicles: Fifty Years of Isaac Asimov, edited by Martin H. Greenberg. Arlington Heights, Illinois, Dark Harvest 1989; London, Legend, 1991.
Robot Visions. New York, Roc, 1990; London, Gollancz, 1991.
The Complete Stories. New York, Doubleday, 2 vols., 1990-92; London, HarperCollins, 2 vols, 1993-94.
Puzzles of the Black Widowers. New York and London, Doubleday, 1990.
Cal. New York, Doubleday, 1991.
Forward the Foundation. New York and London, Doubleday, 1993.
Gold: The Final Science Fiction Collection. New York, HarperPrism, 1995.

Poetry

Lecherous Limericks. New York, Walker, 1975; London, Corgi, 1977.
More Lecherous Limericks. New York, Walker, 1976.
Still More Lecherous Limericks. New York, Walker, 1977.
Asimov's Sherlockian Limericks. Yonkers, New York, Mysterious Press, 1978.
Limericks: Too Gross, with John Ciardi. New York, Norton, 1978.
A Grossery of Limericks, with John Ciardi. New York, Norton, 1981.
Limericks for Children. New York, Caedmon, 1984.

Other

Biochemistry and Human Metabolism, with Burnham Walker and William C. Boyd. Baltimore, Williams and Wilkins, 1952; revised edition, 1954, 1957; London, Ballie Tindall and Cox, 1955.
The Chemicals of Life: Enzymes, Vitamins, Hormones. New York, Abelard Schuman, 1954; London, Bell, 1956.
Races and Peoples, with William C. Boyd. New York, Abelard Schuman, 1955; London, Abelard Schuman, 1958.
Chemistry and Human Health, with Burnham Walker and M.K. Nicholas. New York, McGraw Hill, 1956.
Inside the Atom. New York and London, Abelard Schuman, 1956; revised edition, 1958, 1961, 1966, 1974.
Building Blocks of the Universe. New York, Abelard Schuman, 1957; London, Abelard Schuman, 1958; revised edition, 1961, 1974.
Only a Trillion. New York and London, Abelard Schuman, 1957; as *Marvels of Science,* New York, Collier, 1962.

The World of Carbon. New York and London, Abelard Schuman, 1958; revised edition, New York, Collier, 1962.
The World of Nitrogen. New York and London, Abelard Schuman, 1958; revised edition, New York, Collier, 1962.
The Clock We Live On. New York and London, Abelard Schuman, 1959; revised edition, New York, Collier, 1962; Abelard Schuman, 1965.
The Living River. New York and London, Abelard Schuman, 1959; revised edition, as *The Bloodstream: River of Life*, New York, Collier, 1961.
Realm of Numbers. Boston, Houghton Mifflin, 1959; London, Gollancz, 1963.
Words of Science and the History Behind Them. Boston, Houghton Mifflin, 1959; London, Harrap, 1974.
Breakthroughs in Science (for children). Boston, Houghton Mifflin, 1960.
The Intelligent Man's Guide to Science. New York, Basic Books, 2 vols., 1960; revised edition, as *The New Intelligent Man's Guide to Science*, 1 vol., 1965; London, Nelson, 1967; as *Asimov's Guide to Science*, New York, Basic Books, 1972; London, Penguin, 2 vols., 1975; as *Asimov's New Guide to Science*, Basic Books, 1984.
The Kingdom of the Sun. New York and London, Abelard Schuman, 1960; revised edition, New York, Collier, 1962; Abelard Schuman, 1963.
Realm of Measure. Boston, Houghton Mifflin, 1960.
Satellites in Outer Space (for children). New York, Random House, 1960; revised edition, 1964, 1973.
The Double Planet. New York, Abelard Schuman, 1960; London, Abelard Schuman, 1962; revised edition, 1966.
The Wellsprings of Life. New York and London, Abelard Schuman, 1960.
Realm of Algebra. Boston, Houghton Mifflin, 1961; London, Gollancz, 1964.
Words from the Myths. Boston, Houghton Mifflin, 1961; London, Faber, 1963.
Fact and Fancy. Garden City, New York, Doubleday, 1962.
Life and Energy. Garden City, New York, Doubleday, 1962; London, Dobson, 1963.
The Search for the Elements. New York, Basic Books, 1962.
Words in Genesis. Boston, Houghton Mifflin, 1962.
Words on the Map. Boston, Houghton Mifflin, 1962.
View from a Height. Garden City, New York, Doubleday, 1963; London, Dobson, 1964.
The Genetic Code. New York, Orion Press, 1963; London, Murray, 1964.
The Human Body: Its Structure and Operation. Boston, Houghton Mifflin, 1963; London, Nelson, 1965; revised edition, New York, Mentor, 1992.
The Kite That Won the Revolution. Boston, Houghton Mifflin, 1963.
Words from the Exodus. Boston, Houghton Mifflin, 1963.
Adding a Dimension: 17 Essays on the History of Science. Garden City, New York, Doubleday, 1964; London, Dobson, 1966.
The Human Brain: Its Capacities and Functions. Boston, Houghton Mifflin, 1964; London, Nelson, 1965.
Quick and Easy Math. Boston, Houghton Mifflin, 1964; London, Whiting and Wheaton, 1967.
A Short History of Biology. Garden City, New York, Natural History Press, 1964; London, Nelson, 1965.
Planets for Man, with Stephen H. Dole. New York, Random House, 1964.
Asimov's Biographical Encyclopedia of Science and Technology. Garden City, New York, Doubleday, 1964; London, Allen and Unwin, 1966; revised edition, Doubleday, 1972, 1982; London, Pan, 1975.
An Easy Introduction to the Slide Rule. Boston, Houghton Mifflin, 1965; London, Whiting and Wheaton, 1967.
The Greeks: A Great Adventure. Boston, Houghton Mifflin, 1965.
Of Time and Space and Other Things. Garden City, New York, Doubleday, 1965; London, Dobson, 1967.
A Short History of Chemistry. Garden City, New York, Doubleday, 1965; London, Heinemann, 1972.
The Neutrino: Ghost Particle of the Atom. Garden City, New York, Doubleday, and London, Dobson, 1966.
The Genetic Effects of Radiation, with Theodosius Dobzhansky. Washington, D.C., Atomic Energy Commission, 1966.
The Noble Gases. New York, Basic Books, 1966.
The Roman Republic. Boston, Houghton Mifflin, 1966.
From Earth to Heaven. Garden City, New York, Doubleday, 1966.
Understanding Physics. New York, Walker, 3 vols., 1966; London, Allen and Unwin, 3 vols., 1967; as *The History of Physics*, Walker, 1 vol., 1984.
The Universe: From Flat Earth to Quasar. New York, Walker, 1966; London, Penguin, 1967; revised edition, Walker, and Penguin, 1971; revised edition, as *The Universe: From Flat Earth to Black Holes—and Beyond*, Walker, 1980, Penguin, 1983.
The Roman Empire. Boston, Houghton Mifflin, 1967.
The Moon (for children). Chicago, Follett, 1967; London, University of London Press, 1969.
Is Anyone There? (essays). Garden City, New York, Doubleday, 1967; London, Rapp and Whiting, 1968.
To the Ends of the Universe. New York, Walker, 1967; revised edition, 1976.
The Egyptians. Boston, Houghton Mifflin, 1967.
Mars (for children). Chicago, Follett, 1967; London, University of London Press, 1971.
From Earth to Heaven: 17 Essays on Science. Garden City, New York, Doubleday, 1967; London, Dobson, 1968.
Environments Out There. New York, Abelard Schuman, 1967; London, Abelard Schuman, 1968.
Science, Numbers, and I: Essays on Science. Garden City, New York, Doubleday, 1968; London, Rapp and Whiting, 1969.
The Near East: 10,000 Years of History. Boston, Houghton Mifflin, 1968.
Asimov's Guide to the Bible: The Old Testament, The New Testament. Garden City, New York, Doubleday, 2 vols., 1968-69.
The Dark Ages. Boston, Houghton Mifflin, 1968.
Galaxies (for children). Chicago, Follett, 1968; London, University of London Press, 1971.
Stars (for children). Chicago, Follett, 1968.
Words from History. Boston, Houghton Mifflin, 1968.
Photosynthesis. New York, Basic Books, 1968; London, Allen and Unwin, 1970.
The Shaping of England. Boston, Houghton Mifflin, 1969.
Twentieth Century Discovery (for children). Garden City, New York, Doubleday, and London, Macdonald, 1969.
Opus 100 (selection). Boston, Houghton Mifflin, 1969.
ABC's of Space (for children). New York, Walker, 1969.
Great Ideas of Science (for children). Boston, Houghton Mifflin, 1969.
To the Solar System and Back. Garden City, New York, Doubleday, 1970.

Asimov's Guide to Shakespeare: The Greek, Roman, and Italian Plays; The English Plays. Garden City, New York, Doubleday, 2 vols., 1970.
Constantinople. Boston, Houghton Mifflin, 1970.
The ABC's of the Ocean (for children). New York, Walker, 1970.
Light (for children). Chicago, Follett, 1970.
The Stars in Their Courses. Garden City, New York, Doubleday, 1971; London, White Lion, 1974.
What Makes the Sun Shine. Boston, Little Brown, 1971.
The Isaac Asimov Treasury of Humor. Boston, Houghton Mifflin, 1971; London, Vallentine Mitchell, 1972.
The Sensuous Dirty Old Man (as Dr. A.). New York, Walker, 1971.
The Land of Canaan. Boston, Houghton Mifflin, 1971.
ABC's of Earth (for children). New York, Walker, 1971.
The Space Dictionary. New York, Starline, 1971.
More Words of Science. Boston, Houghton Mifflin, 1972.
Electricity and Man. Washington, D.C., Atomic Energy Commission, 1972.
The Shaping of France. Boston, Houghton Mifflin, 1972.
Asimov's Annotated "Don Juan." Garden City, New York, Doubleday, 1972.
ABC's of Ecology (for children). New York, Walker, 1972.
The Story of Ruth. Garden City, New York, Doubleday, 1972.
Worlds Within Worlds. Washington, D.C., Atomic Energy Commission, 1972.
The Left Hand of the Electron (essays). Garden City, New York, Doubleday, 1972; London, White Lion, 1975.
Ginn Science Program. Boston, Ginn, 5 vols., 1972-73.
How Did We Find Out about Dinosaurs [the Earth Is Round, Electricity, Vitamins, Germs, Comets, Energy, Atoms, Nuclear Power, Numbers, Outer Space, Earthquakes, Black Holes, Our Human Roots, Antarctica, Coal, Oil, Solar Powers, Volcanoes, Life in the Deep Sea, Our Genes, the Universe, Computers, Robots, the Atmosphere, DNA, the Speed of Light, Blood, Sunshine, the Brain, Super Conductivity, Microwaves, Photosynthesis, Pluto] (for children). New York, Walker, 33 vols., 1973-91; 6 vols. published London, White Lion, 1975-76; 1 vol. published London, Pan, 1980; 7 vols. published (as *How We Found Out . . .* series), London, Longman, 1982.
The Tragedy of the Moon (essays). Garden City, New York, Doubleday, 1973; London, Abelard Schuman, 1974.
Comets and Meteors (for children). Chicago, Follett, 1973.
The Sun (for children). Chicago, Follett, 1973.
The Shaping of North America from the Earliest Times to 1763. Boston, Houghton Mifflin, 1973; London, Dobson, 1975.
Please Explain (for children). Boston, Houghton Mifflin, 1973; London, Abelard Schuman, 1975.
Physical Science Today. Del Mar, California, CRM, 1973.
Jupiter, The Largest Planet (for children). New York, Lothrop, 1973; revised edition, 1976.
Today, Tomorrow, and. . . . Garden City, New York, Doubleday, 1973; London, Abelard Schuman, 1974; as *Towards Tomorrow,* London, Hodder and Stoughton, 1977.
The Birth of the United States 1763-1816. Boston, Houghton Mifflin, 1974.
Earth: Our Crowded Spaceship. Garden City, New York, Doubleday, and London, Abelard Schuman, 1974.
Asimov on Chemistry. Garden City, New York, Doubleday, 1974; London, Macdonald and Jane's, 1975.
Asimov on Astronomy. Garden City, New York, Doubleday, and London, Macdonald, 1974.
Asimov's Annotated "Paradise Lost." Garden City, New York, Doubleday, 1974.
Our World in Space. Greenwich, Connecticut, New York Graphic Society, and Cambridge, Patrick Stephens, 1974.
The Solar System (for children). Chicago, Follett, 1975.
Birth and Death of the Universe. New York, Walker, 1975.
Of Matters Great and Small. Garden City, New York, Doubleday, 1975.
Our Federal Union: The United States from 1816 to 1865. Boston, Houghton Mifflin, and London, Dobson, 1975.
The Ends of the Earth: The Polar Regions of the World. New York, Weybright and Talley, 1975.
Eyes on the Universe: A History of the Telescope. Boston, Houghton Mifflin, 1975; London, Deutsch, 1976.
Science Past—Science Future. Garden City, New York, Doubleday, 1975.
Alpha Centauri, The Nearest Star (for children). New York, Lothrop, 1976.
I, Rabbi (for children). New York, Walker, 1976.
Asimov on Physics. Garden City, New York, Doubleday, 1976.
The Planet That Wasn't. Garden City, New York, Doubleday, 1976; London, Sphere, 1977.
The Collapsing Universe: The Story of Black Holes. New York, Walker, and London, Hutchinson, 1977.
Asimov on Numbers. Garden City, New York, Doubleday, 1977.
The Beginning and the End. Garden City, New York, Doubleday, 1977.
Familiar Poems Annotated. Garden City, New York, Doubleday, 1977.
The Golden Door: The United States from 1865 to 1918. Boston, Houghton Mifflin, and London, Dobson, 1977.
Mars, The Red Planet (for children). New York, Lothrop, 1977.
Life and Time. Garden City, New York, Doubleday, 1978.
Quasar, Quasar, Burning Bright. Garden City, New York, Doubleday, 1978.
Animals of the Bible (for children). Garden City, New York, Doubleday, 1978.
Isaac Asimov's Book of Facts. New York, Grosset and Dunlap, 1979; London, Hodder and Stoughton, 1980; abridged edition (for children), as *Would You Believe?* and *More . . . Would You Believe?,* Grosset and Dunlap, 2 vols., 1981-82.
Extraterrestrial Civilizations. New York, Crown, 1979; London, Robson, 1980.
A Choice of Catastrophes. New York, Simon and Schuster, 1979; London, Hutchinson, 1980.
Saturn and Beyond. New York, Lothrop, 1979.
Opus 200 (selection). Boston, Houghton Mifflin, 1979.
In Memory Yet Green: The Autobiography of Isaac Asimov 1920-1954. Garden City, New York, Doubleday, 1979.
The Road to Infinity. Garden City, New York, Doubleday, 1979.
In Joy Still Felt: The Autobiography of Isaac Asimov 1954-1978. Garden City, New York, Doubleday, 1980.
The Annotated Gulliver's Travels. New York, Potter, 1980.
Opus (includes *Opus 100* and *Opus 200*). London, Deutsch, 1980.
Change! Seventy-One Glimpses of the Future. Boston, Houghton Mifflin, 1981.
Visions of the Universe, paintings by Kazuaki Iwasaki. Montrose, California, Cosmos Store, 1981.
Asimov on Science Fiction. Garden City, New York, Doubleday, 1981; London, Granada, 1983.

Venus, Near Neighbor of the Sun (for children). New York, Lothrop, 1981.

The Sun Shines Bright. Garden City, New York, Doubleday, 1981; London, Granada, 1984.

In the Beginning: Science Faces God in the Book of Genesis. New York, Crown, and London, New English Library, 1981.

Exploring the Earth and the Cosmos. New York, Crown, 1982; London, Allen Lane, 1983.

Counting the Eons. Garden City, New York, Doubleday, 1983; London, Granada, 1984.

The Measure of the Universe. New York, Harper, 1983.

The Roving Mind. Buffalo, Prometheus, 1983; Oxford, Oxford Unversity Press, 1987.

Those Amazing Electronic Thinking Machines (for children). New York, Watts, 1983.

X Stands for Unknown (essays). Garden City, New York, Doubleday, 1984; London, Granada, 1985.

Opus 300. Boston, Houghton Mifflin, 1984.

Robots: Where the Machine Ends and Life Begins, with Karen A. Frenkel. New York, Crown, 1985.

The Exploding Suns: The Secrets of the Supernovas. New York, Dutton, 1985.

Asimov's Guide to Halley's Comet. New York, Walker, 1985.

The Subatomic Monster (essays). Garden City, New York, Doubleday, 1985; London, Grafton, 1986.

The Dangers of Intelligence and Other Science Essays. Boston, Houghton Mifflin, 1986.

Future Days: A Nineteenth-Century Vision of the Year 2000. New York, Holt, and London, Virgin, 1986.

Wonderful Worldwide Science Bazaar: Seventy-two Up-to-Date Reports on the State of Everything from Inside the Atom to Outside the Universe. Boston, Houghton Mifflin, 1986.

Bare Bones: Dinosaur (for children), with David Hawcock. New York, Holt, 1986; London, Methuen, 1987.

As Far as the Human Eye Could See (essays). Garden City, New York, Doubleday, 1987; London, Grafton, 1988.

Past, Present, and Future (essays). Buffalo, New York, Prometheus, 1987.

Beginnings: The Story of Origins—of Mankind, Life, the Earth, the Universe. New York, Walker, 1987.

How to Enjoy Writing: A Book of Aid and Comfort, with Janet Asimov. New York, Walker, 1987.

Asimov's Annotated Gilbert and Sullivan. New York, Doubleday, 1988.

Relativity of Wrong: Essays on the Solar System and Beyond. New York, Doubleday, 1988; Oxford, Oxford University Press, 1989.

Library of the Universe (Did Comets Kill the Dinosaurs?; The Asteroids; Ancient Astronomy; Is There Life on Other Planets?; Jupiter, the Spotted Giant; Mercury, the Quick Planet; How Was the Universe Born?; Saturn, the Ringed Beauty; The Space Spotter's Guide; Unidentified Flying Objects; Earth, Our Home Base; The Birth and Death of Stars; Science Fiction, Science Fact; Space Garbage; Astronomy Today; Comets and Meteors, Mythology of the Universe; Pluto, a Double Planet?; Neptune; Piloted Space Flights; Projects in Astronomy; Rockets, Probes, and Satellites; Venus, a Shrouded Mystery; The World's Space Programs; Uranus: The Sideways Planet; Our Milky Way and Other Galaxies; The Earth's Moon; Our Solar System; Mars: Our Mysterious Neighbor; The Sun; Colonizing the Planets and Stars; What Causes Acid Rain?; What's Happening to the Ozone Layer?; Where Does Garbage Can?; Why Are Animals Endangered?; What Is an Eclipse?; Why Does the Moon Change Shape?; Why Are Some Beaches Oily?; Why Are the Rain Forests Vanishing?; Why Are the Whales Vanishing?; Why Does Litter Cause Problems?; Why Is the Air Dirty?; What Is a Shooting Star?; Why Do Stars Twinkle?; Why Do We Have Different Seasons?; Why Do People Come in Different Colors?, with Carrie Dierks; *Why Do Some People Wear Glasses?,* with Carrie Dierks; *Why Do We Need Sleep?,* with Carrie Dierks; *Why Do We Need to Brush Our Teeth?,* with Carrie Dierks; *How Does a Cut Heal?,* with Carrie Dierks; *How Do Airplanes Fly?,* with Elizabeth Kaplan; *How Do Big Ships Float?,* with Elizabeth Kaplan; *What Happens When I Flush the Toilet?,* with Elizabeth Kaplan; *How Does a TV Work?,* with Elizabeth Kaplan; *How Is Paper Made?,* with Elizabeth Kaplan; *The Future in Space,* with Robert Giraud; *The Planet Uranus,* with Francis Reddy). Milwaukee, Wisconsin, Stevens, 57 vols., 1988-94.

The Tyrannosaurus Prescription and 100 Other Essays. Buffalo, New York, Prometheus, 1989.

Asimov's Galaxy: Reflections on Science Fiction. New York, Doubleday, 1989.

Asimov on Science: A Thirty-Year Retrospective. New York, Doubleday, 1989.

Asimov's Chronology of Science and Discovery: How Science Has Shaped the World and How the World has Affected Science from 4,000,000 B.C. to the Present. New York, Harper, 1989.

Think about Space: Where Have We Been and Where Are We Going? (for children), with Frank White. New York, Walker, 1989.

All the Troubles of the World (for children). Mankato, Minnesota, Creative Education, 1989.

Robbie (for children). Mankato, Minnesota, Creative Education, 1989.

Franchise (for children). Mankato, Minnesota, Creative Education, 1989.

Sally (for children). Mankato, Minnesota, Creative Education, 1989.

The Complete Science Fair Handbook: For Teachers and Parents of Students in Grades 4-8, with Anthony D. Fredericks. Glenview, Illinois, Scott Foresman, 1990.

How Did We Find Out about Lasers? New York, Walker, 1990.

How Did We Find Out about Neptune? New York, Walker, 1990.

Secret of the Universe. New York, Doubleday, 1991.

Our Angry Earth, with Frederick Pohl. New York, Tor, 1991.

How Did We Find Out about Pluto? New York, Walker, 1991.

Asimov's Chronology of the World. New York and London, HarperCollins, 1991.

Asimov's Guide to Earth and Space. New York, Dutton, 1991; London, Mandarin, 1992.

Atom: Journey across the Subatomic Cosmos. New York, Dalton, 1991.

Christopher Columbus: Navigator to the New World (for children). Milwaukee, Wisconsin, Gareth Stevens, 1991.

Henry Hudson: Arctic Explorer and North American Adventurer, with Elizabeth Kaplan (for children). Milwaukee, Wisconsin, Gareth Stevens, 1991.

Frontiers: New Discoveries about Man and His Planet, Outer Space, and the Universe. New York, Plume, and London, Mandarin, 1991.

The March of the Millenia: A Key to Looking at History, with Frank White. New York, Walker, 1991.

Asimov Laughs Again: More Than 700 Favorite Jokes, Limericks and Anecdotes. New York, HarperCollins, 1992.

Frontiers II: More Recent Discoveries, with Janet Asimov. New York, Dutton, 1993.

I, Isaac Asimov: A Memoir: New York, Doubleday, 1994.

Yours, Isaac Asimov: A Lifetime of Letters, edited by Stanley Asimov. New York, Doubleday, 1995.

Editor, *The Hugo Winners 1-5.* Garden City, New York, Doubleday, 5 vols., 1962-86; 1 and 3, London, Dobson, 2 vols., 1963-67; 2, London, Sphere, 1973.

Editor, with Groff Conklin, *Fifty Short Fiction Tales.* New York, Collier, 1963.

Editor, *Tomorrow's Children.* Garden City, New York, Doubleday, 1966; London, Futura, 1974.

Editor, *Where Do We Go from Here?* Garden City, New York, Doubleday, 1971; London, Joseph, 1973.

Editor, *Nebula Award Stories Eight.* New York, Harper, and London, Gollancz, 1973.

Editor, *Before the Golden Age: A Science Fiction Anthology of the 1930s.* Garden City, New York, Doubleday, and London, Robson, 1974.

Editor, with Martin H. Greenberg and Joseph D. Olander, *100 Great Science Fiction Short-Short Stories.* Garden City, New York, Doubleday, and London, Robson, 1978.

Editor, with Martin H. Greenberg and Charles G. Waugh, *The Science Fictional Solar System.* New York, Harper, 1979; London, Sidgwick and Jackson, 1980.

Editor, With Martin H. Greenberg and Charles G. Waugh, *The Thirteen Crimes of Science Fiction.* Garden City, New York, Doubleday, 1979.

Editor, with Martin H. Greenberg, *The Great SF Stories 1-21.* New York, DAW, 21 vols., 1979-90.

Editor, with Martin H. Greenberg and Joseph D. Olander, *Microcosmic Tales: 100 Wondrous Science Fiction Short-Short Stories.* New York, Taplinger, 1980.

Editor, with Martin H. Greenberg and Joseph D. Olander, *Space Mail 1.* New York, Fawcett, 1980.

Editor, with Martin H. Greenberg and Joseph D. Olander, *The Future in Question.* New York, Fawcett, 1980.

Editor, with Alice Laurance, *Who Done It?* Boston, Houghton Mifflin, 1980.

Editor, with Martin H. Greenberg and Charles G. Waugh, *The Seven Deadly Sins of Science Fiction.* New York, Fawcett, 1980.

Editor, with Martin H. Greenberg and Joseph D. Olander, *Miniature Mysteries: 100 Malicious Little Mystery Stories.* New York, Taplinger, 1981.

Editor, with Martin H. Greenberg and Charles G. Waugh, *Science Fiction Shorts* series (for children; includes *After the End, Thinking Machines, Travels Through Time, Wild Inventions, Mad Scientists, Mutants, Tomorrow's TV, Earth Invaded, Bug Awful, Children of the Future, The Immortals, Time Warps).* Milwaukee, Raintree, 12 vols., 1981-84.

Editor, *Fantastic Creatures.* New York, Watts, 1981.

Editor, with Charles G. Waugh and Martin H. Greenberg, *The Best Science Fiction [Fantasy, Horror and Supernatural] of the 19th Century.* New York, Beaufort, 3 vols., 1981-83; *Science Fiction,* London, Gollancz, 1983; *Fantasy* and *Horror and Supernatural,* London, Robson, 2 vols., 1985.

Editor, *Asimov's Marvels of Science Fiction.* London, Hale, 1981.

Editor, with Carol-Lynn Rössell Waugh and Martin H. Greenberg, *The Twelve Crimes of Christmas.* New York, Avon, 1981.

Editor, with Charles G. Waugh and Martin H. Greenberg, *The Seven Cardinal Virtues of Science Fiction.* New York, Fawcett, 1981.

Editor, with Martin H. Greenberg and Charles G. Waugh, *TV: 2000.* New York, Fawcett, 1982.

Editor, with Martin H. Greenberg and Charles G. Waugh, *Last Man on Earth.* New York, Fawcett, 1982.

Editor, with Charles G. Waugh and Martin H. Greenberg, *Tantalizing Locked-Room Mysteries.* New York, Walker, 1982.

Editor, with Martin H. Greenberg and Charles G. Waugh, *Space Mail 2.* New York, Fawcett, 1982.

Editor, with J.O. Jeppson, *Laughing Space: Funny Science Fiction Chuckled Over.* Boston, Houghton Mifflin, and London, Robson, 1982.

Editor, with Alice Laurance, *Speculations.* Boston, Houghton Mifflin, 1982.

Editor, with Charles G. Waugh and Martin H. Greenberg, *Science Fiction from A to Z: A Dictionary of the Great Themes of Science Fiction.* Boston, Houghton Mifflin, 1982.

Editor, with Martin H. Greenberg and Charles G. Waugh, *Flying Saucers.* New York, Fawcett, 1982.

Editor, with Martin H. Greenberg and Charles G. Waugh, *Dragon Tales.* New York, Fawcett, 1982.

Editor, *Asimov's Worlds of Science Fiction.* London, Hale, 1982.

Editor, with Martin H. Greenberg and Charles G. Waugh, *Hallucination Orbit: Psychology in Science Fiction.* New York, Farrar Straus, 1983.

Editor, with Martin H. Greenberg, *Magical Worlds of Fantasy* series (*Wizards, Witches*). New York, Signet, 2 vols., 1983-84; as *Magical Worlds of Fantasy: Witches and Wizards,* New York, Bonanza, 1 vol., 1985.

Editor, with Martin H. Greenberg and Charles G. Waugh, *Caught in the Organ Draft: Biology in Science Fiction.* New York, Farrar Straus, 1983.

Editor, *The Big Apple Mysteries.* New York, Avon, 1983.

Editor, with George R.R. Martin and Martin H. Greenberg, *The Science Fiction Weight-Loss Book.* New York, Crown, 1983.

Editor, with Martin H. Greenberg and Charles G. Waugh, *Starships.* New York, Ballantine, 1983.

Editor, *Asimov's Wonders of the World.* London, Hale, 1983.

Editor, with George Zebrowski and Martin H. Greenberg, *Creations: The Quest for Origins in Story and Science.* New York, Crown, 1983; London, Harrap, 1984.

Editor, with Martin H. Greenberg and Charles G. Waugh, *Computer Crimes and Capers.* Chicago, Academy, 1983; London, Viking, 1985.

Editor, with Patricia S. Warrick and Martin H. Greenberg, *Machines That Think: The Best Science Fiction Stories about Robots and Computers.* New York, Holt Rinehart, and London, Allen Lane, 1984; as *War with the Robots,* New York, Wings, 1992.

Editor, with Terry Carr and Martin H. Greenberg, *100 Great Fantasy Short Short Stories.* Garden City, New York, Doubleday, and London, Robson, 1984.

Editor, with Charles G. Waugh and Martin H. Greenberg, *The Best Science Fiction Firsts.* New York, Beaufort, 1984; London, Robson, 1985.

Editor, with others, *Murder on the Menu.* New York, Avon, 1984.

Editor, with Martin H. Greenberg and Charles G. Waugh, *Sherlock Holmes through Time and Space.* New York, Bluejay, 1984; London, Severn House, 1985.

Editor, *Living in the Future.* New York, Beaufort, 1984.
Editor, with Martin H. Greenberg, *Isaac Asimov's Wonderful World of Science Fiction 2: The Science Fictional Olympics.* New York, Signet, 1984.
Editor, with Martin H. Greenberg and Charles G. Waugh, *Young Mutants, Extraterrestrials, Ghosts, Monsters, Star Travelers, Witches and Warlocks* (for children). New York, Harper, 6 vols., 1984-87.
Editor, with Martin H. Greenberg, *Election Day 2084: Stories about the Politics of the Future.* Buffalo, Prometheus, 1984.
Editor, with Martin H. Greenberg and Charles G. Waugh, *Baker's Dozen: 13 Short Science Fiction Novels.* New York, Bonanza, 1984; as *The Mammoth Book of Short Science Fiction Novels,* London, Robinson, 1986.
Editor, with Martin H. Greenberg and Charles G. Waugh, *Baker's Dozen: 13 Short Fantasy Novels.* New York, Greenwich House, 1984; as *The Mammoth Book of Short Fantasy Novels,* London, Robinson, 1986.
Editor, with Martin H. Greenberg and Charles G. Waugh, *Great Science Fiction Stories by the World's Great Scientists.* New York, Fine, 1985.
Editor, with Martin H. Greenberg and Charles G. Waugh, *Amazing Stories: 60 Years of the Best Science Fiction.* Lake Geneva, Wisconsin, TRS, 1985.
Editor, with Martin H. Greenberg and Charles G. Waugh, *Giants.* New York, Signet, 1985.
Editor, *Science Fiction Masterpieces.* New York, Galahad, 1986.
Editor, with Martin H. Greenberg and Charles G. Waugh, *Comets.* New York, Signet, 1986.
Editor, with Martin H. Greenberg and Charles G. Waugh, *Mythical Beasties.* New York, Signet, 1986; as *Mythic Beasts,* London, Robinson, 1988.
Editor, with Carol-Lynn Rössell Waugh and Martin H. Greenberg, *Hound Dunnit.* New York, Carroll and Graf, 1987; London, Robson, 1988.
Editor, with Martin H. Greenberg and Charles G. Waugh, *Cosmic Knights.* London, Robinson, 1987.
Editor, with Martin H. Greenberg and Charles G. Waugh, *The Best Crime Stories of the 19th Century.* New York, Dember, 1988; London, Robson, 1989.
Editor, with Jason A. Shulman, *Book of Science and Nature Quotations.* New York, Weidenfeld and Nicolson, 1988.
Editor, with Martin H. Greenberg and Charles G. Waugh, *Ghosts.* London, Collins, 1988.
Editor, with Martin H. Greenberg and Charles G. Waugh, *The Best Detective Stories of the 19th Century.* New York, Dember, 1988.
Editor, with Martin H. Greenberg and Charles G. Waugh, *The Mammoth Book of Classic Science Fiction: Short Novels of the 1930s.* New York, Carroll and Graf, and London, Robinson, 1988.
Editor, with Martin H. Greenberg and Charles H. Waugh, *Great Tales of Classic Science Fiction.* New York, Galahad, 1988.
Editor, with Martin H. Greenberg and Charles G. Waugh, *Monsters.* New York, Signet, 1988; London, Robinson, 1989.
Editor, with Martin H. Greenberg and Charles G. Waugh, *The Mammoth Book of Golden Age Science Fiction: Short Novels of the 1940s.* New York, Carroll and Graf, and London, Robinson, 1989.
Editor, with Martin H. Greenberg and Charles G. Waugh, *Curses.* New York, Signet, 1989.
Editor, with Martin H. Greenberg and Charles G. Waugh, *Tales of the Occult.* Buffalo, New York, Prometheus, 1989.
Editor, with Martin H. Greenberg and Charles G. Waugh, *Robots.* London, Robinson, 1989.
Editor, *The New Hugo Winners.* New York, Wynwood Press, 1989.
Editor, with Martin H. Greenberg and Charles G. Waugh, *The Mammoth Book of Vintage Science Fiction: Short Novels of the 1950s.* New York, Carroll and Graf, and London, Robinson, 1990.
Editor, with Martin H. Greenberg, *Cosmic Critiques: How and Why Ten Science Fiction Stories Work.* Writer's Digest, Cincinnati, Ohio, 1990.
Editor, with Martin H. Greenberg and Charles G. Waugh, *The Mammoth Book of New World Science Fiction: Short Novels of the 1960s.* London, Robinson, and New York, Carroll and Graf, 1991.
Editor, with Martin H. Greenberg and Charles G. Waugh, *The Mammoth Book of Fantastic Science Fiction: Short Novels of the 1970s.* London, Robinson, and New York, Carroll and Graf, 1992.
Editor, with Martin H. Greenberg and Charles G. Waugh, *The Mammoth Book of Modern Science Fiction: Short Novels of the 1980s.* London, Robinson, and New York, Carroll and Graf, 1993.

*

Bibliography: *Isaac Asimov: A Checklist of Works Published in the United States March 1939-May 1972* by Marjorie M. Miller, Kent, Ohio, Kent State University Press, 1972; in *In Joy Still Felt,* 1980.

Manuscript Collection: Mugar Memorial Library, Boston University.

Critical Studies: *Asimov Analyzed* by Neil Goble, Baltimore, Mirage Press, 1972; *The Science Fiction of Isaac Asimov* by Joseph F. Patrouch, Jr., Garden City, New York, Doubleday, 1974, London, Panther, 1976; *Isaac Asimov* edited by Joseph D. Olander and Martin H. Greenberg, New York, Taplinger, and Edinburgh, Harris, 1977; *Asimov: The Foundations of His Science Fiction* by George Edgar Slusser, San Bernardino, California, Borgo Press, 1980; *Isaac Asimov: The Foundations of Science Fiction* by James Gunn, New York and Oxford, Oxford University Press, 1982; *Isaac Asimov* by Jean Fielder and Jim Mele, New York, Ungar, 1982.

* * *

Isaac Asimov was almost unbelievably prolific in both the number of books he produced and the variety of genres he tackled. He churned out mysteries, young-adult and adult science fiction, young-adult and adult nonfiction, histories, and books of limericks. He also edited a number of anthologies. However, he is best remembered as a master of science fiction, and he more than any other writer popularized science for a vast market. With unshakable faith in science and technology, Asimov, with objectivity and humanity, made comprehensible the cosmological questions that newspaper accounts never seemed to clarify. With the addition of his irrepressible earthy wit, he could make science wondrous and never tedious.

His most famous and certainly most influential book was *I, Ro-*

bot (1950), which laid down his Three Laws of Robotics and changed the nature of robot stories forever. This book introduced Susan Calvin, a robot psychologist, who appeared in many of the robot stories and was one of his best-drawn and most interesting characters. The Three Laws allowed Asimov to engage in puzzles and their clever solutions by placing robots in situations that involved the interplay among the Three Laws. *The Complete Robot* (1982) collected all 31 of his robot tales from 1939 to 1976. Every variety of robot can be seen here, including Multivac the supercomputer, various robot animals, automobiles, walking bombs, immobile robots, and humanoid robots.

Asimov's fascination with puzzles is also evident in the gimmicky Black Widow mysteries, wherein the Widowers discuss crime puzzles over dinner. The mysteries usually involve mathematical or verbal play with some clever twists.

The Caves of Steel (1954), *The Naked Sun* (1957), and *The Robots of Dawn* (1983) combined the detective genre with science fiction. Earth detective Elijah Baley is partnered with a humaniform robot R. Daneel Olivaw. Together they work to solve a murder in each novel. An important irony in these novels is that although the science of robotics had been developed on Earth, it is only on the Outer Worlds inhabited by the Spacers where robotics has flourished with an economy and society heavily dependent on robots. A great hostility towards and restrictions on robots, in contrast, exists on Earth. *Robots and Empire* (1985) allowed Asimov to link his robot series with his other great series dealing with the Galactic Empire and the Foundation.

The Foundation Trilogy consists of *Foundation* (1951), *Foundation and Empire* (1952), and *Second Foundation* (1953). These are not in reality novels but collections of novellas. This series may be the most famous of the so-called hard-core science fiction. In 1966 it was awarded a Hugo and praised as "the greatest all-time science fiction series." The series concerns the imminent collapse of the Galactic Empire which has ruled 25 million planets inhabited by humans. Hari Seldon, through the use of psychohistory which predicts the future, has foreseen the collapse and the dark ages that will follow. He goes about setting up two foundations, one based on physical science and a second on psychology, to keep the dark ages to a minimum. After three decades Asimov continued the series with *Foundation's Edge* (1982). The installment was extremely well-received by critics and praised as stylistically more expansive and mature with a charming cast and a good sense of humor. He continued with *Foundation and Earth* (1987) and *Prelude to Foundation* (1988), both prequels to the series.

Asimov may have been an atrocious literary annotator, but since he succeeded in practically every other area this can be forgiven. He was a science fiction author with a distinctive gift and intelligence, the most readable scientific popularizer of his day, and an incurable humorist. Out of an unbelievable number of books it is truly amazing how many are excellent.

—Jennifer G. Coman

ATWOOD, Margaret (Eleanor)

Nationality: Canadian. **Born:** Ottawa, Ontario, 18 November 1939. **Education:** Victoria College, University of Toronto, 1957-61, B.A. 1961; Radcliffe College, Cambridge, Massachusetts, A.M. 1962; Harvard University, Cambridge, Massachusetts 1962-63, 1965-67. **Family:** Married; one daughter. **Career:** Lecturer in English, University of British Columbia, Vancouver, 1964-65; instructor in English, Sir George Williams University, Montreal, 1967-68; teacher of creative writing, University of Alberta, Edmonton, 1969-70; assistant professor of English, York University, Toronto, 1971-72. Editor and member of board of directors, House of Anansi Press, Toronto, 1971-73. Writer-in-residence, University of Toronto, 1972-73, University of Alabama, Tuscaloosa, 1985, Macquarie University, North Ryde, New South Wales, 1987, and Trinity University, San Antonio, Texas, 1989; Berg Visiting Professor of English, New York University, 1986. President, Writers Union of Canada, 1981-82, and PEN Canadian Centre, 1984-86. **Awards:** E.J. Pratt medal, 1961; President's medal, University of Western Ontario, 1965; Governor-General's award, 1966, 1986; Centennial Commission prize, 1967; Union League Civic and Arts Foundation prize, 1969, and Bess Hogkin prize, 1974 (*Poetry,* Chicago); City of Toronto award, 1976, 1989; St. Lawrence award, 1978; Radcliffe medal, 1980; Molson award, 1981; Guggenheim fellowship, 1981; Welsh Arts Council International Writers prize, 1982; Ida Nudel Humanitarian award, 1986; Toronto Arts award, 1986; Los Angeles *Times* Book award, 1986; Arthur C. Clarke Science-Fiction award, for novel, 1987; Humanist of the Year award, 1987; National Magazine award, for journalism, 1988; Harvard University Centennial medal, 1990; Trillium award, for *Wilderness Tips,* 1992, for *The Robber Bride,* 1994; Commonwealth Writer's prize, 1994, Sunday Times award for literary excellence, 1994, both for *The Robber Bride.* Chevalier dans L'Ordre des arts et des lettres, 1994. D.Litt.: Trent University, Peterborough, Ontario, 1973; Concordia University, Montreal, 1980; Smith College, Northampton, Massachusetts, 1982; University of Toronto, 1983; Mount Holyoke College, South Hadley, Massachusetts, 1985; University of Waterloo, Ontario, 1985; University of Guelph, Ontario, 1985; Victoria College, 1987; University of Leeds, 1994; LL.D.: Queen's University, Kingston, Ontario, 1974. Companion, Order of Canada, 1981. Fellow, Royal Society of Canada, 1987; Honorary Member, American Academy of Arts and Sciences, 1988. **Agent:** Phoebe Larmore, 228 Main Street, Venice, California 90291, U.S.A. **Address:** c/o Oxford University Press, 70 Wynford Drive, Don Mills, Ontario M3C 1J9, Canada.

PUBLICATIONS

Novels

The Edible Woman. Toronto, McClelland and Stewart, and London, Deutsch, 1969; Boston, Little Brown, 1970.

Surfacing. Toronto, McClelland and Stewart, 1972; London, Deutsch, and New York, Simon and Schuster, 1973.

Lady Oracle. Toronto, McClelland and Stewart, and New York, Simon and Schuster, 1976; London, Deutsch, 1977.

Life Before Man. Toronto, McClelland and Stewart, 1979; New York, Simon and Schuster, and London, Cape, 1980.

Bodily Harm. Toronto, McClelland and Stewart, 1981; New York, Simon and Schuster, and London, Cape, 1982.

The Handmaid's Tale. Toronto, McClelland and Stewart, 1985; Boston, Houghton Mifflin, and London, Cape, 1986.

Cat's Eye. Toronto, McClelland and Stewart, 1988; New York, Doubleday, and London, Bloomsbury, 1989.

The Robber Bride. Toronto, McClelland and Stewart, New York, Doubleday, and London, Bloomsbury, 1993.

Short Stories

Dancing Girls and Other Stories. Toronto, McClelland and Stewart, 1977; New York, Simon and Schuster, and London, Cape, 1982.
Encounters with the Element Man. Concord, New Hampshire, Ewert, 1982.
Murder in the Dark: Short Fictions and Prose Poems. Toronto, Coach House Press, 1983; London, Cape, 1984.
Bluebeard's Egg and Other Stories. Toronto, McClelland and Stewart, 1983; Boston, Houghton Mifflin, 1986; London, Cape, 1987.
Unearthing Suite. Toronto, Grand Union Press, 1983.
Hurricane Hazel and Other Stories. Helsinki, Eurographica, 1986.
Wilderness Tips. Toronto, McClelland and Stewart, New York, Doubleday, and London, Bloomsbury, 1991.
Good Bones. Toronto, Coach House Press, 1992; London, Bloomsbury, 1993; New York, Doubleday, 1994.

Plays

Radio Plays: *The Trumpets of Summer,* 1964.

Television Plays: *The Servant Girl,* 1974; *Snowbird,* 1981; *Heaven on Earth,* with Peter Pearson, 1986.

Poetry

Double Persephone. Toronto, Hawskhead Press, 1961.
The Circle Game (single poem). Bloomfield Hills, Michigan, Cranbrook Academy of Art, 1964.
Talismans for Children. Bloomfield Hills, Michigan, Cranbrook Academy of Art, 1965.
Kaleidoscopes: Baroque. Bloomfield Hills, Michigan, Cranbrook Academy of Art, 1965.
Speeches for Doctor Frankenstein. Bloomfield Hills, Michigan, Cranbrook Academy of Art, 1966.
The Circle Game (collection). Toronto, Contact Press, 1966.
Expeditions. Bloomfield Hills, Michigan, Cranbrook Academy of Art, 1966.
The Animals in That County. Toronto, Oxford University Press, 1968; Boston, Little Brown, 1969.
Who Was in the Garden. Santa Barbara, California, Unicorn, 1969.
The Journals of Susanna Moodie. Toronto, Oxford University Press, 1970.
Oratorio for Sasquatch, Man and Two Androids: Poems for Voices. Toronto, Canadian Broadcasting Corporation, 1970.
Procedures for Underground. Toronto, Oxford University Press, and Boston, Little Brown, 1970.
Power Politics. Toronto, Anansi, 1971; New York, Harper, 1973.
You Are Happy. Toronto, Oxford University Press, and New York, Harper, 1974.
Selected Poems. Toronto, Oxford University Press, 1976; New York, Simon and Schuster, 1978.
Marsh, Hawk. Toronto, Dreadnaught, 1977.
Two-Headed Poems. Toronto, Oxford University Press, 1978; New York, Simon and Schuster, 1981.
True Stories. Toronto, Oxford University Press, 1981; New York, Simon and Schuster, and London, Cape, 1982.
Notes Towards a Poem That Can Never Be Written. Toronto, Salamander Press, 1981.
Snake Poems. Toronto, Salamander Press, 1983.
Interlunar. Toronto, Oxford University Press, 1984; London, Cape, 1988.
Selected Poems 2: Poems Selected and New 1976-1986. Toronto, Oxford University Press, 1986; Boston, Houghton Mifflin, 1987.
Selected Poems 1966-1984. Toronto, Oxford University Press, 1990.
Poems 1965-1975. London, Virago Press, 1991.
Morning in the Burned House. Toronto, McClelland and Stewart, Boston, Houghton Mifflin, and London, Virago, 1995.

Other (for children)

Up in the Tree. Toronto, McClelland and Stewart, 1978.
Anna's Pet, with Joyce Barkhouse. Toronto, Lorimer, 1980.
For the Birds. Toronto, Douglas and McIntyre, 1990.
Princess Prunella and the Purple Peanut. London, Workman, 1995.

Other

Survival: A Thematic Guide to Canadian Literature. Toronto, Anansi, 1972.
Days of the Rebels 1815-1840. Toronto, Natural Science of Canada, 1977.
Second Words: Selected Critical Prose. Toronto, Anansi, 1982; Boston, Beacon Press, 1984.
Margaret Atwood: Conversations, edited by Earl G. Ingersoll. Princeton, New Jersey, Ontario Review Press, 1990.
Strange Things: The Malevolent North in Canadian Literature. New York and London, Oxford University Press, 1996.

Editor, *The Canlit Food Book: From Pen to Palate—A Collection of Tasty Literary Fare.* Toronto, Totem, 1987.
Editor, *Barbed Lyres.* Toronto, Key Porter, 1990.

*

Film Adaptations: *The Handmaid's Tale,* 1990.

Bibliography: "Margaret Atwood: An Annotated Bibliography" (prose and poetry) by Alan J. Horne, in *The Annotated Bibliography of Canada's Major Authors 1-2* edited by Robert Lecker and Jack David, Downsview, Ontario, ECW Press, 2 vols., 1979-80.

Manuscript Collection: Fisher Library, University of Toronto.

Critical Studies: *Margaret Atwood: A Symposium* edited by Linda Sandler, Victoria, British Columbia, University of Victoria, 1977; *A Violent Duality* by Sherrill E. Grace, Montreal, Véhicule Press, 1979, and *Margaret Atwood: Language, Text, and System* edited by Grace and Lorraine Weir, Vancouver, University of British Columbia Press, 1983; *The Art of Margaret Atwood: Essays in Criticism* edited by Arnold E. Davidson and Cathy N. Davidson, Toronto, Anansi, 1981; *Margaret Atwood* by Jerome H. Rosenberg, Boston, Twayne, 1984; *Margaret Atwood: A Feminist Poetics* by Frank Davey, Vancouver, Talonbooks, 1984; *Margaret Atwood* by

Barbara Hill Rigney, London, Macmillan, 1987; *Margaret Atwood: Reflection and Reality* by Beatrice Mendez-Egle, Edinburg, Texas, Pan American University, 1987; *Critical Essays on Margaret Atwood* edited by Judith McCombs, Boston, Hall, 1988; *Margaret Atwood: Vision and Forms* edited by Kathryn van Spanckeren and Jan Garden Castro, Carbondale, Southern Illinois University Press, 1988.

* * *

Margaret Eleanor Atwood is one of the most prominent writers in Canada. Born November 18, 1939 in Ottawa, Ontario, she spent many summers in the northern Ontario and Quebec bush where her father, Dr. Carl Edmund Atwood, an entomologist, conducted his research. Atwood has won numerous awards for her poetry and her fiction, including the Governor General's award for *The Circle Game* (1966) and *The Handmaid's Tale* (1985). Her writing has received critical acclaim in Canada, and has been translated into Danish, Finnish, French, German, Japanese, Italian, Spanish, Swedish, Turkish and several other languages.

Atwood's prodigious corpus includes poetry, novels, short stories, literary criticism, and children's literature. Her first volume of poetry, *Double Persephone* (1961), won the E.J. Pratt medal in 1961. Fellow Canadian poet, Dennis Cooley, has commented on the "hurtful connections between people and their environment" in Atwood's *The Circle Game* (1966), *The Animals in That Country* (1968), *Procedures for Underground* (1970), *The Journals of Susanna Moodie* (1970) and *Power Politics* (1971). The poetic speakers in the works that follow this period [*You Are Happy* (1974), *Two-Headed Poems* (1978), *True Stories* (1981), *Interlunar* (1984)] are generally more confident and less ironic. *Morning in the Burned House* (1995) is Atwood's most recent collection of new poems. It incorporates classical as well as popular history and myth.

Despite the powerful nature of her poetry, Atwood is probably best known for her fiction, which foregrounds feminine experience. Her first novel, *The Edible Woman* (1969), portrays a woman aware of rampant consumerism in her society. In *Surfacing* (1972), a nameless female narrator searches for her father in the Canadian wilderness. The novel explores the fusion between woman and nature. *Lady Oracle* (1976), Atwood's third novel, depicts a rather romantic heroine by the name of Joan Foster. She has been called Atwood's funniest and messiest character, because she cannot easily be pinned down. *Life Before Man* (1979) lacks the humorous dimension of *Lady Oracle* and is not typical of Atwood's other texts. It has also been criticized for the weak plot and the dull, flat world it presents. Despite these shortcomings, *Life Before Man* has enjoyed popular success. *Bodily Harm* (1981) offers a unified plot filled with suspense as well as a Caribbean island setting.

Novels published within the last decade reflect Atwood's continued interest in female characters and the construction of story and art. In *The Handmaid's Tale* (1985), for example, Atwood creates a futuristic, religious dystopia where women have virtually no rights. The text includes a story told by a handmaid whose sole function is that of a reproductive vessel. An interesting postscript highlights the self-reflexive or meta-textual elements of texts. *Cat's Eye* (1988) focuses on the childhood, youth, and adulthood of a woman artist who attends an exhibition of her paintings and remembers her past. *The Robber Bride* (1993) explores tensions between three female characters and a manipulative woman by the name of Zenia, described as "the turbulent center of her own never-ending saga."

In addition to her poetry and novels, Atwood has written a variety of other texts. Her short stories include "Dancing Girls" (1977), "Murder in the Dark" (1983), "Bluebeard's Egg" (1983), and "Wilderness Tips" (1991). *Good Bones* (1992) consists of short sketches and prose poems that demonstrate Atwood's humor and mental gymnastics as she experiments with forms other than conventional lyric poetry, shorts stories, and novels. Atwood has also written children's literature, including *Princess Prunella and the Purple Peanut* (1995). In this text, most of the words either begin with or contain a P. *The CanLit Foodbook* (1987), an alternative cookbook, is another of the author's less "serious" texts.

Although Atwood makes a point of distinguishing herself from literary scholars, she has edited anthologies and flirted with academia by writing literary criticism and lecturing at universities. *Survival: A Thematic Guide to Canadian Literature* (1972) focuses on images of victims in Canadian literature. She also analyzes Canadian literature in *Strange Things: the Malevolent North in Canadian Literature* (1995), a book of four essays originally presented as the Clarendon Lectures at Oxford University (England) in 1991. In these essays she discusses the Franklin expedition, the Grey Owl phenomenon of whites turned native, the Wendigo (a giant cannibalistic Algonquin Indian monster), and women writing about the North.

A series of conversations with Atwood can be found in the documentary film *Margaret Atwood: Once in August* (1984), where her inscrutable, compelling yet cutting presence torments the interviewer. She has often been accused of contrariness in her discussions with critics; however, interviewers who insist on explicit parallels between her work and her life are largely to blame for the author's irritation. Numerous interviews with Atwood reveal that she is constantly reinventing herself. She has even entered the realm of cyberspace with the creation of her own home page on the world wide web.

—Karin E. Beeler

AUEL, Jean M(arie)

Nationality: American. **Born:** 18 February 1936, in Chicago, Illinois. **Education:** Attended Portland State University; University of Portland, M.B.A., 1976. **Family:** Married Ray B. Auel, 19 March 1954; children: RaeAnn Marie, Karen Jean, Lenore Jerica, Kendall Poul, Marshall Philip. **Career:** Tektronix, Inc., Beaverton, Ore., clerk, 1965-66, circuit board designer, 1966-73, technical writer, 1973-74, credit manager, 1974-76; writer. **Awards:** Award for Excellence in Writing, Pacific Northwest Booksellers Association, 1980, Vicki Penziner Matson Award, Friends of Literature, 1981, and nomination for best first novel, American Book Awards, 1981, all for *The Clan of the Cave Bear;* Scandinavian Kaleidoscope of Art and Life award, 1982; Golden Plate award, American Academy of Achievement, 1986; Silver Trowel Award, Sacramento Archeology Society, 1990; National Zoo Award, Smithsonian Institution, 1990; Waldo award from Waldenbooks, and Persie Award from WIN, both 1990, both for *Plains of Passage*; honorary degrees from University of Portland, 1983, University of Maine, 1985, and Mt. Vernon College, 1985. **Member:**

Authors Guild, Authors League of America, National Women's Forum. **Agent:** Jean V. Naggar Literary Agency. **Address:** c/o Jean V. Naggar Literary Agency, 336 East 73rd St., New York, New York 10021, U.S.A.

PUBLICATIONS

Novels (series: Earth's Children in all titles)

The Clan of the Cave Bear. Crown, 1980.
The Valley of Horses. Crown, 1982.
The Mammoth Hunters. Crown, 1985.
The Plains of Passage. Crown, 1990.

*

Film Adaptation: *The Clan of the Cave Bear,* 1986.

* * *

Novelist Jean Auel is known for her depictions of early human history in her "Earth's Children" series. Praised for their authenticity, the four novels challenge conventional theories about Neanderthal and Cro-Magnon existence and place their female protagonist, Ayla, at the center of conflicts between both tribes of prehistoric man.

After years of being a "closet" poet, Auel was struck by what she believed was the idea for a short story: a young woman living amongst people who are different from her. The idea blossomed into a 450,000-word novel, *The Clan of the Cave Bear* (1980), which won an American Book Award nomination for best first novel and became a bestseller. Set in the Ukraine around 30,000 B.C. (the Ice Age), the story focuses on Ayla, a five-year-old Cro-Magnon girl who becomes an orphan after an earthquake kills her parents. Adopted by a tribe of Neanderthals, Ayla displays an intelligence and adaptability which allows her to outshine the Neanderthal tribe members, who have reached an evolutionary dead end. As Auel describes them, they possess excellent memories and have several advanced rituals, but their foresight and analytical capacity is almost nonexistent. When a Neanderthal child falls into a stream, for example, the other Neanderthals simply watch it sweep away to be drowned. They are stunned when Ayla dives into the water to save it, having never conceived of this possibility. The differences between Ayla and her tribe come to a head when Broud, the next leader of the Neanderthals, grows insecure and jealous of the tall, blond Ayla—the Neanderthals are short and bow-legged—and initiates a grim showdown.

Some critics, including Barbara Mertz of *Book World,* praised Auel for her writing style but criticized *The Clan of the Cave Bear* for its stock characters and plot: "*Bear* is a prehistoric soap opera—'cave opera' would be an appropriate term. Put the heroine in a bustle instead of a bearskin and she could walk right into one of the 'historical romances' crowding the bookshelves in drugstores and supermarkets." Other critics found Ayla to be a character worthy of Auel's sweeping and ambitious work. As Thomas Hopkins writes in *Maclean's,* "A sort of Cro-Magnon Katharine Hepburn, [Ayla] stoically endures innumerable beatings, a rape and ritual banishment at the hands of oafish and inferior males before finally earning the honorific: The Woman Who Hunts. In Ayla, Auel has an engine both familiar and intriguingly alien enough to drive her next five books."

The Valley of Horses (1982) continues Ayla's epic saga and introduces her mate Jondalar, a six-foot-six-inch Cro-Magnon whose injured leg is healed by Ayla's ministrations. Jondalar and Ayla have been described as archetypal humans, far too superior to those around them to maintain a high level of credibility for long. As Susan Isaacs describes them in *The New York Times Book Review,* "Jondalar is the ultimate civilized Cro-Magnon, a well-muscled, artistic, spear-throwing Cary Grant. And it is Ayla, and Ayla alone, who invents oral sex, horseback riding, a new technique for making fire and a better way of dragging the kill back to the cave." Nevertheless, Isaacs says that *The Valley of Horses* "is great fun to read." Hopkins agrees, adding, "Auel's pedagogy is . . . successful because it illuminates a plausible if melodramatic ancestral world oddly comforting in its richness and diversity."

The Plains of Passage (1990) continues the "Earth's Children" cycle with more adventures of Jondalar and Ayla as they trek through prehistoric Europe. Their encounters with the Neanderthal Clan are reminiscent of *The Clan of the Cave Bear* and offer much in the same way of adventure and meticulous research. While her research has been called into question by both reviewers and anthropologists, Auel's descriptions of prehistoric life have earned praise for their vision of a time period that is little-known and was rarely investigated in fiction before Auel's series. John R. Alden of the *Detroit News* points out this strength and sees Auel's works as possessing a longevity based on its vivid depictions of prehistoric life. Writing about *The Mammoth Hunters* (1985), Alden said that the novel works because its prehistoric characters are presented as "human beings, with the same kinds of emotional conflicts we contemporary earthlings have today. . . .If hunting a herd of mammoth at the base of a mile-high wall of ice doesn't provoke your imagination, I don't know what will." Despite Auel's occasionally heavy-handed prose, readers with a taste for adventure and speculative fiction should enjoy Auel's works.

—Christopher Swann

AXTON, David. *See* **KOONTZ, Dean R(ay).**

B

BACH, Richard (David)

Nationality: American. **Born:** Oak Park, Illinois, 23 June 1936; direct descendant of Johann Sebastian Bach. **Education:** One year at California State University, Long Beach. **Military Service:** United States Air Force, 1956-59, 1961-62: Captain. **Family:** Married 1) Betty Jeanne Franks in 1957 (divorced 1971), three sons and three daughters; 2) Leslie Parrish in 1977. **Career:** Associate editor, West Coast editor, *Flying* magazine, 1961-64; charter pilot, flight instructor, aviation mechanic and barnstormer in Iowa and the American Midwest, 1965-70. **Agent:** Kenneth Littauer, Littauer & Wilkinson, 500 Fifth Avenue, New York, New York 10036, U.S.A.

Publications

Novels

Jonathan Livingston Seagull: A Story, photographs by Russell Munson. New York, Macmillan, 1970; London, Turnstone Press, 1972.
Illusions: The Adventures of a Reluctant Messiah. New York, Delacorte, and London, Heinemann, 1977.
There's No Such Place as Far Away, illustrated by Ronald Wagen. New York, Delacorte, 1979; London, Granada, 1980.
The Bridge Across Forever: A Lovestory (published as non-fiction). New York, Morrow, 1984.
One: A Novel. New York, Morrow, 1988.
Running from Safety: An Adventure of the Spirit. New York, Morrow, 1995.

Short Stories

A Gift of Wings (stories and essays), illustrated by K. O. Eckland. New York, Delacorte, 1974.

Other

Stranger to the Ground. New York, Harper and Row, 1963; London, Cassell, 1964.
Biplane. New York, Harper and Row, 1966; London, Collier Macmillan, 1984.
Nothing by Chance: A Gypsy Pilot's Adventures in Modern America, photographs by Paul E. Hansen. New York, Harper and Row, 1969; London, Collier Macmillan, 1984.

*

Film Adaptation: *Jonathan Livingston Seagull,* 1973.

Biography: *Above the Clouds: A Reunion of Father and Son* (includes letters and afterword by Bach), by Jonathan Bach. New York: Morrow, 1993.

* * *

Richard Bach uses his experiences as a pilot for the basis of his Zen-like novels and travel memoirs. In all of his writing Bach manages to combine beautiful and vivid details of either his own or a character's experiences with his optimistic philosophical outlook.

Stranger to the Ground (1963) and *Biplane* (1966) are both accounts of his flying. They caused critics to compare his writing ability with that of St. Exupery and Ernest K. Gann. *Stranger to the Ground* describes Bach's single flight of a F-64 Thunderstreak from Wetherafield, England, to Chaumount, France. The passage of time is suspended by Bach's rich description of his thoughts and the meticulous details of flying an airplane. The flight described in *Biplane* is a bit more exciting. For this memoir, Bach decided to fly a 1929 Detroit-Ryan biplane across the United States from Lumberton, North Carolina, to Los Angeles. Despite the inevitable sense of adventure the reader encounters as Bach flies an antiquated aircraft across America, it is the philosophical digressions inspired by the changes in landscape that most interest the reader.

Bach's most successful work came with the publication of *Jonathan Livingston Seagull* (1970). The novel is a parable about a young seagull who decides to leave his flock (which is concerned only with eating fish) to discover how high and fast he can really fly. Bach stated that the only message in the novel is the idea that one should discover a dream and pursue it at all costs. Still, popular audiences have turned to the work for other inspiration; passages from the book have been used at momentous occasions of all sorts, such as weddings, funerals, and graduations. The simple story also inspired many different interpretations; some Buddhists felt the story was about the different levels attained through an individual's quest for perfection, for example, while some Catholic priests felt the work dealt with the sin of pride. Despite the confusion the simple story created, most critics and readers enjoyed the book. Yet the popularity eventually annoyed Bach.

Critics and readers received *Illusions: Adventure of a Reluctant Messiah* (1977) with less enthusiasm than his previous novel. One gets the feeling Bach wrote the novel as a reaction against the extreme popularity of *Jonathan Livingston Seagull.* The story deals with Bach's imagined encounter with Shimode, a former self-proclaimed messiah, who decides to give up being a religious leader and make a living selling biplane rides. After Bach meets him, the author decides to become a self-proclaimed messiah when he realizes that he is responsible for his own happiness.

Bach continued the simple format of *Jonathan Livingston Seagull* with *There's No Such Place as Far Away* (1979). The book is a simple story of Bach's imaginary encounters with a hummingbird, owl, eagle, hawk, and seagull on his way to a child's birthday party. The light philosophy and illustrations give the book a juvenile tone.

His most recent novels, *One* (1988) and *Running From Safety: An Adventure of the Spirit* (1995), both deal with the same simple philosophy of his earlier works. Both novels use flashbacks as the springboard for Bach's philosophical assertions. In *One,* the author and his wife, Leslie, are transported into a different world in which they become 16-year-olds again. Each becomes disillusioned until Bach discovers that the only way to achieve happiness is to abandon organized religion and look for truth. Likewise, in *Running from Safety: An Adventure of the Spirit,* Bach is transformed into a nine-year-old child, Dickie. Dickie represents the author's "inner child" and is Bach's key to understanding his current problems. Like Bach's other works, critics were split in their assessment of *Running from Safety,* considering the message and style either dull or uplifting.

Despite the sometimes over-simplistic nature of Bach's works and the triteness of his "lite" philosophy, the sincerity of his writing can make for enjoyable reading.

—Chris Godat

BACHMAN, Richard. *See* **KING, Stephen.**

BAKER, Nicholson

Nationality: American. **Born:** New York, 7 January 1957. **Education:** Eastman School of Music, 1974-75; Haverford College, B.A. 1980. **Family:** Married Margaret Bretano in 1985; one daughter. **Career:** Has held various jobs, including oil analyst, word processor, and technical writer. **Agent:** Melanie Jackson Agency, 250 West 57th St., Suite 1119, New York, New York 10107, U.S.A.

Publications

Novels

The Mezzanine. New York, Weidenfeld and Nicholson, 1988.
Room Temperature. New York, Grove Weidenfeld, and London, Granta, 1990.
Vox. New York, Random House, 1992; London, Puls, 1993.
The Fermata. New York, Random House, 1994; London, Chatto and Windus, 1995.

Other

U and I: A True Story. New York, Random House, and London, Granta, 1991.
Size of Thoughts. London, Chatto and Windus, 1995.

* * *

Few writers would devote several paragraphs puzzling over the gradual disappearance of paper straws or why shoelaces always snap near the top of a shoe's tongue. But in the up-to-the-minutiae world of Nicholson Baker, the extraordinary is teased out from the everyday. To borrow a term coined in his most recent novel, Baker's books are "Fermatas," portraits of a familiar world paused for the purposes of exploration. His narrators, Gullivers of the late 20th century, peer microscopically at the tiniest of objects to discover universes of meaning. Baker's novels magnify the endless clutter of conveniences that characterize contemporary life, making of the banal a startling, new Brodningnag.

An advocate of the subordinate clause, Baker's parenthetical prose can be sampled in his first two short novels. In *The Mezzanine* (1988) the narrator spends his lunch hour puzzling over such topics as the change from linoleum to carpeting as the dominant floor-covering in modern office blocks, the safety of escalators, and the ice-cube tray. *Room Temperature* (1990) shifts from the world of objects to the more subjective world of people and relationships. While bottle-feeding his baby daughter, the narrator, Mike, pieces together a history of his relationship with his wife Patty by exploring the personal associations he has attached to various things. As he argues, "with a little concentration one's whole life [can] be reconstructed from any single 20-minute period randomly or almost randomly selected."

These novels gave Baker cult-status as a quirky chronicler of the microcosm. His third book, *U and I* (1991), brought him a whole new reputation. Self-consciously literary, *U and I* is about Baker's obsession with John Updike. It's an obsession notable for Baker's admission that he has read very little of Updike's canon, and the bits of Updike he *has* read he consistently misquotes. Baker's Updike is as incorporeal an imaginary friend, a literary forefather who Baker admits influences deeply his writing but exists only in his head. The anxiety of influence is an oft-discussed issue in literary circles, but the gravity of this issue is undercut by the refreshing levity of Baker's memoir. Interestingly, the literary academy took Baker more seriously as a result of *U and I,* and the book did much to further his reputation on both sides of the Atlantic.

Baker's most recent work concerns sex, and has done much both to enhance and damage his popular reputation. Highly publicized when first published, *Vox* (1992) concerns a telephone conversation between two "lovers," Abby & Jim, who never meet. They share with each other their experiences and fantasies, each providing the other with the perfect companion for their solitary masturbation. The novel works due to Baker's delight in the erotic possibilities of language. It was a huge bestseller, and not just because of the slick mass-marketing that accompanied it. In a world where safe sex is now imperative, *Vox* touched a nerve. It suggests a possible near-future for our sex lives where intercourse is literally disembodied, with the only contact possible between people occurring in language. For this reason the novel is delightfully stimulating, but also a rather sobering read.

Baker's most recent novel, *The Fermata* (1994) is narrated by Arno Strine, an ordinary office temp who possesses the extraordinary ability to enter "the Fold"; that is, to stop time. Arno uses his gift to remove women's clothes and write erotica. He delights in the erotic potential of just about everything—from transcribing tape-recordings to taking off your watch in public—and the novel is at times triumphantly comic. Yet Arno's activities landed his creator in a very different kind of sticky situation. Undressing women without their consent, some felt, was not an issue to take lightly. If *Vox* had pushed pornography into the main-stream, for some *The Fermata* pulled the reader back down a dark alley. Yet Arno is, for most of the novel, a rather pathetic individual who is patiently satirized. He comes to realize that his sexual obsessions coupled with his gift ultimately function as a kind of paralysis—a no-life—and he doesn't miss his powers when they are eventually lost. As he says at the end of the novel, "you have to time the time-outs, and mix them in with life—that's were the art comes in." Such subtlety was missed by the novel's opponents.

Baker's publisher once told Martin Amis that Baker just wanted to be rich and famous. In an interview in Britain's *Sunday Times Magazine* at the time of *Vox*'s publication, Baker concluded by saying that he just wanted to be liked. At different moments in his short career Baker has certainly been one or the other. But with novels like *The Fermata* offending the sensibilities of some, one wonders whether he will ever be both simultaneously.

—John McLeod

BALDWIN, Alex. *See* **BUTTERWORTH, W. E.**

BALDWIN, James (Arthur)

Nationality: American. **Born:** 2 August 1924, in New York City. **Education:** De Witt Clinton High School, New York, graduated 1942. **Career:** Writer, 1944-87. Youth minister at Fireside Pentecostal Assembly, New York City, 1938-42; variously employed as handyman, dishwasher, waiter, and office boy in New York City, and in defense work in Belle Meade, New Jersey, 1942-46. Lecturer on racial issues at universities in the United States and Europe, 1957-87. **Awards:** Eugene F. Saxton fellowship, 1945; Rosenwald fellowship, 1948; Guggenheim fellowship, 1954; National Institute of Arts and Letters grant for literature, 1956; Ford Foundation grant, 1959; National Conference of Christians and Jews Brotherhood Award, 1962, for *Nobody Knows My Name: More Notes of a Native Son;* George Polk Memorial Award, 1963, for magazine articles; Foreign Drama Critics Award, 1964, for *Blues for Mister Charlie;* National Association of Independent Schools award, 1964, for *The Fire Next Time;* American Book Award nomination, 1980, for *Just Above My Head.* D.Litt. from the University of British Columbia, Vancouver, 1964; Commander of the Legion of Honor (France), 1986. **Member:** Congress on Racial Equality (member of national advisory board), American Academy and Institute of Arts and Letters. **Died:** 1 December 1987, of stomach cancer, in St. Paul de Vence, France.

Publications

Novels

Go Tell It on the Mountain. Knopf, 1953.
Giovanni's Room. Dial, 1956, reprinted, Transworld, 1977.
Another Country. Dial, 1962.
Tell Me How Long the Train's Been Gone. Dial, 1968.
If Beale Street Could Talk. Dial, 1974.
Just above My Head. Dial, 1979.
Harlem Quartet. Dial, 1987.

Short Stories

Going to Meet the Man. Dial, 1965.

Fiction for Children

Little Man, Little Man: A Story of Childhood. M. Joseph, 1976; Dial, 1977.

Plays

The Amen Corner (produced Washington, D.C., 1955; New York, 1965). Dial, 1968.
Giovanni's Room, adaptation of his own novel (produced in New York City at Actors' Studio, 1957).
Blues for Mister Charlie (produced New York, 1964), Dial, 1964.
A Deed for the King of Spain (produced New York, 1974).

Screenplay: *One Day, When I Was Lost,* based on *The Autobiography of Malcolm X* by Alex Haley, 1972.

Nonfiction

Autobiographical Notes. Knopf, 1953.
Notes of a Native Son. Beacon Press, 1955.
Nobody Knows My Name: More Notes of a Native Son. Dial, 1961.
The Fire Next Time. Dial, 1963.
Black Anti-Semitism and Jewish Racism, with others. R. W. Baron, 1969.
A Rap on Race, with Margaret Mead, Lippincott, 1971.
No Name in the Street. Dial, 1972.
Cesar: Compressions d'or, with Françoise Giroud. Hachette, 1973.
A Dialogue, with Nikki Giovanni. Lippincott, 1973.
The Devil Finds Work. Dial, 1976.
The Evidence of Things Not Seen. Holt, 1985.
The Price of the Ticket: Collected Nonfiction 1948-1985. St. Martin's, 1985.

Poetry

Jimmy's Blues: Selected Poems. M. Joseph, 1983, St. Martin's, 1985.

*

Media Adaptations: *Go Tell It on the Mountain* (television play), 1985.

Bibliography: In *Black American Writers: Bibliographical Essays* by Daryl Dance, St. Martin's, 1978.

Critical Studies: *The Furious Passage of James Baldwin* by Fern Marja Eckman, M. Evans, 1966; *James Baldwin: A Critical Study* by Stanley Macebuh, Joseph Okpaku, 1973; *James Baldwin: A Collection of Critical Essays* edited by Kenneth Kinnamon, Prentice-Hall, 1974; *James Baldwin: A Critical Evaluation* by Therman B. O'Daniel, Howard University Press, 1977; *James Baldwin* by Louis Hill Pratt, Twayne, 1978; *James Baldwin* by Carolyn Wedin Sylvander, Frederick Ungar, 1980; *Critical Essays on James Baldwin* edited by Fred Standley and Nancy Burt, G. K. Hall, 1981; *Baldwin: Three Interviews* by Malcolm King, Wesleyan University Press, 1985; *Stealing the Fire: The Art and Protest of James Baldwin* by Horace Porter, Wesleyan University Press, 1989; *James Baldwin: Artist on Fire by W. J. Weatherby,* D. I. Fine, 1989; *James Baldwin: Climbing to the Light* by Robert A.

Lee, St. Martins, 1991; *James Baldwin: Prophet on the Threshing Door* by David Leeming, Knopf, 1994.

Theatrical Activities:

Director: **Play**—*Fortune and Men's Eyes,* 1970. **Film**—*The Inheritance,* 1973.

* * *

James Baldwin's funeral in 1987 was as much a celebration of his life as a lament for his death. Amiri Baraka proclaimed that Baldwin "lived his life as witness." This succinct assessment speaks volumes about both Baldwin's life and his work, which are inextricably linked. As he wrote in 1963, "One writes out of one thing only—one's own experience." While pursuing his calling to witness the turbulence of his times, Baldwin became America's most eloquent spokesman on race, and one of the most prolific and versatile American writers of the 20th century. His frankness about race relations and homosexuality opened a dialogue about America's conflicted identity that continues to be relevant.

Baldwin's reputation rests largely on his first novel, *Go Tell It on the Mountain* (1953), the story of a Harlem youth named John Grimes who discovers his own meaning of religion during a violent struggle with his soul in a Baptist church. In a style that is at once delicate and intense, Baldwin describes how John must undergo a conversion before he can face the struggles that he will encounter in his adult life. Readers of this novel are likely to pick up *Notes of a Native Son* (1955) next. This first collection of essays is personal, yet the themes it embraces are as universal as those in his first novel. Baldwin's first play, *The Amen Corner* (first produced 1955), is similar to these first two books in its subject matter. The protagonist is, like John Grimes, caught between obligation to church and family and the need to forge his own way in the world. These three books, full of passionate intensity and a clear-eyed vision of America from the point of view of a young man in Harlem, deserve their reputation; yet they only begin to reveal Baldwin's versatility and his vision.

The struggle and outrage at social injustice evident in these early efforts develops throughout his work, though the subjects vary greatly. The topics of his writings are the battlegrounds of his world where Americans fought, and often failed, to realize their postwar dream: homosexuality in *Giovanni's Room* (1956), Greenwich Village bohemia in *Another Country* (1962), the lingering racism of the Old South in *Going to Meet the Man* (1965), and contemporary cinema in *The Devil Finds Work* (1976), to name just a few. He moves comfortably among these subjects just as he adapts his vision to a variety of forms. Critics have long debated whether to regard Baldwin primarily as a novelist or as an essayist. The fact is that we need not decide; he is both, as well as a playwright and poet.

Baldwin's novels all deal with the relationship between the victims of modern American society and the tragedy of not learning to love. His most popular novel in terms of sales is the powerful *Another Country,* a bold foray into the racial and sexual issues that plagued America but were generally not discussed in literature prior to Baldwin's time. The novel begins with the decline and suicide of jazz musician Rufus Scott and progresses into a widespread search for identity and meaning in the wake of such a tragedy. His later novels such as *Just Above My Head* (1977) mirror this same structure; the obvious victim is not the only one affected by tragic circumstances. The idea that we are all connected—in our responses to humanity's darker side and in our faulty notion of love—may account for the popularity of Baldwin's fiction across such a broad spectrum of readers.

Baldwin's novels can be read as parables of ideas represented in his essays, as David Leeming illustrates so effectively in his landmark 1994 biography, Baldwin's bestselling nonfiction work, underscores how necessary love is for America to grow the way it should—an important theme of *Another Country.* It was clear from the moment this book was published that Baldwin was to be a lasting voice in American literature. The nation read these essays with the attention due a prophet. The words he uses to conclude this collection ring out with the same intensity as Martin Luther King's speeches do: "If we . . . do not falter in our duty now, we may be able, handful that we are, to end the racial nightmare, and achieve our country, and change the history of the world. If we do not now dare everything, the fulfillment of that prophecy, re-created from the Bible in song by a slave, is upon us: God gave Noah the rainbow sign, No more water, the fire next time!" The voice of witness, preacher, prophet, intellectual, and blues singer combine to make these and all of Baldwin's words as powerful today as they have always been.

—D. Quentin Miller

BARAKA, Amiri

Nationality: American. **Born:** Everett LeRoi Jones in Newark, New Jersey, 7 October 1934; took name Amiri Baraka in 1968. **Education:** Attended Central Avenue School and Barringer High School, Newark; Rutgers University, New Brunswick, New Jersey, 1951-52; Howard University, Washington, D.C., 1953-54, B.A. in English 1954. **Military Service:** United States Air Force, 1954-57. **Family:** Married 1) Hettie Roberta Cohen in 1958 (divorced 1965), two daughters; 2) Sylvia Robinson (now Amina Baraka) in 1967, five children; also two stepdaughters and one other daughter. **Career:** Teacher, New School for Social Research, New York, 1961-64, and summers, 1977-79, State University of New York, Buffalo, Summer 1964, and Columbia University, New York, 1964 and Spring 1980; visiting professor, San Francisco State College, 1966-67, Yale University, New Haven, Connecticut, 1977-78, and George Washington University, Washington, D.C., 1978-79. Assistant professor, 1980-82, associate professor, 1983-84, and since 1985 professor of Africana Studies, State University of New York, Stony Brook. Founder, *Yugen* magazine and Totem Press, New York, 1958-62; editor, with Diane di Prima, *Floating Bear* magazine, New York, 1961-63; founding director, Black Arts Repertory Theatre, Harlem, New York, 1964-66. Since 1966 founding director, Spirit House, Newark; involved in Newark politics: member of the United Brothers, 1967, and Committee for Unified Newark, 1969-75; chair, Congress of Afrikan People, 1972-75. **Awards:** Whitney fellowship, 1961; Obie award, 1964; Guggenheim fellowship, 1965; Yoruba Academy fellowship, 1965; National Endowment for the Arts grant, 1966, award, 1981; Dakar Festival prize, 1966; Rockefeller grant, 1981; Before Columbus Foundation award, 1984; American Book award, 1984. D.H.L.: Malcolm X College, Chicago, 1972. **Member:** Black Academy of Arts and Letters. **Ad-**

dress: Department of Africana Studies, State University of New York, Stony Brook, New York 11794-4340, U.S.A.

PUBLICATIONS (EARLIER WORKS AS LEROI JONES)

Poetry

April 13. New Haven, Connecticut, Penny Poems, 1959.
Spring and Soforth. New Haven, Connecticut, Penny Poems, 1960.
Preface to a Twenty Volume Suicide Note. New York, Totem-Corinth, 1961.
The Disguise. Privately printed, 1961.
The Dead Lecturer. New York, Grove Press, 1964.
Black Art. Newark, Jihad, 1966.
A Poem for Black Hearts. Detroit, Broadside Press, 1967.
Black Magic: Collected Poetry 1961-1967. Indianapolis, Bobbs Merrill, 1970.
It's Nation Time. Chicago, Third World Press, 1970.
In Our Terribleness: Some Elements and Meaning in Black Style, with Fundi (Billy Abernathy). Indianapolis, Bobbs Merrill, 1970.
Spirit Reach. Newark, Jihad, 1972.
African Revolution. Newark, Jihad, 1973.
Hard Facts. Newark, Peoples War, 1976.
Selected Poetry. New York, Morrow, 1979.
AM/TRAK. New York, Phoenix Book Shop, 1979.
Spring Song. Privately printed, 1979.
Reggae or Not! Bowling Green, New York, Contact Two, 1982.
Thoughts for You! Nashville, Winston Derek, 1984.
The Leroi Jones/Amiri Baraka Reader. New York, Thunder's Mouth Press, 1993.
Transbluesency. New York, Marsilio, 1995.

Plays

A Good Girl Is Hard to Find (produced Montclair, New Jersey, 1958; New York, 1965).
Dante (produced New York, 1961; as *The 8th Ditch,* produced New York, 1964). Included in *The System of Dante's Hell,* 1965.
The Toilet (produced New York, 1964). With *The Baptism,* New York, Grove Press, 1967.
Dutchman (produced New York, 1964; London, 1967). With *The Slave,* New York, Morrow, 1964; London, Faber, 1965.
The Slave (produced New York, 1964; London, 1972). With *Dutchman,* New York, Morrow, 1964; London, Faber, 1965.
The Baptism (produced New York, 1964; London, 1971). With *The Toilet,* New York, Grove Press, 1967.
Jello (produced New York, 1965). Chicago, Third World Press, 1970.
Experimental Death Unit #1 (also director: produced New York, 1965). Included in *Four Black Revolutionary Plays,* 1969.
A Black Mass (also director: produced Newark, 1966). Included in *Four Black Revolutionary Plays,* 1969.
Arm Yrself or Harm Yrself (produced Newark, 1967). Newark, Jihad, 1967.
Slave Ship: A Historical Pageant (produced Newark, 1967; New York, 1969). Newark, Jihad, 1967.
Madheart (also director: produced San Francisco, 1967). Included in *Four Black Revolutionary Plays,* 1969.
Great Goodness of Life (A Coon Show) (also director: produced Newark, 1967; New York, 1969). Included in *Four Black Revolutionary Plays,* 1969.
Home on the Range (produced Newark and New York, 1968). Published in *Drama Review* (New York), Summer 1968.
Police, published in *Drama Review* (New York), Summer 1968.
The Death of Malcolm X, in *New Plays from the Black Theatre,* edited by Ed Bullins. New York, Bantam, 1969.
Rockgroup, published in *Cricket,* December 1969.
Four Black Revolutionary Plays. Indianapolis, Bobbs Merrill, 1969; London, Calder and Boyars, 1971.
Insurrection (produced New York, 1969).
Junkies Are Full of (SHHH...), and *Bloodrites* (produced Newark, 1970). Published in *Black Drama Anthology,* edited by Woodie King and Ron Milner, New York, New American Library, 1971.
BA-RA-KA, in *Spontaneous Combustion: Eight New American Plays,* edited by Rochelle Owens. New York, Winter House, 1972.
Black Power Chant, published in *Drama Review* (New York), December 1972.
Columbia the Gem of the Ocean (produced Washington, D.C., 1973).
A Recent Killing (produced New York, 1973).
The New Ark's a Moverin (produced Newark, 1974).
The Sidnee Poet Heroical (also director: produced New York, 1975). New York, Reed, 1979.
S-1 (also director: produced New York, 1976). Included in *The Motion of History and Other Plays,* 1978.
The Motion of History (also director: produced New York, 1977). Included in *The Motion of History and Other Plays,* 1978.
The Motion of History and Other Plays (includes *S-1* and *Slave Ship*). New York, Morrow, 1978.
What Was the Relationship of the Lone Ranger to the Means of Production? (produced New York, 1979).
At the Dim' crackr Convention (produced New York, 1980).
Boy and Tarzan Appear in a Clearing (produced New York, 1981).
Weimar 2 (produced New York, 1981).
Money: A Jazz Opera, with George Gruntz, music by Gruntz (produced New York, 1982).
Primitive World, music by David Murray (produced New York, 1984).
General Hag's Skeezag. New York, Mentor, 1992.

Screenplays: *Dutchman,* 1967; *Black Spring,* 1967; *A Fable,* 1971; *Supercoon,* 1971.

Novel

The System of Dante's Hell. New York, Grove Press, 1965; London, MacGibbon and Kee, 1966.

Short Stories

Tales. New York, Grove Press, 1967; London, MacGibbon and Kee, 1969.

Other

Cuba Libre. New York, Fair Play for Cuba Committee, 1961.
Blues People: Negro Music in White America. New York, Morrow, 1963; London, MacGibbon and Kee, 1965.

Home: Social Essays. New York, Morrow, 1966; London, MacGibbon and Kee, 1968.
Black Music. New York, Morrow, 1968; London, MacGibbon and Kee, 1969.
Trippin': A Need for Change, with Larry Neal and A.B. Spellman. Newark, Cricket, 1969(?).
A Black Value System. Newark, Jihad, 1970.
Gary and Miami: Before and After. Newark, Jihad, n.d.
Raise Race Rays Raze: Essays since 1965. New York, Random House, 1971.
Strategy and Tactics of a Pan African Nationalist Party. Newark, National Involvement 1971.
Beginning of National Movement. Newark, Jihad, 1972.
Kawaida Studies: The New Nationalism. Chicago, Third World Press, 1972.
National Liberation and Politics. Newark, Congress and Afrikan People, 1974.
Crisis in Boston!!!! Newark, Vita Wa Watu-People's War Publishing, 1974.
African Free School. Newark, Jihad, 1974.
Toward Ideological Clarity. Newark, Congress of Afrikan People, 1974.
The Creation of the New Ark. Washington, D.C., Howard University Press, 1975.
Selected Plays and Prose. New York, Morrow, 1979.
Daggers and Javelins: Essays 1974-1979. New York, Morrow, 1984.
The Autobiography of LeRoi Jones/Amiri Baraka. New York, Freundlich, 1984.
The Artist and Social Responsibility. N.p., Unity, 1986.
The Music: Reflections on Jazz and Blues, with Amina Baraka. New York, Morrow, 1987.
A Race Divided. New York, Emerge Communications, 1991.
Conversations with Amiri Baraka. Jackson, Mississippi, University Press of Mississippi, 1994.

Editor, *Four Young Lady Poets*. New York, Totem-Corinth, 1962.
Editor, *The Moderns: New Fiction in America*. New York, Corinth, 1963; London, MacGibbon and Kee, 1965.
Editor, with Larry Neal, *Black Fire: An Anthology of Afro-American Writing*. New York, Morrow, 1968.
Editor, *African Congress: A Documentary of the First Modern Pan-African Congress*. New York, Morrow, 1972.
Editor, with Diane di Prima, *The Floating Bear: A Newsletter, Numbers 1-37*. La Jolla, California, Laurence McGilvery, 1974.
Editor, with Amina Baraka, *Confirmation: An Anthology of African American Women*. New York, Morrow, 1983.

*

Bibliography: *LeRoi Jones (Imamu Amiri Baraka): A Checklist of Works by and about Him* by Letitia Dace, London, Nether Press, 1971; *Ten Modern American Playwrights* by Kimball King, New York, Garland, 1982.

Manuscript Collections: Howard University, Washington, D.C.; Beinecke Library, Yale University, New Haven, Connecticut; Lilly Library, Indiana University, Bloomington; University of Connecticut, Storrs; George Arents Research Library, Syracuse University, New York.

Critical Studies: *From LeRoi Jones to Amiri Baraka: The Literary Works* by Theodore Hudson, Durham, North Carolina, Duke University Press, 1973; *Baraka: The Renegade and the Mask* by Kimberly W. Benston, New Haven, Connecticut, Yale University Press, 1976, and *Imamu Amiri Baraka (LeRoi Jones): A Collection of Critical Essays* edited by Benston, Englewood Cliffs, New Jersey, Prentice Hall, 1978; *Amiri Baraka/LeRoi Jones: The Quest for a Populist Modernism* by Werner Sollors, New York, Columbia University Press, 1978; *Amiri Baraka* by Lloyd W. Brown, Boston, Twayne, 1980; *To Raise, Destroy, and Create: The Poetry, Drama, and Fiction of Imamu Amiri Baraka (LeRoi Jones)* by Henry C. Lacey, Troy, New York, Whitston, 1981; *Theatre and Nationalism: Wole Soyinka and LeRoi Jones* by Alain Ricard, Ife-Ife, Nigeria, University of Ife Press, 1983; *Amiri Baraka: The Kaleidoscopic Torch* edited by James B. Gwynne, New York, Steppingstones Press, 1985; *The Poetry and Poetics of Amiri Baraka: The Jazz Aesthetic* by William J. Harris, Columbia, University of Missouri Press, 1985; *Conscientious Sorcerers: The Black Postmodernist Fiction of Leroi Jones/Amiri Baraka, Ishmael Reed, and Samuel R. Delany* by Robert Elliot Fox, New York, Greenwood Press, 1987; *Amiri Baraka* by Bob Bernotas, New York, Chelsea House, 1991.

* * *

African-American poet, playwright, editor, critic, and outspoken political activist Amiri Baraka was catapulted to fame and acclaim by his play *Dutchman* (1964). In that story, a young, polite, well-educated black man named Clay is goaded and provoked by a white woman named Lula on a New York subway. He finally reveals his repressed anger and hatred toward whites. Once Clay has shown those emotions, Lula stabs him to death and the other passengers on the subway calmly dispose of his body. At the play's end Lula makes eye contact with another unsuspecting young black man.

Often anthologized, winner of the *Village Voice*'s Obie award, and still performed to accolades in the 1990s, *Dutchman* established Baraka's reputation as a major American writer. But the play has also haunted him, as it remains, among the predominantly white critical establishment, his best-known piece of work. *Dutchman* combines a drama of mythic archetypes with a political sensibility which, in 1965, became fully manifested in Baraka's Black Nationalist phase.

Baraka's poetry describes in compelling detail the African-American experience and is considered foundational work in the creation of a modern black aesthetic. But Baraka's provocative stance, at times anti-white and antisemitic, has alienated many readers. His contentious opinions dominated his work in the 1960s, in poetry collections such as *Black Magic* (1970). In 1974, though, Baraka renounced the Black Nationalist period of his life. Declaring himself a Marxist-Leninist, he stated that Black Nationalism was both a racist and fascistic ideology. Furthermore, Baraka has displayed growth beyond the sexism associated with Black Nationalism in the 1960s.

Always political, Baraka's poetry, prose, and plays are designed to promote the cultural liberation of African Americans. His Marxist-Leninist poetry, such as *Hard Facts* (1976), is well-crafted and is generally considered to be some of his best-written work. In this writing as elsewhere, however, Baraka has been criticized for his inflexible insistence on perceiving the world in a Manichean "good and evil" polarity.

Baraka continued to write plays in the 1970s. *What Was the Relationship of the Lone Ranger to the Means of Production?* (1978), for example, presents a surrealist episode using pop culture figures in which a murdering Capitalist exploiter (the Masked Man) provokes a violent worker revolt. Baraka's Marxist work alienated those who did not sympathize with his point of view, provoking comments that he forsook art for politics. On the other hand, those who accept that all art is political admire *Lone Ranger* as an important and influential play.

Baraka sometimes avoids rewriting, and has been criticized for this stylistic holdover from his early experiences amongst the Beat poets. For example, *The Autobiography of LeRoi Jones/Amiri Baraka* (1984) is considered by some to be an exhaustive book that would have benefitted from judicious editing. However, many have hailed the work as an important, brilliant work taking a well-deserved place in the tradition of African-American narratives.

Baraka has continued to write in the 1990s while also teaching at SUNY-Stony Brook, where he is a full professor and chair of African American Studies. The slightly less strident tone of plays such as *The Life and Life of Bumpy Johnson* (1991) and *Meeting Lillie* (1993) elicited a favorable reception by mainstream critics. Baraka nevertheless maintains a political stance, as can be seen in works like *General Hag's Skeezag* (published in *Black Thunder* [1992]). He has edited many anthologies of African-American writing, and has been honored with numerous fellowships, grants, and awards.

—Sean Carney

BARKER, Clive

Nationality: English. **Born:** 1952 in Liverpool, England. **Education:** University of Liverpool. **Career:** Illustrator, painter, actor, playwright, and author. Executive producer of motion pictures. **Awards:** Two British Fantasy awards from British Fantasy Society; World Fantasy award for best anthology/collection from World Fantasy Convention, 1985, for *Clive Barker's Books of Blood.* **Address:** 36 Wimpole St., London W2, England.

PUBLICATIONS

Short Stories

Clive Barker's Books of Blood, Volume One. Sphere, 1984; Berkley Publishing, 1986.
Clive Barker's Books of Blood, Volume Two. Sphere, 1984; Berkley Publishing, 1986.
Clive Barker's Books of Blood, Volume Three. Sphere, 1984; Berkley Publishing, 1986.
Clive Barker's Books of Blood, Volume Four. Sphere, 1985; as *The Inhuman Condition: Tales of Terror,* Poseidon, 1986.
Clive Barker's Books of Blood, Volume Five. Sphere, 1985; as *In The Flesh: Tales of Terror,* Poseidon, 1986.
Clive Barker's Books of Blood, Volume Six. Sphere, 1985.
Cabal (short stories and novella). Poseidon, 1988.
London, Volume One: Bloodline. Fantaco, 1993.

Novels

The Damnation Game. Weidenfeld & Nicolson, 1985; Putnam, 1987.
Weaveworld. Poseidon, 1987.
The Hellbound Heart (novella). Simon & Schuster, 1988.
The Great and Secret Show: The First Book of the Art. HarperCollins, 1989.
Imajica. HarperCollins, 1991.
The Thief of Always: A Fable. HarperCollins, 1993.
Everville: The Second Book of the Art. HarperCollins, 1994.
Sacrament. Ingram, 1996.

Plays

Incarnations: Three Plays by Clive Barker. HarperCollins, 1995.

Screenplays: *Underworld,* 1985; *Rawhead Rex,* 1987; *Hellraiser,* 1987; *Nightbreed,* 1990.

Other

Theatre Games. Heinemann, 1988.
Clive Barker's Shadows in Eden, edited by Stephen Jones, Underwood-Miller, 1991.
Pandemonium: The World of Clive Barker, Eclipse, 1991.

*

Film Adaptations: *Hellraiser,* 1987, from the novella *The Hellbound Heart; Rawhead Rex,* 1987, from the short story of the same title; *Nightbreed,* 1990, from the novella *Cabal.*

Critical Studies: *Clive Barker's Short Stories: Imagination as Metaphor in the Books of Blood & Other Works,* by Gary Hoppenstand, McFarland, 1994.

Theatrical Activities: Director: **Films**—*Hellraiser,* 1987; *Nightbreed,* 1990.

* * *

Clive Barker and the horror genre seem to be traveling side by side in their increasing popularity. Indeed, horror giant Stephen King states in *Publishers Weekly,* "I have seen the future of the horror genre, and his name is Clive Barker." This is a fascinating observation not only because of its prophetic nature, but especially because Barker had originally focused on theatrical work. Only after Barker read *Dark Forces,* a horror anthology edited by King's agent, did he pursue horror as a viable direction for his creative energies.

What quickly followed were six volumes of a short-story collection called *The Books of Blood* (1984-1985). The series, featuring highly graphic stories with such titles as "The Midnight Meat Train," "Pig Blood Blues," "Human Remains," "Down, Satan!," and "How Spoilers Breed," was such a hit in England that the collections were quickly published in the United States. The collection earned two British Fantasy Awards from the British Fantasy Society, as well as the World Fantasy Award for best anthology/collection from the World Fantasy Convention in 1985.

Barker's first novel, *The Damnation Game* (1985) was nominated for the Booker Prize and cracked the *New York Times* best-seller list within a week of the book's publication. The novel centers around the oft-told tale of two enemies with supernatural powers who chase each other for several years. Of course, Barker's rendition of the tale is all the more striking, with his trademark combination of highly literate prose and blood-and-guts horror technique. More recent novels include *The Thief of Always: A Fable* (1993) and *Everville: The Second Book of the Art* (1994).

After a couple of failed film adaptations of his short fiction, Barker realized a huge success with *Hellraiser* (1987) and *The Hellbound Heart: Rawhead Rex* (1989), both adapted from the novella "The Hellbound Heart." Barker told *Contemporary Authors* he attributes the success of the "Hellraiser" movies to his being allowed a significant amount of input into what went into the movies—a chance he was not afforded for *Underworld* (1985) and *Rawhead Rex* (published in 1987 and adapted from his short story of the same title).

Barker has also worked as a playwright, actor, illustrator, and painter, besides writing horror fiction and producing motion pictures.

Barker names as his influences the artists Bosch and Goya and the authors Edgar Allan Poe, Herman Melville, and Ray Bradbury; as well as the movies—and more obvious choices—*Psycho, Night of the Living Dead,* and *Friday the 13th.* Barker sees this background as working to his advantage; he explains in *Contemporary Writers,* "I think the fiction that I write is imagistically richer as a consequence of my painting and graphics background. And it's been observed by others rather than myself that there's a certain cinematic element in the way I put my narratives together."

Why does Barker so enjoy the horror genre? As he explains in *Contemporary Authors,* "I think there's an element of vicarious pleasure to be taken in the reading of horror fiction in the sense that you are watching terrible things happen to people that aren't happening to you."

—Tracy Clark

BARNARD, Judith. *See* **MICHAEL, Judith.**

BARRY, Dave

Nationality: American. **Born:** Armonk, New York, 3 July 1947. **Education:** Haverford College, B.A., 1969. **Family:** Married Elizabeth Lenox Pyle in 1975; one son. **Career:** *Daily Local News,* West Chester, Pennsylvania, reporter, 1971-75; worked for Associated Press, Philadelphia, 1975-76; lecturer on effective writing for businesses for R. S. Burger Associates (consulting firm), 1975-83; free-lance humor columnist, 1980—; *Miami Herald,* humor columnist, 1983—. **Awards:** Distinguished Writing award, American Society of Newspaper Editors, 1986; Pulitzer prize for commentary, 1988. **Agent:** Al Hart, Fox Chase Agency, Public Ledger Bldg., Room 930, Independence Sq., Philadelphia, Pennsylvania, 19106. **Address:** Miami Herald, 1 Herald Plaza, Miami, Florida 33123-1693, U.S.A.

Publications

Humorous Nonfiction

The Taming of the Screw: Several Million Homeowners' Problems Sidestepped. Rodale Press, 1983.
Babies and Other Hazards of Sex: How to Make a Tiny Person in Only Nine Months, with Tools You Probably Have around the Home. Rodale Press, 1984.
Bad Habits: A 100% Fact Free Book. Doubleday, 1985.
Stay Fit and Healthy until You're Dead. Rodale Press, 1985.
Claw Your Way to the Top: How to Become the Head of a Major Corporation in Roughly a Week. Rodale Press, 1986.
Dave Barry's Guide to Marriage and/or Sex. Rodale Press, 1987.
Dave Barry's Greatest Hits. Crown, 1988.
Homes and Other Black Holes: The Happy Homeowner's Guide. Fawcett/Columbine, 1988.
Dave Barry Slept Here: A Sort of History of the United States. Random House, 1989.
Dave Barry Turns Forty. Crown, 1990.
Dave Barry Talks Back. Crown, 1991.
Dave Barry's Guide to Life. Crown, 1991.
Dave Barry Does Japan. Random House, 1992.
Dave Barry Is Not Making This Up. Crown, 1994.
Dave Barry's Guide to Guys: A User's Manual. Random House, 1995.
Dave Barry's Bad Lyrics. Andrews & McMeel, 1996.
Dave Barry in Cyberspace. Crown, 1996.

* * *

Dave Barry, a *Miami Herald* humor columnist who won a Pulitzer Prize in 1988 and was voted "Best in the Business" by the *Washington Journalism Review* in 1989, also writes hysterically funny books. The key element in his writing is his irreverent, youthful attitude which allows him to poke fun at common situations in everyday life.

Typical of Barry's books is his *Dave Barry's Guide to Life* (1991), in which the author gives tongue-in-cheek advice on how to deal with just about every major milestone one will encounter. His advice about credit cards, for example, is "Make your own!" And of dating, he advises; "Go out with a potential mate and do a lot of fun things that the two of you will never do again if you actually get married."

Similarly, *Dave Barry Slept Here: A Sort of History of the United States* (1989) is a spoof of history as most people learned it—or didn't, as the author implies, because they were asleep or daydreaming in class. Therefore, in order to make history less boring, Barry suggests that textbooks be revised to say that all important events actually took place on October eighth, including the Fourth of July. According to Barry, this would also have the benefit of making history easier to remember and improving scholastic test scores. Barry's historical improvisation and misinterpretation includes, for example, discussions of the Revolutionary War (in which the Americans confused the British by singing about how Yankee Doodle stuck a feather in his cap and called it macaroni), and the great early American novelist, Cliff (the author of Cliff Notes).

This book is a historic-satiric delight in the style of Monty Python and Stan Freeburg.

America magazine argues that Barry's satire makes an ironic and perhaps unintentional point about a very real and unfortunate lack of historical knowledge among Americans. However, critics generally like *Dave Barry Slept Here,* as well as most of Barry's other books, calling them zany, ribald, and earthy. Regarding *Dave Barry Does Japan* (1992), in which the author reflects on his vacation in that country, the *New York Times Book Review* praises Barry for making his audience "laugh out loud" and for having "style, grace, true wit, and a sense of humanity (though slightly warped)." On the other hand, in response to Barry's latest book, *Dave Barry's Guide to Guys; A User's Manual* (1995), some critics judge Barry's humor sophomoric and tiresome.

Barry's subject matter is different in each of his books, though none of them has a plot or story-line. Reading his work is like watching a stand-up comedian. Although he often begins by bringing up current issues, he invariably strays onto tangents of the imagination, and winds up doing directionless riffs of comedy. His satire can be biting at times, especially when he discusses politics. But his style is usually more gentle, as when he writes about children and family life. Occasionally he borders on the bawdy, dwelling on sexual themes and bodily functions. He knows that the key to being funny is saying something that is totally unexpected, so he piles up one hilarious nonsequitur after another.

Casual fans may be content to follow Barry's syndicated newspaper column, which appears in the *Living* or *Leisure* section of many Sunday newspapers around the country. But those who can't get enough of his madcap musings read his books. The network television situation comedy called "Dave's World" was inspired by Barry's persona, but it has nothing to do with his life or his writing.

—Bruce Guy Chabot

BAXTER, Charles

Nationality: American. **Born:** 13 May 1947, in Minneapolis, Minnesota. **Education:** Macalester College, B.A., 1969; State University of New York at Buffalo, Ph.D., 1974. **Family:** Married Martha Hauser; children: Daniel. **Career:** High school teacher in Pinconning, Michigan, 1969-70; Wayne State University, Detroit, Michigan, assistant professor, 1974-79, associate professor, 1979-85, professor of English, 1985-89; University of Michigan, Ann Arbor, Michigan, professor of English, 1989—. Warren Wilson College, faculty member, 1986—; University of Michigan, visiting faculty member, 1987. Associate editor of *Minnesota Review,* 1967-69; editor of *Audit/Poetry,* 1973-74; associate editor of *Criticism.* **Awards:** Lawrence Foundation award, 1982, and Associated Writing Programs Award Series in Short Fiction, 1984, both for *Harmony of the World;* National Endowment for the Arts fellowship, 1983; Michigan Council for the Arts fellowship, 1984; Faculty Recognition award, Wayne State University, 1985 and 1987; Guggenheim fellowship, 1985-86; Michigan Council of the Arts grant, 1986; Arts Foundation of Michigan award, 1991; Lawrence Foundation award, 1991; Reader's Digest Foundation fellowship, 1992. **Address:** 1585 Woodland Dr., Ann Arbor, Michigan 48103, U.S.A.

Publications

Novels

First Light. Viking, 1987.
Shadow Play. Norton, 1993.

Short Stories

Harmony of the World. University of Missouri Press, 1984.
Through the Safety Net. Viking, 1985.
A Relative Stranger. Norton, 1990.

Poetry

Chameleon, illustrated by Mary E. Miner. New Rivers Press, 1970.
The South Dakota Guidebook. New Rivers Press, 1974.
Imaginary Paintings and Other Poems. Paris Review Editions, 1990.

* * *

Charles Baxter is much better known as a short-story writer and novelist than as a poet. But his first two books, *Chameleon* (1970) and *South Dakota Guidebook* (1974), are collections of poetry, and he published another fine book of poems, *Imaginary Paintings and Other Poems* in 1990.

So, Baxter, beginning as a poet, later turned to writing fiction, like many of his contemporaries. But unlike most of them he is still an excellent, bold, and experimental poet. As a scholar of the contemporary novel, he has also written brilliant essays on such 20th-century novelists as Nathaniel West and Malcolm Lowry. After receiving his Ph.D. from SUNY at Buffalo, he taught for many years at Wayne State University in Detroit and has taught in the creative writing program at the University of Michigan in Ann Arbor.

His first truly successful book was his award-winning collection of stories called *The Harmony of the World* (1984); he later published two other collections called *Through the Safety Net* (1985) and *A Relative Stranger* (1993).

Baxter's interest in writing stories is reflected in his two published novels, *First Light* (1987) and, more recently, *Shadow Play* (1993) both of which are characterized by superb writing but somewhat arbitrary structures. *First Light,* for instance, is a novel told backwards like a movie run in reverse through a projector. It is best viewed as a series of wonderful, related episodes set in a structural scheme that seems abstract. It lacks the inevitability of action that characterizes the most interesting tragedies and most novels, since we know the outcome of the book at the very beginning. It also tends to be more interesting, because the brother-and-sister protagonists are older, mature people and are generally more interesting than the children they once were. The individual episodes, however, are so powerful that they compensate for any deficiency in structure. *First Light* is the better of the two novels.

Like *First Light, Shadow Play* has some first-class individual episodes, like the visit the protagonist's foster brother Cyril makes to a tattoo parlor (an episode the author is fond of reading at performances). The story of Wyatt Palmer, his fiance Susan and their odd courtship is wonderfully done and would make an excellent piece of short fiction, as would Wyatt's brief affair with Alyce; the suicide of Cyril; Wyatt's attempted arson of Jerry Schwartzwalder's house; and several other segments. But some scenes, especially the tattoo parlor episode, seem almost like tours de force and are isolated from the overall plot.

Unlike *First Light,* however, *Shadow Play* is structured more conventionally, with a regular and intensely engrossing plot. But it's an odd, vaguely disturbing novel—a bit like sleep-walking. "It was the hardest book I've written," Baxter said in an interview. "A number of times it didn't seem to work. I didn't know how people would respond." In fact, there is a real confusion of intention in the novel. If it is meant to make an ecological statement, it does not really work because Wyatt Palmer (the protagonist and the town manager of Five Oaks, a small city in south central Michigan) is altogether lacking in the zeal of the reformer/fanatic. He becomes aware of the problems caused by Jerry's new chemical plant (for which Wyatt has been instrumental in clearing for his economically depressed community, thanks in part to Cyril). He comes to realize that there is very little he can do to stop the chemical plant because of his boss, who points out Cyril's bad habits and reputation as potentially compromising any legal action the town might take. One would think that, as a failed protagonist, Wyatt would somehow disintegrate or be brought to his knees, but nothing like that happens. The chemical plant goes on producing its toxic substances and its victims. Wyatt avoids the problems by moving away and rebuilding his life somewhere else. Nothing works out fine, but nobody, except the nameless victims of the plant, suffers any sort of fall or discomfort. So, as an ecological statement, the novel fails to be either tragic or pointedly satiric.

Where *Shadow Play* may fail in ecological terms, it succeeds unbelievably in artistic ones, because Baxter's interests are subversive and eccentric. He is powerfully drawn towards unusual individuals, including Susan, who is also drawn toward such people, his father, his mother, his foster brother Cyril, and above all his Aunt Ellen (with her new and fascinating "bible"). And it is this interest, and not his politics, that makes him a first-rate writer.

—C. W. Truesdale

BEATTIE, Ann

Nationality: American. **Born:** Washington, D.C., 8 September 1947. **Education:** American University, Washington, D.C., B.A. 1969; University of Connecticut, Storrs, 1970-72, M.A. 1970. **Family:** Married 1) David Gates in 1973 (divorced), one son; 2) Lincoln Perry. **Career:** Visiting assistant professor, 1976-77, visiting writer, 1980, University of Virginia, Charlottesville; Briggs Copeland Lecturer in English, Harvard University, Cambridge, Massachusetts, 1977-78. **Awards:** Guggenheim fellowship, 1977; American University Distinguished Alumnae award, 1980; American Academy award, 1980; L.H.D., American University, 1983. **Member:** American Academy and Institute of Arts and Letters, 1983. **Agent:** International Creative Management, 40 West 57th Street, New York, New York 10019, U.S.A. **Address:** c/o Random House, 201 East 50th Street, New York, New York 10022, U.S.A.

Publications

Novels

Chilly Scenes of Winter. New York, Doubleday, 1976.
Falling in Place. New York, Random House, 1980; London, Secker and Warburg, 1981.
Love Always. New York, Random House, and London, Michael Joseph, 1985.
Picturing Will. New York, Random House, and London, Cape, 1990; New York, Vintage, 1991.
Another You. New York, Random House, 1995.

Short Stories

Distortions. New York, Doubleday, 1976.
Secrets and Surprises. New York, Random House, 1978; London, Hamish Hamilton, 1979.
Jacklighting. Worcester, Massachusetts, Metacom Press, 1981.
The Burning House. New York, Random House, 1982; London, Secker and Warburg, 1983.
Where You'll Find Me and Other Stories. New York, Linden Press, 1986; London, Macmillan, 1987.
What Was Mine and Other Stories. New York, Random House, 1991.

Other

Spectacles (for children). New York, Workman, 1985.
Alex Katz (art criticism). New York, Abrams, 1987.
Americana, photographs by Bob Adelman. New York, Scribner, 1992.

*

Theatrical Activities:

Actress: **Play**—Role in *The Hotel Play* by Wallace Shawn, New York, 1981.

* * *

Ann Beattie has been described as the chronicler of the counterculture world of her generation, a generation which had to translate itself from the idealism of the 1960s into the narcissism of the 1970s. Her collections of short stories deal with the people who must effect these transformations. Taken together these stories chronicle the random comings and leavings of disillusioned young people who do and feel nothing. Her writing style resembles that of a Super-8 camera, documenting all including the insignificant. Her characters are purposely dull with no interest in work, money, or even sex. They sit around listening to music and smoking grass. These pieces are stark studies in domestic depression laced with irony. "Her stories are defiantly underplayed and random, trailing off into inconsequentiality, ending with a whimper or, at best, an embarrassed grin," says Richard Locke.

In her first novel, *Chilly Scenes of Winter* (1976), Beattie applies her remarkable technical skill to material of vast popular appeal. The main character Charles is in love with married Laura and spends the novel waiting for her. During this period of waiting he turns 27, works at a job he despises, endures a crazy mother and a well-meaning but not very smart stepfather, and hangs out with best pal Sam. The waiting is simultaneously painful and humorous. The theme becomes the act of waiting itself. The book is very perceptive and Laura is well worth the wait.

Falling in Place (1980) centers on a 40-year-old ad agency man with a disillusioned wife and a 25-year-old mistress. Other characters include his alcoholic mother, his boss, his cool best friend, Nick, his 15-year-old daughter who failed English, and his overweight ten-year-old son. In a parallel narrative, a washed-out Yale grad student teaches summer school and feels adrift. The novel is built around an accidental shooting and the motif of "falling in place." As many as five characters are given their own point of view, which allows the reader to get inside each of these protagonists. Richard Locke called it "the most impressive American novel of the season."

A third novel, *Love Always* (1985), focuses on Nicole Nelson, a 14-year-old soap-opera star who spends the summer in Vermont with her Aunt Lucy. Critics praised the work for its outrageousness, wit, and inventiveness. Alice Hoffman writes, "Miss Beattie is one of the most graceful writers we have; at times her prose is nothing short of exquisite. It is such sheer pleasure to read the dialogue in *Love Always,* we almost don't care what the characters say to one another. But when we really do listen, the absence of desire is more than unsettling—it's chilling."

Picturing Will (1990) explores the dynamics of family life with the reference point and focus of five-year-old Will. Each section is rendered from a different perspective. The first section, "Mother," is told from the perspective of Will's mother, Jody. Jody, a photographer, has survived a broken marriage with Wayne to become the newest darling of the New York gallery scene. She becomes involved with Mel who is very nurturing and supportive. Beattie constantly shifts the focus and rearranges what we see. In addition, interspersed through the book are a series of italicized sections that speak directly to the reader about the relationship of parent to child and the responsibility inherent within that relationship. The second section, "Father," shows the reader a composite view of Wayne which is extremely unflattering. He comes across as selfish, violent, and completely uncaring towards Will. Finally, "Child" reveals to the reader that the italicized sections were pieces of Mel's journal. So it is Mel who is the real parent to Will. Jody has pushed him aside in pursuit of her career. The traditional nuclear family may have disintegrated, but the different version is just as meaningful.

—Jennifer G. Coman

BEECH, Webb. *See* **BUTTERWORTH, W. E.**

BENCHLEY, Peter (Bradford)

Nationality: American. **Born:** 8 May 1940, in New York. **Education:** Harvard University, A.B. (cum laude), 1961. **Military Service:** U. S. Marine Corps Reserve, 1962-63. **Family:** Married Wendy Wesson, 19 September 1964. **Career:** *Washington Post,* Washington, D.C., reporter, 1963; *Newsweek,* New York City, associate editor, 1964-67; The White House, Washington, D.C., staff assistant to the President, 1967-69; free-lance writer and television news correspondent, beginning 1969. Host of television series, "Expedition Earth," ESPN; host/narrator/writer of more than a dozen wildlife/adventure television shows. **Agent:** International Creative Management, 40 West 57th St., New York, NY 10019.

Publications

Novels

Jaws. Doubleday, 1974.
The Deep. Doubleday, 1976.
The Island. Doubleday, 1979.
The Girl of the Sea of Cortez. Doubleday, 1982.
Q Clearance. Random House, 1986.
Rummies. Random House, 1989.
Beast. Random House, 1991.
Three Complete Novels. Random House Value Publishing, 1993.
White Shark. Random House, 1994.

Plays

Screenplays: *Jaws,* with others, 1975; *The Deep,* with others, 1977; *The Island,* 1980.

Nonfiction

Time and a Ticket. Houghton, 1964.
Ocean Planet. Harry Abrams, 1995.

Children's Fiction

Jonathan Visits the White House. McGraw, 1964.

*

Media Adaptations: Films—*Jaws,* 1975; *The Deep,* 1977; *The Island,* 1980. Television—*Beast,* 1996.

* * *

Perhaps best known for his novel *Jaws* (1974), a *New York Times* bestseller for more than 40 weeks, Peter Benchley has written eight novels, most dealing with adventures and dangers at sea. Criticized for his lack of characterization and often formulaic plotting, Benchley nevertheless offers what many reviewers call a sense of escape for readers fed up with introspective fiction, and in this regard he can be described, much like Michael Crichton, as a modern-day Robert Louis Stevenson.

Despite contrived plots, Benchley's novels bear the hallmark of extensive research. *Jaws,* concerned with the threat of a great white shark near a New England resort town, developed out of Benchley's fascination with sharks, developed during his dives off the Great Barrier Reef of Australia. In the 1970s little was known about great whites, and Benchley capitalized on this with his main character, a twenty-foot great white that attacks several unsuspecting swimmers. Police Chief Martin Brody must contend with frantic citizens and worried town officials who fear that closing the beaches will bankrupt the town. Brody, along with young ichthyologist Matt Hooper and the enigmatic fisherman Quint, sets out to hunt for the great white.

Originally titled *Silence in the Water, Jaws* underwent much editing and revision, including an additional subplot romantically involving Brody's wife and Hooper. Much of the writing is lean and spare, and the scenes with the great white are the most effective. Still, many critics attacked the novel for the subplots, the weak characterization, and what they perceived to be inappropriate allusions to Herman Melville's *Moby Dick*, especially in the final, climactic scene. No one can deny, however, that Benchley created a symbol of fear that lingers in our culture even today. As the *Washington Post* wrote, "Benchley has forged and touched a metaphor that still makes us tingle."

Many of Benchley's subsequent novels follow the same formula of an ocean setting and a menace lurking under the waves. *The Deep* (1976) also includes sharks, but the primary threat comes from drug-dealers who want to protect their cargo of heroin which rests on the sea floor off Bermuda. A pair of treasure seekers locates the stash while on a dive, and the chase begins. *The Island* (1979) deals with Caribbean pirates in the 17th-century, a topic that Benchley researched by consulting scores of books and historical volumes. With the publication of *Beast* (1991), Benchley returned to Bermuda and a story remarkably similar to *Jaws*, this time involving the legendary giant squid.

Not all of Benchley's forays have dealt with a sea-going menace. *The Girl of the Sea of Cortez* (1982) is a slower, more idyllic tale than Benchley's thrillers. Praised for its lyrical descriptions and environmental themes, the novel drew fire for its lack of plot. As Thomas Gifford wrote in the *Washington Post Book World*, "When Benchley sticks to the manta ray, the girl, and the memories of her late father . . . he is often effective, even poignant, moving. But out of water he is quickly beached and gasping his last."

Undaunted, Benchley produced *Q Clearance* (1986), which he described as "a spy comedy." Presidential speech-writer Timothy Burnham gains "Q clearance" and receives confidential information on nuclear energy, earning the enmity of his liberal wife and children. Elaine Kendall of the *Los Angeles Times* praised Benchley for this "prime example of that vanishing literary species, the comic novel." Benchley turned to more satirical wit in *Rummies* (1989), the story of upscale publishing editor Scott Preston's alcoholism and entrance into a substance-abuse center. Preston's initial snobbishness towards his fellow addicts vanishes as he abruptly learns how much in common he has with them. Kendell wrote, "His evolution from a know-it-all, above-it-all, self-deluding lush to a vulnerable human being . . . is told in moving passages." Reviewer David E. Jones added, "Benchley's credentials as a storyteller . . . are only reinforced by this effort, which may be his most ambitious adventure to date."

Three of Benchley's novels have been made into movies, of which Steven Spielberg's *Jaws*, starring Roy Scheider, Robert Shaw, and Richard Dreyfuss, is the most famous and successful. Benchley co-wrote the screenplays for *Jaws* and *The Deep*, and has contributed numerous articles to *The New Yorker, National Geographic*, and several other periodicals.

While Benchley has returned to the formulaic *Jaws*-like storyline in the novels *Beast* and *White Shark* (1994), he has proven to be a competent storyteller whose characterizations have gained strength and substance over time and whose plots have grown increasingly intricate. His sea-thrillers are ultimately of less worth than his land-bound novels, but they do show his deft use of suspense and knowledge of the sea that have intrigued thousands of readers over the past two decades.

—Christopher Swann

BERTON, Pierre

Nationality: Canadian. **Born:** Whitehorse, Yukon, 12 July 1920. **Education:** University of British Columbia, B.A., 1941. **Military Service:** Canadian Army, 1942-45; became captain. **Family:** Married Janet Walker in 1946; five daughters, two sons. **Career:** Vancouver *News Herald*, city editor, 1941-42; *Vancouver Sun*, feature writer, 1946-47; *Maclean's* magazine, Toronto, 1947-58, became managing editor; Toronto *Daily Star*, associate editor and columnist, 1958-62; host of *The Pierre Berton Show*, CBC-TV, 1962-73; *Maclean's* magazine, contributing editor, 1963-64. Television commentator and panelist, *Front Page Challenge;* host of weekly television programs *My Country* and *The Great Debate*. Editor-in-chief, Canadian Centennial Library, beginning 1963. Member of the board of directors, McClelland & Stewart Ltd.; chairman, Heritage Canada. **Awards:** Governor General's award for creative nonfiction, 1956 for *The Mysterious North*, 1958 for *Klondike Fever*, and 1971 for *The Last Spike;* Stephen Leacock Medal for humor, 1959, for *Just Add Water and Stir;* J. V. McAree award for columnist of the year, 1959; National Newspaper awards for feature writing and staff corresponding, 1960; Film of the Year award in Canada and Grand Prix at Cannes for *City of Gold;* Association of Canadian Radio and Television Artists Nellie award for integrity in broadcasting, 1972; LL.D., University of Prince Edward Island, 1973; D.Litt., York University, 1974. **Address:** 21 Sackville St., Toronto, Ontario, Canada M5A 3E1.

Publications

Nonfiction

The Royal Family: The Story of the British Monarchy from Victoria to Elizabeth. McClelland & Stewart, 1954.
The Golden Trail: The Story of the Klondike Gold Rush. Macmillan, 1954; as *Stampede for Gold*, Knopf, 1955.
The Mysterious North. McClelland & Stewart, 1956.
Klondike: The Life and Death of the Last Great Gold Rush. McClelland & Stewart, 1958; as *The Klondike Fever*, Knopf, 1959; revised edition, McClelland & Stewart, 1972.
Just Add Water and Stir. McClelland & Stewart, 1959.
Adventures of a Columnist. McClelland & Stewart, 1960.
The New City: A Prejudiced View of Toronto, photographs by Henry Rossier. Macmillan, 1961.
Fast, Fast, Fast Relief. McClelland & Stewart, 1962.
The Big Sell: An Introduction to the Black Arts of Door-to-Door Salesmanship & Other Techniques. McClelland & Stewart, 1963.
The Comfortable Pew: A Critical Look at Christianity and the Religious Establishment in the New Age. McClelland & Stewart, 1965.
My War with the Twentieth Century. Doubleday, 1965.
Remember Yesterday. Centennial Publishing, 1965.

The Cool, Crazy, Committed World of the Sixties. McClelland & Stewart, 1966.
The Centennial Food Guide, with Janet Berton. Canadian Centennial Publishing, 1966; as Pierre and Janet Berton's Canadian Food Guide, McClelland & Stewart, 1974.
The Smug Minority. McClelland & Stewart, 1968.
The National Dream: The Great Railway, 1871-1881. McClelland & Stewart, 1970.
The Last Spike: The Great Railway, 1881-1885. McClelland & Stewart, 1971.
Drifting Home. McClelland & Stewart, 1973.
Hollywood's Canada: The Americanization of Our National Image. McClelland & Stewart, 1975.
My Country: The Remarkable Past. McClelland & Stewart, 1976.
The Dionne Years: A Thirties Melodrama. McClelland & Stewart, 1977.
The Wild Frontier. McClelland & Stewart, 1978.
The Invasion of Canada, 1812-1813. McClelland & Stewart, 1980.
Flames Across the Border: The Canadian-American Tragedy, 1813-1814. McClelland & Stewart, 1981.
Why We Act Like Canadians. McClelland & Stewart, 1982.
The Klondike Quest: A Photographic Essay, 1897-1899. McClelland & Stewart, 1983.
The Promised Land: Settling the West, 1896-1914. McClelland & Stewart, 1984.
Masquerade. 1985.
Vimy. McClelland & Stewart, 1986.
Starting Out, Volume I: 1920-1947. McClelland & Stewart, 1987.
The Arctic Grail. McClelland & Stewart, 1988.
The Great Depression. McClelland & Stewart, 1990.
Niagara: A History of the Falls. McClelland & Stewart, 1992.
Pierre Berton's Picture Book of Niagara Falls. McClelland & Stewart, 1993.
Winter. McClelland & Stewart, 1994.
My Times: Living. McClelland & Stewart, 1995.

Nonfiction for Children

Bonanza Gold. McClelland & Stewart, 1991.
Canada Under Seige. McClelland & Stewart, 1991.
The Capture of Detroit. McClelland & Stewart, 1991.
The Death of Isaac Brock. McClelland & Stewart, 1991.
The Klondike Stampede. McClelland & Stewart, 1991.
Revenge of the Tribes. McClelland & Stewart, 1991.
Jane Franklin's Obsession. McClelland & Stewart, 1992.
The Men in Sheepskin Coats. McClelland & Stewart, 1992.
Parry of the Arctic. McClelland & Stewart, 1992.
A Prairie Nightmare. McClelland & Stewart, 1992.
The Railway Pathfinders. McClelland & Stewart, 1992.
Steel Across the Plains. McClelland & Stewart, 1992.
Dr. Kane of the Arctic Seas. McClelland & Stewart, 1993.
Trapped in the Arctic. McClelland & Stewart, 1993.
The Battle of Lake Erie. McClelland & Stewart, 1994.

Fiction for Children

The Secret World of Og. McClelland & Stewart, 1961.

Plays

Screenplays: *City of Gold,* 1957.

Editor, *Great Canadians.* McClelland & Stewart, 1967.
Editor, *Historic Headlines.* McClelland & Stewart, 1967.

*

Media Adaptations: *The National Dream, The Last Spike,* and *The Dionne Years* were all filmed for television and broadcast by the CBC.

* * *

For more than 40 years Pierre Berton has been an aggressive and unavoidable presence on the Canadian scene—his voice on radio, his face on TV, and each fall his latest title on the bookshelves. Born in the Yukon and educated in British Columbia, Berton got his start as a newspaper journalist in Vancouver and after 1947 reached national prominence at *Maclean's* magazine in Toronto, roaming the country and the world as a correspondent and rising to become managing editor.

Berton's first book, *The Royal Family* (1954), ably researched and smoothly written, sought to capitalize on the monarchy fever connected with the coronation of Elizabeth I in 1953. Oddly enough, it did better in the United States than in Canada. In any event, Berton was on his way as a bestselling author. There followed in quick succession *The Golden Trail* (1955), a highly successful history for juveniles of the Klondike gold rush, and the exhaustively researched *Klondike* (1958). Similarly, *The Mysterious North* (1956) is a panoramic survey partly based on his travels in the Canadian North.

Berton spun his success in one medium into success in another, with his work at *Maclean's* and as a sometimes-muckraking daily columnist in the *Toronto Star* leading to positions as interviewer, commentator, and panelist on long-running radio and TV shows. That work eventually led to the creation of a TV production company and the syndicated *Pierre Berton Show* (1963-73).

Berton's most controversial book was *The Comfortable Pew* (1965), a denunciation of established religion's social irrelevance in the 1960s. But it was *The National Dream* and *The Last Spike* (1970 and 1971), his two-volume saga of the Canadian Pacific Railway's transcontinental push to the Pacific in the 19th century, that made his reputation as a popular historian. He confirmed that success with such later works as *The Invasion of Canada* (1980); *Flames Across the Border: The Canadian-American Tragedy, 1813-1814* (1981), a patriotic view of the War of 1812; and *The Arctic Grail* (1988), a sweeping account of the attempts to find the Northwest Passage and the North Pole.

As Will Cude noted in *Profiles in Canadian Literature,* "Only a very prominent author, one who felt invulnerable in the security of a well-established reputation, would have ventured either the rushed mediocrity of *Why We Act Like Canadians* (1982) or the pseudo-porn of *Masquerade* (1985) . . . only a highly competent author, one who had full technical control of perception, tone, and material, would have ventured the touchingly reflective reminiscences of *Drifting Home* [Berton's 1973 account of taking his large family by rubber raft down the Yukon waterway to Dawson]."

Plainly, Berton has been unafraid to tackle any form of professional writing. Unlike many writers for adults who turn to books for children, he has the right kind of light touch; *The Secret World of Og* (1961) has sold more than 200,000 copies internationally, and *Adventures in Canadian History* (in 21 short paperback volumes published in 1995) is lively and vivid.

An expert recycler and ferociously hard worker, Berton says in *My Times: Living with History 1947-1995* (1995), the second volume of his memoirs, "I've never set my sights impossibly high. I've attempted to be a good professional writer, not a great one, trying as best I can to understand my times by studying the past." As a reporter, editor, historian, and broadcaster Berton has helped to shape the postwar period in Canada, articulating the liberal and nationalistic myths and ideals that many Canadians, up to the present at least, have held, nurtured, and cherished.

—Fraser Sutherland

BINCHY, Maeve

Nationality: Irish. **Born:** Dublin, 28 May 1940. **Education:** Holy Child Convent, Killiney, County Dublin; University College, Dublin, B.A. in education. **Family:** Married Gordon Snell in 1977. **Career:** History and French teacher, Pembroke School, Dublin, 1961-68. Since 1968 columnist, *Irish Times,* Dublin. **Agent:** Christine Green, 2 Barbon Close, London WC1N 3JX, England.

Publications

Novels

Light a Penny Candle. London, Century, 1982; New York, Viking, 1983.
Echoes. London, Century, 1985; New York, Viking, 1986.
Firefly Summer. London, Century, 1987; New York, Delacorte Press, 1988.
Circle of Friends. London, Century, 1990; New York, Delacorte Press, 1991.
The Copper Beach. London, Orion, 1992; New York, Delacorte Press, 1993.
The Glass Lake. London, Orion, 1994; New York, Delacorte Press, 1995.

Short Stories

Central Line. London, Quartet, 1978.
Victoria Line. London, Quartet, 1980.
Dublin 4. Dublin, Ward River Press, 1982; London, Century, 1983.
London Transports (includes *Central Line* and *Victoria Line*). London, Century, 1983; New York, Dell, 1986.
The Lilac Bus. Dublin, Ward River Press, 1984; London, Century, 1986; New York, Delacorte Press, 1992.
Silver Wedding. London, Century, 1988; New York, Delacorte Press, 1989.
Dublin People. Oxford, Oxford University Press, 1993.

Plays

End of Term (produced Dublin, 1976).
Half Promised Land (produced Dublin, 1979).

Television Plays: *Deeply Regretted By—,* 1976; *Echoes,* from her own novel, 1988; *The Lilac Bus,* from her own story, 1991.

Other

My First Book. Dublin, Irish Times, 1978.
Maeve's Diary. Dublin, Irish Times, 1979.
Dear Maeve: Writings from the "Irish Times." Dublin, Poolbeg Press, 1995.

* * *

Since the early 1980s Irish novelist and journalist Maeve Binchy has written a string of international bestsellers which share several common features: appealing characters, complex storytelling, and heartwarming poignancy. Her sprawling narratives express a moral but tolerant sensibility. Critics either dismiss or applaud her particular genre as "women's fiction," or even, as Helen Birch of *The Independent* writes, "600-page doorstoppers, beach books, fireside books." Most agree that her work transcends these labels. Her accomplished prose contains shrewd, albeit sentimental, social analysis of Irish women's lives in the mid-to-late 20th century.

In various interviews, Binchy acknowledges one main creative principle: write what you know. Her works focus primarily on small town or suburban life, settings in which interaction between characters need not be contrived. Binchy's protagonists are ordinary women through whom she chronicles the nuances of personal development and the intricacies of social relationships. While romance or passion invariably provide the narrative frameworks, Binchy eschews describing sex or violence in favor of the details of friendship and human behavior. Much of her work inhabits the world of the 1950s and 1960s, arguably a more naive time, and one which, in retrospect, is laced with a nostalgic sense of innocence.

Binchy admits that she begins and infuses each novel with a specific emotion. *Light a Penny Candle* (1982) is about an enduring 30-year friendship between an Irish and an English woman. *Firefly Summer* (1987) concerns an American millionaire's desire to return to his Irish roots and the havoc this creates in the village of Mountfern. In *Circle of Friends* (1990) the friendship between three young women—Benny Hogan, Eve Malone, and Nan Mahon—is shaken by betrayal. *The Glass Lake* (1994) tracks the troubled development of a mother-daughter relationship between Kit and Helen McMahon. Binchy's characters are often caught between the circumscribed roles assigned them by church and family and their own need for independence and self-expression. Success and happiness come to those characters who take charge of their own lives. These appealing women are richly conceived, with all of their flaws and strengths carefully articulated.

Binchy's short-story collections—*Lilac Bus* (1984), *Silver Wedding* (1989), and *The Copper Beech* (1992)—profile sets of interconnected characters whose personal stories disclose that they actually know very little about one another. These composite works reveal the subtle complexities or, as Alix Madrigal of *The San Francisco Chronicle* writes, the "gentle epiphanies" of village life and personal experience. As in her novels, Binchy's comfortable and leisurely prose conceals the deft narrative structure linking the stories.

Critics concur on Binchy's abilities as a skillful and entertaining storyteller, one who is almost incapable of writing badly. Negative criticism centers on the impression that she has not realized her potential as a serious writer, that popular women's fiction doesn't allow the flexing of real literary muscle. These critics assert that her works, while manufacturing genuine and moving characters, often lapse into melodrama or otherwise fail to utilize their powerful foundations. Conversely, other critics recognize the politics of chronicling the domestic and personal details of women's lives.

Binchy, while resisting the label of a "romance writer," does not object to having her work described as "comfortable." The easygoing accessibility of her writing may be a factor of this self-described "jokey and benevolent person," who likes to write about people and relationships. "I write very much as I speak," she has said. It is that entertaining and expressive voice which has inspired loyalty among the millions who love a rambling tale.

—Christina Sylka

BLAKE, Walker E. *See* **BUTTERWORTH, W. E.**

BLOCK, Lawrence

Pseudonyms: Chip Harrison, Paul Kavanagh. **Nationality:** American. **Born:** Buffalo, New York, 24 June 1938. **Education:** Attended Antioch College, Yellow Springs, Ohio, 1955-59. **Family:** Married 1) Loretta Ann Kallett in 1960 (divorced 1973); three daughters; 2) Lynne Wood in 1983. **Career:** Editor, Scott Meredith, Inc., New York, 1957-58, and Whitman Publishing Company, Racine, Wisconsin, 1964-66. Since 1977, corresponding editor, *Writer's Digest.* **Awards:** Nero Wolfe award for Best Mystery of 1979, for *The Burglar Who Liked to Quote Kipling;* named Suspense Writer of the Year by the *Romantic Times,* 1984; Shamus award, Private Eye Writers of America, 1983 and 1985; Edgar Allan Poe award, Mystery Writers of America, 1985, 1992, and 1994; Japanese Maltese Falcon award for *When the Sacred Ginmill Closes;* Grand Master award, 1994. **Member:** International Association of Crime Writers, International Narcotics Enforcement Officers Association, International Association for the Study of Organized Crime, Mystery Writers of America, Private Eye Writers of America (president, 1984). **Agent:** Knox Burger, 39½ Washington Square South, New York, New York, 10012, U.S.A.

Publications

Novels

Death Pulls a Doublecross. New York, Fawcett, 1961; as *Coward's Kiss,* New York, Foul Play Press, 1987.
Mona. New York, Fawcett, 1961; London, Muller, 1963; as *Sweet Slow Death,* Berkley, 1986.
Markham: The Case of the Pornographic Photos. New York, Belmont Books, 1961; London, Consul, 1965; as *You Could Call It Murder,* New York, Foul Play Press, 1987.
The Girl with the Long Green Heart. New York, Fawcett, 1965; London, Muller, 1967.
Deadly Honeymoon. New York, Macmillan, 1967; London, Hale, 1981.
After the First Death. New York, Macmillan, 1969; London, Hale, 1981.
The Specialists. New York, Fawcett, 1969; London, Hale, 1980.
No Score, as Chip Harrison. New York, Fawcett, 1970.
Chip Harrison Scores Again, as Chip Harrison, New York, Fawcett, 1971.
Such Men Are Dangerous: A Novel of Violence, as Paul Kavanagh. New York, Macmillan, 1969; London, Hodder and Stoughton, 1971.
Ronald Rabbit Is a Dirty Old Man. New York, Geis, 1971.
The Triumph of Evil, as Paul Kavanagh. Cleveland, World, 1971; London, Hodder and Stoughton, 1972.
Make Out with Murder, as Chip Harrison, New York, Fawcett, 1974; as *Five Little Rich Girls,* as Lawrence Block, London Allison and Busby, 1986.
Not Comin' Home to You, as Paul Kavanagh. New York, Putnam, 1974; London, Hodder and Stoughton, 1976.
The Topless Tulip Caper, as Chip Harrison, New York, Fawcett, 1975; London, Allison and Busby, 1984.
Ariel. New York, Arbor House, 1980; London, Hale, 1981.
Code of Arms, with Harold King. New York, Coward McCann, 1981.
Introducing Chip Harrison, as Chip Harrison, Woodstock, Vermont, Countryman Press, 1984.
Into the Night, with Cornell Woolrich. New York, Mysterious Press, 1987; London, Simon and Schuster, 1989.
Random Walk: A Novel for a New Age. New York, Tor, 1988.

Evan Tanner Series

The Thief Who Couldn't Sleep. New York, Fawcett, 1966.
The Cancelled Czech. New York, Fawcett, 1967.
Tanner's Twelve Swingers. New York, Fawcett, 1967; London, Coronet, 1968.
Two for Tanner. New York, Fawcett, 1967.
Here Comes a Hero. New York, Fawcett, 1968.
Tanner's Tiger. New York, Fawcett, 1968.
Me Tanner, You Jane. New York, Macmillan, 1970.

Matthew Scudder Series

In the Midst of Death. New York, Dell, 1976; London, Hale, 1979.
Sins of the Fathers. New York, Dell, 1976; London, Hale, 1979.
Time to Murder and Create. New York, Dell, 1977; London, Hale, 1979.
A Stab in the Dark. New York, Arbor House, 1981; London, Hale, 1982.
Eight Million Ways to Die. New York, Arbor House, 1982; London, Hale, 1983.
When the Sacred Ginmill Closes. New York, Arbor House, 1986; London, Macmillan, 1987.
Out on the Cutting Edge. New York, Morrow, 1989.
A Ticket to the Boneyard. New York, Morrow, 1990.
A Dance at the Slaughterhouse. New York, Morrow, 1991; London, Orion, 1991.
A Walk among the Tomstones. New York, Morrow, 1992; London, Orion, 1992.

The Devil Knows You're Dead. New York, Morrow, 1993; London, Orion, 1993.
A Long Line of Dead Men. New York, Morrow, 1994; London, Orion, 1994.
Bernie Rhodenbarr Series
Burglars Can't Be Choosers. New York, Random House, 1977; London, Hale, 1978.
The Burglar in the Closet. New York, Random House, 1978; London, Hale, 1980.
The Burglar Who Liked to Quote Kipling. New York, Random House, 1979; London, Hale, 1981.
The Burglar Who Studied Spinoza. New York, Random House, 1981; London, Hale, 1982.
The Burglar Who Painted Like Mondrian. New York, Arbor House, 1983; London, Gollancz, 1984.
The Burglar Who Traded Ted Williams. New York, Dutton, and London, London, Oldcastle, 1994
The Burglar Who Thought He Was Bogart. New York, Dutton, and London, Oldcastle, 1995.

Short Stories

Sometimes They Bite. New York, Arbor House, 1983.
Like a Lamb to the Slaughter. New York, Arbor House, 1984.
Some Days You Get the Bear. New York, Morrow, 1993; London, Orion, 1993.

Nonfiction

Swiss Shooting Talers and Medals, with Delbert Ray Krause. Racine, Wisconsin, Whitman Publishing, 1965.
Writing the Novel: From Plot to Print. Cincinnati, Writer's Digest, 1979; London, Poplar Press, 1986.
Telling Lies for Fun and Profit: A Manual for Fiction Writers. New York, Arbor House, 1981.
Real Food Places, with Cheryl Morrison. Emmaus, Pennsylvania, Rodale Press, 1981.
Spider, Spin Me a Web: Lawrence Block on Writing Fiction. Cincinnati, Writer's Digest, 1988.
After Hours: Conversations with Lawrence Block, with Ernie Bulow. Albuquerque, University of New Mexico Press, 1995.

*

Media Adaptation: Film—*Burglar,* 1987, from the Bernie Rhodenbarr novels.

Manuscript Collection: University of Oregon, Eugene.

* * *

Crime and mystery novelist Lawrence Block has carved a lasting niche in crime fiction over the past four decades, publishing more than 50 novels, short-story collections, and nonfiction books. Compared to Ross Macdonald, John D. MacDonald, and Elmore Leonard for his rise to bestseller status after years of underappreciation, Block is praised for moving beyond his early days of pulp fiction to become an award-winning author. As Peter Gorner of the *Chicago Tribune* writes, "Respected as a writer's writer, [Block is] the rare pro who survived a hack apprenticeship without becoming one."

Block began writing in college, selling short stories to crime magazines. The shrinking market for short fiction led him to become an editor for a New York literary agency rather than attempt a novel. "To make even a marginal living, I would have to write novels, and I didn't think I was ready to do that yet," Block revealed in *Contemporary Authors.* Working as an editor in New York, Block received his first break when he was commissioned to write a detective novel as a tie-in to the television show *Markham.* When he finished the novel, Block decided it was "too good to waste," and after some revision published the novel under the title *Death Pulls a Doublecross* (1961).

Block's Evan Tanner series developed out of *The Thief Who Couldn't Sleep* (1966), a novel about a Korean war veteran whose brain's sleep center is destroyed by shrapnel. Recruited by a mysterious agency, Tanner becomes a globe-hopping spy of sorts; in *The Cancelled Czech* (1967) he must kidnap a former Nazi from Eastern Europe, and in the succeeding five novels he travels to such locales as Lithuania and Central Africa. The novels are humorous and full of quirks; unable to sleep, Tanner spends the nighttime hours learning several foreign languages, associating with many bizarre groups such as the Flat Earth Society, and being followed by the FBI and CIA.

With the success of his Evan Tanner series and various crime novels written under the pseudonyms Chip Harrison and Paul Kavanagh, Block became a full-time writer. His Bernie Rhodenbarr series won widespread critical approval, especially for the central character, a burglar and bibliophile who steals to support his expensive tastes. John McAleer in the *Chicago Tribune Book World* finds Bernie's candor and honesty refreshing: "A man bent on supporting himself by breaking the law finds himself, time and again, compelled by necessity and his own bedrock decency, to restore to society the stability it professes to cherish but which, by its own transgressions, it puts in jeopardy." While many critics responded positively to Bernie's forthrightness and humor, others criticized Block for his confusing plots and unfamiliarity with the art world which Bernie finds so attractive.

Block continued his success with his Matthew Scudder novels about an unlicensed Manhattan private eye struggling with alcoholism. As Jean M. White writes in the *Washington Post Book World,* "Block has turned his considerable talents to the hard-boiled detective school. Through Scudder's eyes, we see a harrowing picture of a naked city's lower depths and a big apple rotting to the core." *Eight Million Ways to Die* (1982) deals with a hooker who wants Scudder's help in getting out of the prostitution racket. *On the Cutting Edge* (1989), which relates two Scudder cases involving a missing young actress and the death of a fellow AA member, earned the following praise from Gary Dretzka in the Chicago *Tribune Books:* "Should crime fiction be taken seriously as literature? To anyone who requires a reply to that query—or has been in hibernation since Raymond Chandler first picked up a pen—[*On the Cutting Edge*] answers . . . with a loud 'yes.'"

A Ticket to the Boneyard (1990) earned widespread praise for its moral complexity and plot about a killer whom Scudder framed and sent to prison years ago when Scudder was a police officer. Richard Lipez in the *Washington Post Book World* found the novel to be "a beautifully modulated and absolutely riveting tale" in which "the social contract is constantly examined and reexamined, always thoughtfully. . . . Scudder discovers that his anguished vigilantism only results in more carnage."

Block has received criticism for his long list of titles, some of which he published under pseudonyms, that even he has called "categorically inferior." Often his writing has been described as slick and too focused on the grisly aspects of crime, especially in his Scudder series. However, most critics agree that Block's accurate portrayal of Scudder as an alcoholic adds an extra dimension of vulnerability to the detective, whose fight to remain sober is as much at the heart of the novels as the crimes he investigates.

—Christopher Swann

BLUME, Judy (Sussman)

Nationality: American. **Born:** 12 February 1938, in Elizabeth, New Jersey. **Education:** New York University, B.A., 1960. **Family:** Married John M. Blume, 15 August 1959 (divorced, 1975); married third husband, George Cooper, 6 June 1987; children: (first marriage) Randy Lee (daughter), Lawrence Andrew; (third marriage) Amanda (stepdaughter). **Career:** Writer of juvenile and adult fiction. Founder of KIDS Fund, 1981. **Awards:** *New York Times* best books for children list, 1970, Nene award, 1975, Young Hoosier Book award, 1976, and North Dakota Children's Choice award, 1979, all for *Are You There God? It's Me, Margaret;* Charlie May Swann Children's Book award, 1972; Young Readers Choice award, Pacific Northwest Library Association, and Sequoyah Children's Book award of Oklahoma, both 1975; Massachusetts Children's Book award, Georgia Children's Book award, and South Carolina Children's Book award, all 1977; Rhode Island Library Association award, 1978; North Dakota Children's Choice award and West Australian Young Readers' Book award, both 1980; United States Army in Europe Kinderbuch award and Great Stone Face award, New Hampshire Library Council, both 1981, for *Tales of a Fourth Grade Nothing;* Arizona Young Readers award, and Young Readers Choice award, Pacific Northwest Library Association, both 1977, and North Dakota Children's Choice award, 1983, all for *Blubber;* South Carolina Children's Book award, 1978, for *Otherwise Known as Sheila the Great;* Texas Bluebonnet List, 1980, Michigan Young Reader's award, and International Reading Association Children's Choice award, both 1981, First Buckeye Children's Book award, Nene award, Sue Hefley Book award, Louisiana Association of School Libraries, United States Army in Europe Kinderbuch award, West Australian Young Readers' Book award, North Dakota Children's Choice award, Colorado Children's Book award, Georgia Children's Book award, Tennessee Children's Choice Book award, and Utah Children's Book award, all 1982, Northern Territory Young Readers' Book award, Young Readers Choice award, Pacific Northwest Library Association, Garden State Children's Book award, Iowa Children's Choice award, Arizona Young Readers' award, California Young Readers' Medal, and Young Hoosier Book award, all 1983, all for *Superfudge;* American Book award nomination, Dorothy Canfield Fisher Children's Book award, Buckeye Children's Book award, and California Young Readers Medal, all 1983, all for *Tiger Eyes.* Golden Archer award, 1974; Today's Woman award, 1981; Eleanor Roosevelt Humanitarian award, Favorite Author—Children's Choice award, Milner award, and Jeremiah Ludington Memorial award, all 1983; Carl Sandburg Freedom to Read award, Chicago Public Library, 1984; Civil Liberties award, Atlanta American Civil Liberties Union, and John Rock award, Center for Population Options, Los Angeles, both 1986; South Australian Youth Media award for Best Author, South Australian Association for Media Education, 1988. D.H.L.: Kean College, 1987. **Member:** Society of Children's Book Writers (member of board), PEN, Authors Guild (member of council), Authors League of America, National Coalition Against Censorship (council of advisors). **Agent:** Harold Ober Associates, Inc., 425 Madison Ave., New York, New York 10017, U.S.A.

Publications

Fiction for Children

The One in the Middle Is the Green Kangaroo. Reilly & Lee, 1969, revised edition, Bradbury, 1981, new revised edition with new illustrations, 1991.
Iggie's House. Bradbury, 1970.
Are You There God? It's Me, Margaret. Bradbury, 1970.
Then Again, Maybe I Won't. Bradbury, 1971.
Freckle Juice. Four Winds, 1971.
Tales of a Fourth Grade Nothing. Dutton, 1972.
Otherwise Known as Sheila the Great. Dutton, 1972.
It's Not the End of the World. Bradbury, 1972.
Deenie. Bradbury, 1973.
Blubber. Bradbury, 1974.
Starring Sally J. Freedman As Herself. Bradbury, 1977.
Superfudge. Dutton, 1980.
Tiger Eyes. Bradbury, 1981.
The Pain and the Great One. Bradbury, 1984.
Just As Long As We're Together. Orchard, 1987.
Fudge-a-Mania. Dutton, 1990.
Here's to You, Rachel Robinson. Orchard, 1993.

Novels for Adults

Forever... Bradbury, 1975.
Wifey. Putnam, 1977.
Smart Women. Putnam, 1984.

Nonfiction

Letters to Judy: What Your Kids Wish They Could Tell You. Putnam, 1986.
The Judy Blume Memory Book. Dell, 1988.

Plays

Screenplay: *Otherwise Known as Sheila the Great,* with Lawrence Blume, 1988.

*

Media Adaptations: *Forever...* (television film), 1978; *Freckle Juice* (animated film), 1987.

Critical Studies: *The Pied Pipers* by Emma Fisher and Justin Wintle, Paddington Press, 1975; *Breakthrough: Women in Writing* by Diana Gleasner, Walker, 1980; *Judy Blume's Story* by Betsey Lee, Dillon Press, 1981; *Presenting Judy Blume* by Maryann Weidt, Twayne, 1989.

* * *

Best known for works such as *Are You There, God? It's Me, Margaret* (1970) and *Superfudge* (1980), Judy Blume is one of America's most controversial writers of young adult fiction. What fuels the interest in her novels are her explicit descriptions of sex and menstruation as well as her depiction of teens. The award-winning Blume writes straightforwardly, cutting to the heart of such issues as puberty, family, and sex. For her candor, Blume has earned much negative criticism and a readership of millions.

Blume scored her first big seller with her third book, *Are You There, God? It's Me, Margaret.* Margaret Simon, the twelve-year-old daughter of a Christian mother and a Jewish father, is in the throes of puberty and religious choice, although for most critics Margaret's religious concerns are a definite sideplot to Margaret's menstrual cycle. Some, such as Lavinia Russ in *Publishers Weekly,* found the book to be realistic and humorous: "With sensitivity and humor, Judy Blume has captured the joys, fears, and uncertainty that surround a young girl approaching adolescence." Others, such as George W. Arthur in *Book Window,* disagreed; Arthur called the descriptions of Margaret's period "excessive, almost obsessive . . . when the author rhapsodizes about the wearing of a sanitary napkin, the effect is banal in the extreme . . . Suddenly a sensitive, amusing novel has been reduced to the level of some of advertising blurb in the 'confidential' section of a teenage magazine." Nevertheless, *Margaret* won three regional awards and a place on the *New York Times* best books for children list.

Blume's books follow a pattern of teenage encounters with a harsh or frightening truth, such as puberty, divorce, relocation, or even loss of virginity. The young narrators tell their stories in first-person, awkwardly yet effectively revealing their own thoughts. This self-revelatory tone and simple diction make an impact on young readers, especially teen girls who came to identify with the narrators. Teens also appreciate the absence of direct moralizing in Blume's works; Blume lets her characters speak for themselves without hitting the reader over the head with a lesson. However, some critics hint at an unspoken moral vision in Blume's works. As Decter writes, "Miss Blume's heroes never have an unacceptable thought; her villains, having once deviated from orthodoxy, are condemned absolutely to their villainy."

Blume's novel *Forever* (1975), considered her first break from young adult fiction, is concerned with Katherine, age 17, and her first sexual encounter. While the descriptions are explicit, they are also stilted, and Katherine and her lover, Michael, are decidedly passionless. Love, Katherine comes to learn, can be a tricky thing, and at the end of the novel she breaks up with Michael, having become attracted to another man. This, in essence, is the plot, and the characters remain relatively unchanged. First love is casually dispensed with. Critic David Rees scathingly portrays *Forever* as "easily [Blume's] worst book . . . Consider the artless banality of this: 'I came right before Michael and as I did I made noises, just like my mother.' It's the same sort of language as 'I went into the kitchen and fixed myself a cup of coffee.'" Lynne Hamilton in *Signal* writes "Sex for Blume is too wholesome and uncomplicated to trigger crises . . . Katherine experiences none of the horrors that usually accompany teenage sex in fiction."

Tiger Eyes (1981), however, is noted by most as Blume's best work. Nominated for an American Book Award, *Tiger Eyes* remains much like Blume's earlier works with its first-person, candid point of view and its 15-year-old female heroine. Yet the situation, dealing with the murder of Davey Wexler's father and her subsequent move from Atlantic City to Los Alamos, has richer possibilities, many of which Blume mines successfully. Davey's uncle in Los Alamos is a weapons scientist who is ironically overprotective of his niece; her boyfriend Wolf, a Hispanic college student, is more of a healer for Davey than a sexual partner. And while Davey does not change substantially by the end of the novel, as Robert Lipsyte writes in *The Nation,* she and her mother "weather a crisis, often helped and hindered by the same well-meaning, mean-spirited people, and now must go forward with their lives."

While many of Blume's books may be considered outdated in their social views, she manages to capture the awkward, transitory years of adolescence and engage young readers. As Faith McNulty writes in *The New Yorker,* "She has convinced millions of young people that truth can be found in a book and that reading is fun. At a time that many believe may be the twilight of the written word, those are things to be grateful for."

—Christopher Swann

BOMBECK, Erma (Louise)

Nationality: American. **Born:** 21 February 1927 in Dayton, Ohio. **Education:** Ohio University; University of Dayton, B.A., 1949. **Family:** married William Lawrence Bombeck (a school administrator), August 13, 1949; children: Betsy, Andrew, Matthew. **Career:** Author, columnist, humorist, and lecturer. Dayton *Journal Herald,* Dayton, Ohio, writer, 1949-53; author of weekly column published in *Kettering-Oakwood Times,* 1963-65; author of thrice-weekly column, "At Wit's End," for Dayton *Journal Herald,* 1965, syndicated to sixty-five newspapers by the Newsday syndicate, 1965-67, and to over nine hundred newspapers by the Field Newspaper syndicate, beginning 1967; columnist with Pubs.-Hall syndicate (now North American syndicate), 1970-85, Los Angeles Times syndicate, 1985-88, and Universal Press syndicate, 1988-96. Appeared twice weekly on "Good Morning America," 1975-86. **Awards:** National Headliner prize from Theta Sigma Phi, 1969; Mark Twain Award for Humor, 1973; American Cancer Society Medal of Honor, 1990. Fifteen honorary doctorates. **Member:** American Academy of Humor Columnists, Women in Communication. **Agent:** Universal Press syndicate, 4900 Main St., Kansas City, Missouri 64112, U.S.A. **Died:** San Francisco, 22 April 1996, of complications from a kidney transplant.

PUBLICATIONS

Humor

At Wit's End. Doubleday, 1967.
Just Wait Till You Have Children of Your Own. Doubleday, 1971.
I Lost Everything in the Post-Natal Depression. Doubleday, 1973.
The Grass Is Always Greener over the Septic Tank. McGraw, 1976.
If Life Is a Bowl of Cherries, What Am I Doing in the Pits? McGraw, 1978.
Aunt Erma's Cope Book: How to Get from Monday to Friday ... in Twelve Days. McGraw, 1979.
Motherhood: The Second Oldest Profession. McGraw, 1983.

Erma Bombeck Giant Economy Size. Doubleday, 1983.
Laugh Along with Erma Bombeck. Fawcett, 1984.
Four of a Kind: A Treasury of Favorite Works by America's Best-Loved Humorist. McGraw, 1985.
At Wit's End. Fawcett, 1986.
Best of Bombeck. Galahad Books, 1987.
Family: The Ties That Bind ... and Gag! McGraw, 1987.
When You Look Like Your Passport Photo, It's Time to Go Home. HarperCollins, 1991.
A Marriage Made in Heaven ..., or, Too Tired for an Affair. HarperCollins, 1993.
All I Know about Animal Behavior I Learned in Loehmann's Dressing Room. HarperCollins, 1995.

Nonfiction

I Want to Grow Hair, I Want to Grow Up, I Want to Go to Boise: Children Surviving Cancer. Harper, 1989.

*

Film Adaptation: *The Grass Is Always Greener over the Septic Tank* (for television), 1978.

* * *

Reading Erma Bombeck's writing is like eating a bowl of chicken noodle soup. It is warm and satisfying, spiced with wit and humor. Known primarily for her syndicated newspaper columns, Bombeck has elevated suburban and domestic life to new heights by using humor, while admitting it's impossible to be a perfect mother, housewife, or worker. She pokes fun at what seems trivial, but has wide appeal because she writes truths from her own experiences. By adding a clever touch of wit, Bombeck can make even the act of thawing a pork chop sound funny (place it under your armpits). While Bombeck writes from the perspective of a housewife, her audience is much broader; she and many feminists see eye to eye, and many men appreciate her dose of good-natured charm.

Bombeck has received mixed reviews on occasion, but the consensus is that she is very talented and successfully manages to convey daily life from a fresh and clever perspective. *People* calls her "America's Housewife-at-Large," while *Time* refers to her as the "female Art Buchwald." Seymour Rothman, of the *Toledo Blade,* says "Erma's role in the column is that of a wife and mother who long ago conceded defeat but can't find anyone to surrender to."

Bombeck writes humorously about being a housewife without making fun of women who stay at home. If anything, she started by drawing from her own experiences and discovered that many women identify with her writing. Says Bombeck, "Basically women work alone when they're at home. They think no one is feeling what they are feeling, that no one understands their daily frustrations. But we do, we all do." Bombeck told Diane Shah, of *Newsweek,* "I spend 90 percent of my time living scripts and ten percent writing them."

Bombeck's first book, *At Wit's End* (1967), is a collection of her syndicated writings. She also wrote *Just Wait Till You Have Children of Your Own* (1971), *I Lost Everything in the Post-Natal Depression* (1973), and *If Life is a Bowl of Cherries, What Am I Doing in the Pits?* (1978). Richard L. Lingeman, reviewer for *The New York Times Book Review,* says of the latter title, "[Bombeck's] humor is precisely targeted on the large number of housewives in this country who share her experiences. Her style is a bit hectic and slapdash, sounding as though she scrawled the column on the back of a laundry list while stirring the evening's Hamburger Helper."

In *The Grass is Always Greener Over the Septic Tank* (1976), Bombeck writes about topics ranging from Ken and Barbie dolls to a little league coach who plays to lose. *Bestseller* critic H. T. Anderson writes, "There are those who write about . . . suburban things with cynicism, snarling, and spleen. Erma Bombeck doesn't. She manages with the deftness of a trapeze artist to come up with a smile on her face in the midst of unaccountable maneuvers. She takes her joy and strength from the things she satirizes—we need more of that!"

Not all critics react as favorably. *Library Journal's* J. W. Powell says, "Bombeck's humor is aimed at pointing up the absurdities of the suburban American middle-class lifestyle, with its trivia, its real or imagined necessities. Sometimes [The Grass . . .] is funny, but unfortunately, Bombeck has become the victim of overexposure through newspaper syndication and TV. However, there is a ready audience for her work." Indeed, *The Grass* sold over 500,000 copies in hardback and was on the bestseller list for over ten months the year Powell wrote that review.

Other of Bombeck's works include *Aunt Erma's Cope Book: How to Get from Monday to Friday . . . in Twelve Days* (1979), *Motherhood: The Second Oldest Profession* (1987), and *A Marriage Made in Heaven—or Too Tired for an Affair* (1993). Susan Mulcahy, of *The New York Times Book Review,* says of *A Marriage,* "Focusing a jovial but analytic eye on their relationship, Mrs. Bombeck determines that she couldn't have done it without Bill, and if she had, it wouldn't have meant much." But the book isn't all yuks. She devotes chapters to such serious episodes as her early difficulties conceiving children, a miscarriage at the age of 40 and, more recently, a mastectomy. But even these jolts are leavened with Mrs. Bombeck's brand of self-deprecatory wit. After her surgery she wrote, "I tortured myself with *Sports Illustrated*'s swimwear edition and I couldn't get Madonna's nuclear-warhead bras out of my mind."

—Liz Mulligan

BOYLE, T(homas) Coraghessan

Nationality: American. **Born:** Thomas John Boyle, 2 December 1948, in Peekskill, New York; changed middle name to Coraghessan when he was seventeen. **Education:** State University of New York at Potsdam, graduated c. 1970; Iowa University, Ph.D., 1977. **Family:** Married Karen Kvashay, c. 1974; children: Kerrie, Milo, Spencer. **Awards:** Coordinating Council of Literary Magazines award for fiction, 1977; National Endowment for the Arts fellowship, 1977; St. Lawrence Prize, 1980; Aga Khan Prize, *Paris Review* magazine, 1981; Faulkner award, PEN American Center, 1989, for *World's End;* PEN Award for short story, PEN American Center, 1990, for "If the River Was Whiskey." **Agent:** Georges Borchardt, 136 East 57th St., New York, New York 10022. **Address:** Department of English, University of Southern California, University Park, Los Angeles, California 90089, U.S.A.

Publications

Novels

Water Music. Atlantic/Little, Brown, 1981.
Budding Prospects: A Pastoral. Viking, 1984.
World's End. Viking, 1987.
East Is East. Viking, 1991.
The Road to Wellville. Viking, 1993.
The Tortilla Curtain. Viking, 1995.

Short Stories

The Descent of Man. Atlantic/Little, Brown, 1979.
Greasy Lake and Other Stories. Viking, 1985.
If the River Was Whiskey. Viking, 1990.
Without a Hero. Viking, 1994.

*

Film Adaptation: *The Road to Wellville,* 1994.

* * *

Since *The Descent of Man* (1979), T. Coraghessan Boyle's first collection of stories, critics have found his dark humor tantalizing and intriguing.

His characters' crazed landings in "rocky gardens, pancake-leafed vegetation, [and] black fountains" would be nonsense without a moral drumskin to unlace. In "Filthy with Things" (*Without a Hero,* 1994), for example, Julian Laxner signs a house-cleaning contract without reading the small print, only to discover that he and his wife have signed away all of their possessions except the few items that the upscale pack rats may reclaim, one each day for thirty days. Besides the social snigger, this twist on the American dream chills; without his signature stuff, Boyle's man has nothing.

Typically, Boyle's main character is a social misfit before his nightmare adventure begins. In *East Is East* (1990), for example, Hiro (no hero) gets picked on by his mates, jumps ship, and swims an impossible distance to the coast of Georgia. He later concludes, "While we live, death is irrelevant; when we are dead we do not exist. There is no reason to fear death." A flashback to his boyhood tormentors shows that nothing much has changed: "They'd gang up on him at the ballfield. . . . When would it end, he asked himself, and the answer was never." Indeed, Hiro struggles through a life of ridiculous repetitions.

Boyle's characters seem always to be backing toward the crumbling cliff, pushing the envelope of possibility, and refiguring the odds of survival. This would be heroically grim if they weren't such clowns and bumblers. In *Water Music* (1981), Ned Rise is "unwashed, untutored, unloved, battered, abused, harassed, deprived, starved, orphaned, impoverished, ignorant, unlucky, and a victim of class prejudice, lack of opportunity, malicious fate, and gin"—a modern litany of reasons why men go wrong.

With the exception of the predictable name games played with Boyle's characters, the expected rarely happens. In *The Road to Wellville* (1993), con artist Charlie Ossining heads for prison while the virtuous Will Lightbody receives enema cures at a sanitarium for the well-heeled, if not healed. An incorrigible prankster, Boyle showers bad luck on everyone with complete impartiality.

The number of twists in his plots is reminiscent of P. G. Wodehouse and his style resembles that of Kurt Vonnegut. For instance, when Charlie Ossining's first get-rich-quick scheme fails, he mourns, "And so it all comes to this." And later, as Kellogg's sanitarium is burning down around him he muses, "And so it goes," straight from Vonnegut's *Slaughterhouse Five.* Deadly fires sweep both novels, but while Vonnegut's villain is Hitler, Boyle's satire shows Dr. John Harvey Kellogg as his own worst enemy, not society's demon (without heroes, there are no monsters). As Jane Smiley said in the *New York Times Book Review,* "the justly deserved fates of his narcissistic and sometimes cruel characters withhold a final portion of pleasurable satisfaction." Even when Boyle seems headed for catharsis or a happy ending, the story turns inside out again.

The 18th-century haiku master Buson said to "use the commonplace to escape the commonplace." That's what Boyle does. Except for an occasional word that even professors would need to look up, his fiction is easy reading (e.g., Dr. Kellogg's "big friendly mitt of a healing hand was pumping Will's limp scrap of wrinkle and bone as if he were trying to draw water from a well"). Boyle's simple words and stereotypes can become, for instance, revelations about two kinds of men everyone vaguely dislikes. An upper-class white male and an illegal Mexican immigrant in *The Tortilla Curtain* (1995) both repeatedly avoid doing the right thing, forgetting their hatred only when faced with worse news: not a fire this time but a flood. We all have days when good deeds are against our better judgment, but that summarizes their lives.

Where are the women and children in Boyle's books? While a few are developed as betrayers or deadweights, most are only roughly sketched or killed. Rarely do good things come to those who love, but in *Without a Hero*'s "Hopes Rise," a city couple discovers passion's pulse and wild rustlings in a sultry surrounding. At an ear-splitting frog concert by a backwoods pond, the mud of human routine turns into a celebration of life. Everyone is guilt-free and in the mood to procreate: the planet isn't dying after all. Few of Boyle's plots end so happily.

Awash in American humor's traditions—brawn, bravado, and ineptitude—the Boylean male sideslips every chance to be a hero. Money mumbles, dumb luck conquers all, scoundrels sleep soundly, and women and children are last. No offense intended, it's just how things go.

—Maril Nowak

BRADBURY, Ray(mond Douglas)

Nationality: American. **Born:** Waukegan, Illinois, 22 August 1920. **Education:** Los Angeles High School, graduated 1938. **Family:** Married Marguerite Susan McClure in 1947; four daughters. **Career:** Since 1943 full-time writer. President, Science-Fantasy Writers of America, 1951-53. Member of the Board of Directors, Screen Writers Guild of America, 1957-61. Lives in Los Angeles. **Awards:** O. Henry prize, 1947, 1948; Benjamin Franklin award, 1954; American Academy award, 1954; Boys' Clubs of America Junior Book award, 1956; Golden Eagle award, for screenplay, 1957; Ann Radcliffe award, 1965, 1971; Writers Guild award, 1974; Aviation and Space Writers award, for television documentary, 1979; Gandalf award, 1980; Nebula Grand Master, 1988; Bram Stoker

Life Achievement award, 1989. D.Litt.: Whittier College, California, 1979. **Agent:** Harold Matson Company, 276 Fifth Avenue, New York, New York 10001. **Address:** c/o Bantam, 666 Fifth Avenue, New York, New York 10103, U.S.A.

PUBLICATIONS

Novels

Fahrenheit 451. New York, Ballantine, 1953; London, Hart Davis, 1954.
Dandelion Wine. New York, Doubleday, and London, Hart Davis, 1957.
Something Wicked This Way Comes. New York, Simon and Schuster, 1962; London, Hart Davis, 1963.
Death Is a Lonely Business. New York, Knopf, 1985; London, Grafton, 1986.
A Graveyard for Lunatics: Another Tale of Two Cities. New York, Knopf, and London, Grafton, 1990.
The Smile. Mankato, Minnesota, Creative Education, 1991.
Green Shadows, White Whale. New York, Knopf, and London, HarperCollins, 1992.

Short Stories

Dark Carnival. Sauk City, Wisconsin, Arkham House, 1947; abridged edition, London, Hamish Hamilton, 1948; abridged edition, as *The Small Assassin,* London, New English Library, 1962.
The Martian Chronicles. New York, Doubleday, 1950; as *The Silver Locusts,* London, Hart Davis, 1951.
The Illustrated Man. New York, Doubleday, 1951; London, Hart Davis, 1952.
The Golden Apples of the Sun. New York, Doubleday, and London, Hart Davis, 1953.
The October Country. New York, Ballantine, 1955; London, Hart Davis, 1956.
A Medicine for Melancholy. New York, Doubleday, 1959.
The Day It Rained Forever. London, Hart Davis, 1959.
The Machineries of Joy. New York, Simon and Schuster, and London, Hart Davis, 1964.
The Vintage Bradbury. New York, Random House, 1965.
The Autumn People. New York, Ballantine, 1965.
Tomorrow Midnight. New York, Ballantine, 1966.
Twice Twenty Two (selection). New York, Doubleday, 1966.
I Sing the Body Electric! New York, Knopf, 1969; London, Hart Davis, 1970.
Bloch and Bradbury, with Robert Bloch. New York, Tower, 1969; as *Fever Dreams and Other Fantasies,* London, Sphere, 1970.
(*Selected Stories*), edited by Anthony Adams. London, Harrap, 1975.
Long after Midnight. New York, Knopf, 1976; London, Hart Davis MacGibbon, 1977.
The Best of Bradbury. New York, Bantam, 1976.
To Sing Strange Songs. Exeter, Devon, Wheaton, 1979.
The Stories of Ray Bradbury. New York, Knopf, and London, Granada, 1980.
The Last Circus, and The Electrocution. Northridge, California, Lord John Press, 1980.
Dinosaur Tales. New York, Bantam, 1983.
A Memory of Murder. New York, Dell, 1984.
The Toynbee Convector. New York, Knopf, 1988; London, Grafton, 1989.

Plays

The Meadow, in *Best One-Act Plays of 1947-48,* edited by Margaret Mayorga. New York, Dodd Mead, 1948.
The Anthem Sprinters and Other Antics (produced Los Angeles, 1968). New York, Dial Press, 1963.
The World of Ray Bradbury (produced Los Angeles, 1964; New York, 1965).
The Wonderful Ice-Cream Suit (produced Los Angeles, 1965; New York, 1987; musical version, music by Jose Feliciano, produced Pasadena, California, 1990).
The Day It Rained Forever, music by Bill Whitefield (produced Edinburgh, 1988). New York, French, 1966.
The Pedestrian. New York, French, 1966.
Christus Apollo, music by Jerry Goldsmith (produced Los Angeles, 1969).
The Wonderful Ice-Cream Suit and Other Plays (includes *The Veldt* and *To the Chicago Abyss*). New York, Bantam, 1972; London, Hart Davis, 1973.
The Veldt (produced London, 1980).
Leviathan 99 (produced Los Angeles, 1972).
Pillar of Fire and Other Plays for Today, Tomorrow, and Beyond Tomorrow (includes *Kaleidoscope* and *The Foghorn*). New York, Bantam, 1975.
The Foghorn (produced New York, 1977).
That Ghost, That Bride of Time: Excerpts from a Play-in-Progress. Glendale, California, Squires, 1976.
The Martian Chronicles, adaptation of his own stories (produced Los Angeles, 1977).
Fahrenheit 451, adaptation of his own novel (produced Los Angeles, 1979).
Dandelion Wine, adaptation of his own story (produced Los Angeles, 1980).
Forever and the Earth (radio play). Athens, Ohio, Croissant, 1984.
On Stage: A Chrestomathy of His Plays. New York, Primus, 1991.

Screenplays: *It Came from Outer Space,* with David Schwartz, 1952; *Moby-Dick,* with John Huston, 1956; *Icarus Montgolfier Wright,* with George C. Johnston, 1961; *Picasso Summer* (as Douglas Spaulding), with Edwin Booth, 1972.

Television Plays: *Shopping for Death,* 1956, *Design for Loving,* 1958, *Special Delivery,* 1959, *The Faith of Aaron Menefee,* 1962, and *The Life Work of Juan Diaz,* 1963 (all *Alfred Hitchcock Presents* series); *The Marked Bullet* (*Jane Wyman's Fireside Theater* series), 1956; *The Gift* (*Steve Canyon* series), 1958; *The Tunnel to Yesterday* (*Trouble Shooters* series), 1960; *I Sing the Body Electric!* (*Twilight Zone* series), 1962; *The Jail* (*Alcoa Premier* series), 1962; *The Groom* (*Curiosity Shop* series), 1971; *The Coffin,* from his own short story, 1988 (U.K.).

Poetry

Old Ahab's Friend, and Friend to Noah, Speaks His Piece: A Celebration. Glendale, California, Squires, 1971.
When Elephants Last in the Dooryard Bloomed: Celebrations for Almost Any Day in the Year. New York, Knopf, 1973; London, Hart Davis MacGibbon, 1975.

That Son of Richard III: A Birth Announcement. Privately printed, 1974.

Where Robot Mice and Robot Men Run round in Robot Towns: New Poems, Both Light and Dark. New York, Knopf, 1977; London, Hart Davis MacGibbon, 1979.

Twin Hieroglyphs That Swim the River Dust. Northridge, California, Lord John Press, 1978.

The Bike Repairman. Northridge, California, Lord John Press, 1978.

The Author Considers His Resources. Northridge, California, Lord John Press, 1979.

The Aqueduct. Glendale, California, Squires, 1979.

The Attic Where the Meadow Greens. Northridge, California, Lord John Press, 1980.

Imagine. Northridge, California, Lord John Press, 1981.

The Haunted Computer and the Android Pope. New York, Knopf, and London, Granada, 1981.

The Complete Poems of Ray Bradbury. New York, Ballantine, 1982.

Two Poems. Northridge, California, Lord John Press, 1982.

The Love Affair. Northridge, California, Lord John Press, 1983.

Other

Switch on the Night (for children). New York, Pantheon, and London, Hart Davis, 1955.

R Is for Rocket (for children). New York, Doubleday, 1962; London, Hart Davis, 1968.

S Is for Space (for children). New York, Doubleday, 1966; London, Hart Davis, 1968.

Teacher's Guide: Science Fiction, with Lewy Olfson. New York, Bantam, 1968.

The Halloween Tree (for children). New York, Knopf, 1972; London, Hart Davis MacGibbon, 1973.

Mars and the Mind of Man. New York, Harper, 1973.

Zen and the Art of Writing, and The Joy of Writing. Santa Barbara, California, Capra Press, 1973.

The Mummies of Guanajuato, photographs by Archie Lieberman. New York, Abrams, 1978.

Beyond 1984: Remembrance of Things Future. New York, Targ, 1979.

About Norman Corwin. Northridge, California, Santa Susana Press, 1979.

The Ghosts of Forever, illustrated by Aldo Sessa. New York, Rizzoli, 1981.

Los Angeles, photographs by West Light. Port Washington, New York, Skyline Press, 1984.

Orange County, photographs by Bill Ross and others. Port Washington, New York, Skyline Press, 1985.

The Art of Playboy (text by Bradbury). New York, van der Marck Editions, 1985.

Zen in the Art of Writing (essays). Santa Barbara, California, Capra Press, 1990.

Yestermorrow: Obvious Answers to Impossible Futures (essays). Santa Barbara, California, Capra Press, 1991.

*

Manuscript Collection: Bowling Green State University, Ohio.

Critical Studies: Interview in *Show* (New York), December 1964; introduction by Gilbert Highet to *The Vintage Bradbury,* 1965; "The Revival of Fantasy" by Russell Kirk, in *Triumph* (Washington, D.C.), May 1968; "Ray Bradbury's *Dandelion Wine:* Themes, Sources, and Style" by Marvin E. Mengeling, in *English Journal* (Champaign, Illinois), October 1971; *The Ray Bradbury Companion* (includes bibliography) by William F. Nolan, Detroit, Gale, 1975; *The Drama of Ray Bradbury* by Benjamin P. Indick, Baltimore, T-K Graphics, 1977; *The Bradbury Chronicles* by George Edgar Slusser, San Bernardino, California, Borgo Press, 1977; *Ray Bradbury* (includes bibliography) edited by Joseph D. Olander and Martin H. Greenberg, New York, Taplinger, and Edinburgh, Harris, 1980; *Ray Bradbury* by Wayne L. Johnson, New York, Ungar, 1980; *Ray Bradbury and the Poetics of Reverie: Fantasy, Science Fiction, and the Reader* by William F. Toupence, Ann Arbor, Michigan, UMI Research Press, 1984; *Ray Bradbury* by David Mogen, Boston, Twayne, 1986.

* * *

A prolific writer of long and short fiction, Ray Bradbury often serves as an introduction to science fiction for elementary and junior high school students (though critics prefer to call him a writer of fantasy, not of science fiction), and with good reason. His short stories are well-written and highly accessible. Still, Bradbury has not received much attention from literary scholars who view him as a popular writer within a popular genre. And he has failed, particularly with his later novels, to achieve the acclaim garnered by his earliest works.

Among those early titles are Bradbury's most noted works *The Martian Chronicles* (1950) and *Fahrenheit 451* (1954). *The Martian Chronicles* depicts a group of Earthlings who colonize Mars. The group meets a sorry fate, not just at the hands of marauding Martians (who kill Captain Black), but also as a result of their unwillingness to adapt to their new surroundings. They hope to merely transfer their small towns and their accompanying lifestyles from Earth to Mars. However, the differences between the two planets are too great to accommodate the colonists' wishes. This juxtaposition of the past and the future is a major theme in Bradbury's writing.

The highly acclaimed *Fahrenheit 451* is centered on the still-lingering effects of the atomic bombs dropped on Hiroshima and Nagasaki at the end of World War II. The plot involves a firefighter whose job is to burn books and therefore discourage people from venturing beyond their four-wall televisions. The firefighter meets a young woman who is curious about the world around her. She influences him to begin reading books, and what follows is a tragic set of circumstances. After he rebels against a society intent on hiding the truths of censorship, government-sanctioned violence, and nuclear war, he commits a murder and is forced to flee into the country. In effect, the light emanating from the fires illuminates a world darkened by suppression.

Bradbury's short stories, though they have not received as much critical attention as his early novels, are perhaps more important because of how widely they are read, particularly by children and teenagers. Nearly every anthology used in language arts classes contains a story or two by Bradbury. Bradbury's precocious children are often disrespectful to their elders, but Lahna Diskin points out that the adults they treat poorly "are people whose authenticity they doubt." Adults who are genuine and whose lives children feel they can emulate are highly respected. Consider "The Veldt," in which George and Lydia Hadley have remodeled their children's playroom to resemble an African veldt, complete with the requisite vegetation and wildlife. "Nothing's too good for our children," George tells his wife. However, in the end the parents' extravagance gets the best of them. The story ends with horrifying, yet deserved, results.

"The Illustrated Man" (1951) is an eerie tale of a man who loses and then regains his job at a circus by transforming from a too-heavy-to-work tent man to a highly decorated freakshow inhabitant via a sudden preponderance of tattoos. Besides being a nuisance to his wife and a wonder to audiences, the tattoos function as mutable fortune tellers. They take the form of conventional tattoos (traced in ink on the man's body), but they are not permanent in that they change shape according to whatever event is being foretold. Not surprisingly, the tattoos are a hit with the circus audiences. However, as with any of Bradbury's stories, they also carry many surprising implications.

Bradbury uses such stories not only to entertain, but to cause readers to think about their own lives. Though Bradbury's topics are hardly true-to-life, they do carry with them themes that we can apply to our daily lives—courteousness, perseverance, flexibility, and self-awareness. These are some of the many lessons that parents and teachers hope to convey to children. The liberal use of adult characters also points toward Bradbury's desire for grown-ups to learn these lessons, sometimes from children.

—Tracy Clark

BRADFORD, Barbara Taylor

Nationality: British. **Born:** 10 May 1933 in Leeds, Yorkshire. **Education:** Studied in private schools. **Family:** Married Robert Bradford, 1963. **Career:** *Yorkshire Evening Post,* Yorkshire, England, reporter, 1949-51, women's editor, 1951-53; *Women's Own,* London, England, fashion editor, 1953-54; *London Evening News,* London, columnist, 1955-57; *Woman,* London, features editor, 1962-64; National Design Center, New York, editor, 1964-65; *Newsday,* Long Island, syndicated columnist; writer. Also served as feature writer for *Today* magazine and executive editor of the *London American.* **Awards:** Dorothy Dawe award, 1970; National Press award, 1971; Matrix award, New York chapter of Women in Communications, 1985; honorary doctorate, Leeds University, 1990. **Member:** Authors Guild (member of council since 1989), American Society of Interior Designers.

PUBLICATIONS

Nonfiction

The Complete Encyclopedia of Homemaking Ideas. Meredith Press, 1968.
How to Be the Perfect Wife: Etiquette to Please Him. Essandess, 1969.
How to Be the Perfect Wife: Entertaining to Please Him. Essandess, 1969.
How to Be the Perfect Wife: Fashions That Please Him. Essandess, 1970.
Easy Steps to Successful Decorating. Simon & Schuster, 1971.
How to Solve Your Decorating Problems. Simon & Schuster, 1976.
Decorating Ideas for Casual Living. Simon & Schuster, 1977.
Making Space Grow. Simon & Schuster, 1979.
Luxury Designs for Apartment Living. Doubleday, 1981.

Novels

A Woman of Substance. Doubleday, 1979.
Voice of the Heart. Doubleday, 1983.
Hold the Dream. Doubleday, 1985.
Act of Will. Doubleday, 1986.
To Be the Best. Doubleday, 1988.
Remember. Ballantine Books, 1992.
Angel. Ballantine Books, 1994.
Everything to Gain. HarperCollins, 1994.
The Women in His Life. Ballantine Books, 1994.
Dangerous to Know. HarperCollins, 1995.
Love in Another Town. HarperCollins, 1995.
Her Own Rules. HarperCollins, 1996.

Other

A Garland of Children's Verse. Lion Press, 1968.

*

Media Adaptations: *A Woman of Substance* (television miniseries); *Hold the Dream* (television miniseries), 1986.

* * *

It is in capturing the complexities within women that Barbara Taylor Bradford succeeds. Truly a commercial storyteller, Bradford adds class to a genre that receives little respect. In her first fiction novel, *A Woman of Substance* (1979), Bradford captures a woman's desire to be respected and noticed for her strong character. Emma Harte is a woman who comes from nothing (in the material sense). As she grows old, however, she acquires all the material possessions she could ever want. What touches the reader is that Harte, because of her pride, nearly dies without finding two everlasting elements of life: love and happiness. Bradford manages to engulf her readers in a gut-wrenching introspective journey into their own motives in life. Bradford demonstrates a deep understanding of what makes "a woman of substance."

The length of a Bradford novel is understandable when one considers both the historical and fictional value. Within each of her novels Bradford takes captive the pains, joys, and fears of her audience and unites them with the struggles of her characters. The historical details add credibility. It is evident after reading her work that she read Charles Dickens and the Bronte sisters as a child.

Bradford's writing career began as a pre-teen when she published her first short story in a children's magazine. From that point forward she was determined to become a professional writer. After foregoing the opportunity for a formal education, Bradford went to work as a typist at the *Yorkshire Evening Post.* It took only two years for her to become editor of the women's page, and another two years before she was the fashion editor of *Women's Own* magazine in London.

In 1963 Bradford married her husband Robert, a producer, and moved to the United States, where she began to publish numerous books. Upon completion of *A Woman of Substance,* Bradford continued the saga of the Harte family by placing Emma Harte's granddaughter in the position of the main character. *Hold the Dream* (1985) and *To Be the Best* (1988) chronicle the life of Paula McGill O'Neill.

Bradford's work includes both nonfiction and fiction. In 1969 and 1970 she wrote three books on how to be a good wife and homemaker. She has also written books on home decorating, including *The Complete Encyclopedia of Homemaking Ideas* (1968).

But it is in fiction that Bradford finds her home, and she continues to write, completing and publishing three recent novels within a two-year period: *Angel* (1994), *The Women in His Life* (1994), and *Dangerous to Know* (1995). Bradford is a great storyteller, as evidenced by sales of her books.

—Tammy J. Bronson

BRADLEY, Marion Zimmer

Pseudonyms: Lee Chapman; John Dexter; Miriam Gardner; Valerie Graves; Morgan Ives; Elfrida Rivers; John J. Wells. **Nationality:** American. **Born:** Albany, New York, 3 June 1930. **Education:** New York State College for Teachers, 1946-48; Hardin-Simmons University, Abilene, Texas, B.A. in English, Spanish, psychology 1964; University of California, Berkeley. **Family:** Married 1) Robert A. Bradley in 1949 (divorced 1964); one son; 2) Walter Henry Breen in 1964 (divorced 1990); one son and one daughter. **Career:** Editor, *Marion Zimmer Bradley's Fantasy Magazine,* since 1988. Singer and writer. **Awards:** *Locus* Award, 1984. **Address:** P.O. Box 72, Berkeley, California 94701, U.S.A.

Publications

Novels (series: Atlantean Chronicles; Leslie Barnes/Claire Moffat; Darkover; Red Moon; Trillium)

The Door through Space. New York, Ace, 1961; London, Arrow, 1979.

I Am a Lesbian (as Lee Chapman). Derby, Connecticut, Monarch, 1962.

Seven from the Stars. New York, Ace, 1962.

The Planet Savers. New York, Ace, 1962; London, Arrow, 1979; expanded edition, Ace, 1976.

The Sword of Aldones (Darkover). New York, Ace, 1962; London, Arrow, 1979; revised as *Sharra's Exile,* New York, DAW, 1981; London, Arrow, 1983.

The Colors of Space (for children). Derby, Connecticut, Monarch, 1963; expanded edition, Norfolk, Virginia, Donning, 1983; London, Lightning, 1989.

Spare Her Heaven (as Morgan Ives). Derby, Connecticut, Monarch, 1963; abridged edition, as *Anything Goes,* Sydney, Stag, 1964.

The Bloody Sun (Darkover). New York, Ace, 1964; London, Arrow, 1978; revised edition, New York, Ace, 1979.

Falcons of Narabedla. New York, Ace, 1964; London, Arrow, 1984.

Castle Terror. New York, Lancer, 1965; Sutton, Surrey, Severn House, 1994.

Star of Danger (Darkover). New York, Ace, 1965; London, Arrow, 1978.

Knives of Desire (as Morgan Ives). San Diego, Corinth, 1966.

No Adam for Eve (as John Dexter). San Diego, Corinth, 1966.

Souvenir of Monique. New York, Ace, 1967.

Bluebeard's Daughter. New York, Lancer, 1968.

The Brass Dragon. New York, Ace, 1969; London, Methuen, 1978.

The Winds of Darkover. New York, Ace, 1970; London, Arrow, 1978.

The World Wreckers: A Darkover Novel. New York, Ace, 1971; London, Arrow, 1979.

Dark Satanic (Barnes/Moffat). New York, Berkley, 1972; Wallington, Surrey, Severn House, 1991.

Darkover Landfall. New York, DAW, 1972; London, Arrow, 1978.

Witch Hill (as Valerie Graves). San Diego, Greenleaf, 1972.

Hunters of the Red Moon. New York, DAW, 1973; London, Arrow, 1979; bylined with Paul Edwin Zimmer, New York, DAW, 1992.

The Spell Sword: A Darkover Novel. New York, DAW, 1974; London, Arrow, 1978.

Endless Voyage. New York, Ace, 1975; expanded edition, as *Endless Universe,* 1979.

The Heritage of Hastur (Darkover). New York, DAW, 1975; London, Arrow, 1979.

Drums of Darkness: An Astrological Gothic Novel: Leo. New York, Ballantine, 1976.

The Shattered Chain: A Darkover Novel. New York, DAW, 1976; London, Arrow, 1978.

The Forbidden Tower (Darkover). New York, DAW, 1977; London, Prior, 1979.

Stormqueen!: A Darkover Novel. New York, DAW, 1978; London, Arrow, 1980.

The Ruins of Isis. Norfolk, Virginia, Donning, 1978; London, Arrow, 1980.

The Catch Trap. New York, Ballantine, 1979; London, Sphere, 1986.

The Survivors (Red Moon), with Paul Edwin Zimmer. New York, DAW, 1979; London, Arrow, 1985.

The House between the Worlds. Garden City, New York, Doubleday, 1980; expanded edition, New York, Ballantine, 1981.

Two to Conquer (Darkover). New York, DAW, 1980; London, Arrow, 1982.

Survey Ship. New York, Ace, 1980.

Hawkmistress! (Darkover). New York, DAW, 1982; London, Arrow, 1985.

The Mists of Avalon. New York, Knopf, 1982; London, Joseph, 1983.

Web of Light (Atlantean). Norfolk, Virginia, Donning, 1983.

Thendara House (Darkover). New York, DAW, 1983; London, Arrow, 1985.

Oath of the Renuciates (includes *The Shattered Chain* and *Thendara House*). Garden City, New York, Doubleday, 1984.

Web of Darkness (Atlantean). New York, Pocket Books, 1984; with *Web of Light,* Glasgow, Drew, 1985; as *The Fall of Atlantis,* New York, Baen, 1987.

The Inheritor (Barnes/Moffat). New York, Tor, 1984; Wallington, Surrey, Severn House, 1992.

City of Sorcery (Darkover). New York, DAW, 1984; London, Arrow, 1986.

Night's Daughter. New York, Ballantine, and London, Inner Circle, 1985.

Warrior Woman. New York, DAW, 1985; London, Arrow, 1987.

The Firebrand. New York, Simon and Schuster, 1987; London, Joseph, 1988.
The Heirs of Hammerfell (Darkover). New York, DAW, 1989; London, Legend, 1991.
Black Trillium, with Julian May and Andre Norton. New York, Doubleday, 1990; London, Grafton, 1991.
Witch Hill. New York, Tor, 1990; Wallington, Surrey, Severn House, 1992.
Rediscovery: A Novel of Darkover, with Mercedes Lackey. New York, DAW, 1993.
The Forest House. London, Joseph, 1993; New York, Viking, 1994.
Lady of the Trillium. New York, Bantam, 1995.
Ghostlight. New York, Tor, 1995.
Tiger Burning Bright, with Andre Norton and Mercedes Lackey. New York, Morrow, 1995.
Exiles Song. New York, DAW, 1996.

Novels as Miriam Gardner

The Strange Women. Derby, Connecticut, Monarch, 1962.
My Sister, My Love. Derby, Connecticut, Monarch, 1963.
Twilight Lovers. Derby, Connecticut, Monarch, 1964.

Short Stories (series: Arwen)

The Dark Intruder and Other Stories. New York, Ace, 1964.
The Jewel of Arwen. Baltimore, T-K Graphics, 1974.
The Parting of Arwen. Baltimore, T-K Graphics, 1974.
Lythande. New York, DAW, 1986; London, Sphere, 1988.
The Best of Marion Zimmer Bradley, edited by Martin H. Greenberg. Chicago, Academy Chicago, 1985; abridged edition, New York, DAW, 1988; London, Orbit, 1990; original version expanded as *Jamie and Other Stories: The Best of Marion Zimmer Bradley,* Chicago, Academy Chicago, 1993.
Marion Zimmer Bradley's Darkover. New York, DAW, 1993.

Other

Songs from Rivendell. Privately printed, 1959.
A Complete, Cumulative Checklist of Lesbian, Variant, and Homosexual Fiction. Privately printed, 1960.
Of Men, Halflings, and Hero-Worship. Rochester, Texas, Fantasy Amateur Press Association, 1961.
The Necessity for Beauty: Robert W. Chambers and the Romantic Tradition. Baltimore, T-K Graphics, 1974.

Editor, *The Keeper's Price and Other Stories.* New York, DAW, 1980.
Editor, *Sword of Chaos and Other Stories.* New York, DAW, 1982.
Editor, *Greyhaven: An Anthology of Fantasy.* New York, DAW, 1983.
Editor, *Sword and Sorceress 1-13.* New York, DAW, 1984-96; vol. 1 published London, Headline, 1988.
Editor, *Free Amazons of Darkover.* New York, DAW, 1985.
Editor, *Other Side of the Mirror.* New York, DAW, 1987.
Editor, *Red Sun of Darkover.* New York, DAW, 1987.
Editor, *Four Moons of Darkover.* New York, DAW, 1988.
Editor, *The Spells of Wonder.* New York, DAW, 1989.
Editor, *Domains of Darkover.* New York, DAW, 1990.
Editor, *Renunciates of Darkover.* New York, DAW, 1991.
Editor, *Leroni of Darkover.* New York, DAW, 1991.
Editor, *Towers of Darkover.* New York, DAW, 1993.
Editor, *Snows of Darkover.* New York, DAW, 1994.
Editor, *The Best of Marion Zimmer Bradley's Fantasy Magazine.* New York, Warner, 1994.

Translator, *El Villano in su Ricon,* by Lope de Vega. Privately printed, 1971.

*

Bibliography: *Leigh Brackett, Marion Zimmer Bradley, Anne McCaffrey: A Primary and Secondary Bibliography* by Rosemarie Arbur, Boston, Hall, 1982.

Manuscript Collection: Boston University.

Critical Studies: *The Gemini Problem: A Study in Darkover* by Walter Breen, Baltimore, T-K Graphics, 1975; *The Darkover Dilemma: Problems of the Darkover Series* by S. Wise, Baltimore, T-K Graphics, 1976.

* * *

Marion Zimmer Bradley is one of the most influential and prolific women writers in the field of science fiction and fantasy. She has written numerous novels as well as books of criticism on science fiction and fantasy. Among other endeavors, she has served as editor of the annual *Sword and Sorceress* anthology as well as *Marion Zimmer Bradley's Fantasy Magazine.* Bradley also writes under the name of Elfrida Rivers, among other undisclosed pseudonyms.

Of her numerous works, Bradley is best known for her *Darkover* series. Beginning with *The Sword of Aldones* and *The Planet Savers,* both published in 1962, *Darkover* was a major success and spawned a number of fanzines and story collections by other authors set in Bradley's universe. The *Darkover* series is a collection of novels that chronicle the history of the planet Darkover over the course of several centuries (Bradley did not write them in chronological order). Soon after settling on Darkover, some of the colonial families interbreed with the telepathically empowered natives to produce the Comyn families, who achieve a level of nobility through their abilities to read minds and prophesy. Over several centuries something of a feudal society develops around blue stones from Darkover that can be psychically keyed to an individual and amplify telepathic brain waves and psychic energies.

Bradley explores the ramifications of a society built on selected breeding and mental powers. She particularly tends to focus on women who are not passive and submissive, but strong and self-actualizing. She is also concerned with the choices that these women make and the consequences of those choices. No decisions on this world are made without risk or without a price. Struggles are not decided easily, but through pain and suffering. Her point seems to be that what is important costs, and the price is to be paid out of the soul rather than out of the pocketbook. Her characters are never black and white but are all shades of gray, making them more compelling and humanized.

Lillian Heldreth in *Survey of Modern Fantasy Literature* has commented that the *Darkover* novels since 1975 give a richer picture of Darkover than the eight previous novels. Indeed, Bradley refuses to be bound by the earlier novels if she discovers that the technology doesn't work as well as it might, or if she's made errors. That strategy has served to strengthen the individual novels and the loyalty of her readers, who appreciate her attentiveness to detail and to the worldbuilding of Darkover. To date, she has rewritten two of the novels in light of later technological developments.

Bradley is also well known for the best-selling *The Mists of Avalon* (1983). That novel is a retelling of the Arthurian legend from the point of view of the women who are central to the story: Igraine, mother of Arthur; Vivaine, Igraine's sister and High Priestess of Avalon; Gwenhwyfar (Guinevere), wife of Arthur; and Morgaine (Morgan le Fay or Morgan of the Fairies), half-sister of Arthur. Morgaine is the principle author, but in drawing on all of the female experiences that make of the tapestry of the legend, Bradley is able to delve into the complexity of their intertwined lives against the tapestry of the undeclared war being waged between the Christians and the Druids. Typical of Bradley is her focus on this battle, which is also a battle between masculine (Christian) and feminine (Druid) values.

Charlotte Spivak has written in *Merlin's Daughters: Contemporary Women Writers of Fantasy,* that *The Mists of Avalon* is "much more than a retelling" of the Arthurian legend, it is "a profound revisioning." Bradley continues this type of revisioning in *The Firebrand* (1987), a retelling of the fall of Troy and of Kassandra, onetime priestess and Amazon.

—Diana Pharaoh Francis

BRISKIN, Jacqueline

Nationality: English. **Born:** Jacqueline Orgell, 18 December 1927, in London. **Education:** University of California, Los Angeles, 1946-47. **Family:** Married Bert Briskin, 9 May 1948; children: Ralph Louis, Elizabeth Ann, Richard Paul. **Career:** Writer. **Awards:** LMV Peer award, 1985. **Address:** 984 Casiano Rd., Los Angeles, California 90049, U.S.A.

Publications

Novels

California Generation. Lippincott, 1970; revised edition, Warner, 1980.
Afterlove. Bantam, 1973.
Rich Friends. Delacorte, 1976.
Paloverde. McGraw, 1978.
The Onyx. Delacorte, 1982.
Everything and More. Putnam, 1983.
Too Much, Too Soon. Berkley Publishing Group, 1985.
Dreams Are Not Enough. Berkley Publishing Group, 1987.
The Naked Heart. Delacorte, 1989.
The Other Side of Love. Dell, 1992.

* * *

Jacqueline Briskin has said that her career in writing developed by chance. After enrolling in an extension course at UCLA, which she assumed was a literature course, Briskin found herself in a creative writing class. It wasn't long until she succumbed to the power of the written word, and success followed quickly. Her first novel, *California Generation* (1970), was purchased by Columbia Pictures, and Lorimar Productions bought the rights to her third novel, *Rich Friends* (1976), for a television miniseries.

In her writing, Briskin includes the elements of many bestsellers: wealth, passion, beauty, and secrets. Common themes appear, but with an exuberance that allows her readers to believe they are experiencing them for the first time. Her skill at capturing her audience and holding them long enough to reach the end of the book without boring them is what allows her novels to inhabit many bedroom night stands. Her readers will never find Briskin in the literary canon, but will wait for her next novel with the same anticipation they had for the one before.

The Naked Heart (1989) is a common story of girls-meet-boy and girls-fight-over-boy. But it is the way in which Briskin tells the story, with uncommon characters, that keeps the reader turning the pages. In *The Naked Heart* two young girls meet in occupied Paris and become lifelong friends. The aristocratic girl is captured, tortured, and forced to watch her parents killed. Before her father dies she makes a promise to hunt down the person and the family of the person who betrayed them. All too familiar, perhaps; but what is not familiar is the way Briskin writes of this victimization. It is truly exceptional how time passes so quickly when reading the plight of this young girl who reunites with her childhood friend only to find they love the same man. How does it end? Briskin keeps the reader wondering with anticipation to the very end.

In Briskin's sixth novel, *Everything and More* (1983), Marylin Wace, the main character, is a young, beautiful, talented actress trying to save her family from poverty. After her father's death in the early 1940s, Wace, along with her mother and sister, moves to Beverly Hills and meets a young girl who will become close friends with Wace's younger sister, Roy. The three girls become successful, and it is the Beverly Hills friend with a secret that threatens the happy existence of the career women. Once again Briskin keeps her readers turning the pages and reaching for the tissue box.

—Tammy J. Bronson

BROOKE-HAVEN, P. *See* **WODEHOUSE, P. G.**

BROOKNER, Anita

Nationality: British. **Born:** London, 16 July 1928. **Education:** James Allen's Girls' School; King's College, University of London; Courtauld Institute of Art, London, Ph.D. in art history. **Career:** Visiting lecturer, University of Reading, Berkshire, 1959-64; lecturer, 1964, and reader, 1977-88, Courtauld Institute of Art; Slade Professor, Cambridge University, 1967-68. Fellow, New Hall, Cambridge; fellow, King's College, 1990. **Awards:** Booker prize,

1984. C.B.E. (Commander, Order of the British Empire), 1990.
Address: 68 Elm Park Gardens, London SW10 9PB, England.

Publications

Novels

A Start in Life. London, Cape, 1981; as *The Debut,* New York, Linden Press, 1981.
Providence. London, Cape, 1982; New York, Pantheon, 1984.
Look at Me. London, Cape, and New York, Pantheon, 1983.
Hotel du Lac. London, Cape, 1984; New York, Pantheon, 1985.
Family and Friends. London, Cape, and New York, Pantheon, 1985.
A Misalliance. London, Cape, 1986; as *The Misalliance,* New York, Pantheon, 1987.
A Friend from England. London, Cape, 1987; New York, Pantheon, 1988.
Latecomers. London, Cape, 1988; New York, Pantheon, 1989.
Lewis Percy. London, Cape, 1989; New York, Pantheon, 1990.
Brief Lives. London, Cape, 1990; New York, Random House, 1991.
A Closed Eye. London, Cape, 1991; New York, Random House, 1992.
Fraud. London, Cape, 1992; New York, Random House, 1993.
A Family Romance. London, Cape, 1993; as *Dolly,* New York, Random House, 1994.
A Private View. London, Cape, 1994; New York, Random House, 1995.
Incidents in the Rue Laugier. London, Cape, 1995; New York, Random House, 1996.

Other

Watteau. London, Hamlyn, 1968.
The Genius of the Future: Studies in French Art Criticism: Diderot, Stendahl, Baudelaire, Zola, the Brothers Goncourt, Huysmans. London, Phaidon Press, 1971; Ithaca, New York, Cornell University Press, 1988.
Greuze: The Rise and Fall of an Eighteenth-Century Phenomenon. London, Elek, and Greenwich, Connecticut, New York Graphic Society, 1972.
Jacques-Louis David: A Personal Interpretation (lecture). London, Oxford University Press, 1974.
Jacques-Louis David. London, Chatto and Windus, 1980; New York, Harper, 1981; revised edition, Chatto and Windus, 1986; New York, Thames and Hudson, 1987.

Translator, *Utrillo.* London, Oldbourne Press, 1960.
Translator, *The Fauves.* London, Oldbourne Press, 1962.
Translator, *Gauguin.* London, Oldbourne Press, 1963.

* * *

Since Anita Brookner's first novel, appropriately entitled *The Debut,* appeared in 1981, her popularity and critical acclaim have continually increased. *The Debut* focuses on a young heroine named Ruth who, neglected by her self-centered actress mother and impractical, dandified father, must adjust to independence and overcome loneliness in order to become successful as a teacher and scholarly researcher. While enduring isolation and frequent misunderstanding, Ruth matures to a well-mannered, disciplined, humane mode of living. Although she ultimately marries somewhat improbably, she becomes a force for a decent, honorable stability in a 20th-century world of disorder and irresponsibility.

The protagonist that Brookner most commonly portrays tends to be well-educated, kindly, and gentle. Although she may have an immensely successful career, like Edith Hope in *Hotel du Lac* (1984), she regards herself as a domestic, security-loving individual. The standard Brookner heroine finds it difficult to be selfish and mean, instead constantly emphasizing a proper, dignified civility.

Brookner's heroines, of course, come in contact and/or in conflict with other viewpoints. For example, Rachel Kennedy, the principal figure in *A Friend from England* (1987), is part owner of a bookstore. She "long ago decided to live her life on the surface" so as to avoid difficult human entanglements and friendships. In a discussion with an acquaintance named Heather, Rachel insists that some women are not cut out for marriage. She extols the life of "being discreet . . . having the strength to do without." Rachel asserts that she lives in the world of reality while Heather lives in a "world of illusions." Rachel had at one time been in love, but the relationship had collapsed. Since then, Rachel has lived a quiet, cautious, polite existence, learning "how to be alone and to put a good face on it." Despite her own choice of lifestyle, Rachel comes to understand that Heather's search for love with a handsome foreigner, while risky, is at least a worthwhile attempt to find her own path. Although Rachel is herself disillusioned with romantic love, she realizes that for Heather it is necessary to prevent despair and frustration.

Frances Hinton in *Look at Me* (1983) is an unmarried librarian. Like Rachel Kennedy, she lives a disciplined, almost spartan, existence. Although she is "pleasant looking," she is not one of those beautiful, spoiled, aggressive women who also populate Brookner's novels and who attract men despite character deficiencies. Frances is tempted to socialize with a stylish, partying group, but she and they come to realize that she is too "orderly" for such an association. Yet Frances writes short stories and novels in her spare time, and she can get attention that will satisfy her by portraying these flawed, superficial snobs in a satirical novel.

In some instances, the reliable, sensible, non-flashy heroines bring men to their more balanced, mature point of view. Blanche Vernon in *A Misalliance* (1986) is recently divorced. She is one of those well-groomed women who is occasionally seen eating alone in restaurants. Blanche considers it a matter of honor to keep busy and perform even ordinary daily tasks in a dedicated, serious manner. In addition, she does volunteer work in a local hospital. Her husband has run off with a petulant, childish computer operator who is lively but demanding. Blanche's friends blame her for being too calm, sweet, and gentle. Although she wishes she could be more aggressive and capricious, she continues her orderly, good-deed-doing life, and eventually her husband returns. He can no longer endure his girlfriend's behavior, realizing that stability and balanced common sense are preferable.

Brookner stresses loyal and dependable love. An open marriage is unacceptable. The heroine of *Hotel du Lac* receives a promising marriage proposal that would give her considerable wealth and social status. Infatuation is not enough; she cannot accept such a marital union without genuine love. Brookner does, however, let some of the characters in her novels espouse the opposite point of view.

In addition to working variations on intriguing themes, Brookner captures the constant attention of the reader with her depth of character analysis. A deeply introspective author, Brookner probes her characters as thoroughly as if she were using the stream-of-consciousness technique. Writing in the third-person, she reveals the activities, habits, and eccentricities of a wide variety of characters in a very detailed psychological manner. Her books are further enhanced by a graceful style that makes exceedingly effective use of metaphor, parallel structure, and rhythmic phrasing. She often uses humor and subtle irony to lighten the mature, deeply meditative nature of her character analysis. In both thought and style, Brookner's novels are decidedly fascinating reading and her future popularity appears assured.

—Paul A. Doyle

BROOKS, Terry

Nationality: American. **Born:** Terence Dean Brooks, Sterling, Illinois, 8 January 1944. **Education:** Hamilton College, Clinton, New York, B.A. 1966; Washington and Lee University, Lexington, Virginia, LL.B. 1969. **Family:** Married Judine Elaine Alba in 1987; one daughter and one son from a previous marriage. **Career:** Partner, Besse, Frue, Arnold, Brooks and Miller, Attorneys at Law, Sterling, Illinois, 1969-86; writer from 1977. **Address:** c/o Ballantine/Del Rey, 201 East 50th Street, New York, New York 10022, U.S.A.

Publications

Novels (series: Magic Kingdom of Landover; Shannara)

The Sword of Shannara. New York, Random House, 1977; London, Futura, 1981.
The Elfstones of Shannara. New York, Del Rey, and London, Futura, 1982.
The Wishsong of Shannara. New York, Del Rey, and London, Futura, 1985.
Magic Kingdom For Sale/Sold! (Landover). New York, Del Rey, 1986; London, Futura, 1987.
The Black Unicorn (Landover). New York, Del Rey, 1987; London, Futura, 1988.
Wizard at Large (Landover). New York, Del Rey, and London, Futura, 1988.
The Scions of Shannara. New York, Del Rey, and London, Orbit, 1990.
The Druid of Shannara. New York, Del Rey, and London, Orbit, 1991.
Hook (novelization of screenplay). London, Arrow, and New York, Fawcett, 1992.
The Elf-Queen of Shannara. New York, Del Rey, and London, Legend, 1992.
The Talismans of Shannara. New York, Del Rey, and London, Legend, 1993.
The Tangle Box (Landover). New York, Del Rey, and London, Legend, 1994.
Witches' Brew. New York, Del Rey, and London, Legend, 1995.
The First King of Shannara. New York, Del Rey, and London, Legend, 1996.

* * *

Perhaps most famous for his *Shannara* novels, Terry Brooks has established himself as one of the most foremost fantasy authors in the world. His first novel, *The Sword of Shannara* (1977), was the first fantasy novel to hit the *New York Times* bestseller list in trade paperback. The impact of this feat on the fantasy publishing world was to prove that fantasy could be profitable in the marketplace, and to pave the way for an influx of new fantasy magazines and novels.

The *Shannara* series is an epic adventure tale. The novels are divided into two groupings, the first comprised of *The Sword of Shannara, The Elfstones of Shannara* (1982), and *The Wishsong of Shannara* (1985). The second grouping, *The Heritage of Shannara,* is comprised of *The Scions of Shannara* (1990), *The Druid of Shannara* (1991), *The Elf Queen of Shannara* (1992), and *The Talismans of Shannara* (1993). A later offering, *First King of Shannara* (1996), is a prequel to the first grouping. All seven take place in the land of Paranor, a land of elves, humans, dwarves and gnomes, where long ago a great war was waged, leaving but a handful of each of the races. But with *The Sword of Shannara,* a new and more devastating war threatens. Shea, a half-human half-elf and the only surviving descendant of the fabled elven house of Shannara, can wield the sword that is capable of stopping the evil Warlock Lord.

Each of the subsequent novels, with the exception of the *First King of Shannara,* take up the adventure of various characters that fight the recurring evil. In *The Elfstones of Shannara,* for instance, the Ellcrys (a tree created by long-lost elven magic to keep the ravening hordes of Demons away from earth) was dying. Shea's grandson Wil must use the elfstones to help create a new Ellcrys with the help of Allanon, his Druid friend, and the elves.

In spite of Brooks' commercial success, critics such as Frank Herbert in his analysis in *New York Times Book Review* found *The Sword of Shannara* to be a derivative of Tolkien. Herbert said that Brooks spends about half the novel "trying on J. R. R. Tolkien's style and subject matter," and that it is impossible for any reader versed in Tolkien's writings to enjoy a sense of suspense in light of glaringly obvious development. Allanon bears a striking resemblance to Tolkien's figures. However, when Brooks reverts to his own style, he pulls in a plethora of myths and legends that work together in a density of unparalleled allegory and storytelling.

Brooks' latest foray into the world of Shannara takes the form of a prequel. In the *First King of Shannara,* Brooks answers many of the questions about the history of Paranor that the rest of the series has generated. In the *Del Rey Internet Newsletter,* he says that in writing the novel he was caught between being able to generate suspense and staying faithful to an ending that the reader would already know. In the end, the book is a fine contribution to the series. Brooks provides detail and revelations concerning previously untold events that set the stage for the earlier novels, but he also maintains the quality of characterizations and tale-telling that make his stories so compelling and engaging.

Other of his writings include the *Magic Kingdom* series. Though that series never gained the huge popularity that characterized the *Shannara* series, they enjoy a solid readership. The *Magic Kingdom* novels combine Brooks' storytelling abilities with a light-hearted fantasy tale that is both engaging and satisfying. Most compelling are his quirky and original characters.

—Diana Pharaoh Francis

BROWN, Dee (Alexander)

Nationality: American. **Born:** 28 February 1908 in Alberta, Louisiana. **Education:** Arkansas State Teachers College (now University of Central Arkansas); George Washington University, B.L.S., 1937; University of Illinois, M.S., 1952. **Military Service:** U.S. Army, 1942-45. **Family:** Married Sara Baird Stroud, 1934; children: James Mitchell, Linda. **Career:** U.S. Department of Agriculture, Washington, D.C., library assistant, 1934-39; Beltsville Research Center, Beltsville, Maryland, librarian, 1940-42; U.S. War Department, Aberdeen Proving Ground, Aberdeen, Maryland, technical librarian, 1945-48; University of Illinois at Urbana-Champaign, librarian of agriculture, 1948-72, professor of library science, 1962-75. **Awards:** Clarence Day award from American Library Association, 1971, for *The Year of the Century: 1876;* Christopher award, 1971; Buffalo award from New York Westerners, 1971, for *Bury My Heart at Wounded Knee;* named Illinoisan of the Year by Illinois News Broadcasters Association, 1972; Best Western for young people award from Western Writers of America, 1981, for *Hear That Lonesome Whistle Blow: Railroads in the West;* Saddleman award from Western Writers of America, 1984. **Member:** Authors Guild, Western Writers of America, Society of American Historians. **Address:** 7 Overlook Dr., Little Rock, Arkansas 72207-1619, U.S.A.

Publications

Novels

Wave High the Banner. Macrae Smith, 1942.
Yellowhorse. Houghton, 1956.
Cavalry Scout. Permabooks, 1958.
They Went Thataway. Putnam, 1960; as *Pardon My Pandemonium,* August House, 1984.
The Girl from Fort Wicked. Doubleday, 1964.
Creek Mary's Blood. Holt, 1980.
Killdeer Mountain. Holt, 1983.
Conspiracy of Knaves. Holt, 1986.

Nonfiction

Fighting Indians of the West, with Martin F. Schmitt. Scribner, 1948.
Trail Driving Days, with Schmitt. Scribner, 1952.
Grierson's Raid. University of Illinois Press, 1954.
The Settlers' West, with Schmitt. Scribner, 1955.
The Gentle Tamers: Women of the Old Wild West. Putnam, 1958.
The Bold Cavaliers: Morgan's Second Kentucky Cavalry Raiders. Lippincott, 1959.
Fort Phil Kearny: An American Saga. Putnam, 1962; as *The Fetterman Massacre,* Barrie & Jenkins, 1972.
The Galvanized Yankees. University of Illinois Press, 1963.
The Year of the Century: 1876. Scribner, 1966.
Action at Beecher Island. Doubleday, 1967.
Bury My Heart at Wounded Knee: An Indian History of the American West. Holt, 1970.
Andrew Jackson and the Battle of New Orleans. Putnam, 1972.
Tales of the Warrior Ants. Putnam, 1973.
The Westerners. Holt, 1974.
Hear That Lonesome Whistle Blow: Railroads in the West. Holt, 1977.
American Spa: Hot Springs, Arkansas. Rose Publishing, 1982.
Wondrous Times on the Frontier. August House, 1991.
When the Century Was Young: A Writer's Notebook. August House, 1993.

Children's Books

Showdown at Little Big Horn. Putnam, 1964.
Teepee Tales of the American Indians. Holt, 1979; as *Dee Brown's Folktales of the Native American, Retold for Our Times,* illustrated by Louis Mofsie, Owl Books, 1993.

*   *   *

Dee Brown's interest in Native American history stems from his childhood in rural Arkansas, where contact with the large local Indian population forced him to question his conventional notions about the history of the American West. While pursuing a lifelong career as a librarian for the U.S. government and the University of Illinois, Brown began writing western novels in the 1940s and produced his first nonfictional history in the mid-1950s.

His first novel, *Wave High the Banner* (1942), dramatized the life of American pioneer Davy Crockett in a tale that *Saturday Review* found unimaginatively "straightforward" but the *New York Times* lauded as "exceptionally shrewd and just." Brown followed it with several traditional westerns, from *Yellowhorse* (1956) and *Cavalry Scout* (1958) to *The Girl from Fort Wicked* (1964). In his more recent western, *Creek Mary's Blood* (1980), Brown chronicles the life of a Creek Indian woman and her two sons as they endure the cruel "manifest destiny" of westward-pushing American settlers. In *Killdeer Mountain* (1983), Brown narrated the tale of 19th-century newspaperman Sam Morrison's efforts to learn the ambiguous truth about a U.S. Army major about to have a fort named after him. *Library Journal* praised the novel as "an intriguing and exciting tale," and *Newsweek* described it as "compelling."

Brown's novel *Conspiracy of Knaves* (1986) is a fictionalized account of the so-called Northwest Conspiracy by Confederate-sympathizing Copperheads during the Civil War; in that conspiracy, a "second Confederacy" of midwestern sympathizers was to be established in Indiana, Illinois, and Ohio. The reviewer for the *New York Times* criticized Brown for narrating the story from the point of view of a purely mercenary double agent and for casting the Copperheads in a wholly negative light; the *Chicago Tribune,* however, described *Conspiracy* as an "energetic, engaging narrative" with a "powerfully lifelike" denouement.

Despite his many novels, Brown's literary reputation is based primarily on his nonfiction and in particular on *Bury My Heart at Wounded Knee,* his highly regarded study of the destruction of Native American civilization in the American West between 1860 and 1890. Relying on original documents from Indian treaty councils and the clear-eyed reminiscences of such Indian leaders as Chief Joseph and Geronimo, Brown painted a grim portrait of the U.S. government's war to drive the Indians from their lands. Critical reception was enthusiastic: *Atlantic* described *Bury My Heart* as "painfully eloquent"; *Best Sellers* called it "an angry book [that] deserves the attention of Americans"; the *New York Times* praised it as "compelling" and "carefully documented"; and the *New Statesman* found it "startling" and "tragic."

Although *Bury My Heart* was Brown's only true bestseller, he is the author of no less than 16 other historical works. In his early histories he explored such subjects as cattle-driving in the American West of the late 1800s (*Trail Driving Days* [1952]); a successful Union cavalry campaign of the Civil War (*Grierson's Raid* [1955]); a history of women's role in the "Wild West" (*The Gentle Tamers* [1958]); a narrative of a highly effective Kentucky cavalry troop during the *Civil War* (Bold Cavaliers [1959]); a history of the Fetterman Massacre of 1866 in which 80 U.S. soldiers were killed by Native Americans in Wyoming (*Fort Phil Kearny* [1962]); and an account of the Confederate prisoners of war who were enlisted into the Union army to fight Indians on the frontier (*The Galvanized Yankees* [1964]). Brown's later nonfictional work has included a chronicle of America's first centennial (*The Year of the Century: 1876* [1966]); an introductory popular history of the American West (*The Westerners* [1975]); a narrative account of transcontinental railroad construction before 1900 (*Hear That Lonesome Whistle Blow* [1977]); a collection of humorous frontier anecdotes that dispel myths about the Old West (*Wondrous Times on the Frontier* [1991]); and a general history of the American frontier between 1838 and 1914 (*The American West* [1995]).

Brown has been praised for his painstaking research and skillful use of source material, highly readable and sometimes gripping prose, and scholarly thoroughness that is nevertheless addressed to the popular reader. Some critics, however, have found fault with Brown's occasionally superficial treatment of his subjects, his sometimes uninspired writing style, and his occasional inability to organize his material effectively.

In addition to his many novels and histories, Brown has written numerous historical articles, three children's books (including *Showdown at Little Big Horn* [1964] and *Teepee Tales of the American Indians* [1979]), and an autobiographical work (*When the Century Was Young* [1993]). He will nevertheless in all likelihood be remembered primarily as the author of *Bury My Heart at Wounded Knee*, a work that so compellingly conveyed the Indians' contemporary perception of their culture's eradication that a Native American once told Brown (a Louisiana-born Caucasian), "You didn't write that book. Only an Indian could have written that book!"

—Paul S. Bodine

BROWN, Rita Mae

Nationality: American. **Born:** Hanover, Pennsylvania, 28 November 1944. **Education:** University of Florida, Gainesville; New York University, B.A. 1968; New York School of Visual Arts, cinematography certificate 1968; Institute for Policy Studies, Washington, D.C., Ph.D. 1976. **Career:** Photo editor, Sterling Publishing Company, New York, 1969-70; lecturer in sociology, Federal City College, Washington, D.C., 1970-71. Since 1973 visiting member, faculty of feminist studies, Goddard College, Plainfield, Vermont. Founding member, Redstockings radical feminist group, New York, 1970s. **Awards:** New York Public Library Literary Lion award, 1986. **Agent:** Julian Bach Literary Agency, 747 Third Avenue, New York, New York 10017. **Address:** American Artists Inc., P.O. Box 4671, Charlottesville, Virginia 22905, U.S.A.

Publications

Novels

Rubyfruit Jungle. Plainfield, Vermont, Daughters, 1973; London, Corgi, 1978.
In Her Day. Plainfield, Vermont, Daughters, 1976.
Six of One. New York, Harper, 1978; London, W.H. Allen, 1979.
Southern Discomfort. New York, Harper, 1982; London, Severn House, 1983.
Sudden Death. New York, Bantam, 1983.
High Hearts. New York and London, Bantam, 1986.
Bingo. New York, Bantam, 1988.
Wish You Were Here, with Sneaky Pie Brown. New York, Bantam, 1990.
Rest in Pieces, with Sneaky Pie Brown. New York, Bantam, 1992.
Venus Envy. New York, Bantam, 1993.
Dolley: A Novel of Dolley Madison in Love and War. New York, Bantam, 1994.
Murder at Monticello; or, Old Sins, with Sneaky Pie Brown. New York, Bantam, 1994.
Pay Dirt. New York, Bantam, 1995.
Riding Shotgun. New York, Bantam, 1996.

Plays

Television and film scripts: *I Love Liberty*, with others, 1982; *The Long Hot Summer*, 1985; *My Two Loves*, 1986; *The Alice Marble Story*, 1986; *Sweet Surrender*, 1986; *The Mists of Avalone*, 1987; *Table Dancing*, 1987; *The Girls of Summer*, 1989; *Selma, Lord, Selma*, 1989; *Rich Men, Single Women*, 1989; *The Thirty Nine Year Itch*, 1989.

Poetry

The Hand That Cradles the Rock. New York, New York University Press, 1971.
Songs to a Handsome Woman. Baltimore, Diana Press, 1973.
Poems. Freedom, California, Crossing Press, 1987.

Other

A Plain Brown Rapper (essays). Baltimore, Diana Press, 1976.
Starting from Scratch: A Different Kind of Writers Manual. New York, Bantam, 1988.

*

Critical Study: *Rita Mae Brown* by Carol M. Ward, New York, Twayne, 1993.

* * *

Although many of her better-known works have lesbian themes, Rita Mae Brown says she would rather be seen as a southern woman of letters than as a lesbian writer. However Brown would like to be regarded, her novels prominently feature both aspects of her life.

Rubyfruit Jungle (1973), for which Brown is best known, provides her readers with a wonderfully meshed combination of the two. The novel features the sometimes depressing, always empowering and rollicking escapades of Molly Bolt, an adventurous Florida girl who grows up into a rebellious New York woman. Though Molly endures much tragedy along the way—endless confrontations with her mother, loss of a full scholarship because of her lesbian romance with her college roommate, and having to live in a car when she first arrives in New York—she manages not only to get by, but to succeed.

Six of One (1978) is a historical novel that takes place in the town of Runnymede, aptly named after the English village in which the Magna Carta was signed in 1215. A revisionist piece, the novel takes a fascinating look at male-centered history through a time period spanning from 1909 to 1980. The narrator, lesbian-feminist Nickel (Nichole), lives in 1980 and recounts her family's history, including, among other things, a fight between two sisters over a hair ribbon. Brown, through Nickel, glosses over the years between 1950 and 1980; not because of lack of development, but because the novel uses a storytelling motif. Nickel simply is not as interested in events occurring during those years. As most any storyteller would do, she skips the boring parts.

Wish You Were Here (1990) marks Brown's foray into the mystery genre. "Co-authored" by her cat, Sneaky Pie Brown, the novel features Mrs. Murphy (modeled on Sneaky Pie), an animal/detective who not only helps to solve a murder case but also teaches readers that animal/human interaction is not only valuable, but also more powerful than humans might believe. Interestingly, Brown breaks from her pattern of positive gay characters with the villainous Josiah DeWitt. Some critics have scolded Brown for this deviation.

Brown returns to lesbian themes with her novels *Venus Envy* (1993) and *Dolley: A Novel of Dolley Madison in Love and War* (1994). *Venus Envy* presents a plucky young woman who, in a single day, receives news that she is dying, writes letters to family members in which she divulges her sexual orientation, and learns the doctor accidentally switched her lab test results with those of another patient (after the confessions have been mailed). The consequences are both humorous and touching.

Although Brown's books characteristically offer their readers a fascinating glimpse of her real life through the filtering lens of fiction, her creative writing how-to book, *Starting From Scratch: A Different Kind of Writer's Manual* (1988), gives us a nuts-and-bolts presentation of her writing technique that few authors have offered. Because the book is presented in Brown's trademark wry, no-nonsense voice, there's something in it not just for creative writers who wish to improve their own craft, but for dedicated readers of her work who would like to see Brown's prose from a more practical perspective—practical, that is, through Brown's satirical eye. For instance, Brown tells her readers that cats are the best judges of a story's worth; she lists them among the essentials of the trade because if a cat will not sit or stand on a freshly typed or printed page, the words on it are mediocre.

Brown's past relationship with tennis superstar Martina Navritalova has sometimes overshadowed critical reception of her work. But Brown—like Molly Bolt in *Rubyfruit Jungle*—has truly been a force to reckon with in that broadly defined genre known as Southern literature.

—Tracy Clark

BROWN, Sandra

Pseudonyms: Laura Jordan, Rachel Ryan, Erin St. Claire. **Nationality:** American. **Born:** Waco, Texas, 12 June 1948. **Education:** Attended Texas Christian University, Oklahoma State University, and University of Texas at Arlington. **Family:** Married Michael Brown in 1968; one daughter, one son. **Career:** Merle Norman Cosmetics Studios, Tyler, Texas, manager, 1971-73; KLTV-TV, Tyler, weather reporter, 1972-75; WFAA-TV, Dallas, weather reporter, 1976-79; Dallas Apparel Mart, Dallas, model, 1976-87; writer. **Address:** 1000 North Bowen, Arlington, Texas 76012, U.S.A.

Publications

Novels (series: Texas!)

Breakfast in Bed. Bantam, 1983.
Heaven's Price. Bantam, 1983.
Relentless Desire. Berkley/Jove, 1983.
Tempest in Eden. Berkley/Jove, 1983.
Temptation's Kiss. Berkley/Jove, 1983.
Tomorrow's Promise. Harlequin, 1983.
In a Class by Itself. Bantam, 1984.
Send No Flowers. Bantam, 1984.
Bittersweet Rain. Silhouette, 1984.
Sunset Embrace. Bantam, 1984.
Riley in the Morning. Bantam, 1985.
Thursday's Child. Bantam, 1985.
Another Dawn. Bantam, 1985.
22 Indigo Place. Bantam, 1986.
The Rana Look. Bantam, 1986.
Demon Rumm. Bantam, 1987.
Fanta C. Bantam, 1987.
Sunny Chandler's Return. Bantam, 1987.
Adam's Fall. Bantam, 1988.
Hawk O'Toole's Hostage. Bantam, 1988.
Slow Heat in Heaven. Warner, 1988.
Tidings of Great Joy. Bantam, 1988.
Long Time Coming. Doubleday, 1989.
Temperatures Rising. Doubleday, 1989.
Best Kept Secrets. Warner, 1989.
A Whole New Light. Doubleday, 1989.
Another Dawn. Warner, 1991.
Breath of Scandal. Warner, 1991.
Mirror Image. Severn, 1991.
French Silk. Warner, 1992.
Honor Bound. Harlequin, 1992.
A Secret Splendor. Harlequin, 1992.
Shadows of Yesterday. Warner, 1992.
Texas! Trilogy. Doubleday, 1992.
  Texas! Lucky, 1990.
  Texas! Sage, 1991.
  Texas! Chase, 1991.
Where There's Smoke. Warner, 1993.
Charade. Warner, 1994.
The Witness. Warner, 1995.
Exclusive. Warner, 1996.

Novels as Laura Jordan

Hidden Fires. Richard Gallen, 1982.
The Silken Web. Richard Gallen, 1982; as Sandra Brown, Warner, 1992.

Novels as Rachel Ryan

Love beyond Reason. Dell, 1981.
Love's Encore. Dell, 1981.
Eloquent Silence. Dell, 1982.
A Treasure Worth Seeking. Dell, 1982.
Prime Time. Dell, 1983.

Novels as Erin St. Claire

Not Even for Love. Harlequin, 1982.
A Kiss Remembered. Harlequin, 1983.
A Secret Splendor. Harlequin, 1983.
Seduction by Design. Harlequin, 1983.
Led Astray. Harlequin, 1985.
A Sweet Anger. Harlequin, 1985.
Tiger Prince. Harlequin, 1985.
Above and Beyond. Harlequin, 1986.
Honor Bound. Harlequin, 1986.
The Devil's Own. Harlequin, 1987.
Two Alone. Harlequin, 1987.
Thrill of Victory. Harlequin, 1989.

* * *

After being fired from her job as a television weatherperson in 1979, Sandra Brown bought a dozen Harlequin romances and several how-to writing guides and began to school herself in the romance novel trade. She proved to be a fast study. Before the year was out Dell Books had purchased her first manuscript (*Love's Encore*), and Brown was launched on an unusually prolific and profitable career as one of America's most bankable romantic suspense novelists.

Writing under the pseudonyms Laura Jordan, Rachel Ryan, and Erin St. Claire (as well as her own name), Brown became adept at generating the "category romances" most often associated with the Harlequin Romance publishing imprint. By 1986 she had published a staggering 27 titles with such genre-determined titles as *Heaven's Price* (1983), *Tempest in Eden* (1983), *A Secret Splendor* (1983), and *Tomorrow's Promise* (1983). In 1990 and 1991, after only a decade in the business, Brown finally reached the *New York Times* bestseller's list with *Mirror Image* (1990) and *Breath of Scandal* (1991), and in the summer of 1992 three of her novels assaulted the *New York Times* bestseller list simultaneously—a feat previously achieved only by Tom Clancy, Stephen King, and Danielle Steel. By the mid-1990s, 40 million Sandra Brown books were in print worldwide, and Warner Books had signed the "Queen of Texas melodrama" to a new three-book contract reported to be worth "well into the multi-millions."

In 1990, Brown embarked on a series of romances for Doubleday Books titled "Texas!" that focused on the exploits of a literary version of television's *Dallas* family, here named the Tylers. The first installment, *Texas! Lucky* (1990), focused on the romantic adventures of Lucky Tyler, one of the two handsome and virile brothers upon whom the continued wealth of the oil-drilling Tylers depends. In the series' second installment, *Texas! Chase* (1991), the younger brother, Chase, loses his wife in a car accident and Brown's heroine swoops in to rescue him from grief-stricken disintegration and, naturally, take his deceased wife's place.

In the trilogy's conclusion, *Texas! Sage* (1992), Brown tells the story of the Tyler brothers' younger sister, Sage, a smart and virginal MBA who finds herself the object of the flirtatious attention of a drifter recently hired by Tyler Drilling. The two eventually find themselves teamed together on a company sales trip, and, after numerous steamy bedroom interludes, Sage learns her suitor is "loaded with a capital L," and Tyler Drilling is saved. *Publishers Weekly* described Chase as a "slick contemporary romance" and Sage as "fluff" with a "factory-made happy ending," while *Kirkus Reviews* dismissed the trilogy as a whole as "lowbrow."

In *French Silk* (1992), later made into a television movie, Brown tells the story of a New Orleans D.A. who, while investigating the murder of an antismut evangelist, finds he is sexually attracted to the crime's principal suspect, the sultry owner of a lingerie company named French Silk. Brown's 1993 novel, *Where There's Smoke,* returned to the Texas oil fields of her Texas! trilogy in the tale of comely physician Lara Mallory, who arrives in East Texas to take over a medical practice willed to her by Congressman Clark Tackett before his unexplained drowning death. While she tries to persuade Clark's brother to help her return to the Third World country where her husband and daughter were killed, several subplots move the reader closer to the truth behind Clark's death and Mallory's central role in the sex scandal that preceded it. In *Charade* (1994), soap opera star Cat Delaney gets a heart transplant and a new boyfriend only to learn that a psycho is killing everyone who might have received his former girlfriend's heart, including, perhaps, Cat herself. Brown published her 57th novel, a legal thriller titled *The Witness,* in 1995 and followed it in 1996 with *Exclusive.* Of her fortuitous choice of careers, Brown has said: "I can't fathom an occupation from which I could derive so much satisfaction as that of writing. It's simply something I must do. Being paid to do it is icing on the cake."

—Paul S. Bodine

BRUNNER, John (Kilian Houston)

Pseudonyms: Gil Hunt; Keith Woodcott. **Nationality:** British. **Born:** Preston Crowmarsh, Oxfordshire, 24 September 1934. **Education:** Cheltenham College, Gloucestershire, 1948-51. **Military Service:** Served in the Royal Air Force, 1953-55. **Family:** Married Marjorie Rosamond Sauer in 1958 (died 1986). **Career:** Technical abstractor, Industrial Diamond Information Bureau, London, 1956; editor, Spring Books, London, 1956-58; writer-in-residence, University of Kansas, Lawrence, 1972; founder, Martin Luther King Memorial prize, 1968; past chairman, British Science Fiction Association. **Awards:** British Fantasy award, 1965; Hugo award, 1969; British Science Fiction Association award, 1970, 1971; Prix Apollo (France), 1973; Cometa d'Argento (Italy), 1976, 1978; Europa award, 1980. **Died:** 25 August 1995.

Publications

Novels (series: Interstellar Empire; Zarathustra Refugee Planet)

Galactic Storm (as Gil Hunt). London, Curtis Warren, 1951.
The Brink. London, Gollancz, 1959.
Threshold of Eternity. New York, Ace, 1959.
The World Swappers. New York, Ace, 1959.
Echo in the Skull. New York, Ace, 1959; revised and expanded as *Give Warning to the World,* New York, DAW, 1974; London, Dobson, 1981.
The 100th Millennium. New York, Ace, 1959; revised and expanded as *Catch a Falling Star,* 1968.
The Atlantic Abomination. New York, Ace, 1960.
Sanctuary in the Sky. New York, Ace, 1960.
The Skynappers. New York, Ace, 1960.
Slavers of Space. New York, Ace, 1960; revised and expanded as *Into the Slave Nebula,* New York, Lancer, 1968; London, Dawson, 1980.
Meeting at Infinity. New York, Ace, 1961.
Secret Agent of Terra (Planet). New York, Ace, 1962; revised and expanded as *The Avengers of Carrig,* New York, Dell, 1969.
The Super Barbarians. New York, Ace, 1962.
Times without Number. New York, Ace, 1962; revised and expanded edition, 1969; Morley, Yorkshire, Elmfield Press, 1974.
The Space-Time Juggler (Empire). New York, Ace, 1963.
The Astronauts Must Not Land. New York, Ace, 1963; revised and expanded as *More Things in Heaven,* New York, Dell, 1973; London, Hamlyn, 1983.
Castaways' World (Planet). New York, Ace, 1963; revised and expanded as *Polymath,* New York, DAW, 1974.
The Rites of Ohe. New York, Ace, 1963.
The Dreaming Earth. New York, Pyramid, 1963; London, Sidgwick and Jackson, 1972.
Listen! The Stars! New York, Ace, 1963; revised and expanded as *The Stardroppers,* New York, DAW, 1972; London, Hamlyn, 1982.
The Crutch of Memory. London, Barrie and Rockliff, 1964.
Endless Shadow. New York, Ace, 1964; expanded as *Manshape,* New York, DAW, 1982.
To Conquer Chaos. New York, Ace, 1964.
The Whole Man. New York, Ballantine, 1964; as *Telepathist: A Science Fiction Novel,* London, Faber, 1965.
The Altar on Asconel (Empire). New York, Ace, 1965.
The Day of the Star Cities. New York, Ace, 1965; revised and expanded as *Age of Miracles,* Ace, and London, Sidgwick and Jackson, 1973.
Enigma from Tantalus. New York, Ace, 1965.
The Repairmen of Cyclops. New York, Ace, 1965.
The Long Result. London, Faber, 1965; New York, Ballantine, 1966.
The Squares of the City. New York, Ballantine, 1965; London, Penguin, 1969.
Wear the Butchers' Medal. New York, Pocket Books, 1965.
A Planet of Your Own. New York, Ace, 1966.
Born under Mars. New York, Ace, 1967.
The Productions of Time. New York, Signet, 1967; revised, London, Penguin, 1970.
Quicksand. Garden City, New York, Doubleday, 1967; London, Sidgwick and Jackson, 1969.
Bedlam Planet. New York, Ace, 1968; London, Sidgwick and Jackson, 1973.
Stand on Zanzibar. Garden City, New York, Doubleday, 1968; London, Macdonald, 1969.
Father of Lies. New York, Belmont, 1968.
Black Is the Color. New York, Pyramid, 1969.
Double, Double. New York, Ballantine, 1969; London, Sidgwick and Jackson, 1971.
The Jagged Orbit. New York, Ace, 1969; London, Sidgwick and Jackson, 1970.
A Plague on Both Your Causes. London, Hodder and Stoughton, 1969; as *Blacklash,* New York, Pyramid, 1969.
Timescoop. New York, Dell, 1969; London, Sidgwick and Jackson, 1972.
The Evil That Men Do. New York, Belmont, 1969.
The Devil's Work. New York, Norton, 1970.
The Gaudy Shadows. London, Constable, 1970; New York, Beagle, 1971.
Good Men Do Nothing. London, Hodder and Stoughton, 1970; New York, Pyramid, 1971.
Honky in the Woodpile. London, Constable, 1971.
The Wrong End of Time. Garden City, New York, Doubleday, 1971; London, Eyre Methuen, 1975.
The Dramaturges of Yan. New York, Ace, 1972; London, New English Library, 1974.
The Sheep Look Up. New York, Harper, 1972; London, Dent, 1974.
The Stone That Never Came Down. Garden City, New York, Doubleday, 1973; London, New English Library, 1976.
Total Eclipse. Garden City, New York, Doubleday, 1974; London, Weidenfeld and Nicolson, 1975.
Web of Everywhere. New York, Bantam, 1974; London, New English Library, 1977.
The Shockwave Rider. New York, Harper, and London, Dent, 1975.
The Infinitive of Go. New York, Ballantine, 1980.
Players at the Game of People. Garden City, New York, Doubleday, 1980.
The Crucible of Time. New York, Ballantine, 1983; London, Arrow, 1984.
The Great Steamboat Race. New York, Ballantine, 1983.
The Tides of Time. New York, Ballantine, 1984; London, Penguin, 1986.
The Shift Key. London, Methuen, 1987.
The Days of March. Worcester Park, Surrey, Kerosina, 1988.
Children of the Thunder. New York, Del Rey, 1989; London, Orbit, 1990.
Victims of the Nova (Planet; includes *Polymath, The Avengers of Carrig,* and *The Repairmen of Cyclops*). London, Arrow, 1989.
A Maze of Stars. Norwalk, Connecticut, Easton Press, 1991.
Muddle Earth. New York, Ballantine, 1993.
The Killing Game. New York, Avon, 1994.
Three Complete Novels (includes *Children of the Thunder, The Tides of Time,* and *The Crucible*). New York, Wings, 1995.

Novels as Keith Woodcott

I Speak for Earth. New York, Ace, 1961.
The Ladder in the Sky. New York, Ace, 1962.
The Psionic Menace. New York, Ace, 1963.
The Martian Sphinx. New York, Ace, 1965.

Short Stories

No Future in It and Other Science Fiction Stories. London, Gollancz, 1962; New York, Doubleday, 1964.
Now Then: Three Stories. London, Mayflower-Dell, 1965; New York, Avon, 1968.
No Other Gods but Me. London, Compact, 1966.
Out of My Mind. New York, Ballantine, 1967; revised as *Out of My Mind: Fantasy and Science Fiction,* London, New English Library, 1968.
Not Before Time: Science Fiction and Fantasy. London, New English Library, 1968.
The Traveler in Black. New York, Ace, 1971; London, Severn House, 1979: expanded as *The Compleat Traveller in Black,* New York, Bluejay, 1986.
From This Day Forward. Garden City, New York, Doubleday, 1972.
Entry to Elsewhen. New York, DAW, 1972.
Time-Jump. New York, Dell, 1973.
The Book of John Brunner. New York, DAW, 1976.
Interstellar Empire. New York, DAW, 1976; London, Hamlyn, 1985.
Foreign Constellations: The Fantastic Worlds of John Brunner. New York, Everest House, 1980.
While There's Hope. Richmond, Surrey, Keepsake Press, 1982.
The Best of John Brunner, edited by Joe Haldeman. New York, Del Rey, 1988.
A Case of Painter's Ear. Eugene, Oregon, Pulphouse, 1991.

Play

Screenplay: *The Terrornauts,* 1967.

Poetry

Trip: A Cycle of Poems. London, Brunner Fact and Fiction, 1966; revised and expanded edition, Richmond, Surrey, Keepsake Press, 1971.
Life in an Explosive Forming Press. London, Poets' Trust, 1971.
A Hastily Thrown-Together Bit of Zork. South Petherton, Somerset, Square House, 1974.

Other

Horses at Home. London, Spring, 1958.
Tomorrow May Be Even Worse: An Alphabet of Science Fiction Cliches. Cambridge, Massachusetts, NESFA Press, 1978.
A New Settlement of Old Scores. Cambridge, Massachusetts, NESFA Press, 1983.

Editor, *The Best of Philip K. Dick.* New York, Ballantine, 1977.
Editor, *John Brunner Presents Kipling's Science Fiction: Stories,* by Rudyard Kipling. New York, Tor, 1992; as *The Science Fiction Stories of Rudyard Kipling,* Secaucus, New Jersey, Carol, 1994.

Translator, *The Overlords of War,* by Gérard Klein, Garden City, New York, Doubleday, 1973.

*

Bibliography: *John Brunner* by Gordon Bensen Jr., Albuquerque, New Mexico, Bensen, 1985.

Critical Study: *The Happening Worlds of John Brunner* (includes bibliography) edited by Joseph W. De Bolt, Port Washington, New York, Kennikat Press, 1975.

* * *

John Brunner was one of the science fiction genre's most prolific and versatile authors, his talents ranging from fantasy and high tech to satire and drama. He authored numerous novels, short stories, poetry, and even a screenplay, *The Terrornauts,* in 1967.

Brunner used his talents to good effect by tackling an old science fiction theme in *More Things in Heaven* (1973) and creating it anew. The story revolves around the crew of the first interstellar space voyage who, after traveling through hyperspace, return as monsters. Brunner is concerned here with the limitations of humanity and its attitudes towards the unknown. Setting aside the limitations of humanity in *The Wrong End of Time* (1971), Brunner suggests that self-sacrifice is still valid in a superbly suspenseful story that combines cultural anthropology and sociology.

The Sheep Look Up (1972) gives a scary, desperate preview of the earth's ruined biosphere. In a world where no inhabitant of the city can venture outside without a protective filtermask, adults are plagued with respiratory illnesses and children with crippling diseases. Although the story line is hard to follow, Brunner's vision of a decaying planet is powerful. The same broad vision comes into play in *The Stone That Never Came Down* (1973). In a war-torn world where fanatical "godheads" own the streets, an underground group comes upon a drug that can expand a person's intelligence. Once again Brunner packs his story with credible characters and suspenseful plotting.

Total Eclipse (1974) centers around a cadre of scientists attempting to solve the puzzle of the extinction of the natives of Sigma Draconis in order to save an increasingly paranoid human race. With believable, sympathetic characters and the appropriate mix of mystery and science, Brunner delivers yet another enlightening and engrossing science fiction tale. In *Web of Everywhere* (1974), the complex plot depends almost entirely upon the complex motivations of characters attempting to rebuild a civilization destroyed by a nuclear war. It was praised by critics as a pleasure to read. Yet another well-received work was *Players at the Game of People* (1980), in which the protagonist Godwin Harpinshield leads an incredibly exotic and exciting life that nevertheless leaves him uneasy and out of touch with reality. He begins to suspect that he is being used by an alien race for their amusement. The novel is well done, and the ending is particularly startling.

The Crucible of Time (1983) contains some of Brunner's best characterization. The book is a wonderfully thought out multi-generational tale of an alien race's progress from the primitive to the reaches of space. The alien personalities are expertly drawn with fascinating speech and thoughts. The saga was hailed as heart-warming and impeccably and logically detailed.

Though Brunner had misses in later works such as *The Tides of Time* (1984) and *A Maze of Stars* (1991)—the former was criticized as a minor work from a major author, and the latter as a series of short stories linked by a framing narrative which never adds up to a novel—he remains in the realm of science fiction a highly regarded writer who never failed to deliver credible characters and engrossing suspense.

—Jennifer G. Coman

BUCKLEY, William F(rank), Jr.

Nationality: American. **Born:** New York City, 24 November 1925. **Education:** Millbrook School, New York, graduated 1943; University of Mexico, 1943-44; Yale University, B.A. (with honors), 1950. **Military Service:** U.S. Army, 1944-46; became second lieutenant. **Family:** Married Patricia Austin Taylor in 1950; one son. **Career:** Instructor in Spanish, Yale University, 1947-51; affiliated with the Central Intelligence Agency (C.I.A.) in Mexico, 1951-52; asssociate editor, *American Mercury* magazine, 1952; freelance writer and lecturer, 1952-55; *National Review* magazine, founder, president, and editor-in-chief, 1955—; syndicated columnist from 1962; host of "Firing Line" weekly television program from 1966. Conservative Party candidate for mayor of New York City, 1965; member of National Advisory Commission on Information, U.S. Information Agency, 1969-72; public member of the U.S. delegation to the United Nations, 1973. Lecturer, New School for Social Research, 1967-68; Froman Distinguished Professor, Russell Sage College, 1973. Chairman of the board, Starr Broadcasting Group, Inc., 1969-78. **Awards:** Freedom award, Order of Lafayette, 1966; George Sokolsky award, American Jewish League against Communism, 1966; Best Columnist of the Year award, 1967; University of Southern California Distinguished Achievement Award in Journalism, 1968; Liberty Bell award, New Haven County Bar Association, 1969; Emmy award, 1969, for "Firing Line"; Man of the Decade award, Young Americans for Freedom, 1970; Cleveland Amory award, *TV Guide*, 1974, for best interviewer/interviewee on television; Bellarmine Medal, 1977; Americanism award, Young Republican National Federation, 1979; Carmel award, American Friends of Haifa University, 1980; American Book award, 1980, for *Stained Glass;* New York University Creative Leadership award, 1981. Honorary degrees: L.H.D. from Seton Hall University, 1966, Niagara University, 1967, Mount Saint Mary's College, 1969, and University of South Carolina, 1985; LL.D. from St. Peter's College, 1969, Syracuse University, 1969, Ursinus College, 1969, Lehigh University, 1970, Lafayette College, 1972, St. Anselm's College, 1973, St. Bonaventure University, 1974, University of Notre Dame, 1978, New York Law School, 1981, and Colby College, 1985; D.Sc.O. from Curry College, 1970; Litt.D. from St. Vincent College, 1971, Fairleigh Dickinson University, 1973, Alfred University, 1974; College of William and Mary, 1981, William Jewell College, 1982, Albertus Magnus College, 1987, College of St. Thomas, 1987, and Bowling Green State University, 1987. **Address:** c/o National Review, 150 East 35th St., New York, New York 10016, U.S.A.

PUBLICATIONS

Nonfiction

God and Man at Yale: The Superstitions of "Academic Freedom." Chicago, Regnery, 1951.
McCarthy and His Enemies: The Record and Its Meaning, with L. Brent Bozell. Chicago, Regnery, 1954.
Up from Liberalism. New York, Obolensky, 1959.
Rumbles Left and Right: A Book about Troublesome People and Ideas. New York, Putnam, 1963.
The Unmaking of a Mayor. New York, Viking, 1966.
The Jeweler's Eye: A Book of Irresistible Political Reflections. New York, Putnam, 1968.
Quotations from Chairman Bill: The Best of William F. Buckley, Jr., compiled by David Franke. New Rochelle, New York, Arlington House, 1970.
The Governor Listeth: A Book of Inspired Political Revelations. New York, Putnam, 1970.
Cruising Speed: A Documentary. New York, Putnam, 1971.
Taiwan: The West Berlin of China. Jamaica, New York, St. John's University Center of Asian Studies, 1971.
Inveighing We Will Go. New York, Putnam, 1972.
Four Reforms: A Guide for the Seventies. New York, Putnam, 1973.
United Nations Journal: A Delegate's Odyssey. New York, Putnam, 1974.
The Assault on the Free Market. Kansas State University, 1974.
Execution Eve and Other Contemporary Ballads. New York, Putnam, 1975.
Airborne: A Sentimental Journey. New York, Macmillan, 1976.
A Hymnal: The Controversial Arts. New York, Putnam, 1978.
Atlantic High: A Celebration. New York, Doubleday, 1982.
Overdrive: A Personal Documentary. New York, Doubleday, 1983.
Right Reason. New York, Doubleday, 1985.
Racing through Paradise: A Pacific Passage. New York, Random House, 1987.
Keeping the Tablets: Modern American Conservative Thought. New York, HarperCollins Publishing, 1988.
On the Firing Line: The Public Life of Our Public Figures. New York, Random House, 1989.
Gratitude: Reflections on What We Owe to Our Country. New York, Random House, 1990.
In Search of Anti-Semitism. New York, Continuum, 1992.
Happy Days Were Here Again. New York, Random House, 1993.
Windfall: End of the Affair. New York, HarperPerennial, 1993.
Lady Chatterly's Lover: Loss & Hope. New York, MacMillan, 1993.

Novels

Saving the Queen. New York, Doubleday, and London, W.H. Allen, 1976.
Stained Glass. New York, Doubleday, and London, Penguin, 1978.
Who's On First. New York, Doubleday, and London, Allen Lane, 1980.
Marco Polo, If You Can. New York, Doubleday, and London, Allen Lane, 1982.
The Story of Henri Tod. New York, Doubleday, and London, Allen Lane, 1984.
See You Later, Alligator. New York, Doubleday, 1985; London, Century, 1986.
High Jinx. New York, Doubleday, and London, Century, 1986.
Mongoose, R.I.P. New York, Random House, and London, Muller, 1988.
Tucker's Last Stand. New York, Random House, 1990; London, Severn House, 1991.
A Very Private Plot. New York, William Morrow, 1994.
Brothers No More. New York, Doubleday, 1995.
Editor, with others, *The Committee and Its Critics: A Calm Review of the House Committee on Un-American Activities.* New York, Putnam, 1963.
Editor, *Odyssey of a Friend: Whittaker Chambers' Letters to William F. Buckley, Jr., 1954-1961.* New York, Putnam, 1970.

Editor, *Did You Ever See a Dream Walking?: American Conservative Thought in the Twentieth Century.* Indianapolis, Bobbs-Merrill, 1970.
Editor, with Charles R. Kesler, *The Tablet Keepers: American Conservative Thought in the 20th Century.* New York, Harper, 1987.

*

Critical Studies: *The Buckleys: A Family Examined* by Charles L. Markmann, New York, Morrow, 1973; *William F. Buckley, Jr.*, by Mark Royden, Boston, Twayne, 1984; *William F. Buckley, Jr.: Patron Saint of the Conservatives* by John Judis, New York, Simon & Schuster, 1988.

* * *

As a columnist, magazine editor and publisher, novelist, and television host, William F. Buckley, Jr., has had a colorful, polemical, and notorious career that has spanned the birth and maturation of the modern American conservative movement, a movement of which he has sometimes been called the "patron saint."

His first book, *God and Man at Yale* (1951) was an attack on the secularist, anti-individualist, and anticapitalist tendencies he detected in the faculty of Yale University. The reviewer for *Atlantic Monthly* claimed the book was "dishonest in its use of facts, false in its theory, and a discredit to its author" while *American Mercury*'s reviewer praised it as "brilliant, sincere, well-informed, keenly reasoned, and exciting to read."

After the pro-McCarthy sentiments of Buckley's second book, *McCarthy and His Enemies* (1954), resulted in almost universal critical silence, Buckley decided to found a magazine in which the conservative viewpoint could gain a national audience. The first issue of *National Review* appeared in 1955, proclaiming its intention to "stand athwart history, yelling 'Stop.'" In *Up from Liberalism* (1959), Buckley defined his conservatism as a body of thought emphasizing "freedom, individuality, the sense of the community, the sanctity of the family, the supremacy of the conscience, [and] the spiritual view of life."

Rumbles Left and Right (1963) showed Buckley further defining and refining his conservative perspective. Following *The Committee and Its Critics* (1963)—that book returned to some of the same issues as *McCarthy and His Enemies*—Buckley began writing syndicated newspaper columns, which over the years were published in such collections as *The Governor Listeth* (1970), *The Jeweler's Eye* (1968), *Inveighing We Will Go* (1972), *Execution Eve* (1975), and *Right Reason* (1985). In 1965, Buckley ran as a Conservative Party candidate for mayor of New York City, later recounting the events of the campaign (which he lost to John Lindsay) in *The Unmaking of a Mayor* (1966).

In *Cruising Speed* (1971), Buckley provided a glimpse into the frenetic activity and concerns of his daily life, a personal memoir that *Harper's* described as "delightful." (In 1983, Buckley used the same diaristic/autobiographical approach in *Overdrive.*) *In Four Reforms* (1973), he advanced proposals for reforms in welfare, aid to education, taxes, and criminal justice, which *Commentary*'s reviewer characterized as "simple, often startling" and—contrary to expectation—displaying little "ideological bias." Reviewing *United Nations Journal* (1974), Buckley's chronicle of his brief tenure as a delegate at the UN, the *Village Voice* called it his "most fully achieved work, the one in which his keen observant eye best serves his moral concerns."

In 1976, Buckley's career took two fresh turns. The first was the publication of *Airborne* (1976), which recounted his adventures and ruminations while indulging his passion for sailing. Such was its reception that he followed it with *Atlantic High* (1982), *Racing through Paradise* (1987), and *Windfall* (1992). The second departure was Buckley's first novel, *Saving the Queen* (1976), the first of a series of spy thrillers featuring Buckley's alter ego, Blackford Oakes. Despite some unenthusiastic reviews, *Saving the Queen* reached the bestseller lists, prompting Buckley to pen nine more novels dramatizing Cold War scenarios.

Some critics have noted that Buckley's spy novels primarily serve a didactic and revisionist purpose: they create fictional scenarios in which the CIA (for which Buckley worked briefly after college) is forced to undertake controversial and ethically problematic means to achieve ends that Buckley believes justify its unorthodox actions. Nevertheless, throughout the series reviewers have praised Buckley for his involving plots, convincing portrayals of historical figures, and unconventional interjection of moral themes in a genre usually characterized by pragmatic, amoral heroes.

In 1990, Buckley stepped down as editor-in-chief of *National Review* but continued his prolific writing career with two major works; *Gratitude* (1990) and *In Search of Anti-Semitism* (1992). In *Gratitude,* Buckley proposed a national program in which most high school graduates would be required to perform a year of civic service. The *New Republic* described the book as "lazily researched and sloppily argued" but praised Buckley's efforts to advance the idea, and the *New York Times Book Review,* also lauding Buckley's intentions, doubted he would be able to convince fellow conservatives that government coercion of the free choice of young adults was justifiable.

In Search of Anti-Semitism arose as a series of articles, responses, and letters appearing in *National Review* concerning the charge that presidential candidate Patrick Buchanan was an anti-Semite and that American conservatives were sympathetic with Buchanan's views. The reviewer for the *New York Times Book Review* praised Buckley for arguing that the unique history of the Jews in the 20th century entitled them to use stricter standards when evaluating the acceptability of unsympathetic statements about Israel or Judaism.

In 1995, Buckley published his eleventh novel and his first devoid of Cold War intrigue, *Brothers No More.* Centering on the friendship between an amoral descendent of FDR and a retiring but principled everyman, the novel evolves into a wide-ranging saga of postwar America that *Playboy* magazine called "irresistible."

—Paul S. Bodine

BUFFETT, Jimmy

Nationality: American. **Born:** Pascogoula, Mississippi, 25 December 1946. **Education:** Attended Auburn University, 1964; University of Southern Mississippi, B.S., 1969. **Family:** Married second wife, Jane Slagsvol, in 1977; two daughters. **Career:** Songwriter and performer, 1960s—; Billboard Publications, Nashville, writer, 1971-73; writer. **Member:** Greenpeace Foundation (honorary director), Cousteau Society, Save the Manatee Commission of Florida (chair). **Agent:** Morton Janklow, 598 Madison Ave., New York, New York 10022. **Address:** Margaritaville Records, 54 Music Sq. E., Suite 303, Nashville, Tennessee 37203; and 1880 Century Park E., Suite 900, Los Angeles, California 90067, U.S.A.

Publications

Novel

Where Is Joe Merchant? A Novel Tale. Harcourt, 1992.

Fiction for Children

The Jolly Mon, with daughter Savannah Jane Buffett, illustrated by Lambert Davis. Harcourt, 1988.
Trouble Dolls, with Savannah Jane Buffett. Harcourt, 1991.

Other

Tales from Margaritaville: Fictional Facts and Factual Fictions. Harcourt, 1989.

* * *

Jimmy Buffett has always been a writer. For years he was best-known as a writer of songs, many of them ballads rich with literary ambition and allusions. However, at the height of his musical career he branched out and became a prose writer as well, publishing two children's books, a short story collection, and a novel.

Crossing boundaries is not surprising in an artist whose work has always defied genres and definitions. Buffett's music is both rock and country, or a fusion of the two, together with reggae and Caribbean. He has recorded 16 albums since his 1973 debut entitled *A White Sport Coat and a Pink Crustacean.* Although his music is not often played on the radio and many people are familiar only with *Margaritaville,* his concerts are legendary for their party atmosphere, and his fans, known as "Parrot-heads," are renowned for their loyalty to the entertainer.

In the mid-1980s Buffett began to deemphasize the allusions to drinking and rowdiness that had occasionally peppered his songs. He began to present a more mature and responsible persona, but without losing his sense of humor. Meanwhile, he decided to try fiction writing as a way to expand the stories embodied in his songs onto a larger canvas. His songs and his books are mainly set in and full of the ambience of the South, especially coastal places like Mobile, Alabama, and Key West, Florida.

Buffett's writing shows respect and affection for many great American authors, especially Mark Twain, to whom he often alludes, and Pat Conroy, with whom he shares the theme of growing up Catholic. The world Buffett creates through his lyrics and his fiction is a world of the senses; the reader can see, hear, feel, and even smell what the author describes. There is magic in Buffett's world, and there is drama, but it is still the real world, so there are also bizarre relatives and memorable fishing trips. Buffett's writing is for people who understand the wisdom of occasionally stepping back from the serious tedium of everyday life in order to better appreciate the beauty and spontaneity that make it worthwhile.

Buffett co-wrote his first book, *The Jolly Mon* (1988) with his daughter Savannah Jane. Father and daughter also collaborated on *Trouble Dolls,* released in 1991. Both are children's books using Buffett's favorite settings—from Florida to the Caribbean—to frame youthful adventures flavored with folklore and fantasy. Both books are beautifully illustrated by Lambert Davis with whimsical seaside scenes that complement the text perfectly. They are ideal for families to read together.

In 1989 Buffett published *Tales From Margaritaville,* a collection of short stories gathered from his many travels. Several of the stories, such as "Son of a Son of a Sailor" and "Off to See the Lizard," are familiar, since they spring from his songs, while others, including "The Swamp Creature Let One In" and "A Gift for the Buccaneer" are completely new.

In 1992 Buffett published *Where is Joe Merchant?,* the story of swashbuckling pilot Frank Bama and his quest to find a long-lost legendary guitarist. It is a light-hearted adventure with liberal doses of intrigue and comic relief. The tone of the book shows the influence of another of Buffett's favorite authors, John D. McDonald (who wrote the Travis McGee mysteries), but with Buffett's unmistakable penchant for boyhood delights like the desire to be a pirate.

Both of Buffett's adult books reached best-seller status. Although they did not receive a great deal of critical attention, most of the reviews they did get were favorable. *Publishers Weekly* and *The New York Times Book Review* agreed that Buffett's work is enjoyable to read. The critics also agree on this: Buffett's books are not Great Literature—he is in no danger of going down in history with William Faulkner or Ernest Hemingway. Yet he is a great storyteller, and his stories, whether printed or sung, allow the audience to have wonderful adventures with colorful friends. Buffett's writings contain few big words or burning social issues, but they do have an unmistakable rhythm that can only be described as the rhythm of life, or at least the kind of rhythm life ought to have. Sometimes it dances and sometimes it skips, but it's always a pleasant motion. Ultimately, Buffett's books are like his music, irresistible and contagious because of their joyful spirit.

—Bruce Guy Chabot

BUKOWSKI, Charles

Nationality: American. **Born:** 16 August 1920, in Andernach, Germany; brought to the United States in 1922. **Education:** Attended Los Angeles City College, 1939-41. **Family:** Married Barbara Fry in 1955 (divorced); married Linda Lee Beighle; children: Marina Louise. **Career:** Worked as an unskilled laborer, beginning 1941, in various positions, including dishwasher, truck driver and loader, mailman, guard, gas station attendant, stock boy, warehouseman, shipping clerk, post office clerk, parking lot attendant, Red Cross orderly, and elevator operator; has also worked in dog biscuit factory, slaughterhouse, cake and cookie factory, and has hung posters in New York subways. Former editor of *Harlequin,* and *Laugh Literary* and *Man the Humping Guns;* columnist ("Notes of a Dirty Old Man"), Open City and L.A. Free Press. **Awards:** National Endowment for the Arts grant, 1974; Loujon Press award; Silver Reel award, San Francisco Festival of the Arts, for documentary film. **Died:** 9 March 1994, in San Pedro, California, of leukemia.

PUBLICATIONS

Poetry

Flower, Fist, and Bestial Wail. Hearse Press, 1959.
Longshot Pomes for Broke Players. 7 Poets Press, 1961.
Run with the Hunted. Midwest Poetry Chapbooks, 1962.
Poems and Drawings. EPOS, 1962.
It Catches My Heart in Its Hands: New and Selected Poems, 1955-1963. Loujon Press, 1963.
Grip the Walls. Wormwood Review Press, 1964.
Cold Dogs in the Courtyard. Literary Times, 1965.
Crucifix in a Deathhand: New Poems, 1963-1965. Loujon Press, 1965.
The Genius of the Crowd. 7 Flowers Press, 1966.
True Story. Black Sparrow Press, 1966.
On Going out to Get the Mail. Black Sparrow Press, 1966.
To Kiss the Worms Goodnight. Black Sparrow Press, 1966.
The Girls. Black Sparrow Press, 1966.
The Flower Lover. Black Sparrow Press, 1966.
Night's Work. Wormwood Review Press, 1966.
2 by Bukowski. Black Sparrow Press, 1967.
The Curtains Are Waving. Black Sparrow Press, 1967.
At Terror Street and Agony Way. Black Sparrow Press, 1968.
Poems Written before Jumping out of an 8-Story Window. Litmus, 1968.
If We Take.... Black Sparrow Press, 1969.
The Days Run Away Like Wild Horses over the Hills. Black Sparrow Press, 1969.
Another Academy. Black Sparrow Press, 1970.
Fire Station. Capricorn Press, 1970.
Mockingbird, Wish Me Luck. Black Sparrow Press, 1972.
Me and Your Sometimes Love Poems. Kisskill Press, 1972.
While the Music Played. Black Sparrow Press, 1973.
Love Poems to Marina. Black Sparrow Press, 1973.
Burning in Water, Drowning in Flame: Selected Poems, 1955-1973. Black Sparrow Press, 1974.
Chilled Green. Alternative Press, 1975.
Africa, Paris, Greece. Black Sparrow Press, 1975.
Weather Report. Pomegranate Press, 1975.
Winter. No Mountain, 1975.
Tough Company, bound with *The Last Poem* by Diane Wakoski. Black Sparrow Press, 1975.
Scarlet. Black Sparrow Press, 1976.
Maybe Tomorrow. Black Sparrow Press, 1977.
Love Is a Dog from Hell: Poems, 1974-1977. Black Sparrow Press, 1977.
Legs, Hips, and Behind. Wormwood Review Press, 1979.
Play the Piano Drunk Like a Percussion Instrument until the Fingers Begin to Bleed a Bit. Black Sparrow Press, 1979.
A Love Poem. Black Sparrow Press, 1979.
Dangling in the Tournefortia. Black Sparrow Press, 1981.
The Last Generation. Black Sparrow Press, 1982.
Sparks. Black Sparrow Press, 1983.
War All the Time: Poems 1981-1984. Black Sparrow Press, 1984.
The Roominghouse Madrigals: Early Selected Poems, 1946-1966. Black Sparrow Press, 1988.
Beauti-ful and Other Long Poems. Wormwood Books and Magazines, 1988.
People Poems: 1982-1991. Wormwood Books and Magazines, 1991.
The Last Night of the Earth Poems. Black Sparrow Press, 1992.
Days Run Away Like Wild Horses over the Hills. Black Sparrow Press, 1993.

Novels

Post Office. Black Sparrow Press, 1971.
Factotum. Black Sparrow Press, 1975.
Women. Black Sparrow Press, 1978.
Ham on Rye. Black Sparrow Press, 1982.
Horsemeat. Black Sparrow Press, 1982.
Hollywood. Black Sparrow Press, 1989.

Short Stories

Notes of a Dirty Old Man. Essex House, 1969; 2nd edition, 1973.
Erections, Ejaculations, Exhibitions, and General Tales of Ordinary Madness. City Lights, 1972; abridged edition published as *Life and Death in the Charity Ward,* London Magazine Editions, 1974; selections, edited by Gail Ghiarello, published as *Tales of Ordinary Madness* and *The Most Beautiful Woman in Town, and Other Stories,* two volumes, City Lights, 1983.
South of No North: Stories of the Buried Life. Black Sparrow Press, 1973.
Bring Me Your Love, illustrated by R. Crumb. Black Sparrow Press, 1983.
Hot Water Music. Black Sparrow Press, 1983.
There's No Business. Black Sparrow Press, 1984.

Other

Confessions of a Man Insane Enough to Live with Beasts. Mimeo Press, 1966.
All the Assholes in the World and Mine. Open Skull Press, 1966.
A Bukowski Sampler, edited by Douglas Blazek, Quixote Press, 1969.
Art. Black Sparrow Press, 1977.
What They Want. Neville, 1977.
We'll Take Them. Black Sparrow Press, 1978.
You Kissed Lilly. Black Sparrow Press, 1978.
Shakespeare Never Did This. City Lights, 1979.
The Bukowski/Purdy Letters: A Decade of Dialogue, 1964-1974, edited by Seamus Cooney, Paget Press, 1983.
You Get So Alone at Times That It Just Makes Sense. Black Sparrow Press, 1986.
A Visitor Complains of My Disenfranchise. Limited edition, Illuminati, 1987.
Septuagenarian Stew: Stories and Poems. Black Sparrow Press, 1990.
Screams from the Balcony: Selected Letters 1960-1970. Black Sparrow Press, 1994.
Pulp. Black Sparrow Press, 1994.

*

Film Adaptations: *Tales of Ordinary Madness,* adapted from *Erections, Ejaculations, Exhibitions and General Tales of Ordinary Madness,* 1983; *Love Is a Dog from Hell,* 1988; *Crazy Love,* adapted from *The Copulating Mermaids of Venice, California,* 1989. The film *Barfly,* 1987, was based on Bukowski's life.

Bibliography: *A Bibliography of Charles Bukowski* by Sanford Dorbin, Black Sparrow Press, 1969; *A Charles Bukowski Checklist,* edited by Jeffrey Weinberg, Water Row Press, 1987.

Manuscript Collection: University of California, Santa Barbara.

Critical Studies: *Charles Bukowski: A Critical and Bibliographical Study* by Hugh Fox, Abyss Publications, 1969; *Bukowski: Friendship, Fame, and Bestial Myth* by Jory Sherman, Blue Horse Press, 1982.

* * *

Best known as the poet of the down-and-out, Charles Bukowski didn't begin to write poetry until the age of 35. He started out writing short stories. But aside from his "Aftermath of a Lengthy Rejection Slip," accepted by *Story* magazine in 1944, Bukowski's publication record was sketchy at best.

Meanwhile, Bukowski worked as an unskilled laborer, moving from city to city until he ended up as a skid-row alcoholic. By then he had given up on his writing. After miraculously recovering from a perforated ulcer in 1955, he again picked up the pen. Four chapbooks of poetry followed in rapid succession, and a collection called *It Catches My Heart in Its Hands: New and Selected Poems, 1955-1963* (1963).

Brutal yet inwardly tender, the collection's persona is in one sense fully invested in macho posturing and in another self-mocking. Firmly located in Los Angeles's underbelly, the persona drinks, gambles, fights, and womanizes, among other things. Throughout, themes that would become common to Bukowski's oeuvre are established: that love is an illusion, life is absurd, and conventional society is insane. These poems, like much of Bukowski's work, are "non-cerebral" and operate on raw emotion. Thus, while critics have largely embraced Bukowski's poetry, academicians have ignored it.

As Bukowski eased more into old-age and respectable living, his poetry had much less of an edge. *War All the Time* (1984), for instance, includes elegiac poems for a cat, poems against war and nuclear technology, and poems about sports and television. The *Last Night on Earth* (1992), his last collection, constitutes the 70-plus-year-old's meditative call back to people who have passed from his life, and forward to visions of his death.

While Bukowski is often remembered as a poet, it was his prose that first brought him a wide, yet largely underground, readership. This began with a collection of disjointed fiction, autobiography, and philosophical musings titled *Notes of a Dirty Old Man.* Culled from a weekly column Bukowski wrote for *Open City,* an alternative newspaper in Los Angeles, *Notes* rode on the cusp of the 1960s counter-culture movements and appealed to cultural exiles who appreciated Bukowski's fiercely anti-authoritarian stance.

The perspective Bukowski establishes in *Notes* carries through his novels of the *Post Office* (1971), *Factotum* (1975), *Women* (1978) and *Ham on Rye* (1982). They feature Henry Chinaski, an alcoholic tough guy whose experiences are based on Bukowski's life. Often a brute displaying hostile and misogynist behavior, Chinaski is, if nothing else, a survivor. *Post Office,* for instance, shows Chinaski surviving the tyrannical nature of paid labor, as embodied in the figure of his mean and petty boss Jonstone. *Ham on Rye* concludes this chronicle of survival by featuring another tyrannical institution, the family. Here, the patriarch is a cruel and brutal man who often beats Chinaski with a razor strap.

Post Office, Factotum, and *Women* are each structured as a series of short, power-packed vignettes. *Ham on Rye,* however, marks a departure in style. As David Montrose noted, this work has "uncharacteristic restraint" which is "hard and exact, [with] the writer's impulse towards egocentricity repressed." Indeed, the "tough guy" persona won't suffice for this story. Its examination of Chinaski's youth, marred by a painful, alienating skin disease and an abusive father, touches deep sorrow.

Bukowski returned to short fiction and other media after *Ham on Rye.* In 1987 director Barbet Schroeder came out with *Barfly.* The movie, a tragicomic look at the bleak life Chinaski shared with another alcoholic, Wanda, solidified Bukowski's role as a cult antihero. At the Cannes Film Festival, *Barfly* was the surprise hit. Bukowski documented the making of the movie in his novel *Hollywood* (1989). Embraced by critics, who noted an uncharacteristic "lightness of touch" in the narration, *Hollywood* comes from a more sober and settled Bukowski.

Nonetheless, it is Bukowski's distinctive, maverick style and the appeal of his writer-as-drinker/drinker-as-writer image that have made Bukowski a popular icon. The span of his career, coupled with translations of his work to the big screen (Dominique Deruddere's *Love is a Dog from Hell,* Marco Ferreri's *Tales of Ordinary Madness,* and Schroeder's *Barfly*) have made Bukowski legendary.

—Aimee M. Houser

BURFORD, Eleanor. *See* **HOLT, Victoria.**

BURNS, Tex. *See* **L'AMOUR, Louis.**

BURROUGHS, William S(eward)

Pseudonym: William Lee. **Nationality:** American. **Born:** St. Louis, Missouri, 5 February 1914. **Education:** John Burroughs School and Taylor School, St. Louis; Los Alamos Ranch School, New Mexico; Harvard University, Cambridge, Massachusetts, A.B. in anthropology 1936; studied medicine at the University of Vienna; Mexico City College, 1948-50. **Military Service:** Served in the U.S. Army, 1942. **Family:** Married 1) Ilse Herzfeld Klapper in 1937 (divorced 1946); 2) Jean Vollmer in 1945 (died 1951), one son (deceased). **Career:** Worked as a journalist, private detective, and bartender; now a full-time writer. Painter: exhibitions at Tony Shafrazi Gallery, New York; October Gallery, London, 1988; Kellas Gallery, Lawrence, Kansas, 1989. Lived for many years in Tangier and New York City; now lives in Lawrence. **Awards:** American Academy award, 1975. **Member:** American Academy, 1983. **Agent:** Andrew Wylie Agency, 250 West 57th Street, New

York, New York 10107. **Address:** William Burroughs Communications, Box 147, Lawrence, Kansas 66044, U.S.A.

Publications

Novels

Junkie: Confessions of an Unredeemed Drug Addict (as William Lee). New York, Ace, 1953; London, Digit, 1957; complete edition, as *Junky,* London, Penguin, 1977.
The Naked Lunch. Paris, Olympia Press, 1959; London, Calder, 1964; as *Naked Lunch,* New York, Grove Press, 1962.
The Soft Machine. Paris, Olympia Press, 1961; New York, Grove Press, 1966; London, Calder and Boyars, 1968.
The Ticket That Exploded. Paris, Olympia Press, 1962; revised edition, New York, Grove Press, 1967; London, Calder and Boyars, 1968.
Dead Fingers Talk. London, Calder, 1963.
Nova Express. New York, Grove Press, 1964; London, Cape, 1966.
The Wild Boys: A Book of the Dead. New York, Grove Press, 1971; London, Calder and Boyars, 1972; revised edition, London, Calder, 1979.
Short Novels. London, Calder, 1978.
Blade Runner: A Movie. Berkeley, California, Blue Wind Press, 1979.
Port of Saints. Berkeley, California, Blue Wind Press, 1980; London, Calder, 1983.
Cities of the Red Night: A Boy's Book. London, Calder, and New York, Holt Rinehart, 1981.
The Place of Dead Roads. New York, Holt Rinehart, 1983; London, Calder, 1984.
Queer. New York, Viking, 1985; London, Pan, 1986.
The Western Lands. New York, Viking, 1987; London, Pan, 1988.
Interzone. London, Picador, 1989.
Ghost of Chance, illustrated by George Condo. New York, Library Fellows of the Whitney Museum of American Art, 1991.

Short Stories

Exterminator! New York, Viking Press, 1973; London, Calder and Boyars, 1974.
Early Routines. Santa Barbara, California, Cadmus, 1981.
The Streets of Chance. New York, Red Ozier Press, 1981.
Junky's Christmas and Other Stories. London, Serpents Tail, 1994.

Uncollected Short Stories

"The Ghost Lemurs of Madagascar," in *Omni* (New York), April 1987.
"The Valley," in *Esquire* (New York), September 1987.
"Twilight's Last Gleamings," in *Paris Review,* Winter 1988.

Play

The Last Words of Dutch Schultz (film script). London, Cape Goliard Press, 1970; New York, Viking Press, 1975.

Other

The Exterminator, with Brion Gysin. San Francisco, Auerhahn Press, 1960.
Minutes to Go, with others. Paris, Two Cities, 1960; San Francisco, Beach, 1968.
The Yage Letters, with Allen Ginsberg. San Francisco, City Lights, 1963.
Roosevelt after Inauguration. New York, Fuck You Press, 1964.
Valentine Day's Reading. New York, American Theatre for Poets, 1965.
Time. New York, "C" Press, 1965.
Health Bulletin: APO-33: A Metabolic Regulator. New York, Fuck You Press, 1965; revised edition, as *APO-33 Bulletin,* San Francisco, Beach, 1966.
So Who Owns Death TV?, with Claude Pelieu and Carl Weissner. San Francisco, Beach, 1967.
The Dead Star. San Francisco, Nova Broadcast Press, 1969.
Ali's Smile. Brighton, Unicorn, 1969.
Entretiens avec William Burroughs, by Daniel Odier. Paris, Belfond, 1969; translated as *The Job: Interviews with William S. Burroughs* (includes *Electronic Revolution*), New York, Grove Press, and London, Cape, 1970.
The Braille Film. San Francisco, Nova Broadcast Press, 1970.
Brion Gysin Let the Mice In, with Brion Gysin and Ian Somerville, edited by Jan Herman. West Glover, Vermont, Something Else Press, 1973.
Mayfair Academy Series More or Less. Brighton, Urgency Press Rip-Off, 1973.
White Subway, edited by James Pennington. London, Aloes, 1974.
The Book of Breeething. Ingatestone, Essex, OU Press, 1974; Berkeley, California, Blue Wind Press, 1975; revised edition, Blue Wind Press, 1980.
Snack: Two Tape Transcripts, with Eric Mottram. London, Aloes, 1975.
Sidetripping, with Charles Gatewood. New York, Strawberry Hill, 1975.
The Retreat Diaries, with *The Dream of Tibet,* by Allen Ginsberg. New York, City Moon, 1976.
Cobble Stone Gardens. Cherry Valley, New York, Cherry Valley Editions, 1976.
The Third Mind, with Brion Gysin. New York, Viking Press, 1978; London, Calder, 1979.
Roosevelt after Inauguration and Other Atrocities. San Francisco, City Lights, 1979.
Ah Pook Is Here and Other Texts (includes *The Book of Breeething, Electronic Revolution*). London, Calder, 1979; New York, Riverrun, 1982.
A William Burroughs Reader, edited by John Calder. London, Pan, 1982.
Letters to Allen Ginsberg 1953-1957. New York, Full Court Press, 1982.
New York Inside Out, photographs by Robert Walker. Port Washington, New York, Skyline Press, 1984.
The Burroughs File. San Francisco, City Lights, 1984.
The Adding Machine: Collected Essays. London, Calder, 1985; New York, Seaver, 1986.
Tornado Alley. Cherry Valley, New York, Cherry Valley Editions, 1988.
Interzone, edited by James Grauerholz. New York, Viking, and London, Pan, 1989.
The Cat Inside. New York, Viking, 1992.
Everything Is Permitted: The Making of Naked Lunch, edited by Ira Silverberg. New York, Grove Weidenfeld, 1992.

The Letters of William S. Burroughs: 1945-1959, edited by Oliver Harris. New York, Viking, and London, Picador, 1993.
My Education: A Book of Dreams. New York, Viking, 1994.

*

Film Adaptation: *Naked Lunch,* directed by David Cronenberg, 1991.

Bibliography: *William S. Burroughs: A Bibliography 1953-1973* by Joe Maynard and Barry Miles, Charlottesville, University Press of Virginia, 1978; *William S. Burroughs: A Reference Guide* by Michael B. Goodman and Lemuel B. Coley, New York, Garland, 1990.

Critical Studies: *William Burroughs: The Algebra of Need* by Eric Mottram, Buffalo, Intrepid Press, 1971, revised edition, as *The Algebra of Need,* London, Boyars, 1991; *Contemporary Literary Censorship: The Case History of Burroughs' Naked Lunch* by Michael B. Goodman, Metuchen, New Jersey, Scarecrow Press, 1981; *With William Burroughs: A Report from the Bunker* edited by Victor Bokris, New York, Seaver, 1981, London, Vermilion, 1982; "William Burroughs Issue" of *Review of Contemporary Fiction* (Elmwood Park, Illinois), vol. 4, no. 1, 1984; *William Burroughs* by Jennie Skerl, Boston, Twayne, 1985; *Literary Outlaw: The Life and Times of William S. Burroughs* by Ted Morgan, New York, Holt, 1988, London, Bodley Head, 1991; *William S. Burroughs at the Front: Critical Reception 1959-1989* edited by Jennie Skerl and Robin Lydenberg, Carbondale, Southern Illinois University Press, 1991; *William Burroughs: El Hombre Invisible: A Portrait* by Barry Miles, London, Virgin, 1992, and New York, Hyperion, 1993.

* * *

Influential and controversial author William S. Burroughs once stated that "all fiction is autobiographical and all autobiography is fiction." The claim holds true for the vast majority of his own writing.

Burroughs achieved literary fame and notoriety simultaneously with the publication of his second book, *Naked Lunch* (1959), a disjointed narrative establishing the hallmarks of his works: alien creatures, strange landscapes, mutating bodies, marginal sexualities, and drug experimentation. *Naked Lunch* is the painful product of Burroughs' addiction to heroin, and is a reflection of his mental landscape. When it appeared in the United States in 1962, the book's dealers were tried for obscenity but were exonerated when the book was successfully defended as an important work of literature. *Naked Lunch* presents a challenge to the vast majority of readers, not only due to the unusual content of the book but also because the writing deliberately frustrates narrative continuity. Instead of a flowing story, the reader is left with a series of strange characters who step in and out of the fragmented scenes. Now canonized, *Naked Lunch* initially polarized and confused critics. The book, intended by Burroughs to be understood as a Swiftean satire attacking the mores of contemporary society, was received as either an exciting and innovative form of "experimental" fiction, or an unreadable, worthless exercise in pornography. What is unarguable is that *Naked Lunch* remains an immensely popular piece of work.

Burroughs followed with *The Soft Machine* (1961), *The Ticket That Exploded* (1962), and *Nova Express* (1964), three books composed of various notes and fragments left out of the final version of *Naked Lunch* and assembled using a random "cut-up" method that forces the reader to piece together the narrative. The story follows the conflict between the Nova Mob, an alien gang which, in the form of viral addictions, has controlled the earth for thousands of years, and the Nova Police, time-travelling agents who try to disrupt the Nova Mob's stranglehold on the human race. Critics have interpreted the alien mob as a metaphor for the forces of government, control, and authority that run the earth. This trilogy attempted to capitalize on the reputation of *Naked Lunch,* but did not generate much interest partly because of the intense unreadability of the "cut-up" method, which requires a form of concentration that is difficult to sustain.

Burroughs abandoned the "cut-up" method with works like *The Wild Boys* (1971), which is considered by some a much more readable novel. The story follows a gang of homosexual warriors who, inhabiting a post-apocalyptic landscape, jaunt through time and space with the intention of disrupting social control at key moments in history. Reception, as always, remained mixed. Alfred Kazin, reviewing the book in the *New York Times,* wrote that "Burroughs is indeed a serious man and a considerable writer, but his books are not really books, they are compositions that astonish, then pall."

Figures from *The Wild Boys* reappear in *The Cities of the Red Night* (1981), a book that provoked a new critical appraisal of Burroughs and once more divided commentators. Panned by some as sensationalistic, derivative of his earlier work, and boring, *The Cities of the Red Night* was praised by others for being as good or better than *Naked Lunch,* and possibly Burroughs' masterpiece. Inspired by a historic figure known only as "Captain Mission," who established an utopic republic named Libertatia, Burroughs tries in this book to "correct retroactively certain fatal errors at crucial turning points in human history." From Burroughs' point of view, the human race is a failure and his role as writer is to attempt to salvage humanity by rewriting history.

Captain Mission returns in the brief novel *The Ghost of Chance* (1991), an apocalyptic narrative in which anti-conservationist terrorism releases upon the human race a host of extinct plagues from an ancient temple in the jungles of Madagascar. The brevity of this narrative and the conciseness of its message concerning the vast error called "humanity" make it a highly lucid and readable distillation of many of Burroughs' predominant themes. The simplicity and directness of the language is characteristic of other recent works, like *The Cat Inside* (1992), a series of poetic contemplations by Burroughs about his cats. The book reveals an aspect of Burroughs that is rarely glimpsed, full of affection and pathos for his non-human companions.

This highly personal side of the author is no more apparent than in *My Education* (1994), a collection of the author's dreams, reflections, and contemplations extending over several years. Figures from his life and his fiction move in and out of the dream fragments that are described in a lucid, direct, and compelling style. In a sense, this book is a return to familiar ground, but it also illustrates that Burroughs' inner landscape has undergone a transformation.

—Sean Carney

BUSCAGLIA, (Felice) Leo(nardo)

Nationality: American. **Born:** 31 March 1924 in East Los Angeles, California. **Education:** University of Southern California, B.A., 1950, M.A., 1954, General Administrative Credential, 1960, Ph.D., 1963. **Military Service:** U.S. Navy, 1941-44; became medical corpsman second class. **Career:** Educator and author. Pasadena City School System, teacher and speech therapist, 1951-60, special education supervisor, 1960-65; University of Southern California, assistant professor, 1965-68, associate professor, 1968-75, professor of education from 1975. Frequent lecturer on television and throughout the United States; has recorded more than a dozen speeches for Public Broadcasting Service (PBS-TV). Newspaper columnist since 1984. President and chairman of the board, Felice Foundation, South Pasadena, California, from 1984. **Awards:** California Governor's award, 1965; elected professor of the year, 1970 and 1972, and received Teaching Excellence award, 1978, University of Southern California; special recognition awards, American Academy of Dentistry for the Handicapped, 1972, and Royal Thai Navy, 1973; Meritorious Service Award, International School (Bangkok), 1973; Outstanding Services award, U.S. Air Force, 1976; certification of appreciation, 5th Air Force, 1976; Appreciation award, Public Broadcasting Service, 1981; Leo F. Buscaglia Day declared, Dunmore, Pennsylvania, 1983. **Address:** P.O. Box 599, Glenbrook, Nevada 89413, U.S.A.

Publications

Nonfiction

Because I Am Human! Charles B. Slack, 1972.
Love. Charles B. Slack, 1972.
The Way of the Bull: A Voyage. Charles B. Slack, 1974.
Personhood: The Art of Being Fully Human. Charles B. Slack, 1978.
Living, Loving, and Learning, edited by Steven Short, introduction by Betty Lou Kratoville. Charles B. Slack/Holt, 1982.
Loving Each Other: The Challenge of Human Relationships. Charles B. Slack/Holt, 1984.
Bus 9 to Paradise: A Loving Voyage, edited by Daniel Kimber. Slack, Inc./Morrow, 1986.
Seven Stories of Christmas Love. Slack, Inc./Morrow, 1987.
Papa, My Father: A Celebration of Dads. Slack, Inc./Morrow, 1989.
Sounds of Love. Nightingale-Conant, 1989.
Profiles in Caring: Advocates for the Elderly. Caring Publishing, 1990.
Born for Love: Thoughts for Lovers. Random House, 1992.
Born for Love: Reflections on Loving. Fawcett Book Group, 1994.
The Love Cookbook. Slack, Inc., 1994.

Children's Fiction

The Fall of Freddie the Leaf: A Story of Life for All Ages. Charles B. Slack/Holt, 1982.
A Memory for Tino, illustrated by Carol Newsom. Slack, Inc./Morrow, 1988.

Editor, *The Disabled and Their Parents: A Counseling Challenge.* Charles B. Slack, 1975; revised edition, Slack, Inc./Holt, 1983.
Editor with Eddie H. Williams, *Human Advocacy and PL94-142: The Educator's Roles.* Charles B. Slack, 1979.

* * *

Writer, lecturer, and public television personality Leo Buscaglia, or "Dr. Hug" as his fans affectionately call him, is known primarily for his promotion of self-acceptance and love as a cure for the confused state of society today. Hugging has become his trademark, as he welcomes members of the audience to come up for a hug after his lectures, some of them waiting in line over an hour to get a dose of the infectious love he spreads. His many books and videos on loving and personal growth have reached out to many more beyond the lecture circuit, making him a wildly popular author; once four of his books appeared on the bestseller lists simultaneously. Buscaglia's other books—children's fiction, personal memoirs of his family, and a tribute to his father and dads in general—have also been of interest to readers, although not as much as his books on loving.

Buscaglia grew up in a large family of Italian immigrants. He was the "love baby," he says, born after the other children had grown. This meant that he had a very special relationship with his father, who was no longer worried about being able to support his family. He was older, more relaxed, and could devote more time and love to his family, as Buscaglia explains in his memoir of his father, *Papa, My Father: A Celebration of Dads* (1989). Pauline Mayer, in a review of the book in the *Los Angeles Times Book Review,* argued that Buscaglia's dad was a kind of model for dad's today: "Dad as nurturer and caretaker, Dad as—well, let's face it—Mom."

Buscaglia began his career as a teacher, a natural choice for him. He once said, "I have always, even as a child, felt a deep responsibility to develop all that I am, not for myself alone, but so I could be more for everyone in my life. This deep desire led me to my chosen profession." He taught in the Pasadena, California school system for many years, working with disadvantaged children. Although he was appointed director of special education, he never felt comfortable with the supervisor's role. When he left his position in the mid-1960s he took the opportunity to travel to the Far East for two years. While there he immersed himself in Eastern religions and the people he met, preserving his experiences in *The Way of the Bull: A Voyage* (1974). "The finest writing I've ever done," he has said, "although no one ever reads it."

When he returned home, Buscaglia joined the USC faculty as a special education expert, winning two teacher of the year awards. When one of his promising students committed suicide, Buscaglia came up with the idea to teach a non-credit course on love to help students build self-esteem. The class, "Love 1A," was wildly popular and eventually blossomed into the book *Love* (1972), which stresses the importance of self-love as a prerequisite to loving others and being loved by others. His many books since then on the topic of love deal with the central theme of sharing affection with others as a way to heal ourselves. "My message is simple," he told *Newsweek.* "Let's get back to a sense of personal dignity and individuality. We should all get in touch with our uniqueness and share it with other people."

Buscaglia's many books are popular with those who find his passionate style and optimism about the healing power of love a much-needed antidote to the mistrust and disconnectedness of contemporary society. But some reviewers have poked fun at Buscaglia's gushy message and what they see as its inexplicable popular appeal. In a 1989 review of his video, *Politics of Love, People* magazine joked about Buscaglia's statement "you've gotta be a zombie not to want to turn around and hug everyone," saying, "Fans will dash out and hug a lamppost; zombies will marvel at his success."

Bernie Zilbergeld of *Psychology Today,* himself a psychologist, had more serious criticism of Buscaglia's message. While he is a "superb entertainer with a knack for getting to us in our most sensitive places, his messages are largely irrelevant to the lives most of us lead." Zilbergeld criticizes Buscaglia for preaching love, marriage, and commitment when he himself has never been married or had children. "It is easy to love everyone when you don't have to be with anyone longer than a few minutes or hours," Zilbergeld quipped. Buscaglia has explained his decision to not marry as a choice to "embrace all personkind rather than concentrate on one single individual." If his sales records are any indication, humanity is hugging back.

—Anne Boyd

BUTLER, Octavia E(stelle)

Nationality: American. **Born:** Pasadena, California, 22 June 1947. **Education:** Pasadena College, 1965-68, A.A. 1968; California State University, 1969. **Career:** Since 1970, freelance writer. **Awards:** Hugo awards, 1984 and 1995; Nebula awards, 1985 and 1995; *Locus* award, 1985; Science Fiction Chronicle award, 1985. **Address:** c/o Warner Books Inc., 666 Fifth Avenue, New York, New York 10103, U.S.A.

Publications

Novels (series: Patternists; Xenogenesis)

Patternmaster (Patternists). Garden City, New York, Doubleday, 1976; London, Sphere, 1978.
Mind of My Mind (Patternists). Garden City, New York, Doubleday, 1977; London, Sidgwick and Jackson, 1978.
Survivor (Patternists). Garden City, New York, Doubleday, and London, Sidgwick and Jackson, 1978.
Kindred. Garden City, New York, Doubleday, 1979; London, Women's Press, 1988.
Wild Seed (Patternists). Garden City, New York, Doubleday, and London, Sidgwick and Jackson, 1980.
Clay's Ark (Patternists). New York, St. Martin's Press, 1984; London, Gollancz, 1991.
Xenogenesis (omnibus). New York, Guild America, 1989.
 Dawn. New York, Warner, and London, Gollancz, 1987.
 Adulthood Rites. New York, Warner, and London, Gollancz, 1988.
 Imago. New York, Warner, and London, Gollancz, 1989.
Parable of the Sower. New York, Four Walls Eight Windows, 1993; London, Women's Press, 1995.

Short Stories

The Evening and the Morning and the Night. Eugene, Oregon, Pulphouse, 1991.
Bloodchild. New York, Four Walls, Eight Windows, 1995.

Critical Study: *Suzy Charnas, Joan Vinge, and Octavia Butler* by Richard Law, with others, San Bernardino, California, Borgo Press, 1986.

* * *

Octavia Butler said in an interview in *Science-Fiction Writers* that she "began writing fantasy and science fiction because these seemed to be the genres in which I could be freest, most creative." She went on to say that her stories are about power—of those who have power, those who do not, and those who want more. She brings together multi-racial groups, not necessarily in the traditional sense, but anyone who has been made "other" than the norm and doesn't fit within the narrow margins of average, normal, proper. She's interested in how these marginalized people cope and interact with one another and their own situations. She consistently attacks racism, sexism, hypocrisy, and class divisions in her writings.

Butler's Patternist (1978-84) novels, the first of her two major groupings of novels, tell the fictional history of a people called Patternists who, by mutation and selective breeding, are developing psionic abilities. The novels are set in a broad range of time periods, from the seventeenth century to the distant future. In these novels Butler dramatizes explicitly and graphically the power struggles between men and women. She never backs away from the harshness or the evil she seeks to portray.

In the chronologically first of the Patternist novels, *Wild Seed* (1980), Butler tells the story of how Doro accumulates his breeding stock. For centuries, before Christ, Doro has been searching for people with mental gifts like his own. When in 1690 he finds a 300-year-old woman who can morph to any form she wishes by manipulating DNA, he humiliates her and arranges for her to produce special children. At her death, Doro links with her, the first time he has used his mental power without killing the other person. This technique enables the later Mary to create the eventual titular pattern.

Mind of My Mind (1977) takes up the task of explaining the vagueness of the Patternmaster concept. In this novel, Mary, Doro's daughter, gathers up and links telepaths together, eventually battling Doro for independence for her people and opposing his individual, self-interested manipulations. *Patternmaster* (1976) develops the system created by Mary, and leads to an eventual duel over who will control it. The final resolution suggests a renewal of society through the union of compassionate patternists. *Survivor* (1978) and *Clay's Ark* (1984) develop this world in greater detail, following other characters in the world set up by Mary. Though many of the protagonists in these novels are black women, Butler does not seek so much to celebrate them as to break down the barriers of race and sexuality, illustrating the inability to evolve and grow for those who are bound by prejudice. Survival and positive progress are key issues for Butler.

The *Xenogenesis* (1987-89) trilogy magnifies and focuses on the differences between humans and aliens, revolving around issues of cultural misunderstanding and antipathy rooted in prejudice. In this series, comprised of *Dawn: Xenogenesis, Adulthood Rites,* and *Imago,* Butler creates a race called the Oankali. These are nomadic aliens who interbreed with other sentient species in an effort to improve their gene pool. They arrive on a postnuclear holocaust earth, offering the handful of survivors the opportunity to combine the best characteristics of both species. This is accomplished through the buffering presence of a third sex, the ooloi, whose function is to create the new species. These novels are a disturbing exploration of race relations between people trying to survive and still trying to retain their humanity.

A recent offering follows on the heels of Butler's successful *The Parable of the Sower* (1994). It is a collection entitled *Bloodchild: Novellas and Stories* (1995). The title story "Blood Child" has won a Nebula award, and "Speech Sounds" has earned a Hugo. In these stories, Butler challenges the traditional, socially constructed roles of women and minorities. Most importantly, Butler makes these characters real and vital, engaging the reader deeply in the outcome of the stories. This collection is an excellent example of Butler's ability as a crafter of story and language.

—Diana Pharaoh Francis

BUTTERWORTH, W(illiam) E(dmund III)

Pseudonyms: Alex Baldwin, Webb Beech, Walker E. Blake, James McM. Douglas, Jack Dugan, W. E. B. Griffin, Eden Hughes, Allison Mitchell, Edmund O. Scholefield, Patrick J. Williams. **Nationality:** American. **Born:** Newark, New Jersey, 10 November 1929. **Military Service:** U.S. Army, 1946-47, 1951-53; served as combat correspondent in Korea; received Expert Combat Infantryman's Badge. **Family:** Married Emma Josefa Macalik in 1950; one daughter, two sons. **Career:** Writer. **Awards:** *LeRoy and the Old Man* was named to the American Library Association's "Best Books for Young Adults" list, 1980; inducted into Alabama Academy of Distinguished Authors, 1982; awarded honorary membership in U.S. Army Otter & Caribou Association, 1985, in U.S. Marine Raider Association, 1988, and in U.S. Marine Corps Combat Correspondents Association, 1991; honorary Doctor of Literature, Norwich University, 1989; Denig award, U.S. Marine Corps Combat Correspondents Association, 1991. **Agent:** Jane Cushman, JCA Literary Agency, Inc., 27 West 20th St., Suite 1103, New York, New York 10011. **Address:** 301 North Creek Dr., Fairhope, Alabama 36532, U.S.A.

Publications

Novels

Comfort Me with Love. New American Library, 1961.
Hot Seat. New American Library, 1961.
Where We Go from Here. New American Library, 1962.
The Court-Martial. New American Library, 1962.
The Love-Go-Round. Berkley Publishing, 1962.
Hell on Wheels. Berkley Publishing, 1962.
The Girl in the Black Bikini. Berkley Publishing, 1962.
Le Falot. Gallimard, 1963.
Fast Green Car. Norton, 1965.
Stock Car Racer. Norton, 1966.
Helicopter Pilot. Norton, 1967.
Road Racer. Norton, 1967.
The Image Makers. Scripts Publishing, 1967.
Air Evac. Norton, 1967.
Orders to Vietnam. Little, Brown, 1968.
Redline 7100. Norton, 1968.
Stop and Search. Little, Brown, 1969.
Wheel of a Fast Car. Norton, 1969.
Grand Prix Driver. Norton, 1969.
Marty and the Micro Midgets. Norton, 1970.
Fast and Smart. Norton, 1970.
Susan and Her Classic Convertible. Four Winds, 1970.
Crazy to Race. Grosset, 1971.
My Father's Quite a Guy. Little, Brown, 1971.
Return to Racing. Grosset, 1971.
Team Racer. Grosset, 1972.
The Narc. Four Winds, 1972.
Dateline: Talladega. Grosset, 1972.
Skyjacked! Scholastic, 1972.
Race Car Team. Grosset, 1973.
Yankee Driver. Grosset, 1973.
Flying Army. Doubleday, 1973.
Dave White and the Electric Wonder Car. Four Winds, 1974.
Stop Thief! Four Winds, 1974.
Return to Daytona. Grosset, 1974.
The Roper Brothers and Their Magnificent Steam Automobile. Four Winds, 1976.
Christina's Passion. Playboy Paperbacks, 1977.
Next Stop Earth. Walker, 1978.
Tank Driver. Four Winds, 1978.
The Air Freight Mystery. Four Winds, 1978.
Under the Influence. Four Winds, 1979.
LeRoy and the Old Man. Four Winds, 1980.
The Wiltons (as Eden Hughes). New American Library, 1981.
The Selkirks (as Eden Hughes). New American Library, 1983.
The Deep Kill (as Jack Dugan). Charter Books, 1984.
Wild Harvest (as Allison Mitchell). New American Library, 1984.
Wild Heritage (as Allison Mitchell). New American Library, 1985.

Nonfiction

The Wonders of Rockets and Missiles. Putnam, 1964.
The Wonders of Astronomy. Putnam 1964.
Soldiers on Horseback: The Story of the United States Cavalry. Norton, 1966.
Grand Prix Racing (as Patrick J. Williams). Four Winds, 1968.
Steve Bellamy. Little, Brown, 1970.
Moving West on 122. Little, Brown, 1970.
Flying Army: The Modern Air Arm of the U.S. Army. Doubleday, 1971.
Wheels and Pistons: The Story of the Automobile. Four Winds, 1971.
The High Wind: The Story of NASCAR Racing. Grosset, 1972.
The Race Driver. Action, 1972.
Tires and Other Things: Some Heroes of Automotive Evolution. Doubleday, 1974.
Mighty Minicycles. Harvey House, 1976.
Black Gold: The Story of Oil. Four Winds, 1975.
Careers in the Services. F. Watts, 1976.
An Album of Automobile Racing. F. Watts, 1977.
Hi-Fi: From Edison's Phonograph to Quadraphonic Sound. Four Winds, 1977.

Novels with Richard Hooker (series: M*A*S*H in all titles)

*M*A*S*H Goes to Paris.* Pocket Books, 1974.
*M*A*S*H Goes to New Orleans.* Pocket Books, 1975.
*M*A*S*H Goes to Morocco.* Pocket Books, 1975.
*M*A*S*H Goes to London.* Pocket Books, 1976.
*M*A*S*H Goes to Las Vegas.* Pocket Books, 1976.
*M*A*S*H Goes to Hollywood.* Pocket Books, 1976.
*M*A*S*H Goes to Vienna.* Pocket Books, 1976.
*M*A*S*H Goes to Miami.* Pocket Books, 1976.
*M*A*S*H Goes to San Francisco.* Pocket Books, 1976.
*M*A*S*H Goes to Texas.* Pocket Books, 1977.
*M*A*S*H Goes to Montreal.* Pocket Books, 1977.
*M*A*S*H Goes to Moscow.* Pocket Books, 1978.

Novels as Alex Baldwin (series: Men at War in all titles)

The Last Heroes. Pocket Books, 1985.
The Secret Warriors. Pocket Books, 1986.
The Soldier Spies. Pocket Books, 1987.
The Fighting Agents. Pocket Books, 1988.

Novels as Webb Beech

No French Leave. Gold Medal, 1960.
Article 92: Murder-Rape. Fawcett, 1965.
Warrior's Way. Fawcett, 1965.
Make War in Madness. Fawcett, 1966.

Novels as Walker E. Blake

The Loved and the Lost. Monarch, 1962.
Heartbreak Ridge. Monarch, 1962.
Once More with Passion. Monarch, 1964.
Doing What Comes Naturally. Monarch, 1965.

Novels as James McM. Douglas

Hunger for Racing. Putnam, 1967.
Racing to Glory. Putnam, 1969.
The Twelve-Cylinder Screamer. Putnam, 1970.
Drag Race Driver. Putnam, 1971.
A Long Ride on a Cycle. Putnam, 1972.

Novels as W. E. B. Griffin (series: Brotherhood of War; Corps; Badge of Honor)

The Lieutenants (Brotherhood). Jove, 1983.
The Captains (Brotherhood). Jove, 1983.
The Majors (Brotherhood). Jove, 1984.
The Colonels (Brotherhood). Jove, 1985.
The Berets (Brotherhood). Jove, 1985.
The Generals (Brotherhood). Jove, 1986.
Semper Fi (Corps). Jove, 1986.
Call to Arms (Corps). Jove, 1987.
Men in Blue (Badge). Jove, 1988.
The New Breed (Brotherhood). Jove, 1988.
Aviators (Brotherhood). Jove, 1989.
Special Operations (Badge). Jove, 1989.
Counterattack (Corps). Putnam, 1990.
Battleground (Corps). Putnam, 1991.
The Victim (Badge). Jove, 1991.
The Assassin (Badge). Jove, 1992.
Close Combat (Corps). Putnam, 1992.
Line of Fire (Corps). Putnam, 1992.
The Witness (Badge). Jove, 1992.
Honor Bound. Putnam, 1994.
The Murderers (Badge). Jove, 1995.
Behind the Lines (Corps). Putnam, 1996.

Novels as Edmund O. Scholefield

Tiger Rookie. World Publishing, 1966.
L'il Wildcat. World Publishing, 1967.
Bryan's Dog. World Publishing, 1967.
Maverick on the Mound. World Publishing, 1968.
Yankee Boy. World Publishing, 1971.

Novels as Patrick J. Williams

Fastest Funny Car. Four Winds, 1967.
Up to the Quarterdeck. Four Winds, 1969.
The Green Ghost. Scholastic, Inc., 1969.
Racing Mechanic. Scholastic, Inc., 1969.

*   *   *

William Edmund Butterworth has penned more than 100 novels and nonfiction works under numerous pseudonyms. Since the early 1960s he has established himself as a top writer of military and war books, although he has also written several novels involving automobile racing. His various nonfiction works in the 1960s and 1970s ranged from *An Album of Automobile Racing* (1977) and *Black Gold: The Story of Oil* (1975) to *The Wonders of Astronomy* (1964) and *Soldiers on Horseback: The Story of the United States Calvary* (1966). But it is his military novels that have made him famous. Those books have appeared under pen names including Jack Duban, Walker E. Blake, Webb Beech, Alex Baldwin, and Patrick J. Williams, among others. Butterworth is most widely known as W.E.B. Griffin, author of the three popular series—Brotherhood of War, The Corps, and Badge of Honor—that he began writing in the 1980s.

Brotherhood of War: The Lieutenants (1982) follows a group of officers through the middle of WWII, peacetime, and into the beginning of the Korean War. If any one of the characters could be considered the main, it would be Lieutenant Robert Bellmon, who is taken prisoner by the Germans. The POW camp commander and Bellmon forge a kind of alliance. Colonel von Grieffenberg shares with Bellmon evidence that the Soviets are implicated in the massacre of several hundred Polish officers. Bellmon eventually escapes with the aid of the colonel and gets back to the States, where his life touches on that of others who become pivotal characters. Critics praised Griffin for a well-written and absorbing account of military life. "In the process, Griffin has captured the rhythms of army life and speech, its rewards and deprivations, the casual racism and anti-Semitism," wrote a reviewer in *Publisher's Weekly.*

The eighth installment in the Brotherhood of War series, which covers 40 years of American military adventure, *The Aviators* (1989) sees Captain Oliver (aide-de-camp to now-General Bellmon, commander of the Army Aviation Center in Alabama) at the hub of the aviation program. Oliver is training flyers, testing equipment, investigating crashes, and serving as a link between officers and brass. Even though the year is 1964, surprisingly there are relatively no references to the Vietnam War. Except for an opening rescue operation in Viet Cong territory, the lion's share of the book takes place at Fort Rucker, Alabama. Although praised for his insights into the minds of military men and their wives, Griffin has been criticized for throwing in far too much military jargon and painfully detailed explications of custom and procedure.

Battleground: The Corps Book IV (1991) takes a handful of marines introduced in the previous books of the Corps series from Midway to Guadalcanal. Navy Captain Fleming Pickering travels to different headquarters, reporting back to the Secretary of the Navy. Captain Charley Galloway is busy forming a new fighter squadron while Sergeant John Moore, a Japanese language expert, is on a top-secret intelligence mission. Griffin's framework of coherent subplots, interesting characters, and sundry WWII arcana creates a fascinating mix. "A surprisingly effective alternative to military fiction's usual foxhole-and-cockpit perspective—he places the characters on the fringes rather than in the thick of the action, skirting familiar events and offering opportunities to explore the Pacific War's less familiar byways," wrote a reviewer in *Publisher's Weekly*.

In 1994 Griffin ventured outside the scope of series writing with *Honor Bound,* set against the background of 1940s South America. In late 1942, marine fighter-ace Clete Frade, army demolitions engineer Anthony Pelosi, and electronics expert David Ettinger are sent by the OSS into neutral Argentina. Their mission is to destroy a merchant ship which has been supplying Nazi submarines. The U.S. hopes to use Clete to gain the influence of his estranged father, who is heavily involved in Argentine politics. One of Griffin's most critically well-received novels, *Honor Bound* has been praised for its tightly constructed plot, credible character development, and excellent attention to details of setting.

Although Griffin may have the tendency to throw in too much logistical information, he never fails to render realistic and moving portraits of American military men and their lives and families.

—Jennifer G. Coman

BYATT, A(ntonia) S(usan)

Nationality: British. **Born:** Antonia Susan Drabble, in Sheffield, Yorkshire, 24 August 1936; sister of Margaret Drabble, *q.v.* **Education:** Sheffield High School; The Mount School, York; Newnham College, Cambridge (open scholarship), B.A. (honours) in English 1957; Bryn Mawr College, Pennsylvania (English-Speaking Union fellow), 1957-58; Somerville College, Oxford, 1958-59, B.A. **Family:** Married 1) I.C.R. Byatt in 1959 (divorced 1969), one daughter and one son (deceased); 2)Peter J. Duffy in 1969, two daughters. **Career:** Teacher, Westminster Tutors, London, 1962-65; lecturer, Central School of Art and Design, London, 1965-69; extramural lecturer, 1962-71, lecturer, 1972-81, and senior lecturer in English, 1981-83, University College, London (assistant tutor, 1977-80, and tutor for admissions, 1980-82, Department of English). British Council Lecturer in Spain, 1978, India, 1981, and Korea, 1985. Deputy chair, 1986, and chair, 1986-88, Society of Authors Committee of Management; member, Kingman Committee, on the teaching of English, 1988-89. Associate, Newnham College, 1977-88. **Awards:** Arts Council grant, 1968; PEN Silver Pen, 1986; Booker prize, 1990, and *Irish Times*-Aer Lingus prize, 1990, both for *Possession.* D.Litt.: University of Bradford, 1987; University of York, 1991; University of Durham, 1991. Fellow, Royal Society of Literature, 1983. C.B.E. (Commander, Order of the British Empire), 1990. **Address:** 37 Rusholme Road, London SW15 3LF, England.

Publications

Novels

Shadow of a Sun. London, Chatto and Windus, and New York, Harcourt Brace, 1964.
The Game. London, Chatto and Windus, 1967; New York, Scribner, 1968.
The Virgin in the Garden. London, Chatto and Windus, 1978; New York, Knopf, 1979.
Still Life. London, Chatto and Windus, and New York, Scribner, 1985.
Possession: A Romance. London, Chatto and Windus, and New York, Random House, 1990.

Short Stories

Sugar and Other Stories. London, Chatto and Windus, and New York, Scribner, 1987.
Angels and Insects (novellas). London, Chatto and Windus, and New York, Random House, 1992.
The Matisse Stories. London, Chatto and Windus, 1993.

Uncollected Short Story

"Art Work," in *The New Yorker,* 20 May 1991.

Other

Degrees of Freedom: The Novels of Iris Murdoch. London, Chatto and Windus, and New York, Barnes and Noble, 1965.
Wordsworth and Coleridge in Their Time. London, Nelson, 1970; New York, Crane Russak, 1973; as *Unruly Times: Wordsworth and Coleridge in Their Time,* London, Hogarth Press, 1989.
Iris Murdoch. London, Longman, 1976.
Passions of the Mind (essays). London, Chatto and Windus, 1991; New York, Turtle Bay, 1992.

Editor, *The Mill on the Floss,* by George Eliot. London, Penguin, 1979.
Editor, with Nicholas Warren, *Selected Essays, Poems, and Other Writings,* by George Eliot. London, Penguin, 1990.

* * *

Since publishing her bestselling, prizewinning novel *Possession* (1990), A.S. Byatt has stepped from the shadow of her sister, Margaret Drabble, to establish her own presence in the British literary world. *Possession* features two scholars who fall in love while tripping over themselves, each other, and a feisty American to obtain never-surfaced manuscripts and biographical data about two fictitious Victorian-era poets (who, as it turns out, had a clandestine love affair). The motif of academics as main characters reflects Byatt's background: she earned her B.A. (with first-class honors) from Newnham College, Cambridge, and took doctoral courses in 17th century English literature at Somerville College, Oxford. She also taught literature at the University of London while writing novels and short stories.

Byatt's first novel, *Shadow of a Sun* (1964), received lukewarm reviews. Critics were unmoved by most of Byatt's characters and tended to focus on comparisons to Drabble. The novel features fictional novelist Henry Severell and his reticent 17-year-old daughter, Anna. Anna—she is only the first in a long series of highly educated Byatt characters—attends Cambridge, gets pregnant, receives a marriage offer from a man who isn't the baby's father, and eventually learns to trust her inner strength.

In 1967 Byatt published *The Game,* about a complex competition for success and attention between two sisters in their thirties. Interestingly, one of the sisters is an Oxford don and the other is a successful novelist and celebrity. Critics naturally wondered whether the novel mimicked Byatt and Drabble—Drabble, incidentally, had published a novel about two sisters four years earlier.

After a hiatus from fiction writing caused, in part, by her divorce from Ian Byatt, remarriage to Peter Duffy, and the death of her son, Charles (all of which took place between 1969 and 1972), Byatt published *The Virgin in the Garden* in 1978. Set at the time of the coronation of Queen Elizabeth II in 1953, the novel contains prominent references to Queen Elizabeth I. This is the first installment of a tetralogy, known as the "Powerhouse Quartet," that follows the Potter children—Stephanie, Frederica, and Marcus—through several decades.

The Virgin in the Garden was followed by *Still Life* (1985), which continues Byatt's exploration of the Potters as they enter adulthood. Character development was much improved in *Still Life,* but incidental conversations about Milton were unrealistic.

A short story collection, *Sugar and Other Stories,* was published in 1987. Many of these stories are autobiographical; "The July Ghost," for example, is about a woman who mourns the loss of her son. Byatt's own son, Charles, was struck and killed by a drunk driver in 1972 when he was 11 years old. Her short fiction contains more passionately charged words than does her longer fiction, which is patently cerebral. But none of the elegance is lost, nor are any of the complex sentence structures.

Byatt has also published several works of nonfiction. The foremost of these is *Passions of the Mind,* (1991). That work is a collection of essays stemming from Byatt's love of reading. In her introduction, she states, "From my early childhood, reading and writing seemed to me to be points on a circle. Greedy reading made me want to write, as if this were the only adequate response to the pleasure and power of books. Writing made me want to read."

More recently, Byatt published *The Matisse Stories* in 1994, inspired by her passion for artist Henri Matisse. The artwork tends to dominate Byatt's prose, but her presence is nevertheless unmistakable.

Much criticism of Byatt's work centers around her devotion to Victorian-era subjects, which are often treated too cerebrally. But Byatt has also been praised for her literary voice, which blends spellbinding creative vision with rigorous academic training. Her word choices, in fact, may send intrigued readers scrambling for their dictionaries. "I am not an academic who happens to have written a novel. I am a novelist who happens to be quite good academically," she has said.

—Tracy Clark

C

CANNON, Curt. *See* **McBAIN, Ed.**

CAPOTE, Truman

Nationality: American. **Born:** Truman Streckfus Persons, 30 September 1924 in New Orleans; name legally changed when he was adopted by Joseph G. Capote. **Education:** Trinity School and St. John's Academy, both in New York City, and public schools in Greenwich, Connecticut. **Career:** Writer. Worked for *New Yorker* magazine as a newspaper clipper and cartoon cataloger, c. 1943-44; also moonlighted as a filmscript reader and freelance writer of anecdotes. **Awards:** O. Henry Award, Doubleday & Co., 1946, for "Miriam," 1948, for "Shut a Final Door," and 1951; National Institute of Arts and Letters creative writing award, 1959; Edgar award, Mystery Writers of America, 1966, and National Book award nomination, 1967, both for *In Cold Blood;* Emmy award, 1967, for television adaptation *A Christmas Memory.* **Member:** National Institute of Arts and Letters. **Died:** 25 August 1984, of liver disease complicated by phlebitis and multiple drug intoxication, in Los Angeles.

Publications

Fiction

Other Voices, Other Rooms. Random House, 1948; reprinted with an introduction by the author, 1968.
A Tree of Night, and Other Stories. Random House, 1949.
The Grass Harp. Random House, 1951.
Breakfast at Tiffany's: A Short Novel and Three Stories. Random House, 1958.
A Christmas Memory. Random House, 1966.
In Cold Blood: A True Account of a Multiple Murder and Its Consequences. Random House, 1966.
The Thanksgiving Visitor. Random House, 1968.
Music for Chameleons: New Writing. Random House, 1983.
One Christmas. Random House, 1983.
Answered Prayers: The Partial Manuscript, edited by Joseph Fox. Random House, 1986.
A Capote Reader. Random House, 1987.

Plays

The Grass Harp, adaptation of his novel (produced New York, 1952; produced as a musical, 1971). Random House, 1952.
The House of Flowers, with Harold Arlen, adaptaton of Capote's short story (produced New York, 1954; rewritten version produced New York 1968). Random House, 1968.

Screenplays: *Beat the Devil,* with John Huston, 1954; *The Innocents,* with William Archibald and John Mortimer, 1961; *Trilogy,* with Eleanor Perry, 1969.

Television Plays: *A Christmas Memory,* 1966; *Among the Paths to Eden,* 1967; *Laura,* 1968; *The Thanksgiving Visitor,* 1968; *Behind Prison Walls,* 1972; *The Glass House,* with Tracy Keenan Wynn and Wyatt Cooper, 1972; and *Crimewatch,* 1973.

Nonfiction

Local Color. Random House, 1950.
The Muses Are Heard: An Account. Random House, 1956; Heinemann, 1957.
The Dogs Bark: Public People and Private Places. Random House, 1973.

*

Film Adaptations: *Breakfast at Tiffany's,* 1961; *In Cold Blood,* 1967.

Bibliography: *Truman Capote: A Primary and Secondary Bibliography* by Robert J. Stanton, G. K. Hall, 1980.

Critical Studies: *The Worlds of Truman Capote* by William L. Nance, Stein & Day, 1970; *Truman Capote* by Helen Garson, Ungar, 1980; *Truman Capote* by Marie Rudisill and James C. Simmons, William Morrow, 1983; *Truman Capote: Dear Heart, Old Buddy* by John Malcolm Brinnin, Delacorte, 1986; *Capote: A Biography* by Gerald Clarke, Simon & Schuster, 1986; *Truman Capote: Conversations* edited by Thomas M. Inge, University Press of Mississippi, 1987; *A Bridge of Childhood: Truman Capote's Southern Years* by Marianne M. Moates, Henry Holt, 1989.

Theatrical Activities: Actor: **Film**—*Murder by Death,* 1976.

* * *

Truman Capote, as obsessed with fame and fortune as with penning great words, was a writer who became as well-known for his late-night talk show appearances as for his prose. With *In Cold Blood,* Capote advanced a new literary form; the "nonfiction novel," while his most anticipated book was the never-finished *Answered Prayers,* which was to reveal the regrets of his rich and famous friends. In his best works, Capote "produced a unique verbal music, a blend of shrewdness and sentimentality that revealed human beings as hybrids both baroque and banal," wrote Jack Kroll in *Newsweek* after Capote's death in 1984.

Capote first gained public attention with the novel *Other Voices, Other Rooms* (1948), the story of a young man who, unable to find his father and unable to adjust to the real world, falls into a relationship with a decadent transvestite. The book was not nearly as provocative as Capote's dustjacket photo, which showed him reclined on a couch, looking "as if he were dreamily contemplating some outrage against conventional morality," as the *Los Angeles Times* reported. Reviewers generally praised the debut, but conservative critics were outraged by what they considered a distasteful homosexual theme.

Over the next ten years, much of it spent traveling in Europe, Capote developed his talent writing nonfiction travel essays, short stories, stage plays, and screenplays. His best works from this period were a droll profile of Marlon Brando and the book *The Muses Are Heard: An Account of the Porgy and Bess Visit to Leningrad* (1957), which subtly mocked a black theatrical troupe's presentation of *Porgy and Bess* to Soviet audiences.

With *Muses,* Capote developed the approach to research that he would later apply to *In Cold Blood.* To gain information from subjects, Capote used neither tape recorder nor note pad. Instead, he conversed freely with subjects and relied upon his memory, then emptied his impressions in notebooks at the end of the day. "Taking notes produces the wrong kind of atmosphere," Capote told *Newsweek*'s Jack Kroll.

Before embarking upon *In Cold Blood,* Capote wrote one last conventional novel, *Breakfast at Tiffany's* (1958), which recounted the absurd adventures of his most memorable character, Manhattan playgirl Holly Golightly. "From her first appearance Holly leaps to life," wrote *New Republic* contributor Stanley Kauffmann. "Her dialogue has the perfection of pieces of mosaic fitting neatly and unassailably in place."

Starting in 1959, Capote embarked on a six-year journey to write *In Cold Blood,* which reported the murder in Holcomb, Kansas, of a wealthy wheat farmer, his wife, and their two teenage children, and the pursuit and eventual execution of the two killers. In writing the nonfiction novel, Capote envisioned "something on a large scale that would have the credibility of fact, the immediacy of film, the depth and freedom of prose, and the precision of poetry," he explained to James Wolcott in the *New York Review of Books.* To achieve this, Capote interviewed the townspeople, the two murderers, and anyone else with any connection to the case. The book ended with a powerful plea for clemency, exploring the irony that though the family was killed in a crime of passion, it was the murderers who were eventually executed in cold blood. "*In Cold Blood* is first-rate entertainment that at moments gives illusory promise of being something more than that," wrote Robert Langbaum in *American Scholar.*

After *In Cold Blood,* Capote's interests turned to his social life, and as he hit writer's block, he turned to finishing his book, *Answered Prayers,* which he had been working on since 1959. Four chapters appeared in *Esquire* magazine in 1975 and 1976, in which Capote revealed the scandalous secrets of his upper-crust friends who had "suffered the worst thing that can befall human beings, to have their prayers answered," wrote Kroll in 1984. *Answered Prayers* became "the most famous unfinished book of our time," wrote Kroll. It was rumored, probably falsely, that Capote had been working on it hours before his death.

—Eric Patterson

CARD, Orson Scott

Pseudonym: Brian Green. **Nationality:** American. **Born:** Richland, Washington, 24 August 1951. **Education:** Brigham Young University, Provo, Utah, B.A. in theatre 1975; University of Utah, Salt Lake City, M.A. in English 1981. **Family:** Married Kristine Allen in 1977; two sons and two daughters. **Career:** Volunteer Mormon missionary in Brazil, 1971-73; operated repertory theatre, Provo, 1974-75; proofreader, 1974, and editor, 1974-76, Brigham Young University Press; assistant editor, *Ensign* magazine, Salt Lake City, 1976-78, and senior editor, Compute! Books, Greensboro, North Carolina, 1983; taught at the University of Utah, 1979-80, 1981, Brigham Young University, 1981, Notre Dame University, Indiana, 1981-82, Clarion Writers Workshop, East Lansing, Michigan, 1982, Appalachian State University (full-time), 1987 (part-time), 1989—. **Awards:** John W. Campbell award, 1978; Nebula award, for novel, 1985, 1986; Hugo award, for novel, 1985, 1986, for novella, 1987, for nonfiction, 1991; *Locus* award, for novel, 1988, 1989; Mythopoeic Fantasy award, 1988. **Agent:** Barbara Bova, 3957 Gulf Shore Blvd. #PH1B, Naples, Florida 33940. **Address:** P.O. Box 18184, Greensboro, North Carolina 27419-8184, U.S.A. **Online Address:** OrsonCard@aol.com.

PUBLICATIONS

Novels (Series: Homecoming; Alvin Maker; Mayflower; Ender Wiggin; Worthing Chronicle)

Hot Sleep: The Worthing Chronicle. New York, Baronet, 1979; London, Futura, 1980.

A Planet Called Treason. New York, St. Martin's Press, 1979; London, Pan, 1981; expanded as *Treason,* New York, St. Martin's Press, 1988.

Songmaster. New York, Dial Press, 1980; London, Futura, 1981.

Hart's Hope. New York, Berkley, 1983; London, Unwin, 1986.

The Worthing Chronicle. New York, Ace, 1983.

Ender's Game. New York, Tor, 1985; London, Unwin, 1985; revised edition, Tor, 1991.

Speaker for the Dead (Ender). New York, Tor, 1986; London, Arrow, 1987; revised edition, Tor, 1991.

Ender's War (includes *Ender's Game* and *Speaker for the Dead*). Garden City, New York, Doubleday, 1986.

Wyrms. New York, Arbor House, 1987; London, Legend, 1988.

Hatrack River: The Tales of Alvin Maker (includes *Seventh Son, Red Prophet,* and *Prentice Alvin*). New York, Guild America, 1987, London, Century, 1988.

Red Prophet. New York, Tor, 1988; London, Legend, 1989.

A Woman of Destiny. New York, Berkley, 1984; as *Saints,* New York, Tor, 1988.

Prentice Alvin. New York, Tor, and London, Legend, 1989.

The Abyss: A Novel (novelization of screenplay). New York, Pocket, and London, Legend, 1989.

The Worthing Saga. New York, Tor, 1990; London, Legend, 1991.

Xenocide (Ender). New York, Tor, and London, Legend, 1991.

The Memory of Earth (Homecoming). New York, Tor, and London, Legend, 1992.

Lost Boys. New York, HarperCollins, 1992.

The Call of Earth (Homecoming). New York, Tor, and London, Legend, 1993.

The Ships of Earth (Homecoming). New York, Tor, and London, Legend, 1994.

Homecoming: Harmony (includes *The Memory of Earth, The Call of Earth,* and *The Ships of Earth*). New York, Guild America, 1994.

Lovelock (Mayflower), with Kathryn H. Kidd. New York, Tor, 1994.
Earthfall (Homecoming). New York, Tor, 1995.
Earthborn (Homecoming). New York, Tor, 1995.
Homecoming: Earth (includes *Earthfall* and *Earthborn*). New York, Guild America, 1995.
Alvin Journeyman (Maker). New York, Tor, 1995.
Children of the Mind. New York, Tor, 1996.

Short Stories

Capitol: The Worthing Chronicle. New York, Ace, 1979.
Unaccompanied Sonata and Other Stories. New York, Dial Press, 1980.
The Folk of the Fringe. West Bloomfield, Michigan, Phantasia Press, 1989; London, Legend, 1990.
Eye for Eye, bound with *The Tunesmith*, by Lloyde Biggle Jr. New York Tor, 1990.
Maps in a Mirror: The Short Fiction of Orson Scott Card. New York, Tor, 1990; London, Legend, 1991; as *The Changed Man, Flux: Tales of Human Futures, Monkey Sonatas*, and *Cruel Miracles*, New York, Tor, 4 vols., 1992-93.
Unaccompanied Sonata. Eugene, Oregon, Pulphouse, 1992.
Turning Hearts: Short Stories on Family Life, with David Dollaite. Salt Lake City, Utah, Bookcraft, 1994.

Plays

The Apostate (produced Provo, Utah, 1970).
In Flight (produced Provo, Utah, 1970).
Across Five Summers (produced Provo, Utah, 1971).
Of Gideon (produced Provo, Utah, 1971).
Stone Tables (produced Provo, Utah, 1973).
A Christmas Carol, adaptation of the story by Dickens (also director; produced Provo, Utah, 1974).
Father, Mother, Mother, and Mom (produced Provo, Utah, 1974). Published in Sunstone, 1978.
Liberty Jail (produced Provo, Utah, 1975).
Rag Mission (as Brian Green), in *Ensign* (Salt Lake City), July 1977.
Fresh Courage Take (also director; produced 1978).
Elders and Sisters (produced 1979).
Wings (produced 1982).

Other

Listen, Mom and Dad. Salt Lake City, Bookcraft, 1978.
Saintspeak. Berkeley, California, Signature, 1981.
Ainge. Midvale, Utah, Signature, 1982.
Compute's Guide to IBM PCjr Sound and Graphics. Greensboro, North Carolina, Compute, 1984.
Cardography. Eugene, Oregon, Hypatia Press, 1987.
Characters and Viewpoint. Cincinnati, Ohio, Writer's Digest, 1988; London, Robinson, 1990.
How To Write Science Fiction and Fantasy. Cincinnati, Ohio, Writer's Digest, 1990.
A Storyteller in Zion: Essays and Speeches. Salt Lake City, Utah, Bookcraft, 1994.

Editor, *Dragons of Darkness*. New York, Ace, 1981.
Editor, *Dragons of Light*. New York, Ace, 1980.
Editor, *Future on Fire*. New York, Tor, 1991.

Manuscript Collection: Brigham Young University, Provo, Utah.

Critical Study: *In the Image of God: Theme, Characterization, and Landscape in the Fiction of Orson Scott Card* by Michael Collings, New York, Greenwood Press, 1990.

* * *

Award-winning author Orson Scott Card has written over a dozen science-fiction and fantasy novels, establishing himself as one of the preeminent authors of these genres. His novels *Ender's Game* (1985) and *Speaker for the Dead* (1986) each won both the Hugo and Nebula awards and are perhaps his best-known works of fiction. A devout Mormon, Card frequently weaves religious and moral concerns into his science fiction tales, distinguishing his novels from others in the genre.

While Card won the John W. Campbell award in 1978 for best new science fiction writer, many of his earliest works received mixed and often sharp criticism. His first book, *Capitol: The Worthing Chronicle* (1978), is a cycle of short stories dealing with the planet-city of Capitol, the center of an empire whose citizens desire immortality in the form of a drug. This premise continues in *Hot Sleep: The Worthing Chronicle* (1978), where the survivors of the empire must begin again on a distant planet. Both novels, along with the collection *Unaccompanied Sonata and Other Stories* (1981), were panned for their reliance on most standard science fiction devices, gratuitous violence, and preachy tone. Nevertheless, most critics agreed that Card showed promise and ambition.

Ender's Game fulfilled this promise and ambition when published as a novel. Developed from the short story of the same name, the novel deals with Andrew "Ender" Wiggin, a six-year-old who is trained to defend Earth from the threat of the "buggers," a largely unknown alien race which has almost successfully invaded Earth twice. Ender's maturation from a young boy into a military genius is manipulated by his superiors and is seen by many as a scathing attack on military systems and operations. However, the novel's popularity is clearly shown by the positive responses it garnered from members of the U.S. military, some of whom use the novel as part of their training courses on tactics and strategy. While the plot seems to be standard science fiction fare, Ender is a sympathetic character who is duped into believing his final annihilation of the buggers is still part of his training, and he reviles what he has done.

The cycle of knowledge, guilt, and atonement continues in *Speaker for the Dead*, where Ender travels the galaxy in search of a new homeworld for the one remaining bugger. He must thwart the extermination of another alien species that poses a viral threat to humanity. The novel sustains the focus on evil and empathy found in *Ender's Game*, yet offers a more complex story with its multiple viewpoints, refined writing devoid of much of Card's earlier violent scenes, and focus on Ender's attempts to redeem himself. In *Xenocide* (1991), the third Ender novel, Ender works with his adopted family to neutralize a virus. While some critics suggested that the action of Card's earlier novels is replaced by philosophical passages, *Xenocide* remains a story of profound moral and intellectual issues.

Following the success of his Ender novels, Card explored several other settings and ideas, not all science fiction. "The Tales of Alvin Maker" series, including *Seventh Son* (1987) and *Red Prophet* (1988), is grounded in Card's use of symbol and allegory, envisioning a pioneer America where the British Restoration never occurred and folk magic is a reality. Card's "Homecoming" series promises the same blend of morality, technology, and action found in his earlier science fiction tales. *The Memory of Earth* (1992), the first "Homecoming" novel, opens on the planet Harmony, where humans have been governed by the global computer Oversoul for forty million years in order to prevent their own self-extermination. *A Woman of Destiny* (1983), later published as *Saints* (1988), is a historical novel centered around Dinah Kirkham, Card's ancestor and an English woman who eventually became the polygamous wife of Mormon founder Joseph Smith.

Card's strengths as a writer lie in the spiritual concerns found in his novels rather than in his attempts to write hard-core science fiction. His best asset as a writer may be his ability to create engaging stories that reach readers at all levels. As critic Michael R. Collings stated in *Fantasy Review*, "*Ender's Game* and *Speaker for the Dead* succeed equally as straightforward SF adventure and as allegorical, analogical disquisitions on humanity, morality, salvation, and redemption." Despite the criticism of his earlier works as conventional and didactic, Card entered the height of his powers with his more recent works and promises to remain among the best writers of 1990s science fiction.

—Christopher Swann

CARR, Philippa. *See* **HOLT, Victoria.**

CARTER, Nick. *See* **SMITH, Martin Cruz.**

CARTLAND, Barbara (Hamilton)

Nationality: English. **Born:** 9 July 1901. **Education:** Attended Malvern Girls' College and Abbey House, Netley Abbey, Hampshire, England. **Military Service:** Chief Lady Welfare Officer for Bedfordshire, 1941-45; Gazetted Honorary Junior Commander, A.T.S. **Family:** Married 1) Alexander George McCorquodale, 1927 (marriage dissolved, 1933); 2) Hugh McCorquodale, 28 December 1936 (died 29 December 1963); children: (first marriage) Raine (Countess Spencer); (second marriage) Ian, Glen. **Career:** Writer, lecturer, historian, political speaker for the Conservatives, newspaper columnist, and television personality. County councillor for Hertfordshire, nine years; chairman of the St. John Council and deputy president of St. John Ambulance Brigade, Hertfordshire, and president of Hertfordshire branch of Royal College of Midwives. **Awards:** Dame of Grace, St. John of Jerusalem, Certificate of Merit, Eastern Command, 1946; National Home Furnishings Association Woman of the Year award, 1981; Bishop Wright Air Industry award for contribution to developing aviation, 1984; Gold Medal of the City of Paris for Achievement, 1988, for selling twenty-five million books in France; Dame of the Order of the British Empire, 1991. **Member:** Oxfam (vice-president), National Association of Health (founder and president, 1965). **Agent:** Rupert Crew Ltd., King's Mews, Gray's Inn Rd., London WC1N 2JA, England. **Address:** Camfield Pl., Hatfield, Hertfordshire, England.

Publications

Novels

Jigsaw. Duckworth, 1925.
Sawdust. Duckworth, 1926.
If the Tree Is Saved. Duckworth, 1929.
For What? Hutchinson, 1930.
Sweet Punishment. Hutchinson, 1931.
A Virgin in Mayfair. Hutchinson, 1932; as *An Innocent in Mayfair,* Pyramid Publications, 1976.
Just off Piccadilly. Hutchinson, 1933; as *Dance on My Heart,* Pyramid Publications, 1977.
Not Love Alone. Hutchinson, 1933.
A Beggar Wished. Hutchinson, 1934; as *Rainbow to Heaven.* Pyramid Publications, 1976.
Passionate Attainment. Hutchinson, 1935.
First Class, Lady? Hutchinson, 1935; as *Love and Linda,* Pyramid Publications, 1976.
Dangerous Experiment. Hutchinson, 1936; as *Search for Love,* Greenberg, 1937.
Desperate Defiance. Hutchinson, 1936.
The Forgotten City. Hutchinson, 1936.
Saga at Forty. Hutchinson, 1937; as *Love at Forty,* Pyramid Publications, 1977.
But Never Free. Hutchinson, 1937; as *The Adventurer,* Pyramid Publications, 1977.
Broken Barriers. Hutchinson, 1938.
Bitter Winds. Hutchinson, 1938; as *The Bitter Winds of Love,* Jove, 1978.
The Gods Forget. Hutchinson, 1939; as *Love in Pity,* Pyramid Publications, 1976.
The Black Panther. Rich & Cowan, 1939; as *Lost Love,* Pyramid Publications, 1970.
Stolen Halo. Rich & Cowan, 1940; as *The Audacious Adventuress,* Pyramid Publications, 1972.
Now Rough, Now Smooth. Hutchinson, 1941.
Open Wings. Hutchinson, 1942.
The Leaping Flame. R. Hale, 1942.
Sleeping Swords. R. Hale, 1942.
The Dark Stream. Hutchinson, 1944; as *This Time It's Love,* Pyramid Publications, 1977.
After the Night. Hutchinson, 1944; as *Towards the Stars,* Pyramid Publications, 1975.
Yet She Follows. R. Hale, 1945; as *A Heart Is Broken,* Pyramid Publications, 1974.
Escape from Passion. R. Hale, 1945.
Armour against Love. Hutchinson, 1945.
Out of Reach. Hutchinson, 1945.
The Hidden Heart. Hutchinson, 1946.
Against the Stream. Hutchinson, 1946.

The Dream Within. Hutchinson, 1947.
If We Will. Hutchinson, 1947; as *Where Is Love?,* Jove, 1978.
Again This Rapture. Hutchinson, 1947.
No Heart Is Free. Rich & Cowan, 1948.
A Hazard of Hearts. Rich & Cowan, 1949.
The Enchanted Moment. Rich & Cowan, 1949.
A Duel of Hearts. Rich & Cowan, 1949.
The Knave of Hearts. Rich & Cowan, 1950.
The Little Pretender. Rich & Cowan, 1950.
Love Is an Eagle. Rich & Cowan, 1951.
A Ghost in Monte Carlo. Rich & Cowan, 1951.
Love Is Mine. Rich & Cowan, 1952.
Love Is the Enemy. Rich & Cowan, 1952.
Cupid Rides Pillion. Hutchinson, 1952; as *The Secret Heart,* Pyramid Publications, 1970.
The Passionate Pilgrim, Rich & Cowan, 1952.
Blue Heather. Rich & Cowan, 1953.
Elizabethan Lover. Hutchinson, 1953.
Love Me for Ever. Hutchinson, 1954.
Desire of the Heart. Hutchinson, 1954.
Wings on My Heart. Rich & Cowan, 1954.
The Enchanted Waltz. Hutchinson, 1955.
The Kiss of the Devil. Hutchinson, 1955.
The Captive Heart. Hutchinson, 1956; as *The Royal Pledge,* 1970.
The Coin of Love. Hutchinson, 1956.
The Kiss of Paris. Rich & Cowan, 1956.
Love Forbidden. Rich & Cowan, 1957.
Sweet Adventure. Hutchinson, 1957.
Stars in My Heart. Hutchinson, 1957.
The Thief of Love. Jenkins, 1957.
The Golden Gondola. Hutchinson, 1958.
Lights of Love. Jenkins, 1958.
The Sweet Enchantress. Jenkins, 1958.
A Kiss of Silk. Jenkins, 1959.
Love in Hiding. Hutchinson, 1959.
The Smuggled Heart. Hutchinson, 1959; as *Debt of Honor,* Pyramid Publications, 1970.
Love under Fire. Hutchinson, 1960.
The Price Is Love. Jenkins, 1960.
Messenger of Love. Hutchinson, 1961.
The Run-Away Heart. Jenkins, 1961.
A Light to the Heart. Ward, Lock, 1962.
The Wings of Love. Hutchinson, 1962.
The Hidden Evil. Hutchinson, 1963.
Love Is Dangerous. Ward, Lock, 1963.
Danger by the Nile. Ward, Lock, 1964.
The Fire of Love. Hutchinson, 1964.
The Unpredictable Bride. Hutchinson, 1964.
Love Holds the Cards. Hutchinson, 1965.
Love on the Run. Ward, Lock, 1965.
Theft of a Heart. Ward, Lock, 1966, Pyramid Publications, 1977.
A Virgin in Paris. Hutchinson, 1966; as *An Innocent in Paris,* 1975.
Love to the Rescue. Hutchinson, 1967.
Love Is Contraband. Hutchinson, 1968.
The Enchanting Evil. Hutchinson, 1968.
The Unknown Heart. Hutchinson, 1969.
The Innocent Heiress. Pyramid Publications, 1970.
The Reluctant Bride. Hutchinson, 1970.
The Secret Fear. Hutchinson, 1970.
The Pretty Horse-Breakers. Hutchinson, 1971.
The Queen's Messenger. Pyramid Publications, 1971.
Stars in Her Eyes. Pyramid Publications, 1971.
Lost Enchantment. Hutchinson, 1972.
A Halo for the Devil. Hutchinson, 1972.
The Irresistible Buck. Hutchinson, 1972.
The Complacent Wife. Hutchinson, 1972.
The Daring Deception. Bantam, 1973.
The Little Adventure. Hutchinson, 1973.
The Wicked Marquis. Hutchinson, 1973.
The Odious Duke. Hutchinson, 1973.
Journey to Paradise. Bantam, 1974.
No Darkness for Love. Bantam, 1974.
The Bored Bridegroom. Bantam, 1974.
The Castle of Fear. Bantam, 1974.
The Cruel Count. Pan Books, 1974.
The Dangerous Dandy. Bantam, 1974.
Lessons in Love. Bantam, 1974.
The Penniless Peer. Bantam, 1974.
The Ruthless Rake. Bantam, 1974.
The Glittering Lights. Bantam, 1974.
A Sword to the Heart. Bantam, 1974.
Fire on the Snow. Hutchinson, 1975.
Bewitched. Bantam, 1975.
The Call of the Heart. Bantam, 1975.
The Devil in Love. Bantam, 1975.
The Flame Is Love. Bantam, 1975.
The Frightened Bride. Bantam, 1975.
The Impetuous Duchess. Bantam, 1975.
The Karma of Love. Bantam, 1975.
Love Is Innocent. Bantam, 1975.
The Magnificent Marriage. Bantam, 1975.
The Mask of Love. Bantam, 1975.
Shadow of Sin. Bantam, 1975.
The Tears of Love. Bantam, 1975.
A Very Naughty Angel. Bantam, 1975.
As Eagles Fly. Bantam, 1975.
Say Yes, Samantha. Bantam, 1975.
The Elusive Earl. Bantam, 1976.
An Angel in Hell. Bantam, 1976.
An Arrow of Love. Bantam, 1976.
The Blue-eyed Witch. Bantam, 1976.
A Dream from the Night. Bantam, 1976.
The Fragrant Flower. Bantam, 1976.
A Frame of Dreams. Bantam, 1976.
A Gamble with Hearts. Bantam, 1976.
The Golden Illusion. Bantam, 1976.
The Heart Triumphant. Bantam, 1976.
Hungry for Love. Bantam, 1976.
The Husband Hunters. Bantam, 1976.
The Incredible Honeymoon. Bantam, 1976.
A Kiss for the King. Bantam, 1976.
Moon over Eden. Bantam, 1976.
Never Laugh at Love. Bantam, 1976.
No Time for Love. Bantam, 1976.
Passions in the Sand. Bantam, 1976.
The Proud Princess. Bantam, 1976.
The Secret of the Glen. Bantam, 1976.
The Slaves of Love. Bantam, 1976.
The Wild Cry of Love. Bantam, 1976.
Conquered by Love. Bantam, 1976.
Love Locked In. Dutton, 1977.
The Mysterious Maid-servant. Bantam, 1977.

The Wild Unwilling Wife. Dutton, 1977.
The Castle Made for Love. Duron Books, 1977.
The Curse of the Clan. Duron Books, 1977.
The Dragon and the Pearl. Duron Books, 1977.
The Hell-cat and the King. Duron Books, 1977.
Look, Listen and Love. Duron Books, 1977.
Love and the Loathsome Leopard. Duron Books, 1977.
The Love Pirate. Duron Books, 1977.
The Marquis Who Hated Women. Duron Books, 1977.
The Naked Battle. Duron Books, 1977.
No Escape from Love. Duron Books, 1977.
The Outrageous Lady. Duron Books, 1977.
Punishment of a Vixen. Duron Books, 1977.
The Saint and the Sinner. Duron Books, 1977.
The Sign of Love. Duron Books, 1977.
The Temptation of Torilla. Duron Books, 1977.
A Touch of Love. Duron Books, 1977.
The Dream and the Glory. Bantam, 1977.
A Duel with Destiny. Bantam, 1977.
Kiss the Moonlight. Pan Books, 1977.
The Magic of Love. Bantam, 1977.
A Rhapsody of Love. Pan Books, 1977.
The Taming of Lady Lorinda. Bantam, 1977.
Vote for Love. Bantam, 1977.
The Disgraceful Duke. Bantam, 1977.
Love at the Helm. Weidenfeld & Nicolson, 1977.
The Chieftain without a Heart. Dutton, 1978.
A Fugitive from Love. Duron Books, 1978.
The Ghost Who Fell in Love. Dutton, 1978.
Love Leaves at Midnight. Duron Books, 1978.
Love, Lords, and Lady-Birds. Dutton, 1978.
The Passion and the Flower. Dutton, 1978.
The Twists and Turns of Love. Duron Books, 1978.
The Irresistible Force. Duron Books, 1978.
The Judgment of Love. Duron Books, 1978.
Lord Ravenscar's Revenge. Duron Books, 1978.
Lovers in Paradise. Duron Books, 1978.
A Princess in Distress. Duron Books, 1978.
The Race for Love. Duron Books, 1978.
A Runaway Star. Duron Books, 1978.
Magic or Mirage? Duron Books, 1978.
Alone in Paris. Hutchinson, 1978.
Flowers for the God of Love. Pan Books, 1978.
The Problems of Love. Duron Books, 1978.
The Drums of Love. Duron Books, 1979.
The Duke and the Preacher's Daughter. Duron Books, 1979.
Imperial Splendor. Dutton, 1979.
Light of the Moon. Duron Books, 1979.
Love in the Clouds. Dutton, 1979.
Love in the Dark. Duron Books, 1979.
The Prince and the Pekingese. Duron Books, 1979.
Love Climbs In. Duron Books, 1979.
The Prisoner of Love. Duron Books, 1979.
A Serpent of Satan. Duron Books, 1979.
The Treasure Is Love. Duron Books, 1979.
The Duchess Disappeared. Duron Books, 1979.
A Nightingale Sang. Duron Books, 1979.
The Dawn of Love. Corgi, 1979.
A Gentleman in Love. Pan Books, 1979.
Only Love. Hutchinson, 1979.
Bride to the King. Corgi, 1979.
Women Have Hearts. Pan Books, 1979.
Terror in the Sun. Bantam, 1979.
Who Can Deny Love? Bantam, 1979.
Love Has His Way. Bantam, 1979.
The Explosion of Love. Bantam, 1979.
A Song of Love. Jove, 1980.
Love for Sale. Dutton, 1980.
Lost Laughter. Dutton, 1980.
Free from Fear. Bantam, 1980.
The Goddess and the Gaiety Girl. Bantam, 1980.
Little White Doves of Love. Bantam, 1980.
Ola and the Sea Wolf. Bantam, 1980.
The Perfection of Love. Bantam, 1980.
The Prude and the Prodigal. Bantam, 1980.
Punished with Love. Bantam, 1980.
Heart Is Stolen. Corgi, 1980.
The Power and the Prince. Bantam, 1980.
Lucifer and the Angel. Bantam, 1980.
Signpost to Love. Bantam, 1980.
From Hell to Heaven. Bantam, 1981.
Pride and the Poor Princess. Bantam, 1981.
Count the Stars. Jove, 1981.
Dollars for the Duke. Bantam, 1981.
Dreams Do Come True. Bantam, 1981.
The Heart of the Clan. Jove, 1981.
In the Arms of Love. Jove, 1981.
Touch a Star. Jove, 1981.
The Kiss of Life. Bantam, 1981.
The Lioness and the Lily. Bantam, 1981.
Love in the Moon. Bantam, 1981.
A Night of Gaiety. Bantam, 1981.
The Waltz of Hearts. Bantam, 1981.
The Wings of Ecstasy. Jove, 1981.
For All Eternity. Jove, 1981.
Afraid. Bantam, 1981.
Enchanted. Bantam, 1981.
Winged Magic. Bantam, 1981.
A Portrait of Love. Bantam, 1981.
The River of Love. Bantam, 1981.
Gift of the Gods. Bantam, 1981.
An Innocent in Russia. Bantam, 1981.
A Shaft of Sunlight. Bantam, 1981.
Pure and Untouched. Bantam, 1981.
Love Wins. Bantam, 1982.
Secret Harbor. Bantam, 1982.
Looking for Love. Bantam, 1982.
The Vibrations of Love. Bantam, 1982.
Lies for Love. Bantam, 1982.
Love Rules. Bantam, 1982.
The Call of the Highlands. Hutchinson, 1982.
Caught by Love. Arrow, 1982.
A King in Love. Everest House, 1982.
Kneel for Mercy. New English Library, 1982.
Love and the Marquis. Pan Books, 1982.
Lucky in Love. Jove, 1982.
Moments of Love. Pan Books, 1982.
The Poor Governess. Jove, 1982.
Riding to the Moon. Everest House, 1982.
Winged Victory. Jove, 1982.
Diona and a Dalmation. Hutchinson, 1983.
A Duke in Danger. Pan Books, 1983.

Fire in the Blood. Pan Books, 1983.
From Hate to Love. New English Library, 1983.
Gypsy Magic. Pan Books, 1983.
Lights, Laughter, and a Lady. New English Library, 1983.
Love and Lucia. Pan Books, 1983.
Love on the Wind. Pan Books, 1983.
A Marriage Made in Heaven. Corgi, 1983.
A Miracle in Music. Corgi, 1983.
Mission to Monte Carlo. Corgi, 1983.
Secrets. Corgi, 1983.
Tempted to Love. Pan Books, 1983.
Wish for Love. Corgi, 1983.
Bride to a Brigand, New English Library, 1984.
Help from the Heart. Arrow, 1984.
The Island of Love. Pan Books, 1984.
Journey to a Star. Corgi, 1984.
Light of the Gods. Corgi, 1984.
Love Comes West. Pan Books, 1984.
Miracle for a Madonna. Hutchinson, 1984.
Moonlight on the Sphinx. Hutchinson, 1984.
The Peril and the Prince. New English Library, 1984.
Revenge of the Heart. Pan Books, 1984.
Royal Punishment. Severn House, 1984.
The Scots Never Forget. Corgi, 1984.
Theresa and a Tiger. New English Library, 1984.
The Unbreakable Spell. Corgi, 1984.
The Unwanted Wedding. Corgi, 1984.
A Very Unusual Wife. Pan Books, 1984.
White Lilac. Pan Books, 1984.
Alone and Afraid. Pan Books, 1985.
The Devilish Deception. Jove, 1985.
Look with Love. Pan Books, 1985.
Paradise Found. Jove, 1985.
Never Forget Love. New English Library, 1985.
A Rebel Princess. Corgi, 1985.
Love Is a Gamble. Pan Books, 1985.
Love Is Heaven. Pan Books, 1985.
Temptation for a Teacher. Pan Books, 1985.
A Witch's Spell. Corgi, 1985.
Safe at Last. Jove, 1986.
Escape. Jove, 1986.
Crowned with Love. Jove, 1986.
The Devil Defeated. Jove, 1986.
A Dream in Spain. Jove, 1986.
The Golden Cage. Jove, 1986.
Haunted. Jove, 1986.
Helga in Hiding. Jove, 1986.
Listen to Love. Jove, 1986.
Love Casts Out Fear. Severn House, 1986.
Love Joins the Clans. Pan Books, 1986.
The Love Trap. Jove, 1986.
Secret of the Mosque. Pan Books, 1986.
Bewildered in Berlin. Jove, 1987.
Dancing on a Rainbow. Jove, 1987.
An Angel Runs Away. Jove, 1987.
The Earl Escapes. Jove, 1987.
Love and Kisses. Jove, 1987.
The Love Puzzle. Jove, 1987.
Forced to Marry. Jove, 1987.
Starlight over Tunis. Jove, 1987.
Wanted—A Wedding Ring. Jove, 1987.
A World of Love. Jove, 1987.
Sapphires in Siam. Jove, 1988.
A Nightingale Sang. Jove, 1988.
Little Tongues of Fire. Jove, 1988.
Saved by Love. Jove, 1988.
Riding to the Sky. Jove, 1988.
Only a Dream. Jove, 1988.
Love Is Invincible. Jove, 1988.
The Herb of Happiness. Jove, 1988.
An Adventure of Love. Jove, 1988.
Lovers in Lisbon. Jove, 1988.
The Goddess of Love. Jove, 1988.
The Bargain Bride. Jove, 1989.
A Circus of Love. Jove, 1989.
Lady and the Highwayman. Pan Books, 1989.
The Perfect Pearl. Jove, 1989.
Solita and the Spies. Jove, 1989.
The Temple of Love. Jove, 1989.
A Knight in Paris. Jove, 1989.
The Perfume of the Gods. Jove, 1989.
A Lovely Liar. Jove, 1989.
Revenge Is Sweet. Jove, 1989.
The Passionate Princess. Jove, 1989.
Love Is a Maze. Jove, 1989.
A Chieftain Finds Love. Jove, 1989.
Paradise in Penang. Pan Books, 1989.
A Game of Love. Severn House, 1989.
The Earl Rings a Belle. Jove, 1990.
The Haunted Heart. Jove, 1990.
Necklace of Love. Jove, 1990.
Kiss from a Stranger. Jove, 1990.
Love at First Sight. Jove, 1990.
Real Love or Fake. Jove, 1990.
A Very Special Love. Jove, 1990.
A Revolution of Love. Jove, 1990.
The Taming of the Tigress. Jove, 1990.
Love Is the Key. Jove, 1990.
The Marquis Wins. Jove, 1990.
Beauty or Brains. Jove, 1991.
Hiding. Jove, 1991.
Just Fate. Jove, 1991
Love Lifts the Curse. Jove, 1991.
A Miracle in Mexico. Jove, 1991.
No Disguise for Love. Jove, 1991.
The Queen Saves the King. Jove, 1991.
A Tangled Web. Jove, 1991.
Too Precious to Lose. Jove, 1991.
Drena and the Duke. Jove, 1992.
The Angel and the Rake. Jove, 1993.
The Dangerous Marriage. Jove, 1993.
Love at the Ritz. Jove, 1993.
Luck Logan Finds Love. Jove, 1993.
Peaks of Ecstasy. Jove, 1993.
The Queen of Hearts. Jove, 1993.
Terror from the Throne. Jove, 1993.
Walking to Wonderland. Jove, 1993.
The Wicked Widow. Jove, 1993.
The Dare-Devil Duke. Jove, 1994.
The Duke Finds Love. Jove, 1994.
Look with the Heart. Jove, 1994.
Never Lose Love. Jove, 1994.

A Royal Rebuke. Jove, 1994.
Running Away to Love. Jove, 1994.
Safe in Paradise. Jove, 1994.
Saved by a Saint. Jove, 1994.
The Spirit of Love. Jove, 1994.
This Is Love. Jove, 1994.
The Wild Cry of Love. Jove, 1994.
The Wonderful Dream. Jove, 1994.
Beyond the Stars. Jove, 1995.
The Eyes of Love. Jove, 1995.
An Icicle in India. Jove, 1995.
The Incomparable. Jove, 1995.
The Innocent Imposter. Jove, 1995.
Love in the Ruins. Jove, 1995.
The Loveless Marriage. Jove, 1995.
A Magical Moment. Jove, 1995.
Passage to Love. Jove, 1995.
The Patient Bridegroom. Jove, 1995.
The Protection of Love. Jove, 1995.
Running from Russia. Jove, 1995.
Someone to Love. Jove, 1995.
Fascination in France. Jove, 1996.
Three Days to Love. Jove, 1996.

Nonfiction

Touch the Stars: A Clue to Happiness. Rider & Co., 1935.
Ronald Cartland (biography of author's brother), with preface by Winston Churchill, Collins, 1942; reprinted with introduction by Arthur Bryant, S.P.C.K., 1980.
The Isthmus Years: Reminiscences of the Years 1919-1939. Hutchinson, 1943.
You—In the Home. Standard Art Book Co., 1946.
The Years of Opportunity: 1939-1945. Hutchinson, 1948.
The Fascinating Forties: A Book for the Over-Forties. Jenkins, 1954; revised edition, Corgi, 1973.
Bewitching Women. Muller, 1955.
Marriage for Moderns. Jenkins, 1955.
Be Vivid, Be Vital. Jenkins, 1956.
Polly: The Story of My Wonderful Mother. Jenkins, 1956.
The Outrageous Queen: A Biography of Christina of Sweden. Muller, 1956.
Love, Life and Sex. Jenkins, 1957; revised edition, Corgi, 1973.
The Scandalous Life of King Carol. Muller, 1957.
Look Lovely, Be Lovely. Jenkins, 1958.
The Private Life of Charles II: The Women He Loved. Muller, 1958.
The Private Life of Elizabeth, Empress of Austria. Muller, 1959.
Vitamins for Vitality. W. & G. Foyle, 1959.
Husbands and Wives. Arthur Barker, 1961; as *Love and Marriage,* Thorson's, 1971.
Josephine, Empress of France. Hutchinson, 1961.
Diane de Poitiers. Hutchinson, 1962.
Etiquette Handbook. Paul Hamlyn, 1962; revised edition published as *Barbara Cartland's Book of Etiquette,* Hutchinson, 1972.
The Many Facets of Love. W. H. Allen, 1963.
Metternich: The Passionate Diplomat. Hutchinson, 1964.
Sex and the Teenager. Muller, 1964.
Living Together. Muller, 1965.
The Pan Book of Charm. Pan Books, 1965.
Woman, the Enigma. Frewin, 1965.
I Search for Rainbows: 1946-1966. Hutchinson, 1967.
The Youth Secret. Corgi, 1968.
The Magic of Honey. Corgi, 1970; revised edition, Corgi, 1977.
We Danced All Night: 1919-1929. Hutchinson, 1970.
Barbara Cartland's Health Food Cookery Book. Hodder & Stoughton, 1972; as *Barbara Cartland's Health Food Cookery,* Pyramid Publications, 1975.
Barbara Cartland's Book of Beauty and Health. Hodder & Stoughton, 1972.
Men Are Wonderful. Corgi, 1973.
Food for Love. Corgi, 1975.
The Magic of Honey Cookbook. Corgi, 1976.
Recipes for Lovers, with Nigel Gordon. Corgi, 1977.
Barbara Cartland's Book of Love and Lovers, Ballantine, 1978.
I Seek the Miraculous. Dutton, 1978.
Barbara Cartland's Scrapbook. Royal Photographic Society, 1981.
Romantic Royal Marriages. Beaufort Book Co., 1981.
Barbara Cartland's Etiquette for Love and Romance. Pocket Books, 1984.
Getting Older, Growing Younger. Dodd, 1984.
The Romance of Food. Doubleday, 1984.
Barbara Cartland's Book of Health. Javelin, 1985.
A Year of Royal Days. Lennard, 1988.
I Reach for the Stars: An Autobiography. Parkwest, 1995.

Fiction for Children

Barbara Cartland's Princess to the Rescue, illustrated by Jane Longmore. F. Watts, 1984.

Editor, *Barbara Cartland's Book of Useless Information,* foreword by Earl Mountbatten. Bantam, 1977.
Editor, *The Light of Love: A Thought for Every Day.* Sheldon Press, 1979; as *The Light of Love: Lines to Live by Day by Day,* Elsevier/Nelson, 1980.

* * *

Barbara Cartland is the world's leading author of romantic fiction. She has sold over 390 million copies of over 300 books, making her the top-selling author in the *Guinness Book of (World) Records.* Cartland rose to her status as a prodigious writer of romance novels during the 1960s and has maintained her rampant writing pace since that time. Her romantic heroes and heroines belong to another era, but their popularity with modern readers shows that people enjoy an escape from impersonal social relationships. Cartland's books are unabashedly escapist. They have nothing to do with social issues; they do not promote feminism nor do they pretend to empathize with a broad range of social classes. Instead, they are about upper-class English men and women who live with manners and ideals in an aristocratic culture. And in that society the intimate male-female relationship is noble, pivotal, and allows the participants gain insight into themselves and the world.

Cartland's books evolved into a pat, though popular, recipe. Starting with her first novel, *Jig-Saw* (1925), Cartland's characters are people of depth with distinctive and engaging personalities. She often interjects her own commentary about life into the characters, so they experience complexity and conflict that result in personal growth. Her early novels master the art of storytelling. Unique characters and settings create an atmosphere that carries the reader effortlessly into action. However, Cartland's later works, such as *Love for Sale* (1980), *Dollars for the Duke* (1981), and *The Perfection of Love* (1980), begin to develop a pattern. The heroines still experience an awakening to life through their romances, but they lose some of their individuality. The stories seem to contain a certain predictability in the plots—even in the dialogue—which diminishes the impact of the story. The novels are still a wonderful escape for the soul, but may not leave the reader with any lasting philosophical considerations about the nature and purpose of life.

Cartland comes by her subject matter naturally, writing about the world she knows well. At age 18 she entered London society, and six years later, in 1925, she was presented at Court. It was during that year that her first novel was published. In fact, she had already started her writing career in 1923 as a gossip columnist for the *Daily Express* in London. In addition to her novels, she has written four autobiographies in which she describes her life and the intriguing people in it, and explores her battles against injustice and her interest in natural health.

One of her most interesting books is not an autobiography but a nonfiction account of personal experiences. It details incidents which she believes reveal evidence of life beyond death. In *I Seek the Miraculous* (1977), Cartland tells of times when she has been inspired, uplifted, or even disillusioned, and has experienced a feeling of intense spirituality more powerful and real than anything physical. She concludes, in the spirit of her earlier, philosophical works, with her own insight into the nature of truth. Truth is love, and those who "give out love become one with the whole living, breathing force of the universe and God."

—Carolyn Eckstein-Soule

CARVER, Raymond

Nationality: American. **Born:** 25 May 1938, in Clatskanie, Oregon. **Education:** Humboldt State College (now California State University, Humboldt), A.B., 1963; University of Iowa, M.F.A., 1966. **Family:** Married Maryann Burk in 1957 (divorced, 1983); married Tess Gallagher in 1988; children: Christine LaRae, Vance Lindsay. **Career:** Manual laborer, c. late 1950s-early 1960s; Science Research Associates, Inc., Palo Alto, California, editor, 1967-70; University of California, Santa Cruz, lecturer in creative writing, 1971-72; University of California, Berkeley, lecturer in fiction writing, 1972-73; Syracuse University, Syracuse, New York, professor of English, 1980-83; writer. Visiting professor of English, Writers Workshop, University of Iowa, 1973-74; member of faculty writing program, Goddard College, 1977-78; visiting distinguished writer, University of Texas at El Paso, 1978-79. **Awards:** National Endowment for the Arts Discovery award for poetry, 1970; Joseph Henry Jackson award for fiction, 1971; Wallace Stegner Creative Writing fellowship, Stanford University, 1972-73; Guggenheim fellowship, 1977-78; National Endowment for the Arts award in fiction, 1979; Carlos Fuentes Fiction award, for short story "The Bath"; Mildred and Harold Strauss Living award, American Academy and Institute of Arts and Letters, 1983; Levinson Prize for poetry, 1985; Los Angeles Times book prize, 1986, for *Where Water Comes Together with Other Water;* inducted into American Academy and Institute of Arts and Letters, 1988. **Died:** 2 August 1988, in Port Angeles, Washington, of lung cancer.

Publications

Poetry

Near Klamath. Sacramento State College, 1968.
Winter Insomnia. Kayak, 1970.
At Night the Salmon Move. Capra, 1976.
Two Poems. Scarab Press, 1982.
Where Water Comes Together with Other Water. Random House, 1985.
This Water. Ewert, 1985.
Ultramarine. Random House, 1986.
In a Marine Light: Selected Poems. Harvill, 1987.
A New Path to the Waterfall. Atlantic Monthly Press, 1989.

Short Stories

Put Yourself in My Shoes. Capra, 1974.
Will You Please Be Quiet, Please? McGraw, 1976.
Furious Seasons. Capra, 1977.
What We Talk about When We Talk about Love. Knopf, 1981.
The Pheasant. Metacom, 1982.
Cathedral. Knopf, 1984.
If It Please You. Lord John, 1984.
The Stories of Raymond Carver. Picador, 1985.
Elephant, and Other Stories. Harvill, 1988.
Where I'm Calling From: New and Selected Stories. Atlantic Monthly Press, 1988.
Short Cuts: Selected Stories. Vintage, 1993.

Plays

Carnations. Engdahl, 1992.

Screenplay: *Dostoevsky,* 1985.

Other

Fires: Essays, Poems, Stories, 1966-1982. Capra, 1983.
Saints. Random House, 1987.
No Heroics, Please: Uncollected Writings. Random House, 1992.

*

Film Adaptation: *Short Cuts,* 1994.

Critical Studies: *Conversations with Raymond Carver,* edited by Marshall B. Gentry and William L. Stull, University Press of Mississippi, 1990; *Raymond Carver: A Study of the Short Fiction* by Ewing Campbell, Macmillan, 1992; *Reading Raymond Carver* by Randolph P. Runyon, Syracuse University Press, 1992; *Remembering Ray: A Composite Biography,* edited by William L. Stull and Maureen P. Carroll, Capra, 1993; *Raymond Carver: An Oral Biography* by Sam Halpert, University of Iowa Press, 1995.

* * *

Raymond Carver climbed through the ropes of the American literary boxing ring with his first collection of short stories, *Will You Please Be Quiet, Please* (1976). By the time of his early death from lung cancer in 1988, he had quite a few knockouts under his belt.

Carver's father was a laborer and saw-sharpener, and his mother was a homemaker. His parents' names were already literary material: Clevie Raymond Carver and Ella Beatrice Casey. The author was born in the logging town of Clatskanie, Oregon, so the mythical material for a working-class writer was already there for the taking.

At heart, Ray Carver was a poet. His first two books were collections of poetry: *Near Klamath* (1968) and *Winter Insomnia* (1970). The American literary marketplace, however, is not kind to poets, and if Carver had gone on writing only poetry he would not have achieved any measurable status. But anyone who has looked closely at the author's career knows that he first learned the writing trade at the feet of two great poets, Ezra Pound and William Carlos Williams.

Pound emphasized going after the *luminous detail;* Williams practiced a doctrine he encapsulated as *write poetry like we talk* (in other words, write plain, American speech and find the significant, telling detail in normal, everyday life). The late novelist John Gardener, one of Carver's first college teachers, emphasized *honesty of sentiment* in writing. Mix in Carver's favorite writer, Anton Chekov; Ernest Hemingway for prose style; and Sherwood Anderson for tone, and you have the writing recipe that Ray Carver used the during the remainder of his life.

As a short-story writer, Carver is very much akin to Sherwood Anderson. Like his Anderson, Carver's characters are lower-middle class or lower class people who are marginal or isolated from the community. And the affect of a Carver story, just as with an Anderson tale, can be strange and unsettling.

In "Jerry and Molly and Sam," from his first collection and also reprinted in *Shortcuts: Selected Stories by Raymond Carver* (1993), Al, a family man and the father of two children, feels that his life is falling apart. He decides that one thing he can do to reestablish some order is to take the bothersome mutt, Suzy, somewhere and drop her off. This action has the opposite result, because his wife and the two children get extremely upset when they find their dog is lost.

Typical of Carver's work is this quote from Al's inner reverie: "Now he was having an *affair,* for Christ's sake, and he didn't know what to do about it. He did not want it to go on, and he did not want to break it off: you don't throw everything overboard in a storm."

A Ray Carver character is usually working out repressed material. Whichever conflict triggers the action, by the end of the story that person's life is altered in some way. Filmmaker Robert Altman, who based his film *Short Cuts* on a selection from Carver's four short-story collections, said in his introduction to *Short Cuts: Selected Stories by Raymond Carver:* "Raymond Carver made poetry out of the prosaic . . . what he really did was capture the wonderful idiosyncrasies of human behavior, the idiosyncracies that exist amid the randomness of life's experiences."

By the time Carver's second collection of stories, *What We Talk about When We Talk about Love* (1981), was published, he had already achieved literary fame and had begun to reap prizes and awards. The last 15 years of his life were financially bountiful. However, anyone who paid close attention to the content of his stories, much of which was taken from the author's life, could not fail to note that cigarettes and booze were standard props in a Carver story or poem.

Carver managed to kick the booze habit—a seemingly common affliction of American authors—through alcohol treatment programs. The title story of *Where I'm Calling From: New and Selected Stories* (1988) is a wonderful tale of what it's like being in one of those programs. Unfortunately, however, he didn't give up the smokes, and cigarettes killed him early. In "My Death" (from the collection *Where Water Comes Together With Other Water* [1985]), a poem he penned before he discovered he had lung cancer, Carver wrote: ". . . I want you to know/ I was happy when I was here./ And remember I told you this a while ago—April 1984./ But be glad for me if I can die in presence/ of friends and family. If this happens, believe me,/ I came out ahead. I didn't lose this one."

—Bill Witherup

CHAPMAN, Lee. *See* **BRADLEY, Marion Zimmer.**

CHAPMAN, Walker. *See* **SILVERBERG, Robert.**

CHATWIN, (Charles) Bruce

Nationality: English. **Born:** 13 May 1940, in Sheffield, Yorkshire. **Education:** Attended private secondary school in Marlborough, England; University of Edinburgh. **Family:** Married Elizabeth Chanler, 1965. **Career:** Sotheby & Co., Great Britain, picture expert, 1958-66, director, beginning 1965. Writer. **Awards:** Hawthornden prize, 1978, and E. M. Forster award, 1979, both for *In Patagonia;* Whitbread Book of the Year Award for First Novel, 1982, and James Tait Black Memorial Prize for Fiction, 1982, both for *On the Black Hill.* **Died:** 18 January 1989, of a rare disease of the bone marrow, in Nice, France.

PUBLICATIONS

Novels

The Viceroy of Ouida. Summit Books, 1980.
On the Black Hill. J. Cape, 1982.
Utz. Viking, 1989.

Other

In Patagonia (travel). J. Cape, 1977, Summit Books, 1978.
The Songlines. Viking, 1987.

What Am I Doing Here (short stories, profiles, essays, and travelogues). Viking, 1989.
Nowhere Is a Place: Travels in Patagonia, with Paul Theroux and Jeff Gnass. Sierra Club Books, 1992.
Far Journeys: Photographs & Notebooks, edited by David King and Francis Wyndham. Viking, 1993.

*

Media Adaptations: *Cobra Verde,* film adaptation of *The Viceroy of Ouiday,* 1987; *On the Black Hill,* stage adaptation by Charles Way, 1986, film adaption by Andrew Greve, 1986.

* * *

When Bruce Chatwin died in 1989, he was still in his 40s and very much a first-rate writer in his prime. Like Herman Melville, not all of his books were equally powerful, but also like Melville he was one of the most gifted writers of his time. Two or three of his books, like *In Patagonia* (1978) and *Songlines* (1987), are among the most remarkable pieces of writing in all of 20th-century literature.

His first book, *In Patagonia,* is about a strange, surreal area in southern Argentina about which many people, including Charles Darwin and even Chatwin's friend Paul Theroux, have written (though none better than Chatwin). Actually, he (with Theroux) wrote yet another book on Patagonia that was published by the Royal Geographical Society in London. Chatwin's last book was *Songlines,* a book about the aboriginal people of Australia that was so real that it is somewhat surprising to learn that he had invented most of what he wrote there. In between, he published several books including his strange and quite wonderful, yet disturbing, novel *On the Black Hill* (1980) about a small rural area of England. He also published *The Viceroy of Ouidah* (1982) about a reverse migration from Brazil to Africa, which some regard as unreadable and outlandish. Along the way, he published many shorter compositions in places like the British travel magazine *Granta.*

The striking thing about his first Patagonia book is how well-suited Chatwin's style is to that strange, forbidding landscape and how it permeates everything there including the odd, eccentric inhabitants. Perhaps the most surprising thing about the book is how, when he comes across a story about Butch Cassidy and the Sundance Kid, he pursues the tale all the way back to the western United States. Doing that might seem extraneous to the book, but it isn't. It is instead a piece of authentic (if weird) scholarship that contributes greatly to the book as a whole. In a curious way it is reminiscent of a story told by a Makedonian about the kind of folktale-telling pursued for centuries in villages in his native country. All the male elders of such a village would gather around and tell one another stories. On one occasion, one of these elders spoke about having lived in the United States for many years and having been in prison in Chicago with the notorious Al Capone. Seeing Capone in this remote context was mind-blowing.

Songlines is full of quotable passages, but none better illustrates his style and quality of perception than this reprise of a conversation he had with his friend Arkady about that country: "In theory, at least, the whole of Australia could be read as a musical score. There was hardly a rock or a creek in the country that could not or had not been sung. One should perhaps visualize the Songlines as a spaghetti of Iliads and Odysseys, writhing this way and that, in which every 'episode' was readable in terms of geology."

Arkady, a funny, bright, eccentric immigrant from Russia, is the real protagonist of *Songlines* (unless Chatwin himself occupies that position). Arkady is the catalyst who brings most of the other eccentrics—aborigines, mixed blood, Anglos, other Europeans—into the book, and his discussions with Chatwin illuminate the nature of the Songlines themselves. It is his second marriage to a blond woman named Marian, who is a major character threaded through this book, that provides the celebration and high spirits near the end. And it is Arkady, more than anyone else, who helps his aboriginal friends, like Titus and Limpy, keep the ancient Songlines alive in a vast region threatened by the encroachment of railroads, mining operations, and other instruments of Progress.

—C. W. Truesdale

CHEEVER, John

Nationality: American. **Born:** Quincy, Massachusetts, 27 May 1912. **Education:** Attended Thayer Academy. **Military Service:** U.S. Army Signal Corps, 1943-45; became sergeant. **Family:** Married Mary M. Winternitz, 22 March 1941; children: Susan, Benjamin Hale, Frederico. **Career:** Novelist and short story writer. Instructor, Barnard College, 1956-57, Ossining, New York, Correctional Facility, 1971-72, and University of Iowa Writers Workshop, 1973; visiting professor of creative writing, Boston University, 1974-75. Member of cultural exchange program to the U.S.S.R., 1964. **Awards:** Guggenheim fellowship, 1951; Benjamin Franklin award, 1955, for "The Five Forty-Eight"; American Academy of Arts and Letters award in literature, 1956; O. Henry award, 1956, for "The Country Husband," and 1964, for "The Embarkment for Cythera"; National Book award in fiction, 1958, for *The Wapshot Chronicle;* Howells Medal, American Academy of Arts and Letters, 1965, for *The Wapshot Scandal;* Editorial Award, *Playboy,* 1969, for "The Yellow Room"; Edward MacDowell medal, MacDowell Colony, 1979, for outstanding contributions to the arts; Pulitzer Prize in fiction, 1979, National Book Critics Circle award in fiction, 1979, and American Book award in fiction, 1981, all for *The Stories of John Cheever;* National Medal for Literature, 1982. Honorary doctorate, Harvard University, 1978. **Member:** National Institute of Arts and Letters. **Died:** 18 June 1982, of cancer.

Publications

Novels

The Wapshot Chronicle. Harper, 1957.
The Wapshot Scandal. Harper, 1964.
Bullet Park. Knopf, 1969.
Falconer. Knopf, 1977.
Oh, What a Paradise It Seems. Knopf, 1982.

Short Stories

The Way Some People Live: A Book of Stories. Random House, 1943.
The Enormous Radio and Other Stories. Funk, 1953.
The Housebreaker of Shady Hill and Other Stories. Harper, 1958.

Some People, Places and Things That Will Not Appear in My Next Novel. Harper, 1961.
The Brigadier and the Golf Widow. Harper, 1964.
Homage to Shakespeare. Country Squire Books, 1965.
The World of Apples. Knopf, 1973.
The Day the Pig Fell into the Well. Lord John Press, 1978.
The Stories of John Cheever. Knopf, 1978.
The Leaves, the Lion-Fish and the Bear. Sylvester and Orphanos, 1980.
Angel of the Bridge. Redpath Press, 1987.
Thirteen Uncollected Stories by John Cheever. Academy Chicago Publishers, 1994.

Other

The Letters of John Cheever, edited by Benjamin Cheever. Simon & Schuster, 1988.
The Journals of John Cheever. Knopf, 1991.
Glad Tidings: A Friendship in Letters, with John D. Weaver. HarperCollins, 1993.

*

Media Adaptations: *The Swimmer*, film adaptation of his short story of the same name, 1968; "The Sorrows of Gin," "The Five Forty-Eight," and "O Youth and Beauty!," teleplays based on short stories of the same names, all 1979.

Bibliography: *John Cheever: A Reference Guide* by Francis J. Bosha, G. K. Hall, 1981.

Critical Studies: *John Cheever* by Samuel Coale, Ungar, 1977; *John Cheever* by Lynne Waldeland, G. K. Hall, 1979; *Critical Essays on John Cheever*, edited by R.G. Collins, G.K. Hall, 1982; *John Cheever: The Hobgoblin Company of Love* by George W. Hunt, Eerdmans Publishing Company, 1983; *Home Before Dark* by Susan Cheever, Houghton Mifflin, 1984; *John Cheever: A Biography* by Scott Donaldson, Random House, 1988; *John Cheever: A Study of the Short Fiction* by James E. O'Hara, Twayne, 1989; *The Critical Response to John Cheever*, edited by Francis J. Bosha, Greenwood Press, 1993; *Dragons and Martinis: The Skewed Realism of John Cheever* by Michael D. Byrne, Borgo Press, 1993; *John Cheever Revisited* by Patrick Meanor, Macmillan, 1994.

* * *

After his death in 1982, John Cheever's uncertain position among the top flight of American writers of serious fiction received a series of jolts that both damaged his reputation and intensified interest in his life and work. First came the biographies and memoirs (including one by his daughter) that laid out the sometimes stunning details of Cheever's not-so-secret life as a bisexual and alcoholic. Those were followed in 1991 by the publication of his private journals, which revealed a level of despair and personal frustration that even those who thought they knew Cheever well found difficult to square with his witty and urbane public persona. Combined with these revelations was the ongoing battle waged by Cheever's family to prevent the publication of his uncollected shorter fiction; stories dating mostly from his pre-World War II apprenticeship years that students of his work maintained would show how extensive and rapid had been Cheever's mastery of the short story form.

While some critics have pointed to such stories as "Of Love: A Testimony," "The Cat," and "Forever Hold Your Peace" as evidence of Cheever's early skill, it was not until his abandonment of the conventional, objective tone of his prewar work for the subjective, lyrical, sometimes fantastic style of his mature fiction that Cheever found his true voice. His ironic, exquisitely written narratives of the private anguish and struggles of middle-class families in suburban New York and Connecticut were occasionally seen as examples of mere "New Yorker school" fiction—pleasantly perceptive entertainments for the well-heeled. More often, however, critics recognized in Cheever's often humorous explorations of marital infidelity, frustrated ambition, and nostalgic yearning the work of a serious artist exposing the underside of the American Dream and the private conflict between good and evil, or hope and despair, in every individual.

Among Cheever's most praised and anthologized stories are "The Enormous Radio" (1947), "O Youth and Beauty" (1953), "The Country Husband" (1954), and "The Swimmer" (1964). In the earliest of these, a conventional middle-class couple purchases a radio that, to their surprise, begins broadcasting the private conversations of their neighbors. Cheever's exposition of the effects of this electronic eavesdropping on the couple's marriage has been called "nearly flawless," an "enduring . . . classic," and "perhaps the most imaginative story Cheever ever wrote."

In 1957 Cheever published his first novel, *The Wapshot Chronicle*, the nostalgic story of Leander Wapshot's fall from familial power and the subsequent misadventures and ultimate survival of his two sons. Although some reviewers took exception to its overabundance of characters and episodic organization, *The Wapshot Chronicle* was generally well received and is widely regarded today as one of Cheever's strongest works. With the publication in 1964 of its less warmly welcomed sequel, *The Wapshot Scandal*, Cheever had apparently completed the successful transition from short story writer to novelist, only to have his third novel, *Bullet Park* (1969), greeted by general critical hostility.

In the mid-1970s, Cheever ended roughly two decades of alcoholism and began work on his last, and some argue his finest, novel, *Falconer* (1977). Cheever's hero, Ezekial Farragut, is a professor and methadone addict imprisoned for murdering his brother. Through Farragut's hellish experiences and eventual escape, Cheever weaves a meditation on the themes of confinement and liberation, crime and punishment, and fear, love, and sin. *Falconer*'s critical reception was mixed: some reviewers found it "forced," "sloppy," and "quite disappointing," while others praised it as "stunning," "beautiful," and "a parable for our times."

Cheever's place in the hierarchy of contemporary American letters is still unclear. Some critics regard him as a minor, sentimental, misogynistic, and finally not very serious writer. At the same time, he attracted the attention of major critics throughout his career, won virtually every major literary award available, and has often been called "the American Chekhov." The most telling indication of his true place, however, may be the esteem in which he was held by his peers: "even at his lowest ebb," John Updike wrote, "Cheever can write like an angel."

—Paul Bodine

CHOPRA, Deepak

Nationality: American. **Born:** India, c. 1946. **Education:** Attended the All-India Medical Institute in New Delhi; internship in the village of Ramgarh, India, 1969; internship in New Jersey, 1970-71; residency in internal medicine at the Rockefeller Institute, Boston. **Family:** Married; wife's name Rita; one son and one daughter. **Career:** Physician specializing in endocrinology; practiced in Boston; currently practices in Los Angeles. **Address:** P.O. Box 344 Lancaster, Massachusetts 01523, U.S.A.

Publications

Nonfiction

Creating Health: Beyond Prevention, Toward Perfection. Houghton Mifflin, 1987; revised edition 1995.
Return to the Rishi: A Doctor's Search for the Ultimate Healer. Houghton Mifflin, 1988.
Quantum Healing: Exploring the Frontiers of Mind/Body Medicine. Bantam, 1989.
Perfect Health: The Complete Mind/Body Guide. Harmony, 1990.
Unconditional Life: Mastering the Forces That Shape Personal Reality: Mastering the Forces That Shape Personal Reality. Bantam, 1991.
Ageless Body, Timeless Mind: The Quantum Alternative to Growing Old. Harmony, 1993.
Creating Affluence: Wealth Consciousness in the Field of All Possibilities. New World Library, 1993.
Escaping the Prison of Intellect: A Journey from Here to Here (audiotape). New World Library, 1994.
Perfect Weight. Harmony, 1994.
Restful Sleep. Harmony, 1994.
Sacred Verses, Healing Sounds: The Bhagavad Gita (audiotape). New World Library, 1994.
Journey into Healing (audiotape). New World Library, 1995.
Boundless Energy. Harmony, 1995.
Perfect Digestion. Harmony, 1995.
The Seven Spiritual Laws of Success. Amber Allen, 1995.
Living without Limits. Ingram, 1995.
The Way of the Wizard. Harmony, 1996.

Novel

The Return of Merlin. Harmony, 1995.

* * *

After meeting Transcendental Meditation guru Maharishi Mahesh Yogi in 1985, Indian-born endocrinologist Deepak Chopra began a new career as the U.S. representative for the Yogi's version of the traditional Indian health regimen Ayurveda. In this view, individuals are seen as divisible into different health types, each of which requires a specific blend of health, dietary, and spiritual measures to remain balanced and youthful.

In his autobiography, *Return of the Rishi* (1988), Chopra recounted his early life as the son of a prominent Indian cardiologist, his years in America as a successful M.D., and his growing awareness that conventional Western medicine lacks a crucial spiritual dimension (the book's title referred to the rishi or sage of the Ayurvedic tradition). *Library Journal* hailed the book as an "engaging, animated account," *The New York Times* found it a "rich and compelling book," and even the *New England Journal of Medicine* declared that Chopra was "a fine and evocative writer."

After the publication of his *Quantum Healing* in 1989, Chopra explored Ayurvedic medicine again in *Perfect Health* (1990), explicating the three basic typologies of human health, the methods for determining one's own type, and the various treatments for each type's characteristic ailments. Chopra placed great emphasis on the practices of meditation, yoga, and self-massage, as well as the ingestion of certain herbs and spices.

In *Unconditional Life* (1991), Chopra mixed aphorisms ("All desires must come true"), case histories, and discussions of such topics as death, consciousness, God, the cosmic whole, bliss, and time, to drive home the theme that listeners must release themselves from their "conditioned" lives and "journey to the true self." In its review, *Publishers Weekly* remarked on the striking resemblance between Chopra's message and "New Age posturing," but applauded Chopra for tackling difficult subjects in a pragmatic way.

After several attempts, Chopra finally burst through to the mass market with the bestselling *Ageless Body, Timeless Mind* (1993), which sold 137,000 copies in one day, after Chopra appeared on *The Oprah Winfrey Show.* The book further advanced Chopra's basic claim that both Eastern and Western medicine demonstrate the clear relationship between the mind, or spirit, and the health of the body and that exercise, diet, relaxation techniques, and the avoidance of "toxic" situations can prolong and even "reverse" the aging process. *Ageless Body* represented Chopra's most definitive attempt to assert through case studies, medical data, and theory a synthesis, however untenable, of Western science and Indian mystical medicine.

By early 1994, *Ageless Body* had sold over one million copies. Chopra quickly followed it with *Creating Affluence* (1993) and *Restful Sleep* (1994). In *Creating Affluence,* Chopra suggested that one can attain "wealth consciousness"—that is, make money—by accessing one's sources of creativity, finding a way to "serve your fellow human beings" rather than yourself, and locating the talent or activity that "causes you to lose track of time." In *Restful Sleep,* Chopra offered an Ayurvedic approach to curing insomnia, which centered on such activities as keeping sleeping logs, performing nonstrenuous physical activity, and attending to one's individual body type.

With the publication of *Restful Sleep* and *Perfect Weight* (1994), Chopra demonstrated that he was not afraid to extend his teachings into mostly unrelated but traditionally profitable corners of the bestseller list; namely, the huge market for books on sleep problems and weight control. With *The Seven Spiritual Laws of Success* (1994), he cannily moved into the positive thinking/self-help/how-to-be-successful market exemplified by such bestsellers as Stephen Covey's *The Seven Habits of Highly Effective People.* Less than a year and a half later more than 850,000 copies of *Seven Spiritual Laws* were in print.

In 1995, Chopra published his first novel, *The Return of Merlin.* Set in contemporary England, it tells the story of two schoolboys who travel back through the "web of time" to the age of King Arthur and Merlin and discover such valuable lessons as the importance of serendipity ("so . . . you can escape the prison of the known"). *People* magazine faulted Chopra for freighting the plot with extended message passages but called it an "imaginative fantasy" and an "intriguing story."

Chopra has been dismissed as the "latest in a line of gurus who have prospered by blending pop science, pop psychology, and pop Hinduism," but Chopra has described himself as just a "bum on the street who has a lot of fun writing."

—Paul S. Bodine

CHRISTIE, Agatha (Mary Clarissa)

Nationality: English. **Born:** 15 September 1890, in Torquay, Devon. **Education:** Tutored at home by her mother until age 16; later studied singing and piano in Paris. **Family:** Married 1) Archibald Christie, 24 December 1914 (divorced 1928); 2) Max Edgar Lucien Mallowan, 11 September 1930 (died 1978); children: (first marriage) Rosalind. **Career:** Writer. During World War I, served as Voluntary Aid Detachment (V.A.D.) nurse in a Red Cross Hospital, Torquay, South Devon, England; after divorce in 1928, traveled for several years; after marriage to Max Mallowan, 1930, helped him with tabulations and photography at his excavations in Iraq and Syria; during World War II, worked in dispensary for University College Hospital, London, England; during postwar 1940s, helped her husband with excavation of Assyrian ruins. **Awards:** Grand Master award, Mystery Writers of America, 1954; New York Drama Critics' Circle award, 1955, for *Witness for the Prosecution;* Commander of the British Empire, 1956; D.Litt., University of Exeter, 1961; Dame Commander, Order of the British Empire, 1971. **Member:** Royal Society of Literature (fellow), Detection Club. **Died:** 12 January 1976, in Wallingford, England.

Publications

Novels

The Secret Adversary. Dodd, 1922.
The Man in the Brown Suit. Dodd, 1924.
The Secret of Chimneys. Dodd, 1925.
The Seven Dials Mystery. Dodd, 1929.
Giant's Bread. Doubleday, 1930.
The Murder at Hazelmoor. Dodd, 1931; as *The Sittaford Mystery,* Collins, 1931.
Unfinished Portrait. Doubleday, 1934.
Why Didn't They Ask Evans?, Collins, 1934; as *The Boomerang Clue,* Dodd, 1935.
Easy to Kill, Dodd, 1939; as *Murder Is Easy,* Collins, 1939.
Ten Little Niggers. Collins, 1939; as *And Then There Were None,* Dodd, 1940; as *Ten Little Indians,* Pocket Books, 1965.
N or M? Dodd, 1941.
Absent in the Spring. Farrar & Rinehart, 1944.
Death Comes as the End. Dodd, 1944.
Towards Zero. Dodd, 1944.
Remembered Death. Dodd, 1945; as *Sparkling Cyanide,* Collins, 1945.
The Rose and the Yew Tree. Rinehart, 1948.
The Crooked House. Dodd, 1949.
They Came to Baghdad. Dodd, 1951.
A Daughter's a Daughter. Heinemann, 1952.
Destination Unknown. Collins, 1954; as *So Many Steps to Death,* Dodd, 1955.
The Burden. Heinemann, 1956.
Ordeal by Innocence. Collins, 1958; Dodd, 1959.
The Pale Horse. Collins, 1961; Dodd, 1962.
Endless Night. Collins, 1967; Dodd, 1968.
By the Pricking of My Thumbs. Dodd, 1968.
Passenger to Frankfurt. Dodd, 1970.
Postern of Fate. Dodd, 1973.
Murder on Board. Dodd, 1974.

Novels (Featuring Hercule Poirot)

The Mysterious Affair at Styles. Lane, 1920; Dodd, 1927.
The Murder on the Links. Dodd, 1923.
The Murder of Roger Ackroyd. Dodd, 1926.
The Big Four. Dodd, 1927.
The Mystery of the Blue Train. Dodd, 1928.
Peril at End House. Dodd, 1932.
Thirteen at Dinner. Dodd, 1933; as *Lord Edgware Dies,* Collins, 1933.
Murder in Three Acts. Dodd, 1934; as *Three Act Tragedy,* Collins, 1935.
Murder on the Calais Coach. Dodd, 1934; as *Murder on the Orient Express,* Collins, 1934.
Death in the Air. Dodd, 1935; as *Death in the Clouds,* Collins, 1935.
The A. B. C. Murders. Dodd, 1936; as *The Alphabet Murders,* Pocket Books, 1966.
Cards on the Table. Collins, 1936; Dodd, 1937.
Murder in Mesopotamia. Dodd, 1936.
Poirot Loses a Client. Dodd, 1937; as *Dumb Witness,* Collins, 1937.
Death on the Nile. Collins, 1937; Dodd, 1938.
Appointment with Death. Peril at End House. Dodd, 1938.
Hercule Poirot's Christmas. Collins, 1938; as *Murder for Christmas,* Dodd, 1939; as *A Holiday for Murder,* Avon, 1947.
One, Two, Buckle My Shoe. Collins, 1940; as *The Patriotic Murders,* Dodd, 1941; as *An Overdose of Death,* Dell, 1953; as *The Patriotic Murders,* edited by Roger Cooper, Berkley, 1988.
Sad Cypress. Dodd, 1940.
Evil Under the Sun. Dodd, 1941.
Murder in Retrospect. Dodd, 1942; as *Five Little Pigs,* Collins, 1942.
The Hollow. Dodd, 1946; as *Murder After Hours,* Dell, 1954.
There Is a Tide .... Dodd, 1948; as *Taken at the Flood,* Collins, 1948.
Mrs. McGinty's Dead. Dodd, 1952; as *Blood Will Tell,* Detective Book Club, 1952.
Funerals Are Fatal. Dodd, 1953; as *After the Funeral,* Collins, 1953; as *Murder at the Gallop,* Fontana, 1963.
Hickory, Dickory, Death. Dodd, 1955; as *Hickory, Dickory, Dock,* Collins, 1955.
Dead Man's Folly. Dodd, 1956.
Cat Among the Pigeons. Collins, 1959; Dodd, 1960.
The Clocks. Collins, 1963; Dodd, 1964.
Third Girl. Collins, 1966; Dodd, 1967.
Hallowe'en Party. Dodd, 1969.
Elephants Can Remember. Dodd, 1972.
Curtain: Hercule Poirot's Last Case. Dodd, 1975.

Novels (Featuring Miss Jane Marple)

The Murder at the Vicarage. Dodd, 1930.
The Body in the Library. Dodd, 1942.
The Moving Finger. Dodd, 1942.
A Murder Is Announced. Dodd, 1950.
Murder with Mirrors. Dodd, 1952; as *They Do It with Mirrors*, Collins, 1952.
A Pocket Full of Rye. Collins, 1953; Dodd, 1954.
What Mrs. McGillicudy Saw! Dodd, 1957; as *4:50 from Paddington*, Collins, 1957; as *Murder She Said*, Pocket Books, 1961.
The Mirror Crack'd from Side to Side. Collins, 1962; as *The Mirror Crack'd*, Dodd, 1963.
A Caribbean Mystery. Collins, 1964; Dodd, 1965.
At Bertram's Hotel. Collins, 1965; Dodd, 1966; revised edition, Pocket Books, 1984.
Nemesis. Dodd, 1971.
Sleeping Murder. Dodd, 1976.

Short Stories

Poirot Investigates. Lane, 1924; Dodd, 1925.
Partners in Crime. Dodd, 1929; abridged edition as *The Sunningdale Mystery*, Collins, 1933.
The Under Dog, and Other Stories, Readers Library, 1929; Dodd, 1951.
The Mysterious Mr. Quin. Dodd, 1930.
The Thirteen Problems. Collins, 1932; as *The Tuesday Club Murders*, Dodd, 1933; abridged edition published as *The Mystery of the Blue Geraniums, and Other Tuesday Club Murders*, Bantam, 1940.
The Hound of Death, and Other Stories. Odhams Press, 1933.
Mr. Parker Pyne, Detective. Dodd, 1934; as *Parker Pyne Investigates*, Collins, 1934.
The Listerdale Mystery, and Other Stories. Collins, 1934.
Dead Man's Mirror, and Other Stories. Dodd, 1937; as *Murder in the Mews, and Three Other Poirot Stories*, Collins, 1937.
The Regatta Mystery, and Other Stories. Dodd, 1939.
The Mystery of the Baghdad Chest. Bantam, 1943.
The Mystery of the Crime in Cabin 66. Bantam, 1943; as *The Crime in Cabin 66*, Vallencey, 1944.
Poirot and the Regatta Mystery. Bantam, 1943.
Poirot on Holiday. Todd, 1943.
Problem at Pollensa Bay [and] Christmas Adventure. Todd, 1943.
The Veiled Lady [and] The Mystery of the Baghdad Chest. Todd, 1944.
Poirot Knows the Murderer. Todd, 1946.
Poirot Lends a Hand. Todd, 1946.
The Labours of Hercules: New Adventures in Crime by Hercule Poirot. Dodd, 1947; as *Labours of Hercules: Short Stories*, Collins, 1947.
Witness for the Prosecution, and Other Stories. Dodd, 1948.
The Mousetrap, and Other Stories. Dell, 1949; as *Three Blind Mice, and Other Stories*. Dodd, 1950.
The Adventure of the Christmas Pudding, and Selection of Entrees. Collins, 1960.
Double Sin, and Other Stories. Dodd, 1961.
13 for Luck!: A Selection of Mystery Stories for Young Readers. Dodd, 1961.
Surprise! Surprise!: A Collection of Mystery Stories with Unexpected Endings. Dodd, 1965.
Star Over Bethlehem, and Other Stories. Dodd, 1965.
13 Clues for Miss Marple. Dodd, 1966.
The Golden Ball, and Other Stories. Dodd, 1971.
Hercule Poirot's Early Cases. Dodd, 1974.
Miss Marple's Final Cases, and Two Other Stories. Collins, 1979.
Hercule Poirot's Casebook: Fifty Stories. Putnam, 1984.
The Agatha Christie Hour. Collins, 1982.
Miss Marple: The Complete Short Stories. Putnam, 1985.

Plays

Black Coffee (produced New York, 1930). Baker, 1934.
Ten Little Niggers, adaptation of her own novel (produced London, 1943; as *Ten Little Indians*, New York, 1944). Samuel French (London), 1944; as *Ten Little Indians*, Samuel French (New York), 1946.
Appointment with Death, adaptation of her own novel (produced London, 1945). Samuel French, 1945.
Little Horizon, adaptation of her novel *Death on the Nile* (produced London, 1945), revised version, as *Murder on the Nile* produced London and New York, 1946). Samuel French, 1948.
The Hollow, adaptation of her own novel (produced London, 1951; Princeton, New Jersey, 1952; New York, 1978). Samuel French, 1952.
The Mousetrap, adaptation of her own short story (produced London, 1952; New York, 1960). Samuel French, 1954.
Witness for the Prosecution, adaptation of her own short story (produced London, 1953; New York, 1954). Samuel French, 1954.
Spider's Web (produced London, 1954; New York, 1974). Samuel French, 1957.
Towards Zero, with Gerald Verner, adaptation of her own novel (produced London, 1956; New York, 1956). Dramatists Play Service, 1957.
The Unexpected Guest (produced London, 1958). Samuel French, 1958.
Verdict (produced London, 1958). Samuel French, 1958.
Go Back for Murder, adaptation of her own novel *Five Little Pigs* (produced London, 1960). Samuel French, 1960.
Rule of Three (includes *Afternoon at the Sea-side; The Patient;* and *The Rats*). Samuel French, 1963.
Akhnaton (produced under title *Akhnaton and Nefertiti*, New York, 1979). Dodd, 1973.
The Mousetrap, and Other Plays (includes *Witness for the Prosecution, Ten Little Indians, Appointment with Death, The Hollow, Towards Zero, Verdict*, and *Go Back for Murder*), with introduction by Ira Levin. Dodd, 1978.

Radio Plays: *The Mousetrap*, 1952; *Personal Call*, 1960.

Poetry

The Road of Dreams. Bles, 1925.
Poems. Dodd, 1973.

Other

Agatha Christie: An Autobiography. Dodd, 1977.
Come, Tell Me How You Live (autobiographical travel book). Dodd, 1946.

Editor with others, *The Times of London Anthology of Detective Stories.* John Day, 1973.

*

Media Adaptations: Films—*Love from a Stranger,* from the short story "Philomel Cottage," 1937 and 1947; *And Then There Were None,* 1945; *Witness for the Prosecution,* 1957; *The Spider's Web,* 1960; *Murder She Said,* 1962; *Murder at the Gallop,* 1963; *Murder Most Foul,* from the novel *Mrs. McGinty's Dead,* 1965; *Ten Little Indians,* 1965; *The Alphabet Murders,* 1967; *Endless Night,* 1971; *Murder on the Orient Express,* 1974; *Death on the Nile,* 1978; *The Mirror Crack'd,* 1980; *Evil Under the Sun,* 1982.

Bibliography: *An A to Z of the Novels and Short Stories of Agatha Christie* by Ben Morselt, David & Charles, 1985.

Critical Studies: *Agatha Christie's Writings* by F. Behre, Adler, 1967; *Agatha Christie: Mistress of Mystery* by Gordon C. Ramsey, Dodd, 1967; *The Mysterious World of Agatha Christie* by Jeffrey Feinman, Award Books, 1975; *A Talent to Deceive: An Appreciation of Agatha Christie* by Robert Barnard, Dodd, 1980; *The Gentle Art of Murder: The Detective Fiction of Agatha Christie* by Earl F. Bargainnier, Bowling Green University Press, 1981; *Agatha Christie and All That Mousetrap* by Hubert Gregg, William Kimber (London), 1981; *Murder She Wrote: A Study of Agatha Christie's Detective Fiction* by Patricia D. Maida and Nicholas B. Spornick, Bowling Green University, 1982; *The Life and Crimes of Agatha Christie* by Charles Osborne, Holt, 1983; *Agatha Christie: A Biography* by Janet Morgan, J. Cape, 1984; *The Agatha Christie Companion: The Complete Guide to Agatha Christie's Life and Work* by Dennis Sanders and Len Lovalio, Delacorte, 1984; *Agatha Christie: The Woman and Her Mysteries* by Gillian Gill, Free Press, 1990.

* * *

The main exponent of what has become known as the "clue-puzzle" genre of crime fiction, Agatha Christie continues to find purchase on a collective imagination and remains one of the world's most popular authors. Christie wrote at least 84 mystery novels and collections of short stories, all of which made use of the same structural and thematic apparatus. Her most famous creations by far are the detectives Hercule Poirot and Miss Jane Marple, both of whom regularly and successfully made the transition from page to screen. Christie is also the author of one of London's longest running plays *The Mousetrap.*

Christie's narratives are mobilized within a fairly strictly circumscribed framework of "Golden Age" conventions. The setting is a cozy and closed environment that contains a limited number of characters and is disrupted by an act of unseen violence. The initial suspect is the second party to be murdered, which emphasizes both the ineptitude of the police and the importance of the assistance of either an amateur (e.g. Miss Marple) or a semi-professional (e.g. Hercule Poirot) detective. Finally, and importantly, the solution of the mystery marks a return to order and well-being.

Indeed, it is from the very adherence to these narrative conventions that Christie's popularity or success is derived, as the project of her fiction is to explode all mystery and make everything accountable to reason, thus providing ideological reassurance to her reader. As crime fiction is a location within which a culture can talk about itself, it is significant that in Christie's work the integral figures of a particular and closed culture find it impossible to reconcile their problems for themselves. Therefore, they require a marginal figure to do so. Moreover, whilst the classic detective novel allows a culture to redeem itself through the discovery of guilt by an outside agency (the perpetrator of the crime always has a guilty secret and is always caught), it refuses to concern itself with the complexities of punishment and possible retribution.

The 4:50 From Paddington (1957), for example, is very deliberately and self-consciously a clue-puzzle mystery, and typically the movement in the novel is backwards to the point of the crime. Yet it is also a book intensely concerned with the condition of England. And whilst it is neither freely xenophobic nor simply English-venerating, it does imply that certain English classes are better than any others. That the bogus Crackenthorpe country house is essentially a new and foreign money mansion implies that the landed gentry have in some way been usurped by lower-class upstarts and foreigners. Christie, then, is keen to present herself as the custodian of high bourgeois culture.

Despite ideological contradictions, Christie's excellent plotting, talent for the surprising twist, and attention to detail will inevitably woo new admirers and thus sustain her popularity.

—Christopher Wigginton

CLANCY, Tom

Nationality: American. **Born:** 1947, in Baltimore, Maryland. **Education:** Graduated from Loyola College, Baltimore, 1969. **Military Service:** U.S. Army Reserve Officers Training Corps. **Family:** Married Wanda Thomas, 1969; children: Michelle, Christine, Tom, Kathleen. **Career:** Insurance agent in Baltimore, Maryland, and Hartford, Connecticut, until 1973; O. F. Bowen Agency (insurance company), Owings, Maryland, agent, beginning in 1973, owner, beginning in 1980; writer. **Agent:** Putnam, 200 Madison Ave., New York, New York 10016 **Address:** P.O. Box 800, Huntingtown, Maryland 20639-0800, U.S.A.

Publications

Novels

The Hunt for Red October. Naval Institute Press, 1984.
Red Storm Rising. Putnam, 1986.
Patriot Games. Putnam, 1987.
The Cardinal of the Kremlin. Putnam, 1988.
Clear and Present Danger. Putnam, 1989.
The Sum of All Fears. Putnam, 1991.
Submarine. Berkley, 1993.
Without Remorse. Putnam, 1994.
Debt of Honor. Putnam, 1994.
Tom Clancy's OP Center. Berkley, 1995.
Tom Clancy's OP Center II: Mirror Image. Berkley, 1995.
Tom Clancy's OP Center III: Games of State. Berkley, 1996.

Nonfiction

Armored Cav: A Guided Tour of an Armored Cavalry Regiment. Berkley, 1994.
Reality Check: What's Going on Out There. Putnam, 1995.
Fighter Wing: A Guided Tour of an Air Force Combat Wing. Berkely, 1995.

*

Film Adaptations: *The Hunt for Red October,* 1990; *Patriot Games,* 1992; *Clear and Present Danger,* 1994.

* * *

Tom Clancy is credited with inventing the techno-military thriller, a genre involving multiple plotlines, extensive description of military personnel and gear, and a large cast of characters ranging from Soviet military officers and CIA directors to the president of the United States. Extremely popular with the U.S. Armed Forces and government officials, including former Secretary of Defense Caspar Weinberger and President Ronald Reagan, Clancy has been hailed by Ross Thomas in *Washington Post Book World* as the "novelist laureate of the military-industrial complex."

A former insurance salesman, Clancy has had a long fascination with machines, systems, and procedures, especially those dealing with the U.S. military. Along with that interest lies a passion for research. So it was after reading several declassified documents on submarine construction, warfare, and deployment that Clancy wrote his first novel, *The Hunt for Red October* (1984). Extrapolating from information available to the public, Clancy created the story of Marko Ramius, a Lithuanian submarine captain who attempts to defect to the United States from the Soviet Union in a new attack submarine. Armed with nuclear warheads and carrying a prototype silent propulsion system, Ramius slips away from Soviet waters and races to America pursued by a Soviet fleet that has orders to sink him.

Critics attacked Clancy for his workman-like prose, his wooden characterizations of characters (particularly Ramius, whose reasons for defecting are treated vaguely), and his too-perfect weaponry. Admirable, though, was his handling of plot and suspense, especially his ability to transform complicated technical subjects such as fleet maneuvers, torpedo guidance systems, and even metallurgy into gripping drama. Ronald Reagan proclaimed the book "a hell of a yarn" and invited Clancy to the White House.

The Hunt for Red October introduced CIA analyst Jack Ryan, the hero of most of Clancy's future novels. Indeed, a subsequent string of bestsellers firmly established Clancy as one of the most popular authors of the last decade. *Red Storm Rising* (1986) deals with a WWIII scenario involving the imminent collapse of the Soviet Union's economy and the country's subsequent attack on NATO forces in Europe. *Patriot Games* (1987) returns to the halls of the CIA and Jack Ryan, who foils an assassination attempt on the Prince and Princess of Wales and earns the enmity of a splinter-group of Irish terrorists. *The Cardinal of the Kremlin* (1988) treats "Star Wars," the controversial Strategic Defense Initiative system developed to combat nuclear attack, and pits the United States against the Soviet Union in a deadly race to complete the first such working system. At the center of the novel is the CIA's highest-placed mole, a Soviet official known only as Cardinal. Other novels have focused on the Colombian drug cartels, Arab terrorist attacks on the United States, and a secret Japanese plot to destroy America's financial system.

Strong adherence to procedural detail gives Clancy's books a sense of realism surpassing most modern suspense fiction. While the soldiers of his books are idealized, Clancy does not turn the CIA into a group of James Bond clones; mistakes are made, plans fail, and characters die. Yet Jack Ryan has emerged as Clancy's hero—a family man, ex-Marine, and CIA analyst who rises through the ranks to become the Deputy Director of Intelligence. Thus, many scenes in which Ryan appears are unrealistic. In *Patriot Games,* for example, Ryan and the Prince of Wales engage in a boat chase with fleeing terrorists. Similarly, in *Clear and Present Danger* (1989), Ryan mans a machine-gun in a helicopter streaking to rescue American soldiers from Colombian drug lords. Readers generally forgive Clancy for these excesses, though, because they are swept toward the startling climax that is a hallmark of his best works.

While several military officials have grown uncomfortable with Clancy's suppositions of top-secret material, charging that the author's fiction is quite close to fact, Clancy has repeatedly insisted that he has never seen any classified material and would report to the Federal Bureau of Investigation anyone who would attempt to show him such documents. In fact, he readily admits that his prose is not his strong point, and stresses that the details and the plots of his novels offset that shortcoming. "I'm not that good a writer. I do a good action scene. I handle technology well," Clancy said in an interview with the *Washington Post.* "Beyond that I'll try to . . . improve what needs improving."

—Christopher Swann

CLARK, Curt. *See* **WESTLAKE, Donald E.**

CLARK, Mary Higgins

Nationality: American. **Born:** New York City, 24 December 1929. **Education:** Attended Villa Maria Academy, Ward Secretarial School, and New York University; Fordham University, B.A. (summa cum laude), 1979. **Family:** Married 1) Warren F. Clark in 1949 (died 1964); 2) Raymond Charles Ploetz, 1978 (marriage annulled); children: Marilyn, Warren, David, Carol, Patricia. **Career:** Remington Rand, New York City, advertising assistant, 1946; stewardess for Pan American Airlines, 1949-50; radio scriptwriter and producer for Robert G. Jennings, 1965-70; Aerial Communications, New York City, vice-president, partner, creative director, and producer of radio programming, 1970-80; David J. Clark Enterprises, New York City, chairman of the board and creative director since 1980. Chairman, International Crime Writers Congress, 1988. **Awards:** New Jersey Author award, 1969, for *Aspire to the Heavens,* 1977, for *Where Are the Children?,* and 1978, for *A Stranger Is Watching;* Grand Prix de Litterature Policière (France), 1980;

honorary doctorate, Villanova University, 1983. **Member:** Mystery Writers of America (president, 1987; member of board of directors), American Academy of Arts and Sciences, American Irish Historical Society (member of executive council). **Agent:** Eugene H. Winick, McIntosh & Otis, Inc., 475 Fifth Ave., New York, New York 10017. **Address:** 210 Central Park South, New York, New York 10019, U.S.A.

Publications

Novels

Where Are the Children? New York, Simon & Schuster, and London, Talmy Franklin, 1975.
A Stranger Is Watching. New York, Simon & Schuster, and London, Collins, 1978.
The Cradle Will Fall. New York, Simon & Schuster, and London, Collins, 1980.
A Cry in the Night. New York, Simon & Schuster, 1982; London, Collins, 1983.
Stillwatch. New York, Simon & Schuster, and London, Collins, 1984.
Murder in Manhattan, with Thomas Chastain and others. New York, Morrow, 1986.
Weep No More, My Lady. New York, Simon & Schuster, and London, Collins, 1987.
While My Pretty One Sleeps. New York, Simon & Schuster, and London, Century, 1989.
Loves Music, Loves to Dance. New York, Simon & Schuster, 1991.
All Around the Town. New York, Simon & Schuster, 1992.
I'll Be Seeing You. New York, Simon & Schuster, 1993.
Remember Me. New York, Simon & Schuster, 1994.
Let Me Call You Sweetheart. New York, Simon & Schuster, 1995.
Silent Night. New York, Simon & Schuster, 1995.
Moonlight Becomes You. New York, Simon & Schuster, 1996.

Short Stories

The Anastasia Syndrome and Other Stories. New York, Simon & Schuster, 1989; London, Century, 1990.
Death on the Cape and Other Stories. London, Arrow Books, 1993.
The Lottery Winner. New York, Simon & Schuster, 1994.

Nonfiction

Aspire to the Heavens: A Biography of George Washington (for children). New York, Meredith Press, 1969.

Editor, *Murder on the Aisle: The 1987 Mystery Writers of America Anthology.* New York, Simon & Schuster, 1987.
Editor, *Bad Behavior.* New York, Harcourt Brace, 1995.

*

Media Adaptations: Films—*A Stranger Is Watching,* 1982; *A Cry in the Night,* 1985; *Where Are the Children?,* 1986. Television—*The Cradle Will Fall,* 1984; *Stillwatch,* 1987.

* * *

Over the last two decades, Mary Higgins Clark has established herself as one of America's most popular authors. Her mystery novels and collections of short fiction have routinely topped the bestseller lists, sometimes even before they have been officially released. With stories about ordinary women who suddenly encounter terrifying situations in their everyday lives, Clark has certainly tapped into what reviewers (both derisively and affectionately) refer to as a successful formula for her mystery-thrillers.

Even as a child, Clark was an avid reader and storyteller, frightening her friends with spine-tingling ghost stories at slumber parties. After the death of her husband in 1964 left her with five children (aged 13 and under) to support, she turned to writing radio scripts for a living. Within five years she had published her first book, a biography of George Washington, *Aspire to the Heavens* (1969). It turned out to be a commercial failure, but Clark remained determined to continue writing, hoping to produce a bestseller.

When Clark decided to write mysteries, she quickly realized that she had found her niche. Her first thriller, *Where Are the Children?* (1975), brought her $100,000 for the paperback rights. Her second mystery novel, *A Stranger Is Watching* (1978), earned her a $500,000 advance and, eventually, $1 million for the paperback rights. Twelve novels and five television and film adaptations later, Clark has become one of the highest paid writers in America. In 1992 she signed a $35 million contract with Simon and Schuster to write four novels, a collection of short stories, and a memoir.

Clark's novels employ a popular formula: a daring heroine is confronted with an evil she must overcome, in the process of which she discovers her inner strength. The core of Clark's novels, though, is sheer terror. In the words of Marilyn Stasio of the *New York Times,* "she taps into some elemental fear that really gives you the willies." In *The Cradle Will Fall* (1980), Katie DeMaio, a young lawyer, witnesses an obstetrician, Dr. Edward Highley, placing a woman's body in the trunk of a car. From the beginning, the reader knows who the killer is, but Clark creates suspense by making the reader wonder if he will kill the heroine, who must go to the doctor for treatment. In a later novel, *I'll Be Seeing You* (1993), the heroine, Meghan Collins, again witnesses a scene which sets the mystery in motion. Meghan sees a woman who could be her identical twin rushed into the emergency room of a hospital, dying of a knife wound. Meghan decides to investigate the stabbing, which seems linked to the mysterious death of her father, whose body was never found.

Critics have responded with mixed reviews to Clark's work. They generally fault Clark for an unimaginative prose and occasional 'contrivances,' but tend to praise her ability to plot a suspenseful story that taps into the reader's deepest fears. In a typical review, Stasio wrote of *Let Me Call You Sweetheart* (1995): "Ms. Clark's style is not subtle ('His eyes, filled with anger and hatred, seemed to be burning through her'), but the no-frills language is so light on its feet that it races the story straight for the cliffs on which every chapter ending hangs." One of Clark's most consistent critics, H.C. Veit of *Library Journal,* wrote of *The Cradle Will Fall*: "There is no point in bothering with Clark's latest novel, a commonplace piece of nonsense. . . . Paralyzingly respectable and stupifyingly ignorant, this rubbish will probably sell like hot cakes." Walter Clemons of *Newsweek,* representing a more common opinion of Clark's work, disagreed: "Sturdy construction, characters to please an aunt of mine who liked to read about 'people I would invite into my own home,' a firm hand at the controls—*The Cradle Will Fall* is sure-fire."

As is typical of much popular fiction, Clark's characters are clearly delineated as good or evil, and in the end good always triumphs, leaving no ambiguity. Her stories provide a kind of social commentary, she has said, fulfilling a need we have to see justice done and to believe that the strength of individuals (particularly women, who are so often portrayed as victims) can overcome evil. Clark told Roy Hoopes of *Modern Maturity*: "We all hang by a thread, and there are many things we cannot choose about our lives. It's how we react to the inevitable that counts. . . . At the end of a suspense novel or a mystery the problem is solved, the culprit is punished, satisfaction has been taken for the victim's life. And I think there is a sense of harmony that we too often don't find in life."

—Anne Boyd

CLARKE, Arthur C(harles)

Nationality: British. **Born:** Minehead, Somerset, 16 December 1917. **Education:** Huish's Grammar School, Taunton, Somerset, 1927-36; King's College, London, 1946-48, B.Sc. (honours) in physics and mathematics 1948. **Military Service:** Flight Lieutenant in the Royal Air Force, 1941-46; served as Radar Instructor, and Technical Officer on the first Ground Controlled Approach radar; originated proposal for use of satellites for communications, 1945. **Family:** Married Marilyn Mayfield in 1954 (divorced 1964). **Career:** Assistant auditor, Exchequer and Audit Department, London, 1936-41; assistant editor, *Physics Abstracts*, London, 1949-50; since 1954, engaged in underwater exploration and photography of the Great Barrier Reef of Australia and the coast of Sri Lanka. Director, Rocket Publishing, London, Underwater Safaris, Colombo, and the Spaceward Corporation, New York. Has made numerous radio and television appearances (as presenter of the television series *Arthur C. Clarke's Mysterious World*, 1980, and *World of Strange Powers*, 1985), and has lectured widely in Britain and the United States; commentator, for CBS-TV, on lunar flights of Apollo 11, 12 and 15; Vikram Sarabhai Professor, Physical Research Laboratory, Ahmedabad, India, 1980. **Awards:** International Fantasy award, 1952; Hugo award, 1956, 1969 (for screenplay), 1974, 1980; Unesco Kalinga prize, 1961; Boys' Clubs of America award, 1961; Franklin Institute Ballantine medal, 1963; Aviation-Space Writers Association Ball award, 1965; American Association for the Advancement of Science-Westinghouse Science Writing award, 1969; *Playboy* award, 1971; Nebula award, 1972, 1973, 1979; Jupiter award, 1973; John W. Campbell Memorial award, 1974; American Institute of Aeronautics and Astronautics award, 1974; Boston Museum of Science Washburn award, 1977; Marconi fellowship, 1982; Science Fiction Writers of America Grand Master award, 1986; Vidya Jyothi medal, 1986; International Science Policy Foundation medal, 1992; Lord Perry award, 1992. D.Sc.: Beaver College, Glenside, Pennsylvania, 1971. D.Litt.: University of Liverpool, 1995. Chair, British Interplanetary Society, 1946-47, 1950-53. Guest of Honor, World Science Fiction Convention, 1956. Fellow, Royal Astronomical Society; Fellow, King's College, London, 1977; Chancellor, University of Moratuwa, Sri Lanka, since 1979. C.B.E. (Commander, Order of the British Empire), 1989. **Agent:** David Higham Associates Ltd., 5-8 Lower John Street, London W1R 4HA, England; or, Scouil, Chichak, Galen Literary Agency, 381 Park Avenue, New York, New York 10016, U.S.A. **Address:** 25 Barnes Place, Colombo 7, Sri Lanka; or, Dene Court, Bishop's Lydeard, Taunton, Somerset TA4 3LT, England.

Publications

Novels

Prelude to Space. New York, Galaxy, 1951; London, Sidgwick and Jackson, 1953; as *Master of Space*, New York, Lancer 1961; as *The Space Dreamers*, Lancer, 1969.

The Sands of Mars. London, Sidgwick and Jackson, 1951; New York, Gnome Press, 1952.

Against the Fall of Night. New York, Gnome Press, 1953; revised edition, as *The City and the Stars*, London, Muller, and New York, Harcourt Brace, 1956.

Childhood's End. New York, Ballantine, 1953; London, Sidgwick and Jackson, 1954.

Earthlight. London, Muller, and New York, Ballantine, 1955.

The Deep Range. New York, Harcourt Brace, and London, Muller, 1957.

Across the Sea of Stars (omnibus). New York, Harcourt Brace, 1959.

A Fall of Moondust. London, Gollancz, and New York, Harcourt Brace, 1961.

From the Oceans, From the Stars (omnibus). New York, Harcourt Brace, 1962.

Glide Path. New York, Harcourt Brace, 1963; London, Sidgwick and Jackson, 1969.

An Arthur C. Clarke Omnibus [and *Second Omnibus*]. London, Sidgwick and Jackson, 2 vols., 1965-68.

Prelude to Mars (omnibus). New York, Harcourt Brace, 1965.

2001: A Space Odyssey (novelization of screenplay). New York, New American Library, and London, Hutchinson, 1968.

The Lion of Comarre, and Against the Fall of Night. New York, Harcourt Brace, 1968; London, Gollancz, 1970.

Rendezvous with Rama. London, Gollancz, and New York, Harcourt Brace, 1973.

Imperial Earth. London, Gollancz, 1975; revised edition, New York, Harcourt Brace, 1976.

The Fountains of Paradise. London, Gollancz, and New York, Harcourt Brace, 1979.

2010: Odyssey Two. New York, Ballantine, and London, Granada, 1982.

The Songs of Distant Earth. London, Grafton, and New York, Ballantine, 1986.

2061: Odyssey Three. New York, Ballantine, and London, Grafton, 1988.

Cradle, with Gentry Lee. London, Gollancz, and New York, Warner, 1988.

Rama II, with Gentry Lee. London, Gollancz, and New York, Bantam, 1989.

Beyond the Fall of Night, with Gregory Benford. New York, Putnam, 1990; with *Against the Fall of Night*, London, Gollancz, 1991.

The Ghost from the Grand Banks. New York, Bantam, and London, Gollancz, 1990.

The Garden of Rama, with Gentry Lee. London, Gollancz, and New York, Bantam, 1991.

Rama Revealed, with Gentry Lee. London, Gollancz, and New York, Bantam, 1993.

The Hammer of God. London, Gollancz, and New York, Bantam, 1993.

Short Stories

Expedition to Earth. New York, Ballantine, 1953; London, Sidgwick and Jackson, 1954.

Reach for Tomorrow. New York, Ballantine, 1956; London, Gollancz, 1962.

Tales from the White Hart. New York, Ballantine, 1957; London, Sidgwick and Jackson, 1972.

The Other Side of the Sky. New York, Harcourt Brace, 1958; London, Gollancz, 1961.

Tales of Ten Worlds. New York, Harcourt Brace, 1962; London, Gollancz, 1963.

The Nine Billion Names of God: The Best Short Stories of Arthur C. Clarke. New York, Harcourt Brace, 1967.

The Wind from the Sun: Stories of the Space Age. New York, Harcourt Brace, and London, Gollancz, 1972.

Of Time and Stars: The Worlds of Arthur C. Clarke. London, Gollancz, 1972.

The Best of Arthur C. Clarke 1937-1971, edited by Angus Wells. London Sidgwick and Jackson, 1973.

The Sentinel. New York, Berkley, 1983; London, Panther, 1985.

A Meeting with Medusa, with *Green Mars,* by Kim Stanley Robinson. New York, Tor, 1988.

Tales from Planet Earth. London, Century, 1989; New York, Bantam, 1990.

Play

Screenplay: *2001: A Space Odyssey,* with Stanley Kubrick, 1968.

Other

Interplanetary Flight: An Introduction to Astronautics. London, Temple Press, 1950; New York, Harper, 1951; revised edition, 1960.

The Exploration of Space. London, Temple Press, and New York, Harper, 1951; revised edition, 1959.

Islands in the Sky (for children). London, Sidgwick and Jackson, and Philadelphia, Winston, 1952.

The Young Traveller in Space (for children). London, Phoenix House, 1954; as *Going into Space,* New York, Harper, 1954; as *The Scottie Book of Space Travel,* London, Transworld, 1957; revised edition, with Robert Silverberg, as *Into Space,* New York, Harper, 1971.

The Exploration of the Moon. London, Muller, 1954; New York, Harper, 1955.

The Coast of Coral. London, Muller, and New York, Harper, 1956.

The Making of a Moon: The Story of the Earth Satellite Program. London, Muller, and New York, Harper, 1957; revised edition, Harper, 1958.

The Reefs of Taprobane: Underwater Adventures Around Ceylon. London, Muller, and New York, Harper, 1957.

Voice Across the Sea. London, Muller, 1958; New York, Harper, 1959; revised edition, London, Mitchell Beazley, and Harper, 1974.

Boy Beneath the Sea (for children). New York, Harper, 1958.

The Challenge of the Spaceship: Previews of Tomorrow's World. New York, Harper, 1959; London, Muller, 1960.

The First Five Fathoms: A Guide to Underwater Adventure. New York, Harper, 1960.

The Challenge of the Sea. New York, Holt Rinehart, 1960; London, Muller, 1961.

Indian Ocean Adventure. New York, Harper, 1961; London, Barker, 1962.

Profiles of the Future: An Enquiry into the Limits of the Possible. London, Gollancz, 1962; New York, Harper, 1963; revised edition, Harper, 1973; Gollancz, 1974, 1982; New York, Holt Rinehart, 1984.

Dolphin Island (for children). New York, Holt Rinehart, and London, Gollancz, 1963.

The Treasure of the Great Reef. London, Barker, and New York, Harper, 1964; revised edition, New York, Ballantine, 1974.

Indian Ocean Treasure, with Mike Wilson. New York, Harper, 1964; London, Sidgwick and Jackson, 1972.

Man and Space, with the editors of *Life.* New York, Time, 1964.

Voices from the Sky: Previews of the Coming Space Age. New York, Harper, 1965; London, Gollancz, 1966.

The Promise of Space. New York, Harper, and London, Hodder and Stoughton, 1968.

First on the Moon, with the astronauts. London, Joseph, and Boston, Little Brown, 1970.

Report on the Planet Three and Other Speculations. London, Gollancz, and New York, Harper, 1972.

The Lost Worlds of 2001. New York, New American Library, and London, Sidgwick and Jackson, 1972.

Beyond Jupiter: The Worlds of Tomorrow, with Chesley Bonestell. Boston, Little Brown, 1972.

Technology and the Frontiers of Knowledge (lectures), with others. New York, Doubleday, 1973.

The View from Serendip (on Sri Lanka). New York, Random House, 1977; London, Gollancz, 1978.

1984: Spring: A Choice of Futures. New York, Ballantine, and London, Granada, 1984.

Ascent to Orbit: A Scientific Autobiography: The Technical Writings of Arthur C. Clarke. New York and Chichester, Sussex, Wiley, 1984.

The Odyssey File, with Peter Hyams. New York, Ballantine, and London, Granada, 1985.

Astounding Days: A Science-Fictional Autobiography. London, Gollancz, 1989; New York, Bantam, 1990.

How the World Was One: Beyond the Global Village. London, Gollancz, and New York, Bantam, 1992.

By Space Possessed: Essays on the Exploration of Space. London, Gollancz, 1993.

The Snows of Olympus: A Garden on Mars. London, Gollancz, 1994.

Editor, *Time Probe: Sciences in Science Fiction.* New York, Delacorte Press, 1966; London, Gollancz, 1967.

Editor, *The Coming of the Space Age: Famous Accounts of Man's Probing of the Universe.* London, Gollancz, and New York, Meredith, 1967.

Editor, with George Proctor, *The Science Fiction Hall of Fame 3: The Nebula Winners 1965-1969.* New York, Avon, 1982.

Editor, *July 20, 2019: A Day in the Life of the 21st Century*. New York, Macmillan, 1986; London, Grafton, 1987.

* * *

Arthur C. Clarke, a science fiction writer and popularizer of scientific theories regarding space exploration and technological development, has achieved lasting fame in both areas because of his ability to envision the possibilities of human innovation and make them plausible to lay readers. His allegiance to scientific accuracy in his fictional portrayals of the future and his sense of wonder at the mystical expanse of the universe have earned him, in the words of David Brin of the *Los Angeles Times,* the title of "the poet laureate of the Space Age." But despite his many fans and stature as an author of some of the classics of science fiction, Clarke also has his detractors, primarily due to what many see as the emphasis on scientific detail and lack of emotional appeal in his works.

Clarke became interested in science fiction at the age of 12, devouring the short pieces in *Amazing Stories* and the longer works of H. G. Wells and Olaf Stapledon. He was also an active member of the British Interplanetary Society. But the turning point for Clarke came with his assignment to ground radar work as a member of the Royal Air Force during World War II. As a result of this work, he published an article called "Extraterrestrial Relays" in which he predicted the feasibility of global radio communications using "rocket stations" a full 20 years before communication satellites began operating. After the war, Clarke earned degrees in physics and applied mathematics.

Clarke has published many nonfiction books which helped to popularize scientific ideas for a broad audience. In *The Exploration of Space* (1951), Clarke summarized the knowledge we possessed about space travel and made predictions about the future development of the world's space programs. His *Profiles of the Future* (1962) particularly dazzled readers with its predictions of technological innovations such as "ground effort machines" (cars that travel on jets of compressed air) and long-distance conveyer-belt roads, as well as his speculation that robots and computers would become the intellectual companions of man. In his *New York Times* review of the book, Isaac Asimov wrote, "This book offers all of us a chance to raise our eyes from the ground and to contemplate the scenery ahead."

Clarke's extensive scientific research as displayed in his nonfiction works provides the impetus for his even more successful fiction, which incorporates his desire to popularize scientific ideas and to explore the spiritual significance of our existence. Most of his science fiction deals with space exploration and the discovery of other intelligent life in the universe. In *Childhood's End* (1953), his most popular and critically acclaimed early work, he portrays the arrival on Earth of a race called the Overlords, who use their superior development to advance the intelligence of humans. In the end, the last generation of Earth's children join the Overmind in a transcendence of material existence in which the Earth itself becomes obsolete.

The collaboration with Stanley Kubrick on the screenplay for *2001: A Space Odyssey* brought Clarke his most lasting fame. The film has been deemed by many to be the classic science fiction film of the 20th century. The story was based on Clarke's 1951 short story "The Sentinel," and Clarke simultaneously wrote the novel as he worked with Kubrick on the script. The novel was released three months after the film and was believed by many to be a more detailed explanation of the somewhat fragmented and complex film version. The story concerns a black monolith that has been discovered on the moon, sending radio signals to distant planets. The spaceship Discovery, equipped with the computer HAL 9000 and a human crew, is sent in the direction of the signal to investigate the possibility of other intelligent life forms, but the computer takes over the mission and the crew, for reasons which are left unexplained.

Despite his assertions that there would be no sequel to *2001,* Clarke has since written two sequels: *2010: Odyssey Two* (1982) and *2061: Odyssey Three* (1988), as well as the popular Rama series.

While Clarke's reputation has remained distinguished, his more recent reception has suffered from the rapid advance of the real world's technological capabilities. As a *Time* reviewer wrote about *2061,* "Clarke's future bears a marked resemblance to the present. . . . by now the mix of imagination and anachronism is wearing as thin as the oxygen layer on Mars." But for most fans, Clarke's ability to portray the fanciful as a reality that is only a step away has made him a master of the genre. As he told Marcia Gauger of *People* magazine, "I'm a hard-core science fiction writer—I have seldom written anything that I thought could not happen."

—Anne Boyd

CLAVELL, James (duMaresq)

Nationality: American. **Born:** 10 October 1925, in Australia; immigrated to United States, 1953, naturalized citizen, 1963. **Education:** University of Birmingham, 1946-47. **Military Service:** Served as captain with the Royal Artillery, 1940-46. **Family:** Married April Stride, 1951; children: Michaela, Holly. **Career:** Worked as a carpenter, 1953; screenwriter, director, and producer, beginning 1954, director of television programs, beginning 1958, novelist, beginning 1962. **Awards:** Writers Guild Best Screenplay award, 1964, for *The Great Escape;* honorary doctorates from the University of Maryland and the University of Bradford. **Died:** 6 September 1994, of cancer, in Vevey, Switzerland.

Publications

Novels

King Rat. Little, Brown, 1962; reprinted as *James Clavell's "King Rat," Delacorte,* 1983.

Tai-Pan: A Novel of Hong Kong. Atheneum, 1966; reprinted, Delacorte, 1983.

Shogun: A Novel of Japan. Atheneum, 1975.

Noble House: A Novel of Contemporary Hong Kong. Delacorte, 1981.

The Children's Story. Delacorte, 1981.

James Clavell's "Whirlwind." William Morrow, 1986.

Gai-jin: A Novel of Japan. Delacorte, 1993.

Plays

Screenplays: *The Fly,* 1958; *Watusi,* 1959; *Five Gates to Hell,* 1959; *Walk Like a Dragon,* 1960; *The Great Escape,* 1963; *633 Squadron,* 1964; *The Satan Bug,* 1965; *Where's Jack?,* 1968; *To Sir with Love,* 1969; *The Last Valley,* 1969.

Fiction for Children

James Clavell's "Thrump-o-moto," with illustrations by George Sharp. Delacorte, 1986.

*

Media Adaptations: Films—*King Rat,* 1965; *Tai-Pan,* 1986. Television—*Shogun,* 1980; *The Children's Story,* 1982; *Noble House,* 1988.

Theatrical Activities:

Director: **Films**—*Five Gates to Hell,* 1959; *To Sir with Love,* 1969.

* * *

Novelist, scriptwriter, director, and author of children's books, James duMaresq Clavell wrote riveting, action-packed historical adventures. Set in the Far and Middle East, these blockbusters combine many genres to give breadth and depth: swashbuckling histories, chronicles of manners, sea adventures, dynasty sagas, lusty romances, Horatio Alger financial fantasies, Bildungsroman, disaster stories, and even spy thrillers. They are all, in part, Englishman-abroad stories that investigate who we as Westerners are and what we can learn from the wisdom of very ancient cultures. They investigate father-son and male-female relationships, the thrill of danger and risk-taking, cultural differences, hypocrisy, class hatreds, the value of capitalism over socialism, and the capitalistic entrepreneur-adventurer as hero in opposition to the rule-bound, authority-oriented supporter of group-think.

Clavell began his writing career with scripts for such films as *The Fly* (1958), *Watusi* (1959), *To Sir with Love* (1969), and, in a collaboration, *The Great Escape* (1963). His first novel, *King Rat* (1962), was his way of coping with the psychological trauma of WWII prison camp survival; it chronicles the physical and moral deterioration of men sadistically starved and abused by a culture that considers them dishonored barbarians, and it sets in opposition rigid adherence to past values with survivalist adaptations. Clavell called the Japanese P.O.W. camp at Changi his "university," one of subhuman living conditions—rats, disease, filth—depersonalized torture and abuse, and a Darwinian struggle for food and dominance. The novel begins with a conventional moral pattern and then twists it the way Changi twisted the prisoners; the resultant morality play teaches the value of capitalistic free enterprise over socialism by smashing rigid class barriers, promoting democracy, and ultimately benefiting the whole community.

In the novels that followed, Clavell reshaped his prison camp experiences into a theory of East-West relationships, culture, and economics tested in the founding and development of Hong Kong (*Noble House* [1981], *Tai-Pan* [1966]), and in Western encounters with Japan (*Shogun* [1975], *Gai-Jin* [1993]) and Iran (*Whirlwind* [1986]). These novels, noted for their energy and scope (sweeping panoramas with as many as thirteen crisscrossing plots), act as fictional laboratories in which Clavell examines issues of economics, personal commitment, and cultural conflict and blending. His other stories include a Japanese-style children's fantasy (*Thrump-O-Moto* [1986]) and a controversial fable about the brainwashing of young people (*The Children's Story* [1981]).

Characterized by cross-cultural business intrigue amid unique, captivating foreign settings, Clavell's adventure novels study Western and Eastern minds in conflict over money, power, and politics. His central characters are enterprising, broad-scale "wheeler-dealers." *Tai-Pan,* set in 1841, is a history of early capitalism at its most exploitative and most daring; it glorifies the business acumen of China traders, who learn to thrive within a cutthroat Chinese business system, and particularly of Scotsman Dirk Struan, who founds Hong Kong. *Gai-Jin,* set in 1862, follows the Struan family to Japan, as Westerners negotiate for trade concessions while Japan undergoes internal rebellions aimed at ousting all foreigners. *Noble House* (set in 1963) sees the Struan business empire continuing to engage clashing cultures and ideologies in a fluctuating and alien market system. Noble House heir Ian Dunross heads the Struan banking house and international shipping firm, juggles international concerns, struggles to protect free enterprise (particularly from a Soviet threat), protects dependent women and children, maintains a lucrative base to support friends and relatives, and fulfills obligations assumed a century before. *Whirlwind* continues the sagas begun in the earlier books, bringing together representatives of the Noble House (protecting helicopter concessions in war-torn Iran) with the descendants of the house of Toranaga (struggling to gain Iranian oil and gas concessions). Westerners caught up in the Islamic reforms of post-Shah Iran encounter an incomprehensible nightmare of irrationality, emotionalism, factionalism, and fanaticism as they find that Iranian wives are medieval and long-time business associates are vehemently anti-Western.

Shogun is Clavell's finest work. In that book, an Elizabethan Englishman, Blackthorne, caught up in the complex intrigues and high civilization of Japanese samurai and warlords, is cleverly manipulated by the Japanese warlord Toranaga and the lovely Lady Mariko, who exploit his knowledge of Westerners to set the stage for expelling them all from Japan. The psychological precision of Blackthorne's cultural assimilation and education is a praiseworthy literary achievement, more so since "our" European "stand-in" is ultimately revealed as the pawn of a clever warlord.

Clavell presaged the modern multicultural movement and took a strong stance on women's rights (particularly in *Whirlwind* and *Gai-Jin*). His novels take readers into other minds and cultures, to precipitate shifts of perception that make Westerners see with Eastern eyes and that indelibly change the interpretation of alien cultures. Clavell argues that cross-cultural contact produces this type of paradigm shift.

—Gina Macdonald

CLEARY, Jon (Stephen)

Nationality: Australian. **Born:** Sydney, New South Wales, 22 November 1917. **Education:** Marist Brothers School, Randwick, New South Wales, 1924-32. **Military Service:** Served in the Australian Imperial Forces in the Middle East and New Guinea, 1940-

45. **Family:** Married Joy Lucas in 1946; two daughters (one deceased). **Career:** Prior to 1939 worked as a commerical traveler, bush worker, and commercial artist. Freelance writer, 1945-48; journalist, Government of Australia News and Information Bureau, London, 1948-49, New York, 1949-51; since 1945, full-time writer. Lives in New South Wales. **Awards:** Australian Broadcasting Commission prize, for radio drama, 1944; Australian Section prize, *New York Herald-Tribune* World Short Story Contest, 1950; Crouch gold medal, 1950; Mystery Writers of America Edgar Allan Poe award, 1974. **Agent:** John Farquharson Ltd., 162-168 Regent Street, London W1R 5TB. **Address:** c/o Harper Collins Publishers, 77-85 Fulham Palace Road, London W6 8JB, England.

PUBLICATIONS

Novels

You Can't See Round Corners. New York, Scribner, 1947; London, Eyre and Spottiswoode, 1949.
The Long Shadow. London, Laurie, 1949.
Just Let Me Be. London, Laurie, 1950.
The Sundowners. New York, Scribner, and London, Laurie, 1952.
The Climate of Courage. London, Collins, 1954; as *Naked in the Night,* New York, Popular Library, 1955.
Justin Bayard. London, Collins, 1955; New York, Morrow, 1956; as *Dust in the Sun,* New York, Popular Library, 1957.
The Green Helmet. London, Collins, 1957; New York, Morrow, 1958.
Back of Sunset. New York, Morrow, and London, Collins, 1959.
North from Thursday. London, Collins, 1960; New York, Morrow, 1961.
The Country of Marriage. New York, Morrow, and London, Collins, 1962.
Forests of the Night. New York, Morrow, and London, Collins, 1963.
A Flight of Chariots. New York, Morrow, 1963; London, Collins, 1964.
The Fall of an Eagle. New York, Morrow, 1964; London, Collins, 1965.
The Pulse of Danger. New York, Morrow, and London, Collins, 1966.
The High Commissioner. New York, Morrow, and London, Collins, 1966.
The Long Pursuit. New York, Morrow, and London, Collins, 1967.
Season of Doubt. New York, Morrow, and London, Collins, 1968.
Remember Jack Hoxie. New York, Morrow, and London, Collins, 1969.
Helga's Web. New York, Morrow, and London, Collins, 1970.
The Liberators. New York, Morrow, 1971; as *Mask of the Andes,* London, Collins, 1971.
The Ninth Marquess. New York, Morrow, 1972; as *Man's Estate,* London, Collins, 1972.
Ransom. New York, Morrow, and London, Collins, 1973.
Peter's Pence. New York, Morrow, and London, Collins, 1974.
The Safe House. New York, Morrow, and London, Collins, 1975.
A Sound of Lightning. New York, Morrow, and London, Collins, 1976.
High Road to China. New York, Morrow, and London, Collins, 1977.
Vortex. London Collins, 1977; New York, Morrow, 1978.
The Beaufort Sisters. New York, Morrow, and London, Collins, 1979.
A Very Private War. New York, Morrow, and London, Collins, 1980.
The Golden Sabre. New York, Morrow, and London, Collins, 1981.
The Faraway Drums. London, Collins, 1981; New York, Morrow, 1982.
Spearfield's Daughter. London, Collins, 1982; New York, Morrow, 1983.
The Phoenix Tree. London, Collins, 1984.
The City of Fading Light. London, Collins, 1985; New York, Morrow, 1986.
Dragons at the Party. London, Collins, 1987; New York, Morrow, 1988.
Now and Then, Amen. London, Collins, 1988; New York, Morrow, 1989.
Babylon South. London, Collins, 1989; New York, Morrow, 1990.
Murder Song. London, Collins, and New York, Morrow, 1990.
Pride's Harvest. London, HarperCollins, and New York, Morrow, 1991.
Dark Summer. New York, William Morrow, 1991; London, HarperCollins, 1992.
Bleak Spring. London, HarperCollins, 1993; New York, William Morrow, 1994.
Autumn Maze. London, HarperCollins, 1994.

Short Stories

These Small Glories. Sydney, Angus and Robertson, 1946.
Pillar of Salt. Sydney, Horwitz, 1963.

Plays

Screenplays: *The Siege of Pinchgut,* with Harry Watt and Alexander Baron, 1959; *The Green Helmet,* 1961; *The Sundowners,* 1961; *Sidecar Racers* (*Sidecar Boys*), 1975.

Radio Play: *Safe Horizon,* 1944.

Television Plays: *Just Let Me Be,* 1957 (England); *Bus Stop* series (2 episodes), 1961 (United States); *Spearfield's Daughter,* from his own novel, 1985 (United States).

* * *

Jon Cleary first appeared in print with a small collection of short stories titled *These Small Glories* (1946), which is based on his experiences as an Australian soldier in the Middle East. Now, almost half a century later, he is the author of some 40 books of fiction and possibly the most successful living Australian author. He writes to a meticulous routine and his novels appear in print runs of 25,000 and 300,000 (paperback), with the paperbacks being reprinted every third year or so.

His first and arguably best novel, *You Can't See Round Corners* (1949), is the graphic documentation of the decline of a smart but hollow young man, Frankie McCoy, who deserts the army into which he has been conscripted and returns to Sydney. The novel captures the ambience of Cleary's beloved city very well and, despite the wisecracking dialogue, the prose carries overtones of a Graham Greene-ish kind of world-weariness; there is a good deal of Greene's Pinky in *Brighton Rock* in Cleary's hero.

Cleary's early novels are mostly set in Australia, or feature Australian protagonists. His first big success came with *The Sundowners* (1952), a novel set in the 1920s that concerns a drover who refuses to settle down and live the stable life his wife and 14-year-old son desire. He followed it with *The Climate of Courage* (1954), which follows a number of soldiers who have returned from fighting in the Middle East and are enjoying a break in Sydney before being sent to New Guinea. The first half of the novel follows their romantic situations while on leave. The second sees them preparing for action and then involved in a disastrous retreat after being ambushed by the Japanese. The agonizing 35 day retreat over land is graphically done. He followed this with *Justin Bayard* (1955); set in the Northwest of Australia, it concerns a conscientious policeman who is forced to investigate the murder of his hostess on a distant station in the Kimberleys.

Both novels mingle realism with conventional romantic elements, but from *The Green Helmet* (1957) onwards Cleary's work becomes both more commercial and more international and topical in tone. He notes rather disarmingly of himself that: "When I first started writing I had two models: Graham Greene and H.E.Bates. Then as time went by I realized I could never be that good. I wasn't aware of the amount of depth one would need to be a really significant writer. But enough people who knew what they were about said I had a natural talent for being a craftsman so I settled for that."

A very sound craftsman is, in fact, what he became. His novels are efficiently plotted, the dialogue is well done though rather plentiful, and it is obvious that careful research goes into the settings (an element on which Cleary prides himself). They range from predictable locations such as Sydney and London to the Middle East, India, China, the Andes and parts of the United States. Most of the novels, though not all, are laced with frequent violent action, whether by men or nature, and the moral dilemmas of the characters are often resolved in this kind of imposed way.

As well as exploring what he calls in the title of one novel "the country of marriage," Cleary examines in his novels the complex and ambivalent bonding of males, like the two astronauts in the ambitious *A Flight of Chariots* (1963) or the two brothers in *The Green Helmet.* Occasionally, and with varying success, Cleary has moved away from the action novel and into the serious probing of *The Country of Marriage* (1962) and its marital and national tensions; he has also done a feebly satirical treatment of the British pop and swingers' scene of the late 1960s. However, his most popular novels deal with topical and public issues—the IRA, the Israel-Egypt six-day war, the outbreak of hostilities between India and China—even if these are usually the background for the romantic entanglings of the protagonists.

More recently, Cleary has turned to the figure of the Australian detective Scobie Malone, whom he first introduced in *The High Commissioner* (1966) with the memorable opening sentence: "'We want you to go to London,' said the Premier, 'and arrest the High Commissioner for murder.'" Scobie appears also in *Helga's Web* (1970) and *Ransom* (1973). But in Cleary's recent work he has used Scobie increasingly to attack what he sees as the elements of corruption in contemporary Australian society. In *Dragons at the Party* (1987), *Now and Then, Amen* (1988), and *Babylon South* (1990), he uses Scobie Malone (in the classic tradition of detective fiction) as an exemplar of the old-fashioned standard of morality that he sees disappearing and which he himself embodies in much of his writing.

—Laurie Clancy

COE, Tucker. *See* **WESTLAKE, Donald E.**

COFFEY, Brian. *See* **KOONTZ, Dean R(ay).**

COLLINS, Hunt. *See* **McBAIN, Ed.**

COLLINS, Jackie

Nationality: English. **Born:** 1941. **Family:** Married 1) Wallace Austin, 1959, (divorced, 1963); 2) Oscar Lerman, 1966; children: has three daughters, Tracy (first marriage), Tiffany, and Rory. **Career:** Novelist and screen actress. **Address:** c/o Simon & Schuster, 1230 Avenue of the Americas, New York, New York, 10020, U.S.A.

Publications

Novels

The World Is Full of Married Men. World Publishing, 1968.
The Stud. W. H. Allen, 1969, World Publishing, 1970.
Sunday Simmons and Charlie Brick. W. H. Allen, 1971; as *The Hollywood Zoo,* Pinnacle Books, 1975.
Lovehead. W. H. Allen, 1974; as *The Love Killers,* Warner Books, 1975.
The World Is Full of Divorced Women. W. H. Allen, 1975.
Lovers and Gamblers. W. H. Allen, 1977, Grosset, 1978.
The Bitch. Pan Books, 1979.
Chances. Warner Books, 1981.
Hollywood Wives. Simon & Schuster, 1983.
Sinners. Pan Books, 1984.
Lucky. Simon & Schuster, 1985.
Hollywood Husbands. Simon & Schuster, 1986.
Rock Star. Pocket Books, 1988.
Lady Boss. Pocket Books, 1990.
American Star: A Love Story. Simon & Schuster, 1993.
Hollywood Kids. Simon & Schuster, 1994.

*

Media Adaptations: Television miniseries—*Hollywood Wives,* 1985; *Lucky/Chances,* 1990; *Lady Boss,* 1992.

* * *

Bestselling novelist Jackie Collins has sold millions of copies of her books. Her novels have been reprinted in over 30 languages, and are noticeably absent from their slots on library shelves. What reviewers and critics cannot explain is why she is so popular.

Collins' novels are known for their thin plots, weak characters, and focus on glamorous lifestyles. All of her books contain generous quantities of sex, drugs, and money; explicit sex scenes are staples in her stories. She does not, however, believe that sex is what makes her books popular. "I don't think the sex sells the books at all . . . it just happens to be in my books," she said in the *Orange County Register.*

Collins' characters are always rich and living big in the fast lane. She is fond of using accents in her writing to attempt realistic conversations between foreign and American characters. This is sometimes confusing to the reader, though it does add some contrast to her characters.

Collins often bases her lead characters on real-life famous personalities. She embellishes them and changes names, but many intrigued readers are able to guess their identities correctly. "Collins insists that their real-life models are every bit as manipulative as the books' characters," the *Orange County Register* said. "There's one very famous manager who, when his rock star wouldn't comply with his wishes, held him out the window by his legs until he agreed to sign the contract." She has had calls from those who recognized themselves in her writings. People even call her with stories about themselves and hoping to be included in one of her books.

One reason her books may be appealing to such a large audience is her basic story lines and plain language. Critics complain that her writing does not use proper grammar. "I don't basically understand grammar . . . I call myself a street writer. I write purely by instinct. I've decided people don't speak in grammatical conversations. . . . The important thing is I get people into the bookstores who probably wouldn't be there otherwise."

Rock Star (1988) is the story of three main characters, nicknamed The Legend, The Survivor, and The Newcomer. The story is set in Hollywood and is filled with drug abuse and casual sex. Critics are turned off by her heavy use of cliches, and her sloppy research. "Her characters . . . are sitting around listening to the Beatles' *Revolver,* and Bob Dylan's *Blonde on Blonde* a year before they were released, seeing punks invade King's Road well before the movement caught on, and worrying about AIDS back when Herpes was on everybody's mind," notes one critic.

Collins has written *Hollywood Wives* (1983), *Hollywood Husbands* (1986), and *Hollywood Kids* (1994), each detailing the torrid, steamy side of their respective subjects. *Hollywood Wives* is by far the most recognized of this set of titles, and was made into a television miniseries. *Hollywood Husbands* covers the sinful lives of the rich and famous men of Tinseltown, and *Hollywood Kids* describes the spoiled, aimless, pleasure-driven life of Hollywood parents' adult offspring. Though the writing may seem weak, there is probably more truth to these tales than readers would believe, making the reading a little more interesting.

Collins is no Shakespeare, but she is a writer who knows exactly what her readers want. She is able to produce it repeatedly, and in slightly different forms for her readers' enjoyment. She writes about what she is familiar with and uses her knowledge to entice her readers to take a break from their mundane, everyday lives, and experience hers.

—Amy Faulkenberry

CONROY, Pat

Nationality: American. **Born:** 26 October 1945, in Atlanta, Georgia. **Education:** The Citadel, B.A., 1967. **Family:** Married 1) Barbara Bolling, 1969 (divorced, 1977); 2) Lenore Gurgewitz, 1981; children: (first marriage) Megan; Jessica, Melissa (stepdaughters); (second marriage) Susannah; Gregory, Emily (stepchildren). **Career:** Writer. Worked as schoolteacher in Daufuski, South Carolina, 1969. **Awards:** Anisfield-Wolf award, Cleveland Foundation, 1972, for *The Water Is Wide.* **Agent:** Julian Bach Literary Agency, 747 Third Ave., New York, New York 10017. **Address:** 1069 Juniper St. N.E., Atlanta, Georgia 30309, U.S.A.

PUBLICATIONS

Novels

The Boo. McClure, 1970.
The Water Is Wide. Houghton, 1972.
The Great Santini. Houghton, 1976.
The Lords of Discipline. Houghton, 1980.
The Prince of Tides. Houghton, 1986.
Beach Music. Doubleday, 1995.

*

Media Adaptations: Films—*Conrack,* adapted from his novel *The Water Is Wide,* 1974; *The Great Santini,* 1979; *The Lords of Discipline,* 1983; *The Prince of Tides,* 1991.

* * *

Pat Conroy became one of the best-selling novelists of the 1980s by focusing on Southern male protagonists caught between oppressive father figures and the culture of the South, both of which he displays in all their myth and actuality. Conroy is credited with ironic, humorous, and often disturbing views of relationships between family and friends in the contemporary South, leading many critics to note a strong autobiographical tendency in his works. His stories alternately romanticize and rail against both southern culture and father figures, leaving the reader with startling and revealing impressions of both.

Conroy's first widely acclaimed book, *The Water Is Wide* (1972), is based on the author's year of teaching on Daufuskie Island, South Carolina. Faced with the poverty and incredible ignorance of the island children, Conroy engaged in a bitter and often futile battle with local school district officials and used unorthodox teaching methods in an attempt to communicate to the children more about the world around them. Eventually fired from the job, Conroy captured the experience in *The Water Is Wide* with incisive and often fervent prose.

The Great Santini (1976) utilized three icons of Conroy's works: fatherhood, the Marines, and the South. Drawing heavily on his family background, Conroy created a tale of initiation and suffering for his protagonist, young Ben Meecham, the son of Marine colonel Bull Meecham. Explosive, profane, and often violent, Bull tests his son's patience and establishes a common Conroy theme of associating love with brutality. During the course of the novel, which is set in South Carolina, Ben must strip away the myths of his own life and those of his father in order to deal with reality. In the end, he rejects his father's professed infallibility. Critics have naturally recognized the parallels with Conroy and his own father, who is also a Marine officer.

Perhaps Conroy's most controversial novel, *The Lords of Discipline* (1980) is a bleak and harrowing look at the Citadel, South Carolina's famous all-male military academy (which Conroy attended). In 1966, Will McLean is a senior cadet at the Carolina Military Institute in Charleston and is charged by the Commandant of Cadets, Colonel "Bear" Berrineau, with protecting the Institute's first black cadet from excessive hazing. The novel explores Conroy's theme of love and brutality with vicious scenes of hazing—referred to by the Institute as "the Taming"—and the subsequent friendships that develop out of such a confrontational setting. The novel contains a twofold conflict: a direct struggle between Will and the legendary cadet group known as the Ten (which has pledged to run the black cadet out of the Institute), and the subtler conflicts between Will and his three roommates—relationships Will treasures yet threatens to destroy by opposing the Ten. While the prose is at times overworked—such as that related to Will's ponderings on the nature of evil—the novel is a suspenseful investigation of both Will McLean's own heart and those of the young men who walk the halls of military academies everywhere.

The Prince of Tides (1986) is Conroy's best known and wildest tale. The protagonist, Tom Wingo, must deal with the dark demons of his family's past when his twin sister Savannah attempts suicide in New York City. Rushing to his sister's side, Tom, aided by Savannah's psychiatrist, Susan Lowenstein, pieces together a life of broken commitments, powerful love, and savage violence, which Tom at first refuses to acknowledge but later reveals in stunning clarity. Following the pattern of *The Great Santini, The Prince of Tides* contains an overbearing father, a hauntingly beautiful and manipulative mother, and a male protagonist who must confront the mythical constructs of his past and his family. Some critics see the novel as overblown and inflated. Others, such as *Detroit News* contributor Ruth Pollack Coughlin, find ". . . spectacular lyrical prose with a bitter sense of humor."

Conroy's prose is never unreadable and at times is fully engaging. However, he can lead a reader to doubt his credibility when he writes at full bore and with raw emotion. While he often touches on something profound at such moments—such as the dangerous love men can have for one another, or the human capacity for self delusion—he occasionally wafts into melodrama and sentimentalism. Nevertheless, there is a strong undercurrent in all of his stories that pulls readers in. As Conroy himself said in an interview, "I do the thing that Southerners do naturally—I tell stories. I always try to make sure there's a good story going on in my books."

—Christopher Swann

COOK, Robin

Nationality: American. **Born:** 4 May 1940 in New York. **Education:** Wesleyan University, B.A., 1962; Columbia University, M.D., 1966; postgraduate study at Harvard University. **Military Service:** U.S. Navy, 1969-71; became lieutenant commander. **Family:** Married Barbara Ellen Mougin, 1979. **Career:** Queen's Hospital, Honolulu, resident in general surgery, 1966-68; Massachusetts Eye and Ear Infirmary, resident in ophthalmology, 1971-75, staff member, 1975—. Clinical instructor at Harvard Medical School, beginning 1972. **Agent:** William Morris Agency, 1350 Avenue of the Americas, New York, New York 10019. **Address:** 6001 Pelican Bay Blvd., Naples, Florida 33963-8166, or c/o G. P. Putnam's Sons, 51 Madison Ave., New York, New York 10010-1603, U.S.A.

Publications

Novels

The Year of the Intern. Harcourt, 1972.
Coma. Little, Brown, 1977.
Sphinx. Putnam, 1979.
Brain. Putnam, 1981.
Fever. Putnam, 1982.
Godplayer. Putnam, 1983.
Mindbend. Putnam, 1985.
Outbreak. Putnam, 1987.
Mortal Fear. Putnam, 1988.
Mutation. Putnam, 1989.
Harmful Intent. Putnam, 1990.
Vital Signs. Putnam, 1990.
Blindsight. Putnam, 1991.
Terminal. Putnam, 1992.
Fatal Cure. Putnam, 1994.
Acceptable Risk. Putnam, 1995.
Contagion. Putnam, 1995.

*

Media Adaptations: Films—*Coma,* 1978; *Sphinx,* 1981; *Mutation,* 1990. Television—*Robin Cook's Virus,* adapted from the novel *Outbreak,* 1995.

* * *

Robin Cook, a practicing doctor, uses events from his medical experience as the basis for his "techno-medical thrillers." Critics generally feel that Cook found a successful formula with *Coma* (1977), but that he has not really developed as a writer since the book's publication. Despite the harsh critical consensus, most reviewers admit that his fiction is fast-paced, and that the experience of reading one of his novels is often enjoyable.

Coma, Cook's first successful novel, is a story that places Susan Wheeler, a heroic young intern, in the world of organized crime. Wheeler discovers that the hospital that employs her has a dubious record concerning the deaths of several of its patients. After a series of frustrating encounters with hospital bureaucrats, the story reaches its climax as Wheeler discovers that the Mafia is running the equivalent of a used body-parts store from the hospital. Critics and readers enjoyed the novel and commented on its incredible, yet frighteningly feasible plot.

Cook continued his formula for success with less favorable results in his next two novels, *Sphinx* (1979), and *Brain* (1981). The second novel received harsh criticism from reviewers who felt that when Cook tried to write about events outside of the hospital, he lost control of the subject matter. Yet many reviewers still acknowledged that both novels had plausible plots.

Throughout the 1980s Cook returned to his steady formula of "techno-medical thrillers," and rarely dealt with events not connected with a hospital mystery. *Fever* (1982) resembles the plot of *Coma*; Dr. Mantel discovers that a 12-year-old boy has been poisoned with benzene, and is thwarted by the entire hospital when he attempts to understand what is going on. Although many critics felt the book's plot was absurd, Christopher Lehman-Haupt wrote in *The New York Times Review of Books*: "I was having far too good a time to be willing to notice."

With *God Player* (1983), *Mortal Fear* (1989), *Mutation* (1990), *Blindsight* (1991), *Terminal* (1993), and *Acceptable Risk* (1995), critics began to feel that Cook's formula was becoming stale. Reviewers considered *God Player* less spectacular than his other thrillers. *Blindsight* continued the exploration of his early novels into medical education and genetic engineering, but critics considered Dr. Lawie Montgomery a "plastic heroine" and found her love interests to be absurd. *Terminal* is fast paced but often stumbles. The story, like his others, is easy to detect within the first 20 pages, and there is little reason to believe that the hero is ever in any danger.

Despite harsh criticism about the content of the books, many critics admit that they can't stop reading after they start one of Cook's books. Clarence Patterson, of the *Chicago Times*, wrote that "the stories work better than most because they don't rely on the supernatural . . . [this]makes the pages turn faster."

—Chris Godat

COOKSON, Catherine (McMullen)

Pseudonym: Catherine Marchant. **Nationality:** British. **Born:** Tyne Dock, South Shields, 20 June 1906. **Family:** Married Thomas H. Cookson in 1940. **Career:** Writer. Lecturer for women's groups and other organizations. **Awards:** Winifred Holtby award for best regional novel from Royal Society of Literature, 1968, for *The Round Tower;* Order of the British Empire, 1985; recipient of Freedom award of the County Borough of South Shields in recognition of her services to the city. **Agent:** Anthony Sheil Associates Ltd., 43 Doughty St., London WC1N 2LF, England. **Address:** White Lodge, 23 Glastonbury Grove, Newcastle upon Tyne NE2 2HB, England.

Publications

Novels (series: Bill Bailey; Mary Ann; Mallen)

Kate Hannigan. Macdonald & Co., 1950.
Fifteen Streets. Macdonald & Co., 1952.
Colour Blind. Macdonald & Co., 1953.
Maggie Rowan. Macdonald & Co., 1954.
The Menagerie. Macdonald & Co., 1958.
Slinky Jane. Macdonald & Co., 1959.
Fenwick Houses. Macdonald & Co., 1960.
The Garment. Macdonald & Co., 1962.
The Blind Miller. Macdonald & Co., 1963.
Hannah Massey. Macdonald & Co., 1964.
The Long Corridor. Macdonald & Co., 1965.
The Unbaited Trap. Macdonald & Co., 1966; revised edition, Bantam, 1995.
Katie Mulholland. Macdonald & Co., 1967.
The Round Tower. Macdonald & Co., 1968.
The Nice Bloke. Macdonald & Co., 1969; as *The Husband,* New American Library, 1976.
The Glass Virgin. Macdonald & Co., 1970.
The Invitation. Macdonald & Co., 1970.
The Dwelling Place. Macdonald & Jane's, 1971.
Fanny McBride. Corgi Books, 1971.
Feathers in the Fire. Macdonald & Co., 1971.
Pure as the Lily. Macdonald & Co., 1972.
The Invisible Cord. Dutton, 1975.
The Gambling Man. Morrow, 1975.
The Tide of Life. Morrow, 1976.
The Girl. Morrow, 1977.
The Cinder Path. Morrow, 1978.
Tilly Trotter. Heinemann, 1978; as *Tilly,* Morrow, 1980.
The Man Who Cried. Morrow, 1979.
The Mallen Novels. Heinemann, 1979.
- *The Mallen Streak.* Heinemann, 1973.
- *The Mallen Girl.* Heinemann, 1974.
- *The Mallen Lot.* Dutton, 1974; as *The Mallen Litter,* Heinemann, 1974.

The Mary Ann Omnibus. Macdonald & Jane's, 1981.
- *A Grand Man.* Macdonald & Co., 1954.
- *The Lord and Mary Ann.* Macdonald & Co., 1956.
- *The Devil and Mary Ann.* Macdonald & Co., 1958.
- *Love and Mary Ann.* Macdonald & Co., 1961.
- *Life and Mary Ann.* Macdonald & Co., 1962.
- *Marriage and Mary Ann.* Macdonald & Co., 1964.
- *Mary Ann's Angels.* Macdonald & Co., 1965.
- *Mary Ann and Bill.* Macdonald & Co., 1966.

Tilly Wed. Morrow, 1981; as *Tilly Trotter Wed,* Heinemann, 1981.
Tilly Alone. Morrow, 1982; as *Tilly Widowed,* Heinemann, 1982.
The Whip. Summit Books, 1982.
Hamilton. Heinemann, 1983.
The Black Velvet Gown. Summit Books, 1984.
Goodbye Hamilton. Heinemann, 1984.
The Bannaman Legacy. Summit Books, 1985; as *A Dinner of Herbs,* Heinemann, 1985.
Harold. Heinemann, 1985.
The Moth. Summit Books, 1986; as *The Thorman Inheritance,* Summit Books, 1989.
Bill Bailey. Heinemann, 1986.
Bill Bailey's Lot. Heinemann, 1987.
The Parson's Daughter. Summit Books, 1987.
Bill Bailey's Daughter. Heinemann, 1988.
The Cultured Handmaiden. Heinemann, 1988.
The Harrogate Secret. Summit Books, 1988.
The Black Candle. Summit Books, 1989.
The Wingless Bird. Bantam, 1990.
The Gillyvors. Bantam, 1990; as *The Love Child,* 1990.
My Beloved Son. Bantam, 1991.
The Rag Nymph. Bantam, 1991.
The House of Women. Bantam, 1992.
The Maltese Angel. Bantam, 1992.
The Year of the Virgins. Bantam, 1993.
The Golden Straw. Bantam, 1993.

Justice Is a Woman. Bantam, 1994.
The Obsession. Bantam, 1994.
Heritage of Folly. Bantam, 1995.
Tinker's Girl. Bantam, 1996.

Fiction for Children

Matty Doolin. Macdonald & Co., 1965.
Joe and the Gladiator. Macdonald & Co., 1968.
The Nipper. Bobbs-Merrill, 1970.
Blue Baccy. Macdonald & Jane's, 1972; as *Rory's Fortune,* Macdonald, 1988.
Our John Willie. Morrow, 1974.
Mrs. Flanagan's Trumpet. Macdonald & Jane's, 1977.
Go Tell It to Mrs. Golightly. Macdonald & Jane's, 1977.
Lanky Jones. Lothrop, 1981.
Nancy Nutall and the Mongrel. Macdonald & Jane's, 1982.

Nonfiction

Our Kate: An Autobiography. Macdonald & Co., 1969.
Catherine Cookson Country. Heinemann, 1986.
Let Me Make Myself Plain. Bantam, 1988.

Novels as Catherine Marchant

Heritage of Folly. Macdonald & Co., 1963.
The Fen Tiger. Macdonald & Co., 1963.
House of Men. Macdonald & Co., 1964.
Evil at Roger's Cross. Lancer Books, 1965; revised edition published as *The Iron Facade,* Heinemann, 1976.
Miss Martha Mary Crawford. Heinemann, 1975.
The Slow Awakening. Heinemann, 1976.

* * *

British-born Catherine Cookson is an amazingly prolific romance novelist. She has written under the pseudonym Catherine Marchant, and has penned three different series of books: the Bill Bailey series, Mary Ann series, and the Mallen series. Most of her novels are historical romances and take place in the farming/mining country of 19th century Northumberland.

An early novel, *Colour Blind* (1953), sets the pattern and background Cookson uses in the majority of her romances. The protagonist Bridget McQueen marries a black man, and, later, their daughter suffers at the hands of classmates and a bitter uncle. The portrait of the British working class Cookson offers us in this novel is seen time and time again in successive books. Class tensions, racism, unemployment—her romances always play out against a realistic social background.

In *The Bannaman Legacy* (1985), Cookson makes use of the favored Northumberland setting to weave a tale of immutable passions. The heroine Mary Ellen suffers from an unrequited love for Roddy Greenbank, who, along with best friend Hal, has been victimized by local squire Bannaman. Roddy escapes to London and pursues an art career while Mary Ellen keeps the home fires burning with Hal. Cookson has become an expert at intertwining many plots to keep the reader entertained.

The Black Candle (1989) again brings the period of 19th-century England to life with vivid detail. Heiress Bridget Mourdant manages the family's factory. She shares a mutual attraction with Joe Skinner who suddenly marries a factory girl. The girl carries the illegitimate child of Lionel Filmore which will lead ultimately to a clash between the Skinners and Filmores. Cookson is at her best when she draws out her story against the class tensions of the time. She excels at shaping colorful characters.

In *The Love Child* (1990), Cookson was praised for her complex heroine Anna Dagshaw. An illegitimate child in 1880s England, she is nonetheless well-educated and cared for by her parents who live together even though her father is still married to a wife who will not give him a divorce. She becomes a tutor to the son of unhappily married Simon and Penella Brodrick. Will she repeat the actions of her mother? Cookson does a fine job detailing Anna's maturation and exploring the moral and social issues of the time.

The trilogy detailing the Mallen family saga begins with *The Mallen Streak* (1973), continues with *The Mallen Girl* (1974), and ends with *The Mallen Lot* (1974). Once again the setting is 19th-century Northumberland. The affairs of the family are played out against a backdrop where the sins of the past continue to haunt the present. At times the mass of events and detail can be too much, but, on the other hand, the series is great escape reading.

This veteran romance writer seems always to hit the mark. Her indomitable heroines may take a lot of hard knocks on their often unconventional way to love and identity, but they always get there.

—Jennifer G. Coman

COONTS, Stephen (Paul)

Nationality: American. **Born:** 19 July 1946, in Morgantown, West Virginia. **Education:** West Virginia University, A.B., 1968; University of Colorado, J.D., 1979. **Military Service:** U.S. Navy, 1968-77, served as aviator in Vietnam, 1971-73; became lieutenant; received Distinguished Flying Cross. **Family:** Married Nancy Quereau, 1971 (divorced, 1984); children: Rachael, Lara, David. **Career:** Cab driver and police officer, 1977-81; Petro-Lewis Corporation (oil and gas company), Denver, Colorado, in-house counsel, 1981-86; full-time writer since 1986. **Awards:** Author award of merit, U.S. Naval Institute, 1986, for *Flight of the Intruder.* **Agent:** Robert Gottlieb, William Morris Agency, 1350 Avenue of the Americas, New York, New York 10019.

Publications

Novels

Flight of the Intruder. U.S. Naval Institute Press, 1986.
Final Flight. Doubleday, 1988.
The Minotaur. Doubleday, 1989.
Under Siege. Pocket Books, 1990.
The Red Horseman. Pocket Books, 1993.
The Intruders. Pocket Books, 1994.

Nonfiction

The Cannibal Queen: An Aerial Odyssey Across America. Pocket Books, 1992.

*

Film Adaptations: *Flight of the Intruder,* 1991; *Under Seige,* 1994.

* * *

Former Navy flyer and bestselling novelist Stephen Coonts relies heavily on his career experiences for the subject matter in his books. Despite mixed reviews, he has amassed a considerable and loyal following since the publication of his first book, *Flight of the Intruder,* in 1986. *Flight,* as well as Coonts' *Under Siege* (1990), were adapted to the screen. Coonts has also penned a nonfiction book, *The Cannibal Queen: An Aerial Odyssey Across America* (1992).

In *Flight of the Intruder,* Coonts details events in the life of A-6 Intruder pilot Jake Grafton, who flies a bomber past enemy flak and surface-to-air missiles in North Vietnam. He then must maneuver the plane at night onto the small deck of an aircraft carrier. He becomes disillusioned after countless raids on seemingly meaningless targets. After his best friend is killed by a random bullet, Grafton plans an unauthorized, solo raid on the Communist Party Headquarters in downtown Hanoi. Critics praised Coonts' excellent depiction of the nerve-wracking aspects of modern air raids. On the ground, however, Coonts seems to be out of his element. M.S. Kaplan nevertheless described the book as a "thrill-a-minute joy ride."

The second installment, *Final Flight* (1988), finds Jake commanding the air wing of a carrier after his failing eyesight precludes any night flying. In Naples, an Arab plot, masterminded by one Colonel Qazi, is detailed which consists of trying to steal the ship's nuclear weapons. Coonts was once again lauded for his well-detailed lives of Navy pilots. The dialogue may be stilted at times, but the plot is riveting.

Jake Grafton returns in *The Minotaur* (1989). This time he is in charge of developing a new tactical aircraft, the Minotaur, which depends on a variation of Stealth technology. He also must track down an information leak at the highest levels of the Defense Department. The book is especially compelling when Coonts looks into the inefficiency and thievery of government military contracts and the pork barrel philosophy of United States senators. The only place this techno-thriller gets bogged down is when Coonts moves into the domestic realm.

Better received was *Under Siege* (1990). The setting is modern-day Washington D.C., where a Colombian drug lord brought there for trial sends killer squads to terrorize the city with a series of mass murders. In addition, a shadowy assassin is running around stalking top officials. The reader is offered a well-drawn, if stereotypical, cast that includes George Bush and Dan Quayle. Jake Grafton is joined in this sprawling plot by journalist Jack Yocke and undercover narcotics officer Harrison Ronald Ford. Coonts may see his world in absolutes, but his gripping portrait of the United States' vulnerability to corruption demands attention.

Coonts' adventure fiction continues with *The Red Horseman* (1993). Jake Grafton is now a rear admiral and deputy director of the Defense Intelligence Agency (DIA). Jake learns that Jewish media big wheel Nigel Keren was poisoned by the CIA. Grafton and sidekick "Toad" Tarkington are threatened with similar fates after discovering, right before a mission to Moscow to oversee the dismantling of their nuclear arsenal, that the DIA offices are bugged. The action, staged on three continents, was heralded by one critic as "one of the most compelling post-glasnost thrillers to date."

More recently, *The Intruders* (1994) picks up Jake Grafton in 1973, right after *Flight of the Intruder.* It has been widely criticized as the weakest in the series. The novel seems to be made up of a hodgepodge of flight scenes which Coonts wasn't able to fit into any of his previous novels.

—Jennifer G. Coman

CORNWELL, Bernard

Pseudonym: Susannah Kells. **Nationality:** British. **Born:** London, 23 February 1944. **Education:** University of London, B.A. 1967. **Family:** Married Judy Acker in 1980. **Career:** Producer, London, 1969-76, and head of current affairs, Belfast, 1976-79, BBC Television; news editor, Thames Television, London, 1979-80.**Agent:** Toby Eady, Toby Eady Associates Ltd, 7 Gledhow Gardens, London SW5 0BL, England.

PUBLICATIONS

Novels (series: Richard Sharpe)

Sharpe's Eagle. London, Collins, and New York, Viking Press, 1981.
Sharpe's Gold. London, Collins, 1981; New York, Viking Press, 1982.
Sharpe's Company. London, Collins, and New York, Viking Press, 1982.
Sharpe's Sword. London, Collins, and New York, Viking Press, 1983.
Sharpe's Enemy. London, Collins, and New York, Viking, 1984.
Sharpe's Honour. London, Collins, and New York, Viking, 1985.
Sharpe's Regiment. London, Collins, and New York, Viking, 1986.
Sharpe's Siege. London, Collins, and New York, Viking, 1987.
Redcoat. London, Joseph, 1987; New York, Viking, 1988.
Sharpe's Rifles. London, Collins, and New York, Viking, 1988.
Wildtrack. London, Joseph, and New York, Putnam, 1988.
Killer's Wake. New York, Putnam, 1989.
Sea Lord. London, Joseph, and New York, Putnam, 1989.
Sharpe's Revenge. London, Collins, and New York, Viking, 1989.
Sharpe's Waterloo. London, Collins, and New York, Viking, 1990.
Crackdown. New York, HarperCollins, 1990; London, Joseph, 1991.
Sharpe's Devil. London and New York, HarperCollins, 1992.
Stormchild. London, Joseph, 1991; New York, HarperCollins, 1992.
Scoundrel. London, Joseph, 1992.
Rebel. London, HarperCollins, 1993.
Copperhead. London, HarperCollins, 1993.
Battle Flag. London, Harpercollins, 1995.
Sharpe's Battle. London, Harpercollins, 1995.
Winter King. London, Harpercollins, 1995.
The Bloody Ground. London, Harpercollins, 1996.

Novels as Susannah Kells (series: Campion)

A Crowning Mercy. London, Collins, 1983.
The Fallen Angels. London, Collins, 1984.
Coat of Arms (based on an idea by Richard Gregson). London, Collins, 1986.

*

Film Adaptations: *Sharpe*, 1993, based on several of the Sharpe books; *Sharpe's Rifles*, 1993.

* * *

One of the best historical action writers around, Bernard Cornwell came to fame with the Sharpe novels, which follow Richard Sharpe, a British officer in the 95th Rifles, through the Napoleonic Wars from Corunna to Waterloo. In the grim, scarred rifleman Sharpe and his giant Irish comrade Patrick Harper, Cornwell created heroes to rank with C.S. Forester's Hornblower or Private Matthew Dodd in *Death to the French.* His readers go with them and their green-jacketed "Chosen Men" through 100 vicious fights against the French Grande Armee, wielding their deadly Baker rifles under Lord Wellington's command.

Sharpe's Eagle (1981) describes the capture of a French battle standard at Talavera, while in *Sharpe's Gold* (1981) they take part in the sack of the citadel at Almeida. In *Sharpe's Revenge* (1989) the plundering of the Emperor's baggage train after Victoria provides the action. Each battle is matched with a struggle to outwit an individual enemy who seeks Sharpe's destruction—the psychotic Sergeant Hakesweill, the crazed bandit El Catolico, the beautiful but faithless Marquesa, and the French spy Major Ducos. Cornwell's masterly description of the horrors of siege warfare at the storm of Badajoz (*Sharpe's Siege,* 1987) and Toulouse (*Sharpe's Revenge,* 1989) are topped by a mind-blowing picture of the final, clinching victory over Napoleon in *Sharpe's Waterloo* (1990). Away from the battlefield he shows his knowledge of the period in both *Sharpe's Regiment* (1986), with its telling account of army corruption and the squalid poverty of London's "rookeries," and *Sharpe's Devil* (1993), where Sharpe and Harper meet the exiled Napoleon en route to South America. His latest book in the series, *Sharpe's Battle* (1995), goes back in time to the campaign of Fuentes d'Onoro in Spain, and rates with his best. Strong in characters, plotlines, and action, the Sharpe series is the core of Cornwell's work and has assured his reputation.

Unwilling to be typecast, Cornwell has been quick to explore other historical fields. Written under the pseudonym "Susannah Kells," his *Crowning Mercy* (1983) and *The Fallen Angels* (1984) are strong, fast-paced adventure stories set in the British Civil War and the French Revolution. *Coat of Arms* (1986), which deals with the efforts of British aristocrats to save their stately home after WWII, lacks the bite of the two earlier books. *Redcoat* (1987, under Cornwell's own name), takes place in Philadelphia in 1777-1778. It describes the Revolutionary conflict through the eyes of a disillusioned British soldier. An excellent historical novel, it is perhaps his best "one-off" work.

Aside from historical novels, Cornwell has written several modern adventure stories. *Wildtrack* (1988), *Sea Lord* (1989), *Killer's Wake* (1989), *Crackdown* (1990), *Stormchild* (1991), *Scoundrel* (1992) and *Eye of the Sea* (1994) are usually set aboard ship, and feature seaborne battles with various terrorist organizations. As action novels they are exciting and well-crafted, but short of his very best fiction.

History has always been Cornwell's strength, and the 1990s have seen him hard at work on two new series. The Starbuck Chronicles have the American Civil War as their background. They focus on Nathaniel Starbuck, a former theology student and the son of an anti-slavery preacher, who finds himself fighting on the side of the Confederates. In the four books of the series—*Rebel* (1993), *Copperhead* (1994), *Battle Flag* (1995), and *The Bloody Ground* (1996)—Cornwell traces the adventures of Starbuck and his comrades of the Faulconer Legion of Virginia from Bull Run to the desperate defense of Richmond. Again, the various campaigns involve Starbuck in deadly encounters with his personal enemies.

The Winter King (1995), first of The Warlord Chronicles, plunges even further back in time to the Dark Age world of Arthur. Action is viewed through the eyes of the warrior Derfel, who serves with Arthur in his struggle against the Saxons and rival British warlords to bring order to the realm. Here, as in the Sharpe and Starbuck novels, Cornwell enters a vanished world and hauls the reader along, pitching him or her headfirst into the fearful scenery of war. Starbuck and Warlord rank with Sharpe as the best of his writing so far.

—Geoff Sadler

CORNWELL, David John. *See* **Le CARRE, John.**

CORNWELL, Patricia Daniels

Nationality: American. **Born:** 9 June 1956, in Portland, Maine. **Education:** Davidson College, B.A., 1979. **Family:** Married Charles Cornwell, 1980 (divorced 1990). **Career:** *Charlotte Observer,* Charlotte, North Carolina, police reporter, 1979-81; Office of the Chief Medical Examiner, Richmond, Virginia, computer analyst, from 1985. Volunteer police officer. **Awards:** Investigative reporting award, North Carolina Press Association, 1980, for a series on prostitution; Gold Medallion Book award for biography, Evangelical Christian Publishers Association, 1985, for *A Time for Remembering*; John Greasy award and Edgar award, best first crime novel, both 1990, for *Postmortem;* Anthony award finalist, best first crime novel, 1990, for *Postmortem;* British Crime Writers Gold Dagger award, 1994. **Member:** Authors Guild, International Crime Writers Association, Mystery Writers of America, National Association of Medical Examiners, Virginia Writers Club. **Agent:** International Creative Management, 40 W. 57th St., New York, New York 10019. **Address:** Cornwell Enterprises, P.O. Box 35686, Richmond, Virginia 23235, U.S.A.

Publications

Novels

Postmortem. New York, Scribner and London, Macdonald 1990.
Body of Evidence. New York, Scribner and London, Macdonald, 1991.
All that Remains. New York, Scribner and London, Little, Brown, 1992.
Cruel & Unusual. New York, Scribner and London, Little, Brown, 1993.
The Body Farm. New York, Scribner and London, Little, Brown, 1994.
From Potter's Field. New York, Simon & Schuster, and London, Little Brown, 1995.
Cause of Death. New York, Putnam, and London, Little Brown, 1996.

Nonfiction

A Time for Remembering (with Charles Cornwell). New York, Harper, 1983.

* * *

Patricia D. Cornwell served as an award-winning crime reporter for the Charlotte *Observer,* then for six years as a volunteer police officer, technical writer, and computer analyst in the chief medical examiner's office. Finally, before taking up fiction writing, she worked as a consultant to the Richmond, Virginia chief medical examiner. Those experiences prepared her for writing highly technical crime novels set in Richmond, which has the second highest per capita homicide rate in the United States. Cornwell also coauthored with her (now former) husband *A Time for Remembering* (1983), a biography of evangelist Billy Graham's wife, Ruth Bell Graham.

Like Herbert Liebermann's *City of the Dead* and John Feegel's *Autopsy,* Cornwell's police procedurals focus on medical autopsies and investigations. The inquiries are conducted by Richmond's chief medical examiner Kay Scarpetta, a fortyish divorcee whose tools are forensic medicine and computer programming. Her analyses focus on the mute biological and chemical testimony of the dead—entry wounds, rigor mortis, lividity, discoloration. Cornwell's crime novels are characterized by the hands-on authenticity of their detail and the compelling psychological study of professionals at work.

Cornwell's first crime story, *Postmortem* (1990), was the only novel ever to win the Edgar, Creasey, Anthony, and Macavity awards, and the French Prix du Roman d'Aventure in the same year. In *Postmortem,* Scarpetta identifies a serial rapist and killer and, at the same time, proves she has the stamina and skill to tackle "a man's job." In *All That Remains* (1992), bones, fragments of clothing, and a jack of hearts are the only remains, making a forensic determination of cause of death difficult. An obstructive FBI heightens the frustration. Then, in *Cruel and Unusual* (1993), the execution of a convicted murderer makes a new murder with the same modus operandi a puzzling problem. Scarpetta's cases hinge on such unromantic forms of evidence as DNA tests, trace evidence, gritty residues, unidentifiable marks, unidentifiable odors, strands of fiber, and special types of duct tape.

When Scarpetta takes on her first cases she must accept ribbing from police officers and detectives uncomfortable with and distrustful of a female medical examiner. But her clear competence and good humor, courageous willingness to place her safety on the line, and valued insights into the cases eventually win their respect and, with time, affection. For example, police detective Pete Marino, with whom Scarpetta works in all her novels, evolves from clear distrust to deep-seated affection and an irritating overprotectiveness. Likewise, a former lover from law school days, FBI agent Mark James, becomes involved with Kay and her case in *Body of Evidence* (1991). He finds himself torn between personal commitments and career in *All that Remains,* and dies from a terrorist bomb in *Cruel and Unusual.* Kay goes on to deal with the pain of that traumatic loss in *The Body Farm* (1994), but finds the potential for new love in *From Potter's Field* (1995).

Through Scarpetta, Cornwell brings legal and medical training, committed professionalism, and a sharp mind to bear on ghastly multiple murders. While distancing herself objectively and dispassionately from the blood, gore, violence of the crime scene, and the tortured bodies of victims, Scarpetta remains sensitive to nuances that involve her intellectually and emotionally. The character's sophistication and civility, says Cornwell, make the senseless cruelty she must confront "all the more horrific." Indeed, her scientific logic and psychological analysis are humanized by personal outrage at the physical and psychological violations of murder. Cornwell notes that struggling with the character of Scarpetta helped her understand an irony central to medical examination: "the more expert one gets in dismantling death, the less he understands it."

Scarpetta's life reflects elements of Cornwell's; both are divorced and childless and have Miami origins, a home in Windsor Farms, an interest in Malibu, professional curiosity, and hard-headed determination. In addition to technical detail, Cornwell's novels include well-plotted narratives, a likable, competent female detective, an unusual perspective, and expert knowledge.

—Gina Macdonald

COUPLAND, Douglas

Nationality: Canadian. **Born:** 30 December 1961, on a Canadian military base in Baden-Sollingen, Germany. **Education:** Emily Carr College of Art and Design, Vancouver, Canada, c. 1984. Completed a two-year course in Japanese business science, Hawaii, 1986. **Address:** c/o Pocket Books, 1230 Ave. of the Americas, New York, New York 10020, U.S.A.

Publications

Novels

Generation X: Tales for an Accelerated Culture. St. Martin's Press, 1991.
Shampoo Planet. Pocket Books, 1992.
Life after God. Pocket Books, 1994.
Microserfs. Pocket Books, 1995.
Polaroids from the Dead. Pocket Books, 1996.

* * *

At the age of 30 Douglas Coupland became the unofficial spokesman for those born between the early 1960s and 1970s, a generation whose label was coined from the title of his first novel, *Generation X* (1991). The scant plot of *Generation X* frames a collection of stories exchanged among three friends—Dag, Andy, and Claire—who have fled society to hang out in Palm Springs. With cartoons along the text margins, countless references to pop culture, and witty neologisms, Coupland gives the reader terse, bitter, and pointed observations of the world of the "twentysomething" generation. He shows us North American kids at the end of the century already world-weary in their dysfunctional culture. They attempt to overcome the lack of meaning in their lives through the trading of stories. The irony comes into play here when the characters' lives are examined. These are people without stories, for they know the endings already by looking at their parents' generation. As John Leland wrote of Generation Xers, "We're alienated from our own alienation."

His second novel, *Shampoo Planet* (1992), again illustrated Coupland's knack for exploring the minds and culture of the cynical young with humor and affection. The narrator Tyler Johnson, a yuppie wanna-be, must learn to balance his concerns with those of his hippie mother Jasmine. Coupland sketches a great assortment of oddball characters in a portrait poised between the idealism of the 1960s and the materialism of the 1980s. These young people are at ease with the apocalypse, laughing at disaster. *Shampoo Planet* was praised as highly entertaining and convincing with an optimism that *Generation X* lacked. Coupland with humor and poignancy evokes the hopes and desires of a generation maturing in a culture of constant change and instant gratification.

His third book, *Life After God* (1994), consists of eight linked sections throughout which the narrator worries about aging and dying. The overall theme of the stories is that of a generation raised on mass culture who end up regarding everything ironically and apathetically. The narrator searches for meaning and spirituality in a society where the prominence of perception has eroded truth into insignificance. This collection of stories was not as critically well-received as his previous works, derided for pretension and a lack of range in character. *Publishers Weekly* pronounced, "they succeed less as an allegory for a postmodern, postironic spiritual life than as an amusing travelogue for jaded, pop-culturally literate couch potatoes."

Coupland's 1995 novel, *Microserfs,* focuses on the lives of young people in a downsizing economy. The narrative follows a group of computer techs who escape Microsoft to found their own multimedia company. The novel is told through the online journal of 26-year-old Daniel Underwood. Using a disjointed style to underline the physical and social alienation of this particular subculture, Coupland sketches a world where the spiritual waits just beyond perception. Praised for his keen observations and witty commentary on mass culture, Coupland was again criticized for characters who come off more as caricatures and who all by novel's end find themselves, fall in love, and bond with their families. The happy endings do not fit with the landscape of angst captured in the novel.

Jay McInerney's description of Coupland sums his work up best. He termed him "slacker sociologist, nonlinear storyteller and pop culture taxonomist." Coupland is uncanny at tapping into the zeitgeist before anyone else. He has brought to life in his fiction a generation who had been previously undefined. Ironically enough, the so-called Generation Xers would have preferred to remain undefined. At the least, though, Coupland's perception of the ennui-ridden generation is perceptively written. It is at times hilarious, at times touching.

—Jennifer G. Coman

COURTENAY, Bryce

Nationality: Australian. **Born:** August 14, 1933, in Redlands, California. **Education:** Attended King's College, 1946. **Family:** Married; three sons (one deceased). **Career:** McCann-Erickson (advertising agency), Sydney, Australia, advertising writer, 1956-66, board member, 1959-66, creative director and southeast Asia chair, 1960-66; J. Walter Thompson Advertising Agency, Sydney, creative director and southeast Asia chair, 1966-71; Courtenay Beirnstein, partner, 1971-76; Harrison, Robinson & Courtenay Ltd. (advertising agency) founder, 1976-87; writer. **Awards:** Hatchard award for best new writer (Great Britain), 1990; Gold award, New York Film Festival, for *The Eleven Powers.* **Address:** c/o 2/29 Benelong Crescent, Bellevue Hill, New South Wales, 2023 Australia.

PUBLICATIONS

Novels

The Power of One. New York, Random House, 1989.
Tandia. London, Heinemann, 1990.

Nonfiction

The Pitch. Gee, 1992.

Film

The Eleven Powers. Frank Heimens, 1986.

*

Media Adaptations: *The Power of One,* Warner Brothers, 1992.

* * *

In just over five years, South African born-and-bred Bryce Courtenay has gone from being a leading but hardly prominent advertising executive to Australia's bestselling author. His first novel, *The Power of One* (1989), earned him a previously unheard of advance of $1 million, which was justified by huge sales in England, South Africa, and Australia, where it remained at or near the top of the bestselling list for several years. Courtenay followed that success with a sequel, *Tandia* (1990), and more recently *The Potato Factory,* which tells the story of early convicts' voyages to Australia. Courtenay also penned two nonfiction works, including the autobiographical *April Fools' Day,* a moving account of the death of his son, a hemophiliac who became infected with AIDS.

Although it deals with racial oppression in South Africa in the 1940s with considerable realism and knowledge, *The Power of One* is a feel-good novel. The title refers to the power of each individual, no matter how tiny, to shape and control his destiny, though in this novel it is a power not given to blacks. At the age of five, white, English-speaking Peekay (as he comes to be called) is parted from his demented mother and affectionate black nanny and placed in a school peopled by Boers. He is tormented there by the other students but slowly learns how to protect himself. Peekay confronts a series of bullies—brutal boxing opponents much larger than himself, and equally brutal policemen—but also profits from a succession of older mentors, including an aging rooster named Grandpa Chook; wise Zulu medicine man Inkosi-Inkosikazi who inspires him with a vision; a boxer called Hoppie Groenewald who gives him a key piece of advice ('First with the head, and then with the heart'); a colored prisoner Geel Piet who coaches him in boxing; a German scholar whom he calls simply Doc; and his best friend Hymie Levy, who eventually helps him reach his lifelong ambition to win the world welterweight championship.

Peekay is, in fact, a prodigy. He refuses to cry no matter what ignominy he suffers, and before he has even turned ten years old he is an expert on a wide-ranging series of subjects ranging from chess and mathematics to language, music, and botany. He wins every fight he enters and by the end of the novel has assumed mystic powers in the eyes of the black South Africans; he is the legendary Tadpole Angel, a slayer of giants who will lead them out of their misery—"the spirit of the great chief who bound Zulu with the Swazi and the Ndebele and the Tsonga and the Sotho."

Although *The Power of One* graphically depicts the violence and racism that permeated South African society, its successor, *Tandia,* is an altogether darker and more somber novel, and one much more explicitly concerned with sexual and racial violence. It opens arrestingly: "On the morning she was raped Tandia had risen just before dawn and come back to the graveside to pay her proper respects to Patel." Nine hundred pages later Tandia finally escapes a South Africa that has increasingly formalized apartheid as an institution. She comes to terms with her feelings about both whites and men sufficiently to acknowledge, belatedly, her love for Peekay. The novel follows their attempt to resist the evils of apartheid—there is a detailed description of the Sharpeville massacre of 1962—and increasing realization of the futility of peaceful opposition. Like Peekay, Tandia is an exceptional person, a woman of breathtaking beauty, immense courage, and scintillating intelligence. But the odds against her succeeding are even greater than those that confronted Peekay, and *Tandia* ends in relative despair with the eponymous heroine fleeing over the border.

In *The Potato Factory,* Courtenay takes the real life figure of Ikey Solomon (perhaps the most notorious criminal of his time and perhaps also the model for Dickens' Fagin) and his mistress Mary Abacus, and follows them both to Australia. The novel is the first part of a trilogy that will take the reader up to the present. It is a lively mess of a novel, laced with a kind of pseudo-19th century argot, piled up with incident upon incident, and liberally splashed with samples from Courtenay's effusive, laissez-faire liberalism and bon mots on the human condition: "If there be a Hell then eternal fire would come but a poor second to an eternity filled with complete solitude, for humans are gregarious creatures, in the main, and not designed to be alone."

—Bryce Courteney

CRICHTON, (John) Michael

Pseudonyms: John Lange; Jeffery Hudson; Michael Douglas. **Nationality:** American. **Born:** 23 October 1942. **Education:** Harvard University, Cambridge, Massachusetts, A.B.(summa cum laude) 1964 (Phi Beta Kappa); Harvard Medical School, M.D. 1969; Salk Institute, La Jolla, California (postdoctoral fellow), 1969-70. **Family:** Married 1) Joan Radam in 1965 (divorced 1971); 2) Kathleen St. Johns in 1978 (divorced 1980); 3) Suzanne Childs (divorced); 4) Anne-Marie Martin in 1987, one daughter. **Career:** Visiting writer, Massachusetts Institute of Technology, Cambridge, 1988. **Awards:** Mystery Writers of America Edgar Allan Poe award, 1968, for *A Case of Need,* and 1980, for *The Great Train Robbery;* Association of American Medical Writers award, 1970, for *Five Patients: The Hospital Explained.* **Agent:** International Creative Management, 40 West 57th Street, New York, New York 10019, U.S.A.

Publications

Novels

A Case of Need (as Jeffery Hudson). Cleveland, World, and London, Heinemann, 1968.
The Andromeda Strain. New York, Knopf, and London, Cape, 1969.
Dealing; or, The Berkeley-to-Boston Forty-Brick Lost-Bag Blues (as Michael Douglas), with Douglas Crichton. New York, Knopf, 1971.
The Terminal Man. New York, Knopf, and London, Cape, 1972.
Westworld. New York, Bantam, 1974.
The Great Train Robbery. New York, Knopf, and London, Cape, 1975.
Eaters of the Dead: The Manuscript of Ibn Fadlan, Relating His Experiences with the Northmen in A.D. 922. New York, Knopf, and London, Cape, 1976.
Congo. New York, Knopf, 1980; London, Allen Lane, 1981.
Sphere. New York, Knopf, and London, Macmillan, 1987.
Jurassic Park. New York, Knopf, 1990; London, Century, 1991.
Rising Sun. New York, Knopf, and London, Century, 1992.
Disclosure. New York, Knopf, 1994.
The Lost World. New York, Knopf, 1995.

Novels as John Lange

Odds On. New York, New American Library, 1966.
Scratch One. New York, New American Library, 1967.
Easy Go. New York, New American Library, 1968; London, Sphere, 1972; as *The Last Tomb* (as Michael Crichton), New York, Bantam, 1974.
The Venom Business. Cleveland, World, 1969.
Zero Cool. New York, New American Library, 1969; London, Sphere, 1972.
Drug of Choice. New York, New American Library, 1970; as *Overkill,* New York, Centesis, 1970.
Grave Descend. New York, New American Library, 1970.
Binary. New York, Knopf, and London, Heinemann, 1972.

Plays

Screenplays: *Westworld,* 1973; *Coma,* 1977; *The Great Train Robbery,* 1978; *Looker,* 1981; *Runaway,* 1984; *Jurassic Park,* with John Koepp, 1993; *Rising Sun,* with Philip Kaufman and Michael Backes, 1993.

Other

Five Patients: The Hospital Explained. New York, Knopf, 1970; London, Cape, 1971.
Jasper Johns. New York, Abrams, and London, Thames and Hudson, 1977.
Electronic Life: How to Think about Computers. New York, Knopf, and London, Heinemann, 1983.
Travels. New York, Knopf, and London, Macmillan, 1988.

*

Film Adaptations: *The Andromeda Strain,* 1971; *The Carey Treatment,* 1973, from the work *A Case of Need; Westworld,* 1973; *The Terminal Man,* 1974; *The Great Train Robbery,* 1978; *Jurassic Park,* 1993; *Rising Sun,* 1993; *Disclosure,* 1994.

Theatrical Activities:

Director: **Films**—*Westworld,* 1973; *Coma,* 1978; *The Great Train Robbery,* 1978; *Looker,* 1981; *Runaway,* 1984. **Television**—*Pursuit,* 1972; *E.R.* (executive producer), 1994.

* * *

Chicago-born John Michael Crichton began writing paperback thrillers on weekends to put himself through Harvard Medical School. After he completed his MD in 1969 and had worked for the respected Salk Institute for Biological Studies for a year, he decided to write full-time (his autobiography describes hospitals as Dantesque infernos). His fictional medical mystery *A Case of Need* (1968) won him the Mystery Writers of America Edgar Award, as did *The Great Train Robbery* (1979); his nonfiction study about psychological qualities as causes of disease, *Five Patients: A Hospital Explained* (1970), won him the Association of American Medical Writers Writer of the Year award in 1970. His medical training brings solid scientific knowledge to his novels, precise technical detail, and a curiosity about biological possibilities; his interest in cultural diversity, for example, raises questions of cross-cultural encounters and ethnocentricity.

Crichton's works are intelligent and informed. They explore issues of ethics, scientific challenge, and responsibility while providing fast-paced adventure and genuine intellectual puzzles. His stories' cinematic quality is influenced by Crichton's other career as a movie director, and their exotic settings were inspired by his travels.

Crichton's initial thrillers, from *Odds On* (1966) to *Grave Descend* (1970), were Ian Fleming imitations written under the pseudonym John Lange, but they provided him the apprenticeship needed to attain the mastery demonstrated in his later books.

In the 1970s Crichton began writing "techno-thrillers," novels that blend technology, suspense, and controversial social issues. Set in contemporary society, Crichton's science fiction plots twist in unexpected directions. In *The Andromeda Strain* (1969), for instance, a satellite returning to earth from the upper atmosphere brings back a mutating micro-organism that wipes out all but two inhabitants of a nearby town; scientists, fearing the threat to all humanity, must act as medical detectives and discover the common biological or chemical factor that has saved a crying infant and the town drunk—when science fails, intuition prevails. Similarly, in *Binary* (1971), a plot to assassinate the President (and most of San Diego along with him) turns on a psychopath's computer skills as he decodes a locked computer code and acquires privileged information about deadly nerve gas shipments. In *The Terminal Man* (1972), an epileptic who believes machines are taking over the world becomes a living bomb when a miniaturized computer and its atomic power pack, implanted under his skin to control his seizures, threaten to rupture because of his biofeedback responses to this experimental treatment.

Sphere (1987) begins with the discovery of a giant spaceship submerged for over 300 years. It reflects Crichton's interest in psychic experiences, in this case the imaginary made real through contact with the alien spheres. *Jurassic Park* (1988) postulates a combination of gene splicing, DNA experiments, computer enhancement allowing the controlled production of dinosaurs from genetic material preserved in amber, and scientific arrogance in the face of natural mutation and adaptation endangering our species. The power of these works derives from convincing technical detail, appropriate scientific jargon, and threats credible enough to fall within the realm of modern possibility. Crichton's style is lean, detached, and clinical. His characters are intelligent and quirky, and his plots are fast-paced and captivating. Crichton's scientific interests are reflected by the screenplays that he chose to write or direct, which include the 1978 film *Coma,* about the harvesting of organs for transplant from doctor-induced coma victims, and the successful television series, *ER,* which debuted in 1994.

Crichton's detective novels all contain convincing detail, credible motivations, and engaging conflicts, but differ in the type of detection. In *A Case of Need* 1968, for example, a doctor turns amateur detective to save a friend, while in *The Great Train Robbery* a clever, likable Victorian criminal outwits the police and the self-righteous hypocrites whom they represent, pulls off a challenging gold heist, and triumphs despite adversity. In the police-procedural *Rising Sun,* Los Angeles detectives with international experience must deal with Japanese inscrutability and hi-tech electronics. They work within an alien social system and solve the murder of an expensive prostitute in the board room of an important Japanese company. *Disclosure* (1994) poses questions about sexual harassment and political correctness, and demonstrates that men and women can be ruthless equals in the workplace; in this crime story, who did it is not as important as proving the truth to prejudiced disbelievers whose ranks are closed by the power structure. Ultimately, it takes a good lawyer and the victim's abilities on the cutting-edge of cyberspace technology to bring justice.

The adventure novels *Eaters of the Dead* (1976) and *Congo* (1981) both postulate a lost and vicious civilization, the former an early evolutionary desert people (possibly Neanderthals) encountered by Vikings, and jungle Gorillas in the latter. Both are basically 19th-century-style adventure stories influenced by Crichton's travels and his experiences with mountain climbing and gorillas. His villains are human greed, indifference to others, and pride in one's own culture and achievements.

—Gina Macdonald

CROSS, Amanda

Pseudonym for Carolyn G(old) Heilbrun. **Nationality:** American. **Born:** East Orange, New Jersey, 13 January 1926. **Education:** Wellesley College, Massachusetts, B.A. 1947 (Phi Beta Kappa); Columbia University, New York, M.A. 1951, Ph.D. in English 1959. **Family:** Married James Heilbrun in 1945; two daughters and one son. **Career:** Instructor, Brooklyn College, 1959-60. Instructor, 1960-62, Assistant Professor, 1962-67, and since 1972, Professor of English, and since 1986 Avalon Foundation Professor of Humanities; Columbia University. Visiting Lecturer, Union Theological Seminary, New York, 1968-70, Swarthmore College, Pennsylvania, 1970, Yale University, New Haven, Connecticut, 1974, University of California, Santa Cruz, 1979, and Princeton University, New Jersey, 1982. Since 1985 coeditor, Gender and Culture series, Columbia University Press. **Member:** Modern Language Association (president, 1984). **Awards:** Guggenheim Fellowship, 1965; Rockefeller Fellowship, 1976; Radcliffe Institute Fellowship, 1976; Nero Wolfe award, 1981; National Endowment for the Humanities Fellowship, 1983; D.H.L.: University of Pennsylvania, 1984; Bucknell University, 1985; Russell Sage College, 1987; Smith College, 1989; D.F.A.: Rivier College, 1986. **Agent:** Ellen Levine Literary Agency, 432 Park Avenue South, Suite 1205, New York, New York 10016. **Address:** 615 Philosophy Hall, Columbia University, New York, New York 10027, U.S.A.

Publications

Novels (series: Professor Kate Fansler in all books)

In the Last Analysis. New York, Macmillan, and London, Gollancz, 1964.
The James Joyce Murder. New York, Macmillan, and London, Gollancz, 1967.
Poetic Justice. New York, Knopf, and London, Gollancz, 1970.
The Theban Mysteries. New York, Knopf, 1971; London, Gollancz, 1972.
The Question of Max. New York, Knopf, and London, Gollancz, 1976.
Death in a Tenured Position. New York, Dutton, 1981; as *A Death in the Faculty,* London, Gollancz, 1981.
Sweet Death, Kind Death. New York, Dutton, and London, Gollancz, 1984.
No Word from Winifred. New York, Dutton, 1986; London, Virago Press, 1987.
A Trap for Fools. New York, Dutton, 1989; London, Virago Press, 1990.
The Players Come Again. New York, Random House, 1990; London, Virago Press, 1991.
An Imperfect Spy. New York, Random House, and London, Virago Press, 1995.

Publications as Carolyn G. Heilbrun

The Garnett Family. New York, Macmillan, and London, Allen and Unwin, 1961.
Christopher Isherwood. New York, Columbia University Press, 1970.
Towards a Recognition of Androgyny: Aspects of Male and Female in Literature. New York, Harper, 1973; as *Towards Androgyny,* London, Gollancz, 1973.
Reinventing Womanhood. New York, Norton, and London, Gollancz, 1979.
Writing a Woman's Life. New York, Norton, 1988; London, Virgo Press, 1989.
Hamlet's Mother and Other Women. New York, Columbia University Press, 1990.

Editor, *Lady Ottoline's Album.* New York, Knopf, 1976; London, Joseph, 1977.
Editor, with Margaret R. Higonnet, *The Representation of Women in Fiction,* Baltimore, John Hopkins University Press, 1983.

*

Manuscript Collection: Smith College, Northampton, Massachusetts.

* * *

As Amanda Cross, Columbia University professor emerita Carolyn Heilbrun has so far written 11 mystery novels that feature a professor/detective named Kate Fansler and her lawyer-husband Reed Amhearst. All her novels are short (seldom more than 200 to 250 pages) and are written in a very plain, almost simple style, yet are exceedingly complex and comprehensive in their range and plots.

There are two basic kinds of mystery novels written in the United States—the so-called hardboiled sort, which was established by Raymond Chandler and is currently represented by such writers as Elmore Leonard, Sarah Paretsky, Patricia Cornwell, and the "police" novelists. The other kind, in which the emphasis is not on violent, crime-ridden streets or serial killers, is represented by such American writers as Elizabeth Peters and Martha Grimes. Cross falls into neither category. There is nothing the least bit hardboiled about her professor/detective Kate Fansler (an English professor at Columbia University) or even about her lover, then husband, the lawyer/district attorney Reed Amhearst. Nor are these characters cute and funky like the array of individuals who populate every Grimes novel (Lord Ardry, his American Aunt Agatha, Marshall Trueblood, Vivian Rivington, and even the Scotland Yard detective, inspector Richard Jury). Kate and Reed, from their very first appearance in a Cross novel to the most recent (where they are married), are literate, well-read, worldly, and sophisticated people whose ongoing relationship develops in interesting ways from novel to novel.

As might be expected, given Cross's academic background, her novels are replete with literary references. An early mystery, *The James Joyce Murder* (1969), has chapters titled throughout after the names of the stories in Joyce's *Dubliners.* And in *An Imperfect Spy* (1955), each chapter has an epigraph from one of the novels of John le Carré, and more often than not from *Smiley's People,* her favorite le Carré book. Even the title of that novel is a take-off on le Carré's *A Perfect Spy.* Her subjects tend to be somewhat literary and/or academic as well. At the very beginning of *The Players Come Again* (1990), for example, Cross says of Kate Fansler, with considerable irony, that, having finished a book of literary criticism, she came to "the realization that she never again wished to publish" that sort of work again.

Nor was she (Fansler) interested in writing memoirs: "Many women and men she knew had abandoned criticism for examination of their personal lives and experience, and while she compulsively read the products of their examinations with interest and occasionally startled recognition, she had no desire or inclination to go and do likewise. Excluded alike from literary studies and memoirs, she wondered if another project would ever occur to her." What the mystery genre allows Cross to do, however, is to voice all sorts of opinions—some of them outrageous, some politically incorrect—on all manner of subjects like the academy itself, the legal profession, literary criticism, current fads in biography writing, and feminism without having to use the single, "true" voice of the memoirist.

Being a "detective" for Fansler, as she says somewhere, is definitely an amateur endeavor. She lets her "cases" come to her in the context of her regular academic profession and does not have to hang her shingle out anywhere. All of this comes together beautifully in her more recent novel, *An Imperfect Spy.* Although there *is* a mysterious death in this book and one that Fansler at first takes to be a probable murder, no murder of any sort actually takes place in the immediate foreground of the novel, which in that sense could then be called an "anti-mystery." Kate is drawn into the "case" by a woman known to her only as "Harriet," who works as a supervisor of secretaries at Schuyler Law School; Schuyler is a minor college much like the John Jay School of Criminal Justice or the Cooper Union for the Advancement of Art and Science, where her husband, Reed, is now a professor and where Kate herself agreed to team-teach a course in Literature and the Law with a regular faculty member named Blair Whitson.

Harriet deliberately models herself after George Smiley, especially in *Smiley's People.* She appears mysteriously at a high school reunion where Kate is giving a speech, later at Kate and Reed's apartment, and still later at a party given at Schuyler Law. Eventually she entices Reed, through Kate, to take up and reopen the case of a woman incarcerated for having killed her abusive husband, a Schuyler Law professor who turns out to be Harriet's estranged daughter.

What is so intriguing about this novel is that it permits Cross to express and develop views on such subjects as the male dominance of colleges and universities, token feminism in such schools, Fansler's marriage to Reed Amhearst (which is very much in a dry period at the beginning of this novel), the politics of sex, and so forth. Most interesting of all, however, is the character of Harriet herself and what it demonstrates about a very atypical view of manipulation as a positive activity.

Unlike many, many "throwaway" mysteries, Cross's bear rereading many times.

—C. W. Truesdale

CUNNINGHAM, E. V. *See* **FAST, Howard (Melvin).**

CUSSLER, Clive (Eric)

Nationality: American. **Born:** 15 July 1931, in Aurora, Illinois. **Education:** Attended Pasadena City College, 1949-1951, Orange Coast College, and California State University, Los Angeles. **Military Service:** U.S. Air Force, 1950-54; became sergeant. **Family:** Married Barbara Knight, 1955; children: Teri, Dirk, Dana. **Career:** Bestgen & Cussler Advertising, Newport Beach, California, owner, 1961-65; Darcy Advertising, Hollywood, copy director, 1965-67; Aquatic Marine Corp., Newport Beach, advertising director, 1967-69; Mefford Advertising, Denver, vice-president and creative director, 1970-75; writer. National Underwater and Marine Agency, Washington, D.C., founder, 1978, currently chairman. **Awards:** Ford Foundation Consumer award, 1965-66, for best promotional presentation; Los Angeles Advertising Club awards, 1965, 1967, both for best sixty-second live commercial; Los Angeles Art Directors' Club certificates of merit, 1965, 1966, distinguished merit award, 1968; First Prize, Chicago Film Festival, 1966, for best thirty-second live action commercial; International Broadcasting awards, 1967, for one of the year's ten best commercials, and 1968, for best sixty-second commercial; New York Art Directors' Club certificate of merit, 1968; Venice Film Festival second place award, 1972, for sixty-second live commercial; Lowell Thomas award, 1986; awarded four Clios and numerous other advertising awards. **Member:** Royal Geographic Society (London; fellow), Writers Guild, Colorado Author's League (president), Explorers Club (New York; fellow). **Agent:** Peter Lampack, The Lampack Agency, 551 Fifth Ave., New York, New York 10017.

Publications

Novels

The Mediterranean Caper. Pyramid Publications, 1973.
Iceberg. Dodd, 1975.
Raise the Titanic. Viking, 1976.
Vixen 03. Viking, 1978.
Night Probe. Bantam, 1981.
Pacific Vortex! Bantam, 1983.
Deep Six. Simon & Schuster, 1984.
Cyclops. Simon & Schuster, 1986.
Treasure. Simon & Schuster, 1988.
Dragon. Simon & Schuster, 1990.
Sahara. Simon & Schuster, 1992.
Inca Gold. Simon & Schuster, 1994.
Shock Wave. Simon & Schuster, 1996.

Plays

Teleplays: Author of story scripts for television series, including *The Courtship of Eddie's Father, I Spy,* and *Twelve O'Clock High.*

Nonfiction

The Sea Hunters. Simon and Schuster, 1996.

*

Media Adaptations: Film—*Raise the Titanic,* 1980.

* * *

Clive Cussler writes adventure novels for the young at heart. The hero of all of his books is Dirk Pitt, a cross between James Bond and Jacques Cousteau. Pitt solves mysteries that take place mostly underwater, working for the United States Government's *National Underwater and Marine Agency* (NUMA), a sort of aquatic CIA. NUMA sends him on missions in which the object of his investigation always somehow winds up underwater in settings such as a submarine, sunken ship, crashed airplane, or submerged atomic bomb.

Cussler's first novel, *Raise the Titanic!* (1976), introduced Dirk Pitt to the public by having him rig a series of gas-filled balloons to the sunken luxury liner. He raises the ship from the ocean floor back to the surface—a feat previously considered impossible by engineers. The resurrection of the ship is necessary because its cargo holds contain a clandestine supply of the rare element byzanium, which the government now needs to use in its modern missile-defense system. Russian agents (reflecting the Cold War setting) are on hand to try and thwart the mission's success.

Reviews of *Raise the Titanic!* were generally favorable. *The Christian Science Monitor* called it a "ripping good story" and the *Library Journal* hailed it as a "spy-spangled thriller." Most critics praised Cussler's exciting, action-filled plot, although some expressed disappointment over what they considered his unrealistic-sounding dialogue (a charge that has been repeated often over the years).

Dirk Pitt returns in Cussler's next book, *Night Probe!* (1981). This time his underwater mission is to retrieve from a sunken ship a lost treaty that proves that the United States actually owns Canada. The excitement is heightened by murder, espionage, and a battle between British and U.S. Marines. Again, reviews of this book were mostly positive; *Quill and Quire,* for example, called the author "an enthralling storyteller who is a master of both sustained action and the misleading clue." Other reviews panned Cussler's unsophisticated writing style and outrageous plots.

Although most critics liked the originality of Cussler's *Cyclops* (1986), many of the usual criticisms emerged, but with some detractors also calling the narrative slow. In *Cyclops,* Pitt encounters a Soviet plot to blow up Havana and prevent Castro from allying with the U.S., as well as a sunken ship containing a priceless jewel-encrusted statue, and a budding war for possession of a secret base set up on the moon by an eccentric millionaire.

Treasure (1988) begins in the year 391, with Roman sailors using their ships to carry away and hide the contents of the famous Alexandrian library to protect them from Emperor Theodosius. The ships are separated and one of them is sealed in Arctic ice with the crew intact, while the rest, as the reader later learns, cross the Atlantic to ancient Mexico and ultimately travel up the Rio Grande to the land that eventually becomes Texas. The plot then jumps ahead to the present, where Pitt must recover the lost scrolls and save the lives of the presidents of both Egypt and Mexico, who have been kidnapped by terrorists. This technique of spanning centuries to depict important events is often used by Cussler, as is the device of conjuring up vessels and people eerily frozen long ago. *The New York Times Book Review* enthusiastically applauded *Treasure,* saying that it would make a great movie.

Cussler uses similar dramatic plotting in *Dragon* (1990), in which Pitt uses a submersible tractor to dig himself out of a landslide on the bottom of the sea, as well as in *Sahara* (1992), in which Pitt searches the Nile river for a 2500-year-old barge and investigates a poisonous red tide that endangers the world's oxygen supply.

Cussler's books have none of the deep political moralizing often found in the works of stodgier novelists like John le Carré. They do, however, have a swashbuckling tone similar to the works of Alistair McLean. Perfect reading for a weekend trip or a plane ride, they represent literary escapism for the type of audiences who go to movie theaters to enjoy Indiana Jones' style of archaeology mixed with adventure. Cussler reliably delivers a brave, likable hero in pursuit of some legendary historical artifact, armed with little more than imagination and a sense of humor.

—Bruce Guy Chabot

D

DAHL, Roald

Nationality: English. **Born:** 13 September 1916, in Llandaff, Wales. **Education:** Graduate of British public schools, 1932. **Military Service:** Royal Air Force, fighter pilot, 1939-45; became wing commander. **Family:** Married the actress Patricia Neal, 1953 (divorced, 1983); married Felicity Ann Crosland, 1983; children: (first marriage) Olivia (deceased), Tessa, Theo, Ophelia, Lucy. **Career:** Shell Oil Co., London, England, member of eastern staff, 1933-37, member of staff in Dar-es-Salaam, Tanzania, 1937-39; writer. Host of a series of half-hour television dramas, *Way Out,* during early 1960s. **Awards:** Edgar award, Mystery Writers of America, 1954, 1959, and 1980; New England Round Table of Children's Librarians award, 1972, and Surrey School award, 1973, both for *Charlie and the Chocolate Factory;* Surrey School award, 1975, and Nene award, 1978, both for *Charlie and the Great Glass Elevator;* Surrey School award, 1978, and California Young Reader Medal, 1979, both for *Danny: The Champion of the World;* Federation of Children's Book Groups award, 1982, for *The BFG;* Massachusetts Children's award, 1982, for *James and the Giant Peach; New York Times* Outstanding Books award, 1983, Whitbread award, 1983, and West Australian award, 1986, all for *The Witches;* World Fantasy Convention Lifetime Achievement award, and Federation of Children's Book Groups award, both 1983; Maschler award runner-up, 1985, for *The Giraffe and the Pelly and Me; Boston Globe/Horn Book* nonfiction honor citation, 1985, for *Boy: Tales of Childhood;* International Board on Books for Young People awards for Norwegian and German translations of *The BFG,* both 1986; Smarties award, 1990, for *Esio Trot.* **Died:** 23 November 1990, in Oxford, England.

Publications

Novels

Sometime Never: A Fable for Supermen. Scribner, 1948.
My Uncle Oswald. M. Joseph, 1979, Knopf, 1980.

Fiction for Children

The Gremlins. Random House, 1943.
James and the Giant Peach: A Children's Story. Knopf, 1961; Allen & Unwin, 1967.
Charlie and the Chocolate Factory. Knopf, 1964; revised edition, 1973, Allen & Unwin, 1967.
The Magic Finger. Harper, 1966; Puffin, 1974.
Fantastic Mr. Fox. Knopf, 1970.
Charlie and the Great Glass Elevator: The Further Adventures of Charlie Bucket and Willy Wonka, Chocolate-Maker Extraordinary. Knopf, 1972; Allen & Unwin, 1973.
Danny: The Champion of the World. Knopf, 1975.
The Enormous Crocodile. Knopf, 1978.
The Complete Adventures of Charlie and Mr. Willy Wonka (contains *Charlie and the Chocolate Factory* and *Charlie and the Great Glass Elevator*). Allen & Unwin, 1978.
The Twits. J. Cape, 1980; Knopf, 1981.
George's Marvelous Medicine. J. Cape, 1981; Knopf, 1982.
The BFG. Farrar, Straus, 1982.
The Witches. Farrar, Straus, 1983.
Boy: Tales of Childhood. Farrar, Straus, 1984.
The Giraffe and Pelly and Me. Farrar, Straus, 1985.
Matilda. Viking Kestrel, 1988.
Esio Trot. Viking, 1990.
The Dahl Diary. Puffin Books, 1991.
The Minpins. Viking, 1991.
The Vicar of Nibbleswicke. Viking, 1992.
My Year. Viking Children's, 1994.

Poetry for Children

Roald Dahl's Revolting Rhymes. J. Cape, 1982; Knopf, 1983.
Dirty Beasts. Farrar, Straus, 1983.
Rhyme Stew. J. Cape, 1989; Viking, 1990.

Short Stories

Over to You: Ten Stories of Flyers and Flying. Reynal, 1946.
Someone Like You. Knopf, 1953.
Kiss, Kiss. Knopf, 1959.
Selected Stories of Roald Dahl. Modern Library, 1968.
Twenty-Nine Kisses from Roald Dahl. M. Joseph, 1969.
Switch Bitch. Knopf, 1974.
The Wonderful World of Henry Sugar and Six More. Knopf and Cape, 1977.
Roald Dahl's Tales of the Unexpected. Vintage, 1979.
Taste and Other Tales. Longman, 1979.
A Roald Dahl Selection: Nine Short Stories, edited and introduced by Roy Blatchford, photographs by Catherine Shakespeare Lane. Longman, 1980.
More Tales of the Unexpected. Penguin and Joseph, 1980; as *Further Tales of the Unexpected,* Chivers, 1981.
Two Fables (contains "Princess and the Poacher" and "Princess Mammalia"). Viking, 1986.
The Roald Dahl Omnibus. Hippocrene Books, 1987.
A Second Roald Dahl Selection: Eight Short Stories, edited by Helene Fawcett. Longman, 1987.
Ah, Sweet Mystery of Life. J. Cape, 1988; Knopf, 1989.

Plays

Screenplays: *You Only Live Twice,* with Jack Bloom, 1967; *Chitty Chitty Bang Bang,* with Ken Hughes, 1968; *The Night-Digger,* adapted from *Nest in a Falling Tree* by Joy Crowley, 1970; *Willie Wonka and the Chocolate Factory,* adaptation of *Charlie and the Chocolate Factory,* 1971; *The Lightning Bug,* 1971.

Nonfiction

Roald Dahl's Book of Ghost Stories. Farrar, Straus, 1983.
Going Solo. Farrar, Straus, 1986.
Memories with Food at Gipsy House, with Felicity Dahl. Viking, 1991.

*

Media Adaptations: Films—*36 Hours,* adaptation of Dahl's short story "Beware of the Dog," 1964; *Willie Wonka and the Chocolate Factory,* 1971; *The Witches,* 1990; *James and the Giant Peach,* 1996; *Matilda,* 1996.

Critical Studies: *Pied Pipers: Interviews with the Influential Creators of Children's Literature* by Justin Wintle and Emma Fisher, Paddington Press, 1975; *Now Upon a Time: A Contemporary View of Children's Literature* by Myra Pollack Sadker and David Miller Sadker, Harper, 1977; *Roald Dahl* by Chris Powling, Hamish Hamilton, 1983.

* * *

Roald Dahl is best-known as an author of children's books such as *Charlie and the Chocolate Factory* (1964) and *James and the Giant Peach* (1961). He first made his mark as a writer for adults, however. As a Royal Air Force (RAF) pilot during WWII, Dahl crashed his plane and almost burned alive in the wreckage; Dahl had to undergo extensive surgery and a lengthy hospital stay to save his life. Dahl described this experience in his first published short story, "A Piece of Cake," which was included in *Over to You: Ten Stories of Flyers and Flying* (1946). Nona Balakian wrote in the *New York Times Book Review* that with *Over to You,* Dahl "has not written the usual postmortem adventure story but tried imaginatively to bring the flier's separate world within the compass of our own."

Through the 1940s and 1950s Dahl wrote stories for adults that "became less and less realistic and more fantastic," as Dahl told Willa Petscheck in the *New York Times Book Review.* These stories are collected in *Someone Like You* (1953) and *Kiss, Kiss* (1959). For example, in "Lamb to the Slaughter," included in *Someone,* a jilted, pregnant wife kills her departing husband with a frozen leg of lamb. In praising Dahl's macabre tales, a *Books and Bookmen* reviewer called Dahl "a master of horror—an intellectual Hitchcock of the writing world."

Dahl produced five children with his wife, actress Patricia Neal. As the children grew older, Dahl began writing stories to entertain them at bedtime. Dahl's first published success came with *James and The Giant Peach,* which depicted a boy who travels across oceans inside an enormous peach while accompanied by four bizarre companions: a centipede, a silkworm, a spider, and a ladybug. *James and the Giant Peach* "lends itself admirably to reading aloud, and its animal characters . . . are most worthy additions to what one may call the *Alice in Wonderland* dynasty," wrote Alasdair Campbell in *The School Librarian.*

In *Charlie and the Chocolate Factory* (1964), Dahl produced his most enduring children's classic. Virtue triumphs and vice fails as Charlie Bucket, the hero, inherits the fantastic chocolate factory of Willy Wonka while four monstrous children—a glutton, a gumchewer, a spoiled brat, and a television addict—meet appropriate fates. "Fertile in invention, rich in humor, acutely observant, [Dahl] depicts fantastic characters who are recognizable as exaggerations of real types, and situations only slightly more absurd than those that happen daily, and he lets his imagination rip in fairyland," wrote Aileen Pippett in *The New York Times Book Review.* Dahl followed *Chocolate Factory* with a weak sequel, *Charlie and the Great Glass Elevator* (1972), that was nonetheless a bestseller.

In many of Dahl's books for children, nasty adults received just desserts. In *The Twits* (1981), for example, a repellent couple is trapped and left to die by the birds and monkeys they have mistreated. In *The Witches* (1983), the young hero, turned into a mouse by witches, saves all of the children in England from the same fate by turning the spell against them. But nice adults also meet sordid fates in Dahl's stories; in *James,* the boy's parents are eaten by a rhinoceros, and in *The Witches,* parents are killed in car crashes.

Some critics believe Dahl's fiction to be too gruesome and that children should be protected from it. Eleanor Cameron, Dahl's most dogged and ferocious critic, wrote in *Children's Literature in Education*: "Because children know what they like, [many people assume] that children automatically know what is good . . . [but] they are by no means always capable of separating by intuition the vapid, the vulgar, the banal, and the tastelessness from what is excellent." Other critics believed that children were perfectly safe in reading Dahl's books. Campbell wrote in *School Librarian* that "normal children are bound to take some interest in the darker side of human nature" and that several of Dahl's books are "ultimately satisfying, with the principles of justice clearly vindicated." Other critics believe Dahl simply wrote in bad taste, to which Dahl replied to interviewer Mark West: "Children are different from adults. Children are much more vulgar than grownups. They have a coarser sense of humor."

—Eric Patterson

DAILEY, Janet (Ann)

Nationality: American. **Born:** 21 May 1944 in Storm Lake, Iowa. **Family:** Married William Dailey; stepchildren: two. **Career:** Writer. Worked as a secretary in Nebraska and Iowa, 1962-74. **Awards:** Received Golden Heart award from the Romance Writers of America, 1981. **Address:** Janbill Ltd., SR 4, Box 2197, Branson, Missouri 65616, U.S.A.

Publications

Novels

No Quarter Asked. Harlequin, 1976.
Boss Man from Ogallala. Harlequin, 1976.
Savage Land. Harlequin, 1976.
Land of Enchantment. Harlequin, 1976.
Fire and Ice. Harlequin, 1976.
The Homeplace. Harlequin, 1976.
After the Storm. Harlequin, 1976.
Dangerous Masquerade. Harlequin, 1977.
Night of the Cotillion. Harlequin, 1977.
Valley of the Vapors. Harlequin, 1977.
Fiesta San Antonio. Harlequin, 1977.
Show Me. Harlequin, 1977.
Bluegrass King. Harlequin, 1977.
A Lyon's Share. Harlequin, 1977.
The Widow and the Wastrel. Harlequin, 1977.
The Ivory Cane. Harlequin, 1978.

The Indy Man. Harlequin, 1978.
Darling Jenny. Harlequin, 1978.
Reilly's Woman. Harlequin, 1978.
To Tell the Truth. Harlequin, 1978.
Sonora Sundown. Harlequin, 1978.
Big Sky Country. Harlequin, 1978.
Something Extra. Harlequin, 1978.
Master Fiddler. Harlequin, 1978.
Beware of the Stranger. Harlequin, 1978.
Giant of Mesabi. Harlequin, 1978.
The Matchmakers. Harlequin, 1978.
For Bitter or Worse. Harlequin, 1979.
Green Mountain Man. Harlequin, 1979.
Six White Horses. Harlequin, 1979.
Summer Mahogany. Harlequin, 1979.
The Bride of the Delta Queen. Harlequin, 1979.
Touch the Wind. Pocket Books, 1979.
Tidewater Lover. Harlequin, 1979.
Strange Bedfellow. Harlequin, 1979.
Low Country Liar. Harlequin, 1979.
Sweet Promise. Harlequin, 1979.
For Mike's Sake. Harlequin, 1979.
Sentimental Journey. Harlequin, 1979.
A Land Called Deseret. Harlequin, 1979.
Kona Winds. Harlequin, 1980.
That Boston Man. Harlequin, 1980.
The Rogue. Pocket Books, 1980.
Bed of Grass. Harlequin, 1980.
The Thawing of Mara. Harlequin, 1980.
The Mating Season. Harlequin, 1980.
Lord of the High Lonesome. Harlequin, 1980.
Southern Nights. Harlequin, 1980.
Ride the Thunder. Pocket Books, 1980.
Enemy in Camp. Harlequin, 1980.
Difficult Decision. Harlequin, 1980.
Heart of Stone. Harlequin, 1980.
One of the Boys. Harlequin, 1980.
Night Way. Pocket Books, 1981.
Wild and Wonderful. Harlequin, 1981.
A Tradition of Pride. Harlequin, 1981.
The Traveling Kind. Harlequin, 1981.
The Hostage Bride. Silhouette Books, 1981.
Dakota Dreamin'. Harlequin, 1981.
This Calder Sky. Pocket Books, 1981.
The Lancaster Men. Silhouette Books, 1981.
For the Love of God. Silhouette Books, 1981.
Northern Magic. Harlequin, 1982.
With a Little Luck. Harlequin, 1982.
Terms of Surrender. Silhouette Books, 1982.
That Carolina Summer. Harlequin, 1982.
This Calder Range. Pocket Books, 1982.
Wildcatter's Woman. Silhouette Books, 1982.
Foxfire Light. Silhouette Books, 1982.
The Second Time. Silhouette Books, 1982.
Mistletoe and Holly. Silhouette Books, 1982.
Stands a Calder Man. Pocket Books, 1983.
Separate Cabins. Silhouette Books, 1983.
Western Man. Silhouette Books, 1983.
Calder Born, Calder Bred. Pocket Books, 1983.
Best Way to Lose. Silhouette Books, 1983.
Leftover Love. Silhouette Books, 1984.
Silver Wings, Santiago Blue. Poseidon, 1984.
The Pride of Hannah Wade. Pocket Books, 1985.
The Glory Game. Poseidon, 1985.
The Great Alone. Poseidon, 1986.
Heiress. Little, Brown, 1987.
Rivals. Little, Brown, 1989.
Masquerade. Little, Brown, 1990.
Aspen Gold. Little, Brown, 1991.
Tangled Vines. Little, Brown, 1992.
The Healing Touch. New Readers Press, 1994.
Riding High. New Readers Press, 1994.
The Proud & the Free. Little, Brown, 1994.
Legacies. Little, Brown, 1995.
Notorious. Ingram, 1996.

Plays

Screenplay: *Foxfire Light,* 1983.

* * *

A loyal following of readers has made romance writer Janet Dailey one of the bestselling female novelists in the United States. With nearly 90 books to her credit since 1976, she has been able to feed the craving of her fans for brief novels of hesitant surrender to passion.

Within a few years of her first novel, Dailey began a foray into longer, more substantial romantic adventures, many with detailed historical settings. The move was welcomed by readers and critics alike. Although some critics remain unimpressed with her work, most have to admit that her overwhelming popularity is the ultimate test of her value as a writer. As Joyce Slater asked in *Tribune Books,* "Can 120 million readers be wrong?"

A self-described "tomboy bookworm" as a child, Dailey left school early to become a secretary for an older, intriguing man who ran a construction business. At the age of 19 she married that man, Bill Dailey, who was 16 years her senior. For Dailey, he is the ultimate romantic hero and she claims that she has modeled many of her male protagonists after him. When Bill retired, ten years after their marriage, they set out in a travel trailer to discover the country. It was on this trip that Dailey became convinced she could write better romance novels than the ones she had brought along to read on the trip. With some encouragement from her husband, she wrote her first novel in six months. To her surprise, Harlequin accepted the novel with no revisions. When *No Quarter Asked* (1976) sold over a million copies, Dailey quickly followed it with others, setting a demanding pace for herself; she worked "six hours a day, ten days a week," a schedule she has kept up for many years. Dailey has never failed to mention to interviewers that she and Bill are a team. He handles the business end and does the research, while she does the writing.

Dailey's novels all employ a fairly standard romance formula: a rich, impassioned man pursues with unswerving loyalty a seemingly reluctant heroine, who manages for a time to resist the temptation of succumbing to the hero's dangerous passion. But the heroine gradually experiences a sexual and emotional awakening that takes the reader, as well as the hero, on a roller coaster ride of prolonged surrender punctuated with rebellion against the hero's magnetism. Ultimately, the hero overpowers her, and after a few frantic cries of "No!" she can resist no longer. This standard plot forms the bare bones of Dailey's Harlequin and Silhouette books, as those publishers demand tight, ten-chapter, formulaic romances. But her longer books, take on more complex subjects and display greater development of both plot and character, although at the core they employ the same pursuit formula.

Some critics have praised Dailey's development as a writer, and applaud her longer novels for their attention to rich, detailed historical settings. Of *The Great Alone* (1986), a novel that adds romance to an adventure in a rugged Alaska setting, Suzan Nightingale of the *Los Angeles Times Book Review* wrote, "Dailey has gone far beyond the spunky heroine formula to incorporate considerable research into Alaska's past." Similarly, Nancy Regan, writing in *Twentieth-Century Romance and Historical Writers,* said that *Night Way* (1981) is her "best book" because it "shows what Dailey can do when she is controlling her romance formula rather than letting it take over her books. In this novel she develops several characters, historically and emotionally, shifts point-of-view and setting, lovingly details place and local culture, and sustains the narrative with greater skill." A more recent review in *Publisher's Weekly* on the novel *Legacies* (1995), sequel to *The Proud & the Free* (1994), also noted Dailey's rich historical detail: "Despite its predictable love story, this Civil War saga provides a fascinating look at Cherokee Indians as plantation owners and slaveholders. . . . Although the on-again, off-again romance between Lije and Diana is as predictable as it is contrived, the fierce intrafamily feud and background material on the Cherokee nation keep the narrative lively and interesting."

Responding to criticism that romance novels are merely escape for women, Dailey told *Redbook,* "Romance novels, don't forget, allow women to see other women moving into jobs and careers, competing with men, having identity crises. But they retain their femininity. They find love—and that's what readers want, so the books are reassuring." Dailey is acutely aware of what her readers want, writing more for them than the critics. She once said, "I write my stories to entertain. That is their purpose for being."

—Anne Boyd

DAVIES, (William) Robertson

Nationality: Canadian. **Born:** Thamesville, Ontario, 28 August 1913. **Education:** Upper Canada College, Toronto; Queen's University, Kingston, Ontario; Balliol College, Oxford, 1936-38, B.Litt. 1938. **Family:** Married Brenda Mathews in 1940; three daughters. **Career:** Teacher and actor, Old Vic Theatre School and Repertory Company, London, 1938-40; literary editor, *Saturday Night,* Toronto, 1940-42; editor and publisher, Peterborough *Examiner,* Ontario, 1942-63. Since 1960 professor of English, since 1962 Master of Massey College, and since 1981 Founding Master, University of Toronto. Governor, Stratford Shakespeare Festival, Ontario, 1953-71. **Awards:** Ottawa Drama League prize, 1946, 1947; Dominion Drama Festival prize, for play, 1948, 1949, for directing, 1949; Leacock medal, 1955; Lorne Pierce medal, 1961; Governor-General's award, for fiction, 1973; World Fantasy Convention award, for fiction, 1984; City of Toronto Book award, 1986; Canadian Authors' Association award, for fiction, 1986; Banff Centre award, 1986; Foundation for the Advancement of Canadian Letters award, 1986, 1990; Toronto Arts Lifetime Achievement award, 1986; U.S. National Arts Club Medal of Honor, 1987 (first Canadian recipient); Molson prize, 1988; Canadian Conference of the Arts diploma, 1988; Scottish Arts Council Neil Gunn International fellowship, 1988. LL.D.: University of Alberta, Edmonton, 1957; Queen's University, 1962; University of Manitoba, Winnipeg, 1972; University of Toronto, 1981; University of Prince Edward Island, Charlottetown, 1989; D.Litt.: McMaster University, Hamilton, Ontario, 1959; University of Windsor, Ontario, 1971; York University, Toronto, 1973; Mount Allison University, Sackville, New Brunswick, 1973; Memorial University of Newfoundland, St. John's, 1974; University of Western Ontario, London, 1974; McGill University, Montreal, 1974; Trent University, Peterborough, Ontario, 1974; University of Lethbridge, Alberta, 1981; University of Waterloo, Ontario, 1981; University of British Columbia, Vancouver, 1983; University of Santa Clara, California, 1985; Trinity College, Dublin, 1990; Oxford University, 1991; University of Wales, 1995; D.C.L.: Bishop's University, Lennoxville, Quebec, 1967; LL.D.: University of Calgary, Alberta, 1975; D.H.L.: Rochester University, Rochester, New York, 1983; Dowling College, New York, 1992; Loyola University, Chicago, 1994; D.S.L.: Thornloe University, Sudbury, Ontario, 1988; Diplome honoris causa: Royal Conservatory of Music, Toronto, 1994. Fellow, Balliol College, Oxford, 1986, and Trinity College, Toronto, 1987. Fellow, Royal Society of Canada, 1967, and Royal Society of Literature, 1984; Honorary Member, American Academy, 1981 (first Canadian elected). Companion, Order of Canada, 1972; Order of Ontario, 1988. **Agent:** Curtis Brown, 10 Astor Place, New York, New York 10003, U.S.A. **Died:** 2 December 1995.

PUBLICATIONS

Novels

The Salterton Trilogy. Toronto and London, Penguin, 1986.
- *Tempest-Tost.* Toronto, Clarke Irwin, 1951; London, Chatto and Windus, and New York, Rinehart, 1952.
- *Leaven of Malice.* Toronto, Clarke Irwin, 1954; London, Chatto and Windus, and New York, Scribner, 1955.
- *A Mixture of Frailties.* Toronto, Macmillan, London, Weidenfeld and Nicolson, and New York, Scribner, 1958.

The Deptford Trilogy. Toronto and London, Penguin, 1983.
- *Fifth Business.* Toronto, Macmillan, and New York, Viking Press, 1970; London, Macmillan, 1971.
- *The Manticore.* Toronto, Macmillan, and New York, Viking Press, 1972; London, Macmillan, 1973.
- *World of Wonders.* Toronto, Macmillan, 1975; New York, Viking Press, 1976; London, W.H. Allen, 1977.

The Cornish Trilogy. Toronto and London, Penguin, 1991.
- *The Rebel Angels.* Toronto, Macmillan, 1981; New York, Viking Press, and London, Allen Lane, 1982.
- *What's Bred in the Bone.* Toronto, Macmillan, and New York, Viking, 1985; London, Viking, 1986.
- *The Lyre of Orpheus.* Toronto, Macmillan, and London, Viking, 1988; New York, Viking, 1989.

Murther & Walking Spirits. Toronto, McClelland and Stewart, New York, Viking, and London, Sinclair Stevenson, 1991.

The Cunning Man. Toronto, McClelland and Stewart, 1994; New York and London, Viking Penguin, 1995.

Short Stories

High Spirits: A Collection of Ghost Stories. Toronto and London, Penguin, 1982; New York, Viking Press, 1983.

Uncollected Short Story

"A Christmas Carol Reharmonized," in *Washington Post Book World,* 1982.

Plays

A Play of Our Lord's Nativity (produced Peterborough, Ontario, 1946).
Overlaid (produced Peterborough, Ontario, 1947). Included in *Eros at Breakfast and Other Plays,* 1949.
The Voice of the People (produced Montreal, 1948). Included in *Eros at Breakfast and Other Plays,* 1949.
At the Gates of the Righteous (produced Peterborough, Ontario, 1948). Included in *Eros at Breakfast and Other Plays,* 1949.
Hope Deferred (produced Montreal, 1948). Included in *Eros at Breakfast and Other Plays,* 1949.
Fortune, My Foe (produced Kingston, Ontario, 1948). Toronto, Clarke Irwin, 1949.
Eros at Breakfast (produced Ottawa, 1948). Included in *Eros at Breakfast and Other Plays,* 1949.
Eros at Breakfast and Other Plays. Toronto, Clarke Irwin, 1949.
At My Heart's Core (produced Peterborough, Ontario, 1950). Toronto, Clarke Irwin, 1950.
King Phoenix (produced Peterborough, Ontario, 1950). Included in *Hunting Stuart and Other Plays,* 1972.
A Masque of Aesop (for children; produced Toronto, 1952). Toronto, Clarke Irwin, 1952; in *Five New One-Act Plays,* edited by James A. Stone, London, Harrap, 1954.
A Jig for the Gypsy (produced Toronto and London, 1954). Toronto, Clarke Irwin, 1954.
Hunting Stuart (produced Toronto, 1955). Included in *Hunting Stuart and Other Plays,* 1972.
Leaven of Malice, adaptation of his own novel (as *Love and Libel,* produced Toronto and New York, 1960; revised version, as *Leaven of Malice,* produced Toronto, 1973). Published in *Canadian Drama* (Waterloo, Ontario), vol. 7, no. 2, 1981.
A Masque of Mr. Punch (for children; produced Toronto, 1962). Toronto, Oxford University Press, 1963.
Centennial Play, with others (produced Lindsay, Ontario, 1967). Ottawa, Centennial Commission, 1967.
Hunting Stuart and Other Plays (includes *King Phoenix* and *General Confession*), edited by Brian Parker. Toronto, New Press, 1972.
Brothers in the Black Art (televised 1974). Vancouver, Alcuin Society, 1981.
Question Time (produced Toronto, 1975). Toronto, Macmillan, 1975.
Pontiac and the Green Man (produced Toronto, 1977).

Television Play: *Brothers in the Black Art,* 1974.

Other

Shakespeare's Boy Actors. London, Dent, 1939; New York, Russell and Russell, 1964.
Shakespeare for Young Players: A Junior Course. Toronto, Clarke Irwin, 1942.
The Papers of Samuel Marchbanks (revised editions). Toronto, Irwin, 1985; New York, Viking, 1986; London, Viking, 1987.
The Diary of Samuel Marchbanks. Toronto, Clarke Irwin, 1947.
The Table Talk of Samuel Marchbanks. Toronto, Clarke Irwin, 1949; London, Chatto and Windus, 1951.
Renown at Stratford: A Record of the Shakespearean Festival in Canada 1953, with Tyrone Guthrie. Toronto, Clarke Irwin, 1953.
Twice Have the Trumpets Sounded: A Record of the Stratford Shakespearean Festival in Canada 1954, with Tyrone Guthrie. Toronto, Clarke Irwin, 1954.
Thrice the Brinded Cat Hath Mew'd: A Record of the Stratford Shakespearean Festival in Canada 1955, with Tyrone Guthrie. Toronto, Clarke Irwin, 1955.
A Voice from the Attic. New York, Knopf, 1960; revised edition, New York and Toronto, Penguin, 1990.
The Personal Art: Reading to Good Purpose. London, Secker and Warburg, 1961.
Marchbanks' Almanack. Toronto, McClelland and Stewart, 1967.
Stephen Leacock. Toronto, McClelland and Stewart, 1970.
What Do You See in the Mirror? Agincourt, Ontario, Book Society of Canada, 1970.
The Revels History of Drama in English 6: 1750-1880, with others. London, Methuen, 1975.
One Half of Robertson Davies: Provocative Pronouncements on a Wide Range of Topics. Toronto, Macmillan, 1977; New York, Viking Press, 1978.
The Enthusiasms of Robertson Davies, edited by Judith Skelton Grant. Toronto, McClelland and Stewart, 1979; London, Viking, 1990.
Robertson Davies, The Well-Tempered Critic: One Man's View of Theatre and Letters in Canada, edited by Judith Skelton Grant. Toronto, McClelland and Stewart, 1981.
The Mirror of Nature (lectures). Toronto, University of Toronto Press, 1983.
Conversations with Robertson Davies, edited by J. Madison Davis. Jackson, University Press of Mississippi, 1989.
Reading and Writing (lectures). University of Utah Press, 1994.

Editor, *Feast of Stephen: An Anthology of Some of the Less Familiar Writings of Stephen Leacock.* Toronto, McClelland and Stewart, 1970; as *The Penguin Stephen Leacock,* London, Penguin, 1981.

*

Bibliography: By John Ryrie, in *The Annotated Bibliography of Canada's Major Authors 3* edited by Robert Lecker and Jack David, Downsview, Ontario, ECW Press, 1981.

Manuscript Collection: National Archives, Canada.

Critical Studies: *Robertson Davies* by Elspeth Buitenhuis, Toronto, Forum House, 1972; *Conversations with Canadian Novelists 1* by Silver Donald Cameron, Toronto, Macmillan, 1975; *Robertson Davies* by Patricia A. Morley, Agincourt, Ontario, Gage, 1977; "Robertson Davies Issue" of *Journal of Canadian Studies* (Peterborough, Ontario), February 1977; *Robertson Davies* by Judith Skelton Grant, Toronto, McClelland and Stewart, 1978; *Here and Now 1* edited by John Moss, Toronto, NC Press, 1979; "The Master of the Unseen World" by Judith Finlayson, in *Quest*

(Toronto), vol. 8, no. 4, 1979; *Studies in Robertson Davies's Deptford Trilogy* edited by Robert G. Lawrence and Samuel L. Macey, Victoria, British Columbia, English Literary Studies, 1980; *The Smaller Infinity: The Jungian Self in the Novels of Robertson Davies* by Patricia Monk, Toronto, University of Toronto Press, 1982; in *Canadian Writers and Their Work* edited by Robert Lecker, Jack David, and Ellen Quigley, Downsview, Ontario, ECW Press, 1985; *Robertson Davies* by Michael Peterman, Boston, Twayne, 1986; *Robertson Davies: Man of Myth* by Judith Skelton Grant, Toronto, Penguin, 1994.

Theatrical Activities:
Actor: **Plays**—Lord Norfolk in *Traitor's Gate* by Morna Stuart, London, 1938; Stingo in *She Stoops to Conquer* by Oliver Goldsmith, London, 1939; Archbishop of Rheims in *Saint Joan* by Shaw, London, 1939; roles in *The Taming of the Shrew* by Shakespeare, London, 1939.

* * *

Robertson Davies has become admired for writing novels that skillfully combine accessibility and literary merit with an intriguing dash of the esoteric, including such subjects as alchemy, saints' legends, Gypsy wisdom, Tarot cards, shamanistic rituals, Anglo-Catholicism, and Jungian psychology. All his work explores the dangers of personal and cultural repression; from the unhappy schoolteacher, Hector Mackilwraith, in the early *Salterton Trilogy* (1986), who makes a fool of himself over a schoolgirl, to the dangerously intense and ultimately murderous priest in *The Cunning Man* (1994). The novels also exhibit a developing interest in Canadian identity—from the anatomizing of provincial life in *The Salterton Trilogy,* to the analysis of the wider cultural effects of the small town in *The Deptford Trilogy* (1983), to the selective but passionate examination of the European heritage of Canada in the later works.

Of *The Salterton Trilogy,* Anthony Burgess wrote in the *British Observer*, "Davies displays all the qualities of a latter-day Trollope." This coveys both the popularity and acute social analysis of these realist comedies of provincial life. *Tempest Tost* (1951) shows amateur dramatics releasing emotions in unfulfilled lives, while *Leaven of Malice* (1954) evokes the world of provincial newspapers, inventive gossip, and repressed young lovers. The final Salterton novel, *A Mixture of Frailties* (1958), initiates a major Davies theme; the redeeming spiritual power of art to combat a stifling bourgeois culture. The novel follows the singing career of Monica Gall as she moves from a repressive upbringing to European sophistication, and simultaneously develops the depth and range of Davies's characterization.

The Deptford Trilogy, better organized, is a web of stories about three boys who leave their small town to exert a profound influence on Canadian culture. On a winter's night in Deptford, Boy Staunton throws a snowball concealing a stone at his friend, Dunstan Ramsay. It misses but hits the pregnant mother of Paul Dempster, causing the premature birth of Paul and his mother's subsequent madness and disgrace. This primal moment haunts the three protagonists of *The Deptford Trilogy* in this psychologically gripping and inventive series of stories. Boy Staunton becomes a famous politician who dies mysteriously in a way that is bizarrely connected to Dunstan Ramsay, a schoolmaster and tracker of saints, and to Paul Dempster (now metamorphosed into Magnus Eisengrim, a master magician).

Personal transformation combined with colorful erotic adventures and psychological truths continue in *The Cornish Trilogy* (1991). Artistically plotted as a trilogy, the two outer novels work around the centerpiece of *What's Bred in the Bone* (1985), which details the extraordinary life of Francis Cornish, including his adventures in war-torn Europe and in the art-faking trade (Francis paints his life secrets into a mock old master called *The Marriage at Cana*). The other two novels, *The Rebel Angels* (1981) and *The Lyre of Orpheus* (1988), approach and then attempt to solve the mysteries of the enigmatic wealthy Francis Cornish. Alan Sillitoe described *The Rebel Angels* accurately as "a cerebral adventure spliced with fantasy, sex, and verbal gymnastics." *The Rebel Angels* centers on the remarkable Maria Magdalena Theotoky, a part-Gypsy doctoral student, learning to accept her complex identity as well as the bizarre sexual needs and displays of the male academic community around her. She reappears in *The Lyre of Orpheus,* where the structure cleverly parallels the production of an opera about King Arthur of Britain with adulterous entanglements between the opera's sponsors and directors.

Davies's career concludes with *Murther and Walking Spirits* (1991) and *The Cunning Man,* clearly a Toronto trilogy in the making interrupted by Davies's death in 1995. *Murther* opens spectacularly with the murder of its narrator, Connor Gilmartin, who then tells the history of his family as the novel explores the European heritage of this Canadian identity. The "cunning man" of the title of Davies's last novel is the narrator, Dr. Jonathan Hullah (godfather of Connor Gilmartin), who combines esoteric medical ideas with western medicine. He describes peculiar rituals in an Anglo-Catholic church peopled with a classic Davies's group of artists and eccentrics.

Davies was an artist of flamboyant plots, psychological depth, strange learning, and surprising wit. His well-earned popularity is rooted in wisdom.

—S. A. Rowland

DEIGHTON, Len

Nationality: British. **Born:** Leonard Cyril Deighton in London, 18 February 1929. **Education:** Marylebone Grammar School, St. Martin's School of Art, and Royal College of Art, 1952-55, all London. **Military Service:** Served in the Royal Air Force. **Family:** Married Shirley Thompson in 1960. **Career:** Has worked as a railway lengthman, pastry cook, dress factory manager, waiter, illustrator, teacher, and photographer; art director of advertising agencies in London and New York; steward, British Overseas Airways Corporation, 1956-57; wrote weekly comic strip on cooking for the *Observer,* London, 1960s; founder, Continuum One literary agency, London. **Agent:** Jonathan Clowes Ltd., Iron Bridge House, Bridge Approach, London NW1 8BD, England.

Publications

Novels

The Ipcress File. London, Hodder and Stoughton, 1962; New York, Simon and Schuster, 1963.

Horse under Water. London, Cape, 1963; New York, Putnam, 1968.

Funeral in Berlin. London, Cape, 1964; New York, Putnam, 1965.
Billion-Dollar Brain. London, Cape, 1966; as *The Billion-Dollar Brain,* New York, Putnam, 1966.
An Expensive Place to Die. London, Cape, and New York, Putnam, 1967.
Only When I Larf. London, Joseph, 1968; as *Only When I Laugh,* New York, Mysterious Press, 1987.
Bomber. London, Cape, and New York, Harper, 1970.
Close-Up. London, Cape, and New York, Atheneum, 1972.
Spy Story. London, Cape, and New York, Harcourt Brace, 1974.
Yesterday's Spy. London, Cape, and New York, Harcourt Brace, 1975.
Twinkle, Twinkle, Little Spy. London, Cape, 1976; as *Catch a Falling Spy,* New York, Harcourt Brace, 1976.
SS-GB: Nazi-Occupied Britain 1941. London, Cape, 1978; New York, Knopf, 1979.
XPD. London, Hutchinson, and New York, Knopf, 1981.
Goodbye Mickey Mouse. London, Hutchinson, and New York, Knopf, 1982.
Game, Set and Match. London, Hutchinson, 1985; New York, Knopf, 1989.
Berlin Game. London, Hutchinson, 1983; New York, Knopf, 1984.
Mexico Set. London, Hutchinson, 1984; New York, Knopf, 1985.
London Match. London, Hutchinson, 1985; New York, Knopf, 1986.
Winter: A Berlin Family 1899-1945. London, Century Hutchinson, and New York, Knopf, 1987.
Spy Hook. London, Century Hutchinson, and New York, Knopf, 1988.
Spy Line. London, Century Hutchinson, and New York, Knopf, 1989.
Spy Sinker. London, Hutchinson, and New York, HarperCollins, 1990.
MAMista. New York, HarperCollins, 1991.
City of Gold. New York, HarperCollins, 1992.
Violent Ward. New York, HarperCollins, 1993.
Blood, Tears & Folly. London, Jonathan Cape, and New York, HarperCollins, 1993.
Faith. Bath, England, Chivers Press, and New York, HarperCollins, 1994.

Short Stories

Declarations of War. London, Cape, 1971; as *Eleven Declarations of War,* New York, Harcourt Brace, 1975.

Plays

Screenplay: *Oh! What a Lovely War,* 1969.

Television Plays: *Long Past Glory,* 1963; *It Must Have Been Two Other Fellows,* 1977.

Other

Action Cook Book: Len Deighton's Guide to Eating. London, Cape, 1965; as *Cookstrip Cook Book,* New York, Geis, 1966.
Ou Est le Garlic; or, Len Deighton's French Cook Book. London, Penguin, 1965; New York, Harper, 1977; revised edition, as *Basic French Cooking,* London, Cape, 1979; revised edition, as *Basic French Cookery,* London, Century, 1990.
Len Deighton's Continental Dossier: A Collection of Cultural, Culinary, Historical, Spooky, Grim and Preposterous Fact, compiled by Victor and Margaret Pettitt. London, Joseph, 1968.
Fighter: The True Story of the Battle of Britain. London, Cape, 1977; New York, Knopf, 1978.
Airshipwreck, with Arnold Schwartzman. London, Cape, 1978; New York, Holt Rinehart, 1979.
Blitzkrieg: From the Rise of Hitler to the Fall of Dunkirk. London, Cape, 1979; New York, Knopf, 1980.
Battle of Britain. London, Cape, and New York, Coward McCann, 1980; revised edition, with Max Hastings, London, Joseph, 1990.
The Orient Flight L.Z. 127-Graf Zeppelin (as Cyril Deighton), with Fred F. Blau. N.p., Germany Philatelic Society, 1980.
The Egypt Flight L.Z. 127-Graf Zeppelin (as Cyril Deighton), with Fred F. Blau. N.p., Germany Philatelic Society, 1981.
ABC of French Food. London, Century Hutchinson, 1989; New York, Bantam, 1990.

Editor, *Drinks-man-ship: Town's Album of Fine Wines and High Spirits.* London, Haymarket Press, 1964.
Editor, *London Dossier.* London, Cape, 1967.
Editor, with Michael Rund and Howard Loxton, *The Assassination of President Kennedy.* London, Cape, 1967.
Editor, *Tactical Genius in Battle,* by Simon Goodenough. Oxford, Phaidon Press, and New York, Dutton, 1979.

*

Bibliography: *Len Deighton: An Annotated Bibliography 1954-85* by Edward Milward-Oliver, Maidstone, Kent, Sammler, 1985.

Critical Studies: *Secret Agents in Fiction: Ian Fleming, John le Carré, and Len Deighton* by L.O. Sauerberg, London, Macmillan, 1984; *The Len Deighton Companion* by Edward Milward-Oliver, London, Grafton, 1987.

* * *

Len Deighton shot to fame at his first attempt, when his debut novel *The Ipcress File* (1962) soared into the bestseller lists. With it, Deighton created a new kind of spy thriller, a world away from James Bond but almost equally popular. His nameless secret agent, a working-class rebel, distrusts his colleagues in British Intelligence as much as his Communist enemies. His suspicions are only too well founded, as he is repeatedly betrayed by his own side. *Ipcress File* has seedy, convincing locations, a mass of factual data, strong characters, and a slick, witty style. The spy with no name continued to star in *Horse Under Water* (1963), *Funeral in Berlin* (1964), *Billion Dollar Brain* (1966) and *An Expensive Place to Die* (1967), all of which feature the same basic mix and vary only in their assignments. After *Ipcress File, Funeral in Berlin* is probably the best, with an interesting plot where a defector is smuggled through the Berlin Wall in a coffin, and a grimly amusing "heavy" in the Russian Colonel Stok.

In the next few years Deighton tried other genres with varying success. *Only When I Larf* (1968), a comic tale of three confidence tricksters and their downfall, is amusing but falls short of his best spy fiction. Far better is *Close-up* (1972), a caustic examination of Hollywood and its backroom maneuvering as seen by an aging British film star, while the epic *Bomber* (1970) rates with his finest work. Describing a night raid over Germany by British bombers, Deighton outlines the suffering and bravery of the crews, the German fighter pilots, and the German and British civilians in a well-researched tribute, while at the same time condemning the butchery of war. He explores this theme again in *Goodbye Mickey Mouse* (1982), which follows the fortunes of an American Mustang squadron, and in such excellent factual works as *Fighter* (1977) and *Blitzkrieg* (1979). *Declarations of War* (1971), which studies soldiers in combat through the ages, has high spots but is less impressive.

Deighton returned to the thriller, fittingly enough, with *Spy Story* (1974), in which agent Peter Armstrong hazards his life in remote areas of Scotland and the Arctic to find a Russian nuclear submarine. *Spy Story,* and its successors *Yesterday's Spy* (1975) and *Twinkle, Twinkle, Little Spy* (1976) have the slick plots, rapid action, and neat dialogue of the earlier books, with a further honing of skills. The third title features the nameless agent in a bid to secure a defecting expert in interstellar communication.

SS-GB (1978) and *XPD* (1981) show Deighton's continuing interest in WWII. The first book presents a 1940s Britain under Nazi rule, and the second describes a secret meeting between Churchill and Hitler. Deighton musters his facts as always, but there's something unsatisfying about these books, which lack the humor and human interest of his best writing. The same is true of *City of Gold* (1992), a tale of espionage in wartime Cairo, and *Mamista* (1991), set in revolutionary South America. His latest departure from the spy novel, *Violent Ward* (1993), is top-class entertainment, a fast-paced Chandlerish tale in which a lawyer uncovers fraud and murder during the Los Angeles riots.

The triple trilogy of spy novels based on the character of Bernard Samson is Deighton's most ambitious effort so far. He builds up a fascinating, complex group of characters and involves them in a tangle of assignments in a style that blends love, humor, and explosive action. Bernard Samson, a tough, working-class agent at odds with his shifty employers has much in common with the nameless spy, but is a more fully developed character. Deighton follows his missions and relationships, from *Berlin Game* (1983), *Mexico Set* (1984) and *London Match* (1985), where Bernard's wife Fiona leaves him and defects to the K.G.B.; through *Spy Hook* (1988), *Spy Line* (1989) and *Spy Sinker* (1990), where Fiona, now revealed as a British "mole", is rescued by him, to *Faith* (1994), *Hope* (1995) and *Charity* (1996), where Bernard is forced to adapt to her return. Deighton's witty, hard-hitting style and the humanity of his characters make these novels his best to date.

Deighton has invented his own brand of spy fiction and made it a mainstay of popular reading. His wartime novels, his factual books, and his "entertainments" add up to an impressive contribution.

—Geoff Sadler

DeLILLO, Don

Nationality: American. **Born:** New York City, 20 November 1936. **Education:** Fordham University, Bronx, New York, 1954-58. **Awards:** Guggenheim fellowship, 1979; American Academy award, 1984; National Book award, 1985; *Irish Times*-Aer Lingus prize, 1989; PEN-Faulkner award for fiction, 1991. **Agent:** Wallace Literary Agency, 177 East 70th Street, New York, New York 10021, U.S.A.

Publications

Novels

Americana. Boston, Houghton Mifflin, 1971; London, Penguin, 1990.
End Zone. Boston, Houghton Mifflin, 1972; London, Deutsch, 1973.
Great Jones Street. Boston, Houghton Mifflin, 1973; London, Deutsch, 1974.
Ratner's Star. New York, Knopf, 1976; London, Vintage, 1991.
Players. New York, Knopf, 1977; London, Vintage, 1991.
Running Dog. New York, Knopf, 1978; London, Gollancz, 1979.
The Names. New York, Knopf, 1982; Brighton, Sussex, Harvester Press, 1983.
White Noise. New York, Viking, 1985; London, Pan, 1986.
Libra. New York and London, Viking, 1988.
Mao II. New York, Viking, and London, Jonathan Cape, 1991.

Uncollected Short Stories

"The River Jordan," in *Epoch* (Ithaca, New York), Winter 1960.
"Spaghetti and Meatballs," in *Epoch* (Ithaca, New York), Spring 1965.
"Take the 'A' Train," in *Stories from Epoch,* edited by Baxter Hathaway. Ithaca, New York, Cornell University Press, 1966.
"Coming Sun. Mon. Tues.," in *Kenyon Review* (Gambier, Ohio), June 1966.
"Baghdad Towers West," in *Epoch* (Ithaca, New York), Spring 1968.
"Game Plan," in *New Yorker,* 27 November 1971.
"In the Men's Room of the Sixteenth Century," in *The Secret Life of Our Times,* edited by Gordon Lish. New York, Doubleday, 1973.
"The Uniforms," in *Cutting Edges,* edited by Jack Hicks. New York, Holt Rinehart, 1973.
"Showdown at Great Hole," in *Esquire* (New York), June 1976.
"The Network," in *On the Job,* edited by William O'Rourke. New York, Random House, 1977.
"Creation," in *Antaeus* (New York), Spring 1979.
"Human Moments in World War III," in *Great Esquire Fiction,* edited by L. Rust Hills. New York, Viking Press, 1983.
"Walkmen," in *Vanity Fair* (New York), August 1984.
"Oswald in the Lone Star State," in *Esquire* (New York), July 1988.
"The Runner," in *Harper's* (New York), September 1988.
"Shooting Bill Gray," in *Esquire* (New York), January 1991.
"Pafko at the Wall," in *Harper's* (New York), October 1992.
"Videotape," in *Antaeus* (Hopewell, New Jersey), Autumn 1994.

Plays

The Engineer of Moonlight, in *Cornell Review* (Ithaca, New York), Winter 1979.
The Day Room (produced Cambridge, Massachusetts, 1986; New York, 1987). New York, Knopf, 1987.

*

Critical Studies: *In the Loop: Don DeLillo and the Systems Novel* by Thomas LeClair, Urbana, University of Illinois Press, 1988; *Introducing Don DeLillo* edited by Frank Lentricchia, Durham, North Carolina, and London, Duke University Press, 1991; *Don DeLillo* by Douglas Keesey, New York, Twayne, 1993.

* * *

The best way to begin to understand Don DeLillo's achievement is to understand the wrongheadedness of those who, judging from a traditional perspective, find his work wanting. Critic Bruce Bawer, for example, acknowledges DeLillo's talent but contends that he does too little with it: juggling jargon rather than developing ideas ("His preoccupation with language generally results in little more than one discouraging battery after another of pointless pretentious rhetoric."); drawing stick figures rather than developing characters worth caring about (their lives just as emotionally rich and varied as Bawer claims his to be); and writing the same lifeless novel over and over rather than maturing both aesthetically and, one assumes, politically (failing to outgrow his liberal funk). But as DeLillo has explained, "My work doesn't provide the comforts of other kinds of fiction that suggest that our lives are no different today than they were 50 or 60 years ago."

Self-conscious but never merely self-indulgent, DeLillo's language is polished and precise, and mysteriously and mockingly elliptical as well as epigrammatic—the bon mots of a postmodern Ben Franklin, tinged with edgy humor. It is a strangely incantatory language that reflects as well as mimics "the way we live now" (Anthony Trollope's phrase from a more innocently realistic age), that creates an atmosphere of comic menace and comprehends the vast surface of contemporary American culture while plumbing the depths of an often obsessive, always deracinated self adrift in a postmodern space in which the relation between word and world is at best problematic, at worst severed. Not content with merely describing this world, DeLillo creates the very texture of life as it is lived in a denatured, discontinuous, doubly mediated consumer culture in which consumerism, "a form of mass anesthesia," fails to protect us from the consequences of "unexpended faith."

The depth of DeLillo's interest in contemporary culture is indicated by the breadth of subjects treated in his novels. There is the television executive who leaves his job to go in search of his and his country's soul (*Americana,* 1971); college football as one organizational system among many in the age of disintegration and entropy (*End Zone,* 1972); celebrity (*Great Jones Street,* 1973); the connection between science and the occult (*Ratner's Star,* 1976); terrorism's allure (*Players,* 1977, and *Running Dogs,* 1978); paranoid plots, multinational corporations, and "risk analysis" (*The Names,* 1982).

White Noise (1984), winner of an American Book Award, was DeLillo's breakthrough novel. It was more accessible and more wide-ranging, an X-ray of the American psyche in the 1980s in which the characters' unease becomes the readers' as well. There is little that DeLillo, working on the garbage compactor principle, does not include; pop icons, higher education, tabloids and television, the restructuring of the family, simulation and nostalgia, the therapeutic society, panic, and drugs. He admirably captures the "feeble" self; wised up, affluent, uncertain, afraid, caught between intolerable drift and maniacal plot in a world in which Hemingway's "clean, well-lighted place" has given way to vast and immaculate but wholly anonymous shopping malls and supermarkets, and where an airborne toxic event is only the most visible sign of a more pervasive toxicity of life lived entirely and entropically in the present.

In *Libra* (1988), DeLillo turned to one of the seminal events in the making of the American postmodern consciousness, the assassination of John Kennedy, in order to further explore the dark side of contemporary American experience in the form of the rootlessness and loneliness and the compensatory megalomania of Lee Harvey Oswald; the way in which a disaffected CIA agent's plot spins out of his control, intersecting with other, deadlier ones; and the efforts of Nicholas Branch, the reader-writer surrogate, trying to find the Jamesian "figure in the carpet" in a world of information- and interpretation-overload.

DeLillo scales the "world of randomness and ambiguity" down a bit in his more recent contribution to "the literature of estrangement and silence." In *Mao II* (1991), DeLillo ponders, only half-jokingly, the fate of a J.D. Salinger-like novelist emerging from his hideaway into a world of mass movements, mass media, and post-Mao cult leaders (the Reverend Moon, the Ayatollah Khomeini, Arab terrorists).

—Robert A. Morace

DeMILLE, Nelson (Richard)

Pseudonyms: Ellen Kay, Kurt Ladner, Brad Matthews. **Nationality:** American. **Born:** 23 August 1943, in New York. **Education:** Hofstra University, B.A., 1970. **Military Service:** U.S. Army Infantry, 1966-69; became first lieutenant; received Bronze Star, Air Medal, combat infantryman's badge, and Vietnamese Cross of Gallantry. **Family:** Married 1) Ellen Wasserman, 1971 (divorced 1987); two children; 2) Virginia Sindel Witte, 1988. **Career:** Has worked variously as a carpenter, electrician's apprentice, house painter, men's clothing salesman, art dealer, stable boy, deck hand, insurance investigator, and editorial assistant. **Awards:** Honorary D.H.L., 1989, and Estabrook award, both from Hofstra University; honorary D.H.L., Long Island University, 1993. **Member:** Mystery Writers of America, Authors Guild, Mensa. **Agent:** Nick Ellison, Sanford J. Greenburger Associates Inc., 55 Fifth Ave., New York, New York 10022. **Address:** 61 Hilton Ave., Ste. 23, Garden City, New York 11530, U.S.A.

Publications

Novels (series: Joe Keller; Joe Ryker)

The Sniper (Ryker). New York, Leisure Books, 1974.
The Hammer of God (Ryker). New York, Leisure Books, 1974.
The Agent of Death (Ryker). New York, Leisure Books, 1974.
The Smack Man (Keller). New York, Manor, 1975.
The Cannibal (Keller). New York, Manor, 1975.
Night of the Phoenix (Keller). New York, Manor, 1975.
Death Squad (Keller). New York, Manor, 1975.
The Quest. New York, Manor, 1975.
Hitler's Children, as Kurt Ladner. New York, Manor, 1976.

By the Rivers of Babylon. New York, Harcourt Brace, and London, Hart Davis, 1978.
Mayday, with Thomas H. Block. New York, Mark, 1979.
Cathedral. New York, Delacorte, and London, Granada, 1981.
The Talbot Odyssey. New York, Delacorte, and London, Granada, 1984.
Word of Honor. New York, Warner, and London, Granada, 1985.
The Charm School. New York, Warner, and London, Gralton, 1989.
The Gold Coast. New York, Warner, and London, Gralton, 1990.
The General's Daughter. New York, Warner, and London, Harpercollins, 1992.
Spencerville. New York, Warner, and London, Harpercollins, 1994.

Nonfiction

The Five Million Dollar Woman: Barbara Walters, as Ellen Kay. New York, Manor, 1976.
Killer Sharks: The Real Story, as Brad Matthews. New York, Manor, 1976.

*

Manuscript Collection: Mugar Memorial Library, Boston.

* * *

Nelson DeMille began his literary career with a series of highly readable, fast-paced, hard-boiled police novels featuring New York homicide detectives Joe Ryker and Joe Keller. But he moved to longer thrillers that are more serious studies of the American psyche—social satires exploring complex moral issues.

The police series depicts with irony and wit a cross-section of violent wrong-doers, crazed Vietnam veterans and clerics, a renegade CIA agent, drug dealers, and vigilante police. DeMille's later novels explore more fully paranoia, conspiracy, class conflicts, and the complexities of human motivation and behavior. DeMille makes the psychology of villains understandable and shows reluctant and unlikely heroes forced against their better judgment into bloody, destructive conflicts as they take on the CIA, rogue intelligence agencies, the Mafia, the Vietnam War machine, the KGB, and even the IRS and members of the justice system. DeMille plays working-class immigrants off against blue-blooded aristocrats, and successfully demonstrates how easily the personal can color perceptions and distort realities. DeMille's writing is hard-edged and honest, confronting disturbing realities head on in rich, literate diction.

DeMille's blockbusters are highly varied. *By the Rivers of Babylon* (1978), inspired by the hijack and rescue at Entebbe, focuses on a passenger jet forced down at a Babylonian archeological site and besieged by Palestinians. It pits a psychotic Arab terrorist against Israeli military and anti-terrorist professionals. Similarly, *Cathedral* (1981) demonstrates the skill, daring, and mixed motives of an IRA terrorist who masterminds the seizure of Saint Patrick's Cathedral and threatens death to his hostages if his conditions are not met. The New York Police Department Hostage Negotiator must also control and overcome the ruthlessness of the police and politicians if he is to save lives. In *The Talbot Odyssey* (1984), high-ranking traitors have penetrated the CIA. The president's top advisor is suspect, and an important defector, a supposedly long-dead war hero, has, like Odysseus, returned from afar to mastermind the conquest of the West. No one can be trusted, as the protagonists struggle to prevent a gigantic, Russian, satellite-induced, electromagnetic pulse from leaving the nation vulnerable.

Word of Honor (1985) grew out of DeMille's personal experiences as a U.S. Army officer in Vietnam. An exposé of war crimes (the massacre of a village) precipitates the court-martial of a former lieutenant, Ben Tyson. DeMille contrasts the court testimony with the wartime reality. *The Charm School* (1988) makes credible a secret compound, which is carefully hidden in the Russian interior, where American MIA's must train Soviet agents to pass as Americans. The KGB Charm School DeMille envisions is the final polishing school, where agents experience a stageset America and learn the "complex matrix of language, habit, nuance, gesture, and shared mythology" necessary to play their "stage parts" around the world. However, a tourist's accidental encounter with an escaped POW sets in motion a dangerous mission to penetrate the compound. DeMille's portrait of Russia and of Russian psychology is convincing and informed.

Sardonic and witty, *The Gold Coast*'s (1990) arrogant, WASP lawyer-narrator, John Sutter, demonstrates DeMille's mastery of narrative voice. Proud of his fading aristocratic legacy and contemptuous of the American masses, he is a rebellious, independent hero of sorts. His unwanted entanglement in the life and affairs of a crass Mafia chieftain who moves in next door seems to suggest the insidious ease with which money and power can corrupt. Yet the dirty dealings of the FBI, the IRS, and the local district attorneys as they ride roughshod over constitutionally protected rights seem to justify Sutter's defense of his infamous neighbor. However, when the Mafia don seduces Sutter's wife he has gone too far, and Sutter's revenge reflects the subtlety of his breeding.

An intriguing, well-plotted murder mystery, *The General's Daughter* (1992) provides a scathing portrait of military corruption as a member of the Army's elite undercover investigative unit teams up with a rape specialist to discover who raped and murdered a general's daughter. *Spencerville* (1994) depicts a fatal triangle (a burned-out Vietnam veteran, his childhood sweetheart, and the sadistic and abusive police chief she married).

DeMille is a skilled and versatile novelist who is cynical, erudite, and compelling. He dissects the rivalries, compromises, and personal egos that endanger the individual, and depicts slightly rebellious but decent human beings caught up in intolerable and life-threatening situations that require intelligence, instinct, and a sense of decency and right to survive and prevail. DeMille believes firmly in democratic values and deplores the dehumanizing conditions that totalitarian regimes (especially Russian) force on people. However, he distrusts all institutions, even democratic ones, and places his hope instead in individuals.

—Gina Macdonald

DEVERAUX, Jude. *See* **WHITE, Jude Gilliam.**

DEXTER, (Norman) Colin

Nationality: English. **Born:** 29 September 1930, in Stamford, Lincolnshire. **Education:** Christ's College, Cambridge, B.A., 1953, M.A., 1958. **Military Service:** National Service, 1949-50. **Family:** Married Dorothy Cooper, 1956; children: Sally, Jeremy. **Career:** Assistant classics master in Leicester, England, 1954-57; sixth form classics master in Loughborough, England, 1957-59; senior classics master in Corby, England, 1959-66; Oxford Local Examination Board, Oxford, England, assistant secretary, 1966-76, senior assistant secretary, 1976-87. **Awards:** Silver Dagger award, Crime Writers Association, for *Service of All the Dead* and *The Dead of Jericho;* Gold Dagger award, 1989, 1992; The Lotos Club of New York Medal of Merit, 1995. Honorary M.A., Oxford University, 1966. **Member:** Crime Writers Association, Detection Club. **Address:** 456 Banbury Rd., Oxford OX2 7RG, England.

Publications

Novels

Last Bus to Woodstock. Macmillan, 1975.
Last Seen Wearing. Macmillan, 1976.
The Silent World of Nicholas Quinn. Macmillan, 1977.
Service of All the Dead. Macmillan, 1979.
The Dead of Jericho. Macmillan, 1981.
The Riddle of the Third Mile. Macmillan, 1983.
The Secret of Annexe 3. Macmillan, 1986.
The Wench Is Dead. Macmillan, 1990.
The Jewel That Was Ours. Macmillan, 1991.
The Way through the Woods. Macmillan, 1992.
Daughters of Cain. Macmillan, 1994.

Short Stories

Morse's Greatest Mystery and Other Stories. Macmillan, 1993.

Nonfiction

Liberal Studies: An Outline Course, two volumes, with E. G. Rayner. Pergamon, 1964; revised edition, 1966.
Guide to Contemporary Politics, with E. G. Rayner. Pergamon, 1966.

* * *

In Colin Dexter's novels, death is the last unexplained phenomenon in the 20th century. Colin Dexter's Chief Inspector Morse is a man who solves cases on unnatural death. The character of Morse draws the reader into the novels, and each successive book fills in another detail of Morse's personality, which is as intriguing as the resolution of the murders themselves.

Dexter's writing career began with *Last Bus to Woodstock* (1975). In that novel, a young woman is brutally killed and Morse, with his faithful helper Sergeant Lewis, is called in to find the murderer. Morse carefully pieces together all the facts and reveals the identity of the murderer in an emotionally charged conclusion. It is this case that sets the pattern for Morse's behavior in the subsequent novels. Morse is shown to be a flawed genius; the best at finding murderers and the worst at personal relationships.

Dexter's skill lies in his depiction of the character of Morse. He ensures that Morse remains a sympathetic character in spite of his alcoholism and womanizing. Dexter makes the situation realistic by focusing upon the relationships between the people involved in the case, from that of Morse and Lewis to that of the murderer and victim.

Dexter follows the usual murder mystery plot; a body is found, the case is investigated, and the murderer brought to justice. Although the basic elements remain the same, each book is significantly different. *The Wench is Dead* (1989), which won the Crime Writers' Association Gold Dagger award, demonstrates Dexter's method of combining the familiar with the new. It is unusual in that there is no corpse to be interrogated for clues, as the murder occurred in the 19th century. A convalescing Morse applies his detecting techniques to the evidence brought to him by Lewis. From his hospital bed Morse is able to solve a complicated case by piecing the facts together. The *Wench is Dead* is one of the more complex Morse stories. The multi-stranded plot is brought to a satisfactory conclusion with the recovery of Morse and the solution of the crime.

An air of sadness pervades *The Daughters of Cain* (1994). The case has two seemingly unconnected murders committed at separate times and of quite different people; an Oxford tutor and an ex-university scout. The sadness comes in and out of the novel as a sub-plot. Morse is older in this novel. He is considering early retirement and is concerned that his ability to solve the increasingly difficult murders will evaporate, as the unsatisfactory nature of his emotional life is intruding on his work. But Dexter has used Morse's drinking and pursuit of women as a continuous motif throughout the 11 books to highlight Morse's humanity. In *The Daughters of Cain,* for example, the motif has assumed a larger importance due to the seriousness with which Morse himself is considering his future.

Dexter uses the character of Morse as the linchpin of his novels. Morse is a fully developed person and readers are attracted to his personality. Dexter owes a lot to the Golden Age of crime fiction. His plots are wholly logical and the reader is able to pit his or her mind against Morse. He includes maps and diagrams of the relevant areas in some of the novels. Morse (and Dexter) are crossword fanatics, a trait reflected in the way in which each case is assembled bit-by-bit to reveal the whole. The same element is found in 1930s crime writing, yet Dexter's novels are not old-fashioned. Furthermore, the novels are realistic whilst being reassuring. The reassurance stems from the determination of Morse to explain seemingly unexplainable instances of death.

—Samantha J. Barber

DEXTER, John. *See* **BRADLEY, Marion Zimmer.**

DEXTER, Pete

Nationality: American. **Born:** 1943, in Pontiac, Michigan. **Education:** Received degree from University of South Dakota, 1970. **Family:** Married to second wife, Dian; children: (second marriage) Casey. **Career:** *West Palm Beach Post,* Palm Beach, Florida, reporter, 1971-72; *Philadelphia Daily News,* Philadelphia, columnist, 1972-84; *Sacramento Bee,* Sacramento, columnist, 1985—; novelist. Has worked as a truck driver, gas station attendant, mail sorter, construction laborer, and salesperson. **Awards:** National Endowment for the Arts grant to write poetry; National Book award, and National Book Critics Circle award nomination, both 1988, both for *Paris Trout.* **Agent:** Esther Newberg, International Creative Management, 40 West 57th St., New York, New York 10019. **Address:** 1170 Markham Way, Sacramento, California 95818; or, c/o *Sacramento Bee,* 21st and Q Streets, Box 15779, Sacramento, California 95852, U.S.A.

Publications

Novels

God's Pocket. Random House, 1984.
Deadwood. Random House, 1986.
Paris Trout. Random House, 1988.
Brotherly Love. Random House, 1993.
The Paperboy. Random House, 1995.

* * *

Raised in Georgia, Illinois, and South Dakota, Pete Dexter turned to writing as a career, he said, "when I found out what it was like to work for a living." After frustrating stints as a truck driver, gas station attendant, and reporter, in the 1970s he began writing a column for the *Philadelphia Daily News,* one of which so offended a local drug gang that they ambushed him and beat him severely with a pipe. The resulting head injuries permanently altered Dexter's sense of taste and he discovered he no longer had his previously hearty appetite for alcohol. "All of a sudden, I had an extra 50 or 60 hours a week with nothing to do. So I started writing more stuff."

One product was Dexter's first novel, *God's Pocket* (1984), set in a Philadelphia working-class neighborhood of the same name and tracing the darkly comic events that unfold when a construction worker's murder by a coworker is passed off as an accident. Mistrusting the official story, the victim's mother enlists the aid of the boy's stepfather in locating the real killer and scaring up money for a respectable coffin. Taking notice of the story, an alcoholic newspaper columnist interviews the grieving mother and eventually falls in love with her. Although some reviewers found it somewhat overloaded and contrived, *God's Pocket* was generally favorably received: The *Washington Post* called it "gritty" and "realistic"; *The Nation* found it "tough, funny," and "articulate"; and the *New York Times* praised it as "nicely written."

Dexter followed it with *Deadwood* (1986), the story of the lives of such historical personages as Wild Bill Hickok, Calamity Jane, and Charley Utter in Deadwood, South Dakota, during the 1870s. Using vivid language and a finely tuned ear for frontier colloquialisms, Dexter created a gritty and comic depiction of the untamed personalities who populated the Old West. Although the *Atlantic* criticized Dexter for not making clear whether he intended to write a Western or a parody of one, *Time* applauded him for "standing the myth of the American West on its head. . . with unusual skill, grace and glee," and the *Washington Post* asserted that Deadwood might be "the best Western ever written."

In *Paris Trout* (1988), Dexter turned to the American South of the 1950s in the Faulknerian story of a psychologically warped loan shark named Paris Trout who exploits the black community of his small Georgian town by lending money at unconscionable rates. After Trout bribes his way out of a conviction for the murder of a young black woman, the novel rises to a violent climax when Trout disintegrates into a homicidal rage. The novel won Dexter a National Book Award in 1988 and was widely seen as a major literary exploration of the evils of racism. *Newsweek* called it Dexter's "big novel," marked by the "touch of mastery"; the *New York Times* lauded Dexter's "exquisite understanding" and "stinging frankness"; and the *Los Angeles Times* extolled it as "a masterpiece, complex and breath-taking."

In *Brotherly Love* (1991), Dexter returned to the Philadelphia streets of his first novel to narrate the story of Peter Flood, a decent man racked by the memories of his passive complicity in the death of his young sister and the Mafia execution of his father for killing the mob-involved policeman responsible for his sister's accidental death. Finding release from his pain only through boxing, Peter falls in with the Philadelphia underworld and moves inexorably closer to his father's violent fate. Critics greeted the novel warmly. *Time* magazine compared it favorably to *Paris Trout,* the *New York Times* described it as a "first-rate novel . . . rendered with rare force," and *People* magazine labeled it "exhilarating."

Northern Florida in the late 1960s is the setting of Dexter's *The Paperboy* (1995), in which Jack Jones, the son of the owner-editor of the local newspaper, is hired by his brother, a star reporter for a Miami paper, and his partner to help them investigate the 1965 murder of a racist policeman by a backwoods redneck named Hillary Van Wetter. Convinced of Van Wetter's innocence, the two reporters eventually win his release and, in dubious fashion, a Pulitzer Prize for their story. *Library Journal* lauded Dexter's exploration of the ambiguous relationships between the Jones brothers and their father as a "chillingly satisfactory new work"; *New Statesman and Society* praised Dexter for creating an "ominous and oppressive" atmosphere; and *People* called it a "searing tale" by "one of America's most original and elegiac voices."

—Paul S. Bodine

DICK, Philip K(indred)

Nationality: American. **Born:** Chicago, Illinois, 16 December 1928. **Education:** Berkeley High School, California, graduated 1945. **Family:** Married 1) Jeanette Dick in 1949 (divorced); 2) Kleo Dick in 1951 (divorced); 3) Ann Dick in 1958 (divorced), one daughter; 4) Nancy Dick in 1967 (divorced), one daughter; 5) Tessa Busby in 1973, one son. **Career:** Announcer, KSMO-AM radio, 1947 and record store manager, 1948-52, both Berkeley. **Awards:** Hugo award, 1963; John W. Campbell Memorial award, 1975. **Died:** 2 March 1982.

Publications

Novels (series: VALIS)

Solar Lottery. New York, Ace, 1955; as *World of Chance,* London, Rich and Cowan, 1956.
The World Jones Made. New York, Ace, 1956; London, Sidgwick and Jackson, 1968.
The Man Who Japed. New York, Ace, 1956; London, Magnum, 1978.
Eye in the Sky. New York, Ace, 1957; London, Arrow, 1971.
The Cosmic Puppets. New York, Ace, 1957; London, Panther, 1985.
Time out of Joint. Philadelphia, Lippincott, 1959; London, Sidgwick and Jackson, 1961.
Dr. Futurity. New York, Ace, 1960; London, Eyre Methuen, 1976.
Vulcan's Hammer. New York, Ace, 1960; London, Arrow, 1976.
The Man in the High Castle: A Novel. New York, Putnam, 1962; London, Penguin, 1965.
The Game-Players of Titan. New York, Ace, 1963; London, Sphere, 1969.
Martian Time-Slip. New York, Ballantine, 1964; London, New English Library, 1976.
The Simulacra. New York, Ace, 1964; London, Eyre Methuen, 1977.
The Penultimate Truth. New York, Belmont, 1964; London, Cape, 1967.
Clans of the Alphane Moon. New York, Ace, 1964; London, Panther, 1975.
The Three Stigmata of Palmer Eldritch. Garden City, New York, Doubleday, 1965; London, Cape, 1966.
Dr. Bloodmoney; or, How We Got Along after the Bomb. New York, Ace, 1965; London, Arrow, 1977.
The Crack in Space. New York, Ace, 1966; London, Eyre Methuen, 1977.
Now Wait for Last Year. Garden City, New York, Doubleday, 1966; London, Panther, 1975.
The Unteleported Man. New York, Ace, 1966; London, Eyre Methuen, 1976; revised edition edited by John Sladek, New York, Berkley, 1983; as *Lies, Inc.,* London, Gollancz, 1984.
Counter-Clock World. New York, Berkley, 1967; London, Sphere, 1968.
The Zap Gun: Being That Most Excellent Account of Travails and Contayning Many Pretie Hystories by Him Set Foorth in Comely Colours and Most Delightfully Discoursed Upon as Beautified and Well Furnished Divers Good and Commendable in the Gesight of Men of That Most Lamentable Wepens Fasoun Deisgners Lars Powderdry and What Nearly Became of Him Due to Certain Most Dreadful Forces. New York, Pyramid, 1967; London, Panther, 1975.
The Ganymede Takeover, with Ray Nelson. New York, Ace, 1967; London, Arrow, 1971.
Do Androids Dream of Electric Sheep? Garden City, New York, Doubleday, 1968; London, Rapp and Whiting, 1969; as *Bladerunner: Do Androids Dream of Electric Sheep?,* New York, Ballantine, 1982.
Ubik. Garden City, New York, Doubleday, 1969; London, Rapp and Whiting, 1970.
Galactic Pot-Healer. New York, Berkley, 1969; London, Gollancz, 1971.
A Maze of Death. Garden City, New York, Doubleday, 1970; London, Gollancz, 1972.
Our Friends from Frolix 8. New York, Ace, 1970; London, Panther, 1976.
A Philip K. Dick Omnibus (includes *The Crack in Space, The Unteleported Man,* and *Dr. Futurity*). London, Sidgwick and Jackson, 1970.
We Can Build You. New York, DAW, 1972; London, Fontana, 1977.
Flow My Tears, The Policeman Said. Garden City, New York, Doubleday, and London, Gollancz, 1974.
Confessions of a Crap Artist. New York, Entwhistle, 1975; London, Magnum, 1979.
Deus Irae, with Roger Zelazny. Garden City, New York, Doubleday, 1976; London, Gollancz, 1977.
A Scanner Darkly. Garden City, New York, Doubleday, and London, Gollancz, 1977.
Radio Free Albemuth (VALIS). New York, Arbor House, 1985; London, Grafton 1987.
Nick and the Glimmung (for children). London, Gollancz, 1988.
The VALIS Trilogy. New York, Quality Paperback Book Club, 1989.
  VALIS. New York, Bantam, and London, Corgi, 1981.
  The Divine Invasion. New York, Timescape, 1981; London, Corgi, 1982.
  The Transmigration of Timothy Archer. New York, Timescape, and London, Gollancz, 1982.
The Man Whose Teeth Were All Exactly Alike. Willimantic, Connecticut, Ziesing, 1984; London, Paladin, 1986.
In Milton Lumky Territory. Hastings-on-Hudson, New York, Dragon Press, and London, Gollancz, 1985.
Puttering about in a Small Land. Chicago, Academy Chicago, 1985; London, Palladin, 1987.
Humpty Dumpty in Oakland. London, Gollancz, 1986.
Mary and the Giant. New York, Arbor House, 1987; London, Gollancz, 1988.
The Broken Bubble. New York, Arbor House, 1988; London, Gollancz, 1989.
The Little Black Box. London, Gollancz, 1990.
Gather Yourselves Together. Herndon, Virginia, WCS Books, 1994.

Short Stories

A Handful of Darkness. London, Rich and Cowan, 1955; Boston, Gregg Press, 1978.
The Variable Man and Other Stories. New York, Ace, 1957; London, Sphere, 1969.
The Preserving Machine and Other Stories. New York, Ace, 1969; abridged edition, London, Gollancz, 1971.
The Book of Philip K. Dick. New York, DAW, 1973; as *The Turning Wheel and Other Stories,* London, Coronet, 1977.
The Best of Philip K. Dick, edited by John Brunner. New York, Ballantine, 1977.
The Golden Man, edited by Mark Hurst. New York, Berkley, 1980; London, Eyre Methuen, 1981.
Robots, Androids, and Mechanical Oddities: The Science Fiction of Philip K. Dick, edited by Patricia S. Warrick and Martin H. Greenberg. Carbondale, Southern Illinois University Press, 1984.
I Hope I Shall Soon Arrive, edited by Mark Hurst and Paul Williams. Garden City, New York, Doubleday, 1985; London, Grafton, 1988.
The Collected Stories of Philip K. Dick. Los Angeles, Underwood Miller, 5 vols., 1987; London, Gollancz, 1988-90.
We Can Remember It for You Wholesale. Berkeley, California, Dark Carnival, 1990.

Play

Screenplay: *Ubik*, 1985.

Other

Philip K. Dick: In His Own Words (interviews), edited by Gregg Rickman. Long Beach, California, Fragments West/Valentine Press, 1984; second edition, 1988.

Philip K. Dick: The Last Testament, with Gregg Rickman. Long Beach, California, Fragments West-Valentine Press, 1985.

Only Apparently Real: The World of Philip K. Dick, with Paul Williams, New York, Arbor House, 1986.

The Dark-Haired Girl. Willimantic, Connecticut, Ziesing, 1988.

Selected Letters of Philip K. Dick, edited by Don Herron. Lancaster, Pennsylvania, Underwood Miller, 1991.

In Pursuit of VALIS: Selections from the Exegesis, edited by Larry Sutin. Novato, California, Underwood Miller, 1991.

The Shifting Realities of Philip K. Dick: Selected Literary and Philosophical Writings, edited by Larry Sutin. New York, Pantheon, 1995.

*

Bibliography: *PKD: A Philip K. Dick Bibliography* by Daniel J.H. Levack, Columbia, Pennsylvania, Underwood Miller, 1981.

Manuscript Collection: California State University, Fullerton.

Critical Studies: *Philip K. Dick and the Umbrella of Light* by Angus Taylor, Baltimore, T-K Graphics, 1975; *Philip K. Dick: Electric Shepherd* (includes bibliography) edited by Bruce Gillespie, Melbourne, Norstrilia Press, 1975; "Philip K. Dick Issue" of *Science-Fiction Studies* (Terre Haute, Indiana), March 1975 (includes bibliography); *Philip K. Dick* by Hazel Pierce, Mercer Island, Washington, Starmont House, 1982; *Philip K. Dick* edited by Martin H. Greenberg and Joseph D. Olander, New York, Taplinger, 1983; *The Novels of Philip K. Dick* by Kim Stanley Robinson, Ann Arbor, Michigan, UMI Research Press, 1984; *Philip K. Dick: The Dream Connection* by D. Scott Apel, San Jose, California, Permanent Press, 1987; *Mind in Motion: The Fiction of Philip K. Dick* by Patricia S. Warrick, Carbondale, Southern Illinois University Press, 1987; *Philip K. Dick* by Douglas A. Mackey, Boston, Twayne, 1988; *Divine Invasions: A Life of Philip K. Dick* by Lawrence Sutin, New York, Harmony, 1989; *To the High Castle: Philip K. Dick, a Life* by Gregg Rickman, Long Beach, California, Fragments West-Valentine Press, 1989.

* * *

Philip K. Dick was one of the most important and influential science fiction writers of the last 30 years, challenging readers with such themes as messianism, existentialism, confusion of identity, control of reality, and the nature of reality. His paranoid and darkly humorous vision is apparent in all of his science fiction, which is riddled with despair and anxiety. Dick's reputation was greatly enhanced when the highly regarded film *Bladerunner*, based on his novel *Do Androids Dream of Electric Sheep?* and directed by Ridley Scott, was released in the year of his death.

In *The Three Stigmata of Palmer Eldritch* (1965), Dick's paranoid vision is evident as he details a dead-on view of an ecologically damaged earth with its decaying society infected with drug abuse. Likewise, in *A Maze of Death* (1970), 14 strangers meet on a distant planet. In time, a homicidal madness begins to infect them. Though a little contrived, the novel was praised as unpredictable and captivating in its suspense. Dick sketched the future society and underground of *Flow My Tears, The Policeman Said* (1974) with his usual credible detail. Though the novel, which follows a famous television performer who loses his identity, closes with an unsatisfying ending, the furious pace and intense action draw the reader in.

The one series Dick created dealt with a godlike character, VALIS, who first appears in *VALIS* (1981). The protagonist Horselover Fat is identified by Dick as himself. Fat is having a hard time reconciling suffering with a belief in God. In a very personal, funny, and painful way, Dick brilliantly portrays Fat's coming apart, reintegration with Dick, and his eventual reappearance after an accidental death. VALIS reappears in *Radio Free Albemuth* (1985), which is set against the familiar Dick background of paranoia, fascism, and thought control. The main character, Nicholas Brady, is friends with Philip K. Dick, a writer. He is guided by VALIS in a plot to topple the fascist government of President Ferris Fremont. Brady is eventually martyred in his attempt. Such a stark political vision is given extra weight through its autobiographical tone. Bleak, well-crafted, and engrossing, this novel allowed Dick to explore his ideas about identity and the purpose of God.

The Transmigration of Timothy Archer (1982) is a fictionalized biography of Bishop Pike of California. Tim Archer, a man of compulsive beliefs, is seen through the eyes of his daughter-in-law Angel. Documents are found that threaten Archer's faith in Jesus as the Messiah. Several tragedies occur, and Archer eventually heads to Israel and dies in the desert. The novel was praised as finely crafted and compelling, and *Transmigration* proved once again Dick's immense knowledge, ironic sense of humor, and penetrating human insight.

After Dick's death, several novels were released that had not been published in his lifetime, all focusing on California during the 1950s as an exemplar of an age of anxiety. *Puttering about in a Small Land* (1985) is a very perceptive novel about the relationships between men and women. The story is written well, and the conclusion is original and unpredictable. *Mary and the Giant* (1987) uses the same backdrop of 1950s California to sketch the tale of a small town girl trying to break out. In *Again in The Broken Bubble* (1988), Dick gives us a quirky love story set against the same background which is alternately hopeful and dark, depressing and humorous. Known previously only for his dark, despairing, yet humorous science fiction, Dick, after his death, became a most compelling chronicler of life in 1950s California.

—Jennifer G. Coman

DICKEY, James (Lafayette)

Nationality: American. **Born:** Atlanta, Georgia, 2 February 1923. **Education:** Clemson College, South Carolina, 1942; Vanderbilt University, Nashville, Tennessee, B.A. (magna cum laude) 1949 (Phi Beta Kappa), M.A. 1950. **Military Service:** pilot in the U.S. Army Air Force during World War II and training officer in the Air Force during the Korean War. **Family:** Married 1) Maxine Syerson in 1948 (died 1976), two sons; 2) Deborah Dodson in 1976, one daughter. **Career:** Teacher at Rice University, Houston, 1950, 1952-54, and University of Florida, Gainesville, 1955-56; copy-writer, McCann-Erickson, New York, 1956-59, and Burke Dowling Adams, Atlanta Georgia, 1960-61; copy chief and creative director, Liller Neal Beattle and Lindsay, Atlanta, 1959-60; poet-in-residence, Reed College, Portland, Oregon, 1963-64, San Fernando Valley State College, Northridge, California, 1964-66, University of Wisconsin, Madison, 1966, and Milwaukee, Summer 1967, and Washington University, St. Louis, Spring 1968; consultant in poetry, Library of Congress, Washington, D.C., 1966-68; Franklin Distinguished Professor, Georgia Institute of Technology, Atlanta, Fall 1968. Since 1969 Professor of English and writer-in-residence, University of South Carolina, Columbia. Associate editor, *Esquire* magazine, early 1970's, and *Sewanee Review;* advisory editor, *Shenandoah* literary review; member of board of directors, *Charleston* magazine. Member of board of governors, South Carolina Academy of Authors. **Awards:** Vachel Lindsay prize, 1959; Longview Foundation award, 1960; Guggenheim fellowship, 1962; Melville Cane award, 1965; National Book award, 1966; American Academy grant, 1966; Médicis prize, for novel, 1971. Has received honorary degrees from 13 American universities. **Member:** American Academy of Arts and Letters. **Address:** 4620 Lelia's Court, Lake Katherine, Columbia, South Carolina 29206, U.S.A.

PUBLICATIONS

Poetry

Into the Stone and Other Poems. New York, Scribner, 1960.
Drowning with Others. Middletown, Connecticut, Wesleyan University Press, 1962; selection, as *The Owl King,* New York, Red Angel Press, 1977.
Helmets. Middletown, Connecticut, Wesleyan University Press, and London, Longman, 1964.
Two Poems of the Air. Portland, Oregon, Centicore Press, 1964.
Buckdancer's Choice. Middletown, Connecticut, Wesleyan University Press, 1965.
Poems 1957-1967. Middletown, Connecticut, Wesleyan University Press, and London, Rapp and Carroll, 1967.
The Achievement of James Dickey: A Comprehensive Selection of His Poems, with a Critical Introduction, edited by Laurence Lieberman. Chicago, Scott Foresman, 1968.
The Eye-Beaters, Blood, Victory, Madness, Buckhead and Mercy. New York, Doubleday, and London, Hamish Hamilton, 1970.
The Zodiac. Bloomfield Hills, Michigan, Bruccoli Clark, 1976; revised edition, New York, Doubleday, 1976; London, Hamish Hamilton, 1977.
The Strength of Fields. Bloomfield Hills, Michigan, Bruccoli Clark, 1977; revised edition, New York, Doubleday, 1979.
Veteran Birth: The Gadfly Poems 1947-1949. Winston-Salem, North Carolina, Palaemon Press, 1978.
Head-Deep in Strange Sounds: Free-Flight Improvisations from the UnEnglish. Winston-Salem, North Carolina, Palaemon Press, 1979.
Falling, May Day Sermon, and Other Poems. Middletown, Connecticut, Wesleyan University Press, 1981.
The Early Motion. Middletown, Connecticut, Wesleyan University Press, 1981.
Puella. New York, Doubleday, 1982.
Värmland. Winston-Salem, North Carolina, Palaemon Press, 1982.
The Central Motion: Poems 1968-1979. Middletown, Connecticut, Wesleyan University Press, 1983.
False Youth: Four Seasons. Dallas, Pressworks, 1983.
For a Time and Place. Columbia, South Carolina, Bruccoli Clark, 1983.
Intervisions, photographs by Sharon Anglin Kuhne. Penland, North Carolina, Visualternatives, 1983.
Bronwen, The Traw, and the Shape-Shifter: A Poem in Four Parts (for children). San Diego, Harcourt Brace, 1986.
The Eagle's Mile. Middletown, Connecticut, Wesleyan University Press, 1990.
The Whole Motion: Collected Poems 1949-1992. Middletown, Connecticut, Wesleyan University Press, 1992.

Recordings: *Poems,* Spoken Arts, 1967; *James Dickey Reads His Poetry,* Caedmon, 1971.

Novels

Deliverance. Boston, Houghton Mifflin, and London, Hamish Hamilton, 1970.
Alnilam. New York, Doubleday, 1987.

Plays

Deliverance: A Screenplay, edited by Matthew J. Bruccoli, Carbondale, Southern Illinois University Press, 1981.

Screenplay: *Deliverance,* 1972.

Television Play: *The Call of the Wild,* from the novel by Jack London, 1976.

Other

The Suspect in Poetry. Madison, Minnesota, Sixties Press, 1964.
A Private Brinksmanship (address). Claremont, California, Pitzer College, 1965.
Spinning the Crystal Ball: Some Guesses at the Future of American Poetry. Washington, D.C., Library of Congress, 1967.
Metaphor as Pure Adventure (lecture). Washington, D.C., Library of Congress, 1968.
Babel to Byzantium: Poets and Poetry Now. New York, Farrar Straus, 1968.
Self-Interviews, edited by Barbara and James Reiss. New York, Doubleday, 1970.
Sorties (essays). New York, Doubleday, 1971.
Exchanges...: Being in the Form of a Dialogue with Joseph Trumbull Stickney. Bloomfield Hills, Michigan, Bruccoli Clark, 1971.
Jericho: The South Beheld, paintings by Hubert Shuptrine. Birmingham, Alabama, Oxmoor House, 1974.
God's Images: The Bible: A New Vision, illustrated by Marvin Hayes. Birmingham, Alabama, Oxmoor House, 1977.
Tucky the Hunter (for children). New York, Crown, 1978; London, Macmillan, 1979.
The Enemy from Eden. Northridge, California, Lord John Press, 1978.

In Pursuit of the Grey Soul (on fishing). Columbia, South Carolina, Bruccoli Clark, 1979.
The Water-Bug's Mittens: Ezra Pound, What We Can Use (lecture). Moscow, University of Idaho, 1979.
The Starry Place Between the Antlers: Why I Live in South Carolina. Columbia, South Carolina, Bruccoli Clark, 1981.
The Eagle's Mile. Columbia, South Carolina, Bruccoli Clark, 1981.
The Poet Turns on Himself. Portree, Isle of Skye, Aquila, 1982.
Night Hurdling: Poems, Essays, Conversations, Commencements, and Afterwords. Columbia, South Carolina, Bruccoli Clark, 1983.
Wayfarer: A Voice from the Southern Mountains, photographs by William A. Bake. Birmingham, Alabama, Oxmoor House, 1988.
The Voiced Connections of James Dickey: Interviews and Conversations, edited by Ronald Baughman. Columbia, University of South Carolina Press, 1989.

Editor, *From the Green Horseshoe: Poems by James Dickey's Students.* Columbia, University of South Carolina Press, 1987.

Translator, *Stolen Apples,* with others, by Yevgeny Yevtushenko. New York, Doubleday, 1971; London, W.H. Allen, 1972.

*

Bibliography: *James Dickey: A Bibliography 1947-1974* by Jim Elledge, Metuchen, New Jersey, Scarecrow Press, 1979; *James Dickey: A Bibliography* by Stuart Wright, Dallas, Pressworks, 1982; *James Dickey: A Descriptive Bibliography* by Matthew J. Bruccoli, Pittsburgh, University of Pittsburgh Press, 1990.

Manuscript Collection: Olin Library, Washington University, St. Louis.

Critical Studies: Introduction by Laurence Lieberman to *The Achievement of James Dickey, 1968; James Dickey: The Expansive Imagination: A Collection of Critical Essays* edited by Richard J. Calhoun, Deland, Florida, Everett Edwards, 1973, and *James Dickey* by Calhoun and Robert W. Hill, Boston, Twayne, 1983; "James Dickey Issue" of *South Carolina Review* (Columbia), April 1978; *James Dickey: Splintered Sunlight* edited by Patricia De La Fuente, Edinburgh, Texas, Pan American University School of Humanities, 1979; *The Imagination as Glory: Essays on the Poetry of James Dickey* edited by Bruce Weigl and T.R. Hummer, Urbana; University of Illinois Press, 1984; *Understanding James Dickey* by Ronald Baughman, Columbia, University of South Carolina Press, 1985; *James Dickey: The Poet as Pitchman* by Neal Bowers, Columbia, University of Missouri Press, 1985.

Theatrical Activities: Actor: **Film**—*Deliverance,* 1972.

* * *

James Dickey's name is commonly associated with the film version of his novel *Deliverance* (1970). In fact, Dickey's dominant medium is poetry, not bestselling fiction. As a poet he is both diligent and patient. "I work slowly, and when I work I mean it," he has said. "Some poems I carry around with me for years, for I have found that working on poems over a long period of time is an integral part of [my] method."

Dickey claims that he "eased into poetry" during an artillery attack in the South Pacific. Narrative mode interested him and in his early poetry he attempted to display the connection between inner and outer states of consciousness that cause a protagonist to recognize one single impression. In his first three books, *Into the Stone* (1960), *Drowning With Others* (1962), and *Helmet* (1964), Dickey reacted against what he considered artificial rhyme and prosodic effects. In these works readers recognized "a unique unmistakable tone, an awareness of physical forces of the world that flow beyond time, beyond history." Similarly, "The Lifeguard," an often anthologized poem from this period, deals with the tension a lifeguard feels after a child drowns. It reveals Dickey's interest in the combination of perceptions and actions: "I knell in the quick of the moon/ At the heart of a distant forest/ And hold in my arms a child/ Of water, water, water." Yet some critics found Dickey's moral messages and repetitive rhythms stale by the time *Helmet* was published.

Dickey's technique advanced with *Buckdancer's Choice* (1965), winner of the National Book Award for Poetry. In this collection Dickey strove for the "conclusionless poem, the open or un-generalizing poem, the un-well-made poem." He became freer with rhythm and confronted his war-time experience to create unsettling poetry. His verse, exampled by the following excerpt from "The Fire Bombing," developed what Dickey calls "split-line," a rapid rhythm in which the poet intentionally leaves gaps to replace both punctuation and words: "Going invisible passing over on/ Over bridges roads for night-walkers/ Sunday night in the country in the enemy's country absolute."

Dickey continued his experiments in technique with the publication of *Poems 1957-67* (1967). Although Dickey was already established as a major poet, his ability to "drag out a poem" and focus on vulgarity neglected the needs of an academic audience in favor of popular reception. One wonders if critics were primarily attacking Dickey's success with the public and his appointment as Consultant on Poetry in English to the Library of Congress. *The Eye-Beaters, Victory, Madness,* and *Buckhead* (all 1970) contained brilliant moments, but were generally criticized for their public tone.

More recent poetry continues to explore issues common to Dickey. For example, the title poem of the collection *Falling* (1988) is a stream-of-conscious narrative of a stewardess as she falls from a plane. Dickey focuses on her attainment of a higher state of existence, which culminates with her death.

Dickey succeeded as a novelist with *Deliverance,* the story of four men on a weekend canoe and hunting trip who deal with both human and natural adversity in backwoods Georgia. Although the novel is not generally acknowledged as serious literature, most readers enjoyed the suspense thriller.

Dickey is also successful as a critic and teacher, having held professorships at the University of South Carolina, the University of Wisconsin, and Washington University. His reviews of contemporary poetry can be found in his *Suspect in Poetry* (1964) and *Babel to Byzantium* (1968). Like the majority of his work, these two collections of essays received mixed reviews; some critics appreciate his refusal to participate in trendy criticism, while others find his views to be unfounded.

An athletic man, Dickey lifts weights and practices archery, and is sometimes referred to by contemporaries as "a jock-strap poet." Yet few critics deny both his rank as a major poet and his development in a relatively brief period of time. Most who personally know Dickey claim there is something very likable about his southern mannerism, and one can't help but smile when he says "[my wife and I] have no permanent home, but plan presently to end up in North Georgia, where, my wife tells me, as though it were her fondest hope, we have the best chance of becoming 'magnificent, witty old people.'"

—Chris Godat

DOCTOROW, E(dgar) L(awrence)

Nationality: American. **Born:** New York City, 6 January 1931. **Education:** The Bronx High School of Science; Kenyon College, Gambier, Ohio, A.B. (honors) in philosophy 1952; Columbia University, New York, 1952-53. **Military Service:** Served in the United States Army, 1953-55. **Family:** Married Helen Setzer in 1954; two daughters and one son. **Career:** Editor, New American Library, New York, 1960-64; editor-in-chief, 1964-69, and publisher, 1969, Dial Press, New York; member of the faculty, Sarah Lawrence College, Bronxville, New York, 1971-78. Adjunct professor of English, 1982-86, and since 1987 Glucksman Professor of American and English Letters, New York University. Writer-in-residence, University of California, Irvine, 1969-70; Creative Writing Fellow, Yale School of Drama, New Haven, Connecticut, 1974-75; visiting professor, University of Utah, Salt Lake City, 1975; Visiting Senior Fellow, Princeton University, New Jersey, 1980-81. Director, Authors Guild of America, and American PEN. Lives in New Rochelle, New York. **Awards:** Guggenheim fellowship, 1972; Creative Artists Public Service grant, 1973; National Book Critics Circle award, 1976, 1990; American Academy award, 1976, and Howells medal, 1990; American Book award, 1986; PEN Faulkner award, 1990. L.H.D.: Kenyon College, 1976; Brandeis University, Waltham, Massachusetts, 1989; Litt.D.: Hobart and William Smith Colleges, Geneva, New York, 1979. **Member:** American Academy, 1984. **Agent:** International Creative Management, 40 West 57th Street, New York, New York 10019, U.S.A. **Address:** c/o Random House Inc., 201 East 50th Street, New York, New York 10022, U.S.A.

Publications

Novels

Welcome to Hard Times. New York, Simon and Schuster, 1960; as *Bad Man from Bodie,* London, Deutsch, 1961.
Big as Life. New York, Simon and Schuster, 1966.
The Book of Daniel. New York, Random House, 1971; London, Macmillan, 1972.
Ragtime. New York, Random House, and London, Macmillan, 1975.
Loon Lake. New York, Random House, and London, Macmillan, 1980.
World's Fair. New York, Random House, 1985; London, Joseph, 1986.
Billy Bathgate. New York, Random House, and London, Macmillan, 1989.
The Waterworks. London, Macmillan, 1994.

Short Stories

Lives of the Poets: Six Stories and a Novella. New York, Random House, 1984; London, Joseph, 1985.

Plays

Drinks Before Dinner (produced New York, 1978). New York, Random House, 1979; London, Macmillan, 1980.

Screenplay: *Daniel,* 1983.

Other

American Anthem, photographs by Jean-Claude Suarès. New York, Stewart Tabori and Chang, 1982.
Eric Fischl: Scenes and Sequences: Fifty-Eight Monotypes (text by Doctorow). New York, Abrams, 1990.

*

Bibliography: *E.L. Doctorow: An Annotated Bibliography* by Michelle M. Tokarczyk, New York, Garland, 1988.

Critical Studies: *E.L. Doctorow: Essays and Conversations* edited by Richard Trenner, Princeton, New Jersey, Ontario Review Press, 1983; *E.L. Doctorow* by Paul Levine, London, Methuen, 1985; *E.L. Doctorow* by Carol C. Harter and James R. Thompson, Boston, Twayne, 1990; *E.L. Doctorow* by John G. Parks, New York, Continuum Press, 1991; *Models of Misrepresentation: The Fiction of E.L. Doctorow* by Christopher D. Morris, Jackson, University Press of Mississippi, 1991.

* * *

E. L. Doctorow's books all address a painful and ongoing rift in American history: the distance between lofty American ideals and the dark and destructive reality of life in America.

Doctorow's approach has been to write historical novels representing different periods in American history. However, these novels tend not to be historical novels in the traditional sense. Consider two brief examples from Doctorow's most popular novel, *Ragtime* (1975). In one case we read that Sigmund Freud came to America with Carl Jung, which we know happened. Later we read that the two "took a boat together through the Tunnel of Love" at Coney Island, which we have no way of knowing or confirming. In the second example, Doctorow presents a conversation between Henry Ford and J. P. Morgan about reincarnation and mass production, a conversation of which no historical record exists.

Thus, Doctorow replaces the traditional historian's concern (or the traditional historical novelist's concern, for that matter) for "what actually happened" with "what possibly happened." It is critical to note that this is not simply a fictional technique that Doctorow employs with a wink and a nod, seeking protection under the definition of "fiction." On the contrary, Doctorow considers his novels to be the truth: "[i]n *Ragtime* I'm satisfied that everything I made up about Morgan, for instance, or Ford, is true, whether it happened or not," he has said.

The principle of history as fiction informs all of Doctorow's novels to a greater or lesser extent, and is a response to a crisis that had been quietly simmering in the field of history until brought to a boil in the 1960s. At that time historians began to acknowledge that books by historians, and the historical records that historians consult, are all written by people with individual biases and concerns. The consequence of this admission is the replacement of "what actually happened" with "what may have happened," and the line between an historical account of Henry Ford and Doctorow's account of Henry Ford disappears. What becomes important is, as Doctorow notes, the truth instead of the reality. There is something true about Freud and Jung in the Tunnel of Love that does not depend on whether or not they actually rode the ride together. (Doctorow is not the most radical author to revise history through fiction: look into the works of John Barth, D. M. Thomas, Robert Coover, and William Styron.)

Doctorow employs the idea of history as ultimately pliable to reveal the destructive nature of American society that still maintains the admirable goals of the Enlightenment as found in the Constitution. Doctorow's novels each occur at a different times in American history. At the same time, Doctorow experiments with narrative within the conventions of various fictional genres in order to confront literature itself. *Welcome to Hard Times* (1960) reworks the typical Western in its account of the destruction of Hard Times, a town in the Dakota Territory during America's westward expansion. *Big As Life* (1966) tackles science fiction as it brings two monstrously large (and monstrously slow-moving) aliens to New York. *Loon Lake* (1980) is slightly science fictional in its confusion of time and slightly historical in its presentation of Depression-era gangsters (a time and theme Doctorow revisits in *Billy Bathgate* [1989]). Finally, Doctorow's *The Waterworks* (1994) is a Gothic mystery set in New York in 1871.

The thread connecting all of Doctorow's works is a disillusionment with idealistic American morality and its inability to stop the miseries of actual American life. This idea is most powerfully told in *The Book of Daniel* (1971), in which Daniel tries to come to terms with his own identity and his relationship to his parents, Paul and Rochelle Isaacson. The Isaacsons are modeled after Julius and Ethel Rosenberg, whose historical actuality is modified as Doctorow sees fit (to the consternation of many critics) in order to highlight the justice of American ideology and the injustice of American practice. They are alienated by their Jewishness and their politics, Daniel is alienated by his relationship to them, and Doctorow portrays the loneliness and confusion of an American life that cannot meet its own standards of justice and equality.

Ultimately, Doctorow wants to confront both the insufficiencies of fiction and the insufficiencies of life in America, and plays each off the other to make his point: "The insufficiency of fiction and the need to reform it, I take as a metaphor for our need to transform our lives and remake ourselves," he says.

—Michael R. Little

DONALDSON, Stephen R.

Pseudonym: Reed Stephens. **Nationality:** American. **Born:** Cleveland, Ohio, 13 May 1947. **Education:** College of Wooster, B.A. in English (departmental honors), 1968; Kent State University, M.A. in English, 1971. **Military Service:** Conscientious objector; assistant dispatcher, Akron City Hospital, Akron, Ohio, 1968-70. **Career:** Teaching fellow, Kent State University, 1971; acquisitions editor, Tapp-Gentz Associates, 1973; associate instructor, Ghost Ranch Writers Workshops, 1973-75; contributing editor, *Journal of the Fantastic in the Arts,* 1993-. **Awards:** British Fantasy Society award, 1979; John W. Campbell award, 1979; Balrog Fantasy award, 1981, 1983, 1985; Saturn award, 1983; Science Fiction Book Club award, 1988, 1989; The College of Wooster Distinguished Alumni award, 1989; Julia Verlanger award, 1990; Department of English Distinguished Alumni award, Kent State University, 1995. **Member:** Board of Directors, United States Karate Alliance. **Agent:** Howard Morhaim, 175 Fifth Ave., Rm. 709, New York, New York 10010, U.S.A.

Publications

Novels (series: Gap; Mordant's Need; Thomas Covenant)

Daughter of Regals. West Kingston, Rhode Island, Donald M. Grant, 1984.
The Mirror of Her Dreams (Mordant's Need). New York, Ballantine, 1987, and London, Collins, 1988.
A Man Rides Through (Mordant's Need). New York, Ballantine, 1987, and London, Collins, 1988.
The Gap into Conflict: The Real Story. London, Collins, 1990, and New York, Bantam, 1991.
The Gap into Vision: Forbidden Knowledge. New York, Bantam, and London, HarperCollins, 1991.
The Gap into Power: A Dark and Hungry God Arises. New York, Bantam, and London, HarperCollins, 1992.
The First Chronicles of Thomas Covenant the Unbeliever. Glasgow, Richard Drew; as *The Chronicles of Thomas Covenant the Unbeliever,* London, Fontana, 1993.
  Lord Foul's Bane. New York, Holt, 1977; Glasgow, Richard Drew, 1983.
  The Illearth War. New York, Holt, 1977; Glasgow, Richard Drew, 1983.
  The Power That Preserves. New York, Holt, 1977; Glasgow, Richard Drew, 1983.
The Second Chronicles of Thomas Covenant the Unbeliever. London, HarperCollins, 1994.
  The Wounded Land. New York, Ballantine, and London, Sidgwick & Jackson, 1980.
  The One Tree. New York, Del Rey, Ballantine, and London, Fontana, 1982.
  White Gold Wielder. New York, Ballantine, and London, Collins, 1983.
The Gap into Madness: Chaos and Order. New York, Bantam, and London, HarperCollins, 1994.
The Gap into Ruin: This Day All Gods Die. New York, Bantam, and London, HarperCollins, 1996.

Novels as Reed Stephens (series: Mick Axbrewder in all titles)

The Man Who Risked His Partner. New York, Ballantine, 1984; London, Fontana, 1987.
The Man Who Killed His Brother. New York, Ballantine, 1986; London, Fontana, 1987.
The Man Who Tried to Get Away. New York, Ballantine, and London, Collins, 1990.

Short Stories

Gilden-Fire (Thomas Covenant). San Francisco and Columbia, Pennsylvania, Underwood-Miller, 1981; London, Collins, 1983.
Daughter of Regals and Other Tales. New York, Ballantine, and London, Collins, 1984.

Other

Epic Fantasy in the Modern World: A Few Observations. Kent, Ohio, Kent State University Libraries, 1986.

Editor, *Strange Dreams: Unforgettable Fantasy Stories.* New York, Bantam, and London, HarperCollins, 1993.

*

Manuscript Collection: Kent State University Libraries, Kent, Ohio.

* * *

Stephen R. Donaldson's first major commercial success as a writer was *The Chronicles of Thomas Covenant, the Unbeliever* (1977), which encompasses two trilogies. These six books tell the story of Thomas Covenant, a man who lives in the "real world" but is mysteriously transported to a strange land of magic and giants. The people there believe that he is their messiah, and he is forced to battle the forces of evil in order to save them.

The Chronicles of Thomas Covenant falls under the category of "epic fantasy," a type of literature featuring such legendary creatures as elves, dwarves, wizards, and dragons. This type of writing has become immensely popular in the second half of the 20th century after being re-introduced by J. R. R. Tolkien, the British linguist, scholar, and author who published *The Lord of the Rings* in 1965. Writing in an epic style, Tolkien revived a literary tradition dating back to Sir Edmund Spenser's *The Faerie Queen* (1590) and ultimately to the ancient Greek *Iliad* of Homer. Now, as the 20th century draws to a close, many contemporary authors write in the epic fantasy, or sword and sorcery, genre. They include Terry Brooks, Anne McAffrey, Ursula K. LeGuin, and David Eddings, to name only a few.

The character Donaldson creates, Thomas Covenant, is an example of the literary figure known as the "anti-hero." This figure is usually understood to be the protagonist, but lacks the moral perfection associated with a stereotypical hero; instead, this person has serious doubts and flaws, and does not do the job of hero quite as expected.

In Donaldson's books, Thomas Covenant exemplifies the common literary practice of having a character's name signify something about him or her. Covenant's name is in fact ironic, because it suggests connotations of a theological covenant between human beings and God, such as those spoken of in the Bible, while his first name calls to mind the New Testament figure of Saint Thomas, who is described in the Gospels as being reluctant to believe in the resurrection of Jesus. Thus, Thomas Covenant in Donaldson's story refuses to accept his role as savior of his new world, and finds it so difficult to believe what is happening to him that the other characters dub him the "Unbeliever."

Many critics have found fault with Donaldson's trilogies because of the dark, pessimistic outlook of his narratives. The *New York Times Book Review,* for example, disliked the anguished, depressed personalities of Donaldson's characters, as well as the author's tendency to be wordy and get tangled up in complex language. However, most critics praise Donaldson for his original ideas, exciting action, and creative imagery.

In Donaldson's next series, consisting of *Mirror of Her Dreams* (1986) and its sequel, *A Man Rides Through* (1987), the protagonist is a young woman taken by a magician into a fantasy world to be its savior; beings in this world are grappling with bizarre problems concerning the interrelationships among illusion, imagination, and reality. Reviews of these books were extremely favorable, citing Donaldson's improving writing style and innovative philosophical questioning.

Then, with the five-volume *Gap Into Conflict* series, beginning with *The Real Story* (1990), Donaldson moves away from fantasy and into the realm of pure science fiction; the *Gap* series, in fact, is often referred to as "space opera." The story is of a future universe ruled by a company that mines the one element needed for survival. Many parts of the story are reminiscent of Frank Herbert's novels, including the technique of "crossing the gap" that *Dune* fans will liken to "folding space." Like many of the main characters, psychopathic cyborg/space-pirate Angus Thermopyle will be disturbing to some readers. But depth of intensity in Donaldson's creations is a hallmark of his science fiction.

In response to the *Gap* books, Faren Miller in *Locus* writes that feminists would be offended by Donaldson's portrayal of some of his women characters. Some reviewers fault Donaldson for overly intricate plots and convoluted prose, while others feel that in spite of such defects his books are easy to understand. Overall, Donaldson's writing is always earthy, and sometimes violent. His favorite themes generally revolve around unusual characters on metaphysical quests. His novels expertly employ alien metaphors to deal with contemporary social issues such as rape, pollution, substance abuse, slavery, cloning, and genetic engineering.

—Bruce Guy Chabot

DOUGLAS, James McM. *See* **BUTTERWORTH, W. E.**

DOUGLAS, Michael. *See* **CRICHTON, (John) Michael.**

DRABBLE, Margaret

Nationality: British. **Born:** Sheffield, Yorkshire, 5 June 1939; sister of A.S. Byatt, *q.v.* **Education:** Mount School, York; Newnham College, Cambridge, B.A. (honours) 1960. **Family:** Married 1) Clive Swift in 1960 (divorced 1975), two sons and one daughter; 2) the writer Michael Holroyd in 1982. **Career:** Deputy chair, 1978-80, and chair, 1980-82, National Book League. **Awards:** Rhys Memorial prize, 1966; James Tait Black Memorial prize, 1968; American Academy E.M. Forster award, 1973. D.Litt: University of Sheffield, 1976; University of Keele, Staffordshire, 1988; University of Bradford, Yorkshire, 1988. C.B.E. (Commander, Order of the British Empire), 1980. **Agent:** Peters Fraser and Dunlop,

503-504 The Chambers, Chelsea Harbour, Lots Road, London SW10 OXF, England.

Publications

Novels

A Summer Bird-Cage. London, Weidenfeld and Nicolson, 1962; New York, Morrow, 1964.
The Garrick Year. London, Weidenfeld and Nicolson, 1964; New York, Morrow, 1965.
The Millstone. London, Weidenfeld and Nicolson, 1965; New York, Morrow, 1966; as *Thank You All Very Much,* New York, New American Library, 1969.
Jerusalem the Golden. London, Weidenfeld and Nicolson, and New York, Morrow, 1967.
The Waterfall. London, Weidenfeld and Nicolson, and New York, Knopf, 1969.
The Needle's Eye. London, Weidenfeld and Nicolson, and New York, Knopf, 1972.
The Realms of Gold. London, Weidenfeld and Nicolson, and New York, Knopf, 1975.
The Ice Age. London, Weidenfeld and Nicolson, and New York, Knopf, 1977.
The Middle Ground. London, Weidenfeld and Nicolson, and New York, Knopf, 1980.
The Radiant Way. London, Weidenfeld and Nicolson, and New York, Knopf, 1987.
A Natural Curiosity. London and New York, Viking, 1989.
The Gates of Ivory. London and New York, Viking, 1991.

Short Stories

Hassan's Tower. Los Angeles, Sylvester and Orphanos, 1980.

Uncollected Short Stories

"A Voyage to Cytherea," in *Mademoiselle* (New York), December 1967.
"The Reunion," in *Winter's Tales 14,* edited by Kevin Crossley-Holland. London, Macmillan, and New York, St. Martin's Press, 1968.
"The Gifts of War," in *Winter's Tales 16,* edited by A.D. Maclean. London, Macmillan, 1970; New York, St. Martin's Press, 1971.
"Crossing the Alps," in *Mademoiselle* (New York), February 1971.
"A Day in the Life of a Smiling Woman," in *In the Looking Glass,* edited by Nancy Dean and Myra Stark. New York, Putnam, 1977.
"A Success Story," in *Fine Lines,* edited by Ruth Sullivan. New York, Scribner, 1981.
"The Dying Year," in *Harper's* (New York), July 1987.

Plays

Bird of Paradise (produced London, 1969).

Screenplays: *Isadora,* with Melvyn Bragg and Clive Exton, 1969; *A Touch of Love (Thank You All Very Much),* 1969.

Television Play: *Laura,* 1964.

Other

Wadsworth. London, Evans, 1966; New York, Arco, 1969.
Virginia Woolf: A Personal Debt. New York, Aloe, 1973.
Arnold Bennett: A Biography. London, Weidenfeld and Nicolson, and New York, Knopf, 1974.
For Queen and Country: Britain in the Victorian Age (for children). London, Deutsch, 1978; New York, Seabury Press, 1979.
A Writer's Britain: Landscape in Literature. London, Thames and Hudson, and New York, Knopf, 1979.
Wordsworth's Butter Knife: An Essay. Northampton, Massachusetts, Catawba Press, 1980.
The Tradition of Women's Fiction: Lectures in Japan, edited by Yukako Suga. Tokyo, Oxford University Press, 1985.
Case for Equality. London, Fabian Society, 1988.
Stratford Revisited: A Legacy of the Sixties. Shipston-on-Stour, Warwickshire, Celandine Press, 1989.
Safe as Houses: An Examination of Home Ownership and Mortgage Tax Relief. London, Chatto and Windus, 1990.
Angus Wilson: A Biography. London, Secker and Warburg, 1995.

Editor, with B.S. Johnson, *London Consequences* (a group novel). London, Greater London Arts Association, 1972.
Editor, *Lady Susan, The Watsons, Sanditon,* by Jane Austen. London, Penguin, 1974.
Editor, *The Genius of Thomas Hardy.* London, Weidenfeld and Nicolson, and New York, Knopf, 1976.
Editor, with Charles Osborne, *New Stories 1.* London, Arts Council, 1976.
Editor, *The Oxford Companion to English Literature.* Oxford and New York, Oxford University Press, 1985; concise edition, edited with Jenny Stringer, 1987.
Editor, *Twentieth Century Classics.* London, Book Trust, 1986.

*

Bibliography: *Margaret Drabble: An Annotated Bibliography* by Joan Garrett Packer, New York, Garland, 1988.

Manuscript Collections: Boston University; University of Tulsa, Oklahoma.

Critical Studies: *Margaret Drabble: Puritanism and Permissiveness* by Valerie Grosvenor Myer, London, Vision Press, 1974; *Boulder-Pushers: Women in the Fiction of Margaret Drabble, Doris Lessing, and Iris Murdoch* by Carol Seiler-Franklin, Bern, Switzerland, Lang, 1979; *The Novels of Margaret Drabble: Equivocal Figures* by Ellen Cronan Rose, London, Macmillan, 1980, and *Critical Essays on Margaret Drabble* (includes bibliography by J.S. Korenman) edited by Rose, Boston, Hall, 1985; *Margaret Drabble: Golden Realms* edited by Dorey Schmidt and Jan Seale, Edinburg, University of Texas-Pan American Press, 1982; *Margaret Drabble: Existing Within Structures* by Mary Hurley Moran, Carbondale, Southern Illinois University Press, 1983; *Guilt and Glory: Studies in Margaret Drabble's Novels 1963-1980* by Susanna Roxman, Stockholm, Almquist & Wiksell, 1984; *Margaret Drabble* by Joanne V. Creighton, London, Methuen, 1985; *The Intertextuality of Fate: A Study of Margaret Drabble* by John Hannay, 1986; *Margaret Drabble* by Lynn Veach Sadler, Boston, Twayne, 1986; *Margaret Drabble: Symbolic Moralist* by Nora Foster Stovel, San Bernardino, California, Borgo Press, 1989.

* * *

Margaret Drabble's realistic, intellectually sophisticated novels have garnered popular approval and critical respect. She began by focusing on the condition and choices of university-educated women like herself in the 1960s, but has developed what has been called a "Dickensian desire" to depict the social complexities and inequalities of contemporary Britain. The voice of a generation of women responding to the development of feminism and the social changes of three decades, Drabble's novels combine social criticism, comedy, vivid characterization, and skillful plotting with an exploration of Zeitgeist.

Drabble's novels of the 1960s focused on the struggle for self-realization by clever young women in a society that seems to offer only marriage and motherhood, or the celibate pursuit of a career. These are the options articulated by Sarah, heroine of *A Summer Bird-Cage* (1963). That novel and the following, *The Garrick Year* (1964), explore the option of marriage, only to find deceit and despair, with children bringing squalor but also a sense of commitment. The redeeming role of children providing meaning to life is considered further in *The Millstone* (1965), which looks at the career option. In that book, Rosamund cannot form real relationships with men but establishes a deep bond with her child as Drabble explores social changes represented by unmarried motherhood.

Jerusalem the Golden (1967) is strengthened by clear autobiographical elements as it follows Clara's flight from the repressed provinciality of Drabble's fictional northern city of Northam to the cosmopolitan life of a charismatic family in London. This is a movement repeated in later books; the intelligent heroine escapes from her dull, lower-middle-class family to form a more exciting, if more fractured, new family in London that often contains ex-spouses and step-children. Such a structure represents Drabble's observation and essential optimism about social changes. The last 1960s novel, *The Waterfall* (1969), is a more poetic evocation of love and adultery with the symbolic splitting of the heroine into the delicate Jane and her alter ego, confident cousin Lucy.

Drabble's 1970s novels focus on themes of middle-age fears. Furthermore, her work broadens beyond mainly female experience to comprehend political and economic realities. *The Realms of Gold* (1975) uses the ideas of its anthropologist heroine, Frances, to comment on the problems of family and social class. *The Ice Age* (1977) is a rarity, as it takes the viewpoint of a male property developer in an attempt to understand some of the emotional and social consequences of economic turmoil. *The Middle Ground* (1980) consolidates the archetypal Drabble heroine in its protagonist, Kate, a spirited, educated, middle-class, divorced mother who is deeply concerned about social ills.

In retrospect, the 1970s novels prepare the way for the ambitious and successful trilogy of *The Radiant Way* (1987), *A Natural Curiosity* (1989), and *The Gates of Ivory* (1991), which together tell the interweaving stories of a huge number of characters in London and Northam in the 1980s. An attempt to chronicle a controversial decade in British political and social history, the trilogy centers on three women, now middle-aged, who met at Oxford in the 1950s. Liz, a psychoanalyst, is left by her media-mogul husband at the beginning of *The Radiant Way*. Alix teaches women in prison and befriends an ex-convict who is murdered by a serial killer. Unmarried art-historian Esther pursues affairs with both men and women. The novels explore family history as Liz discovers the secrets that made her mother a recluse, and Alix investigates the background of her serial killer. The *Gates of Ivory* brings to the fore a particular Drabble theme in the story of Stephen Cox, an unattached intellectual whose adventures in the Far East bring him his desired end. From the fatal Simone (in *A Summer Bird-Cage*) to the more stable wanderer and geologist David Ollerenshaw (in *The Realms of Gold*), the drifting, imperiled, single figure is Drabble's counterpoint to the vivid and usually warm depictions of family life.

Drabble writes of rational people confronting the irrational, and she regards the complexity of contemporary life with intelligence and dread. Her novels combine humor and strong characters with acute social observation, and, in her later novels, exceptionally well-woven plots. Drabble does more than record her times; she helps define them.

—S. A. Rowland

DUGAN, Jack. *See* **BUTTERWORTH, W. E.**

---

du MAURIER, Daphne

Nationality: English. **Born:** 13 May 1907, in London. **Education:** Attended schools in London, England; Meudon, France; and Paris. **Family:** Married Frederick Arthur Montague Browning, 1932 (died, 1965); two daughters and one son. **Career:** Writer, 1931-89. **Awards:** National Book award, 1938, for *Rebecca*; Dame Commander, Order of the British Empire, 1969; Mystery Writers of America Grand Master award, 1977. **Member:** Royal Society of Literature (fellow). **Died:** 19 April 1989, in Par, Cornwall.

Publications

Novels

The Loving Spirit. Doubleday, 1931; reprinted, Pan Books, 1976.
I'll Never Be Young Again. Doubleday, 1932; reprinted, Pan Books, 1975.
The Progress of Julius. Doubleday, 1933; reprinted, Avon, 1973.
Jamaica Inn. Doubleday, 1936; reprinted, Avon, 1977.
Rebecca. Doubleday, 1938; reprinted, Avon, 1988.
Frenchman's Creek. Gollancz, 1941; Doubleday, 1942; reprinted, Pan Books, 1976.
Hungry Hill. Doubleday, 1943; reprinted, Avon, 1974.
The King's General. Doubleday, 1946; reprinted, Avon, 1978.
The Parasites. Gollancz, 1949; Doubleday, 1950; reprinted, Avon, 1974.

My Cousin Rachel. Gollancz, 1951; Doubleday, 1952; reprinted, Buccaneer Books, 1993.
Mary Anne. Doubleday, 1954; reprinted, Dell, 1987.
The Scapegoat. Doubleday, 1957; reprinted, Carroll & Graf, 1988.
Castle d'Or, with Arthur Quiller-Couch. Doubleday, 1962.
The Glass-Blowers. Doubleday, 1963.
The Flight of the Falcon. Doubleday, 1965.
The House on the Strand. Doubleday, 1969; reprinted, Lightyear Press, 1993.
Rule Britannia. Gollancz, 1972; Doubleday, 1973.
Four Great Cornish Novels. Gollancz, 1978.

Short Stories

Come Wind, Come Weather. Heinemann, 1940; Doubleday, 1941.
The Apple Tree: A Short Novel and Some Stories, Gollancz, 1952; as *Kiss Me Again, Stranger: A Collection of Eight Stories,* Long and Short, Doubleday, 1953; reprinted, Avon, 1972; as *The Birds, and Other Stories,* Pan Books, 1977.
The Breaking Point. Doubleday, 1959; as *The Blue Lenses, and Other Stories,* Penguin, 1970.
Early Stories. Todd, 1959.
The Treasury of du Maurier Short Stories. Gollancz, 1960.
Don't Look Now. Doubleday, 1971; as *Not after Midnight,* Gollancz, 1971.
Echoes from the Macabre: Selected Stories. Gollancz, 1976; Doubleday, 1977.
The Rendezvous, and Other Stories. Gollancz, 1980.

Plays

Rebecca (produced London 1940; New York, 1945), Gollancz, 1940; reprinted, 1990.
The Years Between (produced Manchester, 1944; London, 1945), Gollancz, 1945; Doubleday, 1946.
September Tide (produced London, 1948), Gollancz, 1949; Doubleday, 1950.
My Cousin Rachel, edited by Diana Morgan, Dramatists Play Service, 1990.

Screenplays: *Hungry Hill,* adapted from her own novel, 1947.

Nonfiction

Gerald: A Portrait. Gollancz, 1934; Doubleday, 1935; reprinted, Richard West, 1978.
The du Mauriers. Doubleday, 1937.
Happy Christmas. Doubleday, 1940.
Spring Picture. Todd, 1944.
The Infernal World of Branwell Bronte. Gollancz, 1960; Doubleday, 1961.
Vanishing Cornwall. Doubleday, 1967.
Golden Lads: Sir Francis Bacon, Anthony Bacon and Their Friends. Doubleday, 1975.
The Winding Stair: Francis Bacon, His Rise and Fall. Gollancz, 1976; Doubleday, 1977.
Myself When Young: The Shaping of a Writer. Doubleday, 1977; as *Growing Pains: The Shaping of a Writer,* Gollancz, 1977.
The "Rebecca" Notebook, and Other Memories. Doubleday, 1980.
Enchanted Cornwall: Her Pictorial Memoir. Viking Penguin, 1992.

Editor, *The Young George du Maurier: A Selection of His Letters, 1860-1867.* P. Davies, 1951; Doubleday, 1952.

*

Media Adaptations: Films—*Jamaica Inn,* 1939; *Rebecca,* 1940 and 1979; *Frenchman's Creek,* 1944; *Hungry Hill,* 1947; *My Cousin Rachel,* 1953; *The Scapegoat,* 1959; *The Birds,* 1963; *Don't Look Now,* 1973. Television—*Jamaica Inn,* 1985.

Critical Studies: *Daphne: The Life of Daphne Du Maurier* by Judith Cook, Bantam, 1991; *The Private World of Daphne Du Maurier* by Martyn Shallcross, St. Martin's Press, 1992; *Daphne Du Maurier* by Margaret Forster, Chatto and Windus, 1993.

* * *

Daphne du Maurier is probably the most effective practitioner of the art of the modern Gothic novel, and her novels continue to enjoy an avid following. A spiritual descendant of Charlotte Bronte, du Maurier achieved her greatest success with *Rebecca* (1938), a work viewed by some as a minor classic. The book achieved great success; the Hitchcock film based on the book won an Academy Award for Best Picture in 1940. *Rebecca* has remained in print since it was first published.

Du Maurier's first novels were not Gothics; *The Loving Spirit* (1931), *I'll Never Be Young Again* (1932), and *The Progress of Julius* (1933) received lukewarm reviews and were considered to be "bookish" and immature. It was not until the publication of *Jamaica Inn* in 1936 that du Maurier appeared to have found her niche as a writer of romantic novels.

Jamaica Inn is set in 1835 in Cornwall, the locale for most of du Maurier's fiction. Cornwall, in this novel as in many of her others, comes to be a setting integral enough to almost qualify as a character in her books. The story concerns twenty-three-year-old Mary Yellan, who has arrived in Cornwall to live with her mother's sister after the death of her mother. Mary discovers that her aunt is married to a smuggler and possible murderer, Joss Merlyn. She is intrigued and intimidated by Joss, and attracted to his brother Jem. *Jamaica Inn* received favorable reviews, notably from Sean O'Faolain who compared the book to works by Robert Louis Stevenson. The book was late made into a film by Alfred Hitchcock.

Rebecca was published in 1938 and became the most outstanding work du Maurier was to produce. "Last night I dreamt I went to Manderley again," has become one of the best known opening lines in modern literature. Most critics responded to the book with enthusiasm. Comparisons to Charlotte Bronte's *Jane Eyre* were inevitable and accurate. Both books use the now-familiar Gothic formula involving the handsome brooding hero, the mysterious mansion, and the (supposedly) dead wife, but du Maurier somehow managed a twist on the formula that guaranteed her a place in the ranks of noted Gothic authors. It is no small accomplishment to make the most interesting character in a novel one who is dead before the book opens, but that is indeed the case with Rebecca, the late, unlamented wife of Maxim de Winter. De Winter marries the narrator of the story, an unnamed young woman half his age, and brings her to Manderley, his ancestral home. The new Mrs. de Winter is hardly a success in her position as replacement for the remarkable, beautiful, sophisticated Rebecca.

However, things are not as they seem to the narrator. She is to learn that Maxim not only detested Rebecca, but that he killed her for reasons that may have involved the lesbianism hinted at by both Maxim and the wicked Mrs. Danvers, housekeeper for the de Winters, and loyal confidant and servant of Rebecca.

The enormous success of *Rebecca* almost guaranteed that whatever books followed would be considered disappointments. That was, indeed, the case. Books such as *Frenchman's Creek* (1941), *Hungry Hill* (1943), *The King's General* (1946), and *The Parasites* (1949) sold well enough, but were generally ignored by most serious critics.

My Cousin Rachel (1951), however, excited more interest. In some ways, *My Cousin Rachel* is a reversal of the characters in *Rebecca.* As Richard Kelly points out in *Daphne Du Maurier, Rebecca* is the story of a dominating man and a wife who dies before the story begins. *My Cousin Rachel* is about a dominating woman and a husband who dies before the story begins. Philip Ashley tells the story of his cousin Ambrose Ashley, the man who had raised him and who had somewhat mysteriously acquired a wife, Rachel, shortly before he died. Philip is convinced that Rachel has killed Ambrose. But when she appears at his home he becomes less certain. He is both attracted and repelled by Rachel. By the time she dies, readers do not know whether Rachel killed Ambrose, tried to kill Philip, or was even guilty of any criminal intent. The book is ambiguous to the end, leaving the reader to judge Rachel.

The last group of du Maurier's novels dealt more intimately with a theme she'd played with in earlier books; the question of identity and psychological connection. In *The Scapegoat* (1957), she uses a pair of men, virtually identical, to look at the ways the same person might face situations differently. She had used two people to express facets of the same personality before—notably Joss and Jem Merlyn in *Jamaica Inn*—but she began in later novels to deal more closely with that theme.

Du Maurier's work and life have offered intriguing puzzles for scholars and readers, and her books remain favorites of lovers of the Gothic genre.

—June Harris

DUNNE, Dominick

Nationality: American. **Born:** 29 October 1925, in Hartford, Connecticut. **Education:** Williams College, B.A., 1949. **Military Service:** Served in U.S. Army; awarded Bronze Star. **Family:** Married Ellen Griffin (divorced); children: Griffin, Alexander, Dominique (deceased). **Career:** Worked as stage manager, *Howdy Doody Show;* vice-president, Four Star Television; executive producer of television series *Adventures in Paradise;* producer of motion pictures, including *The Boys in the Band,* 1970, *The Panic in Needle Park,* 1971, *Play It as It Lays,* 1972, and *Ash Wednesday,* 1973; full-time writer since 1971. Co-founder of Dunne-Didion-Dunne (film producers). **Agent:** James O. Brown, Curtis Brown Ltd., 575 Madison Ave., New York, New York 10022. **Address:** 24 Fifth Ave., New York, New York 10011, U.S.A.

Publications

Novels

The Winners: Part II of Joyce Haber's "The Users." Simon & Schuster, 1982.
The Two Mrs. Grenvilles. Crown, 1985.
People Like Us. Crown, 1988.
An Inconvenient Woman. Crown, 1990.
A Season in Purgatory. Crown, 1993.

Nonfiction

Fatal Charms, and Other Tales of Today. Crown, 1986.
The Mansions of Limbo. Crown, 1991.

*

Media Adaptations: Television miniseries—*The Two Mrs. Grenvilles,* 1987; *People Like Us,* 1990; *An Inconvenient Woman,* 1991; *A Season in Purgatory,* 1994.

* * *

After drugs and alcohol unraveled his career as a television and film producer in the late 1970s, Dominick Dunne turned to novel writing. In 1982 he published *The Winners,* a sequel to a novel by Joyce Haber. In it, Mona Berg, the ambitious secretary of a big Hollywood agent, saves her boss's life and eventually takes over his agency, using it as a springboard to insinuate herself into the lives of L.A.'s beautiful people. Reviewers greeted *The Winners* lukewarmly at best. The reviewer for the Los Angeles *Times,* for example, criticized Dunne for employing only stock characters but noted that he "somehow . . . manages to keep them moving," while the *Chicago Tribune* viewed the novel as a parody of the lifestyles-of-the-rich-and-homicidal genre.

In *The Two Mrs. Grenvilles* (1985), Dunne turned to the roman-à-clef, or novel-with-a-key, approach, using real-life events and figures to inform the plot, which was based on the 1955 murder of millionaire William Woodward by his wife. The novel chronicles the marriage of mercenary Ann Arden (the first Mrs. Grenville) and wealthy war hero Billy Grenville. After secretly cheating on Billy and then discovering that he has stumbled upon an event in her past that drives him to file for divorce, Ann kills him, then convinces Billy's mother (the second Mrs. Grenville) that she had accidentally mistaken him for a prowler. Although the reviewer for the *New York Times* felt the novel was only "mildly suspenseful," *Publishers Weekly* praised it as "smoothly written and engrossing" and the *Los Angeles Times* called it "a fast and enjoyable piece of reading."

In 1982, Dunne's daughter was murdered by her boyfriend. Dunne's coverage of the trial (which resulted in a mere three-year sentence for the killer) appeared in *Vanity Fair* magazine and was then published along with twelve of Dunne's other *Vanity Fair* pieces in *Fatal Charms, and Other Tales of Today* (1986). In addition to the moving main essay (titled "Justice: A Father's Account of the Trial of His Daughter's Killer"), the collection included profiles of Imelda Marcos, Elizabeth Taylor, and Gloria Vanderbilt, among other prominent figures. The reviewer for the *Washington Post* characterized the celebrity profiles as "slyly irreverent."

Dunne's next two novels, *People Like Us* (1988) and *An Inconvenient Woman* (1990), followed the roman-à-clef approach of *The Two Mrs. Grenvilles:* the former was based on elements of the murder of Dunne's daughter in the story of a celebrity journalist's experiences among New York City's beau monde while waiting for the parole of his daughter's killer; *Inconvenient Woman* was based on the affair between the real-life Alfred Bloomingdale (a friend of Ronald Reagan) and his mistress. Critical opinion was divided on *People Like Us. Time* magazine attacked Dunne for using "unimaginative stock characters" and for capitalizing on his daughter's murder for plot material. Other reviewers praised it as "deliciously witty and wonderfully elegant" (*Chicago Tribune*); "witty, wise, compassionate" (*Publishers Weekly*); and "funny and dead-on target" (*New York Times*). *An Inconvenient Woman* was more uniformly praised: Jill Robinson in the *New York Times* asserted that it was Dunne's "best novel" to date, *Time* labeled it "deliciously wicked," and the Chicago *Tribune* hailed Dunne as "America's preeminent novelist of scandal."

Dunne's second collection of *Vanity Fair* pieces, *The Mansions of Limbo*, appeared in 1991 and featured both celebrity profiles (Jane Wyman, the Duchess of Windsor) and Dunne's burgeoning work as a trial reporter (the Menendez brothers murder trial). His 1993 novel, *A Season in Purgatory*, again worked from real-life parallels, in this case the machinations of a well-to-do New England Catholic family closely resembling the Kennedys. Using his now familiar journalist/outsider narrator to tell a story of murder, cover-up, and guilt, Dunne again won the praise of critics, and *A Season* joined a growing number of Dunne novels made into television miniseries. In 1994, Dunne continued work on his next novel, *The Sins of the Sons.*

Although by 1995 Dunne was by no means unknown, his coverage of the O. J. Simpson murder trial catapulted his career to new levels of celebrity. As *Vanity Fair's* in-the-courtroom observer, Dunne published a series of "insider" reports (a prelude to an expected book-length account of the trial) that established him, in the words of his magazine publisher, as "the premier crime reporter of his time." Although Dunne perhaps only very loosely deserves the appellation "social critic," as a novelist he has fairly been described as occupying a middle ground between the serious social novels of J. P. Marquand and John O'Hara and the supermarket fiction school of Judith Krantz, Danielle Steele, and Sidney Sheldon.

—Paul S. Bodine

DWYER, Deanna. *See* **KOONTZ, Dean R(ay).**

DWYER, K. R. *See* **KOONTZ, Dean R(ay).**

E

ECO, Umberto

Nationality: Italian. **Born:** 5 January 1932, in Alessandria. **Education:** University of Turin, Ph.D., 1954. **Military Service:** Italian Army, 1958-59. **Family:** Married Renate Ramge, 1962; children: Stefano, Carlotta. **Career:** RAI (Italian Radio-Television), Milan, editor for cultural programs, 1954-59; University of Turin, assistant lecturer, 1956-63, lecturer in aesthetics, 1963-64; University of Milan, lecturer in faculty of architecture, 1964-65; University of Florence, professor of visual communications, 1966-69; Milan Polytechnic, professor of semiotics, 1969-71; University of Bologna, associate professor, 1971-75, professor of semiotics, 1975—. Visiting professor, New York University, 1969, 1976, Northwestern University, 1972, University of California, San Diego, 1975, Yale University, 1977, 1980, 1981, and Columbia University, 1978. Lecturer on semiotics at various institutions throughout the world, including University of Antwerp, Ecole Pratique des Hautes Etudes, University of London, Nobel Foundation, University of Warsaw, University of Budapest, University of Toronto, Murdoch University—Perth, and Amherst College. Member of the Council for the United States and Italy. **Awards:** Premio Strega and Premio Anghiari, both 1981, both for *Il nome della rosa;* Prix Medicis for best foreign novel, 1982, for French version of *Il nome della rosa; Los Angeles Times* fiction prize nomination, 1983, and best fiction book award from Association of Logos Bookstores, both for *The Name of the Rose;* McLuhan Teleglobe Canada award from UNESCO's Canadian Commission, 1985, for achievement in communications; honorary degrees from Catholic University, Leuven, 1985, Odense University, 1986, Loyola University, Chicago, 1987, State University of New York at Stony Brook, 1987, Royal College of Arts, London, 1987, and Brown University, 1988. **Member:** International Association for Semiotic Studies (secretary-general, 1972-79, vice-president from 1979), James Joyce Foundation (honorary trustee). **Address:** Piazza Castello 13, 20121 Milano, Italy.

Publications

Novels

Il nome della rosa. Bompiani, 1980; as *The Name of the Rose,* Harcourt, 1983.
Il pendolo di Foucault. Bompiani, 1988; as *Foucault's Pendulum,* Harcourt, 1989.
The Island of the Day Before. Secker, 1995.

Nonfiction

Il problema estetico in San Tommaso. Edizioni di Filosofia, 1956; as *Il problema estetico in Tommaso d'Aquino,* Bompiani, 1970; as *The Aesthetics of Thomas Aquinas,* Harvard University Press, 1988.
Filosofi in liberta. Taylor (Turin), 1958, 2nd edition, 1959.
Sviluppo dell'estetica mediovale. 1959; as *Art and Beauty in the Middle Ages,* Yale University Press, 1986.
Opera aperta: Forma e indeterminazione nelle poetiche contemporanee. Bompiani, 1962; revised edition, 1972; as *The Open Work,* Harvard University Press, 1989.
Diario minimo. Mondadori, 1963; second revised edition, 1976.
Apocalittici e integrati: Comunicazioni di massa e teoria della cultura di massa. Bompiani, 1964; revised edition, 1977.
Le poetiche di Joyce, Bompiani, 1965; second edition, 1966.
Appunti per una semiologia delle comunicazioni visive. Bompiani, 1967.
La struttura assente. Bompiani, 1968; revised edition, 1983.
La definizione dell'arte. U. Mursia, 1968.
Le forme del contenuto. Bompiani, 1971.
Il segno. Isedi, 1971.
Il costume di casa: Evidenze e misteri dell'ideologia italiano. Bompiani, 1973.
Beato di Liebana: Miniature del Beato de Fernando I y Sancha. F. M. Ricci, 1973.
Trattato di semiotica generale. Bompiani, 1975; as *A Theory of Semiotics,* Indiana University Press, 1976.
Il superuomo di massa: Studi sul romanzo popolare. Cooperativa Scrittori, 1976; revised edition, Bompiani, 1978.
Dalla periferia dell'Impero. Bompiani, 1976.
Come si fa una tesi di laurea. Bompiani, 1977.
Lector in fabula: La cooperazione interpretative nei testi narrativa. Bompiani, 1979; as *The Role of the Reader: Explorations in the Semiotics of Texts,* Indiana University Press, 1979.
Perche continuiamo a fare e a insegnare arte?, with others. Cappelli, 1979.
Sette anni di desiderio. Bompiani, 1983.
Postscript to "The Name of the Rose." Harcourt, 1983.
Semiotics and the Philosophy of Language. Indiana University Press, 1984.
Sugli specchi e altri saggi. Bompiani, 1985.
Travels in Hyperreality. Harcourt, 1986.
The Aesthetics of Chaosmos: The Middle Ages of James Joyce. Harvard University Press, 1989.
The Limits of Interpretation. Indiana University Press, 1990.
Interpretation and Overinterpretation. Cambridge University Press, 1992.
Misreadings. Harcourt Brace & Company, 1993.
Apocalypse Postponed: Essays. Indiana University Press, 1994.
How to Travel with a Salmon and Other Essays. Harcourt Brace & Company, 1994.
Six Walks in the Fictional Woods. Harvard University Press, 1994.

For Children

The Bomb and the General, with illustrations by Eugenio Carmi, Harcourt, 1989.
The Three Astronauts. Harcourt, 1989.

Editor with G. Zorzoli, *Storia figurata delle invenzioni: Dalla selce scheggiata al volo spaziali.* Bompiani, 1961; as *The Picture History of Inventions From Plough to Polaris,* Macmillan, 1963.
Editor with Oreste del Buono, *Il caso Bond.* Bompiani, 1965; as *The Bond Affair,* Macdonald, 1966.

Editor with Jean Chesneaux and Gino Nebiolo, *I fumetti di Mao.* Laterza, 1971; as *The People's Comic Book: Red Women's Detachment, Hot on the Trail, and Other Chinese Comics,* Anchor Press, 1973.
Editor with Thomas A. Sebeok, *Sign of the Three: Dupin, Holmes, Peirce.* Indiana University Press, 1984.
Editor with others, *Meaning and Mental Representations.* Indiana University Press, 1988.
Editor with Costantino Marmo, *On the Medieval Theory of Signs.* John Benjamins, 1989.

*

Film Adaptations: *The Name of the Rose,* 1986.

Critical Studies: *Naming the Rose: Essays on Eco's "The Name of the Rose"* edited by Thomas M. Inge, University Press of Mississippi, 1988.

* * *

From the rarefied heights of semiotics to articles in the popular press, from writing about *Finnegans Wake* to writing about James Bond, Umberto Eco has proven remarkably versatile. He is a scholar specializing in medieval aesthetics, theories of sign production, and the philosophy of language who is also an internationally bestselling novelist, "the Pavarotti of the lecture circuit," and arguably as much a cult object as the film *Casablanca* (the subject of one of his semiotic studies).

For all their length, learning, and intricate structure, Eco's three novels, like their author (a kind of postmodern J. R. R. Tolkien), manage to please in various ways. First, they fascinate and entertain, seducing their readers with the depiction of fully realized worlds (whether medieval, late Renaissance, or contemporary). Second, by creating a simulacrum of the real, Eco invites his readers to enter a virtual reality and thus "escape the anxiety that attends us when we try to say something true about the world." Finally, Eco's inviting but essentially demystifying novels do not so much play to the reader as play with him, making him into both prey and accomplice. Strangely enough, this most Borgesian feature of Eco's fiction contributes mightily to the author's essentially humanist agenda. By making the reader more aware of the semiotic "nature" of the world, Eco hopes to make both reader and world more open and tolerant. It is a hope that reflects both Eco's early commitment, along with other members of Italy's Gruppa 63, to the avant-garde novel as an agent of social change, and his later, less politically idealistic interest in the novel as an entertaining, though not necessarily escapist, game.

Because he defines the novel as a machine for generating interpretations, Eco has been reluctant to explain his own work, to speak or write the final word that would preclude any others. Instead of using *Postscript to "The Name of the Rose* (1984), for example, to explain what his novel means, he uses it to explain how he came to write his novel (adopting an approach similar to the one Poe used in "The Philosophy of Composition" to explain how he came to write "The Raven"). As vast and labyrinthine as the library that figures so prominently in its pages, *The Name of the Rose* (1980) is "about" a series of deaths in a monastery only in the most reductive sense. This anti-detective story in which the Holmesian hero concedes that "There was no plot, and I discovered it by mistake" deals more importantly with more general concerns: access to books (and truth), interpretive strategies, and the like. Historically rich, intertextually dense, and intellectually demanding, the novel succeeds so well in large part because Eco narrates all but the first pages from the perspective of a surrogate reader, an 18-year-old novice (as recalled by his 80-year-old self).

The going is a bit rougher in *Foucault's Pendulum* (1988), in which the narrator is an academic Sam Spade with a PhD in philology. Set in the 1980s but harking back all the way to the 15th century, the novel deals more extensively with the question of paranoid plots raised in *The Name of the Rose.* Ambiguous texts breed anxiety and thus the desire to control and limit the play of possible meanings. As one especially paranoid reader says in the novel, "There had to be a plan," or as Eco would add, several of them; a potentially comical situation not without tragic consequences.

The Island of the Day Before (1995) is literally a lighter, brighter book, in part because it deals with a more naive central character; a frail, photophobic hypochrondriac. "Shipwrecked and cast up on a deserted ship" within sight of an island that lies on the other side of the 180th meridian, Roberto della Griva is a jokey version of Robinson Crusoe as well as the frail narrative point upon which Eco heaps a good deal of 17th century history, literary style, and science. The text focuses on various attempts to determine longitude, to locate precisely the kind of fixed point that Eco's machines for generating meanings so assiduously avoid.

Eco's narrative gamesplaying is, of course, not to everyone's taste, but his novels manage to survive (even if not quite refute) the worst that has been said of them; that they are, as Rosemary Dinnage has said of *Island,* more fun to decode than to read, and as Salman Rushdie has said of *Foucault's Pendulum,* "devoid of characters, entirely free of anything resembling a credible spoken word, and mind-numbingly full of gobbledygook of all sorts." Yes, but what high-minded fun, what high-class gobbledygook, what intricately wrought devices for speculating about the origins and consequences of stories and interpretations, science, story, and religion included.

—Robert A. Morace

EDDINGS, David

Nationality: American. **Born:** Spokane, Washington, 7 July 1931. **Education:** Reed College, Portland, Oregon, B.A. in literature 1954; University of Washington, Seattle, M.A. in English 1961. **Military Service:** Served in U.S. Army, 1954-56. **Family:** Married Judith Lee Schall in 1962. **Agent:** Eleanor Wood, Blasingame, McCauley, and Wood, 111 Eighth Avenue, Suite 1501, New York, New York 10011, U.S.A.

Publications

Novels (series: The Belgariad; The Elenium; The Mallorean; The Tamuli)

High Hunt. New York, Putnam, 1973; London, HarperCollins, 1993.
The Belgariad. 2 vols., Garden City, New York, Doubleday, and London, Century, 1985.

Pawn of Prophecy. New York, Ballantine, 1982; London, Century, 1983.
Queen of Sorcery. New York, Ballantine, 1982; London, Century, 1984.
Magician's Gambit. New York, Ballantine, 1983; London, Century, 1984.
Castle of Wizardry. New York, Ballantine, and London, Century, 1984.
Enchanter's Endgame. New York, Ballantine, 1984; London, Century, 1985.
The Mallorean:
Guardians of the West. New York, Ballantine, and London, Bantam, 1987.
King of the Murgos. New York, Ballantine, and London, Bantam, 1988.
Demon Lord of Karanda. New York, Ballantine, and London, Bantam, 1988.
Sorceress of Darshiva. New York, Ballantine, and London, Bantam, 1989.
The Seeress of Kell. New York, Ballantine, and London, Bantam, 1991.
The Losers. New York, Fawcett, 1992; London, HarperCollins, 1993.
The Tamuli:
Domes of Fire. London, HarperCollins, 1992, and New York, Ballantine, 1993.
The Shining Ones. New York, Ballantine, and London, HarperCollins, 1993.
The Hidden City. New York, Ballantine, and London, HarperCollins, 1994.
The Elenium. London, Grafton, 1993.
The Diamond Throne. New York, Ballantine, and London, Grafton, 1989.
The Ruby Knight. New York, Ballantine, and London, Grafton, 1990.
The Sapphire Rose. London, HarperCollins, 1991, and New York, Ballantine, 1992.
Belgarath the Sorcerer. New York, Ballantine, and London, HarperCollins, 1995.

* * *

Of his fantasy writing philosophy, David Eddings jests: "take a bit of magic, mix well with a few open-ended Jungian archetypal myths, make your people sweat and smell and get hungry at inopportune moments, throw in a ponderous prehistory, and let nature take its course."

Though his first novel, *High Hunt* (1973), was a critically well-received science fiction novel, David Eddings has made his mark in the publishing world with his various epic fantasy series: The Belgariad (1982-84), The Malloreon (1987-91), The Elenium (1989-91), and The Tamuli (1991-94). From its appearance on the market, *Pawn of Prophecy* (1982)—the first in the five-book series The Belgariad—was a popular sensation, amassing an immense following of eager readers. Each of the rest of his series shared a similar reception, as well as similar criticisms.

The Belgariad is an appropriate title for this series of books, as none of the individual novels that comprise it are capable of standing alone. This is because The Belgariad is an epic high-fantasy, and therefore requires a lot of space to develop the world, characters, and plot. The story concerns a quest in search of a stolen magic artifact called the "Orb of Aldur." In the course of the story, the main character Garion learns of the hidden secrets of his family and past, and is forced to come to terms at last with what he is and what he has been brought into the world to accomplish. It eventually becomes clear that Garion is not merely a farm boy, but is a powerful image in his own right. Throughout The Belgariad he must strive to come to terms with the astonishing fact that he is the descendent of legends, and the pivotal figure in a mythical quest that will decide the fate of the world. For not only is he a sorcerer, but he is the heir to a throne and the only person who can safely take up the Orb of Aldur against the evil god Torak, who has stolen the Orb.

In The Belgariad Eddings creates a complex and believable world by craftily layering minute details and establishing an elaborate historical background based on an intricate social and political structure. Add to that his amazing ability to make even the smallest characters seem as though they have complete and complex lives, and it is easy to see why The Belgariad is so popular.

Despite the popularity of his books, Eddings has critics. Of the criticisms put forth about his books, the most damaging has been the accusation that they are merely derivatives of J.R.R. Tolkien's works. That accusation is difficult to counter because high fantasy has been largely defined by Tolkien's *The Hobbit* (1965) and *The Fellowship of the Ring* (1965) series, and much of what is considered high fantasy is influenced, at least to some degree, by Tolkien. Eddings does use traditional motifs—the quest, the prophecy, artifacts of magic, and the final arcane duel—but he manages to do so in an interesting and compelling way.

Eddings does, however, seem derivative in The Mallorean series—derivative of himself. In this sequel to The Belgariad, Eddings retells the same story with the same plot. He then repeats the formula in other of his fantasy series, including The Elenium and its sequel series The Tamuli.

The plots in Eddings' novels are fairly straightforward and uncomplicated. The success of the books lies in his ability as a world-builder, and his skill with character and dialogue. In particular, the character of Silk is probably the masterpiece of these series. He is snide and outspoken, with a strange vulnerability and outrageous sense of humor that together are very compelling. But each of Eddings' characters are unique, and he never loses track of any of them—be they major or minor—and never do they appear as mere plot devices. Instead, he breathes humanity into each, complete with quirks, fears, jealousy, pride, and compassion. Furthermore, his plots are intentionally less complex than they could be in order to prevent the stories from overwhelming the richness of the characters.

More recently, Eddings unveiled a prequel to The Belgariad entitled *Belgarath the Sorcerer.* Reviewers of that novel again affectionately criticized it for being derivative of Tolkien, but lauded Eddings' skills related to character development, dialogue, and storytelling. The book must be read with the other ten books of the series, or the reader will be lost.

—Diana Francis

ELKIN, Stanley (Lawrence)

Nationality: American. **Born:** Brooklyn, New York, 11 May 1930. **Education:** The University of Illinois, Urbana, 1948-60,

B.A. 1952, M.A. 1953, Ph.D. in English 1961. **Military Service:** Served in the United States Army, 1955-57. **Family:** Married Joan Jacobson in 1953; two sons and one daughter. **Career:** Instructor, 1960-62, assistant professor, 1962-66, associate professor, 1966-69, since 1969 professor of English, and since 1983 King Professor of Modern Letters, Washington University, St. Louis. Visiting lecturer, Smith College, Northampton, Massachusetts, 1964-65; visiting professor, University of California, Santa Barbara, Summer 1967, University of Wisconsin, Milwaukee, Summer 1969, Yale University, New Haven, Connecticut, 1975, and Boston University, 1976. **Awards:** Longview Foundation award, 1962; *Paris Review* prize, 1965; Guggenheim fellowship, 1966; Rockefeller fellowship, 1968; National Endowment for the Arts grant, 1971; American Academy grant, 1974; Rosenthal Foundation award, 1980; *Southern Review* award, 1981; National Book Critics Circle award, 1983; Brandeis University Creative Arts award, 1986. L.H.D.: University of Illinois, Urbana, 1986. **Member:** American Academy, 1982. **Died:** Of heart failure in St. Louis, Missouri, 31 May 1995.

Publications

Novels

Boswell. New York, Random House, and London, Hamish Hamilton, 1964.
A Bad Man. New York, Random House, 1967; London, Blond, 1968.
The Dick Gibson Show. New York, Random House, and London, Weidenfeld and Nicolson, 1971.
The Franchiser. New York, Farrar Straus, 1976.
George Mills. New York, Dutton, 1982.
The Magic Kingdom. New York, Dutton, 1985.
The Rabbi of Lud. New York, Scribner, 1987.
The Macguffin. New York, Simon and Schuster, 1991.
Mrs. Ted Bliss. New York, Hyperion, 1995.

Short Stories

Criers and Kibitzers, Kibitzers and Criers. New York, Random House, 1966; London, Blond, 1968.
The Making of Ashenden. London, Covent Garden Press, 1972.
Searches and Seizures. New York, Random House, 1973; as *Alex and the Gypsy,* London, Penguin, 1977.
The Living End. New York, Dutton, 1979; London, Cape, 1980.
Early Elkin. Flint, Michigan, Bamberger, 1985.
Van Gogh's Room at Arles: Three Novellas. New York, Hyperion, 1993.

Plays

The Six-Year-Old Man (screeplay). Flint, Michigan, Bamberger, 1987.
The Coffee Room (radio play). Louisville, Kentucky, Contre Coup Press, 1987.

Other

Stanley Elkin's Greatest Hits (omnibus). New York, Dutton, 1980.
Why I Live Where I Live (essay). University City, Missouri, Contre Coup Press, 1983.
Pieces of Soap: Essays. New York, Simon and Schuster, 1990.

Editor, *Stories from the Sixties.* New York, Doubleday, 1971.
Editor, with Shannon Ravenel, *The Best American Short Stories 1980.* Boston, Houghton Mifflin, 1980.

*

Manuscript Collection: Washington University Library, St. Louis.

Critical Studies: *Humanism and the Absurd* by Naomi Lebowitz, Evanston, Illinois, Northwestern University Press, 1971; *City of Words* by Tony Tanner, London, Cape, and New York, Harper, 1971; *The Jewish Writer in America* by Allen Guttman, New York, Oxford University Press, 1971; *Beyond the Wasteland* by Raymond Olderman, New Haven, Connecticut, Yale University Press, 1972; *The Fiction of Stanley Elkin* by Doris G. Bargen, Bern, Switzerland, Lang, 1980; *Reading Stanley Elkin* by Peter J. Bailey, Boston, Houghton Mifflin, 1985; *Stanley Elkin* by David C. Dougherty, Boston, Twayne, 1990; *Comic Sense: Reading Robert Coover, Stanley Elkin, Philip Roth* by Thomas Pughe, Basel, Switzerland, Birkhäuser Verlag, 1994.

* * *

Stanley Elkin was what so many American writers only try to be: an American original. His combination of the storyteller's essentially oral, seemingly artless style with an exemplary and painstaking dedication to craft made him one of the great and certainly one of the most idiosyncratic stylists of the century—the master of an obsessive as well as excessive, fiercely energetic prose. Yet unlike his friend and colleague William Gass's no less rhetorically rich sentences, Elkin's writing is, for all its page-a-day fine-tuning and densely woven texture, wonderfully and at times absurdly, down-to-earth and firmly grounded both in the nuts and bolts of American life and in what Yeats called "the foul rag and bone shop of the heart"—in Elkin's case, the Faulknerian heart in conflict with itself (Elkin wrote his doctoral dissertation on religious themes in Faulkner's fiction).

In Elkin's work rage vies with the ridiculous, grief with grievance, gorgeous prose with comic grotesquerie, "His Pagliaccio clown suit alternat[ing] with his ancient Mariner weeds" (Helen Vendler). His characters suffer the slings and arrows of outrageous fortune ("All books are the Book of Job," Elkin judged), but in a decidedly modern vein, which is to say in a tragi-comic mode. Elkin's own physical ailments—the heart attack at 38 and the onset of Multiple Sclerosis four years later—along with his failure to gain a larger piece of the literary pie fueled his characters' sense of wrongs unfairly inflicted. But it also led Elkin to transform all that is intensely physical and emotional in his and his characters' lives into the purely verbal; the grotesque body into the visionary voice. In this way Elkin rang his variations on a familiar Jewish-American theme, combining as it were the "I want, I want" of Saul Bellow's characters and the wild imaginings of Philip Roth, but in an idiom that was Elkin's own.

Elkin used plot and character the way he used language; according to his own needs, not his reviewers' expectations. His characters are purposely flattened, reduced to their roles or occupations (franchiser, or rather franchisee, bail bondsman, streets commissioner, rabbi, nurse, widow) and to a limited set of quirks, tics, habits, shticks, and riffs that underscore their comic predicament. All feel as the aptly named title character of Elkin's first novel, *Boswell* (1944) does; passed by, second-rate, and either left out or unfairly singled out. They are like Feldman, the department store owner sent to prison for trying to satisfy all his customers' desires; they are all felled men, prone to fantasies of grandeur or victimhood or revenge. For them there is no Boethian consolation of philosophy, but only the relative release of rant, rage, resentment, and remission. Elkin's extravagant style complements, indeed celebrates, the lives of these absurdly obsessive yet strangely likable characters as they try, in outlandish fashion, to retain some shred of dignity. They are versions of Beckett's tramps depicted not against a bleak existential background but instead in all the fullness and specificity of their American lives.

Elkin's plots, like his characters, do not so much develop as accrete. Heeding the siren song of a muse named Serendipity, Elkin follows the simple math of "More is more." Elkin's "more" is at once defiant (see, for example, the 113-page digression in *George Mills*) and celebratory (a variation on a theme from Dylan Thomas's "Do Not Go Gentle into that Good Night"). This "more" is also part of Elkin's larger design; the narrative rhythm of tension and release that helps give Elkin's seemingly cartoonish, essentially Rabelaisian art a surprising emotional intensity, a generosity of spirit, and a sense of obligation that transforms the clearly ridiculous into the quasi-religious. Elkin clearly "shares with comedians a zest for bizarrely elaborated routines, the extended metaphor, prodigious sales pitches, and show-off shaggy-dogging," as Robert Coover has claimed, and, as Gass has written, "Nothing but genre blindness could prevent us from seeing that there is no warmer, wealthier poetry being written in our time."

—Robert A. Morace

ELLIS, Bret Easton

Nationality: American. **Born:** Los Angeles, 7 March 1964. **Education:** Bennington College, Vermont, B.A. 1986. **Agent:** International Creative Management, 40 West 57th Street, New York, New York 10019, U.S.A.

Publications

Novels

Less Than Zero. New York, Simon and Schuster, 1985; London, Pan, 1985.
The Rules of Attraction. New York, Simon and Schuster, 1987; London, Picador, 1988.
American Psycho. New York, Vintage, and London, Picador, 1991.
The Informers. New York, Knopf, and London, Picador, 1994.

* * *

Brat-packer, misogynist, and chronicler of the excesses of the capitalist 1980s are some of the titles Bret Easton Ellis has earned during his short but highly public career. Both praised and damned, Ellis is one of the most controversial and popular novelists to have emerged in recent years. He's the F. Scott Fitzgerald of, as one critic calls it, the "blank generation," or the college-educated children of the rich and famous that are incurably addicted to drugs, clubs, popular music, and sex. His novels capture the vacuity of lives that seem from the outside to be prosperous and full of opportunity. With their vacant present-tense narrators and random plots, they pan across the consumer-frenzy and affluence of 1980s America. But for all their barren emptiness, Ellis's novels constitute some of the most biting social satire to have appeared this century.

Ellis published his first novel *Less Than Zero* (1985) when he was just 20 years old. It soon acquired cult status, ironically with many of the generation Ellis satirizes. It maps the rich kids of Los Angeles at play, endlessly questing for the heights of experience. We travel with Clay, the narrator, in the best cars to the best restaurants and clubs and watch his friends take drugs and have sex. It's soon apparent, however, that this pleasure-seeking never really brings fulfillment. Clay's generation might have BMWs, the latest clothes, and records, but that is *all* they have and all they can ever talk about. Deeper values and emotions, especially love, have disappeared into the void created by a consumer-culture where (for these people at least) virtually anything is affordable.

For Ellis, the pursuit of happiness through drugs and sex is really an attempt to recover more intense and meaningful experiences that have been replaced by a world as flat and two-dimensional as a television screen. This creates an increasingly Sadian spiral of abuse. Clay's friend Rip, for example, keeps a terrified 12-year-old girl tied to his bed for his and his friends' sexual pleasure. What is most disturbing about such spectacles is the sense that, in the worlds Ellis portrays, there no longer exist the moral values with which to condemn them.

Less Than Zero was followed by *The Rules of Attraction* (1987), a depiction of college life that similarly describes a doomed search for stimulation and significance to hide the void of contemporary life. Ellis hit the headlines, however, with the publication of his sensational third novel, *American Psycho* (1991). Its narrator, Patrick Bateman, works on Wall Street, amassing and spending huge sums of money. His narrative is obsessed with the consumer-culture of the late 1980s and is saturated with references to designer clothes, after-shaves, and stereo equipment. He speaks in endless shopping lists. But, like Norman Bates, Bateman has a darker side. He spends significant sections of the novel torturing and murdering children, women, and even a tramp. These activities are described with the same meticulousness and flatness as Bateman's descriptions of his clothes. He shows virtually no remorse and is never brought to justice.

The extremely graphic descriptions of violence—especially against women—outraged many commentators. *American Psycho* was condemned as a how-to-rape guide, an obscene and misogynistic book that relished the seemingly infinite ways the human body could be degraded and eliminated. Support ran along the lines that it showed the consequences of consumerism gone berserk; the desire for bigger, better, more expensive products was slowly making de Sades of us all, forcing us to search desperately for any kind of sensation that would disrupt the anaesthetizing effect of a money-culture. Bateman's actions (if we believe he performs them at all, and there's plenty of evidence in the novel to suggest that they might be fantasies) were perhaps an anguished cry for help in a world where people care more about what others wear than what they do.

Partly due to the furor stirred up by *American Psycho,* it was no surprise that Ellis's next novel would be a low-key affair. In *The Informers* (1994), a series of related short stories, Ellis rounds up all the usual thematic suspects—blankness, consumer-excess, violence. The book is probably his most enjoyable. The narratives are short, snappy vignettes of life in Los Angles in the 1980s, and they combine to make a portrait that is both disturbing yet also extremely amusing. For all his grave insights into the deadness of contemporary American life, Ellis is, above all else, a comic novelist. Like the generation about which he writers, he is having fun with a world that he knows proffers little of real worth and permanence.

—John McLeod

ELLISON, Harlan (Jay)

Nationality: American. **Born:** Cleveland, Ohio, 27 May 1934. **Education:** Attended Ohio State University, Columbus, 1951-53. **Military Service:** Served in the U.S. Army, 1957-59. **Family:** Married 1) Charlotte Stein in 1956 (divorced); 2) Billie Joyce Sanders in 1961 (divorced); 3) Lory Patrick in 1965 (divorced); 4) Lori Horowitz in 1976 (divorced). **Career:** Editor, *Rogue;* founding editor, Regency Books, Evanston, Illinois, 1961-62. Freelance writer and lecturer; editor, Harlan Ellison Discovery Series. Vice-president, Science Fiction Writers of America, 1965-66 (resigned). **Awards:** Nebula award, 1965, 1969, 1977; Writers Guild of America award, for TV play, 1965, 1967, 1973; Hugo award, 1966, 1968 (3 awards), 1972 (for editing), 1974, 1975, 1978; Mystery Writers of America Edgar Allan Poe award, 1973; Jupiter award, 1973; *Locus* award, 1983; Bram Stoker award, for collection, 1988, for nonfiction, 1990. **Address:** 3484 Coy Drive, Sherman Oaks, California 91423, U.S.A.

Publications

Novels

The Deadly Streets. New York, Ace, 1958; London, Digit, 1959; revised edition, New York, Pyramid, 1975.

Rumble. New York, Pyramid, 1958; revised edition as *Web of the City,* 1975.

The Man with Nine Lives, bound with *A Touch of Infinity.* New York, Ace, 1960.

The Juvies. New York, Ace, 1961.

Rockabilly. Greenwich, Connecticut, Fawcett, 1961; London, Muller, 1963; revised edition as *Spider Kiss,* New York, Pyramid, 1975.

Doomsman, bound with *Telepower* by Lee Hoffmann. New York, Belmont, 1967.

Phoenix without Ashes: A Novel of the Starlost, with Edward Bryant. Greenwich, Connecticut, Fawcett, 1975; Manchester, Savoy, 1978.

The City on the Edge of Forever (novelization of TV play). New York, Bantam, 1977.

Short Stories

Sex Gang (as Paul Merchant). San Diego, California, Nightstand, 1959.

A Touch of Infinity, bound with *The Man with Nine Lives.* New York, Ace, 1960.

Gentleman Junkie and Other Stories of the Hung-Up Generation. Evanston, Illinois, Regency, 1961; revised edition, New York, Pyramid, 1975.

Ellison Wonderland. New York, Paperback Library, 1962; as *Earthman, Go Home,* 1964; revised edition, with original title, New York, Bluejay, 1984.

Paingod and Other Delusions. New York, Pyramid, 1965; revised edition, 1975.

I Have No Mouth and I Must Scream. New York, Pyramid, 1967.

From the Land of Fear. New York, Belmont, 1967.

Love Ain't Nothing But Sex Misspelled: Twenty-Two Stories. New York, Trident Press, 1968; revised edition, New York, Pyramid, 1976.

The Beast That Shouted Love at the Heart of the World. New York, Avon, 1969; abridged edition, London, Millington, 1976; revised edition, New York, Bluejay, 1984; further revised, Brooklandville, Maryland, Borderlands Press, 1994.

Over the Edge: Stories from Somewhere Else. New York, Belmont, 1970.

Partners in Wonder, with others (collaborations). New York, Walker, 1971.

Alone against Tomorrow: Stories of Alienation in Speculative Fiction. New York, Macmillan, 1971.

All the Sounds of Fear. St. Albans, Hertfordshire, Panther, 1973.

The Time of the Eye. St. Albans, Hertfordshire, Panther, 1974.

Approaching Oblivion: Road Signs on the Treadmill toward Tomorrow. New York, Walker, 1974; London, Millington, 1976.

Deathbird Stories: A Pantheon of Modern Gods. New York, Harper, 1975; London, Millington, 1977; revised edition, New York, Bluejay, 1984; further revised, Norwalk, Connecticut, Easton Press, 1991.

No Doors, No Windows. New York, Pyramid, 1975; revised edition, Brooklandville, Maryland, Borderlands Press, 1991.

Strange Wine: 15 New Stories from the Nightside of the World. New York, Harper, 1978.

The Book of Ellison, edited by Andrew Porter. New York, Algol Press, 1978.

The Illustrated Harlan Ellison, edited by Byron Preiss. New York, Baronet, 1978.

The Fantasies of Harlan Ellison (omnibus). Boston, Gregg Press, 1979.

All the Lies That Are My Life. San Francisco, Underwood-Miller, 1980.

Shatterday. Boston, Houghton Mifflin, 1980.

Stalking the Nightmare. Huntington Woods, Michigan, Phantasia Press, 1982.

The Essential Ellison: A 35-Year Retrospective, edited by Terry Dowing with Richard Delap and Gil Lamont. Omaha, Nebraska, Nemo Press, 1987.

Angry Candy. Boston, Houghton Mifflin, 1988.

Footsteps. Round Top, New York, Footsteps Press, 1989.

Dreams with Sharp Teeth (omnibus). New York, Quality Paperback Book Club, 3 vols., 1991.

Run for the Stars, bound with *Echoes of Thunder,* by Jack Dann and Jack C. Haldeman II. New York, Tor, 1991.

Mefisto in Onyx. Shingletown, California, Ziesing, 1993.
Mind Fields: The Art of Jacek Yerka, the Fiction of Harlan Ellison. Beverly Hills, California, Morpheus International, 1994.
Slippage: Previously Uncollected, Precariously Poised Stories. Boston, Houghton Mifflin, 1995.

Graphic Novels

Demon with a Glass Hand, illustrated by Marshall Rogers. New York, DC Comics, 1986.
Night and the Enemy, illustrated by Ken Steacy. Norristown, Pennsylvania, Comico, 1987.
Vic and Blood: The Chronicles of a Boy and His Dog, illustrated by Richard Corben. New York, St. Martin's Press, 1989.
Harlan Ellison's Dream Corridor Special. Milwaukie, Oregon, Dark Horse Comics, 1995.

Plays

The City on the Edge of Forever (televised, 1967). Published in *Six Science Fiction Plays,* edited by Roger Elwood, New York, Pocket Books, 1976.
Harlan Ellison's Movie. Westminister, Maryland, Mirage Press, 1991.
I, Robot: The Illustrated Screenplay. New York, Warner, 1994.

Screenplay: *The Oscar,* with Russell Rouse and Clarence Greene, 1966.

Television Plays: *Who Killed Alex Debbs? [Purity Mather?, Andy Zygmunt?, Half of Glory Lee?]* (*Burke's Law* series), 1963-65; *The Soldier* and *Demon with a Glass Hand* (*The Outer Limits* series), 1963-64; *The City on the Edge of Forever* (*Star Trek* series), 1967; and for *Route 66, The Untouchables, The Alfred Hitchcock Hour,* and *The Man from U.N.C.L.E.* series.

Other

Memos from Purgatory. Evanston, Illinois, Regency, 1961.
The Glass Teat: Essays of Opinion on Television. New York, Ace, 1970.
The Other Glass Teat: Further Essays of Opinion on Television. New York, Pyramid, 1975.
Sleepless Nights in the Procrustean Bed: Essays, edited by Marty Clark. San Bernardino, California, Borgo Press, 1984; London, Xanadu, 1990.
An Edge in My Voice. Norfolk, Virginia, Donning, 1985; revised edition, 1987.
Harlan Ellison's Watching. Los Angeles, Underwood-Miller, 1989.
The Harlan Ellison Hornbook (essays). New York, Penzler, 1990.

Editor, *Dangerous Visions: 33 Original Stories.* Garden City, New York, Doubleday, 1967; abridged edition, London, Bruce and Watson, 2 vols., 1967.
Editor, *Nightshade and Damnations,* by Gerald Kersh. Greenwich, Connecticut, Fawcett, 1968.
Editor, *Again, Dangerous Visions.* Garden City, New York, Doubleday, 1972; London, Millington, 1976.
Editor, *Medea: Harlan's World.* Huntington Woods, Michigan, Phantasia Press, 1985.

Recording: *Blood!,* with Robert Bloch, Alternate World, 1976.

*

Bibliography: *Harlan Ellison: A Bibliographical Checklist* by Leslie Kay Swigart, Dallas, Williams, 1973.

Critical Studies: *Harlan Ellison: Unrepentant Harlequin* by George Edgar Slusser, San Bernardino, California, Borgo Press, 1977; "Harlan Ellison Issue" of *Fantasy and Science Fiction* (New York), July 1977; *The Book of Ellison* edited by Andrew Porter, New York, Algol Press, 1978.

* * *

Prolific, outspoken, and controversial, Harlan Ellison writes across a variety of genres. Winner of numerous prestigious awards in the fields of fiction, journalism, and criticism, Ellison has never been afraid to invest each and every piece of his work—he is author or editor of more than 1300 stories, essays, articles, and newspaper columns—with some part of himself. Ellison is most recognized and admired for his short works of fantastic fiction, which he describes as "magic realism." His harsh insights and scathing wit divide readers. Ellison's admirers cherish his exuberant, angry, and unrelenting criticism of the human race, while his detractors condemn him for what they perceive as self-important egotism. Unperturbed by critics, Ellison continues to contribute his unique view of the world in surreal tales that spin from black humor to abject horror, using the imagery of fantasy and science fiction to explore themes of alienation and mortality in modern society.

Ellison was kicked out of college at the age of 21. He started selling fiction in 1955, and in the next year he sold 100 stories. Throughout the 1960s Ellison found his own unique voice. "'Repent, Harlequin!' Said the Ticktockman" (1965), one of the ten most reprinted stories in the English language, presents a world of terminal order in which nonconformism is a crime. Ironic in tone, the tale is a tribute to dystopic works like *1984,* and proposes that there will always be a positive, disruptive force championing individual responsibility.

"I Have No Mouth, and I Must Scream" (1967) is a cautionary tale containing a profoundly humanistic message about the irrepressible power of the human spirit. The last five human beings on Earth are trapped and tortured for all eternity within a vast, worldwide computer system which, consumed with loathing for the race that created it, vengefully provoked a worldwide cataclysm. In these and many other stories Ellison focuses on the pain and danger of isolation and alienation in society.

Ellison has always maintained a love/hate relationship with television and film. His two books of scathing TV criticism, *The Glass Teat* (1970) and *The Other Glass Teat* (1975) are frequently taught in University media courses. He often wrote for television in the 1960s, penning one of the most acclaimed episodes of the TV series *Star Trek,* "The City on the Edge of Forever," for which he won both Writers Guild of America and Hugo awards. This episode, credited as a major inspiration for the film *The Terminator,* uses the idea of time-travel to explore the responsibility of individual human actions and the effect we have upon the human race and its future. Ellison has maintained an interest in television work, antagonistic as he may sometimes be toward the medium. In the mid-1980s he served as creative consultant for the revived *Twi-*

light Zone, and more recently he worked as creative supervisor for the science fiction series *Babylon 5.*

Ellison is a talented and insightful film critic, as can be witnessed in *Harlan Ellison's Watching* (1989), a collection of film essays. Ellison has not met with much success in his own attempts to break into the film medium. The recent publication of *I, Robot: The Illustrated Screenplay* (1994) lets readers judge Ellison's screenwriting talent for themselves. A synthesis of four classic robot stories by Isaac Asimov, *I, Robot* considers the long-term consequences of human actions, and contemplates how technology, as an extension of individual will, shapes and changes the world and the course of history. Never filmed, this epic, enthralling work, a sci-fi homage to *Citizen Kane,* illustrates that Ellison's imagination and originality are perhaps too big for film, and that it is within the theater of the mind where his work will always be most appreciated.

A selection of Ellison's best work is offered in *Angry Candy* (1988), a series of meditations on death and mortality. It contains stunning works of the imagination such as "Eidolons" and "The Function of Dream Sleep" (both winners of Locus awards), and the collection itself was named one of the major works of American literature for 1988. The short novel *Mefisto in Onyx* (1993) manipulates the conventions of the hard-boiled *noir* genre in a gripping tale of psychic powers and the consequences of venturing into the mind of a sociopathic serial killer.

Ellison was included in *The Best American Short Stories 1993,* with "The Man Who Rowed Christopher Columbus Ashore." Structured in thirty-five brief, disjointed narratives, each featuring an enigmatic, god-like trickster figure who calls himself "Levendis," the story vacillates wildly between moments of humor, suffering, pathos, tragedy, absurdity, and extreme violence. The cumulative effect of these aphoristic narrative fragments is to disrupt ideas of fate, causality, or structure in human existence, and to highlight the randomness of life's events. In the end, all that is left is the responsibility of the individual. It is a message in which Ellison clearly has a personal stake, as his career as a writer is infused with a sense of responsibility toward his readers in his self-appointed role as unrelenting social commentator. Following Kleist, Ellison claims, "I only write because I cannot stop."

—Sean Carney

ERDRICH, (Karen) Louise

Nationality: American. **Born:** Little Falls, Minnesota, 7 June 1954. **Education:** Dartmouth College, Hanover, New Hampshire, B.A. 1976; Johns Hopkins University, Baltimore, M.A. 1977. **Family:** Married Michael Anthony Dorris in 1981; three sons and three daughters. **Career:** Visiting poetry teacher, North Dakota State Arts Council, 1977-78; creative writing teacher, Johns Hopkins University, 1978-79; visiting fellow, Dartmouth College, 1981. Member, Turtle Mountain Band of Ojibwa. **Awards:** MacDowell fellowship, 1980; Yaddo fellowship, 1981; Nelson Algren award, for story, 1982; National Book Critics Circle award, 1984; Virginia Sully prize, 1984; Sue Kaufman award, 1984; *Los Angeles Times* Book award, 1985; Guggenheim fellowship, 1985. **Address:** c/o Harper Collins, 10 East 53rd Street, New York, New York 10022, U.S.A.

Publications

Novels

Love Medicine. New York, Holt, 1984; London, Deutsch, 1985.
The Beet Queen. New York, Holt, 1986; London, Hamish Hamilton, 1987.
Tracks. New York, Holt, and London, Hamish Hamilton, 1988.
Crown of Columbus, with Michael Dorris. New York and London, Harper Collins, 1991.
The Bingo Palace. New York and London, Harper Collins, 1994.
The Bluejay's Dance. New York and London, Harper Collins, 1995.

Uncollected Short Stories

"Scales," in *The Best American Short Stories 1983,* edited by Shannon Ravenel and Anne Tyler. Boston, Houghton Mifflin, 1983; as *The Year's Best American Short Stories,* London, Severn House, 1984.
"American Horse," in *Earth Power Coming,* edited by Simon J. Ortiz. Tsaile, Arizona, Navajo Community College Press, 1983.
"Destiny," in *Atlantic* (Boston), January 1985.
"Mister Argus," in *Georgia Review* (Athens), Summer 1985.
"Flesh and Blood," in *Buying Time,* edited by Scott Walker. St. Paul, Minnesota, Graywolf Press, 1985.
"Saint Marie," in *Prize Stories 1985,* edited by William Abrahams. New York, Doubleday, 1985.
"Fleur," in *Prize Stories 1987,* edited by William Abrahams. New York, Doubleday, 1987.
"Snares," in *The Best American Short Stories 1988,* edited by Shannon Ravenel and Mark Helprin. Boston, Houghton Mifflin, 1988.
"A Wedge of Shade," in *Louder than Words,* edited by William Shore. New York, Vintage, 1989.
"Crown of Thorns," in *The Invisible Enemy,* edited by Miriam Dow and Jennifer Regan. St. Paul, Minnesota, Graywolf Press, 1989.
"Matchimanito," in *The Best of the West 2,* edited by James Thomas and Denise Thomas. Layton, Utah, Peregrine Smith, 1989.
"The Bingo Van," in *New Yorker,* 19 February 1990.
"Happy Valentine's Day, Monsieur Ducharme," in *Ladies' Home Journal* (New York), February 1990.
"The Leap," in *Harper's* (New York), March 1990.
"Best Western," in *Vogue* (New York), May 1990.
"The Dress," in *Mother Jones* (San Francisco), July-August 1990.
"The Island," in *Ms.* (New York), January-February 1991.

Poetry

Jacklight. New York, Holt, and London, Sphere, 1990.
Baptism of Desire. New York, Harper Collins, 1991.

* * *

"Contemporary Native American writers have a task quite different," Louise Erdrich has argued, from that of other contemporary American writers. "In the light of enormous loss, they must tell the stories of contemporary survivors while protecting and celebrating the cores of cultures left in the wake of the catastrophe." That Erdrich has accomplished this task while attracting a large mainstream audience attests to both her formidable narrative abilities and her predisposition towards what might be called a kindler, gentler brand of "Indian" story. Hers is a fiction more interested in love and survival than in recrimination. Past wrongs and present hardships do figure in her work but chiefly as the backdrop against which the task of "protecting and celebrating" takes on added force and urgency. (Her non-dogmatic feminism works in much the same way. The strength of many of her female characters does not come at the expense of the males, however weak or foolish or befuddled many of these males may at times be.) Erdrich's sense of loss never gives way to a sense of grievance; her characteristic tone is hopeful, not mournful, and springs from her belief in the persistence and viability of certain Native American values and the vision to which they give rise.

Erdrich succeeds particularly well in creating the sense of some force—spiritual or cultural—capable of binding together an otherwise fragmented and attenuated, even demoralized community, largely but (as *The Beet Queen* [1986] nicely demonstrates) not exclusively tribal in nature. Instead of the single protagonist (and main plot) of the conventional Euro-American novel, Erdrich offers multiple characters who not only share the same narrative space but often appear in more than one work. In a similar vein, Erdrich stresses the almost communal aspect of her writing, giving special credit to her husband and "collaborator" (and in one instance co-author), the fiction writer and Native Americanist, Michael Dorris.

And instead of seeing publication as a final act, Erdrich thinks of it as "temporary storage," the individual story or novel subject to revision and inclusion in some larger, gradually emerging design or kinship system. She shelved the manuscript of a first novel, then wrote a short story that developed into the award-winning *Love Medicine* (1984; read as a novel by some, a collection of interrelated short stories by others). *Love Medicine* spawned *Beet Queen,* set in the same locale but dealing with a mainly non-Native American cast, which in turn led Erdrich back to that first manuscript, which she extensively rewrote and published as *Tracks* (1988), followed by a second, expanded edition of *Love Medicine* and her most contemporary and topical novel to date, *The Bingo Palace* (1993). Thus, a single manuscript grew into a quartet of novels, with the possibility of more to come (see, for example, the story "Night Prayer" in *Granta*'s Winter 1991 issue).

The center of Erdrich's fiction—a fiction that follows many characters over so many generations—lies in her seemingly realistic but in fact poetic, even visionary, and at times grotesquely comic style, and in a sense of place that is at once geographically precise yet mythically resonant. As Erdrich has pointed out, "In a tribal view of the world, where one place has been inhabited for generations, the landscape becomes enlivened by a sense of group or family history."

Erdrich's place is the Turtle Mountain Reservation and the surrounding area in North Dakota, where Erdrich was raised. But what also makes the fiction so interesting is the way in which Erdrich, drawing on her own "mixed" background—Native American (Chippewa) and German-American—addresses the same general identity issue that writers like Chinua Achebe and Salman Rushdie have in their rather different ways. Erdrich's handling of the identity issue at all levels—the personal, the cultural, and the generic—is especially acute in *Tracks.* She plays the oral tradition against the novelistic, communal identity against individual psychology, conservation against assimilation, and the essentially spiritual yet intensely physical nature of Native American life against both the attractions and limitations of Western ways. *Tracks,* like all of Erdrich's novels, opens out and looks affirmatively but problematically ahead, cognizant of the formidable obstacles faced by Native Americans but measured by a sense of mystery and purpose, some supernatural bond, some communal sense of being.

—Robert A. Morace

ERICSON, Walter. *See* **FAST, Howard (Melvin).**

ESTLEMAN, Loren D.

Nationality: American. **Born:** 15 September 1952, in Ann Arbor, Michigan. **Education:** Eastern Michigan University, B.A., 1974. **Family:** Married 1) Carole Ann Ashley in 1987 (divorced 1990); 2) Deborah Ann. **Career:** Writer. *Michigan Fed,* Ann Arbor, cartoonist, 1967-70; *Ypsilanti Press,* Ypsilanti, reporter, 1973; *Community Foto-News,* Pinckney, Michigan, editor in chief, 1975-76; *Ann Arbor News,* special writer, 1976-77; *Dexter Leader,* Dexter, Michigan, staff writer, 1977-80. Has been an instructor for Friends of the Dexter Library, and a guest lecturer at colleges; lives in Whitmore Lake, Michigan. **Awards:** *New York Times Book Review* notable book citations, 1980 for *Motor City Blue* and 1982 for *The Midnight Man;* Golden Spur award for best western historical novel, Western Writers of America, 1982, for *Aces & Eights;* Shamus award nomination for best private eye novel, Private Eye Writers of America, 1984, for *The Glass Highway;* Golden Spur award for best western short story, 1986, for "The Bandit"; Michigan Arts Foundation award for literature, 1987; American Mystery award, 1988. **Member:** Western Writers of America, Private Eye Writers of America. **Agent:** Robin Rue, Anita Diamant Literary Agency, 310 Madison Ave., New York, New York, 10017.

Publications

Novels (series: Amos Walker, Peter Macklin, Page Murdock)

The Oklahoma Punk. Major Books, 1976; as *Red Highway,* Paperjacks, 1987.
The Hider. Doubleday, 1978.
Sherlock Holmes vs. Dracula; or, The Adventure of the Sanguinary Count. Doubleday, 1978.
Dr. Jekyll and Mr. Holmes. Doubleday, 1979.
The High Rocks (Murdock). Doubleday, 1979.
Motor City Blue (Walker). Houghton Mifflin, 1980.
Stamping Ground (Murdock). Doubleday, 1980.
Aces & Eights. Doubleday, 1981.
Angel Eyes (Walker). Houghton Mifflin, 1981.
The Wolfer. Pocket Books, 1981.
The Midnight Man (Walker). Houghton Mifflin, 1982.
Murdock's Law. Doubleday, 1982.
The Glass Highway (Walker). Houghton Mifflin, 1983.

Mister St. John. Doubleday, 1983.
Kill Zone (Macklin). Mysterious Press, 1984.
The Strangers (Murdock). Doubleday, 1984.
Sugartown (Walker). Houghton Mifflin, 1984.
This Old Bill. Doubleday, 1984.
Gun Man. Doubleday, 1985.
Roses Are Dead (Macklin). Mysterious Press, 1985.
Any Man's Death (Macklin). Mysterious Press, 1986.
Every Brilliant Eye (Walker). Houghton Mifflin, 1986.
Lady Yesterday (Walker). Houghton Mifflin, 1987.
Bloody Season. Bantam, 1988.
Downriver (Walker). Houghton Mifflin, 1988.
Red Highway. PaperJacks, 1988.
Peeper. Bantam, 1989.
Silent Thunder (Walker). Houghton Mifflin, 1989.
Western Story. Doubleday, 1989.
Sweet Women Lie. Houghton Mifflin, 1990.
Whiskey River. Bantam, 1990.
Motown. Bantam, 1991.
King of the Corner. Bantam, 1992.
Sudden Country. Bantam, 1992.
Crooked Way. Eclipse Books, 1993.
City of Widows. Tor Books, 1994.
The Judge. Forge, 1994.
Billy Gashade. Tor, 1996.
Edsel. Mysterious Press, 1996.
Stress. Bantam, 1996.

Play

Dr. and Mrs. Watson at Home in *The New Adventures of Sherlock Holmes,* Carroll and Graf, 1987.

Short Stories

General Murders. Houghton Mifflin, 1988.
The Best Western Stories of Loren D. Estleman, edited by Bill Pronzini and Martin H. Greenberg. Ohio University Press, 1989.
People Who Kill. Mystery Scene Press, 1993.

Nonfiction

The Wister Trace: Classic Novels of the American Frontier. Jameson Books, 1987.

Editor, with Martin H. Greenberg, *P. I. Files.* Ivy Books, 1990.

*

Manuscript Collection: Eastern Michigan University, Ypsilanti.

* * *

Widely regarded as perhaps the best contemporary imitator of Raymond Chandler's hard-boiled detective novel style, Loren Estleman began his career in the 1970s as a police reporter for various Michigan newspapers, where, he has said, he "killed a lot of time . . . just listening to cops." The author of over 40 works, Estleman has written mainly in the western and detective novel genres but has also produced artful imitations of Arthur Conan Doyle's Sherlock Holmes stories, two short-story collections, and a serious study of the fiction of the American West.

Estleman published his first western, *The Hider*—a fictionalized account of the last U.S. buffalo hunt—in 1978, and in the following year introduced the first of several "Page Murdock" westerns, *The High Rocks,* which dramatized the efforts of his hero, a crusty Montana lawman, to track down the Indians who murdered his parents. He followed it with *Stamping Ground* (1980), *Murdock's Law* (1982), *The Strangers* (1984), and more recently *City of Widows* (1994), in which Murdock—"Sam Spade with six-shooters," in the words of one reviewer—chases down two homicidal outlaw brothers in New Mexico.

Estleman's other western novels have included *The Wolfer* (1981), *Mister St. John* (1983), *Gun Man* (1985), *Western Story* (1989), and *Sudden Country* (1992) as well as such fictionalized treatments of historical events as *Aces & Eights* (1981), about the murder of Wild Bill Hickok; *This Old Bill* (1984), a depiction of the life of Buffalo Bill Cody; and *Bloody Season* (1988), a dramatization of the gunfight at the O.K. Corral. Several of Estleman's westerns have been nominated for or awarded major literary prizes, and critics have generally praised Estleman's historical accuracy and fictional interpretation of actual events. The *Los Angeles Times* praised *Bloody Season* for presenting a "new vision of what happened in Tombstone," and *Library Journal* lauded *City of Widows* for its "believable dialogue and complex characters."

It is in the heavily tilled field of detective fiction, however, that Estleman has made his deepest mark. Although *The Oklahoma Punk* (1976) was Estleman's first foray into crime fiction, his introduction of the cynical, Vietnam-hardened sleuth Amos Walker in *Motor City Blue* (1980) represented Estleman's first attempt to modernize the ironic, world-weary private eye created by Raymond Chandler and Dashiell Hammett in the 1930s and 1940s. In *Motor City Blue* Walker was hired to locate an ex-gangster's missing ward in Detroit's pornography subculture, and in the other early novels of the series Estleman had Walker search for a nightclub singer who had hired him in expectation of her own disappearance (*Angel Eyes* [1981]); hunt down three cop killers (*The Midnight Man* [1982]); look for a television anchor's missing son in the drug underworld (*The Glass Highway* [1983]); and find an elderly immigrant's long-missing grandson (*Sugartown* [1984]). More recent Amos Walker novels have found him searching for a missing newspaper reporter (*Every Brilliant Eye* [1986]); battling the Colombian drug underworld while looking for an ex-prostitute's father (*Lady Yesterday* [1987]); exonerating an African-American ex-con who insists he was framed for murder (*Downriver* [1988]); and coping with his ex-wife's promiscuity, Mafia romance, and a disaffected CIA spy (*Sweet Women Lie* [1990]).

With *Kill Zone* (1984), Estleman introduced a new (anti)hero, the professional killer Peter Macklin, who Estleman has said satisfied his desire to find out if a decidedly amoral protagonist could sustain the reader's interest and sympathy. Again situating the fiction series in Detroit, Estleman had Macklin attempt to rescue a tour boat seized by terrorists (*Kill Zone*), search for the source of a contract put out on his life (*Roses Are Dead* [1985]), and protect a television evangelist from the Detroit mob and Macklin's own hit man son (*Any Man's Death* [1986]).

Estleman's Walker and Macklin series have repeatedly been criticized for leaning too heavily on the conventions, plots, and language of Raymond Chandler's Philip Marlowe novels, and Estleman has been accused of overwriting and of concocting dubious premises or unsatisfying conclusions. However, praise for his work his grown steadily throughout his career, and critics have been especially appreciative of his gritty evocation of the urban topography of Detroit as well as Estleman's effective recreations of the ambience and humor of the classic "hard-boiled" crime novel.

In his more recent novels, Estleman has continued to practice what he calls "literary crop rotation" (alternating between westerns and detective thrillers), but has turned to new protagonists and subjects. In *Peeper* (1989), he introduced Ralph Poteet, perhaps the most unappealing—and unhygienic—protagonist in all crime fiction, and in *Whiskey River* (1990) he explored the liquor gang wars of Prohibition-era Detroit. The hero of that novel, Connie Minor, a disenchanted newspaper columnist, reappears more recently in *Edsel* (1995), Estleman's imaginative evocation of the world of the "Motor City" in the 1950s and the Ford Motor Company Edsel fiasco.

—Paul S. Bodine

F

FAIN, Michael. *See* **MICHAEL, Judith.**

FALLON, Martin. *See* **HIGGINS, Jack.**

FAST, Howard (Melvin)

Pseudonyms: E.V. Cunningham; Walter Ericson. **Nationality:** American. **Born:** New York City, 11 November 1914. **Education:** George Washington High School, New York, graduated 1931; National Academy of Design, New York. **Military Service:** Served with the Office of War Information, 1942-43, and the Army Film Project, 1944. **Family:** Married Bette Cohen in 1937 (died 1994); one daughter and one son, the writer Jonathan Fast. **Career:** War correspondent in the Far East for *Esquire* and *Coronet* magazines, 1945. Taught at Indiana University, Bloomington, Summer 1947; imprisoned for contempt of Congress, 1947; owner, Blue Heron Press, New York, 1952-57. Since 1989 weekly columnist, New York *Observer.* Founder, World Peace Movement, and member, World Peace Council, 1950-55; member of the Fellowship for Reconciliation. American-Labour Party candidate for Congress for the 23rd District of New York, 1952. Lives in Greenwich, Connecticut. **Awards:** Bread Loaf Writers Conference award, 1933; Schomburg Race Relations award, 1944; Newspaper Guild award, 1947; Jewish Book Council of America award, 1948; Stalin (now Soviet) International Peace prize, 1954; Screenwriters award, 1960; National Association of Independent Schools award, 1962; Emmy award, for television play, 1976. **Agent:** Sterling Lord Literistic Inc., 1 Madison Avenue, New York, New York 10010, U.S.A.

Publications

Novels

Two Valleys. New York, Dial Press, 1933; London, Dickson, 1934.
Strange Yesterday. New York, Dodd Mead, 1934.
Place in the City. New York, Harcourt Brace, 1937.
The Call of Fife and Drum: Three Novels of the Revolution. Secausus, New Jersey, Citadel Press, 1987.
Conceived in Liberty: A Novel of Valley Forge. New York, Simon and Schuster, and London, Joseph, 1939.
The Unvanquished. New York, Duell, 1942; London, Lane, 1947.
The Proud and the Free. Boston, Little Brown, 1950; London, Lane, 1952.
The Last Frontier. New York, Duell, 1941; London, Lane, 1948.
The Tall Hunter. New York, Harper, 1942.
Citizen Tom Paine. New York, Duell, 1943; London, Lane, 1946.
Freedom Road. New York, Duell, 1944; London, Lane, 1946.
The American: A Middle Western Legend. New York, Duell, 1946; London, Lane, 1949.
The Children. New York, Duell, 1947.
Clarkton. New York, Duell, 1947.
My Glorious Brothers. Boston, Little Brown, 1948; London, Lane, 1950.
Spartacus. Privately printed, 1951; London, Lane, 1952.
Fallen Angel (as Walter Ericson). Boston, Little Brown, 1952; as *The Darkness Within,* New York, Ace, 1953; as *Mirage* (as Howard Fast), New York, Fawcett, 1965.
Silas Timberman. New York, Blue Heron Press, 1954; London, Lane, 1955.
The Story of Lola Gregg. New York, Blue Heron Press, 1956; London, Lane, 1957.
Moses, Prince of Egypt. New York, Crown, 1958; London, Methuen, 1959.
The Winston Affair. New York, Crown, 1959; London, Methuen, 1960.
The Golden River, in *The Howard Fast Reader.* New York, Crown, 1960.
April Morning. New York, Crown, and London, Methuen, 1961.
Power. New York, Doubleday, 1962; London, Methuen, 1963.
Agrippa's Daughter. New York, Doubleday, 1964; London, Methuen, 1965.
Torquemada. New York, Doubleday, 1966; London, Methuen, 1967.
The Hunter and the Trap. New York, Dial Press, 1967.
The Crossing. New York, Morrow, 1971; London, Eyre Methuen, 1972.
The Hessian. New York, Morrow, 1972; London, Hodder and Stoughton, 1973.
The Immigrants:
- *The Immigrants.* Boston, Houghton Mifflin, 1977; London, Hodder and Stoughton, 1978.
- *Second Generation.* Boston, Houghton Mifflin, and London, Hodder and Stoughton, 1978.
- *The Establishment.* Boston, Houghton Mifflin, 1979; London, Hodder and Stoughton, 1980.
- *The Legacy.* Boston, Houghton Mifflin, and London, Hodder and Stoughton, 1981.
- *Max.* Boston, Houghton Mifflin, 1982; London, Hodder and Stoughton, 1983.
- *The Outsider.* Boston, Houghton Mifflin, 1984; London, Hodder and Stoughton 1985.
- *The Immigrant's Daughter.* Boston, Houghton Mifflin, 1985; London, Hodder and Stoughton, 1986.

The Dinner Party. Boston, Houghton Mifflin, and London, Hodder and Stoughton, 1987.
The Pledge. Boston, Houghton Mifflin, 1988; London, Hodder and Stoughton, 1989.
The Confession of Joe Cullen. Boston, Houghton Mifflin 1989; London, Hodder and Stoughton, 1990.
The Trial of Abigail Goodman. New York, Crown, 1993.
Seven Days in June. New York, Crown, 1994.
The Bridge Builder's Story. Armonk, New York, M. E. Sharp, 1995.

Novels as E. V. Cunningham

Sylvia. New York, Doubleday, 1960; London, Deutsch, 1962.
Phyllis. New York, Doubleday, and London, Deutsch, 1962.
Alice. New York, Doubleday, 1963; London, Deutsch, 1965.
Lydia. New York, Doubleday, 1964; London, Deutsch, 1965.
Shirley. New York, Doubleday, and London, Deutsch, 1964.
Penelope. New York, Doubleday, 1965; London, Deutsch, 1966.
Helen. New York, Doubleday, 1966; London, Deutsch, 1967.
Margie. New York, Morrow, 1966; London, Deutsch, 1968.
Sally. New York, Morrow, and London, Deutsch, 1967.
Samantha. New York, Morrow, 1967; London, Deutsch, 1968; as *The Case of the Angry Actress,* New York, Dell, 1984.
Cynthia. New York, Morrow, 1968; London, Deutsch, 1969.
The Assassin Who Gave Up His Gun. New York, Morrow, 1969; London, Deutsch, 1970.
Millie. New York, Morrow, 1973; London, Deutsch, 1975.
The Case of the One-Penny Orange. New York, Holt Rinehart, 1977; London, Deutsch, 1978.
The Case of the Russian Diplomat. New York, Holt Rinehart, 1978; London, Deutsch, 1979.
The Case of the Poisoned Eclairs. New York, Holt Rinehart, 1979; London, Deutsch, 1980.
The Case of the Sliding Pool. New York, Delacorte Press, 1981; London, Gollancz, 1982.
The Case of the Kidnapped Angel. New York, Delacorte Press, 1982; London, Gollancz, 1983.
The Case of the Murdered Mackenzie. New York, Delacorte Press, 1984; London, Gollancz, 1985.
The Wabash Factor. New York, Delacorte Press, 1986; London, Gollancz, 1987.

Plays

The Hammer (produced New York, 1950).
Thirty Pieces of Silver (produced Melbourne, 1951). New York, Blue Heron Press, and London, Lane, 1954.
General Washington and the Water Witch. London, Lane, 1956.
The Crossing (produced Dallas, 1962).
The Hill (screenplay). New York, Doubleday, 1964.
David and Paula (produced New York, 1982).
Citizen Tom Paine, adaptation of his own novel (produced Williamstown, Massachusetts, 1985). Boston, Houghton Mifflin, 1986.
The Novelist (produced Williamstown, Massachusetts, 1987).
The Second Coming (produced Greenwich, Connecticut, 1991).

Screenplay: *The Hessian,* 1971.

Television Plays: *What's a Nice Girl Like You . . . ?,* 1971; *The Ambassador* (*Benjamin Franklin* series), 1974; *21 Hours at Munich,* with Edward Hume, 1976.

Poetry

Never to Forget the Battle of the Warsaw Ghetto, with William Gropper. New York, Jewish Peoples Fraternal Order, 1946.
Korean Lullaby. New York, American Peace Crusade, n.d.

Other

The Romance of a People (for children). New York, Hebrew Publishing Company, 1941.
Lord Baden-Powell of the Boy Scouts. New York, Messner, 1941.
Haym Salomon, Son of Liberty. New York, Messner, 1941.
The Picture-Book History of the Jews, with Bette Fast. New York, Hebrew Publishing Company, 1942.
Goethals and the Panama Canal. New York, Messner, 1942.
The Incredible Tito. New York, Magazine House, 1944.
Intellectuals in the Fight for Peace. New York, Masses and Mainstream, 1949.
Tito and His People. Winnipeg, Contemporary Publishers, 1950.
Literature and Reality. New York, International Publishers, 1950.
Peekskill, U.S.A.: A Personal Experience. New York, Civil Rights Congress, and London, International Publishing Company, 1951.
Tony and the Wonderful Door (for children). New York, Blue Heron Press, 1952; as *The Magic Door,* Culver City, California, Peace Press, 1979.
Spain and Peace. New York, Joint Anti-Fascist Refugee Committee, 1952.
The Passion of Sacco and Vanzetti: A New England Legend. New York, Blue Heron Press, 1953; London, Lane, 1954.
The Naked God: The Writer and the Communist Party. New York, Praeger, 1957; London, Bodley Head, 1958.
The Howard Fast Reader. New York, Crown, 1960.
The Jews: Story of a People. New York, Dial Press, 1968; London, Cassell, 1970.
The Art of Zen Meditation. Culver City, California, Peace Press, 1977.
Time and the Riddle: Thirty Zen Stories. Boston, Houghton Mifflin, 1981.
Being Red: A Memoir. Boston, Houghton Mifflin, 1990.
War and Peace. Armonk, New York, Sharpe, 1992.
The Sculpture of Bette Fast. Armonk, New York, Sharpe, 1995.

Editor, *The Selected Work of Tom Paine.* New York, Modern Library, 1946; London, Lane, 1948.
Editor, *The Best Short Stories of Theodore Dreiser.* Cleveland, World, 1947.

*

Manuscript Collections: University of Pennsylvania, Philadelphia; University of Wisconsin, Madison.

Critical Studies: *History and Conscience: The Case of Howard Fast* by Hershel D. Meyer, Princeton, New Jersey, Anvil Atlas, 1958; *Counterpoint* by Roy Newquist, New York, Rand McNally, 1964.

* * *

Howard Fast, a prolific author with nearly one hundred major published works, writes historical novels with dramatic conflicts of ideals, life-like characters, and action-packed narratives. Varying from the highly effective and gripping to the melodramatic or propagandistic, they personalize the famous and show the transformation by circumstance of seemingly "ordinary" characters into people of great accomplishments. Committed to liberal/humanitarian values, Fast brings a social conscience to his fiction, exposing the pitfalls of power and wealth, praising the virtues of simplicity and family, treating women sympathetically, empathizing with cultural outcasts, understanding the pressure to conform, and disdaining prejudice, hypocrisy, and abuse of power, especially if leading to war.

Fast's provocative American Revolutionary War novels explore the price paid for liberty; they humanize historical figures by admitting weaknesses, reversing conventional perspectives, and demonstrating causes of greatness. Among his most compelling works are *Conceived in Liberty* (1939), a grimly realistic study of Valley Forge, *The Unvanquished* (1942), an analysis of how a "confused, humble, indecisive foxhunter" (George Washington) slowly developed into "a leader of men," and *Citizen Tom Paine* (1943), a complex portrait of Paine as a foolish, weak, incompetent politician, and yet a committed visionary and a great radical.

In the 1940s, Fast's antifascist feeling led him to communism and to sometimes one-dimensional, doctrinaire works with capitalist villains and proletarian heroes. *Freedom Road* (1944), for example, portrays a slave's rise to martyred statesman during the traumatic post-Civil War Reconstruction, but is limited by its morality play depiction of virtue and vice. *Clarkton* (1947), *The American* (1946), *Silas Timberman* (1954), and *The Story of Lola Gregg* (1956) all depict political characters and issues from a leftist perspective. *Spartacus* (1951), written while Fast was serving a prison term for contempt of Congress, treats the 71 B.C. slave revolt in Rome. A bestseller and a movie, it brought Fast the Stalin International Peace Prize (1954) and the Screenwriters award (1960). *My Glorious Brothers* (1952) deals with a similar uprising pitting the Maccabean Jews against Greek tyrants. In 1957, tired of communist pressures to change his works to please party functionaries and disenchanted after Khrushchev's revelation of Communist betrayals of principle, Fast wrote *The Naked God* to recant.

Since then he has published at least one book of historical fiction each year (mainly about the American Revolution, immigrants, and biblical figures), science fiction, and thrillers. These are also political, but the doctrinal has given way to the compassionate and the humanistic. Fast always includes people tinged with prejudice against outsiders but convinced they have none. His biblical stories, like Moses, Prince of Egypt, and Agrippa's Daughter, trace the development of Jewish heroes; from spoiled youths and rebels to compassionate and competent leaders. Among his most popular works in this later period is the "Immigrants Quintet" series (published from 1977 to 1980), which together trace the family of a poor French-Italian immigrant who ambitiously builds a corporate empire, only to lose it quickly. Also notable are *April Morning* (a teenager's coming of age at the Battle of Lexington, published in 1961), *The Hessian* (a struggle with conscience over a Hessian youth tried by vengeful townsmen in a kangaroo court, published in 1972), and *The Crossing* (Washington's famous 1776 Christmas crossing of the Delaware, published in 1971). Always an idealist, Fast believes that books "open a thousand doors," shaping lives, widening horizons, and offering "hope for the heart and food for the soul."

Fast's prolific writing still retains the general political and moral interests of the earlier novels, sometimes in relatively experimental literary forms. For example, *The Outsider* (1984) uses a small town in Connecticut to examine the effects of all the major political events of post-war America, from McCarthyism to Vietnam, on the career of a rabbi in a WASP area. *The Dinner Party* (1987), a play-like novel continuing earlier Fast concerns with Central America, takes place in a single day and location, as a U.S. Senator faces the plight of refugees and family turmoil. The Confession of Joe Cullen is a series of guilty "confessions" to the murder of a priest in Central America. Only *The Pledge* (1988) returns to much earlier events, the post WWII years of McCarthyism and the grave repercussions of refusal to cooperate with the House Un-American Activities Committee. Similarly, *Being Red: A Memoir* (1990) is a fascinating nonfiction commentary on the work of the 1940s and 1950s.

Basically, Fast's canon reflects his concern with man's historical and present struggles for liberty. Fast disapproves of all that reduces man to a catchphrase or an ideology. For him, struggle, self-awareness, love, family, privacy, and humane values give life meaning. His politics move from committed Marxism in the 1940s and 1950s to more humanitarian philosophies later on, although Fast has never apologized for his passionate and sometimes extravagant defenses of what he found right. Extreme emotion has informed his political outlook, and thus in his writing his message outweighs all else; as Fast himself says, an artist's "only obligation is to truth."

—Andrew Macdonald

FIERSTEIN, Harvey (Forbes)

Nationality: American. **Born:** 6 June 1954, in Brooklyn, New York. **Education:** Pratt Institute, B.F.A., 1973. **Career:** Actor, producer, and writer for stage and screen. Founding actor in Gallery Players Community Theater, Brooklyn, 1965; female impersonator in New York City; actor in musicals and plays. **Awards:** Four Villager awards, all 1980, all for *Fugue in a Nursery;* Obie award for best off-Broadway play, *Village Voice,* Drama Desk awards for best play and best actor, and George Oppenheimer Playwriting award, *Newsday,* Los Angeles Critics Circle Award, Elizabeth Hull-Kate Warriner award, Dramatists Guild, all 1982, Antoinette Perry (Tony) awards for best play and best actor, 1983, and Oliver award nomination, 1985, all for *Torch Song Trilogy;* Charlie award for "exceptional contribution to the art of comedy," Association of Comedy Artists, 1982; Theater World award, 1983, for Broadway debut; Fund for Human Dignity award, 1983, for volunteer work; Tony awards for best musical and best book of a musical, both 1984, both for *La Cage aux folles;* ACE awards for best dramatic special and for writing, Academy of Cable Excellence, both 1988, both for *Tidy Endings;* grants from Rockefeller Foundation, CAPS, Ford Foundation, and Public Broadcasting System. **Agent:** George Lane, William Morris Agency, 1350 Avenue of the Americas, New York, New York 10019-4701, U.S.A.

Publications

Plays

In Search of the Cobra Jewels (produced in New York, 1973).
Freaky Pussy (produced in New York, 1975).
Flatbush Tosca (produced in New York, 1975).
Torch Song Trilogy (produced New York, 1981). Gay Presses of New York, 1981.
La Cage aux folles, musical; adapted from Jean Poiret's play of the same title, music and lyrics by Jerry Herman (produced in New York, 1983).
Spookhouse (produced New York, 1983; London, 1987).

Safe Sex (trilogy of one-act plays; contains *Manny and Jake, Safe Sex,* and *On Tidy Endings;* produced New York, 1987). Atheneum, 1987.
Forget Him (produced New York, 1988).
Legs Diamond, with Charles Suppon, music and lyrics by Peter Allen (produced New York, 1988).

Screenplays: *Torch Song Trilogy,* adapted from his own play, 1988.
Teleplays: *Tidy Endings,* adapted from his own play, 1988.

*

Theatrical Activities:
Actor: **Plays**—*Pork,* 1971; *Xircus: The Private Life of Jesus Christ; The Trojan Women; Vinyl Visits an FM Station; International Stud,* 1976; *Fugue in a Nursery,* 1979; *Widows and Children First,* 1979; *Torch Song Trilogy,* 1981; *Safe Sex,* 1987; *The Haunted Host,* 1991. **Films**—*Garbo Talks,* 1984; *Torch Song Trilogy,* 1988; *The Harvest,* 1992; *Mrs. Doubtfire,* 1993.

* * *

From childhood, Harvey Fierstein was aware of both his sexual orientation and his desire to act and to write. This vision propelled him in his successful and prolific career. His work as a female impersonator during his teens found its way into *Torch Song Trilogy* (1981), his first acclaimed effort. *Torch* is a bittersweet tale of a drag queen's simultaneous quest for self-actualization and unconditional love from family and friends. The play, which was first performed off-Broadway at the Richard Allen Center, was an instant success and opened on Broadway at the Little Theater in 1982. Sell-out crowds and glowing reviews (from critics who raved over Fierstein's humorous and touching portrayal of Arnold) gained Fierstein numerous acting and production awards, including two Tonys. Fierstein again starred as Arnold when the play was made into a movie in 1988. By this time, though, public awareness of AIDS had increased dramatically. Thus, some reviewers found fault with the film for glorifying the unsafe sexual practices and promiscuity that were characteristic of the 1970s.

Drag queens and female impersonators again took the spotlight in Fierstein's next project, the American version of the French hit play *La Cage Aux Folles* (1983), for which Fierstein wrote the spoken dialogue. The musical takes its name from a transvestite nightclub owned by a gay couple; Georges runs the establishment while his lover, Albin, is the star performer. Georges's son, whom the couple has raised since the young man's birth, is engaged to a woman from a highly conservative family. Rather than confess the truth about their living arrangement, the son hopes to persuade the highly flamboyant Albin to disappear while his future in-laws are present. A hurt Albin balks and poses as his stepson's mother. The result is a rollicking, yet poignant, portrayal of the relationship between parents and child at the tenuous point of transition from active nurturing to detached advice-giving. *La Cage Aux Folles* captured six Tony awards, including Best Musical and Best Book of a Musical. Like *Torch Song Trilogy,* the play was made into a feature-length film called *The Birdcage* (1996), starring Robin Williams as the owner of a Miami nightclub of the same name. Reviews of *The Birdcage* have been generally good.

Another notable Fierstein product is *Safe Sex* (1987), which he described to Glenn Collins of the *New York Times* as his "personal response to living in the time of AIDS." It first appeared at La Mama in 1987 and made it to Broadway's Lyceum Theater later that year. Like *Torch Song,* the play is presented as a trilogy. The three portions feature themes such as modified dating rituals among HIV-positive people and their non-HIV-positive partners, avoidance of intimacy by those who are HIV-positive, and a confrontation between a gay man and his dead lover's former wife. Fierstein starred in the second segment and appeared in HBO's adaptation of the third.

Whatever Fierstein specifically addresses in a given work, he is sure to touch on one or more of many subjects—homosexuality, family, friendships, relationships, AIDS awareness, getting along with others, and laughter in the face of adversity. Whether the audience members are gay or straight, healthy or sick, single or committed, they are sure to learn something new about those around them, humanity in general, or themselves. As John Gilnes, an original producer of *Torch Song Trilogy,* explained to Leslie Bennetts of *The New York Times,* "What Harvey proved was that you could use a gay context and a gay experience and speak in universal truths."

—Tracy Clark

FISHER, Carrie (Frances)

Nationality: American. **Born:** 21 October 1956, in Beverly Hills, California; daughter of the singer Eddie Fisher and the actress Debbie Reynolds. **Education:** Attended Central School of Speech and Drama, London. **Family:** Married singer-songwriter Paul Simon, 1983 (divorced, 1984). **Career:** Writer and actress. **Awards:** *Postcards from the Edge* was named best first novel by PEN Center USA West, 1987. **Address:** c/o Alan Loman, The Authors and Artists Group, 14 East 60th St., New York, New York 10022, U.S.A.

Publications

Novels

Postcards from the Edge. Simon & Schuster, 1987.
Surrender the Pink. Simon & Schuster, 1990.
Delusions of Grandma. Simon & Schuster, 1994.

Plays

Screenplays: *Postcards from the Edge,* adapted from her own novel, 1990.

*

Theatrical Activities:
Actor: **Films**—*Shampoo,* 1975; *Star Wars,* 1977; *The Blues Brothers,* 1980; *The Empire Strikes Back,* 1980; *Under the Rainbow,* 1981; *Return of the Jedi,* 1983; *The Man with One Red Shoe,* 1985; *Hannah and Her Sisters,* 1986; *Appointment with Death,* 1988; *When Harry Met Sally,* 1990.

* * *

Known as the daughter of Eddie Fisher and Debbie Reynolds and for her role as Princess Leia in the Star Wars trilogy, Carrie Fisher swept onto the bestseller scene in 1987 with her hugely successful semi-autobiographical novel, *Postcards from the Edge,* which uses Hollywood as its backdrop. "Maybe I shouldn't have given the guy who pumped my stomach my phone number, but who cares? My life is over anyway." With this the reader is launched into the world of Suzanne Vale, film star and drug addict.

The first section of *Postcards* takes place in a drug rehabilitation clinic. It flips the perspective between the two first-person voices of Suzanne's journal entries and the monologue of a writer named Alex Daniels. In addition, Fisher unconventionally structures the novel by loosely tying together five vignettes. A majority of critics praised the beginning of the novel set in the rehabilitation center as being a bitingly accurate yet comic view of drug addiction. After Suzanne leaves the clinic, however, the novel loses its bite. Fisher seems to lose her way, but at the same time continues to sketch a wonderfully comic, albeit shallow landscape of Hollywood and its players. Hanna Rubin, critiquing for the *New York Times,* saw the novel as "an intermittently funny update of 'Valley of the Dolls.'" Other criticism of the novel concerns the conclusion. Fisher brings in a near-perfect male character named Jesse near the end who is the apparent solution to Suzanne's problems. In fact, he arrives far too late in the novel for the reader to be able to accept him as the panacea for Suzanne's ills. The fairy tale ending is ineffectual and disappointing for the reader.

Postcards was followed three years later by *Surrender the Pink.* This novel centers on Dinah Kaufman, a writer for a soap opera who has recently divorced the intellectual Rudy Gendler. She obsesses on Rudy and ends up chasing him to the Hamptons to spy on him and his girlfriend. The boundary between Dinah's life and the soap she writes becomes confused in some very humorous scenes. Praised for its wit, dialogue, and insider's peek into Hollywood, the novel has been criticized for lack of plotting and a weak climax. The characters may be clever and witty, but they lack substance. Furthermore, the reader is never allowed to approach Dinah's core. Why does she keep latching on to these unattainable men? Such questions are never satisfactorily addressed and the reader is left to wonder.

Fisher's third novel, *Delusions of Grandma* (1994), unfolds once again on the Hollywood scene. The heroine Cora Sharpe engages in an affair with lawyer Ray Beaudrilleaux that ends in his departure and her pregnancy. The last third of the novel has Cora kidnapping her grandfather from a nursing home in Texas. She attempts through comedy to deal with such ponderous issues as birth, death, and Alzheimer's disease. The novel is, like her previous efforts, weakly plotted, but peppered with crackling one-liners.

While Fisher at times misses the mark in plotting and characterization, she more than makes up for those flaws with her acidic, witty, and hip insider's view into the machinations of Hollywood.

—Jennifer G. Coman

FLAGG, Fannie

Nationality: American. **Born:** Patricia Neal, 21 September 1941, in Birmingham, Alabama. **Education:** Attended the University of Alabama; studied at the Pittsburgh Playhouse and the Town and Gown Theatre. **Career:** Actress, comedian, producer, and writer. Producer of *Morning Show* (WBRC-TV), Birmingham, Alabama, 1964-65. Has appeared on numerous television shows and in films. Speaker on the Equal Rights Amendment. Lives in Santa Barbara, California and New York. **Awards:** Fashion award, Ad Club, 1965; named outstanding woman of America, Who's Who in American Women in Radio and Television, 1966; two first place awards in fiction, Santa Barbara Writers Conference.

Publications

Novels

Coming Attractions: A Wonderful Novel. Morrow, 1981; as *Daisy Fay and the Miracle Man,* Warner Books, 1992.

Fried Green Tomatoes at the Whistle Stop Cafe. Random House, 1987.

Plays

Screenplays: *Fried Green Tomatoes,* with Jon Avnet, adapted from her own novel, 1991.

Sound Recordings

Rally 'round the Flagg. RCA Victor, 1967.

My Husband Doesn't Know I'm Making This Phone Call. Sunflower, 1971.

Other

Fannie Flagg's Original Whistle Stop Cafe Cookbook. Fawcett, 1993.

*

Theatrical Activities:
Actor: **Plays**—*Cat on a Hot Tin Roof; Just for Openers,* 1966; *Patio/Porch,* 1977; *Come Back to the Five and Dime, Jimmy Dean, Jimmy Dean,* 1979; *The Best Little Whorehouse in Texas,* 1980. **Films**—*Five Easy Pieces,* 1970; *Some of My Best Friends Are...,* 1971; *Stay Hungry,* 1976; *Grease,* 1978; *Rabbit Test,* 1978.

* * *

Fanny Flagg's success as a writer is based upon two bestselling novels; *Coming Attractions* (1981) and *Fried Green Tomatoes at the Whistle Stop Cafe* (1988). Aside from her writing career, Flagg is a successful actress and has played roles in film, television, and stage drama. Although her writing is generally separated from her acting career, some of her acting roles have inevitably affected the style of her fiction. For example, her use of bittersweet humor in both of her novels resembles the stage work necessary for *The Best Little Whore House in Texas* (1980), while her interest in southern settings places her in the tradition of Tennessee William's *Cat on a Hot Tin Roof* (1966), both of which she has performed. She also helped adapt *Fried Green Tomatoes at the Whistle Stop Cafe* into the Hollywood film version. Film critic Leonard Maltin praised the strength of her adaptation.

Her first novel, *Coming Attractions* (eventually republished as *Daisy Fay and the Miracle Man* [1992]), is based upon Flagg's exploration of coming of age in a southern environment during the 1950s. The novel pretends to be the diary of Daisy Flagg Harper and recounts events in her life from 11 to about 17. The relationship between Daisy and her father becomes the recurrent motif of the novel. Flagg presents a series of touching and humorous scenes as she depicts how Daisy helps her father run the projector at the town theater. Daisy develops a superiority complex and later in life discovers that most of the movies were only "B rate." The novel has a picaresque tone as Daisy encounters one adventure after another, particularly her father's get-rich-quick schemes. Perhaps the funniest of these is her father's bizarre mortgage scam in which he is to come back from the dead. During the seance, his plan backfires as the believers begin to start speaking in tongues and one lady throws off her hearing aid and claims that she can suddenly hear. Critics lauded the work and praised the skill with which Flagg balanced the adventures of Daisy with the harsh realities of growing up.

With the publication of the next novel, *Fried Green Tomatoes at the Whistle Stop Cafe,* Flagg became a bestselling writer. The novel captured the praise of not only critics and the public, but other writers as well. Harper Lee, Erma Bombeck, and Eudora Welty all praised Flagg and recognized her talent as a story teller. Critics enjoyed Flagg's series of recipes at the end of the novel, which contributed to an already enjoyable reading experience.

The narrative is set in a nursing home and is a conversation between Ninny Threadgoode (an 80-year-old woman) and Evelyn Couch (a younger woman visiting another patient). Ninny retells her experiences running a small cafe in Whistle Stop, Alabama. The story hints at a love affair between the two women, and is realistic in its depiction of what would have been acceptable during the 1930s. Yet the novel also incorporates a wide array of adventures that occur in a series of different settings ranging from Valdosta, Georgia, to Chicago, Illinois. Jack Butler, of the *New York Times Review of Books,* called the book "a real novel and a good one," yet he mentioned that Flagg's prose becomes careless and at times she tends to present too many details concerning insignificant events. Regardless of the novel's minor flaws, Butler described the entire work as a relief "in a era plagued by so much trendy experimentalism. [Flagg is] a writer who can end with a genuinely productive innovation."

—Chris Godat

FLEMING, Ian (Lancaster)

Nationality: British. **Born:** London, 28 May 1908. **Education:** Durnford School, Isle of Purbeck, Eton College; Royal Military Academy, Sandhurst; studied languages at the University of Munich and the University of Geneva. **Military Service:** Served in the Royal Naval Volunteer Reserve, as personal assistant to the Director of Naval Intelligence, 1939-45: Lieutenant. **Family:** Married Anne Geraldine Charteris in 1952; one son. **Career:** Moscow correspondent, Reuters news agency, London, 1929-33; worked for Cull and Company, merchant bankers, London, 1933-35; stockbroker, Rowe and Pitman, London, 1935-39; Moscow correspondent, *The Times,* London, 1939; foreign manager, Kemsley, later Thomson, Newspapers, 1945-49: publisher, *Book Collector,* London, 1949-64. Order of the Dannebrog, 1945. **Died:** 12 August 1964.

Publications

Novels (series: James Bond in all titles except *The Diamond Smugglers*)

Casino Royale. London, Cape, and New York, Macmillan, 1954; as *You Asked for It,* New York, Popular Library, 1955.
Live and Let Die. London, Cape, 1954; New York, Macmillan, 1955.
Moonraker. London, Cape, and New York, Macmillan, 1955; as *Too Hot to Handle,* New York, Permabooks, 1957.
Diamonds Are Forever. London, Cape, and New York, Macmillan, 1956.
The Diamond Smugglers. London, Cape, 1957; New York, Macmillan, 1958.
From Russia, with Love. London, Cape, and New York, Macmillan, 1957.
Doctor No. London, Cape, and New York, Macmillan, 1958.
Goldfinger. London, Cape, and New York, Macmillan, 1959.
Thunderball. London, Cape, and New York, Viking Press, 1961.
The Spy Who Loved Me. London, Cape, and New York, Viking Press, 1962.
On Her Majesty's Secret Service. London, Cape, and New York, New American Library, 1963.
You Only Live Twice. London, Cape, and New York, New American Library, 1964.
The Man with the Golden Gun. London, Cape, and New York, New American Library, 1965.
A James Bond Quartet (includes *Casino Royale, Live and Let Die, Moonraker,* and *From Russia, with Love*). London, Cape, 1992.
A James Bond Quintet (includes *Diamonds Are Forever, Doctor No, Goldfinger, For Your Eyes Only,* and *The Spy Who Loved Me*). London, Cape, 1993.
The Essential James Bond (includes *Thunderball, On Her Majesty's Secret Service, You Only Live Twice, The Man with the Golden Gun, Octopussy,* and *The Living Daylights*). London, Cape, 1994.
Ian Fleming's James Bond (includes *Moonraker, From Russia with Love, Dr No, Goldfinger, Thunderball,* and *On Her Majesty's Secret Service*). London, Chancellor Press, 1994.

Short Stories

For Your Eyes Only: Five Secret Occasions in the Life of James Bond. London, Cape, and New York, Viking Press, 1960.
Octopussy, and The Living Daylights. London, Cape, and New York, New American Library, 1966.

Play

Screenplay: *Thunderball,* with Kevin McClory and Jack Whittington. 1965.

Other

Thrilling Cities. London, Cape, 1963; New York, New American Library, 1964.

Chitty-Chitty-Bang-Bang (for children). London, Cape, 3 vols., 1964-65; New York, Random House, 1 vol., 1964; collected edition, Cape, 1971.

Ian Fleming Introduces Jamaica, edited by Morris Cargill. London, Deutsch, 1965; New York, Hawthorn, 1966.

*

Media Adaptations: Films—*Dr. No,* 1962, from the novel; *From Russia with Love,* 1963, from the novel; *Goldfinger,* 1964, from the novel; *Thunderball,* 1965, *Never Say Never Again,* 1983, both from the novel *Thunderball*; *You Only Live Twice,* 1967, from the novel; *Casino Royale* (spoof), 1967, from the novel; *On Her Majesty's Secret Service,* 1969, from the novel; *Diamonds Are Forever,* 1971, from the novel; *Live and Let Die,* 1973, from the novel; *The Man with the Golden Gun,* 1974, from the novel; *The Spy Who Loved Me,* 1977, from an original idea; *Moonraker,* 1979, from the novel; *For Your Eyes Only,* 1981, from the short stories "For Your Eyes Only" and "Risico" (in *For Your Eyes Only*); *Octopussy,* 1983, from the short stories "Octopussy" and "The Property of a Lady" (in *Octopussy and the Living Daylights*); *A View to a Kill,* 1985, from the short story "From a View to a Kill" (in *For Your Eyes Only*); *The Living Daylights,* 1987, from the short story; *License to Kill,* 1989, from an original idea; *Goldeneye,* 1995, from a story by Michael France.

Bibliography: *Ian Fleming: A Catalogue of a Collection: Preliminary to a Bibliography* by Iain Campbell, privately printed, 1978.

Critical Studies: *007 James Bond: A Report* by O.F. Snelling, London, Spearman, 1964, New York, New American Library, 1965; *The James Bond Dossier* by Kingsley Amis, London, Cape, and New York, New American Library, 1965; *The Life of Ian Fleming,* London, Cape, and New York, McGraw Hill, 1966, *007 James Bond,* London, Sidgwick and Jackson, and New York, Morrow, 1973, and *James Bond: The Authorised Biography of 007,* London, Grandar, 1985, New York, Grove Press, 1986, all by John Pearson; *The Bond Affair* by Oreste Del Buono and Umberto Eco, London, Macdonald, 1966; *Ian Fleming: The Spy Who Came In with the Gold* by Henry Zieger, New York, Duell, 1966; *You Only Live Once: Memories of Ian Fleming* by Ivar Bruce, London, Weidenfeld and Nicolson, 1975, Frederick, Maryland, University Publications of America, 1985; *The James Bond Films* by Steven Jay Rubin, London, Arlington, 1982; *Murders in the Millions: Erle Stanley Gardner, Mickey Spillane, Ian Fleming* by J. Kenneth Van Dover, New York, Ungar, 1984; *The James Bond Bedside Companion* by Raymond Benson, New York, Dodd Mead, 1984; *Secret Agents in Fiction: Ian Fleming, John Le Carré, and Len Deighton* by L.O. Saverberg, London, Macmillan, 1984; *James Bond: A Celebration* by Peter Haining, London, W.H. Allen, 1987; *Ian Fleming's James Bond* by John E. Gardner, New York, Avenel, 1987; *The Private Life of James Bond* by David R. Contosta, Lititz, Pennsylvania, Sutter House, 1993; *The Life of Ian Fleming* by Donald McCormick, London, P. Owen, 1993.

* * *

Author Ian Fleming, creator of James Bond, 007 of the British Secret Service, was the first to deny that he had any literary pretensions. Calling his works "trivial piffle," he wanted to entertain readers with his stories and make money in the process. His vehicle for doing so became the famous Bond, described by critics on one hand as boyishly charming, smooth, and unflappable, and on the other as heartless, sadistic, and even misogynistic. Yet Bond has always had his admirers, including President John F. Kennedy (who boosted Fleming's reputation and sales in the United States). Bond came to represent the ideal secret agent; handsome, ruthless when necessary, and always with a girl on his arm as he faced monstrous villains in order to save the world.

The 007 of Fleming's novels became overshadowed by the 007 of Hollywood's movies, played by Sean Connery, Roger Moore, Timothy Dalton and Pierce Brosnan. In the movies, Bond is an invincible agent of British intelligence, relying on fancy gadgets, beautiful leading ladies, and his deadly aim to defeat improbable villains, all megalomaniacs who wish to change the course of history.

In reality, Fleming's view of Bond was quite different—Bond was a rather stupid man to whom things happened. His first novel, *Casino Royale* (1953), shows Bond, a Commander in the British Navy who now works for the British Secret Service, defeating a foreign agent in a high-stakes game of baccarat. Bond is cool and calculating, and comfortable in the posh setting of a Mediterranean casino, yet not especially brilliant in tracking down evil agents, none of whom were British and most of whom were Russian. The novel was panned for its unrealistic plot, sexual content, and scenes of brutality, one of which involved Bond being tied naked to a chair and beaten about the genitals with a carpet brush. Yet other critics admired Fleming's handling of plot and his eye for detail related to espionage; Fleming sounded authentic, having drawn from his own background in British intelligence.

Bond became an instant success and appeared in several more novels, including *From Russia, With Love* (1957), *Dr. No* (1958), and *Goldfinger* (1959). His early antagonists were agents of SMERSH, the actual Soviet espionage agency whose name translated to "Death to Spies." Later, Fleming created SPECTRE (Special Directorate for Counter-intelligence, Terrorism, Revenge and Extortion), an international mafia of criminals, terrorists, and killers run by the mysterious Blofeld. SPECTRE first appeared in *Thunderball* (1961), hijacking a NATO bomber carrying two nuclear weapons and holding the Western world at ransom. In a later novel, *On Her Majesty's Secret Service* (1963), Bond tracks Blofeld to an exclusive resort on top of a Swiss alp with the help of a Mediterranean criminal.

All of the Bond novels deal with foreign locales, shadowy villains, and beautiful women in distress who await salvation in the form of Bond. Fleming's description of action is taut and well-paced, and perhaps more believable than the Bond movies. Also, despite Fleming's eventual distaste for Bond as a "cardboard dummy," in print he occasionally shows a human side. In *Thunderball,* for example, 007 falls in love with the gorgeous Domino, whom he has been using to get close to the SPECTRE villain. Similarly, in *On Her Majesty's Secret Service,* Bond plans to resign from the Secret Service, falls in love with and marries a woman he saves from suicide, and then loses his bride to a SPECTRE assassin.

Most critics recognize Bond as a mythical character drawn from adolescent fantasy—an indestructible hero saving maidens from various evils, and who, for his reward, sleeps with the maidens. In the 1950s Bond was seen as a breath of fresh air to a post-war England seeking escape and excitement. Although he represented the highbrow—with his suits, expensive cars, vodka martinis, and sophisticated women—many readers in the welfare state of Great

Britain responded with rapture. As critic George Grella wrote, "[Bond] lives in the dreams of countless drab people, his gun ready, his honor intact, his morals loose: the hero of our anxiety-ridden, mythless age; the savior of our culture." While modern readers may be disillusioned by Bond's sexist attitudes, they will find the Bond novels to be exciting tales that accurately depict the Cold War fantasy of East-versus-West espionage.

—Christopher Swann

FOLLETT, Ken(neth Martin)

Pseudonyms: Martin Martinsen; Symon Myles; Bernard L. Ross; Zachary Stone. **Nationality:** British. **Born:** Cardiff, Glamorgan, 5 June 1949. **Education:** University College, London, B.A. in philosophy 1970. **Family:** Married 1) Mary Emma Ruth Elson in 1968 (separated 1984), one son and one daughter; 2) Barbara Broer in 1985. **Career:** Reporter and rock music columnist, *South Wales Echo,* Cardiff, 1970-73; reporter, *London Evening News,* 1973-74; editorial director 1974-76, and deputy managing editor, 1976-77, Everest Books, London. Since 1977, full-time writer. **Awards:** Mystery Writers of America Edgar Allan Poe award, 1979. **Agent:** Albert Zuckerman, Writers House Inc., 21 West 26th Street, New York, New York 10010, U.S.A. **Address:** P.O. Box 708, London SW10 ODH, England.

Publications

Novels (series: "Apples" Carstairs in Symon Myles books; Piers Roper)

The Big Black (as Symon Myles). London, Everest, 1974.
The Big Needle (as Simon Myles). London, Everest, 1974; as *The Big Apple,* New York, Zebra, 1975.
The Big Hit (as Symon Myles). London, Everest, 1975.
The Shakeout (Roper). Lewes, Sussex, Harwood Smart, 1975; New York, Armchair Detective Library, 1990.
Amoki: King of Legend (as Bernard L. Ross). London, Futura, 1976.
The Bear Raid (Roper). London, Harwood Smart, 1976; New York, Armchair Detective Library, 1990.
Capricorn One (as Bernard L. Ross). London, Futura, 1976; New York, Fawcett, 1978.
The Modigliani Scandal (as Zachary Stone). London, Collins, 1976; as Ken Follett, New York, Morrow, 1985.
Paper Money (as Zachary Stone). London, Collins, 1977; as Ken Follett, New York, Morrow, 1987.
Storm Island. London, Macdonald, 1978; as *Eye of the Needle,* New York, Arbor House, 1978.
Triple. London, Macdonald, and New York, Arbor House, 1979.
The Key to Rebecca. London, Hamish Hamilton, and New York, Morrow, 1980.
The Man from St. Petersburg. London, Hamish Hamilton, and New York, Morrow, 1982.
On Wings of Eagles. New York, Morrow, and London, Collins, 1983.
Lie Down with Lions. London, Hamish Hamilton, 1985; New York, Morrow, 1986.
The Pillars of the Earth. New York, Morrow, and London, Macmillan, 1989.
Night over Water. New York, Morrow, and London, Macmillan, 1991.
A Dangerous Fortune. New York, Delacorte, 1993; London, Macmillan, 1994.
Churchill's Gold. London, Mandarin, 1993.
A Place Called Freedom. New York, Crown, and London, Macmillan, 1995.
The Third Twin. New York, Crown, and London, Macmillan, 1996.

Fiction for Children

The Secret of Kellerman's Studio. London, Abelard Schuman, 1976; as *The Mystery Hideout,* New York, Morrow, 1990.
The Power Twins and the Worm Puzzle (as Martin Martinsen). London, Abelard Schuman, 1976; as *The Power Twins,* New York, Morrow, 1990.

Play

Television Play: *Fringe Banking* (in *Tagart* series), 1978.

Other

The Heist of the Century (as René Louis Maurice, with others). London, Fontana, 1978; as *The Gentlemen of 16 July,* New York, Arbor House, 1980; as *Under the Streets of Nice; The Bank Heist of the Century,* Bethesda, Maryland, National Press, 1986.
Three Blind Mice: Deportations without Justice. Charter 88 Enterprises, 1992.

*

Media Adaptation: Film—*Eye of the Needle,* 1981, from the novel (also published as *Storm Island*).

* * *

Ken Follett began writing as a reporter and popular music columnist for the *South Wales Echo* in his hometown, Cardiff, and then as a crime reporter for the *London Evening News.* This journalistic beginning infuses his novels with clear, straightforward prose, chains of events in chronological sequence, topicality, an eye on mass readership, and an instinct for a saleable story. Most of his novels involve adventure.

Follett's early efforts were racy and sensational. Typical was *The Big Needle* (1974), in which a vengeful father of a comatose heroin victim punishes those he deems responsible. Among the best of those early stories was *The Modigliani Scandal* (1976), a classic caper novel involving a forged masterpiece, European adventure, and amoral life styles. But his first big success was a war-time spy adventure called *Eye of the Needle* (1978).

A Literary Guild selection and winner of the 1978 Edgar Award from the Mystery Writers of America, *Eye of the Needle* convincingly evokes wartime lifestyles, sensibilities, and attitudes as the German spy (code-named "Die Nadel") discovers that the D-Day attack will occur at Normandy instead of Pas de Calais. With British intelligence in hot pursuit, Faber plans to rendezvous with a German submarine off Aberdeen, Scotland, to document the deception. However, shipwrecked on Storm Island, he finds love in the arms of a strong woman, Lucy, whose husband, the lighthouse keeper, has become embittered by the loss of his legs in a car accident. The perspective shifts at the end as Lucy is torn between love and duty, and between personal feelings and the greater good. Follett's skill is in making the villain well-rounded and understandable. The book was made into a commercially successful movie.

Follett's second bestseller, *Triple,* continues Follett's double vision. In this case, the two sides of the Arab-Israeli conflict are humanized by means of a Mossad agent and PLO terrorists. A fictional account of a 1968 shipboard heist of 200 tons of uranium (the raw material to produce thirty atomic bombs), *Triple* attributes the theft to the Israelis, who were upset at Egypt's nuclear capability. His engaging protagonists include a Palestinian triple agent, an American-born Israeli spy, and a beautiful Lebanese-American with Mafia protectors.

The Key to Rebecca (1980), based on the exploits of the German spy John Eppler and Erwin Rommel's 1942 move toward Alexandria, is one of Follett's most carefully written works. It is psychologically complex and proffers memorable, individualized characters, evocative descriptions of wartime Cairo and desert and nomadic life, and contrasting characters, including a cruel, psychopathic spy and a decent, determined military intelligence officer.

In contrast, *The Man from St. Petersburg* (1982) is the story of a WWII anarchist's plot to assassinate a character who can assure Russian support of England against Germany. The book strains credulity with incredible coincidences and operatic climaxes. *Lie Down with Lions* (1985) is similarly faulty, with its sacrifice of character to plot, heavy-handed culture-clash scenes, and a vexing Western feminist (a leftist whose husband is a deep-cover Soviet operative sent to spy on Afghan freedom fighters, and whose lover is a 1960s radical/poet turned CIA spy).

Follet deviated with *On the Wings of Eagles* (1983), which describes Ross Perot's real-life rescue of two corporate executives imprisoned in Teheran during the 1979 revolution. Likewise, *The Pillars of the Earth* (1989) is a historical romance about the human cost of building a medieval cathedral, the murder of Thomas Beckett, and the whipping of Henry II, while the thrilling, adventure romance, *Night Over Water* (1991), makes credible disturbing political and personal loyalties. *A Dangerous Fortune* (1993), set in Victorian and Edwardian England, exposes hypocrisies and dark secrets behind public facades and the conflict between moral commitment to investors and high-handed, amoral, capitalistic venture.

—Gina & Andrew Macdonald

FOOTE, Shelby

Nationality: American. **Born:** Greenville, Mississippi, 17 November 1916. **Education:** The University of North Carolina, Chapel Hill, 1935-37. **Military Service:** Served in the U.S. Army, 1940-44, and Marine Corps, 1944-45. **Family:** Married Gwyn Rainer in 1956 (second marriage); two children. **Career:** Novelist-in-residence, University of Virginia, Charlottesville, November 1963; playwright-in-residence, Arena Stage, Washington, D.C., 1963-64; writer-in-residence, Hollins College, Virginia, 1968. **Awards:** Guggenheim fellowship, 1955, 1956, 1957; Ford fellowship, for drama, 1963; Fletcher Pratt award, for nonfiction, 1964, 1974; University of North Carolina award, 1975. D.Litt.: University of the South, Sewanee, Tennessee, 1981; Southwestern University, Memphis, Tennessee, 1982; University of North Carolina, Chapel Hill, 1992; University of South Carolina, 1991; University of Notre Dame, South Bend, Indiana, 1994. **Member:** Society of American Historians, 1980; American Academy of Arts and Letters, 1994. **Address:** 542 East Parkway South, Memphis, Tennessee 38104, U.S.A.

Publications

Novels

Tournament. New York, Dial Press, 1949.
Follow Me Down. New York, Dial Press, 1950; London, Hamish Hamilton, 1951.
Love in a Dry Season. New York, Dial Press, 1951.
Shiloh. New York, Dial Press, 1952.
Jordan County: A Landscape in Narrative (includes stories). New York, Dial Press, 1954.
September September. New York, Random House, 1978.
Stars in Their Courses. New York, Random House, 1994.
The Beleaguered City. New York, Random House, 1995.

Play

Jordan County: A Landscape in the Round (produced Washington, D.C., 1964).

Other

The Civil War: A Narrative
Fort Sumter to Perryville. New York, Random House, 1958; London, Bodley Head, 1991.
Fredericksburg to Meridian. New York, Random House, 1963; London, Bodley Head, 1991.
Red River to Appomattox. New York, Random House, 1974; London, Bodley Head, 1991.
The Novelist's View of History. Winston-Salem, North Carolina, Palaemon Press, 1981.
Conversations with Shelby Foote, edited by William C. Carter. Jackson, University Press of Mississippi, 1989.

*

Manuscript Collection: Southern Historical Collection, University of North Carolina, Chapel Hill, North Carolina.

Critical Studies: "Shelby Foote Issue" (includes bibliography) of *Mississippi Quarterly* (State College), October 1971, and *Delta* (Montpellier, France), 1977; *Shelby Foote* by Helen White and Redding Sugg, Boston, Twayne, 1982; *Shelby Foote: Novelist and Historian* by Robert L. Phillips, University of Mississippi Press, 1992.

* * *

Born and raised in the Mississippi Delta, Shelby Foote set his first novel, *Tournament* (1949), in mythical Jordan County, Mississippi, and chronicled the decline and fall of Hugh Bart. Bart, forced to sell his plantation and then swindled in a business deal, resorts to gambling to survive. Foote described the novel's theme as being "that each man . . . is profoundly alone." *Tournament* was well received by critics (the *New York Times Book Review*, for example, described it as "moving" and "freshly and effectively" written), and Foote was, perhaps inevitably, dubbed the next William Faulkner.

Foote's second novel, *Follow Me Down* (1950), was also set on the plantation "Solitaire," introduced in *Tournament*. It tells the story of tenant farmer Luther Eustis and Beulah, the girl he seduces and eventually kills. Some critics noted that Foote used the two characters to represent, respectively, obsolete Protestant moral certainty and decadent sexuality and experience. Foote himself described his intent as "trying to stress the valiance of practically everyone in being able to get through life at all." In 1971, critic Thomas H. Landes described *Follow Me Down* as "perhaps Foote's most powerful work of fiction."

Love in a Dry Season (1951) takes place in Foote's Mississippi Delta between the 1920s and World War II. It also features Foote's portrayal of a 20th-century South scarred and enfeebled by the legacy of the Civil War. Its narrower theme is the absence of love in a rapidly changing southern town where four principal characters, Major Malcolm Barcroft, Harley Drew, and Amy and Jeff Carruthers, represent the amoral and diminished quality of the new South.

The Civil War, which loomed significantly in the background of all Foote's earlier novels, moved to center stage in *Shiloh* (1952), a historical novel in which Foote uses a series of Union and Confederate narrators to provide a full panorama of the crucial Civil War battle in Tennessee. The reviewer for the *New York Times* asserted that *Shiloh* showed that Foote had "arrived" as a novelist, and the *Saturday Review* praised it as "a superb story of war."

On the strength of *Shiloh*, Foote was asked by a publisher to write a short, one-volume history of the Civil War. What resulted was a massive three-volume work published over twenty years. Titled "The Civil War: A Narrative" (1958, 1963, 1974), the work won Foote almost universal acclaim and stands today as perhaps the finest narrative account of the Civil War. The first volume, *Fort Sumter to Perryville,* covers the period 1861 to 1862 and was praised by the reviewer for the *New York Herald Tribune* as a "grand, sweeping narrative." The reviewer for *Commonweal*, however, criticized Foote for eschewing footnotes and using undue license with historical facts.

The second volume of "The Civil War," *Fredericksburg to Meridian,* carried the narrative into 1864 and was praised by T. Harry Williams in the *New York Herald Tribune* as superbly written and astonishing in scope. Some critics faulted Foote for slighting the political dimension of the Civil War in favor of focusing on military events, but his decision to grant equal weight to the campaigns in both the West and the East was cited as one of the narrative's most important accomplishments.

The final volume, *Red River to Appomattox,* drew the ambitious project to a close and allowed critics to assess Foote's accomplishment as a whole. *Time* praised it as "rich in detail and purely exciting," the *New Republic* asserted that the work "surpasses anything on the subject," and the *New York Times Book Review* called it a remarkable achievement. In a comment that may have meant the most to Foote, however, longtime friend and fellow novelist Walker Percy characterized it simply as "an American 'Iliad.'"

In 1978, Foote returned to fiction with *September, September*, the story of the attempt by three whites to kidnap a black youth and extract a large ransom from his wealthy family. Inverting the characteristics stereotypically assigned to whites and blacks and setting the novel against the backdrop of the 1957 racial integration crisis in Arkansas, Foote focused on the theme of "manhood and how it is won" while meditating on the modern condition of the American South.

Although Foote's monumental Civil War series has tended to shift critical attention from his fiction to his historical writing, his novels have been described as "among the best in 20th-century American literature." Through his role as a commentator on the 1991 public television documentary, *The Civil War,* Foote gained renewed attention while he continued work on a novel he described as "a Mississippi *Karamazov.*" "I intend to stop writing," Foote said, "when they let me down into the ground."

—Paul S. Bodine

FORD, Elbur. *See* **HOLT, Victoria.**

FORSYTH, Frederick

Nationality: British. **Born:** Ashford, Kent, in 1938. **Education:** Tonbridge School, Kent. **Military Service:** Served in the Royal Air Force 1956-58. **Family:** Married Carrie Forsyth in 1973; two sons. **Career:** Journalist, *Eastern Daily Press,* Norwich, and in King's Lynn, Norfolk, 1958-61; reporter for Reuters, London, Paris, and East Berlin, 1961-65; reporter, BBC Radio and Television, London, 1965-67; assistant diplomatic correspondent, BBC, 1967-68; freelance journalist in Nigeria, 1968-70; television presenter, *Soldiers* series, 1985, and *Frederick Forsyth Presents* series, 1989-90. Lives in London. **Awards:** Mystery Writers of America Edgar Allan Poe award, 1971, 1983. **Address:** c/o Hutchinson Pub Group Ltd., 62-65 Chandos Pl, London WC2N 4NW, England.

Publications

Novels

The Day of the Jackal. London, Hutchinson, and New York, Viking Press, 1971.

The Odessa File. London, Hutchinson, and New York, Viking Press, 1972.

The Dogs of War. London, Hutchinson, and New York, Viking Press, 1974.

The Shepherd. London, Hutchinson, 1975; New York, Viking Press, 1976.

The Devil's Alternative. London, Hutchinson, 1979; New York, Viking Press, 1980.

The Fourth Protocol. London, Hutchinson, and New York, Viking Press, 1984.
The Negotiator. London and New York, Bantam, 1989.
The Deceiver. London, Corgi, and New York, Bantam, 1991.
The Fist of God. London and New York, Bantam, 1994.

Short Stories

No Comebacks: Collected Short Stories. London, Hutchinson, and New York, Viking Press, 1982.

Play

Screenplay: *The Fourth Protocol,* 1987.

Other

The Biafra Story. London, Penguin, 1969; as *The Making of an African Legend: The Biafra Story,* 1977.
Emeka (biography of Chukwuemeka Odumegwu-Ojukwu). Ibadan, Spectrum, 1982.

*

Media Adaptations: Films—*The Day of the Jackal,* 1973; *The Odessa File,* 1974, *The Dogs of War,* 1981; *The Fourth Protocol,* 1987.

* * *

Frederick Forsyth, among other credits, invented a sub-genre of the suspense thriller. In a typical Forsyth novel, a highly professional man of action (in his 30s in earlier books and 40s in later novels) combats either a lone antagonist or a rigid bureaucratic organization. Often, the hero, though true to his own highly developed professional standards, has trouble conforming to the constricting demands of the modern corporate structure. Scenes typically shift back and forth between the hero and his antagonists, and the action quickens as a collision course perceivable early in the story becomes imminent. The setting is generally European, but may shift to widely varied international locations, especially hotspots of espionage or criminality. This is Eric Ambler territory updated, and, like that earlier spy story writer, Forsyth gives an excellent sense of the mood, manners, and etiquette of a netherworld hardly visible to civilian observers, usually basing his plots on real-life happenings. Finally, Forsyth's impressive command of technical detail creates an "inside story" journalistic appeal that is irresistible.

In fact, Forsyth came to suspense fiction from journalism, and his major nonfiction works, including *The Biafra Story* (1969), reflect that background. Forsyth's first great success was *The Day of the Jackal* (1971), a compelling thriller based on real-life attempts to assassinate French President Charles de Gaulle because of his support for Algerian independence. Probably Forsyth's best book, the novel shifts from the "Jackal," a professional assassin based on the notorious Carlos the Jackal, to the nondescript but equally professional police detective who must foil the plot. Ironically, each recognizes and respects the technical capabilities of the other, allowing a true contest to develop. As with other Forsyth works, this competition in *Jackal* becomes an exploration of professionalism, with amateur emotionalism contrasted to the cool rationality of the pros. A successful 1973 film version starring Edward Fox helped promote Forsyth's signature narration—taut, spare, technical, alternating between opponents—as a modern standard.

The Odessa File (1972) continues the theme of an invisible war between obsessively dedicated opponents. German Peter Miller, a highly competent crime reporter, tracks down a former concentration-camp commander (based on the historical Captain Edward Roschmann), finding a worthy opponent in the Odessa (the organization of former SO members). In another well-written work, *The Dogs of War* (1974), mercenary Cat Shannon leads a coup against an Idi Amin-like African tyrant on behalf of a British mining magnate who wishes to exploit the country's resources. Shannon plays one side against the other in the service of justice, retaining professional independence while exploiting his employer's greed. The story is based on a factual incident, and persistent rumors suggest Forsyth's involvement, especially given the author's contacts with mercenaries after his Biafra experiences.

The *Devil's Alternative* (1979) reflects the hostage-taking and terrorism of the 1970s, focusing on the possibilities of seizing an oil-filled super tanker. Though purely fictional, Forsyth's analogies to real "eco-terrorism" provided a dark vision of future disaster (the title means "no choice at all"). In contrast, *No Comebacks* (1982), a collection of short stories focused on the domestic and everyday, is more conventionally "literary" than Forsyth's other works and surprises with its humor and light ironic touch. *The Fourth Protocol* (1984) concerns the gentleman's agreement between East and West to keep portable nuclear weapons off enemy turf. A rogue Soviet group tries to violate this policy, triggering alternating moves and countermoves reminiscent of *Day of the Jackal.* The popular novel was made into a well-received film starring Pierce Brosnan.

The Negotiator (1989) tracks the attempts of Texas and Russian conservatives to scuttle an unprecedented disarmament agreement by kidnapping the U.S. president's son. In *The Negotiator*, Forsyth introduces a female partner, FBI agent Sam(antha) Somerville. This recognition of new female roles fails to rescue a plot burdened with credibility problems and dated by accelerated changes in U.S.-Soviet relations.

In recognition of changing times, Forsyth offered *The Deceiver* (1991). It featured British superspy Sam McCready, the "deceiver" of the title, who attempts to defend earlier intelligence activity excesses. Again reacting to current events, Forsyth focuses *The Fist of God* (1994) on the Persian Gulf War, with a deep-cover British agent attempting to contact a mole, "Jericho," burrowed far into the Baghdad government of Saddam Hussein. Again we get competing adversaries and shifts of scene in a well-researched and technically informative tale.

Forsyth's novels, while weak in characterization and stylistic grace, are excellent examples of the marriage of high-quality journalism and popular fact-based fiction. Their thorough research informs and teaches even as the page-turning urgency of plot, with Forsyth's characteristic alternation between forces on collision course, keeps readers involved.

—Andrew Macdonald

FOSTER, Alan Dean

Nationality: American. **Born:** New York City, 18 November 1946. **Education:** University of California, Los Angeles, B.A. in political science 1968; M.F.A. in film 1969. **Military Service:** Served in the United States Army Reserve, 1969-75. **Family:** Married JoAnn Oxley in 1975. **Career:** Head copywriter, Headlines Ink Agency, Studio City, California, 1970-71; instructor in English and film, University of California, Los Angeles, intermittently since 1971, and Los Angeles City College, 1972-76. **Awards:** Galaxy award, 1979; Southwest Book award, 1990. **Member:** SFWA, WGAW. **Agent:** (fiction) Virginia Kidd, Box 278, Milford, Pennsylvania 18337; (media) William Morris, 151 El Camino Blvd., Beverly Hills, California. **Address:** P.O. Box 12757, Prescott, Arizona 86301, U.S.A.

Publications

Novels (series: Alien; Commonwealth; The Damned; Spellsinger; Star Wars)

The Tar-Aiym Krang (Commonwealth). New York, Ballantine, 1972; London, New English Library, 1979.
Bloodhype (Commonwealth). New York, Ballantine, 1973; London, New English Library, 1979.
Icerigger (Commonwealth). New York, Ballantine, 1974; London, New English Library, 1976.
Luana (novelization of screenplay). New York, Ballantine, 1974.
Dark Star (novelization of screenplay). New York, Ballantine, 1974; London, Orbit, 1979.
Midworld (Commonwealth). Garden City, New York, Doubleday, 1975; London, Macdonald and Jane's, 1977.
Star Wars: From the Adventures of Luke Skywalker (as George Lucas). New York, Ballantine, 1976.
Orphan Star (Commonwealth). New York, Ballantine, 1977; London, New English Library, 1979.
The End of the Matter (Commonwealth). New York, Ballantine, 1977; London, New English Library, 1979.
Splinter of the Mind's Eye: From the Adventures of Luke Skywalker (Star Wars). New York, Ballantine, and London, Sphere, 1978.
Mission to Moulokin (Commonwealth). Garden City, New York, Doubleday, and London, New English Library, 1979.
The Black Hole: A Novel (novelization of screenplay). New York, Ballantine, 1979.
Cachalot: A Novel (Commonwealth). New York, Ballantine, 1980; London, New English Library, 1987.
Outland (novelization of screenplay). New York, Warner, and London, Sphere, 1981.
Clash of the Titans (novelization of screenplay). New York, Warner, and London, Macdonald, 1981.
The Thing: A Novel (novelization of screenplay). New York, Bantam, and London, Corgi, 1982.
Nor Crystal Tears (Commonwealth). New York, Ballantine, 1982; London, New English Library, 1986.
For Love of Mother-Not (Commonwealth). New York, Ballantine, 1983; London, New English Library, 1984.
Spellsinger at the Gate. Huntington Woods, Michigan, Phantasia Press, 1983.
Spellsinger. New York, Warner, 1983; London, Orbit, 1984.
The Hour of the Gate. New York, Warner, and London Orbit, 1984.
Krull: A Novel (novelization of screenplay). New York, Warner, and London, Corgi, 1983.
The Man Who Used the Universe. New York, Warner, 1983; London, Orbit, 1984.
The I Inside. New York, Warner, 1984; London, Orbit, 1985.
Voyage to the City of the Dead (Commonwealth). New York, Ballantine, 1984; London, New English Library, 1986.
Slipt. New York, Berkley, 1984.
The Last Starfighter (novelization of screenplay). New York, Berkley, and London, W.H. Allen, 1984; adapted for children by Lynn Haney as *The Last Starfighter Storybook,* New York, Putnam, 1984.
The Day of the Dissonance (Spellsinger). Huntington Woods, Michigan, Phantasia Press, 1984; London, Orbit, 1985.
The Moment of the Magician (Spellsinger). Huntington Woods, Michigan, Phantasia Press, 1984; London, Macdonald, 1985.
Starman: A Novel (novelization of screenplay). New York, Warner, 1984; London, Corgi, 1985.
Shadowkeep. New York, Warner, 1984; London, W.H. Allen, 1985.
Sentenced to Prism (Commonwealth). New York, Ballantine, 1985; London, New English Library, 1988.
Pale Rider. New York, Warner, and London, Arrow, 1985.
The Paths of the Perambulator (Spellsinger). West Bloomfield, Michigan, Phantasia Press, 1985; London, Macdonald, 1986.
Season of the Spellsong (includes *Spellsinger, Hour of the Gate,* and *Day of the Dissonance*). Garden City, New York, Doubleday, 1985.
Into the Out Of. New York, Warner, 1986; London, New English Library, 1987.
The Time of the Transference (Spellsinger). West Bloomfield, Michigan, Phantasia Press, 1986; London, Orbit, 1987.
Spellsinger Scherzo (includes *The Moment of the Magician, The Paths of the Perambulator,* and *The Time of the Transference*). Garden City, New York, Doubleday, 1987.
The Deluge Drivers (Commonwealth). New York, Ballantine, 1987; London, New English Library, 1988.
Glory Lane. New York, Ace, 1987; London, New English Library, 1989.
To the Vanishing Point. New York, Warner, 1988; London, Sphere, 1989.
Maori. New York, Berkley, 1988.
Flinx in Flux (Commonwealth). New York, Ballantine, 1988; London, New English Library, 1989.
Alien Nation (novelization of screenplay). New York, Warner, 1988; London, Grafton, 1989.
Quozl. New York, Ace, 1989; London, New English Library, 1991.
Cyber Way. New York, Ace, 1990; London, Orbit, 1992.
A Call to Arms (Damned). Norwalk, Connecticut, Easton Press, 1991.
Cat-a-lyst. New York, Ace, 1991; London, Orbit, 1992.
The False Mirror (Damned). New York, Ballantine, 1992.
Codgerspace. New York, Ace, 1992; London, Orbit, 1993.
Son of Spellsinger. New York, Warner, and London, Orbit, 1993.
The Spoils of War (Damned). New York, Ballantine, 1993.
The Complete Alien Omnibus. London, Warner, 1993.
 Alien (novelization of screenplay). New York, Ballantine, and London, Macdonald and Jane's, 1979.
 Aliens (novelization of screenplay). New York, Warner, and London, Orbit, 1986.
 Alien 3 (novelization of screenplay). New York and London, Warner, 1992.
Greenthieves. New York, Ace, and London, Orbit, 1994.
Chorus Skating (Spellsinger). New York, Warner, 1994; London, Orbit, 1995.

Design for Great Day, with Eric Frank Russell. New York, Tor, 1995.
Life-Form. New York, Ace, 1995.
The Dig. New York, Warner, 1996.
Dinotopia Lost. New York, Warner, 1996.
Mad Amos. New York, Ballantine, 1996.

Short Stories (series: Star Trek)

Star Trek Log One [-Ten] (adaptation of television series). New York, Ballantine, 10 vols., 1974-78; as *Log One [-Log Nine],* 3 vols., 1993; London, Pocket Books, 1995.
With Friends Like These. . . . New York, Ballantine, 1977.
. . . Who Needs Enemies? New York, Ballantine, 1984; London, Orbit, 1986.
The Horror on the Beach: A Tale in the Cthulhu Mythos. San Diego, California, Valcour and Krueger, 1978.
The Metrognome and Other Stories. New York, Ballantine, 1990.
Montezuma Strip. New York, Warner, 1995.

Play

Screenplay: *Star-Trek,* 1979.

Other

Sir Charles Berkley and the Referee Murders (graphic novel). Prescott, Arizona, Hamilton Comics, 1993.

Editor, *The Best of Eric Frank Russell.* New York, Ballantine, 1978.
Editor, *Animated Features and Silly Symphonies.* New York, Abbeville, 1980.
Editor, with Martin H. Greenberg, *Smart Dragons, Foolish Elves.* New York, Ace, 1991.
Editor, with Martin H. Greenberg, *Betcha Can't Read Just One.* New York, Ace, 1993.

*

Critical Studies: *A Guide to the Commonwealth: The Official Guide to Alan Dean Foster's Humanx Commonwealth Universe* by Robert Teague and Michael Goodwin, Roy, Utah, Galagraphics, 1985.

* * *

Popular criticism recognizes Alan Dean Foster, a widely known science fiction author, for his own science fiction stories as well as many novels he adapted from screenplays. Foster's work generally focuses less on exploring his individual style and more on providing a fun-filled, action-packed tale for his fans. Although Foster's novels lack originality, his skill in successfully adapting screenplays into novels is considered more than competent. *Aliens* (1986), *Star Wars* (1976), *Dark Star* (1974), and *Clash of the Titans* (1981) comprise a few of the successful screenplays transformed into novels by Foster.

Foster has produced a number of series that, while not wildly popular, have gained a following anxiously awaiting the next novel. The most popular of these series concentrates on the adventures of a young orphan with psychic powers, Flinx, and his sidekick pet alien, Pip. These novels feature many narrow escapes and near accidents maneuvered by Flinx and Pip as they haphazardly travel throughout Humanx Commonwealth.

In 1995 Foster released another in the Flinx-based series, *Mid-Flinx.* Once again Flinx unwittingly finds himself in a chain reaction of mishaps, requiring all of his brains and Pip's brawn to escape. While escaping, Flinx makes an emergency landing on an unknown planet to find it covered by an exotic rain forest. There he encounters and befriends a civilization of "human descendants of a lost expedition." His peace there is soon shattered as his enemies discover him and force him into making yet one more narrow escape. *Booklist* states that with this novel Foster has finally "honed his narrative style" and that, of all books in this series, *Mid-Flinx* is "so consistently absorbing that newcomers to the Flinx saga will search out earlier installments, and both they and seasoned fans will be gratified by Foster's hints of more to come."

In Quozl (1989), Foster suggests, but does not state, there is hope for mankind. Resembling stuffed animals in appearance, the Quozl race lands on earth and becomes enamored of "flashy clothes, art and sex." However, fearing human response to their presence, they hide in an Idaho valley to contemplate their position. Needless to say, humans discover the Quozl and, on a wave of commercialism and exploitation, the creatures are introduced into the human world. Although Foster does provide an analysis of Quozl and human societies, he reduces all differences and problems between races to responses to uncontrollable psycho-sexual urges (a lesson learned from the wise Quozl) which reads as a convenient ending rather than a legitimate solution to some of humankind's problems.

—Amy Eldridge

FRASER, Jane. *See* **PILCHER, Rosamunde.**

FRENCH, Marilyn

Nationality: American. **Born:** Marilyn Edwards in New York City, 21 November 1929. **Education:** Hofstra College (now University), Hempstead, Long Island, B.A. 1951, M.A. 1964; Harvard University, Cambridge, Massachusetts, Ph.D. 1972. **Family:** Married Robert M. French in 1950 (divorced 1967). **Career:** Instructor, Hofstra University, 1964-68; assistant professor of English, College of the Holy Cross, Worcester, Massachusetts, 1972-76; artist-in-residence, Aspen Institute for Humanistic Study, 1972; Mellon fellow, Harvard University, 1976. **Agent:** Sheedy Literary Agency, 41 King Street, New York, New York 10014, U.S.A.

Publications

Novels

The Women's Room. New York, Summit, 1977; London, Deutsch, 1978.

The Bleeding Heart. New York, Summit, and London, Deutsch, 1980.
Her Mother's Daughter. New York, Summit, and London, Heinemann, 1987.
Our Father. Boston, Little Brown, 1994; New York, Penguin, 1995.

Other

The Book as World: James Joyce's Ulysses. Cambridge, Massachusetts, Harvard University Press, 1976; London, Abacus, 1982.
Shakespeare's Division of Experience. New York, Summit, and, London, Cape, 1981.
Beyond Power: On Women, Men, and Morals. New York, Summit, and London, Cape, 1985.
The War against Women. New York, Summit, and London, Hamilton, 1992.

* * *

Marilyn French's stated life goal is to "change the entire social and economic struture of western civliization, to make it a feminist world." Her fiction and essays make this goal clear. They are unabashedly feminist, unwilling to concede, lie, or euphemize about the roles men and women play in our society.

French attained fame in 1977 with the publication of the best-selling novel, *The Women's Room,* the story of a traditional, submissive married woman who suddenly divorces and realizes the patriarchal nature of the world. Reviews of this book were mixed, since many readers are grateful to recognize in it the world as they know it, while others consider French a male basher. Suzanne Fields wrote, "It behooves us all to arraign those books which exude a destructive hatred of men. Such feelings can infect and calcify in dangerous ways. To intersperse torrid sex scenes with tirades against men for the imagined crime of being men merely allows villains and victims to exchange places."

Like the backlash respondents to *The Color Purple,* French's detractors complain that her work is anti-men and her portraits unrealistic. When asked why she even bothers to deal with men, she replied, "because women and men live on this Earth. And I assume that the Earth is going to go on being peopled." On the other hand, Christopher Lehmann-Haupt, book reviewer for *The New York Times,* confessed that the novel stirred up negative emotions, made him examine his premises, and search for excuses and justifications, but that, in the end, he had to admit the "damnable thing is, she's right."

The outcome of the plot in French's second novel, *The Bleeding Heart* (1980), suggests not only that male-female love is impossible, but that it may even be unethical, according to reviewer Lindsy van Gelder. Given that the male character of this novel, a businessman, "at the very least benefits from an oppressive System buttressed, in part, by women's emotional vulnerability," how can the female protagonist offer her love to him? Is it traitorous to the cause and to herself to open her heart when her mind has struggled so hard to achieve its feminist insights? The protagonist of the novel starts off from a better position than Mira of *The Women's Room,* but she ends up with the same questions. She is a feminist professor of Renaissance literature who has an affair with an unhappily married man. The relationship is volatile and combative. Not, Dolores realizes, one of true equals. Like Van Gelder, Rosellen Brown responds to the message of this novel with questions rather than answers: "Must one wait for love until the world of power changes hands? Is there a difference between accomodation and compromise among lovers? Accomodation and surrender? How to spell out the terms of a partial affirmation?"

Her Mother's Daughter (1987), French's third novel, looks at the heritage of experience, knowledge, and love that mothers pass to their daughters. The narrator, Anastasia, is determined to avoid the oppression of her forbears, but she is haunted by that collective past. Beverly Fields comments that the "novel elaborates a theme that runs more or less quietly through her first two books; the ways in which female submission to male society, with its accompanying suppression of rage, is passed like contagion from mother to daughter." Others see this book as a celebration of motherhood—a thank you note to our mothers for the sacrifices they have made so that we might be free(r).

French's literary and cultural criticism is straightforward, well-researched, and historically grounded. The themes of all of her books are feminist. *Shakespeare's Division of Experience* (1981) laments the historical division of experience into male or female roles, values, and characteristics. *Beyond Power: On Women, Men and Morals* (1986) is a series of essays on the history of the treatment of women by men in the past 2500 years. Since men have always sought power above all else, she argues, they long ago invented the system of patriarchy that now dominates every aspect of our culture. One critic derides this book for romanticizing primitive, matriarchal cultures and for totalizing its vision of patriarchy when, in fact, she believes that patriarchy has produced some good things.

In *The War Against Women* (1993), French argues that physical, economic, and political attacks on women are an intrinsic part of our culture, values, and ideology. The book is well-researched, polemically-worded, compassionate, and sincere. It is proof of the sincerity and persistence of French's stated life goal; to change the world by feminizing our values, institutions, and men.

—Jill Franks

FRENCH, Paul. *See* **ASIMOV, Isaac.**

FULGHUM, Robert (L.)

Nationality: American. **Born:** 4 June 1937, in Waco, Texas. **Education:** University of Colorado; Baylor University, 1957; Starr King (Unitarian) Seminary; studied at Zen Buddhist monastery, 1972. **Family:** Married Marcia McClellan, 1957 (divorced, 1973); married Lynn Edwards, 1976; children: (first marriage) Christian, Hunter, Molly Behen. **Career:** Ordained a Unitarian minister, 1961; part-time Unitarian minister, Bellingham, Washington, beginning in 1961; Edmonds Unitarian Church, Edmonds, Washington, part-time minister, 1966-85, minister emeritus, 1985—;

Lakeside School, Seattle, Washington, art teacher, 1971-88; painter, writer, and lecturer. Worked variously as a sales trainee for International Business Machines (IBM), a singing cowboy and amateur rodeo performer at guest ranches in Montana, Colorado, and Texas, a counselor to mental patients and prison inmates, a creator of motel art, a bartender, and a folk music teacher. Founder of wilderness camp in Canada. **Member:** Greenpeace, Planned Parenthood, American Civil Liberties Union.

Publications

Nonfiction

All I Really Need to Know I Learned in Kindergarten: Uncommon Thoughts on Common Things. Villard Books, 1988.
It Was on Fire When I Lay down on It. Villard Books, 1989.
Uh-Oh: Some Observations from Both Sides of the Refrigerator Door. Villard Books, 1991.
From Beginning to End, Ivy Books, 1996.

* * *

With his greatly successful collections of vignettes and homilies of everyday life, Robert Fulghum has carved out a niche among popular nonfiction writers, emphasizing the beauty and wonder in the ordinary and offering a positive vision of modern existence. Although criticized for his simple style and repetition, Fulghum has struck a chord with readers seeking hopeful messages in today's world.

A Unitarian minister and self-proclaimed philosopher, Fulghum makes no claims to be an intellectual, instead pointing to the importance of basic human values and commonplace rituals that reveal our inherently good natures. His first collections of what he refers to as "stuff," *All I Really Need to Know I Learned in Kindergarten* (1988), grew out of his now-famous Credo which has circulated among kindergarten classes around the country. This list of beliefs grew out of lessons learned in the playground and in kindergarten classrooms, including such directives as "share everything," "play fair," "don't hit people" and "clean up your own mess."

As Ruth Bayard Smith writes in the *New York Times Book Review,* "He knows that the appeal of his message lies in its simplicity. He is acknowledging the inner fears and insecurities that are universal." His stories all share the same qualities of being direct and teaching a universal lesson or moral. Often the topics of his stories are humorous, ranging from hippie lawyers and the delights of meatloaf to a bride who vomits on her wedding guests during the ceremony.

Fulghum went on to publish two more books of a similar nature, including *It Was On Fire When I Lay Down On It* (1989) and *Uh-Oh: Some Observations from Both Sides of the Refrigerator Door* (1991). This repetition of style and substance drew frowns from some critics, including Andrea Cooper who reacted to *Uh-Oh:* "A better editor would have changed that embarrassing title, smoothed the fragmented, ad-copy writing style and encouraged Mr. Fulghum to experiment beyond his predictable format with longer, more substantive reflections." Martin Brady of *Booklist* adds, "Not all of [his message] is pithy . . . sometimes Fulghum comes across as Andy Rooney crossed with Richard Bach." However, others find his loosely-connected homilies refreshing. "He's sincere, and his message feels good," writes *People*'s Louisa Ermelino. "Sure, Fulghum is overbearing, oversimplified and saccharine. But he's also touching, practical, and wise."

Of his own writing style, Fulghum says, "If you notice phrases, ideas, and anecdotes that closely resemble those that appear elsewhere in my writing, it is not a matter of sloppy editing. I'm repeating myself. I'm reshuffling words in the hope that just once I might say something exactly right."

Most readers will delight in Fulghum's wisdom and storytelling, finding uncomplicated answers to many problems of daily life. He does not offer much in the way of implementing his solutions but merely points out reasonable alternatives to the ways we react to life. While his books are largely indistinguishable from one another, they touch on the importance of the mundane and highlight the fragile connections that keep us attached to our loved ones and the human community at large. By focusing on these fragile connections, Fulghum reveals how much we truly need one another.

—Christopher Swann

G

GARCIA MARQUEZ, Gabriel (Jose)

Nationality: Colombian. **Born:** 6 March 1928, in Aracataca, Colombia. **Education:** Attended Universidad Nacional de Colombia, 1947-48, and Universidad de Cartagena, 1948-49. **Family:** Married Mercedes Barcha in 1958; children: two sons. **Career:** Worked as a journalist, 1947-65, including job with *El heraldo,* Baranquilla, Colombia; film critic and news reporter, *El espectador,* Bogota, Colombia, Geneva, Switzerland, Rome, Italy, and Paris, France, Prensa Latina news agency, Bogota, 1959; writer since 1965. Founder, Cuban Press Agency, Bogota; Fundacion Habeas, founder, 1979, president. Mediator between Colombian government and leftist guerrillas in early 1980s. **Awards:** Colombian Association of Writers and Artists award, 1954, for "Un dia despues del sabado"; Premio Literario Esso (Colombia), 1961, for *La mala hora;* Chianciano award (Italy), 1969, Prix de Meilleur Livre Etranger (France), 1969, and Romulo Gallegos prize (Venezuela), 1971, all for *Cien años de soledad;* LL.D., Columbia University, 1971; *Books Abroad* Neustadt International Prize for Literature, 1972; Commonwealth award for Literature, Bank of Delaware, 1980; Nobel prize for literature, 1982; *Los Angeles Times* Book prize for fiction, 1988, for *Love in the Time of Cholera.* **Member:** American Academy of Arts and Letters (honorary fellow), Foundation for the New Latin American Film (Havana; president, since 1985). **Agent:** Agencia Literaria Carmen Balcells, Diagonal 580, Barcelona 21, Spain. **Address:** Apartado Postal 20736 Deleyacion Alvaro bregon 01000, Mexico.

Publications

Fiction

La hojarasca. Ediciones Sipa, 1955.
El coronel no tiene quien le escriba. Aguirre Editor, 1961.
La mala hora. Talleres de Graficas "Luis Perez," 1961; as *In Evil Hour,* Harper, 1979.
Los funerales de la Mama Grande. Editorial Universidad Veracruzana, 1962.
Cien anos de soledad. Editorial Sudamericana, 1967; as *One Hundred Years of Solitude,* Harper, 1970.
Isabel viendo llover en Macondo. Editorial Estuario, 1967.
No One Writes to the Colonel and Other Stories (includes translation of *El coronel no tiene quien le escriba* and stories from *Los funerales de la Mama Grande*), translated by J. S. Bernstein, Harper, 1968.
La increible y triste historia de la candida Erendira y su abuela desalmada. Barral Editores, 1972.
Leaf Storm and Other Stories. Harper, 1972.
El negro que hizo esperar a los angeles. Ediciones Alfil, 1972.
Ojos de perro azul: nueve cuentos desconocidos. Equisditorial, 1972.
El otono del patriarca. Plaza & Janes Editores, 1975; as *The Autumn of the Patriarch,* Harper, 1976.
Todos los cuentos de Gabriel Garcia Marquez: 1947-1972. Plaza & Janes Editores, 1975.
Innocent Erendira and Other Stories (includes translation of *La increible y triste historia de la candida Erendira y su abuela desalmada* and stories from *Ojos de perro azul*). Harper, 1978.
Cronica de una muerte anunciada. La Oveja Negra, 1981; as *Chronicle of a Death Foretold,* J. Cape, 1982, Knopf, 1983.
El rastro de tu sangre en la nieve: El verano feliz de la senora Forbes. W. Dampier Editores, 1982.
Collected Stories. Harper, 1984.
El amor en los tiempos del colera. Oveja Negra, 1985; as *Love in the Time of Cholera,* Knopf, 1988.
El general en su laberinto, Mondadori Espana, 1989; as *The General in His Labyrinth,* Knopf, 1990.
Doce cuentos peregrinos. Mondadori Espana, 1992; as *Strange Pilgrims,* Knopf, 1993.
Del amor y otros demonios. Mondadori Espana, 1994; as *Love and Other Demons,* Knopf, 1995.

Plays

Screenplays: *Erendira,* adapted from his novella *La increible y triste historia de la candida Erendira y su abuela desalmada,* 1983; *A Time to Die,* 1988.

Nonfiction

With Mario Vargas Llosa, *La novela en America Latina: Dialogo.* Lima, Carlos Milla Batres, 1968; as *Dialogo sobre la novela Latinoamericana,* Lima, Peru Andino, 1988.
El relato de un naufrago. Barcelona, Tusquets Editor, 1970; as *The Story of a Shipwrecked Sailor,* Knopf, 1986.
Cuando era feliz e indocumentado. Caracas, Ediciones El Ojo de Camello, 1973.
Cronicas y reportajes. La Oveja Negra, 1978.
Periodismo militante. Bogota, Son de Maquina Editores, 1978.
De viaje por los paises socialistas: 90 dias en las "Cortina de hierro." Colombia, Ediciones Macondo, 1978.
Obra periodistica, edited by Jacques Gilard, Bruguera; Volume 1: *Textos constenos,* 1981; Volumes 2-3: *Entre cachacos,* 1982; Volume 4: *De Europa y America (1955-1960),* 1983.
El olor de la guayaba: Conversaciones con Plinio Apuleyo Mendoza, with P. Mendoza. La Oveja Negra, 1982; as *The Fragrance of Guava,* edited by T. Nairn, Verso, 1983.
Persecucion y muerte de minorias: dos perspectivas, with Guillermo Nolasco-Juarez. Buenos Aires, Juarez Editor, 1984.
La aventura de Miguel Littin, clandestino en Chile: Un reportaje. Editorial Sudamericana, 1986; as *Clandestine in Chile: The Adventures of Miguel Littin,* Holt, 1987.
Primeros reportajes. Consorcio de Ediciones Capriles, 1990.

*

Critical Studies: *Gabriel Garcia Marquez* by George R. McMurray, Ungar, 1977; *Gabriel Garcia Marquez: Revolutions in Wonderland* by Regina Janes, University of Missouri Press, 1981; *Gabriel Garcia Marquez: New Readings,* edited by Bernard McGuirk and Richard Cardwell, Cambridge University Press, 1988.

* * *

With the phenomenal success that greeted *One Hundred Years of Solitude* (1970; *Cien anos de soledad,* 1967), Gabriel Garcia Marquez emerged as the leading literary talent of the Spanish-speaking world. The Nobel Prize for Literature in 1982 clinched his reputation and many began to speak of him as the greatest author in the Spanish language since Cervantes. But like Cervantes after writing *Don Quixote,* Garcia Marquez has subsequently had to contend with critics who are disinclined to acknowledge that his masterpiece can ever be equalled or surpassed.

The omniscient narrator of *One Hundred Years of Solitude* traces with childlike fascination six generations of the Buendia family in the village of their creation, Macondo, which goes from utopia to ruin and is finally swallowed up by the jungle. Despite the novel's earthy humor and satire (which targets the tradition of machismo and Spain's claim to have endowed America with the benefits of European civilization) and its theme of loneliness (all the Buendias living together as a group of solitary individuals) and disintegration, the novel is best known for its imaginative flights of fantasy such as levitation and bodily assumption into heaven. Its prose, said to be accessible to anyone who can read in any language, is straightforward, yet is sophisticated enough to furnish critical analysts with endless amounts of material about which to write.

Years before the publication of *One Hundred Years of Solitude,* Garcia Marquez began writing about his Macondo project in *Leaf Storm* (1972; *La hojarasca,* 1955), which begins by recalling the arrival of a banana company, its boom town, and the "human leaf storm" that follows in its wake and makes aliens of the original inhabitants. This fledgling attempt at fiction won mild critical praise but was eclipsed by controversies involving the author's journalistic work at the time.

When working on his next book after *One Hundred Years of Solitude,* Garcia Marquez sought new techniques and chose to study in *The Autumn of the Patriarch* (1975) the decadence of a hypothetical South American dictator. In preparation he devoured innumerable biographies of Latin American dictators and went to live in Francisco Franco's Spain for firsthand experience. While its single-paragraph chapters, abrupt transitions, interior monologue, and nonlinear form demand far more effort from the reader than its predecessor, it is generally viewed as the author's second-finest work.

Cinematic in presentation and also artistically inventive, his novella *Chronicle of a Death Foretold* (1982; *Cronica de una muerte anunciada,* 1981) reconstructs the events that precede the murder of Santiago Nasar, who has sullied the honor of someone else's bride and who is the only one in town unaware of his fate. It succeeds as a murder mystery despite the reader's foreknowledge of its outcome.

The love so painfully lacking in *The Autumn of the Patriarch* abounds in myriad forms (young love, married love, carnal love, even love with the symptoms of disease) in *Love in the Time of Cholera* (1988; *El amor en los tiempos del colera,* 1985), his most traditional novel. Florentino proposes to Fermina at an inauspicious time and is rejected. They go their separate ways, only to be reunited precisely 50 years, nine months, and four days later.

It is the loveless end of life that he examines in *The General in His Labyrinth* (1990; *El General en su laberinto,* 1989), a foray into historical fiction about the final days of Simon Bolivar, the Liberator of Latin America. Ousted as president of Colombia, he journeys to supposed exile to the sound of jeers and taunts from the same people who had earlier cheered him. Tim Padgett in *Newsweek* complained about the minutiae that clutters the novel, but concluded that while it "might not be quintessential Garcia Marquez," few books bring us closer to "quintessential Bolivar."

In *Of Love and Other Demons* (1995), an 18th-century exorcist becomes infatuated with a nobleman's 12-year-old daughter, who has been bitten by a dog and is now possessed by the demon of hydrophobia. Dubbing it brilliantly moving and a tour de force, A. S. Byatt in the *New York Times Book Review* observes in the novel "all the ineluctable, irrational fatality" of *Chronicle of a Death Foretold* without the comic and inconsequential gentleness of *Love in the Time of Cholera.*

Garcia Marquez writes no criticism and distances himself from the literary establishment. He insists that fiction writing is learned by reading great fiction and not from studying writing theory. And while he claims as mentors such writers as William Faulkner and Virginia Woolf, he is still a man of the people, having been raised in impoverished settlements on Colombia's Caribbean coast. Much of his storytelling ability goes back to his childhood fascination with the history, myth, and legend of his native land.

—Jack Shreve

GARDNER, John (Champlin, Jr.)

Nationality: American. **Born:** Batavia, New York, 21 July 1933. **Education:** De Pauw University, Greencastle, Indiana, 1951-53; Washington University, St. Louis, A.B. 1955; State University of Iowa (Woodrow Wilson Fellow, 1955-56), M.A. 1956, Ph.D. 1958. **Family:** Married 1) Joan Louise Patterson in 1953, two children; 2) Liz Rosenberg in 1980. **Career:** Taught at Oberlin College, Ohio, 1958-59; California State University, Chico, 1959-62, and San Francisco, 1962-65; Southern Illinois University, Carbondale, 1965-74; Bennington College, Vermont, 1974-76; Williams College, Williamstown, Massachusetts, and Skidmore College, Saratoga Springs, New York, 1976-77; George Mason University, Fairfax, Virginia, 1977-78; State University of New York, Binghamton, 1978-82. Visiting professor, University of Detroit, 1970-71, and Northwestern University, Evanston, Illinois, 1973. Editor, *MSS,* and Southern Illinois University Press Literary Structures series. **Awards:** Danforth fellowship, 1970; National Endowment for the Arts grant, 1972; American Academy award, 1975; National Book Critic's Circle award, 1976. **Died:** 4 September 1982.

PUBLICATIONS

Novels

The Resurrection. New York, New American Library, 1966.
The Wreckage of Agathon. New York, Harper, 1970.
Grendel. New York, Knopf, 1971; London, Deutsch, 1972.
The Sunlight Dialogues. New York, Knopf, 1971; London, Cape, 1973.

Jason and Medeia (novel in verse). New York, Knopf, 1973.
Nickel Mountain: A Pastoral Novel. New York, Knopf, 1973; London, Cape, 1974.
October Light. New York, Knopf, 1976; London, Cape, 1977.
In the Suicide Mountains. New York, Knopf, 1977.
Freddy's Book. New York, Knopf, 1980; London, Secker and Warburg, 1981.
Vlemk the Box-Painter. Northridge, California, Lord John Press, 1980.
Mickelsson's Ghosts. New York, Knopf, and London, Secker and Warburg, 1982.

Short Stories

The King's Indian: Stories and Tales. New York, Knopf, 1974; London, Cape, 1975.
Dragon, Dragon and Other Timeless Tales (for children). New York, Knopf, 1975.
Gudgekin the Thistle Girl and Other Tales (for children). New York, Knopf, 1976.
The King of the Hummingbirds and Other Tales (for children). New York, Knopf, 1977.
The Art of Living, and Other Stories. New York, Knopf, 1981; London, Secker and Warburg, 1983.

Plays

William Wilson (libretto). Dallas, New London Press, 1978.
Three Libretti (includes *William Wilson, Frankenstein, Rumpelstiltskin*). Dallas, New London Press, 1979.

Poetry

Poems. Northridge, California, Lord John Press, 1978.

Other

The Gawain-Poet. Lincoln, Nebraska, Cliff's Notes, 1967.
Le Morte D'Arthur. Lincoln, Nebraska, Cliff's Notes, 1967.
The Construction of the Wakefield Cycle. Carbondale, Southern Illinois University Press, 1974.
The Construction of Christian Poetry in Old English. Carbondale, Southern Illinois University Press, 1975.
A Child's Bestiary (for children). New York, Knopf, 1977.
The Poetry of Chaucer. Carbondale, Southern Illinois University Press, 1977.
The Life and Times of Chaucer. New York, Knopf, and London, Cape, 1977.
On Moral Fiction. New York, Basic Books, 1978.
On Becoming a Novelist. New York, Harper, 1983.
The Art of Fiction: Notes on Craft for Young Writers. New York, Knopf, 1984.

Editor, with Lennis Dunlap. *The Forms of Fiction.* New York, Random House, 1962.
Editor, *The Complete Works of the Gawain-Poet in a Modern English Version with a Critical Introduction.* Chicago, University of Chicago Press, 1965.
Editor, with Nicholas Joost, *Papers on the Art and Age of Geoffrey Chaucer.* Edwardsville, Southern Illinois University Press, 1967.
Editor, *The Alliterative Morte Arthure, The Owl and the Nightingale, and Five Other Middle English Poems, in a Modernized Version, with Comments on the Poems, and Notes.* Carbondale, Southern Illinois University Press, 1971.
Editor, with Shannon Ravenel, *The Best American Short Stories 1982.* Boston, Houghton Mifflin, 1982.

Translator, with Nobuku Tsukui, *Tengu Child,* by Kikuo Itaya. Carbondale, Southern Illinois University Press, 1983.
Translator, with John Maier, *Gilgamesh.* New York, Knopf, 1984.

*

Bibliography: *John Gardner: A Bibliographical Profile* by John M. Howell, Carbondale, Southern Illinois University Press, 1980; *John Gardner: An Annotated Secondary Bibliography* by Robert A. Morace, New York, Garland, 1984.

Critical Studies: *John Gardner: Critical Perspectives* edited by Robert A. Morace and Kathryn VanSpanckeren, Carbondale, Southern Illinois University Press, 1982; *Arches and Light: The Fiction of John Gardner* by David Cowart, Carbondale, Southern Illinois University Press, 1983; *A World of Order and Light: The Fiction of John Gardner* by Gregory L. Morris, Athens, University of Georgia Press, 1984.

* * *

John C. Gardner, a remarkably prolific and protean writer, authored 35 books in just 25 years. His works include novels, short stories, poetry, works for young readers, libretti, literary criticism and critical editions, plays, even a biography of Geoffrey Chaucer.

Gardner's fast and lamentably short career as a fiction writer got off to a slow start. Neither *The Resurrection* (published in 1966 when the author was 33 and set in his hometown of Batavia, New York) nor *The Wreckage of Agathon* (published in 1970 and set in ancient Greece) attracted much attention. *Grendel* (1971), on the other hand, was enthusiastically reviewed. This short but wide-ranging retelling of *Beowulf* from the monster's point of view appealed to the temper of an age given to questioning authority and to literary recycling.

The Sunlight Dialogues (1972) was a much longer and more ambitious book, and, like most of Gardner's novels, a literary hybrid; a philosophically inclined detective story and a decidedly contemporary novel that nonetheless had a 19th century feel (and look, as all of Gardner's novels and fiction collections beginning with *Grendel* are illustrated). Its rural realism vying with some inspired clowning and metafictional games, *The Sunlight Dialogues* was Gardner's first commercial success. It spent 15 weeks on the *New York Times* bestseller list.

Jason and Medeia (1973), a novel written in epic-poem form, was at best ill-conceived and at worst "a full-scale literary disaster." But Gardner was soon back on the bestseller list with an adroit reworking of some of his earliest stories in the form of a half-celebratory, half-parodic "pastoral novel" (with a strong if largely comical American Gothic undercurrent) entitled *Nickel Mountain* (1973). The metafictional quality of Gardner's writing—muted but still present in novels like *Nickel Mountain* and more freely displayed in *Grendel*—burst forth in *The King's Indian* (1974), the book that led one reviewer to dub Gardner "the Lon

Chaney of contemporary fiction." These pastiches of Poe, Melville, Kafka, Updike and a host of others constituted an intertextual extravaganza—a celebration of writers and writing. Here was John Barth's "literature of exhaustion" at its most exuberant—a typically post-Freudian way of dealing with what critic Harold Bloom had called "the anxiety of influence."

Not all were pleased with what some clearly felt were pointless academic fictions. As if in response to such criticism Gardner wrote another rural fiction, *October Light* (1976), his third bestseller and winner (after rancorous debate) of the year's National Book Critics Circle Award for fiction. The inclusion of lengthy passages from a deliberately awful paperback sci-fi thriller being read by one of the novel's two main characters was the most obvious precursor of the debate Gardner was soon to initiate with the publication of *On Moral Fiction* (1978). Divorce, colon cancer, troubles with the IRS, and a plagiarism charge (for one of his Chaucer books) had left Gardner feeling pressed and combative. Formerly hailed as a "new fictionist," Gardner now espoused with messianic zeal a seemingly retrograde, Tolstoyan vision of "true art" and its life-enhancing purpose; a vision buttressed with a good many mean-spirited and often wrong-headed comments on the failings of fellow writers.

Neither Gardner nor his fiction ever quite recovered from the publication of a book whose very title seemed to link its author with the Rev. Jerry Falwell's Moral Majority. Reviewers tended to read and often dismiss his later work as poorly conceived efforts to write according to his own theory of moral fiction. And even Gardner's most sympathetic academic critics often praised Gardner on his own terms; as a writer of moral fiction. Gardner's faults are easy to assess: a philosophical pretentiousness, an ambitiousness that at times outstripped his time and talent, a willingness to believe that good ideas and intentions made for good art, and of course a tendency to talk too freely and didactically about his writing and thus establish the terms for judging it. His strengths, however—mainly evident in *Grendel* and *The Sunlight Dialogues*, but still present in works such as "Stillness" in *The Art of Living* (1981), the opening of *Freddy's Book* (1980), and in parts of *Mickelsson's Ghosts* (1982)—are sufficient to ensure his place among the best of postwar American fiction writers.

—Robert A. Morace

GARDNER, John (Edmund)

Nationality: British. **Born:** Seaton Delaval, Northumberland, 20 November 1926. **Education:** Cottham's Preparatory School, Newcastle on Tyne, 1931-34; King Alfred's School, Wantage, Berkshire, 1934-43; St. John's College, Cambridge, 1947-50, B.A. in theology 1950, M.A. 1951; St. Stephen's House, Oxford, 1950-52. **Military Service:** Served in the Royal Navy and the Royal Marines, 1943-47: Commando Service in the Far and Middle East. **Family:** Married Margaret Mercer in 1952; one daughter and one son. **Career:** Entertainer, American Red Cross Entertainments Department, London, 1943; clerk in Holy Orders, Church of England, 1952-58; spent some time as a Chaplain in the Royal Air Force; theatre and cultural reviewer, Stratford upon Avon *Herald*, 1959-67. Lives in the U.S. **Agent:** Desmond Elliot, Kingsbury House, 15-17 King Street, London SW1Y 6QV, England.

Publications

Novels (series: James Bond; Herbie Kruger; Professor Moriarty; Boysie Oakes; Derek Torry)

The Liquidator (Oakes). London, Muller, and New York, Viking Press, 1964.
The Understrike (Oakes). London, Muller, and New York, Viking Press, 1965.
Amber Nine (Oakes). London, Muller, and New York, Viking Press, 1966.
Madrigal (Oakes). London, Muller, 1967; New York, Viking Press, 1968.
Founder Member (Oakes). London, Muller, 1969.
A Complete State of Death (Torry). London, Cape, and New York, Viking Press, 1969; as *The Stone Killer*, New York, Award, 1973.
The Censor. London, New English Library, 1970.
Traitor's Exit (Oakes). London, Muller, 1970.
The Airline Pirates (Oakes). London, Hodder and Stoughton, 1970; as *Air Apparent*, New York, Putnam, 1971.
Every Night's a Bullfight. London, Joseph, 1971; as *Every Night's a Festival*, New York, Morrow, 1973; as *The Director*, London, W.H. Allen, 1982.
The Return of Moriarty. London Weidenfeld and Nicolson, and New York, Putnam, 1974; as *Moriarty*, London, Pan, 1976.
The Corner Men (Torry). London, Joseph, 1974; New York, Doubleday, 1976.
A Killer for a Song (Oakes). London, Hodder and Stoughton, 1975.
The Revenge of Moriarty. London, Weidenfeld and Nicolson, and New York, Putnam, 1975.
To Run a Little Faster. London, Joseph, 1976.
The Werewolf Trace. London, Hodder and Stoughton, and New York, Doubleday, 1977.
The Dancing Dodo. London, Hodder and Stoughton, and New York, Doubleday, 1978.
The Nostradamus Traitor (Kruger). London, Hodder and Stoughton, and New York, Doubleday, 1979.
The Garden of Weapons (Kruger). London, Hodder and Stoughton, 1980; New York, McGraw Hill, 1981.
Golgotha. London, W.H. Allen, 1980; as *The Last Trump*, New York, McGraw Hill, 1980.
Licence Renewed (Bond). London, Cape, and New York, Marek, 1981.
For Special Services (Bond). London, Cape, and New York, Coward McCann, 1982.
The Quiet Dogs (Kruger). London, Hodder and Stoughton, 1982; New York, Berkley, 1989.
Icebreaker (Bond). London, Cape-Hodder and Stoughton, and New York, Putnam, 1983.
Flamingo. London, Hodder and Stoughton, 1983.
Role of Honour (Bond). London, Cape-Hodder and Stoughton, and New York, Putnam, 1984.
The Secret Generations. London, Heinemann, and New York, Putnam, 1985.
Nobody Lives Forever (Bond). London, Cape, and New York, Putnam, 1986.
No Deals, Mr. Bond. London, Cape, and New York, Putnam, 1987.
The Secret Houses (Kruger). New York, Putnam, 1987; London, Bantam, 1988.
Scorpius. London, Hodder and Stoughton, and New York, Putnam, 1988.
The Secret Families (Kruger). New York, Putnam, and London, Bantam, 1989.

Win, Lose, or Die (Bond). London, Hodder and Stoughton, and New York, Putnam, 1989.
Brokenclaw (Bond). New York, Putnam, and London, Hodder and Stoughton, 1990.
The Man from Barbarossa (Bond). New York, Putnam, 1991.
Never Send Flowers (Bond). New York, Putnam, 1993.
Maestro. New York, Simon and Schuster, 1993.
Sea Fire (Bond). New York, Putnam, 1994.
Goldeneye (Bond; from the screenplay by Michael France and Jeffrey Caine). 1995.
Confessor. New York, Simon and Schuster, 1995.

Short Stories

Hideaway. London, Corgi, 1968.
The Assassination File. London, Corgi, 1974.

Other

Spin the Bottle: The Autobiography of an Alcoholic. London, Muller, 1964.
"Smiley at the Circus: Cold War Espionage," in *Murder Ink: The Mystery Reader's Companion,* edited by Dilys Winn. New York, Workman, 1977.

* * *

John E. Gardner is one of the few British espionage writers of the 1960s who has remained an important figure through the 1990s. He views his stories partly as a reaction to those who tried to imitate Ian Fleming.

In his first novel, *The Liquidator* (1964), Gardner's protagonist, Boysie Oakes, is a cowardly and inept agent recruited by mistake. Oakes enjoys the status and privilege of the Bond-like, secret-agent lifestyle, yet contracts Charlie Griffin, who eventually becomes his sidekick, to do his difficult jobs. The anti-hero status of Oakes caused the *Daily Telegraph* to call the work the "cleverest thriller mutation of the year."

The success of his first novel caused him to continue using Oakes as the bumbling protagonist of seven other novels. The Oakes novels effectively sacrificed seriousness in favor of slap-stick routines and misadventures. In *Madrigal* (1968), for example, Oakes deals with weird characters other than his sidekick, including Rosie Puberty. *Traitor's Exit* (1970) often borders on meta-fiction. When the plot becomes intense, Rex Upsdale (the narrator) reminds the audience that Oakes is only fictional. Gardner continues the joke by addressing the narrator: "Careful, laddie, Some people have said that about the Prime Minister." Although *Airline Pirates* (1971) and *Killer for a Song* (1975) contained both surreal and witty moments, they failed to match the wit of *Traitor's Exit.* The waning popularity of spy-fiction and Gardner's interest in widening his horizons caused him to stop using Oakes in his novels.

During the early 1970s Gardner went through a transitional period and was not concerned with espionage. *The Censor* (1970), a serious story of pornography and hypocrisy, and *Every Night's a Bullfight* (1971), based upon a Shakespearean festival, show Gardner's attempts at other genres. In 1981 Gardner produced *The Werewolf of Trace,* a story combining espionage with the supernatural, and then *Golgotha* (1980), a highly experimental account of Britain under Soviet domination. But his desire for popular success caused him to begin writing "pure" espionage fiction. He created Big Herbie Kruger for a series of three novels: *The Nostradamus Traitor* (1979), *The Garden of Weapons* (1981), and *The Quiet Dogs* (1982). The favorable reception of these books led to his being commissioned to update the famous James Bond character.

Gardner's Bond novels received hostile criticism from readers who felt his modern adaptation of 007 in *Licensed Renewed* (1981) was ridiculous. And both critics and fans worried after reading *For Special Services* (1982) that Gardner had lost his edge. However, after fulfilling a contractual obligation with *Flamingo* (1983), Gardner began creating a sprawling trilogy involving two competing families and their fortunes. Critics consider the novels in this trilogy—*The Secret Generations* (1985), *The Secret Houses* (1988), and *The Secret Families* (1989)—to be Gardner's best and most important contributions to fiction. Unlike conventional spy-fiction that depends upon the author's skill in creating fictionalized history, these novels use historically accurate details as a background for understanding the underworld.

Gardner feels that spy fiction is generally not respected, and he resents the critical tendency to lump espionage fiction under the crime category. He believes that some of the best writing of the last two decades has been done by espionage writers, and that the genre can actually escape convention if the writer is willing to explore its boundaries. Indeed, Gardner considers the greatest irony of his career the fact that he was chosen 16 years later to update the Bond character, which he parodied early in his career.

—Chris Godat

GARDNER, Miriam. *See* **BRADLEY, Marion Zimmer.**

GARNER, Alan

Nationality: British. **Born:** Congleton, Cheshire, 17 October 1934. **Education:** Alderley Edge Primary School, Cheshire; Manchester Grammar School; Magdalen College, Oxford. **Military Service:** Royal Artillery: Second Lieutenant. **Family:** Married 1) Ann Cook in 1956 (marriage dissolved), one son and two daughters; 2) Griselda Greaves in 1972, one son and one daughter. **Awards:** Library Association Carnegie Medal, 1968; *Guardian* award, 1968; Chicago International Film Festival prize, 1981; Mother Goose award, 1987. **Address:** "Toad Hall," Blackden, Holmes Chapel, Crewe, Cheshire CW4 8BY, England.

Publications

Novels

The Weirdstone of Brisingamen: A Tale of Alderley. London, Collins, 1960; as *The Weirdstone,* New York, Watts, 1961; revised edition, London, Penguin, 1963; New York, Walck, 1969.

The Moon of Gomrath. London, Collins, 1963; New York, Walck, 1967.
Elidor, illustrated by Charles Keeping. London, Collins, 1965; New York, Walck, 1967.
The Owl Service. London, Collins, 1967; New York, Walck, 1968.
Red Shift. London, Collins, and New York, Macmillan, 1973.

Short Stories

Fairy Tales of Gold (*The Girl of the Golden Gate, The Golden Brothers, The Princess and the Golden Mane, The Three Golden Heads of the Well*), illustrated by Michael Foreman. London, Collins, 4 vols., 1979; 1 vol. edition, Collins, and New York, Philomel, 1980.
Book of British Fairy Tales (retellings), illustrated by Derek Collard. London, Collins, 1984; New York, Delacorte, 1985.

Fiction for Children

The Old Man of Mow, photographs by Roger Hill. London, Collins, 1967; New York, Doubleday, 1970.
The Breadhorse, illustrated by Albin Trowski. London, Collins, 1975.
The Stone Book Quartet, illustrated by Michael Foreman. London, Collins, 1983; New York, Dell, 1988.
The Stone Book. London, Collins, 1976; New York, Collins World, 1978.
Tom Fobble's Day. London, Collins, 1977; New York, Collins World, 1979.
Granny Reardun. London, Collins, 1977; New York, Collins World, 1978.
The Aimer Gate. London, Collins, 1978; New York, Collins World, 1979.
The Lad of the Gad (folktales). London, Collins, 1980; New York, Philomel, 1981.
Jack and the Beanstalk, illustrated by Julek Heller. London, Collins, 1985; New York, Delacorte, 1992.
A Bag of Moonshine (folktales), illustrated by Patrick James Lynch. London, Collins, and New York, Delacorte, 1986.

Plays

Holly from the Bongs: A Nativity Play, music by William Mayne, photographs by Roger Hill (produced Goostrey, Cheshire, 1965). London, Collins, 1966; revised version, music by Gordon Crosse (produced London, 1974), published in *Labrys 7,* 1981.
The Belly Bag, music by Richard Morris (produced London, 1971).
Potter Thompson, music by Gordon Crosse (produced London, 1975). London, Oxford University Press, 1975.
To Kill a King (televised, 1980). Published in *Labrys 7,* 1981.
The Green Mist, in *Labrys 7,* 1981.

Screenplays: *Places and Things,* 1978; *Images,* 1981.

Radio Plays: *Have You Met Our Tame Author?,* 1962; *Elidor,* 1962; *The Weirdstone of Brisingamen,* from his own story, 1963; *Thor and the Giants,* 1965, revised version, 1979; *Idun and the Apples of Life,* 1965, revised version, as *Loki and the Storm Giant,* 1979; *Baldur the Bright,* 1965, revised version, 1979; *The Stone Book, Granny Reardun, Tom Fobble's Day* and *The Aimer Gate,* from his own stories, 1980.

Television Plays: *The Owl Service,* from his own story, 1969; *Red Shift,* from his own story, 1978; *Lamaload,* 1979; *To Kill a King* (*Leap in the Dark* series), 1980; *The Keeper,* 1982.

Other

Editor, *The Hamish Hamilton Book of Goblins: An Anthology of Folklore,* illustrated by Krystyna Turska. London, Hamish Hamilton, 1969; as *A Cavalcade of Goblins,* New York, Walck, 1969; as *A Book of Goblins,* London, Penguin, 1972.

Compiler, *The Guizer: A Book of Fools.* London, Hamish Hamilton, 1975; New York, Greenwillow, 1976.

*

Manuscript Collection: Brigham Young University, Provo, Utah.

Critical Studies: *A Fine Anger: A Critical Introduction to the Work of Alan Garner* by Neil Philip, London, Collins, and New York, Philomel, 1981; *Alan Garner Issue* of *Labrys 7,* 1981.

* * *

Alan Garner's first books, *The Weirdstone of Brisingamen* (1960) and *The Moon of Gomrath* (1963), are magic fantasy tales aimed at the younger reader. They involve battles waged by an alliance of wizards, elves, dwarves and men to defeat the evil powers of the witch-like Morrigan and other assorted monsters. The central characters, however, are two modern youngsters and the stories are set around Alderley Edge, near Manchester. Garner mingles fiery, imaginative writing with descriptions of well-known landmarks, allowing him to bring the fantasy world with its joys and terrors to an actual landscape. Both of these books stand up well 30 years after their first printing.

Elidor (1965) moves forward with a deeper exploration of real and imaginary worlds. A group of children playing on a Manchester demolition site discover and take home various objects from a derelict church. Roland and his friends gradually realize they have found a place where two worlds meet, and are now part of a struggle to restore light to the kingdom of Elidor. Garner's fantasy style is used sparingly, with the "real" world of the Manchester suburb providing a base for the action and characters from Elidor making raids through time in search of their stolen "treasures." This helps to make the supernatural action more powerful and terrifying. The story climaxes with the appearance of the unicorn Findhorn at the demolition site as the "treasures" are returned to Elidor. A subtler, deeper work more likely to appeal to teenage readers, *Elidor* was runner-up for the Carnegie Medal.

Garner topped *Elidor* with *The Owl Service* (1967), where three teenagers on a remote Welsh farm are caught up in a legend of love, betrayal, and death that is reenacted through the ages. This time the action is set entirely in the modern world, with supernatural events breaking in violently at unexpected moments. Garner writes superbly, blending visions and dreams with earthy, modern dialogue as the story moves to an explosive finish. *The Owl Service* won favor from the critics and earned him the Carnegie Medal. It was clear after *The Owl Service* that Garner wasn't writing for children. John Rowe Townsend, in the *Guardian,* commented that: "Alan Garner's novel *The Owl Service* is not meant for children or anyone else; it's a novel, and not many better novels will be published this year." Both *Elidor* and *The Owl Service* have been televised in Britain.

Red Shift (1973) is the most intense and oblique of all Garner's novels. It combines three separate time periods. The story is set in modern Cheshire around the hill of Mow Cop and the village of Bartholmey. The modern love story of Tom and Jan fuses with the adventures of Macey and his fellow legionaries in Roman Britain, and with Margery and Thomas Rowley as Bartholmey prepares for a Royalist attack during the English Civil War. Garner focuses on the visionary, possessed states of Tom, Thomas, and Macey, and on the stone axe handled by them all, the constellation of Orion, and Mow Cop, "the netherstone of the world." His style puts deep thoughts into simple words and powerful feelings into a few terse lines of speech. A complex, moving, tormented work, *Red Shift* is the toughest of his novels. It is also, probably, his finest.

The four stories that make up *The Stone Book Quartet* (1983) describe the lives of five generations of Cheshire craftsmen and their families. The characters are celebrated in a simple but subtle prose that has the depth and force of a fairytale while remaining rooted in real life. The crafts include the stonecutting of the patriarch Robert, who carves the stone book of the title for his daughter Mary. The book also incorporates the musician and blacksmith Joseph and the deadly shooting skills of the sniper Uncle Charlie. The book, which opens with Robert showing Mary the underground cave and its prehistoric remains, ends with William (Joseph's grandson) going out after the old man's death and sledging joyfully under the stars, heedless of the German bombers overhead. A strong, warm, visual work, *The Stone Book Quartet* ranks with the best of Garner's writing.

Speaking in an afterword to *The Moon of Gomrath,* Garner remarked that: "I am convinced that there are no original stories," and that "originality now means the personal coloring of existing themes." A writer steeped in folklore, fairytale, and myth, he has produced several collections of fairytales in recent years. But his ability to mix the fantastic with the everyday, creating a sense of wonder, makes him more original than most.

—Geoff Sadler

GEORGE, Elizabeth

Nationality: American. **Born:** Warren, Ohio, 26 February 1949. **Education:** University of California, Riverside, B.A. in English; California State University, Fullerton, M.S. in counseling. **Family:** Married Ira Tobin in 1971. **Career:** English teacher, Mater Dei High School, Santa Anna, 1974-75, and El Toro High School, 1975-87, both California. Since 1988 creative writing teacher, Coastline College, Costa Mesa, Irvine Valley College, Irvine, 1989, and University of California, Irvine, 1990, all California. **Awards:** Anthony award, 1989; Le Grand Prix de Littérature Policière, 1990. **Agent:** Deborah Schneider, John Farquharson Ltd., 157 West 57th Street, New York, New York 10107; or, Vivienne Schuster, John Farquharson Ltd., 162-168 Regent Street, London W1R 5TB, England. **Address:** 611 13th Street, Huntington Beach, California 92648, U.S.A.

Publications

Novels (series: Inspector Thomas Lynley and Sergeant Barbara Havers in all books)

A Great Deliverance. New York, Bantam, 1988; London, Bantam, 1989.
Payment in Blood. New York and London, Bantam, 1989.
Well-Schooled in Murder. New York and London, Bantam, 1990.
A Suitable Vengeance. New York and London, Bantam, 1992.
For the Sake of Elena. New York and London, Bantam, 1993.
Missing Joseph. New York and London, Bantam, 1993.
Playing for the Ashes. New York and London, Bantam, 1994.
In the Presence of the Enemy. New York and London, Bantam, 1996.

*

Manuscript Collection: Mugar Memorial Library, Boston University.

* * *

Though Ohioan by birth and Californian by choice, Elizabeth George writes convincingly of British values and conflicts in a mystery series set in England. These mysteries are ambitious, multilayered, erudite, and psychologically sound. Key detectives are beautiful and intelligent, and the cast of characters are well-rounded and humanized.

George has taken Dorothy Sayers as her model for an aristocratic detective intrigued by criminal psychology, for romantic tensions intensified by intellectual confrontations, and for the interweaving of the personal problems of her investigators with the demands of plot. However, she is more like P.D. James in the depth of her psychological studies and in the thematic correspondences that interlock her world. Her villains are capable of extreme brutality, but guilt is often shared.

A Great Deliverance (1988) introduces an engaging set of richly drawn upper-class characters: Thomas Lynley, Simon Allcourt-St. James, Deborah Cotter, and Lady Helen Clyde. George plays them off against Lynley's ill-clad, pug-faced, working-class partner, Detective Sergeant Barbara Havers. Where Lynley and friends are witty, educated, delicately restrained, considerate, and perfectly charming, Havers's bad taste, angry fits, and obsession with class differences as the root of all evils offend and irritate.

Lynley is George's Lord Wimsey, a handsome, aristocratic womanizer, a New Scotland Yard detective and the eighth earl of Asherton. Charming on occasion, Lynley cultivates a haughty, aloof manner intensified by contact with Havers. Though their disagreements sum up the broad lines of British class conflict, these two are more than allegorical representations. They change and develop with time, first learning to respect each others' special competencies and then even protecting each other, though their progress is more zig-zag than linear throughout the ongoing series.

Like Agatha Christie and Ruth Rendell, George exposes the violence and hatreds beneath the peaceful facade of village life. In *A Great Deliverance,* for example, incest leads to a headless corpse that shatters the peace of a Yorkshire farm and a retarded girl's assertion of guilt, while in *Missing Joseph* (1993) Lancashire villagers dabble in witchcraft and a vicar with a roving eye ends up poisoned by hemlock in the parsnips. *Playing for the Ashes* (1994) begins with a burned-out 15th century Celandine Cottage in Kent and follows the rippling effect of murder and arson to the world of national cricket.

A Suitable Vengeance (1992) breaks series chronology to give an early glimpse of key characters. It is set in picturesque Cornwall, near the Asherton family estate. The murder in *Payment in Blood* (1989) happens on an isolated estate in the Scottish Highlands when a dirk is driven through the neck of a playwright, while the killing in *Well-Schooled in Murder* (1990) takes place in a prestigious public school in West Sussex, and in *For the Sake of Elena* (1993) the crime is at Cambridge University. Always, as the investigators unlock the secrets of these closed societies they must face their own emotional wounds and combat preconceptions. These works are rich in allusions to music, art, and literature with bits of Dryden, Wilde, Shakespeare, and Sylvia Plath punctuating highly textured descriptions and intensifying meaning. Additionally, George explores the ramifications of a single theme in metaphor, symbol, and layered correspondences.

In all her books, George places complex, fascinating characters in tightly woven plots resonant with history, culture, love, and cruelty.

—Gina Macdonald

GIBSON, William (Ford)

Nationality: American. **Born:** Conway, South Carolina, 17 March 1948. **Education:** University of British Columbia, B.A. 1977. **Family:** Married Deborah Jean Thompson in 1972; one daughter and one son. **Awards:** Hugo award, Philadelphia Science Fiction Society Philip K. Dick memorial award, Nebula award, Porgie award, all 1985, and Australian Science Fiction Convention Ditmar award, all for *Neuromancer*. **Agent:** Martha Millard Literary Agency, 204 Park Avenue, Madison, New Jersey 07940, U.S.A.

PUBLICATIONS

NOVELS

Neuromancer. New York, Ace, 1984, London, HarperCollins, 1994.
Count Zero. New York, Arbor House, 1986.
Mona Lisa Overdrive. New York, Bantam, 1988.
The Difference Engine, with Bruce Sterling. London, Gollancz, 1990; New York, Bantam, 1991.
Virtual Light. New York, Bantam, and London, Viking, 1993.

Short Stories

Burning Chrome. New York, Ace Books, 1986.

Play

Dream Jumbo (text to accompany performance art; produced, Los Angeles, 1989).

*

Film Adaptation: *Johnny Mnemonic,* from the short story, 1995.

Critical Study: *William Gibson* by Lance Olsen, San Bernardino, California, Borgo Press, 1992 (includes bibliography).

* * *

William Gibson has been credited with reinvigorating the science fiction genre, giving it a lean, mean, and utterly contemporary edge. His debut novel, *Neuromancer* (1984), carried off science fiction's three major honors: the Nebula, Hugo, and Philip K. Dick awards. Combining hard science with hardboiled thriller, *Neuromancer* presents a future cityscape of poverty, pollution, and proliferating technology much like that of Ridley Scott's 1982 film, *Blade Runner.* In *Neuromancer,* society has become a cybernetic urban jungle dominated by multinational corporations. Information has replaced money as the most valuable commodity, and the gap between the haves and the have-nots is a yawning chasm. It is a future whose moral decay is as accelerated as its technological progress, portrayed through a high-tech wasteland peopled by streetwise loners, lunatics, junkies, and misfits.

Although Gibson himself rejects the label, he has been hailed as the leading exponent of cyberpunk. *Burning Chrome* (1986) collects the early short stories that established cyberpunk's characteristic features: a slick, spartan, filmic prose style, and vividly realized "grunge futurism." The landscape and themes introduced in "Johnny Mnemonic," "New Rose Hotel," and "Burning Chrome" are progressively explored in Gibson's "Sprawl novels": *Neuromancer, Count Zero* (1986), and *Mona Lisa Overdrive* (1988). It is a terrain of cybernetics, biotechnology, and sophisticated communications networks, a landscape in which the distinctions between human and machine are no longer clear-cut. Moreover, as the trilogy unfolds, even the boundaries between life and death blur as humans project themselves into the matrix of cyberspace in the form of immortal ROM constructs. Cyberspace is, perhaps, Gibson's most innovative contribution to science fiction. The matrix is a "consensual hallucination," a virtual world in which all data is spatialized and where information is transformed into three-dimensional geography. Industrial espionage is carried out by console "cowboys," or surgically-adapted computer hackers who "jack in" to cyberspace to rustle information to sell to the highest corporate bidder. The profession is lucrative but potentially deadly, since the results of being "iced" by security software is brain-death.

Case, the cowboy protagonist of *Neuromancer,* is one such cyberspace victim. At the novel's opening, Case is on skid row, stripped of his "jacking" abilities by his previous employers as punishment for double-crossing them. He is rescued by Molly, a cybernetically enhanced mercenary who offers him restorative surgery in exchange for the use of his hacking talents. Together, they steal contracted data and in the process discover that they are working for Wintermute, one of two Artificial Intelligences owned by a powerful family intent on immortality. Wintermute is a sentient computer with a self-determining agenda. Ironically, their attempts to thwart its plan only aid it. At the novel's conclusion, Wintermute has broken from human control by melding with its alter-ego AI, Neuromancer, in a kind of computer apotheosis.

Neuromancer was criticized by some for its complicated plot and sketchy characterization, and Gibson himself described the novel as "a bit hypermanic." His subsequent Sprawl novels are more deliberately paced and his (recurring) characters are more substantial. Mercenaries and console cowboys still abound, but Gibson broadens his emotional canvas to include innocents and waifs caught up in high-tech corporate maneuverings. He also tantalizingly explores the cyberspace consequences of "The Change" effected at *Neuromancer*'s conclusion. Here, Gibson hints that the matrix itself has become sentient, that it harbors not a god, but a variety of artificial and human ghosts in the machine.

This machinic coming-to-consciousness also marks the conclusion of *The Difference Engine* (1990), Gibson's attempt to confound his cyberpunk categorization. Rather than outlining a not-too-distant future, *The Difference Engine* presents a science fictional rewriting of the past. The title refers to the steam-driven computer designed by 19th century mathematician Charles Babbage. Money was the only barrier to the construction of Babbage's machine; Gibson and Sterling imagine a Victorian England in which his genius was recognized and the Industrial and Information Revolutions occur simultaneously. The plot centers on a ruthless scramble for a mysterious box of punch-cards known as the Modus, a software program eventually used to disable the "great Napoleon"—the largest difference engine of all—by making it run endless loops on itself. Only at the novel's fragmented conclusion does it become apparent that by 1991 the Modus has achieved its designed purpose: the difference engine has become sentient, and the narrative itself constitutes the computer's exploration of its own origins.

While *Virtual Light* (1993) was well-received, Gibson's cyberpunk trilogy remains his most popular and influential work. Whether his fiction is a celebration or a condemnation of the Information Age is a matter of some debate. Gibson himself refuses to label technology as either a blessing or a curse: "I'm neither a technophiliac nor technophobiac . . . I think what I'm writing about is the idea that technology has *already* changed us, and now we have to figure a way to stay sane within that change."

—Jackie Buxton

GILCHRIST, Ellen (Louise)

Nationality: American. **Born:** Vicksburg, Mississippi, 20 February 1935. **Education:** Vanderbilt University, Nashville; Millsaps College, Jackson, Mississippi, B.A. in philosophy 1967; University of Arkansas, Fayetteville, 1976. **Family:** Has three sons. **Career:** Broadcaster on National Public Radio 1984-85; also journalist. **Awards:** Mississippi Arts Festival poetry award, 1968; *New York Quarterly* award, for poetry, 1978; National Endowment for the Arts grant, 1979; *Prairie Schooner* award, 1981; Mississippi Academy award, 1982, 1985; Saxifrage award, 1983; American Book award, 1985; University of Arkansas Fulbright award, 1985; Mississippi Institute Arts and Letters award, for literature, 1985, 1990, 1991. **Address:** c/o Little Brown, 34 Beacon St., Boston, Massachusetts 02108, U.S.A.

Publications

Novels

The Annunciation. Boston, Little Brown, 1983; London, Faber, 1984.
The Anna Papers. Boston, Little Brown, 1988; London, Faber, 1989.
Net of Jewels. Boston, Little Brown, and London, Faber, 1992.
Anabasis: A Journey to the Interior. Jackson, University of Mississippi, 1994.
Starcarbon: A Meditation on Love. Boston, Little Brown, and London, Faber, 1994.
Rhoda: A Life in Stories. Boston, Little, Brown, and London, Faber, 1995.

Short Stories

In the Land of Dreamy Dreams: Short Fiction. Fayetteville, University of Arkansas Press, 1981; London, Faber, 1982.
Victory over Japan. Boston, Little Brown, 1984; London, Faber, 1985.
Drunk with Love. Boston, Little Brown, 1986; London, Faber, 1987.
Light Can Be Both Wave and Particle. Boston, Little Brown, 1989; London, Faber, 1990.
I Cannot Get You Close Enough: Three Novellas. Boston, Little Brown, 1990; London, Faber, 1991.
The Blue-Eyed Buddhist and Other Stories. London, Faber, 1990.

Play

Television Play: *A Season of Dreams,* from stories by Eudora Welty, 1968.

Poetry

The Land Surveyor's Daughter. Fayetteville, Arkansas, Lost Road, 1979.
Riding Out the Tropical Depression: Selected Poems 1975-1985. New Orleans, Faust, 1986.

Other

Falling through Space: The Journals of Ellen Gilchrist. Boston, Little Brown, 1987; London, Faber, 1988.

* * *

Ellen Gilchrist made a splash on the literary scene in 1981 with a well-received collection of short stories entitled *In the Land of Dreamy Dreams.* In these stories Gilchrist details the lives of the beautiful and spoiled in modern New Orleans. She depicts, in an original style, a ruthless code of morality that constricts Southern society. Critics praised the collection as full of promise and talent.

Victory over Japan (1984), which garnered her an American Book Award, deals with similar subject matter. Her lively and clever style serves her material well, and she shows a willingness to take risks. "Without much authorial manicuring or explanation, she allows her characters to emerge whole, in full possession of their considerable stores of eccentricities and passion," says Beverly Lowry of the *New York Times Book Review.*

In 1983 she published her first novel, *The Annunciation.* The protagonist Amanda McCamey, having given up a child for adoption earlier in her life, finds herself childless at 40, living in New Orleans, and married to a wealthy man. Haunted by her past and, consequently, disillusioned with her life, she begins working on translating the manuscript of an 18th-century poetess. After a separation from her husband she falls in love with a younger man, and finds her life paralleling that of the poetess. Although the characterization of the men is weak and the writing is at times self-conscious, the exploration of the mind of a woman who chooses an unconventional path towards finding herself was seen by most critics as original and intelligent.

Drunk with Love (1986) returns again to the background of New Orleans and Fayetteville, but also branches out to such locales as Berkeley, California; Harrisburg, Illinois; and Lincoln, Nebraska. Gilchrist focuses less on hard-drinking Southern belles, but with a wider panorama she seems to lose some of the crackle of her earlier collections.

Her second novel, *The Anna Papers* (1988), proves once again that Gilchrist has an original style and a keen narrative gift. Anna Hand, seen earlier in *Drunk with Love,* is a successful author who, like most of Gilchrist's female characters, is beautiful, rich, and spoiled. By the end of the first part of the novel she has committed suicide after a diagnosis of cancer. The second section details the family at Anna's wake. The third focuses on Anna's sister Helen who transforms herself after reading through Anna's papers. The novel may be uneven, "yet Gilchrist excels in drawing the bonds of love and resentment in sexual and family relationships, and no one who encounters her characters—here or in her earlier works—will want to miss reading about them again," wrote *Publisher's Weekly.*

I Cannot Get You Close Enough (1990) consists of three linked novellas with the focus on the Hand family of Charlotte, North Carolina. "Winter" centers on Anna Hand, sick with cancer at this point. She uses the remnants of her energy to protect her niece Jessie from a neurotic mother. "De Haviland Hand" concerns itself with the other niece, Olivia, the half-Cherokee child of Daniel Hand and Summer Deer. Jessie and Olivia must come to terms with their aging father Daniel. "A Summer in Maine" brings together a mass of relatives and acquaintances to recover Anna's literary papers. They argue, make love, and argue again. Susan Spano Wells described it as a "screwball fugue on the theme of love."

Similarly, Gilchrist's *Starcarbon* (1994), is deemed a "richly textured family fugue" by Sarah Ferguson. The saga of the Hand family continues with the focus on the younger generation introduced in *I Cannot Get You Close Enough.* Olivia returns to her Native American family while Jessie is trapped in New Orleans with a new baby and a failing marriage. Once again, Gilchrist delineates a cluster of sharply accentuated characters rooted in family.

In all of her works Gilchrist is witty and moving. Her works are rich in language and original in structure, and, according to a *Publisher's Weekly* reviewer, "she writes with a distinctive Southern toughness about people who are selfish, demanding, and often cruel to those closest to them, but who invariably gain the reader's sympathy with their total honesty and fierce need for love."

—Jennifer G. Coman

GODWIN, Gail (Kathleen)

Nationality: American. **Born:** Birmingham, Alabama, 18 June 1937. **Education:** Peace Junior College, Raleigh, North Carolina, 1955-57; University of North Carolina, Chapel Hill, 1957-59, B.A. in journalism 1959; University of Iowa, Iowa City, 1967-71, M.A. 1968, Ph.D. in English 1971. **Family:** Married 1) Douglas Kennedy in 1960 (divorced); 2) Ian Marshall in 1965 (divorced 1966). **Career:** Reporter, Miami *Herald,* 1959-60; consultant, U.S. Travel Service, United States Embassy, London, 1962-65; researcher, *Saturday Evening Post,* New York, 1966; instructor in English, 1967-70, and lecturer at the Writers Workshop, 1972-73, University of Iowa; instructor and fellow, Center for Advanced Studies, University of Illinois, Urbana, 1971-72; American specialist, United States Information Service, Brazil, 1976; lecturer, Vassar College, Poughkeepsie, New York, 1977, and Columbia University, New York, 1978, 1981. **Awards:** National Endowment for the Arts grant, 1974, and fellowship, for libretto, 1978; Guggenheim fellowship, 1975; St. Lawrence award, 1976; American Academy award, 1981; Thomas Wolfe Memorial award, 1988; Janet Kafka award, 1988. **Agent:** John Hawkins and Associates, 71 West 23rd Street, Suite 1600, New York, New York 10010. **Address:** P.O. Box 946, Woodstock, New York 12498, U.S.A.

PUBLICATIONS

Novels

The Perfectionists. New York, Harper, 1970; London, Cape, 1971.
Glass People. New York, Knopf, 1972.
The Odd Woman. New York, Knopf, 1974; London, Cape, 1975.
Violet Clay. New York, Knopf, and London, Gollancz, 1978.
A Mother and Two Daughters. New York, Viking, and London, Heinemann, 1982.
The Finishing School. New York, Viking, and London, Heinemann, 1985.
A Southern Family. New York, Morrow, and London, Heinemann, 1987.
Father Melancholy's Daughter. New York, Morrow, and London, Deutsch, 1991.
The Good Husband. New York, Ballantine, and London, Deutsch, 1994.

Short Stories

Dream Children. New York, Knopf, 1976; London, Gollancz, 1977.
Mr. Bedford and the Muses. New York, Viking Press, 1983; London, Heinemann, 1984.

Uncollected Short Stories

"Fate of Fleeing Maidens," in *Mademoiselle* (New York), May 1978.
"The Unlikely Family," in *Redbook* (New York), August 1979.
"Over the Mountain," in *Antaeus* (New York), 1983.

Plays

The Last Lover, music by Robert Starer (produced Katonah, New York, 1975).
Journals of a Songmaker, music by Robert Starer (produced Philadelphia, 1976).
Apollonia, music by Robert Starer (produced Minneapolis, 1979).

Recordings: *Anna Margarita's Will* (song cycle), music by Robert Starer, C.R.I., 1980; *Remembering Felix,* music by Robert Starer, Spectrum, 1987.

Other

Editor, with Shannon Ravenel, *The Best American Short Stories 1985*. Boston, Houghton Mifflin, 1985.

*

Manuscript Collection: Southern Collection, University of Northern Carolina Library, Chapel Hill.

Critical Studies: "*The Odd Woman:* Literature and the Retreat from Life" by Susan E. Lorsch, in *Critique* (Atlanta), vol. 20, no. 2, 1978; "Reaching Out: Sensitivity and Order," in *Recent American Fiction by Women* by Anne Z. Mickelson, Metuchen, New Jersey, Scarecrow Press, 1979; interview and "Gail Godwin and Southern Womanhood" by Carolyn Rhodes, both in *Women Writers of the Contemporary South* edited by Peggy Whitman Prenshaw, Jackson, University Press of Mississippi, 1984; *Gail Godwin* by Jane Hill, New York, Twayne, 1992.

* * *

Gail Godwin's first books share the theme of an unhappily married woman who settles for a traditional solution to her discontent. In *The Perfectionists* (1970), for example, the unmotivated Dane Epson loses interest in her ten-month-old marriage and fails to find meaning in her role as stepmother to her husband's son. In *Glass People* (1972), trophy wife Francesca Bolt, after several misadventures, settles for the role of manipulator and allows her attorney husband to pamper her.

Those first two books failed to gain as much attention as *The Odd Woman* (1974), in which Godwin creates Jane Clifford, a responsible woman who uses teaching, literature, and research to move forward rather than settle for a traditional role. Nominated for a National Book Award, *The Odd Woman* identifies several of Godwin's themes, which Jane Hill explains as modern woman's conflict between career and emotional needs; and the role of the artist to herself, other people, and her art.

In fact, many of Godwin's women use art to create or recreate their worlds and themselves. The eponymous narrator of *Violet Clay* (1978) is roused from complacently illustrating romance novels by the suicide of her Uncle Ambrose (perhaps inspired by Godwin's father's suicide). Understanding his suicide note ("I'm sorry, there is nothing left") to mean inspiration, she plumbs his unfinished written material and recommits to serious painting. That leads her to understand the importance of other people to her work, and to acknowledge that their lives have boundaries which she must not overstep.

In *A Mother and Two Daughters* (1982), Godwin examines three women's intertwined lives. Nell Strickland adjusts to widowhood as her daughters Lydia and Cate work through significant relationships. In this bestseller, also a National Book Award nominee, women readers recognized their own options as the three women confront aging, remarriage, divorce, the need for independence and personal fulfillment, raising teenagers, abortion, and sibling rivalry. Often compromising, each woman settles for a different lifestyle.

With *The Finishing School* (1985), Godwin returns to a first-person narrative and again relies on an artist's need to recreate herself. Now 40, the successful actress Justin Stokes examines her 14th summer when, left behind in North Carolina by her mother, she fell under the instructive spell of Ursula DeVane. Enthralling Justin, the older woman would serve as her life-long inspiration for self creation. Frances Taliaferro praises Godwin's characterization of Justin as "one of the most trustworthy portraits of an adolescent in current literature."

As in earlier novels, Godwin draws upon personal history in *A Southern Family* (1987) by using the suicide of her half-brother as the novel's foundation. Winner of the Janet Heldiger Kafka Award and the Thomas Wolfe Memorial Literary Award, this novel recounts the violent death of novelist Janet Campion's brother while she visits her family in North Carolina.

Father Melancholy's Daughter is set in the small town of Romulus, Virginia. Walter Gower, the rector of St. Cuthbert's Episcopal Church, copes with paralyzing depression after his wife Ruth runs off to New York City with the sophisticated, outrageous Madelyn Farley. Isobel Armstrong suggests that Godwin is fascinated by "unrequited daughters," because Margaret, six when her mother absconds, tells us this part-mystery, part-domestic, part-religious story as she seeks explanations for her mother's abandonment and accidental death a few months later. Brilliant in its secondary characters, the novel wickedly contrasts southern values with New York City sophistication.

The Good Husband (1994) received mixed reviews. Godwin intersects the lives of two academic couples during simultaneous family crises. Magda Evers, the sharp-tongued star of Aurelia College's English Department, is dying of ovarian cancer at 58. Meanwhile, Hugo Henry (an overbearing, blocked writer-in-residence in the same department) and his wife lose their full-term infant to umbilical strangulation during home birth. During visits to the deteriorating Magda, Alice falls in love with Magda's husband, the distraught, sensitive Francis, who trained for the priesthood and now exists only to serve others (especially Magda). So dominant is Magda's personality that after her death the intensity goes out of the book. Yet one critic praised Godwin for risking such unsavory characters as Hugo and Magda.

Along with short stories, Godwin has written four librettos. But she is most successful in her desire to create, as she says, "characters who operate at a high level of intelligence as they go about trying to make sense of the world in which they find themselves, and as they make decisions about how to live their lives."

—Judith C. Kohl

GOUDGE, Eileen

Nationality: American. **Born:** 4 July 1950, in San Mateo, California. **Education:** San Diego State College; California State Vocational Teaching Degree, 1976. **Family:** Married second husband, Roy Bailey, 1974 (divorced); married Albert J. Zuckerman, 1985; children: (first marriage) Michael James; (second marriage) Mary Rose. **Career:** Worked as secretary; Spin Physics, San Diego, California, micro-electronics assembler, 1971-76; writer since 1976. **Agent:** Albert J. Zuckerman, Writers House, 21 West 26th St., New York, New York 10016, U.S.A.

Publications

Novels for Young Adults

It Must Be Magic, under pseudonym Marian Woodruff. Bantam, 1982.
Kiss Me Creep, under pseudonym Marian Woodruff. Bantam, 1984.
Winner All the Way. Dell, 1984.
Smart Enough to Know. Dell, 1984.
'Till We Meet Again, under pseudonym Elizabeth Merrit. Silhouette, 1984.
Too Much Too Soon. Dell, 1984.
Afraid to Love. Dell, 1984.
Bad Girl. Dell, 1985.
Before It's Too Late. Dell, 1985.
Don't Say Goodbye. Dell, 1985.
Forbidden Kisses. Dell, 1985.
Hands Off, He's Mine. Dell, 1985.
Presenting Superhunk. Dell, 1985.
A Touch of Ginger. Dell, 1985.
Against the Rules. Dell, 1986.
Eileen Goudge's Swept Away Number One: Gone with the Wish. Avon, 1986.
Hawaiian Christmas. Dell, 1986.
Heart for Sale. Dell, 1986.
Kiss and Make Up. Dell, 1986.
Life of the Party. Dell, 1986.
Looking for Love. Dell, 1986.
Night after Night. Dell, 1986.
Old Enough: Super Seniors Number One. Dell, 1986.
Sweet Talk. Dell, 1986.
Treat Me Right. Dell, 1986.
Woodstock Magic, with Fran Lantz. Avon, 1986.
Too Hot to Handle. Dell, 1987.
Something Borrowed, Something Blue. Dell, 1988.
Deep-Sea Summer. Dell, 1988.

Adult Novels

Garden of Lies. Viking, 1989.
Such Devoted Sisters. Viking, 1992.
Blessings in Disguise. Viking, 1994.
Trail of Secrets. Viking, 1996.

* * *

Previously known as a teenage paperback romance writer, Eileen Goudge made the leap in 1989 to big-time commercial fiction. In the young-adult market Goudge has written entries for the Bantam Sweet Dreams series and the famously popular Sweet Valley High series. She had her own line at Dell called Seniors, and she packaged Avon's Swept Away line. Goudge admits she enjoys writing in the young adult realm: "My adolescent characters are the embodiment of my teenage angst," she has said. "They were the vehicle by which I could rewrite my own history."

Garden of Lies, Goudge's first adult novel, begins in 1943 after Sylvie Rosenthal takes a baby from a burning hospital; she leaves her own child when she realizes that the child looks more like her Greek lover Nikos than her husband. Pampered Rachel grows up rich and Jewish while the real daughter, Rose Santini, grows up poor and Catholic in Brooklyn. Rose becomes engaged to Brian McClanahan before he is sent off to Vietnam. Rachel, who decided upon a career in medicine, meets Brian in Vietnam and marries him. Goudge takes a very complicated plot and brings it to a nice resolution. Smoothly written and engrossing, the novel was described by *Kirkus Reviews* as "the stuff that mini-series are made of."

Goudge's second novel, *Such Devoted Sisters* (1991), follows the paths of two sisters, Eve and Dolly, in 1950s Hollywood. Eve becomes an overnight success invoking the destructive jealousy of sister Dolly. After Dolly loses her man to Eve, Dolly writes a letter to Senator Joseph McCarthy and the Committee on Un-American Activities. Eve, with her career in ruins, turns to alcohol and eventually commits suicide. Dolly feels obligated to make up for what she has done to Eve's daughters, Annie and Laurel, so she takes them in and gets them jobs in New York. These two sisters also end up at war over the same man. *Sisters* proved to be a successful follow-up to *Garden.* As Joyce R. Slater put it, "Goudge is a gifted writer with an eye for the telling detail, and she understands the difference between a pop-fiction blockbuster and an entertaining novel about genuine ideas and issues."

Blessing in Disguise (1994) continues Goudge's success in the field of adult fiction. The main character, Grace Truscott, recently divorced at 40, decides to write a biography of her deceased father, Senator Eugene Truscott. As she researches her book, she uncovers disturbing information about her father's complicity in a murder. She cannot stop herself from seeking the truth. The theme of privacy versus invasion is an interesting premise. The descriptions may be clichéd and the plot contrived, but overall it's a good read, especially because "Goudge excels at capturing excruciating family dynamics, adolescent tantrums, and emotions that cruise below the surface," according to *Publisher's Weekly.*

Goudge consistently produces highly readable novels that paint intriguing pictures of secret loves and tangled lives. "That's a theme that resonates throughout my novels: how damaging secrets or withheld truths can be within families," she says.

—Jennifer G. Coman

GOULD, Stephen Jay

Nationality: American. **Born:** New York City, 10 September 1941. **Education:** Antioch College, A.B., 1963; Columbia University, Ph.D., 1967. **Family:** Married Deborah Lee in 1965; children: Jesse, Ethan. **Career:** Antioch College, Yellow Springs, Ohio, instructor in geology, 1966; Harvard University, Cambridge, Massachusetts, assistant professor, 1967-71, associate professor, 1971-73, professor of geology and curator of invertebrate paleontology at Museum of Comparative Zoology from 1973—, Alexander Agassiz Professor of Zoology from 1982. Harvard University, assistant curator, 1967-71, associate curator of invertebrate paleontology, 1971-73. Editor, *Evolution,* 1970-72; member of editorial board, *Systematic Zoology,* 1970-72, *Paleobiology,* 1974-76, and *American Naturalist,* 1977-80; member of board of editors, *Science,* since 1986. Member of advisory board, Children's Television Workshop, 1978-81, and *Nova,* since 1980. **Awards:** National Science Foundation, Woodrow Wilson, and Columbia University fellows, 1963-67; Schuchert award, Paleontological Society, 1975; National Magazine Award in essays and criticism, 1980, for "This View of Life"; "Notable Book" citation, American Library Association, 1980, and American Book award in science, 1981, both for *The Panda's Thumb;* "Scientist of the Year" citation, *Discover,* 1981; National Book Critics Circle award in general nonfiction, 1981, and outstanding book award, American Educational Research Association, for *The Mismeasure of Man;* MacArthur Foundation Prize fellowship, 1981-86; medal of excellence, Columbia University, 1982; F. V. Haydn Medal, Philadelphia Academy of Natural Sciences, 1982; Joseph Priestley award and Medal, Dickinson College, 1983; Neil Miner award, National Association of Geology Teachers, 1983; silver medal, Zoological Society of London, 1984; Bradford Washburn award and gold medal, Museum of Science (Boston), 1984; distinguished service award, American Humanists Association, 1984; Tanner Lectures, Cambridge University, 1984, and Stanford University, 1989; meritorious service award, American Association of Systematics Collections, 1984; Founders Council Award of Merit, Field Museum of Natural History, 1984; John and Samuel Bard award, Bard College, 1984; Phi Beta Kappa Book award in science, 1984, for *Hen's Teeth and Horse's Toes;* Sarah Josepha Hale medal, 1986; creative arts award (citation in nonfiction), Brandeis University, 1986; distinguished service award, American Geological Institute, 1986; Glenn T. Seaborg award, International Platform Association, 1986; In Praise of Reason award, Committee for the Scientific Investigation of Claims of the Paranormal, 1986; H. D. Vursell award, American Academy and Institute of Arts and Letters, 1987; Anthropology in Media award, American Anthropological Association, 1987; History of Geology award, Geological Society of America, 1988; T. N. George Medal, University of Glasgow, 1989. Recipient of over twenty honorary degrees from colleges and universities. **Member:** American Association for the Advancement of Science, American Academy of Arts and Sciences, American Society of Naturalists (president, 1979-80), Paleontological Society (president, 1985-86), Society for the Study of Evolution (vice president, 1975, president, 1990), Society of Systematic Zoology, Society of Vertebrate Paleontology, History of Science Society, Linnaean Society of London (foreign member), European Union of Geosciences (honorary foreign fellow). **Address:** Museum of Comparative Zoology, Harvard University, Cambridge, Massachusetts 02138, U.S.A.

Publications

Nonfiction

An Evolutionary Microcosm: Pleistocene and Recent History of the Land Snail P. (Poecilozonites) in Bermuda, 1969.
Ontogeny and Phylogeny. Belknap Press, 1977.
Ever since Darwin: Reflections in Natural History. Norton, 1977.
The Panda's Thumb: More Reflections in Natural History. Norton, 1980.
A View of Life, with Salvador Edward Juria and Sam Singer. Benjamin-Cummings, 1981.
The Mismeasure of Man. Norton, 1981.
Hen's Teeth and Horse's Toes: Further Reflections in Natural History. Norton, 1983.
The Flamingo's Smile: Reflections in Natural History. Norton, 1985.
Illuminations: A Bestiary, with Rosamund Wolff Purcell. Norton, 1986.
Time's Arrow, Time's Cycle: Myth and Metaphor in the Discovery of Geological Time. Harvard University Press, 1987.
An Urchin in the Storm: Essays about Books and Ideas. Norton, 1987.
Wonderful Life. Norton, 1989.
Bully for Brontosaurus. Norton, 1991.
Eight Little Piggies. Norton, 1993.
The Book of Life: An Illustrated History of the Evolution of Life on Earth. Norton, 1995.
Dinosaur in a Haystack: Reflections in Natural History. Harmony, 1996.
Full House: The Spread of Excellence from Plato to Darwin. Harmony, 1996.

Editor with Eldredge, *Mayr, Systematics and the Origin of Species.* Columbia University Press, 1982.
Editor with Eldredge, *Theodosius Dobzhansky, Genetics and the Origin of Species.* Columbia University Press, 1982.

* * *

An intellectually lively scientist and popularizer of his field, Stephen Jay Gould has garnered a prodigious number of awards and honorary degrees for the excellence of his writing, which is primarily centered on evolutionary biology and its ramifications and on the pioneering endeavors of Charles Darwin. The eminent anthropologist, paleontologist, geologist, biologist, and historian of science is connected with Harvard University's Museum of Comparative Zoology and is on the faculty of Harvard's Department of Earth Sciences. Most of his scientific articles have appeared in magazines, particularly *Natural History* and *Discover,* and later have been reprinted in essay collections such as *The Panda's Thumb* (1980), *The Flamingo's Smile* (1985), and *Bully for Brontosaurus* (1991). For breadth of subject matter (baseball included) and felicitous literary style, these writings recall the "grand manner" of scientific and medical writing of past masters. That is, such polymaths as Oliver Wendell Holmes, Thomas Henry Huxley, and Sir William Osler—as well as more recent adepts: Paul de Kruif, Hans Zinsser, Logan Clendening, and Jacob Bronowski.

On the acknowledgments page of his technical book on the history of evolutionary biology, *Ontogeny and Phylogeny* (1977), Gould wrote: ". . . I apologize for forgetting the sources of other [i.e., his unacknowledged] insights; they did not arise *sui generis.* I am a very effective sponge (and a fair manager of disparate information); I am not much of a creator." In his prologue to his essay collection *Ever since Darwin* (1977), he stated that the pieces ranged "broadly from planetary and geological to social and political history," with (he thought) a common element: Darwin's version of evolutionary theory. He added modestly, "I am a tradesman, not a polymath; what I know of planets and politics lies at their intersection with biological evolution." Regarding his erudite yet familiar literary style with its metaphors and literary allusions, as well as possible literary influences on his writing, Gould told a *Contemporary Authors* interviewer in 1988 that he had "always written very intuitively . . . was never trained in writing," and that he was hardly as well read as his quotations might suggest. "I just have the ability not to forget what I've read." The style he developed "more or less grew with . . . practice," and the writers he most admired were Thomas Henry Huxley and Peter Medawar.

Gould's major study, *Ontogeny and Phylogeny,* laid the groundwork for his tracing of the changing extent of acceptance in the scientific community of the cardinal precept of evolutionary biology, *ontogeny recapitulates phylogeny.* That is, the individual organism in embryonic development repeats important ancestral forms indicating a clear line of descent of the group to which the individual belongs. The book also offered Gould's modification of that precept. He attempted to show the extreme importance in evolution of heterochrony: changes in the time-sequence pattern of the individual's embryological development (ontogeny) disrupt the phylogenetic pattern being repeated during the individual's gestation. Reviewers gave the book qualified praise. Gould's highly technical terminology and expository style in enunciating his philosophy of science posed problems for some, despite his contributions to developmental biology.

His essay "Evolution as Fact and Theory," in *Discover* (1981), reprinted in his collection *Hen's Teeth and Horse's Toes* (1983), provides one of his most cogent philosophical statements. He confronts his Creationist adversaries directly, marking their failure to understand terms such as "theory" and "science," as well as "fact" (which does not signify "absolute certainty"), and arguing that their absolutist belief system is unfalsifiable, simply dogma, and by implication outside rational discussion. Among his basic points: "Evolution lies exposed in the *imperfections* that record a history of descent"; the "principle of imperfection extends to all historical sciences"; and "Evolution is one of the half dozen 'great ideas' developed by science," speaking "to the profound issues of genealogy that fascinate all of us." But this essay refers also to Gould's collaborative work on an important modification of classic evolutionary theory, with evolution seen as "a jerky, or episodic, rather than a smoothly gradual, pace of change." He and his colleague Niles Eldredge developed the "punctuated equilibrium" theory, arguing that "two outstanding facts of the fossil record—geologically 'sudden' origin of new species and failure to change thereafter . . . reflect the predictions of evolutionary theory, not the imperfections of the fossil record."

Gould's lavishly illustrated *Wonderful Life: The Burgess Shale and the Nature of History* (1989) concerns the discovery of, and his own reinterpretation of, the fossils found in "the most precious and important of all fossil localities—the Burgess Shale of British Columbia." The Burgess Shale confronts, he says, "our traditional view about progress and predictability in the history of life with the historian's challenge of contingency," whereby evolution is seen "as a staggeringly improbable series of events, sensible" and explainable enough, "but utterly unpredictable and quite unrepeatable." Gould continues to be a major figure in the field of bio-ecological science.

—Samuel I. Bellman

GRAFTON, Sue

Nationality: American. **Born:** Louisville, Kentucky, 24 April 1940; daughter of the writer C.W. Grafton. **Education:** University of Louisville, B.A. in English 1961. **Family:** Married Steven Frederick Humphrey in 1978; three children from previous marriages. **Member:** Writers Guild of America, West; Mystery Writers of America (president, 1994-95); Private Eye Writers of America (president, 1989-90); Crime Writers Association of Great Britain. **Awards:** Christopher award, 1979; Mysterious Stranger award, 1982/83; Private Eye Writers of America Shamus award, 1986, 1991, 1995; Mystery Readers of America Macarity award, for short story, 1986; Anthony award, for novel, 1986, 1987, 1991, and for short story, 1987; Doubleday Mystery Guild award, 1989-94; American Mystery award, 1990, 1992, 1993; Falcon award (Maltese Falcon Society of Japan), 1990. **Agent:** Molly Friedrich, The Aaron Priest Agency, 122 West 42nd Street, No. 3902, New York, New York 10168, U.S.A.

Publications

Novels

Keziah Dane. New York, Macmillan, 1967; London, Owen, 1968.
The Lolly-Madonna War. London, Owen, 1969.
"A" Is for Alibi. New York, Holt, 1982; London, Macmillan, 1986.
"B" Is for Burglar. New York, Holt, 1985; London, Macmillan, 1986.
"C" Is for Corpse. New York, Holt, 1986; London, Macmillan, 1987.
"D" Is for Deadbeat. New York, Holt, and London, Macmillan, 1987.
"E" Is for Evidence. New York, Holt, and London, Macmillan, 1988.
"F" Is for Fugitive. New York, Holt, and London, Macmillan, 1989.
"G" Is for Gumshoe. New York, Holt, and London, Macmillan, 1990.
"H" Is for Homicide. New York, Holt, and London, Macmillan, 1991.
"I" Is for Innocent. New York, Holt, and London, Macmillan, 1992.
"J" Is for Judgment. New York, Holt, and London, Macmillan, 1993.
"K" Is for Killer. New York, Holt, and London, Macmillan, 1994.
"L" Is for Lawless. New York, Holt, and London, Macmillan, 1995.

Short Stories

Kinsey and Me. Columbia, South Carolina, Bench Press, 1992.

Plays

Screenplay: *Lolly-Madonna XXX,* with Rodney Carr-Smith, 1973.

Television Plays: *With Friends Like These* (*Rhoda* series), 1975; *Walking through the Fire,* from the book by Laurel Lee, 1979; *Sex and the Single Parent,* from the book by Jane Adams, 1979; *Nurse,* from the book by Peggy Anderson, 1980; *Mark, I Love You,* from the book by Hal Painter, 1980; *Seven Brides for Seven Brothers, I Love You, Molly McGraw,* and *A House Divided,* with Steven Humphrey (*Seven Brides for Seven Brothers* series), 1982-83; *A Caribbean Mystery,* with Steven Humphrey, from the novel by Agatha Christie, 1983; *A Killer in the Family,* with Steven Humphrey and Robert Aller, 1983; *Sparkling Cyanide,* with Steven Humphrey and Robert Malcolm Young, from the novel by Agatha Christie, 1983; *Love on the Run,* with Steven Humphrey, 1985; *Tonight's the Night,* with Steven Humphrey, 1987.

*

Media Adaptation: Film—*Lolly-Madonna XXX,* 1973, from the novel *The Lolly Madonna War* and the screenplay.

* * *

Through her mystery novels, Sue Grafton has created Kinsey Millhone, a gritty, modern, cop-turned-detective who jogs, eats junk food, and lives in a converted garage. She is also smart and ironic, and contrasts starkly with the characters one would find in, for example, an Agatha Christie novel. In a Christie novel the body is merely the first clue to a big puzzle. In Grafton's novels, violence hurts, chase scenes are action-packed, and dead bodies are treated as former human beings.

Grafton plans to take Millhone all the way through the alphabet in a detective series starting with *"A" Is for Alibi* (1982), in which Millhone is hired to prove a convicted woman's innocence in the murder of a heartless lawyer. It gets complicated when several people have motives. Millhone tracks down the real killer, earning Grafton praise from Katrine Ames of *Newsweek,* who writes that the plot is "smart, well paced, and very funny."

Grafton is, indeed, funny. Yet, in *"B" Is for Burglar* (1984) Grafton's serious consideration of human nature is evident. In that book, Millhone is hired to locate a wealthy woman by the woman's estranged sister so that she might sign a simple legal document. As Millhone scratches the surface of the case, she uncovers a murder. Grafton's philosophy about violence becomes clear. "Mostly what I'm interested in is why we do what we do," Grafton said in an interview with *Modern Maturity.* "Why do we kill each other? Why can't we be happy? I'm looking for answers, looking to figure it out."

Grafton's inspiration comes from varied sources. For instance, one day she was reading *The Gashlycrumb Tinies,* a children's book of cartoons that deals with the alphabet, and realized that she could base a series of novels on the same idea. "Once I was doing research at a coroner's office and they mentioned that they often have bodies around for years," she said about another idea. "I thought, 'A corpse—what an interesting place to hide something,' and used that in *"C" Is for Corpse* (1986)."

To date, Grafton has worked her way through the alphabet to *"L" Is for Lawless* (1995). In between, titles such as *"G" Is for Gumshoe* (1990) and *"J" Is for Judgment* (1993) have received mixed reviews. Alex Kozinski of the *New York Times* said *Gumshoe* is "devoid of intellectual challenge and completely forgettable." Yet, Katrine Ames of *Newsweek* writes: "Wit is the most versatile weapon in Sue Grafton's well-stocked arsenal, and she uses it with disarming precision in her seventh Kinsey Millhone venture." If nothing else, Grafton is prolific. She has written 12 books in 13 years. Prior to mystery writing, Grafton wrote in Hollywood, which she now detests. Her works include "Walking through Fire" (1979) as well as two Agatha Christie novel adaptations; "Caribbean Mystery" and "Sparkling Cyanide."

Grafton learned about writing dialogue and action in Hollywood, but turned to mysteries when her plots were criticized, wanting to prove her critics wrong. Grafton says, "My primary lesson, however, was that I'm happy as a solo writer, happiest when I'm making all the executive decisions. I've always been willing to rise or fall on my own merits."

—Liz Mulligan

GRAHAM, James. *See* **HIGGINS, Jack.**

GRAVES, Valerie. *See* **BRADLEY, Marion Zimmer.**

GRAY, Spalding

Nationality: American. **Born:** 5 June 1941 in Providence, Rhode Island. **Education:** Emerson College, B.A., 1965. **Career:** Actor in Cape Cod, Massachusetts, and Saratoga, New York, 1965-67; actor with Alley Theater, Houston, Texas, 1967; actor with Performance Group (experimental theater company), New York, 1967-79; co-founder of Wooster Group (theater company), New York, 1977; performance artist and writer, 1979—. Visiting instructor at University of California, Santa Cruz, summer, 1978, and at Columbia University, 1985; artist in residence at Mark Taper Forum, Los Angeles, 1986-87. **Awards:** Grants from National Endowment for the Arts, 1978, Rockefeller Foundation, 1979, and Edward Albee Foundation, 1985; fellowships from National Endowment for the Arts, 1978, and Rockefeller Foundation, 1979; Guggenheim fellowship, 1985; Obie award from *Village Voice,* 1985, for *Swimming to Cambodia.* **Agent:** Suzanne Gluck, International Creative Management, 40 West 57th St., New York, New York 10019. **Address:** 22 Wooster St., New York, New York 10013, U.S.A.

Publications

Novel

Impossible Vacation. Knopf, 1992.

Short Stories

Seven Scenes from a Family Album. Benzene Press, 1981.

Other

In Search of the Monkey Girl. Aperture, 1982.
Sex and Death to the Age 14. Random House, 1986.
Swimming to Cambodia: The Collected Works of Spalding Gray. Picador, 1987.
Monster in a Box. Vintage, 1992.

*

Theatrical Activities:
Actor/Performer: **Dramatic Monologues**—*Sex and Death to the Age 14,* 1979; *Booze, Cars, and College Girls,* 1979; *India (And*

After), 1979; *A Personal History of the American Theatre,* 1980; *Interviewing the Audience,* 1981; *In Search of the Monkey Girl,* with Randal Levenson, 1981; *Swimming to Cambodia,* 1985; *Travels through New England,* 1986; *Terrors of Pleasure,* 1986; *Rivkala's Ring,* 1986; *Monster in a Box,* 1992. **Films**—*The Killing Fields,* 1983; *True Stories,* 1987; *Stars and Bars,* 1988; *Clara's Heart,* 1988; *Beaches,* 1989.

Media Adaptations: Films—*Swimming to Cambodia,* 1987; *Monster in a Box,* 1992.

* * *

"Stories seem to fly at me and stick," wrote Spalding Gray in a preface to a collection of his work. "They are always out there, coming in. We exist in a fabric of personal stories. All culture, all civilization is an artful web, a human puzzle, a colorful quilt patched together to lay over a raw indifferent nature. So I never wonder whether, if a tree fell in the forest, will anyone hear it. Rather, who will tell about it."

Never at a loss for words and always finding that he possessed a gift for narration, Gray began his career as a successful actor in mainstream American theater before joining Richard Schechner and the influential avant-garde Performance Group in 1970. He left to form the very successful and controversial Wooster Group in 1980. There, he produced *Three Places in Rhode Island* (*Sakhonnet Point* in 1975; *Rumstick Road* in 1977; and *Nyatt School* in 1978), a trilogy based on his autobiography. *Three Places* was produced under the direction of Elizabeth LeCompte in 1979.

Gray has continued to have an acclaimed theatrical career. But it is as a solo performance artist, delivering his series of monologues drawn from his past, that Gray became popular. He developed an art peculiarly his own, writing monologues (part of an ongoing oral history) based upon his life and delivering them to audiences starting in 1978. His work immediately provoked contrasting criticisms: some viewed them as disjointed and incomplete, while others saw in the performances the work of an artist comparable to Woody Allen, Andy Warhol, or even Mark Twain, reinventing the oral tradition, and breaking new ground.

Among Gray's monologues are "Terrors of Pleasure," "Sex and Death to the Age of 14," "Booze," "A Personal History of the American Theater," "Monster in a Box," "Gray's Anatomy," and more. "Swimming to Cambodia," perhaps his most well-known monologue after being made into a film directed by Jonathan Demme in 1987, recounts the filming of David Putnam's *The Killing Fields* in Thailand. His narrative is preoccupied with details and reflects upon the atrocities perpetrated in Cambodia as well as America's unsavory role in southeast Asia's politics. One reviewer wrote, "The clash between personal and political values becomes a hall of mirrors because nothing is ever quite real." Generally regarded as the best example of transferring Gray's monologues to a written text, "Swimming" retains something of the theatrical despite the absence of visual expressions and verbal emphases.

Gray's novel, *Impossible Vacation,* was organized into a travelogue. Gray, recognizing that his vacation trip to Mexico in 1967 coincided with his mother's death, developed a monologue dealing with the classical themes of a boy killing his mother in order to mature into adulthood. *Impossible Vacation* focuses upon the Oedipal fictions and neurotic picaresque adventures of the character Brewster North. The book follows Brewster's inability to "fly the nest" and examines how this interferes with his ability to form intimate friendships. It also relates Brewster's promise to himself to visit Bali and his various adventures in search of a meaningful existence. The adventures incorporate Zen, drugs, theater, sex, pornography, the Bhagwan, India, Amsterdam, the Himalayas, and California. *Impossible Vacation* was panned by many critics as poorly shaped and rambling.

A more recent monologue is "Gray's Anatomy," which tells of a moderately serious eye ailment that convinced him of the need to marry his girlfriend. After a doctor diagnoses a "puckered macula," Gray's hypochondria sends him in search of alternative treatment to surgery. He encounters a variety of quacks and metaphysical therapists before returning to orthodox medicine, marriage, and a successful operation. Although the observation is precise, few literary niceties are observed in this book, largely because of its origin in an oral tradition.

In addition to his novel and monologues, Gray has written *Seven Scenes From a Family Album* (1981), a series of interrelated autobiographical sketches that satirically depict the sexual tensions and complex emotional relationships of a suburban family.

Gray has always been something of a maverick writer, since much of his writing stems from his role as raconteur, which does not easily fit into tight, conventionally shaped fictional narratives. However, he has managed to remain a popular writer, and much of his success is due to his idiosyncratic view of the world. Gray risks boring readers by revelling in solipsistic, self-indulgent, and narcissistic reflections, but manages to produce work that is generally highly entertaining and stimulating.

—Tim Woods

GREELEY, Andrew M(oran)

Nationality: American. **Born:** Oak Park, Illinois, 5 February 1928. **Education:** St. Mary of the Lake Seminary, A.B. 1950, S.T.B. 1952, S.T.L. 1954; University of Chicago, M.A. 1961, Ph.D. 1962. **Career:** Ordained priest, Roman Catholic Church, 1954; assistant pastor, Church of Christ the King, Chicago, 1954-64; program director, National Opinion Research Center, Chicago, 1961-68; lecturer of sociology, 1963-72; director, Center for the Study of American Pluralism, 1973, all University of Chicago; since 1978 professor of sociology, University of Arizona, Tucson. Since 1985 columnist, *Chicago Sun Times.* **Awards:** Catholic Press Association award, 1965; Thomas Alva Edison award, for radio broadcast, 1963; National Catholic Education Association C. Albert Kobb award, 1977. LL.D: St. Joseph's College, Rensselaer, Indiana, 1967; Litt.D. St. Mary's College, Winona, Minnesota, 1967. Address, c/o Warner Books, 666 Fifth Avenue, New York, New York 10103, U.S.A.

Publications

Novels (series: Monsignor John Blackwood Ryan)

Death in April. New York, McGraw Hill, 1980; London, Macdonald, 1987.

The Cardinal Sins. New York, Warner, and London, W.H. Allen, 1981.

Thy Brother's Wife. New York, Warner, and London, W.H. Allen, 1982.
Ascent into Hell. New York, Warner, and London, W.H. Allen, 1983.
Lord of the Dance. New York, Warner, 1984; Bath, Chivers Press, 1985.
Virgin and Martyr: A Christmas Legend. New York, Warner, and London, Macdonald, 1985.
God Game. New York, Walker, and London, Century Hutchinson, 1986.
Happy Are the Meek (Ryan). New York, Warner, 1985; London, Macdonald, 1986.
Happy Are the Clean of Heart (Ryan). New York, Warner, 1986; London, Macdonald, 1987.
Patience of a Saint. New York, Warner, and London, Macdonald, 1987.
The Final Planet. New York, Warner, 1987; London, Century Hutchinson, 1988.
Rite of Spring. New York, Warner, 1987; London, Macdonald, 1988.
Happy Are Those Who Thirst for Justice (Ryan). New York, Mysterious Press, 1987; London, Severn House, 1988.
Angels of September. New York, Warner, and, London, Macdonald, 1986.
Angel Fire. New York, Warner, 1988.
Love Song. New York, Warner, 1989.
The Cardinal Virtues. New York, Warner, 1990.
St. Valentine's Night. New York, Warner Books, 1990.
Happy Are the Merciful (Ryan). New York, Berkley, 1992.
An Occasion of Sin. New York, Berkley, 1992.
The Search for Maggie Ward. New York, Warner Books, 1992.
Fall from Grace. New York, Putnam, 1993.
Happy Are the Peacemakers (Ryan). New York, Berkley, 1993.
Wages of Sin. New York, Berkley, 1993.
Happy Are the Poor in Spirit (Ryan). New York, Berkley, 1994.
Happy Are Those Who Mourn (Ryan). New York, Berkley, 1995.
Angel Light. New York, Forge, 1995.
Summer at the Lake. New York, Forge, 1996.

Short Stories

All about Women. New York, Tor, 1990.

Other

The Church and the Suburbs. New York, Sheed and Ward, 1959; revised edition, New York, Paulist Press, 1963.
Strangers in the House: Catholic Youth in America. New York, Sheed and Ward, 1961; revised edition, New York, Image, 1967.
The Influence of Religion on the Career Plans and Occupational Values of June, 1961 College Graduates. N.p., 1962.
Religion and Career: A Study of College Graduates. New York, Sheed and Ward, 1963.
Priests for Tomorrow. Notre Dame, Indiana, Ave Maria Press, 1964.
And Young Men Shall See Visions: Letters from Andrew M. Greeley. New York, Sheed and Ward, 1964.
Letters to Nancy from Andrew M. Greeley. New York, Sheed and Ward, 1964; revised edition, New York, Image, 1967.
The Social Effects of Catholic Education, with Peter H. Rossi and Leonard J. Pinto. Chicago, National Opinion Research Center, 1964.
The Education of Catholic Americans, with Peter H. Rossi. Chicago, Aldine, 1966.
The Hesitant Pilgrim: American Catholicism After the Council. New York, Sheed and Ward, 1966.
Stratification and Social Conflict in American White Ethnic Groups, with Joe Spaeth. Chicago, National Opinion Research Center, 1967.
The Changing Catholic College, with William Van Cleve and Grace Ann Carroll. Chicago, Aldine, 1967.
The Catholic Experience: An Interpretation of the History of American Catholicism. New York, Doubleday, 1967.
The Crucible of Change: The Social Dynamics of Pastoral Practice. New York, Sheed and Ward, 1968.
Uncertain Trumpet: The Priest in Modern America. New York, Sheed and Ward, 1968.
What Do We Believe?, with Martin E. Marty. New York, Meredith Press, 1968.
The Future of the Christian Church in the 1970s, with Martin E. Marty. Fort George, Maryland, U.S. Army Chaplain Board, 1969.
Religion in the Year 2000. New York, Sheed and Ward, 1969.
Life for a Wanderer. New York, Doubleday, 1969.
A Future to Hope In: Socio-Religious Speculations. New York, Doubleday, 1969.
From Backwater to Mainstream: A Profile of Catholic Higher Education. New York, McGraw Hill, 1969.
Why Can't They Be Like Us?: Facts and Fallacies About Ethnic Differences and Group Conflicts in America. New York, Institute of Human Relations Press, 1969; revised edition as *Why Can't They Be Like Us?: America's White Ethnic Groups*, New York, Dutton, 1971.
Recent Alumni and Higher Education: A Survey of College Graduates, with Joe H. Spaeth. New York, McGraw Hill, 1970.
The Life of the Spirit Mind (also the Heart, the Libido)... Kansas City, Missouri, National Catholic Reporter, 1970.
Can Catholic Schools Survive?. New York, Sheed and Ward, 1970.
Youth Asks, Does God Still Speak? Camden, New Jersey, Nelson, 1970.
New Horizons for the Priesthood. New York, Sheed and Ward, 1970.
The Friendship Game. New York, Doubleday, 1970.
Come Blow Your Mind with Me. New York, Doubleday, 1971.
The Jesus Myth. New York, Doubleday, 1971.
The Touch of the Spirit. New York, Herder, 1971.
Attitudes Towards Racial Integration, with Paul B. Sheatsley. San Francisco, Freeman, 1971.
A Fresh Look at Vocations. Chicago, Claretian, 197(?).
What a Modern Catholic Believes About God. Chicago, Thomas More Press, 1971.
That Most Distressful Nation: The Taming of the American Irish. Chicago, Quadrangle, 1972.
The Denominational Society: A Sociological Approach to Religion in America. Glenview, Illinois, Scott Foresman, 1972.
Priests in the United States: Reflections on a Survey. New York, Doubleday, 1972.
The Sinai Myth. New York, Doubleday, 1972.
The Church, the National Parish and Immigration: Same Old Mistakes. Staten Island, New York, Center for Migration Studies, 1972.
Teenage World: Its Crises and Anxieties. Techny, Illinois, Divine World, n.d.
Unsecular Man: The Persistence of Religion. New York, Schocken, 1972; London, SCM Press, 1973.

What a Modern Catholic Believes About the Church. Chicago, Thomas More Press, 1972.
The New Agenda. New York, Doubleday, 1973.
The Persistence of Religion. New York, Herder, and London, SCM Press, 1973.
Sexual Intimacy. Chicago, Thomas More Press, 1973.
Ecstasy: A Way of Knowing. Englewood Cliffs, New Jersey, Prentice Hall, 1974.
Ethnicity in the United States: A Preliminary Reconnaissance. New York, Wiley, 1974.
Building Coalitions: American Politics of the 1970s. New York, Viewpoint, 1974.
The Devil, You Say!: Man and His Personal Devil and Angels. New York, Doubleday, 1974.
Church as an Institution, with Gregory Baum. New York, Herder, 1974.
Media: Ethnic Media in the United States, with Douglas J. Zeman. Hanover, New Hampshire. Project Impress, 1974.
Love and Play. Chicago, Thomas More Press, 1975.
May the Wind Be at Your Back: The Prayer of St. Patrick. New York, Seabury Press, 1975.
The Sociology of the Paranormal: A Reconnaissance. Beverly Hills, California, Sage, 1975.
The Sinai Myth. New York, Image, 1975.
Ethnicity, Denomination and Inequality. Beverly Hills, California, Sage, 1976.
The Sociology of the Paranormal: A Reconnaissance. Beverly Hills, California, Sage, 1976.
The Ultimate Values of the American Population, with William C. McCready. Beverly Hills, California, Sage, 1976.
Catholic Schools in a Declining Church, with William C. McCready and Kathleen McCourt. Kansas City, Missouri, Sheed and Ward, 1976.
The Communal Catholic: A Personal Manifesto. New York, Seabury Press, 1976.
Death and Beyond. Chicago, Thomas More Press, 1976.
The Great Mysteries: An Essential Catechism. New York, Seabury, 1976.
Nor, Maeve and Sebi (for children; with Diane Dawson). New York, Paulist Press, 1976.
The American Catholic: A Social Portrait. New York, Basic, 1977.
No Bigger Than Necessary: An Alternative to Socialism, Capitalism, and Anarchy. New York, New American Library, and London, New English Library, 1977.
The Mary Myth: On the Femininity of God. New York, Seabury Press, 1977.
Neighborhood. New York, Seabury Press, 1977.
An Ugly Litle Secret: Anti-Catholicism in North America. Kansas City, Missouri, Sheed Andrews and McMeel, 1977.
Christ for All Seasons, with Nancy McCready. Chicago, Thomas More Press, 1977.
Communication in the Church. New York, Seabury Press, 1978.
Everything You Wanted to Know About the Catholic Church but Were Too Pious to Ask. Chicago, Thomas More Press, 1978.
The Making of the Popes 1978: The Politics of Intrigue in the Vatican. Kansas City, Missouri, Andrews and McMeel, and London, Futura, 1979.
Crisis in the Church: A Study of Religion in America. Chicago, Thomas More Press, 1979.
The Family in Crisis or in Transition. New York, Seabury Press, 1979.
The Magic Cup: An Irish Legend. New York, McGraw Hill, 1979; London, Futura, 1984.
Ethnic Drinking Subcultures, with William C. McCready and Gary Theisen. New York, Praeger, 1980.
The Young Catholic Family. Chicago, Thomas More Press, 1980.
The Irish Americans: The Rise to Money and Power. New York, Harper, 1981.
The Religious Imagination. Los Angeles, Sadlier, 1981.
Religion: A Secular Theory. New York, Free Press, and London, Macmillan, 1982.
The Bottom Line Catechism for Contemporary Catholics. Chicago, Thomas More Press, 1982; London, W.H. Allen, 1983.
A Church to Come Home To, with Mary G. Durkin. Chicago, Thomas More Press, 1982.
Catholic High Schools and Minority Students. New Brunswick, New Jersey, Transaction, 1982.
A Piece of My Mind—On Just About Everything. New York, Doubleday, 1983.
Angry Catholic Women, with Mary G. Durkin. Chicago, Thomas More Press, 1984.
How to Save the Catholic Church. New York, Viking, 1984.
American Catholics Since the Council. Chicago, Thomas More Press, 1985.
Confessions of a Parish Priest. New York, Simon and Schuster, 1986.
Catholic Contributions. Chicago, Thomas More Press, 1987.
The Incarnate Imagination. Bowling Green, Ohio, Popular Press, 1988.
When Life Hurts. Chicago, Thomas More Press, 1988.
Conversations with Andrew M. Greeley. Boston, Quinlan Press, 1988.
God in Popular Culture. Chicago, Thomas More Press, 1988.
Religious Change in America. Cambridge, Massachusetts, Harvard University Press, 1989.
Myths of Religion. New York, Warner, 1989.
The Bible and Us: A Priest and a Rabbi Read Scripture Together, with Jacob Neusner. New York, Warner, 1990.
The Catholic Myth: The Behaviour and Beliefs of American Catholics. New York, Scribner, 1990.

* * *

Andrew Greeley is a controversial and forthright Roman Catholic priest, a trained sociologist, and an entertaining storyteller. Influencing Greeley's work is his belief that the American Catholic Church must respond intelligently and compassionately to its great differences from the European Church. He criticizes the Church for an authoritarian stance that drives away Catholics committed to democracy. He also opposes the Church's stance on birth control, divorce, and the ordination of women, and argues that the Church has, for too long, tolerated the abuse of women. Furthermore, he attacks mean-spirited church careerists as power-hungry, anti-intellectual, and "religiously bankrupt," and admits the pervasiveness of child sexual abuse by the clergy.

At the same time, Greeley challenges readers to reconsider "the religious possibilities in their own lives" and to find the Church's splendor despite its obvious faults and even possible irrelevance. Titles like *Everything You Wanted to Know about the Catholic Church but Were Too Pious to Ask* (1978) and *Angry Catholic Women* (1984) convey his balance of humor, seriousness, and frankness. His novels directly address disturbing issues Greeley believes the modern church must face, as well as such sociological concerns as ethnic divisions, the problems of young people, and the decline of education. Greeley considers his novels parables meant to inculcate moral lessons while providing thrilling and romantic mysteries.

Greeley's fiction grows out of his theological, religious, and social concerns, and sometimes fictionalizes topics from his nonfiction. For example, the murder mystery *The Cardinal Sins* (1981) dramatizes the Machiavellian machinations and infighting of papal elections spelled out in *The Making of the Popes 1978: The Politics of Intrigue in the Vatican* (1979). *Fall from Grace* (1993) tackles the subject of pedophilia among priests, while *Virgin and Martyr* (1985) warns against Berrigan-style radical and charismatic movements and the confusion and frustration produced by Vatican II. Similarly, in *Ascent into Hell* (1983) a parish priest battles senile and psychotic superiors committed to religious repression and hierarchical oppression, while in *Lord of the Dance* (1984) jealous fellow priests undermine a successful talk show host (much like Greeley himself). The priest in *Thy Brother's Wife* (1982) is caught up in the controversies embroiling the modern Church. He confronts the essential human questions of his parishioners, and gradually moves from conservative yes-man to crusading believer. The beatitudes from the Sermon on the Mount unify Greeley's mystery series.

Though called a clerical Harold Robbins because of his stands on human sexuality, his sexual counseling, and his encouragement of inventive marital sex, part of Greeley's moral message is that sexuality is a God-given pleasure which an insensitive Church has sought to deny. He accuses the Church of promoting sexual hysteria and sexual perversions, and, in books like *Sexual Intimacy for America* (1973) and *Faithful Attractions: Discovering Intimacy, Love and Fidelity in American Marriages* (1991), he promotes balance, sanity, and frankness about sexual love, which not only nurtures, but reflects the creative and regenerative powers of the deity.

His novels are full of good sex, lustful clerics, and crimes resulting from repression and guilt. In *Happy Are the Clean of Heart* (1986), the jealousy of a talented, successful movie star spawns hatred that erupts into violence. As they struggle to overthrow the passive, submissive roles imposed on them by Church, convention, family and lovers, Greeley's women are finely and sensitively drawn to seize their own destiny, explore their creative and intellectual capacities, and put past degradation, dehumanization, and brutalization behind them. His Catholics find God's love through accepting their humanity and truly loving each other.

Greeley's provocative science fiction explores present realities in new ways. *God Game* (1986), for example, projects a computer-generated world where human players inspire their programmer with love and compassion. Greeley's series detectives, Father Blackie Ryan and "Ace" McNamara, are both witty, charming, reflective workaholics much like Greeley himself. Limited by flesh and ridden with doubts, they grow and change with experience. They admire resilience and sharp-tongued wit, and relate well to troubled teenagers. Ryan serves as priest/confessor, dealing with death and reconciliation. *Happy Are the Meek* (1983) is a locked room puzzle, only the doors Father Ryan unlocks are the secrets of the heart. *Happy Are Those Who Thirst for Justice* (1987) is a family saga of matriarchal dominance.

Set mainly in Chicago, Greeley's fiction delineates the Church-Mafia connections and the corruption, repression, hatred, and intolerance encouraged by Mayor Daley's political machine. It includes unflattering portraits of thinly disguised local church figures, including archbishops. Usually, an influential Chicago Irish family group tainted by its role in the power structure is at the heart of his novels, and his characters must struggle against social environment, family pressure, and personal insecurities to find self-knowledge and forgiveness. *Death in April* (1980), for instance, depicts Daley politics corrupting the grand jury process, while the Chicago of *St. Valentine's Night* (1989) is a war zone of competing underworld drug lords and volatile politics.

—Gina Macdonald

GRIFFIN, W. E. B. *See* **BUTTERWORTH, W. E.**

GRIMES, Martha

Nationality: American. **Born:** Pittsburgh, Pennsylvania. **Education:** University of Maryland, B.A., M.A. **Family:** Divorced; one son. **Career:** English instructor, University of Iowa, Iowa City; assistant professor of English, Frostburg State College, Maryland; professor of English, Montgomery College, Takoma Park, Maryland. Lives in Silver Spring, Maryland. **Awards:** Nero Wolfe award, 1983. **Address:** c/o Little Brown and Company, 34 Beacon Street, Boston, Massachusetts 02108, U.S.A.

Publications

Novels (series: Inspector Richard Jury in all books except *The End of the Pier*)

The Man with a Load of Mischief. Boston, Little Brown, 1981; London, O'Mara, 1990.

The Old Fox Deceiv'd. Boston, Little Brown, 1982; London, O'Mara, 1990.

The Anodyne Necklace. Boston, Little Brown, 1983; London, O'Mara, 1989.

The Dirty Duck. Boston, Little Brown, 1984; London, O'Mara, 1986.

Jerusalem Inn. Boston, Little Brown, 1984; London, O'Mara, 1987.

Help the Poor Struggler. Boston, Little Brown, 1985; London, O'Mara, 1988.

The Deer Leep. Boston, Little Brown, 1985; London, Headline, 1989.

I Am the Only Running Footman. Boston, Little Brown, and London, O'Mara, 1986.

The Five Bells and Bladebone. Boston, Little Brown, 1987; London, O'Mara, 1988.

The Old Silent. Boston, Little Brown, and London, Headline, 1990.

The Old Contemptibles. Boston, Little Brown, and London, Headline, 1991.

The End of the Pier. New York, Knopf, 1992; London, Headline, 1993.
The Horse You Came in On. New York, Knopf, and London, Headline, 1993.
Rainbow's End. New York, Knopf, and London, Headline, 1995.
Hotel Paradise. New York, Knopf, 1996.

Poetry

Send Bygraves. New York, Putnam, 1989.

* * *

The *New York Times* called Martha Grimes "the Dorothy Sayers of the 1980s." Her novels recreate the classic country-house murder mysteries of the 1930s, setting each case in a modern example of a closed community.

The first novel by Grimes, *The Man with a Load of Mischief* (1981), introduces the reader to two detectives. One, Inspector Richard Jury, is a professional policeman. The other, Melrose Plant, is a part-time academic and an aristocrat who has renounced his title. Each man has his own assistant; Jury has the hypochondriac Wiggins and Plant has the irritating Aunt Agatha. Wiggins and Agatha bring light relief into the novels while they stimulate the two detectives to solve the crimes. In the characters of the two detectives, Grimes alludes to Sayers's aristocratic Lord Wimsey and Christie's refined professional Hercule Poirot.

The murders in *The Man with a Load of Mischief* are centered around the pubs in a small countryside hamlet. They are bizarre and resemble the name of the pub where the body is found. In this story Jury and Wiggins are interlopers intruding into a sleepy village in order to reassert normality. Plant is both an insider and an outsider. He is one of the community, yet he stands apart from the rest of the villagers because of his title. This position makes him the ideal source of information for Jury. Together Jury and Plant discover the identity of the murderer, and the equilibrium village life is restored.

The Old Fox Deceived (1982) maintains Plant's position of police aide. Plant is visiting old friends in Yorkshire when a woman who claimed to be the local aristocrat's long lost ward is found stabbed to death. Jury and Wiggins come to investigate after the local police fail to make progress on the case. In the course of his investigation, Jury discovers and solves a much earlier crime, rescues a young boy who has been deserted by his mother, and discovers an unlikely murderer. The novel is a well-constructed and atmospheric mystery. It contains all the elements from the Golden Age of crime writing; a stranger found dead, mistaken identity, deceit, betrayal, and justice. It is a prime example of modern cozy detective fiction.

A different type of community is infiltrated by Plant and Jury in *The Dirty Duck* (1984). The community in danger is a group of American tourists on a trip to Stratford upon Avon. One of the women on the trip is brutally murdered in a style similar to that of Jack the Ripper. At the same time the adopted son of the tour organizer disappears. The one clue deliberately left on each of the victims is a theater program inscribed with a couplet from a poem. Jury and Plant need to identify the poem to find the murderer before the quotation is complete. The investigation spreads to the States.

The American influence is stronger in *The Horse You Came in On* (1993), in which Jury, Wiggins, and Plant cross the Atlantic to solve the murder of a PhD student. Two communities are explored in this case. One is the academic world of the deceased female student. She had found a manuscript, allegedly written by Edgar Allan Poe, that served to elicit all manner of jealousies and in-fighting at the University. The other world is that of a murdered homeless man whose death increases in importance as the case develops. This world is harder to infiltrate, particularly for the wealthy Plant. The connection between the two communities is surprising.

In her novels, Grimes uses Jury and Plant to delve into small, self-contained communities, and puts a modern twist on country house murders. Jury and Plant work together to find the perpetrator and, by meeting out justice, to restore normality to the community. Grimes fulfills the object of a cozy detective writer by setting a problem and solving it in the contemporary world.

—Samantha J. Barber

GRISHAM, John

Nationality: American. **Born:** Jonesboro, Arkansas, 8 February 1955. **Education:** Mississippi State University, B.S. in accounting 1977; University of Mississippi, LL.D in 1981. **Family:** Married Renee Jones; three children. **Career:** Practiced law, Southaven, Mississippi, 1981-91; member Mississippi House of Representatives, 1984-90. **Address:** c/o Doubleday, 666 Fifth Avenue, New York, New York 10103, U.S.A.

Publications

Novels

A Time to Kill. New York, Wynwood Press, 1989; London, Century, 1993.
The Firm. New York, Doubleday, and London, Century, 1991.
The Pelican Brief. New York, Doubleday, and London, Century, 1992.
The Client. New York, Doubleday, and London, Century, 1993.
The Chamber. New York, Doubleday, and London, Century, 1994.
The Rainmaker. New York, Doubleday, and London, Century, 1995.
The Runaway Jury. New York, Doubleday, and London, Century, 1996.

*

Film Adaptations: *The Firm,* 1993; *The Pelican Brief,* 1993; *The Client,* 1994; *A Time to Kill,* 1996.

* * *

Since publishing his first novel in 1989, John Grisham has established himself as one of the top novelists of the late 20th century. In fact, it was Grisham's second novel, *The Firm* (1991), that launched his rise to stardom. In *The Firm,* a brilliant Harvard Law School graduate named Mitch McDeere accepts a job with a Memphis-based law firm, where he discovers mystery, deceit, and murder. The novel is truly worthy of the oft-used critical phrases "gripping" and "compelling," as evidenced by its long-time status as a *New York Times* bestseller. Grisham keenly keeps the reader one jump ahead of the main character, but a few steps behind the generally unpredictable plot that gradually engulfs him. *The Firm* showcases Grisham's talent for quickly developing intriguing, though uncomplicated, characters—both heroes and villains—to which the reader can relate, and for spinning a fast-unfolding, exciting tale. Those skills compensate for what Bill Brashler, in his review in the *Chicago Tribune,* refers to as a "delicious diet of coincidence" that dilutes the novel's believability.

The stupendous success of *The Firm* sparked interest in Grisham's first novel, *A Time to Kill* (1989), which was soon acclaimed by critics as exciting and thought-provoking. In the novel, Grisham delves into the uncomfortable relationship between whites and blacks in the rural south: a black man is brought to trial for the murder of two white men that raped and tortured his young daughter. Noted for deeper character development, the book provides insight into Mississippi's backwoods culture. The usually sober Grisham even interjects some humor into the dialogue of the salty, down-to-earth characters.

Grisham followed *The Firm* with the best-selling *Pelican Brief* (1992), an explosive, sometimes seamy thriller that involves the White House, the Supreme Court, and a second-year Tulane University law student named Darby Shaw. Shaw's escape from evil mimics that of McDeere's in *The Firm. The Pelican Brief* sustains Grisham's progression from more thoughtful prose and character development in *A Time to Kill* to a more popular, bigger-than-life style designed to wow the reader. Indeed, *The Pelican Brief* captivates with a less believable tale replete with an evil presidential aide and a lunatic billionaire who the reader is asked to believe controls a sort of army of private assassins.

Grisham's move toward the fantastic continues with *The Client* (1993), his fourth novel and smash hit. An 11-year-old boy, Mark Sway, witnesses a suicide that ties him to a case involving the murder of a U.S. Senator. In the course of the story, the boy convinces his lawyer to help him escape from federal detention, scares off a group of Mafia thugs, evades the FBI, and arranges a deal to enter the government witness protection program. Praised as a "fun read," *The Client* can be criticized, perhaps more than Grisham's previous novels, as farfetched and simplistic, but also, in this case, predictable and anticlimactic.

Critical reception was more positive for *The Chamber* (1994). Its plot is centered around the trial of an elderly Ku Klux Klan member in Mississippi who has been sentenced to death for firebombing the office of a Jewish attorney. Commendable is Grisham's use of complex legal details and exploration of controversial issues such as racism and vigilantism.

Grisham excels at the basic task of captivating his readers. Much of his success, though, can be attributed to his ability to weave into his novels parts of his past that make his sensational plots seem more believable. He grew up in the southern United States, earned his law degree at the University of Mississippi, worked as a defense attorney, and was elected to the Mississippi House of Representatives. Elements of the legal profession and the southern lifestyle form the foundation upon which he builds the plot in his books.

Most criticism of Grisham's work centers around shallow character development and simplistic plots. Grisham isn't swayed by such commentary: "I write to grab readers. This isn't serious literature," he has said.

—Dave Mote

GRIZZARD, Lewis (M., Jr.)

Nationality: American. **Born:** 20 October 1946, in Columbus, Georgia. **Education:** University of Georgia, A.B.J., 1967. **Family:** Married, 1966 (divorced, 1969); married Fay Rentz (divorced, 1976); married Kathy Taulman, 1979 (divorced, 1982); married Dedra Kyle, 1994. **Career:** Atlanta *Journal,* 1968-70s, began as sportswriter, became executive sports editor; worked as free-lance writer, staff member of Atlanta *Constitution,* and sports editor of Chicago *Sun-Times,* Chicago, in the 1970s; columnist for Atlanta *Constitution* and Atlanta *Journal,* 1979-94. Commentator for WSB-TV, 1980; owner of Grizzard Enterprises, Atlanta, 1980-94. Lecturer; actor in television programs. **Died:** 20 March 1994, in Atlanta, of brain damage resulting from heart surgery.

Publications

Humorous Essays and Nonfiction

Kathy Sue Loudermilk, I Love You. Peachtree Publishers, 1979.
Won't You Come Home, Billy Bob Bailey? Peachtree Publishers, 1980.
Don't Sit under the Grits Tree with Anyone Else but Me. Peachtree Publishers, 1981.
Glory! Glory! Georgia's 1980 Championship Season: The Inside Story, with Loran Smith. Peachtree Publishers, 1981.
They Tore out My Heart and Stomped That Sucker Flat. Peachtree Publishers, 1982.
If Love Were Oil, I'd Be about a Quart Low: Lewis Grizzard on Women. Peachtree Publishers, 1983.
Elvis Is Dead and I Don't Feel So Good Myself. Peachtree Publishers, 1984.
Shoot Low, Boys—They're Ridin' Shetland Ponies: In Search of True Grit. Peachtree Publishers, 1985.
My Daddy Was a Pistol and I'm a Son of a Gun. Villard Books, 1986.
When My Love Returns from the Ladies Room, Will I Be Too Old to Care? Villard Books, 1987.
Don't Bend over in the Garden, Granny, You Know Them Taters Got Eyes. Villard Books, 1988.
Lewis Grizzard on Fear of Flying: Avoid Pouting Pilots and Mechanics Named Bubba. Longstreet Press, 1989.
Lewis Grizzard's Advice to the Newly Wed ... and the Newly Divorced. Longstreet Press, 1989.
Getting It On: A Down-Home Treasury. Galahad Books, 1989.
Chili Dawgs Always Bark at Night. Villard Books, 1989.
If I Ever Get Back to Georgia, I'm Gonna Nail My Feet to the Ground. Random House, 1990.
Does a Wild Bear Chip in the Woods? Lewis Grizzard on Golf. Longstreet Press, 1990.
You Can't Put No Boogie-Woogie on the King of Rock and Roll. Random House, 1991.
Heapin' Helping of True Grizzard: Down Home Again with Lewis Grizzard. Galahad Books, 1991.
Don't Forget to Call Your Mama—I Wish I Could Call Mine. Longstreet Press, 1991.
Pushing Fifty Is Exercise Enough. Random House, 1993.
I Took a Lickin' and Kept on Tickin': And Now I Believe in Miracles. Random House, 1993.

I Haven't Understood Anything since 1962: And Other Nekkid Truths. Ballantine, 1993.
The Last Bus to Albuquerque: A Commemorative Edition Celebrating Lewis Grizzard. Longstreet Press, 1994.
It Wasn't Always Easy, But I Sure Had Fun: The Best of Lewis Grizzard. Random House, 1994.

* * *

Lewis Grizzard's death in 1994 ended a 26-year career ranging from sportswriter to commentator to actor. He is best remembered, though, for his humorous nonfiction writings. Grizzard has written over 20 books, and his syndicated column appeared in approximately 450 newspapers across the nation. "There's been a Grizzard title in the Upfront section of *Booklist* every year since 1989, a testament to his enduring appeal. . . ." (*Booklist,* 15 September 1994).

Grizzard was accused at different times of being homophobic, racist, sexist, and xenophobic. He described himself as "a quintessential southern male," and took pride in being politically incorrect. Despite those negative labels, Grizzard continued to write with honesty and humor about the things that were important to him.

Grizzard had the incredible ability to make the reader laugh out loud one minute and cry the next. He was obviously a man who loved humor but had a truly sentimental side as well. Whether readers agreed with his opinions or not, they generally respected his talent and unwavering commitment to his opinions.

Written in a comfortable first-person style that uses southern dialect, Grizzard's essays cover topics ranging from sex, food, and music to his relationship with his alcoholic father, and his open heart surgery at age 35. *They Tore Out My Heart And Stomped That Sucker Flat* (1982) tells the life story of his heart from childhood to the day of his surgery. Many heart surgeons have recommended this book to their patients to encourage a positive attitude about heart surgery. Sadness about losses, divorce, regret over past mistakes, and hope for a better life are all discussed in an upbeat manner that wins over even the most critical readers.

My Daddy Was a Pistol and I'm a Son of a Gun (1986) is a memoir of Grizzard's father who died at the age of 56. After fighting in two wars, his father returned home to a world to which he could not adjust. After becoming an alcoholic and divorcing Grizzard's mother, Grizzard's father saw his son only occasionally for the remainder of his life. Despite the hardships in the relationship, Grizzard's book displays love, respect, and honor for the man that was his father. Described as "a heartfelt and hardfelt look at unconditional love," by the *Chicago Tribune,* it is generally considered Grizzard's best effort.

Grizzard penned *I Took a Lickin' and Kept On Tickin', and Now I Believe In Miracles* after his third open-heart surgery. His near-death experience during that time prompted him to put his insights into a book. The work details his diagnosis, surgery, and the miraculous recovery that followed. Though a very serious subject, the story is filled with humorous insights on nurses, doctors, hospitals, and himself. Grizzard shows how to see the positive side in a desperate situation with faith, love, and humor.

—Amy Faulkenberry

GURGANUS, Allan

Nationality: American. **Born:** Rocky Mount, North Carolina, 11 June 1947. **Education:** Rocky Mount Senior High, 1965; Philadelphia Academy of Fine Arts, 1965-66; Sarah Lawrence College, Bronxville, New York, 1970-72. **Military Service:** United States Navy, 1966-70. **Career:** Desk clerk and salesperson of art reproductions, 1969-70; night watchman in a vitamin factory, 1970-72; professor of fiction writing, University of Iowa, Iowa City, 1972-74, Stanford University, Stanford, California, 1974-76, Duke University, Durham, North Carolina, 1976-78, Sarah Lawrence College, Bronxville, New York, 1978-86, and University of Iowa Writers' Workshop, 1989-90. Artist, with paintings in many private and public collections. Member of board, Corporation of Yaddo; cofounder, "Writers for Harvey Gantt." **Awards:** Jones lecturer, Stanford University; PEN prizes for fiction; National Endowment for the Arts grants; Ingram Merrill award; Wallace Stegner fellowship. **Agent:** c/o International Creative Management, 40 West 57th Street, New York, New York 10019, U.S.A.

Publications

Novel

Oldest Living Confederate Widow Tells All. New York, Knopf, and London, Faber, 1989.

Short Stories

Good Help, with illustrations by the author. Rocky Mount, North Carolina Wesleyan College Press, 1988.
Blessed Assurance: A Moral Tale (novella). Rocky Mount, North Carolina Wesleyan College Press, 1990.
White People: Stories and Novellas. New York, Knopf, and London, Faber, 1991.
The Practical Heart. Rocky Mount, North Carolina Wesleyan College Press, 1993.

*

Critical Study: "Black and Blue and Gray: An Interview with Allan Gurganus" by Jeffrey Scheuer, in *Poets and Wrtiers,* November-December 1990.

* * *

The structure of Allan Gurganus's novel, *Oldest Living Confederate Widow Tells All* (1989), is an ambitious one. Lucy Marsden, who married her Civil-War-veteran husband when she was 15 years old, reflects on their lives together from a nursing home bed as she approaches her 100th birthday. But in telling her stories, she tells the stories of others; male and female, black and white, rich and poor. The degree of success Gurganus has with the female narrator is evidence of his own imaginative storytelling skills. The author says that he chose a female narrator in order to produce a new vision of history, that of a woman who was neither rich nor beautiful. In the book, history is made both personal and feminine through her. But at its core, this novel is simply a darn good tale made so by the weaving together of many stories.

That they are often tales "belonging" to other characters and outside Lucy's experiential realm proved controversial at the time of the novel's publication. Some critics found the result cumbersome and improbable. How could Lucy know the ex-slave Castalia's detailed thoughts and dreams of Africa? Why not have Castalia tell her own story? How can the male Gurganus be a credible creator of female experiences? The author defends himself against such accusations by defending creative imagination: "To think that one can write [or narrate] only out of personal experience assumes that literature is a series of statements made out of assurances, rather than a series of questions made out of a need to know."

Oldest Living Confederate Widow Tells All lets us see the connections inherent in all human experiences and the constants we seek as balance in life. For example, there are two such constants that Lucy never abandons: the pot of water on her stove that provides a soothing steam in her otherwise chaotic domestic domain, and her sense of humor. For as poignant as the themes Gurganus deals with can be, in much of his work there is humor.

For example, in *White People* (1991), a collection of stories and novellas, his sense of humor is most farcical and southern in "Nativity, Caucasian," a story about a birth during a bridge party where an antique damask table cloth is graciously sacrificed by the hostess. At the opposite end of the collection, readers are treated to "Blessed Assurance," a story narrated by an aging, white, middle-class man who had sold life insurance to blacks to earn money for college. He has carried the confusion and shame of what he learned about race relations with him for 59 years. It is a powerful tale of regret and hope, sprinkled with wit. In between these two tones lie stories that delineate many of the themes woven into *Oldest Living Confederate Widow Tells All.* Even homosexual issues are addressed briefly in such stories as "Minor Heroism," "Art History," and "Adult Art."

The most prominent aspect of Gurganus's work may be his ability to mimic the voices of so many different people, from elderly women, black women, and ex-debutantes to old men and young boys. The verisimilitude of his characters is often startling.

Gurganus was a friend of John Cheever. The relationship seems to have contributed to his eye for details and his ability to choose just the right balance between specific noted and nuance given. His stories are successful on more than one level; they are at once entertaining and literary, moving and whimsical, hilarious and honorable.

—Maggi R. Sullivan

H

HAILEY, Arthur

Nationality: Canadian. **Born:** Bedfordshire, England, 5 April 1920; emigrated to Canada in 1947: became citizen, 1952. **Education:** Elementary schools in England. **Military Service:** Served as a pilot in the Royal Air Force, 1939-47: Flight Lieutenant. **Family:** Married 1) Joan Fishwick in 1944 (divorced 1950), three sons; 2) Sheila Dunlop in 1951, one son and two daughters. **Career:** Office boy and clerk, London, 1934-39; assistant editor, 1947-49, and editor, 1949-53, *Bus and Truck Transport,* Toronto; sales promotion manager, Trailmobile Canada, Toronto, 1953-56. Since 1956 freelance writer. **Awards:** Canadian Council of Authors and Artists award, 1956; Best Canadian TV Playwright award, 1957, 1958; Doubleday Prize Novel award, 1962. **Address:** Lyford Cay, P.O. Box N. 7776, Nassau, Bahamas.

Publications

Novels

Flight into Danger, with John Castle. London, Souvenir Press, 1958; as *Runway Zero-Eight,* New York, Doubleday, 1959.

The Final Diagnosis. New York, Doubleday, 1959; London, Joseph-Souvenir Press, 1960; as *The Young Doctors,* London, Corgi, 1962.

In High Places. New York, Doubleday, and London, Joseph-Souvenir Press, 1962.

Hotel. New York, Doubleday, and London, Joseph-Souvenir Press, 1965.

Airport. New York, Doubleday, and London, Joseph-Souvenir Press, 1968.

Wheels. New York, Doubleday, and London, Joseph-Souvenir Press, 1971.

The Moneychangers. New York, Doubleday, and London, Joseph-Souvenir Press, 1975.

Overload. New York, Doubleday, and London, Joseph-Souvenir Press, 1979.

Strong Medicine. New York, Doubleday, and London Joseph-Souvenir Press, 1984.

The Evening News. New York, Doubleday, and London, Doubleday-Souvenir Press, 1990.

Plays

Flight into Danger (televised 1956). Published in *Four Plays of Our Time,* London, Macmillan, 1960.

Close-up on Writing for Television. New York, Doubleday, 1960.

Screenplays: *Zero Hour,* with Hall Bartlett and John Champion, 1958; *The Moneychangers,* 1976; *Wheels,* 1978.

Television Plays: *Flight into Danger,* 1956 (USA); *Time Lock* 1962 (UK); *Course for Collision,* 1962 (UK); and plays for *Westinghouse Studio One, Playhouse 90, U.S. Steel Hour, Goodyear-Philco Playhouse,* and *Kraft Theatre* (USA).

* * *

Best-known for his much-spoofed but wildly popular novel *Airport* (1968), Canadian Arthur Hailey was an originator of one of the most successful formulas ever devised for tapping the huge bestseller market. Combining heavily researched portraits of contemporary institutions (airports, hospitals, banks, hotels) with a dizzying variety of characters and subplots and enough violence and sex to keep the whole concoction rolling, Hailey was an early master of the plot-driven, now-a-major-motion-picture action novel.

Hailey's first two novels were based on scripts from his early days as a successful screenwriter for live television theater broadcasts. *Runway Zero Eight* (1958), though actually written by John Castle, was based on Hailey's story of a former fighter pilot (like himself) who safely lands a commercial airliner after its flight crew is felled by food poisoning. In *The Final Diagnosis* (1959), Hailey dramatized the conflict between an aging pathologist whose inability to keep pace with medical advances has led to a patient's death and a young doctor who realizes he must somehow convince his senior colleague to step down.

In Hailey's first original novel, *In High Places* (1962), he depicted an international crisis in which Canada can avert nuclear war with the Soviet Union only by brokering a union with the United States. Hailey's hero, Canadian prime minister James Howden, balances personal political scandals and a national controversy surrounding an illegal immigrant. The action builds to a climactic parliamentary vote on the U.S.-Canada union. *Hotel* (1965) represented Hailey's first attempt to write the slice-of-life "institutional" novel that would become his trademark. Focusing on the behind-the-scenes workings of an elegant but aging New Orleans hotel during a single week in 1964, Hailey dramatizes assistant general manager Peter McDermott's attempts to resolve a number of in-house crises—from attempted rape and racial conflict to burglary—while the old world hotel confronts the threat of new ownership.

It was in *Airport* (1968), however, that Hailey developed his "documentary novel" approach into its most successful and perhaps most effective expression. Made into a popular film in 1970, the novel's action centers on big-city airport manager Mel Bakersfield's efforts to juggle a mammoth snowstorm, a suicidal air traffic controller, a group of local noise-pollution protesters, and an inbound jetliner carrying a bomb-toting terrorist and a romantically preoccupied flight crew. Although *Library Journal* found Airport to be a "vividly portrayed" snapshot of the "excitement and intensity" of a large airport, many reviewers viewed the bestselling novel as an uninspired manipulation. *Time* described it as an "obvious but well-programmed novel," and the *New York Times* dismissed Hailey as a "plodding sort of writer."

In *Wheels* (1971), Hailey focused on a major Detroit car company's attempt to develop, produce, and market a new line of cars whose success or failure will determine the future course of U.S. auto manufacturing. Through the experiences of a company director, a car designer, an African-American executive, a foreman, and a union leader, among other characters, Hailey presented a kaleidoscopic portrait of the workings of a major U.S. industry while dramatizing such issues as racism, corruption, and gambling.

Hailey next attempted to encapsulate the U.S. banking industry in *The Moneychangers* (1975), the story of the struggle for control of a Cleveland bank by a bottom-line-obsessed vice-president and his socially responsible rival. In the course of the novel, Hailey shows the novel's main protagonist, the First Mercantile American Bank, surviving corruption, corporate infighting, currency counterfeiting, and the collapse of a financial empire in a work that amounted to a primer on the stock market, trust funds, electronic funds transfer, and a host of other financial intricacies.

The fertility of his formula evidently on the wane, Hailey published *Overload* in 1979, an account of the conflict between a conservative California utility company executive and his two opponents, a social activist and a scientist concerned with the safety of nuclear power. Although Hailey had announced his intention to retire after *Overload,* a heart operation spurred him to write *Strong Medicine* (1984), a novel about the U.S. pharmaceuticals industry and the social ramifications of a drug that simultaneously cures obesity and enhances the human sex drive. In his most recent work, *The Evening News* (1990), Hailey gave his full-dress "information novel" treatment to the television news industry, telling the story of news anchor Crawford Stone's rescue of his family from Peruvian terrorists.

Throughout his career, critics have consistently praised Hailey for his ability to research and dramatize microcosms of American life that give his readers precisely the right mix of realism, plot twists, violent action, and suspenseful denouements. Hailey, however, has also been consistently faulted for creating cardboard characters and formulaic plots and for failing to probe meaningfully the social and moral issues that lurk beneath the industries and institutions he portrays.

—Paul S. Bodine

HALEY, Alex

Nationality: American. **Born:** 11 August 1921, in Ithaca, New York. **Education:** Alcorn Agricultural & Mechanical College (now Alcorn State University); Elizabeth City Teachers College, 1937-39. **Family:** Married 1) Nannie Branch, 1941 (divorced, 1964); 2) Juliette Collins, 1964 (divorced); children: (first marriage) Lydia Ann, William Alexander; (second marriage) Cynthia Gertrude. **Career:** U.S. Coast Guard, 1939-59, retiring as chief journalist; freelance writer, 1959-92. Founder and president of Kinte Corporation, Los Angeles, 1972-92. Board member of New College of California, 1974; member of King Hassan's Royal Academy. Adviser to African American Heritage Association, Detroit. **Awards:** Litt.D. from Simpson College, 1971, Howard University, 1974, Williams College, 1975, and Capitol University, 1975; honorary doctorate from Seton Hall University, 1974; special citation from National Book award committee, 1977, for *Roots;* special citation from Pulitzer Prize committee, 1977, for *Roots;* Spingarn Medal from NAACP, 1977; nominated to Black Filmmakers Hall of Fame, 1981, for producing *Palmerstown, U.S.A.,* 1981. **Died:** 10 February 1992, in Seattle, Washington, of cardiac arrest.

Publications

Novels

Roots: The Saga of an American Family. Doubleday, 1976.
A Different Kind of Christmas. Doubleday, 1988.
Queen. Morrow, 1993.

Other

The Autobiography of Malcolm X, with Malcolm X. Grove, 1965.

*

Media Adaptations: Television miniseries—*Roots,* 1977, and *Roots: The Next Generations,* 1979; *Malcolm X,* 1992, adapted from *The Autobiography of Malcolm X.*

* * *

Alex Haley's writing career began in the 1960s with The *Autobiography of Malcolm X* (1965). Malcolm, controversial spokesman for the Nation of Islam (Black Muslim) movement, was suspicious of Haley when the two first met, but gradually they became trusting friends. From conversations with Malcolm, Haley builds a compelling account of the black activist's life in his own words, taking in Malcolm's experience of white racism, criminal past as "Detroit Red," and conversion to the Muslim faith. While Haley was writing the book, Malcolm broke with the Nation of Islam and became a target for murderous attacks. His belief that he would not live to see the book proved correct: he was shot dead shortly before it went to press. A powerful, moving work, *Autobiography of Malcolm X* hit the streets to popular acclaim and critical praise, and was later given movie treatment by Spike Lee.

Haley topped this achievement 13 years later with *Roots* (1976), an epic novel tracing his mother's ancestors back to their African beginnings. The book involved him in 12 years of research and a visit to Gambia. *Roots* begins with the story of Kunta Kinte, whose early life is described in detail for the first quarter of the book. Haley shows the advanced spiritual and family-centered African culture and the destructive effect of slavery on its people. Kunta Kinte's capture by slave raiders, his sufferings on the dreaded "Middle Passage," and his life as a plantation slave in Virginia make for harrowing reading. Haley reveals the cruelty of a system that treats men and women like animals, destroying their culture, beliefs, and languages. Kunta's attempts to escape, brutal punishment, and fearless endurance are unforgettably described.

The story continues with his daughter Kizzy, her son the gamecock breeder "Chicken" George, and his son Tom, who carries on the African iron-working tradition as a blacksmith. A massive, stunning novel, *Roots* spans four generations and nearly 200 years, bringing real people and events alive on the page. Its tale of suffering and courage as well as the horrors of racism and slavery are a timely answer to the cozy myths of *Gone with the Wind. Roots* proved a runaway bestseller with 1.5 million hardcover and four million paperback books sold. When it was televised it became the most watched television miniseries ever. It also won Haley the Pulitzer Prize.

A Different Kind of Christmas (1988) is a short novella set in the United States prior to the Civil War. The leading character is young Fletcher Randall, the son of slaveholding Southern parents, who meets a family of Quaker abolitionists while studying at Princeton. Haley gives a true-to-life picture of a young, aggressive man determined to defend the practice of slavery but slowly realizing that it is wrong. Convinced, he returns home and, as an agent of the "Underground Railroad," works with the black slave Harpin' John to spirit a group of slaves to freedom. Not a blockbuster, *A Different Kind of Christmas* shows another side to Haley's talents.

With *Queen* (1993), Haley set out to tell the story of his father's side of the family, tracing them back as he had done his mother's people in *Roots.* Sadly, Haley didn't live to see it finished. The book appeared in 1993, a year after his death (Haley wrote it with the help of David Stevens, who completed the last stages). Like *Roots, Queen* is a huge, epic novel that follows the Irish emigrant James Jackson to success as a merchant in the States. He traces the affair of his son Jass with the slave-girl Easter and the birth of their daughter Queen, from whom the Haley family is descended. Haley once more describes plantation slavery, but also touches on the Cherokee exodus on the "Trail of Tears" and the racism of the Ku Klux Klan. Queen falls short of *Roots*' achievement, but is a strong and thoughtful work in its own right.

With *The Autobiography of Malcolm X* Haley paid tribute to a great black American. In it, and in *Roots,* he celebrates the courage and endurance of African Americans, leaving his countrymen with a positive image of themselves. Judged solely on these two books, his achievement is surely secure.

—Geoff Sadler

HANNON, Ezra. *See* **McBAIN, Ed.**

HARRIS, Thomas

Nationality: American. **Born:** 1940 in Jackson, Mississippi. **Education:** Baylor University, B.A., 1964. **Family:** Has a daughter, Anne. **Career:** Worked as a reporter for the Waco *News-Tribune; Associated Press,* New York City, general assignment reporter and night editor, 1968-74; full-time writer since 1968. **Address:** c/o St. Martin's Press, 175 Fifth Ave., New York, New York 10010, U.S.A.

Publications

Novels

Black Sunday. Putnam, 1975.
Red Dragon. Putnam, 1981.
Silence of the Lambs. St. Martin's, 1988.

*

Film Adaptations: *Black Sunday,* 1977; *Manhunter,* adapted from his novel *Red Dragon,* 1986; *Silence of the Lambs,* 1991.

* * *

Crime-reporter turned novelist, Thomas Harris is perhaps most widely known for the Oscar-winning Jonathan Demme film based on his novel *The Silence of the Lambs* (1988). Harris, however, needs no help from Hollywood to attract an audience; each of his three novels quickly became national bestsellers. All are crime-thrillers: fast-paced, intricately plotted, suspense-charged narratives fuelled by the urgency of a countdown to catastrophe. While *Black Sunday* (1975) operates in the arena of international politics and terrorism, the terrain explored by *Red Dragon* (1981) and *The Silence of the Lambs* is much more intimate. Here, Harris maps the inner landscapes of both detective and criminal, an investigation that suggests some disconcerting correspondences. It is in this area—the realm of human psychology—that Harris works at his chilling best.

Black Sunday establishes some key components of Harris's subsequent work in its examination of the links between violence and madness. A conventional thriller, the novel pits Black September, a Palestinian guerilla group planning a Superbowl massacre, against David Kabakov, a wildcard major in the Israeli Secret Service dispatched to aid an incredulous American government. What distinguishes *Black Sunday* is Harris's imaginative introduction of the terrorists' doomsday weapon (an explosive-laden television blimp), and his careful characterization of the insane Vietnam veteran who pilots it. Indeed, much of the novel's interest lies in the delicate relationship established between the Black September operative and this haunted, volatile madman on whom the success or failure of their mission depends.

Harris's obvious interest in exploring psychological depths is given full fictional rein in his second novel, *Red Dragon.* Trading terrorism for spine-tingling horror, Harris presents the nightmarish exploits of Francis Dolarhyde, a serial killer convinced that the massacre of whole families will aid his transformation into the godlike Red Dragon of the Apocalypse. Intent on catching him before he can repeat his gruesome monthly ritual is Will Graham, an FBI agent with a special aptitude in the area of imaginative projection. This ability enabled him to capture Doctor Hannibal Lecter, a psychiatrist who killed and ate his patients. And it is the psychopathic Lecter to whom Will applies for help in solving the case, a visit that also allows him to regain the mindset required to track the killer. Meticulous in its forensic accuracy and terrifying in its detailed unfolding of the origins of Dolarhyde's obsession, *Red Dragon* is more disturbing in its emphasis on duality and the fine line between sanity and insanity. Harris gives the traditional detective-versus-criminal relationship a subtle edge by establishing an unnerving identification between investigator and psychopathic serial killer. Projecting himself into the mind of a madman, Graham is forced to acknowledge his own heart of darkness. Thus, Lecter's words echo throughout Graham's investigation of Red Dragon, Lecter's symbolic protégé: "The reason you caught me is that we're *just alike.*"

Lecter returns to play a major role in *The Silence of the Lambs,* where his insight is sought by Clarice Starling, an FBI agent in pursuit of a serial killer. Like *Red Dragon,* the novel grips the reader with its psychological intensity and its elegant manipulation of suspense, building to a shattering climax. With serial-killer Jame Gumb, Harris creates an even more macabre madman than Francis Dolarhyde. Gumb too is obsessed with metamorphosis, flaying his victims in order to make himself "a girl suit out of real girls." Again, Harris presents an intimate portrait of derangement. Lecter brings to the novel an added psychoanalytic dimension. Feeding on pain and suffering, he refuses to cooperate with Starling unless she provides him with her formative primal scene: the haunting screams of lambs to the slaughter. His analysis accurately pinpoints Starling's investment in the case, and the empathetic link with Gumb's sacrificial victims that allows her to solve it. As with Will Graham, the self-recognition that Lecter promotes is disconcertingly enabling.

Starling represents something of an anomaly among the heroines of detective fiction because she is intelligent, competent, and highly likable. Nevertheless, it is Hannibal Lecter who has become immortalized in the popular imagination as the hero of Harris's novels. What sets Harris's work apart from most run-of-the-mill crime-thrillers is his exploration of the motivations behind criminal madness. His killers are human monsters whose psychoses can be mapped, but the brilliant Lecter remains frighteningly inexplicable. As a psychiatrist, Lecter is able to accurately plumb the inner depths of those he encounters, but he himself remains ultimately unreadable. What makes Lecter so chilling is his insistence on both detective and reader's confrontation with their own inner demons. Perhaps public fascination with Lecter is the fascination we feel with all serial killers, the attraction of the monster that we could become. Thus, it is fitting that Harris gives Lecter the final word in *The Silence of the Lambs*: "Some of our stars are the same, Clarice."

—Jackie Buxton

HARRISON, Chip. *See* **BLOCK, Lawrence.**

HART, Josephine

Nationality: Irish. **Born:** c. 1942, in Mullingar, Ireland. **Education:** Attended Guildhall School of Music and Drama. **Family:** Married 1) Paul Buckley, 1972 (divorced, 1983); 2) Maurice Saatchi; children: (first marriage) Adam, (second marriage) Edward. **Career:** Haymarket Publications, London, England, started in sales, became publishing director; theater producer; writer. **Agent:** Ed Victor, Ed Victor, Inc., 9255 Sunset Blvd., Suite 301, Los Angeles, California 90069, U.S.A.

PUBLICATIONS

Novels

Damage. Knopf, 1991.
Sin. Knopf, 1992.
Oblivion. Viking, 1995.

*

Film Adaptation: *Damage*, 1992.

* * *

Josephine Hart burst onto the literary scene in 1991 with her novel *Damage*. The book achieved the rare blend of critical admiration and commercial success, receiving favorable reviews and making the *New York Times* bestseller list. "I'd always wanted to write," she told *People* magazine. "For years I paced around composing novels in my head. Everything was there; I just couldn't crash through the brick wall in front of me." Finally, at age 49, the one-time publishing director and theater producer broke through with spectacular success.

Damage is a brief, stylish novel of obsession. In the beginning, we enter an atmosphere of upper-class British civility. The unnamed narrator, a middle-aged man, has the perfect life going for him; he's a wealthy doctor and a member of Parliament, with a lovely wife and two wonderful children. But everything changes when he encounters a magnetic, mysterious woman at a party. The meeting "opens the door to a secret vault." To complicate things, the woman is his son's fiancee, and the narrator can't control his attraction to her. Soon, intense physical relations begin with the unusual, complex woman. "All damaged people are dangerous," she tells him, ". . . because they have no pity. They know that others can survive, as they did." Their liaison sets into motion a life-shattering sequence of events, and the narrator sees himself "falling through layers of power and success, through the membranes of decency and ordinariness into a labyrinth of horror." Rhoda Koenig sums it up nicely: "The result is a climax that is somewhat operatic. . . , but its heartbreaking, confused consequences are real enough."

What makes *Damage* such an affecting novel is the way in which the author's crisp, detached style contrasts with the large themes and major events that are involved. Some reviewers think that Hart's dialogue and scenes are be almost too dramatic to be believable at times, but as Richard Eder wrote in the *Los Angeles Times*, the melodrama is "part of the excitement; it disorients us and leaves us more open to the suspense of her tale . . . she has managed to create a portrait of psychological and erotic obsession that is so compelling as, for a brief moment, to suck all the oxygen out of our air and leave us half-silly."

Hart followed up her stunning debut with another book with a one-word title, *Sin*, in 1992. In Hart's characteristic style, this book explores the sin of envy. The narrator, Ruth, is madly jealous of her cousin Elizabeth, who as an orphan was adopted by Ruth's parents. The gentle Elizabeth becomes a cherished member of the household. From the beginning, Ruth states her life's jealousy: "I came wrapped in a caul of darkness and anger into Elizabeth's kingdom." Ruth's hatred for the innocent and kind Elizabeth grows, and she plots ways to destroy her life. Ruth's envy leads her to actions which have devastating effects on all of the characters in the story.

Critical reception of *Sin* wasn't quite as exuberant as it was for *Damage*. Most critics wondered if the intensity of Ruth's envy was understandable, and argued that the dramatic language and events may have lost some of their power because of this. However, as Dean James wrote in *Library Journal*, "*Sin* remains a disturbing, provocative work, sure to be eagerly sought by readers of *Damage*."

—Doug Dupler

HARVEY, Caroline. *See* **TROLLOPE, Joanna.**

HAWKING, Stephen W(illiam)

Nationality: British. **Born:** Oxford, England, 8 January 1942. **Education:** University College, Oxford, B.A. (with first class honors), 1962; Trinity Hall, Cambridge, Ph.D., 1966. **Family:** Married Jane Wilde in 1965, two sons and one daughter. **Career:** Cambridge University, Cambridge, England, research fellow at Gonville and Caius College, 1965-69, member of Institute of Theoretical Astronomy, 1968-72, research assistant at Institute of Astronomy, 1972-73, research assistant in department of applied mathematics and theoretical physics, 1973-75, reader in gravitational physics, 1975-77, professor of gravitational physics, 1977-79, Lucasian Professor of Mathematics, 1979—. Fairchild Distinguished Scholar at California Institute of Technology, 1974- 75. **Awards:** Eddington medal from Royal Astronomical Society, 1975; Pius IX Gold medal from Pontifical Academy of Sciences, 1975; Dannie Heinemann prize for mathematical physics from American Physical Society and American Institute of Physics, 1976; William Hopkins prize from Cambridge Philosophical Society, 1976; Maxwell medal from Institute of Physics, 1976; Hughes medal from Royal Society of London, 1976; honorary fellow of University College, Oxford, 1977; Albert Einstein award from Lewis and Rosa Strauss Memorial Fund, 1978; Albert Einstein medal from Albert Einstein Society, Berne, 1979; Franklin medal from Franklin Institute, 1981; Commander of the British Empire, 1982; honorary fellow of Trinity Hall, Cambridge, 1984; Royal Astronomical Society Gold Medal, 1985; Paul Dirac medal and prize from Institute of Physics, 1987; Wolf Foundation prize for physics, 1988. Named a Companion of Honour on the Queen's Birthday Honours List, 1989. Received honorary degrees from numerous universities, including Oxford, 1978, Chicago, 1981, Leicester, New York, Notre Dame, and Princeton, all 1982, Newcastle and Leeds, both 1987, and Tufts, Yale, and Cambridge, all 1989. **Member:** Royal Society of London (fellow), Pontifical Academy of Sciences, American Academy of Arts and Sciences, American Philosophical Society, Royal Astronomical Society of Canada (honorary member). **Addresses:** Department of Applied Mathematics and Theoretical Physics, Cambridge University, Silver St., Cambridge CB3 9EW, England.

PUBLICATIONS

Nonfiction

The Large Scale Structure of Space-Time, with G. F. R. Ellis. Cambridge University Press, 1973.
Is the End in Sight for Theoretical Physics? Cambridge University Press, 1980.
A Brief History of Time: From the Big Bang to Black Holes. Bantam, 1988.
Black Holes and Baby Universes, and Other Essays. Bantam, 1993.
The Nature of Space and Time. Princeton University Press, 1995.

*

Film Adaptation: *A Brief History of Time*, 1991.

Critical Study: *Stephen Hawking's Universe* by John Boslough, Quill, 1985.

* * *

The publication of Stephen Hawking's hugely successful *A Brief History of Time* (1988) captured the public's attention—an unusual reception for an astro-physicist—and generated interested in his ideas outside of the scientific community. But long before *A Brief History,* Scientists had praised Hawking because his work with black holes led science closer to an understanding of the origins of the universe.

After receiving a Ph.D. from Cambridge, Hawking held a series of university posts until 1979 when he was appointed to Lucasian Professor of Mathematics. During this period Hawking based his work upon Roger Penrose's understanding of black holes: a collapsing star would eventually form a "singularity," or a point in which the density of matter becomes infinite. Hawking realized that if Penrose's theory were valid, a singularity was necessary for the origin of the universe and would occur if the universe stopped expanding and began to contract. With George Ellis, Hawking summarized this theory in the complex *The Large Scale Structure of Space-Time* (1973).

Hawking altered his emphasis on singularity after he realized that at a point of singularity the theory of relativity becomes invalid. Hawking and other scientists turned their attention to gravitational interactions and began to work on a nonquantum theory of relativity. Although this application has had limited success, Hawking discovered that black holes are not necessarily "black," but do emit energy. The proof for energy emission from black holes is based upon Heisenberg's uncertainty principle; it is impossible for any space to be empty because a point would then have zero energy at a specific time.

Hawking's work with black holes eventually led him to become concerned with cosmology (the study of the origins and ends of the universe). If black holes are collapsed stars, he reasoned, it is possible that their collapse is a smaller scale version of what might happen to the universe. His theory is based upon the idea that although space is infinite and has no boundaries, time is finite and closed by nature. Therefore the universe cannot be considered infinite because of the element of time. But his conception of the origins of the universe are conceptually difficult to follow for the layman, and Hawking readily admits that all of the proof to support his theories has not been attained.

A Brief History of Time is Hawking's attempt at a popular account of his theories of cosmology. Aside from presenting his theories, though, Hawking provides an interesting account of the history of astronomy and the changing perceptions of the universe. His presentation of the basic theories of Galileo, Newton, Einstein, and Planck are easy to understand and help to trace influences on Hawking's understanding of the origins of the universe. Although published, the book is unfinished because Hawking argues that in order for his theories to be validated, there must be a unification of the theory of relativity and the theory of quantum physics. Hawking anticipates that once the two are successfully united "It will be the ultimate triumph of human reason—for then we would know the mind of God."

—Chris Godat

HEAT MOON, William Least. *See* **TROGDON, William.**

HEILBRUN, Carolyn. *See* **CROSS, Amanda.**

HEINLEIN, Robert A(nson)

Nationality: American. **Born:** Butler, Missouri, 7 July 1907. **Education:** University of Missouri, Columbia, 1924-25; United States Naval Academy, Annapolis, Maryland, B.S. 1929; University of California, Los Angeles, 1934-35. **Military Service:** Served in the United States Navy, 1929 until retirement because of physical disability, 1934. **Family:** Married 1) Leslyn McDonald (divorced); 2) Virginia Gerstenfeld in 1948. **Career:** Owned a silver mine, Silver Plume, Colorado, 1934-35; worked in mining and real estate, 1936-39; civilian engineer, Philadelphia Navy Yard, 1942-45. Forrestal Lecturer, United States Naval Academy, 1973. Recipient: Hugo award 1956, 1960, 1962, 1967; Boys' Clubs of America award, 1959; Grand Master Nebula award, 1974; *Locus* award, 1985. Guest of Honor, World Science Fiction Convention, 1941, 1961, 1976. L.H.D.: Eastern Michigan University, Ypsilanti, 1977. **Died:** 8 May 1988.

Publications

Novels (series: Future History; Luna)

Rocket Ship Galileo (for children). New York, Scribner, 1947; London, New English Library, 1971.

Space Cadet (for children). New York, Scribner, 1948; London, Gollancz, 1966.

Beyond This Horizon. Reading, Pennsylvania, Fantasy Press, 1948; London, Panther, 1967.

Sixth Column: A Science Fiction Novel of a Strange Intrigue. New York, Gnome Press, 1949; as *The Day after Tomorrow,* New York, Signet, 1951; London, Mayflower, 1962.

Red Planet: A Colonial Boy on Mars (for children). New York, Scribner, 1949; London, Gollancz, 1963; expanded edition, New York, Ballantine, 1990.

Farmer in the Sky (for children). New York, Scribner, 1950; London, Gollancz, 1962.

Waldo, and Magic Inc. Garden City, New York, Doubleday, 1950; as *Waldo, Genius in Orbit,* New York, Avon, 1958.

The Puppet Masters. Garden City, New York, Doubleday, 1951; London, Museum Press, 1953; expanded edition, New York, Ballantine, 1990; adapted for children by David Fickling, Oxford, Oxford University Press, 1979.

Between Planets (for children). New York, Scribner, 1951; London, Gollancz, 1968.

The Rolling Stones (for children). New York, Scribner, 1952; as *Space Family Stone,* London, Gollancz, 1969; adapted for children by Rosemary Border, Cambridge, Cambridge University Press, 1978.

Starman Jones (for children). New York, Scribner, 1953; London, Sidgwick and Jackson, 1954.

The Star Beast (for children). New York, Scribner, 1954; London, New English Library, 1971.

Tunnel in the Sky (for children). New York, Scribner, 1955; London, Gollancz, 1965.

Time for the Stars (for children). New York, Scribner, 1956; London, Gollancz, 1963.

Double Star. Garden City, New York, Doubleday, 1956; London, Joseph, 1958.

The Door into Summer. Garden City, New York, Doubleday, 1957; London, Panther, 1960.

Citizen of the Galaxy (for children). New York, Scribner, 1957; London, Gollancz, 1969.

Have Space Suit—Will Travel (for children). New York, Scribner, 1958; London, Gollancz, 1970.

Methuselah's Children (Future History). Hicksville, New York, Gnome Press, 1958; London, Gollancz, 1963.

Robert Heinlein Omnibus (includes *The Man Who Sold the Moon* and *The Green Hills of Earth*). London, Science Fiction Book Club, 1958.

Starship Troopers (for children). New York, Putnam, 1959; London, New English Library, 1961.

Stranger in a Strange Land. New York, Putnam, 1961; London, New English Library, 1965; expanded, New York, Putnam, 1990.

Podkayne of Mars: Her Life and Times (for children). New York, Putnam, 1963; London, New English Library, 1969.

Glory Road. New York, Putnam, 1963; London, New English Library, 1965.

Farnham's Freehold: A Novel. New York, Putnam, 1964; London, Dobson, 1965.

Three by Heinlein (includes *The Puppet Masters, Waldo, Magic Inc.*). Garden City, New York, Doubleday, 1965; as *A Heinlein Triad.* London, Gollancz, 1966.

The Robert Heinlein Omnibus (includes *Beyond This Horizon, The Man Who Sold the Moon,* and *The Green Hills of Earth*). London, Sidgwick and Jackson, 1966.

The Moon Is a Harsh Mistress (Luna). New York, Putnam, 1966; London, Dobson, 1967.

I Will Fear No Evil. New York, Putnam, 1970; London, New English Library, 1972.

Time Enough for Love: The Lives of Lazarus Long: A Novel (Future History). New York, Putnam, 1973; London, New English Library, 1974.

The Number of the Beast. New York, Fawcett, and London, New English Library, 1980.

A Heinlein Trio: The Puppet Master; Double Star; The Door into Space. Garden City, New York, Doubleday, 1980.

Friday. New York, Holt Rinehart, and London, New English Library, 1982.

Job: A Comedy of Justice. New York, Ballantine, and London, New English Library, 1984.

The Cat Who Walks through Walls: A Comedy of Manners (Luna). New York, Putnam, 1985; London, New English Library, 1986.

To Sail beyond the Sunset: The Life and Loves of Maureen Johnson (Being the Memoirs of a Somewhat Irregular Lady) (Future History). New York, Putnam, and London, Joseph, 1987.

Short Stories (series: Future History)

The Man Who Sold the Moon. Sidney, American Science Fiction, 1952.

The Man Who Sold the Moon: Harriman and the Escape from Earth to the Moon! (Future History). Chicago, Shasta, 1950; London, Sidgwick and Jackson, 1953.
Universe (Future History). New York, Dell, 1951.
The Green Hills of Earth: Rhysling and the Adventure of the Entire Solar System! (Future History). Chicago, Shasta, 1951; London, Sidgwick and Jackson, 1954.
Revolt in 2100: The Prophets and the Triumph of Reason over Superstition! (Future History). Chicago, Shasta, 1953; London, Digit, 1959.
Assignment in Eternity: Four Long Science Fiction Stories. Reading, Pennsylvania, Fantasy Press, 1953; London, Museum Press, 1955; abridged edition, as *Lost Legacy,* London, Digit, 1960.
The Menace from Earth. Hicksville, New York, Gnome Press, 1959; London, Dobson, 1966.
The Unpleasant Profession of Jonathan Hoag. Hicksville, New York, Gnome Press, 1959; London, Dobson 1964; as *6 x H: Six Stories,* New York, Pyramid, 1961.
Orphans of the Sky (Future History; includes *Universe*). London, Gollancz, 1963; New York, Putnam, 1964.
The Worlds of Robert A. Heinlein. New York, Ace, 1966; London, New English Library, 1970.
The Past through Tomorrow: "Future History" Stories. New York, Putnam, 1967; abridged edition, London, New English Library, 2 vols., 1977.
The Best of Robert Heinlein, edited by Angus Wells. London, Sidgwick and Jackson, 1973.
Destination Moon, edited by David G. Hartwell. Boston, Gregg Press, 1979.
Expanded Universe: The New Worlds of Robert A. Heinlein. New York, Grosset and Dunlap, 1980.
Requiem: New Collected Works by Robert A. Heinlein and Tributes to the Great Master, edited by Yoji Kondo. New York, Tor, 1992.

Plays

Screenplays: *Destination Moon,* with Rip Van Ronkel and James O'Hanlon, 1950; *Project Moonbase,* with Jack Seaman, 1953.

Other

The Discovery of the Future . . . : Speech Delivered by Guest of Honor at 3rd World Science Fiction Convention. Los Angeles, Novacious, 1941.
"On the Writing of Speculative Fiction," in *Of Worlds Beyond: The Science of Science-Fiction Writing,* edited by Lloyd Arthur Eshbach. Reading, Pennsylvania, Fantasy Press, 1947; London, Dobson, 1965.
"Why I selected 'The Green Hills of Earth,'" in *My Best Science Fiction Story,* edited by Leo Margulies and O.J. Friend. New York, Merlin Press, 1949.
"Ray Guns and Rocket Ships," in *Library Journal* (New York), July 1953.
"Science Fiction: Its Nature, Faults, and Virtues," in *The Science Fiction Novel,* edited by Basil Davenport. Chicago, Advent, 1959.
"Heinlein on Science Fiction," in *Vertex* (Los Angeles), April 1973.
The Notebooks of Lazarus Long. New York, Putnam, 1978.
Grumbles from the Grave, edited by Virginia Heinlein. New York, Ballantine, 1989; London, Orbit, 1991.
Tramp Royale. New York, Ace, 1992.
Take Back Your Government: A Practical Handbook for the Private Citizen Who Wants Democracy to Work. Riverdale, New York, Baen, 1992.

Editor, *Tomorrow, The Stars: A Science Fiction Anthology.* Garden City, New York, Doubleday, 1952.

*

Bibliography: *Robert A. Heinlein: A Bibliography* by Mark Owings, Baltimore, Croatan House, 1973.

Manuscript Collection: University of California Library, Santa Cruz.

Critical Studies: *Seekers of Tomorrow* by Sam Moskowitz, Cleveland, World, 1966; *Heinlein in Dimension: A Critical Analysis* (includes bibliography) by Alexei Panshin, Chicago, Advent, 1968; *Robert A. Heinlein, Stranger in His Own Land,* San Bernardino, California, Borgo Press, 1976, and *The Classic Years of Robert A. Heinlein,* Borgo Press, 1977, both by George Edgar Slusser; *Robert A. Heinlein* edited by Martin H. Greenberg and Joseph D. Olander, New York, Taplinger, and Edinburgh, Harris, 1978; *Robert A. Heinlein: America as Science Fiction* by H. Bruce Franklin, New York, Oxford University Press, 1980, London, Oxford University Press, 1981.

* * *

Robert A. Heinlein was one of the most renowned and influential science fiction writers of the modern era, his works marked with their author's provocative, highly opinionated voice. Most of his early books were written for children and young adults. In fact, critics often praised his young adult novels—with their careful plotting and clear, vivid writing—as being more satisfying than much of his adult science fiction. He began writing mainly for adults in the 1960s and continued until his death.

His most famous novel is the satirical *Stranger in a Strange Land* (1961). Considered a classic science fiction novel, it centers on Valentine Michael Smith, a human who is raised to adulthood by Martians. Upon returning to Earth, Michael must contend with the clashing of his completely alien viewpoints and those of his fellow humans. Through this construct Heinlein examines human culture, politics, and religion with a socially critical eye. He attacks contemporary society, in particular the belief in one god and monogamy.

Heinlein was no stranger to serious misfires such as *I Will Fear No Evil* (1970), which was denounced as horrible and trashy, or *Starship Troopers* (1959), which was intensely attacked for its dangerous ideologies. But no doubt exists that he was at the very least thought-provoking. Interestingly enough, in *Time Enough for Love* (1973), which chronicles the life of Lazarus Long (who first appeared in *Methuselah's Children* [1958]), Heinlein somehow manages to make even incest seem perfectly reasonable. The reappearance of Lazarus is another prevailing aspect of Heinlein's work. All of his characters periodically show up scattered throughout his many novels.

Always on the edge of controversy, in *The Number of the Beast* (1980) Heinlein scripts a pair of couples through famous alternate universes of literature, such as Edgar Rice Burroughs's

Barsoom and L. Frank Baum's Oz. In *Job: A Comedy of Justice* (1984), Heinlein, true to his ability to provoke, portrays God as a sadistic fool and Lucifer as the champion of free will and physical pleasure. Praised by some critics as his best effort since *Stranger,* others denigrated it for its slanted religious views.

Heinlein's last novel, *To Sail beyond the Sunset* (1987), reviews the life of Maureen Johnson, the mother of Lazarus Long and the ancestor of several other Heinlein characters. The novel covers time travel, alternate history, and super-longevity. *Kirkus Reviews* described it as "about equal parts hard-nosed homespun wisdom and deliberate provocation, with a sprinkling of pure twaddle." This description applies aptly to most of Heinlein's works.

One thing is certain about Heinlein. He will not be forgotten. He successfully provokes readers' imaginations in every one of his novels. At the same time eclectic, controversial, and interesting, Heinlein's influence on the science fiction genre will continue to be felt.

—Jennifer G. Coman

HELLER, Joseph

Nationality: American. **Born:** Brooklyn, New York, 1 May 1923. **Education:** Abraham Lincoln High School, New York, graduated 1941; University of Southern California, Los Angeles, 1945-46; New York University, B.A. 1948 (Phi Beta Kappa); Columbia University, New York, M.A. 1949; Oxford University (Fulbright scholar), 1949-50. **Military Service:** Served in the United States Army Air Force in World War II: Lieutenant. **Family:** Married 1) Shirley Held in 1945, one son and one daughter; 2) Valerie Humphries. **Career:** Instructor in English, Pennsylvania State University, University Park, 1950-52; advertising writer, *Time* magazine, New York, 1952-56, and *Look* magazine, New York, 1956-58; promotion manager, *McCall's* magazine, New York, 1958-61. **Awards:** American Academy grant, 1963; Médicis prize (France), 1985. **Member:** American Academy, 1977. Hon. fellow, St. Catherine's College, Oxford University, 1991. **Address:** c/o International Creative Management, 40 W. 57th St., New York, New York 10019, U.S.A.

Publications

Novels

Catch-22. New York, Simon and Schuster, 1961; London, Cape, 1962.
Something Happened. New York, Knopf, and London, Cape, 1974.
Good as Gold. New York, Simon and Schuster, and London, Cape, 1979.
God Knows. New York, Knopf, and London, Cape, 1984.
Picture This. New York, Putnam, and London, Macmillan, 1988.
Closing Time: A Sequel to Catch-22. New York and London, Simon and Schuster, 1994.

Uncollected Short Stories

"I Don't Love You Anymore," in *Story* (New York), September-October 1945.
"Castle of Snow," in *Atlantic* (Boston), May 1947.
"Bookies, Beware!," in *Esquire* (New York), March 1948.
"Girl from Greenwich," in *Esquire* (New York), June 1948.
"A Man Named Flute," in *Atlantic* (Boston), August 1948.
"Nothing to Be Done," in *Esquire* (New York), August 1948.
"MacAdam's Log," in *Gentlemen's Quarterly* (New York), December 1959.
"World Full of Great Cities," in *Nelson Algren's Own Book of Lonesome Monsters,* edited by Algren. New York, Lancer, 1962; London, Panther, 1964.
"Love, Dad," in *Playboy* (Chicago), December 1969.
"The Day Bush Left," in *Nation* (New York), 4 June 1990.

Plays

We Bombed in New Haven (produced New Haven, Connecticut, 1967; New York, 1969; London, 1971). New York, Knopf, 1968; London, Cape, 1969.
Catch-22, adaptation of his own novel. New York, Delacorte Press, and London, French, 1973.
Clevinger's Trial, adaptation of chapter 8 of his novel *Catch-22* (produced London, 1974). New York, French, 1973; London, French, 1974.

Screenplays: *Sex and the Single Girl,* adapted from the work by David R. Schwartz, 1964; *Casino Royale* (uncredited), 1967; *Dirty Dingus Magee,* adapted from the work by Tom and Frank Waldman, 1970.

Other

No Laughing Matter (autobiographical), with Speed Vogel. New York, Putnam, and London, Cape, 1986.
The Stern Gang: Idology, Politics, and Terror, 1940-1949. International Specialized Book Services, 1995.

*

Bibliography: *Three Contemporary Novelists: An Annotated Bibliography* by Robert M. Scotto, New York, Garland, 1977; *Joseph Heller: A Reference Guide* by Brenda M. Keegan, Boston, Hall, 1978.

Critical Studies: "Joseph Heller's *Catch-22*" by Burr Dodd, in *Approaches to the Novel* edited by John Colmer, Edinburgh, Oliver and Boyd, 1967; "The Sanity of *Catch-22*" by Robert Protherough, in *Human World* (Swansea), May 1971; *A Catch-22 Casebook* edited by Frederick T. Kiley and Walter McDonald, New York, Crowell, 1973; *Critical Essays on Catch-22,* Encino, California, Dickinson Seminar Series, 1974, and *Critical Essays on Joseph Heller,* Boston, Hall, 1984, both edited by James Nagel; "Something Happened: A New Direction" by George J. Searles, in *Critique* (Atlanta), vol. 18, no. 3, 1977; *From Here to Absurdity: The Moral Battlefields of Joseph Heller* by Stephen W. Potts, San Bernardino, California, Borgo Press, 1982; *Joseph Heller* by Robert Merrill, Boston, Twayne, 1987; *The Fiction of Joseph Heller: Against the Grain* by David Seed, London, Macmillan, 1989; *Understanding Joseph Heller* by Sanford Pinsker, Columbia, University of South Carolina Press, 1991; *Joseph Heller* by Judith Ruderman, New York, Continuum, 1991.

* * *

Joseph Heller is the supreme example of a novelist who had a smash hit with his first book and then struggled unsuccessfully for the rest of his life to repeat it. *Catch-22* (1961), a darkly comic, antiwar novel in the tradition of *The Good Soldier Schweik* and *Journey to the End of Night,* was not a startling success at first with reviewers or readers, but its reputation grew, especially among young people. By the end of the 1960s it had sold over 12 million copies. The novel had become the archetypical work for the decade in the way that *Catcher in the Rye* had for the previous decade, and the term itself had passed into the language.

Catch-22 is the story of Yossarian, an airman stationed in Italy during WWII. Yossarian rebels against the incompetence of military leadership and the indifference to human life he sees all around him, and he refuses to fly any more missions. It is a very funny book but Heller uses puns, paradox, bizarre situations and bewildering non sequiturs to launch a savage attack on war and to pour scorn on the notion that there is any kind of order, divine or otherwise, in the universe.

Although he wrote a play, *We Bombed in New Haven* (1967), and a dramatization of *Catch-22,* Heller waited 13 years before publishing his second novel, *Something Happened* (1974), which seemed to be trying to do to big business what his first had done to the military. It is, however, a very different kind of novel, one that is almost excessively drab and unhappy in its depiction of the unfulfilled life of the advertising executive Robert Slocum.

In *Good as Gold* (1979) Heller returned to the form of black humor (an expression he dislikes)—puns and verbal games, a mixture of anarchy and indignation—that marked his first novel. But the games which in *Catch-22* were the means of suggesting the fundamental insanity of our assumptions of war as a natural and rational form of behavior have here degenerated into facetious and flippant jokes. An additional problem is that Gold is so basically unlikable a character that it is difficult to feel any sympathy for him or his predicaments.

The narrator of *God Knows* (1984) is the dying David, King of the Jews, who has decided that he has been given one of the best parts of the Bible: "I have suicide, regicide, patricide, homicide, fratricide, infanticide, adultery, incest, hanging, and more decapitations than just Saul's." In some respects it is a kind of deconstruction of the Biblical myth; a sort of Woody Allen meets King David as Heller retells the stories in comic and often farcical terms. Though the basic joke is stretched as far as it can go, the best parts of it are very funny.

Picture This (1988) is in many respects is the least characteristic and most interesting of Heller's later novels. Taking as his starting point Rembrandt's painting of *Aristotle Contemplating the Bust of Homer,* Heller draws a series of ironic contrasts between Greek society in the fourth century B.C. and Holland in the 17th century, using both to flay contemporary America. The novel is written in a flatly laconic, laid-back style that is much more typical of the work of his friend Kurt Vonnegut than of Heller himself.

In the significantly titled *Closing Time: A Sequel to Catch-22* (1994), Heller returns to his old stamping ground of *Catch-22.* Yossarian and the gang are now 40 years older and as preoccupied with death as in the earlier novel, but a death by attrition and slow decline rather than violence. Heller's own experiences of the rare but dreaded Guillain-Barre syndrome clearly inform much of the novel's preoccupation with old age, disease, and decay. The entrepreneurial Milo Minderbinder and ex-PFC Wintergreen, two of the least likeable characters in *Catch-22,* return, as does the timid chaplain, his name mysteriously changed from Shipman to Tappman. It is a talky, aimless novel that seems most of the time to be merely going through the motions.

Heller's career after *Catch-22* has not been brilliant. But, in fairness, it must be remembered that he set a very high standard and failed, like some of his contemporaries, to successfully renounce his deeply liberal convictions. He has remained throughout his life a fiercely intransigent critic of the military, corruption in business, and politicians in general.

—Laurie Clancy

HELPRIN, Mark

Nationality: American. **Born:** New York, 28 June 1947. **Education:** Harvard College, A.B. 1969, A.M. 1972; Magdalen College, Oxford, postgraduate study, 1976-77. **Military Service:** Israeli Infantry and Air Corps, border guard, 1972-73. **Family:** Married Lisa Kennedy in 1980; two daughters. **Career:** Briefly merchant seaman; instructor at Harvard University; contributor, *New Yorker* and other magazines. **Awards:** PEN/Faulkner award, National Jewish Book award, American Academy and Institute of Arts and Letters award, Prix de Rome, all 1982.

Publications

Novels

Refiner's Fire: The Life and Adventures of Marshall Pearl, a Foundling. New York, Knopf, 1977.
Winter's Tale. New York, Harcourt, and London, Weidenfeld and Nicolson, 1983.
Swan Lake (for children). Boston, Houghton, 1989.
A Soldier of the Great War. New York, Harcourt Brace, 1991.
Memoir from the Antproof Case. New York, Harcourt Brace, 1995.

Short Stories

A Dove of the East and Other Stories. New York, Knopf, 1975.
Ellis Island and Other Stories. New York, Seymour Lawrence/Delacorte, 1981.

Other

Editor, with Shannon Ravenel, *The Best American Short Stories.* Boston, Houghton, 1988.

* * *

"Everything I write," novelist Mark Helprin has said, "is keyed and can be understood as . . . devotional literature" whose "object" is beauty. Although Helprin's *New Yorker* stories and four novels have explored a wide range of often exotic characters and settings, all have employed an evocative style that injects value and meaning into its subjects through the graceful luminosity of its language. Helprin is widely regarded as master at combining rich narrative textures and oddly resonant details to create dazzling and memorable, though not always thoroughly persuasive, fictional worlds.

Helprin's first collection, *A Dove of the East* (1975), gathered 20 pieces previously published in *New Yorker* magazine and included stories about a soldier in the Civil War assigned to burial duty, a young musician in Paris, a worker in a typewriter ribbon factory, and a Jamaican cattle rancher. Critics praised Helprin's depictions of nature and its force, his focus on characters coping with loss, and his elegant prose. The *Spectator,* for example, observed that "the quality that pervades these stories is love," and *Atlantic Monthly* described Helprin's style as "dreamy" and "antique." A number of reviewers were troubled by the occasionally forced quality of Helprin's style, but *Saturday Review* was typical of critical reaction in finding the collection "immensely readable" and "quite superb."

Helprin's first novel, *Refiner's Fire* (1977), traced the experiences of "foundling" Marshall Pearl from his deathbed on a battlefield in the Middle East in 1973 back through his life in a series of flashbacks that take him from Colorado, Jamaica, New York City, Boston, New Orleans, South Carolina, and Europe to Israel, where the novel concludes with his death. Critics described Helprin's "remembrance of circular time" (in the words of one his characters) as a "fascinating adult fairy tale" (*Harper's*) and a "picaresque tour de force" (*Library Journal*). Some reviewers, however, criticized the novel for its lack of structure, vague symbolism, and airily romantic tone.

In *Ellis Island and Other Stories* (1981), Helprin gathered 11 more *New Yorker* stories, including "Schreuderspitze," about a grieving widower training for a cathartic climb up an Alpine peak; "Ellis Island," involving a romantically successful immigrant's arrival in America; and "Martin Bayer," in which America's loss of innocence in World War I is dramatized in the tale of a young American's prewar remembrances of youth and love. The collection won a PEN/Faulkner Award and was greeted with perhaps the warmest praise of Helprin's career. The *Washington Post* described it as "beautifully written and carefully structured," and *Newsweek* declared Helprin's stories "as good as any being written today."

In 1983, Helprin published *Winter's Tale,* a richly imagined fantasy about a burglar who marries the daughter of a rich New Yorker and, following her death, travels through time on his magical steed Athnasor to help lead the New York City of 1999 into a hopeful future of justice and beauty. Many reviewers were unimpressed by Helprin's imaginative leaps. *Newsweek* called the novel a "disaster," and *Atlantic Monthly* argued that it "verge[d] on the ludicrous." The *New York Times,* however, praised its "moral energy," and the reviewer for the *Detroit News* commended Helprin's richly poetic passages and "fearlessly understated humor."

In 1991, Helprin's modern adaptation of *Swan Lake* appeared to mixed reviews, with some critics praising Helprin's skillful writing and characterization, and others faulting him for freighting the classic tale with irony and philosophical digressions inappropriate for younger readers. In *A Soldier of the Great War* (1991), Helprin narrated the life of Alessandro Guiliani, an artistic descendant of a wealthy Italian family who is dragged into WWI only to encounter desertion, a near execution, lost love, and imprisonment by the enemy. The work's plot served as the platform for some of Helprin's most successful lyrical divagations on life, experience, and meaning.

Helprin's most recent work, *Memoir from the Antproof Case* (1995), is the eccentric memoir of an 80-year-old former fighter pilot living in Brazil to escape real or imaginary assassins. His notes on his life (hidden in an "antproof" chest) detail his career as a convicted murderer, downed American flyer in World War II, billionaire, bank robber, and lover of women. Returning to his characteristic themes of love, redemption, and human endurance, Helprin's novel was called "wonderfully strange and funny," "a grand jigsaw puzzle," and "rich in imagery."

—Paul S. Bodine

HERBERT, Frank (Patrick)

Nationality: American. **Born:** Tacoma, Washington, 8 October 1920. **Education:** Attended the University of Washington, Seattle, 1946-47. **Family:** Married Beverly Ann Stuart in 1946; one daughter and two sons. **Career:** Reporter and editor for West Coast newspapers; lecturer in general and interdisciplinary studies, University of Washington, 1970-72; social and ecological studies consultant, Lincoln Foundation and the countries of Vietnam and Pakistan, 1971. **Awards:** Nebula award, 1965; Hugo award, 1966; Prix Apollo, 1978. **Died:** 12 February 1986.

Publications

Novels (series: Dune; Jorj X. McKie; Pandora)

The Dragon in the Sea. Garden City, New York, Doubleday, 1956; London, Gollancz, 1960; as *21st Century Sub,* New York, Avon, 1956; as *Under Pressure,* New York, Ballantine, 1974.

The Great Dune Trilogy, London, Gollancz, 1979.

Dune. Philadelphia, Chilton, 1965; London, Gollancz, 1966; as *The Illustrated Dune,* New York, Berkley, 1977.

Dune Messiah. New York, Putnam, 1969; London, Gollancz, 1971.

Children of Dune. New York, Berkley, and London, Gollancz, 1976.

Destination: Void (Pandora). New York, Berkley, 1966; London, Penguin, 1967; revised, New York, Berkley, 1978.

The Eyes of Heisenberg. New York, Berkley, 1966; London, Sphere, 1968.

The Green Brain. New York, Ace, 1966; London, New English Library, 1973.

The Santaroga Barrier. New York, Berkley, 1968; London, Rapp and Whiting, 1970.

The Heaven Makers. New York, Avon, 1968; London, New English Library, 1970.

Whipping Star (McKie). New York, Putnam, 1970; London, New English Library, 1972; revised edition, New York, Berkley, 1977.

The God Makers. New York, Putnam, and London, New English Library, 1972.

Soul Catcher. New York, Putnam, 1972; London, New English Library, 1973.

Hellstrom's Hive. Garden City, New York, Doubleday, 1973; London, New English Library, 1974.

The Dosadi Experiment (McKie). New York, Putnam, 1977; London, Gollancz, 1978.

The Jesus Incident (Pandora), with Bill Ransom. New York, Berkley, and London, Gollancz, 1979.

Direct Descent. New York, Ace, 1980; London, New English Library, 1982.
The White Plague. New York, Putnam, 1982; London, Gollancz, 1983.
The Lazarus Effect (Pandora), with Bill Ransom. New York, Putnam, and London, Gollancz, 1983.
Man of Two Worlds, with Brian Herbert. New York, Putnam, and London, Gollancz, 1986.
The Second Great Dune Trilogy. London, Gollancz, 1987.
God Emperor of Dune. New York, Putnam, and London, Gollancz, 1981.
Heretics of Dune. New York, Putnam, and London, Gollancz, 1984.
Chapter House: Dune. London, Gollancz, 1985; as *Chapterhouse: Dune,* New York, Putnam, 1985.
The Ascension Factor (Pandora), with Bill Ransom. New York, Putnam, and London, Gollancz, 1988.

Short Stories

The Worlds of Frank Herbert. London, New English Library, 1970; New York, Ace, 1971.
The Book of Frank Herbert. New York, DAW, 1973; London, Panther, 1977.
The Best of Frank Herbert, edited by Angus Wells. London, Sidgwick and Jackson, 1975.
The Priests of Psi and Other Stories. London, Gollancz, 1980.
Eye, edited by Byron Preiss. New York, Berkley, 1985; London, Gollancz, 1986.

Poetry

Songs of Muad'Dib: Poems and Songs from Frank Herbert's Dune Series and His Other Writings, edited by Brian Herbert. New York, Ace, 1992.

Other

Threshold: The Blue Angels Experience. New York, Ballantine, 1973.
Without Me You're Nothing: The Essential Guide to Home Computers, with Max Barnard. New York, Simon and Schuster, and London, Gollancz, 1980; as *The Home Computer Handbook,* London, New English Library, 1985.
The Maker of Dune: Insights of a Master of Science Fiction, edited by Tim O'Reilly. New York, Berkley, 1987.
The Notebooks of Frank Herbert's Dune, edited by Brian Herbert. New York, Perigee Books, 1988.

Editor, *New World or No World.* New York, Ace, 1970.
Editor, with others, *Tomorrow, and Tomorrow, and Tomorrow.* New York, Holt Rinehart, 1974.
Editor, *Nebula Winners Fifteen.* New York, Harper, 1981; London, W.H. Allen, 1982.

*

Critical Studies: *Frank Herbert* by Timothy O'Reilly, New York, Ungar, 1981; *The Dune Encyclopedia* edited by Willis E. McNelly, New York, Putnam, and London, Corgi, 1984.

* * *

Science-fiction novelist Frank Herbert explored the future of humanity amid distant worlds and alien beings, arguing that change and adversity force needed and sometimes bizarre adaptations, but that stasis brings stagnation and doom. In his books, Herbert sets ideas in opposition: questions of human diversity, singularity, and potential, and of genetic, environmental, and cultural heritage. And he draws on a wide humanistic base of knowledge to argue the need to study the past to avoid absolutist traps, to adjust values to changed circumstances, and to understand our inseparable ties to the ecosystems on which we depend. Though familiar and psychologically credible, Herbert's future humans have evolved physically and intellectually, have discovered latent mystical and psychic abilities nurtured by training and need, and have progressed or retrogressed depending on their willingness to adapt.

Herbert traces the rites of passage through which man evolves god-like intellect and foresight, and faces the dangers such powers bring. Special organic chemicals precipitate evolutionary leaps: "spice" in *Dune* (1965); "Jaspers" in *Santaroga* (1968); kelp hallucinogens in *The Jesus Incident* (1979), *The Lazarus Effect* (1983), and *The Ascension Factor* (1986); a genetic mix of unique strains in *God Makers* (1972) and *Heaven Makers* (1968) and *The Ascension Factor*; and, finally, a special mind or body fuse in *Dosadi Experiment* (1975), *Jesus Incident, Ascension Factor,* and *Man of Two Worlds.*

In *Soul Catcher* (1972), frightening, ancient gods heighten mystic Indian powers gained through ritual. In *The Dosadi Experiment,* humans and aliens caged on an overpopulated, toxic planet, develop mind transference and psi power to avenge themselves on their creators, while in *The God Makers* an interplanetary troubleshooter monitoring planets for signs of aggression develops extrasensory powers, honed by alien philosophers, to help him assure compromises between potential enemies. Similarly, in *Heaven Makers* an immortal movie producer for whom Earth is a film set for full sensory disaster movies interferes with human cycles to provide a blessed loss of immortality for his jaded race. *Man of Two Worlds* (with Brian Herbert) postulates idiot-savant storytellers who can initiate life and interfere in evolution, but whose "story" of Earth results in creatures whose greed, physical obsessions, and lust for power infect their creators with a thirst for destruction. By examining alien intelligence these books more clearly define the human.

Herbert's most famous and most imaginative achievement, the Dune sextet, traces (1) the development and diversification of religion and politics on an alien, feudal desert world where ecology and giant sandworms control destiny, and Bedouin-like Fremen practice scrupulous water conservation and engage in jihads; (2) the intergalactic rise and fall of a great family (the house of Atreides) caught up in revolutionary and messianic convulsions and its legacy to the planet; and (3) human deification through controlled breeding. Of epic proportions, the Dune series, with its Byzantine twists and political intrigues, convincingly captures an entire world in transition, tracing a key political line as it degenerates into perversions (*Dune Messiah* [1969]), until unexpected evolutions (a towering monster who returns the planet to desert in *Children of Dune* [1976]) force the changes necessary for regeneration and for ultimate survival of a people and a world. The God-Emperor of *Dune* (1981) teaches the value of self-reliance as gods and heroes foster lazy thinking, passivity, and inaction, while *Heretics of Dune* (1984) sees the planet turned desert once more, its people forced to revive old skills and deal with questions of genetic variability and uncertainty. Finally,

Chapterhouse: Dune (1985) ends the 50,000-year saga of the House of Atreides, leaping 15,000 years into the future to demonstrate the value of rebellion, diversity, and choice as well as of harmony with the environment.

Herbert's novels reflect careful research into modern concerns and possibilities. They argue the superiority of the intuitive biological organism over the mechanistic, speculate about the nature of deities and the concept of ancestral memory, and suggest future answers in past experiences. Herbert also tackles the problem of human interference in nature in, for example, *The Green Brain* (1966), in which chemical sprays force voracious insects to defensively mutate.

Herbert's experience as a reporter and editor taught him the value of concrete details, and his employment as a social and ecological studies consultant reflects his commitment to the ideals enunciated in his fiction. Skeptic and idealist, Washingtonian Herbert values adaptability, responsibility, and self-reliance. He believes in human potential and evolutionary leaps, but warns against utopias, the destruction of the environment, and the reduction of the human to the mechanical. His provocative, complex creations blend science and imagination.

—Gina Macdonald

HERRIOT, James

Pseudonym of James Alfred Wight. **Nationality:** English. **Born:** 3 October 1916, in Sunderland, County Tyne and Wear. **Education:** Glasgow Veterinary College, M.R.C.V.S., 1938. **Military Service:** Royal Air Force, 1943-45. **Family:** Married Joan Catherine Danbury, 1941; children: James, Rosemary Page. **Career:** Sinclair & Wight, Thirsk, Yorkshire, partner and general practitioner in veterinary medicine, 1938-1992; writer, 1966-95. **Awards:** Best Young Adult Book citations, American Library Association, 1974 for *All Things Bright and Beautiful,* and 1975 for *All Creatures Great and Small;* Order of the British Empire, 1979; D.Litt., Watt University, Scotland, 1979; honorary D.Vsc., Liverpool University, 1984; James Herriot award established by Humane Society of America. **Died:** 23 February 1995, of prostate cancer, in Thirsk, Yorkshire.

Publications

Nonfiction

If Only They Could Talk. M. Joseph, 1970.
It Shouldn't Happen to a Vet. M. Joseph, 1972.
All Creatures Great and Small (contains *If Only They Could Talk* and *It Shouldn't Happen to a Vet*). St. Martin's, 1972.
Let Sleeping Vets Lie. M. Joseph, 1973.
Vet in Harness. M. Joseph, 1974.
All Things Bright and Beautiful (contains *Let Sleeping Vets Lie* and *Vet in Harness*). St. Martin's, 1974.
Vets Might Fly. M. Joseph, 1976.
Vet in a Spin. M. Joseph, 1977.
All Things Wise and Wonderful (contains *Vets Might Fly* and *Vet in a Spin*). St. Martin's, 1977.
James Herriot's Yorkshire, illustrated with photographs by Derry Brabbs. St. Martin's, 1979.
The Lord God Made Them All. St. Martin's, 1981.
The Best of James Herriot. St. Martin's, 1983.
James Herriot's Dog Stories. St. Martin's, 1986.
Every Living Thing. St. Martin's, 1992.
James Herriot's Cat Stories. St. Martin's, 1994.

Fiction for Children

Moses the Kitten, illustrated by Peter Barrett. St. Martin's, 1984.
Only One Woof, illustrated by Barrett, St. Martin's, 1985.
The Christmas Day Kitten, illustrated by Ruth Brown. St. Martin's, 1986.
Bonny's Big Day, illustrated by Brown. St. Martin's, 1987.
Blossom Comes Home, illustrated by Brown. St. Martin's, 1988.
The Market Square Dog, illustrated by Brown. St. Martin's, 1990.
Oscar, Cat-about-Town, illustrated by Brown. M. Joseph, 1990.
Smudge, the Little Lost Lamb, illustrated by Brown. St. Martin's, 1991.
James Herriot's Treasury for Children. St. Martin's, 1992.

*

Media Adaptations: Television series—*All Creatures Great and Small,* 1978. Television film—*All Things Bright and Beautiful* (also released as *It Shouldn't Happen to a Vet*), 1979.

* * *

Since the publication of *If Only They Could Talk* (1970), James Herriot's vet books have been a reliable source of pleasure, invariably earning a place on bestseller lists, especially when recombined for the North American market under the titles *All Creatures Great and Small* (1972), *All Things Bright and Beautiful* (1974), *All Things Wise and Wonderful* (1977), and *The Lord God Made Them All* (1979). They have been filmed, turned into a television series, reissued in large-print formats, and excerpted and illustrated to produce children's picture books.

They are a remarkable achievement. As Alfred C. Ames in *The Chicago Tribune* says, the writing exhibits "a flawless literary control." The comforting, even cozy tone combines with a keen appreciation for the Yorkshire Dales, its dialectal patterns, for food, drink, and other creature comforts, and the eccentricities of the human and animal characters that move through his pages. Not least among his achievements is his sure touch in avoiding the unhappy side of life. Examples of cruelty or soul-destroying failures in the notoriously insecure vocation of farming are never part of his palette. Reading him, one can trust that sorrow will not be unbearable, and that it will illuminate the goodness of life by the courage with which it is borne or by the kindness and generosity which it elicits from others. Part of the enduring appeal of these books is the sense of stability and sanity that they impart.

The series opens with the first-person protagonist, young James Herriot, arriving in Darrowby of the North Yorkshire Dales, fresh from Glasgow Veterinary College and grateful for the chance of a job. The reader meets the charming, contradictory, and eccentric Siegfried Farnon, his boss, as well as Siegfried's scapegrace younger brother Tristan. A host of other characters—among them Mrs. Pumphrey, a comfortably wealthy widow, and her pampered pekinese, Tricky-Woo—begin their march through the chapter-length episodes. We follow this gentle, hardworking, and thoroughly decent man on his rounds, operate with him in his surgery, share his narrow escapes in a variety of dilapidated vehicles, and, above all, laugh with him. All Herriot's books are funny, with a humor that is kind, self-deprecating, and richly appreciative of the variety of human foibles, and of goodness wherever he encounters it.

It Shouldn't Happen to a Vet (1972) uses the same pattern of episodic construction. It introduces us to Helen Anderson, the beautiful daughter of a prosperous farmer, and takes us through the inital stages of Herriot's courtship of her. *Let Sleeping Vets Lie* (1973) gets them married. *Vet in Harness* (1974) continues the formula of the previous books, showing no sign that the convention is growing stale. A sense of enormous happiness breathes from this book in particular, heightened by the parting that is to come. For Herriot's world is not immune to the effects of WWII; the last pages see him heading off to begin training for the Royal Air Force.

Vets Might Fly (1976) and *Vet in a Spin* (1978) mix episodes from Herriot's fighter-pilot training with flashbacks to episodes from his pre-war experiences. For the first time the formula seems unsatisfactory. Richard R. Langeman in the *New York Times Book Review* spoke of "Mechanical plot shifts . . . straining to heighten and point up a diminishing store of materials."

The Lord God Made Them All, which for the first time synchronized the British and U.S. titles and contents, deals with postwar changes in veterinary medicine and Herriot's trips to Russia and Turkey. Despite a loving depiction of his young family and many of the characters from earlier books, the writing becomes increasingly weary. However, *Every Living Thing* (1992), published three years before Herriot's death from prostate cancer, does not seem strained but instead sober and gentle. The magic is not as potent, the humor is less hilarious, and a deep sadness is more evident. Particularly heart-rending is the death in the final pages of the Herriots' cat from a cerebral hemorrhage. Although the craftsmanship and fine writing are still evident, one remembers Herriot's voice from an interview: "a lot of fun has gone from the profession. The past is a sweet, safe place to be."

—Fraser Sutherland

HERSEY, John (Richard)

Nationality: American. **Born:** 17 June 1914, in Tientsin, China, to American parents. **Education:** Yale University, B.A., 1936; attended Clare College, Cambridge, 1936-37. **Family:** Married 1) Frances Ann Cannon, 1940 (divorced, 1958); children: Martin, John, Ann, Baird; 2) Barbara Day Addams Kaufman, 1958; children: Brook (daughter). **Career:** Private secretary, driver, and factotum for Sinclair Lewis, summer, 1937; writer, editor, and correspondent, *Time* magazine, 1937-44, correspondent in China and Japan, 1939, covered South Pacific warfare, 1942, correspondent in Mediterranean theater, including Sicilian campaign, 1943, and in Moscow, 1944-45; editor and correspondent for *Life* magazine, 1944-45; writer for *New Yorker* and other magazines, beginning 1945; made trip to China and Japan for *Life* and *New Yorker,* 1945-46; fellow, Berkeley College, Yale University, 1950-65; master, Pierson College, Yale University, 1965-70, fellow, beginning 1965; writer-in-residence, American Academy in Rome, 1970-71; lecturer, Yale University, 1971-75, professor, beginning 1975. Chairman, Connecticut Volunteers for Stevenson, 1952; member of Adlai Stevenson's campaign staff, 1956. Editor and director of writers' co-operative magazine, *'47.* Member of Westport, Connecticut, School Study Council, 1945-50, of Westport Board of Education, 1950-52, of Yale University Council Committee on the Humanities, 1951-56, of Fairfield, Connecticut, Citizens School Study Council, 1952-56, of National Citizens' Commission for the Public Schools, 1954-56; consultant, Fund for the Advancement of Education, 1954-56; chairman, Connecticut Committee for the Gifted, 1954-57; member of Board of Trustees, Putney School, 1953-56; delegate to White House Conference on Education, 1955; trustee, National Citizens' Council for the Public Schools, 1956-58; member, visiting committee, Harvard Graduate School of Education, 1960-65; member, Loeb Theater Center, beginning 1980; Yale University Council Committee on Yale College, member, 1959-61, chairman, 1964-69; trustee, National Committee for Support of the Public Schools, 1962-68. **Awards:** Pulitzer prize, 1945, for *A Bell for Adano;* Anisfield-Wolf award, 1950, Daroff Memorial Fiction award, Jewish Book Council of America, 1950, and Sidney Hillman Foundation award, 1951, all for *The Wall;* Howland Medal, Yale University, 1952; National Association of Independent Schools award, 1957, for *A Single Pebble;* Tuition Plan award, 1961; Sarah Josepha Hale award, 1963; named honorary fellow of Clare College, Cambridge University, 1967. Honorary degrees: M.A., Yale University, 1947; L.H.D., New School for Social Research, 1950, Syracuse University, 1983; LL.D., Washington and Jefferson College, 1950; D.H.L., Dropsie College, 1950; Litt.D., Wesleyan University, 1954, Bridgeport University, 1959, Clarkson College of Technology, 1972, University of New Haven, 1975, Yale University, 1984, Monmouth College, 1985, William and Mary College, 1987. **Member:** National Institute of Arts and Letters, American Academy of Arts and Letters (secretary, 1961-78, chancellor, beginning 1981), American Academy of Arts and Sciences, Authors League of America (member of council, 1946-70, vice-president, 1949-55, president, 1975-80). **Died:** 23 March 1993, in Key West, Florida.

Publications

Nonfiction

Men on Bataan. Knopf, 1942.
Into the Valley: A Skirmish of the Marines. Knopf, 1943.
Hiroshima. Knopf, 1946.
Here to Stay: Studies on Human Tenacity. Hamish Hamilton, 1962; Knopf, 1963.
The Algiers Motel Incident. Knopf, 1968.
Letter to the Alumni. Knopf, 1970.
The President. Knopf, 1975.
Aspects of the Presidency: Truman and Ford in Office. Ticknor & Fields, 1980.
Blues. Knopf, 1987.
Life Sketches. Knopf, 1989.

Novels

A Bell for Adano. Knopf, 1944.
The Wall. Knopf, 1950.

The Marmot Drive. Knopf, 1953.
A Single Pebble. Knopf, 1956.
The War Lover. Knopf, 1959.
The Child Buyer. Knopf, 1960.
White Lotus. Knopf, 1965.
Too Far to Walk. Knopf, 1966.
Under the Eye of the Storm. Knopf, 1967.
The Conspiracy. Knopf, 1972.
My Petition for More Space. Knopf, 1974.
The Walnut Door. Knopf, 1977.
The Call: An American Missionary in China. Knopf, 1985.
Antonietta. Knopf, 1991.

Short Stories

Fling, and Other Stories. Knopf, 1990.
Key West Tales. Knopf, 1994.

Editor, *Ralph Ellison: A Collection of Critical Essays*. Prentice-Hall, 1973.
Editor, *The Writer's Craft*, Knopf, 1974.

*

Film Adaptations: *A Bell for Adano*, 1945; *The War Lover*, 1962; *The Wall*, 1982.

Bibliography: *John Hersey and James Agee: A Reference Guide* by Nancy Lyman Huse, G. K. Hall, 1978.

Critical Studies: *John Hersey*, Twayne, 1967, and *John Hersey Revisited*, Twayne, 1991, by David Sanders; *The Survival Tales of John Hersey* by Nancy Lyman Huse, Whitston, 1983.

* * *

John Hersey's first novel, *A Bell for Adano* (1944), was a fictionalized account of the real-life efforts of an American Army major to transform a war-ravaged Italian village into a functioning democratic community. The conflict between the captain's humanistic intentions and the impersonal, corporate-style tactics of his army superiors introduced a note of doubt into the euphoria over the coming postwar pax Americana and helped the novel earn Hersey a Pulitzer Prize in 1945. Writing in the *New Republic*, Malcolm Cowley praised *A Bell for Adano* as ". . . an entertaining story, a candid report from behind the lines and an effective tract," a response that encapsulated the critical reaction to most of Hersey's later fiction: entertaining if imperfect storytelling, reflecting thorough research and a reporter's eye, but marred by a penchant for sermonizing.

In 1946, *New Yorker* magazine devoted an entire issue to *Hiroshima*, Hersey's tour de force of understated, artfully crafted journalism, in which Hersey employs the recollections of six survivors of the first atomic bomb blast to graphically illustrate the horrors of the nuclear age. Its impact was enormous (the Book-of-the-Month Club distributed it free, for example, and Albert Einstein was said to have purchased one thousand copies), and it was hailed as "the best reporting" of World War II by a contemporary reviewer.

In *The Wall* (1950), Hersey returned to fiction in the form of a diary kept by a Jewish scholar that recorded the personal thoughts and experiences of doomed Warsaw Jews between 1939 and 1943. Thoroughly researched and regarded by some critics as Hersey's best work, *The Wall*—like *Hiroshima* and some of Hersey's later novels—dealt with the themes of ethnic identity, human survival, and moral responsibility in the face of cataclysmic historical events. In 1959, Hersey produced *The War Lover*, in which the relationship between the two pilots of an Allied bomber crew in World War II dramatizes man's ability—or inability—to understand and cope with his impulse to make war. While some reviewers praised it as a "sophisticated psychological study" and an "exceptionally fine war novel," others noted the novel's failure to rise above Hersey's "reportorial" talents as a journalist and achieve "literary greatness."

Hersey's next novel, *The Child Buyer* (1960), reflected his growing professional involvement with education and told the story of a fictitious corporation's attempts to "buy" a young genius in order to develop his IQ and, once retrained and surgically altered, use him as a sort of superior computer. Despite the novel's whimsical sci-fi plot, the novel represented Hersey's serious attempt to present a satirical parable about the dangers of viewing education as a results-oriented science. He followed it with *White Lotus* (1965), in which the course of African-American history is mirrored in the fanciful story of the Chinese enslavement of American citizens following a war, and *Too Far to Walk* (1966), in which the Faust legend is retold in the contemporary context of a college student's experimentation and eventual rejection of drugs.

In *The Conspiracy* (1972), Hersey used the historical facts surrounding the conspiracy against Roman Emperor Nero in the first century A.D. to present an epistolary debate between the poet Lucan and the philosopher Seneca on freedom and political corruption. The generally poorly received novel *My Petition for More Space* (1974) used a fusion of Kafkaesque touches and a science fiction premise to tell the story of an overcrowded world in which citizens must petition the government for permission to change jobs, marry, or—in the case of the novel's protagonist—obtain more living space. Characteristically, the novel was disparaged as "didactic" and Hersey was criticized for being "more of a reporter than a novelist."

In his last three novels, *The Walnut Door* (1977), *The Call: An American Missionary in China* (1985), and *Antonietta* (1991), Hersey explored material closer to home: education, the American missionary experience in China, and music. But again he failed to gain strong critical acceptance for his fiction. *The Walnut Door* dramatized themes of dependence, nostalgia, genius, and sexual abuse in recounting the relationship between two survivors of the 1960s; *The Call* chronicled the personal transformation of an American missionary confronted by China's poverty and hopelessness; and *Antonietta* told the story of a Stradivarius violin and its history of illustrious owners.

In his long and prolific career, Hersey demonstrated early on that he believed literary art had a moral responsibility to convey the writer's "personal vision and tell someone else what he has seen." In his novels of contemporary history, Hersey consistently showed an uncanny ability to latch onto topical themes and issues and tell them in inventive ways. His inability to curtail his penchant for moralizing or to convince critics that he was not just a journalist masquerading as a novelist suggest, however, that his achievement in *Hiroshima* will be his lasting legacy.

—Paul S. Bodine

HEYER, Georgette

Nationality: British. **Born:** 16 August 1902, in Wimbledon. **Education:** Seminary schools and Westminster College. **Family:** Married George Ronald Rougier, 1925; children: Richard George. **Career:** Writer, 1921-74; lived in Africa, 1925-28, Yugoslavia, 1928-29, and in London after 1942. **Died:** 4 July 1974, in London.

Publications

Romance and Historical Novels

The Black Moth. Houghton, 1921; Bantam, 1976.
The Great Roxhythe. Hutchinson, 1922; Buccaneer Books, 1976.
Instead of the Thorn. Hutchinson, 1923; Buccaneer Books, 1976.
The Transformation of Philip Jettan. n.p., 1923; as *Powder and Patch: The Transformation of Philip Jettan,* Heinemann, 1930; reprinted, Bantam, 1976.
Simon the Coldheart. Small, Maynard, 1925; Dutton, 1979.
These Old Shades. Heinemann, 1926; Dutton, 1966.
Helen. Longmans, Green, 1928; Buccaneer Books, 1976.
The Masqueraders. Heinemann, 1928; Fawcett, 1977.
Beauvallet. Heinemann, 1929; Dutton, 1968.
Pastel. Longmans, Green, 1929; Buccaneer Books, 1976.
The Barren Corn. Longmans, Green, 1930; Buccaneer Books, 1976.
The Conqueror. Heinemann, 1931; Dutton, 1964.
The Convenient Marriage. Heinemann, 1934; Dutton, 1966.
Devil's Cub. Heinemann, 1934; Dutton, 1966.
Regency Buck. Heinemann, 1935; Dutton, 1966.
The Talisman Ring. Heinemann, 1936; Dutton, 1967.
An Infamous Army. Heinemann, 1937; Dutton, 1965.
Royal Escape. Heinemann, 1938; Dutton, 1967.
The Spanish Bride. Heinemann, 1940; Dutton, 1965.
The Corinthian. Heinemann, 1940; Dutton, 1966.
Faro's Daughter. Heinemann, 1941; Dutton, 1967.
Beau Wyndham. Doubleday, 1941.
Friday's Child. Heinemann, 1944; Putnam, 1946; Berkley, 1977.
The Reluctant Widow. Putnam, 1946; Berkley, 1977.
The Foundling. Putnam, 1948.
Arabella. Putnam, 1949; Buccaneer Books, 1978.
The Grand Sophy. Putnam, 1950.
The Quiet Gentleman. Heinemann, 1951; Putnam, 1952.
Cotillion. Putnam, 1953; Buccaneer Books, 1978.
The Toll-Gate. Putnam, 1954.
Bath Tangle. Putnam, 1955; Berkley, 1979.
Sprig Muslin. Putnam, 1956.
April Lady. Putnam, 1957.
Sylvester; or, The Wicked Uncle. Putnam, 1957.
Venetia. Heinemann, 1958; Putnam, 1959.
The Unknown Ajax. Heinemann, 1959; Putnam, 1960.
A Civil Contract. Heinemann, 1961; Putnam, 1962.
The Nonesuch. Heinemann, 1962; Putnam, 1963.
False Colours. Bodley Head, 1963; Dutton, 1964.
Frederica. Dutton, 1965.
Black Sheep. Bodley Head, 1966; Dutton, 1967.
Cousin Kate. Bodley Head, 1968; Dutton, 1969.
Charity Girl. Dutton, 1970.
Lady of Quality. Dutton, 1972.
My Lord John. Dutton, 1975.

Crime and Mystery Novels

Footsteps in the Dark. Longmans, Green, 1932; Buccaneer Books, 1976.
Why Shoot a Butler? Longmans, Green, 1933; Dutton, 1973.
The Unfinished Clue Longmans, Green, 1934; Harmondsworth, 1943; Dutton, 1970.
Merely Murder. Doubleday, 1935; as *Death in the Stocks,* Longmans, Green, 1935; Dutton, 1970.
Behold, Here's Poison! Doubleday, 1936; Fawcett, 1979.
They Found Him Dead. Hodder & Stoughton, 1937; Dutton, 1973.
A Blunt Instrument. Doubleday, 1938; Garland Publishing, 1976.
No Wind of Blame. Hodder & Stoughton, 1939; Dutton, 1970.
Envious Casca. Hodder & Stoughton, 1941; Sun Dial Press, 1942; Bantam, 1978.
Penhallow. Heinemann, 1942; Doubleday, 1943; Dutton, 1971.
Duplicate Death. Heinemann, 1951; Bantam, 1977.
Detection Unlimited. Heinemann, 1953; Dutton, 1969.

Short Stories

Pistols for Two and Other Stories. Heinemann, 1962; Dutton, 1964.

Plays

Radio Play: *The Toll Gate,* from her own novel, 1974.

*

Film Adaptation: *The Reluctant Widow,* 1950.

Critical Studies: *The Private World of Georgette Heyer* by Jane Aiken Hodge, Bodley Head, 1984; *Georgette Heyer's Regency England* by Teresa Chris, Sidgwick and Jackson, 1989.

* * *

Georgette Heyer is one of the most enduringly popular writers of historical romantic fiction, although her detective stories have not lasted. Best known for her Regency romances—she also set some romances in the medieval and Tudor eras—her novels offer a golden world where tragedy, evil, and social miseries are banished. Her stories depict hierarchical but happy societies run by privileged males, with nobly born, spirited heroines confined to the domestic sphere. The fictions combine an absence of social criticism, such as smiling servants devoted to their natural superiors, with meticulous research on the fashions, language, and material accessories of the rich of the period. Heyer particularly admired Jane Austen, whose sparkling humor and fairytale plots reappear in her works.

Three phases can be discerned in Heyer's writing career: the early swashbuckling romances; Regency comedies sometimes combined with a crime story; and late comedies of humor, irony, and family relationships. The early books show a transition between an interest in relationships in a purely masculine world of war or politics to relations between men and women in romance. *Beauvallet* (1929) is a good early example of the hero embroiled in masculine adventures. In that book, an English buccaneer harassing Spanish ships under Queen Elizabeth I becomes distracted by his love for a Spanish protestant noblewoman, fearful of the Inquisition. One of the most remarkable heroines of Heyer's early phase is to be found in *These Old Shades* (1926). Reminiscent of a fairy princess, Leonie enters the novel doubly unqualified to be the hero's object of desire in Heyer's world; she appears to be of servant class and a boy. The novel uncovers her true identity as the noble daughter of the bitter enemy of the man who saved her from the Paris streets. By uncovering the crime that disinherited Leonie of even her gender, a romance is formed that redeems Leonie's cynical savior, the Duke of Avon.

The second phase of Heyer's writing combines Regency comedies of manners with a mystery or a crime. *The Talisman Ring* (1936) is a typical example; the unjustly accused murder suspect, Lord Lavenham, is wounded when smuggling and meets the romantic Eustacie, who is fleeing an arranged marriage with Lavenham's cousin, Sir Tristram. This novel contains what became a typical Heyer device, the doubling of the pair of lovers so that romantic conventions could be commented upon ironically by the older pair observing the naive passions of the younger. It is at this period that Heyer's stock romance heroines and heroes evolve: the hero is either a rakish, formerly dissolute figure to be redeemed by the heroine, or a wealthy, fashionable gentleman who can rescue the heroine from trying circumstances, while heroines tend to be either mature, ironic, humorous ladies or unsophisticated young girls whose innocence causes havoc in polite society, such as the heroines of *Friday's Child* (1946) and *Sprig Muslin* (1956). All the heroines are well-born and virginal, but Heyer continues to place them in unlikely situations. In *Faro's Daughter* (1941), for example, the heroine runs a gaming salon but refuses to exploit a young besotted lord for money, meeting her match in the more sophisticated Max Ravenscar. *An Infamous Army* (1937) is distinctive in Heyer's middle phase in anticipating her later work with a more adult and troubled passion between a soldier, Charles Audley, and Lady Barbara Childe, and also for its remarkably accurate reconstruction of the Battle of Waterloo.

The later novels offer fewer mysteries but are usually comedies of manners and families set in the Regency world of part-myth, part-historical research that Heyer created. Many of these works, such as *Frederica* (1965), center on the initiation of a dangerous and lone but aristocratic male into a domestic world of family relationships through a romance with a woman who is less likely to be young and dazzling but mature and humorous. *False Colours* (1963) and *Sylvester; or The Wicked Uncle* (1957) even hint at a secondary romance structure between mothers and sons. But such perilous ideas never get beyond the fairytale level in Heyer's world.

Heyer remains the archetypal historical romance writer of our times. She is popular for her reassuring but genuinely witty fictions, which employ and satirize romantic conventions. She created neither complex characters nor realistic novels, but her comic dialogue and underlying psychological insight guaranteed that her work responded to deep needs and, furthermore, ensured its enduring success.

—S. A. Rowland

HIAASEN, Carl

Nationality: American. **Born:** Fort Lauderdale, Florida, 12 March 1953. **Education:** Attended Emory University, 1970-72; University of Florida, B.S., 1974. **Family:** Married Constance Lyford in 1970; one son. **Career:** Cocoa Today, Cocoa, Florida, reporter, 1974-76; Miami Herald, reporter from 1976, and columnist from 1985. Professor at Barry College, 1978-79. **Awards:** National Headliners award, distinguished service medallion from Sigma Delta Chi, public service first place award from Florida Society of Newspaper Editors, Clarion award from Women in Communications, Heywood Broun award from Newspaper Guild, all 1980, all for an investigative newspaper series about dangerous doctors; Green Eyeshade award from Sigma Delta Chi, first place award for in-depth reporting from Florida Society of Newspaper Editors, grand prize for investigative reporting from Investigative Reporters and Editors, all 1981, all for a newspaper series on drug smuggling in Key West; Silver Gavel award, American Bar Association, 1982. **Agent:** Esther Newberg, International Creative Management, 40 West 57th St., New York, New York 10019. **Address:** Miami Herald, 1 Herald Plaza, Miami, Florida 33101, U.S.A.

Publications

Novels

Powder Burn, with William D. Montalbano. Atheneum, 1981.
Trap Line, with Montalbano. Atheneum, 1982.
A Death in China, with Montalbano. Atheneum, 1984.
Tourist Season. Putnam, 1986.
Double Whammy. Putnam, 1987.
Skin Tight. Putnam, 1989.
Native Tongue. Knopf, 1991.
Strip Tease. Knopf, 1993.
Stormy Weather. Knopf, 1995.

* * *

The connection between Carl Hiaasen's novels and his career as a journalist is easy to see. Since 1975 Hiaasen has written for the *Miami Herald.* Originally a member of the *Herald's* investigative team, Hiaasen was still, in 1996, writing a twice-weekly column in which he wields his razor sharp wit against politicians and developers who would harm Florida's environmental future. A native of South Florida, Hiaasen has an abiding love for the wetlands and Everglades and is angered by the effects of the tourism industry and overdevelopement. Most of his novels reflect his preoccupation with such issues. His protagonists are often journalists or former journalists struggling against the kinds of evils he writes about in his column. The novels are populated with characters who bear a strong resemblance to real people, but Hiaasen gets to invent the fate he thinks such people deserve.

In *Tourist Season* (1986), a crazed newspaper columnist feeds South Florida tourists to alligators. In *Native Tongue* (1991), protagonist Joe Winder, a newspaper man-turned-public relations hack, takes on a Disney World-type amusement park that wants to build a golf course on 100 acres of pristine wetlands. In *Stormy Weather* (1995), inspired by Hurricane Andrew's devastation, Hiaasen wrote about the aftermath of a hurricane and the unsavory characters who crept out of the wreckage to capitalize on the disaster. Marilyn Stasio of the *New York Times Book Review* called it a "loose piece of writing, but the narrative is driven by gales of laughter and rage," and she noted the "freak show of scavengers, grifters, crooks, con artists and weirdos" that inhabit the book.

Hiaasen's novels resemble those of fellow crime-novelist Elmore Leonard in that he invents vivid characters who drive the action of his novels. Hiaasen, however, is notable for the off-beat humor he brings to the characterizations. In *Skin Tight* (1989), for example, a hit-man disfigured by a bad electrolysis job loses his hand to a barracuda and replaces it with a battery-powered weed wacker. In *Double Whammy* (1987) and *Native Tongue* Hiaasen gives us Skink, a former governor of Florida who now dwells in the Everglades and lives of off roadkill. The novels are not violent, however. Most of the graphic scenes occur "off-camera" or are reserved for "the characters who really have it coming," he told *Writer's Digest* in 1995.

Though widely praised for both his characters and satirical wit, some critics have raised the issue of Hiaasen's misanthropic bent, and he has drawn criticism from Florida's political establishment. Hiaasen reasons that his newspaper column alerts his readers to the exploitation of Florida's resources. His novels are "my own personal therapy for releasing a lot of the venom that I guess builds up naturally when you're a native Floridian and you watch the place [being] paved over," he told *Southern Living* in 1991. "I can write happy endings, which I can't do in real life very often. I can kill off crooked politicians in the most diabolical ways I can conceive of. It gives me great satisfaction."

—Daniel A. Clark

HIBBERT, Eleanor Alice. *See* **HOLT, Victoria.**

HIGGINS, Jack

Pseudonym for Henry Patterson. **Other Pseudonyms:** Martin Fallon; James Graham; Hugh Marlowe. **Nationality:** British and Irish (dual citizenship). **Born:** Newcastle on Tyne, 27 July 1929. **Education:** Leeds Training College for Teachers, Cert. Ed. 1958; University of London, B.Sc. (honours) in sociology 1962. **Military Service:** Served in the Royal Horse Guards, British Army, 1947-49. **Family:** Married 1) Amy Margaret Hewitt in 1958 (dissolved 1984), three daughters and one son; 2) Denise Lesley Anne Palmer in 1985. **Career:** Worked in commercial and civil service posts, 1950-55; history teacher, Allerton Grange Comprehensive School, Leeds, 1958-64; lecturer in liberal studies, Leeds College of Commerce, 1964-68; senior lecturer in education, James Graham College, New Farnley, Yorkshire, 1968-70; tutor, Leeds University, 1971-73. **Awards:** Hon. D. Univ: Leeds Municipal University. **Member:** Royal Society of Arts (fellow). **Agent:** Ed Victor, 6 Bayley St., Bedford Square, London WC1B 3HB, England.

Publications

Novels (series: Liam Devlin; Brigadier Dougal Munro and Captain Jack Carter)

East of Desolation. London, Hodder and Stoughton, 1968; New York, Doubleday, 1969.
In the Hour Before Midnight. London, Hodder and Stoughton, 1969; as *The Sicilian Heritage,* New York, Lancer, 1970.
Night Judgment at Sinos. London, Hodder and Stoughton, 1970; New York, Doubleday, 1971.
The Last Place God Made. London, Collins, 1971; New York, Holt Rinehart, 1972.
The Savage Day. London, Collins, and New York, Holt Rinehart, 1972.
A Prayer for the Dying. London, Collins, 1973; New York, Holt Rinehart, 1974.
The Eagle Has Landed (Devlin). London, Collins, and New York, Holt Rinehart, 1975; revised edition, London, Run, 1982.
Storm Warning. London, Collins, and New York, Holt Rinehart, 1976.
Day of Judgement. London, Collins, 1978; New York, Holt Rinehart, 1979.
Solo. London, Collins, and New York, Stein and Day, 1980.
Luciano's Luck. London, Collins, and New York, Stein and Day, 1981.
Touch the Devil (Devlin). London, Collins, and New York, Stein and Day, 1982.
Exocet. (Villiers). London, Collins, and New York, Stein and Day, 1983.
Confessional (Devlin). London, Collins, and New York, Stein and Day, 1985.
Night of the Fox (Munro and Carter). London, Collins, 1986; New York, Simon and Schuster, 1987.
A Season in Hell. London, Collins, and New York, Simon and Schuster, 1989.
Memoirs of a Dance Hall Romeo. London, Collins, and New York, Simon and Schuster, 1989.
Cold Harbour (Munro and Carter). London, Heinemann, and New York, Simon and Schuster, 1990.
The Eagle Has Flown. London, Chapman, and New York, Simon and Schuster, 1991.
Eye of the Storm. London, Chapman, and New York, Putnam, 1992.
Thunder Point. London, Michael Joseph, and New York, Putnam, 1993.
On Dangerous Ground. London, Michael Joseph, and New York, Putnam, 1994.
Angel of Death. London, Michael Joseph, and New York, Putnam, 1995.
Drink with the Devil. London, Michael Joseph, and New York, Putnam, 1996.

Novels as Harry Patterson (series: Nick Miller; published as Jack Higgins in U.S.)

Sad Wind from the Sea. London, Long, 1959.
Cry of the Hunter. London, Long, 1960.
The Thousand Faces of Night. London, Long, 1961.
Comes the Dark Stranger. London, Long, 1962.
Hell Is Too Crowded. London, Long, 1962; New York, Fawcett, 1976.

Pay the Devil. London, Barrie and Rockliff, 1963.
The Dark Side of the Island. London, Long, 1963; New York, Fawcett, 1977.
A Phoenix in the Blood. London, Barrie and Rockliff, 1964.
Thunder at Noon. London, Long, 1964.
Wrath of the Lion. London, Long, 1964; New York, Fawcett, 1977.
The Graveyard Shift (Miller). London, Long, 1965.
The Iron Tiger. London, Long, 1966; New York, Fawcett, 1974.
Brought in Dead (Miller). London, Long, 1967.
Hell Is Always Today. London, Long, 1968; New York, Fawcett, 1979.
Toll for the Brave. London, Long, 1971; New York, Fawcett, 1976.
The Valhalla Exchange. New York, Stein and Day, 1976; London, Hutchinson, 1977.
To Catch a King. New York, Stein and Day, and London, Hutchinson, 1979.
Dillinger. London, Hutchinson, and New York, Stein and Day, 1983.

Novels as Martin Fallon (series: Paul Chavasse in all books)

The Testament of Caspar Schultz. London and New York, Abelard Schuman, 1962.
Year of the Tiger. London and New York, Abelard Schuman, 1963.
The Keys of Hell. London and New York, Abelard Schuman, 1965.
Midnight Never Comes. London, Long, 1966; New York, Fawcett, 1975.
Dark Side of the Street. London, Long, 1967; New York, Fawcett, 1974.
A Fine Night for Dying. London, Long, 1969.

Novels as Hugh Marlowe

Seven Pillars to Hell. London and New York, Abelard Schuman, 1963; as *Sheba,* London, Michael Joseph, and New York, Putnam, 1994.
Passage by Night. London and New York, Abelard Schuman, 1964.
A Candle for the Dead. London and New York, Abelard Schuman, 1966; as *The Violent Enemy,* London, Hodder and Stoughton, 1969.

Novels as James Graham

A Game for Heroes. London, Macmillan, and New York, Doubleday, 1970.
The Wrath of God. London, Macmillan, and New York, Doubleday, 1971.
The Khufra Run. London, Macmillan, 1972; New York, Doubleday, 1973.
Bloody Passage. London, Macmillan, 1974; as *The Run to Morning,* New York, Stein and Day, 1974.

Play

Radio Scripts: *The Island City,* 1987; *Dead of Night,* (1 episode), 1990.

*

Media Adaptations: Films—*The Violent Enemy,* 1968, from the novel *A Candle for the Dead*; *The Wrath of God,* 1972; *The Eagle Has Landed,* 1977; *A Prayer for the Dying,* 1987. Television films—*To Catch a King,* 1984; *Night of the Fox,* 1990; *On Dangerous Ground,* 1995; *Midnight Man,* 1995, from the novel *Eye of the Storm; Thunderpoint,* 1996.

* * *

Author Jack Higgins (a pseudonym for Henry Patterson) has produced a stunning number of books under various names since his first published novel, *Sad Wind from the Sea* (1959). A former British soldier and teacher, Higgins has become a perennial writer of thriller fiction, spawning several media adaptations of his works and intriguing readers with his complex plots.

Having published over 30 novels by 1975, Higgins had not won widespread acclaim until *The Eagle Has Landed* (1975), a WWII thriller dealing with a secret German invasion of England in 1943. Operation Eagle, a Nazi plan to abduct and/or assassinate British Prime Minister Winston Churchill, becomes reality when German paratroopers, led by Colonel Kurt Steiner, infiltrate England with the aid of likable IRA man Liam Devlin. Remarkable for its suspense and surprising plot twists, the novel depicts the German soldiers in a sympathetic light; Steiner is a career soldier, not a Nazi, and he goes to great lengths to keep civilians from harm. The novel also introduces Devlin, a character who appears in Higgins' later works, including *Touch the Devil* (1982) and *Confessional* (1985).

Many readers fault Higgins for occasionally flat prose and superficial characters and situations, yet few criticize his handling of suspenseful plots. *Confessional* deals with Mikhail Kelly, a half-Irish, half-Russian "maker of disorder" for the KGB who constantly disrupts the tentative peace of Northern Ireland for his Russian masters. Believed by some British intelligence agents to be mad, Kelly breaks all rules when he seems to be planning to shoot Pope John Paul II, who is visiting Canterbury. D. G. Meyers of the *New York Times Book Review* praises Higgins for his "tense" and "riveting" story, adding, "If Mr. Higgins' prose is dull and his understanding of humanity shallow, it may only be because good prose and a deeper understanding would inhibit the race to the plot's final twist."

Higgins' longevity and productivity as a writer may have taken its toll on the credibility and overall quality of his stories. The Greek protagonist of *Solo* (1980) is a world-famous pianist and killer-for-hire. In one instance, he sneaks into a victim's villa and confronts and makes love to the maid in a closet before lovingly tying her up. He then commits his murder before vanishing into the night. *Night of the Fox* (1987), the story of an American philosopher-turned-patriotic killer during WWII, pits the hero against Germans who have captured one Allied soldier who has extensive knowledge of the approaching Normandy invasion. The characters reveal their motives far too early in the novel and clumsily point out obvious ironies.

A Season in Hell (1989) deals with a wide variety of incongruous characters: a murdered man; his wealthy and vengeful American stepmother; her lethal British Secret Services ally; the Sicilian Mafia; a secretive drug czar with various assassins; and a *capo* with a heart of gold, all adding plot twists that lead to the required climactic shootout. As the *New York Times Book Review*'s critic Newgate Callendar points out, "Too much depends upon likely coincidence. But Mr. Higgins is a real pro, and he keeps things moving so fast the reader is apt to forget and forgive." Callendar pans *Eye of the Storm* (1992), saying that the novel "represents Mr. Higgins at his worst . . . the characters have as much credibility as Saturday morning cartoons." Yet *The Eagle Has Flown* (1991), the sequel to *The Eagle Has Landed* which deals with the German plan to rescue the captured Steiner from the Tower of London, is seen by many as reminiscent of Higgins at his best.

Higgins does not claim to be a writer of literary fiction: "I look upon myself primarily as an entertainer" he told *Contemporary Authors*. "Even in my novel *A Phoenix in Blood* (1964), which deals with the color-bar problem in England, I still have tried to entertain, to make the events interesting as a story—not just the ideas [and] ethics of the situation. I believe that at any level a writer's only success is to be measured by his ability to communicate." Fans of Robert Ludlum and Frederick Forsythe looking for a lively thriller can do far worse than picking up a Jack Higgins novel, providing they don't require extensive plot realism or character development beyond a few revealing, well-chosen phrases and the obligatory pistol-waving.

—Christopher Swann

HIGHSMITH, Patricia

Pseudonym: Claire Morgan. **Nationality:** American. **Born:** Mary Patricia Plangman in Fort Worth, Texas, 19 January 1921; took stepfather's name. **Education:** Julia Richmond, High School, New York; Barnard College, New York, B.A. 1942. Lived in Europe since 1963. **Awards:** Grand Prix de Littérature Policière, 1957; Crime Writers Association Silver Dagger award, 1964. **Died:** 5 February 1995.

Publications

Novels

Strangers on a Train. New York, Harper, and London, Cresset Press, 1950.
The Price of Salt (as Claire Morgan). New York, Coward McCann, 1952; as *Carol* (as Patricia Highsmith), London, Bloomsbury, 1990.
The Blunderer. New York, Coward McCann, 1954; London, Cresset Press, 1956; as *Lament for a Lover*, New York, Popular Library, 1956.
The Talented Mr. Ripley. New York, Coward McCann, 1955; London, Cresset Press, 1957.
Deep Water. New York, Harper, 1957; London, Heinemann, 1958.
A Game for the Living. New York, Harper, 1958; London, Heinemann, 1959.
This Sweet Sickness. New York, Harper, 1960; London, Heinemann, 1961.
The Cry of the Owl. New York, Harper, 1962; London, Heinemann, 1963.
The Two Faces of January. New York, Doubleday, and London, Heinemann, 1964.
The Glass Cell. New York, Doubleday, 1964; London, Heinemann, 1965.
The Story-Teller. New York, Doubleday, 1965; as *A Suspension of Mercy*, London, Heinemann, 1965.
Those Who Walk Away. New York, Doubleday, and London, Heinemann, 1967.
The Tremor of Forgery. New York, Doubleday, and London, Heinemann, 1969.
Ripley Under Ground. New York, Doubleday, 1970; London, Heinemann, 1971.
A Dog's Ransom. New York, Knopf, and London, Heinemann, 1972.
Ripley's Game. New York, Knopf, and London, Heinemann, 1974.
Edith's Diary. New York, Simon and Schuster, and London, Heinemann, 1977.
The Boy Who Followed Ripley. New York, Lippincott, and London, Heinemann, 1980.
People Who Knock on the Door. London, Heinemann, 1983; New York, Mysterious Press, 1985.
Found in the Street. London, Heinemann, 1986; New York, Atlantic Monthly Press, 1987.
Ripley Under Water. London, Bloomsbury, 1991.
The Talented Mr. Ripley; Ripley Under Ground; Ripley's Game; The Boy Who Followed Ripley. London, Chancellor, 1994.
Small g: Summer Idyll. London, Bloomsbury, 1995.

Short Stories

The Snail-Watcher and Other Stories. New York, Doubleday, 1970; as *Eleven*, London, Heinemann, 1970.
Kleine Geschichten für Weiberfeinde. Zurich, Diogenes, 1974; as *Little Tales of Misogyny*, London, Heinemann, 1977, New York, Mysterious Press, 1986.
The Animal-Lover's Book of Beastly Murder. London, Heinemann, 1975; New York, Mysterious Press, 1986.
Slowly, Slowly in the Wind. London, Heinemann, 1979; New York, Mysterious Press, 1987.
The Black House. London, Heinemann, 1981.
Mermaids on the Golf Course and Other Stories. London, Heinemann, 1985; New York, Mysterious Press, 1988.
Tales of Natural and Unnatural Catastrophes. London, Bloomsbury, 1987; New York, Atlantic Monthly Press, 1989.

Other

Miranda the Panda Is on the Veranda (for children), with Doris Sanders. New York, Coward McCann, 1958.
Plotting and Writing Suspense Fiction. Boston, The Writer, 1966; London, Poplar Press, 1983; revised edition, New York, St. Martin's Press, 1990.

*

Media Adaptations: Films—*Strangers on a Train*, 1951, *Once You Kiss a Stranger*, 1969, both from the novel *Strangers on a Train*; *Purple Noon* (French-Italian), 1960, from the novel *The Talented Mr. Ripley*; *The American Friend* (U.S.-French-German), 1977, from the novel *Ripley's Game*; several other foreign film adaptations.

* * *

Fort Worth-born Patricia Highsmith wrote 22 novels and numerous short stories before her death in 1995 at age 74. Respected for their literacy, psychological insights, and irony, Highsmith's intensely engaging stories also challenge conventional ethics by examining moral values from very unusual and unexpected perspectives, including not only those of amoral killers and pathological cases but also (in a short story series) those of goats, elephants, and other animals under the control of man. Her studies of the criminal mind, particularly of murderers, focus on human psychology rather than on detection or suspense, and many of her works depend on one-on-one relationships. The clinically detached voice and amoral point of view of her narrators compel, disturb, challenge, and chill, for they make the psychopathic not simply understandable but fascinating and amusing. Highsmith is, as renowned novelist Graham Greene says, a "poet of apprehension." Her spare prose is as incisive as her portraits of human folly are haunting.

Highsmith's explorations of questions of guilt and culpability, their evocation of aggression, self-doubt, and alienation spring in part from her unhappy childhood; her mother drank turpentine to try to miscarry Patricia, her parents divorced shortly after her birth, and her stepfather was alternately indifferent or antagonistic. Highsmith's characterization of the family of one of her doomed heroines as "blind" and "uncaring" describes her own family, except for her Texas grandmother with whom she spent her early years. Her grandmother taught her that reading could be an escape from uncomfortable realities.

Writing allowed her to face those realities in a fictive format. Highsmith published her first short story, "The Heroine," in *Harper's Bazaar* in 1945, and her first novel, *Strangers on a Train,* a suspense classic popularized by the Alfred Hitchcock film of the same title, in 1949. Truman Capote helped her enter the Yaddo artists' colony in upstate New York and get her start as a professional writer. Highsmith's narrative voice and thematic interests proved distinctive from the beginning, surfacing in a terse style that depicted irrational compulsions beneath exterior calm.

Strangers on a Train, a perceptive psychological thriller, introduces a theme that has become a cliche of the detective story—an agreement by strangers to exchange murder victims to prevent police detection based on an investigation of the obvious suspect. Her highly popular, prize-winning Ripley series continues the exploration of charming, amoral psychopaths. Tom Ripley is a criminal protagonist who commits terrible acts without a shred of guilt, yet readers inevitably cheer for him even as the law pursues him. Anthony Hilfer's insightful study in "Not Really Such a Monster: Highsmith's Ripley as Thriller Protagonist and Protean Man," explores the psychological dimensions and unconventional morality of Ripley (*Midwest Quarterly,* 25, Summer, 1984), while Alain Delon, in the French film "Plein Soleil," based on *The Talented Mr. Ripley,* successfully captures the charm that makes Ripley so likable.

Other Highsmith novels deal with the concept of the doppelganger and the interplay of hunter and hunted. *The Glass Cell* (1964) explores the negative effects of incarceration on an individual and the social implications of these effects, while one of her finest novels and Highsmith's personal favorite, *The Tremor of Forgery* (1969), set in Tunisia, which Highsmith visited, probes the moral judgments of Howard Ingham, who is never quite sure whether he killed, inadvertently, an unknown intruder one evening. By conjuring up interior worlds and by providing no pat answers, Highsmith gives the suspense novel a deeper social and moral significance.

It was under the pseudonym Claire Morgan that Highsmith confronted questions of sexually orthodoxy, first in a lesbian love story (*The Price of Salt* [1952]), then in a tale of political activism (like Highsmith's own) in *Edith's Diary* (1977), and finally in her posthumously published novel, *Small g: A Summer Idyll* (1995), about a youthful love triangle in which girl gets girl. In an interview with *Village Voice* reporter Joan Dupont, Highsmith asserted her belief that a writer should talk about "adult human emotions," and "anger and a sense of injustice." She also expressed her irritation that, because of her interest in the unorthodoxies of the criminal mind, American critics have not given her the literary recognition accorded her by Europeans.

Overall, Highsmith makes the conventional seem the abnormal, and the unconventional normal. She explores the dark potentials of the human psyche, traces controversial modern issues to horrifying conclusions, and challenges moral complacency by forcing readers to participate in unconventional mind-sets and perspectives. She is a truly unique literary talent.

—Gina Macdonald

HIJUELOS, Oscar

Nationality: American. **Born:** New York, 24 August 1951. **Education:** City College of the City University of New York, B.A., 1975, M.A., 1976. **Family:** Married; two children. **Career:** Transportation Display, Inc., Winston Network, New York, advertising media traffic manager, 1977-84; writer, 1984—. **Awards:** Received "outstanding writer" citation from Pushcart Press, 1978, for the story "Columbus Discovering America"; Oscar Cintas fiction writing grant, 1978-79; Breadloaf Writers Conference scholarship, 1980; fiction writing grant from Creative Artists Programs Service, 1982, and from Ingram Merrill Foundation, 1983; Fellowship for Creative Writers award from National Endowment for the Arts, and American Academy in Rome Fellowship in Literature from American Academy and Institute of Arts and Letters, both 1985, for *Our House in the Last World*; Pulitzer prize for fiction, 1990, for *The Mambo Kings Play Songs of Love.* **Agent:** Harriet Wasserman Literary Agency, 137 East 36th St., New York, New York, 10016, U.S.A. **Address:** 211 West 106th St., New York, New York 10025, U.S.A.

PUBLICATIONS

Novels

Our House in the Last World. Persea Books, 1983.
The Mambo Kings Play Songs of Love. 1989.
The Fourteen Sisters of Emilio Montez O'Brien. Farrar, Straus and Giroux, 1993.
Mr. Ives' Christmas. HarperCollins, 1995.

* * *

Since publishing his first novel, *Our House in the Last World,* in 1983, Oscar Hijuelos has become an increasingly popular figure in contemporary American literature. *Our House* tells the story of the Santinio family coming to New York City from Cuba in the 1940s. Hijuelos didn't have to look far to find the inspiration for his tale of Cuban immigrants; his parents emigrated from Cuba and settled in New York City, where Hijuelos was born in 1951.

At the center of *Our House* is Hector Santinio, who must attempt to come to terms with the inability of his mother and father to adjust easily to life in America. The struggle of this family to deal with the memories of Cuba ("the last world") is at the center of this tragic story of love and loss. Cultural identity is another theme in this novel. Santinio family members must try to maintain their Cuban heritage while assimilating into American culture. Critics have applauded Hijuelos's rich descriptions of life in Cuba and his ability to incorporate elements of magical realism (a Latin literary tradition) into the novel. Despite the initial positive critical attention given to Hijuelos for this novel, *Our House in the Last World* achieved only spotty commercial success.

Published in 1989, *The Mambo Kings Play Songs of Love* provided Hijuelos with both commercial and critical success. Most notably, the novel was awarded the Pulitzer Prize in 1990, the first time a Cuban-American was awarded the prize. *The Mambo Kings* continues the theme of the search for cultural identity that is present in *Our House in the Last World.* The reader is introduced to the Castillo brothers, Nestor and Cesar, who have emigrated to New York City. Framed by the narrative of Nestor's son, Eugenio, we are told the story of Nestor and Cesar's immigration from Havana and their search for the American dream in the 1950s. Driven by a desire to preserve some sense of their Cuban identity, the brothers form an orchestra known as the Mambo Kings. Through this orchestra Cesar and Nestor gain some fame, but the success isn't enough to help them overcome their sense of longing for their native Cuba. Critics had plenty of good words for this novel; Hijuelos was praised, particularly, for his romantic descriptions of Cuban culture and for the sometimes lyrical language of the novel. The novel gained further attention when it was made into a motion picture (in both English and Spanish).

Following *The Mambo Kings Plays Songs of Love,* Hijuelos published *The Fourteen Sisters of Emilio Montez O'Brien* (1993). In this novel, Hijuelos attempts to branch out from his usual setting of New York City by placing the family in Pennsylvania. The novel is a chronicle of the lives of the children of an Irish-immigrant father and a Cuban-immigrant mother. The O'Brien family story is often presented through the narrative of Emilio, who will begin to tell the family history while taking new photos of the family or reminiscing about old photos. Thus, we are led through a figurative scrapbook of O'Brien family history. Elements of magical realism are again present in this novel as the O'Brien sisters are responsible for many strange happenings due to their feminine wiles. This novel received fair reviews. Some critics enjoyed Hijuelos's mix of Irish and Cuban heritage while others criticized that very element. Negative reviews also faulted Hijuelos for unkind portrayals of women, a weak plot, and a poor premise.

The blending of Cuban and American cultural traditions makes Hijuelos's novels unique. Readers are allowed to escape to a different culture and a different time through the lush imagery and language contained within the pages of his works. Ironically, much criticism of Hijuelos's work concerns his knowledge of Cuban culture as an American-born citizen. These criticisms haven't had much of an effect on Hijuelos. As he once said of his first novel's concern with cultural identity, "Although I am quite Americanized, my book focuses on many of my feelings about identity and my 'Cubanness.' I intended for my book to commemorate at least a few aspects of the Cuban psyche [as I know it]."

—Melissa L. Evans

HILL, John. *See* **KOONTZ, Dean R(ay).**

HILLERMAN, Tony

Nationality: American. **Born:** Sacred Heart, Oklahoma, 27 May 1925. **Education:** Raised among Pottawatomie and Seminole Indians; attended Indian boarding school for eight years; Oklahoma State University, Stillwater; University of Oklahoma, Norman, B.A. in journalism 1948; University of New Mexico, Albuquerque, M.A. in English 1965. **Military Service:** Served in the U.S. Army Infantry during World War II: Silver Star, Bronze Star, Purple Heart. **Family:** Married Marie E. Unzner in 1948; three daughters and three sons. **Career:** Reporter, *News Herald,* Borger, Texas, 1948; news editor, *Morning Press,* 1949, and city editor, *Constitution,* 1950, Lawton, Oklahoma; political reporter, United Press, Oklahoma City, 1952; bureau manager, United Press, Santa Fe, New Mexico, 1953; executive editor, *The New Mexican,* Santa Fe, 1954. Associate Professor 1965-66, Professor of Journalism and Chairman of Department, 1966-88, Assistant to the President, University of New Mexico, 1975-88. **Awards:** Burrows award, for journalism; Shaffer award, for reporting, 1952; Mystery Writers of America Edgar Allan Poe award, 1974; Grand Master award, 1991; U.S. Department of Interior Public Service award; Navajo Tribe award; Center for the American Indian Ambassador award; Western Writers of America Silver Spur award; Anthony award, 1995. Honorary doctorates: Arizona State University, University of New Mexico. **Agent:** Curtis Brown Ltd., 10 Astor Place, New York, New York 10003. **Address:** 1632 Francisca Rd. NW, Albuquerque, New Mexico 87107-7118, U.S.A.

Publications

Novels (series: Sergeant Jim Chee; Lieutenant Joe Leaphorn)

The Blessing Way (Leaphorn). New York, Harper, and London, Macmillan, 1970.

The Fly on the Wall. New York, Harper, 1971.

Dance Hall of the Dead (Leaphorn). New York, Harper, 1973.

Listening Woman (Leaphorn). New York, Harper, 1978; London, Macmillan, 1979.

People of Darkness (Chee). New York, Harper, 1980; London, Gollancz, 1982.

The Dark Wind (Chee). New York, Harper, 1982; London, Gollancz, 1983.

The Ghostway (Chee). New York, Harper, and London, Gollancz, 1985.

Skinwalkers (Chee and Leaphorn). New York, Harper, 1987; London, Joseph, 1988.

A Thief of Time (Chee and Leaphorn). New York, Harper, 1988; London, Joseph, 1989.

Talking God (Chee and Leaphorn). New York, Harper, 1989; London, Joseph, 1990.

The Joe Leaphorn Mysteries (omnibus). New York, Harper, 1989.
Coyote Waits (Chee and Leaphorn). New York, Harper, 1990.
Sacred Clowns (Chee and Leaphorn). New York, Harper, 1993.
Finding Moon (Chee and Leaphorn). New York, Harper, 1995.

Other

The Boy Who Made Dragonfly: A Zuni Myth. New York, Harper, 1972.
The Great Taos Bank Robbery and Other Indian Country Affairs. Albuquerque, University of New Mexico Press, 1973.
New Mexico, photographs by David Muench. Portland, Oregon, Belding, 1974.
Rio Grande, photographs by Robert Reynolds. Portland, Oregon, Graphic Arts Center, 1975.
Indian Country: America's Sacred Land, photographs by Béla Kalman. Flagstaff, Arizona, Northland Press, 1987.

Editor, *The Spell of New Mexico.* Albuquerque, University of New Mexico Press, 1977.
Editor, *The Best of the West.* New York, Harper, 1993.
Editor, *The Mysterious West.* New York, Harper, 1995.

*

Media Adaptation: Film—*The Dark Wind,* 1991, from the novel.

Manuscript Collection: Zimmerman Library, University of New Mexico.

Critical Studies: *Words, Weather and Wolfmen: Conversations with Tony Hillerman* by Tony Hillerman and Ernie Bulow, 1989, revised as *Talking Mysteries: A Conversation with Tony Hillerman* by Tony Hillerman and Ernie Bulow, Albuquerque, University of New Mexico Press, 1991; *The Tony Hillerman Companion: A Comprehensive Guide to His Life and Work,* New York, Harper, 1995.

* * *

Born in Oklahoma, Tony Hillerman learned the craft of storytelling at an early age. As a child, he attended a Catholic school for Seminole and Potawatomie pupils, where he gained knowledge of Native American lifestyles. Later moving to New Mexico, he encountered the Navajo people, whose lives and landscape form the basis of his fiction. His first novel, *The Blessing Way* (1970) is a tense, exciting adventure that mixes espionage and witchcraft. It introduces Lt. Joe Leaphorn, Hillerman's Navajo Tribal Police detective.

Hillerman's second novel, The *Fly on the Wall* (1971) is a murder mystery set outside Navajo country. But in his third book, *Dance Hall of the Dead* (1973), he returns to the Reservation, and Leaphorn. The story opens with the murder of a Zuni boy preparing for the Shalako ceremony, and involves a hippie commune, drugs, and an archaeological dig. Operating in his calm, methodical way, Leaphorn unravels the threads of the mystery. *Dance Hall* won the Mystery Writers of America Edgar Allan Poe Award, but nevertheless fell short of Hillerman's next novel, *The Listening Woman* (1978). In that story, Leaphorn, investigating two homicides, finds himself trapped in an underground cavern with armed terrorists and their hostages. The novel combines clever plotlines with sharp character insights and a taut, nail-biting payoff.

People of Darkness (1980) introduces Jim Chee. Chee, like Leaphorn, is a Tribal Police officer, but younger and more traditional than the experienced lieutenant. Chee is studying to become a "hataali" and perform the sacred ceremonies, but as a policeman is an impulsive loner whose rule-bending sometimes gets him in trouble. *People of Darkness* explores a fatal oil-rig explosion and takes on a murderous hit man. Moving forward, *The Dark Wind* (1982) finds Chee accused of murder and struggling to expose a cocaine-smuggling ring while pursued by federal agents. Then, in *The Ghostway* (1984), he tracks a missing Navajo girl to Los Angeles and encounters large-scale car theft and a ruthless hired killer.

In *Skinwalkers* (1986) Hillerman pairs Leaphorn and Chee together in the same novel, a method used in all four later books. He explores the contrast in their characters: Leaphorn, the calm experienced "supercop," looking for a pattern in every mystery; and Chee, the quick-thinking, rebellious loner, prone to act on impulse. Here, as in all his work, he presents the Navajo way of life—the adaptability and the strong family ties of "The People"—while looking more sadly at the scourges of witchcraft and alcoholism. "Skinwalkers" is Navajo for witches, and the story, which begins with a vicious shotgun attack on Chee, has witchcraft at its center. A strong, neatly worked novel with a shocking climax, it won the Golden Spur Award from the Western Writers of America.

It was *A Thief of Time* (1988) that propelled Hillerman to fame, running eleven weeks on the bestseller lists in the United States. Opening with a murder on an Anasazi historical site, it also features a psychopathic killer and the personal relationships of both Leaphorn and Chee. *Talking God* (1989) is one of Hillerman's finest, and has both Chee and Leaphorn travelling to Washington D.C. in a plot including missing artifacts, Chilean murder squads, and an undersized hired gunman. Hillerman condemns the displays of Native American skeletons still held by the Smithsonian, while writing an excellent imaginative novel.

In *Coyote Waits* (1990) a fellow officer is murdered. Once more Hillerman keeps the reader riveted with several neatly spun plotlines that fuse together in the end. Similarly, *Sacred Clowns* (1993) tries to find a link between the deaths of a Hopi koshare (sacred clown) and a schoolteacher. It shows Hillerman at his best. The unravelling of the mystery and the friendships of Chee and Leaphorn are adroitly blended with touches of humor. Unforgettable is the scene where Chee, lawyer Janet Pete, and Cheyenne cop Harold Blizzard watch "Cheyenne Autumn," and translate the ribald comments of the Navajo extras.

An early influence on Hillerman was Australian writer Arthur Upfield, whose "outback" novels appealed to him. But Hillerman's characters and plots, and his masterly descriptions of the New Mexico terrain, are very much his own. Hillerman's affection for the Navajo has been recognized by the Navajo themselves: his proudest possession is the plaque given to him by the tribal council in 1987, signifying him "Special Friend" of the Navajo. His novels are a fitting tribute to them, and to his own writing skills.

—Geoff Sadler

HINTON, S(usan) E(loise)

Nationality: American. **Born:** 1950, in Tulsa, Oklahoma. **Education:** University of Tulsa, B.S., 1970. **Family:** Married David

E. Inhofe, 1970; children: Nicholas David. **Career:** Writer. **Awards:** *New York Herald Tribune* best teenage books citation, 1967, *Chicago Tribune Book World* Spring Book Festival Honor Book, 1967, *Media & Methods* Maxi award, American Library Association (ALA) Best Young Adult Books citation, both 1975, and Massachusetts Children's Book award, 1979, all for *The Outsiders;* ALA Best Books for Young Adults citation, 1971, *Chicago Tribune Book World* Spring Book Festival Honor Book, 1971, and Massachusetts Children's Book award, 1978, all for *That Was Then, This Is Now;* ALA Best Books for Young Adults citation, 1975, *School Library Journal* Best Books of the Year citation, 1975, and Land of Enchantment award, New Mexico Library Association, 1982, all for *Rumble Fish;* ALA Best Books for Young Adults citation, 1979, *School Library Journal* Best Books of the Year citation, 1979, New York Public Library Books for the Teen-Age citation, 1980, American Book award nomination for children's paperback, 1981, Sue Hefly honor book, Louisiana Association of School Libraries, 1982, California Young Reader Medal nomination, California Reading Association, 1982, and Sue Hefly award, 1983, all for *Tex;* Golden Archer award, 1983; Recipient of first ALA Young Adult Services Division/*School Library Journal* Author award, 1988. **Address:** c/o Press Relations, Delacorte Press, One Dag Hammarskjold Plaza, New York, New York 10017, U.S.A.

Publications

Young Adult Novels

The Outsiders. Viking, 1967.
That Was Then, This Is Now. Viking, 1971.
Rumble Fish. Delacorte, 1975.
Tex. Delacorte, 1979.
Taming the Star Runner. Delacorte, 1988.

Plays

Screenplay: *Rumble Fish,* adapted from her novel, with Francis Ford Coppola, 1983.

Other

Big David, Little David, illustrated by Alan Daniel. Doubleday, 1994.
The Puppy Sister, illustrated by Jacqueline Rogers. Delacorte, 1995.

*

Media Adaptations: Films—*Tex,* 1982; *The Outsiders,* 1983; *That Was Then, This Is Now,* 1985. Television series—*The Outsiders,* 1990.

Critical Studies: *Presenting S. E. Hinton* by Jay Daly, Twayne, 1987.

* * *

Susan Eloise Hinton was 16 when she wrote *The Outsiders* (1967). She has said that she wrote the book because she was unhappy with what was available for teens at the time and she wanted something to read. Whatever her motives, the book made an indelible impression on the world of young adult fiction.

The Outsiders is the story of Ponyboy Curtis, his brothers Darrell and Sodapop, and the gang with which they associate. The book was among the first to focus on the kids from the other side of the tracks (the "outsiders"), rather than the popular kids. Before Hinton's book, young adult fiction had dealt with upper-middle-class young people, and primarily football players, cheerleaders, and other popular and successful students. Hinton shifted the focus to outcasts, gang members, and less socially acceptable students. All of her books use young males as protagonists, and all but one are told from the first-person perspective. Her female characters tend to be weak and ill defined. She has said that she does not do women well, and tends to avoid portraying them.

Hinton's second book, *That Was Then, This Is Now* (1971), was published four years after her first. Hinton acknowledges that she had a major case of writer's block after her first book and that the second took considerably more time to write. The book may be the weakest of all her novels. The adult characters are unrealistic and ill-defined, and much of the so-called drug information is outdated or demonstrably incorrect. Nevertheless, like her other books, it was enormously popular with young adult readers.

Rumble Fish (1975) has been called an "interesting failure." The book is thin, has forced symbolism, and proffers weak plotlines hung on preposterous coincidences. Although the book does have some strengths in its depiction of characters that make it an interesting project, some of the plot turns are just silly. What is the reader to make, for instance, of the fact that the "Motorcycle Boy" locates his mother after seeing her on television in the audience of an awards show? Yet the book has life, and readers.

Tex (1979) is a better book. For the first time Hinton uses an interesting female in the character of Jamie. *Tex* tries to jam too much action into too short a time span, which is probably the book's major flaw. But *Tex* also raises an interesting question about Hinton's work. Tex uses a line that is almost verbatim the same line used by Mark in *That Was Then, This Is Now*: "Nothing that bad ever happened to me." *Tex* also suffers from the same sort of unexplained nightmares as Ponyboy Curtis in *The Outsiders.* Is such repetition simply a dearth of imagination, or does Hinton cannibalize her own work for plot ideas?

Taming the Star Runner (1988), Hinton's most recent young adult book, is different in some ways from her previous works. For one thing, the point of view is third person. *Taming the Star Runner* seems to make the break from a perspective that identifies with the protagonist to a perspective that stands outside and views the protagonist. In *The Outsiders,* Hinton and Ponyboy, the narrator, are inseparable. They are the same person. By the time an older Hinton reaches *Taming the Star Runner,* she is observing the action, telling the reader about a situation in which she is not involved. It's an interesting difference, but a telling one; the move from a participant to an observer is a significant step and seems to mark the fact that Hinton is past the age at which she can closely identify with her characters.

Whatever the assessment of her work in literary terms, there is no doubt that S. E. Hinton had an impact on young adult fiction that was major, indelible, and lasting. If there are flaws in her writing, they have been overlooked by two generations of young adult readers.

—June Harris

HITE, Shere

Nationality: American. **Born:** Shirley Diana Gregory in St. Joseph, Missouri, 2 November 1942. **Education:** University of Florida, B.A. (cum laude), 1964, M.A., 1968; further graduate study at Columbia University, 1968-69. **Family:** Married Friedrich Hoericke in 1985. **Career:** Model for Wilhelmina Agency, late 1960s; National Organization for Women (NOW), New York City, director of Feminist Sexuality Project, 1972-78; Hite Research International, New York City, director, 1978—. Instructor in female sexuality, New York University, 1977—; lecturer, Harvard University, McGill University, Columbia University, and women's groups, 1977-83. Member of advisory board, American Foundation of Gender and Genital Medicine, Johns Hopkins University. **Member:** National Organization for Women (NOW), American Historical Association, American Sociological Association, American Association for the Advancement of Science, Society for the Scientific Study of Sex, Women's Health Network, Academy of Political Science, Women's History Association. **Address:** P.O. Box 5282, FDR Station, New York, New York 10022, U.S.A.

Publications

Nonfiction

The Hite Report: A Nationwide Study of Female Sexuality. Macmillan, 1976.

The Hite Report on Male Sexuality. Knopf, 1981.

Women and Love: A Cultural Revolution in Progress. Knopf, 1987.

Good Guys, Bad Guys: The Hite Guide to Smart Choices, with Kate Colleran. Colleran & Graf, 1991.

The Hite Report on the Family: Growing Up under Patriarchy. Grove, 1994.

Women as Revolutionary Agents of Change: The Hite Reports and Beyond. University of Wisconsin Press, 1994.

Novel

The Divine Comedy of Ariadne and Jupiter. Dufour, 1994.

Editor, *Sexual Honesty: By Women for Women.* Warner Paperback Library, 1974.

* * *

The "Hite reports" have proved to be controversial, provocative, and immediate bestsellers over the years, and have been placed within the company of such reports on sexuality as the Kinsey Report and the Masters and Johnson report. While the Hite reports contain statistics and conclusions, the bulk of them consist of quotations from the people who answered questionnaires. Indeed, Shere Hite's standard method has been to issue a vast number of questionnaires to targeted groups of people, and then to compile her findings by processing the answers.

The first report was *A Nationwide Study of Female Sexuality* (1976), which was the culmination of a trend toward more freedom for women to speak for themselves. Erica Jong praised the simplicity of Hite's initial project, which contrasted strongly with the "inscrutable prose of Masters and Johnson." Criticizing the male-oriented reproductive pattern of sexual expression as the genesis of many of women's sexual difficulties, it presented a revision of the current notions of female sexuality and sexual fulfillment. Hite concluded that men have constructed sexuality to their own advantage. However, despite Jong's forceful defense of the report, many reviewers were put off by what was perceived to be Hite's feminist bias. Furthermore, the report was dismissed by some as pseudo-science.

Undaunted, Hite produced several more reports. *The Hite Report on Male Sexuality* (1981) sought to smash "any remaining myths about 'normal' male sexuality that [had] not been reduced to dust by earlier reports." Although comparisons with the Kinsey report are frequently made, Kinsey measured the frequency of sexual behaviors rather than reporting attitudes or feelings about sex. Nevertheless, although the report argued for a redefinition of masculinity based on its findings, statistical problems remained. The representative nature of the sample was questioned, and it was pointed out that it was difficult to distinguish between fact and fantasy in the male returns to the questionnaire.

Hite's report entitled *Women and Love: A Cultural Revolution in Progress* (1987) was the third instalment of her inquiries into the intimate lives of men and women. According to one reviewer, it produced a "valuable, provocative, loosely argued, searching meditation on how culture influences love." The conclusion was that women's unhappiness about male love for them was due to the fact that male emotion was impoverished, inarticulate, and discriminatory, resulting in female insecurity and neediness. The report concluded that "male ideology discourages them from trying harder" to love women. One critic noted that Hite "suggests that women have more power than they really do," and thus avoided a closer study of their economic situation. Michael Ignatieff described it as "shrill pontification," but conceded that the women's testimonies bear witness to the real misery of women in the United States.

A more recent report, *Growing Up Under Patriarchy* (1994) was proffered as a study of family life. It concluded that new family forms are emerging that are not solely dominated by the patriarchal model. The report attracted the usual controversy. One reviewer announced that it was of limited use, since the results were unsurprising and that it suffered from a post-Freudian fallacy; Hite had not understood "that it may be better for people to keep their family grievances to themselves."

Overall, Hite's reports have proved to be successful largely because they have popularized sexual mores and given a voice to what people feel to be the average citizen's perspective. They have received similar amounts of acclaim and criticism, negative criticism most often focusing on the anecdotal nature of her data.

More recently, Hite has branched out into fiction, with her first novel *The Divine Comedy of Aridane and Jupiter* (1994). A mixture of fantasy and ideas, the narrative tells of the trip Ariadne and her magic dog Jupiter make to earth. What follows is a fast-paced political satire in which Ariadne seeks enlightenment from a panoply of historical figures. The book is a cultural critique, written in something of a postmodern style, and has been hailed as a great comic and satirical success. One waits to see whether this literary *hors d'ouevre* marks a radically new departure for Shere Hite.

—Tim Woods

HOFFMAN, Alice

Nationality: American. **Born:** New York City, 16 March 1952. **Education:** Adelphi University, Garden City, New York, B.A. 1973; Stanford University, California (Mirelles fellow), M.A. 1975. **Family:** Married to Tom Martin; two sons. Lives in Boston, Massachusetts. **Awards:** Bread Loaf Writers Conference Atherton scholarship, 1976. **Address:** c/o Putnam, 200 Madison Avenue, New York, New York 10016, U.S.A.

Publications

Novels

Property Of. New York, Farrar Straus, 1977; London, Hutchinson, 1978.
The Drowning Season. New York, Dutton, and London, Hutchinson, 1979.
Angel Landing. New York, Putnam, 1980; London, Severn House, 1982.
White Horses. New York, Putnam, 1982; London, Collins, 1983.
Fortune's Daughter. New York, Putnam, and London, Collins, 1985.
Illumination Night. New York, Putnam, and London, Macmillan, 1987.
At Risk. New York, Putnam, and London, Macmillan, 1988.
Seventh Heaven. New York, Putnam, and London, Virago Press, 1991.
Turtle Moon. New York, Putnam, and London, Macmillan, 1992.
Second Nature. New York, Putnam, and London, Macmillan, 1994.
Practical Magic. New York, Putnam, and London, Macmillan, 1995.

Uncollected Short Stories

"Blue Tea," in *Redbook* (New York), June 1982.
"Sweet Young Things," in *Mademoiselle* (New York), June 1983.
"Sleep Tight," in *Ploughshares* (Cambridge, Massachusetts), vol. 15, no. 2-3, 1989.

* * *

Novelist Alice Hoffman meshes fantasy and reality to illustrate the bizarre or troubled lives of her characters. She writes about family relationships, misplaced love, faith, and friendship. Her hallmark is the use of folklore and symbolism to create a sense of mythology in everyday modern life. Hoffman accomplishes this through vividly descriptive language that explores people's inner lives.

Certain themes appear regularly in Hoffman's works. She develops influential female characters who are the major source of action in the plots. Men play minor roles; mostly they exist to fulfill the women's fantasies. The men, while sometimes dangerous characters, are not usually the creators of the drama. Opinions vary as to Hoffman's success in developing her characters. For example, William C. Bamberger wrote that her use of conversation to develop personalities is "unrealistic candor between characters who hardly know one another."

Current issues and trends influence Hoffman's writing, with sexual longings and fears occupying a major portion of her characters' experiences. In *Fortune's Daughter* (1985), for instance, she explores the life of a pregnant woman abandoned by the baby's father. Teenage sexual recklessness is portrayed in *Illumination Night,* (1987) and *At Risk* (1988) tells the story of a young girl who innocently contracts AIDS. Hoffman frequently uses magical symbols and talismans to bridge fantasy and reality. One of the main characters in *Fortune's Daughter,* in fact, is a fortune teller.

Another unique feature of Hoffman's novels is their use of mythology as an influence in people's fantasies. *White Horses* (1982) is a tale of arias (supernatural men who lead women out of unfulfilling lives into romance and adventure). In this case, the women are a mother and daughter who believe their son/brother is an aria. An incestuous relationship results between the daughter and son.

Hoffman's first work, *Property Of,* was published in 1977 when she was 25 years old. Perhaps due to her own youth, it is not surprising that the heroine of the novel is a 17-year-old who falls in love with a street gang leader. The story takes place in suburban New York City, and is told through the eyes of the nameless girl. She is attracted to the gang leader's "honor" as exemplified by the gang's code of behavior. Drugs, violence, and young love are explored. These predictable topics are enriched when Hoffman "creates characters touched by legend" (Edith Milton, *Yale Review*).

Many of Hoffman's characters are alienated individuals who achieve some form of redemption through human contact and commitment. *The Drowning Season* (1979) is about a girl whose parents are emotionally unavailable to her because of their own psychological problems. Her grandmother attempts to help her confront the emptiness in her life. In *Angel Landing* (1982) a young woman, Natalie, discovers the identity of a disenchanted nuclear power plant worker who sabotages the construction of the plant. Natalie falls in love with him and commits herself to helping him overcome his alienation by expressing his feelings to her.

Hoffman, born and educated in New York City, uses settings familiar to Easterners, including Long Island, New York City, the eastern seacoast, and Martha's Vineyard. In a symposium on writing in the *New York Times Book Review* in 1984, Hoffman explains that her goal is to take everyday realities and transform them into something fabulous.

—Colin Maiorano and Carolyn Eckstein-Soule

HOLT, Victoria

Pseudonym for Eleanor Alice Hibbert. **Other Pseudonyms:** Eleanor Burford; Philippa Carr; Elbur Ford; Kathleen Kellow; Jean Plaidy; Ellalice Tate. **Nationality:** British. **Born:** Eleanor Alice Burford, London, 1906. **Education:** Educated privately. **Family:** Married G.P. Hibbert. **Died:** 20 January 1993.

Publications

Novels

Mistress of Mellyn. New York, Doubleday, 1960; London, Collins, 1961.

Kirkland Revels. New York, Doubleday, and London, Collins, 1962.
Bride of Pendorric. New York, Doubleday, and London, Collins, 1963.
The Legend of the Seventh Virgin. New York, Doubleday, and London, Collins, 1965.
Menfreya in the Morning. New York, Doubleday, 1966; as *Menfreya,* London, Collins, 1966.
The King of the Castle. New York, Doubleday, and London, Collins, 1967.
The Queen's Confession. New York, Doubleday, and London, Collins, 1968.
The Shivering Sands. New York, Doubleday, and London, Collins, 1969.
The Secret Woman. New York, Doubleday, 1970; London, Collins, 1971.
The Shadow of the Lynx. New York, Doubleday, 1971; London, Collins, 1972.
On the Night of the Seventh Moon. New York, Doubleday, 1972; London, Collins, 1973.
The Curse of the Kings. New York, Doubleday, and London, Collins, 1973.
The House of a Thousand Lanterns. New York, Doubleday, and London, Collins, 1974.
Lord of the Far Island. New York, Doubleday, and London, Collins, 1975.
The Pride of the Peacock. New York, Doubleday, and London, Collins, 1976.
The Devil on Horseback. New York, Doubleday, and London, Collins, 1977.
My Enemy the Queen. New York, Doubleday, and London, Collins, 1978.
The Spring of the Tiger. New York, Doubleday, and London, Collins, 1979.
The Mask of the Enchantress. New York, Doubleday, and London, Collins, 1980.
The Judas Kiss. New York, Doubleday, and London, Collins, 1981.
The Demon Lover. New York, Doubleday, and London, Collins, 1982.
The Time of the Hunter's Moon. New York, Doubleday, and London, Collins, 1983.
The Landower Legacy. London, Collins, and New York, Doubleday, 1984.
The Road to Paradise Island. London, Collins, and New York, Doubleday, 1985.
Secret for a Nightingale. London, Collins, and New York, Doubleday, 1986.
The Silk Vendetta. London, Collins, and New York, Doubleday, 1987.
The Indian Fan. London, Collins, and New York, Doubleday, 1988.
The Captive. London, Collins, and New York, Doubleday, 1989.
Snare of Serpents. London, Collins, and New York, Doubleday, 1990.
Daughter of Deceit. London, HarperCollins, 1991.
Seven for a Secret. London, HarperCollins, and New York, Doubleday, 1992.

Novels as Elbur Ford

Flesh and the Devil. London, Laurie, 1950.
Poison in Pimlico. London, Laurie, 1950.
The Bed Disturbed. London, Laurie, 1952.
Such Bitter Business. London, Heinemann, 1953; as *Evil in the House,* New York, Morrow, 1954.

Novels as Eleanor Burford

Daughter of Anna. London, Jenkins, 1941.
Passionate Witness. London, Jenkins, 1941.
The Married Lover. London, Jenkins, 1942.
When All the World Is Young. London, Jenkins, 1943.
So the Dreams Depart. London, Jenkins, 1944.
Not in Our Stars. London, Jenkins, 1945.
Dear Chance. London, Jenkins, 1947.
Alexa. London, Jenkins, 1948.
The House at Cupid's Cross. London, Jenkins, 1949.
Believe the Heart. London, Jenkins, 1950.
The Love Child. London, Jenkins, 1950.
Saint or Sinner? London, Jenkins, 1951.
Dear Delusion. London, Jenkins, 1952.
Bright Tomorrow. London, Jenkins, 1952.
Leave Me My Love. London, Jenkins, 1953.
When We Are Married. London, Jenkins, 1953.
Castles in Spain. London, Jenkins, 1954.
Heart's Afire. London, Jenkins, 1954.
When Other Hearts. London, Jenkins, 1955.
Two Loves in Her Life. London, Jenkins, 1955.
Begin to Live. London, Mills and Boon, 1956.
Married in Haste. London, Mills and Boon, 1956.
To Meet a Stranger. London, Mills and Boon, 1957.
Pride of the Morning. London, Mills and Boon, 1958.
Blaze of Noon. London, Mills and Boon, 1958.
The Dawn Chorus. London, Mills and Boon, 1959.
Red Sky at Night. London, Mills and Boon, 1959.
Night of Stars. London, Mills and Boon, 1960.
Now That April's Gone. London, Mills and Boon, 1961.
Who's Calling. London, Mills and Boon, 1962.

Novels as Jean Plaidy

Together They Ride. London, Swan, 1945.
Beyond the Blue Mountains. New York, Appleton Century, 1947; London, Hale, 1948.
Murder Most Royal. London, Hale, 1949; New York, Putnam, 1972; as *The King's Pleasure,* New York, Appleton Century Crofts, 1949.
The Goldsmith's Wife. London, Hale, and New York, Appleton Century Crofts, 1950; as *The King's Mistress,* New York, Pyramid, 1952.
Catherine de' Medici. London, Hale, 1969.
  Madame Serpent. London, Hale, and New York, Appleton Century Crofts, 1951.
  The Italian Woman. London, Hale, 1952; New York, Putnam, 1975.
  Queen Jezebel. London, Hale, and New York, Appleton Century Crofts, 1953.
Daughter of Satan. London, Hale, 1952; New York, Putnam, 1973; as *The Unholy Woman,* Toronto, Harlequin, 1954.
The Sixth Wife. London, Hale, 1953; New York, Putnam, 1969.
The Spanish Bridegroom. London, Hale, 1954; Philadelphia, Macrae Smith, 1956.
St. Thomas's Eve. London, Hale, 1954; New York, Putnam, 1970.

Gay Lord Robert. London, Hale, 1955; New York, Putnam, 1972.
Royal Road to Fotheringay. London, Hale, 1955; New York, Putnam, 1968.
Charles II. London, Hale, 1972.
The Wandering Prince. London, Hale, 1956; New York, Putnam, 1971.
A Health unto His Majesty. London, Hale, 1956; New York, Putnam, 1972.
Here Lies Our Sovereign Lord. London, Hale, 1957; New York, Putnam, 1973.
Flaunting Extravagant Queen (Marie Antoinette). London, Hale, 1957.
Lucrezia Borgia. London, Hale, 1976.
Madonna of the Seven Hills. London, Hale, 1958; New York, Putnam, 1974.
Light on Lucrezia. London, Hale, 1958; New York, Putnam, 1976.
Louis, The Well-Beloved. London, Hale, 1959.
The Road to Compiègne. London, Hale, 1959.
Isabella and Ferdinand. London, Hale, 1970.
Castile for Isabella. London, Hale, 1960.
Spain for the Sovereigns. London, Hale, 1960.
Daughters of Spain. London, Hale, 1961.
Katherine of Aragon. London, Hale, 1968.
Katherine, The Virgin Widow. London, Hale, 1961.
The Shadow of the Pomegranate. London, Hale, 1962.
The King's Secret Matter. London, Hale, 1962.
The Captive Queen of Scots. London, Hale, 1963; New York, Putnam, 1970.
The Thistle and the Rose. London, Hale, 1963; New York, Putnam, 1973.
Mary, Queen of France. London, Hale, 1964.
The Murder in the Tower. London, Hale, 1964; New York, Putnam, 1974.
Evergreen Gallant. London, Hale, 1965; New York, Putnam, 1973.
The Last of the Stuarts. London, Hale, 1977.
The Three Crowns. London, Hale, 1965; New York, Putnam, 1977.
The Haunted Sisters. London, Hale, 1966; New York, Putnam, 1977.
The Queen's Favourites. London, Hale, 1966; New York, Putnam, 1978.
The Pleasures of Love. London, Hale, 1991.
Kisses of Death. London, Hale, 1993.

Georgian Saga:
The Princess of Celle. London, Hale, 1967; New York, Putnam, 1985.
Queen in Waiting. London, Hale, 1967; New York, Putnam, 1985.
The Prince and the Quakeress. London, Hale, 1968; New York, Putnam, 1986.
Caroline, The Queen. London, Hale, 1968; New York, Putnam, 1986.
The Third George. London, Hale, 1969; New York, Putnam, 1987.
Perdita's Prince. London, Hale, 1969; New York, Putnam, 1987.
Sweet Lass of Richmond Hill. London, Hale, 1970; New York, Putnam, 1988.
Indiscretions of the Queen. London, Hale, 1970.
The Regent's Daughter. London, Hale, 1971; New York, Putnam, 1989.
Goddess of the Green Room. London, Hale, 1971; New York, Putnam, 1989.

Victorian Saga:
The Captive of Kensington Palace. London, Hale, 1972; New York, Putnam, 1976.
Victoria in the Wings. London, Hale, 1972, New York, Putnam, 1990.
The Queen and Lord M. London, Hale, 1973; New York, Putnam, 1977.
The Queen's Husband. London, Hale, 1973; New York, Putnam, 1978.
The Widow of Windsor. London, Hale, 1974; New York, Putnam, 1978.

Norman Trilogy:
The Bastard King. London, Hale, 1974; New York, Putnam, 1979.
The Lion of Justice. London, Hale, 1975; New York, Putnam, 1979.
The Passionate Enemies. London, Hale, 1976; New York, Putnam, 1979.

Plantagenet Saga:
The Plantagenet Prelude. London, Hale, 1976; New York, Putnam, 1980.
The Revolt of the Eaglets. London, Hale, 1977; New York, Putnam, 1980.
The Heart of the Lion. London, Hale, 1977; New York, Putnam, 1980.
The Prince of Darkness. London, Hale, 1978; New York, Putnam, 1980.
The Battle of the Queens. London, Hale, 1978; New York, Putnam, 1981.
The Queen from Provence. London, Hale, 1979; New York, Putnam, 1981.
Edward Longshanks. London, Hale, 1979; as *Hammer of the Scots,* New York, Putnam, 1981.
The Follies of the King. London, Hale, 1980; New York, Putnam, 1982.
The Vow on the Heron. London, Hale, 1980; New York, Putnam, 1982.
Passage to Pontefract. London, Hale, 1981; New York, Putnam, 1982.
The Star of Lancaster. London, Hale, 1981; New York, Putnam, 1982.
Epitaph for Three Women. London, Hale, 1981; New York, Putnam, 1983.
Red Rose of Anjou. London, Hale, 1982; New York, Putnam, 1983.
The Sun in Splendour. London, Hale, 1982; New York, Putnam, 1983.
Uneasy Lies the Head. London, Hale, 1982; New York, Putnam, 1984.

Queens of England series:
My Self, My Enemy. London, Hale, 1983; New York, Putnam, 1984.
Queen of This Realm: The Story of Queen Elizabeth I. London, Hale, 1984; New York, Putnam, 1985.
Victoria Victorious. London, Hale, 1985; New York, Putnam, 1986.
The Lady in the Tower. London, Hale, and New York, Putnam, 1986.
The Courts of Love. London, Hale, 1987; New York, Putnam, 1988.
In the Shadow of the Crown. London, Hale, 1988; New York, Putnam, 1989.
The Queen's Secret. London, Hale, 1989; New York, Putnam, 1990.
The Reluctant Queen. London, Hale, 1990.
William's Wife. London, Hale, 1990.

Novels as Kathleen Kellow

Danse Macabre. London, Hale, 1952.
Rooms at Mrs. Oliver's. London, Hale, 1953.
Lilith. London, Hale, 1954.
It Began in Vauxhall Gardens. London, Hale, 1955.
Call of the Blood. London, Hale, 1956.
Rochester, The Mad Earl. London, Hale, 1957.
Milady Charlotte. London, Hale, 1959.
The World's a Stage. London, Hale, 1960.

Novels as Ellalice Tate

Defenders of the Faith. London, Hodder and Stoughton, 1956.
The Scarlet Cloak. London, Hodder and Stoughton, 1957.
The Queen of Diamonds. London, Hodder and Stoughton, 1958.
Madame du Barry. London, Hodder and Stoughton, 1959.
This Was a Man. London, Hodder and Stoughton, 1961.

Novels as Philippa Carr

Daughters of England series:
The Miracle at St. Bruno's. London, Collins, and New York, Putnam, 1972.
The Lion Triumphant. London, Collins, and New York, Putnam, 1974.
The Witch from the Sea. London, Collins, and New York, Putnam, 1975.
Saraband for Two Sisters. London, Collins, and New York, Putnam, 1976.
Lament for a Lost Lover. London, Collins, and New York, Putnam, 1977.
The Love-Child. London, Collins, and New York, Putnam, 1978.
The Song of the Siren. London, Collins, and New York, Putnam, 1980.
The Drop of the Dice. London, Collins, and New York, Putnam, 1981.
The Adulteress. London, Collins, and New York, Putnam, 1982.
Zipporah's Daughter. London, Collins, 1983; as *Knave of Hearts*. New York, Putnam, 1983.
Voices in a Haunted Room. London, Collins, and New York, Putnam, 1984.
The Return of the Gypsy. London, Collins, and New York, Putnam, 1985.
Midsummer's Eve. London, Collins, and New York, Putnam, 1986.
The Pool of St. Branok. London, Collins, and New York, Putnam, 1987.
The Changeling. London, Collins, and New York, Putnam, 1989.
The Black Swan. London, HarperCollins, and New York, Putnam, 1991.
A Time for Silence. London, HarperCollins, and New York, Putnam, 1991.
The Gossamer Card. London, HarperCollins, and New York, Putnam, 1992.
The Black Opal. London, HarperCollins, and New York, Doubleday, 1993.

Other as Jean Plaidy

The Triptych of Poisoners. London, Hale, 1958.
The Rise [Growth, End] of the Spanish Inquisition. London, Hale, 3 vols., 1959-61; as *The Spanish Inquisition: Its Rise, Growth, and End*, New York, Citadel Press, 1 vol., 1967.
The Young Elizabeth (for children). London, Parrish, and New York, Roy, 1961.
Meg Roper, Daughter of Sir Thomas More (for children). London, Constable, 1961; New York, Roy, 1964.
The Young Mary Queen of Scots (for children). London, Parrish, 1962; New York, Roy, 1963.
Mary, Queen of Scots, The Fair Devil of Scotland. London, Hale, and New York, Putnam, 1975.

* * *

Victoria Holt was one of the many pseudonyms that Eleanor Burford Hibbert used during her illustrious writing career. A woman who believed writing to be the most exciting thing she could ever do, she was willing to conceal her identity to increase the mysterious allure of her books. Her work over a period of more than 40 years includes more than 150 novels. She died in 1993 on a cruise ship in the Mediterranean.

Hibbert began her writing career with the publication of short stories. She believed that a writer's work should be for the audience, not the critics, and it was in the traditional style that she found her success. She said that she wrote with great feeling and excitement, and felt compelled to elicit an emotional response from her audience.

It was under the pseudonyms Victoria Holt and Jean Plaidy that Hibbert crafted to near perfection her traditional style of fiction. Her agent nudged and directed her towards the writing of romance novels, while Doubleday established for the writer a pseudonym, Victoria Holt. Hibbert's authorship of the Holt works remained a closely guarded secret, and upon the release of her first work under the pseudonym, many in her audience believed the author of *Mistress of Mellyn* (1960) to be Daphne du Maurier. Hibbert assumed that the mistaken identity was attributable to the fact that both du Maurier and Hibbert lived in Cornwall and had written about that region. Hibbert agreed that the two women both wrote atmospheric suspense novels, but she also believed that was the only similarity between the two.

Hibbert wrote a vast number of historical novels which wove fascinating facts drawn from English history into simply written, compelling tales of mystery, intrigue, and of course, passion. Reading one of Hibbert's books is like sitting down for a good gossip, Jean Stubbs of the *Books and Bookmen* wrote. Hibbert was not malicious in her gossip, but she was a writer who told all. She gave credit to the Victorians for influencing her the most. She was a self-disciplined career writer who believed that writing everyday was important, because practice makes perfect. She also believed research to be an important fundamental of fiction writing, a fact that is reflected in the meticulous detail of her historical stories.

—Tammy J. Bronson

HOWATCH, Susan

Nationality: English. **Born:** 14 July 1940, in Leatherhead, Surrey. **Education:** Kings College, London, bachelor of laws, 1961. **Family:** Married Joseph Howatch, 1964 (legally separated); children: Antonia. **Career:** Writer. Masons of London, law clerk, 1961-62; R.C.A. Victor Record Corp., secretary, 1964-65. **Agents:**

Harold Ober Associates, Inc., 40 East 49th St., New York, New York 10017, U.S.A.; Aitken & Stone, 29 Fernshaw Rd., London SW10 0TG, England.

Publications

Novels

The Dark Shore. Ace Books, 1965.
The Waiting Sands. Ace Books, 1966.
Call in the Night. Ace Books, 1967.
The Shrouded Walls. Ace Books, 1968.
April's Grave. Ace Books, 1969.
The Devil on Lammas Night. Ace Books, 1971.
Penmarric. Simon & Schuster, 1971.
Cashelmara. Simon & Schuster, 1974.
The Rich Are Different. Simon & Schuster, 1977.
A Susan Howatch Treasury. Stein & Day, 1978.
Sins of the Fathers. Simon & Schuster, 1980.
The Wheel of Fortune. Simon & Schuster, 1984.
Glittering Images. Knopf, 1987.
Glamorous Powers. Knopf, 1988.
Ultimate Prizes. Knopf, 1990.
Scandalous Risks. Knopf, 1990.
Mystical Paths. David McKay, 1992.
Absolute Truths. David McKay, 1995.

* * *

Susan Howatch began writing Gothic novels in the 1960s. Her first novels, including *The Dark Shore* (1965), *April's Grave* (1969), and *The Devil on Lammas Night* (1972), were popular with readers of the Gothic genre.

Beginning in 1971, however, Howatch began writing a series of family sagas that gained her more readers. The books are largely updated versions of the true stories of historical families, Howatch has said. *Penmarric* (1971), deals with Henry II; *Cashelmara* (1974) is about the three Edwards; *The Rich Are Different* (1977), is about Julius Caesar, Mark Antony, and Cleopatra; *The Sins of the Fathers* (1980) is the story of Julia, the daughter of Augustus; and *The Wheel of Fortune* (1984) recreates aspects of the lives of Edward the Black Prince, John of Gaunt, Richard II and Henry IV and Henry V.

Howatch has said that she is interested in the people behind the historical sagas, and that she retells these stories without the historical details that get in the way of the people themselves. There is no doubt that Howatch tells a mesmerizing story. Her family sagas were very popular with the reading public and regularly made the bestseller lists.

In 1987, Howatch moved into the third phase of her writing career. With the publication in 1987 of *Glittering Images,* she began what would eventually become a six-volume series of novels about clergy in the Church of England. The books are intertwined in many ways. They are all set in or around the fictional Starbridge, in which is located Starbridge Cathedral. Characters who are featured in one of the novels may reappear as minor characters in others; their children grow and assume major roles in the books as the plots move forward in time.

Glittering Images sets the tone for the series in many ways. A young Anglican priest has been sent to investigate the noted Bishop of Starbridge. What he uncovers is a *menage a trois* involving the bishop, his wife, and his wife's young companion, as well as strange distortions of the church's teachings.

The books are interesting for their portrayal of the struggles of the clergy with problems of their humanity, faith, and calling. One reviewer suggests that no one writing today can match Howatch's ability to write "compelling novels that combine theology and psychology in a complex, fast-moving plot." Complex the novels certainly are, but they aren't necessarily compelling. Indeed, the rather implausible plots seem to drag so in places that the reader may simply wish that Howatch would get on with it. One wonders whether the problems of the Anglican clergy are of more interest to readers in England than in the United States. Presumably, a familiarity with the workings of the Church of England might make some of these books more readable. Certainly such familiarity might make the sometimes silly situations more understandable.

Howatch is a good writer and her way with a story is undeniable. Still, they would be the staunchest of readers who could fight their way through all of her Church of England novels with their sometimes contrived plots and less-than-credible moral dilemmas.

—June Harris

HUBBARD, L(aFayette) Ron(ald)

Nationality: American. **Born:** Tilden, Nebraska, 13 March 1911. **Education:** George Washington University, Washington, D.C., B.S. in civil engineering 1934; Princeton University, New Jersey, 1945; Sequoia University, Ph.D. 1950. **Family:** Married Mary Sue Whipp; two daughters and two sons. **Career:** Wrote travel and aviation articles in the 1930s; explorer: Commander, Caribbean Motion Picture Expedition, 1931, West Indies Mineral Survey Expedition, 1932, and Alaskan Radio-Experimental Expedition, 1940. Director, Hubbard Foundation; founding director, Church of Scientology, 1952; director, Dianetics and Scientology, 1952-66; resigned all directorships, 1966. **Died:** 29 January 1986.

Publications

Novels (series: Mission Earth)

Buckskin Brigades. New York, Macaulay, 1937; London, Wright and Brown, 1938.
Death's Deputy. Los Angeles, Fantasy, 1948.
Final Blackout. Providence, Rhode Island, Hadley, 1948.
Slaves of Sleep. Chicago, Shasta, 1948.
Triton, and Battle of Wizards. Los Angeles, Fantasy, 1949.
The Kingslayer (includes "The Beast" and "The Invaders"). Los Angeles, Fantasy, 1949; as *Seven Steps to the Arbiter,* Chatsworth, California, Major, 1975.
Two Science Fantasy Novels by L. Ron Hubbard: Typewriter in the Sky, Fear. New York, Gnome Press, 1951; as *Fear, and Typewriter in the Sky,* New York, Popular Library, 1977.
From Death to the Stars (includes *Death's Deputy* and *The Kingslayer).* Los Angeles, Fantasy, 1953.
Return to Tomorrow. New York, Ace, 1954; London, Panther, 1957.

Fear: An Outstanding Psychological Science Fiction Novel. New York, Galaxy, 1957.
Fear, and Ultimate Adventure. New York, Berkley, 1970.
Battlefield Earth: A Saga of the Year 3000. New York, St. Martin's Press, 1982; London, Quadrant, 1984.
Mission Earth:
The Invaders Plan. Los Angeles, Bridge, 1985; London, New Era, 1986.
Death Quest. Los Angeles, Bridge, 1985; London, New Era, 1987.
Black Genesis: Fortress of Evil. Los Angeles, Bridge, 1986; London, New Era, 1986.
The Enemy Within. Los Angeles, Bridge, 1986; London, New Era, 1987.
An Alien Affair. Los Angeles, Bridge, 1986; London, New Era, 1987.
Fortune of Fear. Los Angeles, Bridge, 1986; London, New Era, 1987.
Voyage of Vengeance. Los Angeles, Bridge, 1987; London, New Era, 1988.
Disaster. Los Angeles, Bridge, 1987; London, New Era, 1988.
Villany Victorious. Los Angeles, Bridge, 1987; London, New Era, 1988.
The Doomed Planet. Los Angeles, Bridge, 1987; London, New Era, 1988.

Short Stories

Ole Doc Methuselah. Austin, Texas, Theta Press, 1970.
Lives You Wished to Lead But Never Dared, edited by V.S. Wilhite. Clearwater, Florida, Theta Press, 1978.
Arctic Wings. Hollywood, Author Services, 1991.
Black Towers to Danger. Hollywood, Author Services, 1991.
The Carnival of Death. Hollywood, Author Services, 1991.
The Case of the Friendly Corpse. Hollywood, Author Services, 1991.
The Ghoul. Hollywood, Author Services, 1991.
Guns of Mark Jardine. Hollywood, Author Services, 1991.
Hell's Legionnaire, The Conroy Diary, Buckley Pays a Hunch: A Special Collecton of Short Stories. Hollywood, Author Services, 1991.
The Red Dragon. Hollywood, Author Services, 1991.
Six-Gun Caballero. Hollywood, Author Services, 1991.
Adventure Short Stories. Hollywood, Author Services, 5 vols., 1992-94.
The Chee-Chalker. Hollywood, Author Services, 1992.
Empty Saddles. Hollywood, Author Services, 1992.
Forbidden Gold. Hollywood, Author Services, 1992.
Hot Lead Payoff. Hollywood, Author Services, 1992.
Inky Odds. Hollywood, Author Services, 1992.
The Kilkenny Cats Series. Hollywood, Author Services, 1992.
Sea Fangs. Hollywood, Author Services, 1992.
The Tramp. Hollywood, Author Services, 1992.
The Ultimate Adventure. Hollywood, Author Services, 1992.
Western Short Stories. Hollywood, Author Services, 6 vols., 1992-95.
Wild-Gone-Mad, and Hurricane's Roar. Hollywood, Author Services, 1992.
The Battling Pilot. Hollywood, Author Services, 1993.
Brass Keys to Murder. Hollywood, Author Services, 1993.
Fantasy Short Stories. Hollywood, Author Services, 1993.
Hurtling Wings. Hollywood, Author Services, 1993.
The Indigestible Triton. Hollywood, Author Services, 1993.
Science Fiction Short Stories. Hollywood, Author Services, 2 vols., 1993-94.
The Sky-Crasher. Hollywood, Author Services, 1993.
The Automatic Horse (for children). Hollywood, Author Services, 1994.
Branded Outlaw. Hollywood, Author Services, 1994.
The Falcon Killer. Hollywood, Author Services, 1994.
Hostage to Death; and, Killer Ape. Hollywood, Author Services, 1994.
The Iron Duke. Hollywood, Author Services, 1994.
Mystery/Suspense Short Stories. Hollywood, Author Services, 1994.
Sabotage in the Sky. Hollywood, Author Services, 1994.
Trouble on His Wings. Hollywood, Author Services, 1994.
To the Stars. Hollywood, Author Services, 1995.

Poetry

Hymn of Asia: An Eastern Poem. Los Angeles, Church of Scientology, 1974.

Other

Dianetics: The Modern Science of Mental Health. New York, Hermitage House, 1950; London, Ridgway, 1951.
Science of Survival. Wichita and East Grinstead, Sussex, Hubbard, 1951.
Self Analysis. Wichita, International Library of Arts and Science, 1951.
Dianetics: The Original Thesis. Wichita, Wichita Publishing, 1951.
Handbook for Preclears. Wichita, Scientic Press, 1951.
Notes on the Lectures of L. Ron Hubbard. Wichita, Hubbard, 1951.
Advanced Procedure and Axioms. Wichita, Hubbard, 1951.
Scientology 8-80. Phoenix, Hubbard, and East Grinstead, Sussex, Scientology, 1952.
A Key to the Unconscious. Phoenix, Scientic Press, 1952.
Dianetics: The Evolution of a Science. London, Hubbard, 1953; Phoenix, Hubbard, 1955.
Scientology: A History of Man. London, Hubbard, 1953.
How to Live Though an Executive. Phoenix, Hubbard, 1953.
Self-Analysis in Dianetics. London, Ridgway, 1953.
Scientology 8-8008. London, Hubbard, 1953.
Dianetics 1955! Phoenix, Hubbard, 1954.
The Creation of Human Ability: A Handbook for Scientologists. Phoenix, Hubbard, and London, Scientology, 1955.
This Is Scientology: The Science of Certainty. London, Hubbard, 1955.
The Key to Tomorrow (selections), edited by U. Keith Gerry. Johannesburg, Hubbard, 1955.
Scientology: The Fundamentals of Thought. London, Hubbard, 1956.
Problems of Work. Johannesburg, Hubbard, 1957.
Fortress in the Sky (on the moon). Washington, D.C., Hubbard, 1957.
Have You Lived Before This Life? London, Hubbard, 1958; New York, Vantage, 1960.
Self-Analysis in Scientology. London, Hubbard, 1959.
Scientology: Plan for World Peace. East Grinstead, Sussex, Scientology, 1964.

Scientology Abridged Dictionary. East Grinstead, Sussex, Hubbard, 1965.
A Student Comes to Saint Hill. Bedford, Sidney Press, 1965.
Scientology: A New Slant on Life. London, Hubbard, 1965.
East Grinstead. East Grinstead, Sussex, Hubbard, 1966.
Introduction to Scientology Ethics. Edinburgh, Scientology, 1968; Los Angeles, Bridge, 1985.
The Phoenix Lectures. Edinburgh, Scientology, 1968.
How to Save Your Marriage. Copenhagen, Scientology, 1969.
When in Doubt, Communicate: Quotations from the Work of L. Ron Hubbard, edited by Ruth Minshull and Edward M. Lefshon. Ann Arbor, Michigan, Scientology, 1969.
Scientology 0-8. Copenhagen, Scientology, 1970.
Mission into Time. Copenhagen, Scientology, 1973.
The Management Series 1970-1974. Los Angeles, American Saint Hill Organization, 1974.
The Organization Executive Course. Los Angeles, American Saint Hill Organization, 8 vols., 1974.
Dianetics Today. Los Angeles, Scientology, 1975.
Dianetics and Scientology Technical Dictionary. Los Angeles, Scientology, 1975.
The Technical Bulletins of Dianetics and Scientology. Los Angeles, Scientology, 1976-86.
The Volunteer Minister's Handbook. Los Angeles, Scientology, 1976.
Axioms and Logics. Los Angeles, Scientology, 1976.
A Summary of Scientology for Churches. Los Angeles, Scientology, 1977.
The Book of Case Remedies. Los Angeles, Scientology, 1977.
What Is Scientology. Los Angeles, Scientology, 1978.
The Research and Discovery Series. Los Angeles, Scientology, 1980-86.
The Second Dynamic (selection), edited by Cass Pool. Portland, Oregon, Heron, 1981.
Self-Analysis. Los Angeles, Bridge, 1982.
Scientology: Fundamentals of Thought. Los Angeles, Bridge, 1983.
Dianetics: The Evolution of a Science. Los Angeles, Bridge, 1983.
The Problems of Work. Los Angeles, Bridge, 1983.
The Dynamics of Life. Los Angeles, Bridge, 1983.
The Way to Happiness. Los Angeles, Bridge, 1984.
Purification: An Illustrated Answer to Drugs. Los Angeles, Bridge, 1984.
The Learning Book. Copenhagen, New Era, 1984.
Child Dianectics. Los Angeles, Bridge, 1989.
The Book of Case Remedies. Los Angeles, Bridge, 1991.
Art. Los Angeles, Bridge, 1991.
Assists Processing Handbook. Los Angeles, Bridge, 1992.

*

Critical Studies: *Bare-Faced Messiah: The True Story of L. Ron Hubbard* by Russell Miller, London, Joseph, 1987; New York, Holt, 1988; *A Piece of Blue Sky: Scientology, Dianetics, and L. Ron Hubbard Exposed* by Jon Atack, London, Lyle Stuart, and New York, Carol, 1990.

* * *

L. Ron Hubbard began by writing aviation and travel articles, mysteries, westerns, and science fiction in the 1930s, then founded the Church of Scientology in 1952, which led to dozens of non-fiction books related to Scientology and its practices.

Hubbard's science fiction career began with titles including *Final Blackout* (1948), *The Kingslayer* (1949), *Typewriter in the Sky (and) Fear: Two Novels* (1951), and *Seven Steps to the Arbiter* (1975). He also contributed many short stories to various magazines. He received wide acclaim for his science fiction writings, and was considered a trendsetter for modern science fiction with his early writings.

One of Hubbard's first novels was *Buckskin Brigade* (1937). It is a tale of the Northwest fur trade in the days of the Lewis and Clark expedition. The book tells the story of the hero, Yellow Hair, a white child brought up by the Blackfeet Indians, and the villain, Alexander McGlincy, a drunk. It was described as "romantic and picturesque," and one *New York Times* reviewer said: "While novels glorifying the fur traders have been plentiful, it has been admitted in fiction before this that there were mercenary rascals among them, white men who robbed . . . and sometimes murdered Indians for their own aggrandizement. Nevertheless, the violence of Mr. Hubbard's convictions lends to his writings an enthusiasm, even a freshness and a sparkle, decidedly rare in this type of romance."

After years of writing, Hubbard became famous in 1950 when he published his nonfiction *Dianetics: The Modern Science of Mental Health* (1950). The book has been on the bestseller list for many of the years since. It draws from nuclear physics, holistic medicine, Eastern religion, and Freud, as well as Hubbard's own experiences. It concludes that mental and physical problems can be cured through clear thinking and establishes simple practices for enabling the mind to think clearly. The book has been controversial form the beginning, and many believe it is potentially dangerous: "The mixture of some oversimplified truths, half-truths, and plain absurdities, the propagandic technique of impressing the reader with the greatness, infallibility and newness of the author's system, the promise of unheard of results attained by the simple means of following Dianetics is a technique which has had most unfortunate results in the fields of patent medicines and politics: applied to psychology and psychiatry it will not be less harmful," wrote Erich Fromm in *New York Herald Tribune* in 1950. "It is either one of the most important [books] ever published, or a vast and inexcusable hoax," wrote the *San Francisco Chronicle* in the same year.

Two years after the publication of *Dianetics,* Hubbard established the Church of Scientology on three principles: Wisdom is meant for anyone who reaches for it; it must be capable of being applied; and any philosophical knowledge is only valuable if it is true or if it works. His ideas have had great appeal, and the Church of Scientology continues to attract converts worldwide with its offer of spiritual peace and personal fulfillment, despite numerous reports of coercive tactics and illegal practices among church leaders.

In the 1980s, Hubbard published his "Mission Earth" series. The stories are told in the first-person viewpoint of a character confessing his crimes to an unseen omnipotent prosecutor. Filled with satire, humor, and raunchy sexual innuendos, the stories center on Voltar, a planet in the Voltar confederacy and its quest to take over the entire galaxy. Each of the ten volumes became a bestseller.

—Amy Faulkenberry

HUDSON, Jeffery. *See* **CRICHTON, (John) Michael.**

HUGHES, Eden. *See* **BUTTERWORTH, W. E.**

HUNT, Gil. *See* **BRUNNER, John.**

HUNTER, Evan. *See* **McBAIN, Ed.**

I-J

IRVING, John (Winslow)

Nationality: American. **Born:** Exeter, New Hampshire, 2 March 1942. **Education:** Phillips Exeter Academy, Exeter, graduated 1962; University of Pittsburgh 1961-62; University of Vienna, 1963-64; University of New Hampshire, Durham, B.A. (cum laude), 1965; University of Iowa, Iowa City, M.F.A. 1967. **Family:** Married 1) Shyla Leary in 1964 (divorced 1981), two sons; 2) Janet Turnbull in 1987. **Career:** Taught at Windham College, Putney, Vermont, 1967-69; lived in Vienna, 1969-71; writer-in-residence, University of Iowa, 1972-75; assistant professor of English, Mount Holyoke College, South Hadley, Massachusetts, 1975-78. **Awards:** Rockefeller grant, 1972; National Endowment for the Arts grant, 1974; Guggenheim grant, 1976; American Book Award, for paperback, 1980. **Agent:** Sterling Lord Literistic, 1 Madison Avenue, New York, New York 10010. **Address:** c/o William Morrow Inc., 105 Madison Avenue, New York, New York 10016, U.S.A.

PUBLICATIONS

Novels

Setting Free the Bears. New York, Random House, 1969; London, Corgi, 1979.
The Water-Method Man. New York, Random House, 1972; London, Corgi, 1980.
The 158-Pound Marriage. New York, Random House, 1974; London, Corgi, 1980.
The World According to Garp. New York, Dutton, and London, Gollancz, 1978.
The Hotel New Hampshire. New York, Dutton, and London, Cape, 1981.
The Cider House Rules. New York, Morrow, and London, Cape, 1985.
A Prayer for Owen Meany. New York, Morrow, and London, Bloomsbury, 1989.
A Son of the Circus. New York, Random House, and London, Bloomsbury, 1994.

Short Stories

Trying to Save Piggy Snead. London, Bloomsbury, 1993.

*

Manuscript Collection: Phillips Exeter Academy, Exeter, New Hampshire.

Critical Studies: Introduction by Terrence DuPres to *3 by Irving* (omnibus), New York, Random House, 1980; *Fowles, Irving, Barthes: Canonical Variations on an Apocryphal Theme* by Randolph Runyon, Columbus, Ohio State University Press, 1982; *John Irving* by Gabriel Miller, New York, Ungar, 1982; *Understanding John Irving* by Edward C. Reilly, Columbia, South Carolina, University of South Carolina Press, 1991.

Theatrical Activities:
Actor: **Film**—*The World According to Garp,* 1982.

* * *

John Irving is a university-trained writer who with his fourth novel, *The World According to Garp* (1978), achieved the fame usually reserved for authors of commercial blockbusters. His transformation from what publishers call a "mid-list" producer of serious fiction to the type of novelist who sets trends and influences lives on a season-to-season basis indicates a shift in priorities among the Masters of Fine Arts programs of American universities. As a graduate of the University of Iowa's Writers Workshop, Irving was able to grow beyond the academic careerism that had characterized other creative writing departments and take advantage of the marketing skills that the Workshop taught along with more conventional schooling in sentence structure and character development.

Irving's first three novels, none of them widely successful, address critically pertinent but popularly irrelevant concerns. *Setting Free the Bears* (1969) introduces two items he would later reshape into more accessible interests: the pathos of bears in captivity and the museum-like quality of otherwise modern Vienna. The first 100 pages of this work were accepted for his MFA project at Iowa, but it is in *The Water-Method Man* (1972) that Irving shows the influence of his teachers, among them Kurt Vonnegut, especially in the talent for advancing several minimally intersecting story lines at the same time. In counterpointing a graduate student's preposterous academic work in Iowa with his other lives in New England, New York City, and abroad, Irving writes a rollicking comedy having great appeal to others in his narrator's situation. But in *The 158-pound Marriage* (1974) this Vonneguttian tendency fades in favor of a more arcane, metafictional attack on real-life novelists Donald Barthelme and John Barth, who much like Irving's character Helmbart write narratives that explore the conditions of their own making.

It is with the issues of male sensitivity and critical feminism that Irving scores big in *The World According to Garp.* Here, as well, the author introduces a plot element he would exploit successfully in subsequent novels: the suspense building around a subtly foreshadowed catastrophe (in this case the protagonist's wife's inadvertent castration of her schoolboy lover during oral sex). As a widely discussed bestseller with notoriously outrageous scenes and themes, *Garp* propelled its author onto the cover of *Time* magazine and into the comfortably remunerative world of film-rights sales and mass-market paperback contracts. Although some momentum was lost in the simultaneous failures of the Robin Williams movie of *Garp* and Irving's next novel, *The Hotel New Hampshire* (1981), career matters stabilized with the more considered attention paid to *The Cider House Rules* (1985), the author's unflamboyant treatment of the same New England heritage featured more extravagantly in each of his previous works.

In *A Prayer for Owen Meany* (1989) John Irving adds a new dimension to his work, having a narrator reexamine a New England childhood memory from the distance of Toronto, where he (like John Irving himself) now lives. Although the story's action is set within the climate of American violence, the novel's voice strives to speak with a sense of Canadian peacefulness and High Church order. *A Son of the Circus* (1994) embraces British Commonwealth attitudes even more emphatically; for this novel Irving creates a protagonist who, as a native Indian and present-day Canadian citizen, finds his homeland utterly foreign. In this character's often slapstick attempts to reconnect with his roots, Irving is able to rechoreograph the comic dance of human futility from an even fresher perspective.

—Jerome Klinkowitz

ISAACS, Susan

Nationality: American. **Born:** 7 December 1943, in Brooklyn, New York. **Education:** Attended Queens College. **Family:** Married Elkan Abramowitz, 1968; children: Andrew, Elizabeth. **Career:** Novelist and screenwriter. *Seventeen* magazine, New York City, 1966-70, began as assistant editor, became senior editor; political speech writer for Democratic candidates in Brooklyn and Queens, New York, and for the president of the borough of Queens, New York City; movie producer. **Member:** International Association of Crime Writers, Mystery Writers of America, National Book Critics Circle, Queens College Foundation (trustee), North Shore Child and Family Guidance Association (trustee). **Agent:** Owen Laster, William Morris Agency, 1350 Avenue of the Americas, New York, New York 10019, U.S.A.

Publications

Novels

Compromising Positions. Times Books, 1978.
Close Relations. Lippincott & Crowell, 1980.
Almost Paradise. Harper, 1984.
Shining Through. Harper, 1988.
Magic Hour. HarperCollins, 1991.
After All These Years. HarperCollins, 1993.

Plays

Screenplays: *Compromising Positions,* adapted from her own novel, 1985; *Hello Again,* adapted from her own novel, 1987.

*

Film Adaptations: *Compromising Postions,* 1985; *Hello Again,* 1987; *Shining Through,* 1992.

* * *

The six novels by Susan Isaacs are modern fairy tales. Each chronicles the development of a relationship between the main character and their ideal partner. They are novels of empowerment as the hero or, more usually, heroine discovers his or her true self and true love, and where he or she belongs in society.

Isaac's first novel, *Compromising Positions* (1978), is a romantic crime story. A society dentist is found murdered at his practice. The heroine, Judith Singer, is in a stale but convenient marriage. She dislikes being a suburban housewife and feels that she does not belong in that world. Judith finds clues missed by the police and then is threatened by the killer. As the case progresses and she becomes more involved in helping the police solve the crime, she and the main investigator fall in love. She has found someone and something that make her feel worthwhile.

Judith Singer is the first in a series of people who are in a relationship with the wrong person. *Close Relations* (1981) is a story of political life. Marcia Green is a speech writer who lives with campaign leader Jerry Morrisey. A new man enters her life as the political debate becomes frantic, and suddenly politics and Jerry pale in comparison. Marcia finds in her new lover her ideal partner and a comfortable social place as his equal. He is Prince Charming to her emotionally deprived Cinderella as he frees her to be exactly whom she wants.

In her third book, *Almost Paradise* (1984), Isaacs changes her usual practice of telling the story by a first-person narrator. This book has a structure that demands a less singular narration. The novel begins with a section set in the present time before embarking on a protracted flashback showing how Jane and Nicholas Cobleigh loved then lost each other. Each chapter is headed with a piece of information about what is happening in the present. This book is less optimistic that the others, as Jane and Nicholas realize too late that the person who best suits them is precisely the person they divorced.

Isaacs sets *Shining Through* (1988) in a different era. This novel is a WWII romance combined with a spy story. Secretary Linda Voss dreams about her handsome boss John Berringer. Her dreams come true when they have an affair and get married. The fairy tale appears to have become reality, but the marriage does not last long. Linda begins to work for the scarred war hero Edward Leland, which leads her to become a spy in Europe sending crucial messages to the allies. When she needs to escape, Edward arrives to help her. This novel retells the Beauty and the Beast tale as Edward proves his love and virtue in the same way as the Beast. A proverb is added as Berringer demonstrates that all that glitters is not gold.

Magic Hour (1991) is the only novel by Isaacs which has a male narrator. Policeman Stephen Brady is searching for a killer and for a place where he belongs. He is a Vietnam veteran and a reformed substance abuser who still has not found emotional tranquillity. This novel subverts the Hollywood fairy tale. A top movie director is shot dead at his home. The people who are not corrupt are those outside or on the periphery of the movie business like Brady and the prime suspect Bonnie. As the investigation progresses he realizes that Bonnie is innocent and that he is in love with her. Bonnie fulfills his emotional needs and it is with her that he belongs. The novel concludes with an unexpected twist that shows the pervasive pollution of the film industry.

Although *Magic Hour* is a good romantic crime story, it lacks the tension of the sixth novel, *After All These Years* (1993). In it, Rosie Meyers learns a lot about herself as she gathers clues to prove her innocence when her estranged husband is found murdered. She reveals the identity of the killer to the disbelieving police in a dramatic conclusion. Rosie is free to continue her life and to reclaim the love she had once lost.

Isaacs expands the romantic formula of "boy meets girl" by making her characters discover true love as they go through a process of personal development. The novels are romantic and most have fairy tale endings. At the same time, Isaacs is "a witty, wry observer of the contemporary scene" (*New York Times*), exploring the characters and the society that shapes them.

—Samantha J. Barber

IVES, Morgan. *See* **BRADLEY, Marion Zimmer.**

JAKES, John (William)

Pseudonyms: William Ard; Alan Payne; Jay Scotland. **Nationality:** American. **Born:** Chicago, Illinois, 31 March 1932. **Education:** DePauw University, Greencastle, Indiana, A.B. 1953; Ohio State University, Columbus, M.A. in American literature 1954. **Family:** Married Rachel Ann Payne in 1951; three daughters and one son. **Career:** Copywriter, then promotion manager, Abbott Laboratories, North Chicago, 1954-60; copywriter, Rumrill Company, Rochester, New York, 1960-61; freelance writer, 1961-65; copywriter, Kircher Helton and Collett, Dayton, Ohio, 1965-68; copy chief, then vice-president, Oppenheim Herminghausen and Clarke, Dayton, 1968-70; creative director, Dancer Fitzgerald Sample, Dayton, 1970-71. Writer-in-Residence, DePauw University, fall 1979. Since 1971, freelance writer. LL.D.: Wright State University, Dayton, Ohio, 1976; Litt.D.: DePauw University, 1977; L.H.D., Winthrop College, 1985. **Address:** c/o Rembar and Curtis, Attorneys, 19 West 44th Street, New York, New York 10036, U.S.A.

Publications

Novels (series: Brak; Dragonard; Klekton)

The Texans Ride North (for children). Philadelphia, Winston, 1952.
Wear a Fast Gun. New York, Arcadia House, 1956; London, Ward Lock, 1957.
A Night for Treason. New York, Bouregy, 1956.
The Devil Has Four Faces. New York, Bouregy, 1958.
This'll Slay You (as Alan Payne). New York, Ace, 1958.
The Imposter. New York, Bouregy, 1959.
Johnny Havoc. New York, Belmont, 1960; London, Severn, 1990.
Johnny Havoc Meets Zelda. New York, Belmont, 1962; as *Havoc for Sale,* New York, Armchair Detective Library, 1990.
Johnny Havoc and the Doll Who Had "It." New York, Belmont, 1963; as *Holiday for Havoc,* New York, Armchair Detective Library, 1991.
G.I. Girls. Derby, Connecticut, Monarch, 1963.
When the Star Kings Die (Dragonard). New York, Ace, 1967.
Brak the Barbarian. New York, Avon, 1968; London, Tandem, 1970.
Making It Big. New York, Belmont, 1968; as *Johnny Havoc and the Siren in Red,* New York, Armchair Detective Library, 1991.
The Asylum World. New York, Paperback Library, 1969; London, New English Library, 1978.
The Hybrid. New York, Paperback Library, 1969.
The Planet Wizard (Dragonard). New York, Ace, 1969.
Secrets of Stardeep (for children). Philadelphia, Westminster Press, 1969.
Tonight We Steal the Stars (Dragonard). New York, Ace, 1969.
Brak the Barbarian Versus the Sorceress. New York, Paperback Library, 1969, London, Tandem, 1970.
Brak Versus the Mark of the Demons. New York, Paperback Library, 1969, London, Tandem, 1970.
The Last Magicians. New York, Signet, 1969.
Black in Time. New York, Paperback Library, 1970.
Mask of Chaos. New York, Ace, 1970.
Master of the Dark Gate (Klekton). New York, Lancer, 1970.
Monte Cristo #99. New York, Curtis, 1970.
Six-Gun Planet. New York, Paperback Library, 1970; London, New English Library, 1978.
Mention My Name in Atlantis—Being, at Last, the True Account of the Calamitous Destruction of the Great Island Kingdom, Together with a Narrative of Its Wondrous Intercourses with a Superior Race of Other-Worldlings, as Transcribed from the Manuscript of a Survivor, Hoptor the Vintner, for the Enlightenment of a Dubious Posterity. New York, DAW, 1972.
Time Gate (for children). Philadelphia, Westminster Press, 1972.
Witch of the Dark Gate (Klekton). New York, Lancer, 1972.
On Wheels. New York, Warner, 1973.
Conquest of the Planet of the Apes (novelization of screenplay). New York, Award, 1974.
Kent Family Chronicles:
- *The Bastard.* New York, Pyramid, 1974; as *Fortune's Whirlwind* and *To an Unknown Shore,* London, Corgi, 2 vols., 1975.
- *The Rebels.* New York, Pyramid, 1975; London, Corgi, 1979.
- *The Seekers.* New York, Pyramid, 1975; London, Corgi, 1979.
- *The Furies.* New York, Pyramid 1976; London, Corgi, 1979.
- *The Titans.* New York, Pyramid 1976; London, Corgi, 1979.
- *The Warriors.* New York, Pyramid, 1977; London, Corgi, 1979.
- *The Lawless.* New York, Jove, 1978; London, Corgi, 1979.
- *The Americans.* New York, Jove, 1980; London, Fontana, 1989.

Brak: When the Idols Walked. New York, Pocket Books, 1978.
Excalibur!, with Gil Kane. New York, Dell, 1980.
North and South trilogy:
- *North and South.* New York, Harcourt Brace, and London, Collins, 1982.
- *Love and War.* New York, Harcourt Brace, 1984; London, Collins, 1985.
- *Heaven and Hell.* New York, Harcourt Brace, 1987; London Collins, 1988.

California Gold. New York, Random House, 1989; London, Collins, 1990.
Homeland. New York, Doubleday,and London, Little Brown, 1993.

Novels as Jay Scotland

The Seventh Man. New York, Bouregy, 1958.
I, Barbarian. New York, Avon, 1959; revised edition, as *John Jakes,* New York, Pinnacle, 1976.
Strike the Black Flag. New York, Ace, 1961.
Sir Scoundrel. New York, Ace, 1962; revised edition, as *King's Crusader,* New York, Pinnacle 1977.

Veils of Salome. New York, Avon, 1962.
Arena. New York, Ace, 1963.
Traitors' Legion. New York, Ace, 1963; revised edition, as *The Man from Cannae,* New York, Pinnacle, 1977.

Novels as William Ard

Make Mine Mavis. Derby, Connecticut, Monarch, 1961.
And So to Bed. Derby, Connecticut, Monarch, 1962.
Give Me This Woman. Derby, Connecticut, Monarch, 1962.

Short Stories

The Best of John Jakes, edited by Martin H. Greenberg and Joseph D. Olander. New York, DAW, 1977.
Fortunes of Brak. New York, Dell, 1980
The Best Western Stories of John Jakes, edited by Martin H. Greenberg and Bill Pronzini. Athens, Ohio University Press, 1991; as *In the Big Country: The Best Western Stories of John Jakes,* Thorndike, Maine, Hall, 1993.

Plays

Dracula, Baby (lyrics only). Chicago, Dramatic Publishing Company, 1970.
Wind in the Willows. Elgin, Illinois, Performance, 1972.
A Spell of Evil. Chicago, Dramatic Publishing Company, 1972.
Violence. Elgin, Illinois, Performance, 1972.
Stranger with Roses, adaptation of his own story. Chicago, Dramatic Publishing Company, 1972.
For I Am a Jealous People, adaptation of the story by Lester del Rey. Elgin, Illinois, Performance, 1972.
Gaslight Girl. Chicago, Dramatic Publishing Company, 1973.
Pardon Me, Is This Planet Taken? Chicago, Dramatic Publishing Company, 1973.
Doctor, Doctor!, music by Gilbert M. Martin, adaptation of a play by Molière. New York, McAfee Music, 1973.
Shepherd Song. New York, McAfee Music, 1974.

Other

Tiros: Weather Eye in Space. New York, Messner, 1966.
Famous Firsts in Sports. New York, Putnam, 1967.
Great War Correspondents. New York, Putnam, 1968.
Great Women Reporters. New York, Putnam, 1969.
The Bastard Photostory. New York, Jove, 1980.
Susanna at the Alamo: A True Story (for children). New York, Harcourt Brace, 1986.

Editor, with Martin H. Greenberg, *New Trails: Twenty-Three Original Stories of the West from Western Writers of America.* New York, Doubleday, 1994.

*

Bibliography: In *The Best Western Stories of John Jakes,* edited by Martin H. Greenberg and Bill Pronzini, Athens, Ohio University Press, 1991.

Manuscript Collections: University of Wyoming, Laramie; DePauw University, Greencastle, Indiana.

Critical Study: *The Kent Family Chronicles Encyclopedia* edited by Robert Hawkins, New York, Bantam, 1979.

* * *

Beginning as a writer of pulp Western novels and science fiction tales, John Jakes earned widespread fame with his historical fiction, which includes the American Bicentennial Series and his North and South trilogy. The thorough research, vivid prose, and lively plots of these works have gained much praise for Jakes from readers and critics alike, making him one of the most widely read American novelists.

Jakes wrote over 20 novels in both the western and science fiction genres, including his first novels *The Texans Ride North* (1952) for children and *Brak the Barbarian* (1968). Jakes's breakthrough was with *The Bastard* (1974), the first of eight historical novels that make up the American Bicentennial Series, otherwise known as the Kent Family Chronicles. Each volume of the series deals with a particular era in American history, from colonial times to the end of the 19th century. *The Bastard* and *The Rebels* (1975) focus on the adventures of Philip Kent in the American Revolution, while the remaining volumes turn to Kent's relatives as they move through the Northwest territory, participate in the War of 1812, and witness the battle for Texas independence, among other historical events. *The Lawless* (1978) and *The Americans* (1980) complete the massive, sweeping saga of the Kent family as America is poised on the brink of the 20th century.

Most critics applauded the series; Bruce Cook of *Book World* compared Jakes's series to Alex Haley's bestselling *Roots* for the novels' investigation of ancestry and family history portrayed against the background of a young and violent America. In an earlier *Book World* review, Jakes was praised for his handling of historical fact: "The history (except for a minor manipulation of chronology) is as accurate as Jakes can make it and seems to interest all sorts of people from housewives to convicts to assembly-line workers in some fairly obscure aspects of America's past." *Publishers Weekly* said of the series, "Jakes's characterizations and lively historical detail entirely envelop the reader, who will be left with the hope that the author decides to bring the Kent family into the 20th century."

What would seem to be the pinnacle of Jakes's success was only the beginning. His North and South trilogy chronicled the lives of two families, the Southern Mains, slave-owning aristocrats, and the Northern Hazards, Pennsylvania industrialists, against the gallantry and violence of the Civil War era. *North and South* (1982) continued to mine the rich success Jakes had garnered with his earlier series of historical fiction; while most critics described his story as melodramatic, they also praised the fast pace of the narrative and, again, Jakes's use of historical fact.

In *North and South,* the Mains and the Hazards are bound together by both love and hate in the 1840s and 1850s and exemplify the divisive feelings and ideological differences that led to the Civil War. *Publishers Weekly* said of Jakes's novel, "His villains are so villainous you love to hate them, his women wild and passionate (mostly), his action fast and often lurid." Mel Watkins of the *New York Times Book Review* said that while the characters are easily forgotten, the focus on the time period outweighs this potential weakness: "As one might expect in a novel played out on so vast a canvas, few characters are memorable. The focus here is on the momentous events of an era . . . if one is looking for a novel with purposefulness of craft, vivid characterization or an insightful, revelatory vision of human events, *North and South* will be a disappointment. If, however, one is looking for an entertaining, popularized, and generally authentic dramatization of American history . . . then the first installment of John Jakes's trilogy covering the events before, during, and after the Civil War will meet his expectations." The immense popularity behind *North and South* led to a successful television miniseries and the remaining two volumes of the trilogy, *Love and War* (1985) and *Heaven and Hell* (1987).

Discussing his writing, Jakes has said that the research is what takes the most time, and he believes that his books "may be the only shot some people have at history." Gay Andrews Dillin in the *Christian Science Monitor* also promoted this view: "Remember how easy it was to doze off in your American history class? Well, if John Jakes had been the teacher, you wouldn't have!"

—Christopher Swann

JAMES, Clive (Vivian Leopold)

Nationality: Australian. **Born:** 7 October 1939, in Kogarah, New South Wales. **Education:** Sydney University, B.A., 1960; Pembroke College, Cambridge, M.A., 1967. **Military Service:** Australian National Service, 1958-60. **Career:** Sydney *Morning Herald*, assistant editor, 1961; *Observer*, London, television critic, 1972-82, feature writer, 1972—; television performer and writer. Worked as a streetcar conductor, librarian, factory hand, statistician, copy editor, and copy writer. President of Footlights (dramatic society) at Cambridge University. **Agent:** A.D. Peters & Co., The Chambers, Chelsea Harbour, Lots Rd., London SW10 0XF, England. **Address:** 8 St. Andrew's Hill, London EC4V 5JA, England.

Publications

Novels

Brilliant Creatures. J. Cape, 1983.
The Remake. J. Cape, 1987.
Brrm! Brrm! J. Cape, 1991; as *The Man from Japan*, Random House, 1993.

Nonfiction

The Metropolitan Critic. Faber, 1974.
Visions before Midnight. J. Cape, 1977.
At the Pillars of Hercules. Faber, 1979.
First Reactions (contains essays previously published in *The Metropolitan Critic, Visions before Midnight,* and *At the Pillars of Hercules).* Knopf, 1980.
Unreliable Memoirs. J. Cape, 1980; Knopf, 1981.
The Crystal Bucket. J. Cape, 1981.
From the Land of Shadows. J. Cape, 1982.
Glued to the Box. J. Cape, 1983.
Flying Visits. J. Cape, 1984; Norton, 1986.
Falling towards England (Unreliable Memoirs Continued). J. Cape, 1985.
Snakecharmers in Texas. J. Cape, 1988.

Poetry

Peregrine Prykke's Pilgrimage through the London Literary World. New Review, 1974; revised version published as *The Improved Version of Peregrine Prykke's Pilgrimage through the London Literary World: A Tragic Poem in Rhyming Couplets,* illustrations by Russell Davies, J. Cape, 1976.
The Fate of Felicity Fark in the Land of the Media, illustrations by Marc. J. Cape, 1975.
Britannia Bright's Bewilderment in the Wilderness of Westminster, illustrations by Marc. J. Cape, 1976.
Fan-Mail. Faber, 1977.
Charles Charming's Challenges on the Pathway to the Throne, illustrations by Marc. New York Review of Books, 1981.
Poem of the Year. J. Cape, 1983.
Other Passports. J. Cape, 1986.

* * *

A prolific and protean writer, Clive James has published well over 20 books in two decades in areas ranging from mock-heroic poetry, reviews, and literary criticism to television journalism, travel books, fiction, and autobiography. He is even better known as a television performer, where he employs his gravelly delivery and perfectly timed one-liners to great effect.

James grew up in Sydney, Australia, and moved to London in 1962. Though he settled in England he travels frequently and has made repeated visits back to Australia. His best and most popular book, the autobiography *Uncertain Memoirs* (1980), gives a hilariously funny account of growing up in Australia. It was followed by two volumes of equally homourous memoirs, *Falling towards England* (1985) and *May Week Was in June* (1990), covering respectively his experiences in London during the 1960s and at Cambridge before that. James also published several mock-epic poems that drew mixed reviews from critics unsure, for instance, (as perhaps he himself was) whether he was for the royal family or against it, courtier or satirist.

Unceasingly witty, playful, and self-referring, James's critical essays reveal, as well, a mind of considerable critical distinction and immense erudition. He has written thoughtfully on subjects as disparate as the Italian poet Eugenio Montale, Formula One car racing, and the World Disco Dancing Championships, as well as about a large number of Australian writers.

More recently, James has turned to fiction. But the dazzling qualities that make him a fine reviewer are stretched thinly over the length of a novel. *Brilliant Creatures* (1983), for instance, is not so much a novel as a presentation pack. The text comes surrounded by an introduction, a set of extensive and very boring notes, and an index at the back. The introduction reveals his ambivalence about the novel, which parodies the English literary scene. On the one hand he recognizes it for what it is; a funny, broadly drawn caricature of English intellectual life. On the other, there is still a sneaking element in him that wants the book to be taken as a serious contribution to contemporary fiction.

The Remake (1988) has a number of brilliant one-liners that read as if they are meant to be spoken out loud. Again, the book satirizes the English literary scene in terms that suggest an ambivalent intimacy with it. The name-dropping and in-jokes are almost incessant, but James' knack of anticipating criticism and deflecting it in advance is even more evident here than usual. He even has a peripheral character named Clive James (this, of course, after saying "God save me from the novel in which the author gets a mention") who is spoken of disparagingly by the protagonists. He is usually depicted as a fat man jogging laboriously around the edge of the narrative, but as the initials suggest bestows aspects of himself on the main characters, Chance Jenolan and Joel Court. Even his self-denigration is preening.

James' third novel, *Brrm! Brrm!* (1992), takes a Japanese man, Akira Suzuki, (hence the title) as its central character, and uses him as a stick to beat London cultural life and the reign of Mrs. Thatcher with a flaccid stick.

James's literary output is as uneven as it is considerable. His talents are so great and so many that perhaps he finds difficulty in applying himself to any of them sufficiently. His facetiousness, in-house allusions, and penchant for preposterous names for his characters may stem from his days with Cambridge's Footlights theater. In any case, they continually prevent the genuine rage he occasionally hints at (as in *Brrm! Brrm!*'s depiction of England in the late 1980s). Only in the autobiographies, particularly the first of them, does the mask of humor drop at times.

Still, one can forgive a lot to the man who describes the sunbathing bimbos at Birarritz as "jailbait teriyaki [who] glowed on the seawall, like Playboy's version of classical entablature," or a group of punks in the street as "a loose pack of homicidally accoutred youths whose heads looked as if birds of paradise had been placed on them and hit with a mallet."

—Laurie Clancy

JAMES, P(hyllis) D(orothy)

Nationality: British. **Born:** Oxford, 3 August 1920. **Education:** Cambridge Girls' High School, 1931-37. During World War II worked as a Red Cross nurse and at the Ministry of Food. **Family:** Married Ernest Connor Bantry White in 1941 (died 1964); two daughters. **Career:** Prior to World War II, assistant stage manager, Festival Theatre, Cambridge; principal administrative assistant, North West Regional Hospital Board, London, 1949-68; principal, Home Office, in police department, 1968-72, and criminal policy department, 1972-79. Justice of the Peace, Willesden, London, 1979-82, and Inner London, 1984. Chair, Society of Authors, 1984-86; governor, BBC, and board of the British Council, 1988-93; chair, Arts Council Literature Advisory Panel, 1989-92. Lives in London. **Awards:** Crime Writers Association award, 1967, Silver Dagger award, 1971, 1975, 1986, Diamond Dagger award, 1987. D.Litt.: Buckingham, 1992; London, 1993; Hertfordshire, 1994; Glasgow, 1995. Associate Fellow, Downing College, Cambridge, 1986; Fellow, Institute of Hospital Administrators, Royal Society of Literature, 1987, and Royal Society of Arts. O.B.E., 1983. Baroness, 1991. **Agent:** Greene & Heaton, Ltd., 37 Goldhawk Road, London W12 8QQ, England.

PUBLICATIONS

Novels

Cover Her Face. London, Faber, 1962; New York, Scribner, 1966.
A Mind to Murder. London, Faber, 1963; New York, Scribner, 1967.
Unnatural Causes. London, Faber, and New York, Scribner, 1967.
Shroud for a Nightingale. London, Faber, and New York, Scribner, 1971.
An Unsuitable Job for a Woman. London, Faber, 1972; New York, Scribner, 1973.
The Black Tower. London, Faber, and New York, Scribner, 1975.
Death of an Expert Witness. London, Faber, and New York, Scribner, 1977.
Innocent Blood. London, Faber, and New York, Scribner, 1980.
The Skull Beneath the Skin. London, Faber, and New York, Scribner, 1982.
A Taste for Death. London, Faber, and New York, Knopf, 1986.
Devices and Desires. London, Faber, 1989; New York, Knopf, 1990.
The Children of Men. London, Faber, 1992; New York, Knopf, 1993.
Original Sin. London, Faber, 1994; New York, Knopf, 1995.

Uncollected Short Stories

"Moment of Power," in *Ellery Queen's Murder Menu.* Cleveland, World, 1969.
"The Victim," in *Winter's Crimes 5,* edited by Virginia Whitaker. London, Macmillan, 1973.
"Murder, 1986," in *Ellery Queen's Masters of Mystery.* New York, Davis, 1975.
"A Very Desirable Residence," in *Winter's Crimes 8,* edited by Hilary Watson. London, Macmillan, 1976.
"Great-Aunt Ellie's Flypapers," in *Verdict of Thirteen,* edited by Julian Symons. London, Faber, and New York, Harper, 1979.
"The Girl Who Loved Graveyards," in *Winter's Crimes 15,* edited by George Hardinge. London, Macmillan, and New York, St. Martin's Press, 1983.
"Memories Don't Die," in *Redbook* (New York), July 1984.
"The Murder of Santa Claus," in *Great Detectives,* edited by D.W. McCullough. New York, Pantheon, 1984.
"The Mistletoe Murder," in *The Spectator* (London), 1991.
"The Man Who Was 80," in *The Man Who.* London, Macmillan, 1992.

Play

A Private Treason (produced Watford, Hertfordshire, 1985).

Other

The Maul and the Pear Tree: The Ratcliffe Highway Murders, 1811, with Thomas A. Critchley. London, Constable, 1971; New York, Mysterious Press, 1986.

*

Critical Study: *P.D. James* by Norma Siebenheller, New York, Ungar, 1981; *P.D. James* by Richard B. Gidez, Boston, Hall, 1986.

* * *

P.D. James (later Baroness James) has said, "after I had done three or four detective novels, I realized that in fact the restriction [of the genre] could almost help by imposing discipline, and that you could be a serious novelist within it." Her work as a whole is testament to her ability to find the formal constraints of crime-genre writing "liberating rather than inhibiting of [the] creative imagination."

Indeed, James's creative play within the circumscribed boundaries of crime fiction manifests itself in various diverse formulations. Consequently, in her fiction can be found graphically detailed accounts of violence, a policeman and published poet whose actions occasionally transgress the system of law which he is there to uphold, and a female private detective who refuses to conform to stereotyped sex roles. Each is an example of writing against the previous conventions of her chosen genre. Furthermore, she makes explicit and distinct the crime novel and the detective story, with *Innocent Blood* (1980) an example of the former, and *Shroud for a Nightingale* (1971) the latter.

The one constant that she refuses to compromise is setting, manipulating to brilliant effect the Audenesque notion, posited in his essay *The Guilty Vicarage,* that: "Nature should reflect its human inhabitants, i.e. it should be the Great Good Place, for the more Eden-like it is the greater the contradiction of murder." Thus, *An Unsuitable Job for a Woman* (1972), the novel that introduces the reader to James's female private detective, Cordelia Gray, sets the appalling death of the victim against the beautiful backdrop of Cambridge in midsummer, evoking the type contrast Auden had in mind. Likewise, *Death of an Expert Witness* (1977) ironically locates murder within an institution created to enable its very solution; a forensic science laboratory.

In James's more recent novel, *Original Sin* (1994), which features Commander Adam Dalgliesh for the ninth time, location is again of paramount importance, as the imagined landscape of London plays host to an absorbing who-and-whydunnit. Equally from this particular can be discerned one of the predominant thematic concerns of James's work; what space is religion to occupy in contemporary society? In fact her novels seem to both chart a society that is in decline because of its lack of faith (the violators and occasionally the violated are explicitly noted as sinning), and highlight the consequential importance and concomitant difficulties of maintaining faith and belief in a violent world.

Thus, James's novels concern themselves with the nature and function of policing, and consequently become locations where all of its institutional problems surface. However, the author infuses the police force, which often represents an index of constantly shifting social values, with dignity, and mobilizes its members as, in some ways, the custodians of morality.

In *Criminal Practices* (1994), Julian Symons explains that "P.D. James is as firmly British as steak and kidney pie, a realistic practical novelist concerned with social morality." While this is certainly true, her ability to take firm hold of the reader's interest by ingenious plotting, detailed characterization, and a commitment to social values have won, and will continue to win, the author an extensive global following.

—Christopher Wigginton

JANOWITZ, Tama

Nationality: American. **Born:** San Francisco, California, 12 April 1957. **Education:** Barnard College, New York, B.A. 1977; Hollins College, Virginia, M.A. 1979; Yale University, New Haven, Connecticut, 1980-81. **Career:** Model, Vidal Sassoon, London and New York, 1975-77; assistant art director, Kenyon and Eckhardt, Boston, Massachusetts, 1977-78; writer-in-residence, Fine Arts Works Center, Provincetown, Massachusetts, 1981-82; since 1985 freelance writer. **Awards:** Bread Loaf Writers fellowship, 1975; Janoway Fiction prize, 1976, 1977; National Endowment award, 1982. **Agent:** Jonathan Dolger, 49 East 96th Street, New York, New York 10028. **Address:** c/o Crown Publishers, 201 E. 50th St., New York, New York 10022, U.S.A.

Publications

Novels

American Dad. New York, Putnam, 1981; London, Picador, 1988.
A Cannibal in Manhattan. New York, Crown, 1987; London, Pan, 1988.
The Male Cross-Dresser Support Group. New York, Crown, and London, Picador, 1992.

Short Stories

Slaves of New York. New York, Crown, 1986; London, Picador, 1987.

Uncollected Short Stories

"Conviction," in *The New Generation,* edited by Alan Kaufman. New York, Doubleday, 1987.
"Case History No.179: Tina," in *Between C and D,* edited by Joel Rose and Catherine Texier. New York, Penguin, 1988.

* * *

Associated early in her writing career with the "brat pack" of "yuppie" novelists, Tama Janowitz has been part of a new wave of writers influenced by mass culture in the 1980s dubbed "post-punk urban realist." Some have perceived this loose group of writers as redressing the experimental cul-de-sac into which the high postmodernists like John Barth and Donald Barthelme had led American fiction, although for a long time people regarded Janowitz's fiction as too shallow, too hip, and too smug. However, many readers have praised Janowitz for her sharp sexual satire and refreshing humor.

Her first novel, *American Dad* (1981), was generally regarded as a fine comic first novel. The Dad is Robert Abraham Przepasniak, a psychiatrist, three-time husband, and father of Earl and Bobo. However, it has been suggested that the real star is Mom (Mavis Przepasniak), since many of the best comic moments belong to her. After she dies halfway through, the story tends to become somewhat flat. Narrated by Earl, an odd misfit (rather like Holden Caulfield or Alex Portnoy), the novel is full of comic invention. Although one critic felt that *American Dad* would have been better structured as a series of short stories, since its humor is "consistently undermined by the lack of grace . . . in her language, . . . a lack of narrative elision."

Her second work, *Cannibal in Manhattan* (1987), generally received very lukewarm attention. Narrated by Mgungu Yabba Mgungu, a South Sea Islander who is brought to Manhattan by Peace Corps volunteer Maria Fishburn, the novel follows his various social trials and intrigues in much the same manner as Crocodile Dundee in Manhattan. Self-consciously playing with the image of the "noble savage," the novel ironically implies that New Yorkers can teach lessons in savagery, as Janowitz explores the sheer barbarity of the most chic and sophisticated of social arrangements. The problem with the novel was that Mgungu was perceived to be cartoonish, leaving the book with no emotional center.

However, *Slaves of New York* (1986) received rave reviews for its "crystalline" precision. A collection of short stories which focus upon the art culture of New York, the work was described by novelist Jay McInerny as one that "anatomizes a class of Philistine Esthetes." With a mischievous sense of humor, it tells of characters who are in the grip of various sexual crises and who are "slaves of fashion." Of the 22 stories, the majority are narrated by two characters, Eleanor and Morley Martello, and it is through them that we watch the minor humiliations of New Yorkers. Some of the stories are realistic and ironic in tone, while others verge on fantasy and fable. McInerny remarks that characteristically, her characters "do not experience catharsis or epiphany," and most of her narratives are static, with "seldom much in way of closure."

Janowitz's triumph with *Slaves of New York* was succeeded by yet another comic success, *The Male Cross-Dresser Support Group.* The book deals with the misadventures and tribulations of Pamela Trowel after her gradual dissatisfaction with her New York job and her abandonment of her life in Manhattan for a life on the road. To complicate matters, she develops a maternal bond with the young boy Abdhul who follows her home one day. After adventures "on the road," she returns to Manhattan in drag, and with the aid of the eponymous Male Cross-Dresser Support Group encounters her old enemies on new terms. As one reviewer has noted, Janowitz manages to show that deviancy can occur without depravity, and concludes that the novel is a "funny, disturbing, anti-*Bildungsroman,* something more than literary junk food." With this latest success, Janowitz appears to have thrown off the millstone around the neck of her fiction—that it was merely designed to attract the young and trendy—and donned the mantle of a comic novelist.

—Tim Woods

JONES, LeRoi. *See* **BARAKA, Amiri.**

JONG, Erica

Nationality: American. **Born:** Erica Mann in New York City, 26 March 1942. **Education:** High School of Music and Art, New York; Barnard College, New York (George Weldwood Murray fellow, 1963), 1959-63, B.A. 1963 (Phi Beta Kappa); Columbia University, New York (Woodrow Wilson fellow, 1964), M.A. 1965; Columbia School of Fine Arts, 1969-70. **Family:** Married 1) Michael Werthman in 1963 (divorced 1965); 2) Allan Jong in 1966 (divorced 1975); 3) the writer Jonathan Fast in 1977 (divorced 1983), one daughter; 4) Kenneth David Burrows in 1989. **Career:** Lecturer in English, City College, New York, 1964-66, 1969-70, and University of Maryland European Division, Heidelberg, Germany, 1967-68; instructor in English, Manhattan Community College, New York, 1969-70. Since 1971 instructor in poetry, YM-YWHA Poetry Center, New York. Member of the literary panel, New York State Council on the Arts, 1972-74. Since 1991 president of Author's Guild. **Awards:** Academy of American Poets award, 1963; Bess Hokin prize (*Poetry,* Chicago), 1971; New York State Council on the Arts grant, 1971; Madeline Sadin award (*New York Quarterly*), 1972; Alice Fay di Castagnola award, 1972; National Endowment for the Arts grant, 1973; Creative Artists Public Service grant, 1973; International Sigmund Freud prize, 1979. **Agent:** Ed Victor Ltd., 162 Wardour Street, London W1V 3AT, England.

Publications

Novels

Fear of Flying. New York, Holt Rinehart, 1973; London, Secker and Warburg, 1974.

How to Save Your Own Life. New York, Holt Rinehart, and London, Secker and Warburg, 1977.

Fanny, Being the True History of the Adventures of Fanny Hackabout-Jones. New York, New American Library, and London, Granada, 1980.

Parachutes and Kisses. New York, New American Library, and London, Granada, 1984.

Serenissima: A Novel of Venice. Boston, Houghton Mifflin, and London, Bantam, 1987.

Any Woman's Blues. New York, Harper, and London, Chatto and Windus, 1990.

Uncollected Short Stories

"From the Country of Regrets," in *Paris Review,* Spring 1973.

"Take a Lover," in *Vogue,* April 1977.

Poetry

Fruits and Vegetables. New York, Holt Rinehart, 1971; London, Secker and Warburg, 1973.

Half-Lives. New York, Holt Rinehart, 1973; London, Secker and Warburg, 1974.

Here Comes and Other Poems. New York, New American Library, 1975.

Loveroot. New York, Holt Rinehart, 1975; London, Secker and Warburg, 1977.

The Poetry of Erica Jong. New York, Holt Rinehart, 1976.

Selected Poems 1-2. London, Panther, 2 vols., 1977-80.

At the Edge of the Body. New York, Holt Rinehart, 1979; London, Granada, 1981.

Ordinary Miracles: New Poems. New York, New American Library, 1983; London, Granada, 1984.

Becoming Light: Poems: New and Selected. New York, HarperCollins, 1991.

Other

Four Visions of America, with others. Santa Barbara, California, Capra Press, 1977.
Witches (miscellany). New York, Abrams, 1981; London, Granada, 1982.
Megan's Book of Divorce: A Kid's Book for Adults. New York, New American Library, 1984; London, Granada, 1985.
The Devil at Large: Erica Jong on Henry Miller. New York, Turtle Bay, and London, Chatto and Windus, 1993.
Fear of Fifty: A Midlife Memoir. New York, HarperCollins, 1994.

*

Critical Studies: Interviews in *New York Quarterly 16,* 1974, *Playboy* (Chicago), September 1975, and *Viva* (New York), September 1977; article by Emily Toth, in *Twentieth-Century American-Jewish Fiction Writers* edited by Daniel Walden, Detroit, Gale, 1984; "Isadora and Fanny, Jessica and Erica: The Feminist Discourse of Erica Jong" by Julie Anne Ruth, in *Australian Women's Book Review* (Melbourne), September 1990.

* * *

Erica Jong shocked the world with her frank and explicit descriptions of women's sexual desire in her first novel, *Fear of Flying* (1973). In her many works of fiction and poetry since then, she has detailed the sexual fantasies and frustrations of female characters and narrators whom many reviewers (and the author herself) see as representative of the sexually liberated generation of women in the 1970s and 1980s, although some critics, most of them women, disagree. Her fame rests on the fact that she almost single-handedly brought the difficulties of women trying to balance love, self-development, and creativity to the attention of a mass audience.

In her semi-autobiographical trilogy—*Fear of Flying* (1973), *How to Save Your Own Life* (1977), and *Parachutes and Kisses* (1984)—Jong traces the adulthood of Isadora Wing, a writer who struggles with her need for both sexual fulfillment and self-development through sexual experimentation and a series of failed relationships with flawed men. In the first novel, Isadora temporarily leaves her psychologist husband for a no-guilt affair with a man who turns out to be impotent and devoted to his family. In the second installment, Isadora becomes a highly successful author, decides to end her stifling marriage, falls in love with a young screenwriter, settles down with him, and has a baby. In the final book, she finds herself deserted by the father of her child and must learn how to be a single, working mother.

Fear of Flying has sold 12 million copies and has received more popular and critical attention than any of Jong's subsequent works. It received some spectacular reviews from Henry Miller, who compared it to his own *Tropic of Cancer,* and John Updike, who compared the novel to Chaucer and J.D. Salinger's *Catcher in the Rye.* Many have praised the novel for its liberating attitude towards sex, while others have denounced it as crude. Over the years, many women scholars and critics have been disturbed by the novel's depiction of sexuality in what they see as male terms. Anne Z. Mickelson has written in her book, *Reaching Out: Sensitivity and Order in Recent American Fiction by Women,* "Instead of a woman finding her own self-worth, language and scene crystallize in the kind of male fantasy found in girlie magazines. . . . By adopting the male language of sexuality, Jong is also fooling herself that she is preempting man's power."

The novel made such a stir that Jong once called the success of *Fear of Flying* a curse, adding that "it typecast me in a way that I've been trying to get free of ever since. I'm enormously grateful to it, and yet very eager to be seen as a woman of letters and not just Erica 'Zipless' Jong." Unfortunately for her, reviewers have since compared almost every subsequent book she has written to *Fear of Flying,* inevitably coming to the conclusion that they fail to measure up to her first success. In a representative review, Benjamin DeMott, in the *New York Times Book Review,* wrote about *Any Woman's Blues* (1990), "What's missing is what won the author of *Fear of Flying* a place among the true and unforgettable headliners of late-20th-century literary vaudeville: gorgeous, saving sass." Perhaps one reason reviewers insist on comparing all of her novels to *Fear* is that they all focus on such similar issues and female protagonists. Michael Malone, writing for the *New York Times Book Review,* said, "Erica Jong has one fictional heroine, brave, bookish, beautiful and indefatigably libidinous."

Interestingly, since so many have believed Jong's heroines to be various slightly veiled versions of herself, her latest book is a self-styled memoir. And once again, reviewers can't help comparing the book to *Fear of Flying,* perhaps because the book's title, *Fear of Fifty* (1994), indicates how closely Jong identifies with Isadora Wing. Nancy Mairs wrote in the *New York Times Book Review,* "Two decades is a long time to go on playing the naughty girl . . . What might have been outre at age 30 seems passe at age 50." What reviewers seem to object to most, though, is Jong's claims of representativeness for her life; Jong has said, "In the process of telling my own story, I tell the story of my generation." Patricia Chisholm of *MacCleans* has argued that the book "claims to provide insights into female sexuality, feminism and aging—and offer[s] none." Mairs insisted that "her global pronouncements," like, "Every liberated woman needs a gigolo from time to time," do not ring true for all women. The mixed responses Jong has received from women over the years indicate that her depictions of female sexuality are not universally representative of all women.

—Anne Boyd

JORDAN, Laura. *See* **BROWN, Sandra.**

JORGENSEN, Ivar. *See* **SILVERBERG, Robert.**

JOVIAL BOB STINE. *See* **STINE, R. L.**

K

KAVANAGH, Paul. *See* **BLOCK, Lawrence.**

KAY, Ellen. *See* **DeMILLE, Nelson.**

KEILLOR, Garrison

Nationality: American. **Born:** Gary Edward Keillor, 7 August 1942, in Anoka, Minnesota. **Education:** University of Minnesota, B.A., 1966, graduate study, 1966-68. **Family:** Married 1) Mary C. Guntzel, 1965 (divorced May, 1976); 2) Ulla Skaerved, 1985; children: (first marriage) Jason. **Career:** Writer. KUOM-Radio, Minneapolis, staff announcer, 1963-68; Minnesota Public Radio, St. Paul, producer and announcer, 1971-74, host and principal writer for weekly program "A Prairie Home Companion," 1974-87; host of "Garrison Keillor's American Radio Company of the Air," since 1989. **Awards:** George Foster Peabody Broadcasting award, 1980, for "A Prairie Home Companion"; Edward R. Murrow award from Corporation for Public Broadcasting, 1985, for service to public radio; *Los Angeles Times* Book award nomination, 1986, for *Lake Wobegon Days;* Grammy award for best non-musical recording, 1987, for *Lake Wobegon Days*; Gold Medal for spoken English, American Academy of Arts and Letters. **Agent:** American Humor Institute, 80 Eighth Ave., No. 1216, New York, New York 10011, U.S.A.

Publications

Humorous Fiction

G.K. the DJ. Minnesota Public Radio, 1977.
The Selected Verse of Margaret Haskins Durber. Minnesota Public Radio, 1979.
Happy to Be Here: Stories and Comic Pieces. Atheneum, 1982; expanded edition, Penguin, 1983.
Lake Wobegon Days. Viking, 1985.
Leaving Home: A Collection of Lake Wobegon Stories. Viking, 1987.
We Are Still Married: Stories and Letters. Viking, 1989.
WLT: A Radio Romance. Viking, 1991.
The Book of Guys. Viking, 1993.

Children's Fiction

Cat, You Better Come Home. Viking, 1995.
The Old Man Who Loved Cheese. Little Brown, 1996.

*

Media Adaptations: Sound Recording—*Lake Wobegon Days,* 1985. Many episodes of "The Prairie Home Companion" have also been recorded and released by Minnesota Public Radio.

Critical Studies: *Garrison Keillor: A Voice of America* by Judith Lee Tavoss, University Press of Mississippi, 1991.

* * *

Garrison Keillor—radio humorist, American icon, and host of the long-running *Prairie Home Companion*—has enjoyed great critical success with his books *Lake Wobegon Days* (1985) and *Happy To Be Here* (1981). *Lake Wobegon Days* is a collection of short stories based on the comedy monologues that Keillor performs every week in the portion of his radio show entitled *News from Lake Wobegon.* In these stories, Keillor speaks with warm humor and gentle satire about the beauty and strangeness of life in the fictional town of Lake Wobegon, Minnesota. Keillor, because of his "story-telling" writing style, has been likened to American literary icons such as Mark Twain and James Thurber. Roy Blount, Jr., in *The New York Times Book Review,* calls Keillor's writing talent "down to earth . . . good-hearted . . . spiritual" and "redemptive."

In *Lake Wobegon Days,* Keillor spins tales of family, school, growing up, swimming, fishing, Scouting, and many other experiences with which most readers can easily relate. Some critics describe his narrative as rambling, but most applaud the author's relaxed, reflective tone as both well-suited to his subject matter and pleasant for the reader. Keillor's writing is emotionally evocative and rich with details appealing to all the senses.

Lake Wobegon Days also contains many stories of the history of Lake Wobegon, as well as its social conventions. Keillor often writes about religion in ways that strike home with Americans of Judeo/Christian denominations. For example, he frequently caricatures the almost Puritan morality of the predominantly Lutheran citizens of the town; for them piety requires habitual humility and self-effacement. The characters' religious attitudes are distinct, but usually tolerant and not divisive; "Clarence is Lutheran, but he sometimes drops in at the [Catholic] rectory for a second opinion."

Some critics detect in the voice of *Lake Wobegon*'s speaker an undercurrent of wry irony, hinting at an artist's need to escape from the restrictive provincial setting in order to grow up and assert his own identity. Reviewers almost unanimously find Keillor touching and funny. The *Washington Post* asserts that *Lake Wobegon* will leave the reader "weeping with laughter."

Happy To Be Here is a collection of essays and stories similar in tone, if not subject matter, to those in *Lake Wobegon Days.* Several of the pieces in *Happy To Be Here* are about baseball, using the sport to lampoon popular "New Age" and self-help movements by expounding on the holistic implications of "Atbatness." The book also includes in its comic suggestions a plea for "shy people's rights" ("Why Not Pretty Soon?"), a take-off on current special interest groups.

Keillor's work is sometimes viewed as sentimental, though most commend the author for the comfortable, conversational feel of his prose. Many of Keillor's contemporaries admire his ability to point out people's foibles without condemning them. *Rolling Stone* praised Keillor for speaking to peoples hearts, and *National Review* commended him for celebrating diversity, declaring Keillor "damn brilliant" and "one of out most original writers."

Keillor has also had some critical failures. *WLT: A Radio Romance* (1991) received almost universally poor reviews. Critics strongly disliked this novel about the radio industry, calling the style disappointing, the tone harsh, and the characters unsympathetically drawn. *The Book of Guys* (1993) received mixed reviews. Some critics fault both of these efforts for an unexpected subtext of sarcasm.

Keillor's most lasting fame will likely center around the *Prairie Home Companion.* With this radio show, Keillor has made a lasting contribution to the literary world, the art of story-telling, public broadcasting, and American culture in general by reviving in the 1980s and 1990s the pre-television tradition of gathering around the radio to listen to variety shows, comedies, and dramas. In this way, Keillor has answered the public's need for old-fashioned, wholesome, family-style entertainment, as well as for nostalgia for a simpler time and a less complicated lifestyle. In addition to the famous *News From Lake Wobegon* segment, the show features eclectic music including folk, gospel, and ballads, as well as a variety of comedy sketches such as "Guy Noir, Private Eye" and parody commercials for imaginary sponsors like Ralph's Pretty Good Grocery ("If you can't find it here, you can probably get along without it") and Bertha's Kitty Boutique ("For persons who care about cats").

—Bruce Guy Chabot

KELLERMAN, Jonathan

Nationality: American. **Born:** New York City, 9 August 1949. **Education:** University of California, Los Angeles, A.B. in psychology 1971; University of Southern California, Los Angeles, A.M. in psychology 1973, Ph.D. 1974; Fellowship in clinical psychology, University of Southern California Medical School, 1975. **Family:** Married the writer Faye Marder in 1972; one son and two daughters. **Career:** Freelance illustrator, 1966-72; staff psychologist, Children's Hospital of Los Angeles, 1975-81; assistant clinical professor, pediatrics, 1978-79. Since 1979, associate clinical professor, University of Southern California School of Medicine; head, Jonathan Kellerman Ph.D and Associates, Los Angeles, 1981-85; director, Psychosocial Program, Children's hospitals of Los Angeles, 1970-81. Mystery Writers of America, Southern Chapter California (board of directors, 1989—). **Awards:** Mystery Writers of America Edgar Allan Poe award, 1985; Anthony Boucher award, 1986. **Agent:** Barney Karpfinger, 500 Fifth Avenue, New York, New York 10110, U.S.A.

Publications

Novels (series: Alex Delaware in all books except *The Butcher's Theatre*)

When the Bough Breaks. New York, Atheneum, 1985; as *Shrunken Heads,* London, Macdonald, 1985.

Blood Test. New York, Atheneum, and London, Macdonald, 1986.

Over the Edge. New York, Atheneum, and London, Macdonald, 1987.

The Butcher's Theatre. New York, Bantam, and London, Macdonald, 1988.

Silent Partner. New York, Bantam, and London, Macdonald, 1989.

Time Bomb. New York, Bantam, and London, Macdonald, 1990.

Private Eyes. New York, Bantam, 1992.

Devil's Waltz. New York, Bantam, 1993.

Bad Love. New York, Bantam, 1994.

Self-Defense. New York, Bantam, 1995.

The Web. New York, Bantam, 1996.

Other

Psychological Aspects of Childhood Cancer. Springfield, Illinois, C.C. Thomas, 1980.

Helping the Fearful Child: A Parent's Guide to Everyday and Problem Anxieties. New York, Norton, 1981.

Daddy, Daddy, Can You Touch the Sky (for children). 1994.

Jonathan Kellerman's ABC of Weird Creatures. 1995.

*

Media Adaptation: Television—*When the Bough Breaks,* from the novel, 1986.

* * *

Californian Jonathan Kellerman abandoned a ten-year career as a child psychologist to become a highly successful writer. The sensitivity to childhood psychology that guides his nonfictional studies (*Psychological Aspects of Childhood Cancer,* [1980], and *Helping the Fearful Child: A Parent's Guide,* [1981]) infuses his fiction as well, for their pleasure comes in part from the author's clear expertise, genuine concern with timely topics in child psychology, and compelling mix of analytical, clinical detachment and humanistic, nurturing commitment to the innocent and helpless.

Kellerman's main series character is 33-year-old child psychologist and amateur investigator Dr. Alex Delaware, who, similar to Kellerman, works with cancer-stricken children. In *When the Bough Breaks* (1985), Delaware has retired from private practice to recover from the emotional stress of sharing the nightmares of stricken children. Sergeant Milo Sturgis, a homosexual homicide detective and friend, challenges Delaware to break out of his typically California malaise (health food, jogging, and emotional detachment) and put his skills to work helping solve a double homicide by eliciting testimony from the only witness: an uncommunicative abused child. The success of that effort leads to a working team, with Sturgis consulting Delaware on special cases needing a child psychologist's special sensitivity. Also important to the team is Delaware's commitment to traumatized patients and his ability to delve into the horrors of self-denial.

Kellerman educates readers about psychology in a way that is entertaining and emotionally accessible. Through Delaware he makes sympathetic and understandable the emotional burn-out mental health workers can suffer. Through the behavior of children traumatized by adults and adults traumatized as children he demonstrates the antisocial results of victimization. One theme is that psychologists cannot walk away from the problems of their clients the way other professionals can. In *Private Eyes* (1992), for example, a patient Delaware treated at age seven returns for therapy and protection at age eighteen. Similarly, in *Bad Love* (1994), a psychotic seeking vengeance for imagined wrongs stalks the psychologist. Kellerman explores the destructive power of secrets, the paralyzing effects of fear, and the interlocking psychoses of several generations, and strongly advocates facing harsh truths with gentleness, humanity, firmness, and knowledge.

Unlike authors who take advantage of headline tragedies to win readership, Kellerman anticipates potential problems. His topics are credibly timely and not exploitative of his themes. For example, the child molesting in *When the Bough Breaks* prefigured rather than followed the McMartin Preschool workers case. In *Blood Test* (1986), a dangerously ill five-year-old is kidnapped by his own parents, while *Over the Edge* (1987) features child persecution and *Devil's Waltz* (1993) Munchausen abuse. In *Time Bomb* (1990) Delaware performs a psychological "autopsy" to discover why a shy, reclusive suburbanite would purposely gun down children playing in a schoolyard. *Silent Partner* (1989) tackles the question of twins, and *Self-Defense* (1995) deals with repressed childhood memories.

Kellerman novels share a strong psychology of place. Like Ross Macdonald, he brings to life a modern Los Angeles with its striking divisions between the barrios of East L.A. and the riches of Mulholland Drive. Sometimes his descriptions are satiric, particularly of Hollywood types, would-be film makers, arrogant academic "geniuses," con artists, and gurus. *The Web* (1996) contrasts an idyllic Pacific island setting with ritual slaying, mutilation, and dark conspiracy, while *The Butcher's Theater* (1988), a captivating break from the Delaware series, is set in Jerusalem, where Kellerman lived from 1968 to 1969. This story of a serial murderer who targets young Arab women in a city where this sort of homicide is rare is one of Kellerman's finest works.

Kellerman probes the perversions of the human mind and the essence of terror. Though suspenseful and tense, with double murders, intriguing relationships, and a progression of stunning revelations, his novels are also intellectually challenging and emotionally satisfying. Kellerman brings his characters to life as rounded individuals, at times eccentric and driven, but always humanized and interesting. His contribution to the genre is to make family concerns central to understanding and preventing crime.

—Gina Macdonald

KELLOW, Kathleen. *See* **HOLT, Victoria.**

KELLS, Susannah. *See* **CORNWELL, Bernard.**

KENEALLY, Thomas (Michael)

Nationality: Australian. **Born:** Sydney, New South Wales, 7 October 1935. **Education:** St. Patrick's College, Strathfield, New South Wales; studied for the priesthood 1953-60, and studied law. **Military Service:** Australian Citizens Military Forces. **Family:** Married Judith Mary Martin in 1965; two daughters. **Career:** High-school teacher in Sydney, 1960-64; lecturer in drama, University of New England, Armidale, New South Wales, 1968-69; lived in the U.S., 1975-77; visiting professor of English, University of California, Irvine, 1985; Berg Professor of English, New York University, 1988. **Member:** Australia-China Council, 1978-83; member of the advisory panel, Australian Constitutional Commission, 1985-88; member, Australian Literary Arts Board, 1985-88; president, National Book Council of Australia, 1985-89; chairman, Australian Society of Authors, 1987. **Awards:** Commonwealth Literary Fund fellowship, 1966, 1968, 1972; Miles Franklin award, 1968, 1969; Captain Cook Bicentenary prize, 1970; Royal Society of Literature Heinemann award, 1973; Booker prize, 1982; Los Angeles *Times* award, 1983;. Fellow, Royal Society of Literature, 1973, American Academy of Arts and Sciences, 1993; Officer, Order of Australia, 1983. **Agent:** Deborah Rogers, Rogers, Colleridge and White, 20 Powis Mews, London W11 1JN, England.

Publications

Novels

The Place at Whitton. Melbourne and London, Cassell, 1964; New York, Walker, 1965.

The Fear. Melbourne and London, Cassell, 1965; as *By the Line,* St. Lucia, University of Queensland Press, 1989.

Bring Larks and Heroes. Melbourne, Cassell, 1967; London, Cassell, and New York, Viking Press, 1968.

Three Cheers for the Paraclete. Sydney, Angus and Robertson, 1968; London, Angus and Robertson, and New York, Viking Press, 1969.

The Survivor. Sydney, Angus and Robertson, 1969; London, Angus and Robertson, and New York, Viking Press, 1970.

A Dutiful Daughter. Sydney and London, Angus and Robertson, and New York, Viking Press, 1971.

The Chant of Jimmie Blacksmith. Sydney and London, Angus and Robertson, and New York, Viking Press, 1972.

Blood Red, Sister Rose. London, Collins, and New York, Viking Press, 1974.

Moses the Lawgiver (novelization of television play). London, Collins-ATV, and New York, Harper, 1975.

Gossip from the Forest. London, Collins, 1975; New York, Harcourt Brace, 1976.

Season in Purgatory. London, Collins, 1976; New York, Harcourt Brace, 1977.

A Victim of the Aurora. London, Collins, 1977; New York, Harcourt Brace, 1978.

Passenger. London, Collins, and New York, Harcourt Brace, 1979.

Confederates. London, Collins, 1979; New York, Harper, 1980.

The Cut-Rate Kingdom. Sydney, Wildcat Press, 1980; London, Allen Lane, 1984.

Schindler's Ark. London, Hodder and Stoughton, 1982; as *Schindler's List,* New York, Simon and Schuster, 1982.

A Family Madness. London, Hodder and Stoughton, 1985; New York, Simon and Schuster, 1986.
The Playmaker. London, Hodder and Stoughton, and New York, Simon and Schuster, 1987.
Towards Asmara. London, Hodder and Stoughton, 1989; as *To Asmara,* New York, Warner, 1989.
Flying Hero Class. London, Hodder and Stoughton, and New York, Warner, 1991.
Woman of the Inner Sea. New York, Doubleday, and London, Hodder, 1992.
Jacko. London, Heinemann, 1993.
A River Town. London, Reed Books, 1995.

Uncollected Short Story

"The Performing Blind Boy," in *Festival and Other Stories,* edited by Brian Buckley and Jim Hamilton. Melbourne, Wren, 1974; Newton Abbot, Devon, David and Charles, 1975.

Plays

Halloran's Little Boat, adaptation of his novel *Bring Larks and Heroes* (produced Sydney, 1966). Published in *Penguin Australian Drama 2,* Melbourne, Penguin, 1975.
Childermass (produced Sydney, 1968).
An Awful Rose (produced Sydney, 1972).
Bullie's House (produced Sydney, 1980; New Haven, Connecticut, 1985). Sydney, Currency Press, 1981.
Gossip from the Forest, adaptation of his own novel (produced 1983).

Screenplays: *The Priest* (episode in *Libido*), 1973; *Silver City,* with Sophia Turkiewicz, 1985.

Television Writing (UK): *Essington,* 1974; *The World's Wrong End* (documentary; *Writers and Places* series), 1981; *Australia* series, 1987.

Other

Ned Kelly and the City of Bees (for children). London, Cape, 1978; Boston, Godine, 1981.
Outback, photographs by Gary Hansen and Mark Lang. Sydney and London, Hodder and Stoughton, 1983.
Australia: Beyond the Dreamtime, with Patsy Adam-Smith and Robyn Davidson. London, BBC Publications, 1987; New York, Facts on File, 1989.
Child of Australia (song), music by Peter Sculthorpe. London, Faber Music, 1987.
Now and in Time to Be: Ireland and the Irish, photographs by Patrick Prendergast. Panmacmillan, Ryan, and, Norton, 1992.

*

Media Adaptations: Film—*Schindler's List,* 1993.

Manuscript Collections: Mitchell Library, Sydney; Australian National Library, Canberra.

Critical Study: *Thomas Keneally* by Peter Quartermaine, London, Arnold, 1991.

Theatrical Activities:
Actor: **Films**—*The Devil's Playground,* 1976; *The Chant of Jimmie Blacksmith,* 1978.

* * *

Thomas (or Tom, as he now signs himself) Keneally is one of Australia's most popular and prolific authors. He first came to prominence with his third novel, *Bring Larks and Heroes* (1967). The story is set in an unnamed penal colony in the late 18th century that bears close similarities to Sydney's Port Jackson. It explores the fate of the doomed Corporal Halloran and his bride, Ann, and the divided allegiance Halloran feels between his duty as a soldier in the king's service and his allegiance as an Irishman to the brutally mistreated convicts. Writing in a powerfully rhetorical style, Keneally exhibits his characteristic fascination with moral questions of conscience (he studied for the priesthood for six years).

Keneally has plundered history for his themes many times since then. Often it is Australian history in which he tries to find lessons for the present. *The Chant of Jimmie Blacksmith* (1972), for example, deals with the uprising of the two Governor brothers, Aborigines who went on a rampage in northern New South Wales in 1900. The novel makes ironic comparisons between whites' brutal mistreatment of Aborigines and their eagerness to join in fighting the Boers in South Africa; and the bright hopes they have for the coming Federation, a coming together which will ignore all of Australia's original citizens. *The Cut-Rate Kingdom* (1980) deals with the more recent history of Australia's ambivalently subservient relationship with the United States during WWII, while *The Playmaker* (1987) goes much further back, its subject being a performance of Farquhar's play *The Recruiting Officer* by convicts in 1789. A more recent novel, *A River Town* (1995), returns to the period of the coming Federation, but in a much more affectionate and evocative way than in *The Chant.*

Keneally's interest in the past extends to the international area. With remarkable eclecticism he has dealt with Joan of Arc, an Antarctic exploration of 1909, the American Civil War, the signing of the Armistice in 1918, and Yugoslav resistance fighters at the end of WWII. But his biggest success and finest novel, *Schindler's Ark* (1982), tells the true story of a German businessman named Oskar Schindler who risked his otherwise undistinguished life, for reasons that will always remain mysterious, to save Jews from the gas chamber. *Schindler's Ark* is, in fact, hardly a novel at all but merely the factual retelling of a story Keneally heard by accident. In a prose that is humbled by its subject and devoid of the purple passages that mark much of his work, Keneally frankly confesses the point at which his understanding of his subject ceases.

Especially in his more recent work, Keneally seems less at home with contemporary subjects. *Towards Asmara* (1989) is a worthy but lamely written account of the Eritrean conflict, while *Flying Hero Class* (1991) is a grossly and farcically implausible novel about a troupe of touring Aboriginal dancers whose plane is hijacked over the Atlantic by Palestinian terrorists. *Jacko* (1994) is even more risible with its spot-the-celebrity air and its narrator who is not too modest to mention casually "the occasional eccentric voices (none of them from my homeland, Australia) who said I might one day be worth a Nobel."

As that comment reveals, Keneally has always felt ambivalent about the tension between popular success and critical acceptance, and many of the reviews of his work exhibit a similar uneasiness:

"One of the minor mysteries of the local literary rating scene is why Thomas Keneally's' novels have been treated as serious 'literature' by Australian critics," Dorothy Green said indignantly many years ago. The issue has been raised many times since. He is often spoken of as a high-class journalist rather than a genuine writer of fiction, and he has spoken many times in interviews of the difficulties of straddling the line between popular and quality fiction, and between writing for a home audience and an international one. At the same time, he has complained about the poor reviews he consistently receives in Australia as compared to those overseas, and has listed the considerable number of international prizes he has won.

Keneally has also written several plays. More recently he tried his hand at nonfiction with books about the Australian Outback, his Irish roots, an autobiographical memoir, and the desirability of Australia becoming a Republic (a cause to which he has firmly committed himself). Although his achievement is wildly eclectic and uneven, his best work will ensure that he continues to be widely read.

—Laurie Clancy

KEROUAC, Jack

Nationality: American. **Born:** 12 March 1922, in Lowell, Massachusetts. **Education:** Attended Horace Mann School for Boys, New York City; attended Columbia College, 1940-42; attended New School for Social Research, 1948-49. **Military Service:** U.S. Navy, 1943. **Family:** Married 1) Frankie Edith Parker, 1944 (marriage annulled, 1945); 2) Joan Haverty, 1950 (divorced); 3) Stella Sampas, 1966; children: (second marriage) Jan Michele Hackett. **Career:** Writer. Worked at odd jobs in garages and as a sports reporter for the Lowell *Sun,* 1942; railroad brakeman with the Southern Pacific Railroad, San Francisco, 1952-53; traveled around the United States and Mexico; fire lookout for the U.S. Agriculture Service in northwest Washington, 1956. **Awards:** American Academy of Arts and Sciences grant, 1955. **Died:** 21 October 1969, of a stomach hemorrhage, in St. Petersburg, Florida.

PUBLICATIONS

Novels

The Town and the City. Harcourt, 1950.
On the Road. Viking, 1957.
The Dharma Bums. Viking, 1958.
The Subterraneans. Grove, 1958; second edition, 1981.
Doctor Sax: Faust Part Three. Grove, 1959.
Maggie Cassidy: A Love Story. Avon, 1959.
Excerpts from Visions of Cody. New Directions, 1959; enlarged edition published as *Visions of Cody,* McGraw, 1972.
Tristessa. Avon, 1960.
Big Sur. Farrar, Straus, 1962.
Visions of Gerard. Farrar, Straus, 1963.
Desolation Angels. Coward, 1965.
Satori in Paris. Grove, 1966.
Vanity of Duluoz: An Adventurous Education. Coward, 1968.
Pic. Grove, 1971.

Poetry

Mexico City Blues: Two Hundred Forty-Two Choruses. Grove, 1959.
Hugo Weber. Portents, 1967.
Someday You'll Be Lying. Privately printed, 1968.
A Lost Haiku. Privately printed, 1969.
Scattered Poems. City Lights, 1971.
Trip Trap: Haiku along the Road from San Francisco to New York, with Albert Saijo and Lew Welch. Grey Fox, 1973.
Heaven and Other Poems. Grey Fox, 1977.
San Francisco Blues. Beat Books, 1983.
Hymn: God Pray for Me. Caliban, 1985.
American Haikus. Caliban, 1986.

Other

Rimbaud. City Lights, 1959.
The Scripture of the Golden Eternity. Corinth Books, 1960.
Book of Dreams. City Lights, 1961.
Lonesome Traveler. McGraw, 1960.
A Memoir in Which Is Revealed Secret Lives and West Coast Whispers. Giligia, 1970.
Home at Christmas. Oliphant, 1973.
Old Angel Midnight. Unicorn Bookshop, 1976.
Take Care of My Ghost, Ghost. Ghost Press, 1977.
Une veille de Noel. Knight, 1980.
Dear Carolyn: Letters to Carolyn Cassady. Unspeakable Visions, 1983.

*

Film Adaptation: *The Subterraneans,* 1960.

Bibliography: *A Bibliography of Works by Jack Kerouac, 1939-1975* by Ann Charters, Phoenix Book Shop, 1975; *Jack Kerouac: A Bibliography of Biographical and Critical Material, 1950-1979* by T. E. Nisonger, Bull Bibliography, 1980; *Jack Kerouac: An Annotated Bibliography of Secondary Sources, 1944-1979* by Robert J. Milewski, Scarecrow, 1981; *Jack Kerouac, The Bootleg Era: A Bibliography of Pirated Editions* edited by Rod Anstee, Water Row Press, 1994.

Critical Studies: *Kerouac: A Biography* by Ann Charters, Straight Arrow, 1973; *Kerouac's Town* by Barry Gifford, Capra, 1973, revised edition, Creative Arts Book Co., 1977; *Visions of Kerouac* by Charles E. Jarvis, Ithaca Press, 1973; *Heart Beat: My Life with Jack and Neal* by Carolyn Cassady, Creative Arts Book Co., 1977; *Jack Kerouac: Prophet of the New Romanticism* by Robert A. Hipkiss, University of Kansas Press, 1977; *Jack Kerouac: The New Picaroon* by Luc Gaffie, Postillion Press, 1977; *Jack's Book: An Oral Biography of Jack Kerouac* by Barry Gifford and Lawrence Lee, St. Martin's, 1978; *Desolate Angel: Jack Kerouac, the Beat Generation, and America* by Dennis McNally, McGraw, 1979; *Jack Kerouac* by Harry Russell Huebel, Boise State University, 1979; *On the Road: Text and Criticism* edited by Scott Donaldson, Viking, 1979; *The Beats: Essays of Criticism* by Lee Bartlett, McFarland, 1981; *Kerouac's Crooked Road: Development of a Fiction* by Tim Hunt, Archon Books, 1981; *Memory Babe: A Critical Biography of Jack Kerouac* by Gerald Nicosia, Grove, 1983; *Jack Kerouac* by Tom Clark, Harcourt, 1984; *Quest* *for Kerouac* by Chris Challis, Faber, 1984; *Kerouac and His Friends: A Beat Generation Album* by Fred W. McDarragh, William Morrow, 1985; *Jack Kerouac* by Warren French, Twayne, 1986; *The Spontaneous Poetics of Jack Kerouac: A Study of Fiction* by Regina Weinreich, Southern Illinois University Press, 1987.

* * *

Having coined the word "beat," Jack Kerouac defined the Beat Generation for the *Random House Dictionary* as "members of the generation that came of age after WWII, who, supposedly as a result of disillusionment stemming from the Cold War, espouse mystical detachment and relaxation of social and sexual tensions." For most, Jean-Louis Lebrid de Kerouac is the quintessential Beat, the "poet of the pads," the "bard of the bebops," and his novel *On The Road* (1957) is the quintessential record of that counterculture.

Churned out in three weeks (according to one source), *On the Road* is a *roman a clef* recounting the adventures of Sal Paradise (a.k.a. Kerouac), Carlo Marx (Allen Ginsberg), Old Bull Lee (William Burroughs), and especially Dean Moriarty (Kerouac's life-transforming friend, Neal Cassady). So seductive were the compulsive continental road trips, the jazz, and the experiments with sex and drugs that the novel became the back-pocket bible for restless late-1950s youth. Sven Birkerts claims that even in 1968, it "could not have felt more present tense."

Despite fans' adulation making the novel a bestseller and Gilbert Millstein calling it "a major novel," dismissive early criticism saw only the high-energy, Bohemian lifestyle, labeling it an immoral "sideshow." Critics, however, now look at Kerouac and his novels in new ways; they read for his descriptions and use of women, jazz, marginalized groups, and particularly his "spontaneous prose," or the exhausting, confessional, high-speed writing Kerouac developed as a way to capture his careening consciousness.

Multiculturalism also calls for a fresh reading. According to Ann Charters, Kerouac's books, arranged chronologically rather than in order of composition, tell the story of a life "deeply marked by the different cultural experience of his [never assimilated] French Canadian family." Kerouac called his Proustian sequence "The Legend of Dulouz"; he was "Dulouz" (the "louse").

Kerouac's first published novel, *The Town and the City* (1950), dramatizes an idyllic New England immigrant life shattered by war and a move to the city. At story's end, the favored son takes to the road. Despite cool reception of his first attempt, Kerouac feverishly produced 12 books between 1951-1957, many of which were at first considered unpublishable.

On The Road was followed by two other "Beat" novels. *The Subterraneans* (1958), spontaneously written in three days in 1953, immediately became a poorly conceived 1960 movie. *The Dharma Bums* (1958), written in ten days and set in 1955-56 when Kerouac was deep into Buddhism, introduces Japhy Ryder (the poet Gary Snyder), who prophetically calls for "a great rucksack revolution" anticipating, as Joan Goldsworthy points out, the 1960s hippies.

Other novels fictionalize Kerouac's earlier life in a French-Canadian community in Lowell, Massachusetts. *Visions of Gerard* (1963) tenderly honors his older brother Gerard and the emotional impact of his 1926 death. *Doctor Sax* (1959), which combines Kerouac's mother's strong Quebec Catholicism, youthful fantasies nourished by pulp fiction, and idealized memories, is a valuable document about French-Canadian acculturation. Two others show a young man's partially successful struggle to break from his immigrant background: *Maggie Cassidy* (1959) records his high school football career and love for an Irish girl, while *Vanity of Dulouz* (1968) covers his leaving home for college and the city.

To these and subsequent works critics remained hostile, despite Ann Charters' evaluation that the above novels are "some of his strongest and most original spontaneous extended narrative." In them, French Canadian critics see Kerouac seeking a balance between his family's marginal status and his personal desire for participation in American life. He never lost sight of his immigrant heritage. As late as 1965 he traveled to France in search of his ancestry. He immediately fictionalized the journey in *Sartori in Paris* (1966).

Other novels in the autobiographical "Dulouz Legend" include *Tristessa* (1960), about his 1955 Mexico City affair with a morphine-addicted prostitute, and *Desolation Angels* (1965) which includes the group's famous trip to visit Burroughs in Tangier. The *Big Sur* (1962) account of a previous summer's alcoholic madness could only have reinforced the critics' distaste for Kerouac's lifestyle.

Reevaluation, however, strengthened with the posthumous republication of the complete *Visions of Cody* (1960), a reworking of *On The Road*, which Aaron Latham reassessed as "*The Huckleberry Finn* of the mid-20th century." Others attribute Kerouac's work with language as a "liberating influence" on authors such as Ken Kesey, Thomas Pynchon, Bob Dylan, and Hunter S. Thompson. Finally, in 1991, *On The Road* was republished as an American "classic."

—Judith C. Kohl

KESEY, Ken (Elton)

Nationality: American. **Born:** La Junta, Colorado, 17 September 1935. **Education:** A high school in Springfield, Oregon; University of Oregon, Eugene, B.A. 1957; Stanford University, California (Woodrow Wilson fellow), 1958-59. **Family:** Married Faye Haxby in 1956; four children (one deceased). **Career:** Ward attendant in mental hospital, Menlo Park, California; president, Intrepid Trips film company, 1964. Since 1974 publisher, *Spit in the Ocean* magazine, Pleasant Hill, Oregon. Served prison term for marijuana possession, 1967. **Awards:** Saxton Memorial Trust award, 1959. **Address:** 85829 Ridgeway Road, Pleasant Hill, Oregon 97455, U.S.A.

Publications

Novels

One Flew over the Cuckoo's Nest. New York, Viking Press, 1962; London, Methuen, 1963.

Sometimes a Great Notion. New York, Viking Press, 1964; London, Methuen, 1966.

Demon Box. New York, Viking, and London, Methuen, 1986.

Caverns, with others. New York, Viking, 1990.

The Further Inquiry. New York, Viking, 1990.

Sailor Song. New York, Viking, 1992; London, Black Swan, 1993.

Last Go Round, with Ken Babbs. New York, Viking, 1994.

Short Story

The Day Superman Died. Northridge, California, Lord John Press, 1980.

Uncollected Short Stories

"The First Sunday in October," in *Northwest Review* (Seattle), Fall 1957.
"McMurphy and the Machine," in *Stanford Short Stories 1962,* edited by Wallace Stegner and Richard Scowcroft. Stanford, California, Stanford University Press, 1962.
"Letters from Mexico," in *Ararat* (New York), Autumn 1967.
"Excerpts from Kesey's Jail Diary," in *Ramparts* (Berkeley, California), November 1967.
"Correspondence," in *Tri-Quarterly* (Evanston, Illinois), Spring 1970.
"Once a Great Nation," in *Argus* (College Park, Maryland), April 1970.
"Dear Good Dr. Timothy," in *Augur* (Eugene, Oregon), 19 November 1970.
"Cut the Motherfuckers Loose," in *The Last Whole Earth Catalog.* San Francisco, Straight Arrow, 1971.
"The Bible," "Dawgs," "The I Ching," "Mantras," "Tools from My Chest," in *The Last Supplement to the Whole Earth Catalog-The Realist* (New York), March-April 1971.
"Over the Border," in *Oui* (Chicago), April 1973.
"'Seven Prayers' by Grandma Whittier," in *Spit in the Ocean 1-5* (Pleasant Hill, Oregon), 1974-79.

Other

Kesey's Garage Sale (miscellany; includes screenplay *Over the Border*). New York, Viking Press, 1973.
Little Tricker the Squirrel Meets Big Double the Bear (for children). New York, Viking, 1990.
The Sea Lion: A Story of the Sea Cliff People (for children). New York, Viking, 1991.

*

Manuscript Collection: University of Oregon, Eugene.

Critical Studies: *The Electric Kool-Aid Acid Test* by Tom Wolfe, New York, Farrar Straus, 1968, London, Weidenfeld and Nicolson, 1969; *Ken Kesey* by Bruce Carnes, Boise, Idaho, Boise State College, 1974; Ken Kesey Issue of *Northwest Review* (Eugene, Oregon), vol. 16, nos. 1-2, 1977; *Ken Kesey* by Barry H. Leeds, New York, Ungar, 1981; *The Art of Grit: Ken Kesey's Fiction,* Columbia, University of Missouri Press, 1982, and *One Flew over the Cuckoo's Nest: Rising to Heroism,* Boston, Twayne, 1989, both by M. Gilbert Porter; *Ken Kesey* by Stephen L. Tanner, Boston, Twayne, 1983; *On the Bus: The Legendary Trip of Ken Kesey and the Merry Pranksters* by Ken Babbs, photographs by Rob Bivert, New York, Thunder's Mouth Press, 1989, London, Plexus, 1991.

* * *

Novelist Ken Kesey received the Western Literature Association annual award for Distinguished Achievement in Writing in 1988 for works that capture the maverick frontier spirit—independence, individualism, and toughness—in opposition to authoritarian repression, group-think, and conformity. His strict, Baptist, Oregon-dairy-farm family taught him a love of the outdoors, physical competition, and down home anecdotes and yarns. His spunky grandmother provided the model for Grandma Whittier in an unfinished novel serialized in Kesey's magazine *Spit in the Ocean.* Kesey's autobiographical short fiction depicts affectionate, respectful father-son relationships.

Studying under Malcolm Cowley (alongside Larry McMurtry and Robert Stone) at Stanford University, Kesey adopted a radical perspective and bohemian existence and became a leader in the 1960s psychedelic counterculture movement, predating Timothy Leary in using LSD and experimenting with other hallucinogenics. Employment as a night attendant in the VA psychiatric ward inspired Kesey's most widely known novel, *One Flew Over the Cuckoo's Nest* (1962)—he reportedly underwent electroconvulsive therapy so he could describe it accurately. Along with Joseph Heller's *Catch-22* and Richard Farina's *Been Down So Long It Looks Like Up to Me, Cuckoo's Nest* became one of the artistic totems of the 1960s, epitomizing, according to Pauline Kael, in *New Yorker* (1975), "the prophetic essence of that whole period." The novel can be read as a tall tale, a reformist social tract attacking the inhumane treatment of mental patients, and a microcosm, with the insane asylum representing conflict between individual freedom and social restraint and between nature and technology.

The book's point of view is the confused, schizophrenic musings of the supposedly deaf and dumb native American Chief Broom, a "chronic" committed to an insane asylum for life. The narrative itself focuses on the tough, swaggering, ex-marine McMurphy, who battles the efficient, machine-like head nurse, "Big Nurse," and the Combine she represents: all systems (governments, schools, churches, etc.) that limit human nature. Big Nurse turns the inmates against each other, preys on their fears, and weakens their nerve, while McMurphy uses laughter, comic exaggeration, impudence, and absurdist acts (watching a blank television screen when Big Nurse cuts off a promised World Series) to teach independence and self-reliance. Ultimately, McMurphy dooms himself to give his fellow inmates hope and self-assurance. The proof of the value of his sacrifice is the escape of Chief Broom, who, coming to terms with his nightmares, strikes out alone to meet the challenges of life. *Cuckoo's Nest* will remain a classic American novel.

Cuckoo's Nest financed the famed 1964 cross-country ride of the Merry Pranksters in a psychedelic school bus, and the "happenings" enroute inspired hippies worldwide and led Tom Wolfe to record the escapades in *The Electric Kool-Aid Acid Test* (1968). Afterwards, Kesey moved back to Oregon and drank and fraternized with loggers to research *Sometimes a Great Notion* (1964). A stylistic experiment, *Notion* frequently shifts perspective and point of view (including those of a dog and a ghost) to depict long-time community rebel Hank Stamper's opposition to a union strike. The national union agent, Jonathan Draeger, brings strong pressure to bear (both legal and illegal) to keep the local community from completing a nearly expired contract, but is ultimately overpowered by Stamper's pig-headed defiance. The novel also chronicles Hank's conflict with his Yale-educated, younger half-brother, Lee Stamper. Kesey has called the brothers sides of himself—pretentious urban intellectual versus woodsy, homespun hick.

After drug arrests and run-ins with the law, Kesey settled in Oregon and published autobiographical sketches, essays, travelogues, and film scripts, but no novels. His writings of this period include *Kesey's Garage Sale* (1973), *Demon Box* (1986), and contributions to the *Whole Earth Catalog* (particularly in 1971). Since his son Jed's 1984 death in a car accident, Kesey has devoted himself to his farm, saying, "I got a kid buried on this land. They'll have to get me off with a bulldozer."

—Gina Macdonald

KING, Stephen (Edwin)

Pseudonyms: Richard Bachman. **Nationality:** American. **Born:** 21 September 1947, in Portland, Maine. **Education:** University of Maine at Orono, B.Sc., 1970. **Family:** Married Tabitha Jane Spruce, 1971; children: Naomi Rachel, Joseph Hill, Owen Phillip. **Career:** Writer. Has worked as a janitor, a laborer in an industrial laundry, and in a knitting mill. Hampden Academy (high school), Hampden, Maine, English teacher, 1971-73; University of Maine, Orono, writer in residence, 1978-79. Owner, Philtrum Press and WZON-AM, Bangor, Maine. Served as judge for 1977 World Fantasy awards, 1978. **Awards:** *School Library Journal* Book List citation, 1975, for *Carrie;* Balrog awards, second place in best novel category for *The Stand,* and second place in best collection category for *Night Shift,* both 1979; American Library Association best books for young adults citation, 1979, for *The Long Walk,* and 1981, for *Firestarter;* World Fantasy award, 1980, for contributions to the field, and 1982, for story "Do the Dead Sing?"; Career Alumni award, University of Maine at Orono, 1981; Nebula award nomination, Science Fiction Writers of America, 1981, for story "The Way Station"; special British Fantasy award for outstanding contribution to the genre, British Fantasy Society, 1982, for *Cujo;* Hugo award, World Science Fiction Convention, 1982, for *Stephen King's Danse Macabre;* named Best Fiction Writer of the Year, *Us* Magazine, 1982; Locus award for best collection, Locus Publications, 1986, for *Stephen King's Skeleton Crew.* **Agent:** Arthur Greene, 101 Park Ave., New York, New York 10178. **Address:** P.O. Box 1186, Bangor, Maine 04001, U.S.A.

PUBLICATIONS

Novels

Carrie: A Novel of a Girl with a Frightening Power. Doubleday, 1974.
'Salem's Lot. Doubleday, 1975.
The Shining. Doubleday, 1977.
The Stand. Doubleday, 1978; revised edition with illustrations by Berni Wrightson, 1990.
The Dead Zone. Viking, 1979.
Firestarter. Viking, 1980.
Cujo. Viking, 1981.
Pet Sematary. Doubleday, 1983.
Christine. Viking, 1983.
The Dark Tower Trilogy: The Gunslinger; The Drawing of the Three; The Waste Lands, NAL/Dutton, 1993.
The Dark Tower: The Gunslinger. New American Library, 1988.
The Drawing of Three. New American Library, 1989.
The Dark Tower III: The Waste Lands. NAL/Dutton, 1992.
The Talisman, with Peter Straub. Viking Press/Putnam, 1984.
The Eyes of the Dragon. Limited edition with illustrations by Kenneth R. Linkhauser, Philtrum Press, 1984; new edition with illustrations by David Palladini, Viking, 1987.
It. Viking, 1986.
Misery. Viking, 1987.
The Tommyknockers. Putnam, 1987.
The Dark Half. Viking, 1989.
Needful Things: The Last Castle Rock Story. Viking Penguin, 1991.
Gerald's Game. Viking Penguin, 1992.
Dolores Claiborne. Viking Penguin, 1992.
Insomnia. Viking Penguin, 1994.
The Langoliers. NAL/Dutton, 1995.
Rose Madder. Viking Penguin, 1995.

Novels under Pseudonym Richard Bachman

Rage. New American Library/Signet, 1977.
The Long Walk. New American Library/Signet, 1979.
Roadwork: A Novel of the First Energy Crisis. New American Library/Signet, 1981.
The Running Man. New American Library/Signet, 1982.
Thinner. New American Library, 1984.

Novellas

Different Seasons (contains: *Rita Hayworth and Shawshank Redemption: Hope Springs Eternal; Apt Pupil: Summer of Corruption; The Body: Fall from Innocence;* and *The Breathing Method: A Winter's Tale*). Viking, 1982.
Cycle of the Werewolf. New American Library, 1985.
Four Past Midnight. Viking Penguin, 1990.

Short Stories

Night Shift, with introduction by John D. MacDonald. Doubleday, 1978.
Stephen King's Skeleton Crew. Viking, 1985.
My Pretty Pony, illustrations by Barbara Kruger. Knopf, 1989.
Nightmares and Dreamscapes. Viking Penguin, 1993.

Plays

Screenplays: *Stephen King's Creep Show,* adapted from his stories "Father's Day," "The Lonesome Death of Jordy Verrill," "The Crate," and "They're Creeping Up on You"; *Cat's Eye,* adapted from his stories "Quitters, Inc.," "The Ledge," and "The General," 1984; *Silver Bullet,* adapted from his novella *Cycle of the Werewolf,* 1985; *Maximum Overdrive,* adapted from his story "Trucks," 1986; *Pet Sematary,* adapted from his own novel, 1989; *Sleepwalkers,* Columbia, 1992. Teleplay: *The Stand,* 1994.

Poetry

Another Quarter Mile: Poetry. Dorrance, 1979.

Nonfiction

Stephen King's Danse Macabre. Everest House, 1981.

Nightmares in the Sky: Gargoyles and Grotesques, photographs by f.Stop FitzGerald. Viking, 1988.

*

Media Adaptations: Films—*Carrie*, 1976; *The Shining*, 1980; *The Boogeyman*, 1982; *Cujo*, 1983; *The Dead Zone*, 1983; *Christine*, 1983; *The Woman in the Room*, 1983; *Firestarter*, 1984; *Children of the Corn*, 1984; *Creepshow 2*, adapted from "The Raft" and two unpublished stories, "Old Chief Woodn'head" and "The Hitchhiker," 1987; *Stand by Me*, adapted from his novella *The Body*, 1986; *The Running Man*, 1987; *Return to 'Salem's Lot*, 1987; *Misery*, 1990; *Graveyard Shift*, 1990; *Tales from the Darkside—The Movie*, three-part anthology, one segment based on King's story "The Cat from Hell," 1990; *The Dark Half*, 1991; *The Lawnmower Man*, 1992; *Needful Things*, 1993; *Children of the Corn II: The Final Sacrifice*, 1993; *The Shawshank Redemption*, 1994; *The Mangler*, 1995; *Dolores Claiborne*, 1995. Television miniseries—*'Salem's Lot*, 1979; *Stephen King's It*, 1990; *The Tommyknockers*, 1993; *The Stand*, 1994; *The Langoliers*, 1995.

Bibliography: *The Annotated Guide to Stephen King: A Primary and Secondary Bibliography of the Works of America's Premier Horror Writer* by Michael R. Collings, Starmont House, 1986.

Critical Studies: *Fear Itself: The Horror Fiction of Stephen King* by Tim Underwood and Chuck Miller, Underwood-Miller, 1982; *Stephen King: The Art of Darkness* by Douglas E. Winter, New American Library, 1984; *Discovering Stephen King* edited by Darrell Schweitzer, Starmont House, 1985; *Stephen King as Richard Bachman, The Many Facets of Stephen King, The Shorter Works of Stephen King*, all 1985, and *The Films of Stephen King*, 1986, by Michael R. Collings, Starmont House; *Stephen King: At the Movies* by Jessie Horsting, Signet/Starlog, 1986; *Kingdom of Fear: The World of Stephen King*, Underwood-Miller, 1986, and *Bare Bones: Conversations on Terror with Stephen King*, McGraw-Hill, 1988, edited by Tim Underwood and Chuck Miller; *The Stephen King Phenomenon* by Michael R. Collings and David Engebretson, Starmont House, 1987; *The Stephen King Companion* edited by George Beahm, Andrews and McMeel, 1989; *Scaring Us to Death: The Impact of Stephen King on Popular Culture* by Michael R. Collins, Borgo, 1995.

Theatrical Activities:
Director: **Film**—*Maximum Overdrive*, 1986. Actor: **Films**—*Knightriders*, 1980; *Creepshow*, 1982; *Maximum Overdrive*, 1986, *Pet Sematary*, 1989, *Sleepwalkers*, 1992. **Television miniseries**—*The Stand*, 1994; *The Langoliers*, 1995.

* * *

Stephen King is a master of the horror genre, skillfully interweaving elements of the supernatural with popular culture and thereby refreshing the standard elements of horror fiction. Immensely scary and frequently violent, King's stories portray believable characters faced with the most appalling circumstances. As a result of his compelling storytelling abilities, King has become one of the bestselling authors of all time and has exerted a profound influence not only on the development of popular literature but also on American popular culture.

King began writing fiction very early in his life, and in 1965 his first published story appeared in *Comics Review* magazine. After graduating in 1970 from the University of Maine, where he majored in English and created a seminar on popular literature and culture, he continued to write short horror fiction; in 1974 Doubleday published his first novel, *Carrie*. The book was an immediate success, and since that time King has published a novel roughly every year, several under the pseudonym Richard Bachman. King's popularity has continued to increase with every new release: of *Publishers Weekly*'s 25 bestselling books of the 1980s, seven were written by King. His reputation has also been enhanced by a number of extremely popular films and television miniseries based on his works, beginning with the highly regarded film adaptation of *Carrie*, directed by Brian DePalma.

King's popularity is based primarily on his ability to create interesting or quirky characters, to construct a compelling plot, and on his keen awareness of what terrifies his readers. King has often discussed the experiences in his own life that have led to this awareness, including being abandoned by his father as a young child and living through the cold-war nuclear paranoia of the 1950s. In the essay "The Horror Writer and the Ten Bears" (1973), King ranked his own worst fears as fear for someone else, fear of others, death, insects, closed-in places, rats, snakes, deformity, "squishy" things, and the dark. Introducing elements designed to provoke such primal fears into well-drawn contemporary milieus, King creates a portrait of everyday life that is at once familiar and terrifying.

His concern for realism has enabled King to transcend the boundaries of traditional horror fiction. His stories take place in contemporary settings filled with details drawn from King's own experiences and frequently contain specific references to cultural and political events of the twentieth century. Having spent much of his life in a small town in Maine, King has with particular skill created the fictional town of Castle Rock, the setting for seven of his stories, and the introduction of violence and the supernatural into this ostensibly idyllic world is an effective device for horror. This realistic technique also allows King to poke fun at what he considers the more absurd aspects of contemporary society, and many readers cite King's sense of humor as one of the more appealing aspects of his work.

—Susan Kraft

KINGSOLVER, Barbara

Nationality: American. **Born:** 8 April 1955, in Annapolis, Maryland. **Education:** DePauw University, B.A. (magna cum laude), 1977; University of Arizona, M.S., 1981, and additional graduate study. **Family:** Married Joseph Hoffmann, 1985; daughter: Camille. **Career:** University of Arizona, Tucson, research assistant in department of physiology, 1977-79, technical writer in office of arid lands studies, 1981-85; free-lance journalist, 1985-87; full-time writer, 1987 to present. **Awards:** Feature-writing award, Arizona Press Club, 1986; American Library Association awards, 1988, for *The Bean Trees*, and 1990, for *Homeland;* citation of accomplishment from United Nations National Council of Women, 1989; PEN fiction prize and Edward Abbey Ecofiction award, both 1991, for *Animal Dreams*. **Member:** International Women's Writing Guild, Amnesty International, Committee for Human Rights in Latin America, Phi Beta Kappa. **Agent:** Frances Goldin, 305 East Eleventh St., New York, New York 10003. **Address:** PO Box 5275, Tucson, Arizona 85703, U.S.A.

Publications

Novels

The Bean Trees. Harper, 1988.
Animal Dreams. Harper, 1990.
Pigs in Heaven. HarperCollins, 1994.

Short Stories

Homeland and Other Stories. Harper, 1989.

Poetry

Another America. Seal Press, 1994.

Nonfiction

Holding the Line: Women in the Great Arizona Mine Strike of 1983. ILR Press, 1989.
High Tide in Tucson: Essays from Now or Never. HarperCollins, 1995.

* * *

Lively, engaging, and sane, Barbara Kingsolver's work centers around the theme of reconciliation. In each of her works, even her nonfiction *Holding the Line: Women in the Great Arizona Mine Strike of 1983* (1989), an opposition is found, explored, and finally acknowledged and resolved. In *The Bean Trees* (1988), for example, a child, Turtle, is adopted and she and her new mother must find a way to unite and communicate. Likewise, in *Animal Dreams* (1990), a woman returns home to confront her past and her village's complexities, and to find a way past her isolation. The theme continues in Kingsolver's more recent work. The collection of poetry, *Another America* (1994), for example, contains translations into Spanish, thereby reconciling the "America" that means the United States for those of us within its borders with the real America that includes both North and South America.

Kingsolver's characters grapple with real concerns of living in fin-de-siècle America. Her poems describe some of the most harrowing experiences known to humanity, as they speak of rape, abuse, and war. They also find joy in the little things, such as a hen's egg. *Pigs in Heaven* returns to the difficult question of identity concerning so many peoples in the world today, as Turtle is claimed by both her adoptive mother and her Native American family. Kingsolver teaches her readers the language of tolerance and negotiation through characters with human failings and human nobility.

However, some readers have taken Kingsolver to task for presenting difficult issues when they turned to her direct and graceful work for an escape from real-life concerns. In her collection of essays, *High Tide in Tucson* (1995), Kingsolver opens a window into a writer's mind as she mulls over these and other reactions she has received from readers, trying to use them to more finely hone her reflections on our world, rather than to silence herself. However, it is Ursula K. LeGuin who puts it best, writing about *Another America*: "Out of this century's dark last years rises a kind of dawn chorus of voices speaking with urgent beauty, clarity, and generosity. Barbara Kingsolver['s] . . . pure American voice, chorded in both the great American languages, is rich with political and human resonance."

That quality in Kingsolver becomes apparent with rereading. In short, her books are fun and real, and give hope to life. We read her for the homey quality of her writing. The characters are like someone we know, or would like to know, living on the interstates and small towns we grew up in or drive through. Kingsolver's short stories offer windows into such towns and people, and her essays finally locate her in that imaginary world, as well. She tells us about the pond she created in her backyard, school-day insecurities, and her daughter Camille, who has, she says, "an imaginary mom" when Kingsolver must go on book tours. The only danger with reading Kingsolver is that you have to wait with excruciating patience for her next book.

—Victoria Carchidi

KINSELLA, W(illiam) P(atrick)

Nationality: Canadian. **Born:** Edmonton, Alberta, 25 May 1935. **Education:** Eastwood High School, Edmonton, graduated 1953; University of Victoria, British Columbia, B.A. in creative writing 1974; University of Iowa, Iowa City, 1976-78, M.F.A. 1978. **Family:** Married 1) Myrna Salls in 1957, two children; 2) Mildred Clay in 1965 (divorced 1978); 3) Ann Knight in 1978. **Career:** Clerk, Government of Alberta, 1954-56, and manager, Retail Credit Co., 1956-61, both Edmonton; account executive, City of Edmonton, 1961-67; owner, Caesar's Italian Village restaurant, 1967-72, editor, *Martlet,* 1973-74, and cab driver, 1974-76, all Victoria, British Columbia; assistant professor of English, University of Calgary, Alberta, 1978-83. Since 1983 full-time writer. **Awards:** *Edmonton Journal* prize, 1966; *Canadian Fiction* award, 1976; Alberta Achievement award, 1982; Houghton Mifflin Literary fellowship, 1982; *Books in Canada* prize, 1982; Canadian Authors Association prize, 1983; Leacock medal, for humor, 1987. **Address:** 14881 Marine Drive, no. 201, White Rock, British Columbia V4B 1C2, Canada.

Publications

Novels

Shoeless Joe. Boston, Houghton Mifflin, 1982; London, Allison and Busby, 1988.
The Iowa Baseball Confederacy. Boston, Houghton Mifflin, 1986.
Box Socials. Toronto, HarperCollins, 1991; New York, Ballantine, 1992.

Short Stories

Dance Me Outside. Ottawa, Oberon Press, 1977; Boston, Godine, 1986.
Scars. Ottawa, Oberon Press, 1978.
Shoeless Joe Jackson Comes to Iowa. Ottawa, Oberon Press, 1980; Dallas, Southern Methodist University Press, 1993.

Born Indian. Ottawa, Oberon Press, 1981.
The Ballad of the Public Trustee. Vancouver, Standard, 1982.
The Moccasin Telegraph and Other Indian Tales. Toronto, Penguin, 1983; Boston, Godine, 1984; London, Arrow, 1985.
The Thrill of the Grass. Toronto and London, Penguin, 1984; New York, Viking, 1985.
The Alligator Report. Minneapolis, Coffee House Press, 1985.
The Fencepost Chronicles. Toronto, Collins, 1986; Boston, Houghton Mifflin, 1987.
Red Wolf, Red Wolf. Toronto, Collins, 1987; Dallas, Southern Methodist University Press, 1990.
Five Stories. Vancouver, Hoffer, 1987.
The Further Adventures of Slugger McBatt. Toronto, Collins, and Boston, Houghton Mifflin, 1988.
The Miss Hobbema Pageant. Toronto, Harper Collins, 1989.
The Dixon Cornbelt League and Other Baseball Stories. Toronto, HarperCollins, 1993.
Go the Distance: Baseball Stories. Dallas, Southern Methodist University Press, 1995.

Poetry

Rainbow Warehouse, with Ann Knight. Lawrencetown Beach, Nova Scotia, Potterfield Press, 1989.

Other

Two Spirits Soaring: The Art of Allen Sapp, The Inspiration of Allan Ganor. Toronto, Stoddart, 1990.
The First and Last Annual Six Towns Area Old Timers' Baseball Game, with wood engravings by Gaylord Schanilec. Minneapolis, Coffee House Press, 1991.

*

Bibliography: *W.P. Kinsella: A Partially-Annotated Bibliographic Checklist (1953-1983)* by Ann Knight, Iowa City, Across, 1983.

Manuscript Collection: National Library of Canada, Ottawa.

Critical Studies: "Down and Out in Montreal, Windsor, and Wetaskiwin" by Anthony Brennan in *Fiddlehead* (Fredericton, New Brunswick), Fall 1977; "Don't Freeze Off Your Leg" Spring 1979, and "Say It Ain't So, Joe" Spring-Summer 1981, both by Frances W. Kaye in *Prairie Schooner* (Lincoln, Nebraska); article by Brian E. Burtch in *Canadian Journal of Sociology* (Edmonton), Winter 1980; essay by Anne Blott in *Fiddlehead* (Fredericton, New Brunswick), July 1982; Marjorie Retzleff in *NeWest Review* (Edmonton), October 1984; "Search for the Unflawed Diamond" by Don Murray in *NeWest Review* (Edmonton), January 1985; *The Fiction of W.P. Kinsella: Tall Tales in Various Voices* by Don Murray, Fredericton, New Brunswick, York Press, 1987.

* * *

W. P. Kinsella is probably best known for his stories that use baseball as a backdrop; the movie *Field of Dreams,* which starred Kevin Costner, was based upon his novel *Shoeless Joe* (1982). However, Kinsella's first story collections centered on the Native North Americans of the Ermineskin Reservation in Alberta, Canada.

Dance Me Outside (1977) consists of 17 tales narrated by Silas Ermineskin, a 19-year-old Cree whose naiveté about life belies a keen intelligence and vulnerability. Lying just beneath the surface comedy of these stories is an edgy tension resulting from a clash between native ways and a desire to experience the world. *Born Indian* (1981) continued Silas' narration. A third collection was praised for the credible speech patterns and realistic detail, but criticized for stereotyped emotion and shallow moralizing. His fourth collection of stories guided by Silas Ermineskin appeared in 1983 as *The Moccasin Telegraph and Other Stories.* The stories ring with local color and naturalness, giving the reader an unsentimental look at daily life on the reservation. Although the stories become repetitious, they are full of the drama and humor of the folk tale.

Kinsella also has story collections which cohere on the idea of baseball. Baseball itself never becomes the subject of these stories but merely supplies the context. Kinsella respects baseball as baseball, not as a metaphor for other things. From the title story "Shoeless Joe Jackson Comes to Iowa" (1980) came the later novel *Shoeless Joe.* Kinsella is adept at blurring the line between fantasy and reality. These stories mainly deal with men struggling with life choices.

The Further Adventures of Slugger McBatt (1988) was lauded as a home-run by critics. Kinsella is exceptional at creating believable, realistic characters and depicting the bonds and tensions between people that force them apart. With a graceful style and quirky characterization, Kinsella invokes both naturalism and fantasy and strikes a lovely balance between the two. *Red Wolf, Red Wolf* (1987) gives the reader several striking and fascinating slices of everyday life. Kinsella has a particular talent for telling these stories of ordinary lives simply and without moral judgment. Even quirky characters are presented with such naturalness that readers find they must readjust their ideas of normalcy.

Shoeless Joe is an inviting mixture of baseball and fantasy. It celebrates innocence, but without achieving sentimentality like Kinsella's best short fiction. Praised as the most imaginative and original baseball novel since *The Natural,* the fanciful if lightweight material seduces the reader into its sweet fantasy. *The Iowa Baseball Confederacy* (1986) did not fare quite as well critically with its similar mix of baseball and fantasy concerning a 2000-inning baseball game that lasts 40 days and nights. *Box Socials* (1991) fared much better. Set in the 1930s in a rural farming community 60 miles from Edmonton, Kinsella draws on the conventions of the oral folktale to sketch this multi-ethnic farm society. The narrator, Jamie O'Day, eavesdrops on the adults. The real story here is his coming-of-age, which is handled sensitively and with great tenderness.

Kinsella's whimsical tales and surreal sketches are deceptively sweet. Upon a second look, however, the reader will be surprised to see just how much pain underlies many of the stories told in his charming, naturalistic style.

—Jennifer G. Coman

KNOX, Calvin M. *See* **SILVERBERG, Robert.**

KOONTZ, Dean R(ay)

Pseudonyms: Aaron Wolfe; David Axton; Brian Coffey; Deanna Dwyer; K.R. Dwyer; John Hill; Leigh Nichols; Anthony North; Richard Paige; Owen West. **Nationality:** American. **Born:** Everett, Pennsylvania, 9 July 1945. **Education:** Shippensburg State College, B.A. in English 1966. **Family:** Married Gerda Ann Cerra in 1966. **Career:** Worked in a federal government poverty-alleviation program in Appalachia, then high school English teacher. Since 1969, full-time writer. **Agent:** Harold Ober Associates, 425 Madison Avenue, New York, New York 10017. **Address:** P.O. Box 9529, Newport Beach, California 92658-9529, U.S.A.

PUBLICATIONS

Novels

Star Quest. New York, Ace, 1968.
The Fall of the Dream Machine. New York, Ace, 1969.
Fear That Man. New York, Ace, 1969.
The Dark Symphony. New York, Lancer, 1970.
Hell's Gate. New York, Lancer, 1970.
Dark of the Woods. New York, Ace, 1970.
Beastchild. New York, Lancer, 1970.
Anti-Man. New York, Paperback Library, 1970.
The Crimson Witch. New York, Curtis, 1971.
The Flesh in the Furnace. New York, Bantam, 1972.
A Darkness in My Soul. New York, DAW, 1972; London, Dobson, 1979.
Time Thieves. New York, Ace, 1972; London, Dobson, 1977.
Warlock. New York, Lancer, 1972.
Starblood. New York, Lancer, 1972.
Demon Seed. New York, Bantam, 1973; London, Corgi, 1977.
Hanging On. New York, Evans, 1973; London, Barrie and Jenkins, 1974.
The Haunted Earth. New York, Lancer, 1973.
A Werewolf Among Us. New York, Ballantine, 1973.
After the Last Race. New York, Atheneum, 1974.
Strike Deep (as Anthony North). New York, Dial Press, 1974.
Invasion (as Aaron Wolfe). Don Mills, Ontario, Laser Books, 1975; as *Winter Moon* (as Dean Koontz), London, Headline, and New York, Ballantine, 1994.
The Long Sleep (as John Hill). New York, Popular Library, 1975.
Nightmare Journey. New York, Berkley, 1975.
Night Chills. New York, Atheneum, 1976; London, W.H. Allen, 1977.
Prison of Ice (as David Axton). Philadelphia, Lippincott, and London, W.H. Allen, 1976; revised under name Dean Koontz as *Icebound,* New York, Ballantine, and London, Headline, 1995.
The Face of Fear (as Brian Coffey). Indianapolis, Bobbs Merrill, 1977; as K.R. Dwyer, London, Davies, 1978; as Dean Koontz, London, Headline, 1989.
The Funhouse: Carnival of Terror (novelization of screenplay; as Owen West). New York, Jove, 1980; London, Sphere, 1981.
The Vision. New York, Putnam, 1977; London, Corgi, 1980.
The Voice of the Night (as Brian Coffey). New York, Doubleday, 1980; London, Hale, 1981; as Dean Koontz, London, Headline, 1991.
Whispers. New York, Putnam, 1980; London, W.H. Allen, 1981.
Heartbeeps (as John Hill). New York, Jove, 1981.
The Mask (as Owen West). New York, Jove, 1981; London, Coronet, 1983; as Dean Koontz, London, Headline, 1989.
Phantoms. New York, Putnam, and London, W.H. Allen, 1983.
Darkness Comes. London, W.H. Allen, 1984; as *Darkfall,* New York, Berkley, 1984.
The Door to December (as Richard Paige). New York, Signet, 1985; as Leigh Nichols, London, Fontana, 1987; as Dean Koontz, London, Headline, 1991.
Twilight Eyes. Plymouth, Michigan, Land of Enchantment, 1985.
Strangers. New York, Putnam, and London, W.H. Allen, 1986.
Watchers. New York, Putnam, and London, Headline, 1987.
Lightning. New York, Putnam, and London, Headline, 1988.
Oddkins: A Fable for All Ages. New York, Warner, and London, Headline, 1988.
Midnight. New York, Putnam, and London, Headline, 1989.
The Bad Place. New York, Putnam, and London, Headline, 1990.
Cold Fire. New York, Putnam, and London, Headline, 1991.
Hideaway. New York, Putnam, and London, Headline, 1992.
Dean R. Koontz: A New Collection (omnibus). New York, Wings, 1992.
Dragon Tears. New York, Putnam, and London, Headline, 1992.
Dean Koontz Omnibus. London, Headline, 1993.
Mr. Murder. London, Headline, and New York, Putnam, 1993.
Dark Rivers of the Heart. Lynbrook, New York, Charnal House, and London, Headline, 1994.
Tick-Tock. New York, Random House, 1995.
Intensity. New York, Random House, 1996.

Novels as Brian Coffey

Blood Risk. Indianapolis, Bobbs Merrill, 1973; London, Barker, 1974.
Surrounded. Indianapolis, Bobbs Merrill, 1974; London, Barker, 1975.
The Wall of Masks. Indianapolis, Bobbs Merrill, 1975.

Novels as Deanna Dwyer

The Demon Child. New York, Lancer, 1971.
Legacy of Terror. New York, Lancer, 1971.
Children of the Storm. New York, Lancer, 1972.
The Dark of Summer. New York, Lancer, 1972.
Dance with the Devil. New York, Lancer, 1973.

Novels as K.R. Dwyer

Chase. New York, Random House, 1972; London, Barker, 1974.
Shattered. New York, Random House, 1973; London, Barker, 1974.
Dragonfly. New York, Random House, 1975; London, Davies, 1977.

Novels as Leigh Nichols

The Key to Midnight. New York, Pocket Books, 1979; London, Magnum, 1980; as Dean Koontz, Arlington Heights, Illinois, Dark Harvest, 1989.
The Eyes of Darkness. New York, Pocket Books, 1981; London, Fontana, 1982; as Dean Koontz, Arlington Heights, Illinois, Dark Harvest, 1989.
The House of Thunder. New York, Pocket Books, 1982; London, Fontana, 1983; as Dean Koontz, Arlington Heights, Illinois, Dark Harvest, 1988.

Twilight. New York, Pocket Books, and London, Fontana, 1984; as *The Servants of Twilight* (as Dean Koontz), Arlington Heights, Illinois, Dark Harvest, 1988.
Shadowfires. New York, Avon, and London, Collins, 1987; as Dean Koontz, Arlington Heights, Illinois, Dark Harvest, 1990.

Short Stories

Soft Come the Dragons. New York, Ace, 1970.
Strange Highways. London, Headline, and New York, Warner, 1995.

Other

The Pig Society, with Gerda Koontz. Los Angeles, Aware Press, 1970.
The Underground Lifestyles Handbook, with Gerda Koontz. Los Angeles, Aware Press, 1970.
Writing Popular Fiction. Cincinnati, Writer's Digest, 1973.
How to Write Best-Selling Fiction. Cincinnati, Writer's Digest, and London, Poplar Press, 1981.

Editor, with Paul Mikol, *Night Visions 6: All Original Stories.* Arlington Heights, Illinois, Dark Harvest, 1988; as *The Bone Yard,* New York, Berkley, 1991.

*

Media Adaptations: *Demon Seed,* 1977.

Critical Studies: *Sudden Fear: The Horror and Dark Suspense Fiction of Dean R. Koontz,* edited by Bill Munster, Mercer Island, Washington, Starmont House, 1988, second edition as *Discovering Dean Koontz,* San Bernardino, Borgo Press, 1995; *The Dean Koontz Companion,* edited by Martin H. Greenberg, Ed Gorman, and Bill Munster, New York, Berkley, 1994.

* * *

Dean Ray Koontz is one of the lesser-known best-selling authors in America. By 1995, after 22 years of writing, he had published more than 60 books (19 of which were published under various pseudonyms). Ten of those novels had become number-one best sellers, leading to a three-book-deal worth $18.9 million.

Koontz started writing at the age of eight, and eventually set a goal of writing one book each year—an apparently easy task for a man who claims to have "reverse writers block." "It's almost as if story ideas are beamed to me. I can sit down for 15 minutes and come up with a dozen ideas," he has said.

Koontz's books are notorious for their dark, terror-filled story lines. He rarely writes about the supernatural; instead he ". . . focuses on possible aberrations and mutations in nature." But Koontz shuns the idea of being a horror writer, preferring instead to be identified with the word terror. His books are consistently filled with a combination of psychological terror, love, science fiction, and happy endings.

A prime example of his work is *Cold Fire* (1991), in which his lead character, Jim Ironheart, finds himself able to transport himself all over the world in order to save lives when he arrives at his destinations. After being followed by a relentless reporter named Holly Thorne, who is present at one of his rescues, they find themselves returning to Ironheart's home town to trace the roots of his powers. Like all of his books, *Cold Fire* is a fast-paced, engrossing tale that holds most readers from start to finish.

A more popular novel, *Demon Seed* (1973), was made into a science-fiction movie in 1977. It tells the tale of Susan, who is raped by a computer named Proteus that her estranged husband built. The computer self-destructs and her resulting pregnancy initiates a wild tale of the birth of a metal baby 28 days later. Susan and her husband reconcile before discovering beneath the metal a baby who is an identical recreation of their deceased daughter. It turns out to be a baby that Proteus reincarnated—classic Koontz.

In *Hideaway* (1992), Hatch and Lindsey Harrison are seriously injured in an automobile accident. After Hatch dies, he is incredibly brought back to life by a brilliant physician. Hoping to start anew after the accident and the death of their child four years earlier, the Harrisons adopt an intelligent, handicapped ten-year-old named Regina. Regina brings them the joy and happiness for which they yearned, until they encounter a frightening sequence of events that brings them in contact with a mysterious unknown. When people who have wronged them suffer violent deaths, and horrendous visions disrupt his thoughts, Hatch begins to think he has brought an evil entity back with him from the afterlife. In order to save their own lives and the life or their daughter, Hatch and Lindsey find and confront the evil entity in an abandoned amusement park.

Hideaway was a best seller in 1992 and was praised by the *San Diego Union* as "Koontz's best effort to date."

More recently, *Mr. Murder* (1993) is the story of Martin Stillwater, a successful mystery writer who is married and the father of two beautiful young daughters. When a maniacal psychotic breaks into his home one stormy night, the terror begins. The stranger claims to be the real Marty Stillwater who wants to eliminate Martin and reclaim the life and family he claims was his in the past. When the police refuse to take Martin's story seriously, the danger escalates. Martin and his family go on the run, only to encounter the impostor in each place they try to hide. It is a harrowing tale of their fight and flight for freedom from their stalker.

Koontz attributes the results of his writing efforts, at least in part, to his disturbing childhood. The only child of a loving mother and an abusive alcoholic father, he became terrified of his father's rage. He took to writing to dispel his fearful, violent thoughts. Though dark and terrifying, his work also includes romance, hope, and happy endings, much like his own adult life. His books are gripping, intriguing, and enjoyable.

—Amy Faulkenberry

KORDA, Michael (Vincent)

Nationality: British. **Born:** London, 8 October 1933. **Education:** Magdalene College, Cambridge, B.A., 1958. **Military Service:** Royal Air Force, 1952-54. **Family:** Son of film art director Vincent Korda and nephew of film producer and director Alexander Korda; married Carolyn Keese in 1958 (divorced), one son; married Margaret Mogford. **Career:** Columbia Broadcasting System, Inc. (CBS-TV), New York City, script reader, 1957; Simon & Schuster, Inc., New York City, 1958—, began as editorial assistant, currently editor-in-chief; author, 1973—. **Member:** National Society of Film Critics. **Address:** 440 East 56th St., New York, New York 10020, U.S.A.

Publications

Novels

Worldly Goods. Random House, 1982.
Queenie. Linden Press/Simon & Schuster, 1985.
The Fortune. Summit, 1988.
Curtain. Summit, 1991.
The Immortals. Simon & Schuster, 1992.

Other

Male Chauvinism! How It Works. Random House, 1973.
Power! How to Get It, How to Use It. Random House, 1975; as *Power in the Office,* Weidenfeld & Nicolson, 1976.
Success! How Every Man and Woman Can Achieve It. Random House, 1977.
Charmed Lives: A Family Romance. Random House, 1979.
Man to Man: Surviving Prostate Cancer. Random House, 1996.

* * *

The flamboyant editor-in-chief of New York publisher Simon & Schuster, Michael Korda is almost as well known for editing such writers as Graham Greene, Richard Nixon, Ronald Reagan, and Jacqueline Susann as he is for his own published work, which has included treatises on Yuppie lifestyle issues, a personal memoir of the rich and famous, potboiling Hollywood novels, and a candid account of his battle with cancer.

His first work was *Male Chauvinism! How It Works* (1973), a guide, primarily for men, to the ways society discriminates against women financially and professionally. Korda focused on such issues as how male chauvinism is inculcated in young males, its psychological origins (namely, fear of virility loss), the reasons it still exists (control and convenience), how it manifests itself at home and in the office, and what can be done to eliminate it. *Atlantic* found the book "earnest," "well-intentioned," and "pleasantly written"; *Library Journal* complained that Korda offered little that was truly new but praised its style; and *Newsweek* lauded Korda for offering concrete examples of chauvinistic office practices and advice for women wishing to force management to address the issue.

In *Power! How to Get It, How to Use It* (1975), which Korda later claimed was meant to be a satire on office politics, he advocated such career-enhancing stratagems as power dressing, advancing "by expansion" rather by traditional promotion, speaking softly to senior colleagues to make them think they're going deaf, and painting one's office in "power colors" like red and blue. Despite Korda's claim of humorous intent many reviewers deplored the book as a Machiavellian succeed-at-any-cost manual: the reviewer for the *New York Times,* for example, derided Korda for forever banishing "talent . . . work . . . [and] kindness" from the workplace and concluded: "God help the people who work with him." Among the reviewers who detected Korda's satirical thrust, the *Times Literary Supplement* called *Power!* "sharp, intelligent, and uncommonly funny."

In 1977, Korda published *Success!,* a recycling of sorts of the material in *Power!* but now from the perspective of middle managers rather than executives. If Korda had intended to resume the satire of the earlier work even fewer reviewers noticed it this time: *Choice* viewed the book as a mere "compendium of cliches," the *New York Times* criticized Korda for extolling the virtues of being successful when "not everyone can do it," and *Newsweek* complained that all three of Korda's exclamatory books were "hysterical and gimmicky."

Korda's next work was a personal biography of his uncle, British film producer Alex Korda (*The Third Man*), and Sir Alex's two brothers: film director Zoltan, and Michael's father, film art director, Vincent. *Charmed Lives* (1979) was distinguished by Korda's revealing personal memories of his father and uncles, as the narrative of Sir Alex's rags-to-riches rise from Hungarian poverty to wealth and fame becomes Korda's account of his search for his own roots and his hero worship of his worldly Uncle Alex ("I longed to be like him in every respect"). *Time* called *Charmed Lives* "warm, well structured, humorous . . . [and] shrewdly observed"; the *New York Times* lauded it as "a rare, intimate portrait"; and *Newsweek* praised it as a "first-rate entertainment."

In 1982, Korda published his first novel, *Worldly Goods,* the story of Holocaust survivor Paul Foster's ruthless pursuit of revenge against his uncle for abandoning his father in a Nazi death camp 35 years earlier. Despite mostly negative reviews, Korda returned in 1985 with *Queenie,* a fictionalized account of the life of actress Merle Oberon, the second wife of Korda's Uncle Alex. Made into a television miniseries, *Queenie* was in many ways a conventional Hollywood scandal novel, replete with a beautiful, ambitious, man-killing heroine; thinly disguised portraits of Hollywood personages; and lurid subplots featuring homosexuality, rape-incest, gangsters, and murder. A runaway success, it was followed by *The Fortune* (1988), the story of a young widow's battle with her husband's family to claim his fortune; *Curtain* (1991), in which the very public marriage of renowned Thespians Robert Vane and Felicia Lisle hides a grim past, a joyless present, and a violent future; and *The Immortals* (1992), a fictionalized account of the relationship between John F. Kennedy and Marilyn Monroe and the underworld schemes that lead to their deaths.

Korda's latest work, *Man to Man: Surviving Prostate Cancer* (1996), is a personal, sometimes affecting account of Korda's treatment for and subsequent recovery from prostate cancer, "the male equivalent," he asserts, "of breast cancer." Although Korda's descriptions of the trials and setbacks of cancer treatment were aimed at a general audience, Korda's case was unique: he was operated on by a physician who he admits is "the Michelangelo of prostate surgery" and immediately afterward he is chauffeured by medivac helicopter to recover at his New York farm. *Publishers Weekly* praised *Man to Man* as an "intensely candid, engaging, and sharply witty memoir."

—Paul S. Bodine

KRANTZ, Judith

Nationality: American. **Born:** 9 January 1927, in New York. **Education:** Wellesley College, B.A., 1948. **Family:** Married to Stephen Krantz; children: Nicholas, Anthony. **Career:** Novelist.

Fashion publicist in Paris, France, 1948-49; *Good Housekeeping,* New York City, fashion editor, 1949-56; contributing writer, *McCall's,* 1956-59, and *Ladies Home Journal,* 1959-71; contributing West Coast editor, *Cosmopolitan,* 1971-79. **Agent:** Morton Janklow, 598 Madison Ave., New York, New York 10022. **Address:** c/o Stephen Krantz Productions, 9601 Wilshire Blvd., Suite 343 Beverly Hills, California 90210, U.S.A.

Publications

Novels

Scruples. Crown, 1978.
Princess Daisy. Crown, 1980.
Mistral's Daughter. Crown, 1982.
I'll Take Manhattan. Crown, 1986.
Till We Meet Again. Crown, 1988.
Dazzle. Crown, 1990.
Scruples 2. Crown, 1992.

*

Media Adaptations: Television miniseries—*Scruples,* 1980; *Princess Daisy,* 1983. Television film—*Mistral's Daughter,* 1984.

* * *

The novels of Judith Krantz involve three major elements: glamour, sex, and money—not necessarily in that order. Krantz had her first "blockbuster" novel with the publication of *Scruples* in 1978. That novel and all of the books she's written since have been bestsellers.

Krantz has carved out a niche for herself in the world of bestselling fiction, and it is one she is uniquely qualified to fill. The ingredients of a Krantz novel are: a heroine who is young, gorgeous, ultimately (if not originally) wealthy, and talented; a handsome consort; high fashion, the best restaurants, and all the right locations; sex, both heterosexual and homosexual; fame; and sympathetic characters who generally revel in all of the good things in life.

In her first novel, *Scruples,* Krantz effectively delineated her territory. Billy Winthop, the young heroine, is, when the reader first encounters her, somewhat overweight and a wallflower. A stay in Paris takes care of all her flaws, and when she returns to the United States she meets and marries an aging multimillionaire, Ellis Ikehorn. When Ellis dies of a stroke, she spends a great deal of money consoling herself and ultimately opens an exclusive boutique called Scruples. By the end of the book she has seemingly found happiness with an Italian filmmaker named Vito Orsini. She becomes pregnant and is waiting for the presentation of Vito's Oscar for the picture on which they've worked together.

Scruples largely set the pattern for Krantz's other books, which vary in their locales, the presentation of their protagonists, and the ways in which those protagonists ultimately arrive at happiness. Readers know what to expect from her books, and they are seldom disappointed. The heroine of *Princess Daisy* (1980) is indeed a Russian princess. The women of *Mistral's Daughter* (1982) are all involved with a French painter who bears more than a passing resemblance to Picasso. The protagonist of *Till We Meet Again* (1988) flies a plane in World War II. The heroine of *Dazzle* (1990) is a renowned photographer. The heroine of *I'll Take Manhattan* (1986) starts her own magazine. All of her women are brilliant, talented, hard working, and ultimately rewarded with riches, love, and happiness. In *Scruples Two* (1992), for example, Krantz returns to Billy Ikehorn Orsini, whose marriage to Vito Orsini quickly falls apart. Nevertheless, Billy somehow manages to make do with her millions and her fabulous face.

Judith Krantz novels feature multifaceted plots and a large cast of characters. She doesn't skimp on the details of the lives of her characters, including more than would seem necessary for any purpose except to put the reader in touch with the fact that she knows the world—or worlds—about which she writes. Her audience enjoys the details, and the verisimilitude they offer is clearly a major appeal of her stories.

Indeed, Krantz's familiarity with the world about which she writes is a major selling point of her fiction. If she dramatizes that world or glamorizes it for professional purposes, she considers it creative license. Krantz worked in the fashion industry for some years in her early career—as a fashion publicist in Paris and as a fashion editor and contributing writer for women's magazines—and she is married to an independent film producer and author. Rodeo Drive would seem to be her natural habitat, and those who read her works look for the closeup view of the glamorous ambience she seems to know intimately.

—June Harris

L

LADNER, Kurt. *See* **DeMILLE, Nelson.**

L'AMOUR, Louis (Dearborn)

Pseudonyms: Jim Mayo; Tex Burns. **Nationality:** American. **Born:** 28 March 1908, in Jamestown, North Dakota. **Education:** Self-educated. **Military Service:** U.S. Army, 1942-46; became first lieutenant. **Family:** Married Katherine Elizabeth Adams in 1956; children: Beau Dearborn, Angelique Gabrielle. **Career:** Author and lecturer. Held numerous jobs, including positions as longshoreman, lumberjack, miner, elephant handler, hay shocker, boxer, flume builder, and fruit picker. Lecturer at many universities including University of Oklahoma, Baylor University, University of Southern California, and University of Redlands. **Awards:** Western Writers of America award, 1969, for *Down the Long Hills;* Theodore Roosevelt Rough Rider award, North Dakota, 1972; American Book award, 1980, for *Bendigo Shafter,* Buffalo Bill award, 1981; Distinguished Newsboy award, 1981; National Genealogical Society award, 1981; Congressional Gold Medal, 1983; Presidential Medal of Freedom, 1984. LL.D.: Jamestown College, 1972; Pepperdine University, 1984. **Died:** 10 June 1988, of lung cancer, in Los Angeles.

Publications

Novels

Westward the Tide, World's Work. Surrey, England, 1950; Bantam, 1984.
Hondo. Gold Medal, 1953.
Crossfire Trail. Ace Books, 1954.
Heller with a Gun. Gold Medal, 1954; Bantam, 1985.
Kilkenny. Ace Books, 1954.
Showdown at Yellow Butte (as Jim Mayo). Ace Books, 1954; reprinted with introduction by Scott R. McMillan, Gregg, 1980; Bantam, 1983.
Utah Blaine (as Jim Mayo). Ace Books, 1954; reprinted with introduction by Wayne C. Lee, Gregg, 1980; Bantam, 1984.
Guns of the Timberlands. Jason, 1955; Bantam, 1985.
To Tame a Land. Fawcett, 1955; Bantam, 1985.
The Burning Hills. Jason, 1956; Bantam, 1985.
Silver Canyon. Avalon, 1956; Bantam, 1981.
Last Stand at Papago Wells. Gold Medal, 1957; Bantam, 1986.
Sitka. Appleton, 1957; Bantam, 1986.
The Tall Stranger. Fawcett, 1957; Bantam, 1986.
Radigan. Bantam, 1958.
The First Fast Draw. Bantam, 1959.
Taggart. Bantam, 1959.
Flint. Bantam, 1960.
High Lonesome. Bantam, 1962.
Killoe. Bantam, 1962.
Shalako. Bantam, 1962.
Catlow. Bantam, 1963.
Dark Canyon. Bantam, 1963.
Fallon. Bantam, 1963.
How the West Was Won. Bantam, 1963; Thorndike, 1988.
Hanging Woman Creek. Bantam, 1964.
The High Graders. Bantam, 1965.
The Key-Lock Man. Bantam, 1965.
Kiowa Trail. Bantam, 1965.
The Broken Gun. Bantam, 1966.
Kid Rodelo. Bantam, 1966.
Kilrone. Bantam, 1966.
Matagorda. Bantam, 1967.
Chancy. Bantam, 1968.
Down the Long Hills. Bantam, 1968.
Conagher. Bantam, 1969.
The Empty Land. Bantam, 1969.
The Man Called Noon. Bantam, 1970.
Reilly's Luck. Bantam, 1970, reprinted, 1985.
Brionne. Bantam, 1971.
Tucker. Bantam, 1971.
Under the Sweetwater Rim. Bantam, 1971.
Callaghen. Bantam, 1972.
The Man from Skibbereen. G. K. Hall, 1973.
The Quick and the Dead. Bantam, 1973; revised edition, 1979.
The Californios. Saturday Review Press, 1974.
The Rider of Lost Creek. Bantam, 1976.
Where the Long Grass Blows. Bantam, 1976.
Bendigo Shafter. Dutton, 1978.
The Mountain Valley War. Bantam, 1978.
The Iron Marshall. Bantam, 1979.
The Proving Trail. Bantam, 1979.
Lonely on the Mountain. Bantam, 1980.
Comstock Lode. Bantam, 1981.
The Cherokee Trail. Bantam, 1982.
The Shadow Riders. Bantam, 1982.
The Lonesome Gods. Bantam, 1983.
Son of a Wanted Man. Bantam, 1984.
The Walking Drum. Bantam, 1984.
Passin' Through. Bantam, 1985.
Last of the Breed. Bantam, 1986.
A Trail to the West. Bantam, 1986.
West of the Pilot Range. Bantam, 1986.
The Haunted Mesa. Bantam, 1987.
Sackett Family Series
- *The Daybreakers.* Bantam, 1960.
- *Sackett.* Bantam, 1961.
- *Lando.* Bantam, 1962.
- *Mojave Crossing.* Bantam, 1964.
- *The Sackett Brand.* Bantam, 1965.
- *Mustang Man.* Bantam, 1966.
- *The Sky-Liners.* Bantam, 1967; Thorndike, 1986.
- *The Lonely Men.* Bantam, 1969.
- *Galloway.* Bantam, 1970.
- *Ride the Dark Trail.* Bantam, 1972.
- *Treasure Mountain.* Bantam, 1972.

Sackett's Land. Saturday Review Press, 1974.
To the Far Blue Mountains. Dutton, 1976.
Sackett's Gold. Bantam, 1977.
The Warrior's Path. Bantam, 1980.
Ride the River. Bantam, 1983.
Jubal Sackett. Bantam, 1985.

The Chantrys Series
North to the Rails. Bantam, 1971.
The Ferguson Rifle. Bantam, 1973.
Over on the Dry Side. Saturday Review Press, 1975.
Borden Chantry. Bantam 1977.
Fair Blows the Wind. Bantam, 1978.

The Talons Series
The Man from the Broken Hills. Bantam, 1975.
Rivers West. Saturday Review Press, 1974, reprinted, Dutton, 1989.
Milo Talon. Bantam, 1981.

Novels as Tex Burns

Hopalong Cassidy and the Riders of High Rock. Doubleday, 1951; Aeonian, 1974.
Hopalong Cassidy and the Rustlers of West Fork. Doubleday, 1951; Aeonian, 1976.
Hopalong Cassidy and the Trail to Seven Pines. Doubleday, 1951; Aeonian, 1976.
Hopalong Cassidy: Trouble Shooter. Doubleday, 1952; Aeonian, 1976.

Short Stories

War Party. Bantam, 1975.
The Strong Shall Live. Bantam, 1980.
Yondering. Bantam, 1980.
Buckskin Run. Bantam, 1981.
Law of the Desert Born. Bantam, 1983.
Bowdrie. Bantam, 1983.
Bowdrie's Law. Bantam, 1984.
The Hills of Homicide. Bantam, 1984.
Dutchman's Flat. Bantam, 1986.
Night over the Solomons. Bantam, 1986.
The Rider of the Ruby Hills. Bantam, 1986.
Riding for the Brand. Bantam, 1986.
The Trail to Crazy Man. Bantam, 1986.
West from Singapore. Bantam, 1987.
Lonigan. Bantam, 1988.
Long Ride Home. Bantam, 1989.
The Outlaws of Mesquite. Bantam, 1991.

Plays

Screenplays: *East of Sumatra,* with Frank J. Gill, Jr., and Jack Natteford, 1953; *Four Guns to the Border,* with George Van Marter and Franklin Coen, 1954; *Treasure of the Ruby Hills,* with Tom Hubbard and Fred Eggers, 1955; *Stranger on Horseback,* with Herb Meadow and Don Martin, 1955; *Kid Rodelo,* with Jack Natteford, 1966.

Poetry

Smoke from this Altar. Lusk, 1939.

Nonfiction

Frontier, with photographs by David Muench, Bantam, 1984.
The Sackett Companion: A Personal Guide to the Sackett Novels. Bantam, 1988.
The Education of a Wandering Man. Bantam, 1989.

*

Media Adaptations: Films—*Hondo,* 1953; *East of Sumatra,* 1953; *Four Guns to the Border,* 1954; *Treasure of the Ruby Hills,* 1955; *Kilkenny,* 1956; *The Burning Hills,* 1956; *Utah Blaine,* 1956; *Walk Tall,* 1957; *Last Stand at Papago Wells,* Columbia, 1958; *Heller with Pink Tights,* adapted from his *Heller with a Gun,* 1960; *Guns of the Timberlands,* 1960; *Taggart,* 1964; *Kid Rodelo,* 1966; *Shalako,* 1968; *Catlow,* 1971; *The Broken Gun,* 1972; *The Man Called Noon,* 1973; *Down the Long Hills,* 1986; *The Quick and the Dead,* 1987. Television miniseries—*The Sacketts.*

Critical Studies: *Critical Essays on the Western American Novel,* edited by William T. Pilkington, G. K. Hall, 1980.

* * *

Louis Dearborn L'Amour is the best-selling western writer ever, with over 108 books regularly in print worldwide, sales measured in hundred millions, and fans from Glasgow to Paris to Moscow. A L'Amour western guarantees old-fashioned values like honesty, hospitality, stoicism, and responsibility for the weak, as well as respect for women, competence, book-learning, self-knowledge, a good horse, a worthy opponent, and beautiful country. His books also provide accurate details about Western topography, ecology, lifestyle, and cultural interactions, including the period's reading-matter, common knowledge, and practical skills. His books offer fast-paced, gripping plots based on understandable human motivations and credible western situations, and they feature well-delineated main characters that are laconic, capable, rugged survivors torn between wanderlust and an urge to settle. L'Amour sustains a no-nonsense recognition of harsh realities, human cruelty, greed, weakness, intolerance, ambition, and spite.

L'Amour prided himself on knowing his subject, partly from the rough, "knockabout," jobs of his youth, partly from stories told by his father (a North Dakota veterinarian and deputy sheriff) and grandfather (an Indian fighter and Civil War buff), and partly from talking to aged pioneers who helped win the west. He was proud of riding and hunting the land he describes, knowing landmarks personally. His descriptions reflect his employment as sailor, soldier, gold prospector, lumberjack, elephant handler, and professional boxer, among others. Drawing on such knowledge, L'Amour entertains and educates readers about the past, for he firmly believes that strength rests in knowledge. To combat modern misconceptions and stereotypes he repeatedly demonstrates the rarity of gunfights, the importance of careful aim over the quick-draw, the speed at which news traveled in frontier times, the diversity of Westerners, the mingling of races, the transforming power of necessity, the ill-treatment of Southern soldiers after the Civil War, the contributions of Mexican-Americans, and the possibility of encountering world travelers, nobility, and the well-read in remote outposts.

A conservationist who believes we hold the land in trust for our descendants, L'Amour demonstrates the Indians' economical harmony with the environment and the conflict between conservationist ranchers and those who overgrazed with dire consequences. His treatment of Indians is balanced; respectful of their bravery, fighting skills, commitment to family and tribe, sense of humor, and understanding of nature, but open about their savage, ruthless violence, and their quirkiness, and inevitable decline.

L'Amour began writing short stories. He published his first novel, *Westward the Tide* (1950), in England. With the success of *Hondo* (1953) as both novel and film, he began to turn out three novels a year, most of them set in the post-Civil War West. However, *The Daybreakers* (1960), about Tennessee brothers who begin anew in the New Mexico Territory of 1866, marked the beginning of an ambitious saga about the Talon, Chantry, and Sackett families; L'Amour completed 25 of the 40 planned stories before his death in 1988. The saga begins in Elizabethan England and follows the shipping and pioneering adventures of the Sacketts to the Carolina coast, and then ever westward with each new generation of trailblazers and Indian fighters, through the Civil War and the Gold Rush to California and points north over a period of 300 years.

The Sacketts tame the land, the Talons settle and build, and the Chantrys envision future possibilities for a firmly established civilization. The pattern is flight from a morally deficient, class-ridden Europe, to an open society based on ability over accidents of birth. This new society begins with lone males wandering free, but is built by the establishment or renewal of family relationships that tie a man to the land and lead him to build a nation. The women in this pattern must be strong, courageous equals who share the hardships and bring civilizing values to uncivilized surroundings. The most notable Sackett is the large, hulking William Tell Sackett, shy and socially awkward but a graceful, efficient fighter with a deep-rooted sense of justice and family obligations. His tough, resilient mother exemplifies the pioneer woman at her best, and all of the Sacketts "set store by kinfolk."

In his later years, L'Amour began to write longer novels, more experimental than his traditional canon. The *Californianos* (1971), *The Lonesome Gods* (1983), and *The Haunted Mesa* (1987) involve mystical time warps, with Indians from a dead past mysteriously reaching out and affecting lives from other time periods, while The *Walking Drum* (1984) traces a 12th-century adventurer across Asia. *Last of the Breed* (1986) postulates a U.S. Air Force pilot in an experimental spy plane shot down over the Soviet Union. The pilot draws on Sioux-Cheyenne ancestral skills, taught to him by his grandfather, to escape the KGB and survive the Siberian winter wastelands. Whatever their time or setting, L'Amour stories place a strong, engaging survivor in a trying situation that demonstrates his inner fiber and his commitment to deep-rooted values.

—Gina Macdonald

LANGE, John. *See* **CRICHTON, (John) Michael.**

LEAST HEAT MOON, William. *See* **TROGDON, Wiiliam.**

LEAVITT, David

Nationality: American. **Born:** 23 June 1961, in Pittsburgh, Pennsylvania. **Education:** Yale University, B.A., 1983. **Career:** Writer. Viking-Penguin, Inc., New York City, reader and editorial assistant, 1983-84. **Awards:** Willets Prize for fiction, Yale University, 1982, for "Territory"; O. Henry award, 1984, for "Counting Months." **Agent:** Andrew Wylie, Wylie, Aitken and Stone, 250 W. 57th St., Suite 2106, New York, New York 10107, U.S.A.

Publications

Novels

The Lost Language of Cranes. Knopf, 1986.
Equal Affections. Weidenfeld and Nicolson, 1989.
While England Sleeps. Viking, 1993.

Short Stories

Family Dancing. Knopf, 1984.
A Place I've Never Been. Viking, 1990.
Editor with Mark Mitchell, *The Penguin Book of Gay Short Fiction.* Viking, 1994.

* * *

David Leavitt strode onto the literary scene in 1984 at the age of 23 with a collection of short stories entitled *Family Dancing.* With a cool, detached style Leavitt addresses the complexities of family. With a maturity and compassion seemingly beyond his years, Leavitt manipulates the everyday details of daily living into images which endure, and he gives the reader a sense of what causes pain. The collection was praised for its eloquence and intense power, albeit within a somewhat narrow range. His second story collection, *A Place I've Never Been* (1990), explores Leavitt's interest in the gay experience. He is concerned here with love in its infinite variety and human sexuality as a continuum of possibilities. He keeps his prose spare without becoming polemical. As Wendy Marlin put it, "Mr. Leavitt's fiction deftly places the many varieties of love and sexual attraction in perspective, seeing them as part of the vast, complex mosaic of human experience and emotion."

His first novel, *The Lost Language of Cranes* (1986), is at heart a gay coming-out tale. The protagonist Philip Benjamin comes out only to discover that his father is gay also. Leavitt goes on uncompromisingly to reveal aspects of gay life in New York City with an almost documentary feel. This is how the novel fails. The sexual orientation of the characters seems of greater importance than the characters themselves. Ironically, the most sympathetic character in the novel is the mother, Rose, a heterosexual resisting the homosexuality of her men—a definite misstep for the acclaimed short-story writer who seems to have lost the maturity and subtlety of his short fiction.

His second novel, *Equal Affections* (1989), saw Leavitt back on track. The novel concerns a modern family in crisis. Louise Cooper is afflicted with lymphatic cancer. Her illness overshadows all of the family relationships, especially her marriage to Nat. The husband and her two homosexual children, April and David, must come to terms with Louise's death. With his characteristic understated prose, Leavitt sketches a sensitive portrait of an older woman embittered by the course of her life. The novel's main weakness lies in the character of April, who is far too up on every feminist stance to come off as a real human being instead of a cipher.

Leavitt's most recent novel, *While England Sleeps* (1993), moves back in history to the time of the Spanish Civil War. Brian Botsford, a Cambridge graduate, falls in love with working class Edward Phelan. The plot seems to owe a great deal to the 1930s gay literary circle of Auden, Stephen Spender, and Christopher Isherwood, who were very much involved in protesting the Spanish Civil War. The novel seems to be an indictment not only of class exploitation but also of sexual exploitation. What has been written seems to sound a true note, but somehow the reader is never allowed a deep involvement with the characters. The melodrama is gracefully crafted but curiously stilted at the same time. Leavitt's attempt to expand his range falls short.

Leavitt seems to be at his best when detailing in his clean, beautiful prose the contemporary family in crisis. Michiko Kakutani says, "Mr. Leavitt's stories depict an America in which the centrifugal forces of history have been loosed upon the family, flinging children and parents apart and yet drawing them back to the idea of home through the persistence of their memories."

—Jennifer G. Coman

le CARRÉ, John

Pseudonym of David John Moore Cornwell. **Nationality:** British. **Born:** Poole, Dorset, 19 October 1931. **Education:** Sherborne School, Dorset; St. Andrew's Preparatory School; Bern University, Switzerland, 1948-49; Lincoln College, Oxford, B.A. (honours) in modern languages 1956. **Family:** Married 1) Alison Ann Veronica Sharp in 1954 (divorced 1971), three sons; 2) Valerie Jane Eustace in 1972, one son. **Career:** Tutor, Eton College, Berkshire, 1956-58; member of the British Foreign Service, 1959-64: second secretary, Bonn Embassy, 1961-64; consul, Hamburg, 1963-64. **Awards:** British Crime Novel award, 1963; Maugham award, 1964; Mystery Writers of America Edgar Allan Poe award, 1965, and Grand Master award, 1984; Crime Writers Association Gold Dagger, 1978, 1980, and Diamond Dagger, 1988; James Tait Black Memorial prize, 1978; Nikos Kazantzakis prize, 1991. Honorary doctorate: University of Exeter 1990. Honorary fellow, Lincoln College, 1984. **Agent:** David Higham Associates, 5-8 Lower John Street, London W1R 4HA, England.

Publications

Novels

Call for the Dead. London, Gollancz, 1961; New York, Walker, 1962; as *The Deadly Affair,* London, Penguin, 1966.
A Murder of Quality. London, Gollancz, 1962; New York, Walker, 1963.
The Spy Who Came In from the Cold. London, Gollancz, 1963; New York, Coward McCann, 1964.
The Looking-Glass War. London, Heinemann, and New York, Coward McCann, 1965.
A Small Town in Germany. London, Heinemann, and New York, Coward McCann, 1968.
The Naive and Sentimental Lover. London, Hodder and Stoughton, 1971; New York, Knopf, 1972.
The Quest for Karla. London, Hodder and Stoughton, and New York, Knopf, 1982.
Tinker, Tailor, Soldier, Spy. London, Hodder and Stoughton, and New York, Knopf, 1974.
The Honourable Schoolboy. London, Hodder and Stoughton, and New York, Knopf, 1977.
Smiley's People. London, Hodder and Stoughton, and New York, Knopf, 1980.
The Little Drummer Girl. London, Hodder and Stoughton, and New York, Knopf, 1983.
A Perfect Spy. London, Hodder and Stoughton, and New York, Knopf, 1986.
The Russia House. London, Hodder and Stoughton, and New York, Knopf, 1989.
The Secret Pilgrim. London, Hodder and Stoughton, and New York, Knopf, 1991.
The Night Manager. London, Hodder and Stoughton, and New York, Knopf, 1993.
Our Game. London, Hodder and Stoughton, and New York, Knopf, 1995.

Uncollected Short Stories

"Dare I Weep, Dare I Mourn," in *Saturday Evening Post* (Philadelphia), 28 January 1967.
"What Ritual Is Being Observed Tonight?," in *Saturday Evening Post* (Philadelphia), 2 November 1968.

Play

Television Play: *Smiley's People,* with John Hopkins, from the novel by le Carré, 1982.

Other

The Clandestine Muse. Portland, Oregon, Seluzicki, 1986.
Vanishing England, with Gareth H. Davies. Topsfield, Massachusetts, Salem House, 1987.

*

Critical Studies: *John le Carré* by Peter Lewis, New York, Ungar, 1985, London, Lorrimer, 1986; *The Novels of John le Carré: The Art of Survival,* Oxford, Blackwell, 1985, and *Smiley's Circus: A Guide to the Secret World of John le Carré,* London,

Orbis, 1986, both by David Monaghan; *John le Carré* by Eric Homberger, London, Methuen, 1986; *Taking Sides: The Fiction of John le Carré* by Tony Barley, Milton Keynes, Buckinghamshire, Open University Press, 1986; *Corridors of Deceit: The World of John le Carré* by Peter Wolfe, Bowling Green, Ohio, Popular Press, 1987; *The Quest for John le Carré* edited by Alan Bold, London, Vision Press, and New York, St. Martin's Press, 1988.

* * *

John le Carré is best known as a Cold War spy novelist, like his older contemporary Eric Ambler. Le Carré describes in intricate and convincing detail the intelligence service conflicts between the West (represented by Britain and the United States) and the East (represented by the former Soviet Union). More recently, he has tried valiantly and with considerable success to take on other aspects of international conflict, most notably in *The Little Drummer Girl* (an intense and characteristically intricate novel about the Israeli intelligence service, published in 1983) and in such other recent novels including *The Russia House* (1989), *A Perfect Spy* (1986), and *The Night Manager* (one of his most successful novels, published in 1993).

Far and away, le Carré's most interesting character is George Smiley, a most unlikely British intelligence agent who made his first appearance in a le Carré novel as a minor character in *The Spy Who Came in from the Cold* (1963). Smiley is the central character in a sequence of novels beginning with *Tinker, Tailor, Soldier, Spy* (1974) and *The Honourable Schoolboy* (1977), and culminating in what is perhaps his finest work, *Smiley's People* (1980).

Smiley is "unlikely" in the sense that he does not at all fit the stereotype of the spy or international intelligence agent. He has been repeatedly cuckolded by his wealthy, upper class wife Ann and, of course, has a dreadful marriage, lacks the macho flair of most such fictional characters (like James Bond), and is slow, deliberate, and intuitive in his approach to intelligence problems—sometimes really enormous ones—and his adversaries at "Moscow Centre" in the Soviet KGB, especially a man somewhat ambiguously identified as "Karla." Karla appears literally only in the last few pages of *Smiley's People* when he walks across the international bridge then separating Eastern from Western Germany. But, like Kurtz in Conrad's *Heart of Darkness,* Karla moves obsessively through Smiley's imagination and dreams long before his presence manifests itself in the novel.

Smiley's People begins at a very low point in its protagonist's career. This former top agent and then director or "Control" of the Circus (le Carré's name for the center of British intelligence) has been replaced by a bunch of bureaucratic and inconsequential idiots and sent off to investigate the murder of a General Vladimir, a former Soviet general and a defector. His new superiors trust that this will be a busywork assignment, but Smiley senses that there is a great deal more behind this murder than is apparent to the people at Circus and that it is really Karla—the man responsible for Smiley's humiliation in *Tinker, Tailor, Soldier, Spy*—who for some mysterious reason is the one behind the murder of the General. After a long, torturous hunt, Smiley not only avenges himself on Karla (when the latter is forced to defect to the West) but on the new breed at Circus who will be forced to acknowledge the importance of the defection. Though Smiley does not resume his former position, he thoroughly redeems himself.

What makes this novel so phenomenal and a cut above most of le Carré's work is the way in which Smiley is presented, the effectiveness of his old-fashioned methods, and the team of old Circus hands that he assembles for the climactic events which conclude *Smiley's People.* Because Smiley is a complicated man and not a stereotype of the usual detective or secret agent, and because his antagonist Karla (like King Claudius in *Hamlet* or Inspector Porfiry in Dostoievski's *Crime and Punishment*) is his equal in most respects, the image of reality that emerges from this novel corresponds in psychological depth to the reality that any contemporary, literate, moderately perceptive individual experiences over a large time span. In this sense, "reality" is a blend of conscious and unconscious elements, of dream and real event, of text and subtext, darkness and light, perhaps even heaven, earth, and hell—all of which Smiley, that heroic swimmer in the dark and hero (both in the modern and traditional sense) with "a thousand faces," mirrors. The fact that the world he moves through is the familiar one of Cold War politics and "the international Communist conspiracy" should not obscure the other fact; that he does so in surprisingly personal and even traditional ways and that the powers he makes such excellent use of—the intelligence informed and energized by intuition, and the concentration which eludes so many of us—make him a splendid, thoroughly contemporary example of an ancient, fascinating, and enduring tradition.

—C. W. Truesdale

LEE, Laurie

Nationality: British. **Born:** Stroud, Gloucestershire, 26 June 1914. **Education:** Slad Village School, Gloucestershire, and Stroud Central School. **Military Service:** During World War II made documentary films for the General Post Office film unit, 1939-40, and the Crown Film Unit, 1941-43, and traveled as a scriptwriter to Cyprus and India; publications editor, Ministry of Information, 1944-46; member of the Green Park Film Unit, 1946-47. **Family:** Married Catherine Francesca Polge in 1950; one daughter. **Career:** Caption writer-in-chief, Festival of Britain, 1950-51. **Awards:** Atlantic award, 1944; Society of Authors traveling award, 1951; Foyle award, 1956; Smith literary award, 1960. Fellow, Royal Society of Literature. Freeman, City of London, 1982. M.B.E. (Member, Order of the British Empire), 1952. **Address:** 9/40 Elm Park Gardens, London SW10 9NZ, England.

PUBLICATIONS

Poetry

The Sun My Monument. London, Hogarth Press, 1944; New York, Doubleday, 1947.

The Bloom of Candles: Verse from a Poet's Year. London, Lehmann, 1947.

My Many-Coated Man. London, Deutsch, 1955; New York, Coward McCann, 1957.

(Poems). London, Vista, 1960.

Pergamon Poets 10, with Charles Causley, edited by Evan Owen. Oxford, Pergamon Press, 1970.

Selected Poems. London, Deutsch, 1983.

Recording: *Laurie Lee Reading His Own Poems,* with Christopher Logue, Jupiter, 1960.

Plays

The Voyage of Magellan: A Dramatic Chronicle for Radio (broadcast, 1946), London, Lehmann, 1948.
Peasants' Priest (produced Canterbury, 1947). Canterbury, Goulden. 1947.

Screenplays: *Cyprus Is an Island,* 1946; *A Tale in a Teacup,* 1947.

Radio Play: *The Voyage of Magellan,* 1946.

Other

Land at War. London, His Majesty's Stationery Office, 1945.
We Made a Film in Cyprus, with Ralph Keene. London, Longman, 1947.
An Obstinate Exile. Privately printed, 1951.
A Rose for Winter: Travels in Andalusia. London, Hogarth Press, 1955; New York, Morrow, 1956.
Cider with Rosie (autobiography). London, Hogarth Press, 1959; as *The Edge of Day: A Boyhood in the West of England,* New York, Morrow, 1960.
Man Must Move: The Story of Transport (for children), with David Lambert. London, Rathbone, 1960; as The *Wonderful World of Transportation,* New York, Doubleday, 1960; revised edition, 1969; as *The Wonderful World of Transport,* London, Macdonald, 1969.
The Firstborn (essay on childhood). London, Hogarth Press, and New York, Morrow, 1964.
As I Walked Out One Midsummer Morning (autobiography). London, Deutsch, and New York, Atheneum, 1969.
I Can't Stay Long. London, Deutsch, 1975; New York, Atheneum, 1976.
Innocence in the Mirror, photographs by Angelo Cozzi. New York, Morrow, 1978.
Two Women, photographs by the author. London, Deutsch, 1983.
A Moment of War (autobiography). London, Viking, 1991.

Editor, with Christopher Hassall and Rex Warner, *New Poems 1954.* London, Joseph, 1954.

Translator, *The Dead Village,* by Avigdor Dagan. London, Young Czechoslovakia, 1943.

*

Critical Studies: *Brodie's Notes on Laurie Lee's Cider with Rosie* by Kenneth Hardacre, London, Pan, 1986; *Cider with Rosie, Laurie Lee* by Jon Andrews and Timothy Clark, Harlow, Longman, 1991.

* * *

Laurie Lee has been so closely identified in millions of minds as the painter of Gloucestershire rural life in *Cider with Rosie* that many of his other literary achievements have been forgotten, including the other parts of the autobiographical trilogy of which *Cider* was only one part.

Lee began his writing career principally with poetry, publishing several volumes which have won several awards. Lee has noted that his poems "were written by someone I once was and who is so distant to me now that I scarcely recognize him anymore. They speak for a time and feeling which of course has gone from me, but for which I still have a close affection and kinship." Many of his early poems were written during WWII, and such poems as "Invasion Summer" and "A Moment of War" contain all the foreboding of that conflict that one might expect. However, in addition to love and travel poems, his poetry evokes all that Lee's name arouses—the smell of apples and grass, the echo of birdsong, and the celebration of the English countryside.

The rich language of "Apples" reads like a prelude to the blown ripeness of Keats' "Ode to Autumn": "Behold the apples' rounded worlds / juice-green of July rain / the black polestar of flower, the rind / mapped with its crimson stain." Indeed, in many respects, his poetry is about an England and a landscape that has gradually disappeared, evoking a certain nostalgia about the countryside that he depicts.

A Rose for Winter (1955) signalled the beginning of Lee's prose ambitions. The first published volume of his autobiographical trilogy, it is the third in the chronological sequence. It tells of Lee's trip to Spain 15 years after his first visit, finding a country ravaged by war, yet still harboring many of the characteristics—flamenco dancing, gypsy pride, bullfight glory—that made Lee fall in love with places like Andalusia. Lee has written that "autobiography can be the laying to rest of ghosts as well as an ordering of the mind. But for me it is also a celebration of living and an attempt to hoard its sensations." This celebration is most evident in *Cider with Rosie* (1959)—the second in the autobiographical sequence, narrating Lee's life during the second decade of the 20th century, comprising an account of his childhood in his Gloucestershire village Slad, situated on the edge of the Cotswolds. It is a memoir of boyhood and sexual awakening told in a series of sketches which were initially published as magazine articles. The book presents a variety of figures, most centrally his mother but also other relatives, village inhabitants, and schoolfellows. As with his poetry, Lee's prose has a wealth of striking imagery and incorporates skilful use of simile and metaphor.

The third installment of Lee's autobiographical sequence was *As I Walked out One Midsummer Morning* (1969), which acts as a sequel to *Cider with Rosie.* It narrates Lee's first trip to Spain in 1936, during which he walked across the country from Vigo to Granada and met a variety of people, including poet Roy Campbell. It chronicles a period of increasing political tension with the advent of civil war, as the illusions and hopes of a better world explode with the conflict.

In addition to the trilogy, Lee has published a collection of essays written over several decades entitled *I Can't Stay Long* (1975). The book has three sections, embracing reflections on love and the senses, travel, and "some early recollections of my country childhood and my departure from it," which makes it of considerable interest to readers of *Cider with Rosie.* Criticism was polarized over this volume, some regarding it as shallow and superficial while others praised Lee's use of imagery. Lee's florid language has caused several critics some irritation, but as one wrote: "When Lee drops his purple mantle he can write with a vivid, spare imagery that makes one realize how closely allied are the eyes of the poet and the painter."

In 1983 Lee published *Two Women,* an extraordinarily intimate and deeply personal portrait in words and photographs of his romantic meeting and courtship of his wife Cathy, and the birth and growth of their daughter Jessy. A more recent publication was *A Moment of War* (1991), which tells about a young man's walk over the Pyrenees into Spain to join the International Brigades in 1937, narrating the bitter defeat of the Republican army in an elegiac and ironic account of youthful idealism at the end of the 1930s.

—Tim Woods

LEE, William. *See* **BURROUGHS, William S.**

Le GUIN, Ursula K(roeber)

Nationality: American. **Born:** Berkeley, California, 21 October 1929; daughter of the anthropologist Alfred L. Kroeber. **Education:** Radcliffe College, Cambridge, Massachusetts, A.B. in French 1951 (Phi Beta Kappa); Columbia University, New York (Faculty fellow; Fulbright fellow, 1953), M.A. in romance languages 1952. **Family:** Married Charles A. Le Guin in 1953; two daughters and one son. **Career:** Instructor in French, Mercer University, Macon, Georgia, 1954, and University of Idaho, Moscow, 1956; department secretary, Emory University, Atlanta, 1955; taught writing workshops at Pacific University, Forest Grove, Oregon, 1971, University of Washington, Seattle, 1971-73, Portland State University, Oregon, 1974, 1977, 1979, 1995, in Melbourne, Australia, 1975, at the University of Reading, England, 1976, Indiana Writers Conference, Bloomington, 1978 and 1983, and University of California, San Diego, 1979. **Awards:** Boston *Globe-Horn Book* award, 1968; Nebula award, 1969, 1975 (twice), 1990; Hugo award, 1970, 1973, 1974, 1975; National Book award, 1972; Newbery Silver Medal award, 1972; *Locus* award (twice), 1973, 1984; Jupiter award, 1975 (twice), 1976; Gandalf award, 1979; Lewis Carroll Shelf award, 1979; University of Oregon Distinguished Service award, 1981; Janet Kafka award, 1986; Prix Lectures-Jeunesse (France), 1987; Pushcart prize, 1991; Harold Vursell award, 1991; Oregon Institute of Literary Arts H.L. Davis award, 1992; *Hubbub* Annual Poetry award, 1995; *Asimov's* Reader's award, 1995. Guest of Honor, World Science Fiction Convention, 1975. D.Litt.: Bucknell University, Lewisburg, Pennsylvania, 1978; Lawrence University, Appleton, Wisconsin, 1979; D.H.L.: Lewis and Clark College, Portland, 1983; Occidental College, Los Angeles, 1985. Lives in Portland, Oregon. **Agent:** Virginia Kidd, 538 East Harford Street, Milford, Pennsylvania 18337, U.S.A.

Publications

Novels

Rocannon's World. New York, Ace, 1966; London, Tandem, 1972.
Planet of Exile. New York, Ace, 1966; London, Tandem, 1972.
City of Illusions. New York, Ace, 1967; London, Gollancz, 1971.
The Left Hand of Darkness. New York, Ace, and London, Macdonald, 1969.
The Lathe of Heaven. New York, Scribner, 1971; London, Gollancz, 1972.
The Dispossessed: An Ambiguous Utopia. New York, Harper, and London, Gollancz, 1974.
The Word for World Is Forest. New York, Putnam, 1976; London, Gollancz, 1977.
Earthsea. London, Gollancz, 1977; as *The Earthsea Trilogy,* London, Penguin, 1979.
A Wizard of Earthsea. Berkeley, California, Parnassus Press, 1968; London, Gollancz, 1971.
The Tombs of Atuan. New York, Atheneum, 1971; London, Gollancz, 1972.
The Farthest Shore. New York, Atheneum, 1972; London, Gollancz, 1973.
Malafrena. New York, Putnam, 1979; London, Gollancz, 1980.
The Eye of the Heron. New York, Harper, and London, Gollancz, 1983.
Always Coming Home. New York, Harper, 1985; London, Gollancz, 1986.
Tehanu: The Last Book of Earthsea. New York, Atheneum, and London, Gollancz, 1990.
Buffalo Gals, Won't You Come Out Tonight, illustrated by Susan Seddon Boulet, San Francisco, Pomegranate Artbooks, 1994.

Short Stories

The Wind's Twelve Quarters. New York, Harper, 1975; London, Gollancz, 1976.
The Water Is Wide. Portland, Oregon, Pendragon Press, 1976.
Orsinian Tales. New York, Harper, 1976; London, Gollancz, 1977.
The Compass Rose. New York, Harper, 1982; London, Gollancz, 1983.
The Visionary: The Life Story of Flicker of the Serpentine, with *Wonders Hidden,* by Scott Russell Sanders. Santa Barbara, California, Capra Press, 1984.
Buffalo Gals and Other Animal Presences (includes verse). Santa Barbara, California, Capra Press, 1987; as *Buffalo Gals,* London, Gollancz, 1990.
Searoad. New York, HarperCollins, 1991; London, Gollancz, 1992.
A Fisherman of the Inland Sea: Science Fiction Stories, New York, HarperPerennial, 1994.
Unlocking the Air and Other Stories. New York, Harpercollins, 1996.

Fiction for children

Very Far Away from Anywhere Else. New York, Atheneun, 1976; as *A Very Long Way from Anywhere Else,* London, Gollancz, 1976.
Leese Webster. New York, Atheneum, 1979; London, Gollancz, 1981.
The Beginning Place. New York, Harper, 1980; as *Threshold,* London, Gollancz, 1980.
The Adventure of Cobbler's Rune. New York, Virginia, Cheap Street, 1982.
Solomon Leviathan's Nine Hundred and Thirty-First Trip Around the World. New Castle, Virginia, Cheap Street, 1983.
A Visit from Dr. Katz. New York, Atheneum, 1988; as *Dr. Katz,* London, Collins, 1988.

Catwings. New York, Orchard, 1988.
Catwings Return. New York, Orchard, 1989.
Fire and Stone. New York, Atheneum, 1989.
A Ride on the Red Mare's Back. New York, Orchard, 1992.
Fish Soup. New York, Atheneum, 1992.
Wonderful Alexander and the Catwings. New York, Orchard, 1994.

Plays

No Use to Talk to Me, in *The Altered Eye,* edited by Lee Harding. Melbourne, Norstrilia Press, 1976; New York, Berkley, 1980.
King Dog (screenplay), with *Dorstoevsky,* by Raymond Carver and Tess Gallagher. Santa Barbara, California, Capra Press, 1985.

Poetry

Wild Angels. Santa Barbara, California, Capra Press, 1975.
Tillai and Tylissos, with Theodora K. Quinn. N.p., Red Bull Press, 1979.
Torrey Pines Reserve. Northridge, California, Lord John Press, 1980.
Gwilan's Harp. Northridge, California, Lord John Press, 1981.
Hard Words and Other Poems. New York, Harper, 1981.
In the Red Zone. Northridge, California, Lord John Press, 1983.
Wild Oats and Fireweed. New York, Harper, 1988.
Blue Moon over Thurman Street. Portland, Oregon, NewSage Press, 1993.
Going Out with Peacocks and Other Poems. New York, HarperPerennial, 1994.

Other

From Elfland to Poughkeepsie (lecture). Portland, Oregon, Pendragon Press, 1973.
Dreams Must Explain Themselves. New York, Algol Press, 1975.
The Language of the Night: Essays on Fantasy and Science Fiction, edited by Susan Wood. New York, Putnam, 1979; revised edition, London, Women's Press, 1989.
Dancing at the Edge of the World: Thoughts on Words, Women, Places. New York, Grove Press, and London, Gollancz, 1989.
The Way the Water's Going: Images of the Northern California Coastal Range, photographs by Ernest Waugh and Alan Nicolson. New York, Harper, 1989.

Editor, *Nebula Award Stories 11.* London, Gollancz, 1976; New York, Harper, 1977.
Editor, with Virginia Kidd, *Interfaces.* New York, Ace, 1980.
Editor, with Virginia Kidd, *Edges.* New York, Pocket Books, 1980.
Editor, with Brian Attebery, *The Norton Book of Science Fiction: North American Science Fiction, 1960-1990.* New York, Norton, 1993.

Recordings: *The Ones Who Walk Away from Omelas,* Alternate World, 1976; *Gwilan's Harp and Intracom.* Caedmon, 1977; *The Earthsea Trilogy,* Colophone, 1981; *Music and Poetry of the Kesh,* Valley Productions, 1985; *Rigel Nine: An Audio Opera,* Charisma, 1985; *The Left Hand of Darkness,* Warner, 1985; *The Word for World Is Forest,* Book of the Road, 1986.

*

Bibliography: *Ursula K. Le Guin: A Primary and Secondary Bibliography* by Elizabeth Cummins Cogell, Boston, Hall, 1983.

Manuscript Collection: University of Oregon Library, Eugene.

Critical Studies: *The Farthest Shores of Ursula K. Le Guin* by George Edgar Slusser, San Bernardino, California, Borgo Press, 1976; "Ursula Le Guin Issue" of *Science-Fiction Studies* (Terre Haute, Indiana), March 1976; *Ursula Le Guin* by Joseph D. Olander and Martin H. Greenberg, New York, Taplinger, and Edinburgh, Harris, 1979; *Ursula K. Le Guin: Voyage to Inner Lands and to Outer Space* edited by Joseph W. De Bolt, Port Washington, New York, Kennikat Press, 1979; *Ursula K. Le Guin* by Barbara J. Bucknall, New York, Ungar, 1981; *Ursula K. Le Guin* by Charlotte Spivack, Boston, Twayne, 1984; *Approaches to the Fiction of Ursula K. Le Guin* by James Bittner, Ann Arbor, Michigan, UMI Research Press, and Epping, Essex, Bowker, 1984; *Understanding Ursula K. Le Guin* by Elizabeth Cummins Cogell, Columbia, University of South Carolina Press, 1990.

* * *

America's Grande Dame of science fiction, Ursula Le Guin had no easy start to her writing career. Publishers said her early work was neither one genre nor another, so despite its obvious merit, it couldn't be published. But once launched, Le Guin has made a career of breaking down barriers that limit what we read, think, and imagine.

Le Guin has won numerous prizes, including the Boston Globe and Newbery awards for the Earthsea trilogy (1979); Hugo and Nebula awards for "The Ones Who Walk Away From Omelos" (1976) and *The Left Hand of Darkness* (1985); and many more. Favorably compared to C.S. Lewis's Narnia chronicles and J.R.R. Tolkien's Lord of the Rings, Le Guin's efforts share with those works the ability to create new worlds that help us reexamine our own. She proffers serious literature that entertains while educating, blurring the distinction between "merely" fantastic and "real" literature to the infinite benefit of readers and writers alike.

Le Guin's best-known works are included in her Hainish cycle, which focuses on planets loosely knit by having been "seeded" in their early history by the Hainish; and her Earthsea cycle, a trilogy expanded with a fourth volume.

Prompted to write for children, Le Guin began writing about Earthsea with the coming-to-maturity of Ged in *A Wizard of Earthsea* (1971). The second book, *The Tombs of Atuan* (1971), centers on a girl's (Tenar's) development. Some critics see this novel as diverging from the cycle's focus, but the wizard Ged saves Tenar from her service to the nameless forces as she saves him from the labyrinth in which he is locked. The final volume of the trilogy shows Ged using up his magical force in the effort to save the world from unmaking. Many years after the cycle, Le Guin wrote the last book of Earthsea, *Tehanu: The Last Book of Earthsea* (1990). This has had a mixed reception, ranging from high praise to the view that it "sourly" deconstructs the Earthsea world. In it, Le Guin explores why the earlier volumes focus on male action—why, for example, the school for wizards is for boys only. She provides the yin for that vision's yang, and explores the power of the middle-aged Tenar and her young adopted daughter, Tehanu, to reshape their world. Marketed "for children," most critics agree that these works will engage any reader's attention.

Le Guin prefers the metaphor of exploration to that of creation for her Hainish worlds; she did not create, but discovered the planets with their various lifeforms. Starting in 1972 with her most technologically oriented novel, *Rocannon's World* (for which Le Guin bemoans having created an impossible "impermasuit"), Le Guin continues with *Planet of Exile* (1972), *The Dispossessed: An Ambiguous Utopia* (1974), and the controversial *The Left Hand of Darkness*, which is populated by androgynous people.

Le Guin guides readers around cultures that reveal our own qualities. Her warnings become most explicit in *The Word for World is Forest*, born out of Le Guin's despair over U.S. involvement in Vietnam. That more recent work encorages similar love and fascination for Earth's own cultures as she locates her subjects on our own Earth's past-yet-to-happen.

Controversy centering on *Tehanu* and *The Left Hand of Darkness* highlights one of Le Guin's strengths: her ability to grow and show her readers her developing awareness. Le Guin's early writing reflected her own "happily unraised" consciousness. In their article on "feminism for men," Craig and Diana Barrow attribute Le Guin's youthful contentment with sexual roles to "the extent to which the significant men in her life have treated her well." *The Left Hand of Darkness*, then, has been criticized for presenting a male-centered view of androgyny. It uses generic male pronouns for characters that purport to be androgynous. Le Guin first defended that decision, but later saw she had silenced female voices and points of view. The later novel *Tehanu* reaffirms that awareness, as it powerfully critiques the invisibility of women and the consequent dangers for whole social structures.

In an interview, Le Guin was asked which prize she preferred, the Hugo or Nebula. She flippantly replied, the Nobel prize. When her interviewer pointed out that they aren't given for fantasy, she said, "Then I'll have to do something for peace." She already has. Le Guin once described her subject as marriage, and that theme unites much of her work. Sometimes it is explicit. *Planet of Exile* (1972), for example, presents literal marriage between two races of peoples. More often, Le Guin demonstrates that the virtues of a good union—tolerance, love, passion, and pragmatism—are even more important for those people not romantically connected, for those, indeed, who fear others' differences, be they sexual, cultural, or other.

Through her writing, Le Guin allows us the space to see ourselves as we are—and to enhance our lives through compassion, restraint, and, above all, imagination.

—Victoria Carchidi

L'ENGLE, Madeleine

Nationality: American. **Born:** Madeleine L'Engle Camp in New York City, 29 November 1918. **Education:** Smith College, Northampton, Massachusetts, A.B. (honors) 1941; New School for Social Research, New York, 1941-42; Columbia University, New York, 1960-61. **Family:** Married Hugh Franklin in 1946 (died 1986); two daughters and one son. **Career:** Worked in the theater, New York, 1941-47; member of the faculty, University of Indiana, Bloomington, summers 1965-66, 1971; writer-in-residence, Ohio State University, Columbus, 1970, and University of Rochester, New York, 1972. Since 1960, teacher, St. Hilda's and St. Hugh's School, New York; since 1966, librarian, Cathedral of St. John the Divine, New York; since 1970, president, Crosswicks Ltd., New York; since 1976, lecturer, Wheaton College, Illinois; since 1976, member, Board of Directors, Authors League Foundation; president, Authors Guild of America. **Awards:** American Library Association Newbery Medal, 1963; University of Southern Mississippi award, 1978; Smith College Medal, 1980, and Sophie award, 1984; American Book award, for paperback, 1980; *Logos* award, for adult nonfiction, 1981; Catholic Library Association Regina Medal, 1984; National Council of Teachers of English ALAN award, 1986. **Agent:** Robert Lescher, 67 Irving Place, New York, New York 10009, U.S.A. **Address:** Crosswicks, Goshen, Connecticut 06756, U.S.A.

Publications

Novels

The Small Rain. New York, Vanguard Press, 1945; London, Secker and Warburg, 1955.
Ilsa. New York, Vanguard Press, 1946.
And Both Were Young. New York, Lothrop, 1949.
Camilla Dickinson. New York, Simon and Schuster, 1951; London, Secker and Warburg, 1952; as *Camilla*, New York, Crowell, 1965.
A Winter's Love. Philadelphia, Lippincott, 1957.
Meet the Austins. New York, Vanguard Press, 1960; London, Collins, 1966.
The Moon by Night. New York, Farrar Straus, 1963; London, Lion, 1988.
The Love Letters. New York, Farrar Straus, 1966.
The Journey with Jonah. New York, Farrar Straus, 1968.
Prelude. New York, Vanguard Press, 1969; London, Gollancz, 1972.
The Other Side of the Sun. New York, Farrar Straus, 1971; London, Eyre Methuen, 1972.
Dragons in the Waters (Canon Tellis). New York, Farrar Straus, 1976; London, Hodder and Stoughton, 1991.
A Ring of Endless Light. New York, Farrar Straus, 1980; London, Lion, 1988.
A Severed Wasp. New York, Farrar Straus, 1982; London, Faber, 1984.
A House Like a Lotus (Canon Tellis). New York, Farrar Straus, 1984.
Certain Women. New York, Farrar Straus, 1992.
Penguins and Golden Calves. New York, Farrar Straus, 1996.

Novels for Children (series: Canon Tellis; Meg Murry)

The Arm of the Starfish (Canon Tellis). New York, Farrar Straus, 1965; London, Hodder and Stoughton, 1990.
The Young Unicorns (Canon Tellis). New York, Farrar Straus, 1968; London, Gollancz, 1970.
The Time Trilogy (Murry). New York, Farrar Strauss, 1979.
- *A Wrinkle in Time.* New York, Farrar Straus, 1962; London, Constable, 1963.
- *A Wind in the Door.* New York, Farrar Straus, 1973; London, Methuen, 1975.
- *A Swiftly Tilting Planet.* New York, Farrar Straus, 1978; London, Souvenir Press, 1980.

Many Waters (Murry). New York, Farrar Straus, 1986.

An Acceptable Time (Murry). New York, Farrar Straus, 1989.
Troubling a Star. New York, Farrar Straus, 1995.

Short Stories

The Sphinx at Dawn: Two Stories. New York, Seabury Press, 1982.

Plays

18 Washington Square, South (produced Northampton, Massachusetts, 1940). Boston, Baker, 1944.
How Now Brown Cow, with Robert Hartung (produced New York, 1949).
The Journey with Jonah (produced New York, 1970). New York, Farrar Straus, 1967.

Poetry

Lines Scribbled on an Envelope and Other Poems. New York, Farrar Straus, 1969.
Weather of the Heart. Wheaton, Illinois, Shaw, 1978.
A Cry Like a Bell. Wheaton, Illinois, Shaw, 1987.

Other

The Twenty-Four Days before Christmas: An Austin Family Story (for children). New York, Farrar Straus, 1964.
Dance in the Desert (for children). New York, Farrar Straus, and London, Longman, 1969.
A Circle of Quiet (essays). New York, Farrar Straus, 1972.
Everyday Prayers (for children). New York, Morehouse Barlow, 1974.
Prayers for Sunday (for children). New York, Morehouse Barlow, 1974.
The Summer of the Great-Grandmother (essays). New York, Farrar Straus, 1974.
The Irrational Season (essays). New York, Seabury Press, 1977.
Ladder of Angels: Scenes from the Bible Illustrated by Children of the World. New York, Seabury Press, 1979.
The Anti-Muffins (for children). New York, Pilgrim Press, 1980.
Walking on Water (essays). Wheaton, Illinois, Shaw, 1980; Tring, Hertfordshire, Lion, 1982.
And It Was Good: Reflections on Beginnings. Wheaton, Illinois, Shaw, 1983.
Dare to Be Creative. Washington, D.C., Library of Congress, 1984.
Trailing Clouds of Glory: Spiritual Values in Children's Literature, with Avery Brooke. Philadelphia, Westminster Press, 1985.
A Stone for a Pillow. Wheaton, Illinois, Shaw, 1987.
Two-Part Invention: The Story of a Marriage (memoir). New York, Farrar Straus, 1988.
Sold into Egypt: Joseph's Journey into Human Being. Wheaton, Illinois, Shaw, 1989.
The Glorious Impossible (for children). New York, Simon and Schuster, 1990.
Baccalaureate Address. Barre, Vermont, Linfield College Press, 1991.
The Rock That Is Higher: Story as Truth. Wheaton, Illinois, Shaw, 1993.
Anytime Prayers. Wheaton, Illinois, Shaw, 1994.

Editor, with William R. Green, *Spirit and Light: Essays in Historical Theology*. New York, Seabury Press, 1976.

*

Manuscript Collections: Wheaton College, Illinois; Kerlan Collection, University of Minnesota, Minneapolis; de Grummond Collection, University of Southern Mississippi, Hattiesburg.

* * *

Madeleine L'Engle's long literary career has resulted in at least 48 books (she has claimed not to be sure of the exact number) covering an incredible range of subjects and disciplines. She has written fiction for children, young adults, and adults, both fantasy and literary. She has written plays, books on prayer and scripture, poetry, and autobiography.

L'Engle is best known for her trilogy of young-adult books: *A Wrinkle in Time* (1962), *A Wind in the Door* (1973) , and *A Swiftly Tilting Planet* (1978). The books combine science fiction and fantasy with the themes of love and morality. *A Wrinkle in Time* is about young Meg Murray and her brother Charles Wallace who must travel through time and space and use their extrasensory perception to rescue their father from an evil force that threatens the galaxy. Despite the fantastic elements of the story, L'Engle creates characters who undergo the very realistic emotional struggles of adolescence. The other two books in the trilogy further develop the characters and the theme of love's ability to ward off evil and heal the damage evil does.

While the books have been criticized as didactic, many have found them to be rich and complex. L'Engle effectively blends fantasy and science fiction with real science and her own sense of spirituality, especially in *A Wind in the Door*, in which she creates a truly imaginative universe where the protagonist Meg Murray can converse with the mitochondria and farandolae inside of her brother's ailing body. As a young-adult author, L'Engle presents strong, admirable young adult protagonists, and provides particularly strong female characters. As biographer Carole F. Chase notes, L'Engle created strong, intelligent female characters (including one with two Ph.D.s and a Nobel prize) "a few years *before* Betty Friedan's *The Feminine Mystique*."

Though L'Engle is usually thought of as an author for young adults, she claims to make no distinction between writing for children and writing for adults. Her adult fiction is sometimes met with less praise, however. In *Certain Women* (1992), she deals with adult themes as aged actor David Wheaton plays out his final scenes aboard his beloved boat with the members of his family as audience. L'Engle is clearly rewriting the story of King David, with no attempt at subtlety. If this novel fails to develop believable or sympathetic characters, it is at least a sign of L'Engle's willingness to take risks. As author John Rowe Townsend says, "She aims high, and will risk a few misses for the sake of the hits."

It is when writing about scripture, spirituality, and autobiography, that L'Engle seems most comfortable. All of her works are full of questions and are clearly antiauthoritarian, and her personal struggles as she explores her Christian faith are conveyed with almost painful vividness. In Lee E. Snook's review of the third book of the Genesis trilogy *Sold into Egypt: Joseph's Journey into Human Being* (1989), he wrote that "whether or not she is anyone's theologian of choice, she addresses theological themes with clarity and down-to-earth honesty."

While her work is very diverse in term of its audience, a reader who encounters more than one genre of her work will find that her questioning voice is remarkably consistent. Her questions become at times quite complex, and she does not shy away from exploring the implications of the answers she encounters. But there is a touching, almost wide-eyed sincerity and freshness that characterizes nearly everything she does.

—Daniel A. Clark

LEONARD, Elmore

Nationality: American. **Born:** New Orleans, Louisiana, 11 October 1925. **Education:** University of Detroit, 1946-50, Ph.B. in English 1950. **Military Service:** Served in the United States Naval Reserve, 1943-46. **Family:** Married 1) Beverly Cline in 1949 (divorced 1977); 2) Joan Shepard in 1979 (died 1993), two daughters and three sons; 3) Christine Kent in 1993. **Career:** Copywriter, Campbell Ewald advertising agency, Detroit, 1950-61; writer of industrial and educational films, 1961-63; director, Elmore Leonard Advertising Company, 1963-66. Since 1967 full-time writer. **Awards:** Western Writers of America award, 1977; Mystery Writers of America Edgar Allan Poe award, 1984; Michigan Foundation for the Arts award, 1985. **Agent:** Michael Siegel and Associates, 502 Tenth St., Santa Monica, California 90402, U.S.A.

Publications

Novels

The Bounty Hunters. Boston, Houghton Mifflin, 1953; London, Hale, 1956.
The Law at Randado. Boston, Houghton Mifflin, 1955; London, Hale, 1957.
Escape from Five Shadows. Boston, Houghton Mifflin, 1956; London, Hale, 1957.
Last Stand at Saber River. New York, Dell, 1959; as *Lawless River,* London, Hale, 1959; as *Stand on the Saber,* London, Corgi, 1960.
Hombre. New York, Ballantine, and London, Hale, 1961.
Valdez Is Coming. London, Hale, 1969; New York, Fawcett, 1970.
The Big Bounce. New York, Fawcett, and London, Hale, 1969.
The Moonshine War. New York, Doubleday, 1969; London, Hale, 1970.
Forty Lashes Less One. New York, Bantam, 1972.
Mr. Majestyk (novelization of screenplay). New York, Dell, 1974; London, Penguin, 1986.
Fifty-Two Pickup. New York, Delacorte Press, and London, Secker and Warburg, 1974.
Swag. New York, Delacorte Press, 1976; London, Penguin, 1986; as *Ryan's Rules,* New York, Dell, 1976.
The Hunted. New York, Delacorte Press, 1977; London, Secker and Warburg, 1978.
Unknown Man No. 89. New York, Delacorte Press, and London, Secker and Warburg, 1977.
The Switch. New York, Bantam, 1978; London, Secker and Warburg, 1979.
Gunsights. New York, Bantam, 1979.
City Primeval: High Noon in Detroit. New York, Arbor House, 1980; London, W.H. Allen, 1981.
Gold Coast. New York, Bantam, 1980; London, W.H. Allen, 1982.
Split Images. New York, Arbor House, 1982; London, W.H. Allen, 1983.
Cat Chaser. New York, Arbor House, 1982; London, Viking, 1986.
Stick. New York, Arbor House, 1983; London, Allen Lane, 1984.
LaBrava. New York, Arbor House, 1983; London, Viking Press, 1984.
Glitz. New York, Arbor House, and London, Viking, 1985.
Bandits. New York, Arbor House, and London, Viking, 1987.
Touch. New York, Arbor House, 1987; London, Viking, 1988.
Freaky Deaky. New York, Arbor House, and London, Viking, 1988.
Killshot. New York, Arbor House, and London, Viking, 1989.
Get Shorty. New York, Delacorte Press, and London, Viking, 1990.
Maximum Bob. New York, Delacorte Press, and London, Viking, 1991.
Rum Punch. New York, Delacorte Press, and London, Viking, 1992.
Pronto. New York, Delacorte Press, and London, Viking, 1993.
Riding the Rap. New York, Delacorte Press, and London, Viking, 1995.
Out of Sight. New York, Delacorte, and London, Viking, 1996.

Uncollected Short Stories

"Trail of the Apache," in *Argosy* (New York), December 1951.
"Red Hell Hits Canyon Diablo," in *Ten Story Western,* 1952.
"Apache Medicine," in *Dime Western,* May 1952.
"You Never See Apaches," in *Dime Western,* September 1952.
"Cavalry Boots," in *Zane Grey's Western* (New York), December 1952.
"Long Night," in *Zane Grey's Western 18* (London).
"The Rustlers," in *Zane Grey's Western 29* (London), 1953.
"Under the Friar's Ledge," in *Dime Western,* January 1953.
"The Last Shot," in *Fifteen Western Tales,* September 1953.
"Trouble at Rindo's Station," in *Argosy* (New York), October 1953.
"Blood Money" in *Western Story* (London), February 1954.
"Saint with a Six-Gun," in *Frontier,* edited by Luke Short. New York, Bantam, 1955.
"3:10 to Yuma," in *The Killers,* edited by Peter Dawson. New York, Bantam, 1955.
"The Hard Way," in *Branded West,* edited by Don Ward. Boston, Houghton Mifflin, 1956.
"No Man's Gun," in *Western Story* (London), May 1956.
"Moment of Vengeance," in *Colt's Law,* edited by Luke Short. New York, Bantam, 1957.
"The Tall T," in *The Tall T and Other Western Adventures.* New York, Avon, 1957.
"The Rancher's Lady," in *Wild Streets,* edited by Don Ward. New York, Doubleday, 1958.
"Only Good Ones," in *Western Roundup,* edited by Nelson Nye. New York, Macmillan, 1961.
"The Boy Who Smiled," in *The Arbor House Treasury of Great Western Stories,* edited by Bill Pronzini and Martin H. Greenberg. New York, Arbor House, 1982.
"The Nagual," in *The Cowboys,* edited by Bill Pronzini and Martin H. Greenberg. New York, Fawcett, 1985.

"The Captive," in *The Second Reel West,* edited by Bill Pronzini and Martin H. Greenberg. New York, Doubleday, 1985.
"Law of the Hunted Ones," in *Wild Westerns,* edited by Bill Pronzini and Martin H. Greenberg. New York, Walker, 1986.
"The Colonel's Lady," in *The Horse Soldiers,* edited by Bill Pronzini and Martin H. Greenberg. New York, Fawcett, 1987.
"Jugged" in *The Gunfighters,* edited by Bill Pronzini and Martin H. Greenberg. New York, Fawcett, 1987.
"The Tonto Woman," in *The Arizonans,* edited by Bill Pronzini and Martin H. Greenberg. New York, Fawcett, 1989.
"The Big Hunt," in *More Wild Westerns,* edited by Bill Pronzini. New York, Walker, 1989.

Plays

Screenplays: *The Moonshine War,* 1970; *Joe Kidd,* 1972; *Mr. Majestyk,* 1974; *Stick,* with Joseph C. Stinson, 1985.

Television Play: *High Noon, Part II: The Return of Will Kane,* 1980.

*

Manuscript Collection: University of Detroit Library.

Critical Study: *Elmore Leonard* by David Geherin, New York, Ungar-Continuum, 1989.

* * *

For more than 20 years, Elmore Leonard has been among the leading writers of the contemporary 'hard-boiled' school of crime fiction in the United States, and a writer of great popular appeal throughout the world. Distinguished by an extraordinary ear for dialogue, the ability to establish mood and setting with the deftest of touches, and a memorably terse and laconic prose style, Leonard's work has established the paradigm for a whole school of crime writing. Although he is now widely imitated, he remains at the top of the pile.

After writing a number of successful film scripts, including *3:10 to Yuma* (1955) and *Hombre* (1961) as well as several pulp western novels, Leonard turned to crime fiction in the early 1970s. His earliest works, notably *Fifty-Two Pick Up* (1974), *Swag* (1976), *Unknown Man no. 89* (1977), and *The Switch* (1978), are dark and mordant tales of Detroit low-life. His plots are complex and twisting, showing greed and violence to be endemic in modern urban life, and his characters are drawn with precision and economy. At times, the narrative structure seems reminiscent of the classic Western, especially in the climactic showdown in *City Primeval* (1980). But Leonard's real strengths as a writer become increasingly obvious in the incidental felicities of his style and the studied casualness of his delivery.

Moving from Detroit to Florida, Leonard dealt with the absurdities of present-day Miami in novels like *Gold Coast* (1982), *Cat Chaser* (1986), and *Split Images* (1983), before emerging in his most accomplished style in a series of more ambitious and expansive novels. The three novels of the mid-1980s—*LaBrava, Glitz,* and *Bandits*—are extraordinarily confident pieces of writing, and they were instrumental in establishing Leonard's name beyond the limits of genre fiction. Dealing with con-men, ex-actresses, psychopaths, and a whole range of sleazy characters, Leonard weaves a wonderfully enthralling portrait of life on the edges of normality which only his Boston contemporary George V. Higgins has rivaled.

It is characteristic of Leonard that alongside the chilling and somber features of those novels, readers are offered distracting and amusing diversions that really have no bearing on the mechanics of the plot. A good example would be the constant references to the acting career of Warren Oates in *Stick* (1984). By mixing the macabre and the absurd in this way, Leonard achieves the distinctive tonality of his writing, and his later work emphasizes the two features differently. In *Killshot* (1989), the sense of menace and threat is brilliantly conveyed through an account of the witness protection program. In *Freaky Deaky* (1988), a more playful note can be heard amidst the mayhem. And in a relative curiosity, *Touch* (1988) deals with the consequences of having the gift of healing in the urban jungle of today.

In his later novels, the more prominent mood is of dark celebration, where the absurdities of human conduct are celebrated even as they issue into violence. *Get Shorty* (1990) is a wonderfully funny (and frightening) account of Hollywood life, while *Maximum Bob* (1991) presents its account of the professional and domestic life of a Florida judge almost in terms of black comedy. It may be that Leonard's subsequent novels have been a little less inventive, and that *Rum Punch* (1992), *Pronto* (1993), and *Ridin' the Rap* (1995) simply reproduce some of the author's best early work. Nevertheless, they remain the most readable, best-written, and evocative crime novels today.

—Ian A. Bell

LEVIN, Ira

Nationality: American. **Born:** New York City, 27 August 1929. **Education:** Drake University, Des Moines, Iowa, 1946-48; New York University; 1948-50, A.B. 1950. **Military Service:** Served in the United States Army Signal Corps, 1953-55. **Family:** Married 1) Gabrielle Aronsohn in 1960 (divorced 1968), three sons; 2) Phyllis Finkel in 1979 (divorced 1982). **Awards:** Mystery Writers of America Edgar Allan Poe award, 1954, and Special Award, 1980. **Agent:** Harold Ober Associates, 425 Madison Avenue, New York, New York 10017, U.S.A.

PUBLICATIONS

Novels

A Kiss Before Dying. New York, Simon and Schuster, 1953; London, Joseph, 1954.
Rosemary's Baby. New York, Random House, and London, Joseph, 1967.
This Perfect Day. New York, Random House, and London, Joseph, 1970.
The Stepford Wives. New York, Random House, and London, Joseph, 1972.
The Boys from Brazil. New York, Random House, and London, Joseph, 1976.
Sliver. New York, Bantam, and London, Joseph, 1991.

Plays

No Time for Sergeants, adaptation of the novel by Mac Hyman (produced New York, 1955; London, 1956). New York, Random House, 1956.
Interlock (produced New York, 1958). New York, Dramatists Play Service, 1958.
Critic's Choice (produced New York, 1960; London, 1961). New York, Random House, 1961; London, Evans, 1963.
General Seeger (produced New York, 1962). New York, Dramatists Play Service, 1962.
Drat! That Cat!, music by Milton Schafer (produced New York, 1965).
Dr. Cook's Garden (also director: produced New York, 1967). New York, Dramatists Play Service, 1968.
Veronica's Room (produced New York, 1973; Watford, Hertfordshire, 1982). New York, Random House, 1974; London, Joseph, 1975.
Deathtrap (produced New York and London, 1978). New York, Random House, 1979; London, French, 1980.
Break a Leg (produced New York, 1979). New York, French, 1981.
Cantorial (produced Stamford, Connecticut, 1984; New York, 1989). New York and London, French, 1990.

*

Media Adaptations: Films—*Rosemary's Baby,* 1968; *The Stepford Wives,* 1975; *The Boys from Brazil,* 1978; *Sliver,* 1993.

Critical Study: *Ira Levin* by Douglas Fowler, Mercer Island, Washington, Starmont, 1988.

Theatrical Activities:
Director: **Play**—*Dr. Cook's Garden,* New York, 1967.

* * *

From *Rosemary's Baby* (1967) to *Sliver* (1991), horror author Ira Levin has explored the darker side of human, and not-so-human, nature. Popularly considered a "master builder of psychological thrillers," Levin takes readers behind the scenes of seemingly normal situations to see the evil that lurks there.

Rosemary's Baby blends modern and gothic visions of horror in a tale of a young New York couple, their apartment in an old building, their odd neighbors, and a satanic cult. Friendly neighbors mask an evil conspiracy in which the young husband becomes embroiled, the young wife becomes victim, and even the devil himself makes an appearance. It is well written, as is all of Levin's work, and critics dispute only the believability of the demonic presence in this novel, preferring the believable essence of evil in humans that Levin depicts in other novels, including *The Stepford Wives* (1972).

In *The Stepford Wives,* Levin proves that things are not always as they seem by introducing the town of Stepford, a dream come true for the American family. Stepford boasts well-manicured neighborhoods, well-behaved children, a friendly community, and (most importantly) absolutely perfect wives. A new couple moves into Stepford and becomes instantly smitten, only to discover Stepford's horrific recipe for perfection and the grotesque sacrifice required to stay.

Levin's most recent novel, *Sliver,* like *Rosemary's Baby,* takes place in an apartment building suspiciously marked by bad luck. Again, the innocent must fight the forces of evil, but this time the foe is not an unbelievable demon, but more frighteningly a murderer masked as a friend. In response to Levin's *Sliver,* Stephen King remarked, "Mr. Levin, who wove his jittery, compelling magic in such novels as *Rosemary's Baby, The Stepford Wives,* and *The Boys from Brazil,* has in *Sliver* created the apartment dweller's worst nightmare. As always, his characters have a texture and a reality that's almost eerie, and the narrative is as stripped-down and efficient as an automatic weapon."

Levin introduces the reader to a world where the ends justify the means, and where the means are almost always purely evil and immoral. He puts the strength of human vanity and greed on display, and then brings in innocence to battle it, keeping the reader in suspense and raising multitudes of moral questions. Because Levin delivers so skillfully these complex tales of deceit and conspiracy, it goes all the more noticed that he provides himself the opportunity to make large moral statements, or at least serious moral implications, and then fails to do so. Popular criticism, while generally busy singing Levin's praises, reflects frustration at the moral questions asked but not answered by Levin. But, frustrated or not, reviews tend to applaud Levin's efforts as well-written, incredibly suspenseful and, overall, appealing.

—Amy Eldridge

LIMBAUGH, Rush H. III

Nationality: American. **Born:** Cape Girardeau, Missouri, 1951(?). **Education:** Attended Southeast Missouri State University. **Family:** Married 1) Roxie McNeely in 1977 (divorced, 1977); 2) Michelle Sixta in 1985 (divorced, 1991). **Career:** Reporter, disc jockey, and newsreader for radio stations in Kansas City, Pittsburgh, and other cities until 1980; Kansas City Royals, marketing executive, c. 1980-84; WFBK, Sacramento, California, radio talk-show host, 1984-88; WABC, New York City, radio talk-show host, 1988—; host of syndicated television talk-show.

Publications

Nonfiction

The Way Things Ought to Be. Pocket Books, 1992.
See, I Told You So. Pocket Books, 1993.

* * *

The son of a successful attorney in Cape Girardeau, Missouri, Rush Limbaugh rose to national prominence in the late 1980s when he relocated his conservative commentary/call-in radio show from Sacramento to New York City. Combining clever, sometimes puerile pranks and jokes with Baby Boomer music and an energetic verbal barrage of Ronald Reagan Republicanism, Limbaugh's booming voice and chuckling assault on various liberal groups and issues quickly struck a responsive chord in a broad segment of the American populace.

Describing himself as "the epitome of morality and virtue" with "talent on loan from God," Limbaugh's on-air shtick has included poking fun at Democratic political figures (he labeled the Clinton administration's political program "The Raw Deal"), promoting "deficit reduction ribbons" (dollar bills folded up to spoof the AIDS-awareness symbol), and performing "caller abortions" on unwanted telephone calls (in which the sound of a vacuum cleaner is punctuated with an infant's screams). Many have objected to his intentionally outrageous attempts to offend special interest groups ("I love the women's movement, especially when I'm walking behind it") and occasional factual inaccuracies, but by 1995 his three-hour, five-day-a-week radio show claimed 20 million listeners and his nighttime television show boasted a viewership second only to that of Jay Leno and David Letterman.

His first book, *The Way Things Ought to Be* (1992) was written with the help of a Wall Street Journal editorial writer. It mixed autobiographical anecdotes with a vigorous skewering of the usual liberal suspects—from "Communists," "Socialists," "Environmentalist Wackos," and "Feminazis" to "Liberal Democrats," "Militant Vegetarians," "Animal Rights Extremists," and "Liberal Elitists." Alternating between demagogic appeals to readers' prejudices and principled expositions of conservative stands on multiculturalism, the Persian Gulf War, abortion, and AIDS, *The Way Things Ought to Be* sold more than four million copies in its first year and was described as the "fastest selling hardcover in history."

Critical response was mixed. The *Christian Science Monitor* called *The Way Things Ought to Be* "entertaining and informative"; the *Wall Street Journal* praised Limbaugh as "a sensitive fellow, an old-style reformer, . . . a man who is amazingly civil"; and *Fortune* found the book "neither particularly bad nor especially good," though marked by a "dogged thoughtfulness." The *New York Times,* on the other hand, described it as "a rant of opinions, gags and insults" marred by Limbaugh's "relentless self-promotion," while the *Washington Post* faulted it for its unsupported assertions, "offensive generalities," and "mean-spirited and oblivious vision of America."

In 1993, Limbaugh published *See, I Told You So,* in which he abandoned the partly autobiographical approach of *The Way Things Ought to Be* in favor of a mostly straightforward exposition of his conservative positions on American history, feminism, Al Gore, Dan Quayle, education, the New Democrats, the Clintons, the Reagan era, political correctness, and the 1960s. Among its highlights were Limbaugh's occasionally inspired verbal inventiveness (on Ross Perot: "a hand grenade with a bad haircut") and a chapter titled "Politically Correct Liberal Lexicon" in which Limbaugh presented often amusing definitions of liberal buzzwords. Salting his familiar mix of pique and humor with references to such tony thinkers as Theodor Adorno and Antonio Gramsci, Limbaugh offered a manifesto of his conservative values in the book's conclusion while calling for unity and leadership in the Republican Party.

Although *See, I Told You So* enjoyed the largest first printing—two million books—in the history of American publishing, critical reaction was often harsh. *Christianity Today,* for example, announced that "Limbaugh's legendary ego . . . has now reached repulsive levels" and complained that he was "surprisingly ambiguous on what he actually believes." The *Atlantic* characterized the book as a "less interesting conservative tract" than *The Way Things Ought to Be,* and the *Economist* found it "just as insufferably arrogant" as his first work. The *New York Times,* however, saw it as "the best presentation of popular conservatism since Barry Goldwater's *Conscience of a Conservative,* and *Booklist* called it "political and social commentary so lively it cries out to be read."

While Limbaugh's conservative-populist opinions can often claim much common-sense merit, his gleeful baiting of those he disagrees with has sometimes caused the message to be eclipsed by the messenger. Furthermore, he has exacerbated his notorious image by pointlessly attacking long-extinct liberal species ("long-haired, maggot-infested, dope-smoking peace pansies") and lapsing into cruel and tasteless gags (joking, for example, that Chelsea Clinton was the "White House dog"). Because of his persona as the nation's avuncular daily radio companion, Limbaugh has been compared to radio commentator Paul Harvey. But his persistent mean-spiritedness and boorishness more often recall radio "shock jock" vulgarians like Howard Stern and Don Imus.

—Paul S. Bodine

LINDSEY, (Helen) Johanna

Nationality: American. **Born:** Frankfurt, Germany, 10 March 1952. **Education:** Attended high school in Kailua, Hawaii. **Family:** Married Ralph Lindsey in 1970; three sons. **Career:** Writer, 1975—. **Awards:** Historical romance writer of the year award, 1984, and numerous Reviewer's Choice awards, *Romantic Times;* bronze award, West Coast Review of Books, for *So Speaks the Heart;* Waldenbooks Best Historical, 1986-1991; Outstanding Achiever award, 1991, and numerous Favorite Author awards and Silver Pen awards. **Address:** Ahuimanu Hills, 47-598 Puapoo Place, Kaneohe, Hawaii 96744, U.S.A.

PUBLICATIONS

Novels

Captive Bride. Avon, 1977.
A Pirate's Love. Avon, 1978.
Fires of Winter. Avon, 1980.
Paradise Wild. Avon, 1981.
Glorious Angel. Avon, 1982.
So Speaks the Heart. Avon, 1983.
Heart of Thunder. Avon, 1983.
A Gentle Feuding. Avon, 1984.
Brave the Wild Wind. Avon, 1984.
Tender Is the Storm. Avon, 1985.
Love Only Once. Avon, 1985.
When Love Awaits. Avon, 1986.
A Heart So Wild. Avon, 1986.
Hearts Aflame. Avon, 1987.
Secret Fire. Avon, 1987.
Tender Rebel. Avon, 1988.
Silver Angel. Avon, 1988.
Defy Not the Heart. Avon, 1989.
Savage Thunder. Avon, 1989.
Warrior's Woman. Avon, 1990.
Gentle Rogue. Avon, 1990.
Once a Princess. Avon, 1991.
Prisoner of My Desire. Avon, 1991.
Man of My Dreams. Avon, 1992.
Angel. Avon, 1992.

The Magic of You. Avon, 1993.
Keeper of the Heart. Avon, 1993.
Surrender, My Love. Avon, 1994.
You Belong to Me. Avon, 1994.
Love Me Forever. Morrow, 1995.
Until Forever. Avon, 1995.

* * *

Since the publication of her first novel, *Captive Bride* (1977), prolific American novelist Johanna Lindsey has become a phenomenally popular author. Lindsey was selling more than three million books annually in North America alone in the mid-1990s and had nearly 50 million paperbacks in print in 12 different languages. While all of her books have been bestsellers, five of her novels—*Keeper of the Heart* (1993), *Angel* (1992), *Man of My Dreams* (1992), *Defy Not the Heart* (1989), and *A Gentle Feuding* (1984)—have topped the *New York Times* Paperback Bestseller List. Lindsey made her hardcover debut in 1995 with *Love Me Forever.*

The secret of Lindsey's success is that she combines a modern sensibility with popular romance fiction conventions. She has an unabashed enthusiasm for the historical romance genre and, consequently, writes the books that she and her devoted audience love. Critics acknowledge that these books are fast-paced, easy-to-read, and rather far-fetched. The *Romantic Times* has called Lindsey an author who "creates fairy tales that come true." Indeed, the fantastic qualities of fairy tales inform much of her work. *Until Forever* (1995), for example, chronicles a passionate affair between a virginal yet sensual history professor and a handsome 1000-year-old Viking warrior, who, in the course of their romance, travel through time. Lindsey's other narrative worlds are equally varied, ranging from the Wild West (*Savage Thunder* [1989]) to 12th-century England (*Prisoner of My Desire* [1991]) to the year 2139 on the planet Kystran (*Warrior's Woman* [1990]).

Lindsey has explained that her inspiration often begins with a single scene or point in time: "Sometimes I'll begin with a certain period in history and build my story from there. Other times, I suddenly have a scene in my head and then I set it in its proper historical context." Lindsey also acknowledges the importance of research in order to develop a sense of setting and atmosphere. While the language of her novels is modern and accessible, the details of clothing and event provide an historically accurate scaffolding upon which to hang the literary devices of romance.

While critics commend Lindsey's use of historical detail, her narratives are essentially character driven. "I don't use an outline," she has said. "I let the characters go their own way. I don't make them do anything they wouldn't be doing. I never know the ending until it happens." This spontaneity results in vividly drawn, although stereotypical, characters; the heroines are always feisty and beautiful while the heroes are inevitably proud and magnificent. Their development is often shallow and they represent only a certain kind of femininity and masculinity, but the central characters are nonetheless fiery and appealing. While Lindsey's novels are arguably less sexually explicit than others in the genre, the powerful attraction between her lovers smoulders and sparks into both spirited arguments and passionate couplings. Barriers to the happy endings—initial antipathy, mistaken identity, family disapproval—are overcome with sustained erotic energy.

Lindsey's lively, unpretentious prose style also contributes to her success. Many readers appreciate the humour and lightness which Lindsey brings to her tales of sparring, embattled, and impassioned lovers. For them, the works are funny and escapist, an opportunity to enter another place and another time to experience tempestuous emotions and the intensity of romantic love.

—Christina Sylka

LODGE, David (John)

Nationality: British. **Born:** London, 28 January 1935. **Education:** St. Joseph's Academy, London; University College, London, 1952-55, 1957-59, B.A. (honors) in English 1955; M.A. 1959; University of Birmingham, Ph.D. 1967. Military Service: served in the Royal Armoured Corps, 1955-57. **Family:** Married Mary Frances Jacob in 1959; two sons and one daughter. **Career:** Assistant, British Council, London, 1959-60. Assistant lecturer, 1960-62, lecturer, 1963-71, senior lecturer, 1971-73, reader, 1973-76, and professor of modern English literature, 1976-87, University of Birmingham; now honorary professor. Since 1987 full-time writer. Visiting associate professor, University of California, Berkeley, 1969; Henfield Writing Fellow, University of East Anglia, Norwich, 1977. Chairman of the Booker prize judges, 1989. **Awards:** Harkness Commonwealth fellowship, 1964; *Yorkshire Post* award, 1975; Hawthornden prize, 1976; Whitbread award, for fiction and for book of the year, 1980; *Sunday Express* Book-of-the-Year award, 1988. Fellow, Royal Society of Literature, 1976, University College, London, 1982, and Goldsmiths' College, London, (honorary), 1992. **Address:** English Department, University of Birmingham, Birmingham B15 2TT, England.

PUBLICATIONS

Novels

The Picturegoers. London, MacGibbon and Kee, 1960.
Ginger, You're Barmy. London, MacGibbon and Kee, 1962; New York, Doubleday, 1965.
The British Museum Is Falling Down. London, MacGibbon and Kee, 1965; New York, Holt Rinehart, 1967.
Out of the Shelter. London, Macmillan, 1970; revised edition, London, Secker and Warburg, 1985; New York, Penguin, 1989.
Changing Places: A Tale of Two Campuses. London, Secker and Warburg, 1975; New York, Penguin, 1979.
How Far Can You Go? London, Secker and Warburg, 1980; as *Souls and Bodies,* New York, Morrow, 1982.
Small World: An Academic Romance. London, Secker and Warburg, 1984; New York, Macmillan, 1985.
Nice Work. London, Secker and Warburg, 1988; New York, Viking, 1989.
Paradise News. London, Secker and Warburg, 1991.
Therapy. New York, Viking, and London, Secker, 1995.

Uncollected Short Stories

"The Man Who Couldn't Get Up," in *Weekend Telegraph* (London), 6 May 1966.
"My First Job," *London Review of Books,* 4 September 1980.

"Hotel des Boobs," in *The Penguin Book of Modern British Short Stories,* edited by Malcolm Bradbury. London, Viking, 1987; New York, Viking, 1988.
"Pastoral," in *Telling Stories,* edited by D. Minshull. London, Hodder and Stoughton, 1992.

Plays

Between These Four Walls (revue), with Malcolm Bradbury and James Duckett (produced Birmingham, 1963).
Slap in the Middle (revue), with others (produced Birmingham, 1965).
The Writing Game (produced Birmingham, 1990). London, Secker and Warburg, 1991.

Television Writing: *Big Words . . . Small Worlds* (also presenter), 1987; *Nice Work,* from his own novel, 1989; *The Way of St. James* (also presenter), 1993; and *Martin Chuzzlewit* (adapted from Charles Dickens), 1994.

Other

About Catholic Authors (for teenagers). London, St. Paul Publications, 1958.
Graham Greene. New York, Columbia University Press, 1966.
Language of Fiction. London, Routledge, and New York, Columbia University Press, 1966; revised edition, Routledge, 1984.
Evelyn Waugh. New York, Columbia University Press, 1971.
The Novelist at the Crossroads and Other Essays on Fiction and Criticism. London, Routledge, and Ithaca, New York, Cornell University Press, 1971.
The Modes of Modern Writing: Metaphor, Metonymy, and the Typology of Modern Literature. London, Arnold, and Ithaca, New York, Cornell University Press, 1977.
Working with Structuralism: Essays and Reviews on Nineteenth- and Twentieth-Century Literature. London, Routledge, 1981.
Write On: Occasional Essays 1965-1985. London, Secker and Warburg, 1986.
After Bakhtin: Essays on Fiction and Criticism. London and New York, Routledge, 1990.
The Art of Fiction. New York, Viking, and London, Secker and Penguin, 1992.

Editor, *Jane Austen: "Emma": A Casebook.* London, Macmillan, 1968; Nashville, Aurora, 1970(?).
Editor, with James Kinsley, *Emma,* by Jane Austen. London, Oxford University Press, 1971.
Editor, *Twentieth-Century Literary Criticism: A Reader.* London, Longman, 1972.
Editor, *Scenes of Clerical Life,* by George Eliot. London, Penguin, 1973.
Editor, *The Woodlanders,* by Thomas Hardy. London, Macmillan, 1974.
Editor, *The Best of Ring Lardner.* London, Dent, 1984.
Editor, *The Spoils of Poynton,* by Henry James. London, Penguin, 1987.
Editor, *Modern Criticism and Theory: A Reader.* London, Longman, 1988.
Editor, *Lucky Jim,* by Kingsley Amis. London, Penguin, 1992.

*

Media Adaptations: Television miniseries—*Changing Places,* 1989.

Manuscript Collection: University of Birmingham Library.

Critical Studies: Interview with Bernard Bergonzi, in *Month* (London), February 1970, "The Decline and Fall of the Catholic Novel," in *The Myth of Modernism and Twentieth-Century Literature* by Bergonzi, Brighton, England, Harvester Press, 1986, *Exploding English: Criticism, Theory, Culture* by Bergonzi, Oxford, England, n.p., 1990; *David Lodge* by Bergonzi, Plymouth, England, n.p., 1995. "The Novels of David Lodge" by Michael Parnell, in *Madog* (Barry, Wales), Summer 1979; article by Dennis Jackson, in *British Novelists since 1960* edited by Jay L. Halio, Detroit, Gale, 1983; *Novelists in Interview* by John Haffenden, London and New York, Methuen, 1985; *The Dialogic Novels of Malcolm Bradbury and David Lodge* by Robert A. Morace, Carbondale, Southern Illinois University Press, 1989; *Modern Critics in Practice: Critical Portraits of British Literary Critics* by P. Smallwood, London, n.p., 1990; *David Lodge: How Far Can You Go?* by M. Moseley, San Bernardino, California, n.p., 1991; *Faithful Functions: The Catholic Novel in British Literature* by T. Woodman, n.p., Milton Keynes, 1991.

* * *

There is more than a touch of the Irish to David Lodge's fiction, even though the author was born in London and has spent most of his adult life in the midlands city of Birmingham. What politicians see as an Irish-English opposition and literary apologists try to explain as a subtle complementarity, Lodge exploits as "polyglossia," a term coined by the Russian theoritician Mikhail Bakhtin to signify the simultaneous existence of two national languages within a single cultural system. As a critic, Lodge has explained this theory in *After Bakhtin* (1990), but it is in his novels that the richness of such linguistic competition emerges as a natural condition for the British Isles today.

The Picturegoers (1960), David Lodge's first novel, is only partly about characters attending movies. At the same time they are attending church, and in the often contrary but never entirely opposed languages of cinema and religion the author is able to counterpoint the developmental struggles of his young protagonist with the conservative effects of orthodox behavior. That the hero lives in a university world and the religion in question is Catholicism makes the story itself competitive with the more dominant realms of commerce and Protestantism, giving readers an even richer perspective on this novel's action.

In subsequent novels Lodge explores what he describes as other "binary oppositions." *Ginger, You're Barmy* (1962) follows a young man through his compulsory national service in the army, where he is rebellious and opportunistic at the same time. *The British Museum Is Falling Down* (1965) parallels the contradictions within a hoped-for academic career with the trials of domestic life, while *Out of the Shelter* (1970) satirizes Britain as the economic and cultural loser of WWII as opposed to postwar Germany's boom under American influence. The material richness of the United States, especially in its lavishly supported universities, is counterposed with the penury of England's sorry redbrick campuses in *Changing Places* (1975), a theme Lodge would extend into complex structural dimensions a bit later with *Small World* (1984). But first comes the transitional contrast between 1950s Catholic conformity and 1960s religious turbulence in *How*

Far Can You Go? (1980, published in the United States as *Souls and Bodies*), Lodge's last novel in which matters of faith predominate over purely secular concerns.

When David Lodge's seventh novel, *Small World*, was shortlisted for Britain's most prestigious and highly remunerative literary award, the Booker Prize, the author's reputation as a popular writer was assured. In terms of purely critical development, it also signals two new stages in his work: the ability to tell a seemingly infinite number of stories simultaneously (and interestingly), and the talent for dramatizing everday events in profounding religious deimensions. In *Small World* this dramatization is the same as it will be in parts of *Paradise News* (1992) and *Therapy* (1995), that whenever people are removed from their religious compulsions they will reinvent them in secular form, such as feeling driven to undertake pilgrimages to expiate their presumed sins. Yet even here Lodge remains faithful to the source of his literary genius, which is the ability to capture the essense of his characters by discerning how and why they speak. Thus *Small World* revels in the sometimes hilariously competing buzz-word languages of postmodern jet-setting professors and *Paradise News* has great fun with the way travel agents speak and travelers feel obliged to think. Yet Lodge remains a master of simple binary oppositions, as demonstrated by the success (as a novel in 1988 and as a BBC television miniseries in 1989) of *Changing Places*. Here the author borrows a real-life scheme, in which an engineering firm's managing director shares work experiences with a young feminist-socialist professor, with results similar to those experienced in *Changing Places* two decades before.

—Jerome Klinkowitz

LOGAN, Jake. *See* **SMITH, Martin Cruz.**

LUDLUM, Robert

Pseudonyms: Jonathan Ryder; Michael Shepherd. **Nationality:** American. **Born:** New York City, 25 May 1927. **Education:** Rectory School, Pomfret, Connecticut; Kent School, Connecticut; Cheshire Academy, Connecticut; Wesleyan University, Middletown, Connecticut, B.A. in Fine Arts 1951. **Military Service:** Served in the U.S. Marine Corps, 1945-47. **Family:** Married Mary Ryducha in 1951; two sons and one daughter. **Career:** Stage and television actor from 1952; producer, North Jersey Playhouse, Fort Lee, 1957-60, and Playhouse-on-the-Mall, Paramus, New Jersey, 1960-69. Since 1969 freelance writer. **Agent:** Henry Morrison Inc., 58 West 10th Street, New York, New York 10011, U.S.A.

PUBLICATIONS

Novels (series: Bourne)

The Scarlatti Inheritance. Cleveland, World, and London, Hart Davis, 1971.

The Osterman Weekend. Cleveland, World, and London, Hart Davis, 1972.

The Matlock Paper. New York, Dial Press, and London, Hart Davis MacGibbon, 1973.

Trevayne (as Jonathan Ryder). New York, Delacorte Press, 1973; London, Weidenfeld and Nicolson, 1974, as Robert Ludlum, London, Grafton, 1989.

The Cry of the Halidon (as Jonathan Ryder). New York, Delacorte Press, and London, Weidenfeld and Nicolson, 1974.

The Rhinemann Exchange. New York, Dial Press, 1974; London, Hart Davis MacGibbon, 1975.

The Road to Gandolfo (as Michael Shepherd). New York, Dial Press, 1975; London, Hart Davis MacGibbon, 1976.

The Gemini Contenders. New York, Dial Press, and London, Hart Davis MacGibbon, 1976.

The Chancellor Manuscript. New York, Dial Press, and London, Hart Davis MacGibbon, 1977.

The Holcroft Covenant. New York, Marek, and London, Hart Davis, 1978.

The Matarese Circle. New York, Marek, and London, Granada, 1979.

The Bourne Identity. New York, Marek, and London, Granada, 1980.

The Parsifal Mosaic. New York, Random House, and London, Granada, 1982.

The Aquitaine Progression. New York, Random House, and London, Granada, 1984.

The Bourne Supremacy. New York, Random House, and London, Grafton, 1986.

The Icarus Agenda. New York, Random House, and London, Collins, 1988.

The Bourne Ultimatum. New York, Random House, and London, Grafton, 1990.

The Road to Omaha. New York, Random House, and London, HarperCollins, 1992.

The Scorpio Illusion. New York, Bantam Books, and London, HarperCollins, 1993.

The Robert Ludlum Companion (omnibus), edited by Martin H. Greenberg. New York, Bantam Books, and London, HarperCollins, 1993.

The Apocalypse Watch. New York, Bantam Books, and London, HarperCollins, 1995.

*

Media Adaptations: Films—*The Osterman Weekend,* 1983, from the novel; *The Holcroft Covenant,* 1985, from the novel; Television—*The Bourne Identity,* 1988, from the novel.

Critical Studies: In *The Robert Ludlum Companion,* edited by Martin H. Greenberg, New York, Bantam Books, and London, HarperCollins, 1993.

Theatrical Activities:
Actor: **Plays**—Sterling Brown in *Junior Miss* by Jerome Chodorov and Joseph Fields, New York, 1941, and Haskell Cummings on tour, 1943-44; in stock, Canton Show Shop, Connecticut, summer 1952; soldier in *The Strong Are Lonely* by Fritz Hochwalder, New York, 1952; in stock, Ivorytown Playhouse, Connecticut, summer 1953; Third Messenger in *Richard III,* New York, 1953; Spartacus, in *The Gladiator,* New York, 1954; in stock, Cragsmoor

Playhouse, New York, summer 1954; policeman and, later, Cashel Byron in *The Admirable Bashville* by G.B. Shaw, New York, 1956; D'Estivel in *Saint Joan* by G.B. Shaw, New York, 1956; in stock, Olney Theatre, Maryland, summer 1957.

* * *

Robert Ludlum, whose espionage thrillers regularly hit the top of the bestseller charts, is one of the most popular living authors. His experience as an actor and producer has served him well as an author, teaching him about establishing character, setting a scene, making a story work, involving his audience, and whetting their appetite for more. He writes violent, fast-paced stories with complex plots and exotic settings for readers in what he calls "the age of conspiracy."

Because Ludlum believes "arresting fiction is written out of a sense of outrage," he searches for recent situations in which the official explanation is conceivably a coverup that allows him to make a personal statement about a political or historical matter. He is particularly interested in Far Eastern history, politics, psychology, and culture, and his villains include the Mafia and other crime organizations, Fascists, Communists, multinational businesses, terrorists, fanatics, monopolies, and secret organizations that wield power behind the scenes.

His plots are the nightmare possibilities behind the headlines. *The Scarlatti Inheritance* (1971), for example, postulates ruthless western businesses that finance Hitler's Third Reich, while *The Holcroft Covenant* (1978) grew out of Ludlum's distress at an ultraconservatism he equated with international fascism. In *The Gemini Contenders* (1976), spy networks compete for the demoralizing evidence of a 2000-year-old conspiracy to distort disturbing facts behind the crucifixion. The popular Bourne series (1980-1990) features the infamous international assassin "the Jackal," killer of presidents, premiers, and other heads of state. In accordance with their themes of paranoia, Ludlum's three-word titles sound like code names.

Ludlum argues that the hope of a democracy is educated, competent individuals, whose personal loyalties take precedence over national loyalties and who, when pushed to the edge, find within themselves the determination and courage necessary to oppose the nameless faces of tyranny. In a typical Ludlum novel a lone individual (often an academician, historian, or soldier) pits his wits against a giant conspiracy. The schemes of a nebulous, national or international organization force him to reinterpret events, relationships, and motivations, decipher cryptic codes, and engage in challenging confrontations. Exciting cross-country chases and pursuits confirm the power and organization of the enemy. However, the hunted eventually turns the tables on the hunters and develops effective strategies to defeat the seemingly undefeatable.

The hero typically teams up with a strong, supportive heroine, who at first distrusts him but comes to appreciate his honesty and integrity. A collision course is set up early in the action with scenes shifting back and forth from hero to adversary, with the action quickening and the scenes shortening until the inevitable confrontation and denouement. Given Ludlum's focus on conspiracy, it is natural for psychological assessment to be a tool of the enemy, who labels the hero schizophrenic or paranoid. The Bourne series is, in fact, a study in personality disintegration, with the hero a divided self, at times using multiple personalities as a way of coping with amnesia, post-traumatic stress syndrome, and the confusion that results from chemical debriefings.

Ludlum's fiction appeals to readers' fantasy of a split self in the Walter Mitty tradition; the domesticated, middle-class suburbanite who, of necessity, becomes a James-Bond-type hero, battling and defeating evil forces.

—Gina Macdonald

LUSTBADER, Eric van. *See* **VAN LUSTBADER, Eric.**

M

MacDONALD, John D(ann)

Nationality: American. **Born:** Sharon, Pennsylvania, 24 July 1916. **Education:** University of Pennsylvania, Philadelphia, 1934-35; Syracuse University, New York, B.S. 1938; Harvard University, Cambridge, Massachusetts, M.B.A. 1939. **Military Service:** Served with the United States Army, Office of Strategic Services, 1940-46: Lieutenant Colonel. **Family:** Married Dorothy Mary Prentiss in 1937; one son. **Career:** Writer in several genres and under a number of pseudonyms for the pulps and other magazines. **Member:** President, Mystery Writers of America, 1962. **Awards:** Benjamin Franklin award, for short story, 1955; Grand Prix de Littérature Policière, 1964; Mystery Writers of America Grand Master award, 1972; American Book award, 1980. D.H.L.: Hobart and William Smith Colleges, Geneva, New York, 1978; University of South Florida, Tampa, 1980. **Died:** 28 December 1986.

Publications

Novels

The Brass Cupcake. New York, Fawcett, 1950; London, Muller, 1955.
Judge Me Not. New York, Fawcett, 1951; London, Muller, 1964.
Murder for the Bride. New York, Fawcett, 1951; London, Fawcett, 1954.
Weep for Me. New York, Fawcett, 1951; London, Muller, 1964.
Wine of the Dreamers. New York, Greenberg, 1951; as *Planet of the Dreamers,* New York, Pocket Books, 1953; London, Hale, 1955.
Ballroom of the Skies. New York, Greenberg, 1952.
The Damned. New York, Fawcett, 1952; London, Muller, 1964.
Dead Low Tide. New York, Fawcett, 1953; London, Fawcett, 1955.
The Neon Jungle. New York, Fawcett, 1953; London, Fawcett, 1954.
Cancel All Our Vows. New York, Appleton Century Crofts, 1953; London, Hale, 1955.
Contrary Pleasure. New York, Appleton Century Crofts, 1954; London, Hale, 1955.
All These Condemned. New York, Fawcett, 1954.
Area of Suspicion. New York, Dell, 1954; London, Hale, 1956; revised edition, New York, Fawcett, 1961.
A Bullet for Cinderella. New York, Dell, 1955; London, Hale, 1960; as *On the Make,* New York, Dell, 1960.
Cry Hard, Cry Fast. New York, Popular Library, 1955; London, Hale, 1969.
April Evil. New York, Dell, 1956; London, Hale, 1957.
Border Town Girl (novelettes). New York, Popular Library, 1956; as *Five Star Fugitive,* London, Hale, 1970.
Murder in the Wind. New York, Dell, 1956; as *Hurricane,* London, Hale, 1957.
You Live Once. New York, Popular Library, 1956; London, Hale, 1976; as *You Kill Me,* New York, Fawcett, 1961.
Death Trap. New York, Dell, 1957; London, Hale, 1958.
The Empty Trap. New York, Popular Library, 1957; London, Magnum, 1980.
The Price of Murder. New York, Dell, 1957; London, Hale, 1958.
A Man of Affairs. New York, Dell, 1957; London, Hale, 1959.
Clemmie. New York, Fawcett, 1958.
The Executioners. New York, Simon and Schuster, 1958; London, Hale, 1959; as *Cape Fear,* New York, Fawcett, 1962.
Soft Touch. New York, Dell, 1958; London, Hale, 1960; as *Man-Trap,* London, Pan, 1961.
The Deceivers. New York, Fawcett, 1958; London, Hale, 1968.
The Beach Girls. New York, Fawcett, 1959; London, Muller, 1964.
The Crossroads. New York, Simon and Schuster, 1959; London, Hale, 1961.
Deadly Welcome. New York, Dell, 1959; London, Hale, 1961.
Please Write for Details. New York, Simon and Schuster, 1959.
The End of the Night. New York, Simon and Schuster, 1960; London, Hale, 1964.
The Only Girl in the Game. New York, Fawcett, 1960; London, Hale, 1962.
Slam the Big Door. New York, Fawcett, 1960; London, Hale, 1961.
One Monday We Killed Them All. New York, Fawcett, 1961; London, Hale, 1963.
Where Is Janice Gantry? New York, Fawcett, 1961; London, Hale, 1963.
The Girl, the Gold Watch, and Everything. Greenwich, Connecticut, Fawcett, 1962; London, Coronet, 1968.
A Flash of Green. New York, Simon and Schuster, 1962; London, Hale, 1971.
A Key to the Suite. New York, Fawcett, 1962; London, Hale, 1968.
The Drowner. New York, Fawcett, 1963; London, Hale, 1964.
On the Run. New York, Fawcett, 1963; London, Hale, 1965.
I Could Go On Singing (novelization of screenplay). New York, Fawcett, 1963; London, Hale, 1964.
The Deep Blue Goodby. New York, Fawcett, 1964; London, Hale, 1965.
Nightmare in Pink. New York, Fawcett, 1964; London, Hale, 1966.
A Purple Place for Dying. New York, Fawcett, 1964; London, Hale, 1966.
The Quick Red Fox. New York, Fawcett, 1964; London, Hale, 1966.
A Deadly Shade of Gold. New York, Fawcett, 1965; London, Hale, 1967.
Bright Orange for the Shroud. New York, Fawcett, 1965; London, Hale, 1967.
Darker than Amber. New York, Fawcett, 1966; London, Hale, 1968.
One Fearful Yellow Eye. New York, Fawcett, 1966; London, Hale, 1968.
The Last One Left. New York, Doubleday, 1967; London, Hale, 1968.
Three for McGee (omnibus). New York, Doubleday, 1967.
Pale Gray for Guilt. New York, Fawcett, 1968; London, Hale, 1969.
The Girl in the Plain Brown Wrapper. New York, Fawcett, 1968; London, Hale, 1969.
Dress Her in Indigo. New York, Fawcett, 1969; London, Hale, 1971.

The Long Lavender Look. New York and London, Fawcett, 1970.
A Tan and Sandy Silence. New York, Fawcett, 1972; London, Hale, 1973.
The Scarlet Ruse. New York, Fawcett, 1973; London, Hale, 1975.
The Turquoise Lament. Philadelphia, Lippincott, 1973; London, Hale, 1975.
McGee (omnibus). London, Hale, 1975.
The Dreadful Lemon Sky. Philadelphia, Lippincott, 1975; London, Hale, 1976.
Condominium. Philadelphia, Lippincott, and London, Hale, 1977.
The Empty Copper Sea. Philadelphia, Lippincott, 1978; London, Hale, 1979.
The Green Ripper. Philadelphia, Lippincott, 1979; London, Hale, 1980.
Free Fall in Crimson. New York, Harper, and London, Collins, 1981.
Cinnamon Skin. New York, Harper, and London, Collins, 1982.
One More Sunday. New York, Knopf, and London, Hodder and Stoughton, 1984.
The Best of Travis McGee. London, Hale, 1985.
The Lonely Silver Rain. New York, Knopf, and London, Hodder and Stoughton, 1985.
Barrier Island. New York, Knopf, 1986; London, Hodder and Stoughton, 1987.

Short Stories

End of the Tiger and Other Stories. New York, Fawcett, 1966; London, Hale, 1967.
Seven. New York, Fawcett, 1971; London, Hale, 1974.
Other Times, Other Worlds. New York, Fawcett, 1978.
The Good Old Stuff: 13 Early Stories, edited by Martin H. Greenberg and others. New York, Harper, 1982; London, Collins, 1984.
More Good Old Stuff. New York, Knopf, 1984.

Other

The House Guests. New York, Doubleday, 1965; London, Hale, 1966.
No Deadly Drug. New York, Doubleday, 1968.
Nothing Can Go Wrong, with John H. Kilpack. New York, Harper, 1981.
A Friendship: The Letters of Dan Roawan and John D. MacDonald 1967-74. New York, Knopf, 1986.
Reading for Survival. Washington, D.C., Library of Congress, 1987.

Editor, *The Lethal Sex.* New York, Dell, 1959; London, Collins, 1962.

*

Bibliography: *A Bibliography of the Published Works of John D. MacDonald* by Jean and Walter Shine, Gainesville, University of Florida Libraries, 1981.

Manuscript Collection: University of Florida Library, Gainesville.

Critical Studies: *John D. MacDonald* by David Geherin, New York, Ungar, 1982; *Meditations on America; John D. MacDonald's Travis McGee Series and Other Fiction* by Lewis D. Moore, Bowling Green, Bowling Green State University Popular Press, 1994; *John D. MacDonald and the Colorful World of Travis McGee* by Frank D. Campbell Jr., San Bernardino, California, Borgo Press, 1977; *A Special Tribute to John D. MacDonald,* Cedar Rapids, Iowa, Fedora, 1987.

* * *

John D. MacDonald used fiction to comment on wide-ranging contemporary issues including greed, corporate corruption, sleazy real estate scams, ecological dangers, the drug culture, suburban marriages, infidelity, the swinging-singles lifestyle, nearsighted local politics, the mushrooming population, conspicuous consumption, racism, and human irresponsibility in general.

With an MBA from Harvard, he brought to his writing a knowledge of accounting and economics. He used that knowldege to clearly depict corruption and allow his fictional heroes to set up counter ploys to outwit con artists and recover the savings of innocent victims ranging from vulnerable seniors to traumatized widows. As a military man and a former employee of the Office of Strategic Services (precursor of the CIA), MacDonald wrote convincingly of coastal areas, ships, and crime.

MacDonald's early works reflect his literary learning process. He wrote of shapely women, muscular men, lively parties, big capers, and hard-boiled murder, with titles like *The Brass Cupcake* (1950), *A Bullet for Cinderella* (1955), *Death Trap* (1957), and *Soft Touch* (1958). *Deadly Welcome* (1958) sends a Defense Department employee up against his tough home town to rescue a missing scientist, while *A Key to the Suite* (1962) follows a corporation hatchet man to an industry convention and recounts the nasty maneuvering that ends careers and destroys dreams. The feisty heroine of *The Only Girl in the Game* (1960) takes on a Las Vegas crime syndicate, while the heroine of *The Last One Left* (1967) decides to escape the hardware dealers' conventions of her past by going for the big score, $800,000 of unrecorded bribe money. The authenticity of detail about Mexico in *The Damned* (1952) and *Border Town Girl* (1956) reflects MacDonald's life there, and *Dress Her in Indigo* (1971), set in Oaxaca, Mexico, effectively satirizes the drug culture and vividly portrays rich American hippies alienating the poor abroad.

MacDonald's most famous series features Travis McGee, a Florida-based version of Raymond Chandler's detective as knight errant. McGee is a resilient, tall, 200-pound, bronzed beach bum, a former professional football player who disapproves of brutality but enjoys a good fistfight. A drop-out from conventional society, he resides aboard a comfortable houseboat, the "Busted Flush" (won in a card game) in Bahia Mar, Fort Lauderdale. McGee enjoys the beach scene (but not the spring college invasions), rescues maidens in distress, and eventually sweeps them off to private rest and recuperation somewhere in the Caribbean.

McGee's specialty is "salvage"; he recovers stolen goods for hapless victims of confidence men, and, at the same time, tries to restore the confidence and spirit of those who have been cheated. Many of his clients are in some way connected with his past—daughters, sisters, or wives of old friends. McGee is a romantic with a clear moral code. He regularly recites maxims about integrity, honesty, obligation, and commitment. He engages regularly in sexual gymnastics but talks a lot about love and caring. His method of detection seems random, but McGee patiently pieces together information until he discovers a pattern that makes sense of the facts. McGee changes little in the series, but he does come to understand his own potential for greed and violence and the distinction between attraction and love, a self-knowledge that makes him seem more vulnerable.

McGee's relationship with his boating neighbor, retired economist and chess-player Meyer, is like that of Rex Stout's Archie to Nero Wolfe. McGee, like Archie, does all the physical work, takes all the beatings, and regularly suffers numerous injuries, while Meyer (like Wolfe) remains physically aloof from the action but provides the interpretation that makes sense of the details McGee collects related to financial processes and the machinery of finance work. Unlike Archie, McGee is the key detective whose first-person narration dominates perceptions and who ultimately puts his life on the line to battle evil. But Meyer is often essential to working out exactly how a scam works and how greed can be turned against the villains. All twenty-one McGee thriller titles include a color.

MacDonald's tough but sentimental hero, his easy style, his environmental commitments, and his insights into business chicanery make his procedural novels enjoyable. Though the McGee series makes up half MacDonald's canon, the author's more-than-70 books are far ranging. *The Girl, The Gold Watch, and Everything* (1962) proffers delightful science-fiction romance about time travel. *Ballroom of the Skies* (1952) blames alien subversives for an atomic war that leaves India world ruler. In contrast, *Murder in the Wind* (1956) and *Condominium* (1977) provide graphically realistic descriptions of hurricanes; the first in a crime story and the second in a blockbuster exposé of ecologically fatal Florida real estate scams.

—Gina Macdonald

MACDONALD, Ross

Pseudonym for Kenneth Millar. **Nationality:** American. **Born:** Los Gatos, California, 13 December 1915; brought up in Canada. **Education:** Kitchener-Waterloo Collegiate Institute, Ontario, graduated 1932; University of Western Ontario, London, 1933-38, B.A. (honors) 1938; University of Toronto, 1938-39; University of Michigan, Ann Arbor, 1941-44, 1948-49 (Graduate Fellow, 1941-42; Rackham Fellow, 1942-43), M.A. 1942, Ph.D. in English 1951. **Military Service:** Served in the U.S. Naval Reserve in the Pacific, 1944-46: Lieutenant Junior Grade. **Family:** Married Margaret Sturm (the writer Margaret Millar) in 1938; one daughter (deceased). **Career:** Teacher of English and History, Kitchener-Waterloo Collegiate Institute, 1939-41; Teaching Fellow, University of Michigan, 1942-44, 1948-49. Book reviewer, *San Francisco Chronicle,* 1957-60. **Member:** Mystery Writers of America (board of directors, 1960-61, 1964-65, president, 1965). **Awards:** Crime Writers Association Gold Dagger award, 1965; University of Michigan Outstanding Achievement award, 1972; Mystery Writers of America Grand Master award, 1973; Popular Culture Association Award of Excellence, 1973; Private Eye Writers of America Life Achievement award, 1981; *Los Angeles Times* Kirsch award, 1982. **Died:** 11 July 1983.

Publications

Novels (series: Lew Archer in all books except *The Ferguson Affair* and *The Wycherly Woman*)

The Moving Target (as John Macdonald). New York, Knopf, 1949; London, Cassell, 1951; as *Harper,* New York, Pocket Books, 1966.
The Barbarous Coast. New York, Knopf, 1956; as John Ross Macdonald, London, Cassell, 1957.
The Doomsters. New York, Knopf, 1958; as John Ross Macdonald, London, Cassell, 1958.
The Galton Case. New York, Knopf, 1959; as John Ross Macdonald, London, Cassell, 1960.
The Ferguson Affair. New York, Knopf, 1960; London, Collins, 1961.
The Wycherly Woman. New York, Knopf, 1961; London, Collins, 1962.
The Zebra-Striped Hearse. New York, Knopf, 1962; London, Collins, 1963.
The Chill. New York, Knopf, and London, Collins, 1964.
The Far Side of the Dollar. New York, Knopf, and London, Collins, 1965.
Black Money. New York, Knopf, and London, Collins, 1966.
The Instant Enemy. New York, Knopf, and London, Collins, 1968.
The Goodbye Look. New York, Knopf, and London, Collins, 1969.
The Underground Man. New York, Knopf, and London, Collins, 1971.
Sleeping Beauty. New York, Knopf, and London, Collins, 1973.
The Blue Hammer. New York, Knopf, and London, Collins, 1976.

Novels as Kenneth Millar (series: Chet Gordon)

The Dark Tunnel (Gordon). New York, Dodd Mead, 1944; as *I Die Slowly,* London, Lion, 1955.
Trouble Follows Me (Gordon). New York, Dodd Mead, 1946; as *Night Train,* London, Lion, 1955.
Blue City. New York, Knopf, 1947; London, Cassell, 1949.
The Three Roads. New York, Knopf, 1948; London, Cassell, 1950.

Novels as John Ross Macdonald (series: Lew Archer in all books except *Meet Me at the Morgue*)

The Drowning Pool. New York, Knopf, 1950; as John Macdonald, London, Cassell, 1952.
The Way Some People Die. New York, Knopf, 1951; London, Cassell, 1953.
The Ivory Grin. New York, Knopf, 1952; London, Cassell, 1953; as *Marked for Murder,* New York, Pocket Books, 1953.
Meet Me at the Morgue. New York, Knopf, 1953; as *Experience with Evil,* London, Cassell, 1954.
Find a Victim. New York, Knopf, 1954; London, Cassell, 1955.
The Lew Archer Omnibus, vol. 1 (includes *The Drowning Pool, The Chill,* and *The Goodbye Look*). London, Allison and Busby, 1993.
The Lew Archer Omnibus, vol. 2 (includes *Moving Target, Barbarous Coast,* and *Far Side of the Dollar*). London, Allison and Busby, 1994.

Short Stories

The Name Is Archer (as John Ross Macdonald). New York, Bantam, 1955.

Lew Archer, Private Investigator. Yonkers, New York, Mysterious Press, 1977.

Other

On Crime Writing. Santa Barbara, California, Capra Press, 1973.
"Down These Streets a Mean Man Must Go," in *Antaeus* (New York), Spring—Summer 1977.
A Collection of Reviews. Northridge, California, Lord John Press, 1980.
Self-Portrait: Ceaselessly into the Past, edited by Ralph Sipper. Santa Barbara, California, Capra Press, 1981.

Editor, *Great Stories of Suspense.* New York, Knopf, 1974.

*

Media Adaptations: Films—*Harper,* 1966, from the novel *The Moving Target; The Drowning Pool,* 1975, from the novel of the same title.

Bibliography: *Kenneth Millar/Ross Macdonald: A Descriptive Bibliography* by Matthew J. Bruccoli, Pittsburgh, University of Pittsburgh Press, and London, Feller and Simons, 1983.

Manuscript Collection: University of California Library, Irvine.

Critical Studies: *Dreamers Who Live Their Dreams: The World of Ross Macdonald's Novels* by Peter Wolfe, Bowling Green, Ohio, Popular Press, 1976; *Ross Macdonald* by Jerry Speir, New York, Ungar, 1978; *Ross Macdonald/Kenneth Millar* by Matthew J. Bruccoli, New York, Harcourt Brace, 1984; *A Long Way from Solving That One: Psycho, Social and Ethical Implications of Ross Macdonald's Lew Archer Tales* by Jeffrey Howard Mahan, Lanham, University Press of America, 1990; *Ross Macdonald* by Bernard A. Schopen, Boston, Twayne, 1990; *Hard-Boiled Heretic: The Lew Archer Novels of Ross Macdonald* by Mary S. Weinkauf, edited by Mary Wickizer Burgess, San Bernardino, California, Brownstone Books, 1994.

* * *

Ross Macdonald was the the pseudonym of English teacher and scholar Kenneth Millar, a Canadian-educated Californian with a Ph.D. from the University of Michigan. He is undisputedly one of detective fiction's greats; a craftsman and an artist capable of rendering moral complexity in economical prose with the skill of a poet. He has been called an "historian of despair" and a chronicler of "the modern American psyche."

Bearing the mantle of Dashiell Hammett and Raymond Chandler, Macdonald purposefully made his hard-boiled but introspective detective Lew Archer face not only the mean streets of urban California but also the neuroses and psychoses of several generations of fragmented families driven by ruthless compulsions. Hugh Kenner rightly called Macdonald's books "fables of modern identity," for Macdonald's characters are swept up in social changes, twisted by their pasts, and corrupted by dirty politics. His young men are angry and adrift and his women sensual, decadent, and dangerous. Children flee their homes as parents circle each other warily, and guilt taints several generations. Orestes, Oedipus, and Freud provide clues to modern behavior (e.g., *The Three Roads* (1948) alludes to Oedipus Tyrannus), and the fires that burn the California forests and hillsides are outward manifestations of the flames in the souls of his characters.

Macdonald's early novels play rich against poor. Their focus is the personal implications of the class struggle. But his later ones examine the psychological roots of crime, with detective as psychologist collecting different interpretations of events and cutting through illusion to find reality at the core of disparate views. They also explore their author's own troubled roots; a broken home, an embittered mother, a violent war experience in the Navy, and requisite psychoanalysis. For example, the young hero in *The Galton Case* (1959) was born in California, raised in Canada, and then returned to California, mimicking Macdonald's early life, "transformed and simplified." Powerful metaphors, rich symbols, and literary allusions give hard-hitting diction depth and broad significance.

Sea and water, which are recurring images in Macdonald's books, are associated with free, open, powerful natural forces, but also suggest submerged and hidden horrors. Macdonald also uses images of animals, sickness, acting, and role playing. In *Sleeping Beauty* (1973), for example, corporate irresponsibility reflects personal irresponsibility. When a leaking offshore oil platform has "stabbed the world" and spilled "black blood," murder ensues. Similarly, Macdonald's masterpiece, *The Underground Man* (1971), parallels the physical fire that consumes the murdered and hastily buried Stanley Broadhurst with the emotional fire that rages out of control. That novel is typical Macdonald—a story of the sins of the fathers visited upon the children. Adultery, jealousy, psychotic obsessions, materialism, and emotional instabilities over three generations turn wives against husbands and sons against fathers, and result in rape and triple murder with a whole family pattern of betrayal ultimately responsible.

Macdonald's series detective Lew Archer, formerly of the corrupt Long Beach police force, is a self-employed Los Angeles private investigator. He is about 35 years old at the beginning of the series but ages into his sixties as the crime stories continue. He used to do divorce work, adultery, and blackmail, but now, after years of psychoanalysis, specializes in family murders with an Oedipal twist. In his younger days he was rough and violent, but now has a richer clientele and prefers probing questions and a sympathetic ear to get people to talk. A hunter whose chosen study is other men, Archer doesn't believe in coincidences; he seeks the connections that intertwine lives and acts and finds the underlying significance of the parts within a whole. He believes, "We are all guilty. We have to learn to live with it." Over time his goal has changed from justice to mercy.

Macdonald explores social problems produced by failures of responsibility. These include an overuse of escapist drugs (alcohol, barbiturates, marijuana, and LSD), untreated mental illness, the generation gap, dropouts, runaways, and the decay of the family. He blames sexual irresponsibility—divorce, abandonment, rape, teenage pregnancy, adulterous promiscuity, homosexuality—social divisions based on race and income, greed, and an egotism that leads to "me first" values and a welfare state. He also blames cupidity and overpopulation for the pollution and destruction of nature. Given the selfishness and irresponsibility of his characters, crime seems an inevitable by-product.

Macdonald's novels guarantee literacy, compassion, social and psychological insights, and an integrated universe where time and space can't hide the submerged but interlocked ties that bind humanity. His essay "The Writer as Detective Hero," a study of the links between writers and their fictive creations, discusses the detective story as an "imaginative arena" where disturbing realities can be confronted under controlled conditions. Macdonald's wife, Margaret Millar, is a famous mystery writer in her own right.

—Gina Macdonald

MacINNES, Helen (Clark)

Nationality: American. **Born:** Glasgow, Scotland, 7 October 1907; emigrated to the U.S. in 1937; naturalized, 1951. **Education:** Hermitage School, Helensburgh; High School for Girls, Glasgow; Glasgow University, M.A. 1928; University College, London, Diploma in Librarianship 1931. **Family:** Married the writer Gilbert Highet in 1932 (died 1978); one son. **Career:** Special cataloguer, Ferguson Collection, University of Glasgow, 1928-29; employed by the Dunbartonshire Education Authority to select books for county libraries, 1929-30; acted with the Oxford University Dramatic Society and with the Oxford Experimental Theatre, 1934-37. **Awards:** Columbia Prize in Literature, Iona College, New Rochelle, New York, 1966. **Died:** 30 September 1985.

Publications

Novels

Above Suspicion. Boston, Little Brown, and London, Harrap, 1941.

Assignment in Brittany. Boston, Little Brown, and London, Harrap, 1942.

While Still We Live. Boston, Little Brown, 1944; as *The Unconquerable,* London, Harrap, 1944.

Horizon. London, Harrap, 1945; Boston, Little Brown, 1946.

Friends and Lovers. Boston, Little Brown, 1947; London, Harrap, 1948.

Rest and Be Thankful. Boston, Little Brown, and London, Harrap, 1949.

Neither Five Nor Three. New York, Harcourt Brace, and London, Collins, 1951.

I and My True Love. New York, Harcourt Brace, and London, Collins, 1953.

Pray for a Brave Heart. New York, Harcourt Brace, and London, Collins, 1955.

North from Rome. New York, Harcourt Brace, and London, Collins, 1958.

Decision at Delphi. New York, Harcourt Brace, 1963; London, Collins, 1961.

The Venetian Affair. New York, Harcourt Brace, 1963; London, Collins, 1964.

The Double Image. New York, Harcourt Brace, and London, Collins, 1966.

The Salzburg Connection. New York, Harcourt Brace, 1968; London, Collins, 1969.

Message from Màlaga. New York, Harcourt Brace, and London, Collins, 1972.

Snare of the Hunter. New York, Harcourt Brace, and London, Collins, 1974.

Agent in Place. New York, Harcourt Brace, and London, Collins, 1976.

Prelude to Terror. New York, Harcourt Brace, and London, Collins, 1978.

The Hidden Target. New York, Harcourt Brace, and London, Collins, 1980.

Cloak of Darkness. New York, Harcourt Brace, and London, Collins, 1982.

Ride a Pale Horse. New York, Harcourt Brace, and London, Collins, 1984.

Play

Home Is the Hunter. New York, Harcourt Brace, 1964.

Other

Translator, with Gilbert Highet, *Sexual Life in Ancient Rome,* by Otto Kiefer. London, Routledge, 1934; New York, Dutton, 1935.

Translator, with Gilbert Highet, *Friedrich Engels: A Biography,* by Gustav Mayer. London, Chapman and Hall, and New York, Knopf, 1936.

*

Media Adaptations: Films—*Above Suspicion,* 1943, from the novel; *Assignment in Brittany,* 1943, from the novel; *Venetian Affair,* 1967, from the novel; *The Salzburg Connection,* 1972, from the novel.

Manuscript Collection: Princeton University Library, New Jersey.

* * *

Glaswegian Helen MacInnes, author of 21 spy novels and acknowledged "queen" of international suspense, pits decent men and women against the faceless agents of totalitarianism (Nazis, Communists, and terrorists) to argue that goodwill can prevail over the forces of darkness if ordinary people stand up for their convictions. Critics have called her romance adventures "classic travelogues" because of their strong evocations of place based on MacInnes's travels and the integrity of her geographic, cultural, political, and historical details. Typically, a young woman traveling in a romantic foreign setting becomes unwittingly involved in political intrigue, and, aided by a romantic lead (often a British or American agent), flees villainous pursuers and ultimately thwarts them in the defense of democracy and right.

MacInnes began her writing career when she and her husband, scholar Gilbert Highet, visited pre-war Germany and observed firsthand the repressive and threatening climate under Hitler. The experience inspired *Above Suspicion* (1941). Later, her husband's experience as a WWII British intelligence officer provided insights into tyranny and espionage reflected in her canon. *Assignment in Brittany* (1942), a novel that the military used to train Allied undercover agents, dramatizes the rebellious spirit of Nazi-occupied Brittany. Likewise, *While Still We Live* (1944) so convincingly depicted the activities of the Polish Resistance that Washington officials demanded she reveal her sources. The hero of *Horizon*

(1945), a capable mountain climber who has escaped an Italian prison camp and headed off the Germans in the Dolomites, is caught up in the shifting loyalties of the South Tyrol as the Germans march in. These works capture MacInnes's familiarity with the European theater and her insider's knowledge of men at war, in prison camps, and undercover, as well as her personal horror at the changes wrought by Nazis in regions she knew well.

Some of MacInnes's postwar thrillers involve WWII secrets that still threaten: Nazi diamonds financing Communist operations in *Pray for a Brave Heart* (1955); WWII Greek guerrilla fighters thwarting terrorists who kidnap for political ends in *Decision at Delphi* (1960); and secret lists of blackmailable collaborators in *The Salzburg Connection* (1968). However, most are about cold war games. They warn of Communist-financed drug rings (*North from Rome* [1958]), Communist propaganda (the infiltration of New York publishing firms and the college classroom in *Neither Five Nor Three* [1951], for example, and skillfully contrived disinformation in *Ride a Pale Horse* [1984]). Some, like *The Snare of the Hunter* (1974), speculate about the torn allegiances of writers in exile, and others, like *Agent in Place* (1976), explore the effects of newspaper leaks of top-secret information on private lives and public events and the moral dilemma of reporters concerning whether to publish or not.

Her later novels are more complex and more carefully plotted than her early works, with more fully developed characters, but they still depend on a close knowledge of territory (readers can follow events on a map) and on careful research (for instance, interviewing WWII partisans to guarantee accuracy about battles and locales). MacInnes's compelling argument throughout her canon is that politics cannot be ignored, and that naive Americans must open their eyes to hidden dangers and test and defend their received values in the crucible of conflict. Her basic pattern is one of hunter and hunted, chase and pursuit, with all the traditional espionage lore, including cyanide gas in pens, microphones in flowers, double agents, and secret codes. Although critics find these works occasionally preachy and sometimes long on description, their sense of worldwide conspiracy clearly inspired writers from Robert Ludlum to Dean Koontz.

Other MacInnes novels focus on human relations. For example, *Friends and Lovers* (1947) is a partly autobiographical love story, *Rest and Be Thankful* (1949) is a comic satire about an eastern writer learning to value Wyoming on a dude ranch, and *I and My True Love* (1953) combines a poignant, tragic romance with spy games in Washington, D.C. *Home Is the Hunter* (1964), in turn, is a comic modernization of Ulysses' return from the Trojan War, with his activities described as an ancient resistance movement.

The world of the MacInnes novel is typically one of terrifying menace, old-fashioned virtues, ruthless villains, and opposing ideologies. Her key characters are educated and ultimately courageous. WWII made MacInnes take personally the threat of political thugs who viewed human beings as instruments to be manipulated or destroyed in the name of expediency, ambition, or ideology. Later, she found the strategies of the Communist Left duplicating those she had abhorred in the Fascist Right. Although she very much reflects the Red scare of the Fifties, MacInnes brings sincerity and honest fears to her writing, and clearly takes satisfaction from the hope that right will prevail and that good citizenship will thwart tyranny.

—Gina Macdonald

MacLEAN, Alistair (Stuart)

Pseudonym: Ian Stuart. **Nationality:** Scottish. **Born:** Daviot, Invernesshire, 28 April 1922. **Education:** University of Glasgow, M.A., 1953. **Military Service:** Royal Navy, 1941-46; served as torpedo man on convoy escorts. **Family:** Married 1) Gisela Hinrichsen (divorced, 1972), three sons; 2) Mary Marcelle Georgeus in 1972 (divorced, 1977). **Career:** Writer, 1955-87. Former teacher of English and history at Gallowflat Secondary School in Glasgow, Scotland. **Died:** 2 February 1987, of heart failure, in Munich.

Publications

Novels

H.M.S. Ulysses. Collins, 1955; Doubleday, 1956.
The Guns of Navarone. Doubleday, 1957.
South by Java Head. Doubleday, 1958.
The Secret Ways. Doubleday, 1959; as *The Last Frontier,* Collins, 1959.
Night without End. Doubleday, 1960.
The Black Shrike. Scribner, 1961; as *The Dark Crusader,* Collins, 1961.
Fear Is the Key. Doubleday, 1961.
The Golden Rendezvous. Doubleday, 1962.
The Satan Bug. Scribner, 1962.
Ice Station Zebra. Doubleday, 1963.
When Eight Bells Toll. Doubleday, 1966.
Where Eagles Dare. Doubleday, 1967.
Force 10 from Navarone. Doubleday, 1968.
Puppet on a Chain. Doubleday, 1969.
Caravan to Vaccares. Doubleday, 1970.
Bear Island. Doubleday, 1971.
The Way to Dusty Death. Doubleday, 1973.
Breakheart Pass. Doubleday, 1974.
Circus. Doubleday, 1975.
The Golden Gate. Doubleday, 1976.
Goodbye, California. Collins, 1977; Doubleday, 1978.
Seawitch. Doubleday, 1977.
Athabasca. Doubleday, 1980.
River of Death. Collins, 1981; Doubleday, 1982.
Partisans. Collins, 1982; Doubleday, 1983.
Floodgate. Collins, 1983; Doubleday, 1984.
San Andreas. Collins, 1984; Doubleday, 1985.
Santorini. Collins, 1986; Doubleday, 1987.

Short Stories

The Lonely Sea. Collins, 1985; Doubleday, 1986.

Plays

Screenplays: (all adapted from his own novels) *The Guns of Navarone,* 1959; *Where Eagles Dare,* 1969; *When Eight Bells Toll,* 1971; *Puppet on a Chain,* 1971; *Caravan to Vaccares,* 1974; *Breakheart Pass,* 1976; *The Golden Rendezvous,* 1977; *Force 10 from Navarone,* 1978.

Other

Lawrence of Arabia. Random House, 1962; as *All About Lawrence of Arabia,* W. H. Allen, 1962.
Alistair MacLean Introduces Scotland. McGraw-Hill, 1972.
Captain Cook. Doubleday, 1972.
Hostage Tower, with John Denis. Fontana, 1980.
Air Force One Is Down, with John Denis. Fontana, 1981.

*

Media Adaptations: Films—*The Guns of Navarone,* 1959; *South by Java Head,* 1959; *The Secret Ways,* 1961; *The Satan Bug,* 1964; *Ice Station Zebra,* 1968; *Where Eagles Dare,* 1969; *When Eight Bells Toll,* 1971; *Puppet on a Chain,* 1971; *Fear Is the Key,* 1972; *Caravan to Vaccares,* 1974; *Breakheart Pass,* 1976; *The Golden Rendezvous,* 1977; *Force 10 from Navarone,* 1978; *Bear Island,* 1980; *River of Death,* 1990.

Critical Studies: *Alistair MacLean: The Key Is Fear,* by Robert A. Lee, Borgo Press, 1976; *Alistair MacLean: A Life,* by Jack Webster, Chapman, 1991.

* * *

By the early 1970s, Alistair MacLean was one of the top ten best-selling authors in the world. In novels such as *The Guns of Navarone* (1957) and *Ice Station Zebra* (1963), MacLean established himself as an excellent thriller writer with a keen eye for fast-paced, suspenseful narrative. While his novels tend toward a single design—that of a good man fighting evil and struggling against incredible odds—they reveal MacLean's deft use of vivid action, suspense, and plot twists.

Many of MacLean's novels reveal a nostalgia for the days of WWII, a period in which the author's themes of espionage and heroics thrive. His first novel, *H.M.S. Ulysses* (1955), was an immediate best-seller. It deals with the story of a naval convoy in the North Atlantic battling German submarines and foul weather. Although it lacks extensive characterization and plot subtlety, it does contain a taut narrative that is the hallmark of MacLean's stories. It also helps to establish a pattern for his future novels, which each include a hero, band of men, hostile climate, ruthless enemy, and traitor.

The Guns of Navarone, one of MacLean's most famous novels, is the story of a motley group of British and American soldiers who must destroy the German artillery on the Mediterranean island of Navarone so that 1,200 British soldiers stranded on a nearby island can be safely evacuated. The heroes face stormy seas, a blizzard, pursuit by German soldiers and a harrowing climb at night, in the rain, up an almost insurmountable cliff. The Germans are rarely viewed compassionately; one Nazi commander is described starkly as "neat, dapper, debonair and wholly evil." Despite its simply-drawn characters, the story sweeps the reader along to the explosive climax, rallying the reader around its heroes by treating them with pity, hope, and courage.

Ice Station Zebra deals with the Cold War of the 1950s and 1960s, signaling a change in setting for MacLean but continuing the same narrative style. The narrator and protagonist, the mysterious Carpenter, sails on an American nuclear submarine sent to rescue *Ice Station Zebra*, a British weather-monitoring station above the Arctic Circle that has lost contact with England. It soon becomes apparent that Carpenter is not simply a doctor and that Ice Station Zebra is not just a weather-monitoring station. Russian spies, sabotaged torpedo tubes, and a fire onboard the submarine while it is trapped under the ice make for a thrilling tale of Cold War espionage. Cleverly, Carpenter never reveals his true motives to his companions or to the reader until the final pages, and the novel is vintage MacLean with its surprises, harsh environment, and heroics.

MacLean's thrillers differ from those of many of his contemporaries, such as Ian Fleming and Robert Ludlum. There is little if any sex in his stories, and violence is treated briefly and then only to arouse the sympathies of the reader for the hero, who is either attacked by surprise or captured and then cuffed across the face by the despicable villain. Good and evil are not examined in depth but are depicted in black and white. The heroes are all men, all carrying some kind of secret knowledge, and all deadly despite the air of sarcastic good humor they openly display. The villains are brutish, efficient, humorless, and utterly without remorse.

The sea is MacLean's favorite setting, from his first novel to his late collection of short fiction, *The Lonely Sea* (1985). But he also favors the icy north in *Ice Station Zebra* and *Athabasca* (1980), in which the Alaskan Pipeline is held hostage by ruthless businessmen. His fiction translated well onto the movie screen, and MacLean wrote fourteen screenplays, many of which drew big Hollywood actors; Rock Hudson headlined *Ice Station Zebra*, for example, and Clint Eastwood and Richard Burton starred in the movie version of *When Eagles Dare* (1967).

Of his novels, MacLean said, "I'm not a novelist, I'm a storyteller. There's no art in what I do, no mystique." However, his thrillers are among the very best of that often-criticized and rarely-praised genre.

—Christopher Swann

MACLEAN, Norman (Fitzroy)

Nationality: American. **Born:** 23 December 1902, in Clarinda, Iowa. **Education:** Dartmouth College, A.B., 1924; University of Chicago, Ph.D., 1940. **Family:** Married Jessie Burns in 1931 (deceased); children: Jean Snyder, John Norman. **Career:** Dartmouth College, instructor in English, 1924-26; worked in logging camps and U.S. Forest Service in Montana and Idaho, 1926-28; University of Chicago, instructor, 1930-41, assistant professor, 1941-44, associate professor, 1944-54, professor of English, 1954-73, William Rainey Harper Professor of English, 1963-73, professor emeritus, beginning 1973, dean of students, 1941-46, chairman of Committee on General Studies, 1956-64. Member of board of directors of Southeast Chicago Commission. **Awards:** Prize for excellence in undergraduate teaching from University of Chicago, 1932, 1940, and 1973; D. Letters from Montana State University, 1980. **Died:** 1990.

PUBLICATIONS

Short Fiction

A River Runs through It, and Other Stories. University of Chicago Press, 1976.

Nonfiction

Young Men and Fire. University of Chicago Press, 1992.

Editor with R. S. Crane and others, *Critics and Criticism: Ancient and Modern*. University of Chicago Press, 1952.

*

Film Adaptation: *A River Runs through It*, 1992.

Critical Studies: *Norman Maclean*, edited by Ron McFarland and Hugh Nichols, Confluence Press, 1988.

* * *

Norman Maclean did not begin writing fiction until he was in his early 70s, following a 43-year career as a professor of English at the University of Chicago. The Montana-raised son of a Presbyterian minister, Maclean spent his youth fishing, logging, and working for the U.S. Forest Service, experiences he would recount in rich detail—and transform into brilliant literary art—in his fictional works.

Maclean's now classic collection, *A River Runs through It* (1976), began, he said, as his answer to his "homespun anti-shuffleboard philosophy of what to do when I was old enough to be scripturally dead." Rejected by commercial publishers, the book, which consisted of two novellas and a short story, met with unanticipated success and universal critical admiration when published by the University of Chicago Press in 1976. The title novella's first sentence, "In our family, there was no clear line between religion and fly fishing," introduced Maclean's partly fictionalized account of his youthful indoctrination into the art of fly fishing in Montana's Big Blackfoot River and his deeply felt if ambivalent relationships with his father and self-destructive brother Paul. The action of the story is minimal—Maclean watches Paul court and eventually find death and at the same pays tribute to his father and the beauty of the American West. *A River Runs through It*, however, was distinguished by Maclean's dry humor ("Until a man is redeemed, he will always take a fly-rod too far back"), masculine prose, and knowing ruminations on life, art, and the spiritual significance of fishing.

USFS 1919: The Ranger, the Cook, and a Hole in the Sky, the collection's second story, recounted Maclean's experiences as a participant in the Forest Service's end-of-summer practice of "cleaning out the town," in which a saloon fight, a fixed card game, and a prostitute who speaks in iambic pentameter teach Maclean humorous lessons about life and art. "Logging and Pimping and 'Your Pal, Jim,'" the collection's short (and some critics argued least successful) story, dramatized Maclean's encounter with the Paul Bunyan-like Jim Grierson, logger extraordinaire, socialist, and off-season pimp.

Its title story made into an acclaimed Hollywood film in 1992, *A River Runs through It* met with enthusiastic critical praise. The *New Republic* noted that it struck "that magical balance of the particular and the universal that good literature is all about," and the *Sewanee Review* claimed Maclean had "plumbed the waters of memory and . . . recovered a past that is as charged with light as it is with conviction." The *New York Times* argued that Maclean's voice "rings out in the richest American tradition—acerbic, laconic, deadpan," and the *Washington Post* called it "a pass-it-on classic . . . well-crafted prose and familial love sublimated into sport."

Maclean died at age 87 in 1990, leaving an unfinished work, *Young Men and Fire*, which was published in edited form by the University of Chicago Press in 1992. Over the course of roughly 12 summers beginning in the 1970s, Maclean had returned to the site of Montana's Mann Gulch forest fire of 1949 to research the story of a fire that blew out of control, overrunning and immolating a team of crack firefighters parachuted in to quell what was thought to be a relatively minor blaze. In the course of the book's first seven chapters, Maclean vividly and spellbindingly traced the minute details of the fire, whose three lone survivors escaped death only by outrunning the flames or, in the case of the squad's leader, by spontaneously improvising the now widely used tactic of the "defensive" counterfire (intentionally setting a patch of ground ablaze in advance of the fire to deny it fuel and so provide the firefighter with a saving supply of oxygen). In the book's last seven chapters, Maclean analyzed the controversy that followed the disaster and began to develop the story into the full-fledged tragedy he clearly intended the finished book to be: "They were young and did not leave much behind them and need someone to remember them."

Using mathematical models to re-create the fire's course, imagined expositions of the doomed firefighter's experiences, and exhaustive research in Forest Service files, Maclean created a lyrical and authoritative account of the tragedy, "where nothing much was left of the elite who came from the sky but courage struggling for oxygen." Unfinished or not, *Young Men and Fire* was greeted with reverent critical praise. The *New York Times* hailed Maclean's "heroic writing," the *Washington Post* declared the book "a harrowing, mesmerizing story," the *Christian Science Monitor* called it "a remarkable study in persistence and perception," and *Library Journal* described it as "a moving account of humanity, nature, and the perseverance of the human spirit."

—Paul S. Bodine

MAILER, Norman (Kingsley)

Nationality: American. **Born:** Long Branch, New Jersey, 31 January 1923. **Education:** Boys' High School, Brooklyn, New York, graduated 1939; Harvard University, Cambridge, Massachusetts (associate editor, *Harvard Advocate*), 1939-43, S.B. (cum laude) in aeronautical engineering 1943; the Sorbonne, Paris, 1947. **Military Service:** United States Army, 1944-46: Sergeant. **Family:** Married 1) Beatrice Silverman in 1944 (divorced 1951), one daughter; 2) Adele Morales in 1954 (divorced 1961), two daughters; 3) Lady Jeanne Campbell in 1962 (divorced 1963), one daughter; 4) Beverly Bentley in 1963 (divorced 1979), two sons; 5) Carol Stevens in 1980 (divorced 1980); 6) Norris Church in 1980, one son. **Career:** Co-founder, 1955, and columnist, 1956, *Village Voice*, New York; columnist ("Big Bite"), *Esquire*, New York, 1962-63, and *Commentary*, New York, 1962-63. Member of the Executive Board, 1968-73, and president, 1984-86, PEN American Center; independent candidate for mayor of New York City, 1969. Lives in Brooklyn, New York. **Awards:** *Story* prize, 1941; American Academy grant, 1960; National Book award, for nonfiction, 1969; Pulitzer prize, for nonfiction, 1969, 1980; MacDowell medal, 1973;

National Arts Club gold medal, 1976. D.Litt.: Rutgers University, New Brunswick, New Jersey, 1969. **Member:** American Academy, 1985. **Agent:** Scott Meredith Literary Agency, 845 Third Avenue, New York, New York 10022. **Address:** c/o Rembar, 19 West 44th Street, New York, New York 10036, U.S.A.

Publications

Novels

The Naked and the Dead. New York, Rinehart, 1948; London, Wingate, 1949.
Barbary Shore. New York, Rinehart, 1951; London, Cape, 1952.
The Deer Park. New York, Putnam, 1955; London, Wingate, 1957.
An American Dream. New York, Dial Press, and London, Deutsch, 1965.
Why Are We in Vietnam? New York, Putnam, 1967; London, Weidenfeld and Nicolson, 1969.
A Transit to Narcissus: A Facsimile of the Original Typescript, edited by Howard Fertig. New York, Fertig, 1978.
Ancient Evenings. Boston, Little Brown, and London, Macmillan, 1983.
Tough Guys Don't Dance. New York, Random House, and London, Joseph, 1984.
Harlot's Ghost. New York, Random House, and London, Joseph, 1991.

Short Stories

New Short Novels 2, with others. New York, Ballantine, 1956.
Advertisements for Myself (includes essays and verse). New York, Putnam, 1959; London, Deutsch, 1961.
The Short Fiction of Norman Mailer. New York, Dell, 1967.
The Short Fiction of Norman Mailer (not same as 1967 book). New York, Pinnacle, 1981; London, New English Library, 1982.

Plays

The Deer Park, adaptation of his own novel (produced New York, 1960; revised version, produced New York, 1967). New York, Dial Press, 1967; London, Weidenfeld and Nicolson, 1970.
A Fragment from Vietnam (as *D.J.*, produced Provincetown, Massachusetts, 1967). Included in *Existential Errands,* 1972.
Maidstone: A Mystery (screenplay and essay). New York, New American Library, 1971.

Screenplays: *Wild 90,* 1968; *Beyond the Law,* 1968; *Maidstone,* 1971; *The Executioner's Song,* 1982; *Tough Guys Don't Dance,* 1987.

Poetry

Deaths for the Ladies and Other Disasters. New York, Putnam, and London, Deutsch, 1962.

Other

The White Negro. San Francisco, City Lights, 1957.
The Presidential Papers. New York, Putnam, 1963; London, Deutsch, 1964.
Cannibals and Christians. New York, Dial Press, 1966; London, Deutsch, 1967.
The Bullfight. New York, Macmillan, 1967.
The Armies of the Night: The Novel as History, History as a Novel. New York, New American Library, and London, Weidenfeld and Nicolson, 1968.
Miami and the Siege of Chicago: An Informal History of the Republican and Democratic Conventions of 1968. New York, New American Library, and London, Weidenfeld and Nicolson, 1968.
The Idol and the Octopus: Political Writings on the Kennedy and Johnson Administrations. New York, Dell, 1968.
Of a Fire on the Moon. Boston, Little Brown, 1971; as *A Fire on the Moon,* London, Weidenfeld and Nicolson, 1971.
The Prisoner of Sex. Boston, Little Brown, and London, Weidenfeld and Nicolson, 1971.
The Long Patrol: 25 Years of Writing from the Works of Norman Mailer, edited by Robert F. Lucid. Cleveland, World, 1971.
King of the Hill: On the Fight of the Century. New York, New American Library, 1971.
Existential Errands. Boston, Little Brown, 1972; included in *The Essential Mailer,* 1982.
St. George and the Godfather. New York, New American Library, 1972.
Marilyn: A Novel Biography. New York, Grosset and Dunlap, and London, Hodder and Stoughton, 1973.
The Faith of Graffiti, with Mervyn Kurlansky and John Naar. New York, Praeger 1974; as *Watching My Name Go By,* London, Mathews Miller Dunbar, 1975.
The Fight. Boston, Little Brown, 1975; London, Hart Davis MacGibbon, 1976.
Some Honorable Men: Political Conventions 1960-1972. Boston, Little Brown, 1976.
Genius and Lust: A Journey through the Major Writings of Henry Miller, with Henry Miller. New York, Grove Press, 1976.
The Executioner's Song: A True Life Novel. Boston, Little Brown, and London, Hutchinson, 1979.
Of Women and Their Elegance, photographs by Milton H. Greene. New York, Simon and Schuster, and London, Hodder and Stoughton, 1980.
The Essential Mailer. London, New English Library, 1982.
Pieces and Pontifications (essays and interviews). Boston, Little Brown, 1982; London, New English Library, 1983.
Huckleberry Finn: Alive at 100. Montclair, New Jersey, Caliban Press, 1985.
Conversations with Norman Mailer, edited by J. Michael Lennon. Jackson, University Press of Mississippi, 1988.
Portrait of Picasso as a Young Man. New York, Grove Atlantic, 1995.
Oswald's Tale. New York, Grove Atlantic, 1995.

*

Bibliography: *Norman Mailer: A Comprehensive Bibliography* by Laura Adams, Metuchen, New Jersey, Scarecrow Press, 1974.

Critical Studies (selection): *Norman Mailer* by Richard Foster, Minneapolis, University of Minnesota Press, 1968; *The Structured Vision of Norman Mailer* by Barry H. Leeds, New York, New York University Press, 1969; *Sexual Politics* by Kate Millett, New York, Doubleday, 1970, London, Hart Davis, 1971; *Norman Mailer: The Man and His Work* edited by Robert F. Lucid, Boston, Little Brown, 1971; *Norman Mailer* by Richard Poirier, London, Collins, and New York, Viking Press, 1972; *Norman Mailer: A Collection of Critical Essays* edited by Leo Braudy, Englewood Cliffs, New Jersey, Prentice Hall, 1972; *Down Mailer's Way* by Robert Solotaroff, Urbana, University of Illinois Press, 1974; *Norman Mailer: A Critical Study* by Jean Radford, London, Macmillan, and New York, Barnes and Noble, 1975; *Existential Battles: The Growth of Norman Mailer* by Laura Adams, Athens, Ohio University Press, 1976; *Mankind in Barbary: The Individual and Society in the Novels of Norman Mailer* by Stanley T. Gutman, Hanover, New Hampshire, University Press of New England, 1976; *Norman Mailer* by Philip Bufithis, New York, Ungar, 1978; *Norman Mailer*, Boston, Twayne, 1978, and *Norman Mailer Revisited,* New York, Twayne, 1992, both by Robert Merrill; *Norman Mailer: The Radical as Hipster* by Robert Ehrlich, Metuchen, New Jersey, Scarecrow Press, 1978; *Norman Mailer's Novels* by Sandy Cohen, Amsterdam, Rodopi, 1979; *Norman Mailer, Quick-Change Artist* by Jennifer Bailey, London, Macmillan, 1979, New York, Barnes and Noble, 1980; *Acts of Regeneration: Allegory and Archetype in the Work of Norman Mailer* by Robert J. Begiebing, Columbia, University of Missouri Press, 1980; *An American Dreamer: A Psychoanalytic Study of the Fiction of Norman Mailer* by Andrew M. Gordon, Rutherford, New Jersey, Fairleigh Dickinson University Press, 1980; *Mailer: A Biography* by Hilary Mills, New York, Empire, 1982, London, New English Library, 1983; *Mailer: His Life and Times* by Peter Manso, New York, Simon and Schuster, and London, Viking, 1985; *Mailer's America* by Joseph Wenke, Hanover, New Hampshire, University Press of New England, 1987; *Radical Fictions and the Novels of Norman Mailer* by Nigel Leigh, London, Macmillan, 1990; *The Lives of Norman Mailer* by Carl Rollyson, New York, Paragon House, 1991; *Norman Mailer* by Brian Morton, London, Arnold, 1991.

Theatrical Activities:
Director: **Films**—*Wild 90*, 1968; *Beyond the Law*, 1968; *Maidstone*, 1971; *Tough Guys Don't Dance*, 1987. Actor: **Films**—his own films, and *Ragtime*, 1981.

* * *

Norman Mailer found fame early, when *The Naked and the Dead* (1948) stormed the bestseller charts. The story of a reconnaissance platoon's mission on a Pacific island in WWII, it explores the lives of its varied characters in flashback. The fast-paced, exciting novel shows Mailer's love-hate relationship with power-hungry figures like the fascist Sergeant Croft.

Having hit the heights, Mailer saw his next two novels viciously panned by the critics. *The Barbary Shore* (1952), a claustrophobic Cold War tale, focuses on a handful of misfits crammed together in a Brooklyn lodging house. Its tense action and violent finish make for disturbing reading. *The Deer Park* (1955) takes a hard look at the darker side of 1950s Hollywood. A more ambitious effort, it has good scenes but disappoints in comparison. Like *Barbary Shore,* it suffered bad press.

Hit hard by the critics, Mailer quit the novel for a while. His essay, *White Negro* (1957), examines the role of the artist as outsider, and the violence of modern America. With *Advertisements for Myself* (1959) he broke through again, blending essays, autobiography, and fiction in a single narrative. Mailer lashed back at his critics while at the same time breaking down the barriers between factual and fictional writing. *Advertisements* also proffers his belief that every earthly act has a cosmic "echo," and that the world is a battleground between God and the Devil, where maybe the Devil is winning. *The Presidential Papers* (1963) and *Cannibals and Christians* (1966) continued along the same lines. "Superman Comes to the Supermarket," in the first collection, is an inspired essay on J.F.Kennedy as "existential hero."

Mailer returned to the novel with the dark, macabre *An American Dream* (1965). Through the eyes of war-hero celebrity Stephen Rojack, he explores a universe of corruption, sexual perversion, and crime, including the murder by Rojack of his wife Deborah. The nightmarish plot involves gangsters, politics, and black magic, and peaks with Rojack's scary walk around a skyscraper parapet. An uneven, shocking work, *An American Dream* is topped by *Why Are We in Vietnam?* (1967), in which Mailer studies the American psyche and that of his hero D.J. through the action of an Arctic bear hunt. The slangy, expletive-spattered narrative is perfect for the book, which contains scenes of heart-stopping visual action.

With *The Armies of the Night* (1968) Mailer produced one of his finest works. An account of his participation and arrest in the antiwar protest march on the Pentagon, it merges fiction and reportage in compelling fashion. Mailer stars as the leading character of his story, while describing the events. *Miami and the Siege of Chicago* (1968) adopts the same style for the 1968 Democratic Convention, and *Of a Fire On the Moon* (1971) gives a masterly personal view of the 1969 Apollo moon landing. These efforts won him a Pulitzer Prize and show him at his best. His idea of liberation through sex and violence resulted in sharp critical essays in *The Prisoner of Sex* (1971) and in *The Fight* (1975), a brilliant account of Muhammad Ali's victory over George Foreman in Zaire.

The momentum continued in the 1970s and 1980s with *The Executioner's Song* (1979), a documentary novel about murderer Gary Gilmore, with the modern hardboiled thriller *Tough Guys Don't Dance* (1984), which mixes comedy and fast action, and with two massive epic novels *Ancient Evenings* (1980) and *Harlot's Ghost* (1991). The first is set in ancient Egypt, the second has a top C.I.A. man recalling his past for a "ghost" autobiography, and both explore the nature of sex, violence, and fulfillment. *Oswald's Tale* (1996) studies the mind of John F. Kennedy's assassin.

Mailer, who once took pride in surviving as a small Jewish infantryman in a platoon of Southern rednecks, has made a living taking on the world. At times his aggressive posturing may become annoying, but his work for the past 40 years shows a constant, restless search, and it may be that he isn't finished.

—Geoff Sadler

MALAMUD, Bernard

Nationality: American. **Born:** 28 April 1914, in Brooklyn, New York. **Education:** City College of New York, B.A., 1936; Columbia University, M.A., 1942. **Family:** Married Ann de Chiara in 1945; children: Paul, Janna. **Career:** Worked for Bureau of Census, Washington, D.C., 1940; Erasmus Hall High School, New York, evening instructor in English, beginning 1940; instructor in English, Harlem High School, 1948-49; Oregon State University,

1949-61, began as instructor, became associate professor of English; Bennington College, Bennington, Vermont, Division of Language and Literature, member of faculty, 1961-86. Visiting lecturer, Harvard University, 1966-68. Honorary consultant in American letters, Library of Congress, 1972-75. **Awards:** *Partisan Review* fellow in fiction, 1956-57; Richard and Hinda Rosenthal Foundation award, and Daroff Memorial award, both 1958, both for *The Assistant;* Rockefeller grant, 1958; National Book award in fiction, 1959, for *The Magic Barrel,* and 1967, for *The Fixer;* Ford Foundation fellow in humanities and arts, 1959-61; Pulitzer Prize in fiction, 1967, for *The Fixer;* O. Henry Award, 1969, for "Man in the Drawer"; Jewish Heritage award of the B'nai B'rith, 1976; Governor's award, Vermont Council on the Arts, 1979, for excellence in the arts; American Library Association Notable Book citation, 1979, for *Dubin's Lives;* Brandeis University Creative Arts award in fiction, 1981; Gold Medal for fiction, American Academy and Institute of Arts and Letters, 1983; Elmer Holmes Bobst award for fiction, 1983; honorary degree from City College of the City University of New York. **Member:** National Institute of Arts and Letters, American Academy of Arts and Sciences. **Died:** 18 March 1986, in New York.

Publications

Novels

The Natural. Harcourt, 1952; reprinted, Avon, 1980.
The Assistant. Farrar, Straus, 1957; reprinted, Avon, 1980.
A New Life. Farrar, Straus, 1961; reprinted, 1988.
The Fixer. Farrar, Straus, 1966; reprinted, Pocket Books, 1982.
The Tenants. Farrar, Straus, 1971; reprinted, 1988.
Dubin's Lives. Farrar, Straus, 1979.
God's Grace. Farrar, Straus, 1982.

Short Stories

The Magic Barrel. Farrar, Straus, 1958; reprinted, Avon, 1980.
Idiots First. Farrar, Straus, 1963.
Pictures of Fidelman: An Exhibition. Farrar, Straus, 1969; reprinted, New American Library, 1985.
Rembrandt's Hat. Farrar, Straus, 1973.
The Stories of Bernard Malamud. Farrar, Straus, 1983.
The People, and Uncollected Stories, edited by Robert Giroux. Farrar, Straus, 1989.

Other

A Malamud Reader, edited by Philip Rahv. Farrar, Straus, 1967.

*

Film Adaptations: *The Fixer,* 1969; *The Angel Levine,* 1970; *The Natural,* 1984.

Bibliography: *Bernard Malamud: An Annotated Checklist* by Rita Nathalie Kosofsky, Kent State University Press, 1969; *Bernard Malamud: A Reference Guide* by Joel Salzburg, G. K. Hall & Co., 1985.

Manuscript Collection: Library of Congress.

Critical Studies: *Bernard Malamud* by Sidney Richman, Twayne, 1966; *Bernard Malamud and the Critics,* New York University Press, 1970, and *Bernard Malamud: A Collection of Critical Essays,* Prentice-Hall, 1975, edited by Leslie A. Field and Joyce W. Field; *Bernard Malamud and the Trial by Love* by Sandy Cohen, Rodopi, 1974; *Art and Idea in the Novels of Bernard Malamud: Toward "The Fixer"* by Robert Ducharme, Mouton, 1974; *The Fiction of Bernard Malamud,* edited by Richard Astro and Jackson J. Benson, Oregon State University Press, 1977; *Bernard Malamud* by Sheldon J. Hershinow, Ungar, 1980; *The Good Man's Dilemma: Social Criticism in the Fiction of Bernard Malamud* by Iska Alter, AMS Press, 1981; *Understanding Bernard Malamud* by Jeffrey Helterman, University of South Carolina Press, 1985; *Critical Essays on Bernard Malamud,* edited by Joel Salzburg, G. K. Hall, 1987; *Conversations with Bernard Malamud,* edited by Lawrence M. Lasher, University Press of Mississippi, 1991.

* * *

The novels and stories of Bernard Malamud deal with downtrodden losers whose lives consist of facing hardship and humiliation, which they may or may not be able to endure. Many of his characters are Jewish, inhabiting poor ghetto neighborhoods and struggling to survive. Malamud's first story, "The Cost of Living" (1949) tells a bleak, depressing tale of a small shopkeeper put out of business by the arrival of a chain store. The skill of the writing only serves to intensify the grim, pitiless account. His first novel, *The Natural* (1952) describes the fate of baseball star Roy Hobbs, a gifted athlete whose brief success is undermined by flaws in his character that finally destroy him. *The Assistant* (1957) shows the gradual redemption of the racist thief Frank Alpine, who works as assistant to the Jew Morris Bober in his run-down store. Slowly the young racist becomes aware of his and others' humanity, and when Bober dies Alpine carries on running the store, ending the book a better person. *The Assistant* established Malamud as a front-rank novelist.

His mastery of the short story was demonstrated with *The Magic Barrel* (1958) and *Idiots First* (1963), where the tragic hand-to-mouth lives of his characters are lightened by caricatured descriptions and an adroit use of salty Jewish speech. "The Magic Barrel," which mingles both sadness and humor, describes a student's hiring of a marriage broker, only to choose the broker's disowned daughter, while in "Idiots First" a dying father scrapes money together to send his retarded son to relatives in California. Later story collections—*Rembrandt's Hat* (1973), *The Stories of Bernard Malamud* (1983) and *People and Uncollected Short Stories* (1992) show a continuing honing and depth of skill in stories like "God's Wrath," where a devout sexton discovers his daughter has taken up prostitution.

A New Life (1961) follows lecturer Seymour Levin to a college in Oregon, where he searches for a fresh start. Levin, whose name recalls the naive idealist in Tolstoy's Anna Karenina, finds that human nature stays the same wherever it is found. McCarthyite prejudice and personal enmities lead to his dismissal, while his affair with a colleague's wife quickly palls. He finds a new life only when he flees the campus as husband of the woman he has ceased to love. *The Fixer* (1966), Malamud's finest novel, centers on Yakov Bok, a Jewish handyman in anti-Semitic Tsarist Russia who is arrested and accused of ritual murder. Bok, who has always avoided trouble, is faced with the painful choice of whether to sign a false confession and indict his fellow Jews, or suffer alone. The terrible decision summons up an inner strength, and when he is finally released he knows he is a changed man. A powerful, darkly moving book, *The Fixer* won Malamud a National Book Award and the Pulitzer Prize.

Pictures of Fidelman (1969) follows a failed painter's efforts at self-discovery. It is a lighter-toned work, but with *The Tenants* (1972) comes a further darkening of Malamud's vision. He describes the struggle of two novelists, one white and one black, who between writing pursue a bitter feud. The quarrel ends with them hacking each other to death, a savage climax unrelieved by Malamud's sardonic humor. *Dubin's Lives* (1979) explores the mind of a biographer living second-hand through his famous subjects. Seeking his own liberation, he fails, while his wife and children find more fulfilling lives. Dubin hits bottom before struggling to a kind of happiness. In contrast, the ferocious *God's Grace* (1983), Malamud's last novel, shows a world where God has wiped out mankind after they have wrecked of the planet. A Jewish scientist who survives sets up an animal colony on a remote island and begins to teach them civilization in a fable reminiscent of Aldous Huxley. In the end, though, the animals prove as stupid and destructive as men, and massacre each other.

Malamud reveals a hard, unforgiving world where human beings can expect only to be thwarted, ridiculed, and defeated. *The Assistant* and *The Fixer* hold out some kind of hope, but in *The Tenants* and *God's Grace* even that possibility is denied. All that seems left is to face whatever is coming.

—Geoff Sadler

MANCHESTER, William (Raymond)

Nationality: American. **Born:** 1 April 1922, in Attleboro, Massachusetts. **Education:** Massachusetts State College (now University of Massachusetts), A.B., 1946; University of Missouri, A.M., 1947. **Military Service:** U.S. Marine Corps, 1942-45; became sergeant; awarded Purple Heart. **Family:** Married Julia Brown Marshall in 1948; children: John Kennerly, Julie Thompson, Laurie. **Career:** *Daily Oklahoman,* Oklahoma City, reporter, 1945-46; *Baltimore Sun,* reporter, Washington correspondent, and foreign correspondent in the Middle East, India, and Southeast Asia, 1947-54; Wesleyan University, managing editor of Wesleyan University Publications, 1955-64, member of university faculty, 1968-69, member of faculty of East College, 1968—, writer in residence, 1975—, adjunct professor of history, 1979—. Friends of the University of Massachusetts Library, president of board of trustees, 1970-72, trustee, 1970-74. **Awards:** Guggenheim fellow, 1959-60; Wesleyan Center for Advanced Studies fellow, 1959-60; L.H.D., University of Massachusetts, 1965; Prix Dag Hammarskjoeld au merite litteraire, 1967; Overseas Press Club citation for best book on foreign affairs, 1968; University of Missouri honor award for distinguished service in journalism, 1969; Connecticut Book award, 1975; L.H.D., University of New Haven, 1979; President's Cabinet award, University of Detroit, 1981; Frederick S. Troy award, University of Massachusetts, 1981; McConnaughty award, Wesleyan University, 1981; Union League/ Abraham Lincoln Literary award, 1984, for *The Last Lion: Winston Spencer Churchill, Volume 1: Visions of Glory: 1874-1932;* Connecticut Bar Association Distinguished Public Service Award, 1985. **Member:** American Historical Association, Society of American Historians. **Agent:** Don Congdon Associates, Inc., 156 Fifth Ave., Suite 625, New York, New York 10010. **Address:** Wesleyan University, 329 Wesleyan Station, Middletown, Connecticut 06457, U.S.A.

Publications

Nonfiction

Disturber of the Peace: The Life of H. L. Mencken. Harper, 1951; 2nd edition edited by Stephen B. Oates and Paul Mariani, University of Massachusetts Press, 1986.
A Rockefeller Family Portrait: From John D. to Nelson. Little, Brown, 1959.
Portrait of a President: John F. Kennedy in Profile. Little, Brown, 1962; 2nd edition, 1967.
The Death of a President: November 20-November 25, 1963. Harper, 1967.
The Arms of Krupp, 1587-1968. Little, Brown, 1968.
The Glory and the Dream: A Narrative History of America, 1932-1972. Little, Brown, 1974.
Controversy and Other Essays in Journalism. Little, Brown, 1976.
American Caesar: Douglas MacArthur, 1880-1964. Little, Brown, 1978.
Goodbye, Darkness: A Memoir of the Pacific War. Little, Brown, 1980.
One Brief Shining Moment: Remembering Kennedy. Little, Brown, 1983.
The Last Lion: Winston Spencer Churchill, Volume 1: Visions of Glory: 1874-1932. Little, Brown, 1983.
The Last Lion: Winston Spencer Churchill, Volume 2: Alone, 1932-1940. Little, Brown, 1987.
The Last Lion: Winston Spencer Churchill, Volume 3: Defender of the Realm: 1940-1965. Little, Brown, 1988.
In Our Time: The World as Seen by the Photographers of Magnum. Norton, 1989.
A World Lit Only by Fire: The Medieval Mind and the Renaissance: Portrait of an Age. Little, Brown, 1992.

Novels

The City of Anger. Ballantine, 1953; reprinted, Little, Brown, 1987.
Shadow of the Monsoon. Doubleday, 1956.
Beard the Lion. Morrow, 1958.
The Long Gainer. Little, Brown, 1961.

*

Media Adaptations: Television miniseries—*American Caesar,* 1985.

* * *

After sending H. L. Mencken a biographical study he had done of the "Sage of Baltimore" while in graduate school, William Manchester was invited by Mencken himself to join the *Baltimore Evening Sun* as a staff reporter in 1947. The biography was eventually published as *Disturber of the Peace: The Life of H. L. Mencken* (1951), and Manchester's newspaper apprenticeship laid the groundwork for a long and distinguished career as a biographer and historian. Although Manchester's first literary efforts were in fiction, only *The City of*

Anger (1953), an examination of crime and corruption in a large American city, has sustained any critical interest.

Manchester's first two nonfiction works began as magazine articles. Both *A Rockefeller Family Portrait: From John D. to Nelson* (1959) and *Portrait of a President* (1962) were overtly sympathetic to their subjects (a fact few reviewers failed to note), but Manchester's engaging, well-researched prose earned him national critical attention.

On the strength of *Portrait,* Manchester was selected by the Kennedy family to write the authorized account of John F. Kennedy's assassination. The resulting study, *The Death of a President* (1967), secured Manchester's reputation by providing a moving and intensely researched account of the five days surrounding the tragic event. Although some contemporary reviewers faulted Manchester for a subjective style that detracted from the book's historical objectivity, the *Washington Post* argued in 1985 that "it remains without question the best account in print of the assassination."

In 1969 Manchester published *The Arms of Krupp,* a heavily researched history of Germany's notorious family of munitions makers. *Commonweal* complained that Manchester's disclosure that Alfred Krupp had been reprieved from punishment for war crimes in order to lead Germany's postwar revival was "hardly news," and the *Wall Street Journal* lamented that Manchester's history was marred by his "obvious strong dislike for the Krupps and Germans as a whole." The reviewer for *Saturday Review,* however, praised it as a "monumental study."

Manchester's *The Glory and the Dream* (1974) offered a colorful, populist chronicle of the United States from the 1930s to the Nixon era, which the *New York Times* called a "good, gossipy, anecdotal history." The *New York Times Book Review* described it as a "fluent" and "likable" narrative but objected to Manchester's "sentimental" notion that American life became difficult only with the onset of the Depression.

Manchester's 1978 biography of Douglas MacArthur, *American Caesar,* combined an exhaustively researched account of MacArthur's life with a far from uncritical analysis of the general's contradictory personality. Manchester argued that the combination of MacArthur's genuine military genius and his preternaturally vain and jealous temperament resulted in a "thundering paradox of a man." *Saturday Review* praised *American Caesar* as a "thorough and spellbinding" biography, and *Newsweek* described it as a "thrilling and profoundly ponderable piece of work."

In 1980, Manchester published his account of his experiences as a young Marine sergeant in World War II as *Goodbye, Darkness.* The *New York Times* declared that the book's "combat writing stands comparison with the best," and the *Chicago Tribune* praised it as an "intelligent, beautifully crafted but complicated work."

The first two volumes of Manchester's planned three-volume biography of Winston Churchill, *The Last Lion,* appeared in 1983 and 1987, respectively. *Visions of Glory* traced Churchill's experiences from his privileged but lonely youth to his "retirement" from public life in 1932, while *Alone* detailed the eight years before WWII in which Churchill tried to galvanize the British public to face the threat posed by Hitler. (The final volume, subtitled *Defender of the Realm,* was to trace Churchill's tenure as prime minister and elder statesman to his death in 1965.) Some reviewers objected to the "apologetic" tone of the biography, lamented Manchester's occasional historical inaccuracies, or wondered at the need for a new Churchill biography given Martin Gilbert's official and more comprehensive treatment. Praise for *The Last Lion* has generally been enthusiastic, however. *Newsweek,* for example, characterized it as "the best Churchill biography for the plain readers of this generation," and *Booklist* praised it as "a masterful biography, written with great fluidity and insight."

Following his 1983 Kennedy memoir, *One Brief Shining Moment* (1983), which some reviewers faulted for its sentimentality, Manchester embarked on a wide-ranging historical portrait of the 16th century. While focusing on such pivotal figures as da Vinci, Copernicus, and, in particular, Magellan, *A World Lit Only by Fire* (1992) offered a personal interpretation of the main events and currents of medieval European history. *Booklist* praised it as "a wonderfully curmudgeonly and one-sided sketch" and *Publishers Weekly* called it "marvelously vivid." The reviewer for the *Washington Post,* however, faulted Manchester's "extremely shallow" comprehension of medieval life, which was, he argued, outside "Manchester's capacity to explain and analyze."

—Paul Bodine

MARCHANT, Catherine. *See* **COOKSON, Catherine.**

MARLOWE, Hugh. *See* **HIGGINS, Jack.**

MARSH, (Edith) Ngaio

Nationality: New Zealander. **Born:** Christchurch, 23 April 1895. **Education:** St. Margaret's College, Christchurch, 1910-14; Canterbury University College School of Art, Christchurch, 1915-20. Actress in New Zealand, 1920-23; theatrical producer, New Zealand, 1923-27; interior decorator, in partnership with Mrs. Tahu Rhodes, London, 1928-32. **Military Service:** Served in a New Zealand Red Cross transport unit during World War II. **Career:** Producer for D. D. O'Connor Theatre Management, New Zealand, 1944-52; artistic director, British Commonwealth Theatre Company, 1951-52. Honorary lecturer in Drama, Canterbury University. Ngaio Marsh Theatre founded at Canterbury University, 1967. **Awards:** Mystery Writers of America Grand Master award, 1977. D. Litt.: Canterbury University, 1962. Fellow, Royal Society of Arts. Officer, Order of the British Empire), 1948; Dame Commander, Order of the British Empire, 1966. **Died:** 18 February 1982.

Publications

Novels (series: Inspector/Superintendent Roderick Alleyn in all books)

A Man Lay Dead. London, Bles, 1934; New York, Sheridan, 1942.

Enter a Murderer. London, Bles, 1935; New York, Pocket Books, 1941.
The Nursing-Home Murder, with Henry Jellett. London, Bles, 1935; New York, Sheridan, 1941.
Death in Ecstasy. London, Bles, 1936; New York, Sheridan, 1941.
Vintage Murder. London, Bles, 1937; New York, Sheridan, 1940.
Artists in Crime. London, Bles, and New York, Furman, 1938.
Death in a White Tie. London, Bles, and New York, Furman, 1938.
Overture to Death. London, Collins, and New York, Furman, 1939.
Death at the Bar. London, Collins, and Boston, Little Brown, 1940.
Death of a Peer. Boston, Little Brown, 1940; as *Surfeit of Lampreys,* London, Collins, 1941.
Death and the Dancing Footman. Boston, Little Brown, 1941; London, Collins, 1942.
Colour Scheme. London, Collins, and Boston, Little Brown, 1943.
Died in the Wool. London, Collins, and Boston, Little Brown, 1945.
Final Curtain. London, Collins, and Boston, Little Brown, 1947.
Swing, Brother, Swing. London, Collins, 1949; as *A Wreath for Rivera,* Boston, Little Brown, 1949.
Opening Night. London, Collins, 1951; as *Night at the Vulcan,* Boston, Little Brcwn, 1951.
Spinsters in Jeopardy. Boston, Little Brown, 1953; London, Collins, 1954; as *The Bride of Death,* New York, Spivak, 1955.
Scales of Justice. London, Collins, and Boston, Little Brown, 1955.
Death of a Fool. Boston, Little Brown, 1956; as *Off with His Head,* London, Collins, 1957.
Singing in the Shrouds. Boston, Little Brown, 1958; London, Collins, 1959.
False Scent. Boston, Little Brown, and London, Collins, 1960.
Hand in Glove. Boston, Little Brown, and London, Collins, 1962.
Dead Water. Boston, Little Brown, 1963; London, Collins, 1964.
Killer Dolphin. Boston, Little Brown, 1966; as *Death at the Dolphin,* London, Collins, 1967.
Clutch of Constables. London, Collins, 1968; Boston, Little Brown, 1969.
When in Rome. London, Collins, 1970; Boston, Little Brown, 1971.
Tied Up in Tinsel. London, Collins, and Boston, Little Brown, 1972.
Black as He's Painted. London, Collins, and Boston, Little Brown, 1974.
Last Ditch. Boston, Little Brown, and London, Collins, 1977.
Grave Mistake. Boston, Little Brown, and London, Collins, 1978.
Photo-Finish. London, Collins, and Boston, Little Brown, 1980.
Light Thickens. London, Collins, and Boston, Little Brown, 1982.
The Roderick Alleyn Mysteries (includes *A Man Lay Dead, The Nursing Home Murder,* and *Final Curtain*). London, HarperCollins, 1993.

Short Stories

Death on the Air and Other Stories. New York, International Polygonics, 1989; London, HarperCollins, 1995.
The Collected Shorter Fiction of Ngaio Marsh, edited by Douglas G. Greene. New York, International Polygonics, 1989.

Plays

The Nursing-Home Murder, with Henry Jellett, adaptation of their own novel (produced Christchurch, 1935).
False Scent, with Eileen Mackay, adaptation of her own novel (produced Worthing, Sussex, 1961).
The Christmas Tree (for children). London, S.P.C.K., 1962.
A Unicorn for Christmas, music by David Farquhar (produced Wellington, 1962).
Murder Sails at Midnight (produced Auchland, 1963; Bournemouth, Hampshire, 1972).

Television Play: *Evil Liver* (Crown Court series), 1975.

Other

New Zealand, with Randal Matthew Burdon. London, Collins, 1942.
A Play Toward: A Note on Play Production. Christchurch, Caxton Press, 1946.
Perspectives: The New Zealander and the Visual Arts. Auckland, Auckland Gallery Associates, 1960.
New Zealand (for children). New York, Macmillan, 1964; London, Collier Macmillan, 1965.
Black Beech and Honeydew: An Autobiography. Boston, Little Brown, 1965; London, Collins, 1966; revised edition, Collins, 1981.

*

Manuscript Collections: Mugar Memorial Library, Boston University; Alexander Turnbull Library, Wellington.

Critical Studies: *Ngaio Marsh: A Life* by Margaret Lewis, London, Chatto and Windus, 1991; *Ngaio Marsh* by Kathryne Slate McDorman, Boston, Twayne, 1991; *Ngaio Marsh: The Woman and Her Work,* edited by B.J. Rahn, Metuchen, New Jersey, Scarecrow Press, 1995; *Murder Most Poetic: The Mystery Novels of Ngaio Marsh* by Mary S. Weinkauf, edited by Mary A. Burgess, San Bernardino, California, Brownstone Books, 1995.

Theatrical Activities:
Director: **Play**—*Six Characters in Search of an Author* by Pirandello, London, 1950.

* * *

Ngaio Marsh wrote classics of the British whodunnit puzzle school of crime fiction featuring country house murders and gentlemen detectives. This sub-genre was most popular in the interwar years, when Marsh's contemporaries included Dorothy L. Sayers and Agatha Christie, but Marsh's books still enjoy a loyal following.

Characteristics of Marsh's novels include: the charismatic gentleman detective in the form of Roderick Alleyn (a rather upper-class policeman); a murder (usually domestic, and with no violence depicted); a stereotypical group of characters in a confined space, and usually in a country house. The reader gains the cerebral pleasures of following the clues that Alleyn obligingly lays out, allowing them to race the celebrated detective to the inevitable denouement when all the characters are gathered together for the crime to be reconstructed and the perpetrator revealed. These murder mysteries are not realistic depictions of police procedure or life, but are tightly formatted puzzles featuring stereotypes of upper-class manners wittily employed by the use of skilful dialogue.

Perhaps in an attempt to humanize the infallible detective, Marsh brought in a beloved, Agatha Troy, in *Artists in Crime* (1938). Troy's name suggests some of romanticism attached to her subsequent marriage to Alleyn, and she appears in many later novels, occasionally with their son. Despite passionate distractions, the core team of a Marsh detective story consists of Alleyn, his faithful lower-class and slower-brained assistant, Inspector Fox (after the model of Dr. Watson to Conan Doyle's Sherlock Holmes), and the virtually silent crime experts, Bailey and Thompson. The crime is usually initiated by the feuds and desires of a family or group of friends, although later novels did try, none too successfully, to evoke worlds of organized crime (and even politics in *Black As He's Painted* [1974]).

Marsh's style and content were both persistent and open to some changes. There is a continuing concern for class distinctions with a recognizable portrayal of a servant class as late as *Grave Mistake* (1978)—students of the 20th-century British class system would find Marsh invaluable. Other recurring themes are bohemian artists or primadonnas in the theater reflecting Marsh's other careers. Change occurs in the attempt to diversify from upper-class family murders to disturbed criminality. *Singing in the Shrouds* (1958) contains Marsh's nearest portrait of a psychopath but lacks convincing depth or menace. The suspects are isolated onboard ship, and only very peripheral or lower-class characters die before Alleyn saves the day. There is an interesting experiment with political crime in *Black As He's Painted,* but Marsh's work remains in the realms of entertainment and eschews realistic depth.

Regularly praised for dialogue and the puzzle-like nature of her plots, Marsh stays within the strict conventions of her format but has fun with them, often by mocking the stereotypical behavior of her characters. *Final Curtain* (1947) is a good example of an archetypal country house murder that parodies the highly strung characters of its cast, an acting family. Similarly, *False Scent* (1960) centers around the household of an aging leading actress, a figure who recurs in other guises throughout Marsh's writing. Sometimes the narrative is told from the point of view of another character who is only marginally suspect, as occurs in *Surfeit of Lampreys* (1941), or Troy Alleyn herself before Alleyn arrives deus ex machina to sort out the mess. The Lampreys are an impossibly engaging upper-class family and there is an audible sigh of relief when an outsider proves to be the criminal.

Marsh provides the pleasures of texts where crime is a solvable puzzle that can cure the world of violence and disorder. Her plots are not elaborate but provide enough red herrings to keep the readers guessing and to send them back to plans of houses or interviews with Alleyn to tease out that last crucial clue. The occasional taste for the bizarre in murder is shown by *Off With His Head* (1957), where the typical class-ridden characters in a country village find a death in their ancient mummer's play in which five sons behead their patriarch father. Likewise, *In Vintage Murder* (1937) a magnum of champagne proves deadly.

Lacking verisimilitude of plot or characterization, Marsh produced detective stories as highly crafted entertainment capable of ironic amusement about their own genre. Her books contain mysteries to intrigue and delight with a reliable, incorruptible detective to solve crimes and exact justice. They will be read as well for their recording of social class, charm, and effective dialogue.

—S. A. Rowland

MARSTEN, Richard. *See* **McBAIN, Ed.**

MARTINSEN, Martin. *See* **FOLLETT, Ken.**

MATTHEWS, Brad. *See* **DeMILLE, Nelson.**

MAUPIN, Armistead

Nationality: American. **Born:** 13 May 1944, in Washington, D.C. **Education:** University of North Carolina at Chapel Hill, B.A., 1966. **Military Service:** Served in the U.S. armed forces in Vietnam. **Career:** Writer. Charleston *News and Courier,* Charleston, South Carolina, reporter, 1970-71; Associated Press, San Francisco, reporter, 1971-72; public-relations account executive in San Francisco, 1973; *Pacific Sun,* San Francisco, columnist, 1974; San Francisco Opera, publicist, 1975; *San Francisco Chronicle,* author of column "Tales of the City," 1976-77; KRON-TV, San Francisco, commentator, 1979. **Agent:** Amanda Urbin, International Creative Management, 40 West 57th St., New York, New York 10019, U.S.A.

Publications

Novels

Tales of the City. Harper, 1978.
More Tales of the City. Harper, 1980.
Further Tales of the City. Harper, 1982.
Babycakes. Harper, 1984.
Significant Others. Harper, 1987.
Sure of You. Harper, 1989.
The Complete Tales of the City. HarperCollins, 1991.
Back to Barbary Lane: The Final Tales of the City Omnibus. HarperCollins, 1991.
Maybe the Moon. HarperCollins, 1992.

* * *

Armistead Maupin's novels have the feel of a storyteller spinning tales to a rapt live audience sitting in comfortable chairs and couches. That is because Maupin wants it that way. As he has explained: "I think I was a born storyteller, or at least a bred one. I was rotten at sports but I could tell a good ghost story."

The stories Maupin tells these days are not of ghosts, but of everyday people's lives and loves. His "Tales of the City" series started out as a column in the mid-1970s in the *San Francisco Chronicle* and came out in book form in 1978. The novel follows a group of men and women who live in a funky, haphazard-looking apartment house run by a marijuana-smoking, fifty-something landlady. She grows her own crop and hands out joints and sage words of advice to all of her tenants—whether they want them or not. Using a combination of rollicking humor and touching candor, *Tales of the City* illustrates the fact that while some people rise, others fall, and all learn something new along the way. No matter which direction a given character travels, Maupin approaches him or her with a keen eye and a kind heart. The novel was produced as a miniseries that aired on PBS in 1994. However, some PBS affiliates refused to show *Tales of the City* because of its gay themes and depiction of drug use.

More Tales of the City (1980) and *Further Tales of the City* (1982) also received a test-run in the *Chronicle* before being published as novels. As one might guess, these novels follow the house at 28 Barbary Lane through old and new tenants and their trials, tribulations, and celebrations. Interestingly, Mary Ann, the unassuming girl who "runs away" to San Francisco from Cleveland in *Tales of the City,* hardens a bit through the series. Conversely, spoiled debutante DeDe becomes more considerate of others. Meanwhile, Mrs. Madrigal keeps on smoking.

Other members of the "Tales of the City" series include *Babycakes* (1984), *Significant Others* (1987), and *Sure of You* (1989). Maupin has said that *Sure of You* will be the last of the series, and that he would like subsequent works to focus on characters separate from those that readers have met and gotten to know since the "Tales of the City" series began in the mid-1970s.

Besides Maupin's appearances in the *San Francisco Chronicle* and the *San Francisco Examiner,* he has been published in the *Advocate,* the *Los Angeles Times,* the *New York Times,* and the *Village Voice.* Although many of his works have gay themes and have appeared in gay and lesbian forums, Maupin does not wish to consider himself strictly as a "gay writer." "I don't mind being described as a gay writer, because I'm a writer and I am gay," he has said. "But to many people that implies that you're only writing for a gay audience, or you're writing esoteric subject matter. My aim from the very beginning was to create a large framework of humanity and to place gay characters in that framework."

—Tracy Clark

MAYO, Jim. *See* **L'AMOUR, Louis.**

McBAIN, Ed

Pseudonym for Evan Hunter. **Other Pseudonyms:** Curt Cannon; Hunt Collins; Ezra Hannon; Richard Marsten. **Nationality:** American. **Born:** Salvatore A. Lombino, New York City, 15 October 1926. **Education:** Cooper Union, New York, 1943-44; Hunter College, New York, B.A. 1950 (Phi Beta Kappa). **Military Service:** Served in the U.S. Navy, 1944-46. **Family:** Married 1) Anita Melnick in 1949 (divorced), three sons; 2) Mary Vann Finley in 1973, one stepdaughter. **Career:** In the early 1950s taught in vocational high schools, and worked for Scott Meredith Literary Agency, New York. **Awards:** Mystery Writers of America Edgar Allan Poe award, 1957; Grand Master award, 1985. **Agent:** John Farquharson Ltd., 250 West 57th Street, New York, New York 10019, U.S.A., or, 162-168 Regent Street, London WIR 5TB, England. **Address:** Norwalk, Connecticut.

Publications

Novels as Ed McBain (series: Officers of the 87th Precinct; Matthew Hope)

Cut Me In (as Hunt Collins). New York, Abelard Schuman, 1954; London, Boardman, 1960; as *The Proposition,* New York, Pyramid, 1955.
Cop Hater (87th Precinct). New York, Permabooks, 1956; London, Boardman, 1958.
The Mugger (87th Precinct). New York, Simon and Schuster, 1956; London, Boardman, 1959.
The Pusher (87th Precinct). New York, Simon and Schuster, 1956; London, Boardman, 1959.
The Con Man (87th Precinct). New York, Permabooks, 1957; London, Boardman, 1960.
Killer's Choice (87th Precinct). New York, Simon and Schuster, 1957; London, Boardman, 1960.
Killer's Payoff (87th Precinct). New York, Simon and Schuster, 1958; London, Boardman, 1960.
April Robin Murders, with Craig Rice (completed by McBain). New York, Random House, 1958; London, Hammond, 1959.
Lady Killer (87th Precinct). New York, Simon and Schuster, 1958; London, Boardman, 1961.
I'm Cannon—For Hire (as Curt Cannon). New York, Fawcett, 1958; London, Fawcett, 1959.
Killer's Wedge (87th Precinct). New York, Simon and Schuster, 1959; London, Boardman, 1961.
'Til Death (87th Precinct). New York, Simon and Schuster, 1959; London, Boardman, 1961.
King's Ransom (87th Precinct). New York, Simon and Schuster, 1959; London, Boardman, 1961.
Give the Boys a Great Big Hand (87th Precinct). New York, Simon and Schuster, 1960; London, Boardman, 1962.
The Heckler (87th Precinct). New York, Simon and Schuster, 1960; London, Boardman, 1962.
See Them Die (87th Precinct). New York, Simon and Schuster, 1960; London, Boardman, 1963.
Lady, Lady, I Did It! (87th Precinct). New York, Simon and Schuster, 1961; London, Boardman, 1963.
Like Love (87th Precinct). New York, Simon and Schuster, 1962; London, Boardman, 1964.
Ten Plus One (87th Precinct). New York, Simon and Schuster, 1963; London, Hamish Hamilton, 1964.
Ax (87th Precinct). New York, Simon and Schuster, and London, Hamish Hamilton, 1964.
The Sentries. New York, Simon and Schuster, and London, Hamish Hamilton, 1965.

He Who Hesitates (87th Precinct). New York, Delacorte Press, and London, Hamish Hamilton, 1965.
Doll (87th Precinct). New York, Delacorte Press, 1965; London, Hamish Hamilton, 1966.
Eighty Million Eyes (87th Precinct). New York, Delacorte Press, and London, Hamish Hamilton, 1966.
Fuzz (87th Precinct). New York, Doubleday, and London, Hamish Hamilton, 1968.
Shotgun (87th Precinct). New York, Doubleday, and London, Hamish Hamilton, 1969.
Jigsaw (87th Precinct). New York, Doubleday, and London, Hamish Hamilton, 1970.
Hail, Hail, The Gang's All Here! (87th Precinct). New York, Doubleday, and London, Hamish Hamilton, 1971.
Sadie When She Died (87th Precinct). New York, Doubleday, and London, Hamish Hamilton, 1972.
Let's Hear It for the Deaf Man (87th Precinct). New York, Doubleday, and London, Hamish Hamilton, 1973.
Hail to the Chief (87th Precinct). New York, Random House, and London, Hamish Hamilton, 1973.
Bread (87th Precinct). New York, Random House, and London, Hamish Hamilton, 1974.
Where There's Smoke. New York, Random House, and London, Hamish Hamilton, 1975.
Blood Relatives (87th Precinct). New York, Random House, 1975; London, Hamish Hamilton, 1976.
Doors (as Ezra Hannon). New York, Stein and Day, 1975; London, Macmillan, 1976.
Guns. New York, Random House, 1976; London, Hamish Hamilton, 1977.
So Long as You Both Shall Live (87th Precinct). New York, Random House, and London, Hamish Hamilton, 1976.
Long Time No See (87th Precinct). New York, Random House, and London, Hamish Hamilton, 1977.
Goldilocks (Hope). New York, Arbor House, 1977; London, Hamish Hamilton, 1978.
Calypso (87th Precinct). New York, Viking Press, and London, Hamish Hamilton, 1979.
Ghosts (87th Precinct). New York, Viking Press, and London, Hamish Hamilton, 1980.
Rumpelstiltskin (Hope). New York, Viking Press, and London, Hamish Hamilton, 1981.
Heat (87th Precinct). New York, Viking Press, and London, Hamish Hamilton, 1981.
Beauty and the Beast (87th Precinct). London, Hamish Hamilton, 1982; New York, Holt Rinehart, 1983.
Ice (87th Precinct). New York, Arbor House, and London, Hamish Hamilton, 1983.
Jack and the Beanstalk (Hope). New York, Holt Rinehart, and London, Hamish Hamilton, 1984.
Lightning (87th Precinct). New York, Arbor House, and London, Hamish Hamilton, 1984.
Snow White and Rose Red (Hope). New York, Random House, and London, Hamish Hamilton, 1985.
Eight Black Horses (87th Precinct). New York, Arbor House, and London, Hamish Hamilton, 1985.
Another Part of the City (87th Precinct). New York, Mysterious Press, 1985; London, Hamish Hamilton, 1986.
Cinderella. (Hope). New York, Holt, and London, Hamish Hamilton, 1986.
Poison (87th Precinct). New York, Arbor House, and London, Hamish Hamilton, 1987.
Puss in Boots (Hope). New York, Holt, and London, Arbor House, 1987.
Tricks (87th Precinct). New York, Arbor House, and London, Hamish Hamilton, 1987.
The House That Jack Built (Hope). New York, Holt, and London, Hamish Hamilton, 1988.
Lullaby (87th Precinct). New York, Morrow, and London, Hamish Hamilton, 1989.
Downtown. New York, Morrow, and London, Heinemann, 1989.
Three Blind Mice (Hope). New York, Arcade, 1990; London, Heinemann, 1991.
Vespers (87th Precinct). New York, Morrow, and London, Heinemann, 1990.
Widows (87th Precinct). New York, Morrow, and London, Heinemann, 1991.
Kiss (87th Precinct). New York, Morrow, and London, Heinemann, 1992.
Mary, Mary (Hope). New York, Warner Books, and London, Heinemann, 1992.
Mischief (87th Precinct). New York, Morrow, and London, Hodder and Stoughton, 1993.
And All Through the House (87th Precinct). New York, Warner Books, and London, Hodder and Stoughton, 1994.
There Was a Little Girl (Hope). New York, Warner Books, and London, Hodder and Stoughton, 1994.
Romance (87th Precinct). New York, Warner Books, and London, Hodder and Stoughton, 1995.

Novels as Evan Hunter

The Evil Sleep! N.p., Falcon, 1952.
The Big Fix. N.p., Falcon, 1952; as *So Nude, So Dead* (as Richard Marsten), New York, Fawcett, 1956.
Don't Crowd Me. New York, Popular Library, 1953; London, Consul, 1960; as *The Paradise Party*, London, New English Library, 1968.
The Blackboard Jungle. New York, Simon and Schuster, 1954; London, Constable, 1955.
Second Ending. New York, Simon and Schuster, and London, Constable, 1956; as *Quartet in H*, New York, Pocket Books, 1957.
Tomorrow's World. New York, Avalon, 1956; as *Tomorrow and Tomorrow*, New York, Pyramid, 1956; as Ed McBain, London, Sphere, 1979.
Strangers When We Meet. New York, Simon and Schuster, and London, Constable, 1958.
A Matter of Conviction. New York, Simon and Schuster, and London, Constable, 1959; as *The Young Savages*, New York, Pocket Books, 1966.
Mothers and Daughters. New York, Simon and Schuster, and London, Constable, 1961.
Buddwing. New York, Simon and Schuster, and London, Constable, 1964.
The Paper Dragon. New York, Delacorte Press, 1966; London, Constable, 1967.
A Horse's Head. New York, Delacorte Press, 1967; London, Constable, 1968.
Last Summer. New York, Doubleday, 1968; London, Constable, 1969.
Sons. New York, Doubleday, 1969; London, Constable, 1970.
Nobody Knew They Were There. New York, Doubleday, and London, Constable, 1971.

Every Little Crook and Nanny. New York, Doubleday, and London, Constable, 1972.
Come Winter. New York, Doubleday, and London, Constable, 1973.
Streets of Gold. New York, Harper, 1974; London, Macmillan, 1975.
The Chisholms: A Novel of the Journey West. New York, Harper, and London, Hamish Hamilton, 1976.
Walk Proud. New York, Bantam, 1979.
Love, Dad. New York, Crown, and London, Joseph, 1981.
Far from the Sea. New York, Atheneum, and London, Hamish Hamilton, 1983.
Lizzie. New York, Arbor House, and Hamish Hamilton, 1984.
Criminal Conversation. New York, Warner Books, 1994.
Privileged Conversation. New York, Warner Books, 1996.

Novels as Richard Marsten

Runaway Black. New York, Fawcett, 1954; London, Red Seal, 1957.
Murder in the Navy. New York, Fawcett, 1955; as *Death of a Nurse* (as Ed McBain), New York, Pocket Books, 1968; London, Hodder and Stoughton, 1972.
The Spiked Heel. New York, Holt, 1956; London, Constable, 1957.
Vanishing Ladies. New York, Permabooks, 1957; London, Boardman, 1961.
Even the Wicked. New York, Permabooks, 1958; as Ed McBain, London, Severn House, 1979.
Big Man. New York, Pocket Books, 1959; as Ed McBain, London, Penguin, 1978.

Short Stories as Ed McBain

I Like 'em Tough (as Curt Cannon). New York, Fawcett, 1958.
The Empty Hours (87th Precinct). New York, Simon and Schuster, 1962; London, Boardman, 1963.
The McBain Brief. London, Hamish Hamilton, 1982; New York, Arbor House, 1983.
McBain's Ladies: The Women of the 87th Precinct. New York, Mysterious Press, and London, Hamish Hamilton, 1988.
McBain's Ladies Too. New York, Mysterious Press, 1989; London, Hamish Hamilton, 1990.

Short Stories as Evan Hunter

The Jungle Kids. New York, Pocket Books, 1956.
The Last Spin and Other Stories. London, Constable, 1960.
Happy New Year, Herbie, and Other Stories. New York, Simon and Schuster, 1963; London, Constable, 1965.
The Beheading and Other Stories. London, Constable, 1971.
The Easter Man (a Play) and Six Stories. New York, Doubleday, 1972; as *Seven,* London, Constable, 1972.

Plays as Evan Hunter

The Easter Man (produced Birmingham and London, 1964; as *A Race of Hairy Men,* produced New York, 1965). Included in *The Easter Man (a Play) and Six Stories,* 1972.
The Conjuror (produced Ann Arbor, Michigan, 1969).

Screenplays: *Strangers When We Meet,* 1960; *The Birds,* 1963; *Fuzz,* 1972; *Walk Proud,* 1979.

Television Plays: *Appointment at Eleven* (*Alfred Hitchcock Presents* series), 1955-61; *The Chisholms* series, from his own novel, 1978-79.

Other as Evan Hunter

Find the Feathered Serpent (for children). Philadelphia, Winston, 1952.
Rocket to Luna (for children; as Richard Marsten). Philadelphia, Winston, 1952; London, Hutchinson, 1954.
Danger: Dinosaurs! (for children; as Richard Marsten). Philadelphia, Winston, 1953.
The Remarkable Harry. New York and London, Abelard Schuman, 1961.
The Wonderful Button. New York, Abelard Schuman, 1961; London, Abelard Schuman, 1962.
Me and Mr. Stenner. Philadelphia, Lippincott, 1976; London, Hamish Hamilton, 1977.

Editor (as Ed McBain), *Crime Squad.* London, New English Library, 1968.
Editor (as Ed McBain), *Homicide Department.* London, New English Library, 1968.
Editor (as Ed McBain), *Downpour.* London, New English Library, 1969.
Editor (as Ed McBain), *Ticket to Death.* London, New English Library, 1969.

*

Media Adaptations: Films—*High and Low* (Japanese), 1962, from the novel *King's Ransom*; *Fuzz,* 1972, from the novel; *Without Apparent Motive* (French), 1972, from the novel *Ten Plus One*; *Blood Relatives* (French-Canadian), 1978, from the novel.

Manuscript Collection: Mugar Memorial Library, Boston University.

* * *

Prolific author of nearly 50 87th Precinct novels, in addition to other books and short stories, Ed McBain is famous for realistic police procedurals and thrillers. He was awarded the Edgar Allan Poe Award in 1957 and a Grand Masters Award in 1986. His short, fast-moving stories contain little background description, but an array of credible characters and a close-knit team of police detectives dealing with the aftermath of violence to solve crimes and protect citizens. Born Evan Hunter, McBain has written under different pseudonyms (Curt Cannon, Hunt Collins, Ezra Hannon, and Richard Marsten). All of his stories, though, capture the daily frustrations of those involved in making the justice system work, and his description of police methods is precise, convincing, and thorough. His police are hunter-trackers, with keen instincts for the chase and a street-wise intuition that takes over where procedure leaves off. McBain's classic police novels are tough and realistic but tempered by humor, irony and compassion.

As police procedurals, the 87th Precinct novels often follow several ongoing criminal investigations, some interrelated, most not. A number of investigators (as many as seventeen) are led by Senior Police Detective Steve Carella, a tall, athletic Italian of Jewish ancestry, whose courtship of and marriage to a beautiful deaf-mute, Teddy, adds romantic interest. These investigators approach the crime from different directions and perspectives that round out the picture. From the discovery of a crime or a corpse, the narrative follows such routine procedures as the meticulous gathering of scene-of-the-crime evidence, the finding and interviewing of witnesses, the consultation of experts, and the study of forensic reports. The witnesses may range from prostitutes and street people to nosy neighbors, observant children, or cops on the beat—with some readily forthcoming, others reticent, even recalcitrant—so detectives must rely on instinct and human psychology to judge reliability and pry from them details that might otherwise be missed. McBain's detectives are always driven to understand the criminals' motives and compulsions. Their methodology provides a detached, clinical anatomy of violence underscored by terse, economical prose.

Efficiency and routine reduce the irrational and the violent to the manageable and provide the involved officers a distance from the crime, though on rare occasion one or more are personally involved with victim or perpetrator. Carella balances cold intelligence with humanity to guide a team that is slowly developed during the series with personal characteristics and experiences that pile up and are humanized by recurring patterns (jokes about Meyer Meyer's name and toupee, and stories of his embattled childhood; Cotton Hayes' puritanical diatribes and scathing social commentary; rookie Bert Kling's bad-luck women; Dick Genero's stupid blundering).

The novels often end with the final capture and booking of the perpetrator, though sometimes chance takes over and justice is served by other means. The Precinct novels are chronological and linked, with the same set of key personalities recurring. Occasionally, a case like that of the elusive criminal genius, the Deaf Man (*The Heckler* [1962]; *Fuzz* [1968]; *Let's Hear It for the Deaf Man* [1972]) frustrates and puzzles the Precinct investigative team over a number of novels. Among other popular McBain works are: *Ghost* (1980), a Christmas story; *Lullaby* (1990), a witty, suspenseful New Year's tale; and *Vespers* (1991), which is a bizarre and horrifying investigation of the butchering of a troubled priest in his own church.

In a number of books McBain experiments with plot to recapture the freshness and excitement that a predictable pattern can sometimes undercut. *He Who Hesitates* (1965), for example, is told through the eyes of the murderer and police activity is peripheral, while *Downtown* (1989) is from the perspective of the victim (an out-of-towner who is taken repeatedly by urban con artists). The *Killer's Wedge* (1961) alternates between a locked-room mystery and a precinct held hostage with nitroglycerine, while *Hail, Hail, The Gang's All Here* (1971) juggles multiple story lines. In contrast, the Attorney Matthew Hope novels provide a new perspective and a new setting that effectively captures Florida's sleaziness. Hope is a divorce lawyer whose sexual entanglements lead to trouble—a murdered rock star in *Rumpelstiltskin* (1961) and a paranoid schizophrenic in *Snow White and Red Rose* (1985).

However, McBain does not write only about crime. The first novel to bring him success, *The Blackboard Jungle* (1954), grew out of his experiences as a substitute teacher in New York vocational schools; it proffers a tough, scary picture of a devoted teacher's attempts to make attendance at an anarchical New York City high school a genuine educational experience. *Second Ending* (1956) warned of the effects of drug addiction. Furthermore, McBain has tried a number of genres, writing short stories, plays, teleplays, and screenplays (including "The Birds," 1963), as well as editing texts. His children's books range from stories about dinosaurs to rocketry and Aztecs.

—Gina Macdonald

McCAFFREY, Anne

Nationality: Irish (originally American). **Born:** Cambridge, Massachusetts, 1 April 1926. **Education:** Stuart Hall, Staunton, Virginia; Montclair High School, New Jersey; Radcliffe College, Cambridge, Massachusetts, B.A. (cum laude) in Slavonic languages and literature 1947; studied meteorology at City of Dublin University. **Family:** Married E. Wright Johnson in 1950 (divorced 1970); two sons and one daughter. **Career:** Copywriter and layout designer, Liberty Music Shops, New York, 1948-50; copywriter, Helena Rubinstein, New York, 1950-52. Currently runs a thoroughbred horse stud farm in Ireland; since 1978, director, Dragonhold Ltd., and since 1979, director, Fin Film Productions. Has performed in and directed several operas and musical comedies in Wilmington and Greenville, Delaware. Secretary-Treasurer, Science Fiction Writers of America, 1968-70. **Awards:** Hugo award, 1968, 1979; Nebula award, 1968; Gandalf award, 1979; Balrog award, 1980. **Member:** Authors' Guild; SFWA. **Agent:** Virginia Kidd, Box 278, Milford, Pennsylvania 18337, U.S.A. **Address:** Dragonhold, Kilquade, Greystones, County Wicklow, Ireland.

Publications

Novels (series: Doona; Dragonriders of Pern; Ireta; Killashandra; Pegasus; Pern; Harper Hall; Planet Pirate; Power; Rowan; The Ship)

Restoree. New York, Ballantine, 1967; London, Rapp and Whiting, 1968.

Dragonflight (Dragonrider). New York, Ballantine, 1968; London, Rapp and Whiting, 1969.

Decision at Doona. New York, Ballantine, 1969; London, Rapp and Whiting, 1970.

Dragonquest (Dragonrider). New York, Ballantine, 1971; London, Rapp and Whiting-Deutsch, 1973.

The Mark of Merlin. New York, Dell, 1971; London, Millington, 1977.

Ring of Fear. New York, Dell, 1971; London, Millington, 1979.

The Kilternan Legacy. New York, Dell, 1975; London, Millington, 1976.

Dragonsong (for children; Harper Hall). New York, Atheneum, and London, Sidgwick and Jackson, 1976.

Dragonsinger (for children; Harper Hall). New York, Atheneum, and London, Sidgwick and Jackson, 1977.

The White Dragon (Dragonrider). New York, Ballantine, 1978; London, Sidgwick and Jackson, 1979.

The Dragonriders of Pern (omnibus). Garden City, New York, Doubleday, 1978.

Dragondrums (for children; Harper Hall). New York, Atheneum, and London, Sidgwick and Jackson, 1979.

Crystal Singer (Killashandra). New York, Ballantine, and London, Severn House, 1982.
The Coelura (Pern). Lancaster, Pennsylvania, Underwood-Miller, 1983.
Moreta, Dragonlady of Pern. New York, Ballantine, and London, Severn House, 1983.
The Harper Hall of Pern (omnibus). Garden City, New York, Doubleday, 1984.
Stitch in Snow. San Francisco, Brandywine, 1984; London, Corgi, 1985.
The Ireta Adventure. Garden City, New York, Doubleday, 1985.
Dinosaur Planet. London, Orbit, and New York, Ballantine, 1978.
Dinosaur Planet Survivors. New York, Ballantine, and London, Futura, 1984.
Killashandra. New York, Ballantine, 1985; London, Bantam, 1986.
Nerilka's Story (Dragonrider). New York, Ballantine, 1986.
The Year of the Lucy. San Francisco, Brandywine, 1986; London, Corgi, 1987.
The Lady. New York, Ballantine, 1987; as *The Carradyne Touch,* London, Macdonald, 1988.
Dragonsdawn (Pern). Norwalk, Connecticut, Easton Press, and London, Bantam, 1988.
The Renegades of Pern. New York, Ballantine, 1989; London, Bantam, 1990.
Sassinak (Planet Pirate), with Elizabeth Moon. New York, Baen, 1990; London, Orbit, 1991.
The Death of Sleep (Planet Pirate), with Jody Lynn Nye. New York, Baen, 1990; London, Orbit, 1991.
Pegasus in Flight. New York, Ballantine, and London, Bantam, 1990.
The Rowan. New York, Ace, and London, Bantam, 1990.
Three Gothic Novels. Lancaster, Pennsylvania, Underwood-Miller, 1990; as *Three Women,* New York, Tor, 1992.
Generation Warriors (Planet Pirate), with Elizabeth Moon. New York, Baen, 1991; London, Orbit, 1992.
The Wings of Pegasus (omnibus). New York, Guild America, 1991.
Rescue Run. Newark, New Jersey, Wildside Press, 1991.
All the Weyrs of Pern. New York, Ballantine, 1991.
PartnerShip (The Ship), with Margaret Ball. Riverdale, New York, Baen, 1992; London, Orbit, 1994.
Crystal Line (Killashandra). New York, Ballantine, and London, Bantam, 1992.
Damia (Rowan). London, Bantam, and New York, Putnam, 1992.
Crisis on Doona, with Jody Lynn Nye. New York, Ace, 1992; London, Orbit, 1993.
The Ship Who Searched, with Mercedes Lackey. Riverdale, New York, Baen, 1992; London, Orbit, 1994.
The City Who Fought (The Ship), with S. M. Stirling. Riverdale, New York, Baen, 1993; London, Orbit, 1995.
Damia's Children (Rowan). New York, Ace/Punam, and London, Bantam, 1993.
Powers That Be, with Elizabeth Ann Scarborough. New York, Ballantine, and London, Bantam, 1993.
The Planet Pirate, with Elizabeth Moon and Jody Lynn Nye (omnibus). Riverdale, New York, Baen, 1993.
The Ship Who Won, with Jody Lynn Nye. Riverdale, New York, Baen, 1994.
Power Lines, with Elizabeth Ann Scarborough. London, Bantam, and New York, Ballantine, 1994.
Treaty Planet (Doona), with Jody Lynn Nye. London, Orbit, 1994; as *Treaty at Doona,* New York, Ace, 1994.
The Dolphins of Pern. New York, Ballantine, and London, Bantam, 1994.
Lyon's Pride (Rowan). New York, Ace/Putnam, and London, Bantam, 1994.
A Diversity of Dragons (for children). New York, Simon and Schuster, 1995.
Freedom's Landing. New York, Ace/Putnam, 1995.
Power Play, with Elizabeth Ann Scarborough. London, Bantam, and New York, Ballantine, 1995.

Short Stories

The Ship Who Sang. New York, Walker, 1969; London, Rapp and Whiting, 1971.
To Ride Pegasus. New York, Ballantine, 1973; London, Dent, 1974.
A Time When. Cambridge, Massachusetts, NESFA Press, 1975.
Get off the Unicorn. New York, Ballantine, 1977; London, Corgi, 1979.
The Worlds of Anne McCaffrey. London, Deutsch, 1981.
The Girl Who Heard Dragons (for children). New Castle, Virginia, Cheap Street, 1985.
Habit Is an Old Horse. Seattle, Washington, Dryad Press, 1986.
The Dolphins' Bell (Pern). Newark, New Jersey, Wildside Press, 1993.
The Chronicles of Pern: First Fall. Norwalk, Connecticut, Easton Press, and London, Bantam, 1993.
The Girl Who Heard Dragons (collection). New York, Tor, 1994.
An Exchange of Gifts (for children). Newark, New Jersey, Wildside Press, 1995.

Other

The Dragonlover's Guide to Pern, with Jody Lynn Nye. New York, Ballantine, 1989.

Editor, *Alchemy and Academe: A Collection of Original Stories Concerning Themselves with Transmutations, Mental and Elemental, Alchemical and Academic.* Garden City, New York, Doubleday, 1970.
Editor, *Cooking out of This World.* New York, Ballantine, 1973.

*

Bibliography: *Leigh Brackett, Marion Zimmer Bradley, Anne McCaffrey: A Primary and Secondary Bibliography* by Rosemarie Arbur, Boston, Hall, 1982.

Critical Studies: *Anne McCaffrey* by Mary T. Brizzi, Mercer Island, Washington, Starmont, 1986; *Anne McCaffrey: A Critical Companion* by Robin Roberts, Westport, Connecticut, Greenwood, 1996.

Manuscript Collections: Syracuse University, New York; Kerlan Collection, University of Minnesota, Minneapolis.

* * *

Award-winning author Anne McCaffrey has written more than 40 novels, short-story collections, and other manuscripts since her first publication in the 1960s. Creator of the world of Pern and the fantastic Dragonriders who protect the planet, she has been praised for her inventive combination of fantasy and science fiction and her imaginatively drawn heroes and heroines. According to James and Eugene Sloan in *Chicago Tribune Book World,* McCaffrey's Dragonrider books "must now rank as the most enduring serial in the history of science fantasy."

Like J. R. R. Tolkien's Middle-Earth and Ursula K. LeGuin's Earthsea, McCaffrey's Pern has gained a depth and significance far outweighing other fictional settings found in fantasy and science fiction. A former colony of Earth, Pern's knowledge of history and science has vanished into a murky past, replaced by a feudal society plagued by the Threads (deadly spores which fall from a neighboring planet). In order to survive this ecological menace, the human inhabitants of Pern have developed a symbiotic relationship with Pern's fire-breathing, telepathic dragons, each of which, at birth, selects a human partner to be its lifemate. The Dragonriders conjure up medieval images of knights riding to rescue their society; indeed, a hallmark of McCaffrey's world is that the technical elements generally found in science fiction take a back seat to the fantasy setting. This device has earned much praise from critics, including *New York Times Book Review* critic Gerald Jones: "Few are better at mixing elements of high fantasy and hard science in a narrative that disarms skepticism by its open embrace of the joys of wish fulfillment."

Dragonflight (1968), McCaffrey's first Dragonrider novel, won both the Hugo and Nebula awards in 1969 and enchanted readers with its introduction to Pern. *Dragonquest* (1971) finds the dragon population nearly extinct and the humans of Pern embroiled in a civil war. According to Edra C. Bogle in the *Dictionary of Literary Biography, Dragonquest* is "full of action and unexpected twists . . . [it] may be the best of these books. The major theme of all the volumes, how to rediscover and preserve the past while maintaining flexibility, is well brought out here." *Dragonsong* (1976) was praised for its characterization of the young girl Menolly and her struggle to find a place in the male-dominated society of the Dragonriders. *Dragonsdawn* (1988) reverted to a more science-fiction premise, describing the story of how the original colonists of Pern used genetic manipulation to develop the dragons.

One of McCaffrey's strengths as a writer is her social commentary, according to critics like Bogle. "Most of McCaffrey's protagonists are women or children, whom she treats with understanding and sympathy," Bogle says, pointing out that the social injustices the women suffer "are at the heart of most of McCaffrey's books." Most of McCaffrey's novels feature strong heroines, such as the Weyrwomen of the Dragonrider books, the talented psychics of *To Ride Pegasus* (1973), and Helva, the living brain of a starship in *The Ship Who Sang* (1969). With these books, Bogle indicates, "McCaffrey has brought delineations of active women into prominence in science fiction."

While her Dragonrider novels have received the most critical attention, McCaffrey's other novels have drawn praise as well. *The Ship Who Sang,* for example, was compared to Daniel Keyes' moving *Flowers for Algernon.* Likewise, *Get Off the Unicorn* (1977), a collection of short stories, was praised for its warmth and humor, especially in stories such as "Changeling," which deals with homosexual parenting, and "A Proper Santa Claus," which focuses on a small boy's ideal Santa.

The Dragonrider series has been alternately praised and criticized for its tight connections. While the cohesiveness of the novels gives life and further delineation to the world of Pern, many readers suggest that the novels do not stand alone without reading the previous books. Detractors have also criticized McCaffrey's episodic plots and repetition of characters and situations. However, McCaffrey's vision of Pern has sustained itself through over a dozen Dragonrider novels, and readers today should find Pern and its dragons fully accessible and entertaining.

—Christopher Swann

McCARTHY, Cormac

Nationality: American. **Born:** Charles McCarthy, in Providence, Rhode Island, 20 July 1933. **Education:** University of Tennessee. **Military Service:** United States Air Force, 1953-56. **Family:** Married 1) Lee Holman in 1961 (divorced), one child; 2) Anne de Lisle, 1967 (divorced). **Awards:** Ingram-Merrill Foundation grant for creative writing, 1960; William Faulkner Foundation award, 1965, for *The Orchard Keeper*; Rockefeller Foundation grant, 1966; MacArthur Foundation grant, 1981; National Book award, 1992, for *All the Pretty Horses*; Lyndhurst Foundation grant; Institute of Arts and Letters award. American Academy of Arts and Letters traveling fellowship to Europe, 1965-66; Guggenheim fellowship, 1976. **Agent:** Amanda Urban, International Creative Management, 40 West 57th Street, New York, New York 10019, U.S.A.

Publications

Novels

The Orchard Keeper. New York, Random House, 1965; London, Picador, 1994.
Outer Dark. New York, Random House, 1968; London, Picador, 1994.
Child of God. New York, Random House, 1974; London, Chatto and Windus, 1975.
Suttree. New York, Random House, 1979; London, Chatto and Windus, 1980.
Blood Meridian; or, The Evening Redness in the West. New York, Random House, 1985; London, Picador, 1989.
All the Pretty Horses. New York, Knopf, 1992; London, Picador, 1993.
The Crossing. New York, Knopf, and London, Picador, 1994.

Plays

The Stonemason: A Play in Five Acts. Hopewell, New Jersey, Ecco Press, 1994.

Television Play: *The Gardener's Son,* 1977.

*

Critical Studies: *The Achievement of Cormac McCarthy* by Vereen M. Bell, Baton Rouge, Louisiana State University Press, 1988; *Perspectives on Cormac McCarthy* edited by Edwin T. Arnold and Dianne C. Luce, Jackson, University Press of Mississippi, 1993; *Notes on "Blood Meridian"* by John Sepich, Louisville, Kentucky, Bellarmine College Press, 1993.

* * *

Author of seven novels, Cormac McCarthy received little public recognition for his works until his sixth novel, *All the Pretty Horses* (1992), which won both the National Book Award and the National Book Critics Circle Award. His earlier novels are considered Southern Gothic in the tradition of William Faulkner and Flannery O'Connor, with Appalachian settings and dark, brutal stories. In contrast, his most recent novels are set in the American Southwest and Mexico, and focus on boy-heroes undertaking various quests. All of his novels reflect a largely pessimistic world view and a vision of society reduced to primitive levels, yet his characters struggle towards some kind of redemption.

Readers of McCarthy's early novels often find them full of violence and grotesque characters. *Outer Dark* (1968), for example, deals with Culla and Rinthy Holme, a pair of incestuous siblings. Similarly, *Child of God* (1974) is the story of Lester Ballard and his decline into murder and necrophilia. In *Suttree* (1979), however, the protagonist Suttree undergoes both a fall and an ascent. Rejecting his wealthy family, he lives among the Knoxville degenerates on the river bank, yet in the end undergoes a spiritual rejuvenation and reconciles with his family.

Blood Meridian (1985), a departure from McCarthy's Southern tales, parodies the stereotypical western film by exaggerating it with extreme lawlessness and gore. While the novel received critical praise, it drew criticism for its over-the-top scenes of violence (including a long description of a beheading) and was seen largely as a failure to retell convincingly a western tale in McCarthy's dark voice.

All the Pretty Horses, the first of McCarthy's *Border Trilogy,* departed from the gore of *Blood Meridian* and became an overnight success. It is the story of John Grady Cole, a sixteen-year-old who in 1949 finds himself the last of a generation of west-Texas ranchers. With the death of his grandfather, John Grady leaves the ranch with his friend Lacey Rawlins and rides to Mexico. There, he and Rawlins encounter Jimmy Blevins, a comic and loveable figure who embroils them in horse-thieving, prison, and the eventual death of one of the three boys. A romantic subplot involving John Grady and the beautiful daughter of a wealthy Mexican rancher is also new territory for McCarthy. *All the Pretty Horses* won wide acclaim for its style, scope and prose. *Publishers Weekly* proclaimed of the novel that "one searches in vain for comparisons in American literature."

The Crossing (1994) is a darker work that combines the lyricism of *All the Pretty Horses* with the ugly brutality of earlier works like *Outer Dark.* While it follows *All the Pretty Horses* as volume two of the *Border Trilogy,* it has no clear connection with the previous novel other than in its similar hero and settings. In the years before World War II, young Billy Parham sets out to trap a murderous wolf in the New Mexico wilderness. Although the old trappers and their wisdom have vanished into the past, Billy eventually captures the she-wolf, one of the last of her kind, and moves to release it in the mountains of Mexico. He returns home to find his parents have been murdered, and sets out with his brother Boyd to claim revenge. Their personal odyssey carries them again through Mexico, where they experience a vast range of encounters and conflicts with bandits, pilgrims, revolutionaries, and a young girl alone on the road, all of which lead ultimately to their separate fates. More tragic than *All the Pretty Horses, The Crossing* contains a plot that moves in ever-widening circles until its focus becomes obscured. However, Billy Parham continues the McCarthy tradition of heroism embodied in adolescence and signals a possible third young hero in the projected conclusion of the *Border Trilogy.*

McCarthy's prose is his greatest strength, inviting comparison with Melville and Faulkner for its poetic imagery, biblical grandeur, and treatment of the animal world. Of McCarthy's descriptive writing, the citation for the National Book Award read in part: "Not until now has the unhuman world been given its own canon, and never has landscape been so purely and heartbreakingly evoked."

Many readers may be initially discouraged by the density and darkness of McCarthy's prose. "The style comes out of the place, material, characters, etc.," says McCarthy, who argues that his stories demand the kind of writing he produces. Nevertheless, at the heart of his better novels lie stories that are epic in scope and ring clear and true in a reader's ear.

—Christopher Swann

McCULLOUGH, Colleen

Nationality: Australian. **Born:** c.1938 in Wellington, New South Wales. **Education:** Attended University of Sydney. **Family:** Married Ric Robinson in 1984. **Career:** Worked as a teacher, a library worker, and a bus driver in Australia's Outback; journalist; Yale University, School of Internal Medicine, New Haven, Connecticut, associate in research neurology department, 1967-76; writer, 1976-. **Agent:** Frieda Fishbein Ltd., 353 West 57th St., New York, New York 10019, U.S.A.

Publications

Novels

Tim. Harper, 1974.
The Thorn Birds. Harper, 1977.
An Indecent Obsession. Harper, 1981.
A Creed for the Third Millennium. Harper, 1985.
The Ladies of Missalonghi. Harper, 1987.
The First Man in Rome. Morrow, 1990.
The Grass Crown. Morrow, 1991.
Fortune's Favorites. Morrow, 1993.

Other

An Australian Cookbook, Harper, 1982.

*

Media Adaptations: Film—*Tim,* 1981. Television miniseries—*The Thorn Birds,* 1983.

* * *

Born in New Zealand, Colleen McCullough moved to Sydney, Australia, at an early age and later spent ten years working in the Yale School of Medicine. Since her commercial success she has chosen to live on Norfolk Island. Her first novel, *Tim* (1974), concerns the developing relationship between a mentally retarded but physically beautiful young man and a love-shy, plain, middle-aged spinster who risks social disapproval to follow her heart's desires.

However, it was with her second novel, *The Thorn Birds* (1977), that she became a bestseller (more than ten million copies) and instant millionaire. This sprawling saga tells the story of the Cleary family between 1915 and 1969 as they move from New Zealand to New South Wales, with additional forays into other parts of the world. In particular it is the story of the feisty Meg Cleary, who falls in love with handsome Father de Bricassart, who is "put together with a degree of care about the appearance of the finished product God lavished on few of His Creatures." The theme of the novel is pain and the relationship between pain and virtue. Its title comes from "the old Celtic legend of the bird with the thorn in its breast, singing its heart out and dying." Because it has to, it is driven to: "We can know what we do wrong even before we do it, but self-knowledge can't affect or change the outcome, can it?" But in the novel's confused code of ethics it is never clear whether pain is inflicted by God or by the self. Nor does it seem to matter much.

An Indecent Obsession (1981) is set in Ward X of a psychiatric hospital in the south Pacific near the end of WWII. It is the story of Sister Honour Langtry and her testy charges, one of whom she finally marries. Langtry is in the R.D. Laingian tradition of psychotherapy, believing that not one of the men in the ward really deserves to be there. McCullough says that one reason she wrote it was that she wanted to write about a woman who was in charge of a group of men.

McCullough describes *A Creed for the Third Millennium* (1985) as "a political thriller with religious overtones." But it is actually in the dystopian tradition of fiction, which is surprisingly common in Australia. Set in the United States in the year 2032, it depicts a society run by faceless bureaucrats and marked by frequent suicides, an approaching ice age, and families limited to one child each. Into this world comes a newly manufactured Messiah, Dr. Joshua Christian, accompanied by his own personal Judas, the elegant Dr Judith Carriol. Amidst the anguish, the doomed Dr. Christian offers his creed for the third millennium, one of faith, hope, and love. In modernizing the New Testament, the author has done what she says Dr. Joshua tries to do: "to ruminate some particularly knotty concept into smooth mental paste."

Publication of *The Ladies of Missalonghi* (1987) provoked accusations that the novel had been plagiarized from Lucy Maud Montgomery's *Blue Castle.* Set in the Blue Mountains of New South Wales early this century, the novel's familiar heroine is Missy Wright, who persuades a man to marry her by convincing him that she will die within a year. As McCullough has pointed out, four of her first five novels have unmarried women as heroines or villains. However, McCullough fails to heed her hero's warning to "go easy on the soap."

Each of the novels to this point had been a new venture, with the author determined not to repeat herself. In 1990, she embarked on a sextet of carefully researched novels into the Roman empire between the period 110 and 27 BC. The novels are scrupulously researched (by an assistant) and atrociously written. *The First Man in Rome* (1990) traces the rivalry of two men, Lucius Cornelius Sulla and Gaius Marius, for the unfilled, eponymous position. It is filled with action, but the Roman names (which are even more distracting than Russian patronyms), combined with a prose that alternates suet-like exposition with colorful flights of metaphor, makes it hard going. It was followed by a mammoth sequel, *The Grass Crown* (1990), involving huge doses of rapine and battle in the period 99 to 86 BC. It is so dull that one reviewer suggested that for her next work McCullough should do the research and have her assistant write the novel.

—Laurie Clancy

McGINNISS, Joe

Nationality: American. **Born:** New York City, 9 December 1942. **Education:** Holy Cross College, B.S., 1964. **Family:** Married 1) Christine Cooke in 1965 (divorced), two daughters, one son; 2) Nancy Doherty in 1976, two sons. **Career:** Port Chester Daily Item, Port Chester, New York, reporter, 1964; Worcester Telegram, Worcester, Massachusetts, reporter, 1965; Philadelphia Bulletin, reporter, 1966; Philadelphia Inquirer, columnist, 1967-68; free-lance writer since 1968. Lecturer in writing at Bennington College. **Agent:** Morton L. Janklow, 598 Madison Ave., New York, New York, 10022, U.S.A.

Publications

Nonfiction

The Selling of the President, 1968. Trident, 1969.
Heroes. Viking, 1976.
Going to Extremes. Knopf, 1980.
Fatal Vision. Putnam, 1983.
Blind Faith. Putnam, 1988.
Cruel Doubt. Simon & Schuster, 1991.
The Last Brother. Simon & Schuster, 1993.

Novel

The Dream Team. Random House, 1972.

*

Media Adaptations: Television miniseries—*Fatal Vision,* 1984.

* * *

With the publication of his *Selling of the President, 1968* (1969), Joe McGinniss became at age 26 perhaps the youngest American writer ever to claim a national nonfiction title on the bestseller lists. Chronicling the strategies and personalities behind the marketing campaign that helped elect Richard Nixon president, McGinniss focused on the staging of the campaign's TV commercials and publicity events and graphically documented the behind-the-scenes machinations of American presidential elections. *The Selling of the President* topped bestseller lists for seven months and won universal critical praise. *Christian Century* typified American reviews in sounding a note of alarm over the book's startling insights, declaring: "At times this book will scare you." Since the publication of his first book, McGinniss has continued to publish nonfiction explorations of the American dream gone awry, as well as one notably unsuccessful foray into fiction with the novel *The Dream Team.*

In 1976 McGinniss published *Heroes,* in which he interwove reflections on the drinking and marital infidelity arising from his struggles with his early success in a quest to determine if heroism still exists in contemporary America. Interviewing Eugene McCarthy, William Styron, William F. Buckley Jr., and William Westmoreland, among others, McGinniss decides that heroism is impossible today because "there were no heroic acts left to perform." The *New York Times* found *Heroes* an "interesting" book by a "crisp, professional writer," but *Atlantic Monthly* called it "a fascinating disaster," and the *Washington Post* faulted McGinnis for foisting a flawed definition of heroism on his interviewees.

McGinniss's next work was *Going to Extremes* (1980), a travelogue/narrative of the two years he spent exploring Alaska's geography and interviewing the pioneering souls who populate it. In the state's odd assortment of personalities McGinniss discovers that "the boundaries within which the normal range of human activity occurred had been . . . not just extended, but removed." *Time* celebrated *Going to Extremes* as a "poignant, hilarious, and beautifully modulated account"; the *New Republic* praised McGinniss for "succeeding well in capturing Alaska"; and the *New York Times* declared it an insightful success.

If McGinniss had been troubled by his inability to recapture the success of *The Selling of the President,* his next three books established him as perhaps the nation's most bankable craftsman of "true-life crime" narratives. In *Fatal Vision,* McGinniss chronicled the case of Dr. Jeffrey MacDonald, who after murdering his wife and two daughters exploited his reputation to gain acquittal, only to be retried, eventually convicted, and then jailed 13 years after the crime. Although McGinniss was initially engaged by MacDonald to write a book that McDonald thought would exonerate him, McGinniss discovered that the evidence pointed to unquestionable guilt, and thus *Fatal Vision* traced not only the details of the crime and the trial but McGinniss's own journey of personal revelation.

In *Blind Faith* (1989), McGinniss used the same technique to narrate the story of the murder of a New Jersey woman by her husband, who, involved with another woman, sought his wife's life insurance policy. McGinniss also feelingly explored the anguish of the couple's two sons who believed until their father's confession that he was innocent. Two years later, McGinniss produced *Cruel Doubt* (1991), which narrated the murder of a North Carolina man by his son, who on the night of the crime had also unsuccessfully tried to kill his mother in order to gain her $2 million fortune. *Fatal Vision* was generally well received by critics, though some complained of McGinniss' over-reliance on extended quotations from trial transcripts. *Blind Faith* and *Cruel Doubt* were also generally seen as absorbing and affecting stories, but with each book the reviews grew less enthusiastic, suggesting that McGinniss's formula and material were wearing thin.

In 1993 McGinniss gained enormous but unwelcome publicity when his rumination-cum-biography of Senator Ted Kennedy, *The Last Brother,* was greeted by overwhelming critical disdain. By deciding to relate Kennedy's life in part through a novelistic—and thoroughly imagined—creation of Kennedy's supposed thoughts, McGinniss, many critics felt, had crossed the bounds of reasonable biographical practice and had exacerbated the issue by failing to provide any new information on Kennedy's life and, worse, some claimed, plagiarizing from others. *Time* magazine rated it the "worst" book of 1993, and Jonathan Yardley of the *Washington Post* claimed it was the worst book he had encountered in three decades of reviewing.

—Paul S. Bodine

McINERNEY, Jay

Nationality: American. **Born:** Hartford, Connecticut, 13 January 1955. **Education:** Williams College, Williamstown, Massachusetts, B.A. 1976; Syracuse University, New York. **Family:** Married Merry Reymond in 1984. **Career:** Reporter, Hunterdon *Country Democrat*, Flemington, New Jersey, 1977; editor, *Time-Life*, Osaka, Japan, 1978-79; fact checker, *New Yorker*, 1980; reader, Random House, publishers, New York, 1980-81; instructor in English, Syracuse University, 1983. Since 1983 full-time writer. Lives in New York. **Agent:** Deborah Rogers, Rogers Coleridge and White Ltd., 20 Powis Mews, London W11 1JN, England; or, International Creative Management, 40 West 57th Street, New York, New York 10019, U.S.A.

Publications

Novels

Bright Lights, Big City. New York, Vintage, 1984; London, Cape, 1985.

Ransom. New York, Vintage, 1985; London, Cape, 1986.

Story of My Life. London, Bloomsbury, and New York, Atlantic Monthly Press, 1988.

Brightness Falls. New York, Knopf, 1992; London, Penguin, 1993.

Uncollected Short Stories

"The Real Tad Allagash," in *Ms.* (New York), August 1985.

"It's Six a.m. Do You Know Where You Are?," in *Look Who's Talking*, edited by Bruce Weber. New York, Washington Square Press, 1986.

"Reunion," in *Esquire* (New York), March 1987.

"Smoke," in *Atlantic* (Boston), March 1987.

"She Dreams of Johnny," in *Gentlemen's Quarterly* (New York), March 1988.

"Lost and Found," in *Esquire* (New York), July 1988.

Other

Editor, *Cowboys, Indians and Commuters.* London, Viking, 1994.

*

Critical Study: "You Will Have to Learn Everything All Over Again" by Richard Sisk, in *Pacific Review*, Spring 1988.

* * *

Jay McInerney's wildly successful debut, *Bright Lights, Big City* (1984), was a funny and affecting coming-of-age novel about a troubled young New Yorker struggling with his career, drugs, a failed marriage, and the death of his mother. It was distinguished by McInerney's use of second-person singular narration (e.g., "You are at a nightclub talking to a girl with a shaved head"), and his dramatization of his experiences as a fact checker at *New Yorker* magazine. The novel was greeted warmly by critics, who praised McInerney's "expertly polished" style, "spectacularly effective" use of the second person, and "cynical, deadpan, and right-on-target" humor. Some critics, however, faulted the novel for its trendiness, slightness, "increasingly irritating" use of the second-person narrative voice, and unconvincing rendering of the central scene of the mother's death.

In his second novel, *Ransom* (1985), McInerney told the story of Chris Ransom, a young American expatriate teaching English in Osaka, Japan, while immersing himself in the culture of karate. As in *Bright Lights,* McInerney's protagonist is burdened by his family—his interfering TV-producer father who Ransom blames for his mother's death—and his friends, drug smugglers who meet an inglorious end in Pakistan. Ransom looks to the austerities of karate to free him from his past and the sense of unreality he sees in other people's lives, and attempts to evade the provocations of another American karate student who resents him for his privileged upbringing. Some reviewers praised *Ransom* as "wittier and more complex" than *Bright Lights,* but others criticized McInerney for failing to create substantial characters, "trivializing" his story through distracting comic asides, and contriving an oversignificant ending that is "breathtakingly wrong" for the novel.

In *Story of My Life* (1988) McInerney returned to the New York setting of *Bright Lights* in the first-person narrative of Alison Poole, a spoiled and vacuous party girl who pursues drugs, sex, and her own self-destruction with a bitterly comic abandon, fueled by her resentment of her father for killing her favorite horse for the insurance. Like *Ransom,* the novel was almost universally panned by critics. The reviewer for *New Statesman and Society,* for example, characterized it as "another slight tale of moneyed, Stateside dissolution," and the *New York Times Book Review* accused McInerney of "fail[ing] to develop his theme beyond a superficial level." Likewise, *Time* magazine described it as "a prodigal waste of talent." Some critics praised McInerney for successfully depicting a realistic feminine voice, but the consensus was that McInerney's third novel was "trivial" and "disappointing."

In writing his fourth novel, *Brightness Falls* (1992), McInerney recalled that "what was going through my head . . . was: What if [Tom Wolfe's] *Bonfire of the Vanities* had real people in it? . . . In this book I was to trying to wed the psychologically acute domestic fiction of minimalism with the social novels of the authors I've been reading in recent years: Balzac and Dickens, Trollope and Thackeray." The result was an ambitious social drama of a young book editor's attempts to pursue a leveraged buyout of his publishing company in the days before the stock market crash of 1987. Like Tom Wolfe's *Bonfire,* McInerney attempted a wide-ranging, realistic depiction of life in New York City but within a portrayal of the dynamics of the protagonist's marriage to a sensitive Wall Streeter and his friendship with a drug-addicted writer.

Critical opinion was mixed. Several reviewers argued that McInerney had attempted a sharp satire à la Tom Wolfe but did not have the necessary scorn for the satirized to bring it off, while others lamented the indistinctness of the novel's characters and McInerney's "lust for inclusiveness," which finally rendered the novel "overstuffed" and "melodramatic." At the same time, many critics praised *Brightness Falls* for its ambitious scope, "comic touch," "literary vigor," "crispness of dialogue, and "authentic writing." In particular, critic James Atlas claimed that *Brightness Falls* was "incredibly good, even profound. He's captured the spirit of New York in the eighties, and the characters, though comic, are portrayed with real generosity."

In 1992, *Vanity Fair* magazine called McInerney the "most celebrated writer under forty in America," yet McInerney's career has consistently been dogged by the extravagant success of his first novel and by critics' sense that he is writer of distinct and genuine talent who has never completely translated promise into accomplishment. He has been compared to Dorothy Parker, J. D. Salinger, and (perhaps inevitably) F. Scott Fitzgerald, whose elegant style, romanticism, and large themes have plainly influenced his fiction. McInerney's urbane comic flair, his themes of innocence lost or betrayed, and his eye for the "luminous details" of contemporary life have won him a highly visible if still uncertain place in contemporary American fiction.

—Paul S. Bodine

McMILLAN, Terry

Nationality: American. **Born:** 18 October 1951, in Port Huron, Michigan. **Education:** University of California, Berkeley, B.S., 1979; Columbia University, M.F.A., 1979. **Family:** One son, Solomon Welch. **Career:** University of Wyoming, Laramie, instructor, 1987-90; University of Arizona, Tucson, professor, 1990-92; writer. **Awards:** National Endowment for the Arts fellowship, 1988. **Agent:** Molly Friedrich, Aaron Priest Literary Agency, 122 East 42nd St., Suite 3902, New York, New York 10168. **Address:** Free at Last, P.O. Box 2408, Danville, California 94526, U.S.A.

Publications

Novels

Mama. Houghton, 1987.
Disappearing Acts. Viking, 1989.
Waiting to Exhale. Viking, 1992.
How Stella Got Her Groove Thing Back. Viking, 1995.

Editor, *Breaking Ice: An Anthology of Contemporary African-American Fiction.* Viking, 1990.

Contributor, *Five for Five: The Films of Spike Lee.* Stewart, Tabori, 1991.

* * *

Terry McMillan garnered fame with her novel *Waiting to Exhale* (1992), and her popularity was greatly augmented the success of the Whitney Houston film based on that novel. The novel takes the reader on a journey into the intimate lives of four African-American women coming to terms with adulthood, focusing in particular on relationships with lovers, parents, and husbands who are at times extremely trying, humiliating, and repressive. In fact, women of any color are represented by these four well-rounded and superbly developed female characters.

Among McMillan's many accomplishments is her acceptance into the MacDowell Colony in 1983, where she wrote the first draft of her first novel *Mama* (1987), her most autobiographical work. In *Mama,* McMillan defines and explores the tensions and frustrations of a poor African-American family in the 1960s and 1970s while celebrating the resilience and ingenuity of the central character, the strong-willed Mama of the title.

In *Disappearing Act* (1989), McMillan's second novel, she again touches her audience with tense and explosive emotions. The setting for this novel is Brooklyn during the early 1980s. The story is narrated by the two main characters, Zora and Franklin, who relate a tale of love and turmoil that placed McMillan in a landmark legal battle with her former living partner, who sued her for defamation of character. In creating Franklin, the male main character, McMillan wanted to create the voice of a deeply good person plagued with much anger. Her former living partner believed the male character was recognizably himself, and that the depiction was injurious. Fiction writers exhaled a sigh of relief when his claim was dismissed in court.

McMillan is a fascinating woman. After completing her first novel, she published the book and did the selling herself, writing bookstores and African-American organizations stating that she would do readings from her book if they would support her promotions. She was born in Port Huron, Michigan, to Edward McMillan and Madeline Washington, and was educated at Berkeley and Columbia. McMillan has been an instructor at the University of Wyoming and an Associate Professor at the University of Arizona. Not only does she tour extensively reading her works, but she teaches writing workshops nationally.

It is McMillan's strong maternal ties that give her the insight and courage necessary to explore the female psyche the way she does. She has been quoted as saying her mother is the strongest woman she has ever met in her life. From her early writings in *Black Thoughts,* a campus newspaper, it is easily seen how her strong mother-figure encouraged her to break out and find her voice. Other influences included Ishmael Reed, who gave her the courage to write, and the Harlem Writer's Guild, where people encouraged her to extend a short story into what became her first novel. From this encouragement and support grew an accomplished African-American female author who has published not only highly acclaimed fictional works but various critical essays as well.

—Tammy J. Bronson

McMURTRY, Larry (Jeff)

Nationality: American. **Born:** Wichita Falls, Texas, 3 June 1936. **Education:** Archer City High School, Texas, graduated 1954; North Texas State College, Denton, B.A. 1958; Rice University, Houston, 1954, 1958-60, M.A. 1960; Stanford University, California (Stegner fellow), 1960-61. **Family:** Married Josephine Scott in 1959 (divorced 1966); one son. **Career:** taught at Texas Christian University, Fort Worth, 1961-62, Rice University, 1963-64 and 1965, George Mason College, Fairfax, Virginia, 1970, and American University, Washington, D.C., 1970-71. Since 1971 owner, Booked Up Inc., antiquarian booksellers, Washington, D.C., Archer City, Texas, and Tucson, Arizona. Regular reviewer, Houston *Post*, 1960s, and Washington *Post*, 1970s; contributing editor, *American Film*, New York, 1975. President, PEN American Center, 1989. **Awards:** Guggenheim grant, 1964; Pulitzer prize, 1986. **Address:** Booked Up Inc., 2509 North Campbell Avenue, No. 95, Tucson, Arizona 85719, U.S.A.

Publications

Novels

Horseman, Pass By. New York, Harper, 1961; as *Hud,* New York, Popular Library, 1963; London, Sphere, 1971.
Leaving Cheyenne. New York, Harper, 1963; London, Sphere, 1972.
The Last Picture Show. New York, Dial Press, 1966; London, Sphere, 1972.
Moving On. New York, Simon & Schuster, 1970; London, Weidenfeld and Nicolson, 1971.
All My Friends Are Going to Be Strangers. New York, Simon & Schuster, 1972; London, Secker and Warburg, 1973.
Terms of Endearment. New York, Simon & Schuster, 1975; London, W.H. Allen, 1977.
Somebody's Darling. New York, Simon & Schuster, 1978.
Cadillac Jack. New York, Simon & Schuster, 1982.
The Desert Rose. New York, Simon & Schuster, 1983; London, W.H. Allen, 1985.
Lonesome Dove. New York, Simon & Schuster, 1985; London, Pan, 1986.
Texasville. New York, Simon & Schuster, and London, Sidgwick and Jackson, 1987.
Anything for Billy. New York, Simon & Schuster, 1988; London, Collins, 1989.
Some Can Whistle. New York, Simon & Schuster, 1989; London, Century, 1990.
Buffalo Girls. New York, Simon & Schuster, 1990; London, Century, 1991.
Pretty Boy Floyd, with Diana Ossana. New York, Simon & Schuster, 1994; London, Orion, 1995.
Dead Man's Walk. New York, Simon & Schuster, and London, Orion, 1995.
The Late Child. New York, Simon & Schuster, and London, Orion, 1995.

Uncollected Short Stories

"The Best Day Since," in *Avesta* (Denton, Texas), Fall 1956.
"Cowman," in *Avesta* (Denton, Texas), Spring 1957.
"Roll, Jordan, Roll," in *Avesta* (Denton, Texas), Fall 1957.
"A Fragment from Scarlet Ribbons," in *Coexistence Review* (Denton, Texas), vol. 1, no. 2, 1958(?).
"There Will Be Peace in Korea," in *Texas Quarterly* (Austin), Winter 1964.
"Dunlop Crashes In," in *Playboy* (Chicago), July 1975.

Play

Screenplay: *The Last Picture Show*, with Peter Bogdanovich, 1971.

Other

In a Narrow Grave: Essays on Texas. Austin, Texas, Encino Press, 1968.

It's Always We Rambled: An Essay on Rodeo. New York, Hallman, 1974.

Larry McMurtry: Unredeemed Dreams, edited by Dorey Schmidt. Edinburg, Texas, Pan American University, 1980.

Film Flam: Essays on Hollywood. New York, Simon & Schuster, 1987.

*

Manuscript Collection: University of Houston Library.

Critical Studies: *Larry McMurtry* by Thomas Landess, Austin, Texas, Steck Vaughn, 1969; *The Ghost Country: A Study of the Novels of Larry McMurtry* by Raymond L. Neinstein, Berkeley, California, Creative Arts, 1976; *Larry McMurtry* by Charles D. Peavy, Boston, Twayne, 1977; *Larry McMurtry's Texas: Evolution of a Myth* by Lera Patrick Tyler Lich, Austin, Texas, Eakin Press, 1987; *Taking Stock: A Larry McMurtry Casebook* edited by Clay Reynolds, Dallas, Southern Methodist University Press, 1989.

* * *

In his novels, Larry McMurtry draws upon his Texas background to create memorable characters and settings. Though McMurtry is not considered a great writer by critics—he sometimes sports a T-shirt reading, "Minor Regional Novelist"—the reputation of this inarguably entertaining writer continues to grow. "McMurty . . . has given a comical, elegiac view of America past and present," wrote John Gerlach.

McMurtry's first novel was *Horseman, Pass By* (1961), the basis for the popular Paul Newman movie *Hud.* As the narrator, Lonnie Bannon, comes of age, he finds several role models he can follow, among them his fun-worshipping step-uncle, Hud. Lonnie also has an intriguing relationship with Halmea, the black housekeeper, who to him is both a surrogate mother and an object of desire. Charles D. Peavy wrote in his book *Larry McMurtry* that McMurtry introduces in *Horseman* what would become a recurring theme: "the initiation into manhood and its inevitable corollaries—loneliness and loss of innocence."

Adolescent frustration is again borne in *The Last Picture Show* (1966), which director Peter Bogdanovich adapted into a successful movie. The smallness of the Texas town Thalia becomes oppressive to its adolescents, who begin to use sex as an outlet for their boredom and their loneliness. McMurtry patterned Thalia after his hometown and later regretted the bitterness with which he wrote *The Last Picture Show.* Thomas Lask described McMurtry's portrait of Thalia in the *New York Times*: "A sorrier place would be hard to find. It is dessicated and shabby physically, mean and small-minded spiritually. Mr. McMurtry is expert in anatomizing its suffocating and dead-end character."

In his "urban trilogy" of novels—*Moving On* (1970), *All My Friends Are Going to Be Strangers* (1972), and *Terms of Endearment* (1975), all set in Houston—McMurtry creates characters possessing cowboy spirits who, transplanted to the suburbs, engage in aimless pursuits across the country. These novels have not been well-received critically. Ernestine P. Sewell wrote that by focusing on "rootless, restless, directionless, city folk," McMurtry's novels too became meandering. Other critics were more appreciative, particularly of *Terms of Endearment,* which was made into an Academy Award-winning film. *Terms* follows the widow Aurora Greenway, her exploitation of her various "suitors," and her relationship to her married daughter Emma, who in the last quarter of the novel is dying of cancer. *New York Times* critic Christopher Lehmann-Haupt wrote: "One laughs at the slapstick, one weeps at the maudlin, and one likes all of Mr. McMurtry's characters, no matter how delicately or broadly they are drawn."

McMurtry strayed from Texas as a setting to write three critically panned novels known as the "trash trilogy": *Somebody's Darling* (1978), *Cadillac Jack* (1982), and *The Desert Rose* (1983), which were respectively set in Hollywood, Washington, and Las Vegas, "the most placeless places McMurtry could have picked," according to Gerlach. McMurtry returned to Texas as a setting for a trilogy of historical westerns—*Lonesome Dove* (1985), perhaps his best work; *Anything for Billy* (1988), and *Buffalo Girls* (1990)—that served to debunk the myths of the Old West. In *Lonesome Dove,* for which he was awarded the Pulitzer Prize for fiction, McMurtry relates the story of Woodrow Call and Augustus McCrae on a cattle drive, a well-used plot in old movie Westerns. *Lonesome Dove,* however, does not evoke that same romance. Nicholas Lemann wrote in the *New York Times Book Review*: "All of Mr. McMurtry's antimythic groundwork—his refusal to glorify the West—works to reinforce the strength of the traditionally mythic parts of *Lonesome Dove* by making it far more credible than the old familiar horse operas. . . . For now, for the Great Cowboy Novel, *Lonesome Dove* will have to do."

In recent years McMurtry has developed sequels to previous novels that have generally failed to please critics. The most successful of them, *Texasville* (1987), the sequel to *The Last Picture Show,* updates the characters from Thalia, who struck it rich in the Texas oil boom only to flail amidst their material possessions as the wells run dry. Though a funny book, *Texasville* was not satisfying to most critics. Louise Erdrich wrote in the *New York Times Book Review*: "In *The Last Picture Show,* the quest for love was not only for sex, but sex linked to tenderness and mystery, to love. In *Texasville* sex is just sex. It happens everywhere and often."

Because of how successfully McMurtry's books have translated to the screen, some critics contend that as McMurtry writes a novel he has its cinematic adaptation in mind. Julia Cameron wrote in the *Los Angeles Times Book Review*: "It is damning praise to be termed a 'cinematic' writer and McMurtry certainly is."

—Eric Patterson

McPHEE, John (Angus)

Nationality: American. **Born:** Princeton, New Jersey, 8 March 1931. **Education:** Princeton University, A.B., 1953; graduate study at Cambridge University, 1953-54. **Family:** Married Pryde Brown in 1957 (marriage ended), four daughters; married Yolanda Whitman in 1972; two stepsons, two stepdaughters. **Career:** Playwright for "Robert Montgomery Presents" television show, 1955-57; *Time* magazine, New York City, associate editor, 1957-64; New

Yorker magazine, New York City, staff writer, 1964—; Princeton University, Princeton, New Jersey, Ferris Professor of Journalism, 1975—. **Awards:** Award in Literature, American Academy and Institute of Arts and Letters, 1977; American Association of Petroleum Geologists Journalism award, 1982, 1986; Woodrow Wilson award, Princeton University, 1982; John Wesley Powell award, United States Geological Survey, 1988; John Burroughs Medal, 1990; Walton Sullivan award, American Geophysical Union, 1993; Litt.D., Bates College, 1978, Colby College, 1978, Williams College, 1979, University of Alaska, 1980, College of William and Mary, 1988, and Sc.D. Rutgers University, 1988, and Maine Maritime Academy, 1992. **Member:** Geological Society of America (fellow). **Address:** c/o Farrar, Straus and Giroux, 19 Union Sq.W., New York, New York, 10003, U.S.A.

Publications

Nonfiction

A Sense of Where You Are. Farrar, Straus, 1965.
The Headmaster. Farrar, Straus, 1966.
Oranges. Farrar, Straus, 1967.
The Pine Barrens. Farrar, Straus, 1968.
A Roomful of Hovings and Other Profiles. Farrar, Straus, 1969.
The Crofter and the Laird. Farrar, Straus, 1969.
Levels of the Game. Farrar, Straus, 1970.
Encounters with the Archdruid. Farrar, Straus, 1972.
Wimbledon: A Celebration, photographs by Alfred Eisenstaedt. Viking, 1972.
The Deltoid Pumpkin Seed. Farrar, Straus, 1973.
The Curve of Binding Energy. Farrar, Straus, 1974.
Pieces of the Frame. Farrar, Straus, 1975.
The Survival of the Bark Canoe. Farrar, Straus, 1975.
The John McPhee Reader, edited by William Howarth. Farrar, Straus, 1977.
Coming into the Country. Farrar, Straus, 1977.
Giving Good Weight. Farrar, Straus, 1979.
Alaska: Images of the Country, with Rowell Galen. Sierra, 1981.
Basin and Range. Farrar, Straus, 1981.
In Suspect Terrain. Farrar, Straus, 1983.
Annals of the Former World (contains *Basin and Range* and *In Suspect Terrain*), two volumes. Farrar, Straus, 1984.
La Place de la Concorde Suisse. Farrar, Straus, 1984.
Table of Contents. Farrar, Straus, 1985.
Rising from the Plains. Farrar, Straus, 1986.
Outcroppings (includes portions of *Encounters with the Archdruid, Basin and Range,* and *Rising from the Plains*), photographs by Tom Till. Peregrine Smith, 1988.
The Control of Nature. Farrar, Straus, 1989.
Looking for a Ship. Farrar, Straus, 1990.
Assembling California. Farrar, Straus, 1993.
The Ransom of Russian Art. Farrar, Straus, 1994.

* * *

Most of John McPhee's work originally appeared as essays, or sometimes three- and four-part series, in *The New Yorker,* a magazine that has traditionally supported many excellent writers by providing them with generous contracts and encouraging them to go on to book publishers.

Among McPhee's best known books is his *Coming into the Country,* a long work about Alaska that many regard as the best single book about that state ever published. Although he has written over 20 books on various subjects—about the headmaster of his prep school, the Swiss military defense system (or paranoia), and the processing of oranges in Florida, for example—his abiding interest has been on the subject of geology in general and on the geology of the United States in particular. In fact, he has written so many books on this subject that he is doubtless the outstanding lay authority on geology in this country.

Many of the geology-related books, like *Basin and Range* (on the geological formation of the state of Utah, published in 1981), *Assembling California* (1993), and *Rising from the Plains* (1986) deal with the American West. Certainly one of the best of these is *Rising from the Plains,* which blends the human history of Wyoming with its highly complex geological history. McPhee's mentor, guide, and focus in this book is a geologist named David Love, the descendant of a family which settled in Wyoming around the turn of the century and became deeply involved in ranching.

The combination of personal and geological histories is a hallmark of McPhee's writing, and works particularly well in this book. But it works just as well in almost everything he writes, because McPhee invariably seeks out and befriends people who are experts in things that he wants to know and are usually interesting and colorful in themselves. What emerges from *Rising from the Plains* is a compelling and detailed story about the Love family and its struggle with the land, set in the frame of the immense and awesome geological history of that state going back millions of years. The use of the mentor/guide figures makes McPhee a fellow-traveler of that other great contemporary writer of cross-disciplinary works, Oliver Sacks.

More recently, *The New Yorker* (in the issue of 29 January 1996) has published McPhee's long three-section essay on "forensic geology." One of the essays is a study of the FBI's geological work that led to the arrest of the kidnaper and murderer of Adolph Coors III. This would not have been possible without intense geological investigation of the site where the murder happened, the place where the body was discovered in Colorado, and the identification of soil and sand particles in a car eventually recovered in New Jersey.

McPhee, who was born and reared in Ames, Iowa, and lived and wrote in Princeton, New Jersey, in the mid-1990s, calls himself a journalist. But it is hard to think of him as that in any conventional sense of the word. In a delightful essay, "North of the C.P. Line," published in a 1985 book titled *Table of Contents,* (1985), McPhee has this to say of his work: "There is a lot of identification, even transformation, in the work I do—moving along from place to place, as a reporter, a writer, repeatedly trying to sense another existence and in some ways to share it."

In this essay, that other existence comes in the form of a man also named John A. McPhee. The writer takes full advantage of that consanguinity of names and almost certain kinship: "The door [of the float plane] opened. The pilot stepped down and stood on the pontoon. About 40, weathered and slim, he looked like a North-West Mounted Policeman. His uniform jacket was bright red, trimmed with black flaps over the breast pockets, black epaulets. A badge above one pocket said, 'STATE OF MAINE WARDEN PILOT.' Above the other pocket was a brass plate incised in block letters with his name: JOHN MCPHEE. I almost fell into the lake."

This other McPhee becomes a good friend and flies the writer all over the woodlands of northern Maine and fills him (and the reader) with a lifetime of knowledge about the woods, the effect of the big lumber operations and their roads built to haul out timber, and many other things. That whole area of Maine comes vividly alive in this essay, but McPhee (the writer) never loses sight of the humor of the whole situation: "Yet for all practical purposes we are indeed using each other's names, and while I had been making my own professional journeys on lakes and streams through the woods of Maine I had in my ignorance felt no twinge of encroachment and could not have imagined being over myself in the air."

—C.W. Truesdale

MERTZ, Barbara

Pseudonyms: Barbara Michaels; Elizabeth Peters. **Nationality:** American. **Born:** Barbara Louise Gross in Canton, Illinois, 29 September 1927. **Education:** University of Chicago Oriental Institute, Ph.B. 1947, M.S. 1950, Ph.D. 1952. **Family:** Married Richard R. Mertz in 1950 (divorced 1968); one daughter and one son. **Career:** Egyptologist. **Awards:** Grandmaster award, Boucheron, 1986; Agatha award for best mystery novel, 1989, and Malice Domestic Convention, 1989, both for *Naked Once More;* D.H.L.: Hood College, 1989. **Member:** American Crime Writers League, Egypt Exploration Society, American Research Council in Egypt, Society for the Study of Egyptian Antiquities, National Organization for Women. **Agent:** Dominick Abel Literary Agency, 146 West 82nd Street, Suite 1B, New York, New York, 10024, U.S.A.

Publications

Novels as Elizabeth Peters (series: Vicky Bliss; Amelia Peabody Emerson; Jacqueline Kirby)

The Jackal's Head. Meredith, 1968.
The Camelot Caper. Meredith, 1969.
The Dead Sea Cipher. Dodd Mead, 1970.
The Night of Four Hundred Rabbits. Dodd Mead, 1971; as *Shadows in the Moonlight,* Coronet, 1975.
The Seventh Sinner (Kirby). Dodd Mead, 1972.
Borrower of the Night (Bliss). Dodd Mead, 1973.
The Murders of Richard III (Kirby). Dodd Mead, 1974.
Crocodile on the Sandbank (Emerson). Dodd Mead, 1975.
Legend in Green Velvet. Dodd Mead, 1976; as *Ghost in Green Velvet,* Cassell, 1977.
Devil-May-Care. Dodd Mead, 1977.
Street of the Five Moons (Bliss). Dodd Mead, 1978.
Summer of the Dragon. Dodd Mead, 1979.
The Love Talker. Dodd Mead, 1980.
The Curse of the Pharaohs (Emerson). Dodd Mead, 1981.
The Copenhagen Connection. Congdon and Lattes, 1982.
Silhouette in Scarlet (Bliss). Congdon and Weed, 1983.
Die for Love (Kirby). Congdon and Weed, 1984.
The Mummy Case (Emerson). Congdon and Weed, 1985.
Lion in the Valley (Emerson). Atheneum, 1986.
Trojan Gold (Bliss). Atheneum, 1987.
The Deeds of the Disturber (Emerson). Atheneum, 1988.
Naked Once More (Kirby). Warner, 1989.

Novels as Barbara Michaels

The Master of Blacktower. Appleton Century Crofts, 1966.
Sons of the Wolf. Meredith, 1967.
Ammie, Come Home. Meredith, 1968.
Prince of Darkness. Meredith, 1969.
The Dark on the Other Side. Dodd Mead, 1970.
Greygallows. Dodd Mead, 1972.
The Crying Child. Dodd Mead, 1973.
Witch. Dodd Mead, 1973.
House of Many Shadows. Dodd Mead, 1974.
The Sea King's Daughter. Dodd Mead, 1975.
Patriot's Dream. Dodd Mead, 1976.
Wings of the Falcon. Dodd Mead, 1977.
Wait for What Will Come. Dodd Mead, 1978.
The Walker in Shadows. Dodd Mead, 1979.
The Wizard's Daughter. Dodd Mead, 1980.
Someone in the House. Dodd Mead, 1981.
Black Rainbow. Congdon and Weed, 1982.
Here I Stay. Congdon and Weed, 1983.
Dark Duet. Congdon and Weed, 1983.
The Grey Beginning. Congdon and Weed, 1984.
Be Buried in the Rain. Atheneum, 1985.
Shattered Silk. Atheneum, 1986.
Search the Shadows. Atheneum, 1987.
Smoke and Mirrors. Simon and Schuster, 1989.
Into the Darkness. Simon and Schuster, 1990.
Scattered Blossoms. Simon and Schuster, 1992.
Vanish with the Rose. Simon and Schuster, 1992.
Houses of Stone. Simon and Schuster, 1993.
Stitches in Time. Simon and Schuster, 1995.

Other, as Barbara Mertz

Temples, Tombs, and Hieroglyphs: The Story of Egyptology. Coward McCann, 1964; revised edition, Dodd Mead, 1978; second revised edition, Bedrick, 1990.
Red Land, Black Land: The World of the Ancient Egyptians. Coward McCann, 1966; revised edition, Dodd Mead, 1978; second revised edition, Bedrick, 1990.
Two Thousand Years in Rome, with Richard Mertz. Coward McCann, 1968.

*

Manuscript Collections: Mugar Memorial Library; Boston University; University of Wyoming, Laramie.

* * *

As Barbara Michaels and Elizabeth Peters, Barbara Louise Gross Mertz, an Egyptologist with a Ph.D. from the University of Chicago Oriental Institute, writes intriguing, literate novels with strong, practical, no-nonsense heroines and convincing historical, academic, or foreign settings based on personal travel and research. In the mid-1960s she turned from serious scholarly studies about Egypt and Rome to fiction.

As Michaels, she specializes in Gothic romances with supernatural terrors rooted in legend and the human psyche. Her first published novel, *The Master of Blacktower* (1966), establishes her key character types: an educated heroine led into difficulties by innocence or curiosity; and a blunt, rough-hewn male with blazing eyes, who, despite initial antagonism and suspicious behavior, becomes the romantic lead. Often, as in *The Dead Sea Cipher* (1970), an American heroine's travel to exotic places leads to treasure or mystery, an attractive enemy, and an initially irritating future lover.

As Elizabeth Peters, Mertz produces light-hearted mystery romances with tongue-in-cheek repartee, strong deduction, and solidly researched background. The Kirby series follows classical mystery plot patterns but later works employ more unconventional forms, such as the hilarious, euphemistic, erudite diaries of Amelia Peabody Emerson.

The capable, hard-working heroines of the Michaels ghost stories make their incredible experiences credible. Spunky, stubborn Andrea of *Here I Stay* (1983) transforms a rundown Maryland mansion into a country inn and puts to rest its resident ghost. (A ghost reputedly haunts Mertz's 200-year-old stone house outside Frederick, Maryland.) Likewise, Karen, in *Shattered Silk* (1986), erases an unhappy divorce by establishing a thriving antique-clothing store. Then, terrorized by life-threatening ghostly activities, she courageously exposes a crazed murderess.

In the Michaels novels, Mertz infuses the conventional lore of werewolves (*Sons of the Wolf* [1967]), haunted castles/houses (*Greygallows* [1972], *Wait for What Will Come* [1978], *House of Many Shadows* [1974]), black masses and demonic possession (*The Dark on the Other Side* [1970]), psychic powers (*Wizard's Daughter* [1980]), witchcraft and voodoo (*Witch* [1973], *Prince of Darkness* [1969]), and psychological trauma (*The Crying Child* [1973]) with wit, psychological realism, and a fascination with historical manuscripts, archaeology, architecture, and interesting oddities from falconry (*Wings of the Falcon* [1977]) to old roses (*Vanish with the Rose* [1992]). She effectively suspends disbelief but is sometimes arch about her chosen genre, particularly its deus ex machina rescues.

Ironically, the clearheaded heroines of the Peters mysteries scorn the fuzzy-headed thinking perpetuated by superstitious believers in ghosts, demons, ancient gods, resuscitated mummies, and curses, and debunk the supernatural with fact and logic. The conflict between superstition and reason—between true believers and rational thinkers—is a recurring theme, with Michaels/Peters clearly more comfortable as debunker than as mythmaker. She is best at parody and satire, for example, and historical romance writers, backroom politics, antiquarians (the Vicky Bliss series), Victorian types, bogus Egyptologists, archeological hoaxes, parenthood, and domesticity (the Peabody series).

The spirited, academic heroines (anthropologists, librarians, antiquarians, and students) of the Peters books become enmeshed in criminal acts related to history. Undaunted by the physical and intellectual demands of their quests, they compete successfully with antagonistic males, very much like the irritatingly handsome, gruff, unromantic young Scottish laird Jamey Erskine in *Legend in Green Velvet* (1976), though these men are not always as clever as they think they are. Series character Vicky Bliss, for example, a good-looking, good-humored museum art historian, must regularly rescue her beloved art thief, Sir John Smythe, while the copper-tressed series character Jacqueline Kirby, a middle-aged librarian, just as regularly abandons her academic boyfriends for the latest smart cop.

Mertz's most compelling series character, Amelia Peabody Emerson (*Crocodile on the Sandbank* [1975]) is an amateur sleuth with a sharp curiosity and sharper tongue. This Victorian bluestocking snares a hot-blooded, irascible Egyptologist, Radcliffe Emerson, and bears a child progeny who, together with his cat Basset, is a constant center of chaotic activities. The Peabody-Emerson series brings comic romps, tongue-in-cheek high romance, and the excitement of archaeological discovery to the mystery genre.

Whatever her pseudonym, Mertz produces lucid prose, reliable and scholarly details, good humor, and lively, knowledgeable, and unpretentious heroines who are willing to defy conventional manners to pursue intellectual or personal challenges.

—Gina Macdonald

MICHAEL, Judith

Joint pseudonym of Judith Barnard and Michael Fain. **Nationality:** American. **BARNARD—Born:** c. 1934. **Education:** Ohio State University, B.A., Northwestern University, M.F.A. **Family:** Married Michael Fain, 1979 (second marriage); children: (first marriage) one daughter, one son. **Career:** Writer. Worked as a reporter and critic. **Awards:** Award of Excellence from Friends of American Literature. **FAIN—Born:** c. 1937. **Education:** Attended University of Chicago. **Family:** Married Judith Barnard, 1979 (second marriage). **Career:** Writer and photographer. Worked as an engineer for NASA. **Agent:** Poseidon Press, Simon & Schuster Bldg., 1230 Avenue of the Americas, New York, New York 10020, U.S.A.

Publications

Novels as Judith Michael

Deceptions. Poseidon, 1982.
Possessions. Poseidon, 1984.
Private Affairs. Poseidon, 1986.
Inheritance. Poseidon, 1988.
A Ruling Passion. Poseidon, 1990.
Sleeping Beauty. Poseidon, 1991.
Pot of Gold. Simon & Schuster Trade, 1993.
A Tangled Web. Simon & Schuster Trade, 1994.

* * *

Judith Michael is the pseudonym of husband-and-wife writing team Judith Barnard and Michael Fain. Their first novel, *Deceptions,* (1982) inventively traces the lives of twin sisters who decide to switch roles while on vacation in China. Lady Sabrina assumes the duties of housewife Stephanie Anderson, and finds to her surprise that she doesn't miss the fast lane. She begins to feel comfortable in the acceptance and security of Stephanie's family, and even starts to fall for Grant, Stephanie's husband. Meanwhile, Stephanie decides that she never wants to leave the good life behind. A freak accident eventually leaves Sabrina unsure of her identity. Critics praised the heartwarming *Deceptions* for its intensity, which leads to a satisfying ending.

Their second effort, the consistently interesting *Possessions* (1984), focuses on heroine Katherine, who learns of her husband's sordid past only to have him disappear after being charged with embezzlement. She is left with their two kids, and moves from Vancouver to San Francisco to take an entry-level job and get her life back together. In San Francisco she is suddenly swept into the good life of elegance and excitement. This variation of an old gothic/romance formula was praised by *Publisher's Weekly* for being a "believable modern odyssey, a woman's search for identity unburdened by melodrama or undue gimmickry."

Private Affairs (1986) tackles the themes of love, honor, and corruption. Protagonists Elizabeth and Matt Lovell are forced on their wedding day into taking over a family business in Santa Fe, thus squelching their dreams of careers in journalism. Years later they attempt to get back to these dreams by remaking a failing weekly paper. Elizabeth begins writing a column for the paper entitled "Private Affairs." Meanwhile her husband falls under the influence of wealthy Keegan Rourke who offers him the control of a multimillion-dollar newspaper chain. His integrity and marriage become threatened as Matt succumbs to the glitter of a fast-lane lifestyle. Flat descriptions of the good life, though, and padded dialogue prompt *Kirkus Reviews* to deem *Private Affairs* "relatively glitterless."

Continuing their commercial success with *Inheritance* (1988), Barnard and Fain turn to a tightly written tale of betrayal. After their parents' death, Laura and Clay Fairchild are trained in the art of burglary by stepbrother Ben. By setting up the Salinger hotel chain, Ben hopes to avenge wrongs done his father by Felix Salinger. Laura, however, ruins his plans by becoming friends with Salinger patriarch Owen. She joins their family, finding love in the arms of Paul. After the death of Owen, Felix throws her out of the family with the use of her past. She then works on creating a hotel chain that will rival that of the Salingers. The plot twists may be predictable, but animated characterizations and an assured style guarantee good entertainment.

After three additional smoothly written pot-boilers, Barnard and Fain returned to the successful story of their first novel in *A Tangled Web* (1994). A year after the death of Stephanie, Sabrina has been forgiven for her deception and makes a life for herself with Grant. The real Stephanie, however, has been rescued from the explosion by Max, an international smuggler who takes advantage of her memory loss by telling her they are married. Complications ensue and when the twins eventually find each other they must deal with the consequences of their deceptions.

At times this husband and wife team overwrites and relies on predictable plots. But their stories move along smoothly and with style, and end in exciting conclusions that assure great commercial success.

—Jennifer G. Coman

MICHAELS, Barbara. *See* **MERTZ, Barbara.**

MICHENER, James A(lbert)

Nationality: American. **Born:** 1907(?); brought up by foster parents. **Education:** Doylestown High School, Pennsylvania; Swarthmore College, Pennsylvania, A.B. (summa cum laude) 1929 (Phi Beta Kappa); University of Northern Colorado, Greeley, A.M. 1935; University of St. Andrews, Fife, Scotland. **Military Service:** United States Navy, 1944-45: Lieutenant Commander. **Family:** Married 1) Patti Koon in 1935 (divorced 1948); 2) Vange Nord in 1948 (divorced 1955); 3) Mari Yoriko Sabusawa in 1955. **Career:** Master, Hill School, Pottstown, Pennsylvania, 1929-31, and George School, Newtown, Pennsylvania, 1934-36; professor, University of Northern Colorado, 1936-40; visiting professor, Harvard University, Cambridge, Massachusetts, 1940-41; associate editor, Macmillan Company, New York, 1941-49. Since 1949 freelance writer. **Awards:** Pultizer prize, 1948; National Association of Independent Schools award, 1954, 1958; Einstein award, 1967; National Medal of Freedom, 1971. D.H.L.: Rider College, Lawrenceville, New Jersey, 1950; Swarthmore College, 1954; LL.D.: Temple University, Philadelphia, 1957; Litt.D.: Washington University, St. Louis, 1967; Yeshiva University, New York, 1974; D.Sc.: Jefferson Medical College, Philadelphia, 1979. Lives in Austin, Texas. **Member:** Advisory Committee on the Arts, United States Department of State, 1957; chair, President Kennedy's Food for Peace Program, 1961; secretary, Pennsylvania Constitution Convention, 1967-68; member of the Advisory Committee, United States Information Agency, 1970-76, and NASA, 1980-83. Since 1983 member of the Board, International Broadcasting. **Address:** 2719 Mount Laurel Lane, Austin, Texas 78703, U.S.A.

Publications

Novels

The Fires of Spring. New York, Random House, 1949; London, Corgi, 1960.

The Bridges at Toko-Ri. New York, Random House, and London, Secker & Warburg, 1953.

Sayonara. New York, Random House, and London, Secker & Warburg, 1954.

The Bridge at Andau. New York, Random House, and London, Secker & Warburg, 1957.

Hawaii. New York, Random House, 1959; London, Secker & Warburg, 1960.

Caravans. New York, Random House, 1963; London, Secker & Warburg, 1964.

The Source. New York, Random House, and London, Secker & Warburg, 1965.

The Drifters. New York, Random House, and London, Secker & Warburg, 1971.

Centennial. New York, Random House, and London, Secker & Warburg, 1974.

Chesapeake. New York, Random House, and London, Secker & Warburg, 1978; selections published as *The Watermen*, Random House, 1979.

The Covenant. New York, Random House, and London, Secker & Warburg, 1980.

Space. New York, Random House, and London, Secker & Warburg, 1982.

Poland. New York, Random House, 1983; London, Secker & Warburg, 1984.

Texas. New York, Random House, and London, Secker & Warburg, 1985.

Legacy. New York, Random House, and London, Secker & Warburg, 1987.

Alaska. New York, Random House, and London, Secker & Warburg, 1988.

Journey. New York, Random House, and London, Secker & Warburg, 1989.

Caribbean. New York, Random House, and London, Secker & Warburg, 1989.

The Eagle and the Raven, with drawings by Charles Shaw. Austin, Texas, State House Press, 1990; London, Secker & Warburg, 1992.

The Novel. New York, Random House, and London, Secker & Warburg, 1991.

Mexico. New York, Random House, and London, Secker & Warburg, 1992.

Recessional. New York, Random House, 1994; London, Secker & Warburg, 1995.

Miracle in Seville. New York, Random House, 1995.

Short Stories

Tales of the South Pacific. New York, Macmillan, 1947; London, Collins, 1951.

Return to Paradise. New York, Random House, and London, Secker & Warburg, 1951.

Creatures of the Kingdom: Stories of Animals and Nature, illustrated by Karen Jacobsen. New York, Random House, and London, Secker & Warburg, 1993.

Other

The Unit in the Social Studies, with Harold M. Long. Cambridge, Massachusetts, Harvard University Graduate School of Education, 1940.

The Voice of Asia. New York, Random House, 1951; as *Voices of Asia*, London, Secker & Warburg, 1952.

The Floating World (on Japanese art). New York, Random House, 1954; London, Secker & Warburg, 1955.

Rascals in Paradise, with A. Grove Day. New York, Random House, and London, Secker & Warburg, 1957.

Selected Writings. New York, Modern Library, 1957.

Japanese Prints from the Early Masters to the Modern. Rutland, Vermont, Tuttle, and London, Paterson, 1959.

Report of the County Chairman. New York, Random House, and London, Secker & Warburg, 1961.

The Modern Japanese Print: An Introduction. Rutland, Vermont, Tuttle, 1962.

Iberia: Spanish Travels and Reflections. New York, Random House, and London, Secker & Warburg, 1968.

The Subject Is Israel: A Conversation Between James A. Michener and Dore Schary. New York, Anti-Defamation League of B'nai B'rith, 1968.

Presidential Lottery: The Reckless Gamble in Our Electoral System. New York, Random House, and London, Secker & Warburg, 1969.

The Quality of Life. Philadelphia, Lippincott, 1970; London, Secker & Warburg, 1971.

Facing East: A Study of the Art of Jack Levine. New York, Random House, 1970.

Kent State: What Happened and Why. New York, Random House, and London, Secker & Warburg, 1971.

A Michener Miscellany 1950-1970, edited by Ben Hibbs. New York, Random House, 1973; London, Corgi, 1975.

About "Centennial": Some Notes on the Novel. New York, Random House, 1974.

Sports in America. New York, Random House, 1976; as *Michener on Sport*, London, Secker & Warburg, 1976.

Testimony. Honolulu, White Knight, 1983.

Collectors, Forgers—and a Writer: A Memoir. New York, Targ, 1983.

Six Days in Havana, with John Kings. Austin, University of Texas Press, 1989; London, Souvenir Press, 1990.

Pilgrimage: A Memoir of Poland and Rome. Emmaus, Pennsylvania, Rodale Press, 1990.

James A. Michener's Writer's Handbook: Explorations in Writing and Publishing. New York, Random House, 1992.

My Lost Mexico, with photographs by the author. Austin, Texas, State House Press, and London, Secker & Warburg, 1992.

The World Is My Home: A Memoir. New York, Random House, 1992.

Editor, *The Future of the Social Studies: Proposals for an Experimental Social-Studies Curriculum*. New York, National Council for the Social Studies, 1939.

Editor, *The Hokusai Sketch Books: Selections from the Manga*. Rutland, Vermont, Tuttle, 1958.

Editor, *Firstfruits: A Harvest of 25 Years of Israeli Writing*. Philadelphia, Jewish Publication Society of America, 1973.

*

Manuscript Collection: Library of Congress, Washington, D.C.

Critical Studies: *James Michener* by A. Grove Day, New York, Twayne, 1964, revised edition, 1977; *James Michener* by George J. Becker, New York, Ungar, 1983; *James A. Michener: A Biography* by John P. Hayes, Indianapolis, Bobbs Merrill, and London, W.H. Allen, 1984.

* * *

James Michener is best know for his scholarly representations of family sagas based in a particular region. Michener's interest in the setting of his fiction is linked to the vast amount of traveling he has done. He has studied at several universities, received more than 20 honorary degrees, and has been awarded both the Navy Gold Cross and the Medal of Freedom. Aside from novels, Michener writes nonfiction and articles for various periodicals.

Michener based his first fiction, *Tales of the South Pacific* (1947), on his WWII experience touring Pacific islands. Critics classified the work as a series of short fiction, yet Michener considers it a novel because of the unified setting and the recurrence of several characters throughout the book. The stories depict a wide panorama of life in the South Pacific during WWII, from the love affair between Joe Cable (a young G.I.) and Liat (an island resident) to the allied invasion. It is usually considered one of the best novels about Americans in the Pacific theater. In 1949 a musical adaptation of the novel, *South Pacific,* increased Michener's popularity.

Michener continued writing semi-autobiographical fiction with *The Fires of the Spring* (1949), a story about a young orphan.

The book marked a turning point in Michener's career because of Macmillan's refusal to publish it. Michener went to Random House and met Bennett Cerf and Albert Erskine, who became his publisher and editor, respectively.

Michener returned to the Pacific and wrote a prolific amount of non-fiction, including *Return to Paradise* (1951), a collection of travel sketches; *The Voice of Asia* (1951), a series of 53 interviews with various Asians; *The Floating World* (1954), a study of Japanese prints; and *Rascals in Paradise* (1957), a collaboration with Grove Day about various figures in Pacific history.

Michener stayed in Honolulu in 1956 and began writing a chronicle of Hawaii. The novel *Hawaii* (1959) began as a history of the islands and eventually developed into a million-word historical novel. The novel is not traditional historical-fiction because Michener does not focus upon specific names and places, but instead chooses to highlight the continual influx of settlers. The novel was praised for its thesis that paradise is not an end in itself but a means achieved through a constant mixing of various peoples and cultures.

Michener's travel's to Israel inspired another chronicle, *The Source* (1965). Like *Hawaii,* the book begins with the history of the place before humans arrived and ends with contemporary events, such as Israel's War of Independence. This novel is one of his longest, and many critics consider it to be his best because of its unification of theme, particularly religion in the region, and the limited setting.

Centennial (1974) and *Chesapeake* (1978), are reminiscent of *The Source,* but lack the previous work's clear definition of theme (although ecological concerns and discussion of the American annexation of the wilderness abound in both novels).

Michener's most financially successful novels are those that follow his formula of mixing fictional characters with the history of a particular place. *Poland* (1983), *Texas* (1985), *Alaska* (1988), and *Mexico* (1994) all received less-than-favorable reviews; critics generally felt that although the works are readable, they are encumbered by excessive attention to historical details. For example, some reviewers wrote the main problem with *Alaska* was that the book needed editing. Some critics are also cynical of his financial success. Larry L. King, of the *Chicago Tribune,* wrote that *Texas* "will sell no matter what we say about it."

Aside from Michener's interest in writing weighty historical tomes, he has published smaller books with similar concerns. *Legacy* (1987) is a short essay-like novel that criticizes the United States' tendency to criticize the world, and *The Novel* (1991) is a story of the settlement of Pennsylvania by the Dutch. Like his longer works, these generally received mixed critical reception. Peter C. Newman, of the *Chicago Tribune,* perhaps best summarizes the reading of Michener's books: "They are truly awful, but you can't stop reading them." Regardless of their aesthetic merit, Michener's novel sell.

—Chris Godat

MILLAR, Kenneth. *See* **MACDONALD, Ross.**

MITCHELL, Allison. *See* **BUTTERWORTH, W. E.**

MOMADAY, N(avarre) Scott

Nationality: American. **Born:** Lawton, Oklahoma, 27 February 1934. **Education:** University of New Mexico, Albuquerque, A.B. 1958; Stanford University, California (creative writing fellow, 1959), A.M. 1960, Ph.D. 1963. **Family:** Married 1) Gaye Mangold in 1959 (divorced), three daughters; 2) Regina Heitzer in 1978, one daughter. **Career:** Assistant professor, 1963-67, and associate professor, 1967-69, University of California, Santa Barbara; professor of English and comparative literature, University of California, Berkeley, 1969-72; professor of English, Stanford University, 1972-80. Since 1980 professor of English and comparative literature, University of Arizona, Tucson. Professor, University of California Institute for the Humanities, 1970; Whittall Lecturer, Library of Congress, Washington, D.C., 1971; visiting professor, New Mexico State University, Las Cruces, 1972-73, State University of Moscow, Spring 1974, Columbia University, New York, 1979, and Princeton University, New Jersey, 1979; writer-in-residence, Southeastern University, Washington, D.C., 1985, and Aspen Writers' Conference, Colorado, 1986. Artist: has exhibited drawings and paintings. Since 1978 member of the Board of Trustees, Museum of the American Indian, New York. **Awards:** Academy of American Poets prize, 1962; Guggenheim grant, 1966; Pulitzer prize, 1969; American Academy award, 1970; Western Heritage award, 1974; Mondello prize (Italy), 1979; Western Literature Association award, 1983. D.H.L.: Central Michigan University, Mt. Pleasant, 1970; University of Massachusetts, Amherst, 1975; Yale University, New Haven, Connecticut, 1980; Hobart and William Smith Colleges, Geneva, New York, 1980; College of Santa Fe, New Mexico, 1982; D.Litt.: Lawrence University, Appleton, Wisconsin, 1971; University of Wisconsin, Milwaukee, 1976; College of Ganado, 1979; D.F.A.: Morningside College, Sioux City, Iowa, 1980. **Address:** Department of English, University of Arizona, Tucson, Arizona 85721, U.S.A.

Publications

Novels

House Made of Dawn. New York, Harper, 1968; London, Gollancz, 1969.
The Ancient Child. New York, Doubleday, 1989.

Poetry

Angle of Geese and Other Poems. Boston, Godine, 1974.
Before an Old Painting of the Crucifixion, Carmel Mission, June 1960. San Francisco, Valenti Angelo, 1975.
The Gourd Dancer. New York, Harper, 1976.

In the Presence of the Sun: Stories and Poems, 1961-1991, illustrated by the author. New York, St. Martin's Press, 1992.

Other

Owl in the Cedar Tree (for children). Boston, Ginn, 1965.
The Journey of Tai-me (Kiowa Indian tales). Privately printed, 1967; revised edition, as *The Way to Rainy Mountain*, Albuquerque, University of New Mexico Press, 1969.
Colorado: Summer, Fall, Winter, Spring, photographs by David Muench. Chicago, Rand McNally, 1973.
The Names: A Memoir. New York, Harper, 1976.
Circle of Wonder (for children). Santa Fe, New Mexico, Clear Light, 1994.

Editor, *The Complete Poems of Frederick Goddard Tuckerman*. New York, Oxford University Press, 1965.
Editor, *American Indian Authors*. Boston, Houghton Mifflin, 1976.
Editor, *A Coyote in the Garden*, by An Painter. Lewiston, Idaho, Confluence Press, 1988.

*

Manuscript Collection: Bancroft Library, University of California, Berkeley.

Critical Studies: *Four American Indian Literary Masters* by Alan R. Velie, Norman, University of Oklahoma Press, 1982; *N. Scott Momaday: The Cultural and Literary Background* by Matthias Schubnell, Norman, University of Oklahoma Press, 1986; *Approaches to Teaching Momaday's "The Way to Rainy Mountain"* edited by Kenneth M. Roemer, New York, Modern Language Association of America, 1988; *Ancestral Voice: Conversations with N. Scott Momaday* (includes bibliography) by Charles L. Woodard, Lincoln, University of Nebraska Press, 1989; *Landmarks of Healing: A Study of "House Made of Dawn"* by Susan Scarberry-Garcia, Albuquerque, University of New Mexico Press, 1990; *Place and Vision: The Function of Landscape in Native American Fiction* by Robert M. Nelson, New York, Lang, 1993.

* * *

Scott Momaday's poetry and prose reflect his Kiowa Indian heritage. He grew up on the reservations of the Southwest and lived amongst people who were deeply involved in the traditional life. At a young age Momaday was aware of the strength and beauty that were missing in modern culture, and even today seeks to involve the modern world in the celebration of cultural tradition through his writings. In his poetry, such as "The Bear" (1961), it is the Indian oral tradition that brings to life not only the subject, but the intensity of the culture and the strength of the poet himself. Momaday's works combines myth, history, and memories into literary masterpieces about the Kiowa tribe.

The spirituality of the Kiowa infiltrates the reader in all the works of Momady. Momady beautifully crosses back and forth between the Anglo-American heritage and the Kiowa traditional heritage. His mother, Mayme Natachee Scott, is a descendant of both Native Americans and American pioneers, but she preferred to identify herself using her Indian heritage. Her son has chosen to do the same. Momady has been quoted as saying he prefers to think of himself as all Indian, and to imagine himself living emotionally and spiritually with his native ancestors.

Language, for Momady, is used not only to describe the physical environment, but also to give it shape. In *Names: A Memoir* (1976), for example, Momady refers to the names given his people as the objects, forms, and features of the land. Names for the Kiowa mean much more than just an identifying tag; they are an ideal that determines the source of a man's or woman's character and course in life.

House Made of Dawn has as its foundation the conflict of acceptance between Indians and Anglos. The hero of the novel is a victim of the frustrations of living in both worlds. Abel, the hero, leaves the reservation for a tour in the Army during WWII. Upon returning home, he commits a murder and is sentenced to a Los Angeles relocation center where he struggles to adapt to a factory job. Due to his inability to cope, Abel succumbs to his frustrations and the result is a brutal beating by a Los Angeles policeman. Abel returns to the reservation and, as the novel ends, we find the hero running in the ancient ritual dawn race against evil and death.

Momady views himself as a poet, not a novelist. In fact, it was 20 years after the publication of *House Made of Dawn* that he wrote his second novel, *The Ancient Child* (1989). *The Ancient Child* is a story of a modern Indian artist's search for his identity. The novel has been called an autobiography, since it is based on the legend surrounding Momady's Indian name, Tsoailee.

The Way Of Rainy Mountain (1969) is considered Momady's best literary work. As the subject for his novel, Momady uses the disappearance of the sacred buffalo. The buffalo was seen as an animal representation of the sun. When the buffalo began to disappear, therefore, the blessings of the sun god disappeared with them because there were no sacrificial victims for the Sun Dance. Momady, in depicting the reality in the loss of tradition of the American Indian caused by the uncaring and insensitive American government, represents superbly a very sad part of American history.

Momady is passionately aware of the struggle between the Indian and Anglo-American culture, and seeks not to reflect on the negative, but to challenge his audience to use their senses to capture the endless spiritual benefits that a merging of such cultures can bring.

—Tammy J. Bronson

MORGAN, Claire. *See* **HIGHSMITH, Patricia.**

MORRISON, Toni

Nationality: American. **Born:** Chloe Anthony Wofford, Lorain, Ohio, 18 February 1931. **Education:** Howard University, Washington, D.C., B.A. 1953; Cornell University, Ithaca, New York, M.A. 1955. **Family:** Married Harold Morrison in 1958 (divorced

1964); two sons. **Career:** Instructor in English, Texas Southern University, Houston, 1955-57, and Howard University, 1957-64; senior editor, Random House, publishers, New York, 1965-84; associate professor, State University of New York, Purchase, 1971-72; visiting lecturer, Yale University, New Haven, Connecticut, 1976-77, Rutgers University, New Brunswick, New Jersey, 1983-84, and Bard College, Annandale-on-Hudson, New York, 1986-88; Schweitzer Professor of the Humanities, State University of New York, Albany, 1984-89; Regents' Lecturer, University of California, Berkeley, 1987; Santagata Lecturer, Bowdoin College, Brunswick, Maine, 1987. Since 1989 Golheen Professor of the Humanities, Princeton University, New Jersey. **Awards:** American Academy award, 1977; National Book Critics Circle award, 1977; New York State Governor's award, 1985; Book of the Month Club award, 1986; Before Columbus Foundation award, 1988; Robert F. Kennedy award, 1988; Melcher award, 1988; Pulitzer prize, 1988; MLA Commonwealth award in literature, 1989; Nobel prize, 1993, for literature; Pearl Buck award, 1994; Condorcet medal (Paris), 1994; Rhegium Julii prize, 1994, for literature. Honorary degree: College of Saint Rose, Albany, 1987. **Agent:** International Creative Management, 40 West 57th Street, New York, New York 10019. **Address:** Department of Creative Writing, Princeton University, Princeton, New Jersey 08544, U.S.A.

PUBLICATIONS

Novels

The Bluest Eye. New York, Holt Rinehart, 1970; London, Chatto and Windus, 1980.
Sula. New York, Knopf, and London, Allen Lane, 1974.
Song of Solomon. New York, Knopf, 1977; London, Chatto and Windus, 1978.
Tar Baby. New York, Knopf, and London, Chatto and Windus, 1981.
Beloved. New York, Knopf, and London, Chatto and Windus, 1987.
Jazz. New York, Knopf, and London, Chatto and Windus, 1992.

Play

Dreaming Emmett (produced Albany, New York, 1986).

Other

Playing in the Dark: Whiteness and the Literary Imagination. Cambridge, Massachusetts, and London, Harvard University Press, 1992.
Conversations with Toni Morrison, edited by Danille Taylor-Guthrie. Jackson, University Press of Mississippi, 1994.
Lecture and Speech of Acceptance upon the Award of the Nobel Prize for Literature. London, Chatto and Windus, 1994.

Editor, *Race-ing Justice, En-gendering Power: Essays on Anita Hill, Clarence Thomas, and the Construction of Social Reality.* New York, Pantheon, 1992; London, Chatto and Windus, 1993.

*

Bibliography: *Toni Morrison: An Annotated Bibliography* by David L. Middleton, New York, Garland, 1987.

Critical Studies: *The Crime of Innocence in the Fiction of Toni Morrison* by Terry Otten, Columbia, University of Missouri Press, 1989; *Toni Morrison* by Wilfred D. Samuels and Clenora Hudson-Weems, Boston, Twayne, 1990; *Toni Morrison* edited by Harold Bloom, Chelsea House, 1990; *Fiction and Folklore: The Novels of Toni Morrison* by Trudier Harris, Knoxville, University of Tennessee Press, 1991; *The Voices of Toni Morrison* by Barbara Hill Rigney, Columbus, Ohio State University Press, 1991; *The Novels of Toni Morrison: The Search for Self and Place Within the Community* by Patrick Bryce Bjork, New York, Lang, 1992; *Toni Morrison: Critical Perspectives Past and Present* edited by Henry Louis Gates Jr. and K.A. Appiah, New York, Amistad, 1993; *Toni Morrison* by Douglas Century, New York, Chelsea House, 1994; *Bridging the Americas: The Literature of Paule Marshall, Toni Morrison, and Gayl Jones* by Stelamaris Coser, Philadelphia, Temple University Press, 1994; *A World of Difference: An Inter-Cultural Study of Toni Morrison's Novels* by Wendy Harding and Jacky Martin, Westport, Greenwood Press, 1994; *Toni Morrison's Fiction* edited by Matthew J. Bruccoli, University of South Carolina Press, 1996.

* * *

Nobel laureate Toni Morrison transcends racial and class boundaries to appeal to readers of all ages and educational backgrounds. Though she has written six novels, two books of critical commentary, and was commissioned by the New York State Writers Institute to write the play *Dreaming Emmett,* her most discussed work is her Pulitzer Prize-winning novel, *Beloved.*

Beloved was inspired by the life of Margaret Garner, a black American slave woman who chose to kill her children rather than have them endure slavery. While researching material for a historical project, *The Black Book,* Morrison came across the account of Garner's life. She later drew upon her reading to develop protagonist Sethe, who tried to kill her children but was successful only in murdering the unnamed infant, "Beloved." This daughter comes back to haunt Sethe and her kinfolk. "Beloved" quite possibly is responsible for the death of Sethe's mother, Baby Suggs, who gives up on life to contemplate harmless colors in her coverlet. This book, like all of Morrison's novels, is brimming with African-American folk wisdom and celebrates African-American community values. Its historical accuracy lends an authentic air to this piece of fiction, which the protagonist declares to be a story "not to be passed on."

Morrison was educated at Howard and Cornell Universities. She began writing during the late 1960s when American attitudes about race and the condition of women were undergoing a radical transformation. She learned her storytelling abilities at the knee of her father, George, who wanted to impress his children with a sense of black heritage by telling them the folktales of the black community. Morrison was brought up with a strong distrust of whites since Ramah, her mother, and her father moved to the North to escape the problems of southern racism.

In 1966 Morrison was employed as a textbook editor at Random House. She was promoted to tradebook editor in 1968 and then to senior editor. While at Random House, Morrison helped Gayl Jones, Toni Cade Bambara, John McCluskey, Andrew Young, and Muhammad Ali become published. She went on to teach at

Southern University and Howard University. Morrison compiled her highly acclaimed critical work, *Playing in the Dark: Whiteness and the Literary Imagination* (1992), from her lectures as a Harvard Massey Lecturer.

Morrison was married to Jamaican architect Harold Morrison; they had two sons before they divorced. Perhaps Harold and his Caribbean background served as influences for Morrison's novel, *Tar Baby*. Set in the Caribbean, *Tar Baby* is the story of the spoiled and pampered American, Jadine, who falls in love with the earthy Caribbean "Son." Jadine takes advantage of an old uncle and aunt who have endured racial insubordination as servants in a white household so that Jadine can have the best of everything. "Son" is a mysterious criminal type who sneaks into the white household and catches everyone, including Jadine, off guard. Ultimately, Jadine falls in love with "Son" and makes some startling realizations about her life, her assumptions about race, and her aunt and uncle.

Morrison's bestselling work was her *Song of Solomon* (1977), a Book-of-the-Month Club Selection that sold three million copies. This African-American folk myth-saturated novel depicts the story of a young man who travels back to his family home to gain wisdom about his family heritage, but is hindered by his repressed, middle-class, dysfunctional family. The novel spent 16 weeks on the *New York Times* bestseller list and won the National Book Critic's Circle Award as well as the American Academy and Institute of Arts and Letters Award (1978).

Carolyn Denard describes Morrison as a "'literary Moses' who believes that the story, the novel, is the mode through which African Americans can be led out of the cultural confusion and complexity of contemporary society." (*Black Women in America*). She is a writer whose great power and skill appeal to the general reader and scholar alike.

—Bennis Blue

MORTIMER, John (Clifford)

Nationality: British. **Born:** Hampstead, London, 21 April 1923. **Education:** Harrow School, Middlesex, 1937-40; Brasenose College, Oxford, 1940-42, B.A. 1947; called to the bar, 1948; Queen's Counsel, 1966; Master of the Bench, Inner Temple, 1975. **Military Service:** Served with the Crown Film Units as scriptwriter during World War II. **Family:** Married 1) Penelope Dimont in 1949 (divorced 1971), one son and one daughter; 2) Penny Gollop in 1972, one daughter. **Career:** Drama critic, *New Statesman, Evening Standard,* and *Observer,* 1972, all London; member of the National Theatre Board, 1968-88; president, Berkshire, Buckinghamshire, and Oxford Naturalists' Trust, from 1984; chairman, League of Dramatists; chairman of the council, Royal Society of Literature for 1989; chairman, Royal Court Theatre since 1990; president, Howard League for Penal Reform since 1991; chairman, the Royal Society of Literature since 1992. Lives in Henley-on-Thames, Oxfordshire. **Awards:** Italia prize, for radio play, 1958; Screenwriters Guild award, for television play, 1970; BAFTA award, for television series, 1980; *Yorkshire Post* award, 1983. D. Litt.: Susquehanna University, Selinsgrove, Pennsylvania, 1985; University of St. Andrews, Fife, 1987; University of Nottingham, 1989; LL.D.: Exeter University, 1986. Commander, Order of the British Empire, 1986. **Agent:** Peters Fraser and Dunlop, 503-504 The Chambers, Chelsea Harbour, Lots Road, London SW10 0XF, England.

Publications

Novels

Charade. London, Lane, 1948.
Rumming Park. London, Lane, 1948.
Answer Yes or No. London, Lane, 1950; as *The Silver Hook,* New York, Morrow, 1950.
Like Men Betrayed. London, Collins, 1953; Philadelphia, Lippincott, 1954.
The Narrowing Stream. London, Collins, 1954; New York, Viking, 1989.
Three Winters. London, Collins, 1956.
Will Shakespeare: The Untold Story. London, Hodder and Stoughton, 1977; New York, Delacorte Press, 1978.
Paradise Postponed. London and New York, Viking, 1985.
Summer's Lease. London and New York, Viking, 1988.
Titmuss Regained. London and New York, Viking, 1990.
Dunster. London and New York, Viking Penguin, 1992.

Short Stories

Rumpole. London, Allen Lane, 1980.
Rumpole of the Bailey. London, Penguin, 1978; New York, Penguin, 1980.
The Trials of Rumpole. London, Penguin, 1979; New York, Penguin, 1981.
Regina v. Rumpole. London, Allen Lane, 1981.
Rumpole's Return. London, Penguin, 1980; New York, Penguin, 1982.
Rumpole for the Defence. London, Penguin, 1982.
Rumpole and the Golden Thread. New York, Penguin, 1983.
The First Rumpole Omnibus (includes *Rumpole of the Bailey, The Trials of Rumpole, Rumpole's Return).* London, Penguin, 1983.
Rumpole's Last Case. London, Penguin, 1987; New York, Penguin, 1988.
The Second Rumpole Omnibus (includes *Rumpole for the Defence, Rumpole and the Golden Thread, Rumpole's Last Case).* London, Viking, 1987; New York, Penguin, 1988.
Rumpole and the Age of Miracles. London, Penguin, 1988; New York, Penguin, 1989.
Rumpole à la Carte. London and New York, Viking Penguin, 1990.
Rumpole on Trial. London and New York, Viking Penguin, 1992.
The Best of Rumpole. London and New York, Viking Penguin, 1993.
Rumpole and the Angel of Death. London and New York, Viking Penguin, 1996.

Plays

The Dock Brief (broadcast 1957; produced London, 1958; New York, 1961). In *Three Plays,* 1958.
I Spy (broadcast 1957; produced Salisbury, Wiltshire, and Palm Beach, Florida, 1959). In *Three Plays,* 1958.
What Shall We Tell Caroline? (produced London, 1958; New York, 1961). In *Three Plays,* 1958.

Three Plays: The Dock Brief, What Shall We Tell Caroline?, I Spy. London, Elek, 1958; New York, Grove Press, 1962.
Call Me a Liar (televised 1958; produced London, 1968). In *Lunch Hour and Other Plays,* 1960; in *The Television Playwright: Ten Plays for B.B.C. Television,* edited by Michael Barry, New York, Hill and Wang, 1960.
Sketches in *One to Another* (produced London, 1959). London, French, 1960.
The Wrong Side of the Park (produced London, 1960). London, Heinemann, 1960.
Lunch Hour (broadcast 1960; produced Salisbury, Wiltshire, 1960; London, 1961; New York, 1977). In *Lunch Hour and Other Plays* 1960; published separately, New York, French, 1961.
David and Broccoli (televised 1960). In *Lunch Hour and Other Plays,* 1960.
Lunch Hour and Other Plays (includes *Collect Your Hand Baggage, David and Broccoli, Call Me a Liar*). London, Methuen, 1960.
Collect Your Hand Baggage (produced Wuppertal, Germany, 1963). In *Lunch Hour and Other Plays,* 1960.
Sketches in *One over the Eight* (produced London, 1961).
Two Stars for Comfort (produced London, 1962). London, Methuen, 1962.
A Voyage round My Father (broadcast 1963; produced London, 1970). London, Methuen, 1971.
Sketches in *Changing Gear* (produced Nottingham, 1965).
A Flea in Her Ear, adaptation of a play by Feydeau (produced London, 1966; Tucson, Arizona, 1979). London and New York, French, 1967.
A Choice of Kings (televised 1966). In *Playbill Three,* edited by Alan Durband, London, Hutchinson, 1969.
The Judge (produced London, 1967). London, Methuen, 1967.
Desmond (televised 1968). In *The Best Short Plays 1971,* edited by Stanley Richards, Philadelphia, Chilton, 1971.
Cat among the Pigeons, adaptation of a play by Feydeau (produced London, 1969; Milwaukee, 1971). New York, French, 1970.
Come As You Are: Four Short Plays (includes *Mill Hill, Bermondsey, Gloucester Road, Marble Arch)* (produced London, 1970). London, Methuen, 1971.
Five Plays (includes *The Dock Brief, What Shall We Tell Caroline?, I Spy, Lunch Hour, Collect Your Hand Baggage*). London, Methuen, 1970.
The Captain of Köpenick, adaptation of a play by Carl Zuckmayer (produced London, 1971). London, Methuen, 1971.
Conflicts, with others (produced London, 1971).
I, Claudius, adaptation of the novels *I, Claudius* and *Claudius the God* by Robert Graves (produced London, 1972).
Knightsbridge (televised 1972). London, French, 1973.
Collaborators (produced London, 1973). London, Eyre Methuen, 1973.
The Fear of Heaven (as *Mr. Lucy's Fear of Heaven,* broadcast 1976; as *The Fear of Heaven,* produced with *The Prince of Darkness* as *Heaven and Hell,* London, 1976). London, French, 1978.
Heaven and Hell (includes *The Fear of Heaven* and *The Prince of Darkness*) (produced London, 1976; revised version of *The Prince of Darkness,* as *The Bells of Hell* produced Richmond, Surrey, and London, 1977). *The Bells of Hell* published London, French, 1978.
The Lady from Maxim's, adaptation of a play by Feydeau (produced London, 1977). London, Heinemann, 1977.
John Mortimer's Casebook (includes *The Dock Brief, The Prince of Darkness, Interlude*) (produced London, 1982).
When That I Was (produced Ottawa, 1982).
Edwin (broadcast 1982). In *Edwin and Other Plays,* 1984.
A Little Hotel on the Side, adaptation of a play by Feydeau and Maurice Desvalliers (produced London, 1984). In *Three Boulevard Farces,* 1985.
Edwin and Other Plays (includes *Bermondsey, Marble Arch, The Fear of Heaven, The Prince of Darkness*). London, Penguin, 1984.
Three Boulevard Farces (includes *A Little Hotel on the Side, A Flea in Her Ear, The Lady from Maxim's*). London, Penguin, 1985.
Die Fledermaus, adaptation of the libretto by Henri Meihac and Ludovic Halévy, music by Johann Stauss (produced London, 1989). London, Viking, 1989.
A Christmas Carol, adaptation of the novel by Charles Dickens (produced London, 1994).

Screenplays: *Ferry to Hong Kong,* with Lewis Gilbert and Vernon Harris, 1959; *The Innocents,* with Truman Capote and William Archibald, 1961; *Guns of Darkness,* 1962; *I Thank a Fool,* with others, 1962; *Lunch Hour,* 1962; *The Running Man,* 1963; *Bunny Lake Is Missing,* with Penelope Mortimer, 1964; *A Flea in Her Ear,* 1967; *John and Mary,* 1969.

Radio Plays: *Like Men Betrayed,* 1955; *No Hero,* 1955; *The Dock Brief,* 1957; *I Spy,* 1957; *Three Winters,* 1958; *Lunch Hour,* 1960; *The Encyclopedist,* 1961; *A Voyage round My Father,* 1963; *Personality Split,* 1964; *Education of an Englishman,* 1964; *A Rare Device,* 1965; *Mr. Luby's Fear of Heaven,* 1976; *Edwin,* 1982; *Rumpole,* from his own stories, 1988; *Glasnost,* 1988.

Television Plays: *Call Me a Liar,* 1958; *David and Broccoli,* 1960; *A Choice of Kings,* 1966; *The Exploding Azalea,* 1966; *The Head Waiter,* 1966; *Hughie,* 1967; *The Other Side,* 1967; *Desmond,* 1968; *Infidelity Took Place,* 1968; *Married Alive,* 1980; *Swiss Cottage,* 1972; *Knightsbridge,* 1972; *Rumpole of the Bailey,* 1975, and series, 1978, 1979, 1987, 1988; *A Little Place off the Edgware Road, The Blue Film, The Destructors, The Case for the Defence, Chagrin in Three Parts, The Invisible Japanese Gentlemen, Special Duties,* and *Mortmain,* all from stories by Graham Greene, 1975-76; *Will Shakespeare,* 1978; *Rumpole's Return,* 1980; *Unity,* from the book by David Pryce-Jones, 1981; *Brideshead Revisited,* from the novel by Evelyn Waugh 1981; *Edwin,* 1984; *The Ebony Tower,* from the story by John Fowles, 1984; *Paradise Postponed,* from his own novel, 1986; *Summer's Lease,* from his own novel, 1989; *The Waiting Room,* 1989.

Other

No Moaning of the Bar (as Geoffrey Lincoln). London, Bles, 1957.
With Love and Lizards (travel), with Penelope Mortimer. London, Joseph, 1957.
Clinging to the Wreckage: A Part of Life (autobiography). London, Weidenfeld and Nicolson, and New Haven, Connecticut, Ticknor and Fields, 1982.

Murderers and Other Friends (autobiography). London and New York, Viking Penguin, 1994.
In Character (interviews). London, Allen Lane, 1983.
The Liberty of the Citizen (lecture), with Franklin Thomas and Lord Hunt of Tanworth. London, Granada, 1983.
Character Parts (interviews). London, Viking, 1986.

Editor, *Famous Trials,* edited by Harry Hodge and James H. Hodge. London, Viking, and New York, Penguin, 1984.
Editor, *Great Law and Order Stories.* London, Bellew, 1990.

*

Manuscript Collections: Boston University; University of California, Los Angeles.

* * *

John Mortimer may have been undervalued from his sheer versatility, for he is equally television playwright (a much more distinguished occupation in Britain than in the United States), dramatist, and novelist. He has also published two enjoyable autobiographies and two collections of interviews with celebrities. He has maintained a commitment to socialism; he explained that he adapted *A Christmas Carol* for the Royal Shakespeare Company in 1994 because the novel was "a denunciation of poverty." He maintained his work as a lawyer for most of his life.

Mortimer's best-known and most entertaining creation is Horace Rumpole, memorably played by Leo McKern, who he has taken through several television series in the years since 1978. Rumpole is a scruffy, aging barrister who is always for the defence, fighting pomposity and self-satisfaction, a lover of cheap claret, devoted to the *Oxford Book of English Verse,* and doomed to a home life in a South Kensington apartment with She Who Must Be Obeyed. Each Rumpole story interweaves his domestic story with the small change of the daily round in his Temple Chambers (including the intrusion of the first woman), and his triumphs and failures in court. Rumpole, as J.W. Lambert wrote in the *Sunday Times,* is "the first of television's multifarious brood to achieve the dignity of literature." Marcel Berlins, writing in the same paper in 1990, goes further: "Rumpole has customarily been described as a great comic creation. He deserves to lose the limiting adjective, comic. He is simply one of the great fictional characters of modern English literature." In the stories, Mortimer succeeds in doing more than adapting his scripts into fiction. His style and intelligence enable him to bring dignity to the limited form of prose-based-on-script.

Paradise Postponed (1985) and its sequel, *Titmuss Regained* (1990), were written simultaneously as novel and television serial (eleven parts for the first and only three for the second). This dual aim does not weaken the novels, which attempt an ambitious Condition of England study from post-war dreams in the 1940s to Thatcher's 1980s. Mortimer sees the England he loves as anticipating the creation of a paradise after victory in war and the election of a Labor government, and questions why that paradise had so conspicuously failed to arrive over the next 40 years.

The issue posed in *Paradise Postponed* is the reason the socialist vicar left his fortune to an exceptionally obnoxious Conservative MP, and not to his sons, a trendy novelist and a worthy doctor. A rural village provides a large supporting cast, from the titled, with ugly duckling daughter, to token farm laborer. The outstanding figure is Leslie Titmuss, embodied on television by David Threlfall. Titmuss, a grammar school boy made good, is a self-righteous opportunist who finds his natural home in the new look Tory Party. In the sequel Titmuss is observed in love (a classy second wife, lured by his purchase of an old manor house) and in the Cabinet, responsible for the creation of new towns, a Thatcherite enterprise he supports—except when on his doorstep. As Penny Perrick wrote in the *Sunday Times,* Mortimer presents "a gritty and immensely satisfying plot which is mercilessly funny in its observations on the way we live now."

Several other television series were published as novels, not in the little-read form of the script. The best was *Summer's Lease* (1989), which involved mysteries around a family vacation in an Italian villa. *Will Shakespeare* (1977) and *Under the Hammer* (1994), about an art auction house, met with less success.

The best of Mortimer's numerous plays is the autobiographical *A Voyage round my Father* (1970). The characters are labelled Father, Mother, the Boy. The focus is a portrait of his larger-than-life father, a barrister who continued working when blind and whose blindness was never to be mentioned; who enjoyed stalking earwigs and hid from visitors; who knew quantities of verse by heart; and who interrupted a solemn Remembrance Day service singing "Sweet Polly Perkins." This anecdotal ramble is an unsentimental homage to his father, while also sketching the English middle class from 1935 to 1960. On the London stage, Mark Dignam created the part, followed by Alec Guinness and then by Laurence Olivier, who played it on television in 1982. Another noteworthy play is the two-hander, *The Dock Brief* (1957).

Mortimer's autobiographies are funny and sometimes moving memories, dreams, and experiences that gradually build to give the reader a sense of the writer's personality, or the personality which he wants publicly known. Mortimer provides insights into people he has known in the theater, like John Gielgud, and to politicians such as Harold Wilson.

The best of Mortimer's work is both intelligent and popular, and embodies qualities of the Victorian novelists he admires as well as the virtues of 20th-century authors such as Somerset Maugham.

—Malcolm Page

MOSLEY, Walter

Nationality: American. **Born:** Los Angeles, 1952. **Education:** Attended Goddard College; received degree from Johnson State College; attended City College of the City University of New York, beginning 1985. **Family:** Married Joy Kellman. **Career:** Formerly a computer programmer; now a full-time writer. **Awards:** Shamus award, Private Eye Writers of America, and Edgar Award nomination, best new mystery, Mystery Writers of America, 1990, both for *Devil in a Blue Dress.* **Agent:** c/o W. W. Norton, 500 Fifth Ave., New York, NY 10110.

Publications

Novels

Devil in a Blue Dress. Norton, 1990.
A Red Death. Norton, 1991.

White Butterfly. Norton, 1992.
Black Betty. Norton, 1994.
R. L.'s Dream. Norton, 1995.
Little Yellow Dog. Norton, 1996.

Plays

Screenplays: *Devil in a Blue Dress,* 1995.

* * *

At first glance, Walter Mosley's mysteries seem to represent the hardboiled school of detective fiction. His detective, Ezekiel "Easy" Rawlins, is a shrewd and wary soul who is trying to survive in a Darwinian world. Mosley's intricate plots are filled with betrayals, double-crossings, multiple murders, and steamy sex within the tough urban landscape of Watts and Los Angeles. The dialogue is blunt, swift, and often brutal, a product of the nightmarish and marginal underworld of the American city. Like several mystery writers, he has developed titles which suggest, in this case, a color-coded series: *Devil in a Blue Dress* (1990), *A Red Death* (1991), *White Butterfly* (1992), and *Black Betty* (1994).

But Mosley's landscape and vision are decidedly his own. As a black writer he explores black urban experience and culture—its music, its nightlife, its mean streets, and its secrets. The visible horrors of racism permeate his world in an intricately realized realm of slang, comradeship, and futility. Within each novel he explores the social dimensions of the times: in *Devil in a Blue Dress* the flight of blacks from the South to work in Los Angeles in the aircraft industry in 1948; the communist-baiting paranoia of 1953 in *A Red Death*; the real-estate and economic boom of 1956 in *White Butterfly*; and in *Black Betty* the spreading poverty and despair of Watts in 1961.

Typical of his carefully structured and elaborate mysteries is *Devil in a Blue Dress,* which was made into a critically acclaimed film in 1995. A black woman passing for white is the devil. She sexually ignites every male around her, becomes the mistress of an important and wealthy white man, seduces Easy Rawlins, discovers the dead body of a former lover, and murders a homosexual candidate for mayor. In the tempestuous and tortuous plot that swirls around her—Easy has been hired to find her—Daphne is revealed to be the half-sister of a notorious gangster and the childhood victim of incest.

In his four mysteries Mosley also traces Easy Rawlins' life. Having fled from a sharecropper's family and the violent streetworld of Houston to work in an aircraft factory in 1948, Easy goes on to adopt Jesus, the young boy whom the homosexual mayor has brought for his own amusement. He finds himself relying on his extremely sociopathic friend, Raymond Alexander "Mouse," when caught in excruciatingly dangerous circumstances. In later novels Easy marries and has a daughter, but Regina, his wife, runs off with their daughter and one of his best friends because Easy refuses to confide in her. He goes on to adopt the daughter of a murdered stripper and, with money given to him by Daphne from what she stole from her white rich lover in the first mystery, continues to make money in the real-estate business, pretending that he works for his own apartment manager.

In 1995 Mosley broke with his cycle of mysteries to write the critically acclaimed *R. L.'s Dream,* a contemporary tale set in the doomed Lower East Side of New York. It is about a dying blues singer and guitar-player, Atwater "Soupspoon" Wise, who is taken in by Kiki Waters, a white Southern woman barely recovering from her father's violent incestuous acts. The two of them try to prop one another up, despite Soupspoon's cancer and Kiki's alcoholism. Before he dies, Soupspoon wants to tape his and others' memories of the famous Robert Johnson, the Delta blues singer whom he befriended in his youth. Soupspoon's life becomes the dream or nightmare that Johnson may have lived, had he not died violently and young in 1938.

Throughout *R. L.'s Dream* Mosley weaves a fascinating tapestry of contemporary racism and hope, childhood encounters and death-haunted tales of the Mississippi Delta, and the sad but strangely noble relationship between Soupspoon, Kiki, and their friends—Mavis, Soupspoon's former wife, and Randy, one of Kiki's present lovers. The novel is filled with stories (a legacy, Mosley insists, from the oral tradition passed on to him by his father and other relatives). Sentiment may overburden individual episodes at times, but the tone and tenor of the book are crisply authentic, heartwarming, at times terrifying, and always moving.

—Samuel Coale

MOWAT, Farley (McGill)

Nationality: Canadian. **Born:** 12 May 1921, in Belleville, Ontario. **Education:** University of Toronto, B.A., 1949. **Military Service:** Canadian Army Infantry, 1939-45; became captain. **Family:** Married Frances Thornhill in 1947 (marriage ended, 1959); married Claire Angel Wheeler in 1964; children: (first marriage) Robert Alexander, David Peter. **Career:** Author. **Awards:** President's medal for best short story, University of Western Ontario, 1952, for "Eskimo Spring"; Anisfield-Wolfe award for contribution to interracial relations, 1954, for *People of the Deer;* Governor General's medal, 1957, and Book of the Year award, Canadian Association of Children's Librarians, both for *Lost in the Barrens;* Canadian Women's Clubs award, 1958, for *The Dog Who Wouldn't Be;* Hans Christian Andersen International award, 1958; Boys' Clubs of America Junior Book award, 1962, for *Owls in the Family;* National Association of Independent Schools award, 1963, for juvenile books; Hans Christian Andersen Honours List, 1965, for juvenile books; Canadian Centennial medal, 1967; Stephen Leacock medal for humor, 1970, and L'Etoile de la Mer Honours List, 1972, both for *The Boat Who Wouldn't Float;* Vicky Metcalf award, 1970; Mark Twain award, 1971; Curran award, 1977, for "contributions to understanding wolves"; Queen Elizabeth II Jubilee medal, 1978; Knight of Mark Twain, 1980; Officer, Order of Canada, 1981; Author's award, Foundation for the Advancement of Canadian Letters, 1985, for *Sea of Slaughter;* Book of the Year designation, Foundation for the Advancement of Canadian Letters, and named Author of the Year, Canadian Booksellers Association, both 1988, both for *Virunga;* Gemini award for best documentary script, 1989, for *The New North;* Take Back the Nation award, Council of Canadians, 1991. Honorary degrees: D.Lit., Laurentian University, 1970; Doctor of Law from Lethbridge University, 1973, University of Toronto, 1973, and University of Prince Edward Island, 1979; Doctor of Literature, University of Victoria, 1982, and Lakehead University, 1986. **Address:** c/o Key Porter Books Ltd., 70 The Esplanade, Toronto, Ontario M5E 1R2, Canada.

Publications

Nonfiction

People of the Deer. Little, Brown, 1952; revised edition, McClelland & Stewart, 1975.
The Regiment. McClelland & Stewart, 1955; revised edition, 1973.
The Dog Who Wouldn't Be. Little, Brown, 1957.
The Grey Seas Under. Little, Brown, 1958.
The Desperate People. Little, Brown, 1959; revised, McClelland & Stewart, 1976.
The Serpent's Coil. McClelland & Stewart, 1961, Little, Brown, 1962.
Never Cry Wolf. Little, Brown, 1963; revised edition, McClelland & Stewart, 1973.
Westviking: The Ancient Norse in Greenland and North America. Little, Brown, 1965.
Canada North. Little, Brown, 1967.
This Rock within the Sea: A Heritage Lost, photographs by John de Visser. Little, Brown, 1969; new edition, McClelland & Stewart, 1976.
The Boat Who Wouldn't Float. McClelland & Stewart, 1969, Little, Brown, 1970.
Sibir: My Discovery of Siberia. McClelland & Stewart, 1970; revised edition, 1973; as *The Siberians*, Little, Brown, 1971.
A Whale for the Killing. Little, Brown, 1972.
Wake of the Great Sealers, illustrated by David Blackwood. Little, Brown, 1973.
The Great Betrayal: Arctic Canada Now. Little, Brown, 1976; as *Canada North Now: The Great Betrayal*, McClelland & Stewart, 1976.
And No Birds Sang. McClelland & Stewart, 1979; Little, Brown, 1980.
The World of Farley Mowat: A Selection from His Works, edited by Peter Davison. Little, Brown, 1980.
Sea of Slaughter. Atlantic Monthly Press, 1984.
My Discovery of America. Little, Brown, 1985.
Woman in the Mists: The Story of Dian Fossey and the Mountain Gorillas of Africa. Warner Books, 1987; as *Virunga: The Passion of Dian Fossey*, McClelland & Stewart, 1987.
The New Founde Land: A Personal Voyage of Discovery. McClelland & Stewart, 1989.
Rescue the Earth. McClelland & Stewart, 1990.
Born Naked: The Early Adventures of the Author of "Never Cry Wolf." Key Porter, 1993; Houghton, 1994.
My Father's Son: Memories of War and Peace. Houghton, 1993.

Plays

Television Plays: *Sea Fare*, 1964; *Diary of a Boy on Vacation*, 1964.

Novels for Young Adults

Lost in the Barrens, illustrated by Charles Geer. Little, Brown, 1956; as *Two Against the North*, illustrated by Alan Daniel. Scholastic-TAB, 1977.
The Black Joke, illustrated by D. Johnson. McClelland & Stewart, 1962; illustrated by Victory Mays, Little, Brown, 1963.
The Curse of the Viking Grave, illustrated by Geer. Little, Brown, 1966.

Nonfiction for Young Adults

Owls in the Family, illustrated by Robert Frankenberg. Little, Brown, 1961.

Short Stories

The Snow Walker. McClelland & Stewart, 1975; Little, Brown, 1976.

Editor, *Top of the World Trilogy*. McClelland & Stewart, 1976.
Ordeal by Ice. McClelland & Stewart, 1960; Little, Brown, 1961.
The Polar Passion: The Quest for the North Pole, with Selections from Arctic Journals. McClelland & Stewart, 1967; Little, Brown, 1968; revised edition, 1973.
Tundra: Selections from the Great Accounts of Arctic Land Voyages. McClelland & Stewart, 1973; Peregrine Smith, 1990.

*

Media Adaptations: Film—*Never Cry Wolf*, 1983. Television films—*A Whale for the Killing*, 1980; *Lost in the Barrens*, 1990; *Curse of the Viking Grave*, 1992. Television documentaries—*The New North*, 1989; *Sea of Slaughter* ("The Nature of Things" series), 1990.

Manuscript Collection: McMaster University, Hamilton, Ontario.

Critical Study: *Farley Mowat* by Alex Lucas, McClelland & Stewart, 1976.

* * *

Farley Mowat has become Canada's best-known defender of nature. In his books, Mowat makes clear that unless humankind stops its overexploitation of natural resources, wild species, and indigenous peoples, it faces certain extinction. Mowat often conveys this serious message, however, with pointed humor, particularly in skewering governments for not responding to this crisis. Though the emotional force of Mowat's work has won him many readers, critics often dismiss Mowat as too passionate and too loose in style to be considered a serious author. Such criticism never fazed Mowat. He has described himself as "a storyteller who is far more concerned with reaching his audience than with garnering kudos from the arbiters of literary greatness."

After witnessing brutal killing as a World War II soldier in Italy, Mowat took a respite from humanity to serve as a government biologist in remote northern Canada, where he was sent to document the role of the wolf in the region's dwindling number of caribou. There, Mowat befriended and learned the language of the Ihalmiuts, an inland Eskimo people who, because they depended on the caribou for survival, were also dying off. Mowat wrote of the Ihalmiuts in his first book, *People of the Deer* (1952). In telling the story of this gentle tribe and of the Canadian government's indifference toward its preservation, Mowat "contrived the most damning indictment of his own government and country, the so-called white race and its Anglo-Saxon branch in particular, the Christian religion, and civilization as a whole, that had ever been written," wrote *Saturday Review* contributor Ivan T. Sanderson.

When Mowat reported to the government that its wildlife mismanagement, not the wolf, was causing the caribou's decline, his report was quickly dismissed. Mowat instead fashioned his interpretation into an often funny work of fiction, *Never Cry Wolf* (1963), which forever transformed many a reader's image of the wild. David Graber wrote in the *Los Angeles Times Book Review* that "by writing *Never Cry Wolf,* [Mowat] almost single-handedly reversed the public's image of the wolf, from feared vermin to romantic symbol of the wilderness."

Through the 1960s, Mowat continued to write about the North in books that recounted early Arctic explorations, Mowat's trips to Siberia, and tales of sea adventure. Mowat returned to the strong defense of wildlife after an 80-ton fin whale became caught in a tidal pond near his home of Burgeo, Newfoundland. To Mowat's horror, townspeople amused themselves by shooting at the whale with rifles. But in writing *A Whale for the Killing* (1972), Mowat reserved his harshest words for the government and for scientists, who reacted too slowly—or didn't react at all—to save the whale's life.

Mowat's most important work was *Sea of Slaughter* (1984), where he explained humanity's clear role in the extinction or near-extinction of many North Atlantic land and sea animals which, just four centuries before, had been plentiful in number. Mowat followed with a biography of primatologist Dian Fossey, *Woman in the Mists: The Story of Dian Fossey and the Mountain Gorillas of Africa* (1987), which was commissioned after her murder in 1985. Unfortunately, Mowat stayed too true to her journals and used weak narrative to bridge between the entries. As a result, wrote *Chicago Tribune* contributor Anita Susan Grossman, "the central drama of Fossey's life remains as murky as the circumstances of her death."

Mowat has also written more light-hearted children's books such as *Lost in the Barrens* (1956), about two teenaged boys forced to brave the winter in the Arctic wilderness, and *The Dog Who Wouldn't Be* (1957), a humorous recollection of an odd family pet. Alec Lucas writes in *Canadian's Children's Literature,* "Mowat's children's books . . . demonstrate his desire on the one hand to indoctrinate boys with his social concepts and values and, on the other, to retain the pleasant memories of his childhood."

—Eric Patterson

MYLES, Symon. *See* **FOLLETT, Ken.**

N-O

NAYLOR, Gloria

Nationality: American. **Born:** New York City, 25 January 1950. **Education:** Brooklyn College, New York, B.A. in English 1981; Yale University, New Haven, Connecticut, 1981-83, M.A. in Afro-American Studies 1983. **Career:** Missionary for the Jehovah's Witnesses, New York, North Carolina, and Florida, 1968-75; telephone operator, New York City hotels, 1975-81. Writer-in-residence, Cummington Community of the Arts, Massachusetts, Summer 1983; visiting professor, George Washington University, Washington, D.C., 1983-84, University of Pennsylvania, Philadelphia, 1986, New York University, 1986, Princeton University, New Jersey, 1986-87, and Boston University, 1987; Fannie Hurst Visiting Professor, Brandeis University, Waltham, Massachusetts, 1988; United States Information Agency Cultural Exchange Lecturer, India, Fall 1985. Columnist, *New York Times,* 1986. Since 1988 judge, Book-of-the-Month Club. **Awards:** American Book award, 1983; National Endowment for the Arts fellowship, 1985; Guggenheim fellowship, 1988. **Address:** c/o One Way Productions, 638 Second Street, Brooklyn, New York 11215, U.S.A.

PUBLICATIONS

Novels

The Women of Brewster Place: A Novel in Seven Stories. New York, Viking Press, 1982; London, Hodder and Stoughton, 1983.
Linden Hills. New York, Ticknor and Fields, and London, Hodder and Stoughton, 1985.
Mama Day. New York, Ticknor and Fields, and London, Hutchinson, 1988.
Bailey's Café. New York, Harcourt Brace, 1992; London, Minerva, 1993.

Uncollected Short Story

"Life on Beekman Place," in *Essence* (New York), March 1980.

*

Media Adaptations: Television series—*Brewster Place,* 1989-90.

Critical Study: *Gloria Naylor: Critical Perspectives Past and Present* edited by Henry Louis Gates and K. A. Appiah, New York, Amistad, 1993.

* * *

Beginning with her first novel, *The Women of Brewster Place* (1983), Gloria Naylor has tried to capture the black female experience for both black and white readers. She told *Contemporary Writers,* "I wanted to become a writer because I felt that my presence as a black woman and my perspective as a woman in general had been underrepresented in American literature."

The Women of Brewster Place, an intergenerational tale of seven black women's triumphs and struggles, is an illustration of how women who vastly differ in age, social background, personal strength, and sexual orientation can be close friends. Extended and chosen families are also key in the novel; we meet and get to know—or at least hear about—the women's husbands, ex-husbands, lovers, children, parents, and other relatives and significant people. In short, *The Women of Brewster Place* is about life. But the novel is also about death and the painful journey faced by those left behind. The novel was adapted into a miniseries in 1989, and became a weekly series on ABC in 1990.

Naylor's second novel, *Linden Hills* (1985), portrays a more affluent area from which an idealistic, disenchanted young woman flees to the inner city. She is a carryover from *The Women of Brewster Place.* Indeed, Naylor makes a habit of carrying at least one character from each novel into the next. In *The Women of Brewster Place* we see a glimpse of the spiritual decay and material greediness that drove the woman out of her posh surroundings. In *Linden Hills* we receive the whole story, not from the woman's chosen refuge, but from her surroundings of origin. The novel is presented as a stark comparison between the noble-hearted poor and the often selfish motivations of the wealthy.

Mama Day (1988), named for its main character, features a 90-year-old fortune teller. She, too, appears in one of Naylor's previous works. She is portrayed in *Linden Hills* as a toothless eccentric. The setting of *Mama Day* is an island off the coast of Georgia and South Carolina that has been in Mama Day's family since before the Civil War. Rita Mae Brown contends that Naylor turns the world upside down by portraying slaves as property owners. Actually, it is Mama Day herself, more than anyone, who turns the world upside down; her magical powers not only make life easier for those she helps, but she saves the life of her grandniece when she falls dangerously ill.

Some critics have found fault with Naylor because, although they enjoy her wonderfully presented characters, they at times believe her technique to be flawed. Jewelle Gomez believes that Naylor's work "often feels like a literary exercise rather than a groundbreaking adaptation." Indeed, pulling off well-executed modern renditions of Dante's *The Inferno* (*Linden Hills*) and Shakespeare's *Hamlet* and *The Tempest* (*Mama Day*) is a tough task. But Naylor's ambitions are admirable and her fans numerous.

—Tracy Clark

NICHOLS, Leigh. *See* **KOONTZ, Dean R(ay).**

NIVEN, Larry

Nationality: American. **Born:** Laurence Van Cott Niven, Los Angeles, California, 30 April 1938. **Education:** California Institute of Technology, Pasadena, 1956-58; Washburn University, Topeka, Kansas, A.B. 1962; University of California, Los Angeles, 1962-63. **Family:** Married Marylin Wosowati in 1969. **Career:** Since 1964, freelance writer. **Awards:** Hugo award, for story, 1967, 1972, 1975, 1976, for novel, 1971; Nebula award, 1970; Ditmar award, 1971; *Locus* award, 1985. **Address:** c/o Baen Publishing Enterprises, 260 Fifth Avenue, Suite 35, New York, New York 10001, U.S.A.

PUBLICATIONS

Novels (series: Dream Park; Known Space; Magic; Moat; Buck Rogers)

World of Ptavvs (Space). New York, Ballantine, 1966; London, Macdonald, 1968.
A Gift from Earth (Space). New York, Ballantine, 1968; London, Macdonald, 1969.
Ringworld (Space). New York, Ballantine, 1970; London, Gollancz, 1972.
The Flying Sorcerers, with David Gerrold. New York, Ballantine, 1971; London, Corgi, 1975.
Protector (Space). New York, Ballantine, 1973; Tisbury, Wiltshire, Compton Russell, 1976.
The Mote in God's Eye, with Jerry Pournelle. New York, Simon and Schuster, 1974; London, Weidenfeld and Nicolson, 1975.
Inferno, with Jerry Pournelle. New York, Pocket Books, 1976; London, Wingate, 1977.
A World out of Time. New York, Holt Rinehart, 1976; London, Macdonald and Jane's 1977.
Lucifer's Hammer, with Jerry Pournelle. Chicago, Playboy Press, 1977.
The Magic Goes Away. New York, Ace, 1978; London, Futura, 1982.
The Ringworld Engineers (Space). West Bloomfield, Michigan, Phantasia Press, 1979; London, Gollancz, 1980.
Mordred (Buck Rogers), with Jerry Pournelle and John Eric Holmes. New York, Ace, 1980.
The Patchwork Girl (Space). New York, Ace, 1980; London, Macdonald, 1982.
Dream Park, with Steven Barnes. Huntington Woods, Michigan, Phantasia Press, 1981; London, Macdonald, 1983.
Oath of Fealty, with Jerry Pournelle. Huntington Woods, Michigan, Phantasia Press, 1981; London, Macdonald, 1982.
Warrior's Blood (Buck Rogers), with Jerry Pournelle and Richard S. McEnroe. New York, Ace, 1981.
Warrior's World (Buck Rogers), with Jerry Pournelle and Richard S. McEnroe. New York, Ace, 1981.
The Descent of Anansi, with Steven Barnes. New York, Tor, 1982; London, Orbit, 1992.
Rogers' Rangers (Buck Rogers), with Jerry Pournelle and John Silbersack. New York, Ace, 1983.
The Integral Trees (Space). New York, Ballantine, and London, Macdonald, 1984.
Footfall, with Jerry Pournelle. New York, Ballantine, and London, Gollancz, 1985.
The Legacy of Heorot, with Jerry Pournelle and Steven Barnes. London, Gollancz, and New York, Simon and Schuster, 1987.
The Smoke Ring (Space). New York, Ballantine, and London, Macdonald, 1987.
The Man-Kzin Wars, with Poul Anderson and Dean Ing. New York, Baen, 1988; London, Orbit, 1989.
The Man-Kzin Wars II, with Dean Ing, Jerry Pournelle, and S.M. Stirling. New York, Baen, 1989; London, Orbit, 1991.
The Barsoom Project (Dream Park), with Steven Barnes. New York, Ace, 1989; London, Pan, 1990.
The Man-Kzin Wars III, with Poul Anderson, Jerry Pournelle, and S.M. Stirling. New York, Baen, 1990.
Achilles' Choice, with Steven Barnes. New York, Tor, 1991; London, Pan, 1993.
Fallen Angels, with Jerry Pournelle and Michael Flynn. Norwalk, Connecticut, Easton Press, 1991; London, Pan, 1993.
The Voodoo Game (Dream Park). London, Pan, 1991; as *The California Voodoo Game*, New York, Ballantine, 1992.
The Gripping Hand (Moat), with Jerry Pournelle. New York, Pocket Books, 1993; as *The Moat around Murcheson's Eye*, London, HarperCollins, 1993.
Beowulf's Children, with Jerry Pournelle and Steve Barnes. New York, Pocket Books, 1995.

Short Stories (series: Known Space)

Neutron Star (Space). New York, Ballantine, 1968; London, Macdonald, 1969.
The Shape of Space (Space). New York, Ballantine, 1969.
All the Myriad Ways. New York, Ballantine, 1971.
The Flight of the Horse. New York, Ballantine, 1973; London, Futura, 1975.
Inconstant Moon. London, Gollancz, 1973.
A Hole in Space. New York, Ballantine, 1974; London, Futura, 1975.
Tales of Known Space: The Universe of Larry Niven. New York, Ballantine, 1975; London, Orbit, 1992.
The Long ARM of Gil Hamilton (Space). New York, Ballantine, 1976; London, Futura, 1980.
Convergent Series (Space). New York, Ballantine, 1979; London, Orbit, 1986.
The Time of the Warlock, illustrated by Dennis Wolf. Minneapolis, Steel Dragon Press, 1984.
Niven's Laws (includes articles). Philadelphia, Philadelphia Science Fiction Society, 1984.
Limits. New York, Ballantine, 1985; London, Orbit, 1986.
N-Space. New York, Tor, 1990; London, Orbit, 1992.
Playgrounds of the Mind. New York, Tor, 1991.
Man-Kzin Wars IV, with Donald Kingsbury, Greg Bear, and S.M. Stirling. Riverdale, New York, Baen, 1991.
Man-Kzin Wars V, with Jerry Pournelle, S.M. Stirling, and Thomas T. Thomas. Riverdale, New York, Baen, 1992.
Bridging the Galaxies. San Francisco, ConFrancisco, 1993.
Crashlander (Space). New York, Ballantine, 1995.
Man-Kzin Wars VI, with Donald Kingsbury, Mark O. Martin, and Gregory Benford. Riverdale, New York, Baen, 1994.
Flatlander (Space). New York, Ballantine, 1995.

Other

Editor, *The Magic May Return*. New York, Ace, 1981.
Editor, *More Magic*. New York, Berkley, 1984.

*

Bibliography: *The Guide to Larry Niven's Ringworld* by Kevin Stein, Riverdale, New York, Baen, 1994.

Manuscript Collection: George Arents Research Library, Syracuse University, New York.

* * *

Larry Niven is a prolific science fiction writer who loves to mix hard science with mind-blowing ideas about time and space. He has collaborated with several authors, particularly Jerry Pournelle. He also has five science fiction series under his belt: Dream Park, Magic, Moat, Buck Rogers, and Known Space, his most popular.

The Known Space series includes *Ringworld* (1970) and *The Ringworld Engineers* (1979). These two novels are concerned with an artificial world which consists of a titanic wheel with a sun at its hub. With a clever speculative science, Niven sketches an intriguing alien race in a clear and efficient style. *Ringworld* was more highly regarded than its sequel due to shallow plotting in the latter. *The Protector* (1973), also of the series, was praised as hard core science fiction at its best. Aliens slip into the colonized Solar System to inform humanity that they are merely a larval stage for a more advanced species. The novel is peppered with good dialogue and well-drawn characters.

Two entries in the Known Space series detail life in a band of breathable air surrounding a decaying neutron star within which float strange flora and fauna and tribes of tree-dwelling people. *The Integral Trees* (1984) follows the travels of the migrating Quinn tribe who must vacate after their tree dies. The alien environment, in true Niven fashion, is superbly detailed. The plot may be unoriginal but the premise is inventive and well-paced. The sequel *The Smoke Ring* (1987) was praised by many for being even better than its predecessor. The novel showcases Niven's talent for placing humans in extremely original settings and confronting them with unusual problems. Most criticism relates to Niven's most prevalent weakness, indistinguishable characters.

Niven has collaborated numerous times with fellow science fiction writer Jerry Pournelle. Their first collaboration, *The Mote in God's Eye* (1974), is about the first contact between humans and another sentient species. It was well-received critically. The conflict exists between the humans' desire for knowledge and the fear of the unknown. The most highly praised aspect of the novel was the highly original characterization of the alien race, the Moties. The view of alien life is outstanding in its inventiveness and realism. Niven and Pournelle cooked up a wonderful stew of adventure, war, science, politics, and sociology with an added dash of humor besides. The sequel to *Mote,* entitled *The Gripping Hand,* came in 1993. Two characters surviving from the first novel become convinced that the Moties are attempting to break out of the quarantine surrounding their system. As with the first installment, the aliens are still far more interesting than the humans.

Niven has also published several short story collections. His short stories mirror his novels in their strengths and weaknesses. Like his novels, his stories are long on concept and short on characterization. Niven focuses so intensely on scientific detail and the nuances of his fantasy worlds that literary style and characterization often lose out. Nevertheless, few hard science fiction writers are as inventive or have such a keen eye for detail.

—Jennifer G. Coman

NORTH, Anthony. *See* **KOONTZ, Dean R(ay).**

OATES, Joyce Carol

Pseudonym: Rosamond Smith. **Nationality:** American. **Born:** Millersport, New York, 16 June 1938. **Education:** Syracuse University, New York, 1956-60, B.A. in English 1960 (Phi Beta Kappa); University of Wisconsin, Madison, M.A. in English 1961; Rice University, Houston, 1961. **Family:** Married Raymond J. Smith in 1961. **Career:** Instructor, 1961-65, and assistant professor of English, 1965-67, University of Detroit; member of the Department of English, University of Windsor, Ontario, 1967-78. Since 1978 writer-in-residence, and currently Roger S. Berlind Distinguished Professor, Princeton University, New Jersey. Since 1974 publisher, with Raymond J. Smith, *Ontario Review,* Windsor, later Princeton. **Awards:** National Endowment for the Arts grant, 1966, 1968; Guggenheim fellowship, 1967; O. Henry award, 1967, 1973, and Special Award for Continuing Achievement, 1970, 1986; Rosenthal award, 1968; National Book award, 1970; Rea award, for short story, 1990; Bobst Lifetime Achievement award, 1990; Heideman award, 1990, for one-act play; Walt Whitman award, 1995. **Member:** American Academy, 1978. **Agent:** John Hawkins and Associates, 71 West 23rd Street, Suite 1600, New York, New York 10010. **Address:** 185 Nassau Street, Princeton, New Jersey 08540, U.S.A.

PUBLICATIONS

Novels

With Shuddering Fall. New York, Vanguard Press, 1964; London, Cape, 1965.
A Garden of Earthly Delights. New York, Vanguard Press, 1967; London, Gollancz, 1970.
Expensive People. New York, Vanguard Press, 1968; London, Gollancz, 1969.
Them. New York, Vanguard Press, 1969; London, Gollancz, 1971.
Wonderland. New York, Vanguard Press, 1971; London, Gollancz, 1972.
Do with Me What You Will. New York, Vanguard Press, 1973; London, Gollancz, 1974.
The Assassins: A Book of Hours. New York, Vanguard Press, 1975.
Childwold. New York, Vanguard Press, 1976; London, Gollancz, 1977.
Son of the Morning. New York, Vanguard Press, 1978; London, Gollancz, 1979.
Cybele. Santa Barbara, California, Black Sparrow Press, 1979.
Unholy Loves. New York, Vanguard Press, 1979; London, Gollancz, 1980.
Bellefleur. New York, Dutton, 1980; London, Cape, 1981.
Angel of Light. New York, Dutton, and London, Cape, 1981.

A Bloodsmoor Romance. New York, Dutton, 1982; London, Cape, 1983.
Mysteries of Winterthurn. New York, Dutton, and London, Cape, 1984.
Solstice. New York, Dutton, and London, Cape, 1985.
Marya: A Life. New York, Dutton, 1986; London, Cape, 1987.
You Must Remember This. New York, Dutton, 1987; London, Macmillan, 1988.
American Appetites. New York, Dutton, and London, Macmillan, 1989.
Because It Is Bitter, and Because It Is My Heart. New York, Dutton, 1990; London, Macmillan, 1991.
I Lock My Door upon Myself. New York, Ecco Press, 1990.
The Rise of Life on Earth. New York, New Directions, 1991.
Black Water. New York, Dutton, 1992.
Foxfire: Confessions of a Girl Gang. New York, Dutton, 1993.
What I Lived For. New York, Dutton, 1994.
Zombie. New York, Dutton, 1995.
First Love: A Gothic Tale. New York, Dutton, 1996.

Novels as Rosamond Smith

Lives of the Twins. New York, Simon and Schuster, 1987.
Soul-Mate. New York, Dutton, 1989.
Snake Eyes. New York, Dutton, 1992.
You Can't Catch Me. New York, Dutton, 1995.

Short Stories

By the North Gate. New York, Vanguard Press, 1963.
Upon the Sweeping Flood and Other Stories. New York, Vanguard Press, 1966; London, Gollancz, 1973.
The Wheel of Love and Other Stories. New York, Vanguard Press, 1970; London, Gollancz, 1971.
Cupid and Psyche. New York, Albondocani Press, 1970.
Marriages and Infidelities. New York, Vanguard Press, 1972; London, Gollancz, 1974.
A Posthumous Sketch. Los Angeles, Black Sparrow Press, 1973.
The Girl. Cambridge, Massachusetts, Pomegranate Press, 1974.
Plagiarized Material (as Fernandes/Oates). Los Angeles, Black Sparrow Press, 1974.
The Goddess and Other Women. New York, Vanguard Press, 1974; London, Gollancz, 1975.
Where Are You Going, Where Have You Been? Stories of Young America. Greenwich, Connecticut, Fawcett, 1974.
The Hungry Ghosts: Seven Allusive Comedies. Los Angeles, Black Sparrow Press, 1974; Solihull, Warwickshire, Aquila, 1975.
The Seduction and Other Stories. Los Angeles, Black Sparrow Press, 1975.
The Poisoned Kiss and Other Stories from the Portuguese (as Fernandes/Oates). New York, Vanguard Press, 1975; London, Gollancz, 1976.
The Triumph of the Spider Monkey. Santa Barbara, California, Black Sparrow Press, 1976.
The Blessing. Santa Barbara, California, Black Sparrow Press, 1976.
Crossing the Border. New York, Vanguard Press, 1976; London, Gollancz, 1978.
Daisy. Santa Barbara, California, Black Sparrow Press, 1977.
Night-Side. New York, Vanguard Press, 1977; London, Gollancz, 1979.
A Sentimental Education. Los Angeles, Sylvester and Orphanos, 1978.
The Step-Father. Northridge, California, Lord John Press, 1978.
All the Good People I've Left Behind. Santa Barbara, California, Black Sparrow Press, 1979.
The Lamb of Abyssalia. Cambridge, Massachusetts, Pomegranate Press, 1979.
A Middle-Class Education. New York, Albondocani Press, 1980.
A Sentimental Education (collection). New York, Dutton, 1980; London, Cape, 1981.
Funland. Concord, New Hampshire, Ewert, 1983.
Last Days. New York, Dutton, 1984; London, Cape, 1985.
Wild Saturday and Other Stories. London, Dent, 1984.
Wild Nights. Athens, Ohio, Croissant, 1985.
Raven's Wing. New York, Dutton, 1986; London, Cape, 1987.
The Assignation. New York, Ecco Press, 1988.
Heat and Other Stories. New York, Dutton, 1991.
Where Is Here? Hopewell, New Jersey, Ecco, 1992.
Haunted: Tales of the Grotesque. New York, Dutton, 1994.
Will You Always Love Me? and Other Stories. New York, Dutton, 1996.

Plays

The Sweet Enemy (produced New York, 1965).
Sunday Dinner (produced New York, 1970).
Ontological Proof of My Existence, music by George Prideaux (produced New York, 1972). Included in *Three Plays,* 1980.
Miracle Play (produced New York, 1973). Los Angeles, Black Sparrow Press, 1974.
Daisy (produced New York, 1980).
Three Plays (includes *Ontological Proof of My Existence, Miracle Play, The Triumph of the Spider Monkey*). Windsor, Ontario Review Press, 1980.
The Triumph of the Spider Monkey, from her own story (produced Los Angeles, 1985). Included in *Three Plays,* 1980.
Presque Isle, music by Paul Shapiro (produced New York, 1982).
Lechery, in *Faustus in Hell* (produced Princeton, New Jersey, 1985).
In Darkest America (*Tone Clusters* and *The Eclipse*) (produced Louisville, Kentucky, 1990; *The Eclipse* produced New York, 1990).
American Holiday (produced Los Angeles, 1990).
I Stand Before You Naked (produced New York, 1991).
How Do You Like Your Meat? (produced New Haven, Connecticut, 1991).
Twelve Plays. New York, Dutton, 1991.
Black (produced Williamstown, 1992).
The Secret Mirror (produced Philadelphia, 1992).
The Perfectionist (produced Princeton, New Jersey, 1993). In *The Perfectionist and Other Plays,* 1995.
The Truth-Teller (produced New York, 1995).
Here She Is! (produced Philadelphia, 1995).
The Perfectionist and Other Plays. Hopewell, New Jersey, Ecco, 1995.

Poetry

Women in Love and Other Poems. New York, Albondocani Press, 1968.

Anonymous Sins and Other Poems. Baton Rouge, Louisiana State University Press, 1969.
Love and Its Derangements. Baton Rouge, Louisiana State University Press, 1970.
Woman Is the Death of the Soul. Toronto, Coach House Press, 1970.
In Case of Accidental Death. Cambridge, Massachusetts, Pomegranate Press, 1972.
Wooded Forms. New York, Albondocani Press, 1972.
Angel Fire. Baton Rouge, Louisiana State University Press, 1973.
Dreaming America and Other Poems. New York, Aloe Editions, 1973.
The Fabulous Beasts. Baton Rouge, Louisiana State University Press, 1975.
Public Outcry. Pittsburgh, Slow Loris Press, 1976.
Season of Peril. Santa Barbara, California, Black Sparrow Press, 1977.
Abandoned Airfield 1977. Northridge, California, Lord John Press, 1977.
Snowfall. Northridge, California, Lord John Press, 1978.
Women Whose Lives Are Food, Men Whose Lives Are Money. Baton Rouge, Louisiana State University Press, 1978.
The Stone Orchard. Northridge, California, Lord John Press, 1980.
Celestial Timepiece. Dallas, Pressworks, 1980.
Nightless Nights: Nine Poems. Concord, New Hampshire, Ewert, 1981.
Invisible Woman: New and Selected Poems 1970-1982. Princeton, New Jersey, Ontario Review Press, 1982.
Luxury of Sin. Northridge, California, Lord John Press, 1984.
The Time Traveller: Poems 1983-1989. New York, Dutton, 1989.

Other

The Edge of Impossibility: Tragic Forms in Literature. New York, Vanguard Press, 1972; London, Gollancz, 1976.
The Hostile Sun: The Poetry of D.H. Lawrence. Los Angeles, Black Sparrow Press, 1973; Solihull, Warwickshire, Aquila, 1975.
New Heaven, New Earth: The Visionary Experience in Literature. New York, Vanguard Press, 1974; London, Gollancz, 1976.
The Stone Orchard. Northridge, California, Lord John Press, 1980.
Contraries: Essays. New York, Oxford University Press, 1981.
The Profane Art: Essays and Reviews. New York, Dutton, 1983.
Funland. Concord, New Hampshire, Ewert, 1983.
On Boxing, photographs by John Ranard. New York, Doubleday, and London, Bloomsbury, 1987; expanded edition, Hopewell, New Jersey, Ecco, 1994.
(Woman) Writer: Occasions and Opportunities. New York, Dutton, 1988.
Conversations with Joyce Carol Oates, edited by Lee Milazzo. Jackson, University Press of Mississippi, 1989.
George Bellows: American Artist. Hopewell, New Jersey, Ecco, 1995.

Editor, *Scenes from American Life: Contemporary Short Fiction.* New York, Vanguard Press, 1973.
Editor, with Shannon Ravenel, *The Best American Short Stories 1979.* Boston, Houghton Mifflin, 1979.
Editor, *Night Walks: A Bedside Companion.* Princeton, New Jersey, Ontario Review Press, 1982.
Editor *First Person Singular: Writers on Their Craft.* Princeton, New Jersey, Ontario Review Press, 1983.
Editor, with Boyd Litzinger, *Story: Fictions Past and Present.* Lexington, Massachusetts, Heath, 1985.
Editor, with Daniel Halpern, *Reading the Fights* (on boxing). New York, Holt, 1988.

*

Bibliography: *Joyce Carol Oates: An Annotated Bibliography* by Francine Lercangée, New York, Garland, 1986.

Manuscript Collection: Syracuse University, New York.

Critical Studies: *The Tragic Vision of Joyce Carol Oates* by Mary Kathryn Grant, Durham, North Carolina, Duke University Press, 1978; *Joyce Carol Oates* by Joanne V. Creighton, Boston, Twayne, 1979; *Critical Essays on Joyce Carol Oates* edited by Linda W. Wagner, Boston, Hall, 1979; *Dreaming America: Obsession and Transcendence in the Fiction of Joyce Carol Oates* by G.F. Waller, Baton Rouge, Louisiana State University Press, 1979; *Joyce Carol Oates* by Ellen G. Friedman, New York, Ungar, 1980; *Joyce Carol Oates's Short Stories: Between Tradition and Innovation* by Katherine Bastian, Bern, Switzerland, Lang, 1983; *The Image of the Intellectual in the Short Stories of Joyce Carol Oates* by Hermann Severin, New York, Lang, 1986; *Joyce Carol Oates: Artist in Residence* by Eileen Teper Bender, Bloomington, Indiana University Press, 1987; *Understanding Joyce Carol Oates* by Greg Johnson, Columbia, University of South Carolina Press, 1987.

* * *

The short stories in *By the North Gate* (1963) began a writing career for Joyce Carol Oates so prolific that criticizing her for her abundant output of novels, essays, short stories, poems, and drama became fashionable, despite praise as a "writer's writer" and her winning of the National Book Award for *Them* (1969), the last of a trilogy that included *Garden of Earthly Delights* (1967) and *Expensive People* (1968). This trilogy characterizes Oates' style of psychological realism through exploration of the "darker aspects of the human condition" and "the excesses of American culture" as seen from distinct social levels and geographic regions. She achieves verisimilitude for each work's time period by weaving into its setting real events, such as the McCarthy Hearings or Watergate.

One of her geographic settings, Eden County, New York, is a fictionalized Lockport, New York, which she uses with Detroit, a city that she says "made me the person I am, consequently the writer I am." This urban setting figures in *Do With Me What You Will* (1973) and *Them,* and in some stories in *Marriages and Infidelities* (1972).

Many hold Oates as "America's preeminent master of the short story," citing her chilling *Heat and Other Stories* (1992) and surrealistic, macabre *Haunted: Tales of the Grotesque* (1994). Those books include essays that explore American society's fascination with frightening, degrading, and violent things; a fascination explored in the psychological thriller *You Can't Catch Me* (1994), one of five books published using her pseudonym Rosamond Smith.

Oates' trademarks of physical and psychological violence fuse in *Wonderland* (1971). Greg Johnson calls this haunting study of the human brain a turning point for Oates. *Wonderland's* narrative of Dr. Jesse Vogel begins a series that probes American institutions through the conflict of "emotionally needy intellectuals" with their social environments. In addition to medicine, Oates looks at law in *Do With Me What You Will*; politics in *The Assassins: A Book of Hours* (1975); religion in *Son of the Morning* (1978); and academics in *Unholy Loves* (1979).

Oates also penned a Gothic trilogy that is "parodic" of 19th-century techniques. Dean Flower chastises her for this "costume fiction," but the million-seller *Bellefleur* (1980)—a "magnificent piece" according to John Gardner—*A Bloodsmore Romance* (1982), and *Mysteries of Winterthurn* (1984) attracted feminist critics, as did her next novels *Solstice* (1985) and *Marya: A Life* (1986). The latter work was constructed in penetrating episodes about a woman academic and the people and events that define her life.

Not surprisingly, but to the consternation of some sports enthusiasts, Oates published *On Boxing* (1987); Oates calls boxing "America's tragic theater." In "Golden Gloves" (1986) Oates gets inside "the skin and the muscle" of a boxer. Equally praised are her descriptions of boxing events in *You Must Remember This* (1987), a "blatantly sexual book" that includes attempted suicides, abortion, car accidents, and a brutally passionate affair between adolescent Enid Stevick and her Uncle Felix, a prizefighter.

In the 1990s, Oates continues grappling with contemporary America. *Because It Is Bitter and Because It Is My Heart* (1990) uses the Vietnam War as as the setting for a story in which murder entangles a black and a white family. Nominated for a National Book Award, *Black Water* (1992) fictionalizes the sensational events involving Senator Edward Kennedy at Chappaquiddick. Richard Bausch ranked this "powerfully imagined" novel with her best. Her play *The Gulf War* was staged Off-Broadway.

With *Foxfire: Confessions of a Girl Gang* (1993), Oates returns to adolescent angst. James Carroll sees the lengthy *What I Lived For* (1994), set in upstate New York, as a "savage dissection of our national myths of manhood and success." Murder and madness dominate the stories in *What Is Here?* (1994). Finally, *Zombie* (1995), her entry into the growling sub-genre about serial killers, assures us that her poetry, fiction, and criticism will continue to respond to America's obsessions.

John Updike writes, "if the phrase 'woman of letters' existed, she would be, foremost in this country, entitled to it."

—Judith C. Kohl

O'BRIAN, Patrick

Nationality: Irish. **Born:** Ireland, 1914. **Family:** Married; wife's name Mary. **Career:** Writer and translator. **Address:** c/o Sheil Land Associates, 43 Doughty St., London WC1N 20S England.

PUBLICATIONS

Novels (series: Aubrey-Maturin)

Three Bear Witness. Secker and Warburg, 1952; as *Testimonies,* Harcourt, 1952.
The Frozen Flame. Hart-Davis, 1953; as *The Catalans,* Harcourt, 1953.
The Road to Samarkand. Hart-Davis, 1954.
The Golden Ocean. Hart-Davis, 1956; revised edition, Macmillan, 1970.
The Unknown Shore. Hart-Davis, 1959.
Richard Temple. Macmillan, 1962.
Master and Commander (Aubrey). Lippincott, 1969.
Post Captain (Aubrey). Lippincott, 1972.
H.M.S. Surprise (Aubrey). Lippincott, 1973.
The Mauritius Command (Aubrey). Collins, 1977.
Desolation Island (Aubrey). Collins, 1978.
The Fortune of War (Aubrey). Collins, 1979.
The Surgeon's Mate (Aubrey). Collins, 1980.
The Ionian Mission (Aubrey). Collins, 1981.
Treason's Harbour (Aubrey). Collins, 1983.
The Far Side of the World (Aubrey). Collins, 1984.
The Reverse of the Medal (Aubrey). Collins, 1986.
The Letter of Marque (Aubrey). Collins, 1988.
The Thirteen-Gun Salute (Aubrey). Collins, 1989.
The Nutmeg of Consolation (Aubrey). Norton, 1991.
The Truelove (Aubrey). Norton, 1992; as *Clarissa Oakes,* HarperCollins, 1992.
The Wine-Dark Sea (Aubrey). Norton, 1993.

Short Stories

The Last Pool and Other Stories. Secker and Warburg, 1950.
The Walker and Other Stories. Harcourt, 1955; as *Lying in the Sun and Other Stories.* Hart-Davis, 1956.
The Chian Wine and Other Stories. Collins, 1974.

Other

Men-of-War. Collins, 1974.
Picasso: A Biography. Putnam, 1976.
Joseph Banks: A Life. Harvill, 1987.

Editor, *A Book of Voyages.* Home and Van Thal, 1947.

Translator, *The Daily Life of the Aztecs on the Eve of the Spanish Conquest,* by Jacques Soustelle. Weidenfeld and Nicolson, 1961.
Translator, *St. Bartholomew's Night: The Massacre of Saint Bartholomew,* by Philippe Erlanger. Pantheon, 1962.
Translator, *The Wreathed Head,* by Christine de Rivoyre. Hart-Davis, 1962.
Translator, *A History of the U.S.A.: From Wilson to Kennedy,* by Andre Maurois, Weidenfeld and Nicolson, 1964; as *From the New Freedom to the New Frontier: A History of the United States from 1912 to the Present,* McKay.
Translator, *A History of the USSR: From Lenin to Kruschev,* by Louis Aragon, McKay, 1964.
Translator, *A Letter to Myself,* by Françoise Mallet-Joris, Farrar, Straus, 1964.
Translator, *When the Earth Trembles,* by Haroun Tazieff, Harcourt, 1964.
Translator, *Munich: Peace in Our Time,* by Henri Nogueres. McGraw-Hill, 1965.
Translator, *The Uncompromising Heart,* by Françoise Mallet-Joris, Farrar, Straus, 1966.
Translator, *A Very Easy Death,* by Simone de Beauvoir. Putnam, 1966.

Translator, *The Delights of Growing Old,* by Maurice Goudeket, Farrar, Straus, 1966.
Translator, *The Italian Campaign,* by Michel Mohrt. Viking, 1967.
Translator, *Memoirs,* by Clara Malraux. Farrar, Straus, 1967.
Translator, *The Quicksand War: Prelude to Vietnam,* by Lucien Bodard. Little, Brown, 1967.
Translator, *The Horsemen,* by Joseph Kessel. Farrar, Straus, 1968.
Translator, *Les Belles Images,* by Simone de Beauvoir. Putnam, 1968.
Translator, *Louis XVI; or, The End of the World,* by Bernard Faae. Regnery, 1968.
Translator, *The Woman Destroyed,* by Simone de Beauvoir. Putnam, 1969.
Translator, *The Japanese Challenge,* by Robert Guillian. Lippincott, 1970.
Translator, *A Life's Full Summer,* by Andre Martinerie. Harcourt, 1970.
Translator, *Papillon,* by Henri Charriere. Hart-Davis, 1970.
Translator, *The Coming of Age,* by Simone de Beauvoir. Putnam, 1972; as *Old Age,* Deutsch-Weidenfeld and Nicolson, 1972.
Translator, *The Assassination of Heydrich,* by Miroslav Ivanov. Hart-Davis, 1973.
Translator, *The Further Adventures of Papillon,* by Henri Charriere. Morrow, 1973.
Translator, *All Said and Done,* by Simone de Beauvoir. Putnam, 1974.
Translator, *The Paths of the Sea,* by Pierre Schoendoerffer. Collins, 1977.
Translator, *Obsession: An American Love Story,* by Yves Berger. Putnam, 1978.
Translator, *When Things of the Spirit Come First: Five Early Tales,* by Simone de Beauvoir. Pantheon, 1982.
Translator, *Adieux: A Farewell to Sartre,* by Simone de Beauvoir. Pantheon, 1984.
Translator, *De Gaulle,* by Jean Lacouture. Norton, 1990.

* * *

Patrick O'Brian's popularity is based upon the success of his Aubrey/Maturin novels. In each novel, Captain Jack Aubrey, a British naval officer during the Napoleonic Wars, and Maturin, his intellectual ship surgeon, encounter a series of fantastic adventures and participate in naval battles. Yet the fantastic events generally serve as a backdrop for the more important depictions of life aboard the *Surprise.* Although each may be read as an independent work, together the novels are an ongoing saga of the professional and personal conflicts encountered by the two characters. Although the novels are unrealistic, O'Brian wields control over his prose and is a gifted storyteller. The *New York Times* considered the series to be "the best historical novels ever written," and most of the contemporary fans of his fiction claim that after finishing one of the Aubrey/Maturin novels, the reader will become obsessed with reading the others.

Critics immediately recognized that *Master Commander* (1969) was a significant work of adventure literature. In this novel O'Brian managed to balance nautical details of a 19th-century British man-o-war with philosophical, political, and sensual digressions. In *Master,* Aubrey looses sight of the other crew members and looses his ship to mutiny. O'Brian adds original plot twists that make the unbelievable account almost seem credible, such as Aubrey and Maturin's pro-Irish political feelings and the navigator/peddler who eventually develops a crush on Aubrey.

Of the following novels, no one book stands out as either great or terrible. The plots are generally predictable, and one reads for the details and account of Aubrey's and Maturin's friendship. Perhaps the greatest example of an intriguing yet unrealistic adventure story is found with *Wine Dark Sea* (1993). In this book, O'Brian combines Maturin's relationship problems with Clarissa Oaks with a series of oversized adventures, including a volcanic eruption, an open-boat jaunt through a storm, an exciting chase through the icebergs of Cape Horn, and a South American revolution.

Aside from the Aubrey/Maturin works, two early novels of note appeared early in O'Brian's career. *Testimonies* (1952) deals with a farming community in Northern Wales and the conflicts which arise when Pugh, an outsider, enters the community and falls in love with Bronwen, a farmer's wife. Critics consider the novel rare and beautiful, and praised the book for the quality of its visual images. His second novel, *Catalans* (1953), is set in Spain. It evidences O'Brian's unique ability to depict folk culture and customs. Though less acclaimed than *Catlans,* the book was an important step towards his historical research for the Aubrey/ Maturin novels.

—Chris Godat

O'BRIEN, Tim

Nationality: American. **Born:** William Timothy O'Brien in Austin, Minnesota, 1 October 1946. **Education:** Macalaster College, St. Paul, Minnesota, B.A. in political science (summa cum laude) 1968; Harvard University, Cambridge, Massachusetts, 1970-76. **Military Service:** Served in the United States Army during the Vietnam war; discharged wounded 1970: Purple Heart. **Career:** Reporter, Washington *Post,* 1971-74. **Awards:** National Book award, 1978; National Endowment for the Arts award; Bread Loaf Writers Conference award. **Agent:** International Creative Management, 40 West 57th Street, New York, New York 10019, U.S.A.

Publications

Novels

Northern Lights. New York, Delacorte Press, and London, Calder and Boyars, 1975.
Going after Cacciato. New York, Delacorte Press, and London, Cape, 1978.
The Nuclear Age. Portland, Oregon, Press 22, 1981; London, Collins, 1986.
In the Lake of the Woods. Boston, Houghton Mifflin, 1994.

Short Stories

The Things They Carried. Boston, Houghton Mifflin, and London, Collins, 1990.

Uncollected Short Stories

"Keeping Watch by Night," in *Redbook* (New York), December 1976.
"Night March," in *Prize Stories of 1976,* edited by William Abrahams. New York, Doubleday, 1976.

"Fisherman," in *Esquire* (New York), October 1977.
"Calling Home," in *Redbook* (New York), December 1977.
"Speaking of Courage," in *Prize Stories of 1978,* edited by William Abrahams. New York, Doubleday, 1978.
"Civil Defense," in *Esquire* (New York), August 1980.
"The Ghost Soldiers," in *Prize Stories of 1982,* edited by William Abrahams. New York, Doubleday, 1982.
"Quantum Jumps," in *The Pushcart Prize 10,* edited by Bill Henderson. Wainscott, New York, Pushcart Press, 1985.
"Underground Tests," in *The Esquire Fiction Reader 2,* edited by Rust Hills and Tom Jenks. Green Harbor, Massachusetts, Wampeter Press, 1986.
"The Lives of the Dead," in *Esquire* (New York), January 1989.
"Sweetheart of the Song Tra Bong," in *Esquire* (New York), July 1989.
"In the Field," in *Gentlemen's Quarterly* (New York), December 1989.
"Enemies and Friends," in *Harper's* (New York), March 1990.
"Field Trip," in *McCall's* (New York), August 1990.
"Speaking of Courage," in *The Other Side of Heaven: Post-War Fiction by Vietnamese and American Writers,* edited by Wayne Karling. Williamatic, Connecticut, Curbstone Press, 1995.

Other

If I Die in a Combat Zone, Box Me Up and Ship Me Home (memoirs). New York, Delacorte Press, and London, Calder and Boyars, 1973; revised edition, Delacorte Press, 1979.
Speaking of Courage. Santa Barbara, California, Neville, 1980.

*

Critical Studies: "Imagining the Real: The Fiction of Tim O'Brien" by Daniel L. Zins, in *Hollins Critic* (Hollins College, Virginia), June 1986; "Tim O'Brien's Myth of Courage" by Milton J. Bates, in *Critique* (Washington, D.C.), Summer 1987; *Understanding Tim O'Brien* by Steven Kaplan, Columbia, University of South Carolina Press, 1994.

* * *

Tim O'Brien must be frustrated, in a way, that he is associated so strongly with the Vietnam War. True enough, he is the most famous and enduring author of the Vietnam experience, and Vietnam does touch all of his works, some more obliquely than others. Yet he is also an author who writes with tremendous insight into the dark side of the human mind, and one who speculates with serious consideration about the nature of truth and its relationship to both fact and fiction.

This is not to say that Vietnam is merely incidental in O'Brien's work; the war in which he served obviously had a lasting and unresolved effect on his own identity, as well as on American identity in general. His writings often blur the lines between what actually happened during the War and what our imaginations have created to help us understand it. His first work, *If I Die in a Combat Zone* (1973), is his most overtly factual. It consists of magazine and newspaper journalism which provides a direct account of the War at its worst. His first novel, *Northern Lights* (1975), remains obscure, but O'Brien fans have unearthed it to find the roots of his fictional vision. It is the story of two brothers—one of whom served in Vietnam—who must rely on each other to survive a disastrous skiing trip in the wilds of Minnesota.

The factual nature of his first book and the relatively conventional narrative methods of his second give way to a much more imaginative account of Vietnam in *Going After Cacciato* (1978), the book that launched him to stardom. The members of a platoon stationed in Vietnam pursue a deserter, but the chase occurs more in their minds than in reality. Of particular interest is the imaginative capacity of the soldiers who endure the terrifying reality that was Vietnam. It is not only a vivid portrait of the experience of a soldier, but an evocative inquiry into the relationship between storytelling and history.

These same concerns are evident in his award-winning short-story cycle *The Things They Carried* (1990), powerful tales so much like memoirs that O'Brien feels compelled to emphasize in a prefatory note that what follows is "a work of fiction." Fiction is a complicated term in O'Brien's world, though; the stories are deemed true sometimes because they happened that way and sometimes because they convey some larger truth about the Vietnam experience. This book suggests that stories often communicate a more accurate notion of the truth than even experience can, which makes them compelling whether or not the reader experienced the War first-hand.

The Nuclear Age (1986) is an imaginative and broad-reaching account of anxieties which have seized our world in the latter half of the 20th century. The panic of the Vietnam world is applied to the more widespread condition of life with the Bomb. William Cowling, the protagonist, is haunted from a young age by the apocalyptic terror of his world. Despite his awareness that his parents, his wife, and his daughter all think he is insane, he acts out his life as a drama of paranoia and nuclear dread, fashioning an impromptu shelter out of a ping-pong table as a youth and digging a hole for a larger shelter as an adult. This novel clearly demonstrates how O'Brien's Vietnam anxieties are actually versions of the anxiety that we all feel in the nuclear age.

O'Brien treats the Vietnam War even more obliquely in his novel *In the Lake of the Woods* (1994), the story of Kathy Wade's disappearance from a secluded Minnesota cottage in 1986. Her husband John, having recently lost a senatorial election, retreats with her to reconstruct their lives in the wake of his career as a politician. Events such as John's terrible experience in Vietnam, his father's suicide, his lifetime hobby as a magician, and his habit of spying on Kathy during college begin to cast light onto what may have happened on that mysterious night. The book is more about uncertainty than it is about Vietnam, but the two are connected; Kathy's fate and Vietnam are both unknowable, in some senses, but storytelling can bring us closer to such knowledge. O'Brien's initial popularity can be attributed to America's fascination with the Vietnam War. But as he begins to locate this topic within broader contexts, his continued popularity can be attributed to his gifts as a master storyteller, his willingness to grapple with the relevant intellectual issues of our time, and his reminder of the continued need for fiction in a world which increasingly tends to look elsewhere for the truth about itself.

—D. Quentin Miller

OLDS, Sharon

Nationality: American. **Born:** San Francisco, California, 19 November 1942. **Education:** Stanford University, California, B .A.

(honors) 1964; Columbia University, New York, Ph.D. 1972. **Career:** Lecturer-in-residence on poetry, Theodor Herzl Institute, New York, 1976-80; visiting teacher of poetry, Manhattan Theatre Club, New York, 1982, Nathan Mayhew Seminars, Martha's Vineyard, Massachusetts, 1982, YMCA, New York, 1982, Poetry Society of America, 1983, Squaw Valley Writers' Conference, 1984-90, Sarah Lawrence College, Bronxville, New York, 1984, Goldwater Hospital, Roosevelt Island, New York, since 1985, Columbia University, New York, 1985-86, and State University of New York, Purchase, 1986-87; Fanny Hurst Chair in literature, Brandeis University, Waltham, Massachusetts, 1986-87; adjunct professor, 1983-90, director, 1988-91, and since 1990, associate professor, Graduate Program in Creative Writing, New York University. **Awards:** Creative Arts Public Service award, 1978; Madeline Sadin award, 1978; Guggenheim fellowship, 1981-82; National Endowment for the Arts fellowship, 1982-83; Lamont prize, 1984; National Book Critics Circle award, 1985; Lila Wallace/Reader's Digest fellowship grant, 1993-96. **Address:** 250 Riverside Drive, New York, New York 10025, U.S.A.

Publications

Poetry

Satan Says. Pittsburgh, Pennsylvania, University of Pittsburgh Press, and London, Feffer and Simons, 1980.
The Dead and the Living. New York, Knopf, 1984.
The Gold Cell. New York, Knopf, 1987.
The Matter of This World: New and Selected Poems. Nottingham, Slow Dancer Press, 1987.
The Sign of Saturn. London, Martin Secker and Warburg, 1991.
The Father. New York, Knopf, 1992; London, Martin Secker and Warburg, 1993.
The Wellspring. New York, Knopf, 1996.

Recording—*Coming Back to Life,* Watershed, 1984.

*

Critical Studies: "Sharon Olds: Painful Insights and Small Beauties" by Jonah Bornstein, in *Literary Cavalcade* (New York), January 1989; "American Visionaries: Helen Keller and the Poets Muriel Rukeyser, Denise Levertov, and Sharon Olds," in *Women Against the Iron Fist: Alternatives to Militarism 1900-1989,* by Sybil Oldfield, Cambridge, Massachusetts, Blackwell, 1989; "Talking to Our Father: The Political and Mythical Appropriations of Adrienne Rich and Sharon Olds" by Suzanne Matson, in *American Poetry Review* (Philadelphia), November/December 1989.

* * *

Intimate and candid in her writing, which is usually drawn from her own life, Sharon Olds creates poetry that is precise and concrete in its use of imagery. Many critics have commented on the exhilarating, vibrant, and celebratory quality of her language, despite the often morbid and unhappy subjects of her poetry. Although Olds uses language very explicitly, which has occasionally raised some eyebrows, this nevertheless establishes her poetry within the American modernist tradition of poets like Whitman, Stein, Williams, and Olson, who have sought to use the contemporary idiom of language in poetry.

This blunt use of language is evident in her first collection, *Satan Says* (1980), which was hailed as an impressive debut. One critic described it as "harsh and shockingly truthful," and another as "a graph of pain." In this passionate volume, a variety of selves appear, with the collection divided into sections entitled "Daughter," "Woman," "Mother," and "Journey." The poems explore the central meanings of love and shared experience. This is achieved through an investigation of the "other," which is estranged from the self, such as the alter ego, family, friends, and lovers. The poems explore the difficulties of finding a language sufficiently broad and expansive with which to define one's relationship with others without compromising the complexities and differences of those relationships.

Anticipating a "sizeable following" for Olds' work on the strength of this initial collection, her critics' high expectations were substantiated by her next collection, *The Dead and the Living* (1984). Again, many of the poems focused on the family, especially reproachful childhood reminiscences, as in "Possessed." Despite their frequent honesty and intimacy, these poems manage to transcend the confessional as they move outward to an inclusive understanding of suffering based upon the family as an analogue of the world. In her range of the exploration of people, both the famous like the Shah of Iran and Marilyn Monroe, and the not-so-famous, Olds uses complex and sharp images as she attempts to recreate the past as a means of liberating the present and future. The poems are about processing experience and "saving the past." The integrity of Olds' voice emerges as a call for justice, in which there are "no ideas but in beings."

The Gold Cell (1987) followed, again concentrating on personal relationships with poems about motherhood, love, and lust, as well as life in New York. Never refraining from pulling her punches, Olds can write tenderly about her children in poems like "Boy Out in the World" and "Looking at Them Asleep," but can also consider the strained racial tensions in New York, as in "On the Subway." In the latter, political reflections are sparked by a meeting between a black man and a white woman on a subway, echoing Amiri Baraka's *Dutchman.* These are poems of clarity and precision, with engrossing metaphors and similes and a carefully crafted tone that runs the risk of sentimentality but does not fall into it, rescued by truthfulness and integrity. *The Sign of Saturn, 1980-1987* (1991) collects poems from the three previous collections, under the baleful influence of Saturn, the father who ate his children.

It is with *The Father* (1992) that Olds made her biggest impression. It is a sequence of poems that explore the responses of a daughter to her unloving father's slow death. The poems chart a gradual acceptance based on an appreciation of the body as matter, as physical substance. As Clair Wills observed in the *Times Literary Supplement,* these poems are not elegies in the usual manner, since they are always "superseded by an unaffected and humorous refusal to be fooled about God, life after death, or the meaning of the father's life." Wills praises Olds' ability to transform the sordid into the sublime, as she "turns her subject matter, inexorable death, into something touching and strangely comforting." Generally regarded as an enthralling volume, *The Father* has secured Olds an established position. Although sometimes found to be jarring and unexpected, the variety of emotions in Olds' work, her "lyrical acuity" as one critic has put it, and her ability to push against the boundaries of acceptability without appearing merely sensationalist have marked her as a skillful poet.

—Tim Woods

O'ROURKE, P(atrick) J(ake)

Nationality: American. **Born:** 14 November 1947, in Toledo, Ohio. **Education:** Miami University, Oxford, Ohio, B.A., 1969; Johns Hopkins University, M.A., 1970. **Family:** Married Amy Lumet in 1990. **Career:** Writer and editor with underground newspapers, 1968-71; *New York Herald,* feature editor, 1971-72; freelance writer, 1972-73; *National Lampoon,* New York City, executive editor and managing editor, 1973-77, editor-in-chief, 1978-81; *Rolling Stone,* New York City, head of international affairs desk, 1981—. Speaker at universities and colleges. **Awards:** Woodrow Wilson fellow, 1969-70; Merit award, Art Directors Club, 1973; Gold award, 1975; Merit award, Society of Publication Designers, 1976; received other awards for visual excellence for *National Lampoon.* **Address:** c/o *Rolling Stone,* 1290 Avenue of the Americas, New York, New York 10104, U.S.A.

Publications

Humorous Nonfiction

Modern Manners: An Etiquette Book for Rude People. Dell, 1983; revised edition, Atlantic Monthly Press, 1989.
Republican Party Reptile. Atlantic Monthly Press, 1987.
The Bachelor's Home Companion: A Practical Guide to Keeping House Like a Pig. Pocket Books, 1987; revised edition, Atlantic Monthly Press, 1993.
Holidays in Hell. Atlantic Monthly Press, 1988.
Parliament of Whores: A Lone Humorist Attempts to Explain the Entire U.S. Government. Atlantic Monthly Press, 1991.
Give War a Chance: Eyewitness Accounts of Mankind's Struggle against Tyranny, Injustice and Alcohol-Free Beer. Atlantic Monthly Press, 1992.
Everybody Had His Own Gringo: The CIA and the Contras. Brassey's, 1992.
All the Trouble in the World: The Lighter Side of Overpopulation, Famine, Plague, Ecological Disaster, Ethnic Hatred, and Poverty. Grove/Atlantic Monthly Press, 1994.
Age and Guile Beat Youth, Innocence and a Bad Haircut. Grove/Atlantic Monthly Press, 1995.
P. J.'s Very Own Public Enemies List: Flushing out Liberals in the Age of Clinton. Grove/Atlantic Monthly Press, 1996.

Poetry

Our Friend the Vowel. Stone House, 1975.

Plays

Screenplay: *Easy Money,* with Rodney Dangerfield, Michael Endler, and David Blain, 1983.

* * *

Educated at Miami University of Ohio and the Johns Hopkins University, P. J. O'Rourke began his career as a somewhat stereotypical 1960s counterculture journalist, apprenticing with the now defunct *Baltimore Harry* until a group of local radicals called the "Balto-Cong" raided the newspaper's offices to, in O'Rourke's words, "liberate us." Discovering that they liked an undercover policeman masquerading as one of their photographers more than the militants who held them hostage, O'Rourke and his colleagues all promptly "cut our hair and got jobs," he later recalled.

After masterminding two bestselling parody books for *National Lampoon* magazine as well as dozens of humorous articles, O'Rourke penned his first book, *Modern Manners: An Etiquette Book for Rude People* (1983), a deeply tongue-in-cheek guide to contemporary etiquette for an age in which "[a]ll existence is in disarray." Tackling such abstruse issues as how to regurgitate decorously ("Actually, there is no way to make vomiting courteous"), when to refuse alcohol (never), and what to say when being led to the electric chair ("'See you in Hell, Mom,' is nice"), O'Rourke employed wicked satire to demonstrate that good manners, though seldom practiced, can disguise a multitude of sins.

In 1987 O'Rourke followed *Modern Manners* with *The Bachelor Home Companion,* a user-friendly guide to neglecting one's apartment that discussed the psychological ramifications of upholstery slipcovers, how to explain the empty beer cans under your couch, and a variety of other housekeeping tips. *Republican Party Reptile* (1987), a collection of 21 magazine "essays and outrages," appeared the same year and seemed to announce O'Rourke's intention to assume Hunter S. Thompson's mantle as America's preeminent "gonzo journalist," though with an avowedly Republican point of view. Typical chapters saw O'Rourke updating ancient mythology ("Myths Made Modern"), satirizing the media ("A Long, Thoughtful Look Back at the Last Fifteen Minutes"), and documenting the Third World quality of New York City ("Just One of Those Days"). In the collection's other pieces, O'Rourke focused a jaundiced eye on the baroque highlights of trips to Manila, Beirut, the Carribbean, and the Soviet Union.

In *Holidays in Hell* (1988), O'Rourke spun his growing stature as *Rolling Stone*'s "investigative humorist" of international affairs into a book-length world trip through South Korea, Poland, Israel, South Africa, Nicaragua, the Phillippines, and Panama. Finding little in foreign cultures to compete with life in the United States, O'Rourke added chapters on Jim and Tammy Faye Bakker's Heritage USA resort, Disney's Epcot Center, and Hollywood to demonstrate that Americans needn't leave home to experience the culture shock of the foreign traveler. Despite his claim that "[t]here are no earnest messages in this book," O'Rourke made his preference for American culture and freedoms palpable throughout the book.

In his next work, *Parliament of Whores* (1991), O'Rourke turned his sights on the labyrinthine and often unfathomable activities of the U.S. Government. In chapters with such titles as "The Three Branches of Government: Money, Television, and Bullshit" and "Graft for the Millions," he examined the American welfare lobby, environmentalists, farm policy, the savings and loan crisis, and federal housing projects and concluded that the U.S. Government is "huge, stupid, [and] greedy" and that although every government is a "parliament of whores . . . in a democracy the whores are us."

Give War a Chance (1992) collected previously published pieces on liberals ("mealy-mouthed, bullying, irresponsible, and victimized"), the elections in Nicaragua, the Persian Gulf War, and

O'Rourke's personal abandonment of 1960s idealism for an updated version of Reaganite Republicanism. Acknowledging that he currently believes in nothing save "Western civilization," O'Rourke took often hilarious potshots at Dan Quayle and George Bush, leftist lawyer William Kunstler, modern celebrities, and America's role as the world's policeman.

In *All the Trouble in the World* (1994), O'Rourke again focused on the sorry state of the world outside America's borders, addressing the problems of overpopulation, famine, environmental decay, ecology, multiculturalism, and "plague" as seen through trips to such international garden spots as Bangladesh, Somalia, Peru, the Czech Republic, the former Yugoslavia, Haiti, and Vietnam. Beginning with an impassioned assault on the spirit of complaint that pervades American culture despite its economic and political advantages ("This is a moment of hope in history. Why doesn't anybody say so?"), O'Rourke provided a richly amusing global travelogue punctuated by often astute observations on the world's major social problems.

Critics have generally viewed O'Rourke's work favorably, although his unabashed rock-and-roll-flavored conservatism has drawn predictable fire from left-leaning reviewers. While his humor has occasionally been labeled offensive, mean-spirited, immature, and uneven, a number of critics have unqualifiedly labeled him the "funniest writer in America," capable of "downright exhilarating" comic epiphanies. Indeed, if H. L. Mencken has a modern heir, O'Rourke's barbed style and brutal insightfulness have probably established him as the most likely contender.

—Paul S. Bodine

OSBORNE, David. *See* **SILVERBERG, Robert.**

OZICK, Cynthia

Nationality: American. **Born:** New York City, 17 April 1928. **Education:** New York University, B.A. (cum laude) in English 1949 (Phi Beta Kappa); Ohio State University, Columbus, M.A. 1951. **Family:** Married Bernard Hallote in 1952; one daughter. **Career:** Instructor in English, New York University, 1964-65; Distinguished Artist-in-Residence, City University, New York, 1982; Phi Beta Kappa Orator, Harvard University, Cambridge, Massachusetts, 1985. Lives in New Rochelle, New York. **Awards:** National Endowment for the Arts fellowship, 1968; Wallant award, 1972; B'nai B'rith award, 1972; Jewish Book Council Epstein award, 1972, 1977; American Academy award, 1973; Hadassah Myrtle Wreath award, 1974; Lamport prize, 1980; Guggenheim fellowship, 1982; Strauss Living award, 1982-1987; Distinguished Alumnus award, New York University, 1984; Rea award, for short story, 1986; Lucy Martin Donnelly award, Bryn Mawr College, 1991-92. D.H.L.: Yeshiva University, New York, 1984; Hebrew Union College, Cincinnati, 1984; Williams College, Williamstown, Massachusetts, 1986; Hunter College, New York, 1987; Jewish Theological Seminary, New York, 1988; Adelphi University, Garden City, New York, 1988; State University of New York, 1989; Brandeis University, Waltham, Massachusetts, 1990; Bard College, Annandale-on-Hudson, New York, 1991; Skidmore College, 1992. **Agent:** Raines and Raines, 71 Park Avenue, New York, New York 10016. **Address:** c/o Knopf Inc., 201 East 50th Street, New York, New York 10022, U.S.A.

Publications

Novels

Trust. New York, New American Library, 1966; London, MacGibbon and Kee, 1967.
The Cannibal Galaxy. New York, Knopf, 1983; London, Secker and Warburg, 1984.
The Messiah of Stockholm. New York, Knopf, and London, Deutsch, 1987.

Short Stories

The Pagan Rabbi and Other Stories. New York, Knopf, 1971; London, Secker and Warburg, 1972.
Bloodshed and Three Novellas. New York, Knopf, and London, Secker and Warburg, 1976.
Levitation: Five Fictions. New York, Knopf, and London, Secker and Warburg, 1982.
The Shawl: A Story and a Novella. New York, Knopf, 1989.

Uncollected Short Stories

"The Sense of Europe," in *Prairie Schooner* (Lincoln, Nebraska), June 1956.
"Stone," in *Botteghe Oscure* (Rome), Autumn 1957.
"The Laughter of Akiva," in *New Yorker,* 10 November 1980.
"At Fumicaro," in *New Yorker,* 6 August 1984.
"Puttermesser Paired," in *New Yorker,* 8 October 1990.

Plays

Blue Light (produced Long Island, 1994).

Other

Art and Ardor (essays). New York, Knopf, 1983.
Metaphor and Memory (essays). New York, Knopf, 1989.
What Henry James Knew, and Other Essays on Writers. Bennington, Vermont, Bennington College, 1993.

*

Bibliography: "A Bibliography of Writings by Cynthia Ozick" by Susan Currier and Daniel J. Cahill, in *Texas Studies in Literature and Language* (Austin), Summer 1983.

Critical Studies: "The Art of Cynthia Ozick" by Victor Strandberg, in *Texas Studies in Literature and Language* (Austin), Summer 1983; *Cynthia Ozick, Texas Studies in Literature and Language,* edited by Catherine Rainwater and William J. Scheick, University Press of Kentucky, 1983; *Crisis and Covenant: The Ho-*

locaust in American Jewish Fiction, by Alan L. Berger, State University of New York, 1985; *Cynthia Ozick* edited by Harold Bloom, New York, Chelsea House, 1986, and *Cynthia Ozick: Modern Critical Views,* by Bloom, Chelsea Publishers, 1986; *The World of Cynthia Ozick: Studies in American Jewish Literature,* edited by Daniel Walden, Kent State University Press, 1987; *Since Flannery O'Conner: Essays on the Contemporary Short Story,* by Loren Logsdon and Charles W. Mayer, Western Illinois University Press, 1987; *The Uncompromising Fictions of Cynthia Ozick* by Sanford Pinsker, Columbia, University of Missouri Press, 1987; *Cynthia Ozick* by Joseph Lowin, Boston, Twayne, 1988; *Understanding Cynthia Ozick* by Lawrence S. Friedman, University of South Carolina Press, 1991; *Cynthia Ozick: Tradition and Invention* by Elaine M. Kasuvar, Indiana University Press, 1993; *Greek Mind, Jewish Soul* by Victor Strandberg, University of Wisconsin Press, 1994; *Cynthia Ozick's Comic Art,* by Sarah Blacher Cohen, Indiana University Press, 1994.

* * *

Cynthia Ozick's Jewish background has served her well as a fiction writer; it appears prominently and with heart and soul in most of her work. She was born in 1928 to Russian-Jewish immigrant parents and grew up in the Bronx, where she was subjected to much degradation because of her religion. Ozick escaped the taunts by reading as much and as often as she could; writing was, as she saw it, a natural progression. She told Eve Ottenberg, "Even at age six—no, as soon as I was conscious of being alive—I knew I was a writer."

Henry James was a major influence on Ozick, and detoured Ozick early in her career. For several years she had attempted to complete a Jamesian novel, *Mercy, Pity, Peace, and Love.* Though the piece, modeled on James's *The Ambassadors,* was unwieldy to begin with, Ozick had held out hope that she would eventually complete her celebration of James. Instead, as Ozick observed 20 years later, her obsession with James threatened to end her own career before it really began.

Over six years would elapse between Ozick's final abandonment of *Mercy, Pity, Peace, and Love* and the completion of her first published novel, *Trust* (1966). Although *Trust* was equal in length to its failed predecessor, it was a superior work in that it contained as much of Ozick's own voice as James's influence. Like James's works, *Trust* features upper-class characters who jaunt between Europe and America. Money and the corruption it often spawns is also at the heart of the novel. But unlike James and much like the fiction that Ozick would later produce, the Jewish influence is the driving force behind the novel.

The Europe in *Trust* is a far cry from the Europe in James's novels. Ozick's novel takes place in 1946, when Europe is just beginning to assess and repair the physical and emotional damage of WWII, and when Europe and the rest of the world are just beginning to learn of the atrocities inflicted upon the Jews by Adolf Hitler's Nazi regime. Wealthy Allegra travels to Europe from America to imbibe what she believes to be a more established, cultured atmosphere, a la James. But when she arrives, she pouts about continued rationing, comparatively poor food quality, and accommodations that she considers substandard. Fellow American Enoch, whose job is to account for displaced and deceased Jews, is just as oblivious to Allegra's grandiose rendition of Europe as she is to his all-too-stark impression of the continent. Somehow, he cannot escape the stench of the camps. She, on the other hand, does not seem to notice at all.

It seems that no one who reads the "The Shawl" (the title story in a collection of short fiction [1989]) can escape the horrors faced by those who lived through, or died in, the Holocaust. The depictions of suffering and brutality are particularly poignant, such as the episode when Rosa bundles her infant, Magda, into a shawl to hide her from the guards; Magda is so hungry that she attempts to feed herself by sucking at the shawl, which smells and tastes like cinnamon and almonds. Rosa, who is equally malnourished, is unable to nurse the baby because her milk has dried up. In a harrowing illustration of brutality born of adversity, Rosa's 14-year-old niece, Stella, snatches the shawl from the baby because she is cold. Magda, who had been quiet, begins wailing and attracts the attention of a guard, who then hurls the starving baby into an electrified fence. Rosa is then left to suck at the shawl in imitation of her lost baby. Rosa and Stella survive their ordeal and make their way to America. However, the experience has left Rosa broken and unwilling to adapt to new circumstances.

Although Ozick's works have Jewish themes, she balks at being called "a Jewish writer." Robert Harris, in the *Saturday Review,* tells us that Ozick is simply a writer who is "obsessed with the words she puts on paper, with what it means to imagine a story and to tell it, with what fiction is."

—Tracy Clark

P-Q

PAGLIA, Camille (Anna)

Nationality: American. **Born:** Endicott, New York, 2 April 1947. **Education:** State University of New York, Binghamton, B.A., 1968; Yale University, M.Phil., 1971, Ph.D., 1974. **Career:** Bennington College, Bennington, Vermont, faculty member in Literature and Languages Division, 1972-80; Wesleyan University, Middletown, Connecticut, visiting lecturer in English, 1980; Yale University, New Haven, Connecticut, fellow of Ezra Stiles College, 1981, visiting lecturer in comparative literature, 1981 and 1984, visiting lecturer in English, 1981-83, fellow of Silliman College, 1984; Philadelphia College of Performing Arts, Philadelphia, assistant professor, 1984-86, associate professor, 1987-91; professor of humanities, 1991—. **Agent:** Lynn Nesbit, Janklow and Nesbit, 598 Madison Ave., New York, New York 10022. **Address:** Department of Humanities, University of the Arts, 320 South Broad St., Philadelphia, Pennsylvania 19102, U.S.A.

Publications

Nonfiction

Sexual Personae: Art and Decadence from Nefertiti to Emily Dickinson. Yale University Press, 1990.
Sex, Art, and American Culture: Essays. Vintage Books, 1992.
Vamps and Tramps: New Essays. Vintage Books, 1994.

* * *

Chronologically speaking, Camille Paglia is still somewhat new to book publishing since her first book came out in 1990. However, some might find that fact surprising, since her inaugural appearance—*Sexual Personae: Art and Decadence from Nefertiti to Emily Dickinson*—evoked such an explosive reaction from academics and casual readers that whenever a new work appears, supporters and critics have flocked to bookstores and libraries just to see what she has to say.

Sexual Personae traces the sexual development of women via Western art from antiquity to the present, with special focus on such erotic figures as the femme fatale, the vampire, and the hermaphrodite. It also represents Paglia's interest in the relationship between sex and beauty. For instance, Paglia chides Western culture for being "a distortion of reality" and suggests that "the glory of art lies in its power to extemporize fictive identities—the personae—that swerve away from biology's literal insistence on what we are." Feminists were outraged because they saw Paglia's work as a sensationalist denigration of women as sex objects. Their ire was particularly raised by Paglia's contention, "If civilization had been left in female hands, we would still be living in grass huts."

Sex, Art, and American Culture: Essays (1992) focuses on more contemporary subjects such as Madonna and date rape, the latter being covered in two separate chapters. As the title suggests, the subject of sex in general receives lots of attention. Paglia appears fascinated by the topics of sadomasochism and homosexuality. As a result, *Sex, Art, and American Culture* sparked controversy and was consequently treated by critics as a sequel to *Sexual Personae.* But reviewers were even less kind to *Sex, Art, and American Culture* because they considered it a continuation of what they saw as unsubstantiated ravings.

Paglia's *Vamps & Tramps: New Essays* (1994) is so titled because, as Paglia explains in her introduction, "I want a revamped feminism. Putting the vamp back means the lady must be a tramp." The book is a continuation of the shock-intellectual theme that has been Paglia's since *Sexual Personae.* Paglia continues her attack on the methods of feminists and gay activists, whom she calls "self-destructive" in their "habit of jeering at the church and trying to twist it to their own purposes." Paglia further suggests that nonviolent sexual conduct should not be legislated. "Neither women nor gays should plead for special protections or preferential treatment," she states. In another essay, Paglia gives us a twisted comparison of Princess Di to Cinderella. She tells us that Di has not been rescued by her Prince; rather, he and his family are the wicked step-relations from whom she must protect herself. Paglia tells us that Di's friends joke that POW means not "Princess of Wales," but "prisoner of war." Other essays feature Barbra Streisand, Hillary Clinton, D.H. Lawrence's novel *Women In Love,* Edward Said's *Culture and Imperialism,* and John and Lorena Bobbitt.

So many groups have been offended by Paglia's contentions that some readers might wonder which groups, if any, Paglia champions. Indeed, Paglia does not support any particular group; rather, she supports and defends her own free speech. Paglia tells us in her introduction to *Vamps & Tramps* that *Sex, Art, and American Culture* "was secretly aimed toward students and seems to have succeeded in its mission," which is to help them find their own voices as the 1960s radicals were able to do for the youth of that time. Not surprisingly, Paglia considers herself a Libertarian. In *Vamps and Tramps* she suggests that sexual conduct—based on her libertarian position—"in the absence of physical violence cannot and must not be legislated from above, that all intrusion by authority figures into sex is totalitarian."

—Tracy Clark

PAIGE, Richard. *See* **KOONTZ, Dean R(ay).**

PALEY, Grace

Nationality: American. **Born:** Grace Goodside in New York City, 11 December 1922. **Education:** Evander Childs High School, New York; Hunter College, New York, 1938-39. **Family:** Married 1) Jess Paley in 1942, one daughter and one son; 2) the playwright Robert Nichols in 1972. **Career:** Has taught at Columbia University, New York, and Syracuse University, New York. Since 1966 has taught at Sarah Lawrence College, Bronxville, New York, and since 1983 at City College, New York. New York State Author, 1986-88. **Awards:** Guggenheim grant, 1961; National Endowment for the Arts grant, 1966; American Academy award, 1970; Edith Wharton award, 1988, 1989. **Member:** American Academy, 1980. **Address:** Box 620, Thetford Hill, Vermont 05074, U.S.A.

Publications

Short Stories

The Little Disturbances of Man: Stories of Men and Women in Love. New York, Doubleday, 1959; London, Weidenfeld and Nicolson, 1960.
Enormous Changes at the Last Minute. New York, Farrar Straus, 1974; London, Deutsch, 1975.
Later the Same Day. New York, Farrar Straus, and London, Virago Press, 1985.

Uncollected Short Story

"Two Ways of Telling," in *Ms.* (New York), November-December 1990.

Poetry

Leaning Forward. Penobscot, Maine, Granite Press, 1985.
New and Collected Poems. Maine, Tilbury Press, 1991.

Other

365 Reasons Not to Have Another War. Philadelphia and New York, New Society Publications—War Resisters' League, 1989.
Long Walks and Intimate Talks. New York, Feminist Press, 1991.

*

Critical Studies: *Grace Paley: Illuminating the Dark Lives* by Jacqueline Taylor, Austin, University of Texas Press, 1990; *Grace Paley: A Study of the Short Fiction* by Neil Isaacs, Boston, Twayne, 1990.

* * *

Grace Paley's literary career anticipates the emergence of feminism among both intellectuals and creative writers in the American 1960s, 1970s, and 1980s. In nearly all of her stories one senses the presence of a woman writing, for references to gender are overt as well as subtly directive. As popular culture caught up with her innovations and accorded her, in her mid-50s, a measure of fame, her stated presence became that of an older woman writing. Yet never has her position been one of an ideological spokesperson. Instead, she has closed the distance between social pertinence and imaginative fancy by giving her fiction a poetic voice that expresses women's concerns in a uniquely artistic way. At the same time she has taken a more actively social posture in her personal life, demonstrating against the Vietnam War and participating in other protest actions that have led to arrest and detention. Only when she writes as an essayist does direct social statement become a factor in her work.

With her short stories appearing in such mainline magazines as *Esquire* and *The New Yorker,* Paley has never lacked a middle-class readership. Yet her fiction has always pushed conventional sensibilities beyond accepted norms. Single mothers appeared in her work years before such status became popularly accepted—men serve as boyfriends and nuisances more often that as husbands; and children, while respected, are never sentimentalized, but instead are encouraged to stand on their feet and find their own way as soon as reasonably possible.

The paradigm for Paley's most typical character is "The Long Distance Runner," collected in *Enormous Changes at the Last Minute* (1974). Here, "A woman inside the steamy energy of middle age runs and runs," somewhat fantastically but ultimately realistically to "the houses and the streets where her childhood happened." To do so she must leave her own children minimally attended for three weeks ("I told Mrs. Raftery to look in now and then and give them some of that rotten Celtic supper she makes") and place herself in a marginally dangerous situation (seeking shelter in her old immigrant neighborhood that has now become an African-American ghetto). Returning from her adventure, she recounts it for her sometimes boyfriend and teenage sons, none of whom comprehend what she has learned, which is, "as though she were a child...what in the world is coming next."

All of Grace Paley's fiction is driven by language as much as it is by event. Just as her narrator's experiences in "The Long Distance Runner" are characterized by artful conversations with the strangers she meets, so too are other women's perspectives expressed in uncommonly crafted prose. In the title story from *Enormous Changes at the Last Minute,* Alexandra explains her father to a new lover in these words: "He remembered the first time he'd seen the American flag on wild Ellis Island. Under its protection and working like a horse, he'd read Dickens, gone to medical school, and shot like a surface-to-air missile right into the middle class." In "Mother," from *Later the Same Day* (1985), another narrator hears a lyric on the radio and wishes she could once again see her mother standing in the doorway, as the song says—and then, in two quick pages, recounts four brief scenes that capture the mother forever in memory, locked there by the language chosen so carefully for each moment.

In her author's note to *Long Walks and Intimate Talks,* Paley describes herself as "a cooperative anarchist and combative pacifist." What more literal writers see as contradictions, she sees as complexities resolved by the reader's ability to hold differing ideas in one's mind without demanding a hasty resolution.

—Jerome Klinkowitz

PALMER, Michael

Nationality: American. **Born:** New York City, 11 May 1943. **Education:** Harvard University, Cambridge, Massachusetts, 1961-68, B.A. in French 1965, M.A. in comparative literature 1967. **Family:** Married Cathy Simon in 1972; one daughter. **Career:** Editor, *Joglars Magazine,* Providence, Rhode Island, 1964-66; contributing editor, *Sulfur* magazine, Los Angeles. **Awards:** National Endowment for the Arts fellowship, 1975. **Address:** 265 Jersey Street, San Francisco, California 94114, U.S.A.

PUBLICATIONS

Poetry

Plan of the City of O. Boston, Barn Dream Press, 1971.
Blake's Newton. Los Angeles, Black Sparrow Press, 1972.
C's Songs. Berkeley, California, Sand Dollar, 1973.
Six Poems. Los Angeles, Black Sparrow Press, 1973.
The Circular Gates. Los Angeles, Black Sparrow Press, 1974.
Without Music. Santa Barbara, California, Black Sparrow Press, 1977.
Alogon. Berkeley, California, Tuumba Press, 1980.
Notes for Echo Lake. Berkeley, California, North Point Press, 1981.
First Figure. Berkeley, California, North Point Press, 1984.
For a Reading: A Selection of Poems. New York, Dia Art Foundation, 1988.
Sun. Berkeley, California, North Point Press, 1988.
An Alphabet Underground: Poems. Viborg, Denmark, After Hand, 1993.

Plays

Radio Plays: *Idem l-4,* 1979.
Dance Scenarios (collaborations with Margaret Jenkins Dance Company): *Interferences,* 1975; *Equal Time,* 1976; *Video Songs,* 1976; *About the Space in Between,* 1977; *No One But Whitington,* 1978; *Red, Yellow, Blue,* 1978; *Straight Words,* 1980; *Versions by Turns,* 1980; *Cortland Set,* 1982; *First Figure,* 1984.

Novels

Side Effects. New York, Bantam, 1985; London, Severn House, 1987.
Flashback. Toronto and New York, Bantam, 1988.
Extreme Measures. Piatkus, 1991.
Natural Causes. New York, Bantam, 1994.
Silent Treatment. New York, Bantam, 1996.

Other

Editor, *Code of Signals: Recent Writings in Poetics.* Berkeley, California, North Atlantic, 1983.

Translator, with Geoffrey Young, *Relativity of Spring: 13 Poems,* by Vicente Huidobro. Berkeley, California, Sand Dollar, 1976.
Translator, *Jonah Who Will Be 25 in the Year 2000* (screenplay), by Alain Tanner and John Berger. Berkeley, California, North Atlantic, 1983.

*

Critical Studies: By Michael Davidson, in *Caterpillar 20* (Sherman Oaks, California), 1973; Steve McCaffery, in *Open Letter* (Toronto), Fall 1975, April 1978, and Fall 1978; David Chaloner, in *Poetry Information* (London), Summer 1976; William Corbett, in *L=A=N=G=U=A=G=E 2* (New York), 1978; Martin Dodman in *Montemora* 5 (New York), June 1979; George Lakoff, in *Poetics Journal 2* (Berkeley, California), 1982; Alan Soldofsky, in *Ironwood 19* (Tucson), 1982; *Language Poetry: Writing as Rescue* by Linda Reinfeld. Baton Rouge and London, Louisiana State University Press, 1992.

* * *

Novelist and physician Michael Palmer has followed the same path as writers Michael Crichton and Robin Cook, taking his knowledge of medicine and using it to construct elaborate thrillers. A graduate of Wesleyan University (as is Cook), Palmer practices internal medicine in Massachusetts when he isn't penning his next bestseller.

Palmer's four novels are all layered with technical jargon and hidden conspiracies uncovered by astute young doctors. *Side Effects* (1987), a story of a hospital's use of female patients as unsuspecting guinea pigs for a Nazi doctor's sterility drug, was called "topical, fast-paced and scary" by *Publishers Weekly.* Its hero is pathologist Kate Bennett, who struggles in a male-dominated field and whose strict ethics and stubbornness have earned her several enemies who may pose danger to her when she stumbles across the experimentations.

Flashback (1988) is written in a similar vein, although here the hospital of a small New Hampshire town is conducting surgeries without the benefit of anesthesia, the memories of which surface as painful flashbacks for the patients. Young surgeon Zack Iverson, who grew up in the town and has returned to practice medicine, must race to discover the culprit and save the lives of other patients. *Booklist* praised *Flashback* as "a lively medical thriller."

Palmer continued to hone his skills with *Extreme Measures* (1991), which centers around a Boston hospital's emergency room chief resident Eric Najarian and the mysterious group Caduceus, which promises Najarian a promotion if he will help them with unspecified research. Then dead patients begin to revive due to a voodoo-like zombie drug, and Najarian and the beautiful Laura Enders, whose brother Scott was subjected to the drug, team up to bring Caduceus to justice. Ray Olson of *Booklist* praised the novel stating that "the nail-biting befuddlement caused by the many plot twists is what puts this neat, eminently filmable thriller out in front of other recent members of its pack, including Cook's *Vital Signs.*" *Kirkus Reviews* was less praiseworthy, calling *Extreme Measures* "Not as much sheer fun as Cook—the tone here is darker, more solemn—but with strong narrative drive geared by myriad plot twists, this is brisk, hard-working entertainment for fans of medical mischief."

Palmer's *Natural Causes* (1994) received less favorable reviews for its story of Dr. Sarah Baldwin, a third-year OB/GYN resident in Boston who utilizes acupuncture and herbal medicine along with more Western methods. When two of her pregnant patients die, suspicion mounts until Baldwin saves her third patient, and then the blame for the two deaths hovers over several suspects, including an unctuous attorney, an embittered ex-boyfriend, a dissatisfied surgeon, and the president of the hospital. While *Kirkus Reviews* called the story "intriguing," it said the dialogue "reads like speechmaking" and called the novel "mildly entertaining, but without much verve or suspense."

Fans of Michael Crichton's *Five Patients* and Robin Cook's medical mysteries should find Palmer to be equal to the task, creating engaging stories with surprise endings in realistic medical settings.

—Christopher Swann

PARETSKY, Sara

Nationality: American. **Born:** Ames, Iowa, 8 June 1947. **Education:** University of Kansas, Lawrence, B. A. in political science (summa cum laude) 1967; University of Chicago, Ph.D. in history 1977. **Family:** Married Courtenay Wright in 1976; three children. **Career:** Publications and conference manager, Urban Research Corporation, Chicago, 1971-74; freelance business writer, 1974-77; manager of direct mail marketing programs, CNA Insurance, Chicago, 1977-86. Since 1986 full-time writer. **Member:** Sisters in Crime (cofounder and president). **Awards:** Crime Writers Association Silver Dagger award, 1988. **Agent:** Dominick Abel, 146 West 82nd Street, New York, New York 10024. **Address:** 5831 South Blackstone, Chicago, Illinois 60637, U.S.A.

Publications

Novels (series: V. I. Warshawski in all books)

Indemnity Only. New York, Dial Press, and London, Gollancz, 1982.
Deadlock. New York, Dial Press, and London, Gollancz, 1984.
Killing Orders. New York, Morrow, 1985; London, Gollancz, 1986.
Bitter Medicine. New York, Morrow, and London, Gollancz, 1987.
Blood Shot. New York, Delacorte Press, 1988; as *Toxic Shock,* London, Gollancz, 1988.
Burn Marks. New York, Delacorte Press, and London, Chatto and Windus, 1990.
Guardian Angel. New York, Delacorte Press, and London, Hamish Hamilton, 1992.
Tunnel Vision. New York, Delacorte Press, and London, Hamish Hamilton, 1994.
Windy City Blues. New York, Delacorte Press, 1995; as *V. I. for Short,* London, Hamish Hamilton, 1995.

Other

Case Studies in Alternative Education. Chicago Center for New Schools, 1975.

Editor, *Eye of a Woman* (short stories). New York, Delacorte Press, 1990.

*

Media Adaptation: Film—*V. I. Warshawski,* 1991, from the V. I. Warshawski novels.

* * *

Sharp-tongued, sharp-shooting female private detective V. I. Warshawski is the hugely popular creation of Sara Paretsky. The *Los Angeles Times* wrote of her novel *Tunnel Vision* (1994) that it offered the reader "a story of non-stop immediacy and action, peopled with vivid and often tragically affecting characters." The statement provides a clue to her formula for success: tightly plotted, fast-paced sleuthing thrillers combined with richly imagined characters in realistic and diverse social settings.

V. I. herself is a fiercely independent single woman with strong emotional ties to her real family and a capacity for forming surrogate families through deep friendships, some of which continue through the novels. Her beat is the Chicago mean streets, but V. I. is equally at home with scions of inherited wealth, big businessmen, and politicians, as well as pimps, prostitutes, and the working poor. Through V. I.'s narration, Paretsky uses the hardboiled private eye format for feminist and political ends as the novels discover corruption in different ares of society (such as industrial pollution in *Toxic Shock* [1988] and the inequities in healthcare in *Bitter Medicine* [1987]). Frequently, the crime stories also uncover abuses of power in the traditional nuclear family: child abuse has been explored twice; once in *Toxic Shock* and more recently in *Tunnel Vision.*

Readers also follow the cast of intriguing and sympathetic characters who surround the embattled V. I. These include: Dr. Lotty Herschel, doctor to the poor and mother figure to V. I.; My Contreras, geriatric neighbor and over enthusiastic protector; Bobby Mallory, exasperated but caring police officer; and a strong cast of women friends.

The typical V. I. Warshawski novel opens with one or two simple mysteries that gradually reveal a more complex web of corruption linking organized crime with respectable institutions. Paretsky's work is remarkable for the realistic portrayal of diverse forms of American working life from insurance offices to shipping, waitressing to industrial plants, and construction sites to police procedure. V. I. always reveals the labyrinthine criminal connections, although justice is sometimes harder to achieve. What is satisfying about these detective stories is V. I.'s determination to fix the moral guilt where it belongs, despite the tragic sense that solving the crime does not put the world to rights as more conservative detective novelists sometimes intimate.

With union bosses in hock to organized crime, *Indemnity Only* (1982) and *Deadlock* (1984) depict corporate corruption leading to murder in the worlds of insurance and shipping companies. Social concern is stepped up in *Killing Orders* (1985) when the Catholic church's emotional, social, and political hold on American society is criticized, while *Bitter Medicine*'s strong plot examines the healthcare system and the pro-life movement. The plight of industrial workers in the chemical industry is the subject of *Toxic Shock* when a voice from V. I.'s past, now an environmental campaigner, wants V. I.'s help in challenging an industrial giant. Despite threats, violence, and attempts to buy her off, V. I. uncovers a horrifying conspiracy to conceal from the workers just how the pollutants are killing them.

Burn Marks (1990) deals with the mingling of police, political, and corporate corruption, with the unlikely figure of V. I.'s drunken aunt, Elena, precipitating the drama. Family tensions meld perfectly with the wider connections of crime and violence in Chicago in this example of how Paretsky combines strong feeling, complex characters, and intricate crime plots. *Guardian Angel* (1992) develops Paretsky's concern with society's forgotten loners, the elderly poor. This novel links yuppies persecuting an old woman and her dogs in V. I.'s neighborhood with insurance fraud, industrial crime, and murder. There is also a delightful dog giving birth. Consummate plotting skill is maintained in *Tunnel Vision,* as V. I.'s trails lead her to the homeless through middle-class domestic violence and corrupt construction companies.

Poised between tragedy and reassurance, Paretsky's work offers the comforts of unravelling complex cases, fast-moving action, and a strong cast of engaging characters. Realistic depictions of working America are infused with feminist passion and humor.

Tough yet vulnerable, V. I. Warshawski is a popular heroine commanding affection and respect.

—S. A. Rowland

PARKER, Robert B(rown)

Nationality: American. **Born:** Springfield, Massachusetts, 17 September 1932. **Education:** Colby College, Waterville, Maine, B.A. 1954; Boston University, M.A. 1957, Ph.D. 1971. **Military Service:** Served in the U.S. Army, 1954-56. **Family:** Married Joan Hall in 1956; two sons. **Career:** Technical writer and group leader, Raytheon Company, 1957-59; copy writer and editor, Prudential Insurance Company, Boston, 1959-62; partner, Parker Farman Company, advertising, Boston, 1960-62; teaching fellow and lecturer, Boston University, 1962-64; instructor, Massachusetts State College, Lowell, 1964-66; lecturer, Suffolk University, Boston, 1965-66; instructor, Massachusetts State College, Bridgewater, 1964-68; assistant professor, 1968-74, associate professor, 1974-77, and professor, 1977-79, Northeastern University, Boston. **Awards:** Mystery Writers of America Edgar Allan Poe award, 1976. LiH.D: Northeastern University, Boston, 1987. **Agent:** Helen L. Brann Agency, 94 Curtis Road, Bridgewater, Connecticut 06752, U.S.A. **Address:** Cambridge, Massachusetts.

Publications

Novels (series: Spenser in all books)

The Godwulf Manuscript. Boston, Houghton Mifflin, 1973; London, Deutsch, 1974.
God Save the Child. Boston, Houghton Mifflin, 1974; London, Deutsch, 1975.
Mortal Stakes. Boston, Houghton Mifflin, 1975; London, Deutsch, 1976.
Promised Land. Boston, Houghton Mifflin, 1976; London, Deutsch, 1977.
The Judas Goat. Boston, Houghton Mifflin, 1978; London, Deutsch, 1982.
Wilderness. New York, Delacorte Press, 1979.
Looking for Rachel Wallace. New York, Delacorte Press, 1980; Loughton, Essex, Piatkus, 1982.
A Savage Place. New York, Delacorte Press, 1981; Loughton, Essex, Piatkus, 1982.
Early Autumn. New York, Delacorte Press, 1981; London, Severn House, 1987.
Ceremony. New York, Delacorte Press, 1982; Loughton, Essex, Piatkus, 1983.
The Widening Gyre. New York, Delacorte Press, 1983; London, Severn House, 1991.
Love and Glory. New York, Delacorte Press, 1983.
Valediction. New York, Delacorte Press, 1984; London, Penguin, 1985.
A Catskill Eagle. New York, Delacorte Press, 1985; London, Viking, 1986.
Taming a Sea-Horse. New York, Delacorte Press, 1986; London, Viking, 1987.
Pale Kings and Princes. New York, Delacorte Press, 1987; London, Viking, 1988.
Crimson Joy. New York, Delacorte Press, 1988; London, Viking, 1989.
Playmates. New York, Putnam, 1989; London, Viking, 1990.
Poodle Springs (completion of novel by Raymond Chandler). New York, Putnam, 1989; London, Macdonald, 1990.
Stardust. New York, Putnam, 1990; London, Viking, 1991.
Pastime. New York, Putnam, and London, Viking, 1991.
Perchance to Dream (sequel to *The Big Sleep* by Raymond Chandler). New York, Putnam, and London, Macdonald, 1991.
Double Deuce. New York, Putnam, and London, Viking, 1992.
Paper Doll. New York, Putnam, and London, Viking, 1993.
All Our Yesterdays. New York, Delacorte, and London, Viking, 1994.
Walking Shadow. New York, Putnam, and London, Viking, 1994.
Thin Air. New York, Putnam, and London, Viking, 1995.

Short Stories

Surrogate. Northridge, California, Lord John Press, 1982.

Other

Sports Illustrated Training with Weights, with John R. Marsh. Philadelphia, Lippincott, 1974.
"Marlowe's Moral Code," in *Popular Culture Scholar* (Frostburg, Maryland), 1976.
"Marxism and the Mystery," in *Murder Ink: The Mystery Reader's Companion,* edited by Dilys Winn. New York, Workman, 1977.
Three Weeks in Spring, with Joan H. Parker. Boston, Houghton Mifflin, and London, Deutsch, 1978.
The Private Eye in Hammett and Chandler. Northridge, California, Lord John Press, 1984.
Parker on Writing. Northridge, California, Lord John Press, 1985.
A Year at the Races, with Joan H. Parker. New York, Viking, 1990.
Spenser's Boston. New York, Otto Penzler Books, 1994.

Editor, *The Personal Response to Literature.* Boston, Houghton Mifflin, 1971.
Editor, *Order and Diversity.* New York, Wiley, 1973.

* * *

Robert B. Parker received his Ph.D. in 1971 from Boston University with a dissertation dissecting the private eye in the novels of Dashiell Hammett, Raymond Chandler, and Ross Macdonald. Two years later his first novel, *The Godwulf Manuscript,* was published. The novel focuses on a gumshoe named Spenser (with no first name). While he pays tribute to Hammett's Sam Spade, Chandler's Philip Marlowe, and Macdonald's Lew Archer, Parker manages to create a style all his own expanding on the hard-boiled tradition. "Like Sam Spade, he is tough and often cynical. Like Philip Marlowe, he has a quick wit, an insolent tongue, and an observant eye for the pompous and absurd. Like Lew Archer, he frequently finds himself drawn into the personal lives of his clients," says David Geherin in his book *Sons of Sam Spade.* Spenser, however, unlike his predecessors who remain lonely and isolated after the close of a case, has a private life separate from his work.

In his second novel, *God Save the Child* (1974), Parker introduces Susan Silverman, who becomes Spenser's lover. In *God Save the Child,* Parker moves away from the self-conscious nod at the hard-boiled tradition in his first novel, and develops his style more fully. Parker handles the plot better than in his first effort, and sketches even minor characters brilliantly. Throughout all of his novels, even when his plotting is less than satisfactory, Parker's characterization, wit, and dialogue serve to captivate the reader to the end.

The popularity of this ex-cop, ex-soldier, ex-boxer, gourmet detective (who spouts literary allusions as often as he's called a wise-cracking bum) earned Parker an Edgar award for best mystery novel of 1976. The book *Promised Land* was the fourth in the series. Whether Spenser is chasing after international terrorists in *The Judas Goat* (1978), protecting a lesbian writer in *Looking for Rachel Wallace* (1980), or investigating drug smuggling in *Pale Kings and Princes* (1987) and *Pastime* (1991), he is building a code of behavior. This code will enable him to deal with a chaotic world. Ernest Hemingway laid out such a code in *The Sun Also Rises*; Parker is doing the same in his Spenser series. The measure of a man is in his response to situations.

Spenser usually must deal with a moral or ethical dilemma by the close of each novel. For example, *Ceremony* (1982) deals with the sexual exploitation of children. By the end of the novel Spenser must decide with whom April, a young prostitute, should live, uncaring parents or a high-class bordello. His choice would seem reprehensible by society's standards, but Spenser lives by a code which at times must supersede society's moral code.

In *Promised Land,* Parker introduces the character of Hawk, an enforcer for the mob. Newgate Callendar describes him as "a black angel of death who strikes terror into all who cross him." Hawk is the perfect foil for Spenser. Hawk serves to remind Spenser that he doesn't have that far to fall to become Hawk. The relationship between Spenser and Hawk also becomes an excellent source of witty banter.

Where Parker has differed from the hard-boiled tradition most is the extended family that Spenser clearly has throughout the series. Paul Giacomin, who first appeared in *Early Autumn* (1981), plays the role of Spenser's surrogate son again in *The Widening Gyre* (1983) and *Pastime* (1991). Hawk, his friend, and Susan, his lover, appear in almost every novel in the series. Spenser also has contact with Lieutenant Martin Quirk, Sergeant Frank Belson, and Lieutenant Healy over the course of the series. All of these characters form an extended family on which Spenser relies. This is a definite break from the tradition of the detective who returns after a case—alone, desperate to escape from the chaos of the world, and unwilling to connect with another human being—to his shabby apartment.

Although Parker has written a few books not connected with the character of Spenser, including a panned sequel to Chandler's *The Big Sleep* entitled *Perchance to Dream* (1991), these forays outside the Spenser series have not been as well received. In Spenser, Parker has created a character to not only continue the hard-boiled detective tradition, but to expand its boundaries. As Robin S. Winks puts it, "There are a dozen claimants to follow Hammett, Chandler, and Ross Macdonald; Parker alone has done it."

—Jennifer G. Coman

PATTERSON, Henry. *See* **HIGGINS, Jack.**

PAYNE, Alan. *See* **JAKES, John.**

PECK, M(organ) Scott

Nationality: American. **Born:** 22 May 1936, in New York. **Education:** Middlebury College, 1954-56; Harvard University, A.B., 1958; Case Western Reserve University, M.D., 1963. **Family:** Married Lily Ho in 1959; children: Belinda, Julia, Christopher. **Career:** U.S. Army, 1963-72, intern at Tripler Medical Center, Honolulu, Hawaii, 1963-64, resident in psychiatry at Letterman General Hospital, San Francisco, 1967-70, chief of department of psychology at U.S. Army Medical Center, Okinawa, Japan, 1967-70, assistant chief of psychiatry and neurology at office of surgeon general, Washington, D.C., 1970-72, leaving service as lieutenant colonel; private practice of psychiatry in New Preston, Connecticut, 1972-84. Medical director of New Milford Hospital Mental Health Clinic, 1973-81, and 1974-83; vice-chairman of the board, Foundation for Community Encouragement; board member, Ouroborus, Inc. Consultant to U.S. surgeon general, 1970-72. **Awards:** Meritorious service medal with Oak Leaf Cluster. **Address:** Bliss Rd., New Preston, Connecticut 06777, U.S.A.

Publications

Nonfiction

The Road Less Traveled: A New Psychology of Love, Traditional Values and Spiritual Growth. Simon & Schuster, 1978.
People of the Lie: The Hope for Healing Human Evil. Simon & Schuster, 1983.
What Return Can I Make?: The Dimensions of the Christian Experience, with Marilyn von Waldener and Patricia Kay. Simon & Schuster, 1985; revised as *Gifts for the Journey,* 1995.
The Different Drum: Community Making and Peace. Simon & Schuster, 1987.
Creating Community Anywhere: Finding Support in a Fragmented World. Putnam, 1993.
Further Along the Road Less Traveled. Simon & Schuster, 1993.
Meditations from the Road. Simon & Schuster, 1993.
A World Waiting to Be Born: Rediscovering Civility. Bantam, 1993.
In Search of Stones: A Pilgrimage of Faith, Reason, and Discovery. Simon & Schuster, 1995.
A Place Reserved: A Vision of the Afterlife. Simon & Schuster, 1996.

Novels

A Bed by the Window: A Novel of Mystery and Redemption. Bantam, 1990.
The House of Charon. Bantam, 1990.

* * *

M. Scott Peck wrote one of the most popular self-help books of all time, *The Road Less Traveled* (1978). The book has sold nearly ten million copies and spent over a decade on the *New York Times* bestseller list. The popularity of his work has made the Connecticut psychiatrist highly in demand as a physician, speaker, and spiritual teacher.

The Road Less Traveled is essentially an optimistic discussion of the process of human growth and problem solving. Peck states that there is no difference between psychological healing and spiritual growth. The book contains an appealing mixture of common sense, psychoanalytical theory, and ideas from an assortment of religions and philosophers. Peck writes in a warm, honest style, and gives plenty of examples from his own life and psychiatric practice. The main tool that we can use to overcome our problems in life, Peck argues, is discipline, and the greatest motivating factor behind discipline should be love. Peck outlines the ways in which we can apply discipline to our lives. Then he addresses the broad subject of love, in the context of relationships and religion. Such topics as evil, power, mental illness, psychotherapy, and the nature of God are also discussed in the book. Peck's uncommon insight and knowledge prompted Phyllis Theroux of the *Washington Post* to acclaim that it was "not just a book, but a spontaneous act of generosity."

In 1983 Peck published *People of the Lie: The Hope for Healing Human Evil.* In it, Peck focuses upon the nature of evil within individuals and throughout society. Peck defines evil as "the imposition of one's will upon others by overt or covert coercion—in order to avoid spiritual growth." The book is written in Peck's characteristic style, mixing personal stories, clinical cases, and various religious and philosophical ideas. Paul Huss in *Library Journal* called it a "superb job of integrating psychology, theology, and therapeutic practice." Peck also raises some controversial points in the book, such as using exorcism to rid individuals of evil. Leo O'Donovan in *Commonweal* wrote that the book was "at once instructive, persuasive—and distressingly idiosyncratic."

In *The Different Drum: Community Making and Peace* (1985), Peck analyzes how people come together in communities and institutions. Peck argues that communities function just like the individuals within them, and are subject to the same behaviors. He then suggests ways in which we can make the world a better place to live. Elise Chase of *Library Journal* said that the book "draws exciting analogies between the ways communities emerge and the dynamics of individual spiritual development." Lillian Rubin in the *New York Times* wrote that Peck is a "compelling preacher" and that "the life he entreats us to seek is surely worth pursuing," but Rubin found Peck's proposed solutions to world problems "simple-minded."

In 1990, Peck tried his hand at fiction in *The Bed by the Window: A Novel of Mystery and Redemption.* The book is set in a midwestern nursing home, where a transplanted New York police officer tries to solve a homicide and meets a cast of unique characters in the process. It is a combination murder mystery, psychological case study, and spiritual sermon, and readers will recognize Peck's favorite themes. Most critics agreed with Mary Kay Blakely of the *New York Times,* who wrote that the book was "overtly didactic and opaquely religious," but was also "moving and brave."

Peck continued in 1993 with *Further Along the Road Less Traveled: The Unending Journey Toward Spiritual Growth.* The book discusses more big topics; adult maturation, death, forgiveness, self-esteem, good and evil, and addiction, within Peck's usual context of religion and psychology. Peck makes the point that the contemplation of death is part of the spiritual journey, and ultimately our acceptance of death will give life its full meaning. He also argues that contemporary psychiatry too often turns to biochemical solutions instead of spiritual guidance. John Mort of *Booklist* wrote that, "while it contains no startling revelations," the book has "accessible common sense full of winning anecdotes."

Peck is also a speaker and teacher, and sometimes works with large corporations. He is so popular for his ideas that he seriously considered running for president in the 1980s. His admirers are attracted by the wisdom they find in his writings, but Peck has been criticized for expressing some eccentric, far-out ideas as well. John Skow in *Time* summed up Peck's wise and eccentric combination: "Both qualities are evident in his writings and his personality, though a surprising range of critics clearly feel that what predominates is wisdom." That wisdom has made *The Road Less Traveled* a beloved guidebook for many people.

—Doug Dupler

PERCY, Walker

Nationality: American. **Born:** 28 May 1916, in Birmingham, Alabama. **Education:** University of North Carolina, B.A., 1937; Columbia University, M.D., 1941. **Family:** Married Mary Bernice Townsend in 1946; children: Ann Boyd, Mary Pratt. **Career:** Full-time writer, 1943-90. Bellevue Hospital, New York City, intern, 1942. **Awards:** National Book award for fiction, 1962, for *The Moviegoer;* National Institute of Arts and Letters grant, 1967; National Catholic Book award, 1971, for *Love in the Ruins; Los Angeles Times* Book prize, 1980, National Book Critics Circle citation, 1980, American Book Award nomination, 1981, Notable Book citation from American Library Association, 1981, all for *The Second Coming; Los Angeles Times* Book prize for current interest, 1983, for *Lost in the Cosmos: The Last Self-Help Book;* St. Louis Literary award, 1986; Ingersoll prize from Ingersoll Foundation, 1988. **Member:** American Academy and Institute of Arts and Letters (fellow). **Died:** 10 May 1990, of cancer, in Covington, Louisiana.

Publications

Novels

The Moviegoer. Knopf, 1961; reprinted, Avon, 1980.
The Last Gentleman. Farrar, Straus, 1966; reprinted, Avon, 1978.
Love in the Ruins: The Adventures of a Bad Catholic at a Time near the End of the World. Farrar, Straus, 1971; reprinted, Avon, 1978.
Lancelot. Farrar, Straus, 1977.
The Second Coming. Farrar, Straus, 1980.
The Thanatos Syndrome. Farrar, Straus, 1987.

Nonfiction

The Message in the Bottle: How Queer Man Is, How Queer Language Is, and What One Has to Do with the Other. Farrar, Straus, 1975.

Lost in the Cosmos: The Last Self-Help Book. Farrar, Straus, 1983.
Novel-Writing in an Apocalyptic Time. Faust Publishing Company, 1986.
State of the Novel: Dying Art or New Science. Faust Publishing Company, 1988.

*

Bibliography: *Walker Percy: A Bibliography: 1930-1984* by Stuart Wright, Meckler, 1986; *Walker Percy: A Comprehensive Descriptive Bibliography* by Linda Whitney Hobson, Faust, 1988.

Critical Studies: *The Sovereign Wayfarer: Walker Percy's Diagnosis of the Malaise* by Martin Luschei, Louisiana State University Press, 1972; *Walker Percy: An American Search* by Robert Coles, Little, Brown, 1978; *The Art of Walker Percy: Stratagems for Being,* edited by Panthea Reid Broughton, Louisiana State University Press, 1979; *Walker Percy: Art and Ethics,* edited by Jac Tharpe, University Press of Mississippi, 1980; *Walker Percy* by Tharpe, Twayne, 1983; *Percy and the Old Modern Age* by Patricia Lewis Poteat, Louisiana State University Press, 1985; *In Search of Self: Life, Death, and Walker Percy* by Jerome L. Taylor, Cowley, 1986; *Walker Percy: A Southern Wayfarer* by William Rodney Allen, University Press of Mississippi, 1986; *The Fiction of Walker Percy* by John Edward Hardy, University of Illinois Press, 1987; *Following Percy: Essays on Walker Percy's Work,* Whitson, 1987, and *Still Following Percy,* University Press of Mississippi, 1995, by Lewis A. Lawson; *Walker Percy and the Postmodern World* by Mary K. Sweeney, Loyola University Press, 1987; *Understanding Walker Percy* by Linda Whitney Hobson, University of South Carolina Press, 1988; *Walker Percy: Critical Essays,* edited by Donald J. and Sue Mitchell Crowley, G. K. Hall, 1989; *Walker Percy: The Making of an American Moralist,* 1990, and *Pilgrim in the Ruins,* 1992, by Jay Tolson, Simon & Schuster; *Walker Percy: Novelist and Philosopher,* edited by Jan Nordby Gretlund and Karl-Heinz Westarp, University Press of Missippi, 1991; *Walker Percy: Books of Revelations* by Gary M. Ciuba, University of Georgia Press, 1992; *The Myth of the Fall & Walker Percy's Last Gentleman* by Bernadette Prochaska, Peter Lang, 1993; *The Signs of Christianity in the Work of Walker Percy* by Ann M. Futrell, Catholic Scholarly Press, 1994.

* * *

His death in 1990 leaves us to ponder what Walker Percy would have said about the cultural corruptions of the 1990s. Percy is a satirist extraordinaire whose work reflects a post-1950s alienation from American society with which many readers and critics can identify. His protagonists are lusty, thirsty, apathetic-yet-questing, self-mythologizing, and irreverent. They carry too much cultural baggage to ever be content to live in America, or even to live. Yet, Percy has many dedicated fans and scholars. Numerous dissertations, books, and articles have been written on such topics as the nature of Percy's Catholicism and the techniques of his satiric-fantastic realism. Readership is not confined to the southeastern states, but is nationwide and international, with translations in a dozen languages.

Although not his first novel, *The Moviegoer* (1961) was the first to receive publication. It won the prestigious National Book Award for 1962. Its hero finds the movies more real than life, because they at least engage in a search for meaning. Yet it is questionable whether Binx Bolling, *The Moviegoer*'s protagonist, finds the meaning he was looking for when, in the end of the novel, he marries his neurotic, suicidal cousin and promises his aunt that he will apply to medical school. The book was most praised for its tight structure, characters, and symbolism, but some critics found Binx's search pretentious. Samuel Hyman commented that it was the search of a neurotic rather than a spiritual person.

The second book, *The Last Gentleman* (1966), drew more varied critical response. It was different in form and complexity, using an episodic, picaresque plot in which the antihero Will Barrett follows the family of the girl he loves from New York to the South to New Mexico. The book ends with the death of the girlfriend's brother. Again, the ending leaves questions unanswered: did Will's witnessing of the death help him to carve out an identity from his many experiences, or did he only absorb it and move on, forgetting the pain as he had forgotten much of his past?

Percy also wrote philosophical essays. His main interest is the role of language in communicating or failing to communicate. His essays are "ambitious, dense, and difficult," according to J. Donald Crowley. Their publication in *The Message in the Bottle* (1975) helped critics understand the ideas and motivations for the novels. Hugh Kenner called Percy's theory of language a "Copernican breakthrough."

The most memorable Percy novel is *Lancelot* (1977) because it humorously anatomizes the symbolically named antihero and his neurotic obsession with his wife's infidelity. In the throes of his agony upon discovering his wife's affair, he asks himself how a five-inch piece of flesh entering another person can turn the world into chaos. Like all Percy's protagonists, Lancelot's vision is apocalyptic. His wife's affair with a movie producer spells the corruption of the entire gender and of civilization itself. To express his distaste, Lancelot burns his wife and her cohorts to death.

The later novels show a trend towards stereotyping women and blacks, but they also bring Percy's religious and philosophical beliefs to the fore, clarifying the driving ideology of these books. The public remains intrigued and perplexed by this uncategorizable writer, who has called himself a "southern philosophical Catholic existentialist."

—Jill Franks

PERRY, Anne

Nationality: British. **Born:** London, 28 October 1938. **Education:** Privately educated. **Career:** Has had a variety of jobs, including airline stewardess, 1962-64; asssistant buyer, Newcastle uopn Tyne, 1964-66; property underwriter, Muldoon and Adams, Los Angeles. Since 1972 full-time writer. Lived in California, 1967-72. **Agent:** Meg Davis, MBA Literary Agency Ltd., 45 Fitzroy Street, London, W1P 5HR, England. **Address:** 1 Seafield, Portmabomack, Rosshire IY20 IYB, Scotland.

Publications

Novels (series: Charlotte and Thomas Pitt in all books except as indicated)

The Cater Street Hangman. St. Martin's Press, 1979.
Callander Square. St. Martin's Press, 1980.

Paragon Walk. St. Martin's Press, 1981.
Resurrection Row. St. Martin's Press, 1981.
Rutland Place. St. Martin's Press, 1983.
Bluegate Fields. St. Martin's Press, 1984.
Death in the Devil's Acre. St. Martin's Press, 1985.
Cardington Crescent. St. Martin's Press, 1987.
Silence in Hanover Close. St. Martin's Press, 1988.
Bethlehem Road. St. Martin's Press, 1990.
Face of a Stranger (Monk William). Fawcett, 1990.
A Dangerous Mourning (Monk William). Fawcett, 1991.
Highgate Rise. Fawcett, 1991.
Belgrave Square. Fawcett, 1992.
Defend and Betray (Monk William). Fawcett, 1992.
Farriers' Lane. Fawcett, 1993.
A Sudden, Fearful Death (Monk William).Fawcett, 1993.
The Hyde Park Headsman. Fawcett, 1994.
The Sins of the Wolf (Monk William). Fawcett, 1994.
Cain and His Brother. Fawcett, 1995.
Traitor's Gate. Fawcett, 1995.
Pentecost Alley. Fawcett, 1996.

*

Manuscript Collection: Mugar Memorial Library, Boston University.

* * *

Anne Perry is famous for two sets of engaging detective novels set in Victorian London. While each of her novels involves a unique and separate investigation, both sets follow a chronological sequence with key characters and their maturing relationships developed from book to book. The result is both continuity and a growing awareness of the limited size of "respectable" society and the restrictive social power this limit entailed, particularly on women, whose reputations could be ruined with a whisper. To the crime genre Perry brings the fascination of historical novels—their ability to sum up the fears, beliefs and ideals of an age in a handful of representative characters—and a humanistic belief in the consistency of human nature that makes the excesses and lies of the past illuminate our own.

The Cater Street Hangman (1979) introduces the Ellison sisters; Emily, who marries above her station (a lord), and amateur detective Charlotte, who marries beneath her station (police officer Thomas Pitt). Through Thomas, Charlotte sees a seamier side of society than does her family, while she uses family connections to gather information unavailable to her husband because of his social standing. She is occasionally assisted by various good-natured elderly relatives with peerless social credentials and a firm grasp of the codes by which proper society is conducted. Charlotte Pitt provides a mirror into both social worlds and the murky netherworld of peccadillos, perversions, and cruelties where these worlds overlap. As family members, neighbors, and acquaintances caught in compromising situations and suspected of crime close ranks, the Pitts typically encounter secret sins, from opium addiction and child abuse to slum lords and Jew baiting. Often, the domestic and the governmental are intertwined, as in *Traitors Gate* (1995), which turns on a husband's interpretation of his wife's political questions as personal betrayal.

The Monk/Hester series involves seamier views of London, greater violence, and more courtroom drama than the Pitt series, which is set thirty years later. The morose London detective William Monk is a complex, Byronic figure, stricken with amnesia and unable to rediscover his past self. His hunt for villains leads to private truths about his own identity (his ruthless ambition and calculated sacrifices) and to repeated contact with the strong-willed, competent, and committed Hester Latterly. Latterly, a friend and associate of Florence Nightingale, served as nurse/surgeon's assistant in the Crimea during the Charge of the Light Brigade, and Monk's antagonism for her hides a deep love that his conscious mind denies. *The Face of a Stranger* (1990), a haunting psychological suspense story, centers on the brutal murder of a Crimean war "hero" with feet of clay, while *Defend and Betray* (1992) exposes a respected individual who is in fact a child abuser. In *A Sudden, Fearful Death* (1993) nurses are strangled, while in *The Sins of the Wolf* (1994) Latterly is charged with poisoning a patient and Monk must restore her reputation.

Perry comments on the limited education of most Victorian women as well as the social climate that excluded women from serious concerns, bound behavior by rigid patterns of politeness, prevented most women from developing any vision of a potential self, and made fathers and husbands official guardians of their wealth and well-being. Thus, the fathers and husbands were potential tyrants with the legal and financial authority to enforce their prejudices. Perry's dominant themes grow out of her construct of Victorian society, a hypocritical world that boxes, categorizes, separates, euphemizes, and obfuscates, while behind the facade of respectability it taints and twists all relationships, including familial and sexual ones.

Perry criticizes the constraints and restraints imposed by class and by sex, and creates crimes that allow her to explore wide-ranging social concerns including child prostitution, workhouse labor, incest, institutions for the insane, overprescription of laudanum, the brutal squalor of Victorian hospitals, unequal property rights in divorce, and the deadly effects of venereal disease on the social fabric. *In Bethlehem Road* (1990), for example, a prominent suffragist accused of murdering a Parliamentarian who opposed women's voting rights raises questions about the subjugation of women.

Perry's strengths are her firm understanding of Victorian repressions and the effects of a secret shame, and her drive to tear down the facades of the very proper. Her own real-life teenage experiences with a forbidden sexual liaison, with pent-up emotions unleashed in violence (matricide with a brick), and with the legal, social, and personal repercussions have given her a deep sympathy with social outcasts, rebels, and murderers. The New Zealand film *Heavenly Creatures* dramatizes Perry's past.

While firmly placing blame, Perry skillfully humanizes the most hideous crime. Distancing graphic, bloody description with Victorian propriety, she captures the motivations and psychology of the criminal and helps the reader understand the social conditions, repressions, and frustrations that often produce violence.

—Gina Macdonald

PETERS, Elizabeth. *See* **MERTZ, Barbara.**

PILCHER, Rosamunde

Pseudonym: Jane Fraser. **Nationality:** English. **Born:** 22 September 1924, in Lelant, Cornwall. **Education:** Educated at public schools in England and Wales. **Military Service:** Women's Royal Naval Service, 1942-46. **Family:** Married Graham Hope Pilcher in 1946; children: Fiona, Robin, Philippa, Mark. **Career:** Writer. **Agent:** Curtis Brown, 62-68 Regent St., London W1, England. **Address:** Over Pilmore, Invergowrie, by Dundee DD2 5EL, Scotland.

Publications

Novels

A Secret to Tell. Collins, 1955.
April. Collins, 1957.
On My Own. Collins, 1965.
Sleeping Tiger. Collins, 1967.
Another View. Collins, 1969.
The End of the Summer. Collins, 1971.
Snow in April. St. Martin's, 1972.
The Empty House. Collins, 1973.
The Day of the Storm. Collins, 1975.
Under Gemini. Collins, 1976.
Wild Mountain Thyme. St. Martin's, 1979.
The Carousel. St. Martin's, 1982.
Voices in Summer. St. Martin's, 1982.
The Shell Seekers. St. Martin's, 1988.
September. St. Martin's, 1990.
Coming Home. St. Martin's, 1995.

Novels as Jane Fraser

Halfway to the Moon. Mills & Boon, 1949.
The Brown Fields. Mills & Boon, 1951.
Dangerous Intruder. Mills & Boon, 1951.
Young Bar. Mills & Boon, 1952.
A Day Like Spring. Mills & Boon, 1953.
Dear Tom. Mills & Boon, 1954.
Bridge of Corvie. Mills & Boon, 1956.
A Family Affair. Mills & Boon, 1958.
A Long Way from Home. Mills & Boon, 1963.
The Keeper's House. Mills & Boon, 1963.

Short Stories

The Blue Bedroom and Other Stories. St. Martin's, 1985.
Flowers in the Rain and Other Stories. St. Martin's, 1992.
Love Stories. St. Martin's, 1996.

Plays

The Dashing White Sergeant, with Charles C. Gairdner (produced London, 1955). Evans, 1955.

* * *

English romanticist Rosamunde Pilcher, author of more than two dozen novels, has fashioned a strong place for herself among women's fiction with her tales of family and romance, all written without the silly pretension of much of that genre. Pilcher's greatest strength seems to be her ability to pace her tales and bring her several subplots together for happy and believable endings. A resident of Scotland, Pilcher was born in Cornwall and has set most of her stories in these two places, which she uses successfully for atmosphere without overshadowing her strong characters.

Under Gemini (1976), her 20th novel (ten were written under her pseudonym Jane Fraser), gained her much favorable criticism for its story of twin sisters Flora and Rose, who are separated at birth and 22 years later switch places. While Rose happily abandons her fiance Anthony and runs off to Greece, the honest Flora takes Rose's place just as Anthony's dying grandmother, Tuppy, wishes to see the couple once more. Flora, of course, proves to be everything Anthony could wish for—except his true fiance. *Kirkus Reviews* called *Under Gemini* "utterly agreeable," and the *New York Times Book Review* described the novel as "warmed with honest sentiment, lubricated with tears of happiness and souped up by an ace romanticist."

Pilcher continued her success with her next two novels, *Wild Mountain Thyme* (1979) and *The Carousel* (1982). *Wild Mountain Thyme* is especially witty, concerned with angry British playwright Oliver and his kidnapping of his motherless two-year-old son Tommy from the maternal grandparents, whom Oliver finds insufferable. Oliver takes both his son and an old girlfriend, Victoria, to call on his author friend Roddy in Scotland, where Oliver grows increasingly irritable and the hapless Victoria falls for Roddy's nephew John, an international banker. "Pilcher demonstrates just what can be done with a mini-romance when fueled by coincidence and happy accident," *Kirkus Reviews* wrote of *Wild Mountain Thyme*; "she idles this with such affectionate involvement in personages and scenery that you're shamelessly delighted when everything sorts out nicely in the end."

It was not until her novel *The Shell Seekers* (1988) that Pilcher, at the age of 60, became a hit in America. The novel was a departure in other ways as well, turning from the comfortable love stories of young English women to the chronicle of an aging and unyielding widow, Penelope Keeling, age 64, whose late husband Lawrence Stern was a famous English painter. It is easy to dislike Penelope's children, particularly the social-climbing Nancy and the self-centered, immature Noel, though the tough-minded Olivia is far better. All three want Penelope to sell the last-remaining canvases of her husband, yet she stubbornly keeps them as they remind her of her youth and of her lover, Richard Lomax, who died at Normandy in WWII. She befriends a young and likable couple, Antonia and Danus, who become rivals in the minds of Penelope's children, particularly when Penelope's will is revealed. While *Kirkus Reviews* criticized the book's slim plot and sometimes illogical Penelope, author and columnist Maeve Binchy praised *The Shell Seekers,* writing in *The New York Times Book Review* that "Penelope could enter and win any number of 'unforgettable character' competitions . . . *The Shell Seekers* is a deeply satisfying story, written with love and confidence."

September (1990) is perhaps Pilcher's best novel, in which the venal son of Penelope Keeling, Noel from *The Shell Seekers,* returns. Violet Aird, an elderly gentlewoman, has retired to a cottage on the local laird's estate in the Scottish Highlands, and views the painful affairs of her son Edmund and her granddaughter Alexa. Edmund's second marriage, to the beautiful Virginia, is headed for trouble due to arguments over the future of their son Henry. Alexa, meanwhile, has fallen in love for the first time, but it is with Noel

Keeling. The laird's daughter, vivacious Pandora Blair who had an affair with Edmund 20 years earlier, picks this timely moment to return from gallivanting across the world. In the center of the emotional maelstrom is Violet, who maintains her independent life yet dispenses sound, practical wisdom to her wayward family. A Literary Guild Dual Selection, *September* won praise from *Kirkus Reviews* with its "easy intimacy created between character and reader."

Readers who enjoy a good tale without ornate language or cumbersome philosophy should respond well to Pilcher's character-driven novels which, while dabbed with romantic affections, avoid the reefs of melodrama and ostentation on which other novels of this genre founder and then sink.

—Christopher Swann

PIRSIG, Robert M(aynard)

Nationality: American. **Born:** Minneapolis, Minnesota, 6 September 1928. **Education:** University of Minnesota, B.A., 1950, M.A., 1958. **Military Service:** U.S. Army, 1946-48. **Family:** Married Nancy Ann James in 1954 (divorced August, 1978); married Wendy L. Kimball in 1978; children: (first marriage) Christopher (deceased November 17, 1979), Theodore; (second marriage) Nell. **Career:** Montana State College, Bozeman, instructor in English composition, 1959-61; University of Illinois, Chicago, instructor in rhetoric, 1961-62; technical writer at several Minneapolis, Minnesota electronic firms, 1963-67; Century Publications, Minneapolis, contract technical writer, 1967-73; writer. Minnesota Zen Meditation Center, member of board of directors from 1973, vice-president, 1973-75. **Awards:** Guggenheim fellowship, 1974; Friends of Literature award, 1975; outstanding achievement award, University of Minnesota, 1975; American Academy and Institute of Arts and Letters award, 1979. **Member:** Society of Technical Communicators (secretary, 1970-71; treasurer, 1971-72). **Address:** c/o Bantam Books, 1540 Broadway, New York, New York 10036, U.S.A.

Publications

Nonfiction

Zen and the Art of Motorcycle Maintenance: An Inquiry into Values. Morrow, 1974.
Lila: An Inquiry into Morals. Bantam, 1991.

*

Critical Studies: *The Cosmic Web: Scientific Field Models and Literary Strategies in the Twentieth Century* by Katherine N. Hayles, Cornell University Press, 1984; McCaffery, Larry, *Postmodern Fiction: A Bio-Bibliographical Guide* by Larry McCaffery, Greenwood Press, 1986; *Guidebook to "Zen and the Art of Motocycle Maintenance"* by Ronald L. Di Santo and Thomas J. Steele, William Morrow, 1990.

* * *

With the publication of *Zen and the Art of Motorcycle Maintenance: An Inquiry into Values* in 1974, Robert Pirsig quickly attained a cult following and established himself as a fixture of popular culture. The book won several awards and was a major bestseller of the 1970s and 1980s.

The unusual autobiography details a fractured man's search for wholeness in a world which eventually drove him to insanity. On a motorcycle trip from Minnesota to California with his 11-year-old son, the narrator/Phaedrus uses his free time in meditations upon the relations of art and technology, subject and object, romanticism and classicism, substance and value, and myth and science. In the past, the narrator had become obsessed with the idea of quality, which he defines as the meeting point of subject and object. This obsession led to the collapse of his mind. The narrator spends the journey trying to understand his disturbing past. Through a loose framework of recollections, observations, and events, the narrator comes to understand that quality cannot be abstracted from experience. He discards the idea that technology degrades values. By working on the motorcycle, he works on himself. Implicit in this is the Zen idea that the self and the external world are not separate objects but two manifestations of the cosmic essence.

Zen became one of the most influential books of popular philosophy in recent times. Although praised for raising compelling and original questions, Pirsig was criticized for his flat repertorial style and a certain amount of tedium. While some critics saw Pirsig's arguments as penetrating and absorbing, others felt he gave shallow treatment to the issues. "Beneath the complexity of disorganization, the picture of society which the book presents and the panaceas it offers are distressingly naive and reductive, evading the very difficulties the book pretends to confront," said Eva Hoffman. Nevertheless, the book sustained its cult following into the 1990s.

Seventeen years after *Zen,* Pirsig continued the story of Phaedrus in *Lila: An Inquiry into Morals* (1991). A boat sailing down the Hudson River takes the place of the motorcycle this time around. Phaedrus is busy composing a metaphysics of quality which will be the key to all intellectual problems—something he believed impossible in *Zen*—when he encounters Lila. He becomes intrigued by Lila, and uses her to test his system. Does Lila have quality? Through Lila, Phaedrus addresses such issues as the nature of morals and values, insanity versus normality, Native Americans, Zen, and Victorian society. *Lila* differs from *Zen* in that the philosophy is less interesting than the actual narrative. Lila, a wonderfully complex character, is far more interesting than the tedium of Phaedrus's lectures. At the end, Phaedrus, with Lila's help, constructs his metaphysics of quality, which evaluates actions according to four evolutionary levels: natural, biological, social, and intellectual. Once again Pirsig manages to amalgamate the novel, the autobiography, and a personal philosophy into an original mix of thought and traditional narrative.

Throughout Pirsig's attempt to integrate the divided Western consciousness, he ranges widely in his philosophical ramblings which are at times provoking and incisive. Chris Goodrich explained, "At bottom, it's his asides, meditations, dissenting appraisals, and passionate search for 'the good' that make his work so attractive."

—Jennifer G. Coman

PLAIDY, Jean. *See* **HOLT, Victoria.**

PLAIN, Belva

Nationality: American. **Born:** 9 October 1919, in New York. **Education:** Graduated from Barnard College. **Family:** Married Irving Plain in 1941 (died 1982); children: three. **Career:** Writer. **Agent:** c/o Delacorte Press, 666 Fifth Ave., New York, New York 10103. **Address:** 77 Slope Drive, Short Hills, New Jersey 07078, U.S.A.

Publications

Novels

Evergreen. Delacorte, 1978.
Random Winds. Delacorte, 1980.
Eden Burning. Delacorte, 1982.
Crescent City. Delacorte, 1984.
The Golden Cup. Delacorte, 1987.
Tapestry. Delacorte, 1988.
Blessings. Delacorte, 1989.
Harvest. Delacorte, 1990.
Treasures. Delacorte, 1992.
Whispers. Delacorte, 1993.
Daybreak. Delacorte, 1994.
The Carousel. Dell, 1995.

*

Media Adaptation: Television miniseries—*Evergreen,* 1985.

* * *

Bestselling author Belva Plain has entertained readers for decades with her stories of forbidden love and romance. Plain began writing short stories for women's magazines such as *Cosmopolitan* and *Good Housekeeping* in the 1940s, publishing tales of women who consider extramarital affairs yet remain devoted to their marriages. From this beginning, she has become a novelist with a large audience that delights in her intricate plots and rich sense of setting.

Tiring of the formula fiction of her early short stories, Plain published nothing for nearly 12 years until she grew tired of stereotypes of Jewish characters in fiction. Recognizing what *Contemporary Authors* described as "the dominating, hysterical Jewish mothers of contemporary myth" and rejecting that image as inaccurate, Plain wrote her first novel, *Evergreen* (1978), the story of a young immigrant maid, Anna, who falls in love with her boss's son Paul. Later produced as a miniseries, *Evergreen* was the first in a long line of successful, bestselling novels. Most readers responded positively to her strong female characters and their secret, unfulfilled loves. As Laura Kavesh explains in the *Chicago Tribune,* "Plain's characters march through life courageously and usually with great success—but bearing private, searing aches over love just out of reach, the kind that sneaks along behind its slaves forever, jumping out in front of them now and again to shake things up."

One of Plain's goals in writing is to rid readers of stereotypes that have been advanced in other fiction. As Plain herself stated in an interview with *Contemporary Authors,* "I think so many novelists stereotype their characters: the Jewish mother is a demanding woman who has a heart attack every time her children want to do something that she doesn't like; the Irish family always has a perennial drunk; the Italians are always burdened with somebody who's in the Mafia. These things get to be sickening after a while." Her novels also uncover little-known historical facts that she hopes will pique the reader's interest; for example, *Crescent City* (1984), set in the Civil War era, depicts Jews on both sides of the slave issue, and reveals that only Confederate Jews were allowed to have chaplains until Lincoln recognized this discrepancy. Gay Courter in the *Washington Post* also remarked on the evocative setting and situations of *Crescent City*: "It's all here, moss and mansions, languid afternoons and clandestine evenings, repressed old maids and irresistible quadroons, the glamour and gore of war, chance encounters and missed opportunities."

Plain continued to be intrigued by her character Anna in *Evergreen* and continued her story in *The Golden Cup* (1987), this time exploring her story from Paul Werner's point of view. *Tapestry* (1988), the third book in the cycle, focuses on Anna's grandchildren, and *Harvest* (1990) follows the grandchildren through New York, California, and Israel in the 1960s. *Treasures* (1992) picks up on a new set of characters, three Ohio siblings dealing with the aftermath of their alcoholic father's death, and deals with their greed and accumulation of wealth.

While Plain has been praised for breaking stereotypical molds and creating multilayered plots, some critics see this as a weakness of her writing. Webster Schott of the *New York Times Book Review* says of Plain's novels, "They're easy, consoling works of generous spirit, fat with plot and sentiment, thin in nearly every other way and almost invisible in character development." However, most critics agree that Plain is a strong craftswoman whose engaging stories keep many readers wanting more.

—Christopher Swann

POPCORN, Faith (Beryl)

Nationality: American. **Born:** Faith Plotkin in New York City, c. 1947; name legally changed in 1969. **Education:** Attended New York University. **Career:** BrainReserve, New York, marketing and trend analysis firm, founder and operator, 1974—. **Address:** c/o BrainReserve, 1 Madison Ave., New York, New York 10010, U.S.A.

Publications

Nonfiction

The Popcorn Report: Faith Popcorn on the Future of Your Company, Your World, Your Life. Doubleday, 1991.

Clicking: 16 Trends to Future-Fit Your Life, Your Work, and Your Business. Doubleday, 1996.

* * *

Professional futurist and trend-spotter Faith Popcorn (born Faith Plotkin) began to emerge as a national figure in the mid-1970s when her New York-based research and marketing organization, BrainReserve, began offering major corporate clients—at up to $1 million a shot—customized trend analysis services on which to base their product marketing strategies. Unlike traditional marketing research organizations, however, Popcorn relied little on exhaustive consumer interviewing. Instead, she claimed a special "proprietary methodology" that combined conventional consumer sampling techniques with the careful sifting of the cultural clues buried in movies, newspapers, and magazines.

By the 1990s, BrainReserve was pitching an arsenal of trend information products to willing buyers, including: a $12,000-a-year "TrendPack" subscription to clients, which consisted of a monthly rundown of the latest trends spotted, cataloged, and packaged by Popcorn and her staff; a "TrendFlash" fax service; "TrendBank," which was the latest compilation of Popcorn's top 12 trends; "TrendView" seminars, and more. To her credit, Popcorn accurately predicted that Coca-Cola's "New Coke" formula would fail, "Obession" would prove a popular name for a perfume line, and corporations should exploit an emerging trend among consumers for stay-at-home dining and recreation.

As fellow futurist John Naisbitt's (*Megatrends* [1982]) star began to fade in the mid-1980s, Popcorn stepped into the vacuum, adeptly salting the media with her catchy, zeitgeist-encompassing phrases, the most famous of which—"cocooning"—soon became a cultural byword. Other trend-terms followed, such as "grazing" and cocooning's evil twin, "burrowing." But only her 1993 formulation, "pleasure revenge," which described the move by American consumers toward increased smoking, drinking, and other health-endangering activities as a release from society's pressures, came as close to permeating the culture.

In 1991, her *Popcorn Report: On the Future of Your Company, Your World, Your Life* provided what Popcorn described as "an everyday guide to the 1990s that could be useful to anyone." Essentially an exposition of the ten key trends Popcorn saw as shaping American social change in the 1990s, *The Popcorn Report* devoted chapters to such concepts as "99 lives" (the acceleration of social life that leads consumers to juggle an ever increasing multitude of lives), "cocooning" (shutting out the world through absorption in one's private life), "fantasy adventure" (recreational risk-taking), "small indulgences" (spending money on small but more sophisticated enjoyments), and "cashing out" (trading down in salary for increased personal fulfillment). Rounding out the book were sections containing quotations from Popcorn's friends and clients, as well as a glossary of Popcornian terminology.

Critical reception for *The Popcorn Report* was generally unfavorable. While *Publishers Weekly* lauded the book's "refreshingly original concepts" and Popcorn's "quick and easy" presentation of her ideas, the *Christian Science Monitor* faulted her for using the "pounding prose of modern-day business-speak," though finding "grains of gut-truth . . . worth sorting out." *Library Journal* also criticized the "barrage of futurespeak" in *The Popcorn Report* as well as Popcorn's "woeful ignorance of business history." But it praised her for crafting a "thoughtful book . . . guaranteed to stimulate creative thinking." *Inc.* magazine's reviewer, however, blistered the *Report* as "the silliest, most pretentious little book I've come across in ages," offering little more than "a relentless sales pitch for herself and her company."

In 1996, Popcorn published *Clicking: 16 Trends to Future-Fit Your Life, Your Work, and Your Business.* Focusing this time on the individual's need to find his or her niche (or "clicking"), Popcorn delineated 16 trends shaping modern life. Those trends ranged from "anchoring" (finding personal balance by seeking spiritual roots in the past) and "female-think" (the shift from patriarchal social relations to more communal, nonhierarchical practices) to "icon toppling" (the trend toward rejecting authority). Popcorn combined personal and corporate success stories with chapters on finding a new career and helping children make positive choices. She also emphasized the feasibility of leading a profitable, ethical, and passionate life. *Publishers Weekly* praised the book for its plethora of practical ideas and its potential to "jolt those stuck in a rut."

Critics have rightly faulted Popcorn for the sometimes airy generality of her predictions (on boxer shorts: "people think, maybe if I wear them, everything will be all right"), which sometimes create the impression that Popcorn may in reality be only a kind of Madison Avenue version of the Psychic Friends Network. But many major corporations have invested heavily in her prognostications, and her appeal may finally be traced to the quintessentially American combination of directness and optimism at the heart of her forecasts.

—Paul S. Bodine

PRATCHETT, Terry

Nationality: British. **Born:** 1948. **Education:** Wycombe Technical High School. **Career:** Journalist in Buckinghamshire, Bristol, and Bath, then press officer, Central Electricity Board Western Region, until 1987. **Awards:** British Science Fiction award, 1990. **Agent:** Colin Smythe Ltd., P.O. Box 6, Gerrards Cross, Buckinghamshire SL9 8XA, England.

Publications

Novels (series: Discworld; Truckers/Bromeliad)

Carpet People. Gerrards Cross, Buckinghamshire, Smythe, 1971; revised edition, London, Doubleday, 1992.

The Dark Side of the Sun. Gerrards Cross, Buckinghamshire, Smythe, 1976.

Strata. Gerrards Cross, Buckinghamshire, Smythe, and New York, St. Martin's Press, 1981.

The Colour of Magic (Discworld). Gerrards Cross, Buckinghamshire, Smythe, and New York, St. Martin's Press, 1983.

The Light Fantastic (Discworld). Gerrard's Cross, Buckinghamshire, Smythe, and New York, St. Martin's Press, 1986.

Mort (Discworld). London, Gollancz, and New York, New American Library, 1987.

Sourcery (Discworld). London, Gollancz, 1988; New York, New American Library, 1989.
Pyramids (Discworld). London, Gollancz, and New York, Penguin, 1989.
Guards! Guards! (Discworld; with Gray Jolliffe). London, Gollancz, 1989; New York, Roc, 1991.
Truckers (first of the Truckers trilogy; in the U.S. as the Bromeliad trilogy). London, Doubleday, 1989; New York, Delacorte, 1990.
Eric (Discworld). London, Gollancz, 1989.
Good Omens: The Nice and Accurate Predictions of Agnes Nutter, Witch, with Neil Gaiman. London, Gollancz, and New York, Workman, 1990.
Moving Pictures (Discworld). London, Gollancz, 1990.
Diggers (Truckers/Bromeliad). London, Doubleday, and New York, Delacorte, 1990.
Wings (Truckers/Bromeliad; with Neil Gaiman). London, Doubleday, 1990; New York, Delacorte, 1991.
Reaper Man (Discworld). London, Gollancz, 1991.
Lords and Ladies. London, Gollancz, 1992.
Only You Can Save Mankind. London, Doubleday, 1992.
Small Gods (Discworld). London, Gollancz, and New York, HarperCollins, 1992.
Men at Arms (Discworld). London, Gollancz, 1993.
Johnny and the Dead. London, Doubleday, 1993.
Interesting Times. London, Gollancz, 1994.
Soul Music (Discworld). London, Gollancz, 1994; New York, HarperPrism, 1995.
The Witches Trilogy (Discworld). London, Gollancz, 1995.
Equal Rites. London, Gollancz, 1986; New York, New American Library, 1987.
Wyrd Sisters. London, Gollancz, and New York, Penguin, 1988.
Witches Abroad. London, Gollancz, 1991.

Other

The Unadulterated Cat, with illustrations by Gray Jolliffe. London, Gollancz, 1989.
The Discworld Companion, with Stephen Briggs. London, Gollancz, 1994.

* * *

The Colour of Magic (1983) really marks the beginning of British author Terry Pratchett's popularity, as this was the first novel in his wildly successful Discworld series. The Discworld is a flat world carried on the back of four giant elephants on the back of a giant turtle swimming through space. It is the home of a hilarious variety of characters and creatures that have sprung from world mythologies and legends as well as Pratchett's own wit and imagination.

The Discworld novels are some of the best humorous fantasy novels published. In these novels, Pratchett parodies just about everything, from the fantasy genre to Shakespeare to popular culture. For example, *Wyrd Sisters* (1988) is his take on *MacBeth,* while *Witches Abroad* (1991) parodies fairy tales, particularly "Cinderella." Other novels satirize such things as Hollywood, rock and roll, and religion.

The Discworld novels are not all direct sequels. Instead, they tend to feature groups of characters that reappear periodically. The most popular reoccurring main characters are Rincewind the Inept; the three witches Granny Weatherwax, Nanny Ogg, and Magrat; and Death. Other minor characters appear with frequency as well; among these are the Librarian, an orangutan who was once human; Cut-Me-Own-Throat Dibbler, the consummate salesman; and Cohen the Barbarian.

Though funny, many of the Discworld novels lack depth, and many are just novel-length gags (a fact Pratchett admits). However, some are remarkable stories with subtle and touching characterization. A perfect example of both these modes is *Reaper Man* (1991). This is the second novel featuring Death, a typical scythe-carrying, skull-faced, black-robed specter. But Pratchett's Death is much more than that. In the main plot of *Reaper Man,* Death retires and moves to a small village where he takes up farming. He eventually partakes in a John Henry-type contest against a harvesting machine. But he also learns about life and compassion. Knowing his former landlady is about to die, Death arrives and takes her in style to the Harvest Dance. She has the best time of her life and death. And then Death reunites her with her long-dead and long-missing fiancé. Death is skillfully handled and the ending is touching. However, the sub-plot featuring Windle Poons, a wizard who is undead because of Death's retirement, is simply a gag about shopping malls being the death of cities. This novel demonstrates Pratchett at both his strongest and his weakest.

Besides the Discworld series, Pratchett's other successful series is the young-adult science fiction trilogy featuring the Nomes. The three books in the series are *Truckers* (1989), *Diggers* (1990), and *Wings* (1990), though they were also collected and published in the United States under the title *The Bromeliad* (1993). These novels feature the Nomes, a race of little people who initially inhabit a store. In fact, they think the store is the whole world and are devastated when they have to move. In the course of the novels, Pratchett explores the human foibles of prejudice, narrow-mindedness (particularly when it comes to religion), and blind tradition through the Nomes. He also explores the nature of language since the Nomes read everything literally, providing a great souce of humor. For instance, they believe that when a sign reads "Road Work Ahead," that the road should work. The humor, along with the adventure and likable characters, make these novels fun for both adults and children. The Nome series is also more than just gags. It contains both romantic and coming of age themes.

Terry Pratchett has published other works as well. *The Carpet People* (1971, revised 1992) is another children's fantasy. *The Dark Side of the Sun* (1976) and *Strata* (1981) are science fiction parodies, with *Strata* also featuring a flat planet. *Good Omens* (1990), a collaboration with Neil Gaiman, parodies the *Omen* movies and Armageddon stories in general. But Pratchett will probably always be best known for the Discworld novels. This series has provided him with his biggest success, and it continues to grow.

—P. Andrew Miller

PRICE, Eugenia

Nationality: American. **Born:** 22 June 1916, in Charleston, West Virginia. **Education:** Attended Ohio University, 1932-35; Northwestern University, dental student, 1935-37. **Career:** National Broadcasting Co., Chicago, serial writer for "In Care of Aggie

Horn," 1939-42; Proctor and Gamble, Cincinnati, Ohio, serial writer for "Joyce Jordan, M.D.," 1944-46; owner, Eugenia Price Productions (radio), 1945-49; WGN, Chicago, writer, producer, and director of "Unshackled," 1950-56; free-lance writer. Lecturer in the United States and Canada, 1949-63. **Awards:** Litt.D., Alderson-Broaddus College, 1967; award from Coastal Georgia Historical Society, 1968, for the "St. Simons Trilogy"; Distinguished Service award in literature from Georgia College, 1974; Belles-lettres citation from St. Augustine Historical Society, 1974; Matson award from Chicago Friends of Literature, 1978, for *Maria*; Governor's Award in the Arts for literature, 1978. **Died:** Of congestive heart failure, 28 May 1996.

PUBLICATIONS

Novels

The Beloved Invader. Lippincott, 1965.
New Moon Rising. Lippincott, 1969.
Lighthouse. Lippincott, 1971.
Don Juan McQueen. Lippincott, 1974.
Maria. Lippincott, 1977.
Margaret's Story. Lippincott, 1980.
Savannah. Doubleday, 1983.
To See Your Face Again. Doubleday, 1985.
Before the Darkness Falls. Doubleday, 1987.
Stranger in Savannah. Doubleday, 1989.
Bright Captivity. Doubleday, 1991.
Beauty from Ashes. Doubleday, 1995.

Nonfiction

Discoveries Made from Living My New Life. Zondervan, 1953.
The Burden Is Light: The Autobiography of a Transformed Pagan Who Took God at His Word. Revell, 1955; revised edition, Pillar Books, 1975.
Never a Dull Moment: Honest Questions by Teen Agers, with Honest Answers by Eugenia Price. Zondervan, 1956.
Early Will I Seek Thee: Journal of a Heart That Longed and Found. Revell, 1957.
Share My Pleasant Stones Every Day for a Year. Zondervan, 1958.
Woman to Woman. Zondervan, 1959.
Strictly Personal: The Adventure of Discovering What God Is Really Like. Zondervan, 1960; as *What Is God Like?*, Oliphants, 1965.
Beloved World: The Story of God and People as Told from the Bible. Zondervan, 1961.
A Woman's Choice: Living through Your Problems. Zondervan, 1962.
God Speaks to Women Today. Zondervan, 1964.
The Wider Place: Where God Offers Freedom from Anything That Limits Our Growth. Zondervan, 1966; as *Where God Offers Freedom,* Oliphants, 1966.
Make Love Your Aim. Zondervan, 1967.
Just as I Am. Zondervan, 1968.
Learning to Live from the Gospels. Lippincott, 1968.
The Unique World of Women in Bible Times and Now. Zondervan, 1969.
Learning to Live from the Acts. Lippincott, 1970.
No Pat Answers. Zondervan, 1972.
St. Simons Memoir: The Personal Story of Finding the Island and Writing the St. Simons Trilogy of Novels. Lippincott, 1978.
Leave Your Self Alone. Zondervan, 1979.
Diary of a Novel. Lippincott, 1980.
At Home on St. Simons. Peachtree Publishers, 1981.
Getting through the Night. Doubleday, 1982.
What Really Matters. Doubleday, 1983.
Another Day. Doubleday, 1984.
Inside One Author's Heart: A Deeply Personal Sharing with My Readers. Doubleday, 1992.
Where Shadows Go. Doubleday, 1993.

*

Critical Studies: *Eugenia Price's South: A Guide to the People and Places of Her Beloved Region* by Mary B. Wheeler, Longstreet Press, 1993.

Manuscript Collection: Boston University.

* * *

Eugenia Price had essentially three careers, as the originator of and primary force behind radio soap opera in the 1940s, as a popular dispenser of spiritual advice during the 1950s and 1960s, and as the author of hugely successful romance novels set in the American South from the 1970s until the time of her death in 1996.

After attending Ohio University and studying dentistry at Northwestern University, Price decided to try her hand at writing, and she began her career at the National Broadcasting Company in Chicago as a serial writer for "In Care of Aggie Horn." Her keen sense of what would appeal to daytime radio listeners ensured her success, and she subsequently developed a number of radio serials for Procter & Gamble.

In the late 1940s, Price claimed to have undergone an intense religious conversion, and in 1953 she published her first book, *Discoveries Made from Living My New Life,* to chronicle her experiences and explain her faith. She followed it with a string of mostly successful and insightful nonfiction books numbering about 30 between the 1950s and early 1990s. Titles ranged from *Never a Dull Moment: Honest Questions by Teenagers, with Honest Answers by Eugenia Price* (1956) to *Learning to Live from the Acts* (1970). Most were self-help and inspirational books written from a Christian perspective. The books earned her a reputation as a leading religious writer.

However, it is for her sweeping historical romance novels that Price is best known. Set against the picturesque backdrop of the American South, her novels create compelling sagas that blend personal stories of love and tragedy (as in her earlier radio serials) with the dramatic events of the region's history. Her first series of novels was inspired by a trip to St. Simon's Island, off the coast of Georgia, where she later settled. Price's great love for and sympathy with the area were manifest in her lyrical, detailed descriptions, while her understanding of the region's history gave the books an authenticity which immediately appealed to readers. The St. Simon's books were a huge success, and Price followed them with a Florida trilogy and a Savannah quartet. A final St. Simon's trilogy was completed just before her death.

—Tammy J. Bronson

PROULX, E(dna) Annie

Nationality: American. **Born:** Norwich, Connecticut, 22 August 1935. **Education:** University of Vermont, Burlington, B.A.(cum laude), 1969 (Phi Beta Kappa); Sir George Williams University, Montreal, M.A., 1973. **Family:** Married James Hamilton Lang in 1969 (divorced 1990); three children. **Awards:** Kress Fellow, Harvard University, Boston, 1974; Vermont Council of the Arts fellowship, 1989, National Endowment for the Arts fellowship, 1991, Guggenheim Foundation fellowship, 1992; PEN/Faulkner award, 1993, for *Postcards*; National Book award, 1993, *Chicago Tribune* Heartland award, 1993, *Irish Times International* award, 1993, and Pulitzer prize, 1994, all for *The Shipping News*. D.H.L.: University of Maine, Orono, 1994. **Address:** c/o Scribners Publishing Co., 866 Third Avenue, 7th floor, New York, New York 10022, U.S.A.

Publications

Novels

Postcards. New York, Scribner, 1992; London, Fourth Estate, 1993.
The Shipping News. New York, Scribner, 1993; London, Fourth Estate, 1994.
Accordion Crimes. New York, Simon & Schuster, 1996.

Short Stories

Heart Songs, and Other Stories. New York, Scribner, 1988; London, Flamingo, 1989.

Other

Sweet and Hard Cider: Making It, Using It, and Enjoying It, with Lew Nichols. Charlotte, Vermont, Garden Way, 1980.
"What'll You Take for It?": Back to Barter. Charlotte, Vermont, Garden Way, 1981.
The Complete Dairy Foods Cookbook: How to Make Everything from Cheese to Custard in Your Kitchen, with Lew Nichols. Emmaus, Pennsylvania, Rodale Press, 1982.
The Gardener's Journal and Record Book. Emmaus, Pennsylvania, Rodale Press, 1983.
Plan and Make Your Own Fences and Gates, Walkways, Walls and Drives. Emmaus, Pennsylvania, Rodale Press, 1983.
The Fine Art of Salad Gardening. Emmaus, Pennsylvania, Rodale Press, 1985.
The Gourmet Gardener: Growing Choice Fruits and Vegetables with Spectacular Results, illustrated by Robert Byrd. New York, Fawcett Columbine, 1987.

* * *

E. Annie Proulx published a series of how-to gardening and cooking books during the 1980s before publishing her first novel, *Postcards*, which was awarded the PEN/Faulkner award in 1992. She garnered international fame for her second novel, *The Shipping News* (1993), which won that year's National Book Award and went on to win the 1994 Pulitzer Prize for fiction. Her works of fiction are characterized by her inventive use of language, vivid evocations of landscape, and precise dialect. While her works all focus on themes of heredity, desperation, and hope, each examines these themes with fresh insight and perspective.

In *Postcards*, Proulx's doomed protagonist Loyal Blood flees from his home and family in Vermont on a 40-year odyssey on the road. The Bloods degenerate into a feuding clan who fight over petty hatreds and end up as suicides or freaks, disillusioned or imprisoned. As critic Dwight Garner points out, the characters suffer from "heredity's crushing burden," and "Proulx's ambivalence about family and home gives the book its complexity. The Bloods may be at each other's throats when they're together, but separately they're utterly lost."

The Shipping News concerns Quoyle, an astonishingly unsuccessful man whose wife, the sexually ravenous Petal Bear, constantly cheats on him and ends up dying with a lover in a flaming car wreck. Quoyle retreats with his two daughters to Killick-Claw, Newfoundland, his ancestral home, and attempts to rebuild his shattered life. The eccentric citizens of Killick-Claw and the rugged, demanding Newfoundland coast provide Proulx with a rich source of material, much of it tinged with dark humor. Quoyle lands a job at *The Gammy Bird*, a local paper which specializes in reporting sexual abuse cases and whose editor assigns stories that play on the worst fears of the reporters. Quoyle also discovers that his family ancestors were pirates who scavenged off shipwrecks that they caused, and that his grandfather sired his father at age 12 just before drowning. Perhaps most ironically, he is faced with the daunting responsibility of raising two daughters when he has never adequately cared for himself. The local characters, including his aunt Agnis Hamm, editor Jack Buggit, and journalist friend Nutbeem, attempt in various good-natured ways to assist Quoyle in his search for significance and love without pain. They also introduce several subplots that enhance the story.

Proulx's use of language is the most remarkable element of the novel, distilling each sentence to its most essential message, at times reducing sentences to a list of fragmented images and statements that initially distract a reader but eventually add to the story. Her use of metaphors occasionally borders on the grotesque—"The bay crawled with whitecaps like maggots seething in a broad wound"—but they add to the bleakness of Quoyle's plight, as do the forbidding place-names of the Newfoundland coast; Lost All Hope, Bad Fortune, Port Anguish, and Go Aground. The dialect and local words such as skreel, marl, and glutch, along with regional delicacies such as cod cheeks and fried bologna, give the setting its own weight and resonance, as does the tempestuous atmosphere and brutal weather.

Many readers might find Proulx's tale—full of howling storms, premonitory dreams, decapitations and the "resurrection" of a drowned man—improbable. At times her use of language can be stifling and off-putting. Characters with names like Al Catalog and Diddy Shovel become cartoonish. But in *New Statesman and Society*, critic Roz Kaveney argues that this is part of Proulx's skill as a writer: "Her work not only describes, but is imbued with, a chancy decency that looks us forthright in the eye and challenges disbelief. . . . What risks being mere whimsy has steel behind it, because there is passion here and a real potential for tragedy." The passion and potential for tragedy in *The Shipping News* reside in Quoyle, who, in all his physical incompetence and heartache, grounds the novel for the reader and provides a center, albeit unstable, for this story set at the wintry, ragged edge of civilization.

—Christopher Swann

PUZO, Mario

Nationality: American. **Born:** New York City, 15 October 1920. **Education:** New School for Social Research, New York; Columbia University, New York. **Military Service:** Served in the United States Army Air Force during World War II. **Family:** Married Erika Lina Broske in 1946; three sons and two daughters. **Career:** Administrative assistant in U.S. Government offices, in New York and overseas, for 20 years; assistant editor of a magazine, late 1960s. Lives on Long Island, New York. **Awards:** Oscar, for screenplay for *The Godfather,* 1972, and *The Godfather, Part 2,* 1974. **Agent:** Candida Donadio and Associates, Inc., 111 West 57th St., New York, New York 10019. **Address:** c/o G.P. Putnam and Sons Inc., 200 Madison Ave., New York, New York 10022, U.S.A.

PUBLICATIONS

Novels

The Dark Arena. New York, Random House, 1955; London, Heinemann, 1971.
The Fortunate Pilgrim. New York, Atheneum, 1965; London, Heinemann, 1966.
The Godfather. New York, Putnam, and London, Heinemann, 1969.
Fools Die. New York, Putnam, and London, Heinemann, 1978.
The Sicilian. New York, Linden Press, 1984; London, Bantam Press, 1985.
The Fourth K. New York, Random House, and London, Heinemann, 1991.
The Last Don. New York, Random House, 1996.

Uncollected Short Stories

"Last Christmas," in *American Vanguard 1950,* edited by Charles I. Glicksberg. New York, Cambridge, 1950.
"First Sundays," in *Redbook* (New York), February 1968.

Plays

Screenplays: *The Godfather,* with Francis Ford Coppola, 1972; *The Godfather, Part 2,* with Francis Ford Coppola, 1974; *Earthquake,* with George Fox, 1974; *Superman,* with others, 1978; *Superman II,* with David Newman and Leslie Newman, 1981.

Other

The Runaway Summer of Davie Shaw (for children). New York, Platt and Munk, 1966; Kingswood, Surrey, World's Work, 1976.
The Godfather Papers and Other Confessions. New York, Putnam, and London, Heinemann, 1972.
Inside Las Vegas. New York, Grosset and Dunlap, 1977.

*

Critical Study: *The Italian-American Novel* by Rose B. Green, Fairleigh Dickinson University Press, 1974.

Manuscript Collection: Boston University.

* * *

Money and its corruption in American cities are recurring themes in the fiction of Mario Puzo. Puzo considers himself a naturalistic writer and tries to imitate the tragic tone of other naturalists, especially Theodore Dreiser. Almost all of his fiction has tragic overtones as the characters discover that after money is acquired one must still work to attain reputation, power, and respect.

The Dark Arena (1955), Puzo's first novel, is different from the course of the rest of his work in that the action occurs in Occupied Germany. The novel deals with the relationship between Mosca, a soldier, and Hella, a German native, and explores the problems created by the characters' different backgrounds. Mosca's story is often seen as a parable of America's failed occupation policy; the tone of work suggests that occupation ignored the feelings of the natives.

The Fortunate Pilgrim (1965) is considered to be Puzo's greatest artistic achievement. Its plot is centers around an Italian peasant woman's perceptions of the "American dream." Puzo juxtaposes her honest and determined progress with that of Larry Angeluzzi, who justifies becoming a corrupt collection agent for Mr. di Lucca. Puzo manages to weave details of city life with his moralizing to create a balanced work of fiction. The novel has been called "one of the two or three best novels on American city life ever written." Although the book received critical acclaim, it sold only moderately well and spurred Puzo to target his fiction toward a larger audience.

Puzo decided to establish himself as a bestselling author with *The Godfather* (1969), which allowed him to become financially secure. The novel was the top bestseller in New York for over 67 weeks and was successful in both Germany and France. That success, combined with the film production, earned Puzo more than $1 million. Puzo achieved his financial goals, but admits that "I wrote below my gifts in that book."

Like *The Fortunate Pilgrim, The Godfather* explores the New York City underworld. Its main protagonist, Don Corleone, resembles di Lucca, yet in this novel Corleone is seen in his domestic life. Corleone has a particular style and grace that make the reader feel uneasy, creating great sympathy for a man who is essentially a murderer. The work has an underlying political tone; some suggest that Corleone's charming family life, paralleled by his life in organized crime, is said to represent the American intervention in Vietnam. Puzo answered mixed critical response by suggesting that "the novelist's job [is] not to be a moralist, but to make you care about the people in his book."

Fools Die (1978) is set in Las Vegas, Hollywood, Tokyo, and New York during the 1950s and 1960s. The plot is centered around John Merlyn, a dishonest fiction writer who considers himself a modern-day magician. Artistically, the novel is considered Puzo's weakest. Merlyn's characterization is difficult, and the extended structure of the book fails to present authentic experiences. Yet novel was commercially successful (Puzo earned $2.5 million dollars).

More recently, Puzo perfected soap-opera fiction with the *4thK* (1991), a wild and outlandish story of Kennedy's nephew becoming president. It contains a series of crises that occur after the assassination of the Pope with a warmonger Arab sultan. Reviewers cynically compared the experience of reading the book to reading a miniseries.

Puzo represents one of the great ironies of modern popular fiction, as many consider it unfortunate that he is remembered and appreciated by the public for *The Godfather* rather than for his more accomplished work.

—Chris Godat

PYNCHON, Thomas

Nationality: American. **Born:** Glen Cove, New York, 8 May 1937. **Education:** Cornell University, Ithaca, New York, 1954-58, B.A. 1958. **Military Service:** United States Naval Reserve. **Career:** Former editorial writer, Boeing Aircraft, Seattle. **Awards:** Faulkner award, 1964; Rosenthal Memorial award, 1967; National Book award, 1974; American Academy Howells medal, 1975. **Agent:** Candida Donadio and Associates, 231 West 22nd Street, New York, New York 10011. **Address:** c/o Little Brown, 34 Beacon Street, Boston, Massachusetts 02106, U.S.A.

Publications

Novels

V. Philadelphia, Lippincott, and London, Cape, 1963.
The Crying of Lot 49. Philadelphia, Lippincott, 1966; London, Cape, 1967.
Gravity's Rainbow. New York, Viking Press, and London, Cape, 1973.
Vineland. Boston, Little Brown, and London, Secker and Warburg, 1990.

Short Stories

Mortality and Mercy in Vienna. London, Aloes, 1976.
Low-lands. London, Aloes, 1978.
The Secret Integration. London, Aloes, 1980.
The Small Rain. London, Aloes, 1980(?).
Slow Learner: Early Stories. Boston, Little Brown, 1984; London, Cape, 1985.

Other

A Journey into the Mind of Watts. London, Mouldwarp, 1983.
Deadly Sins, illustrations by Etienne Delessert. New York, Morrow, 1994.

*

Bibliography: *Thomas Pynchon: A Bibliography of Primary and Secondary Materials* by Clifford Mead, Elmwood Park, Illinois, Dalkey Archive Press, 1989.

Critical Studies: *Mindful Pleasures: Essays on Thomas Pynchon* edited by George Levine and David Leverenz, Boston, Little Brown, 1976; *The Grim Phoenix: Reconstructing Thomas Pynchon* by William M. Plater, Bloomington, Indiana University Press, 1978; *Pynchon: A Collection of Critical Essays* edited by Edward Mendelson, Englewood Cliffs, New Jersey, Prentice Hall, 1978; *Pynchon: Creative Paranoia in Gravity's Rainbow* by Mark Richard Siegel, Port Washington, New York, Kennikat Press, 1978; *Thomas Pynchon: The Art of Allusion* by David Cowart, Carbondale, Southern Illinois University Press, 1980; *The Rainbow Quest of Thomas Pynchon* by Douglas A. Mackey, San Bernardino, California, Borgo Press, 1980; *Pynchon's Fictions: Thomas Pynchon and the Literature of Information* by John O. Stark, Athens, Ohio University Press, 1980; *A Reader's Guide to Gravity's Rainbow* by Douglas Fowler, Ann Arbor, Michigan, Ardis, 1980; *Critical Essays on Thomas Pynchon* edited by Richard Pearce, Boston, Hall, 1981; *Pynchon: The Voice of Ambiguity* by Thomas H. Schaub, Urbana, University of Illinois Press, 1981; *Thomas Pynchon* by Tony Tanner, London, Methuen, 1982; *Signs and Symptoms: Thomas Pynchon and the Contemporary World* by Peter L. Cooper, Berkeley, University of California Press, 1983; *Approaches to Gravity's Rainbow* edited by Charles Clerc, Columbus, Ohio State University Press, 1983; *Ideas of Order in the Novels of Thomas Pynchon* by Molly Hite, Columbus, Ohio State University Press, 1983; *The Style of Connectedness: Gravity's Rainbow and Thomas Pynchon* by Thomas Moore, Columbia, University of Missouri Press, 1987; *A Gravity's Rainbow Companion* by Steven C. Weisenburger, Athens, University of Georgia Press, 1988; *The Fictional Labyrinths of Thomas Pynchon* by David Seed, London, Macmillan, 1988; *A Hand to Turn the Time: The Menippean Satires of Thomas Pynchon* by Theodore D. Kharpertian, Rutherford, New Jersey, Fairleigh Dickinson University Press, 1989; *Writing Pynchon: Strategies in Fictional Analysis* by Alec McHoul and David Wills, London, Macmillan, 1990; *The Gnostic Pynchon* by Dwight Eddins, Bloomington, Indiana University Press, 1990; *Thomas Pynchon* by Joseph V. Slade, New York, Lang, 1990; *Thomas Pynchon: Allusive Parables of Power* by John Dugdale, London, Macmillan, and New York, St. Martin's Press, 1990; *New Essays on "The Crying of Lot 49"* edited by Patrick O'Donnell, Cambridge, Cambridge University Press, 1991; *The Postmodernist Allegories of Thomas Pynchon* by Deborah L. Madsen, New York, St. Martin's Press, and Leicester, Leicester University Press, 1991; *Marginal Forces/Cultural Centers: Tolson, Pynchon, and the Politics of the Canon* by Michael Bérubé, Ithaca, New York, Cornell University Press, 1992; *Thomas Pynchon* by Judith Chambers, New York, Twayne, 1992; *Pynchon's Poetics: Interfacing Theory and Text* by Hanjo Berressem, Urbana, University of Illinois Press, 1993; *The Vineland Papers: Critical Takes on Pynchon's Novel* edited by Geoffrey Green, Donald Greiner, and Larry McCaffery, Normal, Illinois, Dalkey Archive Press, 1994.

* * *

Like a Cheshire Cat, Thomas Pynchon has somehow managed to maintain invisibility in the contemporary literary scene, leaving his substantial body of fans only a mocking grin and four exquisitely wrought novels. In the literary world, where invasive interviewers and book-length biographers lurk in every shadow, Pynchon has raised privacy to an art form, allowing nothing of himself to be scrutinized except a grainy high-school yearbook photo and his fiction.

The details of Pynchon's life might not matter as much if readers did not cry out for some sort of clue to understanding the mysteries and secrets of the extraordinary mind behind his fiction. His massive masterpiece, *Gravity's Rainbow* (1973), is considered by many to be the most arresting and mystifying novel written in the latter half of the 20th century. Rich and complex in texture and style, *Gravity's Rainbow* explores the psychology of a world gone mad with information. From the famous first sentence—"A screaming comes across the sky"—the reader is taken on a chaotic journey beginning in London besieged by German V-2 rockets, then into "the zone," an unreal postwar landscape in which everything, including the character we had thought was the protagonist, literally and irrevocably falls apart. The intellectual layers of the novel run deep, but something prevents us from penetrating the ever-expanding surface, informed as it is by cinematic flourishes and surreal fantasies. We come away from the book unsure of what we just experienced, but certain enough that paranoia is the pervasive condition of the contemporary world, and that we are all at the mercy of some manipulative System. The anti-establishment overtones of this most cryptic of novels might explain why it has captured the imagination of the baby-boomer generation despite its complexity.

Less dedicated readers can find the same theme of paranoia in *V.* (1963) and *The Crying of Lot 49* (1966), novels which showcase Pynchon's celebrated style to considerably shorter and easier degrees than does *Gravity's Rainbow.* Pynchon's playfulness is evident from even a quick glimpse at these novels; readers delight in his tendency to move his self-consciously fictional characters with names like Oedipa Maas and Benny Profane through absurd scenarios, such as shooting alligators in the New York sewer system. These hapless ciphers bumble across their changing landscapes on a perpetual quest for something that will inevitably mutate before it can be discovered. Pynchon's narrators break gleefully into hilarious song lyrics and limericks, or they address the reader directly just as things have begun to become somewhat understandable. "You want cause-and-effect?" the narrator of *Gravity's Rainbow* asks us, and we know full well that he's not going to give it to us. There is nothing conventionally logical about these works. We must give in to the whims and humorous caprices of a storyteller whose imagination is more entertaining than realism could ever hope to be.

These three novels set up high expectations for Pynchon's reading public, who waited breathlessly for 17 years for *Vineland* (1990). In the meantime, Pynchon released *Slow Learner* (1984), a collection of his early stories published in the late 1950s and early 1960s. The significant contribution in this collection is the title essay in which Pynchon talks about himself as a young writer. Acknowledging such influences as Jack Kerouac, Saul Bellow, and the surrealist art movement, Pynchon comes closest to revealing an official statement about his work. He also seems to communicate the weariness he feels after completing *Gravity's Rainbow,* leaving the public to speculate whether he would ever write anything again. Despite the excessive wait, *Vineland* does not hold a candle to *Gravity's Rainbow* in terms of scope or sheer virtuosity, and reviews of it communicate disappointment. Still, it is an entertaining romp through disillusioned post-1960s America in classic Pynchon style, focusing on a logging community in California rather than war-torn Europe.

Besides paranoia, Pynchon's novels are all governed by the law of entropy (the idea that all systems eventually lose their energy). This condition is an apt metaphor for his own writing career, which is evidently ending with a whimper rather than a bang. Rumor has it that Pynchon is now done with writing for good, but with such an erratic past, who could hope to predict his future? Perhaps he's waiting to fire another devastating masterpiece in our direction. The chief delight in anticipating such an event is like reading Pynchon in general; we finally have no definite idea what he is up to.

—D. Quentin Miller

QUINN, Martin. *See* **SMITH, Martin Cruz.**

QUINN, Simon. *See* **SMITH, Martin Cruz.**

R

RAMPLING, Anne. *See* **RICE, Anne.**

See RICE, Anne.

RAND, Ayn

Nationality: American. **Born:** Alice Rosenbaum in St. Petersburg, Russia, 2 February 1905; emigrated to the United States in 1926; naturalized, 1931. **Education:** University of Leningrad: graduated in history 1924. **Family:** Married Frank O'Connor in 1929. **Career:** Screenwriter, 1932-34, 1944-49. Editor, *The Objectivist,* New York, 1962-71, and *The Ayn Rand Letter,* New York, 1971-82. Visiting lecturer at several universities, including Yale University, New Haven, Connecticut, Princeton University, New Jersey, Columbia University, New York, Harvard University and Massachusetts Institute of Technology, both Cambridge, and Johns Hopkins University, Baltimore. D.H.L.: Lewis and Clark College, Portland, Oregon, 1963. **Died:** 6 March 1982.

Publications

Novels

We the Living. New York, Macmillan, and London, Cassell, 1936.
Anthem. London, Cassell, 1938; revised edition, Los Angeles, Pamphleteers, 1946.
The Fountainhead. Indianapolis, Bobbs-Merrill, 1943; London, Cassell, 1947.
Atlas Shrugged. New York, Random House, 1957.

Short Stories

The Early Ayn Rand: A Selection from Her Unpublished Fiction, edited by Leonard Peikoff. New York, New American Library, 1984.

Plays

Night of January 16th (as *Woman on Trial,* produced Hollywood, 1934; New York, 1935; London, 1936; *as Penthouse Legend,* produced New York, 1973). New York, Longman, 1936; revised edition, New York, New American Library, 1987.
The Unconquered, adaptation of her own novel *We the Living* (produced New York, 1940).

Screenplays: *You Came Along,* with Robert Smith, 1945; *Love Letters,* 1945; *The Fountainhead,* 1949.

Other

Textbook of Americanism. New York, Branden Institute, 1946.
Notes on the History of American Free Enterprise. New York, Platen Press, 1959.
Faith and Force: The Destroyers of the Modern World. New York, Branden Institute, 1961.
For the New Intellectual. New York, Random House, 1961.
The Objectivist Ethics. New York, Branden Institute, 1961.
America's Persecuted Minority: Big Business. New York, Branden Institute, 1962.
Conservatism: An Obituary (lecture). New York, Branden Institute, 1962.
The Fascist "New Frontier." New York, Branden Institute, 1963.
The Virtue of Selfishness: A New Concept of Egoism. New York, New American Library, 1965.
Capitalism: The Unknown Ideal, with others. New York, New American Library, 1966.
Introduction to Objectivist Epistemology. New York, *The Objectivist,* 1967; revised edition by Leonard Peikoff and Harry Binswanger, New York, New American Library, 1990.
The Romantic Manifesto: A Philosophy of Literature. Cleveland, World, 1970.
The New Left: The Anti-Industrial Revolution. New York, New American Library, 1971.
Philosophy: Who Needs It? Indianapolis, Bobbs-Merrill, 1982.
The Voice of Reason: Essays in Objectivist Thought. New York, New American Library, 1989.

*

Manuscript Collection: Library of Congress, Washington, D.C.

Critical Studies: *Who Is Ayn Rand? An Analysis of the Novels of Ayn Rand* by Nathaniel Branden, New York, Random House, 1962; *The Philosophic Thought of Ayn Rand* edited by Douglas J. Den Uyl and Douglas B. Rasmussen, Urbana, University of Illinois Press, 1984; *The Ayn Rand Companion* by Mimi Reisel Gladstein, Westport, Connecticut, Greenwood Press, 1984; *The Passion of Ayn Rand: A Biography* by Barbara Branden, New York, Doubleday, 1986, London, W.H. Allen, 1987; *The Ayn Rand Lexicon: Objectivism from A to Z* edited by Harry Binswanger, New York, New American Library, 1986; *Judgment Day: My Years with Ayn Rand* by Nathaniel Branden, New York, Houghton Mifflin, 1989.

*   *   *

In 1957, Russian immigrant Ayn Rand described the essence of her philosophy as "the concept of man as a heroic being, with his own happiness as the moral purpose of his life, with productive achievement as his noblest activity, and reason as his only absolute." Rand's creed of "Objectivism," which rejected Christian and Marxist views of society with equal contempt, espoused a life of radical individualism and earthly self-fulfillment in which all "altruistic" notions bonding individuals and societies together were seen as self-destructive illusions.

In the first of her two major novels, *The Fountainhead* (1943), Rand tells the story of genius architect Howard Roarke whose refusal to compromise his personal and aesthetic ideas consigns him to a lonely 20-year struggle to realize his architectural vision. When he discovers that his design for a public housing project has been tampered with by his enemies (the "second-handers"), he destroys it and during his trial proclaims his philosophy of enlightened selfishness ("All that which proceeds from man's independent ego is good. All that which proceeds from man's dependence upon men is evil.") At the novel's conclusion, Roarke is acquitted and marries the ex-wife of his two arch rivals.

Contemporary reviews of *The Fountainhead* were generally unkind. Although some reviewers described Rand as a "writer of great power," critic Diana Trilling wrote that the novel "[s]urely . . . is the curiosity of the year, and anyone who is taken in by it deserves a stern lecture on paper rationing." It sold well, however, and grew in popularity over the years, forcing later critics to try to diagnose its appeal. It has been variously interpreted as a "heroic" admonishment, "not to sacrifice the self but to remain true to it at all costs," an "impeccably conservative novel of ideas," a "ripe and fanciful mixture of politics and sex," and Rand's "fullest explication of the primacy of the individual."

Fourteen years later Rand followed it with *Atlas Shrugged* (1957), the story of inventor John Galt's efforts to convince America's creative and technical elite that the only way to resist the gradual destruction of society at the hands of the "looters" or "Destroyers" (Rand's term for the purveyors of mediocrity and mass thinking) is, in essence, to go on strike, cease creating and thinking, and retreat from society in anticipation of the inevitable annihilation of the economy when the looters are left on their own. Finally cornering the Galtians in their Colorado fortress, the looters torture Galt to force him to rescue the collapsing economy only to find that they also need his technical expertise to keep their instrument of torture running.

Although the *New York Herald Tribune* praised *Atlas Shrugged* as "a piece of inspired and thoroughly exciting story-telling," *The Christian Science Monitor* described it as a "polemic . . . disguised as a novel" and the *Catholic World* dismissed it as "completely bad, from conception to expression." In a famous review that led to Rand's excommunication from the American conservative movement, Whittaker Chambers argued that the philosophical upshot of the novel's message was "To a gas chamber—go!"

Like *The Fountainhead,* it took years of brisk word-of-mouth sales to convince critics that *Atlas Shrugged* was worthy of serious explication. Critics have variously interpreted it as less a novel than a modern-day myth or morality play; a manifesto for a hypercapitalist "religion of finance"; a drama of romantic utopianism; a feminist "science fiction romance"; and a philosophical "detective story" combining elements of the thriller, the mystery, and the political parable.

As Rand's almost cultlike popularity peaked in the 1960s, her earlier works found new audiences. *Night of January 16th* (1934) is a courtroom drama in which the audience acts as the jury in the trial of a woman charged with pushing her rich lover/employer out an office building window. In the novel *We the Living* (1936) Rand tells the story of a Russian woman loved by two men; one communist, the other an aristocrat. The novel's heroine entices her communist suitor to help his aristocratic rival get into a hospital reserved only for trade union members, but both are fatally betrayed when the aristocrat becomes involved in the black market and abandons the heroine for another woman. Set in a postapocalyptic future, *Anthem* (1938) takes place in a barbaric collectivist society in which individuality is suppressed. Rand's rebellious hero undergoes a physical and spiritual dark night of the soul before discovering a land unaffected by the holocaust where he can found a society based on love and freedom. Rand used such later works as *For the New Intellectual* (1961), *The Virtue of Selfishness* (1965), and *Introduction to Objectivist Epistemology* (1967) to elaborate her theory of rational individualism in more rigorous philosophical terms.

—Paul S. Bodine

RANDALL, Robert. *See* **SILVERBERG, Robert.**

RENDELL, Ruth (Barbara)

Pseudonym: Barbara Vine. **Nationality:** British. **Born:** Ruth Barbara Grasemann, London, 17 February 1930. **Education:** Loughton High School, Essex. **Family:** Married Donald Rendell in 1950 (divorced 1975); remarried in 1977; one son. **Career:** Reporter and sub-editor, *Express* and *Independent* newspapers, West Essex, 1948-52. **Awards:** Mystery Writers of America Edgar Allan Poe award, for short story, 1975, 1984; Crime Writers Association Silver Dagger award, 1984, and Gold Dagger award, 1976, 1986, 1987; Arts Council National Book award, 1981; Arts Council bursary, 1981; Popular Culture Association award, 1983. **Agent:** Peters Fraser and Dunlop, 503-504 The Chambers, Chelsea Harbour, Lots Road, London SW10 0XF. **Address:** Nussteads, Polstead, Colchester, Essex CO6 5DN, England.

PUBLICATIONS

Novels

From Doon with Death. London, Hutchinson, 1964; New York, Doubleday, 1965.

To Fear a Painted Devil. London, Long, and New York, Doubleday, 1965.

Vanity Dies Hard. London, Long, 1965; New York, Beagle, 1970; as *In Sickness and in Health,* New York, Doubleday, 1966.

A New Lease of Death. London, Long, and New York, Doubleday, 1967; as *Sins of the Fathers,* New York, Ballantine, 1970.

Wolf to the Slaughter. London, Long, 1967; New York, Doubleday, 1968.

The Secret House of Death. London, Long, 1968; New York, Doubleday, 1969.

The Best Man to Die. London, Long, 1969; New York, Doubleday, 1970.

A Guilty Thing Surprised. London, Hutchinson, and New York, Doubleday, 1970.

No More Dying Then. London, Hutchinson, 1971; New York, Doubleday, 1972.

One Across, Two Down. London, Hutchinson, and New York, Doubleday, 1971.

Murder Being Done Once. London, Hutchinson, and New York, Doubleday, 1972.

Some Lie and Some Die. London, Hutchinson, and New York, Doubleday, 1973.
The Face of Trespass. London, Hutchinson, and New York, Doubleday, 1974.
Shake Hands for Ever. London, Hutchinson, and New York, Doubleday, 1975.
A Demon in My View. London, Hutchinson, 1976; New York, Doubleday, 1977.
A Judgement in Stone. London, Hutchinson, 1977; New York, Doubleday, 1978.
A Sleeping Life. London, Hutchinson, and New York, Doubleday, 1978.
Make Death Love Me. London, Hutchinson, and New York, Doubleday, 1979.
The Lake of Darkness. London, Hutchinson, and New York, Doubleday, 1980.
Put On by Cunning. London, Hutchinson, 1981; as *Death Notes,* New York, Pantheon, 1981.
Master of the Moor. London, Hutchinson, and New York, Pantheon, 1982.
The Speaker of Mandarin. London, Hutchinson, and New York, Pantheon, 1983.
The Killing Doll. London, Hutchinson, and New York, Pantheon, 1984.
The Tree of Hands. London, Hutchinson, 1984; New York, Pantheon, 1985.
An Unkindness of Ravens. London, Hutchinson, and New York, Pantheon, 1985.
Live Flesh. London, Hutchinson, and New York, Pantheon, 1986.
A Warning to the Curious. London, Hutchinson, 1987.
Heartstones. London, Hutchinson, and New York, Harper, 1987.
Talking to Strange Men. London, Hutchinson, and New York, Harper, 1987.
Wexford: An Omnibus. London, Hutchinson, 1988.
The Veiled One. London, Hutchinson, and New York, Pantheon, 1988.
The Bridesmaid. London, Hutchinson, and New York, Mysterious Press, 1989.
The Fourth Wexford Omnibus. London, Hutchinson, 1990.
Going Wrong. London, Hutchinson, and New York, Mysterious Press, 1990.
The Fifth Wexford Omnibus. London, Hutchinson, 1991.
Kissing the Gunner's Daughter. London, Hutchinson, and New York, Mysterious Press, 1992.
The Crocodile Bird. London, Hutchinson, and New York, Crown, 1993.
Inspector Wexford. London, Cresset, 1993.
Simisola. London, Hutchinson, 1994; New York, Crown, 1995.
Brimstone Wedding. London, Hutchinson, 1995; New York, Crown, 1996.
The Keys to the Street. London, Hutchinson, and New York, Crown, 1996.
Blood Lines. London, Hutchinson, and New York, Crown, 1996.

Novels as Barbara Vine

The Dark-Adapted Eye. London, Viking, and New York, Bantam, 1986.
A Fatal Inversion. London, Viking, and New York, Bantam, 1987.
The House of Stairs. London, Viking, and New York, Crown, 1989.
Gallowglass. London, Viking, and New York, Crown, 1990.
King Solomon's Carpet. London, Viking, 1991.
Asta's Book. London, Viking, 1993.
No Night Is Too Long. London, Viking, 1994.

Short Stories

The Fallen Curtain and Other Stories. London, Hutchinson, and New York, Doubleday, 1976.
Means of Evil and Other Stories. London, Hutchinson, 1979; New York, Doubleday, 1980.
The Fever Tree and Other Stories. London, Hutchinson, and New York, Pantheon, 1982.
The New Girl Friend. London, Hutchinson, 1985; New York, Pantheon, 1986.
Collected Short Stories. London, Hutchinson, 1987; New York, Pantheon, 1988.
The Strawberry Tree (with *Flesh and Grass* by Helen Simpson). London, Pandora Press, 1990.
The Copper Peacock and Other Stories. London, Hutchinson, and New York, Mysterious Press, 1991.

Other

Ruth Rendell's Suffolk, photographs by Paul Bowden. London, Muller, 1989.

Editor, *A Warning to the Curious: The Ghost Stories of M.R. James.* London, Century Hutchinson, 1987; Boston, Godine, 1989.
Editor, with Colin Ward, *Undermining the Central Line.* London, Chatto and Windus, 1989.

* * *

Since her first novel, *From Doon with Death* (1964), Ruth Rendell has published more than 40 books and become one of the United Kingdom's most popular crime writers, although her work transcends the genre. She has won numerous awards for novels, which show how "humanity walks ever on a thin crust over terrifying abysses."

Her work falls into three categories. The "Wexford" books form a series in which the wise and avuncular Chief Inspector Reg Wexford and his uptight and narrow-minded assistant Mike Burden solve a series of murders in the apparently tranquil Sussex town of Kingsmarkham. Burden's wife dies halfway through the series, and in *No More Dying Then* (1971) Burden is shown to be as vulnerable to sexual obsession as many of Rendell's criminals, falling for a young woman whose child has disappeared. These novels often engage in a rather stereotypical way with contemporary issues—*An Unkindness of Ravens* (1985) with militant feminism, and *Simisola* (1995) with racism and domestic slavery. In the Wexford books, order is generally restored, but Rendell says that this is not her main concern: "I like dramatic rather than moral satisfaction."

In the second category of Rendell novels crimes are committed, but the focus is less on the solution than on the psyche of the criminal. In novels such as *Live Flesh* (1986) Rendell takes the reader inside the mind of the disturbed, obsessive, or psychopathic individual (here a rapist). Rendell has a deep awareness of the lives of the disadvantaged: Wexford tells Burden, after they have interviewed a series of child molesters, "You might have been one of them if your parents had rejected you. . . . They sit in darkness, they're born, as Blake or some clever sod said, to endless night." In the Wexford novels such explanations seem rather simplistic—Rendell has said that she believes that "evil exists inside people, inside human nature"—but in more complex novels, such as *The Crocodile Bird* (1993), Rendell provides more satisfying social and psychological contexts for her plots. In that book, Eve keeps her daughter Liza in isolation in the remote country mansion where she works, telling her the world outside is evil. But it is Eve who has committed murder. Liza is the bird who lives inside the mouth of the crocodile, feeding off the scraps left in its teeth until her mother kills again, and sends Liza away. She goes to her secret lover Sean and tells him the fairytale story of her life, whilst in the present an inexorable chain of events leads Liza back to the truth about her mother.

In 1986 Rendell initiated her third category of books by publishing her first novel under the name Barbara Vine, *A Dark-Adapted Eye.* It is intricately plotted study of the battle of wills between two sisters, Eden and Vera, over possession of a child. The novel opens on the morning of Vera's execution for murder, and 35 years later her niece Faith reconstructs the events of the past whilst leaving the reader to do much of the work of reconstruction. Plot construction, close observation of human relationships, and social difference are more important than the solution of the crime. The reader is often unsure who the victim is, let alone the perpetrator. "I'm interested in guilt," Rendell says, "and the fictional process of moving back and forward in time."

The second Vine novel, *A Fatal Inversion* (1987), opens with the discovery of the skeletons of a young woman and a baby in the grounds of a country house in Suffolk: 11 years earlier Adam had inherited the house from his uncle, called it Ecalpemos (a "fatal inversion") and spent a summer there with a group of young people including the rootless Zosie, who steals a child. Not until the end do we know who was killed and buried there, and in the meantime the past which Adam thought he had buried threatens to destroy his carefully reconstructed life.

In *Asta's Book* (1993), a mystery (a "quest for an identity and for a lost child") is created and solved through the writing and reading of diaries, letters, and trial transcripts. The narrator is Anne, the niece of Swanny. Swanny is the daughter of Asta, whose diaries were found and published after her death; before she dies, Asta tells Swanny that she is not her child. Anne inherits the original diaries and attempts to solve the mystery of Swanny's identity. The quest leads her to the murder of two women and the disappearance of a child in 1905.

Reading Rendell is compulsive. Some of her books leave a nasty taste in the mouth, as if one has been complicit in the crime by reading about it. But her reply is that "people who refuse to confront the horror are part of the problem." Her capacity for invention seems inexhaustible. She often says that the next Wexford will be the last, but he has not been killed off yet. "People say the Rendells are starting to resemble the Vines," she says. "But it was bound to happen. There is, after all, only one of me."

—Nicola King

RICE, Anne

Pseudonyms: Anne Rampling; A. N. Roquelaure. **Nationality:** American. **Born:** Howard Allen O'Brien, New Orleans, Louisiana, 4 October 1941; name changed to Anne c.1947. **Education:** Texas Women's University, Denton, Texas, 1959-60; San Francisco State College (now University), California, B.A. 1964, M.A. 1971; graduate study at University of California, Berkeley, 1969-70. **Family:** Married Stan Rice in 1961; one daughter (deceased), and one son. **Career:** Has held a variety of jobs, including waitress, cook, theater usherette, and insurance claims examiner. Currently, a full-time writer. **Awards:** Joseph Henry Jackson award honorable mention, 1970. **Address:** 1239 First St., New Orleans, Louisiana 70130, U.S.A.

Publications

Novels

The Feast of All Saints. New York, Simon and Schuster, 1980; Harmondsworth, Penguin, 1982.
Cry to Heaven. New York, Knopf, 1982; London, Chatto and Windus, 1990.
Exit to Eden (as Anne Rampling). New York, Arbor House, and London, Futura, 1985.
Belinda (as Anne Rampling). New York, Arbor House, 1986; London, Macdonald, 1987.
The Mummy; or, Ramses the Damned. New York, Ballantine, and London, Chatto and Windus, 1989.
Vampire Chronicles.
 Interview with the Vampire. New York, Knopf, and London, Raven, 1976.
 The Vampire Lestat. New York, Ballantine, and London, Macdonald, 1985.
 The Queen of the Damned. New York, Knopf, 1988; London, Macdonald, 1989.
 The Tale of the Body Thief. New York, Knopf, and London, Chatto and Windus, 1992.
 Memnoch the Devil. New York, Random House, and London, Chatto and Windus, 1995.
The Mayfair Witches
 The Witching Hour. New York, Knopf, 1990; London, Chatto and Windus, 1991.
 Lasher. New York, Knopf, and London, Chatto and Windus, 1993.
 Taltos: Lives of the Mayfair Witches. New York, Knopf, and London, Chatto and Windus, 1994.
The Servant of the Bones. New York, Knopf, and London, Chatto and Windus, 1996.

Novels as A. N. Roquelaure

The Sleeping Beauty Novels. New York, New American Library/Dutton, 1991.
 The Claiming of Sleeping Beauty. New York, Dutton, and London, Macdonald, 1983.
 Beauty's Punishment. New York, Dutton, 1984.
 Beauty's Release. New York, Dutton, 1985; London, Warner, 1994.

*

Film Adaptations: *Interview with the Vampire,* 1994; *Exit to Eden,* 1994.

Critical Studies: *Prism of the Night: A Biography of Anne Rice* by Katherine M. Ramsland, New York, Dutton, 1991; *Anne Rice* by Bette B. Roberts, New York, Twayne, and Oxford, Maxwell Macmillan, 1994.

* * *

Anne Rice is one of those rare phenomena; a writer who has been able to attain a level of success in more than one genre. She has done well both economically and critically with novels that appear on bookshelves with works of fantasy, historical fiction, and erotic fiction. However, the discerning reader will immediately notice that all of her works contain elements of more than one of these three sub-groups. Two of her novels have been made into high-budget motion pictures [*Interview with the Vampire* (1994) and *Exit to Eden* (1994)] and her work is the subject of extensive discussion on the Internet. Of course, Rice's work has not received universal approbation. There are many critics who consider it all "popular literature" with few, if any, redeeming artistic values. In fact, it is possible to observe a certain degradation in the artistic quality of Rice's work, because she is overextending herself, some argue.

Rice's first published novel, *Interview with the Vampire* (1976), managed to fire the imagination of readers and develop a cult-like following. This book, with its brooding, self-conscious hero, Louis, represents many of the aspects of the common consciousness of North American youth of the 1970s. Louis is an outsider, unable to integrate with normal human existence or the shadowy community of other vampires. It chronicles Louis' life from the time of his conversion to vampirism in 1791 until the date of the interview in the 1970s. As well as its engaging historical setting, this novel has strong homoerotic overtones that have helped to establish its cult status.

It is interesting to note that in the 1990s, a period gripped by revivals of the fashions and music of the 1970s, *Interview with the Vampire* appeared as a relatively successful motion picture. Rice continued to publish novels based upon the characters and situations from *Interview with the Vampire* under the title of "The Vampire Chronicles [*The Vampire Lestat* (1985), *The Queen of the Damned* (1988), *The Tale of the Body Thief* (1992), *Memnoch the Devil* (1995)] although none of them live up to the artistic promise of the initial text. There is, however, a great deal of popular interest in the continuing series. The character of Louis, which may represent some aspects of the artist herself, has been relegated to the role of a background figure, and the swashbuckling figure of Lestat, Louis' first vampire companion, is the focus of much attention. Lestat even does a stint as a rock star in *The Vampire Lestat.* The latest of the group, *Memnoch the Devil*, is reported to be the last. Rice's novels in the genre of the fantastic also include *The Mummy* (1989) and a series entitled "The Mayfair Witches" [*The Witching Hour* (1990), *Lasher* (1993), and *Taltos* (1994)].

Rice's historical fiction includes *The Feast of All Saints* (1980) and *Cry to Heaven* (1982). *The Feast of All Saints* is set in pre-Civil War New Orleans and is concerned with the lives of free people of color in a time of slavery. *Cry to Heaven* is the story of an 18th century Italian castrato. In both of these texts, as in the vampire novels, there is an underlying current of sado-masochism and sexuality that cannot, for one reason or another, be fully expressed.

The sado-masochistic elements of Rice's creative fiction are most explicitly present in her trilogy of erotic fiction; *The Claiming of Sleeping Beauty* (1983), *Beauty's Punishment* (1984) and *Beauty's Release* (1985). These three works were published under the pseudonym A.N. Roquelaure—A roquelaure is kind of cloak, hence A.N. (Anne) cloaked. Though not so explicitly sexual, her novels *Exit to Eden* (1985) and *Belinda* (1986), which were published under the pseudonym Anne Rampling, also deal with the world of alternate sexual experience.

Unlike many contemporary authors, Rice seems to have a genuine interest in her fans and to actually enjoy the public attention attracted by her work. This, rather than simple avarice, may be the reason for her massive publication record and the concomitant waning of artistic quality in her work.

—Stan Beeler

RIVERS, Elfrida. *See* **BRADLEY, Marion Zimmer.**

ROBBINS, Tom

Nationality: American. **Born:** Thomas Eugene Robbins in Blowing Rock, North Carolina, 22 July 1936. **Education:** High school in Warsaw, Virginia; Hargarve Military Academy; Washington and Lee University, Lexington, Virginia; Richmond Professional Institute (now Virginia Commonwealth University), graduated 1960. **Military Service:** Served in the United States Air Force in Korea. **Family:** Married Terrie Robbins (second marriage; divorced); one child. **Career:** Copy editor, Richmond *Times-Dispatch,* 1960-62, and Seattle *Times* and *Post-Intelligencer,* 1962-63; reviewer and art columnist, *Seattle Magazine,* and radio host, 1964-68. **Agent:** Phoebe Larmore, 228 Main Street, Venice, California 90291, U.S.A.

Publications

Novels

Another Roadside Attraction. New York, Doubleday, 1971; London, W.H. Allen, 1973.

Even Cowgirls Get the Blues. Boston, Houghton Mifflin, 1976; London, Corgi, 1977.

Still Life with Woodpecker. New York, Bantam, and London, Sidgwick and Jackson, 1980.

Jitterbug Perfume. New York, Bantam, 1984.

Skinny Legs and All. New York, Bantam, 1990; London, Bantam, 1991.

Half Asleep in Frog Pajamas. New York, Bantam, 1994.

Uncollected Short Story

"The Chink and the Clock People," in *The Best American Short Stories 1977,* edited by Martha Foley. Boston, Houghton Mifflin, 1977.

Other

Guy Anderson. Seattle, Gear Works Press, 1965.
Guy Anderson (exhibition catalogue), with William Ivey and Wallace S. Baldinger. Seattle, Seattle Art Museum, 1977.

*

Critical Study: *Tom Robbins* by Mark Siegel, Boise, Idaho, Boise State University, 1980.

* * *

Tom Robbins has made a name for himself by writing novels that defy the ordinary in terms of plot, language, characterization, and theme, and by cultivating a following of countercultural groupies (who have receded in number since the 1970s). His six novels display his trademarks: an episodic, nonlinear structure that Robbins has called "psychedelic," based on his early LSD experiences; a cast of bizarre characters with names like Bonanza Jellybean and Marx Marvelous who search for the meaning of life; a style characterized by outrageous metaphors and absurd images; and an optimistic philosophy based on Eastern mysticism, quantum physics, antimaterialism, feminism, and above all, playfulness. But for most critics it is Robbins's style that stands out the most, at times stealing the show from his quirky plots and characters and usually delighting the reader with flamboyant images, such as one from *Skinny Legs and All* (1990) in which the sound of a quarter being dropped into a pay phone is described as "a hollow yet musical clink, like a robot passing a kidney stone."

Robbins's first book, *Another Roadside Attraction* (1971), became a cult classic with its 1973 paperback edition that was marketed largely by word-of-mouth among college students. In this book, a group of eccentrics discover Christ's mummified body. They bring it to a hot dog stand called Capt. Kendrick Memorial Hot Dog Wildlife Preserve, where they try to disprove Christianity. "The point of *Another Roadside Attraction,*" according to Jerome Klinkowitz in *The Practice of Fiction in America,* "is the reinvention (through perception) of reality, a revitalization of life which logic and authority have dulled beyond appreciation." The book repudiates the authority of Christianity, reflecting Robbins's belief, as he once said, that "religion is spirituality in which the spiritual has been killed. . . . Spirituality doesn't lend itself to organization."

His second and most popular book, *Even Cowgirls Get the Blues* (1976), is about a beautiful woman, Sissy Hankshaw, who learns to live with her socially unacceptable, oversized thumbs by becoming the best hitchhiker in the country. When she arrives at the Rubber Rose Ranch in South Dakota, a former cosmetic farm for women that has been taken over by cowgirl feminists, she discovers the path to wisdom with the help of Chink, a Japanese hermit. Chink teaches Sissy that Americans must learn to reach back to their spiritual roots in Pantheism, which is characterized by feminine receptivity rather than masculine aggression. Mark Siegel has written in his study of Tom Robbins that the novel "posits the abandonment of out-worn mainstream social roles that are destructive in their rigidity."

Robbins's first two novels were received enthusiastically by most critics. But by the time his next novel, *Still Life with Woodpecker* (1980), was published, reviewers were tiring of his style. Julie B. Peters wrote in the *Saturday Review* that Robbins's writing "is marbled with limping puns heavily splattered with recurrent motifs and a boyish zeal for the scatological." Another reviewer criticized the novel for being too "cute." In addition, some critics disliked the fact that, instead of the larger social messages of his previous works, the novel centered on the personal relationship between a princess and a "good-hearted terrorist."

The publication of his next three novels brought Robbins relatively little critical praise. It appears that his style and message have largely lost their appeal for a generation of critics who have outgrown their attraction to playfulness and countercultural ethics. In his review of *Skinny Legs and All* for the *New York Times Book Review,* Joe Queenan wrote, "Mr. Robbins is still a very funny guy, but he—and we—are getting a bit old for comic books." Others find that the old philosophical enlightenment of his first books had turned into didacticism. Karen Karbo of the *New York Times Book Review* argued that "unless his work was imprinted on you when you were 19 and stoned, you'll find him forever unreadable. A sober 21-year-old is already too steely-eyed and seasoned to frolic in Mr. Robbins's trademark cuckoo plots, woo-woo philosophizing, overwrought metaphors and cheerful misogyny."

But Robbins continues to craft his quirky and ultimately optimistic novels of the search for the meaning of life, convinced that our culture remains as materialistic, conformist, and confused as ever. He once wrote, "social action on the political/economic level is wee potatoes. Our great human adventure is the evolution of consciousness. We are in this life to enlarge the soul and light up the brain." This is what Robbins tries to achieve with his writing.

—Anne Boyd

ROGERS, Rosemary

Nationality: American. **Born:** 7 December 1932, in Panadura, Ceylon (now Sri Lanka); immigrated to United States in 1962, naturalized citizen. **Education:** University of Ceylon, B.A. **Family:** Married 1) Summa Navaratnam (divorced), children: Rosanne, Sharon; 2) Leroy Rogers (divorced), children: Michael, Adam; 3) Christopher Kadison, children: Christopher. **Career:** Associated Newspapers of Ceylon, Colombo, writer of features and public affairs information, 1959-62; Travis Air Force Base, Fairfield, California, secretary in billeting office, 1964-69; Solano County Parks Department, Fairfield, secretary, 1969-74; writer. Part-time reporter for *Fairfield Daily Republic.* **Address:** c/o Avon Books, 105 Madison Ave., New York, New York 10016, U.S.A.

Publications

Sweet Savage Love. Avon, 1974.
The Wildest Heart. Avon, 1974.
Dark Fires. Avon, 1975.
Wicked Loving Lies. Avon, 1976.
The Crowd Pleasers. Avon, 1978.
The Insiders. Avon, 1979.
Lost Love, Last Love. Avon, 1980.
Love Play. Avon, 1981.

Surrender to Love. Avon, 1982.
The Wanton. Avon, 1985.
Bound by Desire. Avon, 1988.
The Tea Planter's Bride. Avon, 1995.

*

Critical Study: *Love's Leading Ladies* by Kathryn Falk, Pinnacle Books, 1982.

* * *

Rosemary Rogers is a classic American success story. She was born in Sri Lanka. Although she was raised in an atmosphere of wealth and privilege, Rogers rebelled against the restrictive nature of her comfortable yet bland existence. She was the first woman in her family to get a job, as a feature writer for a Ceylon newspaper. She married, divorced, married again, and then moved to California with her second husband. While she raised her four children she wrote for her own entertainment, the way many people watch television.

When her second marriage ended in divorce, Rogers worked as a secretary for a very low wage. Her parents left Ceylon during the Marxist rebellion to join her. That was when she knew she had to do something to improve her financial status. Out of desperation she took one of her old stories, rewrote it several times, and sent it to Avon Books. Her manuscript arrived at the right time. Avon had just experienced great success with a similar novel, *The Flame and the Flower* by Kathleen Woodiwiss. Avon offered Rogers a contract immediately and she was on her way to a new career.

Rogers's story was unique because she added a twist to the conventional historical romance novel. There were more explicit sexual accounts than ever before, and lots of them. In fact, some critics say her novels are pornographic. The characters are mostly interested in sex, which often takes the form of a rape fantasy for the heroine. The "romance" is generally of a violent and forceful nature, not the soft, poetic longings of the typical romance novel's hero and heroine. Rogers justifies her theme by saying "Most women *do* have a rape fantasy. But there is a difference between actual rape, which is horrifying, and fantasy. In the rape fantasy, you pick the man and the circumstances. It's not at all scary."

Rogers injects an element of adventure into her plots. She writes the kind of books she would like to read. She isn't particularly bothered by unfavorable reviews, because she writes to please her reading audience. The audience, by the way, contains a sizable number of men, not just women who are presumed to have an interest in romantic fiction. Rogers knows her writing is escapist. It is not the kind to win literary prizes. But it has purpose because it gives ordinary individuals an outlet from their mundane, ordinary lives. Her heroines do what many women long to do. They travel, meet famous people, and have passionate romances with intriguing men.

The sexual revolution was widely established by the mid-1970s, which undoubtedly played a factor in the success of her first novel, *Sweet Savage Love* (1974). She soon followed with another bestseller, *Dark Fires,* in 1975 and then wrote *Lost Love, Last Love* (1980). These three books chronicled the long, passionate, and occasionally violent relationship between Steven Morgan, a womanizing adventurer, and Virginia Brandon, the spirited heroine. In between and following those were other successes including *Wicked Loving Lies* (1976), *The Insiders* (1979), and *Bound by Desire* (1988).

To the delight of her fans, Rogers wrote *The Tea Planter's Bride* (1995) after a six-year sabbatical. It went to the top of the national charts even before Avon began its print campaign, selling over one million copies by May 1995.

—Carolyn Eckstein-Soule

ROOKE, Leon

Nationality: American. **Born:** 11 September 1934, in Roanoke Rapids, North Carolina. **Education:** University of North Carolina, 1955-58, 1961-62. **Military Service:** U.S. Army, Infantry, 1958-60; served in Alaska. **Career:** Short story writer, novelist, and dramatist. University of North Carolina at Chapel Hill, writer-in-residence, 1965-66; University of Victoria, Victoria, British Columbia, lecturer in creative writing, 1971-72, visiting professor, 1980-81; Southwest Minnesota State College, Marshall, writer-in-residence, 1975-76; University of Toronto, Toronto, Ontario, writer-in-residence, 1984-85. **Awards:** MacDowell fellowship, 1974; Canada Council theatre and fiction grants, 1974, 1975, 1976, 1979, 1983, and 1985; Epoch prize, 1975; National Endowment for the Arts fellowship, 1978; Yaddo fellowship, 1979; Best Paperback Novel of the Year, 1981, for *Fat Woman*; Canada/Australia prize, 1981, for overall body of work; Governor General's Literary award for fiction, Canada Council, 1984, for *Shakespeare's Dog*; Periodical Distributors First prize for magazine fiction, 1986; Author's award for short fiction, Foundation for the Advancement of Canadian Letters, 1986. **Agent:** Liz Darhansoff, 1220 Park Ave., New York, New York 10128, U.S.A. **Address:** 1019 Terrace Ave., Victoria, British Columbia, Canada V8S 3V2.

Publications

Short Stories

Last One Home Sleeps in the Yellow Bed. Louisiana State University Press, 1968.
Vault, a Story in Three Parts: Conjugal Precepts, Dinner with the Swardians, and Break and Enter. Lillabulero Press, 1973.
The Love Parlour. Oberon, 1977.
The Broad Back of the Angel. Fiction Collective, 1977.
Cry Evil. Oberon, 1980.
Death Suite. ECW Press, 1981.
The Birth Control King of the Upper Volta. ECW Press, 1982.
Sing Me No Love Songs, I'll Say You No Prayers. Ecco Press, 1984.
A Bolt of White Cloth. Ecco Press, 1985.
The Happiness of Others. Porcupine's Quill, 1992.

Novels

The Magician in Love. Aya Press, 1981.
Fat Woman. Knopf, 1981.

Shakespeare's Dog. Knopf, 1983.
A Good Baby. Knopf, 1990.

* * *

Leon Rooke is one of Canada's most prolific and inventive writers. Playwright, novelist, and editor, he is probably best known for the several hundred short stories he has written. He later said that when he began writing, "many young writers were insisting that the old short-story imperatives of beginning, middle, and end—as with other rigid conventions—needed revitalization. . . . We were seeking more open forms, fresh angles of approach to material."

The key to his art is versatility. Rather than adopting a single mode or narrative voice, he has created a whole theater of voices. Arenas in which he has worked include black humor, fantasy, surrealism, political satire, and the gritty realism of writers like Raymond Carver and Frederic Barthelme. A large number of his stories are written in the first person, but in different voices and using a heavy reliance on dialogue and especially on colloquial speech. Some stories are even told through a medley of voices. Without abandoning older conventions such as narrative and characterization, Rooke attempts to marry them to new forms and fresh insights.

Rooke's first successful novel, *Fat Woman* (1981), captured the idiom of a woman who is all too aware of how her eating disorder has alienated her husband in a compassionate but comic way. Ella Mae is a highly original characterization, pathetic but also admirable in her romanticism as the truth about her physical self confronts her on the weighing machine: "She carried it, the weight, but it was not her. . . . She could forget everything, she could be as slender as a thread, a soft wind could lift her up and blow her along and put her down again with nothing broken, with no leaf damaged, no skin bruised."

In *Shakespeare's Dog* (1983) Rooke displays even greater virtuosity. This inventive work has the whimsical notion of telling part of the life of Shakespeare through the eyes of his dog, Hooker. The novel views Shakespeare at the age of 21 (in 1585), tricked into marriage by "the noxious Hathaway," burdened with three children, and as desperately anxious to escape from the village and seek fame as Anne is to keep him there. Rooke carries the jape off in brilliantly virtuosic style in a language that sounds like a kind of Elizabethan gone slightly askew. Earthy and richly imaginative, his prose is full of the sounds and smells of Elizabethan life.

Rooke's early stories are filled with mordant humor, which gave him an undeserved reputation for pessimism; he particularly regretted the title of his second collection, *Cry Evil* (1980). The first story in that book, "The Deacon's Tale," is an ironic, partly self-mocking narrative that sends up the idea of narrative itself. One suspects the author is making an ironic commentary on his own predicament when his narrator, speaking of his wife, says, "According to her, the people in my stories are never polite and nice the way people really are. In my stories it's always hocus-pocus, slam-bang, and someone has a knife at your throat."

But the stories in the later collection, *A Bolt of White Cloth* (1985), are more magnanimous in tone and for all the grimness of their material are marked often at the end by a Joycean kind of epiphany. "The Only Daughter," for instance, a triumph of vernacular language, concerns a young girl who has been sent by her dying mother to see if her father will look after her. Raw and gritty in its account of the girl's sufferings, it ends on a slightly upbeat note; after watching him unseen for several days, the girl finally decides to give her father a chance to look after her. "Dirty Heels of the Fine Young Children" similarly shows a father unexpectedly reconciled with his children, while the ironically titled "The Woman's Guide to Home Companionship" mingles humor with tragedy in its account of two women who finally turn on their brutal husbands and murder them.

In *How I Saved the Province*, Rooke turns more directly to political satire—of British Columbia and in one story of Reagan's America—but the humor is even more bizarre and surreal than in his earlier work. He is a difficult writer to pin down precisely because he refuses to repeat himself and is always looking for new challenges and new ways of expressing himself. "My conception of what a fiction writer ought to be," he says, "is one who can move into and occupy all sorts of human frames—and take on all sorts of vastly opposed human voices." This is precisely what he does.

—Laurie Clancy

ROQUELAURE, A. N. *See* **RICE, Anne.**

ROSS, Bernard L. *See* **FOLLETT, Ken.**

ROTH, Philip (Milton)

Nationality: American. **Born:** Newark, New Jersey, 19 March 1933. **Education:** Weequahic High School, New Jersey; Newark College, Rutgers University, 1950-51; Bucknell University, Lewisburg, Pennsylvania, 1951-54; A.B. 1954 (Phi Beta Kappa); University of Chicago, 1954-55, M.A. 1955. **Military Service:** Served in the United States Army, 1955-56. **Family:** Married 1) Margaret Martinson in 1959 (separated 1962; died 1968); 2) the actress Claire Bloom in 1990. **Career:** Instructor in English, University of Chicago, 1956-58; visiting writer, University of Iowa, Iowa City, 1960-62; writer-in-residence, Princeton University, New Jersey, 1962-64; visiting writer, State University of New York, Stony Brook, 1966, 1967, and University of Pennsylvania, Philadelphia, 1967-80. Since 1988 Distinguished Professor, Hunter College, New York. General editor, Writers from the Other Europe series, Penguin publishers, London, 1975-80. Member of the Corporation of Yaddo, Saratoga Springs, New York. **Awards:** Houghton Mifflin literary fellowship, 1959; Guggenheim fellowship, 1959; National Book award, 1960; Daroff award, 1960; American Academy grant, 1960; O Henry award, 1960; Ford Foundation grant, for drama, 1965; Rockefeller fellowship, 1966; National Book Critics Circle award, 1988, for *The Counterlife*, 1992, for *Patrimony;* National Jewish Book award, 1988; PEN-Faulkner award, 1993, for *Operation Shylock.* Honorary degrees: Bucknell University, 1979; Bard College, Annandale-on-Hudson, New York, 1985; Rutgers University, New Brunswick, New Jersey, 1987; Columbia University, New York, 1987. **Member:** American Academy, 1970. **Address:** c/o Simon and Schuster, 1230 Avenue of the Americas, New York, New York 10020, U.S.A.

Publications

Novels

Letting Go. New York, Random House, and London, Deutsch, 1962.
When She Was Good. New York, Random House, and London, Cape, 1967.
Portnoy's Complaint. New York, Random House, and London, Cape, 1969.
Our Gang (Starring Tricky and His Friends). New York, Random House, and London, Cape, 1971.
The Breast. New York, Holt Rinehart, 1972; London, Cape, 1973; revised edition in *A Philip Roth Reader,* 1980.
The Great American Novel. New York, Holt Rinehart, and London, Cape, 1973.
My Life as a Man. New York, Holt Rinehart, and London, Cape, 1974.
The Professor of Desire. New York, Farrar Straus, 1977; London, Cape, 1978.
Zuckerman Bound (includes *The Prague Orgy*). New York, Farrar Straus, 1985.
The Ghost Writer. New York, Farrar Straus, and London, Cape, 1979.
Zuckerman Unbound. New York, Farrar Straus, and London, Cape, 1981.
The Anatomy Lesson. New York, Farrar Straus, 1983; London, Cape, 1984.
The Prague Orgy. London, Cape, 1985.
The Counterlife. New York, Farrar Straus, and London, Cape, 1987.
Deception. New York, Simon and Schuster, and London, Cape, 1990.
Operation Shylock: A Confession. New York, Simon and Schuster, and London, Cape, 1993.
Sabbath's Theater. New York, Houghton Mifflin, 1995.

Short Stories

Goodbye, Columbus, and Five Short Stories. Boston, Houghton Mifflin, and London, Deutsch, 1959.
Penguin Modern Stories 3, with others. London, Penguin, 1969.
Novotny's Pain. Los Angeles, Sylvester and Orphanos, 1980.

Uncollected Short Stories

"Philosophy, or Something Like That," May 1952, "The Box of Truths," October 1952, "The Fence," May 1953, "Armando and the Frauds," October 1953, and "The Final Delivery of Mr. Thorn," May 1954, all in *Et Cetera* (Lewisburg, Pennsylvania).
"The Day It Snowed," in *Chicago Review,* Fall 1954.
"The Contest for Aaron Gold," in *Epoch* (Ithaca, New York), Fall 1955.
"Heard Melodies Are Sweeter," in *Esquire* (New York), August 1958.
"Expect the Vandals," in *Esquire* (New York), December 1958.
"The Love Vessel," in *Dial* (New York), Fall 1959.
"Good Girl," in *Cosmopolitan* (New York), May 1960.
"The Mistaken," in *American Judaism* (New York), Fall 1960.
"Psychoanalytic Special," in *Esquire* (New York), November 1963.
"On the Air," in *New American Review 10,* edited by Theodore Solotaroff. New York, New American Library, 1970.
"Smart Money," in *New Yorker,* 2 February 1981.
"His Mistress's Voice," in *Partisan Review* (Boston), vol. 53, no. 2, 1986.

Play

Television Play: *The Ghost Writer,* with Tristram Powell, from the novel by Roth, 1983.

Other

Reading Myself and Others. New York, Farrar Straus, and London, Cape, 1975; revised edition, London, Penguin, 1985.
A Philip Roth Reader. New York, Farrar Straus, 1980; London, Cape, 1981.
The Facts: A Novelist's Autobiography. New York, Farrar Straus, 1988; London, Cape, 1989.
Patrimony: A True Story. New York, Simon and Schuster, and London, Cape, 1991.
Conversations with Philip Roth, edited by George J. Searles. Jackson, University Press of Mississippi, 1992.
The Conversion of the Jews (for children). Mankato, Minnesota, Creative Education, 1993.
A Philip Roth Reader. London, Vintage, 1993.

*

Bibliography: *Philip Roth: A Bibliography* by Bernard F. Rodgers, Jr., Metuchen, New Jersey, Scarecrow Press, 1974; revised edition, 1984.

Manuscript Collection: Library of Congress, Washington, D.C.

Critical Studies: *Bernard Malamud and Philip Roth: A Critical Essay* by Glenn Meeter, Grand Rapids, Michigan, Eerdmans, 1968; "The Journey of Philip Roth" by Theodore Solotaroff, in *The Red Hot Vacuum,* New York, Atheneum, 1970; *The Fiction of Philip Roth* by John N. McDaniel, Haddonfield, New Jersey, Haddonfield House, 1974; *The Comedy That "Hoits": An Essay on the Fiction of Philip Roth* by Sanford Pinsker, Columbia, University of Missouri Press, 1975, and *Critical Essays on Philip Roth* edited by Pinsker, Boston, Twayne, 1982; *Philip Roth* by Bernard F. Rodgers, Jr., Boston, Twayne, 1978; "Jewish Writers" by Mark Shechner, in *The Harvard Guide to Contemporary American Writing* edited by Daniel Hoffman, Cambridge, Massachusetts, Harvard University Press, 1979; introduction by Martin Green to *A Philip Roth Reader,* New York, Farrar Straus, 1980, London, Cape, 1981; *Philip Roth* by Judith Paterson Jones and Guinevera A. Nance, New York, Ungar, 1981; *Philip Roth* by Hermione Lee, London, Methuen, 1982; *Reading Philip Roth* edited by A.Z. Milbauer and D.G. Watson, London, Macmillan, 1988; *Understanding Philip Roth* by Murray Baumgarten and Barbara Gottfried, Columbia, University of South Carolina Press, 1990; *Philip Roth Revisited* by Jay L. Halio, New York, Twayne, 1992; *Comic Sense: Reading Robert*

Coover, Stanley Elkin, Philip Roth by Thomas Pughe, Basel, Birkhäuser, 1994; *Philip Roth and the Jews* by Alan Cooper, State University of New York Press, 1996.

* * *

Philip Roth is one of the leading writers of contemporary fiction. He is often called the funniest and most innovative contemporary American writer and has been referred to as the "American Franz Kafka." Humor based on Roth's Jewish heritage is the most striking element of his fiction.

Goodbye, Columbus (1959) is a collection of short fiction that depicts the integration and assimilation of Jewish individuals into mainstream American culture. "Defender of the Faith," considered to be the strongest story in the collection, depicts a young U.S. Army sergeant's conflict between a strict religious background and emerging personal opinions felt during training camp. In this story, Roth established the use of a first-person narrative voice that becomes central to all of his better fiction; a voice torn between sensitivity towards one's situation and the desire to act in a blindly rebellious manner.

Roth's early novels, *Letting Go* (1962) and *When She Was Good* (1967), continued his interest in maturing intellectuals. These two novels show his debt to F. Scott Fitzgerald, especially the attention to details of middle-class American life during the 1950s and the nostalgic depiction of naive romantic dreams. Yet the conventional structure and realism of these novels led critics to view them as unexceptional.

Portnoy's Complaint is perhaps the best aesthetic, and certainly financial, success of his early career. Alexander Portnoy's vivid recollections of adolescent traumas are both daring in theme and precise in technique. Roth's descriptions of a stand-up comic's act caused the *Chicago Sun-Times* to laud the work as one of the funniest books in America. Despite the generally favorable reception, some critics consider the book too crude and note that the crass humor may offend more conservative tastes.

During the 1970s Roth's writing developed a science-fiction tone and received less critical acclaim: *Our Gang* (1970) is a satire about Richard Nixon; *The Breast* (1971) is a bizarre Kafkaesque story about a man's transformation into a breast; and *The Great American Novel* (1973) is a strange combination of baseball folklore and bad jokes.

My Life as a Man (1974) and *The Professor of Desire* (1977) marked Roth's return to fiction based on the concerns of *Portnoy's Complaint,* including psychoanalysis, relationships, and Jewish Americans. *Zuckerman Bound* (1985), *Zuckerman Unbound* (1981), and *The Counterlife* (1987), which won the National Book Critics Circle, show a marked advance in Roth's style. These three novels escape the self-indulgent tone of *Portnoy's Complaint* and succeed in combining humor with sentimentality.

Patrimony (1991), winner of the National Book Critics Circle, is a true account of the death of Roth's father. Roth expresses mixed emotions, such as love, anxiety, and relief, as he watches his father slowly struggle with a brain tumor, yet the account is saved from melodrama by Roth's humor and objectivity.

In *Operation Shylock* (1993) Roth manages to combine a sense of humor with Israel's political conflicts. In that novel, Roth meets a man claiming to be Philip Roth. Roth's double chooses to live an active political lifestyle, which creates a series of problems for the author. Philosophy and political concerns are combined with a suspenseful plot-line and several vivid characters, such as exiles, war villains, other writers, a seductive member of an organization called Anti-Semites Anonymous, and of course, his doppelganger to create what critics consider his most innovative and important work. Roth's meta-fiction is a frightening portrayal of an individual who loses control of both physical and psychological security. It is reminiscent of two writers alluded to in the novel: Franz Kafka and Bruno Schulz.

Sabbath's Theater (1995) reveals a Roth who has become concerned with the fear of death and loneliness of aging. In that book, Mickey Sabbath, a retired puppeteer, fruitlessly searches his past for meaning only to reveal a series of disconnected and offensive acts. Its poignancy led a *Time* reviewer to call the novel one of the best-written works of 1995.

—Chris Godat

ROYKO, Mike

Nationality: American. **Born:** Chicago, Illinois, 19 September 1932. **Education:** Attended Wright Junior College, 1951-52. **Military Service:** U.S. Air Force, 1952-56. **Family:** Married Carol Joyce Duckman in 1954 (died, 1979); two sons. **Career:** Chicago North Side Newspapers, reporter, 1956; Chicago City News Bureau, reporter and assistant city editor, 1956-59; Chicago *Daily News,* reporter and columnist, 1959-78, associate editor, 1977-78; Chicago *Sun-Times,* columnist, 1978-84; Chicago *Tribune,* syndicated columnist, 1984—. **Awards:** Heywood Brown award, 1968; Pulitzer prize, 1972, for commentary; Man of the Year award from City of Hope Medical Center and medal for service to journalism from University of Missouri School of Journalism, both 1979; named to Chicago Press Club Journalism Hall of Fame, 1980. **Addresses:** Chicago Tribune, 435 N. Michigan Ave., Chicago, Illinois 60611, U.S.A.

Publications

Nonfiction

Up Against It. Regenery, 1967.
I May Be Wrong, but I Doubt It. Regnery, 1968.
Boss: Richard J. Daley of Chicago. Dutton, 1971.
Slats Grobnik and Some Other Friends. Dutton, 1973.
Sez Who? Sez Me. Dutton, 1982.
Like I Was Sayin'. Dutton, 1984.
Dr. Kookie, You're Right! Dutton, 1989.

* * *

Mike Royko began his journalism career as a reporter in 1956, moving in 1959 to the *Chicago Daily News,* where he began writing his now famous column. He moved to the *Chicago Sun-Times* in 1978 and finally to the rival *Chicago Tribune* in 1984. The focus of his contentious, call-'em-like-I-see-'em column ranges from the quotidian details of urban life to the broad themes of national politics. But he has remained the common man's columnist, the practitioner of a "beer-and-a-shot journalism" whose ideal reader has always been more blue-collar than intellectual.

The 60 columns gathered in *Up Against It* (1967), Royko's first collection, featured Royko's skeptically sardonic take on such topics as Mayor Daley, politics, the mob, religion, urban life, the Women's Christian Temperance Union, and the lives of everyday Chicagoans—including the down-on-his-luck Chicago cabbie discussed in the collection's title essay. *Booklist* lauded the book's "effectively sarcastic" style; *Library Journal,* though noting that Royko's Chicago focus limited the book to a regional audience, praised Royko as a fine writer; and the reviewer for *Editor and Publisher* applauded Royko's "simple tastes, . . . feeling for people, and . . . fantastic sense of humor," which he consistently used to "devastating" effect.

Royko's second collection, *I May Be Wrong, but I Doubt It* (1968), featured his Daily News columns on such topics as the scene in a Chicago bar shortly after Martin Luther King's assassination, a fanciful movie script about Adolf Hitler and Eva Braun, and the tale of four men whose fathers were killed by Bonnie and Clyde. In its review, *Christian Century* praised the "humane purpose" lurking behind the collection's pieces, *Publishers Weekly* found many of the pieces "amusing" and "sizzling," and *Library Journal,* while again noting Royko's regional appeal, extolled Royko as "a writer of uncommon talent, and uncommon social conscience."

Long a target of Royko's columns, Richard Daley was by 1971 serving his 16th year as Chicago's mayor when Royko's *Boss: Richard J. Daley of Chicago* (1971) leveled an unstintingly critical blast at the notorious mayor's career. Daley emerged as a brutal and corrupt figure with a blindness to the effect of racism on Chicago's African-American community and a fatal inability to rise above the blue-collar worldview of his Chicago neighborhood. *Saturday Review* praised *Boss* as "devastating"; the *New York Times* called it "pungent and precise" and a "remorseless book that bites and tears"; and the *Times Literary Supplement* embraced its "marvelously detailed analysis." The *Washington Post Book World,* on the other hand, faulted Royko for his "thorough, steely contempt" for Daley, who emerged as only "a two-dimensional villain," and for failing to convey a sense of Daley's internal motivations.

Royko returned to collections of columns in his next four books. *Slats Grobnik and Some Other Friends* (1973) collected selected *Daily News* columns from 1966-73, which in the first part of the book center on Royko's "alter ego," Slats Grobnik, a boyhood friend and archetypal blue-collar Chicagoan who over the years emerged as a kind of version of Royko himself. *Sez Who? Sez Me* (1982) gathered more than 90 columns written for the *Daily News* and the *Sun-Times* in which he returned to his traditional subjects—sports, bureaucracy, and bars—as well as several new ones, humorously dissecting Jane Fonda, Margaret Trudeau, Phyllis Schafley, designer jeans, and such topics as the number of rodent hairs permitted in peanut butter jars. *Like I Was Sayin'* (1984) featured another 100 of Royko's columns from 1966 on, and, in addition to his signature subjects, Royko took on such contemporary trends as jogging, roller-skating, and the lifestyles of Chicago's beau monde—with predictably scathing effect. In *Dr. Kookie, You're Right* (1990), Royko ruminated on the world's worst curses, rush-hour traffic, and, in the collection's title piece, Dr. I. M. Kookie, who Royko describes as "one of the world's leading experts on a lot of things."

Royko has found a wide and faithful audience among those who often feel disenfranchised by American politics and journalism, which they view as competing elites. Often controversial, his ideas reflect the frustration experienced by those who see themselves as the strong backbone of American society, and he provides a refreshing tonic to the endless intellectual angst of contemporary journalism.

—Paul S. Bodine

RULE, Ann

Pseudonym: Andy Stack. **Nationality:** American. **Born:** 22 October 1935, in Lowell, Michigan. **Education:** University of Washington, B.A., 1954; graduate study at University of Washington; received degree in police science. **Family:** Married Bill Rule (divorced, 1972); children: Laura, Leslie, Andy, Mike. **Career:** Writer. Has worked as a police officer in Seattle, Washington, and as a caseworker for the Washington State Department of Public Assistance. **Awards:** Achievement award, Pacific Northwest Writers Conference, 1991. **Agent:** Foley Agency, 34 East 38 St., New York, New York 10016, U.S.A.

Publications

Nonfiction

Beautiful Seattle. Beautiful America, 1979; reprinted as *Beautiful America's Seattle,* Beautiful America, 1989.
The Stranger beside Me. Norton, 1980.
Small Sacrifices: A True Story of Passion and Murder. New American Library, 1987.
If You Really Loved Me: A True Story of Desire and Murder. Simon & Schuster, 1991.
Everything She Ever Wanted: A True Story of Obsessive Love, Murder, and Betrayal. Simon & Schuster, 1992.
A Rose for Her Grave and Other Cases. Pocket Books, 1993.
You Belong to Me and Other True Cases: Ann Rule's Crime Files. Pocket Books, 1994.
Dead by Sunset: Perfect Husband, Perfect Killer? Simon & Schuster, 1995.

Novels

Possession. Norton, 1983.
Lust Killer, as Andy Stack. New American Library, 1983.
Want-Ad Killer, as Andy Stack. New American Library, 1983.
The I-Five Killer, as Andy Stack. New American Library, 1984.

*

Media Adaptation: Television film—*Small Sacrifices,* 1989.

* * *

Drawing heavily from her background as a policewoman and case worker, Ann Rule delivers horrifying stories of manipulation and murder. The most horrifying aspect of her stories is their truth. Rule gives the reader a complete picture of the people and events associated with real murder cases by following the development of the victims and the perpetrators from childhood. She even includes personal information about the investigators and lawyers involved. A personal interview with the killer is often included to give the reader a glimpse inside the mind of a person capable of committing the most heinous crimes while appearing completely ordinary. She includes just enough technical information and details of the investigation to emphasize the truth of the stories without making them difficult to read or boring. "Rule makes the story of each victim as fascinating as the pathology of the killer," wrote the *Indianapolis Star,* and John Saul refers to Rule as "the undisputed master crime writer of the 1980s and 1990s."

Rule has written several novels under the name Andy Stack, but the majority of her critical acclaim is for her nonfiction. One of the first books to gain nationwide acclaim was *The Stranger Beside Me* (1980), which is the story of the notorious serial killer Ted Bundy. Her next book, *Small Sacrifices: A True Story of Passion and Murder* (1987) was made into a television film in 1989. This book tells the chilling story of Diane Downs, who, along with her three children, came to a hospital emergency room one night, apparent victims of a highway robber. The smallest child is dead on arrival, the other two children are seriously injured, and Diane has been shot in the arm. After an extensive search for the "shaggy-haired stranger" yields no clues, the police become suspicious that Ms. Downs shot her own children and herself. As the case unfolds, the intelligent, beautiful, seemingly good mother is revealed as a cold-blooded killer so wrapped up in her own destructive forces that she is able to attempt the murder of her children because they no longer fit in with her life. Rule looks deeply into the psychological profile and background of Diane Downs and presents the investigation, trial, and incarceration with clarity and bone-chilling detail.

In *If You Really Loved Me: A True Story of Desire and Murder* (1991), David Brown appears to be an ordinary guy who owns a very successful business, until his very young wife is murdered and his 14-year-old daughter is convicted and incarcerated for the crime. Though it seems to be an open and shut case, one investigator can't let it rest. As he continues to probe, he uncovers details that show Brown to be an obsessive and manipulative psychopath who controls his family so completely that they are willing to do anything to keep his love. Though he is finally arrested, he continues his manipulation from jail, trying to prevent witnesses from testifying and the prosection from convicting him by having them all killed.

Dead by Sunset (1995) is another story of a charming, successful businessman who brutally murders one of his ex-wives. *Publishers Weekly* states "Rule provides a perceptive character analysis of a malignant, self-centered, charismatic con artist."

Rule "brings to her work the passion, the prodigious research and the narrative skill necessary to create suspense," wrote Walter Walker in the *New York Times Book Review.* Her books are compelling and intense as they explore the frightening realities of human nature.

—Jane Conkright

RUSHDIE, (Ahmed) Salman

Nationality: British. **Born:** Bombay, India, 19 June 1947. **Education:** Cathedral School, Bombay; Rugby School, Warwickshire, 1961-65; King's College, Cambridge, 1965-68, M.A. (honours) in history 1968. **Family:** Married 1) Clarissa Luard in 1976 (divorced 1987), one son; 2) the writer Marianne Wiggins in 1988. **Career:** Worked in television in Pakistan and as actor in London, 1968-69; freelance advertising copywriter, London, 1970-81; council member, Institute of Contemporary Arts, London, from 1985. Sentenced to death for *The Satanic Verses* in a religious decree (*fatwa*) by Ayatollah Khomeini, and forced to go into hiding, February 1989. **Awards:** Arts Council bursary; Booker prize, 1981; English-Speaking Union award, 1981; James Tait Black Memorial prize, 1982; Foreign Book prize (France), 1985; Whitbread prize, 1988. Fellow, Royal Society of Literature, 1983. **Agent:** Viking Penguin, 27 Wright's Lane, London W8 5TZ, England.

Publications

Novels

Grimus. London, Gollancz, 1975; New York, Overlook Press, 1979.
Midnight's Children. London, Cape, and New York, Knopf, 1981.
Shame. London, Cape, and New York, Knopf, 1983.
The Satanic Verses. London, Viking, 1988; New York, Viking, 1989.
The Moor's Last Sigh. London, Cape, 1995; New York, Pantheon, 1996.

Short Stories

East, West: Stories. New York, Pantheon, 1994.

Uncollected Short Stories

"The Free Radio," in *Firebird 1,* edited by T. J. Binding. London, Penguin, 1982.
"The Prophet's Hair," in *The Penguin Book of Modern British Short Stories,* edited by Malcolm Bradbury. London, Viking, 1987; New York, Viking, 1988.
"Good Advice Is Rarer than Rubies," in *New Yorker,* 22 June 1987.
"Untime of the Imam," in *Harper's* (New York), December 1988.

Fiction (for children)

Haroun and the Sea of Stories. London, Granta, 1990; New York, Viking, 1991.

Plays

Television Writing: *The Painter and the Pest,* 1985; *The Riddle of Midnight,* 1988.

Other

The Jaguar Smile: A Nicaraguan Journey. London, Pan, and New York, Viking, 1987.
Is Nothing Sacred? (lecture). London, Granta, 1990.
Imaginary Homelands: Essays and Criticism 1981-1991. London, Granta, and New York, Viking, 1991.
The Wizard of Oz. London, BFI, 1992.

*

Critical Studies: *Three Contemporary Novelists: Khushwant Singh, Chaman Nahal, and Salman Rushdie* edited by R. K. Dhawan, New Delhi, Classical, 1985; *The Perforated Sheet: Essays on Salman Rushdie's Art* by Uma Parameswaran, New Delhi, Affiliated East West Press, 1988; *The Rushdie File* edited by Lisa Appignanesi and Sara Maitland, London, Fourth Estate, 1989, Syracuse, New York, Syracuse University Press, 1990; *Salman Rushdie and the Third World: Myths of the Nation* by Timothy Brennan, London, Macmillan, 1989; *A Satanic Affair: Salman Rushdie and the Rage of Islam* by Malise Ruthven, London, Chatto and Windus, 1990; *The Rushdie Affair: The Novel, The Ayatollah, and the West* by Daniel Pipes, New York, Birch Lane Press, 1990; *Salman Rushdie: Sentenced to Death* by W. J. Weatherby, New York, Carroll and Graf, 1990; *Distorted Imagination: Lessons from the Rushdie Affair* by Ziauddin Sardar and Merryl Wyn Davies, London, Grey Seal, 1990; *The Novels of Salman Rushdie* edited by G. R. Tanefa and R. K. Dhawan, New Delhi, Indian Society for Commonwealth Studies, 1992; *Salman Rushdie* by James Harrison, New York, Twayne, 1992; *Salman Rushdie's Fiction: A Study* by Madhusudhana Rao, New Delhi, Sterling, 1992; *For Rushdie: A Collection of Essays by 100 Arabic and Muslim Writers*, New York, Braziller, 1994.

* * *

Perhaps the world's most famous and controversial living novelist, Salman Rushdie entered the literary spotlight in 1981 when his second book, *Midnight's Children* (1981), won the Booker Prize. A political and media spotlight has beamed intensely on him since February of 1989, when his fourth novel, *The Satanic Verses* (1988), earned the wrath of Iran's Ayatollah Khomeini for allegedly blaspheming against Islam. Rushdie, an Indian Muslim by birth, became the target of an international *fatwa,* or death sentence. He has lived in hiding ever since, as sensationally ambushed by politics as any of his own beleaguered characters.

Rushdie's first novel, *Grimus* (1975), is an ambitious but flawed experimental fantasy. Its hero is an androgynous 777-year-old Amerindian trying to solve the puzzles of K, a timeless communal utopia. Although it prefigures themes and techniques that bear fruit in later novels, most critics agree with Rushdie's own retrospective view of *Grimus* as an apprentice work "too clever for its own good."

In *Midnight's Children* Rushdie found his fictional voice and place. The story of Saleem Sinai, born at the moment of India's independence in 1947 and consequently "handcuffed to history," is an allegorical *tour-de-force.* Saleem's narrative sweeps exuberantly through 63 years of the subcontinent's recent past with a profusion of inventive stories. Rushdie ingeniously links eccentric personal lives with explosive public events, and displays the verbal dazzle and bizarre imagination for which his work is renowned. By turns hilarious, horrifying, scandalous and bitterly satiric, *Midnight's Children* has been widely hailed as a masterpiece, and was recently named "the Booker of Bookers" (the best novel to win the prize in 25 years).

Shame (1983) is set among Pakistan's ruling elite. It satirizes the power struggles between Zia ul-Haq and Zulfikar Ali Bhutto, turning real-life politicians into fictionalized grotesques whose buffoonery is exceeded only by their outsize cruelty. Not surprisingly, it was banned by Zia's government. As outrageously fantastic as its predecessor, *Shame* culminates in a spectacular apocalypse. As Rushdie's narrator grimly says, "Shamelessness, shame: the roots of violence."

The Satanic Verses shifts locale from South Asia to England. Two Indian men, Saladin Chamcha and Gibreel Farishta, survive a mid-air aircraft explosion only to be transformed into a goatish devil and a would-be angel. Their surreal journeys through London's immigrant communities show a city that is itself transformed, revolutionized by its new global citizenry. The novel's theme—how does newness come into the world?—becomes a refrain, and Rushdie splices into the main narrative two separate story lines that tackle the question from different perspectives. Framed as dreams of the schizophrenic Gibreel, they tell of Ayesha, a mysterious girl clothed only in butterflies who leads Indian villagers on a doomed pilgrimage, and of Mahound, Islam's founding prophet by another name. It is the latter segment that incited the *fatwa.* Its playful flouting of sacred history and its portrayal of Mohammad as an opportunistic "businessman" were deemed an unforgivable affront to Islam.

The *fatwa* provoked noisy debates about religion, censorship, imaginative freedom, international diplomacy, and the writer's responsibility. But these arguments overwhelmed what Rushdie saw as the novel's real concern; to celebrate "hybridity, impurity, intermingling, the transformation what comes of new and unexpected combinations of human beings, cultures, ideas . . . the great possibility that mass migration gives the world." The political and cultural themes of his novels are argued directly and elegantly in his essays, collected in *Imaginary Homelands* (1991). He speaks strongly against racist, authoritarian, and purist worldviews, and for a secular, inclusive, cosmopolitan revisioning of Western and Eastern societies.

Even as it gets harder to disentangle Rushdie's life, art, and high-profile activism, he continues to write compelling fiction. His first post-*fatwa* novel, *Haroun and the Sea of Stories* (1990), is ostensibly an adventure-fantasy for children. But Haroun's mission to overcome Khattam-Shud, "the Arch-Enemy of all Stories . . . the Prince of Silence and the Foe of Speech," has obvious connections with Rushdie's plight, and the book has delighted many adult readers.

In 1994 Rushdie published *East, West,* a collection of nine stories, and in 1995 another novel, *The Moor's Last Sigh.* The latter, like *Midnight's Children,* is an intricate, sprawling epic set in India. Its narrator, Moor, ages twice as fast as normal, his life reflecting and intersecting with tumultuous national events. In its devastating portrayals of fundamentalist bullies and shady capitalists it brings Rushdie's disgruntled politics up to date. *The Moor's Last Sigh* has been hailed in the West for its "profligate passion" and "linguistic brilliance" (*Boston Review*), and damned in the East as "a tawdry, artless melodrama told in sophomoric language" (*IndiaStar*). For as long as Rushdie hangs on to his life and voice, it seems, his books will be flashpoints for political and aesthetic disputes. But as he says, that's what literature is for: it "tells us there are no answers; or . . . that answers are easier to come by, and less reliable, than questions."

—John Clement Ball

RYAN, Rachel. *See* **BROWN, Sandra.**

RYDER, Jonathan. *See* **LUDLUM, Robert.**

S

SACKS, Oliver (Wolf)

Nationality: British. **Born:** London, England, 9 July 1933; immigrated to the United States in 1960. **Education:** Queen's College, Oxford, B.A., 1954, M.A., B.M., and B.Ch., all 1958; attended University of California, Los Angeles, 1962-65. **Career:** Yeshiva University, Albert Einstein College of Medicine, Bronx, New York, 1965—, began as instructor, currently clinical professor of neurology; Beth Abraham Hospital, Bronx, staff neurologist, 1966—. Visiting professor, University of California, Santa Cruz, 1986. Consultant neurologist, Bronx State Hospital, from 1966, and at the Little Sisters of the Poor in New York City. **Awards:** Hawthornden prize, 1974, for *Awakenings;* Oskar Pfister award, American Psychiatric Association, 1988; Guggenheim fellowship, 1989; Harold D. Vursell Memorial award, American Academy and Institute of Arts and Letters, 1989. **Member:** American Academy of Neurology (fellow). **Agent:** International Creative Management, 40 West 57th St., New York, New York 10019. **Address:** 119 Horton St., Bronx, New York 10464, U.S.A.

PUBLICATIONS

Nonfiction

Migraine: Evolution of a Common Disorder. University of California Press, 1970; revised and enlarged edition published as *Migraine: Understanding a Common Disorder,* 1985.
Awakenings. London, Duckworth, 1973.
A Leg to Stand On. New York, Summit Books, 1984.
The Man Who Mistook His Wife for a Hat, and Other Clinical Tales. London, Duckworth, 1985.
Seeing Voices: A Journey into the World of the Deaf. University of California Press, 1989.
An Anthropologist on Mars: Seven Paradoxical Tales. London, Duckworth, 1995.

*

Film Adaptation: *Awakenings,* 1990.

* * *

Oliver Sacks is best known in the United States, perhaps, for the film version of his 1973 book *Awakenings* (released in 1990, starring Robert DeNiro as one of the patients and Robin Williams as the young doctor). This book is now a classic study of the surviving victims of an encephalitis (or "sleeping sickness") epidemic that struck down many people early in the 20th century. Some of the patients had survived (in a sleeping state) into the 1960s, when they came to Sacks' attention as a young neurologist in a hospital in New York. He gave the patients a medicine called L-DOPA, which had produced extraordinary results in the treatment of a related disease, Parkinsons. When Sacks' encephalitis victims received this new treatment, many of them "woke up" for the first time in 40 or more years, only to lapse back into a sleeping condition after various periods of awakening. *Awakenings* is occasionally burdened by excessive medical terminology, as if Sacks had not yet quite figured out whether he was writing for fellow doctors or a more general audience. The problem does not occur in later books.

Sacks has never confined himself to writing about his profession as a clinical neurologist. He could be faulted for this, but such a judgment would be a grave error. When Sacks writes about deaf students at Gallaudet University as he did in *Seeing Voices* (1989), he is really writing about the human, social, and political implications of deafness and about the extraordinary development of American Sign Language. This book offers the reader a thoroughly researched history of the treatment of deafness and chronicles the demonstration by deaf students at that university that resulted in the appointment of its first deaf president. What he is doing is simply and beautifully extending the observations he has made in his own practice and specialty to another subject and demonstrating a unique and invaluable approach to medicine that is complex, unreductive, unmechanistic, and compassionate. Because he has been so deeply involved in the medical and human aspects of his own neurological specialty, he has no problem visualizing and extending his own approaches by analogy to such other human conditions as Tourette's Syndrome, autism, and the like, which he does with great insight in his most recent book, *An Anthropologist on Mars.*

That book is in some ways his most ambitious, yet it contains seven essays (which he calls "paradoxical tales") all published previously in either the *New Yorker* or the *New York Review of Books.* Each of these essays concentrates on one individual—each of them quite extraordinary—who is afflicted with a grave, and one would think utterly crippling, malady. One essay in this collection, for instance, involves a painter, previously known as a gifted colorist, who suddenly went colorblind. Another deals with a painter from Italy who reproduces from memory nothing but nearly exact reproductions of the village in Italy where he had grown up. Still another deals with a surgeon, Dr. Carl Bennett, afflicted with Tourette's Syndrome.

Sacks begins that essay with a clear, concise, and illuminating account of that syndrome: "The syndrome . . . [is] characterized, above all, by convulsive tics, by involuntary mimicry or repetition of others' words or actions . . . and by the involuntary or compulsive utterances of curses and obscenities. . . . Some individuals (despite their affliction) showed an odd insouciance or nonchalance; some a tendency to make strange, often witty, occasionally dreamlike associations; some extreme impulsiveness and provocativeness, a constant testing of physical and social boundaries; some a constant, restless reacting to the environment, a lunging at and sniffing of everything or a sudden flinging of objects; and yet others an extreme stereotypy and obsessiveness—no two patients were ever quite the same."

How such a man as Bennett, afflicted as he is with Tourette's Syndrome, could practice so well in such an intricate and demanding profession as surgery is infinitely curious to Sacks. As is the autistic biologist, Temple Grandin, of whom he was initially suspicious because she defied so completely the conventional stereotype of the autistic individual as "incapable of self-understanding." She had written, of all things, an autobiography.

What seems to interest Sacks the most in this book, and elsewhere in his writing, is how individuals such as these can transcend afflictions one would assume to be crippling to achieve works or develop professional skills (as did Dr. Bennett and Ms. Grandin) far beyond anyone's expectations.

—C. W. Truesdale

SAGAN, Carl (Edward)

Nationality: American. **Born:** New York City, 9 November 1934. **Education:** University of Chicago, A.B. (with general and special honors), 1954, B.S., 1955, M.A., 1956, Ph.D., 1960. **Family:** Married 1) Lynn Alexander in 1957 (divorced, 1963), two sons; 2) Linda Salzman in 1968 (divorced), one son; 3) Ann Druyan, two daughters, one son. **Career:** Scientist, author. University of California, Berkeley, Miller research fellow in astronomy, 1960-62; Harvard University, 1962-68, assistant professor of astronomy; Smithsonian Institution, Astrophysical Observatory, Cambridge, Massachusetts, astrophysicist, 1962-68; Cornell University, Ithaca, New York, associate professor, 1968-70, professor of astronomy and space sciences, 1970—, David Duncan Professor of Astronomy and Space Sciences, 1976—, director of Laboratory for Planetary Studies, 1968—, associate director of Center for Radiophysics and Space Research, 1972-81. Visiting professor and lecturer at numerous colleges and universities, as well as at the National Aeronautics and Space Administration astronaut training program, the Motion Picture Academy of Arts and Sciences, the U.S. Air Force Academy, the American Psychiatric Association, and the National Geographic Society. President, Carl Sagan Productions, Inc. (television programming), 1981— . President, Planetary Society, 1979—. Fellow, Robotics Institute, Carnegie-Mellon University, 1982—; Distinguished Visiting Scientist, Jet Propulsion Laboratory, California Institute of Technology, 1986—. Member of Committee to Review Project Blue Book (U.S. Air Force), 1956-66. Experimenter, Mariner 2 mission to Venus, 1962, Mariner 9 and Viking missions to Mars, Voyager mission to the outer solar system, Galileo mission to Jupiter; designer of Pioneer 10 and 11 and Voyager 1 and 2 interstellar messages. Member of council, Smithsonian Institution, 1975-85; member, board of directors, Council for the Advancement of Science Writing, 1972-77; member, Usage Panel, American Heritage Dictionary of the English Language, 1976—; member, Fellowship Panel, John S. Guggenheim Memorial Foundation, 1976-81; chairman, Study Group on Machine Intelligence and Robotics, NASA, 1977-79; member, board of directors, Council for a Livable World Education Fund, 1980—; member, board of advisors, Children's Health Fund, 1988—; co-chairman, Science, Global Forum of Spiritual and Parliamentary Leaders on Human Survival, 1988—; member, International Board of Advisors, Asahi Shimbun, Tokyo, 1991—; member, Advisory Council, National Institutes for the Environment, 1991—; member, American Committee on U.S.-Soviet Relations, 1983—. Member of various advisory groups of National Aeronautics and Space Administration; consultant to National Academy of Science; member of advisory panel, Civil Space Station Study, Office of Technology Assessment, U.S. Congress, 1982—. **Awards:** National Science Foundation pre-doctoral fellowship, 1955-58; Alfred P. Sloan Foundation research fellowship at Harvard University, 1963- 67; A. Calvert Smith prize, Harvard University, 1964; National Aeronautics and Space Administration, Apollo Achievement award, 1970, medal for exceptional scientific achievement, 1972, medal for distinguished public service, 1977, 1981; Prix Galabert (international astronautics prize), 1973; Klumpke-Roberts prize, Astronomical Society of the Pacific, 1974; John W. Campbell Memorial award, World Science Fiction Convention, 1974, for *The Cosmic Connection;* Golden Plate award, American Academy of Achievement, 1975; Joseph Priestly award, Dickinson College, 1975; Pulitzer prize, 1978, for *The Dragons of Eden: Speculations on the Evolution of Human Intelligence;* Washburn Medal, Boston Museum of Science, 1978; Rittenhouse medal, Franklin Institute/Rittenhouse Astronomical Society, 1980; 75th Anniversary award, Explorers Club, 1980; Academy of Family Films and Family Television award for Best Television Series of 1980, American Council for Better Broadcasts Citation for Highest Quality Television Programming of 1980-81, Silver Plaque from Chicago Film Festival, President's Special award from Western Educational Society for Telecommunication, 1981, George Foster Peabody award for excellence in television programming, University of Georgia, 1981, and Ohio State University annual award for television excellence, 1982, all for *Cosmos* television series; Humanist of the Year award, American Humanist Association, 1981; Glenn Seaborg prize for communicating science from the lecture platform, American Platform Association, 1981; Ralph Coats Roe medal, American Society of Mechanical Engineers, 1981; Hugo award, World Science Fiction Convention, 1982, for the book *Cosmos;* Stony Brook Foundation award, with Frank Press, for distinguished contributions to higher education, 1982; John F. Kennedy Astronautics award, American Astronautical Society, 1983; Locus Award, 1986, for *Contact;* Honda prize, Honda Foundation, 1985; Arthur C. Clarke award for exploration and development of space, 1984; Peter Lavan award for humanitarian service, Bard College, 1984; New Priorities award, Fund for New Priorities in America, 1984; Sidney Hillman Foundation Prize award, for "outstanding contributions to world peace," 1984; SANE National Peace award, 1984; Regents Medal for Excellence, Board of Regents, University of the State of New York, 1984; Olive Branch award, New York University, 1984, 1986, and 1989; Physicians for Social Responsibility Annual award for Public Service, 1985; Leo Szilard award for physics in the public interest, with Richard P. Turco and others, for "the discovery of nuclear winter," American Physical Society, 1985; Distinguished Service award, World Peace Film Festival, Marlboro College, 1985; Nahum Goldmann Medal, "in recognition of distinguished service to the cause of peace and many accomplishments in science and public affairs," World Jewish Congress, 1986; Brit HaDorot award, Shalom Center, 1986; annual award of merit, American Consulting Engineers Council, 1986; Maurice Eisendrath award for Social Justice, Central Conference of American Rabbis and the Union of American Hebrew Congregations, 1987; In Praise of Reason award, Committee for the Scientific Investigation of Claims of the Paranormal, 1987; Konstantin Tsiolkovsky medal, Soviet Cosmonautics Federation, 1987; George F. Kennan Peace award, SANE/Freeze, 1988; Helen Caldicott Peace Leadership award, with Ann Druyan, Women's Action for Nuclear Disarmament, 1988; Distinguished Service award for innovation in higher education, University Without Walls International Council, 1988; Roger Baldwin award, Massachusetts Civil Liberties Union, 1989; Oersted Medal, American Association of Physics Teachers, 1990; Annual award for outstanding television script, Writers Guild of

America, 1991; Presidential award, National Science Supervisors Association, 1991; UCLA Medal, University of California at Los Angeles, 1991. Numerous honorary dictorates. **Member:** American Academy of Arts and Sciences (fellow), Council on Foreign Relations, International Astronomical Union (member of organizing committee, Commission of Physical Study of Planets), International Council of Scientific Unions (vice chairman, working group on moon and planets, committee on space research), International Academy of Astronautics, International Society for the Study of the Origin of Life (member of council, 1980—), American Astronomical Society (councillor; chairman, division of planetary sciences, 1975-76), American Physical Society (fellow), American Geophysical Union (fellow; president, planetology section, 1980-82), American Association for the Advancement of Science (fellow; chairman, astronomy section, 1975), American Institute of Aeronautics and Astronautics (fellow), American Astronautical Society (fellow; member of council, 1976-81), Federation of American Scientists (member of council, 1977-81, 1984-88; sponsor), Society for the Study of Evolution, British Interplanetary Society (fellow), Astronomical Society of the Pacific, Genetics Society of America. **Agent:** Scott Meredith Literary Agency, 845 Third Ave., New York, New York 10022. **Address:** Laboratory for Planetary Studies, Space Science Building, Cornell University, Ithaca, New York 14853, U.S.A.

Publications

Nonfiction

The Atmospheres of Mars and Venus, with W. W. Kellogg. National Academy of Sciences, 1961.
Intelligent Life in the Universe, with I. S. Shklovskii. Holden-Day, 1963; reprinted, 1978.
Planets, with Jonathan Leonard. Time-Life Science Library, 1966.
Planetary Exploration: The Condon Lectures. University of Oregon Press, 1970.
The Air War in Indochina, with R. Littauer and others. Center for International Studies, Cornell University, 1971.
Mars and the Mind of Man, with Ray Bradbury, Arthur C. Clarke, Bruce Murray, and Walter Sullivan. Harper, 1973.
Life beyond Earth and the Mind of Man, with R. Berendzen, A. Montagu, P. Morrison, K. Stendhal, and G. Wald. U.S. Government Printing Office, 1973.
The Cosmic Connection: An Extraterrestrial Perspective. Doubleday, 1973.
Other Worlds. Bantam, 1975.
The Dragons of Eden: Speculations on the Evolution of Human Intelligence. Random House, 1977.
Murmurs of Earth: The Voyager Interstellar Record, with F. D. Drake, A. Druyan, J. Lomberg, L. Sagan, and T. Ferris. Random House, 1978.
Broca's Brain: Reflections on the Romance of Science. Random House, 1979.
Cosmos. Random House, 1980.
The Fallacy of Star Wars, with R. Garwin and others. Vintage Books, 1984.
The Cold and the Dark, with Paul R. Ehrlich, Donald Kennedy, and Walter Orr Roberts. Norton, 1984.
Comet, with Ann Druyan. Random House, 1985.
A Path Where No Man Thought: Nuclear Winter and the End of the Arms Race, with Richard Turco. Random House, 1989.
Shadows of Forgotten Ancestors: A Search for Who We Are, with Ann Druyan. Random House, 1992.
Pale Blue Dot: A Vision of the Human Future in Space. Random House, 1994.
The Demon-Haunted World: Science as a Candle in the Dark. Random House, 1996.

Novel

Contact. Random House, 1985.

Editor with T. Owen and H. J. Smith, *Planetary Atmospheres.* D. Reidel, 1971.
Editor with K. Y. Kondratyev and M. Rycroft, *Space Research XI.* Two volumes, Akademie Verlag, 1971.
Editor with T. Page, *UFOs: A Scientific Debate.* Cornell University Press, 1972.
Editor, *Communication with Extraterrestrial Intelligence.* MIT Press, 1973.

*

Film Adaptation: *Planets* has been adapted as a film; the television series upon which the book *Cosmos* was based aired on public television in 1980.

Critical Study: *Carl Sagan: Superstar Scientist* by Daniel Cohen, Dodd, Mead, 1987.

* * *

Carl Sagan is one of the most well-known science writers of our age. His books on the evolution of human intelligence and the probability of other intelligent life forms in the universe have opened up a world of scientific and philosophical inquiry to millions of lay readers, young and old. For Sagan, space travel is a vital part of contemporary human existence because we have run out of earth to discover and must satisfy our urge to explore the unknown. This urge accounts for the popularity of Sagan's books and his television series *Cosmos,* which seek to inject science with an excitement and wonder that many people lack in their everyday lives. Sagan once said, "I think that science has been separated artificially from feelings. One of the objectives of *Cosmos* is to heal that breach."

In 1963, Sagan worked on a translation of I. S. Schlovskii's book *Intelligent Life in the Universe* and added ten new chapters to the book, more than doubling its size. The book, according to Stuart Bauer of *New York* magazine, is "the first comprehensive treatment of the entire panorama of natural evolution." Sales of the book revealed the strong interest the public had in such theoretical studies of evolution. So in addition to his many scientific articles for academic journals, Sagan began to produce books on science for a popular audience.

Over the next decade he wrote books primarily on astronomy. But it was *The Dragons of Eden: Speculations on the Evolution of Human Intelligence* (1977) that gained him a popular audience and a Pulitzer Prize. In this book, Sagan presents the theory of the "triune brain," which was anything but new, but "nevertheless appeals to popularizers," R. J. Herrnstein wrote in *Commen-*

tary. The theory posits that three evolutionary components made up the human brain: reptilian ancestry, pre-human mammalian ancestry, and an original, rational component. In addition, according to Peter Stoler in *Time,* Sagan "offers some idiosyncratic thoughts on why man's neurological legacy makes him behave the way he does." For instance, Sagan speculates that our fear of falling might have derived from our "arboreal ancestors, who lived in trees and suffered when they forgot the effects of gravity," Stoler wrote. Most reviewers tended to agree that Sagan's speculations detracted from the book. Richard Restak wrote in *The New York Times Book Review* that "while it is often insightful and challenges several scientific paradigms, it is also sometimes embarrassingly naive and on occasion just plain fantastic."

Sagan's next book, *Broca's Brain: Reflections on the Romance of Science* (1979) again elicited a mixed response from critics. This collection of essays on a broad range of unusual scientific topics, such as ancient astronauts and mathematically gifted horses, prompted reviewers again to charge Sagan with overspeculation. According to Robert Jastrow in the *New York Times Book Review,* Sagan "soars all too often on flights of meaningless fancy." But Richard Berendzen of *Science* found rewards in the book worth the effort of difficult reading. Despite "uneven technical detail, loose connections, and an overabundance of polysyllabic jargon," he finds that the book "can answer old questions, raise new ones, open vistas, become unforgettable. In short, Sagan has done it again. The book's title might be *Broca's Brain,* but the subject is Sagan's."

The eight-million-dollar television series *Cosmos,* which aired on public television in 1980, brought Sagan his greatest fame, reaching four million viewers. The program used special effects and elaborately designed sets to create the illusion of various aspects of the universe, essentially bringing to life the unknown, from the smallest cell to the immensity of a black hole. A book version followed the series, becoming Sagan's most popular book. William J. O'Malley writing in *America* found that "[Sagan's] ability to explain the complex in terms of the commonplace is mesmerizing; his encyclopedic knowledge is humbling; his articulateness captivates."

Despite the debates surrounding Sagan, he remains one of the most effective popularizers of science in our age. And his popularity has convinced him, he once said, that "the public is a lot brighter and more interested in science than they're given credit for. . . . They're not numskulls. Thinking scientifically is as natural as breathing."

—Anne Boyd

SALINGER, J(erome) D(avid)

Nationality: American. **Born:** New York City, 1 January 1919. Has lived in New Hampshire since 1953. **Education:** McBurney School, New York, 1932-34; Valley Forge Military Academy, Pennsylvania (editor, *Crossed Sabres*), 1934-36; New York University, 1937; Ursinus College, Collegetown, Pennsylvania, 1938; Columbia University, New York, 1939. **Military Service:** Served in the 4th Infantry Division of the United States Army, 1942-45: Staff Sergeant. **Family:** Married 1) Sylvia Salinger in 1945 (divorced 1946); 2) Claire Douglas in 1955 (divorced 1967), one daughter and one son. **Agent:** Dorothy Olding, Harold Ober Associates, 425 Madison Avenue, New York, New York 10017, U.S.A.

Publications

Novel

The Catcher in the Rye. Boston, Little Brown, and London, Hamish Hamilton, 1951.

Short Stories

Nine Stories. Boston, Little Brown, 1953; as *For Esmé—With Love and Squalor and Other Stories,* London, Hamish Hamilton, 1953.

Franny and Zooey. Boston, Little Brown, 1961; London, Heinemann, 1962.

Raise High the Roof Beam, Carpenters, and Seymour: An Introduction. Boston, Little Brown, and London, Heinemann, 1963.

Uncollected Short Stories

"The Young Folks," in *Story* (New York), March-April 1940.

"The Hang of It," in *Collier's* (Springfield, Ohio), 12 July 1941.

"The Heart of a Broken Story," in *Esquire* (New York), September 1941.

"Personal Notes on an Infantryman," in *Collier's* (Springfield, Ohio), 12 December 1942.

"The Varioni Brothers," in *Saturday Evening Post* (Philadelphia), 17 July 1943.

"Both Parties Concerned," in *Saturday Evening Post* (Philadelphia), 26 February 1944.

"Soft-Boiled Sergeant," in *Saturday Evening Post* (Philadelphia), 15 April 1944.

"Last Day of the Last Furlough," in *Saturday Evening Post* (Philadelphia), 15 July 1944.

"Once a Week Won't Kill You," in *Story* (New York), November-December 1944.

"A Boy in France," in *The Saturday Evening Post Stories 1942-45,* edited by Ben Hibbs. New York, Random House, 1945.

"Elaine," in *Story* (New York), March-April 1945.

"The Stranger," in *Collier's* (Springfield, Ohio), 1 December 1945.

"I'm Crazy," in *Collier's* (Springfield, Ohio), 22 December 1945.

"Slight Rebellion Off Madison," in *New Yorker,* 21 December 1946.

"A Young Girl in 1941 with No Waist at All," in *Mademoiselle* (New York), May 1947.

"The Inverted Forest," in *Cosmopolitan* (New York), December 1947.

"Blue Melody," in *Cosmopolitan* (New York), September 1948.

"The Long Debut of Lois Taggett," in *Story: The Fiction of the Forties,* edited by Whit and Hallie Burnett. New York, Dutton, 1949.

"A Girl I Knew," in *The Best American Short Stories 1949,* edited by Martha Foley. Boston, Houghton Mifflin, 1949.

"This Sandwich Has No Mayonnaise," in *The Armchair Esquire,* edited by Arnold Gingrich and L. Rust Hills. New York, Putnam, 1958.

"Hapworth 16, 1924," in *New Yorker,* 19 June 1965.

"Go See Eddie," in *Fiction: Form and Experience,* edited by William M. Jones. Lexington, Massachusetts, Heath, 1969.

*

Bibliography: *J.D. Salinger: A Thirty Year Bibliography 1938-1968* by Kenneth Starosciak, privately printed, 1971; *J.D. Salinger: An Annotated Bibliography 1938-1981* by Jack R. Sublette, New York, Garland, 1984.

Critical Studies (selection): *The Fiction of J.D. Salinger* by Frederick L. Gwynn and Joseph L. Blotner, Pittsburgh, University of Pittsburgh Press, 1958, London, Spearman, 1960; *Salinger: A Critical and Personal Portrait* edited by Henry Anatole Grunwald, New York, Harper, 1962, London, Owen, 1964; *J.D. Salinger and the Critics* edited by William F. Belcher and James W. Lee, Belmont, California, Wadsworth, 1962; *J.D. Salinger* by Warren French, New York, Twayne, 1963, revised edition, 1976, revised edition, as *J.D. Salinger Revisited,* 1988; *Studies in J.D. Salinger* edited by Marvin Laser and Norman Fruman, New York, Odyssey Press, 1963; *J.D. Salinger* by James E. Miller, Jr., Minneapolis, University of Minnesota Press, 1965; *J.D. Salinger: A Critical Essay* by Kenneth Hamilton, Grand Rapids, Michigan, Eerdmans, 1967; *Zen in the Art of J.D. Salinger* by Gerald Rosen, Berkeley, California, Creative Arts, 1977; *J.D. Salinger* by James Lundquist, New York, Ungar, 1979; *Salinger's Glass Stories as a Composite Novel* by Eberhard Alsen, Troy, New York, Whitston, 1984; *In Search of J.D. Salinger* by Ian Hamilton, London, Heinemann, and New York, Random House, 1988; *Brodie's Notes on J.D. Salinger's The Catcher in the Rye,* by Catherine Madinaveitia, London, Pan, 1987; *Critical Essays on Salinger's The Catcher in the Rye* edited by Joel Salzberg, Boston, Hall, 1990; *Holden Caulfield* edited by Harold Bloom, New York, Chelsea House, 1990; *Alienation in the Fiction of Carson McCullers, J.D. Salinger, and James Purdy* by Anil Kumar, Amritsar, Guru Nanak Dev University Press, 1991; *J.D. Salinger: A Study of the Short Fiction* by John Wenke, Boston, Twayne, 1991; *New Essays on The Catcher in the Rye* by Jack Salzman, Cambridge, Cambridge University Press, 1991; *The Catcher in the Rye: Innocence Under Pressure* by Sanford Pinsker, New York, Twayne, 1993.

* * *

J. D. Salinger has published only one novel, *The Catcher in the Rye* (1951), and a few volumes of short stories. Yet even with such a limited output, he has become not only a spokesman for several generations of dissaffected youth, but also one of the most significant and often-discussed figures in modern American literature.

Salinger's achievement, throughout his oeuvre, lies in the skillful expression of the increasing sense of alienation felt by young people in post-World War II America as they reluctantly faced an ominous future of enforced and thoroughly superficial conventionality. One of the most powerful and controversial aspects of this depiction is Salinger's use of colloquial speech—including what many regard as obscenity—to create convincing, accessible protagonists who voice their concerns in a way many can understand.

The Catcher in the Rye is an intimate examination of basic human issues such as honesty, love, and religion, within Salinger's larger theme of alienation. Salinger's characters are often forced to react to—accept, rebel against, or withdraw from—a less-than-perfect society. The novel tells the story of a sensitive 16-year-old named Holden Caufield who gets kicked out of prep school. Caufield detests "phonies" and is quick to expose gestures that reveal them. In the course of the book he spends two days in New York City killing time, observing, and seeking direction. Phoebe, his little sister, gives direct and sensible advice, while his favorite teacher, in contrast, is drunk when Caufield goes to talk with him. Caufield actually grows toward adulthood, although in a painfully sensitive way. The book is filled with examples of how the honesty of childhood is tainted by the realities of adult life, and the chief appeal of the novel is its honest, though tortured, expression of Caulfield's angst.

Nine Stories (1953) is a collection of short pieces that range from the desperate to the sublime, as evidenced by three examples. In "A Perfect Day for Bananafish," Seymour Glass has an easier time talking to a little girl on the beach than to his socially acceptable wife. As with most of Salinger's works, the ending leaves much for the reader to decide. "For Esme with Love and Squalor" is the beautiful story of a young, precocious English girl whose father was "s-l-a-i-n" in Africa—she spells the word for the benefit of her younger brother. The story demonstrates how her act of selfless caring helps restore the "f-a-c-u-l-t-i-e-s" of an American soldier whose nerves were shattered in battle. Finally, "Teddy" deals with a boy genius who embraces mysticism. He accepts things as they are, showing a Zen influence to which Salinger refers at the beginning of the book.

Franny and Zooey (1961) details the lives of the Glass family and its search for honesty. As with Holden Caufield, these characters can't abide pretentious, plastic characters who seem to be everywhere. They keep searching for truth, both in ideas and in people. The character Franny, for example, collapses in the lady's room of a restaurant because she can't tolerate her superficial boyfriend. Zooey reassures her that there is good in everyone, and posits that searching for honesty and accepting others is the solution.

In *Raise High the Roof Beam, Carpenters and Seymour: An Introduction* (1963), Salinger has Seymour Glass too "keyed up" to show up for his own wedding. Seymour is convinced that there is a plot to make him happy. He sees things differently than most people. While characters such as Holden Caufield seem to speak the truth for many of us, Seymour follows his own truth. To Salinger, this makes him a hero; a larger-than-life character who simply prefers honest innocence to the compromises of adult life.

Salinger was among the first writers to expose the seamy underside of the American dream in the 1950s; his works were immediately popular and their popularity grew along with the rise of the counterculture throughout the late 1950s and 1960s. Despite his own dogged silence—he has refused to comment on his works and has not published a book since 1963—Salinger has been called one of the most influential writers since World War II, and an ever-increasing legion of fans has come to trust his honest observations.

—Liz Mulligan

SANDERS, Lawrence

Pseudonym: Lesley Andress. **Nationality:** American. **Born:** Brooklyn, New York, 1920. **Education:** Wabash College. Crawfordsville, Indiana, B.A. 1940. **Military Service:** Served in the U.S. Marine Corps, 1943-46: Sergeant. **Career:** Staff member, Macy's department store, New York, 1940-43; journalist: staff member, *Mechanix Illustrated;* editor, *Science and Mechanics.*

Awards: Mystery Writers of America Edgar Allan Poe award, 1970. **Address:** c/o G.P. Putnam's Sons, 200 Madison Avenue, New York, New York 10016, U.S.A.

Publications

Novels (series: Timothy Cone; Edward X. Delaney; Peter Tangent; Archy McNally)

The Anderson Tapes. New York, Putnam, and London, W.H. Allen, 1970.
The Pleasures of Helen. New York, Putnam, 1971.
Love Songs. New York, Putnam, 1972.
The First Deadly Sin (Delaney). New York, Putnam, 1973; London, W.H. Allen, 1974.
The Tomorrow File. New York, Putnam, 1975; London, Corgi, 1977.
The Tangent Objective. New York, Putnam, 1976; London, Hart Davis, 1977.
The Marlow Chronicles. New York, Putnam, 1977; Loughton, Essex, Piatkus, 1979.
The Second Deadly Sin (Delaney). New York, Putnam, 1977; London, Hart Davis, 1978.
The Tangent Factor. New York, Putnam, and London, Hart Davis, 1978.
The Sixth Commandment. New York, Putnam, and London, Granada, 1979.
Caper (as Lesley Andress). New York, Putnam, and London, Granada, 1980.
The Tenth Commandment. New York, Putnam, 1980; London, Granada, 1981.
The Third Deadly Sin (Delaney). New York, Putnam, and London, Granada, 1981.
The Case of Lucy Bending. New York, Putnam, 1982; London, New English Library, 1983.
The Seduction of Peter S. New York, Putnam, 1983; London, New English Library, 1984.
The Passion of Molly T. New York, Putnam, 1984; London, New English Library, 1985.
The Fourth Deadly Sin (Delaney). New York, Putnam, and London, New English Library, 1985.
The Loves of Harry Dancer. New York, Berkley, 1986; as *The Loves of Harry D,* London, New English Library, 1986.
The Eighth Commandment. New York, Putnam, and London, New English Library, 1986.
Tales of the Wolf. New York, Avon, 1986; London, Severn House, 1988.
The Dream Lover. New York, Berkley, 1987.
The Timothy Files (Cone). New York, Putnam, 1987; London, New English Library, 1988.
Timothy's Game (Cone). New York, Putnam, and London, New English Library, 1988.
Capital Crimes. New York, Putnam, and London, New English Library, 1989.
Stolen Blessings. New York, Berkley, 1989; London, New English Library, 1990.
Sullivan's Sting. New York, Putnam, and London, New English Library, 1990.
The Seventh Commandment. 1991.
McNally's Secret. New York, Putnam, 1992.
McNally's Luck. New York, Putnam, 1992.
McNally's Risk. New York, Putnam, 1993.
McNally's Caper. New York, Putnam, 1994.
Private Pleasures. 1994.
McNally's Trial. New York, Putnam, 1995.
McNally's Puzzle. New York, Putnam, 1996.

Other

Handbook of Creative Crafts, with Richard Carol. New York, Pyramid, 1968.

Editor, *Thus Be Loved: A Book for Lovers.* New York, Arco, 1966.

*

Media Adaptations: Films—*The Anderson Tapes,* 1972, from the novel; *The First Deadly Sin,* 1980, from the novel.

* * *

Lawrence Sanders has been characterized as a pulp-fiction writer who has captivated his audience by successfully mastering his genre. He began his writing career as an editor of war stories, men's adventure stories, and detective stories for several magazines. He was a feature editor for *Mechanix Illustrated* and an editor for *Science and Mechanics* in New York before becoming a novelist in 1969. Sanders, who has written under a variety of pseudonyms, admits he lives the life of a Walter Mitty; he has no hobbies, does not drive, and is completely obsessed with writing.

Sanders's success came with the publication of his first novel, *The Anderson Tapes* (1970). Electronic surveillance played a big part in the storyline, a fact which is both ironic and prophetic considering that the Watergate scandal was about to rock the nation. America found it fascinating that governmental agencies could wiretap anyone anywhere. Sanders won the Edgar Allen Poe Award for the best first mystery novel, and *Tapes* was pronounced a bestseller upon publication and later made into a movie by Columbia Pictures.

Sanders also gained recognition for his Deadly Sin series of novels. The main character is Edward X. Delaney, a New York City police detective with a good reputation. Delaney is a well-rounded character; we see him at work, but also in the warmly explored relationship between him and his wife. In the Deadly Sin series Delaney finds himself hunting human animals who commit gruesome murders and act in sexually deviant ways. Some critics have faulted Sanders with delivering to his audience too much sensationalism, but if the reader looks beyond the written text they will find a great paradox; in trying to balance his psyche, Delaney is forced to juggle his work and the nightmares it entails with his passion towards his wife and concern for her well-being.

In *The Tangent Objective* (1976) and *The Tangent Factor* (1978), Sanders takes a risk and jumps into the world of international politics. Again he captures the imagination and piques the curiosity of his audience, first by inventing a West African Nation and then by developing two evil protagonists. An American businessman with no morals and an African leader manipulate the fictitious African nation's government for their own powerful and financial interests. Sanders uses violence and treachery to create two novels that are tightly composed, quick, exciting reads.

Sanders has said that he learned his trade as a novelist by editing the work of pulp magazines and realizing that he could write just as well or better. At age 50 he decided to go out and do it.

—Tammy J. Bronson

SAUL, John

Nationality: American. **Born:** 25 February 1942, in Pasadena, California. **Education:** Antioch College, 1959-60; Montana State University, 1961-62; and San Francisco State College, 1963-65. **Career:** Writer. Spent several years traveling about the United States, writing and supporting himself by odd jobs; worked for a drug and alcohol program in Seattle, Washington; director of Tellurian Communities, Inc., 1976-78, member of board of Governors; Seattle Theater Arts, Seattle, director, 1978-80. Vice-president of Chester Woodruff Foundation. **Agent:** Jane Rotrosen, 318 East 51st St., New York, New York 10022, U.S.A.

Publications

Novels

Suffer the Children. New York, Dell, 1977.
Punish the Sinners. New York, Dell, 1978.
Cry for the Strangers. New York, Dell, 1979.
Comes the Blind Fury. New York, Dell, 1980.
When the Wind Blows. New York, Dell, 1981.
The God Project. New York, Bantam, 1982.
Nathaniel. New York, Bantam, 1984.
Brainchild. New York, Bantam, 1985.
Hellfire. New York, Bantam, 1986.
The Unwanted. New York, Bantam, 1987.
The Unloved. New York, Bantam, 1988.
The Fear Factor. New York, Bantam, 1988.
Creature. New York, Bantam, 1989.
Sleepwalk. New York, Bantam, 1990.
Second Child. New York, Bantam, 1990.
Darkness. New York, Bantam, 1991.
Shadows. New York, Bantam, 1992.
Guardian. New York, Fawcett, 1994.
The Homing. New York, Fawcett, 1994.
Black Lightning. New York, Fawcett, 1995.

* * *

Since publishing his first novel, *Suffer the Children* (1977), an immediate million-copy bestseller that he wrote in a single month, John Saul has written a new novel each year with such horror-oriented titles as *Punish the Sinners* (1978), *Comes the Blind Fury* (1980), *Hellfire* (1986), *Creature* (1989), *Darkness* (1991), *Shadows* (1992) and *Black Lightning* (1995). In most of these he relies on a typically formulaic gothic plot that involves an isolated setting—an old New England town, a decaying Southern mansion, a Louisiana swamp, an Idaho ranch—several adolescent characters (both victims and victimizers and often members of dysfunctional families), and the return of a ghost from some violent past who seeks revenge in the present. He also creates a tantalizing ambiguity in his fiction that often lingers beyond the conclusion of the plot, suggesting that the presence of a ghost may be real or it might also be the projection of some psychic disturbance in one of the characters. In some cases these two possibilities overlap, adding to the layered intensity of his novels.

Several of his books begin with violent prologues—nightmarish visions or memories of murder, assault, flight—that set the scene and the pattern of revenge in motion. With *The God Project* (1982), his sixth book and the first novel published in hard back, Saul entered the realm of "techno-thrillers," complete with secret government projects, deadly scientific experiments that go wrong, evil doctors and brain surgeons, and his own contemporary social commentary about such phenomena. *Creature* (1989), for instance, involves steroid abuse with a Dr. Frankenstein character, an isolated town in Colorado, and a satiric look at the American obsession with high school football heroes. *Brainchild* (1985) combines both the ghost's-revenge plot and a futuristic tale of brain damage, recovery, and murder. Later novels, such as *The Homing* (1994) and *Guardian* (1993), have focused on deadly swarms of bees and strange transformations between humans and animals.

An earlier work, *Nathaniel* (1984), reveals Saul at his best. A curse haunts the ominously isolated landscape of Prairie Bend where the several descendents of Abby Randolph have either been killed as babies or are born dead. The ghost of Nathaniel, her son who killed her with a pitchfork after she may or may not have boiled her other children alive in order to eat during a terrible winter in 1884, may still inhabit the deserted barns in the area, eager to kill newborns. When the recently widowed Janet Hall and her son Michael move in with her in-laws, the autocratic Amos, and the wheelchair-ridden Anna, family tensions awaken past horrors. The plot keeps you turning pages.

Saul has admitted that his favorite book is *Sleepwalk* (1990) because of his interest in certain social and environmental issues. Futuristic technology is represented by microtransmitters planted in the bloodstreams of the people in Borrego, New Mexico, which can either control or kill them. The plot focuses on the teenaged hero, Jed Arnold (a half-breed), his Native American grandfather, Brown Eagle, and Rakantoh, a legendary eagle and totem of Brown Eagle's clan who has been deprived of his home by the lake created by the new dam near a collapsing oil refinery. All of this culminates in the dam's collapse and the resulting doom of the oil villains who are swept away in the catastrophe.

Critics have continually upbraided Saul for his formulaic plots, reliance on children as victims and perpetrators, and often-colorless dialogue. Saul, however, has cannily used that formula to shape his own swift twists of breathless plotting in a crisp clean style. He is also very adept at describing the psychic growing pains, wounds, and grievances of his younger characters. He is delighted by the fact that many of his younger readers find his work particularly attractive and that he has introduced millions of them to reading, according to school librarians. Why do his horror stories sell so well? "You see," he has said, "I'm a natural coward. I think that's why I can write a scary book." Despite his lack of critical success, Saul's gothic tales continue to sell millions of copies on an annual basis and he continues to "find horror in the commonplace" in the next work-in-progress.

—Samuel Coale

SCHOLEFIELD, Edmond O. *See* **BUTTERWORTH, W. E.**

SCOTLAND, Jay. *See* **JAKES, John.**

SEBASTIAN, Lee. *See* **SILVERBERG, Robert.**

SEGAL, Erich (Wolf)

Nationality: American. **Born:** 16 June 1937, in Brooklyn, New York. **Education:** Harvard University, A.B., 1958, A.M., 1959, Ph.D., 1965. **Family:** Married Karen Llona Marianne James in 1975; children: Francesca. **Career:** Yale University, visiting lecturer, 1964-65, assistant professor, 1965-68, associate professor of classics and comparative literature, 1968-72, adjunct professor of classics since 1981. Visiting professor at University of Munich, 1973, Princeton University, 1974-75, Tel Aviv University, spring, 1976, and Dartmouth College, fall, 1976, and 1977; visiting fellow, Wolfson College, Oxford University, 1978, 1979, 1981, and 1986; honorary research fellow, University College, University of London, 1983. Member of National Advisory Council of Peace Corps, 1970; jury member, Cannes Film Festival, 1971, and National Book award for Arts and Letters, 1971. Sports commentator at Olympic Games, for American Broadcasting Companies, Inc. (ABC-TV), 1972, and 1976, and during pre-Olympic coverage, for National Broadcasting Company, Inc. (NBC-TV), 1980; French-language radio commentator at Olympic Games for RT-Radio (Paris, France), 1972, and 1976; occasional commentator on NBC-TV's "Sports World" and ABC-TV's "Wide World of Sports." **Awards:** Guggenheim fellowship, 1968; Golden Globe award for screenplay, Hollywood Foreign Press Association, 1971, for *Love Story*; Presidential commendation, 1972, for service to the Peace Corps; Humboldt Stiftung award (West Germany), 1973; Premio Bancarella (Italy) and Prix Deauville (France), both 1986, for *The Class.* **Agent:** Ed Victor Ltd., 162 Wardour St., London W1V 4AB, England. **Address:** c/o Lazarow, Rm. 1106, 119 West 57th St., New York, New York 10019, U.S.A.

Publications

Novels

Love Story. Harper, 1970.
Oliver's Story. Harper, 1977.
Man, Woman and Child. Harper, 1980.
The Class. Bantam, 1985.
Doctors. Bantam, 1987.
Acts of Faith. Bantam, 1992.
Prizes. Ivy Books, 1996.

Plays

Screenplays: *Yellow Submarine,* with others, 1968; *Love Story,* adapted from his own novel, 1970; *The Games,* 1970; *R.P.M.,* 1970; *Jennifer on My Mind,* 1971; *Oliver's Story,* adapted from his own novel, with John Korty, 1978; *A Change of Seasons,* 1981; *Man, Woman and Child,* adapted from his own novel, with David Z. Goodman, 1983.

Fiction for Children

Fairy Tale. Harper, 1973.

Nonfiction

Roman Laughter: The Comedy of Plautus. Harvard University Press, 1968, revised and expanded edition, Oxford University Press, 1987.

Editor, *Euripides: A Collection of Critical Essays.* Prentice-Hall, 1968.
Editor and translator, *Plautus: Three Comedies.* Harper, 1969; revised edition, Bantam, 1985.
Editor, *Scholarship on Plautus,* 1965-1976, Classical World Surveys, 1981.
Editor, with Fergus Millar, *Caesar Augustus: Seven Essays.* Clarendon Press, 1984.
Editor, *Greek Tragedy: Modern Essays in Criticism.* Harper, 1983; as *Oxford Readings in Greek Tragedy,* Oxford University Press, 1983.
Editor, *Plato's Dialogues.* Bantam, 1986.
Editor, *Oxford Readings in Aristophanes.* Oxford University Press, 1996.

*

Film Adaptations: *Love Story,* 1970; *Oliver's Story,* 1978; *Consenting Adults,* adapted from his story "Frost on the Apples," written with Martin Ransohoff, 1979.

* * *

Erich Segal has known the ups and downs of the writing life. Before he was a popular novelist he was a professor of classics and comparative literature at Yale. Despite having proved himself a scholar, Segal often has been criticized for his unintellectual writing style. For example, Laura Shapiro in *Newsweek* called Segal "the most successful translator of Plato and Plautus who ever wrote junk fiction."

Love Story is a short, poignant novel set against the backdrop of an Ivy League campus. A wealthy Harvard student-athlete, Oliver Barrett IV, falls in love with Jenny Cavilleri, a poor but spirited young woman. Oliver decides to marry Jenny against the wishes of his domineering father, who cuts Oliver out of the family. The novel features a heartbreaking ending that has left millions of readers teary-eyed and made Segal a literary celebrity.

Critics were divided over the merits of *Love Story.* S. A. Haffner in *Library Journal* called it "a very professionally crafted short first novel . . . it is funny and sad and generally recommended." Other critics, like S. K. Oberbeck in *Newsweek*, thought the story was too predictable, skipping "from cliche to cliche with abandon." Segal recognized the criticism and played it up, telling Oberbeck: "Everyone is tired of being shocked. We're on the threshold of a new romanticism, a sentimental age." Segal's writing had perfect timing. Nora Ephron, in *Esquire*, wrote that the book's success was "something of a mystery . . . it makes readers cry . . . it encourages people to believe the world has not changed. . . . And, yes, it has come at a time when young people are returning to earlier ways."

Segal followed *Love Story* in 1977 with *Oliver's Story*, another short, sentimental novel which continues in the sad life of Oliver Barrett IV. It was also a bestseller, and it too was coolly received by critics. In 1980 Segal published *Man, Woman, and Child*, the story of a Boston professor whose marriage and family is drastically changed by the news that he has a son from a long-forgotten affair. Undaunted by criticism, Segal next turned his efforts to writing long, epic novels, which continued to make the bestseller lists. *The Class* (1985) chronicles the lives of five members of the Harvard class of 1958. Susan Isaacs in the *New York Times* called Segal "a good enough storyteller that, despite the dead language, the reader still wants to find out what happens to his characters." *Doctors* (1987) is another long saga, this time centered around the lives of five doctors, all members of the Harvard Medical School class of 1962. It reached the top of the *New York Times* bestseller list, but critics continued to assault Segal's work. Joanne Kaufman in *People* wrote that the book "is 674 pages long, boring, banal, bloated, and badly written. . . . Segal seems to believe that assigning characteristics is creating characters."

In 1992 Segal published *Acts of Faith*, which the jacket cover declares to be "master storyteller Erich Segal's most moving and ambitious work to date." This time Segal focuses his attention on the subject of religion. Tim Hogan is an Irish Catholic tough guy, and Daniel and Deborah Luria are a brother and sister from an old Orthodox Jewish family. These lives and religions intersect when Deborah and Tim fall madly in love, and ultimately each character must either defy their religion (or make an "act of faith"). The book raises some interesting questions, including some related to sexuality and gender issues within religions. In fact, controversy surrounded the book when several Catholic newspapers refused to run its advertisements. Critics generally found the book to be less dangerous; John Ottenhoff wrote in *Library Journal* that, "promising as his themes may be, Segal . . . fails to deliver anything more than formula fiction." Likewise, Kaufman criticized the book for being "protracted, predictable, and pretentious."

Segal has taught at Harvard, Yale, Princeton, and Oxford, and occasionally publishes scholarly work. He has won literary prizes in France and Italy, and has even worked as a network sports commentator during the Olympic Games. He continues to enjoy a successful and varied career.

—Doug Dupler

SHAW, Irwin

Nationality: American. **Born:** 27 February 1913, in New York City. **Education:** Brooklyn College, B.A., 1934. **Military Service:** U.S. Army, 1942-45; became warrant officer. **Family:** Married Marian Edwards in 1939 (divorced, 1970); remarried, 1982; children: Adam. **Career:** Novelist and playwright. Script writer for the "Andy Gump" and "Dick Tracy" radio shows, 1934-36; *New Republic*, Washington, D.C., drama critic, 1947-48; New York University, instructor in creative writing, 1947-48. **Awards:** O. Henry awards, 1944, for "Walking Wounded" (first prize), and 1945, for "Gunner's Passage" (second prize); National Institute of Arts and Letters grant, 1946; *Playboy* award, 1964, 1970, and 1979; Brooklyn College, honorary doctorate. **Died:** 16 May 1984, in Davos, Switzerland.

Publications

Novels

The Young Lions. Random House, 1948.
The Troubled Air. Random House, 1950.
Lucy Crown. Random House, 1956.
Two Weeks in Another Town. Random House, 1960.
Voices of a Summer Day. Delacorte, 1965.
Rich Man, Poor Man. Delacorte, 1970.
Evening in Byzantium. Delacorte, 1973.
Nightwork. Delacorte, 1975.
Beggarman. Thief, Delacorte, 1977.
The Top of the Hill. Delacorte, 1979.
Bread upon the Waters. Delacorte, 1981.
Acceptable Losses. Arbor House, 1982.

Plays

Bury the Dead (produced New York, 1936). Random House, 1936.
Siege (produced New York, 1937).
The Gentle People: A Brooklyn Fable (produced New York and London, 1939). Random House, 1939.
Quiet City (produced New York, 1939).
Retreat to Pleasure (produced New York, 1940).
Sons and Soldiers (produced New York, 1943). Random House, 1944.
The Assassin (produced New York and London, 1945). Random House, 1946.
The Survivors, with Peter Viertel (produced New York, 1948).
Children from Their Games (produced New York, 1963).

Screenplays: *The Big Game*, 1936; *Commandos Strike at Dawn*, 1942; *The Hard Way*, with Daniel Fuchs and Jerry Wald, 1942; *Talk of the Town*, with Sidney Buchman, 1942; *Easy Living*, with Charles Schnee, 1949; *Take One False Step*, with Chester Erskine and David Shaw, 1949; *I Want You*, 1951; *Act of Love*, 1953; *Ulysses*, with others, 1955; *Fire Down Below*, 1957; *Desire under the Elms*, 1958; *This Angry Agė*, with Rene Clement, 1958; *The Big Gamble*, 1961; *In the French Style*, 1963; *Survival 1967*, 1968. Teleplay: *The Top of the Hill*, adapted from his own novel, 1980.

Short Stories

Sailor Off the Bremen and Other Stories. Random House, 1939.
Welcome to the City and Other Stories. Random House, 1942.
Act of Faith and Other Stories. Random House, 1946.

Mixed Company: Collected Short Stories. Random House, 1950.
Tip on a Dead Jockey and Other Stories. Random House, 1957.
Selected Short Stories. Modern Library, 1961.
In the French Style. MacFadden, 1963.
Love on a Dark Street and Other Stories. Delacorte, 1965.
Short Stories. Random House, 1966.
Retreat and Other Stories. New English Library, 1970.
Whispers in Bedlam: Three Novellas. Weidenfeld & Nicolson, 1972.
God Was Here, But He Left Early. Arbor House, 1973.
Short Stories: Five Decades. Delacorte, 1978.

Nonfiction

Report on Israel. Simon & Schuster, 1950.
In the Company of Dolphins. Geis, 1964.
Paris! Paris!. Harcourt, 1977.
Paris/Magnum: Photographs, 1935-1981. Harper, 1981.

* * *

By the time he passed away in 1984, Irwin Shaw had become a respected writer. He established himself as a serious writer early on; Richard Schickel noted that "his first play, *Bury the Dead* (1936), was an emblematic work of social-protest theater in the 1930s. His lyrically realistic *New Yorker* stories in the same era . . . made it look easy—almost fun—to be so good . . . they became inspiring, formative experiences for several generations of writers."

Shaw catapulted to worldwide fame with the publication of *The Young Lions* (1948). This ambitious, epic novel remains one of the best works to come out of the WWII era. The book follows the lives of three soldiers in the war (two Americans and a German), and provides a realistic and panoramic view of the European struggle. Shaw spent most of the war in Europe, where he served on a documentary film unit. His position enabled him to rub shoulders with the powerful and famous, and to see the war close-up, which makes *The Young Lions* such an exciting, authentic work. The book sold millions of copies and Shaw began to concentrate his efforts on writing other big, epic novels.

Shaw's monetary success enabled him to live a life as epic as his work. He remained in Europe most of his life, living in Paris, the Riviera, Swiss resorts, and other exotic locations. His novels often feature similar ritzy locales, and sometimes portray wealthy, jet-setting characters. Many of Shaw's critics have observed that the effort Shaw put into living the good life and writing commercial fiction might have hurt his literary reputation. As Schickel wrote, "Preoccupied by productivity and the demands of his lifestyle, he had no time left to develop the guiding vision of self and world a major novelist needs."

Rich Man, Poor Man, published in 1970, was Shaw's most commercially successful novel. It sold nearly seven million copies and inspired a television miniseries. It is a huge, sprawling saga, featuring a cornucopia of characters centered around the rags-to-riches story of an American family, the Jordaches. Over the next nine years, Shaw wrote six more novels, all of them plotted, entertaining, bestselling reads. *Evening in Byzantium* (1973) features a once-famous Hollywood producer who goes to Cannes to test his screenplay. He has a romance there, and looks wistfully upon his passing life. *Nightwork* (1975) is about a night clerk in a seedy New York hotel who finds a dead body and $100,000, and runs off to underworld adventures in Europe. Schickel called the book "very intelligent entertainment." *Beggerman, Thief* (1977) is the sequel to *Rich Man, Poor Man,* while *The Top of the Hill* (1979) features a young man who quits his successful life in the city and risks it all by pursuing dangerous outdoor sports. Eventually, in the mountains, the young man confronts himself and his past life.

Critics generally agreed that Shaw was a masterful storyteller, and that his epics could portray a rich spectrum of the human experience. Mark Goodman in *Time* wrote that Shaw had the "ability to create a bestseller with moral resonance." But many critics also felt that Shaw never lived up to his considerable literary talents, as he only seemed to write for popular acceptance. John Leggett, in the *Saturday Review,* wrote that Shaw should have been "confirmed as one of our great writers," but concluded that it was his "agonizing duty to report that *Rich Man, Poor Man* does not redeem his long-standing promise." Shaw reacted to the growing criticism, once telling the *New York Times*: "I cringe when critics say . . . I'm just a popular writer, but so were Tolstoy, Dickens, and Balzac."

—Doug Dupler

SHEEHY, Gail

Nationality: American. **Born:** Gail Henion in Mamaroneck, New York, 25 November 1936. **Education:** University of Vermont, B.S., 1958; Columbia University, graduate study, 1970. **Family:** Married Albert Sheehy in 1960 (divorced, 1968); one daughter, one foster daughter. **Career:** Democrat and Chronicle, Rochester, New York, fashion editor, 1961-63; New York Herald Tribune, New York City, feature writer, 1963-66; *New York* magazine, New York City, contributing editor, 1968-77; free-lance writer. Has worked as a traveling home economist. **Awards:** Front Page award from Newswomen's Club of New York, 1964, for most distinguished feature of interest to women, and 1973, for best magazine feature; National Magazine award, 1972, for reporting excellence; Alicia Patterson Foundation fellowship, 1974. **Agent:** Paul R. Reynolds Inc., 12 East 41st St., New York, New York 10017. **Address:** c/o William Morrow & Co., 105 Madison Ave., New York, New York 10016.

Publications

Novel

Lovesounds. Random House, 1970.

Nonfiction

Panthermania: The Clash of Black against Black in One American City. Harper, 1971.
Speed Is of the Essence. Pocket Books, 1971.
Hustling: Prostitution in Our Wide Open Society. Delacorte, 1973.
Passages: Predictable Crises of Adult Life. Dutton, 1976.
Pathfinders. Morrow, 1981.
Spirit of Survival. Morrow, 1986.
Character: America's Search for Leadership. Morrow, 1988.

The Man Who Changed the World: The Lives of Mikhail Gorbachev. HarperCollins, 1990.
The Silent Passage: Menopause. Random House, 1992.
New Passages. Random House, 1995.

* * *

Gail Sheehy first exhibited her writing skill in the novel *Lovesounds* (1970), a story of a needless divorce. There are no major faults in the main characters, a good wife and a good husband who have rewarding careers and love their child. Sheehy demonstrates that there is no perfection; what looks perfect may be unfulfilling and meaningless, making the quest for perfection a senseless goal. The novel is a study of emotions, and of what to do when all goes seemingly right, yet wrong. Critical appraisal of *Lovesounds* varied widely. The book was a precursor to a series of nonfiction works by Sheehy, most of them dealing with the human condition, with subject matter ranging from prostitution and racial strife to menopause, leadership, and Mikhail Gorbachev.

Sheehy's most renowned work is *Passages: Predictable Crises of Adult Life* (1976). She divides life into four stages: "Pulling Up Roots," "The Trying Twenties," "Passage To The Thirties," and "The Deadline Decade: Setting Off on the Mid-life Passage." Sheehy feels that each of us, in order to successfully complete adulthood, must confront the four stages and break through them. It is the understanding of the human element of fear regarding the uncertainties of change and growing old that makes this book a success.

Controversy plagued *Passages* when contributors Daniel Levinson (a Yale Psychologist), Margaret Hennig, and Roger Gould spoke out about the way that Sheehy used their information. Hennig said that she had no complaints, but Gould sued Sheehy and her publisher, Dutton, for plagiarism. Gould eventually walked away with $10,000 and ten percent of the royalties. Despite those setbacks, the book was extremely popular. Roderick MacLeish of the *Washington Post* defended Sheehy and *Passages* and praised the work as a "stunning accomplishment" and a "revelation for the layman as he tries to understand the inevitable movement in his life." Indeed, this seems to be the essence of Sheehy's accomplishment; despite criticism of her methods and her writings from the scientific community, Sheehy has touched millions of readers with her concise explanations and reassuring wisdom.

—Tammy J. Bronson

SHELDON, Sidney

Nationality: American. **Born:** 11 February 1917, in Chicago, Illinois. **Education:** Attended Northwestern University, 1935-36. **Military Service:** U.S. Army Air Forces, 1941. **Family:** Married Jorja Curtright in 1951 (died, 1985); children: Mary Sheldon Dastin. **Career:** Writer. Former script reader for Universal and Twentieth Century-Fox Studios; creator, producer, and writer of television shows, including *The Patty Duke Show, I Dream of Jeannie, Nancy,* and *Hart to Hart.* **Awards:** Academy award ("Oscar") for best original screenplay, Academy of Motion Picture Arts and Sciences, 1948, for *The Bachelor and the Bobby-Soxer*; Screen Writers' Guild award for best musical of the year, 1948, for *Easter Parade,* and 1950, for *Annie Get Your Gun*; Antoinette Perry award ("Tony"), 1959, for *Redhead*; Emmy awards for *I Dream of Jeannie*; Edgar award for best first mystery novel, Mystery Writers of America, and *New York Times* citation for best first mystery novel, both 1970, both for *The Naked Face.* **Member:** Freedom to Read Foundation. **Address:** c/o Press Relations, William Morrow, 1350 Avenue of the Americas, New York, New York 10016, U.S.A.

Publications

Novels

The Naked Face. Morrow, 1970.
The Other Side of Midnight. Morrow, 1974.
A Stranger in the Mirror. Morrow, 1976.
Bloodline. Morrow, 1977.
Rage of Angels. Morrow, 1980.
Master of the Game. Morrow, 1982.
If Tomorrow Comes. Morrow, 1985.
Windmills of the Gods. Morrow, 1987.
The Sands of Time. Morrow, 1988.
Memories of Midnight. Morrow, 1990.
The Doomsday Conspiracy. Morrow, 1991.
The Stars Shine Down. Morrow, 1992.
Nothing Lasts Forever. Morrow, 1994.
Morning, Noon, & Night. Morrow, 1995.

Plays

Jackpot, with Ben Roberts (produced New York, 1944).
Dream with Music, with Roberts and Dorothy Kilgallen (produced New York, 1944).
Alice in Arms, with Ladislaus Bush-Fekete and Mary Helen Fay (produced New York, 1945).
Redhead, with Dorothy and Herbert Fields, and David Shaw (produced New York, 1959).
Roman Candle (produced New York, 1960).

Screenplays: *Borrowed Hero,* with Roberts, 1941; *Dangerous Lady,* with Jack Natteford, 1941; *Gambling Daughters,* with Roberts, 1941; *South of Panama,* with Roberts, 1941; *Fly by Night,* with Roberts, 1942; *She's in the Army,* 1942; *The Carter Case,* with Roberts, 1947; *The Bachelor and the Bobby-Soxer,* 1947; *Easter Parade,* with Albert Hackett and Frances Goodrich, 1948; *Annie Get Your Gun,* 1950; *Nancy Goes to Rio,* 1950; *Rich, Young, and Pretty,* with Dorothy Cooper, 1951; *No Questions Asked,* 1951; *Three Guys Named Mike,* 1951; *Just This Once,* 1952; *Dream Wife,* with Herbert Baker and Alfred L. Levitt, 1953; *Remains to Be Seen,* 1953; *You're Never Too Young,* 1955; *Anything Goes,* 1956; *Pardners,* 1956; *The Buster Keaton Story,* with Robert Smith, 1957; *All in a Night's Work,* 1961; *Jumbo,* 1962; *The Birds and the Bees,* with Preston Sturges, 1965.

*

Media Adaptations: Films—*The Other Side of Midnight,* 1977; *The Naked Face,* 1985. Television miniseries—*Bloodline,* 1982; *Rage of Angels,* 1983; *Master of the Game,* 1984; *If Tomorrow Comes,* 1986; *Windmills of the Gods,* 1988.

Theatrical Activities:
Director: **Films**—*Dream Wife,* 1952; *The Buster Keaton Story,* 1957.

* * *

Before he began writing novels, Sidney Sheldon was a hugely successful television producer and writer of plays and screenplays. He had won an Academy Award in 1948 for the best original screenplay for *The Bachelor and the Bobbysoxer,* for example, and among his successful television shows were *I Dream of Jeannie, The Patty Duke Show,* and *Hart to Hart.* He turned to writing novels at the age of 50 when, he says, he got an idea that simply would not adapt well to the media with which he had been successful. His first novel-writing effort, *The Naked Face* (1970), received the Edgar Award from the Mystery Writers of America and a *New York Times* citation for the best first mystery novel published that year.

The Naked Face didn't sell very well, but Sheldon achieved great commercial success with his second effort, *The Other Side of Midnight* (1974). The book was a runaway bestseller, and since that success virtually all of his books have made the bestseller lists. *The Other Side of Midnight* is about revenge, a recurring theme in Sheldon's books. Sheldon also likes to use intricate plot lines, female protagonists, and surprising plot twists, all of which are used to good effect in *The Other Side of Midnight.* The novel features an Aristotle Onassis-type tycoon, his mistress, her lovers, and a richly woven plot that doesn't reveal its secrets until the very end. All of these elements are typical of Sheldon's work, and all pop up in various combinations throughout his novels.

Sheldon likes to use women as protagonists. A typical Sheldon plot will put a beautiful but bright woman in a situation in which she is brutally and unjustly violated in some way, whether physically, emotionally, or legally. She will fight back, finding unique and satisfying ways of gaining revenge on those who have mistreated her. *Rage of Angels* (1980) uses this format quite successfully. Sheldon may also put a woman who is rich and successful in a position of some jeopardy from forces that are clever and virtually undetectable. *Windmills of the Gods* (1987) puts a woman who is an American ambassador in this situation, and *Bloodline* (1977) uses a very wealthy and quite vulnerable young woman.

In 1990 Sheldon penned *Memories of Midnight,* a sequel to *The Other Side of Midnight.* While the book managed to tie up plot lines from the first, the rule that sequels are seldom as effective as their predecessors definitely came into play here. The book was one of his least effective.

While most critics dismiss Sheldon's work as "potboilers" and "airport novels," he succeeds in telling a fine, well-crafted story. Sheldon's novels are deliberately written to hook the reader. Once begun, the books are hard to put down, and his years as a writer of fast-moving plots for films and television is apparent in his fiction writing; his quick scene changes, interesting characters, and exotic locales are as addictive as salted peanuts.

Furthermore, no one has ever faulted Sheldon's research. For *Master of the Game* (1982) he traveled to South Africa to research diamond mining. For *The Sands of Time* (1988), a story set in Spain and based in the internal strife between the government and the Basque rebels, he studied Cistercian convents to achieve intimate knowledge of the workings of the nuns who observe strict silence. His books read as though he has been to his locations and studied his subjects, which he has.

Sidney Sheldon's books are light reading; after digesting one of his novels, it's hard to remember much about what the story involved. Still, Sheldon accomplishes his chief goal, which is to entertain.

—June Harris

SHEPHERD, Michael. *See* **LUDLUM, Robert.**

SHIELDS, Carol

Nationality: Canadian and American. **Born:** Carol Warner, Oak Park, Illinois, 2 June 1935. **Education:** Hanover College, Indiana, 1953-57, A.B.; University of Ottawa, 1969-75, M.A. **Family:** Married Donald Shields, 1957; four daughters, one son. **Career:** Editorial assistant, *Canadian Slavonic Papers,* 1972-74; faculty member, University of Ottawa, 1976-77, and University of British Columbia, 1978-79. Since 1980, faculty member, University of Manitoba. **Awards:** Canada Council grant, 1972, 1974, 1976; Canadian Authors Association prize, 1976, for *Small Ceremonies;* Governor General's award for fiction, 1993; National Book Critics Circle award, 1994; Pulitzer prize for fiction, 1995. Honorary doctorate: University of Ottawa, 1995. **Agent:** Bella Pomer, 22 Shallmar Blvd., Toronto, Ontario M5N 2Z8, Canada. **Address:** 701-237 Wellington Cr., Winnipeg, Manitoba R3M 0A1, Canada.

Publications

Novels

Small Ceremonies. McGraw Hill Ryerson, 1976.
The Box Garden. McGraw Hill Ryerson, 1977.
Happenstance. McGraw Hill Ryerson, 1980; Fourth Estate, 1993; Viking, 1994.
A Fairly Conventional Woman. Macmillan Canada, 1982; Fourth Estate, 1993; Viking, 1994.
Swann: A Mystery. Stoddart, 1987.
A Celibate Season, with Blanche Howard. Coteau, 1991.
The Republic of Love. Random House Canada, 1992.
The Stone Diaries. Random House Canada, 1993.

Short Stories

Various Miracles. Stoddart, 1985.
The Orange Fish. Random House Canada, 1989.

Plays

Arrivals and Departures. Blizzard, 1990.
Thirteen Hands. Blizzard, 1993.

Poetry

Others. Borealis Press, 1972.
Intersect. Borealis Press, 1974.
Coming to Canada. Carleton University Press, 1992.

Other

Susanna Moodie: Voice and Vision. Borealis Press, 1976.

*

Manuscript Collection: National Library of Canada.

* * *

Carol Shields published her first novel, *Small Ceremonies,* in 1976, and in 1993 was awarded the Pulitzer Prize for her sixth book, *The Stone Diaries.* Her writing is perceptive, witty, and subtle, and every sentence is clear and precise. "I like to work on sentences and make them feel right," she says. "I will tinker with them all day." Yet the result seems effortless, as if Shields is able to transmit reality directly to the page.

This reality is, usually, the domestic life of married couples living in Canadian cities, or the stories of those who are yet to meet and become those couples. Although her novels have been described as "celebrations of the domestic," they resonate with wider implications. In *Happenstance* (1980), for example, the events of the same few days are narrated twice, once from the point of view of Jack, a historian, and once from that of his wife, Brenda, who has become well known for her quilts (described so that their shapes and colors glow on the page). Brenda goes away alone for the first time, to a quiltmakers' symposium, and both husband and wife, who love and still feel sexual desire for each other, must confront the fact that they are, nevertheless, strangers: "I wanted to write about two people who were . . . happily married, but who were, in fact, strangers to each other and always would be, and the value of that strangeness."

Small Ceremonies also charts the lives of a married couple who live together affectionately but whose lives are partly concealed from each other. Judith Gill is a biographer writing about the life of the 19th-century Canadian writer Susannah Moodie (a biography which has actually been written by Shields herself); when she tries to branch out into fiction writing she finds herself involved in the complex ethics of plagiarism and literary ownership. The stability of her married life is threatened by her husband's apparently crazy idea of demonstrating the themes and images of Milton's *Paradise Lost* in a tapestry, which he plans to exhibit at a conference. She fears his humiliation but he is a great success.

Intertextuality, literary research, and the problems of biography are recurrent themes in Shields' work, often presented with a light and humorous touch. In *Swann: A Mystery* (1987), Sarah, an ambitious young academic, is researching the life of Mary Swann, a poet who lived in poverty and obscurity until she was brutally murdered by her husband. Shields is also a poet, and the poems she gives Mary combine the domestic with a bleak despair: "Feet on the winter floor / Beat flowers to blackness / Making a corridor / Named helplessness." Sarah and three other disparate characters become involved in a game of literary detection which is often funny, but which also conveys the brutality of Swann's life and the impossibility of fully reconstructing it.

That "the recounting of a life is a cheat, of course" is also the theme of *The Stone Diaries* (1993), the meticulous and moving story of the fictitious Daisy Flett, nee Stone, whose life spans the century. It is hard to define as either biography or autobiography, as it is written mostly in the third-person but occasionally in the first. It is also hard to believe that it is not "true," especially since Flett provides a full family tree and photographs from a family album, several of which apparently are her own. Daisy is born in 1905 in a Manitoba kitchen to a mother who did not even know she was pregnant, and who dies in childbirth. Well-cared for and apparently successful—in middle age she writes a popular gardening column for a local paper—Daisy goes through life feeling that she lacks a self. In old age she wonders: "What is the story of a life? A chronicle of fact or a skillfully wrought impression? . . . or the adding up of what has been off-handedly revealed, those tiny allotted increments of knowledge?" It is Shields' gift to make us ponder these questions whilst also convincing us of the concrete reality of the lives she narrates, often illuminated, especially in *The Republic of Love* (1992), by the transfiguring power of love.

—Nicola King

SIDDONS, (Sybil) Anne Rivers

Nationality: American. **Born:** 9 January 1936, in Atlanta, Georgia. **Education:** Auburn University, B.A.A., 1958; attended Atlanta School of Art, c. 1958. **Family:** Married Heyward L. Siddons in 1966; children: (stepsons) Lee, Kemble, Rick, David. **Career:** Worked in advertising with Retail Credit Co., c. 1959, Citizens & Southern National Bank, 1961-63, Burke-Dowling Adams, 1967-69, and Burton Campbell Advertising, 1969-74; full-time writer since 1974. Senior editor, *Atlanta* magazine. Member of governing board, Woodward Academy; member of publications board and arts and sciences honorary council, Auburn University, 1978-83. **Awards:** Alumna achievement award in arts and humanities, Auburn University, 1985. **Address:** 3767 Vermont Rd. N.E., Atlanta, Georgia 30319; and (summer) Haven Colony, Brooklin, Maine 04616, U.S.A.

PUBLICATIONS

Nonfiction

John Chancellor Makes Me Cry. Doubleday, 1975.
Go Straight on Peachtree. Dolphin Books, 1978.

Novels

Heartbreak Hotel. Simon & Schuster, 1976.
The House Next Door. Simon & Schuster, 1978.
Fox's Earth. Simon & Schuster, 1980.
Homeplace. Harper, 1987.
Peachtree Road. Harper, 1988.
King's Oak, HarperCollins, 1990.
Outer Banks. HarperCollins, 1991.
Colony. HarperCollins, 1992.

Hill Towns. HarperCollins, 1993.
Downtown. HarperCollins, 1994.
Fault Lines. HarperCollins, 1995.

*

Film Adaptation: *Heart of Dixie,* adapted from her novel *Heartbreak Hotel,* 1989.

* * *

In *John Chancellor Makes Me Cry* (1975), Anne Rivers Siddons relates the every day choices of her life in Atlanta, a southern setting she knows intimately and recreates often in her fiction. The memoir's humor is often compared to that of Erma Bombeck, who called Siddons "unique" and "original in her essays." Chancellor's name in the title points to Siddons's liberal use of popular culture references.

These popular references continue in the title of her first novel *Heartbreak Hotel* (1976); throughout, lyrics from Elvis Presley's hit song establish the 1956 time period, as do civil rights activities in Montgomery and references to Martin Luther King. Maggie Deloach, a protected Alabama college girl, defies convention and chooses a liberal journalist over her Delta-raised fraternity gentleman. Critics admired the novel's "anything but nostalgic" detail.

Over the past two decades Siddons's writings have become more complex and ambitious as signature techniques and motifs develop related to her women characters—who must make choices between two ways of life—and her superb evocation of time and place.

After the poorly received horror novel *The House Next Door* (1978), Siddons wrote *Fox's Earth* (1980), which introduced a signature theme: an out-of-her-element woman, usually working class, either conquers or is defeated by the wealthy society into which she marries. *Homeplace* (1987) introduces another Siddons's motif. New York journalist Mike Winship returns to Georgia after 20 years to confront and make peace with her past. Both themes will recur in Siddons's bestsellers.

In the mesmerizing *Peachtree Road* (1988), the names say it all. Sheppard Gibbs Bondurant III tells of his obsession with, and the South's destruction of, Lucy Bondurant Chastain Venable, his passionate, emotion-ridden cousin. Critics labeled the story "every bit as fascinating as . . . [that other Atlanta] story of Scarlett and Rhett." Prefaced by James Dickey's "Looking for the Buckhead Boys," this book authentically recreates 1960s Atlanta and the Buckhead wealthy who strove to build the leading city of the new South, sometimes at their own peril. The highly praised novel launched Siddons onto the bestseller list and earned awards and comparisons to Pat Conroy, Truman Capote, and Tennessee Williams.

Named Georgia Author of the Year in 1988, Siddons also has been awarded the American Psychological Association's first media award, which cites her "insightful, intelligent, and compassionate" depiction of "people with emotional illnesses of personal crises." This award-winning talent is also reflected in later novels.

Horses, nuclear waste, sacred woodlands and a traumatized daughter tangle up the new life of recently divorced Andy Calhoun, another Siddons woman who must choose between men and contrasting lifestyles in *King's Oak* (1990), named for the huge tree that dominates the wooded tract adjacent to the Big Silver bomb plant in Pemberton, Georgia. The more popular *Outer Banks* (1991) finds cancer sufferer Kate Abrams rejuvenated after a confrontational reunion with three sorority sisters in North Carolina when the truth comes out about their college vacations. Her depictions of the power of old friendships are right on target.

The "absorbing" multigenerational saga bestseller *Colony* (1992) captivates readers as it follows South Carolinian Maude Gascoigne from bride of Princeton man Peter Chambliss through 70 summers to a time when she is matriarch of his family's Maine camp. The breathtaking descriptions of Maine attest to Siddons's eye for authentically rendered settings. Rome and Tuscany are described in *Hill Towns* (1993), another bestseller which looks at the nature of love and leads an emotionally scarred woman to independence. With the crises and triumphs of Catherine Gaillard, Siddons is at the height of her storytelling powers.

Through poems, song lyrics, and political events, Siddons's novels resonate with recognizable events from her era, but *Downtown* (1994) is her most autobiographical. The innocent Smoky O'Donnell leaves Savannah to assume her position on *Downtown,* a hot Atlanta magazine patterned after *Atlanta* magazine, where Siddons served as senior editor. Through career, moral, and political choices, Smoky's innocence disappears with that of America's.

In *Fault Lines* (1995), Merritt Fowler, living in wealthy Atlanta, is about to crack like the California earthquake at novel's end, but through flight and a bittersweet adulterous affair she rescues herself from the role of perpetual caretaker of her younger sister, dictatorial husband, anorexic daughter, and Alzheimer-debilitated mother-in-law for the benefit of them all. In *Fault Lines,* Siddons avoids fluff fiction with her excellent landscapes and characters, who are believable and for whom we care.

—Judith C. Kohl

SILKO, Leslie Marmon

Nationality: American. **Born:** 1948. **Education:** Board of Indian Affairs schools, Laguna, New Mexico, and a Catholic school in Albuquerque; University of New Mexico, Albuquerque, B.A. (summa cum laude) in English 1969; studied law briefly. **Family:** Has two sons. **Career:** Taught for 2 years at Navajo Community College, Tsaile, Arizona; lived in Ketchikan, Alaska, for 2 years; taught at University of New Mexico. Since 1978 professor of English, University of Arizona, Tucson. **Awards:** National Endowment for the Arts award, 1974; *Chicago Review* award, 1974; Pushcart prize, 1977; MacArthur Foundation grant, 1983. **Address:** Department of English, University of Arizona, Tucson, Arizona 85721, U.S.A.

Publications

Novels

Ceremony. New York, Viking Press, 1977.
Almanac of the Dead. New York, Simon and Schuster, 1991.

Uncollected Short Stories

"Bravura" and "Humaweepi, the Warrior Priest," in *The Man to Send Rain Clouds: Contemporary Stories by American Indians,* edited by Kenneth Rosen. New York, Viking Press, 1974.

"Laughing and Loving," in *Come to Power,* edited by Dick Lourie. Trumansburg, New York, Crossing Press, 1974.
"Private Property," in *Earth Power Coming,* edited by Simon J. Ortiz. Tsaile, Arizona, Navajo Community College Press, 1983.

Play

Lullaby, with Frank Chin, adaptation of the story by Silko (produced San Francisco, 1976).

Poetry

Laguna Woman. Greenfield Center, New York, Greenfield Review Press, 1974.
Storyteller (includes short stories). New York, Seaver, 1981.

Other

The Delicacy and Strength of Lace: Letters Between Leslie Marmon Silko and James A. Wright, edited by Anne Wright. St. Paul, Minnesota, Graywolf Press, 1986.
Yellow Woman, edited by Melody Graulich. New Brunswick, New Jersey, Rutgers University Press, 1993.

*

Manuscript Collection: University of Arizona, Tucson.

Critical Studies: *Leslie Marmon Silko* by Per Seyersted, Boise, Idaho, Boise State University, 1980; *Four American Indian Literary Masters* by Alan R. Velie, Norman, University of Oklahoma Press, 1982.

* * *

After the publication of her first novel, *Ceremony,* in 1977, Leslie Marmon Silko's work began to gain substantial critical acclaim. The novel chronicles a young Native American's struggle to readapt to society following imprisonment by the Japanese in WWII. Tayo returns to his Laguna Pueblo reservation only to be haunted by the events he has witnessed and experienced as a soldier overseas. The struggle to find an identity and a will to survive lead him to the traditions of his Native American culture. The beliefs and practices of his Indian past are revealed to him as he searches for a ritual, or ceremony, that will bring back his desire to live. Critics hailed Silko as gifted in her ability to combine Native American legends and traditions in a novel about post-WWII America.

The critical attention surrounding *Ceremony* brought new respect to earlier works by Silko. A collection of her poems titled *Laguna Woman* (1974), for example, and several of her short stories found new audiences and recognition. "Yellow Woman," "Lullaby," and "Tony's Story" are three of her most noted short stories. They deal with the situations of Native Americans in contemporary society. Silko designs the stories to reflect the difficulties Native Americans have had to face in the continuing struggle to maintain a balance between the traditions associated with Native American culture and the demands of modern society.

Silko's second novel, *Almanac of the Dead,* was published in 1991. In this novel, Native Americans are aided by their ancestors' spirits to take back the land seized from them during the colonization of the New World. Critics found this novel to be a passionate and compelling indictment of any culture or person who destroys another culture for the enjoyment of seeing others suffer. Despite its release date coinciding with the anniversary celebration of Columbus' landing in the Caribbean, *Almanac* was not Silko's commentary against Western European colonization. Instead, many critics saw it as her way of trying to honor the culture and determination of Native Americans.

Readers of *Ceremony* can begin to appreciate the skills that Silko employs in all her stories. We are drawn into Tayo's search and want to know, as he does, more about the magic and spiritualism of Native American culture. Silko is a storyteller in the true sense of the word; just as her Native American ancestors told stories to pass on the traditions of their culture, so does she. As her narrator states at the beginning of *Ceremony,* "I will tell you something about stories, they aren't just entertainment. Don't be fooled. They are all we have, you see, all we have to fight off illness and death. You don't have anything if you don't have the stories."

—Melissa L. Evans

SILVERBERG, Robert

Pseudonyms: Walker Chapman; Ivar Jorgenson; Calvin M. Knox; David Osborne; Robert Randall; Lee Sebastian. **Nationality:** American. **Born:** New York City, 15 January 1935. **Education:** Columbia University, New York, A.B. 1956. **Family:** Married Barbara H. Brown in 1956. **Career:** Full-time writer. Associate editor, *Amazing,* January 1969 issue, and associate editor, *Fantastic,* February-April 1969 issues. President, Science Fiction Writers of America, 1967-68. **Awards:** Hugo award, 1956, 1969; Nebula award, for story, 1969, 1971, 1974, for novel, 1971, for novella, 1985; Jupiter award, 1973; Prix Apollo, 1976; *Locus* award, 1981. Guest of Honor, 28th World Science Fiction Convention, 1970. **Agent:** Ralph Vicinanza, 432 Park Avenue South, Room 1205, New York, New York 10016, U.S.A.

PUBLICATIONS

Novels (series: Majipoor; Nidor)

The 13th Immortal. New York, Ace, 1957.
Master of Life and Death. New York, Ace, 1957; London, Sidgwick and Jackson, 1977.
The Shrouded Planet (Nidor; as Robert Randall, with Randall Garrett). New York, Gnome Press, 1957; London, Mayflower, 1964.
Invaders from Earth. New York, Ace, 1958; London, Sidgwick and Jackson, 1977.
Invincible Barriers (as David Osborne). New York, Avalon, 1958.
Stepsons of Terra. New York, Ace, 1958.
Aliens from Space (as David Osborne). New York, Avalon, 1958.
Starhaven (as Ivar Jorgenson). New York, Avalon, 1958.
The Dawning Light (Nidor; as Robert Randall, with Randall Garrett). New York, Gnome Press, 1959; London, Mayflower, 1964.
The Planet Killers. New York, Ace, 1959.

Collision Course. New York, Avalon, 1961.
The Seed of Earth. New York, Ace, 1962; London, Hamlyn, 1978.
Recalled to Life. New York, Lancer, 1962; revised edition, New York, Doubleday, 1972; London Gollancz, 1974.
The Silent Invaders. New York, Ace, 1963; London, Dobson, 1975.
Regan's Planet. New York, Pyramid, 1964.
A Pair from Space. New York, Belmont, 1965.
To Open the Sky. New York, Ballantine, 1967; London, Sphere, 1970.
Thorns. New York, Ballantine, 1967; London, Rapp and Whiting, 1969.
Those Who Watch. New York, New American Library, 1967; London, New English Library, 1977.
The Time-Hoppers. New York, Doubleday, 1967; London, Sidgwick and Jackson, 1968.
Planet of Death. New York, Holt Rinehart, 1967.
Hawksbill Station. New York, Doubleday, 1968; as *The Anvil of Time,* London, Sidgwick and Jackson, 1969.
The Masks of Time. New York, Ballantine, 1968; as *Vornan-19,* London, Sidgwick and Jackson, 1970.
Up the Line. New York, Ballantine, 1969; London, Gollancz, 1987.
Nightwings. New York, Avon, 1969; London, Sidgwick and Jackson, 1972.
To Live Again. New York, Doubleday, 1969; London, Sidgwick and Jackson, 1975.
Downward to the Earth. New York, Doubleday, 1970; London, Gollancz, 1977.
Tower of Glass. New York, Scribner, 1970; London, Panther, 1976.
A Robert Silverberg Omnibus. London, Sidgwick and Jackson, 1970.
The World Inside. New York, Doubleday, 1971; London, Millington, 1976.
A Time of Changes. New York, Doubleday, 1971; London, Gollancz, 1973.
Son of Man. New York, Ballantine, 1971; London, Panther, 1979.
The Book of Skulls. New York, Scribner, 1971; London, Gollancz, 1978.
Dying Inside. New York, Scribner, 1972; London, Sidgwick and Jackson, 1974.
The Second Trip. New York, Doubleday, 1972; London, Gollancz, 1979.
The Stochastic Man. New York, Harper, 1975; London, Gollancz, 1976.
Shadrach in the Furnace. Indianapolis, Bobbs Merrill, 1976; London, Gollancz, 1977.
Lord Valentine's Castle (Majipoor). New York, Harper, and London, Gollancz, 1980.
The Desert of Stolen Dreams. Columbia, Pennsylvania, Underwood Miller, 1981.
A Robert Silverberg Omnibus. New York, Harper, 1981.
Majipoor Chronicles. New York, Arbor House, and London, Gollancz, 1982.
Valentine Pontifex. New York, Arbor House, 1983; London, Gollancz, 1984.
Lord of Darkness. New York, Arbor House, and London, Gollancz, 1983.
The Conglomeroid Cocktail Party. New York, Arbor House, 1984; London, Gollancz, 1985.
Gilgamesh the King. New York, Arbor House, 1984; London, Gollancz, 1985.
Tom O'Bedlam. New York, Fine, 1985; London, Gollancz, 1986.
Sailing to Byzantium. Columbia, Pennsylvania, Underwood Miller, 1985.
Star of the Gypsies. New York, Fine, 1986; London, Gollancz, 1987.
At Winter's End. New York, Warner, and London, Gollancz, 1988.
The Secret Sharer (novella). Los Angeles, California, Underwood Miller, 1988.
The Mutant Season, with Karen Haber. New York, Doubleday, 1989.
Time Gate, with Bill Fawcett. New York, Baen, 1989.
To the Land of the Living. London, Gollancz, 1989; Norwalk, Connecticut, Easton Press, 1990.
The Queen of Springtime. London, Gollancz, 1989.
The New Springtime. New York, Warner, 1990.
Nightfall, with Isaac Asimov. New York, Doubleday, and London, Gollancz, 1990.
The Man in the Maze. London, Gollancz, 1990.
In Another Country, with *Vintage Season* by C.L. Moore. New York, Tor, 1990.
Child of Time, with Isaac Asimov. London, Gollancz, 1991.
The Face of the Waters. New York, Bantam, and London, Grafton, 1991.
The Ugly Little Boy, with Isaac Asimov. New York, Doubleday, 1992.
Thebes of the Hundred Gates. London, HarperCollins, 1993.
The Positronic Man, with Isaac Asimov. London, Gollancz, 1992; New York, Doubleday, 1993.
Kingdoms of the Wall. London, HarperCollins, 1992; New York, Bantam, 1993.
Hot Sky at Midnight. New York, Bantam, and London, HarperCollins, 1994.
The Mountain of Majipoor. New York, Bantam, and London, Macmillan, 1995.
Starborne. New York, Bantam, and London, Macmillan, 1996.

Novels as Calvin M. Knox

Lest We Forget Thee, Earth. New York, Ace, 1958.
The Plot Against Earth. New York, Ace, 1959.
One of Our Asteroids Is Missing. New York, Ace, 1964.

Short Stories

Next Stop the Stars. New York, Ace, 1962; London, Dobson, 1979.
Godling, Go Home! New York, Belmont, 1964.
To Worlds Beyond. Philadelphia, Chilton, 1965; London, Sphere, 1969.
Needle in a Timestack. New York, Ballantine, 1966; London, Sphere, 1967; revised edition, Sphere, 1979.
To Open the Sky. New York, Ballantine, 1967.
Dimension Thirteen. New York, Ballantine, 1969.
Parsecs and Parables. New York, Doubleday, 1970; London, Hale, 1973.
The Cube Root of Uncertainty. New York, Macmillan, 1970.
Moonferns and Starsongs. New York, Ballantine, 1971.
The Reality Trip and Other Implausibilities. New York, Ballantine, 1972.
Valley Beyond Time. New York, Dell, 1973.
Unfamiliar Territory. New York, Scribner, 1973; London, Gollancz, 1975.
Earth's Other Shadow. New York, New American Library, 1973; London, Millington, 1977.

Born with the Dead (three novellas). New York, Random House, 1974; London, Gollancz, 1975.
Sundance and Other Science Fiction Stories. Nashville, Nelson, 1974; London, Abelard Schuman, 1975.
The Feast of St. Dionysus. New York, Scribner, 1975; London, Gollancz, 1976.
The Shores of Tomorrow. Nashville, Nelson, 1976.
The Best of Robert Silverberg. New York, Pocket Books, 1976; London, Sidgwick and Jackson, 1977.
Capricorn Games. New York, Random House, 1976; London, Gollancz, 1978.
The Songs of Summer and Other Stories. London, Gollancz, 1979.
World of a Thousand Colors. New York, Arbor House, 1982.
Beyond the Safe Zone: Collected Short Fiction. New York, Fine, 1986.

Fiction (for children)

Revolt on Alpha C. New York, Crowell, 1955.
Starman's Quest. New York, Gnome Press, 1959.
Lost Race of Mars. Philadelphia, Winston, 1960.
Time of the Great Freeze. New York, Holt Rinehart, 1964.
Conquerors from the Darkness. New York, Holt Rinehart, 1965.
The Calibrated Alligator. New York, Holt Rinehart, 1969.
The Gate of Worlds. New York, Holt Rinehart, 1967; London, Gollancz, 1978.
Across a Billion Years. New York, Dial Press, 1969; London, Gollancz, 1977.
The Man in the Maze. New York, Avon, and London, Sidgwick and Jackson, 1969.
Three Survived. New York, Holt Rinehart, 1969.
World's Fair 1992. Chicago, Follett, 1970.
Sunrise on Mercury. Nashville, Nelson, 1975; London, Gollancz, 1983.
Project Pendulum. New York, Walker, 1987; London, Hutchinson, 1989.
Letters from Atlantis. New York, Atheneum, 1990.

Other (for children)

Treasures Beneath the Sea. Racine, Wisconsin, Whitman, 1960.
Lost Cities and Vanished Civilizations. Philadelphia, Chilton, 1962.
Sunken History: The Story of Underwater Archaeology. Philadelphia, Chilton, 1963.
Home of the Red Man: Indian North America Before Columbus. Greenwich, Connecticut, New York Graphic Society, 1963.
The Great Doctors. New York, Putnam, 1964.
The Man Who Found Nineveh: The Story of Austen Henry Layard. New York, Holt Rinehart, 1964; Kingswood, Surrey, World's Work, 1968.
The World of Coral. New York, Duell, 1965.
The Mask of Akhnaten. New York, Macmillan, 1965.
Socrates. New York, Putnam, 1965.
Niels Bohr, the Man Who Mapped the Atom. Philadelphia, Macrae Smith, 1965.
Forgotten by Time: A Book of Living Fossils. New York, Crowell, 1966.
Kublai Kahn, Lord of Xanadu (as Walker Chapman). Indianapolis, Bobbs Merrill, 1966.
Rivers (as Lee Sebastian). New York, Holt Rinehart, 1966.
To the Rock of Darius: The Story of Henry Rawlinson. New York, Holt Rinehart, 1966.
Four Men Who Changed the Universe. New York, Putnam, 1968.
The South Pole (as Lee Sebastian). New York, Holt Rinehart, 1968.
Bruce of the Blue Nile. New York, Holt Rinehart, 1969.

Other

First American into Space. Derby, Connecticut, Monarch, 1961.
The Fabulous Rockefellers. Derby, Connecticut, Monarch, 1963.
15 Battles That Changed the World. New York, Putnam, 1963.
Empires in the Dust. Philadelphia, Chilton, 1963.
Akhnaten, The Rebel Pharaoh. Philadelphia, Chilton, 1964.
Man Before Adam. Philadelphia, Macrae Smith, 1964.
The Loneliest Continent (as Walker Chapman). Greenwich, Connecticut, New York Graphic Society, 1965; London, Jarrolds, 1967.
Scientists and Scoundrels: A Book of Hoaxes. New York, Crowell, 1965.
The Old Ones: Indians of the American Southwest. Greenwich, Connecticut, New York Graphic Society, 1965.
Men Who Mastered the Atom. New York, Putnam, 1965.
The Great Wall of China. Philadelphia, Chilton, 1965.
Frontiers of Archaeology. Philadelphia, Chilton, 1966.
The Long Rampart: The Story of the Great Wall of China. Philadelphia, Chilton, 1966.
Bridges. Philadelphia, Macrae Smith, 1966.
The Dawn of Medicine. New York, Putnam, 1967.
The Adventures of Nat Palmer, Antarctic Explorer. New York, McGraw Hill, 1967.
The Auk, the Dodo, and the Oryx. New York, Crowell, 1967; Kingswood, Surrey, World's Work, 1969.
The Golden Dream: Seekers of El Dorado. Indianapolis, Bobbs Merrill, 1967.
Men Against Time: Salvage Archaeology in the United States. New York, Macmillan, 1967.
The Morning of Mankind. Greenwich, Connecticut, New York Graphic Society, 1967; Kingswood, Surrey, World's Work, 1970.
The World of the Rain Forest. New York, Meredith Press, 1967.
Light for the World: Edison and the Power Industry. Princeton, New Jersey, Van Nostrand, 1967.
Ghost Towns of the American West. New York, Crowell, 1968.
Mound Builders of Ancient America. Greenwich, Connecticut, New York Graphic Society, 1968.
Stormy Voyager: The Story of Charles Wilkes. Philadelphia, Lippincott, 1968.
The World of the Ocean Depths. New York, Meredith Press, 1968; Kingswood, Surrey, World's Work, 1970.
The Challenge of Climate: Man and His Environment. New York, Meredith Press, 1969; Kingswood, Surrey, World's Work, 1971.
Vanishing Giants: The Story of the Sequoias. New York, Simon and Schuster, 1969.
Wonders of Ancient Chinese Science. New York, Hawthorn, 1969.
The World of Space. New York, Meredith Press, 1969.
If I Forget Thee, O Jerusalem: American Jews and the State of Israel. New York, Morrow, 1970.
Mammoths, Mastodons, and Man. New York, McGraw Hill, 1970; Kingswood, Surrey, World's Work, 1972.
The Pueblo Revolt. New York, Weybright and Talley, 1970.
The Seven Wonders of the Ancient World (for children). New York, Crowell Collier, 1970.

Before the Sphinx. New York, Nelson, 1971.
Clocks for the Ages: How Scientists Date the Past. New York, Macmillan, 1971.
To the Western Shore: Growth of the United States 1776-1853. New York, Doubleday, 1971.
Into Space, with Arthur C. Clarke. New York, Harper, 1971.
John Muir: Prophet among the Glaciers. New York, Putnam, 1972.
The Longest Voyage: Circumnavigation in the Age of Discovery. Indianapolis, Bobbs Merrill, 1972.
The Realm of Prester John. New York, Doubleday, 1972.
The World Within the Ocean Wave. New York, Weybright and Talley, 1972.
The World Within the Tide Pool. New York, Weybright and Talley, 1972.
Drug Themes in Science Fiction. Rockville, Maryland, National Institute on Drug Abuse, 1974.
The Ultimate Dinosaur, with Byron Preiss, edited by Peter Dodson. New York, Bantam, 1992.

Editor, *Great Adventures in Archaeology.* New York, Dial Press, 1964; London, Hale, 1966.
Editor, *Earthmen and Strangers.* New York, Duell, 1966.
Editor (as Walker Chapman), *Antarctic Conquest.* Indianapolis, Bobbs Merrill, 1966.
Editor, *Voyagers in Time.* New York, Meredith Press, 1967.
Editor, *Men and Machines.* New York, Meredith Press, 1968.
Editor, *Mind to Mind.* New York, Meredith Press, 1968.
Editor, *Tomorrow's Worlds.* New York, Meredith Press, 1969.
Editor, *Dark Stars.* New York, Ballantine, 1969; London, Ballantine, 1971.
Editor, *Three for Tomorrow.* New York, Meredith Press, 1969; London, Gollancz, 1970.
Editor, *The Mirror of Infinity: A Critics' Anthology of Science Fiction.* New York, Harper, 1970; London, Sidgwick and Jackson, 1971.
Editor, *Science Fiction Hall of Fame 1.* New York, Doubleday, 1970; London, Gollancz, 1971.
Editor, *The Ends of Time.* New York, Hawthorn, 1970.
Editor, *Great Short Novels of Science Fiction.* New York, Ballantine, 1970; London, Pan, 1971.
Editor, *Worlds of Maybe.* New York, Nelson, 1970.
Editor, *Alpha 1-9.* New York, Ballantine, 5 vols., 1970-74; New York, Berkley, 4 vols., 1975-78.
Editor, *Four Futures.* New York, Hawthorn, 1971.
Editor, *The Science Fiction Bestiary.* New York, Nelson, 1971.
Editor, *To the Stars.* New York, Hawthorn, 1971.
Editor, *New Dimensions 1-12* (vols. 11 and 12 edited with Marta Randall). New York, Doubleday, 3 vols., 1971-73; New York, New American Library, 1 vol., 1974; New York, Harper, 6 vols., 1975-80; New York, Pocket Books, 2 vols., 1980-81; *5-7* published London, Gollancz, 3 vols., 1976-77.
Editor, *The Day the Sun Stood Still.* Nashville, Nelson, 1972.
Editor, *Invaders from Space.* New York, Hawthorn, 1972.
Editor, *Beyond Control.* Nashville, Nelson, 1972; London, Sidgwick and Jackson, 1973.
Editor, *Deep Space.* Nashville, Nelson, 1973; London, Abelard Schuman, 1976.
Editor, *Chains of the Sea.* Nashville, Nelson, 1973.
Editor, *No Mind of Man.* New York, Hawthorn, 1973.
Editor, *Other Dimensions.* New York, Hawthorn, 1973.
Editor, *Three Trips in Time and Space.* New York, Hawthorn, 1973.
Editor, *Mutants.* Nashville, Nelson, 1974; London, Abelard Schuman, 1976.
Editor, *Threads of Time.* Nashville, Nelson, 1974; London, Millington, 1975.
Editor, *Infinite Jests.* Radnor, Pennsylvania, Chilton, 1974.
Editor, *Windows into Tomorrow.* New York, Hawthorn, 1974.
Editor, with Roger Elwood, *Epoch.* New York, Berkley, 1975.
Editor, *Explorers of Space.* Nashville, Nelson, 1975.
Editor, *The New Atlantis.* New York, Hawthorn, 1975.
Editor, *Strange Gifts.* Nashville, Nelson, 1975.
Editor, *The Aliens.* Nashville, Nelson, 1976.
Editor, *The Crystal Ship.* Nashville, Nelson, 1976; London, Millington, 1980.
Editor, *Triax.* Los Angeles, Pinnacle, 1977; London, Fontana, 1979.
Editor, *Trips in Time.* Nashville, Nelson, 1977; London, Hale, 1979.
Editor, *Earth Is the Strangest Planet.* Nashville, Nelson, 1977.
Editor, *Galactic Dreamers.* New York, Random House, 1977.
Editor, *The Infinite Web.* New York, Dial Press, 1977.
Editor, *The Androids Are Coming.* New York, Elsevier Nelson, 1979.
Editor, *Lost Worlds, Unknown Horizons.* New York, Elsevier Nelson, 1979.
Editor, *The Edge of Space.* New York, Elsevier Nelson, 1979.
Editor, with Martin H. Greenberg and Joseph D. Olander, *Car Sinister.* New York, Avon, 1979.
Editor, with Martin H. Greenberg and Joseph D. Olander, *Dawn of Time: Prehistory through Science Fiction.* New York, Elsevier Nelson, 1979.
Editor, *The Best of New Dimensions.* New York, Simon and Schuster, 1979.
Editor, with Martin H. Greenberg, *The Arbor House Treasury of Modern Science Fiction.* New York, Arbor House, 1980; as *Great Science Fiction of the 20th Century,* New York, Avenel, 1987.
Editor, with Martin H. Greenberg, *The Arbor House Treasury of Great Science Fiction Short Novels.* New York, Arbor House, 1980; as *Worlds Imagined,* New York, Avenel, 1989.
Editor, with Martin H. Greenberg and Charles G. Waugh, *The Science Fictional Dinosaur.* New York, Avon, 1982.
Editor, *The Best of Randall Garrett.* New York, Pocket Books, 1982.
Editor, with Martin H. Greenberg, *The Arbor House Treasury of Science Fiction Masterpieces.* New York, Arbor House, 1983; as *Great Tales of Science Fiction,* New York, Galahad, 1985.
Editor, with Martin H. Greenberg, *Fantasy Hall of Fame.* New York, Arbor House, 1983; as *The Mammoth Book of Fantasy All-Time Greats,* London, Robinson, 1988.
Editor, *The Nebula Awards 18.* New York, Arbor House, 1983.
Editor, with Martin H. Greenberg, *The Time Travelers: A Science Fiction Quartet.* New York, Fine, 1985.
Editor, with Martin H. Greenberg and Charles G. Waugh, *Neanderthals.* New York, New American Library, 1987.
Editor, *Robert Silverberg's Worlds of Wonder.* New York, Warner, 1987; London, Gollancz, 1988.
Editor, with Karen Haber, *Universe 1.* New York, Doubleday, 1990.
Editor, with Martin H. Greenberg, *The Horror Hall of Fame.* New York, Carroll and Graf, 1991.
Editor, *Murasaki: A Novel in Six Parts,* by Poul Anderson. New York, Bantam, 1992; London, Grafton, 1993.

*

Bibliography: In *Fantasy and Science Fiction* (New York), April 1974.

Manuscript Collection: Syracuse University, New York.

Critical Studies: "Robert Silverberg Issue" of *SF Commentary* (Melbourne), March 1977; *Robert Silverberg* by Thomas D. Clareson, Mercer Island, Washington, Starmont House, 1983; *Robert Silverberg's Many Trapdoors: Critical Essays on His Science Fiction* edited by Charles L. Elkins and Martin Harry Greenberg, Westport, Connecticut, Greenwood Press, 1992.

* * *

Robert Silverberg has written so much over the last five decades that Barry M. Malzberg of the *Magazine of Fantasy and Science Fiction* wrote, "he may be, in terms of accumulation of work per working year, the most prolific writer who ever lived." Silverberg, who may also be the most well-known science fiction writer alive today, has also written prolifically in nonfiction, primarily on archeology and science. But he has become a giant in the field of science fiction writing by creating stories and novels that speak to the emotional and spiritual aspects of humankind, in contrast to the merely high-tech novels of scientific futurism that flood the genre.

Silverberg began to write for a living in the 1950s when science fiction magazines proliferated. His output was immense from the outset. The editorial practice of publishing only one story per byline per issue led Silverberg to begin publishing under various pseudonyms so that he could submit as many stories as he was capable of producing. He has admitted that many of his stories of this period were hack work. "Some of the stuff—a fair amount of it—was such junk that I really didn't want to take credit for it," he said.

By the late 1950s, many science fiction magazines folded, and Silverberg responded to the changing market by writing nonfiction, much of it for children. Through the mid-1960s Silverberg maintained his frenetic pace of production until a hyperactive thyroid gland and a fire at his home caused him to slow his pace considerably. He went back to writing science fiction, this time with a much more serious commitment to producing quality work. He began to incorporate the techniques used in the modern literature being produced in other genres, experimenting with form and structure, and exploring the themes of religion, morality, and modern alienation.

It was during the late 1960s and early 1970s that Silverberg produced some of his best work, including *Nightwings* (1969), *A Time of Changes* (1971), and *Dying Inside* (1972). In *Nightwings,* Silverberg presents a vision of the future in which the Earth has progressed scientifically, but regressed politically. *A Time of Changes* explores the theme of psychedelic drugs, and *Dying Inside* depicts a man who, having lived for 40 years with the curse of being able to read others' thoughts, is now losing that power. Critics responded with what Silverberg saw as uninformed commentary to the works of this period. Despite some credit for "stretch[ing] both the genre and himself" (from Gerald Jones in *The New York Times Book Review*) most of the critical response focused on the darkness of Silverberg's work. For example, Joanna Russ wrote in the *Magazine of Fantasy and Science Fiction,* "I don't like his feverishness or his intense, mad romanticism, and I suspect Mr. Silverberg . . . needs some time to get out of his system all the sophomoric dark doom that most of us . . . dealt with during our apprenticeships." Such responses, and the fact that by 1975 all of his most important novels were out of print, led Silverberg to announce that he was ending his career as a science fiction writer.

By the beginning of the 1980s Silverberg was back, partially because the success of the *Star Wars* and *Star Trek* movies had brought science fiction back into vogue, and also because he needed the money to buy a house for his wife, from whom he was separated. So he wrote what he thought would be one last book, *Lord Valentine's Castle* (1980). The novel was such a popular and critical success that he resumed his career. In the book (for which he received $127,500, a record for a science fiction novel), Silverberg depicts the planet Majipoor, which abounds with over 20 million species and serves as a glorious backdrop to Valentine's quest for his identity after he loses his memory. Silverberg went on to write three more books about Majipoor: *Majipoor Chronicles,* a short story collection (1982); *Valentine Pontifex* (1983); and *The Mountains of Majipoor* (1995).

While Silverberg's collaborations with Isaac Asimov on such novels as *Nightfall* (1990) and *The Positronic Man* (1992) have disappointed some critics, his solo efforts have continued to satisfy, particularly *At Winter's End* (1988) and its sequel, *The New Springtime* (1990). In the introduction to one of his many edited collections of great science fiction stories, *Galactic Dreamers* (1977), Silverberg wrote that his aim was "[t]o show the reader something he has never been able to see with his own eyes, . . . which draws him for a moment out of himself, places him in contact with the vastness of the universe, . . . and leaves him forever transformed, forever enlarged."

—Anne Boyd

SIMMONS, Dan

Nationality: American. **Born:** 1948. **Career:** Writer. Worked as an elementary school teacher. **Awards:** Fulbright scholarship, 1977; award from *Twilight Zone* for "The River Styx Runs Upstream"; World Fantasy award for best first novel, 1985, for *Song of Kali;* Hugo award, 1989, for *Hyperion; Locus* award for best science fiction novel, 1989, for *Hyperion,* 1990, for *The Fall of Hyperion,* and for best horror/dark fantasy novel, 1991, for *Summer of Night;* Bram Stoker award for best horror novel, 1990, for *Carrion Comfort,* and for best horror collection, 1991, for *Prayers to Broken Stones.*

Publications

Novels

Song of Kali. Tor Books, 1985.
Phases of Gravity. Bantam, 1989.
Hyperion. Doubleday, 1989.
The Fall of Hyperion. Doubleday, 1990.
Carrion Comfort. Warner Books, 1990.
Summer of Night. Putnam, 1991.
Children of the Night. Putnam, 1992.

The Hollow Man. Bantam, 1992.
Fires of Eden. Putnam, 1994.
Endymion. Bantam, 1996.

Short Stories and Novellas

Prayers to Broken Stones. Dark Harvest, 1990.
Lovedeath. Warner, 1993.

* * *

In his novella collection *Lovedeath* (1993), fantasist Dan Simmons writes, "the themes of love, death, and the act of dealing with the sense of loss so common to these human experiences, are almost obsessive topics in my fiction. I do not plan it so. It is what stirs me deep within and I write about it." Over the past decade Simmons has methodically left his mark on the varied genres of fantasy, horror, and science fiction. He concocts compulsive page-turners, liberally laced with the exotic and the grisly. His books are notorious for their graphic violence, but Simmons' defenders maintain that he uses the trappings of horror fantasy to convey messages of profound morality.

Simmons received the World Fantasy Award for his first novel, *Song of Kali* (1985), a staggering tale of suspense about American journalist Robert Luczak and his family, who are terrorized in Calcutta by a malign cult. The tale moves at breakneck speed as the journalist races to save his kidnapped daughter from the Hindu goddess Kali. Simmons effectively manipulates the universal fear of loss of family, bringing the book to a wrenching climax. *Song of Kali* was a great success and immediately established Simmons as a force to be reckoned with.

Nothing could prepare readers, however, for Simmons' next major foray into the horror genre, *Carrion Comfort* (1990). A monstrous epic, *Carrion Comfort* is disturbing, ultra-violent, and impossible to put down. The novel posits that the human race is infested with mutants with a frightening psychic power; the ability to invade the minds of normal humans and seize control. Absolute power, in this book, corrupts absolutely, and the mutants use their abilities for obsessive, sadistic personal gain. Puppet-humans are manipulated as pawns in a metaphoric chess-game as these psychic vampires war amongst each other for control of the human race. The only hope comes from a small group of normal humans dedicated to wiping this evil from the face of the planet. Much admired for its careful plotting and gripping suspense, *Carrion Comfort* garnered for the author the Bram Stoker Award.

Simmons branched out into the field of science fiction space opera with the two-part opus *Hyperion* (1989, Hugo award winner in 1990) and *The Fall of Hyperion* (1990). Together, the Hyperion Cantos stand as required reading in late-1980s mainstream science fiction. Far in the future, long after a black hole has consumed the Earth, the human race has broken into two rival factions: a vast galactic civilization called the Hegemony, and a band of interstellar barbarians called the Ousters. A robot-based civilization called the Technocore has broken from humanity and pursues its own unknown ends. War between the Hegemony and the Ousters sends a band of seven pilgrims to a planet called Hyperion, where a fearsome, godlike figure called the Shrike may provide salvation in the face of stellar war. Borrowing themes and motifs from Chaucer and Keats, the Hyperion Cantos is a highly praised sci-fi tour de force.

Simmons' further explorations into the genre of horror include *Summer of Night* (1991), a Stephen King-esque adventure about a group of youngsters who find their summer vacation far from relaxing: an evil force has inhabited the belfry of their school, and they alone must find the resources to do battle with it. The book covers well-trodden ground, but is saved by Simmons' suspenseful plotting and thorough characterizations.

A slight departure for Simmons is *The Hollow Man* (1992), in which a brilliant mathematician, Jeremy Bremen, is plagued by telepathic powers which he cannot control. The book opens with the death of his wife, the only person able to shield his mind from the thoughts of humanity at large. Simmons here abandons epic plot in favor of a personal, inner journey. Although *The Hollow Man* is marred by a strange central episode that degenerates into shocking horror, the book stands as a moving search for meaning in the universe, with an emotional denouement.

The novella collection *Lovedeath* (1993) is notable for tales such as "Sleeping with Teeth Women," an intriguing amalgamation of Native American lore into a fantastic story of a young Sioux Warrior's reluctant coming-of-age. In a similar vein, the more recent novel *Fires of Eden* (1994) adopts the myths and legends of native Hawaiians in a mixture of horror and subtle humor. Inspired in part by Mark Twain's "Letters from the Sandwich Islands," the motley characters in *Fires* find themselves caught up in a modern day conflict with the gods of Hawaii over a multimillion-dollar resort which has destroyed ancient sacred grounds. Although an engaging read, *Fires of Eden* lacks the punch and drive of Simmons' earlier works, and indicates that, for the moment, the author may be marking time.

—Sean Carney

SMILEY, Jane

Nationality: American. **Born:** Los Angeles, 26 September 1949. **Education:** Vassar College, B.A. in English 1971; University of Iowa, M.A. 1975, M.F.A. 1976, Ph.D. 1978. **Family:** Married 1) John Whiston, 1970 (divorced 1975); 2) William Silag, 1978 (divorced), two daughters; 3) Stephen Mark Mortensen, 1987. **Career:** Assistant professor, 1981-84, associate professor, 1984-89, professor, 1989-90, and since 1992, Distinguished Professor, all Iowa State University. Visiting assistant professor, University of Iowa, 1981, 1987. **Awards:** Fulbright grant, 1976-77; Pushcart prize, 1977, for "Jeffrey, Believe Me"; O. Henry award, 1982, for "The Pleasure of Her Company," 1985, for "Lily," and 1988; NEA grant, 1978, 1987; Friends of American Writers prize, 1981; Pulitzer prize, 1992, and National Book Critics Circle award, 1992, both for *A Thousand Acres;* Midland Author's award, 1992; Heartland prize, 1992; **Address:** Department of English, Iowa State University, 201 Ross, Ames, Iowa 50011-1401, U.S.A.

Publications

Novels

Barn Blind. New York, Harper and Row, 1980; London, Flamingo, 1994.

At Paradise Gate. New York, Simon and Schuster, 1981.
Duplicate Keys. New York, Knopf, and London, Cape 1984.
The Greenlanders. New York, Knopf, and London, Collins, 1988.
A Thousand Acres. New York, Knopf, and London, Flamingo, 1991.
Moo. New York, Knopf, and London, Flamingo, 1995.

Short Stories

The Age of Grief. New York, Knopf, 1987; London, Collins, 1988.
Ordinary Love and Good Will (novellas). New York, Knopf, 1989; London, Collins, 1990.
The Life of the Body, with linoleum cuts by Susan Nees. Minneapolis, Minnesota, Coffee House Press, 1990.

Other

Catskill Crafts: Artisans of the Catskill Mountains. New York, Crown, 1988.

Editor, *Best American Short Stories 1995.* Boston, Houghton Mifflin, 1995.

* * *

Jane Smiley writes sweeping novels that, whether set in the colonies of 14th century Greenland, as in *The Greenlanders* (1988) or on a declining family farm, as in *A Thousand Acres* (1991) center on families and their struggles to stay together. Joanne Kaufman wrote in *People* that Smiley "has an unerring, unsettling ability to capture the rhythms of family life gone askew."

Smiley made an impressive debut as a novelist with *Barn Blind* (1980), the story of Kate Karlson, a rancher's wife obsessed with raising her four troubled teenagers to become equestrian stars; they will fulfill what Kate herself could not achieve. Even when the story ends in tragedy, "Kate is barn blind to grief and loss; she is thrown, but never falls," wrote Michael Malone in the *New York Times Book Review.* Smiley followed with *At Paradise Gate* (1981), in which the elderly Anna Robinson faces the death of her violent husband. When their three daughters return home and begin to bicker among themselves, the household's long-repressed tension resurfaces. Valerie Miner wrote in the *New York Times Book Review* that "[*At Paradise Gate* is] about families and death and the deathlessness of families . . . [Smiley considers] the afterlife of survivors who, in their grief, encounter both sides of mortality—their relatives' deaths and their own continuing lives."

With *Duplicate Keys* (1984), Smiley wrote a murder mystery novel that transcended the genre. Set in Manhattan, 1980, *Duplicate Keys* reveals a close circle of transplanted New Yorkers who have become lost in the big city and alienated from each other emotionally. "No one has any kids; they have become each other's. No one gets to say no anymore about sharing; they just do—keys, beds, trouble, loss of faith, murder. . . . The operating condition here is affectlessness, formerly known as cool," wrote Lois Gould in the *New York Times Book Review.*

Smiley took five years to write *The Greenlanders,* a 558-page historical novel set in the 14th century Greenland colonies established by Eric the Red. *The Greenlanders* centers on the farmer Gunnar Asgeirsson and his family as they persist through hundreds of episodes, including curses, marriages, feuds, and death. "*The Greenlanders* is a grim book, and yet in its austerity and the caliber of its art it is jubilant, its effect that of a prayer," wrote Verlyn Klinkenborg in the *New Republic.*

With *A Thousand Acres,* for which Smiley won the Pulitzer Prize for fiction, the author creates what Laura Shapiro of *Newsweek* termed "a brilliant twist on the [King Lear] story." Larry Cook decides to give his Iowa farm to his three daughters, Ginny, Rose, and Caroline. When Caroline hesitates, Larry becomes angry and removes her from the grant at the last minute. Smiley details the struggle to keep the family farm alive, telling the story from the point of view of Ginny, the oldest daughter. Donna Rifkind wrote in the *Washington Post:* "Smiley's novel is about the power and the entrapment of the land. . . . It is also about the power and the entrapment of love, which, along with bitterness and hatred, keeps the Cook family writhing poisonously, desperately together to the end." Some critics found fault with the novel's wealth of detail, which is a trademark of Smiley's work. "We learn far too much about hogs and slurry systems and combine harvesters. . . . The idea is that America-the-poem . . . will write the novel for you if you let it overwhelm you. It sinks [*A Thousand Acres*]," wrote James Wood in the *London Review of Books*:

Smiley moved from tragedy to academic farce with *Moo* (1995), in which she details the eccentric machinations within a midwestern university. "Moo U," so-nicknamed for its agricultural program, likely resembles Iowa State University, where Smiley teaches. "For a satirist, Ms. Smiley is remarkably fair-minded and kind," wrote Alison Lurie in the *New York Times Book Review.* "[Her] target, of course, is larger than just one midwestern university. Moo U is, in microcosm, a version of America today: it is both well-meaning and mercenary, devoted to the truth and to noble ideals, but also eager for money and power and perks."

—Eric Patterson

SMITH, Martin Cruz

Pseudonyms: Nick Carter; Jake Logan; Martin Quinn; Simon Quinn. **Nationality:** American. **Born:** Martin William Smith, Reading, Pennsylvania, 3 November 1942. **Education:** University of Pennsylvania, Philadelphia, B.A. 1964. **Family:** Married Emily Stanton Arnold in 1968; two daughters and one son. **Career:** Reporter, *Philadelphia Daily News,* 1965, and Magazine Management, 1966-69. **Awards:** Crime Writers Association Gold Dagger award, 1982. **Agent:** Knox Burger Associates, 39½ Washington Square South, New York, New York, 10012, U.S.A. **Address:** 240 Cascade Drive, Mill Valley, California 94941, U.S.A.

Publications

Novels (series: Roman Grey; Arkady Renko)

The Indians Won (as Martin Smith). New York, Belmont Tower, 1970; London, Star, 1982.
Gypsy in Amber (Grey). New York, Putnam, 1971; London, Barker, 1975.
The Analog Bullet. New York, Belmont Tower, 1972; London, W.H. Allen, 1982.

Canto for a Gypsy (Grey). New York, Putnam, 1972; London, Barker, 1975.
The Adventures of the Wilderness Family (as Martin Quinn; novelization of screenplay). New York, Ballantine, 1976; London, Arrow, 1977.
Nightwing. New York, Norton, and London, Deutsch, 1977.
Gorky Park (Renko). New York, Random House, and London, Collins, 1981.
Stallion Gate. London, Collins Harvill, and New York, Random House, 1986.
Polar Star (Renko). London, Collins, and New York, Random House, 1989.
Red Square (Renko). London, Collins, and New York, Random House, 1992.
Rose. London, Collins, and New York, Random House, 1996.

Novels as Nick Carter (series: Nick Carter in all books)

The Inca Death Squad. New York, Award, 1972; London, Tandem, 1973.
Code Name: Werewolf. New York, Award, and London, Tandem, 1973.
The Devil's Dozen. New York, Award, 1973; London, Tandem, 1974.

Novels as Simon Quinn (series: The Inquisitor [Francis Xavier Killy] in all books except *The Human Factor*)

His Eminence, Death. New York, Dell, 1974.
Nuplex Red. New York, Dell, 1974.
The Devil in Kansas. New York, Dell, 1974.
The Last Time I Saw Hell. New York, Dell, 1974.
The Midas Coffin. New York, Dell, 1975.
Last Rites for the Vulture. New York, Dell, 1975.
The Human Factor (novelization of screenplay). New York, Dell, and London, Futura, 1975.

Novels as Jake Logan

North to Dakota. Chicago, Playboy Press, 1976.
Ride for Revenge. Chicago, Playboy Press, 1977.

Play

Screenplay: *Nightwing,* with Steve Shagan and Bud Shrake, 1981.

*

Media Adaptations: Films—*Nightwing,* 1979, from the novel; *Gorky Park,* 1983, from the novel.

* * *

Suspense writer Martin Cruz Smith stands at the pinnacle of his genre, praised not only for his thrilling stories but also for the quality of his writing. The *New York Times Book Review* described his novel *Polar Star* (1989) as "not merely the work of our best writer of suspense, but of one of our best writers, period." Smith stands out for his unique characters, his deft use of dialogue and metaphor, and his ability to evoke settings.

Smith has written over 30 crime and detective novels, many under pseudonyms. Suffering under financial strain like most beginning writers, Smith got his break with the publication of *Nightwing* (1977), a melodramatic tale of vampire bats in the Southwest which became a surprise hit and earned close to half a million dollars. While *Nightwing* was lurid and somewhat unrealistic, it did offer a fresh locale and much detail on Indian life and lore.

Smith's best-known works are his Arkady Renko novels, which are set in the former Soviet Union. Renko is a Moscow investigator whose wry insights into Soviet life are a window into the actual day-to-day existence in the communist nation. After a one-week trip to Moscow, Smith interviewed several Russian émigrés and defectors to prepare for *Gorky Park* (1981), the first Arkady Renko novel. When three corpses are found frozen in Moscow's Gorky Park, their faces and fingertips removed by a knife blade, Renko investigates to uncover a tale of corruption and greed that involves the KGB, the FBI, New York police, and a wealthy American businessman. The sense of place and atmosphere are superb, but the real achievement is the very human Renko, a fallible yet doggedly determined investigator who must succeed despite the interference of the Soviet bureaucratic machine. The plot is complex and places Renko in several ethical dilemmas, including his falling in love with Irina Asanova, a beautiful Russian dissident who may be connected with the murders. While the final section of the novel, set in New York, ends in a gun battle that seems formulaic and unnecessary, Smith's characterization of Renko and description of Moscow are witty, ironic, and well-chosen.

Stallion Gate (1986) deals with the Manhattan Project and the weeks and months just prior to the detonation of the first atomic bomb in New Mexico during WWII. The novel is similar in its constructs to *Gorky Park*; the protagonist, here a Native American in the U.S. Army, recognizes the convoluted plots of his superiors and investigates. Yet the book lacks the strong characterization and central plot of the Arkady Renko novels. Still, Smith's setting and use of Indian folklore add weight to the novel, a work of historical fiction that explores the theory that Oppenheimer, the inventor of the A-bomb, was a Soviet sympathizer.

Polar Star, the second Arkady Renko novel, returns to the Soviet Union to find the now ex-investigator Renko on the run in the Pacific, where he works anonymously aboard a Soviet factory ship. When a fish net hauls up a dead crew member, Renko is called upon to investigate and discovers smuggling, espionage and possible murder. The sense of place—above the fog-drenched Arctic Circle—is even more palpable than the Moscow of *Gorky Park,* and some critics even noted that the setting threatens to overshadow the plot. Nevertheless, the characters, including a dedicated sea captain, a distrustful political officer, and a muscular criminal from Renko's past, are sharply drawn and have surprising depth, and the insight into Soviet culture is as keen as ever.

Red Square (1992) is the third Arkady Renko novel. Reinstated as an investigator, Renko now moves among the new Russian mafias and the fledgling black markets of Moscow in the aftermath of the democratic overthrow of the communist regime. An informant of Renko's dies from a car bomb, leading Renko from the outskirts of Moscow to Munich and Berlin on the trail of the murderer. When fate brings Renko within reach of his long-lost love Irina Asanova, he must decide between her and the duty he cannot ignore, the investigation of a crime that may result in his losing Irina once more. Redolent with intrigue and the death-throes of the communist empire, the novel rushes to a climax that incorporates the real-life hard-line coup of August 1991. Moreover, it bears witness to the troubled pasts of both Arkady Renko and the actual Russian republic, and the writing is again superb.

His ability to endure the labels of both "crime fiction" and "literary work" sets Smith apart from his contemporaries. At the heart of his novels lie human characters in all their weakness and strength who must grapple with the dilemmas of love, responsibility, and truth.

—Christopher Swann

SMITH, Rosamond. *See* **OATES, Joyce Carol.**

SMITH, Wilbur (Addison)

Nationality: South African. **Born:** 9 January 1933, in Broken Hill, Northern Rhodesia (now Zambia). **Education:** Rhodes University, Bachelor of Commerce, 1954. **Family:** Married Jewell Slabbert, 1964; married second wife, Danielle Thomas, 1971; two sons and one daughter. **Career:** Affiliated with Goodyear Tire & Rubber Co., Port Elizabeth, South Africa, 1954-58, and H. J. Smith & Son, Ltd., Salisbury, Rhodesia (now Zimbabwe), 1958-63; full-time writer, 1964—. **Member:** South African Wildlife Society (trustee), Friends of Conservation (trustee), Rhodesian Wildlife Conservation Association. **Agent:** Charles Pick Consultancy, Flat 3, 3 Bryanston Place, London W1H 7FN, England. **Address:** Sunbird Hill, 34 Klaassens Road, Constantia 7800, South Africa.

Publications

Novels

When the Lion Feeds. Viking, 1964.
The Train from Katanga. Viking, 1965; as *The Dark of the Sun,* Heinemann, 1965.
Shout at the Devil. Coward, 1968.
Gold Mine. Doubleday, 1970.
The Diamond Hunters. Heinemann, 1971; Doubleday, 1972.
The Sunbird. Heinemann, 1972; Doubleday, 1973.
Eagle in the Sky. Doubleday, 1974.
Eye of the Tiger. Doubleday, 1974.
Cry Wolf. Doubleday, 1975.
A Sparrow Falls. Doubleday, 1976.
Hungry as the Sea. Doubleday, 1977.
Wild Justice. Doubleday, 1978.
A Falcon Flies. Doubleday, 1979; as *Flight of the Falcon,* Doubleday, 1982.
Men of Men. Doubleday, 1980.
The Delta Decision. Doubleday, 1981.
The Angels Weep. Doubleday, 1983.
The Leopard Hunts in Darkness. Doubleday, 1984.
The Burning Shore. Doubleday, 1985.
Power of the Sword. Little, Brown, 1986.
Rage. Little, Brown, 1987.
The Courtneys. Little, Brown, 1988.
A Time to Die. Random House, 1989.
Golden Fox. Random House, 1990.
Elephant Song. Random House, 1991.
The Sound of Thunder. Fawcett, 1991.
River God. St. Martin's, 1994.
The Seventh Scroll. St. Martin's, 1994.

*

Film Adaptation: *The Dark of the Sun,* Metro-Goldwyn-Mayer, 1968; *Gold Mine,* Hemdale, 1974.

* * *

Smith has sold more than 70 million copies of his swashbuckling adventure novels set against the historical backdrop of Africa. As a white African, Smith had a hard time gaining acceptance in America, despite the fact that his books were banned in his homeland of South Africa for a time. But since Nelson Mandela's election, *Publisher's Weekly* reports, his sales have quadrupled.

As a boy, Smith lived on a 90,000-acre ranch in northern Rhodesia and, in his words, "lived like a prince." As he describes his youth in a 1995 *Publisher's Weekly* interview with Michele Field, he experienced plenty of adventure to supply himself with a lifetime's supply of imaginative material to write his novels. As Field wrote, "Half of Smith's adult life continues in this romantic 'boy's own adventure' fashion—not only on his own ranch in the South African Karoo but also in his novels, which are about searching for hidden treasures and keeping the 'gang' together."

Smith has written two trilogies. The first, which includes *When the Lion Feeds* (1964), *The Sound of Thunder* (1966), and *A Sparrow Falls* (1976), follows the life of Sean Courtney from the 1860s to the 1930s. It includes many of the events of South Africa's history during that time period, including the Anglo-Boer War and the first gold rush on the Witswatersrand. Peggy Crane, in *Books and Bookmen,* compares the trilogy to Ian Fleming's Bond novels, saying that "some of [Smith's] heroes could well be styled the Bond of the Bush." She goes on to describe the last book in the series as "the perfect fairytale."

The second trilogy, which includes *A Falcon Flies* (1979), *Men of Men* (1980), and *The Angels Weep* (1982), chronicles the Ballantyne family, who challenge the ambitious Cecil Rhodes and link their destiny with that of Rhodesia itself. In this series, the novels' plots are intertwined with the tumultuous history of Rhodesia, including the slave trade, diamond mining, and tribal warfare. William Bradley Hooper of *Booklist* explains that "[g]reed is the theme that has linked the individual novels of the trilogy, specifically the greed for African gems and minerals that reduced so many British imperialists to moral midgets, indifferent to the destruction of land and people that their pursuit of riches unfailingly entailed." Hooper concludes, "All three of Smith's Ballantyne books combine adventure and melodrama with sex and violence on a grand scale—a time-honored formula for bestsellerdom."

Smith's books have received contradictory responses from critics. Many have found Smith's novels to be highly entertaining, some of the best pulp fiction has to offer. John Brosnahan of *Booklist* reviewed *Flight of the Falcon* (the American release of *A*

Falcon Flies) very favorably, saying "All the risky entanglements, treacherous enemies, exotic locales, impetuous desires, and high-spirited action make for a fine stew of adventure and lust." Roger Manvell of *British Book News*, in his review of the same novel, wrote that "Wilbur Smith must surely be considered an author in the grand tradition of the picaresque novel of travel and adventure to which he brings a modern quality of research." But others find Smith's novels rife with flat, one-dimensional characters and clichés. For example, in his review of *Hungry as the Sea* (1977) for the *New York Times Book Review*, Newgate Callendar charged that "as a writer, Mr. Smith can be very tacky. At moments of emotional stress, his characters fall back on the worst soap-opera conventions." And Michael Healy, in a review of *The Angels Weep* for *Best Sellers*, regretted the way Smith handled some very serious material. Healy wrote, "the toll on those who suffered under the imperialists and their legacy in Zimbabwe makes this a story that deserves more than trivializing and stereotyping."

But if the popularity of his more recent efforts in the United States is any indication, Smith's career will continue to be nothing but "bright lights and big money," as Field wrote it has been up until this point. His most recent books, *River God* (1994) and *The Seventh Scroll* (1994) portray the Quenton-Harper family and their involvement in the historical events of Egypt and Africa during ancient times. The two novels form a new series, which has led readers to expect a third novel to complete the trilogy. Smith himself told Field, "Any time I want to go back, they (the Quenton-Harper family) are there. As an old dog, practically my only advice to young writers is this: don't kill off good characters."

—Anne Boyd

SONTAG, Susan

Nationality: American. **Born:** New York City, 16 January 1933. **Education:** The University of California, Berkeley, 1948-49; University of Chicago, 1949-51, B.A. 1951; Harvard University, Cambridge, Massachusetts, 1954-57, M.A. 1955; St. Anne's College, Oxford, 1957. **Family:** Has one son. **Career:** Instructor in English, University of Connecticut, Storrs, 1953-54; teaching fellow in philosophy, Harvard University, 1955-57; editor, *Commentary*, New York, 1959; lecturer in philosophy, City College of New York, and Sarah Lawrence College, Bronxville, New York, 1959-60; instructor in religion, Columbia University, New York, 1960-64; writer-in-residence, Rutgers University, New Brunswick, New Jersey, 1964-65. President, PEN American Center, 1987-89. Lives in New York City. **Awards:** American Association of University Women fellowship, 1957; Rockefeller fellowship, 1965, 1974; Guggenheim fellowship, 1966, 1975; American Academy award, 1976; Brandeis University Creative Arts award, 1976; Ingram Merrill Foundation award, 1976; National Book Critics Circle award, 1977; Academy of Sciences and Literature award (Mainz, Germany), 1979; MacArthur Foundation fellowship, 1990-95; Premio Malaparte award (Italy), 1992. **Member:** American Academy, 1979; Officer, Order of Arts and Letters (France), 1984. **Address:** c/o Wylie, Aitken & Stone, 250 West 57th Street, New York, New York 10107, U.S.A.

Publications

Novels

The Benefactor. New York, Farrar Straus, 1963; London, Eyre and Spottiswoode, 1964.
Death Kit. New York, Farrar Straus, 1967; London, Secker and Warburg, 1968.
The Volcano Lover. New York, Farrar Straus, and London, Cape, 1992.

Short Stories

I, etcetera. New York, Farrar Straus, 1978; London, Gollancz, 1979.
The Way We Live Now, illustrated by Howard Hodgkin. New York, Farrar Straus, and London, Cape, 1991.

Uncollected Short Stories

"Man with a Pain," in *Harper's* (New York), April 1964.
"Description (of a Description)," in *Antaeus* (New York), Autumn 1984.
"The Letter Scene," in *The New Yorker*, 18 August 1986.
"Pilgrimage," in *The New Yorker*, 21 December 1987.

Plays

Duet for Cannibals (screenplay). New York, Farrar Straus, 1970; London, Allen Lane, 1974.
Brother Carl (screenplay). New York, Farrar Straus, 1974.
Alice in Bed. New York, Farrar Straus, 1993.

Screenplays: *Duet for Cannibals*, 1969; *Brother Carl*, 1971.

Other

Against Interpretation and Other Essays. New York, Farrar Straus, 1966; London, Eyre and Spottiswoode, 1967.
Trip to Hanoi. New York, Farrar Straus, and London, Panther, 1969.
Styles of Radical Will (essays). New York, Farrar Straus, and London, Secker and Warburg, 1969.
On Photography. New York, Farrar Straus, 1977; London, Allen Lane, 1978.
Illness as Metaphor. New York, Farrar Straus, 1978; London, Allen Lane, 1979.
Under the Sign of Saturn (essays). New York, Farrar Straus, 1980; London, Writers and Readers, 1983.
A Susan Sontag Reader. New York, Farrar Straus, 1982; London, Penguin, 1983.
Aids and Its Metaphors. New York, Farrar Straus, and London, Allen Lane, 1989.

Editor, *Selected Writings of Artaud*, translated by Helen Weaver. New York, Farrar Straus, 1976.
Editor, *A Barthes Reader*. New York, Hill and Wang, and London, Cape, 1982; as *Barthes: Selected Writings*, London, Fontana, 1983.
Editor, *Best American Essays: 1992*. New York, Ticknor and Fields, 1992.
Editor, with Danilo Kis, *Homo Poeticus*. New York, Farrar Straus, 1995.

*

Critical Study: *Susan Sontag: The Elegiac Modernist* by Sohnya Sayres, New York, Routledge Chapman and Hall, 1989; London, Routledge, 1990.

Theatrical Activities:
Director: **Plays**—*As You Desire Me* by Pirandello, Turin and Italian tour, 1979-80; *Jacques and His Master* by Milan Kundera, Cambridge, Massachusetts, 1985; *Waiting for Godot* by Samuel Beckett, Sarajevo, 1993-94. **Films**—*Duet for Cannibals,* 1969; *Brother Carl,* 1971; *Promised Lands* (documentary), 1974; *Unguided Tour,* 1983.

* * *

With the nickname "The Dark Lady of Letters," Susan Sontag can proclaim that she has made her mark on the intellectual world and a name for herself in popular literature. Possible reasons for the association of her name with darkness are many. She writes about grave topics such as AIDS, cancer, the Vietnam war and the holocaust, for example, and about other serious intellectuals such as Walter Benjamin, Jean-Paul Sartre, Roland Barthes, Jean Genet, and Ingmar Bergman. Furthermore, her style is polemical, maverick and aggressive. However, in the last several years she has softened, if not lightened, professing the desire to be more self-revealing. Comparing Sontag to Camille Paglia clarifies some of the Dark Lady's characteristics: she is as well-educated and far-ranging in references as Paglia, and both want to turn mainstream assumptions about culture, gender, and America on their heads, but Sontag is more detached from her reader, more serious, and less focused on sexuality as the ultimate metaphor of the self.

Sontag's best-known works are *On Photography,* winner of the 1978 National Book Critics Award for criticism, *Illness as Metaphor* (1978), *and AIDS and Its Metaphors* (1990). In the first book, she critiques photography as an act that appropriates images to the use of the photographer, who mistakes this capturing for knowledge and power. It is not that she is against photography. She is a hobbyist herself. But she believes that photography ignores distinctions between subjects, pretending to a false democratization. Diane Arbus' photos of monsters and outcasts, and Edward Steichen's 1955 exhibit "Family of Man" suggest that humanity is ugly and desperate on the one hand, or beautiful and romantic on the other, ignoring the reality of the lives behind the photographs. Sontag also believes that photography gives us a false sense of history. It "actively promotes nostalgia" and privileges the gap between events and things while pretending to give a linear and true account. Her bottom line criticism is one that recurs in various forms throughout her work: photographs and photojournalism often pretend to give a moral reading to their images, but, she says, a record is only that, not a reading. Using examples of photographs taken during the Vietnam War, she points out that the presence of the photographer qua photographer implies the absence of the person as intervenor or helper to the victims of war tragedies. Photography, then, is voyeuristic.

Applying a similar line of reasoning to how we romanticize illness, Sontag protests that we have historically made illness represent moral corruption by our use of the metaphors of military warfare, thereby marginalizing other sick people and blaming ourselves for our own illnesses. It was her personal struggle against breast cancer that gave Sontag the insight to write this book. Later, she applied the theory to AIDS. Critics have found her AIDS essay unsympathetic to homosexuality because she uses loaded words, as in the following excerpt: "Promiscuous homosexual men practicing their vehement sexual customs under the illusory conviction, fostered by medical ideology with its cure-all antibiotics, of the relative innocuousness of all sexually transmitted diseases, could be viewed as dedicated hedonists—though it's now clear that their behavior was no less suicidal." Throughout the book, Sontag blends sympathy for the victims with apparent, though perhaps unconscious, scorn.

But Sontag, like any great intellectual, is no stranger to self-contradiction. In an early essay on American imperialism in 1966, she used illness as metaphor, saying "the white race is the cancer of human history . . . which eradicates autonomous civilizations wherever it spreads." In addition, she has historically wavered between the position that art is separate from morality and the position that they are inseparable.

Sontag's fiction is less admired than her essays, although her latest novel, *The Volcano Lover* (1993), shows a more playful mind and heart at work than her two 1960s novels. Similarities of focus and style remain, however, the most curious being her continual choice of male protagonists. This choice parallels the focus of her nonfiction work on male figures and "male" fields such as philosophy, history, and war. Some feminist readers consider Sontag too male-identified for their tastes. When questioned by Adrienne Rich about why she did not explore the feminist implications of fascist aesthetics, Sontag replied that "most of history is patriarchal history, so distinctions will have to be made, and it is not possible to keep the feminist thread running through the explanations all the time." Although her essay "The Third World of Women" (1976) asks for no less than a radical transformation of society and consciousness to transcend gender and advocate "genuine bisexuality," her real priorities, she admits, lie elsewhere.

—Jill Franks

SPENCER, LaVyrle

Nationality: American. **Born:** 17 August 1943, in Browerville, Minnesota. **Education:** Attended high school in Staples, Minnesota. **Family:** Married Daniel F. Spencer in 1962; children: Amy Elizabeth, Beth Adair. **Career:** Seamstress in Minneapolis, Minnesota, 1969-72; Osseo Junior High School, Osseo, Minnesota, instructional aide, 1974-78; writer. **Awards:** Historical Romance of the Year award, Romance Writers of America, for *The Endearment, Hummingbird,* and *Twice Loved.* **Agent:** c/o Putnam, 200 Madison Ave., New York, New York 10016. **Address:** 6701 79th Ave., Brooklyn Park, Minnesota 55445, U.S.A.

Publications

Novels

The Fulfillment. Avon, 1979.
The Endearment. Pocket Books, 1982.
Hummingbird. Jove, 1983.
The Hellion. Jove, 1984.
Twice Loved. Jove, 1984.

Sweet Memories. Harlequin, 1984.
A Heart Speaks. Jove, 1986.
Tears. Jove, 1986.
Years. Jove, 1986.
The Gamble. Jove, 1987.
Separate Beds. Jove, 1987.
Vows. Jove, 1988.
Morning Glory. Putnam, 1988.
Spring Fancy. Jove, 1989.
Bitter Sweet. Putnam, 1990.
November of the Heart. Putnam, 1992.
Forgiving. Putnam, 1991.
Bygones. Putnam, 1993.
Family Blessings. Putnam, 1993.
Home Song. Putnam, 1995.
That Camden Summer. Putnam, 1996.

*

Media Adaptations: Television film—*The Fulfillment of Mary Gray,* adapted from her novel *The Fulfillment,* 1989.

* * *

That LaVyrle Spencer writes "love stories" is the simple truth behind the amazing success she has enjoyed as one of today's most prolific and successful romance novelists. Her goal is not to create a literary masterpiece, but to use the basic elements of "tenderness, sensuality, and love" to "entertain and to leave the reader feeling good." Judging by the fact that she has produced bestsellers at the rate of nearly one per year since the publication of *The Fulfillment* in 1979, she seems to have accomplished her goal. Though her novels are fairly simple and predictable, Spencer keeps the reader engrossed by creating believable situations and realistic characters. She invents people with whom the reader can identify as she explores their thoughts and emotions with sensitivity and compassion. Her novels are filled with warmth and sensuality, and just enough anticipation that they are difficult to put down. The characters travel through the story to the inevitable happy ending.

Although Spencer's novels are set in many different places and times, love is the common theme. She explores love in all of its forms: physical, romantic, and familial. Many of her novels have historical settings, including *The Endearment* (1982), *The Gamble* (1987), and *Hummingbird* (1983), the last of which "launched (her) stunning career" according to *Affaire de Coeur. Hummingbird* is the story of a very prim and proper spinster who learns from an alleged train robber how to enjoy life and love. Spencer makes the reader feel the inner turmoil the heroine experiences as she struggles to abandon her rigid codes of behavior and morality and learns not only how to love but how to be loved.

Spencer also deals with the complexities of marriage and families. In *November of the Heart* (1992), a girl from a wealthy society family falls in love with a laborer and must make the difficult decision whether to follow the wishes of her family or the desires of her heart. Spencer presents the story from all sides so the reader can identify both with the impulsive young lover's anger and sorrow and the family's fear and difficulty in letting their daughter become an independent adult. *Kirkus Reviews* calls this novel "one of Spencer's best." *Home Song* (1995) is another novel that deals with family issues. The Gardeners seem to have the perfect family—two happily married parents with two well-adjusted, happy children—until a mistake from Tom Gardener's past arrives in the form of a son he didn't know he had. This story is truly heart-wrenching as all of the characters have to evaluate and redefine their relationships while coming to terms with this situation.

Spencer's work has received many glowing reviews from both romance publications and sources such as the New York *Daily News* and the *Los Angeles Times*. Her strength lies not so much in the content of her stories as in the feelings of empathy and compassion she provokes in the reader. Her novels are geared toward the ordinary person that may need a little injection of faith in the innate goodness of people. Though her characters face many trials and tribulations, in the end love and goodness always triumph. "(Her) legions of fans are drawn to her fiction because of its uncalculated emotion and the author's almost old-fashioned sense of integrity," according to the *Chicago Tribune*.

In a world where happy endings are rare, sometimes it's nice to be drawn into someone else's world—to experience their joys and sorrows and to be assured that all will be well in the end. Above all, Spencer gives the reader a chance to believe in love.

—Jane Conkright

ST. CLAIRE, Erin. *See* **BROWN, Sandra.**

STACK, Andy. *See* **RULE, Ann.**

STARK, Richard. *See* **WESTLAKE, Donald E.**

STEEL, Danielle (Fernande)

Nationality: American. **Born:** 14 August 1947 in New York City. **Education:** Educated in France; attended Parsons School of Design, 1963, and New York University, 1963-67. **Family:** Married second husband in 1977 (divorced); married to third husband, John Traina; children: (first marriage) one daughter; (second marriage) one son; (third marriage) two stepsons, four daughters, one son. **Career:** Supergirls, Ltd. (public relations firm), vice president of public relations, 1968-71; Grey Advertising, San Francisco, copywriter, 1973-74; has worked at other positions in public relations and advertising; writer.

Agent: Morton L. Janklow Associates, Inc., 598 Madison Ave., New York, New York 10022, U.S.A.

PUBLICATIONS

Novels

Going Home. Pocket Books, 1973.
Passion's Promise. Dell, 1977.
The Promise. Dell, 1978.
Now and Forever. Dell, 1978.
Season of Passion. Dell, 1979.
Summer's End. Dell, 1979.
The Ring. Delacorte, 1980.
Loving. Dell, 1980.
Remembrance. Delacorte, 1981.
Palomino. Dell, 1981.
To Love Again. Dell, 1981.
Crossings. Delacorte, 1982.
Once in a Lifetime. Dell, 1982.
A Perfect Stranger. Dell, 1982.
Changes. Delacorte, 1983.
Thurston House. Dell, 1983.
Full Circle. Delacorte, 1984.
Secrets. Delacorte, 1985.
Family Album. Delacorte, 1985.
Wanderlust. Delacorte, 1986.
Fine Things. Delacorte, 1987.
Kaleidoscope. Delacorte, 1987.
Zoya. Delacorte, 1988.
Star. Delacorte, 1989.
Daddy. Delacorte, 1989.
Message from Nam. Delacorte, 1990.
Heartbeat. Delacorte, 1991.
No Greater Love. Delacorte, 1991.
Mixed Blessings. Delacorte, 1992.
Jewels. Delacorte, 1992.
Vanished. Delacorte, 1993.
The Gift. Delacorte, 1994.
Accident. Delacorte, 1994.
Wings. Delacorte, 1994.
Lightning. Delacorte, 1994.
Five Days in Paris. Delacorte, 1995.
Malice. Delacorte, 1996.
Days of Shame. Delacorte, 1996.

Fiction for Children

Martha's Best Friend. Delacorte, 1989.
Martha's New Daddy. Delacorte, 1989.
Martha's New School. Delacorte, 1989.
Max and the Baby-Sitter. Delacorte, 1989.
Max's Daddy Goes to the Hospital. Delacorte, 1989.
Max's New Baby. Delacorte, 1989.
Martha's New Puppy. Delacorte, 1990.
Max Runs Away. Delacorte, 1990.
Max and Grandma and Grandpa Winky. Delacorte, 1991.
Martha and Hillary and the Stranger. Delacorte, 1991.
Freddie's Trip. Dell, 1992.
Freddie's First Night Away. Dell, 1992.
Freddie's Accident. Dell, 1992.
Freddie and the Doctor. Dell, 1992.

Poetry

Love Poems: Danielle Steel. Dell, 1981; abridged edition, Delacorte, 1984.

*

Media Adaptations: Films—*Now and Forever,* 1983. Television miniseries—*Crossings,* 1986. Television films—*Kaleidoscope,* 1990; *Fine Things,* 1990; *Changes,* 1991; *Daddy,* 1991; *Palomino,* 1991.

* * *

The writings of Danielle Steel are best classified as romance novels. Her storylines are fairly predictable, containing love, tragedy, loss, healing, and love found anew. Her characters are vulnerable yet strong, suffering yet hopeful, and sophisticated yet simple. Her endings are always happy. Judging by book sales, Steel is unarguably a master in a huge, highly competitive niche of the fiction industry.

Steel has written many novels over the span of her career, most of which have made the bestseller list and several of which have become television miniseries. In 1986, in fact, she got into the *Guiness Book World of World Records* for having at least one of her books on the *New York Times* bestseller list for 225 consecutive weeks. Despite consistently weak, even negative reviews, she continues to sell millions of books with each new release.

Reading one of her novels has been likened to watching a television miniseries. Travel, intrigue, untimely deaths, and love abound in her stories. Though the reader can be guaranteed a happy ending, the roller-coaster ride of emotions leading up to that point can be tantalizing, or excruciating, depending on the reader's perception of soap-opera-style writing.

Steel typically receives raves from critics who enjoy light, easy romance stories. These reviewers tend to appreciate her storytelling abilities and her talent for creating intriguing characters. For example, in her review of *Zoya* (1988), Mary Ellen Kent in the *Indianapolis Star* said "Zoya has a wonderful fairy-tale-like quality. The heroine, Zoya, is not only a Russian countess but also a beautiful ballerina, so the elements for daydreams are in place from the beginning."

But some reviewers of Steel's writings have used words like "brain-dead" to describe her plots.

Heartbeat (1991) is the story of Bill Thigpen, a writer and producer of a top daytime soap opera. His wife, feeling neglected and hating his long work hours, divorces him when Bill's show and Bill are moved to California. Once in Hollywood, Bill meets a married, pregnant news show producer whose husband does not want their baby. They immediately fall in love. The development of their relationship makes up the storyline of this tale of two rejected characters who find each other, and the hurdles they must overcome to stay together. This is definitive Danielle Steel; a quick read and moderately entertaining.

Zoya (1988) tells the life story of Zoya, a Russian countess and ballerina. Her parents and brother are killed in the revolution, leaving her to provide for her grandmother and an elderly servant. Zoya escapes to Paris and uses her dancing talent to earn a living.

She meets and marries an American soldier and moves to New York after the war. They start a family and build a fortune only to lose everything in the stock market crash. Her husband then dies of a heart attack and she is once again alone and poor with children to support. She eventually works her way back to being a countess again. Though the reader becomes fond of the lead character, the pace of this story becomes tiring and the plot twists unbelievable.

A more recent novel titled *The Gift* (1994) is one of Steel's best efforts. This story depends less on death and tragedy, and focuses more on making a positive out of a negative. Though not lacking in tragic circumstances, this book contains believable characters, real-life situations, and a bittersweet ending. The reader is drawn into the story by the lead characters, Tommy and Maribeth. These two young people come together by accident and find in each other the strength and unconditional love they need to get through their respective difficulties. This one is hard to put down. The reader cannot help feeling for all of the characters, and hoping for the best for each of them. This is Steel's 33rd bestselling book, and worth reading.

Since 1989 Steel has also written several children's books. But it is with romance novels that she continues to accrue a huge and loyal following.

—Amy Faulkenberry

STEPHENS, Reed. *See* **DONALDSON, Stephen R.**

STEWART, Mary (Florence Elinor)

Nationality: British. **Born:** Mary Rainbow, Sunderland, County Durham, 17 September 1916. **Education:** Eden Hall, Penrith, Cumberland; Skellfield School, Ripon, Yorkshire; St. Hilda's College, University of Durham, B.A. (honours) 1938, M.A. 1941. **Military Service:** Royal Observer Corps during World War II. **Family:** Married Sir Frederick Henry Stewart in 1945. **Career:** Lecturer in English, Durham University, 1941-45. **Awards:** Crime Writers Association Silver Dagger, 1961; Frederick Niven award, 1971; Scottish Arts Council award, 1975. Fellow, Royal Society of Arts, 1968; Fellow, Newnham College, Cambridge, 1986. **Address:** c/o Hodder Headline PLC, 338 Euston Road, London NW1 3BH, England.

Publications

Novels (series: Merlin)

Madam, Will You Talk? Hodder and Stoughton, 1955.
Wildfire at Midnight. Hodder and Stoughton, 1956.
Thunder on the Right. Hodder and Stoughton, 1957.
Nine Coaches Waiting. Hodder and Stoughton, 1958.
My Brother Michael. Hodder and Stoughton, 1960.
The Ivy Tree. Hodder and Stoughton, 1961.
The Moon Spinners. Hodder and Stoughton, 1962.
This Rough Magic. Hodder and Stoughton, 1964.
Airs above the Ground. Hodder and Stoughton, 1965.
The Gabriel Hounds. Hodder and Stoughton, 1967.
The Wind Off the Small Isles. Hodder and Stoughton, 1968.
Touch Not the Cat. Hodder and Stoughton, 1976.
Merlin Trilogy. Morrow, 1980.
  The Crystal Cave. Hodder and Stoughton, 1970.
  The Hollow Hills. Hodder and Stoughton, 1973.
  The Last Enchantment. Hodder and Stoughton, 1979.
The Wicked Day (Merlin). Hodder and Stoughton, 1983.
Thornyhold. Hodder and Stoughton, 1988.
Stormy Petrel. Hodder and Stoughton, 1991.
The Prince and the Pilgrim. Hodder and Stoughton, 1995.

Poetry

Frost on the Window and Other Poems. Hodder and Stoughton, 1990.

Plays

Radio Plays: *Lift from a Stranger, Call Me at Ten-Thirty, The Crime of Mr. Merry,* and *The Lord of Langdale,* 1957-58.

Other (for children)

The Little Broomstick. Brockhampton Press, 1971.
Ludo and the Star Horse. Brockhampton Press, 1974.
A Walk in Wolf Wood. Hodder and Stoughton, 1980.

*

Film Adaptation: *The Moon-Spinners,* 1964.

Manuscript Collection: National Library of Scotland, Edinburgh.

* * *

Mary Stewart appeared on the popular fiction scene in 1956 with her romantic adventure *Madam, Will You Talk?* James Sandoe coined the term "Eurydicean" for the kind of novel, which when looked back upon, reveals such tremendous inconsistencies and coincidences that the novel seems to disappear. *Madam* to some extent fits this term neatly; but as Anthony Boucher allowed, ". . . so unusually skillful is this young Englishwoman in her first novel that you don't really care."

Without exception, her romantic thrillers center upon an attractive, intelligent, likable, young lady who with the help of a love interest solves a mystery. These stories are set in exotic or mysterious locales with a pervading atmosphere of ambiguity. Who is good? Who is evil? These questions are not easily answered until the heart-pounding climax brings the story to its close.

The reader is whisked to such atmospheric locales as the Isle of Skye in *Wildfire at Midnight* (1956), where the practice of an ancient ritual murder has been revived; the French Pyrenees in *Thunder on the Right* (1958); Haute Savoie near the Swiss border in *Nine Coaches Waiting* (1959); Delphi in *My Brother Michael* (1960); a farm in Northumberland in *The Ivy Tree* (1961); Crete's White Mountains in *The Moon-Spinners* (1963); the Isle of Corfu in *This Rough Magic* (1964); Styria, Austria in *Airs above the Ground* (1965); and the Near East in *The Gabriel Hounds* (1967).

No one writes the damsel-in-distress tale with more charm and urgency than Stewart. She crams her novels thick with action and suspense. Her chase scenes are brilliantly cinematic. In fact, in 1964 *The Moon-Spinners* was made into a Disney movie starring Hayley Mills. As Anthony Boucher points out, "her heroines are always spirited, intelligent, resolute—quite free from the vapid idiocy which mars most books of this type."

In 1970 Stewart diverged from her path by tackling the Arthurian myth in the first novel of her Merlin trilogy, *The Crystal Cave*. She expands the myth into a first-person history told from the perspective of Merlin. The story follows six-year-old Merlin up to his role in the conception of Arthur in Ygraine by Uther Pendragon. She sets the romantic adventure in the more historically accurate fifth-century Britain. Stewart provides the reader with so many historically accurate details of the daily life of the period that the legend is given an authentic feel. Once again Stewart excels at distilling the mystic romance out of the locale; in this case, Wales, Cornwall, and Brittany. The second of the trilogy, *The Hollow Hills,* followed in 1973. In this chapter Merlin sets out to teach Arthur about kingship, and to maneuver events so Arthur will pull the sword from the stone. Stewart closed the trilogy in 1979 with *The Last Enchantment,* which moves from Arthur's coronation to the phasing out of Merlin's role.

The Wicked Day (1983) followed the trilogy with the story of Mordred, son of Arthur and Morgause (Arthur's half-sister). In this entertaining romance, Stewart recasts Mordred as a sort of Hamlet helpless before his fate, instead of the evil, power-driven, illegitimate son most readers have seen before.

All of Stewart's novels, though they may fail in originality, give the reader much urgent action and suspense sketched on gorgeous and mysterious locales.

—Jennifer G. Coman

STINE, R(obert) L(awrence)

Pseudonyms: Jovial Bob Stine. **Nationality:** American. **Born:** Columbus, Ohio, 8 October 1943. **Education:** Ohio State University, B.A., 1965; graduate study at New York University, 1966-67. **Family:** Married Jane Waldhorn in 1969; one son. **Career:** Social Studies teacher at junior high schools in Columbus, Ohio, 1967-68; *Junior Scholastic* magazine, New York City, associate editor, 1969-71; *Search* magazine, New York City, editor, 1972-75; *Bananas* magazine, New York City, editor, 1972-83; *Maniac* magazine, New York City, editor, 1984-85; freelance writer, 1982—; head writer for *Eureeka's Castle,* Nickelodeon cable network. **Awards:** Several Children's Choice awards, American Library Association. **Address:** 225 West 71st St., New York, New York 10023, U.S.A.

Publications

Fiction for Children and Young Adults

The Time Raider, illustrations by David Febland. Scholastic, 1982.
The Golden Sword of Dragonwalk, illustrations by Febland. Scholastic, 1983.
Horrors of the Haunted Museum. Scholastic, 1984.
Instant Millionaire, illustrations by Jowill Woodman. Scholastic, 1984.
Through the Forest of Twisted Dreams. Avon, 1984.
The Siege of the Dragonriders, as Eric Affabee. Avon, 1984.
Indiana Jones and the Curse of Horror Island. Ballantine, 1984.
Indiana Jones and the Giants of the Silver Tower. Ballantine, 1984.
Indiana Jones and the Cult of the Mummy's Crypt. Ballantine, 1985.
The Badlands of Hark, illustrations by Bob Roper. Scholastic, 1985.
The Invaders of Hark. Scholastic, 1985.
Demons of the Deep, illustrations by Fred Carrillo. Golden Books, 1985.
Challenge of the Wolf Knight. Avon, 1985.
James Bond in Win, Place, or Die. Ballantine, 1985.
Conquest of the Time Master. Avon, 1985.
Attack on the King, as Eric Affabee. Avon, 1986.
Blind Date. Scholastic, 1986.
Cavern of the Phantoms. Avon, 1986.
G.I. Joe and the Everglades Swamp Terror, as Eric Affabee. Ballantine, 1986.
G.I.Joe: Operation Star Raider, as Eric Affabee. Ballantine, 1986.
Mystery of the Imposter. Avon, 1986.
Operation: Deadly Decoy. Ballantine, 1986.
The Dragon Queen's Revenge, as Eric Affabee. Avon, 1986.
Twisted. Scholastic, 1987.
The Jet Fighter Trap, as Zachary Blue. Scholastic, 1987.
The Petrova Twist, as Zachary Blue. Scholastic, 1987.
Broken Date. Simon & Schuster, 1988.
Jungle Raid. Ballantine, 1988.
The Baby-Sitter. Scholastic, 1989.
Phone Calls. Archway, 1990.
How I Broke Up with Ernie. Archway, 1990.
Curtains. Archway, 1990.
The Boyfriend. Scholastic, 1990.
Beach Party. Scholastic, 1990.
Snowman. Scholastic, 1991.
The Girlfriend. Scholastic, 1991.
Baby-Sitter II. Scholastic, 1991.
Beach House. Scholastic, 1992.
Hit and Run. Scholastic, 1992.
Be Careful What You Wish For. Scholastic, 1993.
Hitchhiker. Scholastic, 1993.
Baby-Sitter III. Scholastic, 1993.
The Dead Girl Friend. Scholastic, 1993.
Halloween Night. Scholastic, 1993.
The Beast. Minstrel, 1994.
Call Waiting. Scholastic, 1994.
Halloween Night II. Scholastic, 1994.
Horrors of the Haunted Museum. Scholastic, 1994.
I Saw You That Night. Scholastic, 1994.
Baby-Sitter IV. Scholastic, 1995.
The Beast II. Minstrel, 1995.
Cataluna Chronicles: The Deadly Fire. Pocket Books, 1995.
Superstitious. Warner, 1995.
Time Raiders. Scholastic, 1995.

Fear Street Series
The New Girl. Archway, 1989.

The Surprise Party. Archway, 1990.
The Stepsister. Archway, 1990.
Missing. Archway, 1990.
Halloween Party. Archway, 1990.
The Wrong Number. Archway, 1990.
The Sleepwalker. Archway, 1991.
Ski Weekend. Archway, 1991.
The Secret Bedroom. Archway, 1991.
The Overnight. Archway, 1991.
Lights Out. Archway, 1991.
Haunted. Archway, 1991.
The Fire Game. Archway, 1991.
Prom Queen. Archway, 1992.
The Knife. Archway, 1992.
First Date. Archway, 1992.
The Best Friend. Archway, 1992.
Sunburn. Archway, 1993.
The Cheater. Archway, 1993.
Bad Dreams. Archway, 1994.
The Dare. Archway, 1994.
The Dead Lifeguard. Archway, 1994.
Double Date. Archway, 1994.
The Mind Reader. Archway, 1994.
The New Boy. Archway, 1994.
One Evil Summer. Archway, 1994.
Thrill Club. Archway, 1994.
College Weekend. Archway, 1995.
Final Grade. Archway, 1995.
The Stepsister II. Archway, 1995.
Switched. Archway, 1995.
Truth or Dare. Archway, 1995.
Wrong Number II. Archway, 1995.
The Boy Next Door. Archway, 1996.
The Face. Pocket Books, 1996.
House of Whispers. Pocket Books, 1996.
A New Fear. Pocket Books, 1996.
The Perfect Date. Pocket Books, 1996.
Secret Admirer. Pocket Books, 1996.
What Holly Heard. Pocket Books, 1996.

Fear Street: Super Chiller Series
Party Summer. Archway, 1991.
Silent Night. Archway, 1991.
Goodnight Kiss. Archway, 1992.
Silent Night II. Archway, 1992.
Broken Hearts. Archway, 1993.
Bad Moonlight. Archway, 1995.
Dead End. Archway, 1995.
The New Year's Party. Archway, 1995.

Fear Street: Cheerleaders Series
The First Evil. Archway, 1992.
The Second Evil. Archway, 1992.
The Third Evil. Archway, 1992.
The New Evil. Archway, 1994.

Fear Street Chronicles Series
Evil Moon. Pocket Books, 1995.

Fear Street Saga Series
The Betrayal. Archway, 1993.
The Secret. Archway, 1993.
The Burning. Archway, 1993.

99 Fear Street: The House of Evil Series
The First Horror. Archway, 1994.
The Second Horror. Archway, 1994.
The Third Horror. Archway, 1994.

Ghosts of Fear Street Series
The Attack of the Aqua Apes. Pocket Books, 1995.
The Bugman Lives. Pocket Books, 1996.
The Eye of the Fortunteller. Pocket Books, 1996.
Fright Knight. Pocket Books, 1996.
Revenge of the Shadow People. Pocket Books, 1996.
Stay Away from the Three House. Pocket Books, 1996.

Goosebumps Series (all from Scholastic Press)
Welcome to Dead House. 1992.
Stay out of the Basement. 1992.
Monster Blood. 1992.
Say Cheese and Die. 1992.
The Curse of the Mummy's Tomb. 1993.
Let's Get Invisible. 1993.
Night of the Living Dummy. 1993.
The Girl Who Cried Monster. 1993.
Welcome to Camp Nightmare. 1993.
The Ghost Next Door. 1993.
The Haunted Mask. 1993.
Piano Lessons Can Be Murder. 1993.
The Werewolf of Fever Swamp. 1993.
Attack of the Mutant. 1994.
Deep Trouble. 1994.
Ghost Beach. 1994.
Go Eat Worms! 1994.
My Hairiest Adventure. 1994.
Monster Blood II. 1994.
Phantom of the Auditorium. 1994.
Return of the Mummy. 1994.
The Scarecrow Walks at Midnight. 1994.
Why I'm Afraid of Bess. 1994.
You Can't Scare Me. 1994.
The Abominable Snowman of Pasadena. 1995.
The Barking Ghost. 1995.
The Cuckoo Clock of Doom. 1995.
Escape from the Carnival of Horrors. 1995.
The Haunted Mask II. 1995.
The Headless Ghost. 1995.
The Horror at Camp Jellyjam. 1995.
It Came from Beneath the Sink. 1995.
Monster Blood III. 1995.
More Tales to Give You Goosebumps. 1995.
A Night in Terror Tower. 1995.
Revenge of the Lawn Gnomes. 1995.
Bad Hare Day. 1996.
Beast from the East. 1996.
Egg Monster from Mars. 1996.
Ghost Camp. 1996.
The Girl Who Cried Monster. 1996.
How I Got My Shrunken Head. 1996.
Night of the Living Dummy III. 1996.
Say Cheese and Die! Again. 1996.

Give Yourself Goosebumps Series (all from Scholastic Press)
Tick Tock, You're Dead. 1995.
Trapped in Batwing Hall. 1995.
Beware of the Purple Peanut Butter. 1996.
The Magician's Spell. 1996.
Night in Werewolf Woods. 1996.
Space Cadets Series
Jerks-in-Training. Scholastic, 1991.
Losers in Space. Scholastic, 1991.
Bozos on Patrol. Scholastic, 1992.

Fiction for Children and Young Adults as Jovial Bob Stine

The Absurdly Silly Encyclopedia and Flyswatter, illustrations by Bob Taylor. Scholastic Book Services, 1978.
How To Be Funny: An Extremely Silly Guidebook, illustrations by Carol Nicklaus. Dutton, 1978.
The Complete Book of Nerds, illustrations by Sam Viviano. Scholastic Book Services, 1979.
The Dynamite Do-It-Yourself Pen Pal Kit, illustrations by Jared Lee. Scholastic Book Services, 1980.
Dynamite's Funny Book of the Sad Facts of Life, illustrations by Lee, Scholastic Book Services, 1980.
Going Out! Going Steady! Going Bananas!, photographs by Dan Nelken, Scholastic Book Services, 1980.
The Pigs' Book of World Records, illustrations by Peter Lippman, Random House, 1980.
The Sick of Being Sick Book, with Jane Stine, edited by Ann Durrell, illustrations by Nicklaus. Dutton, 1980.
Bananas Looks at TV. Scholastic Book Services, 1981.
The Beast Handbook, illustrations by Taylor. Scholastic Book Services, 1981.
The Cool Kids' Guide to Summer Camp, with Jane Stine, illustrations by Jerry Zimmerman, Scholastic Book Services, 1981.
Gnasty Gnomes, illustrations by Lippman. Random House, 1981.
Don't Stand in the Soup, illustrations by Nicklaus. Bantam Books, 1982.
Bored with Being Bored!: How to Beat the Boredom Blahs, illustrations by Zimmerman. Four Winds, 1982.
Blips!: The First Book of Video Game Funnies, illustrations by Bryan Hendrix. Scholastic, 1983.
Everything You Need to Survive: Brothers and Sisters, with Jane Stine. Random House, 1983.
Everything You Need to Survive: First Dates, with Jane Stine. Random House, 1983.
Everything You Need to Survive: Homework, with Jane Stine, Random House, 1983.
Everything You Need to Survive: Money Problems, with Jane Stine. Random House, 1983.
Jovial Bob's Computer Joke Book. Scholastic, 1985.
Miami Mice, illustrations by Eric Gurney. Scholastic, 1986.
One Hundred and One Silly Monster Jokes. Scholastic, 1986.
The Doggone Dog Joke Book. Parachute Press, 1986.
Pork and Beans: Play Date, illustrations by Jose Aruego and Ariane Dewey. Scholastic, 1989.
Ghostbusters II Storybook. Scholastic, 1989.
One Hundred and One Vacation Jokes, illustrations by Rick Majica. Scholastic, 1990.
The Amazing Adventures of Me, Myself, and I. Bantam, 1991.

*

Media Adaptations: Television series—*Goosebumps.*

* * *

Elementary and middle-school teachers rue what he has wrought, but R. L. Stine's fans—pre-teens and young adults—seem spellbound by this Ohio-born writer's craft. Stine has penned more than 100 books for young people and is among the most successful writers in his niche. He started churning out books in the early 1980s, achieving acclaim with numerous books of adventure, young love, and various youth-related issues like baby-sitting. He is perhaps best known for his "Fear Street" and "Goosebumps" series, which he started publishing in 1989. He has also published numerous books, including many young people's joke books, under the name Jovial Bob Stine.

When, as an adult, he visited the elementary school that he attended as a boy, Stine's teacher, Mrs. Drugan, greeted him with a hug and a pet name of "my Bobby." One young second grader declared Stine his favorite author and asserted that he was the proud owner of 38 Stine books, which his mother read to him. Yet another young Stine reader, a 14-year-old, explained his addiction to Stine's books as having started when he was a fifth grader. He declared Stine to be the Stephen King of the teen set.

What do young people find so spellbinding about Stine's successful "Fear Street" and "Goosebumps" books? Look at the covers of any of these books or at the Fox television series *Goosebumps,* and it will be clear that Stine appeals to young people's desire to be frightened out of their wits—what literary critics call "the gothic" when they speak of writers such as Edgar Allan Poe and Charles Brockden Brown. R. L. Stine cautions readers that none of the things that happen on his "Fear Street" are true, they are just intended to be scary.

Typical of Stine's work is his Fear Street Saga trilogy, which revolves around teen relationships that are complicated by murder or potential murder. The Fear Street books are usually set at Shadyside High School, and each chapter of each book ends with a cliffhanger that compels the youthful reader to pick up the book again for another reading. The Saga stories are set in the burned out Fear Mansion, which is all that is left of the Fear family. *The Betrayal* (1993) tells of an innocent young girl who was burned at the stake as a witch, setting off a bloody 200-year feud. The story continues in the sequel, *The Secret* (1993), where Simon Fear learns a mighty secret which may save his teenage daughters from the family curse. *The Burning* (1993) concludes the series with Simon Fear trying to save his daughters and Nora, the last of the Fear family.

Stine has written numerous funny novels and joke books for young children. *How I Broke Up With Ernie* (1990), for example, is the comical story of young Amy and her attempts to break up with Ernie. Likewise, in *Phone Calls* (1990), Stine portrays five teens engaged in a deadly game of phone war.

Robert Stine, who also served as head writer for Nickelodeon's television show "Eureeka's Castle," lives in New York with his wife Jane and their teenage son Matt.

—Bennis Blue

STONE, Irving

Nationality: American. **Born:** Irving Tannenbaum, 14 July 1903, in San Francisco; name legally changed to Stone. **Education:** University of California, Berkeley, B.A., 1923, graduate study, 1924-26; University of Southern California, M.A., 1924. **Family:** Married Jean Factor in 1934; children: Paula Hubbell, Kenneth. **Career:** University of Southern California, Los Angeles, instructor in economics, 1923-24; University of California, Berkeley, instructor in economics, 1924-26; writer, 1926—. Visiting professor of creative writing, University of Indiana, 1948, University of Washington, 1961, and Gustavus Adolphus College, 1982; lecturer, University of Southern California and California State Colleges, 1966, New York University and Johns Hopkins University, 1985. Specialist on cultural exchange for U.S. State Department to Soviet Union, Poland, and Yugoslavia, 1962; contributing member, American School of Classical Studies, Athens, Greece, from 1965. Member of advisory board, University of California Institute for Creative Arts, from 1963; founder, California State Colleges Committee for the Arts, 1967; member, Center for the Study of Evolution and the Origin of Life, University of California, Los Angeles, 1985. Member, U.S. delegation to Writers Conference, Kiev, Soviet Union, 1982; panelist, Nobel Conference on "Darwin's Legacy"; member, Soviet-American Writers Conference, Pepperdine University, 1984; Regents' professor, University of California, Los Angeles, from 1984. **Awards:** Christopher award and Silver Spur award from Western Writers of America, both 1957, for *Men to Match My Mountains*; Golden Lily of Florence, Rupert Hughes award from Author's Club, Gold Medal from Council of American Artist Societies, and Gold Medal from Commonwealth Club of California, all for *The Agony and the Ecstasy*; named commendatore of Republic of Italy; American Revolution Round Table award and Literary Father of the Year award, both 1966, for *Those Who Love*; Gold Trophy from American Women in Radio and Television, 1968; Herbert Adams Memorial medal from National Sculpture Society, 1970; Golden Plate award from American Academy of Achievement, 1971; Alumnus of the Year from University of California, Berkeley, 1971; Corpus Litterarum award from Friends of the Libraries, University of California, Irvine, 1975; Author of the Year award from Book Bank USA, 1976; distinguished body of work annual award, Los Angeles PEN Center, 1980; Rupert Hughes award for excellence in writing from Author's Club, 1980; Call Achievement award from University of Southern California, 1980; named Grand Ufficiale of the Italian Republic, 1982; Neil H. Jacoby award from International Student Center, University of California at Los Angeles, 1983; honorary citation from Union of Soviet Writers, 1983. Commandeur dans l'Ordre des Arts et des Lettres from French Ministry of Culture, 1984. D.L. from University of Southern California, 1965; D.Litt. from Coe College, 1967, and California State Colleges, 1971; LL.D. from University of California, Berkeley, 1968; H.H.D. from Hebrew Union College, 1978. **Member:** Society of American Historians, National Society of Arts and Letters (member of advisory council, from 1976), Academy of American Motion Picture Arts and Sciences, Academy of Political Science, Academy of American Poets (founder), Renaissance Society of America, Historical Society of Southern California, Fellows for Schweitzer (founder and president, from 1955), Berkeley Fellows (charter member), Los Angeles Dante Alighieri Society (president, 1968-69). **Died:** 26 August 1989 in Los Angeles, of heart failure.

PUBLICATIONS

Novels

Lust for Life. Longmans, Green, 1934.
Sailor on Horseback. Houghton, 1938; as *Jack London, Sailor on Horseback*, Doubleday, 1947.
False Witness. Doubleday, 1940.
Immortal Wife. Doubleday, 1944.
Adversary in the House. Doubleday, 1947.
The Passionate Journey. Doubleday, 1949.
The President's Lady: A Biographical Novel of Rachel and Andrew Jackson. Doubleday, 1951.
Love Is Eternal: A Biographical Novel of Mary Todd and Abraham Lincoln. Doubleday, 1954.
The Agony and the Ecstasy. Doubleday, 1961.
Those Who Love. Doubleday, 1965.
The Passions of the Mind. Doubleday, 1971.
The Greek Treasure: A Biographical Novel of Henry and Sophia Schliemann. Doubleday, 1975.
The Origin. Doubleday, 1980.
Depths of Glory: A Biographical Novel of Camille Pissaro. Doubleday, 1985.

Nonfiction

Pageant of Youth. A. H. King, 1933.
Clarence Darrow for the Defense. Doubleday, 1941; reprinted, New American Library, 1971.
They Also Ran: The Story of the Men Who Were Defeated for the Presidency. Doubleday, 1945.
Earl Warren: A Great American Story. Prentice-Hall, 1948.
We Speak for Ourselves: A Self-Portrait of America. Doubleday, 1950.
Men to Match My Mountains: The Opening of the Far West, 1840-1900. Doubleday, 1956.
The Story of Michelangelo's Pieta. Doubleday, 1964.
The Science, and the Art, of Biography. Division of Honors, University of California, Los Angeles, 1986.
The Composition and Distribution of British Investment in Latin America, 1865-1913. Garland, 1987.
Keeping Spirit Journal. Doubleday, 1987.

Editor, with Jean Stone, *Dear Theo: The Autobiography of Vincent van Gogh*. Doubleday, 1937.
Editor and author of introduction, *The Drawings of Michelangelo*. Borden Publishing, 1961.
Editor, with Stone, *I, Michelangelo, Sculptor: An Autobiography through Letters*. Doubleday, 1962.
Editor, with Allan Nevins, *Lincoln: A Contemporary Portrait*. Doubleday, 1962.
Editor and author of introduction, *There Was Light: Autobiography of a University; Berkeley*. Doubleday, 1970.

Plays

The Dark Mirror (produced New York, 1928).
The White Life (produced New York, 1929).
Truly Valiant (produced New York, 1936).

Screenplays: *Magnificent Doll*, 1946.

*

Film Adaptations: *Arkansas Judge*, adapted from his novel *False Witness*, 1941; *The President's Lady*, adapted from his novel *Immortal Wife*, 1953; *Lust for Life*, 1956; *The Agony and the Ecstasy*, 1963.

* * *

Irving Stone claimed that he wrote "bio-history." He identified the genre as "bringing history to life in terms of the tremendous human stories that have made history." For each of his books, Stone did extensive research. *The Agony and the Ecstasy* (1961), for example, required over four years of research and extensive interviews with the founder of UCLA's Italian Department to translate Michelangelo's letters into English. Yet Stone still acknowledged that his research was limited by the impossibility of knowing what went on inside a man's head, and noted that this is the point at which the novelist must become creative.

Lust for Life (1934), Stone's first work to receive popular acclaim, is an intimate study into the life of Vincent van Gogh. Aside from van Gogh, the characters that interested Stone were generally found in American history: *Sailor on Horseback* (1938) about Jack London, *Adversary in the House* (1947) about Eugene Debs, and *The President's Lady* (1951) about Rachael Jackson. Some of his work attempts to focus upon more than one individual. *They Also Ran* (1943), for example, is an account of the lives of defeated Presidential candidates.

Critical reception to Stone's work is often mixed. Although *The Agony and Ecstasy* is considered Stone's best work, reviewer's have criticized its "optimistic" narrative method; Stone often discovers facts about Michelangelo's life then alters them to fit his fiction. Robert J. Clements in the *Saturday Review* called Stone's Michelangelo "an idealized version purged . . . of egotism, fault-finding, harsh irony, and ill temper." *Those Who Love* (1965), a novel about Abigail Adams, also received mixed reviews, and critics accused Stone of ignoring Adam's faults and idealizing her.

The Passions of the Mind (1971), a novel about Sigmund Freud, received the harshest critical response. Reviewers described the novel as a failure in historical fiction and surmised that the work was aimed only at people with no knowledge of Freud. Steven Marcus of the *Atlantic Monthly* wrote that "Stone's incapacities as a novelist are inseparable from his ineptitudes as a biographer, even as a popular one; actually, he is not even a biographer but a simple chronicler." *The Greek Treasure* (1975), based on letters between Heinrich Schliemann (the archeologist who unearthed Troy) and his wife, Sophia, received more favorable reviews.

Stone wrote *Depths of Glory* (1987) shortly before his death. It is an account of Camille Pissarro and his contributions to the Impressionist movement. The novel has a more realistic tone in its depiction of a struggling artist in 19th-century Paris. The *Los Angeles Times* felt the novel possessed an understanding of an artist's obsession with achieving greatness and accurately depicted the realities of living in poverty and unhappiness.

Some critics attribute Stone's popular reception to the challenging nature of his fiction. One must spend time with a Stone work, but when one has completed it one feels a sense of accomplishment not found in less thorough works. Stone admitted that at times he is complex and long-winded (some manuscripts were half a million words before his late wife edited them). Stone's response to harsh critical reception was that he had "a passionately optimistic nature," which inevitably affected the presentation of his characters. Stone also felt most of the negative criticism was based upon a lack of respect for the genre. He once declared, "the great school of historical novelists is a thing of the past, with some of them dead and others no longer working in the field."

—Chris Godat

STONE, Zachary. *See* **FOLLETT, Ken.**

STRAUB, Peter (Francis)

Nationality: American. **Born:** Milwaukee, Wisconsin, 2 March 1943. **Education:** University of Wisconsin-Madison, B.A., 1965; Columbia University, M.A., 1966; attended University College, Dublin, 1969-72. **Family:** Married Susan Bitker, 1966; one son, one daughter. **Career:** University School, Milwaukee, Wisconsin, English teacher, 1966-69; writer, 1969—. **Awards:** British Fantasy award and August Derleth award, both 1983, for *Floating Dragon.* **Member:** Writers Action Group. **Address:** P.O. Box 395, Greens Farms, Connecticut 06436, U.S.A.

Publications

Novels

Marriages. Coward, 1973.
Julia. Coward, 1975.
If You Could See Me Now. Coward, 1977.
Ghost Story. Coward, 1979.
Shadowland. Coward, 1980.
Floating Dragon. Putnam, 1983.
The Talisman, with Stephen King. Viking, 1984.
Blue Rose. Underwood/Miller, 1985.
Under Venus. Berkley, 1985.
Koko. Dutton, 1988.
Mystery. Dutton, 1991.
Mrs. God. Donald Grant, 1991.
The Throat. Dutton, 1993.
The Hellfire Club. Random House, 1996.

Short Stories

The General's Wife. D. M. Grant, 1982.
Houses without Doors. Dutton, 1991.

Poetry

Ishmael. Turret Books, 1972, Underwood/Miller, 1973.
Open Air. Irish University Press, 1972.
Leeson Park and Belsize Square: Poems 1970-1975. Underwood/Miller, 1983.

*

Film Adaptations: *The Haunting of Julia,* 1981, from *Julia; Ghost Story,* 1981.

* * *

Novelist and poet Peter Straub has frightened millions of readers with his tales of horror and suspense, being especially good at what *Maclean's* Barbara Matthews calls "stark cold horror—the kind worshippers of the genre love to spirit away and read quickly, inhaling fright and holding it in their lungs until it becomes brittle enough to shatter if so much as a telephone rings." What pervades Straub's best writing, however, is his examination of the realistic roots of the fantastic and his treatment of suspense.

Dissatisfied with his academic career, Straub abandoned his doctoral work at the University of Ireland in 1972 and published his first novel, *Marriages* (1973), about an American businessman's extramarital affair in Europe. Already a published poet, Straub received favorable criticism for his novel, and many critics noted the lyrical qualities of his writing. As a *Times Literary Supplement* critic wrote, "It may be this [poetic] skill which enables him to place so securely the sense of gesture, and the texture of atmosphere, which characterizes *Marriages.*"

When his attempts at a second novel met with rejection, Straub despaired until his agent suggested he try to write a gothic novel. The result, *Julia* (1975), proved that Straub had a flair for the genre. It also intrigued the author with the thought of manipulating the stock conventions of horror writing. *Julia* describes the tale of an American woman in London who is haunted by the ghost of a murdered child and comes to learn of her responsibility for the death of her own child. Criticized for its inconsistent and often clumsy writing, *Julia* nevertheless displays Straub's adept use of horror conventions. As critic Michael Mason wrote in the *Times Literary Supplement,* "In the last resort *Julia* . . . [succeeds] in the brutal business of delivering supernatural thrills . . . [Straub] has thought of a nasty kind of haunting, and he presses it upon the reader to a satisfying point of discomfort."

Straub's novel *Ghost Story* (1979) proved to be his breakthrough work. A bestseller, *Ghost Story* is the tale of four elderly New Englanders who make up the Chowder Society. They are terrorized by the ghost of a young woman whose death they were responsible for years earlier. The novel earned criticism for its overt reference to such influences as Nathaniel Hawthorne and Edgar Allan Poe, and Christopher Lehmann-Haupt in the *New York Times* referred to it as "horror-cliché and campfire trash." But it also won praise for its complex plot and use of horror story motifs. As Valerie Lloyd noted in *Newsweek,* "with considerable technical skill, Peter Straub has constructed an extravagant entertainment which, though flawed, achieves in its second half some awesome effects. . . . It is, I think, the best thing of its kind since Shirley Jackson's 'The Haunting of Hill House.'"

Other bestselling novels of Straub's include *Shadowland* (1980), which relates the story of two boys involved in magic and fantasy; and *Floating Dragon* (1983), the tale of a destructive spirit which periodically visits an affluent Connecticut suburb. *The Talisman* (1984), which Straub co-wrote with his friend and fellow horror writer Stephen King, was an instant bestseller. Concentrating on a young boy's search for a magical talisman to cure his dying mother, the novel focused in general on the struggle between good and evil in a strange world. While many critics felt the novel contained too many special effects and digressive story elements, Frank Herbert in the *Washington Post Book World* wrote, "*The Talisman* is exactly what it sets out to be—a fine variation on suspense and horror filled with many surprises, a ground King and Straub have plowed before with great success, together and individually."

Perhaps the most positive response Straub has received was for *Koko* (1988), a psychological suspense thriller that departs from Straub's supernatural novels. The story of four Vietnam War veterans who track down a former platoon member whom they believe is now a deranged killer, *Koko* is remarkable for what Emily Tennyson in the *Detroit Free Press* called "an examination of fear in the human soul." Lucius Shepard added in the *Washington Post Book World,* "Judged as a thriller, *Koko* deserves to be compared with the best of the genre, to novels such as *Gorky Park* and *The Honorable Schoolboy* . . . [it] is vastly entertaining, often brilliantly written, full of finely realized moments and miniatures of characterization. . . . What all this most hearteningly signals is that Peter Straub is aspiring toward a writerly range which may cause his future novels to face more discriminating judgments yet."

—Christopher Swann

STUART, Ian. *See* **MacLEAN, Alistair.**

STYRON, William

Nationality: American. **Born:** Newport News, Virginia, 11 June 1925. **Education:** Christchurch School, Virginia; Davidson College, North Carolina, 1942-43; Duke University, Durham, North Carolina, 1943-44, 1946-47, B.A. 1947 (Phi Beta Kappa). **Military Service:** Served in the United States Marine Corps, 1944-45, 1951: 1st Lieutenant. **Family:** Married Rose Burgunder in 1953; three daughters and one son. **Career:** Associate editor, McGraw Hill, publishers, New York, 1947. Since 1952 advisory editor, *Paris Review,* Paris and New York; member of the editorial board, *American Scholar,* Washington, D.C., 1970-76. Since 1964 fellow, Silliman College, Yale University, New Haven, Connecticut. **Awards:** American Academy Prix de Rome, 1952; Pulitzer prize, 1968; Howells Medal, 1970; American Book award, 1980; Connecticut Arts award, 1984; Cino del Duca prize, 1985; MacDowell Medal, 1988; Bobst award, 1989; National Magazine award, 1990; National Medal of Arts, 1993; National Arts Club Medal of Honor, 1995. Litt.D.: Duke University, 1968; Davidson College, Davidson, North Carolina, 1986. **Member:** American Academy, American Academy of Arts and Sciences, and American Academy of Arts and Letters; Commander, Order of Arts and Letters (France), and Legion of Honor (France). **Address:** 12 Rucum Road, Roxbury, Connecticut 06783, U.S.A.

Publications

Novels

Lie Down in Darkness. Indianapolis, Bobbs Merrill, 1951; London, Hamish Hamilton, 1952.

The Long March. New York, Random House, 1956; London, Hamish Hamilton, 1962.

Set This House on Fire. New York, Random House, 1960; London, Hamish Hamilton, 1961.

The Confessions of Nat Turner. New York, Random House, 1967; London, Cape, 1968.

Sophie's Choice. New York, Random House, and London, Cape, 1979.

Short Story

Shadrach. Los Angeles, Sylvester and Orphanos, 1979.

Uncollected Short Stories

"Autumn," and "Long Dark Road," in *One and Twenty,* edited by W.M. Blackburn. Durham, North Carolina, Duke University Press, 1945.

"Moments in Trieste," in *American Vanguard 1948,* edited by Charles I. Glicksburg. New York, Cambridge, 1948.

"The Enormous Window," in *American Vanguard 1950,* edited by Charles I. Glicksburg. New York, Cambridge, 1950.

"The McCabes," in *Paris Review 22,* Autumn-Winter 1959-60.

"Pie in the Sky," in *The Vintage Anthology of Science Fantasy,* edited by Christopher Cerf. New York, Random House, 1966.

Play

In the Clap Shack (produced New Haven, Connecticut, 1972). New York, Random House, 1973.

Other

The Four Seasons, illustrated by Harold Altman. University Park, Pennsylvania State University Press, 1965.

Admiral Robert Penn Warren and the Snows of Winter: A Tribute. Winston-Salem, North Carolina, Palaemon Press, 1978.

The Message of Auschwitz. Blacksburg, Virginia, Press de la Warr, 1979.

Against Fear. Winston-Salem, North Carolina, Palaemon Press, 1981.

As He Lay Dead, A Bitter Grief (on William Faulkner). New York, Albondocani Press, 1981.

This Quiet Dust and Other Writings. New York, Random House, 1982; London, Cape, 1983.

Conversations with William Styron (interviews), edited by James L. W. West III. Jackson, University Press of Mississippi, 1985.

Darkness Visible (memoirs). New York, Random House, 1990; London, Cape, 1991.

A Tidewater Morning (Three Tales from Youth). Helsinki, Eurographica, 1991; New York, Random House, 1993; London, Cape, 1994.

Editor, *Best Short Stories from the Paris Review.* New York, Dutton, 1959.

*

Bibliography: *William Styron: A Descriptive Bibliography* by James L. W. West III, Boston, Hall, 1977; *William Styron: A Reference Guide* by Jackson R. Bryer and Mary B. Hatem, Boston, Hall, 1978; *William Styron: An Annotated Bibliography of Criticism* by Philip W. Leon, Westport, Connecticut, Greenwood Press, 1978.

Manuscript Collections: Library of Congress, Washington, D.C.; Duke University, Durham, North Carolina.

Critical Studies: *William Styron* by Robert H. Fossum, Grand Rapids, Michigan, Eerdmans, 1968; *William Styron* by Cooper R. Mackin, Austin, Texas, Steck Vaughn, 1969; *William Styron* by Richard Pearce, Minneapolis, University of Minnesota Press, 1971; *William Styron* by Marc L. Ratner, New York, Twayne, 1972; *William Styron* by Melvin J. Friedman, Bowling Green, Ohio, Popular Press, 1974; *The Achievement of William Styron* edited by Irving Malin and Robert K. Morris, Athens, University of Georgia Press, 1975, revised edition, 1981; *Critical Essays on William Styron* edited by Arthur D. Casciato and James L. W. West III, Boston, Hall, 1982; *The Root of All Evil: The Thematic Unity of William Styron's Fiction* by John K. Crane, Columbia, University of South Carolina Press, 1985; *William Styron* by Judith Ruderman, New York, Ungar, 1989; *The Novels of William Styron* by Gavin Cologne-Brookes, Baton Rouge, Louisiana State University Press, 1995.

* * *

Three male writers emerged after WWII who would stand head and shoulders above their contemporaries: Norman Mailer, Ralph Ellison, and William Styron. Styron's first novel, *Lie Down in Darkness* (1951), published when he was only 26 years old, announced the arrival of an author who was to become both a complex, literary novelist *and* a popular novelist. The book follows the dissolution of a Port Virginia family and ends with the suicide of Peyton, one of the daughters. Harvey Breit, in *Atlantic Monthly,* favorably compared *Lie Down in Darkness* with Thomas Mann's first novel, *Buddenbrooks.*

Lie Down in Darkness is, indeed, Styron's benchmark. The reader will find in these pages what were to be the author's main concerns over the course of his writing life: the grand themes of love and death, the nature of evil, suicide, and race relations. Peyton Loftis' suicide soliloquy foreshadows Styron's own emotional exhaustion and struggle with suicidal wishes, which he was later to reveal in his memoir of manic-depressive illness, *Darkness Visible* (1990).

Lie Down in Darkness was followed by *The Long March* (1956), a novella based on Styron's Marine Corps experience, moving with the economy of Greek tragedy. The author, in the collection of essays *This Quiet Dust and Other Writings* (1982), cited this story as the one in which everything had "gone right."

The Long March was frequently anthologized in English language short-story anthologies, as well as publications in France, Germany, Italy, Portugal, and Romania, to name only some of the countries where it appeared in translation, helping to establish Styron's international reputation.

Styron won the Prix de Rome for *Lie Down in Darkness,* providing him with funds to travel in Europe, where he stayed for a time both in Paris and a small Italian village. Italy was the setting for his second big novel, *Set This House on Fire* (1960). The book was a sprawling, overwritten work. For the most part, it received a critical flailing. If *Set This House on Fire* was an artistic failure, it was a significant one, because it laid the foundation for his fourth novel, *Sophie's Choice* (1979). A European commentator on the American novel, G. A. M. Janssens, said, "it might be argued that *Sophie's Choice* is a rewriting of the earlier novel."

Styron's third novel, *The Confessions of Nat Turner* (1967), was to be his most controversial book. A fictional treatment of an 1831 slave revolt in Tidewater, Virginia, the novel drew heat from black activists who felt that the author's recreation of Nat Turner was both historically false and racist (see *William Styron's Nat Turner: Ten Black Writers Respond*, 1968). Though Styron won the Pulitzer Prize in 1967 for this book and received $800,000 for movie rights, the film was never made. The furor caused by the Nat Turner book was very painful for Styron. It should be pointed out that the great African-American writer, Ralph Ellison, stood up for him and for every writer's authorial freedom to reimagine and recreate historical persons.

Sophie's Choice, Styron's fourth novel, was a huge success and was made into a movie in 1982. Meryl Streep starred as the Polish refugee, Sophie Zawitowska, who had been in the concentration camp at Auschwitz. Kevin Kline played her lover, Nathan Landau, and Peter MacNicol acted the part of Stingo. Stingo is the novel's narrator, a writer who just happens to move into a Brooklyn rooming house where he meets the tragic lovers. It is a very literary book, including in its 626 pages references to his earlier novels and themes, while at the same time keeping the reader hooked on the story. This is the source of William Styron's strength and staying power as a writer: his ability to grapple with the big questions and yet spin a good story as well.

In his most recent collection, *A Tidewater Morning* (1993), Styron returns to home ground. The three stories here, "Love Day," "Shadrach," and the title story, "A Tidewater Morning," are as beautifully executed and perfect as *The Long March*. The title story is about a young boy's reaction to the death of his mother by cancer, an event that occurred in the author's own life. Once again, Styron has looked a painful, personal experience in the face and transformed it into art.

—Bill Witherup

SUTCLIFF, Rosemary

Nationality: English. **Born:** East Clanden, Surrey, 14 December 1920. **Education:** Educated privately and at Bideford School of Art, 1935-39. **Career:** Writer, 1945-92. **Awards:** Carnegie Medal commendation, 1955, and American Library Association (ALA) Notable Book, both for *The Eagle of the Ninth;* Carnegie Medal commendation, *New York Herald Tribune*'s Children's Spring Book Festival honor book, both 1957, and ALA notable book, all for *The Shield Ring;* Carnegie Medal commendation, and *New York Herald Tribune*'s Children's Spring Book Festival honor book, both 1958, both for *The Silver Branch;* Carnegie Medal commendation, 1959, Hans Christian Andersen award honor book, 1959, International Board on Books for Young People honor list, 1960, Highly Commended Author, 1974, and ALA notable book, all for *Warrior Scarlet;* Carnegie Medal, 1960, and ALA notable book, both for *The Lantern Bearers;* ALA notable book, 1960, for *Knight's Fee*; *New York Herald Tribune's* Children's Spring Book Festival award, 1962, ALA notable book, and *Horn Book* honor list, all for *Dawn Wind;* ALA notable book, and *Horn Book* honor list, both 1962, both for *Beowulf;* ALA notable book, and *Horn Book* honor list, both 1963, both for *The Hound of Ulster;* ALA notable book, *Horn Book* honor list, both 1965, and Children's Literature Association Phoenix award, 1985, all for *The Mark of the Horse Lord*; *Horn Book* honor list, 1967, for *The High Deeds of Finn MacCool;* Lewis Carroll Shelf award, 1971, ALA notable book, and *Horn Book* honor list, all for *The Witch's Brat*; *Boston Globe-Horn Book* award for outstanding text, Carnegie Medal runner-up, both 1972, ALA notable book, and *Horn Book* honor list, all for *Tristan and Iseult*; *Heather, Oak, and Olive: Three Stories* was selected one of Child Study Association's "Children's Books of the Year," 1972, and *The Capricorn Bracelet* was selected, 1973; *Boston Globe-Horn Book* honor book for fiction, 1977, and *Horn Book* honor list, both for *Blood Feud*; *Children's Book Bulletin* Other Award, 1978, for *Song for a Dark Queen*; *Horn Book* honor list, 1978, for *Sun Horse, Sun Moon;* Children's Rights Workshop Award, 1978; ALA Notable Book, 1982, for *The Road to Camlann: The Death of King Arthur;* Royal Society of Literature fellow, 1982. Officer, 1975, and Commander, 1992, Order of the British Empire. **Member:** National Book League, Society of Authors, Royal Society of Miniature Painters. **Died:** 23 July 1992.

Publications

Novels

Three Legions: A Trilogy. Oxford University Press, 1980.
The Eagle of the Ninth, illustrated by C. Walter Hodges. Oxford University Press, 1954.
The Silver Branch, illustrated by Charles Keeping. Oxford University Press, 1957.
The Lantern Bearers, illustrated by Charles Keeping. Walck, 1959.
Lady in Waiting. Hodder & Stoughton, 1956.
The Rider of the White Horse. Hodder & Stoughton, 1959; published in the United States as *Rider on a White Horse*. Coward, 1960.
Rudyard Kipling. Bodley Head, 1960.
Sword at Sunset, illustrated by John Vernon Lord. Coward, 1963.
The Flowers of Adonis. Hodder & Stoughton, 1969.
The Light beyond the Forest: The Quest for the Holy Grail, illustrated by Shirley Felts. Bodley Head, 1979.
The Sword and the Circle: King Arthur and the Knights of the Round Table, illustrated by Shirley Felts. Dutton, 1981.
The Road to Camlann: The Death of King Arthur, illustrated by Shirley Felts. Bodley Head, 1981.
Blood and Sand. Hodder & Stoughton, 1987.

Plays

Mary Bedell (produced Chichester, England, 1986).

Children's Fiction

The Chronicles of Robin Hood, illustrated by C. Walter Hodges. Walck, 1950.
The Queen Elizabeth Story, illustrated by C. Walter Hodges. Walck, 1950.
The Armourer's House, illustrated by C. Walter Hodges. Walck, 1951.

Brother Dusty-Feet, illustrated by C. Walter Hodges. Walck, 1952.
Simon, illustrated by Richard Kennedy. Walck, 1953.
Outcast, illustrated by Richard Kennedy. Walck, 1955.
The Shield Ring, illustrated by C. Walter Hodges. Walck, 1956.
Warrior Scarlet, illustrated by Charles Keeping. Walck, 1958.
The Bridge-Builders. Blackwell, 1959.
Knight's Fee, illustrated by Charles Keeping. Walck, 1960.
Houses and History, illustrated by William Stobbs. Batsford, 1960.
Dawn Wind, illustrated by Charles Keeping. Oxford University Press, 1961.
Dragon Slayer, illustrated by Charles Keeping. Bodley Head, 1961; published as *Beowulf,* Dutton, 1962; published as *Dragon Slayer: The Story of Beowulf,* Macmillan, 1980.
The Hound of Ulster, illustrated by Victor Ambrus. Dutton, 1963.
Heroes and History, illustrated by Charles Keeping. Putnam, 1965.
A Saxon Settler, illustrated by John Lawrence. Oxford University Press, 1965.
The Mark of the Horse Lord, illustrated by Charles Keeping. Walck, 1965.
The High Deeds of Finn MacCool, illustrated by Michael Charlton. Dutton, 1967.
The Chief's Daughter, illustrated by Victor Ambrus. Hamish Hamilton, 1967.
A Circlet of Oak Leaves, illustrated by Victor Ambrus. Hamish Hamilton, 1968.
The Witch's Brat, illustrated by Richard Lebenson. Walck, 1970; same title illustrated by Robert Micklewright, Oxford University Press, 1970.
Tristan and Iseult, illustrated by Victor Ambrus. Dutton, 1971.
The Truce of the Games, illustrated by Victor Ambrus. Hamish Hamilton, 1971.
Heather, Oak, and Olive: Three Stories (includes *The Chief's Daughter, A Circlet of Oak Leaves,* and *A Crown of Wild Olive*), illustrated by Victor Ambrus. Dutton, 1972.
The Capricorn Bracelet, illustrated by Richard Cuffari. Walck, 1973.
The Changeling, illustrated by Victor Ambrus. Hamish Hamilton, 1974.
We Lived in Drumfyvie, with Margaret Lyford-Pike. Blackie, 1975.
Blood Feud, illustrated by Charles Keeping. Oxford University Press, 1976, Dutton, 1977.
Shifting Sands, illustrated by Laszlo Acs. Hamish Hamilton, 1977.
Sun Horse, Moon Horse, illustrated by Shirley Felts. Bodley Head, 1977, Dutton, 1978.
Song for a Dark Queen. Pelham Books, 1978.
Frontier Wolf. Oxford University Press, 1980.
Eagle's Egg. illustrated by Victor Ambrus, Hamish Hamilton, 1981.
Bonnie Dundee. Bodley Head, 1983.
Flame-Coloured Taffeta. Oxford University Press, 1985.
The Roundabout Horse, illustrated by Alan Marks. Hamilton Children's, 1986.
The Best of Rosemary Sutcliff. Chancellor, 1987.
Little Hound Found. Hamilton Children's, 1989.
A Little Dog Like You, illustrated by Jane Johnson. Simon & Schuster, 1990.
The Shining Company. Farrar, Straus, 1990.
Chess-Dream in a Garden, illustrated by Ralph Thompson. Candlewick Press, 1993.
The Minstrel and the Dragon Pup, illustrated by Emma Chichester. Candlewick Press, 1993.
Black Ships before Troy: The Story of the Iliad, illustrated by Alan Lee. Delacorte, 1993.

Other

Blue Remembered Hills: A Recollection. Bodley Head, 1983.

Editor, with Monica Dickens, *Is Anyone There?* Penguin, 1978.

*

Manuscript Collections: Kerlan Collection, University of Minnesota, Minneapolis.

Critical Studies: *Treasure Seekers and Borrowers: Children's Books in Britain 1900-1960* by Marcus Crouch, Library Association, 1962; *Rosemary Sutcliff* by Margaret Meek, Walck, 1962; *Tellers of Tales: British Authors of Children's Books from 1800 to 1964* by Roger Lancelyn Green, Kaye & Ward, 1965; *The Green and Burning Tree: On the Writing and Enjoyment of Children's Books* by Helen Cameron, Little, Brown, 1969; *Horn Book Reflections: On Children's Books and Reading, Selected from Eighteen Years of The Horn Book Magazine—1949-1966,* Horn Book, 1969; *Children and Their Literature* by Constantine Georgiou, Prentice-Hall, 1969; *A Sense of Story: Essays on Contemporary Writing for Children* by John Rowe Townsend, Lippincott, 1971; *Children and Books* by May Hill Arbuthnot and Zena Sutherland, *Scott, Foresman, 1972; The Nesbit Tradition: The Children's Novel in England, 1945-1970* by Marcus Crouch, Benn, 1972.

* * *

For 40 years Rosemary Sutcliff has been a leading name in historical fiction, and many of her books for teenage and adult readers are now regarded as classics. First published in 1950, her early works showed her still searching for a style and voice of her own, but gave hints of the later, mature artist.

Sutcliff's breakthrough came with *The Eagle of the Ninth* (1954), a landmark novel which established her name on the historical scene. Set in Roman Britain, it describes the journey of former centurion Marcus Aquila to recover the eagle standard of his father's 9th Hispana Legion after both eagle and legion vanish mysteriously in the country north of Hadrian's Wall. The adventures of Marcus and his Celtic comrade Esca display the full range of Sutcliff's talents, with rapid action, strong characters, lively speech, and stunning description of the Scottish highland terrain. Sutcliff brings the past to life, her words capturing the scent of flowers, the colors of heather and bracken, and the wooded hills under rain. Best of all, she gets inside the minds of the people, as well as their thoughts and feelings, making their long-lost world as real and immediate as our own. *Eagle of the Ninth* also makes use of familiar objects—the capricorn bracelet, the emerald signet ring—that reappear in later novels, linking one generation with the next.

In the ten years that followed, Sutcliff hit a creative peak, turning out an impressive series of historical novels. *Outcast* (1955) gives powerful treatment to the theme of the orphan surviving among strangers, with Beric, the central character, struggling to adapt between the warring nations of Rome and Britain. *The Shield Ring* (1956) has Viking settlers fighting off a Norman invasion in England's Lake District, and its two leading figures are again orphans. *The Silver Branch* (1957) and *The Lantern Bearers* (1959) return to the Roman world, and focus on the adventures of later generations of the Aquila family. The first deals with the internal warfare of the late Empire, while *Lantern Bearers* follows the struggle of Romanized Britons against the invading Saxons. One of Sutcliff's finest works, it won her the Carnegie Medal, Britain's top award for teenage fiction. *Warrior Scarlet* (1958) reaches back into the Bronze Age, describing a young boy's initiation into manhood. *Lady in Waiting* (1956) and *The Rider of the White Horse* (1959) were aimed at adult readers. In *Dawn Wind* (1962), Owain, a Roman-British boy left alone after the death of his family, slowly comes to terms with life in an Anglo-Saxon world. Violent change is continuous in Sutcliff's books, and most of her characters have to adapt. They fight hard to hold on to what they have known, but in the end change is inevitable, and former enemies must learn to live together.

Perhaps the best of all Sutcliff's writing is found in two novels of the 1960s, *The Sword at Sunset* (1963), which tells of the life and death of the Celtic warlord Artos (Arthur) and his doomed fight against the Saxons, and *The Mark of the Horse Lord* (1965), where a freed gladiator impersonates a Scottish chieftain and inherits his highland kingdom. Both stories end in tragedy, but contain an unforgettable blend of action, deep thinking, and eye-blasting landscapes.

The 1970s and 1980s have seen a smaller amount of work by Sutcliff, but no lack of quality. *The Capricorn Bracelet* (1973), a collection of stories first used as radio broadcasts, covers 300 years and six generations of Aquila descendants fighting for Rome in the Scottish border country, and is full of sharp, beautiful writing. *Blood Feud* (1977) is the story of the Anglo-Saxon Jestyn, captured by marauding Vikings, who journeys with them to Constantinople to fight for the Byzantine Emperor. *Frontier Wolf* (1980) returns to Roman Britain, where Alexios Aquila commands a body of frontier scouts against Scottish tribesmen along the Wall. Both novels are fine examples of Sutcliff's work. *Song for a Dark Queen* (1978) has all the old skill, but lacks some of the familiar fire and passion.

An autobiography, *Blue Remembered Hills* (1983) has Sutcliff recalling her early life and her own brave struggle against the crippling arthritis which has afflicted her from childhood. Sutcliff's creations inhabit a world of battles and violent death, always superbly described; but this isn't what concerns her most. What matters to her is the people involved, and what becomes of them afterwards. It's a measure of her skill as a writer that readers feel they know these people too, and care about them.

—Geoff Sadler

T

TAN, Amy (Ruth)

Nationality: American. **Born:** Oakland, California, 19 February 1952. **Education:** San Jose State University, California, B.A. in linguistics and English, 1973, M.A. in linguistics, 1974; University of California, Berkley, 1974-76. **Family:** Married Louis M. DeMattei in 1974. **Career:** Specialist in language development, Alameda County Association for Mentally Retarded, Oakland, 1976-80; project director, MORE Project, San Francisco, 1980-81; reporter, managing editor, and associate publisher, *Emergency Room Reports,* 1981-83; technical writer, 1983-87. **Awards:** Commonwealth Club gold award, 1989, and Bay Area Book Reviewers award, 1990, both for *The Joy Luck Club;* Best American Essays award, 1991. Honorary D.H.L.: Dominican College, San Rafael, 1991. **Address:** c/o Random House, Inc., Publicity, 201 E. 50th St., 22nd Floor, New York, New York 10022, U.S.A.

Publications

Novels

The Joy Luck Club. New York, Putnam, and London, Heinemann, 1989.
The Kitchen God's Wife. New York, Putnam, and London, Collins, 1991.
The Hundred Secret Senses. New York, Putnam, and London, Collins, 1995.

Play

Screenplay: *The Joy Luck Club,* 1993.

Other

The Moon Lady (for children). New York, Macmillan, 1992.
The Chinese Siamese Cat, illustrated by Gretchen Shields (for children). New York, Macmillan, and London, Hamilton, 1994.

*

Film Adaptation: *The Joy Luck Club,* 1993.

* * *

Novelist Amy Tan was born in Oakland, California in 1952, two-and-a-half years after her parents immigrated from China. Her father was educated as an engineer in Beijing, but eventually became a Baptist minister. Her mother came from a wealthy Shanghai family and left three children in China while escaping from an unhappy arranged marriage. Tan's brother Peter and her father John both died of brain cancer within six months of each other between 1967 and 1968 (The tragic irony is that her parents had wanted their daughter to become a brain surgeon). Amy Tan moved to Europe with her widowed mother Daisy at age 15, but later returned to California, where she pursued a double major in English and linguistics, received an MA in linguistics from San Jose State University, and began a doctoral program at Berkeley. She discontinued her doctoral studies to work as a freelance writer and as a consultant to programs for disabled children.

The Joy Luck Club, Tan's first effort, was a bestseller and received the 1990 Bay Area Reviewers Award for Fiction. It was also a finalist for the National Book Award and the National Book Critics Circle Award. Tan has said that she wrote *The Joy Luck Club* in four months: "I wrote from nine to six and took weekends off. I said, 'You have to get this done by a certain day because if you don't this chance may go away.'" It is often called a novel, but it is perhaps more correctly identified as a series of interlocking stories told by seven different Chinese-American women. In this collection, the author presents generational and cultural differences between Chinese mothers who immigrated to America and their American-born daughters. The author frequently draws on her own family's experiences in *The Joy Luck Club.* For example, one of Tan's key characters, Jing-mei or June, describes an embarrassing piano recital. Tan herself started piano lessons at the age of five. June's mother, Suyuan Woo, who abandoned two daughters in China, is an echo of Tan's mother who had to leave three children behind in China. Individual stories from this text have been widely anthologized, and *The Joy Luck Club* has been released as a successful film (directed by Wayne Wang). Tan assisted in the writing of the screenplay.

The author's second book, *The Kitchen God's Wife* (1991), also became a leading bestseller. It also portrays Chinese immigrants in California. In this novel, Tan draws on the story of her own grandmother, who was raped and forced to be a concubine; she subsequently committed suicide. Tan describes the effect of male domination and class structures on women.

The Hundred Secret Senses (1995) returns to the concept of secrecy, but is quite a departure from the realistic mode of fiction. Through a Chinese-born woman named Kwan, Tan explores reincarnation and communication with spirits. Kwan sees visions of ghosts and introduces her American half-sister, Olivia, to Chinese tradition and the value of the past.

One of the strengths of Tan's fictional craft is her ability to weave a story seamlessly from past to present and from one setting to another. In fact, reviewers have commented that her stories almost tell themselves. She has given a voice to women of Chinese ancestry, foregrounding the special bond and conflicts between mothers and daughters: "The feeling is in Chinese culture that [the bond] can never be broken." Tan also believes that men and women view life differently: "Men pan the whole scene and describe a wide panorama; their world is larger, but the sense of intimacy is not there. In my fiction and that of many women, the focus starts close-up, then the world pans out."

Despite the prominence of Chinese-American culture in her works, Tan has cautioned against the use of the label "ethnic literature." She has argued that the term can prevent critics from reading a text for its aesthetic merits. Instead they may focus solely on its historical and cultural features. Although Asian-American literature is a growing field of interest in academic circles, Tan's fiction has not received the kind of scholarly attention that the writing of another Chinese-American author, Maxine Hong Kingston, has generated. This may be due to the unfair assumption of some academics that her work must be less serious or complex because of its incredible popularity.

—Karin E. Beeler

TATE, Ellalice. *See* **HOLT, Victoria.**

THEROUX, Paul (Edward)

Nationality: American. **Born:** Medford, Massachusetts, 10 April 1941; brother of Alexander Theroux. **Education:** Medford High School; University of Maine, Orono, 1959-60; University of Massachusetts, Amherst, B.A. in English 1963. **Family:** Married Anne Castle in 1967; two sons. **Career:** Lecturer, University of Urbino, Italy, 1963; Peace Corps lecturer, Soche Hill College, Limbe, Malawi, 1963-65; lecturer, Makerere University, Kampala, Uganda, 1965-68, and University of Singapore, 1968-71; writer-in-residence, University of Virginia, Charlottesville, 1972. **Awards:** *Playboy* award, 1971, 1977, 1979; American Academy award, 1977; Whitbread award, 1978; *Yorkshire Post* award, 1982; James Tait Black Memorial prize, 1982; Thomas Cook award, for travel book, 1989. D. Litt.: Tufts University, Medford, Massachusetts, 1980; Trinity College, Washington, D.C., 1980; University of Massachusetts, 1988. **Member:** Fellow, Royal Society of Literature, and Royal Geographical Society; American Academy, 1984. **Address:** c/o Hamish Hamilton Ltd., 27 Wright's Lane, London W8 5TZ, England.

Publications

Novels

Waldo. Boston, Houghton Mifflin, 1967; London, Bodley Head, 1968.
Fong and the Indians. Boston, Houghton Mifflin, 1968; London, Hamish Hamilton, 1976.
Girls at Play. Boston, Houghton Mifflin, and London, Bodley Head, 1969.
Murder in Mount Holly. London, Ross, 1969.
Jungle Lovers. Boston, Houghton Mifflin, and London, Bodley Head, 1971.
Saint Jack. London, Bodley Head, and Boston, Houghton Mifflin, 1973.
The Black House. London, Hamish Hamilton, and Boston, Houghton Mifflin, 1974.
The Family Arsenal. London, Hamish Hamilton, and Boston, Houghton Mifflin, 1976.
Picture Palace. London, Hamish Hamilton, and Boston, Houghton Mifflin, 1978.
The Mosquito Coast. London, Hamish Hamilton, 1981; Boston, Houghton Mifflin, 1982.
Doctor Slaughter. London, Hamish Hamilton, 1984.
Half Moon Street: Two Short Novels (includes *Doctor Slaughter* and *Doctor DeMarr*). Boston, Houghton Mifflin, 1984.
O-Zone. London, Hamish Hamilton, and New York, Putnam, 1986.
My Secret History. London, Hamish Hamilton, and New York, Putnam, 1989.
Chicago Loop. London, Hamish Hamilton, 1990; New York, Random House, 1991.
Doctor DeMarr. London, Hutchinson, 1990.
Millroy the Magician. London, Hamish Hamilton, 1993; New York, Random House, 1994.

Short Stories

Sinning with Annie and Other Stories. Boston, Houghton Mifflin, 1972; London, Hamish Hamilton, 1975.
The Consul's File. London, Hamish Hamilton, and Boston, Houghton Mifflin, 1977.
World's End and Other Stories. London, Hamish Hamilton, and Boston, Houghton Mifflin, 1980.
The London Embassy. London, Hamish Hamilton, 1982; Boston, Houghton Mifflin, 1983.

Plays

The Autumn Dog (produced New York, 1981).
The White Man's Burden. London, Hamish Hamilton, 1987.

Screenplay: *Saint Jack,* with Peter Bogdanovich and Howard Sackler, 1979.

Television Play: *The London Embassy,* from his own story, 1987.

Other

V.S. Naipaul: An Introduction to His Work. London, Deutsch, and New York, Africana, 1972.
The Great Railway Bazaar: By Train through Asia. London, Hamish Hamilton, and Boston, Houghton Mifflin, 1975.
A Christmas Card (for children). London, Hamish Hamilton, and Boston, Houghton Mifflin, 1978.
London Snow (for children). Salisbury, Wiltshire, Russell, 1979; Boston, Houghton Mifflin, 1980.
The Old Patagonian Express: By Train through the Americas. London, Hamish Hamilton, and Boston, Houghton Mifflin, 1979.
Sailing through China. Salisbury, Wiltshire, Russell, 1983; Boston, Houghton Mifflin, 1984.
The Kingdom by the Sea: A Journey around the Coast of Great Britain. London, Hamish Hamilton, and Boston, Houghton Mifflin, 1983.
The Imperial Way: Making Tracks from Peshawar to Chittagong, photographs by Steve McCurry. London, Hamish Hamilton, and Boston, Houghton Mifflin, 1985.
Patagonia Revisited, with Bruce Chatwin. Salisbury, Wiltshire, Russell, 1985; Boston, Houghton Mifflin, 1986.
Sunrise with Seamonsters: Travels and Discoveries 1964-1984. London, Hamish Hamilton, and Boston, Houghton Mifflin, 1985.
The Shortest Day of the Year: A Christmas Fantasy. Leamington, Warwickshire, Sixth Chamber Press, 1986.

Riding the Iron Rooster: By Train through China. London, Hamish Hamilton, and New York, Putnam, 1988.
Travelling the World. London, Sinclair Stevenson, 1990.
The Happy Isles of Oceania: Paddling the Pacific. London, Hamish Hamilton, and New York, Putnam, 1992.
The Pillars of Hercules: A Grand Tour of the Mediterranean. New York, Putnam, 1995.

* * *

"The difference between travel writing and fiction is the difference between recording what the eye sees and discovering what the imagination knows," Paul Theroux has written.

In his fiction, his solitary characters, who are outsiders in an alien culture or displaced strangers in a strange land, espouse a romance of solitude that continuously haunts them and resembles Theroux's own state of mind in his nonfiction travel books. Individual characters (such as Jack Flowers, the pimp in *Saint Jack* [1973]; Maude Coffin Pratt, the photographer in *Picture Palace* [1978]; the very American, larger-than-life Allie Fox, the obsessive inventor in *The Mosquito Coast* [1981]; and Millroy in *Millroy the Magician* [1993]) attempt to impose their own order on the world around them but usually fail in their often violent and presumptuous designs.

In all of his travel narratives, in contrast, Theroux himself is the solitary wanderer, escaping the tyranny of the ordinary and the usual tourist myths by focusing on improvisation, the timetable of travel itself, and the incidents, images, and incongruities that assault him. As in his fiction he proclaims, "Being alive is being alone," and "this intense and lonely concentration" occupies the heart of the journey. As a stylist, Theroux displays a caustic and often scornful wit, merciless in its precision and iconoclastic in its tone, fueled by skepticism and irony in an attempt to see the world and its creatures as clearly as possible. He delights in subverting fashionable assumptions, skewering any "politically correct" dogma or edict, and revealing the arduous and difficult task of life itself, stripped of self-deception and self-delusion. The solitary self becomes a wary observer, trusting only in his senses and his imagination, ever on the alert for the telling conversation or the suggestive incident. Tourism bores him and travel propels him and becomes its own destination. Only in distant, often bleak and barren places—the desert, Tibet, Cape Wrath on the northwestern tip of Scotland, Patagonia—does he come upon a kind of raw beauty and redemption that speaks directly to his own brooding solitude. "As long as there is wilderness there is hope," he has written.

In recent years Theroux's fiction has darkened. Sexual obsessions and nightmares, a pervasive sense of guilt and despair, and the duplicity bred into characters who lead double lives pervade such novels as *Half Moon Street* (1984), *My Secret History* (1989) and *Chicago Loop* (1990). These grimmer but strangely exhilarating tales reveal the more demonic side of solitude and loneliness and seem to build on his earlier, more violent and often gothic novels such as *The Black House* (1974) and *The Family Arsenal* (1976).

In many of his novels, but especially in *The Mosquito Coast* and *Millroy the Magician,* Theroux creates a kind of ultimate American anti-hero who rises out of the culture to castigate and attack it but goes on to create his own chaos and confusion as a result of this. Allie Fox in *The Mosquito Coast* reminds the reader of American self-reliance and ingenuity writ large, from Benjamin Franklin to Melville's Captain Ahab, as his quest to transplant American values and technology to the jungles of Honduras ends in disaster. Millroy courts but escapes disaster when he falls in love with the narrator of his novel, Jilly Farina, a kind of romantic redemption that seems to have occurred in Theroux's own life. In both these beguiling and beautifully crafted books, a child tells the tale and the disaster or triumph plays itself out through his or her eyes.

Theroux's novels display intricate and scrupulously designed plots that at times threaten to overpower his characters. He relies on more or less conventional realistic methods to generate his fiction, but this works well in terms of a strong central character amid a Third World or post-colonial culture. When he is at his best, such tales take on mythic and social dimensions that illuminate and comment upon a vision of the late twentieth century that can be chaotic, violent, and frightening. At such times, both in his fiction and in his non-fiction, Theroux's impeccable art dazzles.

—Samuel Coale

THOMPSON, Hunter S(tockton)

Nationality: American. **Born:** 18 July 1939 in Louisville, Kentucky. **Education:** Attended public schools in Louisville; studied journalism at Columbia University. **Military Service:** U.S. Air Force, 1956-58. **Family:** Married Sandra Dawn in 1963 (divorced); children: one son. **Career:** Writer and journalist. Began as a sports writer in Florida; *Time,* Caribbean correspondent, 1959; *New York Herald Tribune,* Caribbean correspondent, 1959-60; *National Observer,* South American correspondent, 1961-63; *Nation,* West Coast correspondent, 1964-66; *Ramparts,* columnist, 1967-68; *Scanlan's Monthly,* columnist, 1969-70; *Rolling Stone,* national affairs editor, 1970-84; *High Times,* global affairs correspondent, 1977-82; *San Francisco Examiner,* media critic, 1985-90; *Smart,* editor at large, 1988—. Political analyst for various European magazines (including *London Observer, Tempo, Time Out, Das Magazine, Nieuwe Revu,* and *Die Woche*), 1988—. Candidate for sheriff of Pitkin County, Colorado, 1968; member, Sheriff's Advisory Committee, Pitkin County, 1976-81; executive director, Woody Creek Rod and Gun Club. **Member:** Overseas Press Club, National Press Club, American Civil Liberties Union, Fourth Amendment Foundation (founder), National Rifle Association, U.S. Naval Institute, Air Force Association, National Organization for the Reform of Marijuana Laws (NORML; member of national advisory board, 1976—), Hong Kong Foreign Correspondents Club. **Agent:** c/o Janklow & Nesbit, 598 Madison Ave., New York, New York 10022. **Address:** Owl Farm, Woody Creek, Colorado 81656.

Publications

Novels

Prince Jellyfish. n.p., 1960.
The Rum Diary. n.p., 1967.
Untitled Novel. David McKay, 1992.

Nonfiction

Hell's Angels: A Strange and Terrible Saga. Random House, 1966.
Fear and Loathing in Las Vegas: A Savage Journey to the Heart of the American Dream, illustrated by Ralph Steadman. Random House, 1972.
Fear and Loathing on the Campaign Trail '72, illustrated by Ralph Steadman. Straight Arrow Books, 1973.
The Great Shark Hunt: Strange Tales from a Strange Time; Gonzo Papers, Volume One. Summit Books, 1979.
The Curse of Lono, illustrated by Ralph Steadman. Bantam, 1983.
Generation of Swine: Tales of Shame and Degradation in the '80s; Gonzo Papers, Volume Two. Summit Books, 1988.
Songs of the Doomed: More Notes on the Death of the American Dream; Gonzo Papers, Volume Three. Summit Books, 1990.
Silk Road: Thirty-Three Years in the Passing Lane. Simon & Schuster, 1990.
Better than Sex: Fear and Loathing on the Campaign Trail, 1992. Random House, 1993.

*

Film Adaptation: *Where the Buffalo Roam,* 1980 (from several works, including *Fear and Loathing in Las Vegas* and *Fear and Loathing on the Campaign Trail '72*).

Critical Studies: *Wampeters Foma & Granfalloons* by Kurt Vonnegut, Jr., Delacorte, 1974; *Gates of Eden: American Culture in the Sixties* by Morris Dickstein, Basic Books, 1977; *The Life of Fiction* by Jerome Klinkowitz, University of Illinois Press, 1977; *Fables of Fact: The New Journalism as New Fiction* by John Hellman, University of Illinois Press, 1981.

* * *

As a participatory journalist (one who covers a news story by becoming part of it), Hunter S. Thompson has gained a following as much for his hilarious antics as for his sharp observations of U.S. culture and politics. After years of struggling as a conventional journalist, Thompson's breakthrough came in covering the Hell's Angels, a California motorcycle gang being painted as savage rapists and thugs by the hysterical mainstream press. Thompson gained the trust of several gang members, then rode with the Hell's Angels for a year to research a *Nation* article and his book, *Hell's Angels: A Strange and Terrible Saga* (1966). *Hell's Angels* is a piece of strong journalism that is more conventional than his later works. Elmer Bendiner wrote in the *Nation:* "Thompson's point of view remains eminently sane and honest. He does not weep for the Angels or romanticize them or glorify them. Neither does he despise them." In riding with this notorious gang, Thompson's reputation as a daredevil was sealed.

Thompson unveiled his brand of participatory journalism, which he labeled "gonzo journalism," in "The Kentucky Derby Is Decadent and Depraved" (1970), an article for *Scanlan's Monthly.* In covering this decaying remnant of Southern gentility, Thompson had collected a number of Faulkner-like impressions. But when deadline came, Thompson froze. "I'd blown my mind, couldn't work," he recalled in a *Playboy* interview. "So finally I just started jerking pages out of my notebook and numbering them and sending them to the printer. I was sure it was the last article I was ever going to do for anybody." Instead, many praised the article as a breakthrough in journalism. Thompson continued: "And I thought . . . if I can write like this and get away with it, why should I keep trying to write like the *New York Times?*"

Thompson later produced his gonzo classic, *Fear and Loathing in Las Vegas: A Savage Journey to the Heart of the American Dream* (1972). Sent to Las Vegas to cover a desert motorcycle race and a district attorney's conference on drugs, Thompson did neither. Instead, he recounts, in first person, the adventures of Raoul Duke (Thompson's guise) and his "300-pound Samoan attorney," Dr. Gonzo (actually, a Chicano lawyer named Oscar Zeta Acosta), who ingest heavy quantities of alcohol and drugs, sit in at law-and-order conventions, and otherwise run amok in the desert glitter city. By getting so high that they can't see or think straight, Duke and Dr. Gonzo find truths about 1970s America following the countercultural rebellion. *National Observer* contributor Michael Putney called the book "a trip, literally and figuratively, all the way to bad craziness and back again. It is . . . an acid, wrenchingly funny portrait of straight America's most celebrated and mean-spirited pleasure-dome, Las Vegas."

In proposed jacket copy for *Fear and Loathing in Las Vegas,* later published in *The Great Shark Hunt: Strange Tales from a Strange Time; Gonzo Papers, Volume One* (1979), Thompson described "gonzo journalism": "My idea was to buy a fat notebook and record the whole thing as it happened, then send in the notebook for publication—without editing. That way, I felt the eye and the mind of the journalist would be functioning as a camera. True Gonzo reporting needs the talents of a master journalist, the eye of an artist/photographer, and the heavy balls of an actor. Because the writer must be a participant in the scene, while he's writing it—or at least taping it, or even sketching it. Or all three."

Thompson took the gonzo approach to covering the 1972 Presidential election campaign in *Fear and Loathing on the Campaign Trail '72* (1973). As a press outsider covering the campaign for *Rolling Stone* magazine, Thompson had the freedom to produce the first straight coverage of a political campaign, though *Campaign Trail* contains his usual fine-tunings of the truth. Still, Thompson "recorded the nuts and bolts of a presidential campaign with all the contempt and incredulity that other reporters must feel but censor out," noted Morris Dickstein in *Gates of Eden: American Culture in the Sixties.*

After *Fear and Loathing on the Campaign Trail,* Thompson's output dropped off. With the *Curse of Lono* (1983), Thompson returned to gonzo journalism after a decade hiatus. Here, Thompson's coverage of the Honolulu Marathon takes back seat to the narrator's delusion that he has become a Hawaiian god. Critics found the book hilarious, though not as well written as his 1970s work. Reviews have been more mixed for his hodgepodge compendiums of previously published material, among them *The Great Shark Hunt.*

With his fondness for firearms and his legendary capacity for alcohol and drug use, Thompson may be better remembered for his renegade behavior than for his talent as a writer. Nevertheless, "for all of the charges against him, Hunter S. Thompson is an amazingly insightful writer," wrote Jerome Klinkowitz in *The Life of Fiction.* "His 'journalism' is not in the least irresponsible. On the contrary, in each of his books he's pointed out the lies and gross distortions of conventional journalism . . . Moreover, his books are richly intelligent."

—Eric Patterson

THOMPSON, Jim

Nationality: American. **Born:** Oklahoma, 1906. **Education:** University of Nebraska, B.A. **Family:** Married Alberta Thompson in 1931; two children. **Career:** Had a variety of jobs including oil pipeline worker, steeplejack, burlesque actor, and professional gambler. Journalist for the *New York Daily News* and the *Los Angeles Times Mirror*. Associated with the Federal Writers Project in Oklahoma in the 1930s. **Died:** 7 April 1977.

Publications

Novels

Now and On Earth. Modern Age, 1942.
Heed the Thunder. Greenberg, 1946.
Nothing More Than Murder. Harper, 1949.
Cropper's Cabin. Lion, 1952.
The Killer inside Me. Lion, 1952.
The Alcoholics. Lion, 1953.
Bad Boy. Lion, 1953.
The Criminal. Lion, 1953.
Recoil. Lion, 1953; London, Corgi, 1988.
Savage Night. Lion, 1953.
A Swell-Looking Babe. Lion, 1954.
The Golden Gizmo. Lion, 1954.
A Hell of a Woman. Lion, 1954.
The Nothing Man. Dell, 1954.
Roughneck. Lion, 1954.
After Dark, My Sweet. Popular Library, 1955.
The Kill-Off. Lion, 1957.
Wild Town. New American Library, 1957.
The Getaway. New American Library, 1959.
The Transgressors. New American Library, 1961.
The Grifters. Regency, 1963.
Pop. 1280. Fawcett, 1964.
Texas by the Tail. Fawcett, 1965.
Ironside (novelization of television series). Popular Library, 1967.
South of Heaven. Fawcett, 1967.
The Undefeated (novelization of screenplay). Popular Library, 1969.
Nothing but a Man (novelization of screenplay). Popular Library, 1970.
Child of Rage. Lancer, 1972.
King Blood. Sphere, 1973.
Hard Core (omnibus). Fine, 1986.
More Hardcore (omnibus). Fine, 1987.

Plays

Screenplay: *Paths of Glory*, with Stanley Kubrick and Calder Willingham, 1957.

Television Writing: scripts for *Dr. Kildare* series.

*

Media Adaptations: Films—*The Getaway*, 1972 (Peckinpah) and 1993 (Donaldson); *The Killer inside Me*, 1976; *Coup de Torchon*, based on his novel *Pop. 1280*, 1981; *After Dark, My Sweet*, 1990; *The Grifters*, 1990; *The Kill-Off*, 1990.

Theatrical Activities:
Actor: **Film**—*Farewell, My Lovely*, 1975.

Critical Studies: *Jim Thompson: The Killers inside Him* by Max Allan Collins and Ed Gorman, Cedar Rapids, Iowa, Fedora Press, 1983; *Jim Thompson: Sleep with the Devil*, by Michael J. McCauley, 1990.

* * *

Jim Thompson's career has followed an ironic trajectory that only a pulp novelist could imagine. After failing in the more acceptable venue of hardcover fiction, he toiled in the ghettos of tough-guy writing for the usual minuscule payments and low-rent audience. He then climbed to the somewhat less squalid neighborhood of paperback originals and dwelled there obscurely for the rest of his writing life. Although he attained some success with his novels and stories (and enjoyed a degree of notoriety in Hollywood), his writing found its most appreciative audience after his death in 1977.

Like some of his predecessors in the bloody arena of pulp fiction, Thompson found some acceptance in France, but remained a minor figure until some astute academic critics and publishers like Mysterious Press and Black Lizard Press resurrected his work. Now the arty crowd has discovered his novels and turned him into something like a cult figure; aside from the usual incorrect comparisons to Hammett and Chandler, he has been more accurately located in the pulp pantheon alongside the best "pure" American hardboiled writers like James M. Cain and Horace McCoy. The books sell, inspiring several new movies including *Coup de Torchon, After Dark, My Sweet, The Grifters*, and the remake of *The Getaway*. Thompson's audience increases and the superlatives accumulate, all too late for the author to benefit from the attention and accompanying loot.

Most of his novels and some of his uncollected short fiction have been reprinted for the delectation of a new generation of readers who may never have seen the coarse yellowish paper of a pulp magazine or the garish, sexy cover of a typical paperback original. Although his work depends upon the illustrious traditions of American plain style, stretching back to Mark Twain, Stephen Crane, and Ernest Hemingway, as well as to those writers Edmund Wilson called "the boys in the back room," Thompson speaks to us in his own special voice about his often terrifying vision. The best of his books illustrate just how bleak, ironic, and uncompromising tough American writing can be. In addition, they express the peculiar twist he applies to the conventions of his chosen form.

The Getaway (1959) provides a telling example of just how Thompson can alter the boundaries of normal crime fiction; it begins as a relatively orthodox big caper novel about the usual daring and capable crook who plans a perfect crime that inevitably goes awry. He takes the premise much further, however, when the criminal mastermind, Doc, must escape by, among other difficulties, being buried alive and tunneling through excrement—a characteristic Thompson touch—before ending up at the perfect hideout, an expensive resort designed especially for crooks on the lam. Once there, however, Doc realizes that he has descended into a version of Hell itself, truly a last resort.

Some of Thompson's titles, like *A Swell-Looking Babe* (1954) and *A Hell of a Woman* (1954), suggest the rather quaint raciness and directness of his pulp antecedents; others, like *The Killer inside Me* (1952) and *The Nothing Man* (1954), neatly sum up the perversity and emptiness of his vision. Like the later *Pop. 1280* (1964), which it resembles in plot, narrator, and murder-by-murder progression, *The Killer inside Me* details the virtually motiveless violence of a pure psychopath, a man who is almost beautiful in his entirely conscious, unsullied madness. The narrator-protagonist, Deputy Lou Ford, beats women for his (and sometimes their) sexual pleasure, commits a series of brutal murders, and, most horribly, enjoys conversing in a series of exaggeratedly idiotic platitudes that mock his listeners, readers, and perhaps even himself. His thoroughly insincere harangue about sending black people back to Africa, as well as his reiteration of sentiments about clouds with silver linings, heat and humidity, rain bringing rainbows, and so forth, betray his cunning madness and his wholesale hatred better than all his terrible violence. Even worse than the banality of evil, for Thompson, is the conscious banality of its utterance.

Extending its despair even further than *The Killer inside Me, The Nothing Man* may serve as the best example of Thompson's vaunted nihilism. Its protagonist, a newspaperman named Clinton Brown, who talks occasionally like Lou Ford, has suffered essentially the same war wound as Jake Barnes; his lack of a penis defines his nothingness and impels him to destruction. He drinks, scorns, hurts, and kills, but is so much a nothing man that he cannot even get himself blamed for the crimes he commits; his doom is to continue his life as a nothing man.

Although his style often breaks down into the mixture of urgent pacing and heavy facetiousness of too many pulp writers, and his dialogue seems less acceptable than his narration, Thompson's characters, actions, and themes underline the originality of his achievement. Within a narrow and violent world his work attains a special and most disturbing originality; some of his peers write better, but none, like it or not, attains so bleak a vision of human emptiness.

—George Grella

TOFFLER, Alvin

Nationality: American. **Born:** New York City, 28 October 1928. **Education:** New York University, B.A., 1949. **Family:** Married Adelaide Farrell, 1950; one daughter. **Career:** Washington correspondent for various newspapers and magazines, 1957-59; *Fortune* magazine, New York, N.Y., associate editor, 1959-61; freelance writer since 1961. Member of faculty, New School for Social Research, 1965-67; visiting professor, Cornell University, 1969; visiting scholar, Russell Sage Foundation, 1969-70. Member of board of trustees, Antioch University. Consultant to organizations, including Rockefeller Brothers Fund, American Telephone & Telegraph Co., Institute for the Future, and Educational Facilities Laboratories, Inc. **Awards:** Award from National Council for the Advancement of Educational Writing, 1969, for *The Schoolhouse in the City*; McKinsey Foundation Book award, 1970, and Prix du Meilleur Livre Etranger (France), 1972, both for *Future Shock; Playboy* magazine best article award, 1970; Doctor of Laws from University of Western Ontario, D.Litt. from University of Cincinnati, D.Sc. from Rensselaer Polytechnic Institute, and D.Litt. from Miami University, all 1972; Doctor of Letters, Ripon College, 1975; Author of the Year Award, American Society of Journalists and Authors, 1983; American Association for the Advancement of Science fellow, 1984; Centennial award, Institute of Electrical and Electronics Engineers, 1984; Officier de l'Ordre des Arts et des Lettres, 1984; Doctor of Laws, Manhattan College, 1984. **Member:** American Society of Journalists and Authors, Society for the History of Technology (member of advisory council). **Agent:** c/o Bantam Books, 666 Fifth Ave., New York, New York 10103.

Publications

Nonfiction

The Culture Consumers: A Study of Art and Affluence in America. St. Martin's, 1964.
Future Shock. Random House, 1970.
The Eco-Spasm Report. Bantam, 1975.
The Third Wave. Morrow, 1980.
Previews and Premises. Morrow, 1983.
The Adaptive Corporation. McGraw, 1984.
Order Out of Chaos: Man's New Dialogue with Nature. Bantam, 1984.
Powershift: Knowledge, Wealth, and Violence at the Edge of the 21st Century. Bantam, 1991.
War and Anti-War in the Twenty-First Century. Little, Brown, 1993; as *War and Anti-War: Making Sense of Today's Global Chaos,* Warner, 1995.

Editor, *The Schoolhouse in the City.* Praeger, 1968.
Editor, *The Futurists.* Random House, 1972.
Editor, *Learning for Tomorrow: The Role of the Future in Education.* Random House, 1974.

* * *

Alvin Toffler's works present his hypotheses about the future developments of our society and suggest ways of coping with the unprecedented rate of change and its attendant problems. He is best known for his trilogy, *Future Shock* (1970), *The Third Wave* (1980), and *Powershift: Knowledge, Wealth, and Violence at the Edge of the Twenty-first Century* (1991), which is essentially optimistic about the ability of Americans to shape their future rather than be overwhelmed and manipulated by it. Each of his books, in the words of Rosalind Williams of *Technology Review,* acts as "a manual of survival strategies" as we face the future and its difficulties.

In *Future Shock,* which became a popular bestseller, Toffler argued that Americans were experiencing "future shock," a concept he derived from the anthropological concept of "culture shock," which means the inability of members of one culture to adapt to the rapid introduction of features of another culture. Very similarly, Toffler argued, Americans were experiencing severe problems in coping with the societal effects of advanced technology, and that growing divorce rates and crime rates were signs that Americans were being pushed past their capacity for adapting to change. Toffler offered remedies to future shock, namely that children should read more science fiction and that the study of the future should become a standard part of American education.

Future Shock created quite a stir and prompted some critics to challenge its self-proclaimed authority. Many reviewers criticized the book for oversimplifying complex issues and overstating its case, but many others felt that it offered constructive suggestions for dealing with change. Neil Millar of the *Christian Science Monitor* wrote, "If it oversimplifies some issues (and it does) it also opens bright vistas of hope." And P. M. Grady of *Book World* wrote, "I think that *Future Shock,* despite its problems, might assist us not only in preparing for a softer landing into the future, but also in diagnosing more keenly some of today's social puzzles."

The next installment of the trilogy, *The Third Wave,* focused more on signs of positive change and a brighter future. Toffler identified the first two waves of history as the agricultural and industrial revolutions, and argued that the third wave will be a restructuring of our society to offer more humane ways of living. He predicted that we will increase our utilization of renewable energy resources, that the media will become more responsive to individual needs, and that more people will have access to decision-making, effectively eliminating social hierarchies.

Again, the critical response to *The Third Wave* was mixed, with most of the criticism focusing on Toffler's writing style and argumentation. Langdon Winner of the *New York Times Book Review* found that "*The Third Wave* contains the same kind of titillating but slipshod analysis" as *Future Shock.* He also felt that Toffler was "in such a hurry to package his ideas in flashy conceptual wrappers that he seldom completes a thought." But H. G. Shane, writing for *Phi Delta Kappan,* decided that "the work merits an A+ for Toffler's lucid reviews of intricate problems of the present and for the way he defends the thesis that a new era of civilization is bursting into being in our midst."

The final book of the trilogy, *Powershift,* concerned the shifting of political power and how it will affect individuals, corporations, and the government. Toffler accounted for this powershift with the prevalence of computers and communications technology, which he believed would allow business and government to use knowledge as a powerful tool to control the information age.

Reviews of *Powershift* differed. Some critics found the work enlightening. Diane Cole of the *New York Times Book Review* wrote, "By placing the accelerated changes of our current information age in the larger perspective of history, Mr. Toffler helps us to face the future with less weariness and more understanding." Curt Suplee offered a conflicted view about the book that characterizes many of the responses to Toffler's work: "It is pretentious, bombastic, repetitive, infuriatingly facile, shamefully simplistic, and more or less entirely right."

Toffler's works elicit volatile responses, not only because of his tendency to generalize about the future, but also because of the sensitive nature of his subject. As a reviewer from the *Economist* asserted about *Future Shock,* "People are ready, willing and eager to be frightened about the future and Mr. Toffler . . . has written a scarifying book." It is exactly this fear and curiosity we have about our future which has made Toffler such a popular author.

—Anne Boyd

TOLKIEN, J(ohn) R(onald) R(euel)

Nationality: British. **Born:** Bloemfontein, Orange Free State, South Africa, 3 January 1892; immigrated to England, 1895. **Education:** King Edward VI School, Birmingham, 1900-02, 1903-11; St. Philip's School, Birmingham, 1902-03; Exeter College, Oxford (open classical exhibitioner; Skeat prize, 1914), 1911-15, B.A. (honors), 1915, M.A. 1919. **Military Service:** Served in the Lancashire Fusiliers, 1915-18: lieutenant. **Family:** Married Edith Mary Bratt in 1916 (died 1971); three sons and one daughter. **Career:** Assistant, Oxford English Dictionary, 1919-20; reader in English, 1920-23, and professor of the English language, 1924-25, University of Leeds, Yorkshire; at Oxford University: Rawlinson and Bosworth Professor of Anglo-Saxon, 1925-45; fellow, Pembroke College, 1926-45; Leverhulme research fellow, 1934-36; Merton Professor of English language and literature, 1945-59; honorary fellow, Exeter College, 1963, and Merton College, 1973. Andrew Lang lecturer, University of St. Andrews, Fife, 1939; W.P. Ker lecturer, University of Glasgow, 1953; lived in Bournemouth, Dorset, 1968-71, and Oxford, 1971-73. Artist: one-man show: Ashmolean Museum, Oxford, 1977. **Awards:** International Fantasy award, 1957; Royal Society of Literature Benson medal, 1966; Foreign Book prize (France), 1973; World Science Fiction Convention Gandalf award, 1974; Hugo award, 1978. D.Litt.: University College, Dublin, 1954; University of Nottingham, 1970; Oxford University, 1972; Dr. en Phil et Lettres: Liège, 1954; honorary degree: University of Edinburgh, 1973. Fellow, Royal Society of Literature, 1957. C.B.E. (Commander, Order of the British Empire), 1972. **Died:** 2 September 1973.

Publications

Novels (series: Lord of the Rings)

The Hobbit; or, There and Back Again, illustrated by the author. London, Allen and Unwin, 1937; Boston, Houghton Mifflin, 1938; revised edition, 1951; revised edition, 1966.

The Lord of the Rings. London, Allen and Unwin, 1968.

- *The Lord of the Rings: The Fellowship of the Ring.* London, Allen and Unwin, and Boston, Houghton Mifflin, 1954; revised edition, New York, Ballantine, 1965; London, Allen and Unwin, 1966.
- *The Two Towers.* London, Allen and Unwin, 1954; Boston, Houghton Mifflin, 1955; revised edition, New York, Ballantine, 1965; London, Allen and Unwin, 1966.
- *The Return of the King.* London, Allen and Unwin, 1955; Boston, Houghton Mifflin, 1956; revised edition, New York, Ballantine, 1965; London, Allen and Unwin, 1966; excerpted as *The Grey Havens,* Brookline, Massachusetts, Pilcrow, 1990.

The Silmarillion, edited by Christopher Tolkien. London, Allen and Unwin, and Boston, Houghton Mifflin, 1977.

Novels for children

Farmer Giles of Ham, illustrated by Pauline Baynes. London, Allen and Unwin, 1949; Boston, Houghton Mifflin, 1950.

Smith of Wootton Major, illustrated by Pauline Baynes. London, Allen and Unwin, and Boston, Houghton Mifflin, 1967.

Mr. Bliss, illustrated by the author. London, Allen and Unwin, 1982.

The History of Middle Earth, edited by Christopher Tolkien

The Book of Lost Tales 1-2. London, Allen and Unwin, 2 vols., 1983-84; Boston, Houghton Mifflin, 2 vols., 1984.
Lays of Beleriand. London, Allen and Unwin, and Boston, Houghton Mifflin, 1985.
The Shaping of Middle-Earth: The Quenta, the Ambarkanta, and the Annals, Together with the Earliest 'Silmarillion' and the First Map. London, Allen and Unwin, and Boston, Houghton Mifflin, 1986.
The Lost Road and Other Writings. London, Unwin Hyman, and Boston, Houghton Mifflin, 1987.
The History of the Lord of the Rings:
The Return of the Shadow. London, Unwin Hyman, 1988; Boston, Houghton Mifflin, 1989.
The Treason of Isengard. London, Unwin Hyman, and Boston, Houghton Mifflin, 1989.
The War of the Ring. London, Unwin Hyman, and Boston, Houghton Mifflin, 1990.
Sauron Defeated: The End of the Third Age, The Notion Club Papers, and, The Drowning of Anadûnê. London, Unwin Hyman, and Boston, Houghton Mifflin, 1991.
Morgoth's Ring: The Later Silmarillion Part 1, The Legends of Aman. London, Unwin Hyman, and Boston, Houghton Mifflin, 1993.
The War of the Jewels: The Later Simarillion Part 2, The Legends of Beleriand. London, Unwin Hyman, and Boston, Houghton Mifflin, 1994.

Short Stories

Unfinished Tales of Númenór and Middle-Earth, edited by Christopher Tolkien. London, Allen and Unwin, and Boston, Houghton Mifflin, 1980.

Play

The Homecoming of Beorhtnoth Beorhthelm's Son (broadcast, 1954). Included in *The Tolkien Reader,* 1966; in *Tree and Leaf, Smith of Wootton Major, The Homecoming of Beorhtnoth Beorhthelm's Son,* 1975.

Radio Play: *The Homecoming of Beorhthnoth Beorhthelm's Son,* 1954.

Poetry

Songs for the Philologists, with others. Privately printed, 1936.
The Adventures of Tom Bombadil and Other Verses from the Red Book, illustrated by Pauline Baynes. London, Allen and Unwin, 1962; Boston, Houghton Mifflin, 1963.
The Road Goes Ever On: A Song Cycle, music by Donald Swann. Boston, Houghton Mifflin, 1967; London, Allen and Unwin, 1968; revised edition, Houghton Mifflin, 1978.
Bilbo's Last Song, illustrated by Pauline Baynes. London, Allen and Unwin, and Boston, Houghton Mifflin, 1974.
Poems and Stories. London, Allen and Unwin, 1980.

Other

A Middle English Vocabulary. Oxford, Clarendon Press, and New York, Oxford University Press, 1922.
Beowulf: The Monsters and the Critics. London, Oxford University Press, 1937.
Tree and Leaf (includes short story "Leaf by Niggle" and essay "On Fairy-Stories"). London, Allen and Unwin, 1964; Boston, Houghton Mifflin, 1965; revised edition, London, Unwin Hyman, 1988.
The Tolkien Reader. New York, Ballantine, 1966.
Tree and Leaf, Smith of Wootton Major, The Homecoming of Beorhtnoth Beorhthelm's Son. London, Allen and Unwin, 1975.
The Father Christmas Letters, edited by Baillie Tolkien, illustrated by the author. London, Allen and Unwin, and Boston, Houghton Mifflin, 1976.
Pictures. London, Allen and Unwin, and Boston, Houghton Mifflin, 1979.
The Letters of J.R.R. Tolkien: A Selection, edited by Humphrey Carpenter and Christopher Tolkien. London, Allen and Unwin, and Boston, Houghton Mifflin, 1981.
Finn and Hengest: The Fragment and the Episode, edited by Alan Bliss. London, Allen and Unwin, and Boston, Houghton Mifflin, 1983.
The Monsters and the Critics and Other Essays, edited by Christopher Tolkien. London, Allen and Unwin, 1983; Boston, Houghton Mifflin, 1984.

Editor, with E.V. Gordon, *Sir Gawain and the Green Knight.* Oxford, Clarendon Press, and New York, Oxford University Press, 1925.
Editor, *Ancrene Wisse.* London, Oxford University Press, 1962; New York, Oxford University Press, 1963.

Translator, *Sir Gawain and the Green Knight, Pearl, and Sir Orfeo,* edited by Christopher Tolkien. London, Allen and Unwin, and Boston, Houghton Mifflin, 1975.
Translator, *The Old English Exodus,* edited by Joan Turville-Petre. Oxford, Clarendon Press, 1981.

*

Bibliography: *Tolkien Criticism: An Annotated Checklist* by Richard C. West, Kent, Ohio, Kent State University Press, 1970; revised edition, 1981.

Manuscript Collections: Wade Collection, Wheaton College, Illinois; Marquette University, Milwaukee.

Critical Studies (selection): *Master of Middle-Earth: The Fiction of J.R.R. Tolkien* by Paul Kocher, Boston, Houghton Mifflin, 1972, London, Thames and Hudson, 1973; *Tolkien's World,* London, Thames and Hudson, and Boston, Houghton Mifflin, 1974, and *Tolkien and the Silmarils,* Thames and Hudson, 1981, both by Randel Helms; *J.R.R. Tolkien: A Biography* (includes bibliography) by Humphrey Carpenter, London, Allen and Unwin, and Boston, Houghton Mifflin, 1977; *The Mythology of Middle-Earth* by Ruth S. Noel, London, Thames and Hudson, and Boston, Houghton Mifflin, 1977; *The Complete Guide to Middle-Earth* by Robert Foster, London, Allen and Unwin, and New York, Ballantine, 1978; *Tolkien's Art: A Mythology for England* by Jane C. Nitzche, London, Macmillan, 1979; *Tolkien: New Critical Per-*

spectives edited by Neil D. Isaacs and Rose A. Zimbardo, Lexington, University Press of Kentucky, 1981; *The Road to Middle-Earth* by T.A. Shippey, London, Allen and Unwin, 1982, Boston, Houghton Mifflin, 1983; *J.R.R. Tolkien: This Far Land* edited by Robert Giddings, London, Vision, 1983; *The Song of Middle-Earth; J.R.R. Tolkien's Themes, Symbols, and Myths* by David Harvey, London, Allen and Unwin, 1985; *The Magical World of the Inklings: J.R.R. Tolkien, C.S. Lewis, Charles Williams, Owen Barfield* by Gareth Knight, Shaftesbury, Element, 1990; *A Tolkien Thesaurus* by Richard E. Blackwelder, New York, Garland, 1990.

* * *

Few authors have enjoyed as much international and long-lasting popularity as J.R.R. Tolkien. Creator of the imaginary land of Middle-earth, this Oxford professor of linguistics and medieval literature is also the father of modern fantasy. His tales are not of the sword-and-sorcery variety, however, but have a depth that is unmatched by any recent works of the imagination.

Tolkien's work with ancient northern languages and poems such as "Beowulf" greatly influenced his stories, which contain many mythical icons such as dwarves and wizards. Primarily a philologist, Tolkien claimed that his work was "fundamentally linguistic in inspiration" and delighted in inventing new languages for the nonhuman races of his tales, and in drawing names from the northern texts he researched all his life.

The Hobbit (1937) was written to please Tolkien's children as a simple bedtime fairy tale. While the dwarves and elves in the story are recognizable from legend, the protagonist, Bilbo Baggins, is a hobbit, wholly the invention of the author. Hobbits are the size of children, with cheerful personalities and a great love for eating and singing. In the novel, Bilbo becomes embroiled in the quest for a group of dwarves who, advised by the wizard Gandalf, seek to regain their ancient halls in the Lonely Mountain from Smaug, a wicked dragon who has stolen their home and treasure. Bilbo is prodded by Gandalf into joining the party as their burglar, and sets out reluctantly on the adventure. While much of the world Tolkien describes is fantastic—including goblins, spider-infested forests, and Bilbo's discovery of a magic ring of invisibility—the lovable Bilbo grounds the tale into reality and gives the reader a clear and recognizable perspective on Tolkien's world.

While *The Hobbit* is said to be a work of fantasy for children, the sweeping *Lord of the Rings* trilogy contains a much richer and more complex tale. The plot, however, is relatively straightforward. The magic ring Bilbo acquired years before in *The Hobbit* is discovered by Gandalf to be the One Ring wrought ages ago by the evil Sauron (the Dark Lord), who wishes to recover it and use its hidden power to enslave all of Middle-earth. Now held by Bilbo's nephew Frodo, the Ring must be destroyed by casting it into the furnace in which it was created: Mount Doom, at the center of Sauron's kingdom of Mordor. Once again, Tolkien is concerned with the heroic quest. But while *The Hobbit* deals only with Bilbo Baggins' fate, this epic has a far more dire and perilous concern; the subjugation of the free world. Hobbits are again at the center of the story, their simple courage and earnest goodwill set against the machinations of the Dark Lord. Aided by a group of companions, including Gandalf and Frodo's loyal servant Sam Gamgee, Frodo bears yet another burden: all who carry and use the Ring eventually become corrupted by it. Therefore the trilogy deals with evil on both a personal level and a grander world scale.

What gives the epic its depth and majestic vision is not only its sheer size—over 600,000 words in length, it was published as three separate novels, *The Fellowship of the Ring* (1954), *The Two Towers* (1954), and *The Return of the King* (1955)—but also the fact that the tale is steeped in an ancient history of Tolkien's devising that reaches back to the dawn of Middle-earth and appears at every point in the novel, from place names and characters and their ancestries to objects such as the Ring. This history appears in several appendices in *The Return of the King* and in a more complete version in *The Silmarillion* (1977), and gives the story an iceberg effect—what the reader sees is the culmination of a vast sweep of events that takes place over centuries. One of the great accomplishments of Tolkien is his imaginative ability to create this history, as well as his implementation of it in his novels; they enrich the tale rather than drown it amid a sea of dates and historical facts.

Tolkien repeatedly rejected a popular view that his trilogy was an allegory of the events of WWII, insisting instead that it was a "fundamentally religious and Catholic work" examining the dual nature of evil, defined as both the attempt to separate one's self from God and as a separate force distinct from God, with the physical world as their battleground. The symbol of evil in the book is the shadow, which is an absence of light that does not exist in and of itself but is still visible and perceptible as if it did. In the end, however, it is not the symbolism or the mythical history that we remember; it is the hobbits, with their child-like innocence and steadfast courage, who impress themselves upon our hearts and minds.

—Christopher Swann

TOWNSEND, Susan Elaine

Nationality: English. **Born:** Leicester, Leicestershire, 2 April 1946. **Education:** Attended English secondary school. **Career:** Worked in various capacities, including garage attendant, hot dog saleswoman, dress shop worker, factory worker, and trained community worker; full-time writer, 1982—. Writer and presenter, "Think of England," British Broadcasting Corporation (BBC-TV), 1991. **Awards:** Thames Television Bursary, 1979, for *Womberang*. **Agent:** Giles Gordon, Anthony Sheil Associates, 43 Doughty Street, London WC1N 2LF, England. **Address:** Bridge Works, Knighton Fields Road West, Leicester LE2 6LH, England.

Publications

Novels

The Secret Diary of Adrian Mole, Aged 13 3/4. Methuen, 1982.
The Growing Pains of Adrian Mole. Methuen, 1984.
The Adrian Mole Diaries (includes *The Secret Diary of Adrian Mole, Aged 13 3/4* and *The Growing Pains of Adrian Mole*). Methuen, 1985, Grove Press, 1986.
Rebuilding Coventry: A Tale of Two Cities. Methuen, 1988.
Mr. Bevan's Dream. Trafalgar Square, 1990.
The Queen and I. Methuen, 1992, Soho Press, 1993.
Adrian Mole: The Wilderness Years. Methuen, 1993.

Plays

Womberang (produced Leicester, England, 1979).
Groping for Words (produced London, 1983).
The Great Celestial Cow (produced Leicester, England, 1984).
Bazaar and Rummage (play collection includes *Groping for Words* and *Womberang*), Methuen, 1984.
The Secret Diary of Adrian Mole, Aged 13 3/4 (produced London, 1984). Methuen, 1985.
Ear, Nose, and Throat (produced Cambridge, England, 1989).
Ten Tiny Fingers, Nine Tiny Toes. Heinemann, 1991.

* * *

Formerly a moderately successful left-wing playwright, British satirist Sue Townsend established herself as what critic Michael Elliott, in the *New York Times,* calls "a one-woman cottage industry" with her immensely successful *Secret Diary of Adrian Mole Aged 13 3/4* (1982). This first and most satisfying installment of the Adrian Mole series introduced millions of readers to the titular "diarist and juvenile philosopher" who mingles adolescent angst, sex obsession, and intellectual pretention with sardonic social observations. The sequel, *The Growing Pains of Adrian Mole* (1984), elaborates on Adrian's self-absorbed musings on family life, spotty skin, penis size, love, and Margaret Thatcher's England.

British critical and public response to the diaries was phenomenal. Critics have said that Adrian Mole's appeal for readers lies in his absurd contradictions; he is self-absorbed but compassionate, tidy but unfashionable, stingy but generous, and shallow but philosophical. The diaries have had strong international success, and some American critics have drawn parallels to *Catcher in the Rye,* another teenage novel which has appealed to a wide cross-section of adults.

Townsend has published subsequent volumes of the Adrian Mole diaries, following him up to age 25 and tracing his efforts to get published and to get a sex life in post-Thatcher England. Adrian remains, however, emotionally short sighted, and consequently a nerdy vehicle for Townsend's acidic brand of social satire. Critical response to the later volumes has been mixed, with American critics in particular finding that Mole's adolescent charm wears thinner upon his having reached adulthood.

In her other work, Townsend continues to articulate the insanity and inertia of England's decaying social structure through the voices of uncomprehending outcast figures. She employs memorable characters and sometimes one-dimensional caricatures to attack institutions and authority figures as well as individual pretensions and self-delusions. *Rebuilding Coventry* (1988) follows a beautiful middle-aged woman who kills a loutish neighbor, abandons her family, and flees to London, where she finds a kind of liberation from her circumscribed suburban life. The novel is speedily paced, and the brevity of its chapters are reminiscent of long diary entries (but entries from a diverse set of contributors). Townsend demonstrates humorous compassion for the sheer misery of being poor, while concomitantly skewering suburban and urban posturings, emotional sterility, and officious authoritarians.

The Queen & I (1992), an uncannily prophetic dissection of the dissolution of the British Royal family, was another significant bestseller for Townsend. The novel's premise is that the monarchy has been overturned and that its members, suddenly on welfare, move into a housing project. Much of the humor comes from the fact that the Royals behave as public preconceptions would assume; the Queen endures with dignity, Philip goes mad, Charles delights in the opportunities for organic gardening, and Diana finds a new boyfriend. There are in this work, as the *Washington Post's* Nina King points out, some serious targets as well, including the inequities of wealth and class and the degradation imposed by "the decaying welfare state."

Most clearly in *The Queen and I,* but also throughout her work, Townsend focuses on the way people try to live in a deluded and uncaring society. She has a unrelenting eye for detail and incisively sketches out the hilarious and bathetic contradictions of life. Some critics point out that Townsend's rather slapdash style often leaves loose ends and that her satiric acuity occasionally betrays a tendency to sneer. While she has a keen awareness of human foibles, she is nevertheless a compassionate and funny observer of human life.

—Christina Sylka

TROGDON, William (Lewis)

Pseudonym: William Least Heat Moon. **Nationality:** American. **Born:** Kansas City, Missouri, 27 August 1939. **Education:** University of Missouri-Columbia, B.A. in literature, 1961, M.A., 1962, Ph.D., 1973, B.A. in photo-journalism, 1978. **Military Service:** U.S. Navy, served on USS Lake Champlain, 1963-65; became personnelman third class. **Family:** Married 1) Lezlie Trogdon in 1967 (divorced, 1978); 2) Linda Keown. **Career:** Stephens College, Columbia, Missouri, teacher of English, 1965-78; writer. Lecturer at University of Missouri School of Journalism, 1984—. **Award:** Christopher award, 1984, and Books-Across-the-Sea award, 1984, both for *Blue Highways; Blue Highways* was named a notable book by the New York Times and one of the five best nonfiction books of 1983 by *Time; PrairyErth* was selected as the best work of nonfiction by the American Library Association and was named a notable book of 1991 by the *New York Times.* **Agent:** Lois Wallace, 177 East 70th St., New York, New York 10021. **Address:** 222 Berkeley St., Boston, Massachusetts 02116, U.S.A.

Publications

Nonfiction as William Least Heat Moon

Blue Highways. Little, Brown, 1982.
PrairyErth (A Deep Map). Houghton, 1991.

* * *

William Least Heat Moon says a Missourian, as he is, "gets used to Southerners thinking him a Yankee, a Northerner considering him a cracker, a Westerner sneering at his effete Easternness, and an Easterner taking him for a cowhand." This self-characterization is from his first book, *Blue Highways* (1982), which describes people, places, and things of America in an uncommonly personal manner.

A blue highway, Heat Moon writes, is how older roadmaps indicate a secondary road. These are the routes he travelled in a

Ford Econoline van, navigating his way along the perimeters of the United States in a journey taking him as far as he could get from his home in the heartland. Left behind were his wife (from whom he had been separated for nine months), his college teaching job (from which he was being dismissed because of declining enrollment), and his legal name, William Trogdon. What he found includes a better understanding of his partly Osage Native American heritage. But the emphasis in *Blue Highways* is how Americans of all varieties live their lives in contexts that have escaped the homogenization of interstate travel and nationalized communications.

In the idiosyncracies of others Heat Moon discovers an America many commentators have considered lost, yet he steadfastly refuses to romanticize what his writing recovers. Instead, he delights in the offbeat but ultimately happy juxtapositions of times and cultures that a present-day trip can yield. A typical example is in St. Martinsville, Louisiana, where a statue of three women—Emmeline Labiche (a heroic pioneer of Acadian days), Evangeline Bellefontaine (the heroine of Henry Wadsworth Longfellow's poem), and Dolores Del Rio (who starred in the 1929 Hollywood Film, *Evangeline,* parts of which were filmed on location near St. Martinsville)—symbolizes the town's meagre claims to fame. Throughout *Blue Highways* there are enough fortunate accidents to make the reading experience a continual adventure. Yet in the ultimate isolation of the people he meets, Heat Moon is able to better understand his own loneliness and return to Missouri realizing that nothing material can fill a void in one's self.

Loneliness and isolation are also the themes of *The Red Couch* (1984), a series of photographs by Kevin Clarke and Horst Wackerbarth for which William Least Heat Moon wrote the preface and captions. In a neorealistic experiment, the photographers carried a large, plushly upholstered sofa across the United States for five years, photographing it in the company of distinctive individuals and scenery. Heat Moon's accompanying narrative reminds readers that every picture tells a story, and also supplies information from the photographers' notebooks that confirms how the constant presence of the red couch is the only consistent element in a world where a Hell's Angels motorcycle club chapter creates more red tape than a government bureau and a crew of slaughterhouse workers and their employer exude great openness and friendliness among the hideously evident carnage.

It is in the writing of *PrairyErth* (1991) that Heat Moon finds an antidote to loneliness in literary art. Here he concentrates his focus on a single, sparsely settled county in Kansas that happens to be the geographical center of the United States. For 624 closely set pages he studies Chase County in its historical, demographical, and even geological dimensions, making the story of a rock as interesting and compelling as the biography of a colorful local character. From all perspectives this small square of land is an eternal place of "energy transfer," with the most reenergized person being the author himself.

—Jerome Klinkowitz

TROLLOPE, Joanna

Pseudonym: Caroline Harvey. **Nationality:** British. **Born:** Gloucestershire, 9 December 1943. **Education:** St Hugh's College, Oxford (Gamble scholar), 1962-65, M.A. in English 1972. **Family:** Married 1) David Potter in 1966, two daughters; 2) the playwright Ian Curteis in 1985. **Career:** Research assistant, Foreign Office, London, 1965-67; teacher in preparatory schools and adult foreign student classes, 1968-78. **Awards:** Romantic Novelists Association Major award, 1980. **Agent:** A.D. Peters, Fifth Floor, The Chambers, Chelsea Harbour, Lots Road, London SW10 0XF, England. **Address:** The Mill House, Coln St Aldwyns, Cirencester, Gloucestershire, England.

Publications

Novels

Eliza Stanhope. London, Hutchinson, 1978; New York, Dutton, 1979.
Parson Harding's Daughter. London, Hutchinson, 1979; as *Mistaken Virtues*, New York, Dutton, 1980.
Leaves from the Valley. London, Hutchinson, 1980; New York, St Martin's Press, 1984.
The City of Gems. London, Hutchinson, 1981.
The Steps of the Sun. London, Hutchinson, 1983; New York, St Martin's Press, 1984.
The Taverners' Place. London, Hutchinson, 1986; New York, St Martin's Press, 1987.
The Choir. London, Hutchinson, 1988.
The Village Affair. London, Bloomsbury, and New York, HarperCollins, 1989.
A Passionate Man. London, Bloomsbury, 1990.
The Rector's Wife. London, Bloomsbury, 1991.
Castle in Italy. London, Bloomsbury, 1992.
The Men and the Girls. London, Bloomsbury, 1992.
A Second Legacy. London, Corgi, 1992.
A Spanish Lover. London, Bloomsbury, 1993.
The Country Habit. London, Bantam, 1993.
The Best of Friends. London, Bantam, 1995.

Novels as Caroline Harvey (series: Legacy of Love)

Legacy of Love. London, Octopus, 1983.
Charlotte. London, Sundial, 1980.
Alexandra. London, Sundial, 1980.
Cara. London, Octopus, 1983.

Other

Britannia's Daughters: Women of the British Empire. London, Hutchinson, 1983.

Editor, *The Country Habit: An Anthology*. London, Bantam, 1993.

* * *

A descendant of Victorian novelist Anthony Trollope, Joanna Trollope deals with the problems of modern living and loving. But she started by writing historical novels. *Eliza Stanhope* (1978) tells of Eliza's love for cavalry officer Francis Beaumont and their journey to the battlefield of Waterloo, where Francis is wounded and Eliza assists the surgeons in their grisly work. In *Parson Harding's Daughter* (1979), Catherine Harding leaves England for Calcutta as the promised bride of her childhood sweetheart Johnnie Gates, only to find that he has become a hopeless drunkard. Their "marriage of convenience" runs into trouble when she meets and falls in love with the aloof Sir Edward Ashton. Both novels are sharply written and peopled with interesting characters. They score over some of Trollope's later historical works, which are well researched but seem to lack the bite and liveliness of these first two books. *Leaves from the Valley* (1980), *City of Gems* (1981) and *The Steps of the Sun* (1983), are set respectively in India, 19th century Burma, and the South Africa of the Boer War. They are capably written but somehow less striking than her previous work.

In addition to books under her own name, Trollope has produced three historical novels as "Caroline Harvey." The first of these, *Legacy of Love* (1983), is a family saga featuring heroines from three successive generations. Its sequel, *A Second Legacy* (1993), takes the action from Afghanistan in the 1840s to the present day. Both novels are strong, ambitious works and rank with the best of her historical fiction. *Castle in Italy* (1992) has its merits, but does not quite equal them.

With *The Choir* (1988), Trollope entered an entirely new phase, turning from history to the present with her first contemporary novel. It was an inspired decision that found her writing at her best. Aldminster Cathedral needs expensive repairs, and the powerful Dean suggests that the choir be disbanded to save money. The resulting quarrel involves a variety of characters as Trollope explores power struggles and intrigue, not only through the eyes of the Dean and the opposing headmaster, but also from the viewpoint of Sally Ashworth, the mother of star choirboy Henry, who turns from a loveless marriage to organist Leo Beckford; and Frank Ashworth, the socialist councillor who is Henry's grandfather. The tangle of plots is brilliantly woven and neatly solved, but Trollope avoids the happy ending, and the victory is achieved only at a cost.

One of her finest works, *The Choir* showed Trollope at her peak. She followed up with *A Village Affair* (1989), a deep and thoughtful treatment of a love affair between two women and its effect on them and their village community. *A Passionate Man* (1990) was followed by *The Rector's Wife* (1991), which describes Anna Bouverie's struggle to fulfil herself as a person in her own right (and not merely as "the rector's wife") in a country parish. Bitter at being refused promotion, her clergyman husband withdraws from her into his parish duties. Anna is forced to make her own life without him. *The Choir, A Village Affair,* and *The Rector's Wife* have been adapted for television and broadcast in the United Kingdom.

The Men and the Girls (1992) is equally good, and explores the traumas of two young women living with older male partners whose lives are changed by a chance accident and career changes. Trollope's superb cast of characters extends from punk teenager Joss to the elderly, keen-witted Miss Bachelor. The ending again takes in grief and loss as well as joy. *A Spanish Lover* (1993) is the story of twin sisters, one a married mother whom is successful in business, and the other single and seemingly unfulfilled. When Frances, the single sister, meets her Spanish lover and Lizzie's business hits trouble, their world is changed and both have to adapt. Trollope describes their struggles with wit and understanding. *The Best of Friends* (1995), finds her as skilled as ever, this time studying the disrupted lives of two families when one couple separates. She examines the nature of love between young adults, teenagers, and the elderly with equal sympathy and conviction. *The Best of Friends* is more proof that Joanna Trollope leads the way among contemporary novelists in the field of human relationships.

—Geoff Sadler

TRUMAN, (Mary) Margaret

Nationality: American. **Born:** Independence, Missouri, 17 February 1924; daughter of President Harry S. Truman. **Education:** George Washington University, A.B., 1946. **Family:** Married E. Clifton Daniel, Jr., 1956; children: four sons. **Career:** Writer. Opera coloratura, touring nationwide and appearing on radio and television, 1947-54; host of radio program *Authors in the News,* 1954-61; cohost, with Mike Wallace, of radio program *Weekday,* 1955-56; host of television program *CBS International Hour,* 1965; summer stock actress. Director of Riggs National Bank, Washington, DC; trustee of Harry S. Truman Institute at Georgetown University; secretary of Harry S. Truman Scholarship Fund. **Awards:** L.H.D., Wake Forest University, 1972; Litt.D., George Washington University, 1975; H.H.D., Rockhurst College, 1976. **Agent:** Scott Meredith, Scott Meredith Literary Agency, Inc., 845 Third Ave., New York, New York 10022.

PUBLICATIONS

Novels

Murder in the White House. Arbor House, 1980.
Murder on Capitol Hill. Arbor House, 1981.
Murder in the Supreme Court. Arbor House, 1982.
Murder in the Smithsonian. Arbor House, 1983.
Murder on Embassy Row. Arbor House, 1984.
Murder at the FBI. Arbor House, 1985.
Murder in Georgetown. Arbor House, 1986.
Murder in the CIA. Random House, 1987.
Murder at the Kennedy Center. Random House, 1989.
Murder at the National Cathedral. Random House, 1990.
Murder at the Pentagon. Fawcett, 1992.
Murder on the Potomac. Random House, 1994.
Murder at the National Gallery. Random House, 1996.

Short Stories

Margaret Truman: Three Complete Stories. Random House, 1994.

Other

Souvenir: Margaret Truman's Own Story, with Margaret Cousins, McGraw, 1956.
White House Pets. McKay, 1969.
Harry S. Truman. Morrow, 1972, Avon, 1993.
Women of Courage. Morrow, 1976.
Bess W. Truman. Macmillan, 1986.
Where the Buck Stops: The Personal & Private Writings of Harry S. Truman. Warner, 1990.
First Ladies. Random House, 1995.

Editor, *Letters from Father: The Truman Family's Personal Correspondence.* Arbor House, 1981.

* * *

Margaret Truman not only surprised her audience with her creativity and success as a mystery writer, she surprised herself. After publishing a succession of biographical books, she found herself chatting with her agent and heard herself agree to try her hand at writing fiction. Mystery readers are still thanking her.

Truman began her literary career by writing her autobiography, entitled *Souvenir: Margaret Truman's Own Story* (1956). The title accurately suggests that someone else was thinking about writing Truman's story. Co-writing the autobiography with Margaret Cousins, Truman smothered the success of the unauthorized biography, which was her intention. *Souvenir* relates incidents from her childhood in Missouri and later in the White House, and it follows her successful career as a concert singer. Reviews typically cast her work as graceful, simple, warm, genuine, and modest, revealing a midwest girl barely affected by the rest of the world.

The success Truman achieved with *Souvenir* was matched when she took on the task of writing her father's biography, *Harry S. Truman* (1972). The president's daughter gave the world an intimate view of a great, gentle family man in a way no other biographer could. Truman gave the nation and the world a view of the president through the eyes of a "loving and loyal daughter," as Pamela Marsh from the *Christian Science Monitor* put it. The biography sold well over a million copies.

Truman continued to give the world an inside view of her family by publishing another biography, this time of her mother, Bess W. Truman. Bess Truman destroyed much of her correspondence and little is known of the First Lady's thoughts and emotions. But Truman captures her mother's intimate nature in this biography and opens the door into the White House from the perspective of the often forgotten First Lady.

In her mystery novels, Truman has given the world a close and private look into the heartbeat of American politics. Her mystery novels are set in Washington, D.C., at familiar agencies and buildings. Truman credits the success of her first mystery novel to her name and the book's setting. *Murder In the White House* (1980) was optioned for a television movie and earned Truman over $200,000 for the paperback rights alone.

In spite of her success, Truman has said that she does not find writing a pleasant activity: "Writing is the hardest and most exacting career I've ever had."

—Tammy J. Bronson

TRYON, Thomas

Nationality: American. **Born:** Hartford, Connecticut, 14 January 1926. **Education:** Yale University, B.A. (with honors), 1949; further study at Art Students League, New York City, 1950; studied acting with Sanford Meisner, Neighborhood Playhouse, New York City. **Military Service:** U.S. Navy, 1943-46. **Family:** Married Ann Lilienthal in 1955 (divorced, 1958). **Career:** Actor under name Tom Tryon, 1952-71; writer and producer, beginning 1971. Set painter and assistant stage manager, Cape Playhouse, Dennis, Cape Cod, Mass., 1950. Production assistant, Columbia Broadcasting System, Inc. (CBS-TV); worked occasionally as an extra on television shows. **Awards:** Prix Femina de Belgique for outstanding male performance, and Laurel award, Motion Picture Exhibitors, both 1964, both for *The Cardinal;* Ann Radcliffe award, Count Dracula Society, 1974. **Died:** 4 September 1991.

PUBLICATIONS

Novels and Novellas

The Other. Knopf, 1971, reprinted, Fawcett, 1987.
Harvest Home. Knopf, 1973.
Lady. Knopf, 1974.
Crowned Heads (novellas; includes *Fedora, Bobbitt, Lorna,* and *Willie*). Knopf, 1976.
All That Glitters: Five Novellas. Knopf, 1986.
The Night of the Moonbow. Knopf, 1988.
The Wings of the Morning. Knopf, 1990.
In the Fire of Spring. Knopf, 1992.

Fiction for Children

The Adventures of Opal and Cupid. Viking, 1990.

Plays

Screenplays: *The Other,* 1972.

*

Media Adaptations: Films—*The Other,* 1972; *Fedora,* 1978. Television film—*Harvest Home,* 1973.

Theatrical Activities:

Actor: **Plays**—*Wish You Were Here,* 1952; *Cyrano de Bergerac,* 1953; *Richard III,* 1953. **Films**—*The Scarlet Hour,* 1956; *Screaming Eagles,* 1956; *Three Violent People,* 1958; *The Unholy Wife,* 1958; *I Married a Monster from Outer Space,* 1958; *The Story of Ruth,* 1960; *Marines, Let's Go!,* 1961; *Moon Pilot,* 1962; *The Longest Day,* 1962; *Something's Got to Give,* 1962; *The Cardinal,* 1963; *In Harm's Way,* 1965; *The Glory Guys,* 1965; *Momento Mori,* 1968; *Color Me Dead,* 1969; *The Narco Men,* 1971. **Television series**—*Texas John Slaughter,* 1958.

* * *

Thomas Tryon was educated at Yale and studied art in New York, but his early fame came from his acting. He appeared in some Broadway plays before moving in 1955 to California, where he appeared in several less-than-memorable films. In 1963 he starred in *The Cardinal* and received good reviews for his performance. He continued to make films and to appear on television until the early 1970s. However, he later told an interviewer that he had essentially chosen the wrong career when he had turned to acting, and that eventually he "lost his actor's nerve."

Tryon then turned to writing novels, and in 1971 published *The Other.* The book was a hit, remaining on the bestseller list for seven months. *The Other* is a Gothic novel; a story of twins who are separated by the death of one of the boys (or perhaps the personalities of both boys come to inhabit the body of the remaining twin). Tryon holds the reader in considerable suspense as the plot unfolds one layer at a time. *The Other* was filmed in 1972, with Tryon serving as the executive producer.

Tryon's second novel, *Harvest Home* (1973), reads a bit as if Shirley Jackson had written "The Lottery" as a novel instead of a short story. Tryon set the novel in his native New England, and the book was again a bestseller, although the critics gave it mixed reviews. *Harvest Home* details the story of a young couple who move to rural New England and find themselves caught up in a community dedicated to pagan ritual. The book was alternately panned and praised, but Stephen King, in the *New York Times Book Review*, said that it was a "true book; it says exactly what Tryon wanted it to say." A television movie based on *Harvest Home* was produced in 1973.

Tryon moved away from the Gothic with *Lady* (1974), his third book. This is the story of a fascinating woman, seen through the eyes of a young man who worshipped her when he was a boy. *Crowned Heads*, published in 1976, is a collection of four novellas, all based in Hollywood (a long-departed Hollywood). A movie based on one of the novellas, *Fedora*, was filmed in 1978. Tryon used Hollywood as his base again when he published *All That Glitters: Five Novellas* in 1986. He followed that work in 1988 with *The Night of the Moonbow*.

With the publication of *The Wings of the Morning* in 1990, Tryon made another switch in genre. With this novel, he turned from the Gothic novel and the Hollywood novella to historical fiction. Again, he found commercial success. Tryon set the story in the fictional Pequot Landing in pre-Civil War New England. The story follows the conflict between the Grimes family, whose stance is proslavery, and the Talcott family, dedicated to abolition. Tryon had intended this to be the first of a trilogy set in historical New England, but this was not to be. The second novel in the trilogy, *In the Fire of Spring*, was published in 1992, shortly after Tryon's death from cancer in September, 1991. Tryon also published a children's book, *The Adventures of Opal and Cupid* (1990).

—June Harris

TUCHMAN, Barbara W(ertheim)

Nationality: American. **Born:** New York City, 20 January 1912. **Education:** Radcliffe College, B.A., 1933. **Family:** Married Lester R. Tuchman in 1940; children: three daughters. **Career:** Institute of Pacific Relations, New York City, research and editorial assistant, 1933, Tokyo, 1934-35; *Nation* magazine, New York City, staff writer and foreign correspondent, 1935-37, correspondent in Madrid, 1937-38; *The War with Spain* (magazine), London, England, staff writer, 1937-38; *New Statesman* magazine and *Nation*, London, U.S. correspondent, 1939; Office of War Information, New York City, editor for Far Eastern Affairs, 1943-45; author, 1938—. Trustee, Radcliffe College, 1960-72. Appointed Jefferson Lecturer for the National Endowment for the Humanities, 1980. Lecturer at Harvard University, University of California, U.S. Naval War College, and other institutions. **Awards:** Pulitzer prize, 1963, for *The Guns of August*, and 1972, for *Stilwell and the American Experience in China, 1911-1945;* gold medal for history, American Academy of Arts and Sciences, 1978; Regent Medal of Excellence, University of the State of New York, 1984; Sarah Josepha Hale award, 1985; Abraham Lincoln Literary award, Union League Club, 1985; received Order of Leopold from the Kingdom of Belgium. D.Litt. from Yale University, Columbia University, New York University, Williams College, University of Massachusetts, Smith College, Hamilton College, Mount Holyoke College, Boston University, Harvard University, and other schools. **Member:** Society of American Historians (president, 1970-73), Authors Guild (treasurer), Authors League of America (member of council), American Academy of Arts and Letters (president, 1979), American Academy of Arts and Sciences, Cosmopolitan Club. **Died:** 6 February 1989.

Publications

Nonfiction

The Lost British Policy: Britain and Spain since 1700. United Editorial, 1938.
Bible and Sword: England and Palestine from the Bronze Age to Balfour. New York University Press, 1956.
The Zimmermann Telegram. Viking, 1958; revised edition, Macmillan, 1966.
The Guns of August. Macmillan, 1962.
The Proud Tower: A Portrait of the World before the War, 1890-1914. Macmillan, 1966.
Stilwell and the American Experience in China, 1911-1945. Macmillan, 1971.
Notes from China. Collier Books, 1972.
A Distant Mirror: The Calamitous Fourteenth Century. Knopf, 1978.
Practicing History: Selected Essays. Knopf, 1981.
The March of Folly: From Troy to Vietnam. Knopf, 1984.
The First Salute: A View of the American Revolution. Knopf, 1988.

*

Critical Study: *New Women in Social Sciences* by Kathleen Bowman, Creative Education Press, 1976.

* * *

Unlike most contemporary historians, Barbara Tuchman has enjoyed both public and critical attention. Shortly before the publication of *The Guns of August* (1962), the *New York Times* advertised the book by printing the entire introduction followed by a favorable review. If all of her works have not received the same critical acclaim and attention, they have still attracted much attention and sold well.

The Guns of August, considered by most critics to be her best work, is Tuchman's discussion of events during the first month of WWI. Although historians generally contest the thesis of the work (that the outcome of the war was decided during the first month), many critics consider it a classic of historical writing. Tuchman's focus on people rather than events is found throughout this work. For example, she explains events by calling William II "notable but stupid," and describes Czar Nicholas as having "the indifference of a mind so shallow as to be all surface." Clifton Fadiman of the *New York Times* described the book as "a story never before told with such depth and penetration . . . [it] has the effect of sheer, tense drama."

Tuchman's next work, *The Proud Tower* (1966), continues her focus on the origins of WWI. The book is divided into eight chapters that chart the development of diplomacy, culture, and art in Western Europe and the United States between 1890-1914. Although critics claim the book raises fundamental questions about both the origins of the war and the nature of historical inquiry, they also claim the work leaves the reader formulating his or her own evaluation of events because there is no connection between chapters. She is also accused of using both anecdotes with no relationship to historical contexts, and clichés, such as her description of Nietzsche: "[he] rolled and billowed like storm clouds." Yet Tuchman still managed to paint vivid pictures of individual characters, and critics praised her for "not being afraid to tell a story."

Stilwell and the American Experience in China (1971), winner of the Pulitzer Prize, focuses on the United States' involvement with China from early in the twentieth century to WWII. The tone of the account is darker than her previous works because of its emphasis on the failure of the United States to make intelligent decisions. With regard to U.S. foreign policy in China, it prompts a pertinent question: "how could America act so confidently when it knew it was wrong?"

A Distant Mirror (1978) deals with Europe in the fourteenth century. Although the work began as an attempt to understand the effects on society of the catastrophic outbreak of Bubonic plague, Tuchman claims the work is also instructive for our times because "it is reassuring to know the human race has lived through worse before." Like all of her other works, it is not merely a study of causes, but a detailed account of the Black Death, Church corruption, and the beginnings of the Hundred Years War, as seen through the eyes of one family. Critics lauded the account as a "tapestry that brings many disembodied details to life."

The First Salute (1988) analyzes the relationship between the American Revolution and international politics. Tuchman begins with the Dutch involvement at the island of St. Eustatius and eventually shows how European diplomacy affected British colonial interests. Although John Grass of the *New York Times* felt "there is a point where the reader wonders where she is going [with the history]," it is a genuine attempt to place the American Revolution in the context of European perspectives. Tuchman's focus on individuals and select episodes allows her to create lasting scenes, particularly Washington's 500-mile march from Yonkers to Yorktown.

Practicing History (1981), a collection of essays written throughout Tuchman's life, is an effort to give insight into the art of historical writing. She presents the historian as a storyteller who discovers a thesis only after he or she understands the material. "In Search of History," an essay in the collection, encourages historians to work from primary materials. Although she sometimes romanticizes the task, her descriptions of historical writing help one perceive her as an artist, not merely a dry academic. She writes that historical writing is "often painful, sometimes agony. It means rearrangement, revision, adding, cutting, rewriting. But it brings a sense of excitement, almost a rapture."

—Chris Godat

TUROW, Scott

Nationality: American. **Born:** Chicago, Illinois, 12 April 1949. **Education:** Amherst College, B.A., 1970; Stanford University, M.A., 1974; Harvard University, J.D., 1978. **Family:** Married Annette Weisberg in 1971; children: two daughters and one son. **Career:** Stanford University, Stanford, California, E. H. Jones Lecturer in Creative Writing, 1972-75; Suffolk County District Attorney's Office, Boston, Massachussetts, clerk; United States Court of Appeals (7th District), Chicago, Illinois, assistant United States attorney, 1978-86; Sonnenschein Carlin Nath & Rosenthal, Chicago, Illinois, partner, 1986—. Writer, 1972—. **Awards:** Writing award, College English Association and Book-of-the-Month Club, 1970; Edith Mirrielees fellow, 1972; Silver Dagger award, Crime Writers Association, 1988, for *Presumed Innocent*. **Address:** c/o Sonnenschein, Carlin, Nath and Rosenthal, Sears Tower, Suite 8000, Chicago, Illinois 60606, U.S.A.

Publications

Novels

Presumed Innocent. New York, Farrar, Straus, 1987.
The Burden of Proof. New York, Farrar, Straus, 1990.
Pleading Guilty. New York, Farrar, Straus, 1993.

Nonfiction

One L: An Inside Account of Life in the First Year at Harvard Law School. Putnam, 1977.

*

Film Adaptations: *Presumed Innocent*, 1990; *The Burden of Proof*, 1992.

* * *

Upon completing his Harvard Law School training, Scott Turow began his writing career with a nonfiction report on his experiences as a first-year law student in *One L* (1977). Since then his practice as a Chicago lawyer with the firm of Sonnenschein Nath & Rosenthal has provided a solid legal foundation for insider studies of the justice system, the inner workings of the legal trade, its deceptions and trade secrets, and the Byzantine psychology and loyalties of professionals at all levels of the legal system. Turow writes convincingly of daily routines, courtroom encounters, behind-the-scenes investigations, and trial procedures. His crime novels are characterized by skillful misdirection, unforgettably powerful metaphors, vivid detail, and elegant prose that reveals the hidden darker selves of its characters and the illusory nature of reality while questioning "justice" and the ability of man and his institutions to find even simple truths.

Turow builds on familiar territory, specializing in psychological studies of clever, cynical lawyers, humanized by confessions of private fears and doubts. His three provocative novels, *Presumed Innocent* (1987), *Burden of Proof* (1990) and *Pleading Guilty* (1993), depend on narrative voice to obfuscate guilt and responsibility. All three are set in a fictionalized Chicago area called

"Kindle County," and gain depth and interest from studies of those caught up in the justice system, from street cops, pathologists, judges, and attorneys to lonely wives, angry children, cynical jurors, and ruthless politicians.

All three books depict total truth as unknowable, betrayal as inevitable, and legal officialdom as having more in common with criminals than with decent citizens. Their narrators mourn the fate of those close to them: the first the murdered former lover for whom the narrator was a stepping-stone to success; the second, the suicide of his wife of many years; and the third, the loss of his wife to a lesbian lover. All three love their sons, but worry about them being maladjusted. The devious, unreliable narrators of *Presumed Innocent* (a prosecuting attorney) and *Pleading Guilty* (an ex-cop turned corporate lawyer) seem to unburden their souls to the readers as they manipulate evidence and interpret events to make themselves seem like victims, and their colleagues, associates, and lovers seem like conspirators and possible criminals. The first justifies murder, and the second justifies stealing stolen money. In contrast, the narrator of *Burden of Proof* is a family man and dedicated defense lawyer who is sympathetic to human frailty and driven to understand motive and make sense of the seemingly senseless.

As its title suggests, *Presumed Innocent* turns on the question of a presumption of innocence and on the idea that circumstantial evidence might incriminate an innocent man. It is a psychological study of a morose man, Rusty Sabich, beset by inescapable pain, corruption, and guilt, engaging in introspective Dostoevsky-like monologues and manipulating the justice system for personal ends. Sabich is the chief deputy prosecuting attorney who understands the inner workings of the system and who has loyal friends in important places. The victim, his former lover, is an amoral prosecuting attorney who has slept with Sabich's boss and possibly even the judge on her way to the top. The key facts never become clear-cut, and perceptions change rapidly as the narration progresses and the final understanding is the impossibility of ever really knowing the full truth. Instead, the reader has a series of possible scenarios, all initially convincing but somehow flawed, and the human heart remains hidden. There seem to be no real innocents—only a presumption of innocence.

Sabich's enigmatic defense attorney, Sandy Stern, is the key figure in *Burden of Proof,* a psychologically and emotionally complicated novel more concerned with human frailty and inescapable family ties than with guilt or innocence. Where *Presumed Innocent* takes places in the headlines, Burden occurs behind the scenes where it explores complex interplays of love and betrayal, misunderstanding, and sacrifice. Stern must face his wife's seemingly inexplicable suicide, a missing $850,000 check, an embarrassing social disease, and his maverick brother-in-law's grand jury indictment for business fraud in a commodity-futures firm. Unspoken family codes conflict with the more formal legal codes. Stern the lawyer must judge witnesses and evidence, weigh options, and formulate legal strategy, but Stern the man must reevaluate his life, come to terms with his dead wife and his alienated offspring, make sense of acts that seem out-of-character, and reestablish meaningful human relationships.

In *Pleading Guilty,* Mack Malloy, partner-on-the-wane at a top-notch law firm, has been assigned to find the firm's star litigator, who, along with $5.6 million designated to settle a class-action suit against the firm's largest client, has been missing for weeks. As narrator of a set of transcribed tapes (his report to his company), he guides readers into a world of moral ambiguity, cut-throat alliances, corpses, and scams.

Turow's novels proffer suspenseful, masterfully contrived plots that bring style and vision to indepth analyses of the justice system and of human interaction.

—Gina Macdonald

TYLER, Anne

Nationality: American. **Born:** Minneapolis, Minnesota, 25 October 1941. **Education:** Duke University, Durham, North Carolina, 1958-61, B.A. 1961; Columbia University, New York, 1961-62. **Family:** Married Taghi Modarressi in 1963; two daughters. **Career:** Russian bibliographer, Duke University Library, 1962-63; assistant to the librarian, McGill University Law Library, Montreal, 1964-65. **Awards:** American Academy award, 1977; Janet Kafka prize, 1981; PEN Faulkner award, 1983; National Book Critics Circle award, 1986; Pulitzer prize, 1989. **Agent:** Russell and Volkening Inc., 50 West 29th Street, New York, New York 10001. **Address:** 222 Tunbridge Road, Baltimore, Maryland 21212, U.S.A.

Publications

Novels

If Morning Ever Comes. New York, Knopf, 1964; London, Chatto and Windus, 1965.

The Tin Can Tree. New York, Knopf, 1965; London, Macmillan, 1966.

A Slipping-Down Life. New York, Knopf, 1970; London, Severn House, 1983.

The Clock Winder. New York, Knopf, 1972; London, Chatto and Windus, 1973.

Celestial Navigation. New York, Knopf, 1974; London, Chatto and Windus, 1975.

Searching for Caleb. New York, Knopf, and London, Chatto and Windus, 1976.

Earthly Possessions. New York, Knopf, and London, Chatto and Windus, 1977.

Morgan's Passing. New York, Knopf, and London, Chatto and Windus, 1980.

Dinner at the Homesick Restaurant. New York, Knopf, and London, Chatto and Windus, 1982.

The Accidental Tourist. New York, Knopf, and London, Chatto and Windus, 1985.

Breathing Lessons. New York, Knopf, 1988; London, Chatto and Windus, 1989.

Saint Maybe. New York, Knopf, and London, Chatto and Windus, 1991.

Ladder of Years. New York, Knopf, 1995.

Uncollected Short Stories

"I Play Kings," in *Seventeen* (New York), August 1963.

"Street of Bugles," in *Saturday Evening Post* (Philadelphia), 30 November 1963.

"Nobody Answers the Door," in *Antioch Review* (Yellow Springs, Ohio), Fall 1964.

"I'm Not Going to Ask You Again," in *Harper's* (New York), September 1965.
"Everything but Roses," in *Reporter* (New York), 23 September 1965.
"As the Earth Gets Old," in *New Yorker,* 29 October 1966.
"Feather Behind the Rock," in *New Yorker,* 12 August 1967.
"Flaw in the Crust of the Earth," in *Reporter* (New York), 2 November 1967.
"Common Courtesies," in *McCall's* (New York), June 1968.
"With All Flags Flying," in *Redbook* (New York), June 1971.
"Bride in the Boatyard," in *McCall's* (New York), June 1972.
"Respect," in *Mademoiselle* (New York), June 1972.
"Misstep of the Mind," in *Seventeen* (New York), October 1972.
"Knack for Languages," in *New Yorker,* 13 January 1975.
"Some Sign That I Ever Made You Happy," in *McCall's* (New York), October 1975.
"Your Place Is Empty," in *New Yorker,* 22 November 1976.
"Holding Things Together," in *New Yorker,* 24 January 1977.
"Average Waves in Unprotected Waters," in *New Yorker,* 28 February 1977.
"Foot-Footing On," in *Mademoiselle* (New York), November 1977.
"The Geologist's Maid," in *Stories of the Modern South,* edited by Ben Forkner and Patrick Samway. New York, Penguin, 1981.
"Laps," in *Parents' Magazine* (New York), August 1981.
"The Country Cook," in *Harper's* (New York), March 1982.
"Teenage Wasteland," in *The Editors' Choice 1,* edited by George E. Murphy, Jr. New York, Bantam, 1985.
"Rerun," in *New Yorker,* 4 July 1988.
"A Street of Bugles," in *Saturday Evening Post* (Indianapolis), July-August 1989.
"A Woman like a Fieldstone House," in *Louder than Words,* edited by William Shore. New York, Vintage, 1989.

Other

Tumble Tower (for children). New York, Orchard, 1993.

Editor, with Shannon Ravenel, *The Best American Short Stories 1983.* Boston, Houghton Mifflin, 1983; as *The Year's Best American Short Stories,* London, Severn House, 1984.

*

Critical Studies: *Art and the Accidental in Anne Tyler* by Joseph C. Voelker, Jackson, University Press of Mississippi, 1989; *The Fiction of Anne Tyler* edited by C. Ralph Stephens, Jackson, University Press of Mississippi, 1990; *Understanding Anne Tyler* by Alice Hall Petty, Columbia, University of South Carolina Press, 1990.

* * *

Ann Tyler (Modarressi) began writing at age 21 for "something to do." An intensely private person (she conducts interviews by mail), Tyler, who studied with Reynolds Price, denies literary influences with the possible exception of Eudora Welty. Her work resists classification.

Often labeled a Southern writer, Tyler set her first three novels in North Carolina; marriage took her to Baltimore, the minutely depicted, nearly southern locale of her subsequent books. Defined through small, graphic details and gestures, Tyler's characters, which she often draws before writing, cope in what Alice Petry has called "a messy chaotic world of happenstance," usually within a quirky, eccentric, unhappy, yet nurturing family.

Tyler's characters are urban survivors often adopting surrogate families, as in *The Clock Winder* (1972). *Celestial Navigation* (1974)—a "difficult book to write," according to Tyler—was praised for its five women's accounts of the agoraphobic, alienated Jeremy Pauling. Critically acclaimed for its wit, *Searching for Caleb* (1976) looks at rebellion and conformity. It covers a century of the Peck family and reveals what Walter Sullivan calls Tyler's innocent view of life and "abiding affection for her own flaky characters." The disorganized Morgan Gower in *Morgan's Passing* (1980), her first award winner, generated exuberant debate. Peter S. Prescott admired the comic characterization; others thought Morgan maddening as he role plays his way around Baltimore by donning various hats.

The bestseller and Pulitzer nominee *Dinner at the Homesick Restaurant* (1982) opens with the deathbed meditation of Pearl Tull, who was deserted by her husband, left to raise her three children singlehandedly. Ezra, her favorite, so wants a complete, happy family dinner that he opens a restaurant to serve warm, comforting meals. In this "gentle masterpiece," flashbacks tell the bittersweet comedy of false starts and rivalries as Tyler works through the homesick metaphor. Her next novels use more traditionally structured story lines.

Tyler's popularity reached a pinnacle with the 1988 motion picture of her award-winning *Accidental Tourist* (1985). The superorganized Macon Leary writes guidebooks for travelers who, like himself, want to avoid surprise and change. Divorced by his wife after the accidental murder of their son and forced by a broken leg to return to his equally maladjusted siblings, Macon blunders into a romance with garish Muriel Pritchett via his well-drawn Welsh Corgi Edward.

Funnier but not as popular, *Breathing Lessons* (1988) nevertheless won the Pulitzer Prize and became a TV movie. Continuing Tyler's focus on family, this thin novel gently probes marriage and its accompanying romantic complications, children, and responsibilities through three couples. Maggie and Ira Moran drive to Pennsylvania for Max's funeral, which his widow Serena turns into a reenactment of their wedding, reception film included. Maggie's meddling creates two long detours: one is an unannounced visit to convince their daughter-in-law Fiona and grandchild to return to son Jesse, a failed rock star; and the other is to accompany an elderly black man to a gas station after Maggie, taking umbrage at his driving, lies by shouting that his car's tire is flat. The detours highlight Tyler's skill at "brilliantly funny set pieces," although some critics saw them as a "200 page denouement."

The comic *Saint Maybe* (1991) shows Tyler's ability to "do" children and surprised fans as a "secular tale of holy redemption." Here, Tyler also introduces foreigners for the first time. Consumed by false guilt over his brother Danny's suicide, 17-year-old Ian Bedloe sacrifices 24 stuffy years in assuming responsibility for Danny's oddball family and joins the storefront Church of the Second Chance. Some reviewers took the opportunity to criticize Tyler's many "boring" men calling them "regimenters" who "bury themselves in routine" and are attracted to "inappropriate" women.

Tyler carried her skill at creating children into *Tumble Tower* (1993), a whimsical children's book told from a child's viewpoint, written in collaboration with her younger daughter Mitra Modarressi as illustrator.

In the minimalist *Ladder of Years* (1995), Delia Grinstead continues Tyler's use of "accident" as she wanders from her vacationing family, hitchhikes to a small Delaware town, and builds a new personality. Her husband Sam, a lackluster family MD (similar to Tyler's other ineffective men), doesn't come after her, but the pull of a family wedding lures her back to Baltimore. Joyce Carol Oates sees Tyler as having "a vision of a middle-class, suburban-Caucasian world of interchangeable husbands," and calls her "the poet of the family."

—Judith C. Kohl

U-V

UPDIKE, John (Hoyer)

Nationality: American. **Born:** Shillington, Pennsylvania, 18 March 1932. **Education:** Public schools in Shillington; Harvard University, Cambridge, Massachusetts, A.B. (summa cum laude) 1954; Ruskin School of Drawing and Fine Arts, Oxford (Knox fellow), 1954-55. **Family:** Married 1) Mary Pennington in 1953 (marriage dissolved), two daughters and two sons; 2) Martha Bernhard in 1977. **Career:** Staff reporter, *New Yorker*, 1955-57. **Awards:** Guggenheim fellowship, 1959; Rosenthal award, 1960; National Book award, 1964; O. Henry award, 1966; Foreign Book prize (France), 1966; New England Poetry Club Golden Rose, 1979, MacDowell medal, 1981; Pulitzer prize, 1982, 1991; American Book award, 1982; National Book Critics Circle award, for fiction, 1982, 1991, for criticism, 1982; Union League Club Abraham Lincoln award, 1982; National Arts Club Medal of Honor, 1984; National Medal of the Arts, 1989. **Member:** American Academy, 1976. **Address:** 675 Hale Street, Beverly Farms, Massachusetts 01915, U.S.A.

Publications

Novels

The Poorhouse Fair. New York, Knopf, and London, Gollancz, 1959
Rabbit, Run. New York, Knopf, 1960; London, Deutsch, 1961
The Centaur. New York, Knopf, and London, Deutsch, 1963.
Of the Farm. New York, Knopf, 1965.
Couples. New York, Knopf, and London, Deutsch, 1968
Rabbit Redux. New York, Knopf, 1971; London, Deutsch, 1972.
A Month of Sundays. New York, Knopf, and London, Deutsch, 1975.
Marry Me: A Romance. New York, Knopf, 1976; London, Deutsch, 1977.
The Coup. New York, Knopf, 1978; London, Deutsch, 1979.
Rabbit Is Rich. New York, Knopf, 1981; London, Deutsch, 1982.
The Witches of Eastwick. New York, Knopf, and London, Deutsch, 1984.
Roger's Version. New York, Knopf, and London, Deutsch, 1986.
S. New York, Knopf, and London Deutsch, 1988.
Rabbit at Rest. New York, Knopf, 1990; London, Deutsch, 1991.
Memories of the Ford Administration. New York, Knopf, 1992; London, Hamish Hamilton, 1993.
Brazil. New York, Knopf, and London, Hamish Hamilton, 1994.
In the Beauty of the Lilies. New York, Knopf, and London, Hamish Hamilton, 1992.

Short Stories

The Same Door. New York, Knopf, 1959; London, Deutsch, 1962.
Pigeon Feathers and Other Stories. New York, Knopf, and London, Deutsch, 1962.
Olinger Stories: A Selection. New York, Knopf, 1964.
The Music School. New York, Knopf, 1966; London, Deutsch, 1967.
Penguin Modern Stories 2, with others. London, Penguin, 1969.
Bech: A Book. New York, Knopf, and London, Deutsch, 1970.
The Indian. Marvin, South Dakota, Blue Cloud Abbey, 1971.
Museums and Women and Other Stories. New York, Knopf, 1972; London, Deutsch, 1973.
Warm Wine: An Idyll. New York, Albondocani Press, 1973.
Couples: A Short Story. Cambridge, Massachusetts, Halty Ferguson, 1976.
Three Illuminations in the Life of an American Author. New York, Targ, 1979.
Too Far to Go: The Maples Stories. New York, Knopf, 1979; London, Deutsch, 1980.
The Chaste Planet. Worcester, Massachusetts, Metacom Press, 1980.
The Beloved. Nothridge, California, Lord John Press, 1982.
Bech Is Back. New York, Knopf, and London, Deutsch, 1982.
Getting Older. Helsinki, Eurographica, 1985.
The Afterlife. Leamington, Warwickshire, Sixth Chamber Press, 1987.
Going Abroad. Helsinki, Eurographica, 1987
Trust Me. New York, Knopf, and London, Deutsch, 1987.
Baby's First Step. Huntington Beach, California, Cahill, 1993.
The Afterlife and Other Stories. New York, Knopf, and London, Hamish Hamilton, 1994.

Uncollected Short Stories

"Morocco," in *Atlantic* (Boston), November 1979.

Plays

Three Tests from Early Ipswich: A Pageant. Ipswich, Massachusetts, 17th Century Day Committee, 1968.
Buchanan Dying. New York, Knopf, and London, Deutsch, 1974.

Poetry

The Carpentered Hen and Other Tame Creatures. New York, Harper, 1958; as *Hoping for a Hoopoe,* London, Gollancz, 1959.
Telephone Poles and Other Poems. New York, Knopf, and London, Deutsch, 1963.
Dogs Death. Cambridge, Massachusetts, Lowell House, 1965.
Verse. New York, Fawcett, 1965.
The Angels. Pensacola, Florida, King and Queen Press, 1968.
Bath after Sailing. Monroe, Connecticut, Pendulum Press, 1968.
Midpoint and Other Poems. New York, Knopf, and London, Deutsch, 1969.
Seventy Poems. London, Penguin, 1972.
Six Poems. New York, Aloe, 1973.
Query. New York, Albondocani Press, 1974.
Cunts (Upon Receiving the Swingers Life Club Memberships Solicitation). New York, Hallman, 1974.
Tossing and Turning. New York, Knopf, and London, Deutsch, 1977.

An Oddly Lovely Day Alone. Richmond, Virginia, Waves Press, 1979.
Sixteen Sonnets. Cambridge, Massachusetts, Halty Ferguson, 1979.
Five Poems. Cleveland Bits Press, 1980.
Spring Trio. Winston-Salem, North Carolina, Palaemon Press, 1982.
Jester's Dozen. Northridge, California, Lord John Press, 1984.
Facing Nature. New York, Knopf, 1985; London, Deutsch, 1986.
A Pear Like a Potato. Northridge, California, Santa Susana Press, 1986.
Two Sonnets. Austin, Texas, Wind River Press, 1987.
Collected Poems, 1953-1993. New York, Knopf, and London, Hamish Hamilton, 1993.

Other

The Magic Flute (for children), with Warren Chappell. New York, Knopf, 1962.
The Ring (for children), with Warren Chappell. New York, Knopf, 1964.
Assorted Prose. New York, Knopf, and London, Deutsch, 1965.
A Child's Calendar. New York, Knopf, 1965.
On Meeting Authors. Newburyport, Massachusetts, Wickford Press, 1968.
Bottom's Dream: Adapted from William Shakespeare's "A Midsummer Nights Dream" (for children). New York, Knopf, 1969.
A Good Place. New York, Aloe, 1973.
Picked-Up Pieces. New York, Knopf, 1975; London, Deutsch, 1976.
Hub Fans Bid Kid Adieu. Northridge, California, Lord John Press, 1977.
Talk from the Fifties. Northridge, California, Lord John Press, 1979.
Ego and Art in Walt Whitman. New York, Targ, 1980.
People One Knows: Interviews with Insufficiently Famous Americans. Northridge, California, Lord John Press, 1980.
Invasion of the Book Envelopes. Concord, New Hampshire, Ewert, 1981.
Hawthorne's Creed. New York, Targ, 1981.
Hugging the Shore: Essays and Criticism. New York, Knopf, 1983; London, Deutsch, 1984.
Confessions of a Wild Bore (essay). Newton, Iowa, Tamazunchale Press, 1984.
Emersonianism (lecture). Cleveland, Bits Press, 1984.
The Art of Adding and the Art of Taking Away: Selections from John Updike's Manuscripts, edited by Elizabeth A. Falsey. Cambridge, Massachusetts, Harvard College Library, 1987.
Just Looking: Essays on Art. New York, Knopf, and London, Deutsch, 1989.
Self-Consciousness: Memoirs. New York, Knopf, and London, Deutsch, 1989.
Odd Jobs: Essays and Criticism. New York, Knopf, and London, Deutsch, 1991.
Concerts at Castle Hill. Northridge, California, Lord John Press, 1993.
The Twelve Terrors of Christmas. New York, Gotham Book Mart, 1993.
A Helpful Alphabet of Friendly Objects (for children). New York, Knopf, 1995.
Golf Dreams: Writings on Golf. New York, Knopf, 1996.

Editor, *Pens and Needles*, by David Levine. Boston, Gambit, 1970.

Editor, with Shannon Ravenel, *The Best American Short Stories 1984*. Boston, Houghton Mifflin, 1984; as *The Year's Best American Short Stories*, London, Severn House, 1985.

*

Bibliography: *John Updike: A Bibliography* by C. Clarke Taylor, Kent, Ohio, Kent State University Press, 1968; *An Annotated Bibliography of John Updike Criticism 1967-1973, and a Checklist of His Works* by Michael A. Olivas, New York, Garland, 1975; *John Updike: A Comprehensive Bibliography with Selected Annotations* by Elizabeth A. Gearhart, Norwood, Pennsylvania, Norwood Editions, 1978.

Manuscript Collection: Harvard University, Cambridge, Massachusetts

Critical Studies: Interviews in *Life* (New York), 4 November 1966, *Paris Review*, Winter 1968, and *New York Times Book Review*, 10 April 1977; *John Updike* by Charles T. Samuels, Minneapolis, University of Minnesota Press, 1969; *The Elements of John Updike* by Alice and Kenneth Hamilton, Grand Rapids, Michigan, Eerdmans, 1970; *Pastoral and Anti-Pastoral Elements in John Updike's Fiction* by Larry E. Taylor, Carbondale, Southern Illinois University Press, 1971; *John Updike: Yea Sayings* by Rachael C. Burchard, Carbondale, Southern Illinois University Press, 1971; *John Updike* by Robert Detweiler, New York, Twayne, 1972, revised edition, 1984; *Rainstorms and Fire: Ritual in the Novels of John Updike* by Edward P. Vargo, Port Washington, New York, Kennikat Press, 1973; *Fighters and Lovers: Theme in the Novels of John Updike* by Joyce B. Markle, New York, New York University Press, 1973; *John Updike: A Collection of Critical Essays* by Suzanne H. Uphaus, New York, Ungar, 1980; *The Other John Updike: Poems/Short Stories/Prose/Play*, 1981, and *John Updike's Novels*, 1984, both by Donald J. Greiner, Athens, Ohio University Press; *John Updike's Images of America* by Philip H. Vaughan, Reseda, California, Mojave, 1981; *Married Men and Magic Tricks: John Updike's Erotic Heroes* by Elizabeth Tallent, Berkeley, California, Creative Arts, 1982; *Critical Essays on John Updike* edited by William R. Macnaughton, Boston, Hall, 1982; *John Updike* by Judie Newman, London, Macmillan, 1988; *Conversations with John Updike* edited by James Plath, Jackson, Mississippi, University Press, 1994.

* * *

Novelist, short-story writer, poet, playwright, and essayist are some of the titles John Updike has garnered for himself over the past four decades. He is that rare combination of celebrity and high literary merit, winner of virtually every American literary award and a best-selling author who has been described as a successor to Hemingway and Faulkner. Focusing on what he describes as "the despair of the daily," Updike has become our preeminent chronicler of the life of middle America.

It is his choice of subjects that has polarized Updike's readers and critics into two camps. As Joseph Kanon wrote in the *Saturday Review*, "Those who admire the work consider him one of the keepers of the language; those who don't say he writes beautifully about nothing very much." Most readers agree that Updike possesses a superb style and a mastery of language, observation, and wit. But some see the author as too fluent, and as a writer whose arrangement of words takes precedence over the narrative thread. Updike disagrees, saying, "There is a great deal to be said about almost anything. Everything is as interesting as every other thing. An old milk carton is worth a rose. . . . My subject is the American Protestant small town middle class. I like middles. It is in middles that extremes clash, where ambiguity restlessly rules. . . ."

Many of Updike's novels, including *Couples* (1968) and *S.* (1988), deal with the sexual mores and habits of middle-class Americans. His "Rabbit" books have earned the most fame, beginning with *Rabbit, Run* (1960), continuing with *Rabbit Redux* (1971) and *Rabbit Is Rich* (1981), and culminating in *Rabbit at Rest* (1990). The novels reveal the saga of Harry "Rabbit" Angstrom, a Pennsylvania home-town basketball star whose life is examined at ten-year intervals; he tries to leave his marriage, discovers his wife's infidelity, loses his blue-collar job, and confronts middle age. The stories are not tragic, but view Rabbit's fortunes and misfortunes with a clear wit, laying bare all of Rabbit's flaws and blunderings so that readers are both amused by him and recognize something of themselves in his travails.

Rabbit at Rest received the Pulitzer Prize, the National Book Critics Circle Award, and the American Book Award for its magnificent prose, its stunning and accurate portrayal of America in the late 1980, and its treatment of Rabbit himself, now a grandfather with heart trouble whose family has become more and more incomprehensible to him. Like most of Updike's heroes, Rabbit is slowly and carefully drawn, suffering from guilt even as he plunges into the sins of adultery and selfishness. And, like all of Updike's heroes, Rabbit yearns for salvation, even if he is not quite sure from what it is he needs to be saved.

Updike has proven to be an extremely inventive writer, challenging the conventions of the realistic novel. *The Centaur* (1963), for example, interweaves the legend of Prometheus and Chiron, the noblest centaur of Greek myth, with the story of schoolteacher George Caldwell, who in the 1940s sees his teenage son grow and change as he himself begins to lose touch with his own life. The *Witches of Eastwick* (1984) is the tale of three gorgeous women who are seduced by a wickedly handsome incarnation of the devil.

Updike's short stories have been collected in nearly a dozen volumes, including *Pigeon Feathers* (1962) and *The Afterlife* (1987), and have appeared in several editions of the Best American Short Stories series. He has long been a contributor to *The New Yorker* as a short story writer, poet, and reviewer.

Almost all of Updike's works deal with the inherent tensions in all people—the buried desires of men versus the pressures of civilized society. These tensions typically result in an act or at least contemplation of adultery, a breakdown in relationships, and the reestablishment of priorities and connections with the world at large. Despite his reputation as an accurate portrayer of America in its various eras, Updike has received criticism for the marked absence of violence in his works, which many argue is unrealistic in today's society. Updike says that he has seen or engaged in little violence himself and feels that to write about it would seem more literary or constructed and less real.

Readers will find Updike an intelligent, thoughtful, and humorous writer who does not let his humor get in the way of his sometimes scathing insights into American culture. His sexual explicitness is not lurid or pornographic but carefully and—for the most part—tastefully executed. Furthermore, few authors can capture the agonies and triumphs of American life with such stunning precision.

—Christopher Swann

URIS, Leon (Marcus)

Nationality: American. **Born:** Baltimore, Maryland, 3 August 1924. **Education:** Schools in Baltimore. **Military Service:** Served in the United States Marine Corp, 1942-45. **Family:** Married 1) Betty Beck in 1945 (divorced 1965); 2) Margery Edwards in 1968 (died 1969); 3) Jill Peabody in 1970; three children. **Career:** Newspaper driver for the San Francisco *Call-Bulletin,* late 1940s. Full-time writer since 1950. Lives in Aspen, Colorado. **Awards:** Daroff Memorial award, 1959; American Academy grant, 1959. **Address:** c/o Doubleday, 666 Fifth Avenue, New York, New York 10103, U.S.A.

Publications

Novels

Battle Cry. New York, Putnam, and London, Wingate, 1953.
The Angry Hills. New York, Random House, 1955; London, Wingate, 1956.
Exodus. New York, Doubleday, 1958; London, Wingate, 1959.
Mila 18. New York, Doubleday, and London, Heinemann, 1961.
Armageddon: A Novel of Berlin. New York, Doubleday, and London, Kimber, 1964.
Topaz. New York, McGraw Hill, 1967; London, Kimber, 1971.
Q.B. VII. New York, Doubleday, 1970; London, Kimber, 1971.
Trinity. New York, Doubleday, and London, Deutsch, 1976.
The Haj. New York, Doubleday, and London, Deutsch, 1984.
Mitla Pass. New York, Doubleday, 1988; London, Doubleday, 1989.
Redemption. New York, HarperCollins, 1995.

Plays

Ari, music by Walt Smith and William Fisher, adaptation of his own novel *Exodus* (produced New York, 1971).

Screenplays: *Battle Cry,* 1955; *Gunfight at the OK Corral,* 1957; *Israel* (documentary), 1959.

Other

Exodus Revisted. New York, Doubleday, 1960; as *In the Steps of Exodus,* London, Heinemann, 1962.
The Third Temple, with *Strike Zion,* by William Stevenson. New York, Bantam, 1967.
Ireland, A Terrible Beauty: The Story of Ireland Today, with Jill Uris. New York, Doubleday, 1975; London, Deutsch, 1976.
Jerusalem: Song of Songs, with Jill Uris. New York, Doubleday, and London, Deutsch, 1981.

* * *

Leon Uris's *Exodus* (1958) is one of the great success stories in American publishing. The novel immediately went through 50 translations, was distributed secretly into communist countries, and had an immense effect on public perceptions of Israel. A story about the Jewish experience during WWII, *Exodus* was surrounded by controversy. Uris was accused of libel for his depictions of

Dr. Wladislav Dering, a war criminal from Auschwitz, and although the resulting lawsuit was eventually dropped, the controversy served as free publicity, contributing to the book's commercial success and finally establishing the author as a popular writer.

"It took me all my life to become an overnight success," Uris quipped in a 1984 interview. In fact, Uris flunked English three times, never graduated from high school, and lived an erratic life during his military experience in the South Pacific. His first novel, *Battle Cry* (1953), received favorable reception from both critics and readers who were becoming tired of cynical WWII novels. Uris admits that he hated the war, but "unlike most novelists, I did not hate the men who fought the war." His next book, *The Angry Hills* (1955), is a spy-chase novel based upon Uris's uncle, who fought in Greece. It received less praise and Uris had difficulty getting it published. Then came *Exodus.*

After *Exodus,* Uris became interested in Jewish ghettos. He began traveling throughout Eastern Europe interviewing Holocaust survivors. The experience placed Uris at great personal risk and critics were less than enthusiastic about a novel of ghetto life, but Uris considers *Mila 18* (1961) to be his greatest accomplishment. Uris feels that "it was the one thing I wrote not caring if it sold ten copies or ten thousand. I simply had to tell a story."

Uris remained a controversial figure with the publication of *Topaz* (1967). Phillipe Thyraud de Vosjoli, an exiled French diplomat protesting DeGaulle, approached Uris with papers containing information about the French Intelligence Service. Vosjoli agreed to let Uris use the notes for a novel, the publication of which caused serious conflict inside the French government.

Uris Dedicated *QBVII* (1970) to his new wife Jill, who changed Uris's career when she also became his chief editor. The novel is based loosely on his own experiences (particularly the libel suit surrounding *Exodus*) and deals with British legal practices.

Ireland fascinated Uris, and he began to work on a photo-essay entitled *Ireland, a Terrible Beauty* (1975) while living in a flat in Dublin. The work was lauded as "perhaps the most definitive book of its kind ever done on Ireland," yet his publishers were uneasy with the work until he began a marketing tour to increase sales. *Trinity* (1976), a novel based upon his Irish experiences, became an instant bestseller and was compared with *Exodus* for its impact on popular perceptions of a particular people.

Like much of his previous work, *The Haj* (1984) was a difficult novel to research and received mixed critical reception. Although the novel was an instant bestseller, Uris was criticized for his attempt to speak honestly about Islamic people and was actually threatened by some extremist Arab groups. The author commented that "Americans are reluctant to believe ill about other people." The story consists of the struggles of Ibrahim, an Islamic patriarch who tries to maintain control of his family in the midst of conflict in the Middle East. The book is biased towards Jewish people and has been criticized as Israeli jingoism at the expense of Arab nations.

Uris's next novel, *Mitla Pass* (1988), received less attention. The story is a semiautobiographical account of a writer's life. The novel's form is experimental, having little direction and containing less interesting subject matter than his historical fiction.

Uris excels as the basic task of creating controversial situations in his fiction that ultimately captivate his readers. He has always been a dedicated novelist (before he published he would often write 18 hours a day), and is willing to risk his life when doing research on a particular project. When asked in a 1984 interview if he had advice for young writers he answered, "If you spend the rest of your life digging 16 tons of coal a day, it will be easier than becoming a novelist."

—Chris Godat

VAN LUSTBADER, Eric

Nationality: American. **Born:** New York City, 24 December 1946. **Education:** Stuyvesant High School, New York, 1960-64; Columbia University, 1964-68, B.A. in sociology. **Family:** Married Victoria Schochet in 1982. **Career:** Teacher, Project Head Start and All-Day Neighborhood Schools, New York, 1967-69; editor, *Cash Box* magazine, New York, 1970-72; assistant to president for A&R, Elektra Records, New York, 1972-73; director of publicity and creative services, Dick James Music (USA), New York, 1973-76; manager of creative services, CBS Records, New York, 1977-79; freelance writer from 1980. **Agent:** Henry Morrison, Inc., PO Box 235, Bedford Hills, NY 10507, USA.

Publications

Novels (series: Sunset Warrior)

The Sunset Warrior. New York, Doubleday, 1977; London, Star, 1979.
Shallows of Night (Sunset Warrior). New York, Doubleday, 1978; London, Star, 1979.
Dai-San (Sunset Warrior). New York, Doubleday, 1978; London, Star, 1980.
Beneath an Opal Moon (Sunset Warrior). New York, Doubleday, 1980.
The Ninja. New York, Evans, and London, Granada, 1980.
Sirens. New York, Evans, and London, Granada, 1981.
Black Heart. New York, Evans, and London, Granada, 1984.
The Miko. New York, Villard, and London, Granada, 1984.
Jian. New York, Villard, and London, Granada, 1985.
Zero. New York, Random House, and London, Grafton, 1986.
Shan. New York, Random House, and London, Grafton, 1987.
French Kiss. New York, Fawcett, and London, Grafton, 1988.
White Ninja. New York, Fawcett, and London, Grafton, 1990.
Angel Eyes. New York, Fawcett, and London, HarperCollins, 1991.
Black Blade. New York, Fawcett, and London, HarperCollins, 1992.
The Kaisho. New York, Pocket, and London, HarperCollins, 1993.
Floating City. New York, Pocket, and London, HarperCollins, 1994.
Second Skin. New York, Pocket, and London, HarperCollins, 1995.

* * *

Eric Van Lustbader, author of such thrillers as *The Ninja* (1980) and *Floating City* (1994), writes a blend of detective fiction, Japanese history, and eroticism flavored with the Orient—ritual suicides, steamy sex scenes, and shuriken and other bladed Japanese weaponry, all overlayed with a Buddhist spirituality that concerns his characters more than his readers. Still, with several bestsellers to his name, Van Lustbader has made a name for himself among writers of action-adventure in the tradition of Trevanian's *Shibumi,* James Clavell's *Shogun,* and Ridley Scott's film *Black Rain,* a shake-and-bake mixture of Western sleuthing and Eastern philosophy.

The hero of many of Van Lustbader's novels is Nicholas Linnear, son of a British colonel and a Japanese-Chinese beauty, who lives in America yet retains his inherently Japanese soul. A shadow warrior or ninja himself—ninja means "in stealth" in Japanese—Linnear is first introduced in *The Ninja* when a corporate millionaire hires Linnear to protect him against another, more murderous ninja. The writing is somewhat ornate, as is the plot which pits Linnear against a childhood foe. Yet the detailed passages of violence and erotic passion, as well as the brief glimpses into what appears to be an Oriental mystique, lure readers throughout the tangled web of red herrings to the dramatic conclusion. *Booklist* described the novel as "a beautifully written, exotic adventure rooted in Japanese tradition and then transplanted in the West," while *Kirkus Reviews* passed *The Ninja* off as "bloody pages strewn with haiku."

Van Lustbader's follow-up novel, *Sirens* (1981), fared worse with critics. The story of Hollywood star Daina Whitney and her terrorization by a group of violent murderers (who kill Daina's best friend Maggie and stuff her into a stereo speaker) falters from the very first pages and quickly descends into a gruesome tale of sex and violence. *Kirkus Reviews* described the novel as "lurid junk of the lowest order," while Peter Andrews in the *New York Times Book Review* wrote "Mr. Lustbader writes much the way Howard Cosell speaks: as if English were a language with which he is neither familiar nor comfortable."

Linnear's return in *The Miko* (1984) is therefore welcome, if not wholly successful. The plot revolves around a Japanese oil-extracting robot and the sensual sorceress Akiko, a miko whose powers threaten not only an international business merger but Linnear as well. With several violent confrontations and ritual killings galore, Van Lustbader is back on familiar ground, and he earned a Literary Guild main selection for this sequel to *The Ninja.* Martin Levin writes in *The New York Times Book Review,* "Eric Van Lustbader knows how to move things along at such a thundering clip that everything seems right on course."

White Ninja (1990) offers up more Linnear-based action. MANTIS, a computer virus, threatens to decimate Linnear's newly-developed electronic chip and render his American/Japanese corporation bankrupt. On a more personal level, Linnear's three-year-old daughter dies, his wife and he become estranged, and (most importantly to the plot) he loses his ninja powers and becomes shiro ninja, or white ninja. In a typical Van Lustbader plot twist, both threats are related, in this case through a psychotic rapist-murderer, Senjin, who is also a Japanese homicide police commander and who has robbed Linnear of his abilities. The main focus is Linnear's struggle to reestablish his ninja powers. The book is written in the same fashion as Van Lustbader's earlier novels.

Angel Eyes (1991) departs again from the Linnear novels, this time with more success than *Sirens* but with no more plot credibility. Tori Nunn, agent of a secret U.S. intelligence agency known as the Mall, resigns when her brother Greg dies on a joint Russian/American space mission. However, Greg has not died but has merely been transformed by something extraterrestrial into a peaceful semi-dolphin who is kept hidden in a Russian prison and runs an underground group called White Star, which plots, among other things, to save Gorbachev from assassination. Tori is lured back into the Mall to stop the Medellin drug cartel and its new, lethal brand of cocaine. Through subplots, she eventually encounters her brother Greg in his Russian pool. *Kirkus Reviews* hailed the novel as "stupendous trash from a master hand."

Van Lustbader has not finished with Nicholas Linnear, as is made apparent by *Floating City* (1994), which features Yakuza criminals, illegal arms trading, government corruption, and more ninja mysticism. Thomas Gaughan in *Booklist* criticized the novel as uncompelling: "There are too many characters to keep track of and too much over-the-top, mystical-meganinja nonsense. There's also too little mayhem, and what there is is written more flatly than in earlier Linnears." However, the unresolved loose ends of the novel promise more of the same, which should delight readers who enjoy Van Lustbader's earlier work.

—Christopher Swann

VIDAL, Gore

Nationality: American. **Born:** Eugene Luther Gore Vidal, Jr. in West Point, New York, 3 October 1925. **Education:** Los Alamos School, New Mexico, 1939-40; Phillips Exeter Academy, New Hampshire, 1940-43. **Military Service:** Served in the United States Army, 1943-46: Warrant Officer. **Career:** Editor, E.P. Dutton, publishers, New York, 1946. Lived in Antigua, Guatemala, 1947-49, and Italy, 1967-76; member, advisory board, *Partisan Review,* New Brunswick, New Jersey, 1960-71; Democratic candidate for congress, New York, 1960; member, President's Advisory Committee on the Arts, 1961-63; co-chairman, New Party, 1968-71. **Awards:** Mystery Writers of America award, for television play, 1954; Cannes Film Critics award, for screenplay, 1964; National Book Critics Circle award, for criticism, 1983. **Addresses:** La Rondinaia, Ravello, Salerno, Italy; or c/o Random House Inc., 201 East 50th Street, New York, New York 10022, U.S.A.

Publications

Novels

Williwaw. New York, Dutton, 1946; London, Panther, 1965.

In a Yellow Wood. New York, Dutton, 1947; London, New English Library, 1967.

The City and the Pillar. New York, Dutton, 1948; London, Lehmann, 1949; revised edition, Dutton, and London, Heinemann, 1965.

The Season of Comfort. New York, Dutton, 1949.

Dark Green, Bright Red. New York, Dutton, and London, Lehmann, 1950.

A Search for the King: A Twelfth Century Legend. New York, Dutton, 1950; London, New English Library, 1967.

The Judgment of Paris. New York, Dutton, 1952; London, Heinemann, 1953; revised edition, Boston, Little Brown, 1965; Heinemann, 1966.

Messiah. New York, Dutton, 1954; London, Heinemann, 1955; revised edition, Boston, Little Brown, 1965; Heinemann, 1968.

Three: Williwaw, A Thirsty Evil, Julian the Apostate. New York, New American Library, 1962.

Julian. Boston, Little Brown, and London, Heinemann, 1964.

Washington, D.C. Boston, Little Brown, and London, Heinemann, 1967.
Myra Breckenridge. Boston, Little Brown, and London, Blond, 1968.
Two Sisters: A Memoir in the Form of a Novel. Boston, Little Brown, and London, Heinemann, 1970.
Burr. New York, Random House, 1973; London, Heinemann, 1974.
Myron. New York, Random House, 1974; London, Heinemann, 1975.
1876. New York, Random House, and London, Heinemann, 1976.
Kalki. New York, Random House, and London, Heinemann, 1978.
Creation. New York, Random House, and London, Heinemann, 1981.
Duluth. New York, Random House, and London, Heinemann, 1983.
Lincoln. New York, Random House, and London, Heinemann, 1984.
Empire. New York, Random House, and London, Deutsch, 1987.
Hollywood. New York, Random House, and London, Deutsch, 1990.
Live from Golgotha. New York, Random House, 1992.

Novels as Edgar Box

Death in the Fifth Position. New York, Dutton, 1952; London, Heinemann, 1954.
Death Before Bedtime. New York, Dutton, 1953; London, Heinemann, 1954.
Death Likes It Hot. New York, Dutton, 1954; London, Heinemann, 1955.

Short Stories

A Thirsty Evil: Seven Short Stories. New York, Zero Press, 1956; London, Heinemann, 1958.

Plays

Visit to a Small Planet (televised 1955). Included in *Visit to a Small Planet and Other Television Plays,* 1956; revised version (produced New York, 1957; London, 1960), Boston, Little Brown, 1957; in *Three Plays,* 1962.
Honor (televised 1956). Published in *Television Plays for Writers: Eight Television Plays,* edited by A. S. Burack, Boston, The Writer, 1957; revised version as *On the March to the Sea: A Southron Comedy* (produced Bonn, Germany, 1961), in *Three Plays,* 1962.
Visit to a Small Planet and Other Television Plays (includes *Barn Burning, Dark Possession, The Death of Billy the Kid, A Sense of Justice, Smoke, Summer Pavilion, The Turn of the Screw*). Boston, Little Brown, 1956.
The Best Man: A Play about Politics (produced New York, 1960). Boston, Little Brown, 1960; in *Three Plays,* 1962.
Three Plays (includes *Visit to a Small Planet, The Best Man, On the March to the Sea*). London, Heinemann, 1962.
Romulus: A New Comedy, adaptation of a play by Friedrich Dürrenmatt (produced New York, 1962). New York, Dramatists Play Service, 1962.
Weekend (produced New York, 1968). New York, Dramatists Play Service, 1968.
An Evening with Richard Nixon and . . . (produced New York, 1972). New York, Random House, 1972.

Screenplays: *The Catered Affair,* 1956; *I Accuse,* 1958; *The Scapegoat,* with Robert Hamer, 1959; *Suddenly, Last Summer,* with Tennessee Williams, 1959; *The Best Man,* 1964; *Is Paris Burning?,* with Francis Ford Coppola, 1966; *Last of the Mobile Hot-Shots,* 1970; *The Sicilian,* 1970; *Gore Vidal's Billy the Kid,* 1989.

Television Plays: *Barn Burning,* from the story by Faulkner, 1954; *Dark Possession,* 1954; *Smoke,* from the story by Faulkner, 1954; *Visit to a Small Planet,* 1955; *The Death of Billy the Kid,* 1955; *A Sense of Justice,* 1955; *Summer Pavillion,* 1955; *The Turn of the Screw,* from the story by Henry James, 1955; *Honor,* 1956; *The Indestructible Mr. Gore,* 1960; *Vidal in Venice* (documentary), 1985; *Dress Gray,* from the novel by Lucian K. Truscott IV, 1986.

Other

Rocking the Boat (essays). Boston, Little Brown, 1962; London, Heinemann, 1963.
Sex, Death, and Money (essays). New York, Bantam, 1968.
Reflections upon a Sinking Ship (essays). Boston, Little Brown, and London, Heinemann, 1969.
Homage to Daniel Shays: Collected Essays 1952-1972. New York, Random House, 1972; as *Collected Essays 1952-1972,* London, Heinemann, 1974.
Matters of Fact and of Fiction: Essays 1973-1976. New York, Random House, and London, Heinemann, 1977.
Sex Is Politics and Vice Versa (essay). Los Angeles, Sylvester and Orphanos, 1979.
Views from a Window: Conversations with Gore Vidal, with Robert J. Stanton. Secaucus, New Jersey, Lyle Stuart, 1980.
The Second American Revolution and Other Essays 1976-1982. New York, Random House, 1982; as *Pink Triangle and Yellow Star and Other Essays,* London, Heinemann, 1982.
Vidal in Venice, edited by George Armstrong, photographs by Tore Gill. New York, Summit, and London, Weidenfeld and Nicolson, 1985.
Armegeddon? Essays 1983-1987. London, Deutsch, 1987; as *At Home,* New York, Random House, 1988.
A View from the Diners Club. London, Deutsch, 1991.
The Decline and Fall of the American Empire. Berkeley, California, Odonian Press, 1992.
Screening History. Cambridge, Harvard University Press, and London, Deutsch, 1992.
United States: Essays, 1952-1992. New York, Random House, and London, Deutsch, 1993.
Palimpsest: A Memoir. New York, Random House, 1995.

*

Bibliography: *Gore Vidal: A Primary and Secondary Bibliography* by Robert J. Stanton, Boston, Hall, and London, Prior, 1978.

Manuscript Collection: University of Wisconsin, Madison.

Critical Studies: *Gore Vidal* by Ray Lewis White, New York, Twayne, 1968; *The Apostate Angel: A Critical Study of Gore Vidal* by Bernard F. Dick, New York, Random House, 1974; *Gore Vidal* by Robert F. Kiernan, New York, Ungar, 1982; *Gore Vidal: Writer against the Grain* edited by Jay Parini, New York, Columbia University Press, and London, Deutsch, 1992.

* * *

Although Gore Vidal is famous for his controversial characters and historical novels, his reputation as a writer is also based upon his success as a screenwriter, essayist, mystery writer, and playwright. As both a public figure and artist, he has managed to reach popular audiences; so effectively, in fact, that he was almost elected to Congress in 1960. His ability to understand the basic tendencies and motivations of the American public and to convey his ideas in straightforward prose accounts for much of his popularity.

In 1943 Vidal enlisted in the U.S. Army and began to write as a means of dealing with the tedium of service life. His first two novels were *Williwaw* (1946), the story of a crew on a military transport ship who fail to bring a murderer to justice; and *In a Yellow Wood* (1947), the story of a man's re-adaptation to civilian life. Both are influenced by Vidal's military experience, and both blame war for the characters' selfishness and survivalist tendencies. The novels also show Vidal's stylistic debt to Hemingway and Crane.

The City and the Pillar (1948) deals with the then extremely controversial subject of homosexuality. After writing the novel, Vidal said, "I was bored with playing it safe. I wanted to take risks, to try something no American had done before." The original plot deals with the relationship between two men, involving jealousy and murder. Critical response to the novel was mixed; some claimed the novel was too preachy in tone, and that the protagonist's becoming a killer was an inconsistent character development. Vidal eventually agreed with the negative criticism and rewrote the novel in 1965, adding a more realistic and less dramatic ending with the protagonist merely leaving without committing murder.

Seasons of Comfort (1949), *Search for the King* (1950), and *Dark Green, Bright Red* (1950) are transitional pieces for Vidal. During the writing of these works, Vidal began to search for a new medium for his stories and eventually refined the use of historical fiction. Although the above novels were financially unsuccessful, they anticipate the historical and philosophical direction of his later works.

Vidal secluded himself in a New York mansion and composed *The Judgment of Paris* (1952) and *Messiah* (1954). Critical reception of the two novels was very favorable. Ray Lewis White wrote that Vidal "demonstrated the firm control of his medium that had been present in promise more than in execution in his earlier works." In *Messiah* Vidal deals with the exile of Eugene Luther, a preacher of the newly created religion Caveswood, after he attempts to preach a more humanistic version of the religion. Some consider this to be Vidal's best work of fiction because of his insight into contemporary religious behavior.

During the next ten years Vidal's chief concern was financial, so he wrote television and stage plays. In the mid-1960s he returned to fictional and political concerns. His American trilogy—*Washington DC* (1967), *Burr* (1973), and *1876* (1976)—shows the relish with which Vidal portrays American politics. The last two novels are based upon conventions of historical fiction, yet convey a sense of the moral ambiguity of historical events. For example, in *Burr* Vidal presents Aaron Burr as a hero at the expense of the founding fathers and the American Republic.

Vidal's fame is also based in part on the disappointing screen adaptation of his novel *Myra Breckinridge* (1968). Vidal's novel is a complex, satirical story of sexual ambiguity and aggression. The film production, however, focused primarily on the titillating aspects of the plot and starred Raquel Welch and Rex Reed. Unfortunately for Vidal, he received much of the blame for the tasteless film.

Live from Golgotha (1992), is an interesting portrayal of the media juxtaposed with the religious concerns found in *Messiah*. The satire is both sharp and humorous as Vidal looks at Christ's crucifixion from a new and original perspective.

—Chris Godat

VINE, Barbara. *See* **RENDELL, Ruth.**

VIORST, Judith (Stahl)

Nationality: American. **Born:** Newark, New Jersey, 2 February 1931. **Education:** Rutgers University, B.A. (with honors), 1952; Washington Psychoanalytic Institute, graduate, 1981. **Family:** Married Milton Viorst, 1960; children: three sons. **Career:** Poet, journalist, and writer of books for adults and children. *True Confessions*, New York City, secretary, 1953-55; *Women's Wear Daily*, New York City, secretary, 1955-57; William Morrow, New York City, children's book editor, 1957-60; Science Service, Washington, D.C., science book editor and writer, 1960-63. Contributing editor, *Redbook* magazine. **Awards:** New Jersey Institute of Technology awards, 1969, for *Sunday Morning*, and 1970, for *I'll Fix Anthony*; Emmy award (with others) for writing a comedy, variety, or music program, 1970, for CBS special, *Annie: The Women in the Life of a Man*; *School Library Journal* citation for one of the best books of the year, 1972, and Georgia Children's Picture Book award, 1977, for *Alexander and the Terrible, Horrible, No Good, Very Bad Day*; Silver Pencil award, 1973, for *The Tenth Good Thing about Barney*; Penney-Missouri award, 1974, for article in *Redbook*: Albert Einstein College of Medicine award, 1975; American Academy of Pediatrics award, 1977, for article in *Redbook*; American Association of University Women award, 1980, for article in *Redbook*; Christopher award, 1988. **Agent:** Robert Lescher, 67 Irving Place, New York, New York 10003. **Address:** 3432 Ashley Terrace N.W., Washington, D.C. 20008, U.S.A.

PUBLICATIONS

Plays

Happy Birthday and Other Humiliations (produced Pasadena, California, 1989).

Love and Guilt and the Meaning of Life (produced Pasadena, California, 1989).

Teleplay: *Annie: The Women in the Life of a Man*, with others, 1970.

Poetry

The Village Square. Coward, 1965.

It's Hard to Be Hip over Thirty and Other Tragedies of Married Life. World Publishing, 1968.

People and Other Aggravations. World Publishing, 1971.
How Did I Get to Be Forty and Other Atrocities. Simon & Schuster, 1976.
If I Were in Charge of the World and Other Worries: Poems for Children and Their Parents. Atheneum, 1981.
When Did I Stop Being Twenty and Other Injustices: Selected Poems from Single to Mid-Life. Simon & Schuster, 1987.
Forever Fifty and Other Negotiations. Simon and Schuster, 1989.

Other

The Washington, D.C. Underground Gourmet, with Milton Viorst, Simon & Schuster, 1970.
Yes, Married: A Saga of Love and Complaint. Saturday Review Press, 1972.
Love and Guilt and the Meaning of Life, Etc. Simon & Schuster, 1979.
A Visit from St. Nicholas (To a Liberated Household). Simon & Schuster, 1979.
Necessary Losses. Simon & Schuster, 1986.
Murdering Mr. Monti: A Merry Little Tale of Sex and Violence. Simon & Schuster, 1994.

Fiction for Children

Sunday Morning. Harper, 1968.
I'll Fix Anthony. Harper, 1969; reprinted, Macmillan, 1988.
Try It Again, Sam: Safety When You Walk. Lothrop, 1970.
The Tenth Good Thing about Barney. Atheneum, 1971; reprinted, Macmillan, 1988.
Alexander and the Terrible, Horrible, No Good, Very Bad Day. Atheneum, 1972; reprinted, Macmillan, 1987.
My Mama Says There Aren't Any Zombies, Ghosts, Vampires, Creatures, Demons, Monsters, Fiends, Goblins or Things. Atheneum, 1973; reprinted, Macmillan, 1988.
Rosie and Michael. Atheneum, 1974.
Alexander, Who Used to Be Rich Last Sunday. Atheneum, 1978.
The Good-bye Book. Atheneum, 1988.
Earrings, illustrated by Nola Langner Malone, Atheneum. 1990.
The Alphabet from Z to A: With Much Confusion on the Way. Macmillan, 1994.
Alexander, Who's Not (Do You Hear Me? I Mean It!) Going to Move. Simon & Schuster, 1995.
Sad Underwear and Other Complications. Macmillan, 1995.

Nonfiction for Children

Projects: Space. Washington Square Press, 1962.
One Hundred and Fifty Science Experiments, Step-by-Step. Bantam, 1963.
Natural World. Bantam, 1965.
The Changing Earth. Bantam, 1967.
Editor, with Shirley Moore, *Wonderful World of Science.* Science Service, 1961.

* * *

To read Judith Viorst is to know her, and to know her is good fun because she writes about the things that touch us where we live, both figuratively and literally. The warmth, wisdom, and good humor of her work make everyday burdens a bit lighter by taking potentially serious family situations and giving them a light perspective. Viorst allows us to laugh at ourselves.

Her career began with poetry, which she has been writing since childhood; "terrible poems about dead dogs, mostly," she says. Her first book, *Village Square* (1965), was written in the voice of a Greenwich Village bachelorette. Viorst compares her exotic new neighborhood with her traditional upbringing, poking fun at both, and the poems remain fresh today. "I'll Never Teach My Parents to Be Village Intellectuals," for example, develops the emotional security she gains by finding herself finally on equal ground with her parents, who "like gin rummy better than they like Jean Jacques Rosseau / . . . [and] listen quite politely while I clarify world thought for them / [but] laugh at me the minute that I go." Viorst is never too proud to tell a joke on herself.

In what would become a series, her poetry books represent stages of life. "Nice Baby," from *It's Hard to Be Hip over Thirty and Other Tragedies of Married Life* (1968) profiles the evolution of a career woman, from worrying about her appearance to parenting "a nice baby, drooling over our antique satin spread." Motherhood means wearing socks to bed when she has a cold because she knows she'll have to "bring the children one more glass of water." In *Yes, Married: A Saga of Love and Complaint* (1972) she finds herself in a family of males "where the seat of the toilet is always lifted up"—and loving it.

Parenting is also the ritual of not letting the kids out of the house without a warning to "watch out for cars and pay attention to traffic lights . . . [and] if you get into any trouble, . . . turn right around and come back home," as the child in *Try it Again, Sam: Safety When You Walk* (1970) discovers. Viorst's children's books are as much a wealth of humor for parents as they are for the kids. If readers have not been a midnight glass-of-water carrier or a hausfrau in tired socks, we have all been thirsty in the night or have gone through similar house-leaving rituals with our own parents in a comedy of the familiar circumstance.

Viorst admits that most of her ideas originate in her own or her friends' families. " For example, the "dead dogs" theme of her childhood grew up into *The Tenth Good Thing about Barney* (1971). For that book's gentle, sensible treatment of talking to children about death, Viorst earned the 1971 Junior Literary Guild's Selection of the Year. The book was closely followed by what has become another American classic, *Alexander and the Terrible, Horrible, No Good, Very Bad Day,* which received the same honor in 1972.

Viorst was one of the first children's authors to challenge outmoded gender stereotypes by allowing little boys to show fears and tears or girls to be strong and self-confident. Even so, she waits to hear "I love you, Mom," knowing the actual words of a child are more often something like "yesterday we cut a worm in half . . . and Iggy Halpern ate it."

To Viorst, every relationship is a story, every incident a slice of life waiting to be told. The warmth of her character, her open approach, and ingenuous humor abound in the nonfictional *Necessary Losses* (1986). As with her other works, the theme is embodied in the title. It is a rich collection of other psychoanalysts' and authors' views, as well as Viorst's observations. Without becoming saccharine, she sweetens the human pain that comes from feelings of loss and fears about aging.

Similar wisdom—but with laughs added—comes from the main character in *Murdering Mr. Monti: A Merry Little Tale of Sex and Violence* (1994), Brenda Kovner, who finds murder in her heart when she believes Monti is "doing harm to my family." The novel is a comedy of eros and errors from beginning to end, with so many plot twists and firecrackers it would keep any adult up late enough to still be wearing shoes when the kids call for water.

—Maril Nowak

VOLLMANN, William T.

Nationality: American. **Born:** Santa Monica, California, 28 July 1959. **Education:** Deep Springs College, 1977-79; Cornell University, B.A. (summa cum laude), 1981; graduate study at University of California, Berkeley, 1982-83. **Career:** Writer. Founder, CoTangent Press. **Awards:** Ella Lyman Cabot Trust fellowship grant, 1982; regent's fellow, University of California, Berkeley, 1982-83; Aid for Afghan Refugees grant-in-aid, 1983; Ludwig Vogelstein award, 1987; corecipient of Maine Photographic Workshops grant, 1987; Whiting Writers' award, 1988, for *You Bright and Risen Angels: A Cartoon*; Shiva Naipaul Memorial prize, 1989, for an excerpt from *Seven Dreams: A Book of North American Landscapes.* **Member:** Center for Book Arts. **Address:** c/o Viking-Penguin, 375 Hudson St., New York, New York 10014, U.S.A.

Publications

Novels

You Bright and Risen Angels: A Cartoon. Atheneum, 1987.
The Ice Shirt: A Book of North American Landscapes. Viking, 1990.
Whores for Gloria; or, Everything Was Beautiful until the Girls Got Anxious. Pan-Picador, 1991.
Butterfly Stories. Grove/Atlantic, 1993.
Fathers and Crows: A Book of North American Landscapes. Viking, 1993.
The Rifles. Viking, 1994.
The Atlas: People, Places, and Visions. Viking, 1996.

Short Stories

The Rainbow Stories. Atheneum, 1989.
Thirteen Stories and Thirteen Epitaphs. Deutsch, 1991.

Nonfiction

An Afghanistan Picture Show: Or How I Saved the World. Farrar, Straus, 1992.
Open All Night, with photographs by Ken Miller. Overlook Press, 1995.

* * *

William Vollmann's rise has been meteoric, but not free of harsh criticism. He burst upon the scene with *You Bright and Risen Angels* (1987), which was acclaimed as an inventive first novel. The reviewer of the *New York Times Book Review* described it as "a social and political satire that critiques America in technological terms, a computer cartoon that is both a product of technology and a comment on it."

Angels is like an elaborate computer game in which "bright and risen angels" are characters brought to life by electricity. The subject of the novel, power in America, is embedded in the metaphor of electricity. A struggle for domination occurs between electricity and insects, and this becomes a running battle between reactionaries, revolutionaries, and bugs. Although regarded as an ingenious and clever book, a predominant feature in the reception of Vollmann's work was already noticeable; it was regarded as a sprawling and somewhat disorderly novel in which the digression hampers the narrative, as "whole episodes seem extraneous."

Vollmann's next effort, *Rainbow Stories* (1989), began to establish Vollmann's style as lying somewhere between the journalism of Tom Wolfe and the postmodern symbolism of Thomas Pynchon. Vollmann pays particular attention to the grotesque details of murder and anatomy. Again, the stories were regarded by some reviewers as overwritten rhetoric that blunted the precision of his observation. While many readers admired Vollmann's ambition and talent, others found his style to be baggy and unshaped; as one critic put it, "hyperventilating paragraphs run on endlessly."

Vollmann's major project, Seven Dreams, is an epic and complex series of novels about the symbolic history of the settlement of the North American landscape. The first novel in the series was *The Ice-Shirt: A Book of North American Landscapes* (1990), an ambitious and often enthralling novel about the Vikings' arrival in North America. Experimental in form, it contained notes and glossaries, effortlessly interweaving characters, voyages, murders, and supernatural horrors, with some modern interpolations. The central image was of the "ice-shirt," which refers to the way in which white people "infected" the American continent by bringing frost with them. Although there were the usual reservations about the nature of his experimental form, praise for the novel was high, with one reviewer announcing "Mr. Vollmann has a knack for stringing a sentence with simple words in a way that transports the reader. . . . [*Ice-Shirt*] impresses mightily in its scope, its scene-painting and its enciphered social messages."

The second volume in the Seven Dreams sequence was *Fathers and Crows: A Book of North American Landscapes* (1993), another gargantuan novel with footnotes, maps, and drawings embedded within the text. This somewhat hybrid novel is narrated by William the Blind. It chronicles the establishment of colonial settlements in Canada, with intricate histories of the Indian tribal politics and warfare, particularly that of the Hurons. Yet readers were getting impatient with Vollmann's historical excursions and digressions, and one reader suggested that a greater degree of editorial surgery was required: "The hundreds of pages of historical background included to bulk up the narrative subvert rather than enhance this novel of faith, desire, and the tragedy of spiritual imperialism."

The third book in the series, *The Rifles* (1994), incurred similar reservations. With all the usual blends of history, illustrations, and documentary sources, the novel is structured as a parallel narrative, moving backwards and forwards between Sir John Franklin's fatal expedition to find the Northwest Passage in 1846, and his modern counterpart in 1989, an American novelist having an affair with an Inuit woman. Revelling in a narrative dislocation, the novel has been described as a "documentary prose poem," albeit as a "dream logic" with an "appalled, hyperactive, unhomogenized vision." However, another reviewer has stated that "for all his stylistic quirkiness, [Vollmann] is the master of his material."

In addition to the Seven Dreams project are other novels, including *Whores for Gloria; or, Everything Was Beautiful Until the Girls Got Anxious* (1991). It initiated a series of books about prostitutes for which he received much criticism. *Butterfly Stories* (1993) continued this focus, comparing the author and the prostitutes to butterflies, of which there are "billions of species." In a series of linked short stories, it focuses on queasy relationships in a number of very precisely observed cases. Responses have varied, but dissatisfaction appears regularly: "uninformative, distanced, flat," with "something so juvenile about Mr. Vollmann's assumption that we will be shocked by his subject matter."

His other work, *Thirteen Stories and Thirteen Epitaphs* (1991), also juggles reportage with fictional forays as it explores urban subcultures (such as the Tenderloin prostitutes in San Francisco) in a number of different journeys. Although his precision of observation is again recognized, he has been criticized here for "a failure of global imagination. Experiences feel undifferentiated, all given equal weight. Journeys lack momentum. Everywhere starts to seem the same."

—Tim Woods

VONNEGUT, Kurt, Jr.

Nationality: American. **Born:** Indianapolis, Indiana, 11 November 1922. **Education:** Shortridge High School, Indianapolis, 1936-40; Cornell University, Ithaca, New York, 1940-42; Carnegie Institute, Pittsburgh, 1943; University of Chicago, 1945-47. **Military Service:** Served in the United States Army Infantry, 1942-45: Purple Heart. **Family:** Married 1) Jane Marie Cox in 1945 (divorced 1979), one son and two daughters, and three adopted sons; 2) the photographer Jill Krementz in 1979, one daughter. **Career:** Police reporter, Chicago City News Bureau, 1946; worked in public relations for the General Electric Company, Schenectady, New York, 1947-50. Since 1950 freelance writer. After 1965, teacher, Hopefield School, Sandwich, Massachusetts. Visiting lecturer, Writers Workshop, University of Iowa, Iowa City, 1965-67, and Harvard University, Cambridge, Massachusetts, 1970-71; visiting professor, City University of New York, 1973-74. Lives in New York City. **Awards:** Guggenheim fellowship, 1967; American Academy grant, 1970. M.A.: University of Chicago, 1971; D.Litt.: Hobart and William Smith Colleges, Geneva, New York, 1974. **Member:** American Academy, 1973. **Address:** c/o Donald C. Farber, Tanner Gilbert Propp and Sterner, 99 Park Avenue, 25th Floor, New York, New York 10016, U.S.A.

Publications

Novels

Player Piano. New York, Scribner, 1952; London, Macmillan, 1953; as *Utopia 14,* New York, Bantam, 1954.
The Sirens of Titan. New York, Dell, 1959; London, Gollancz, 1962.
Mother Night. New York, Fawcett, 1962; London, Cape, 1968.
Cat's Cradle. New York, Holt Rinehart, and London, Gollancz, 1963.
God Bless You, Mr. Rosewater; or, Pearls Before Swine. New York, Holt Rinehart, and London, Cape, 1965.
Slaughterhouse-Five; or, The Children's Crusade. New York, Delacorte Press, 1969; London, Cape, 1970.
Breakfast of Champions; or, Goodbye, Blue Monday. New York, Delacorte Press, and London, Cape, 1973.
Slapstick; or, Lonesome No More! New York, Delacorte Press, and London, Cape, 1976.
Jailbird. New York, Delacorte Press, and London, Cape, 1979.
Deadeye Dick. New York, Delacorte Press, 1982; London, Cape, 1983.
Galápagos. New York, Delacorte Press, and London, Cape, 1985.
Bluebeard. New York, Delacorte Press, 1987; London, Cape, 1988.
Hocus Pocus; or, What's the Hurry, Son? New York, Putnam, and London, Cape, 1990.

Short Stories

Canary in a Cat House. New York, Fawcett, 1961.
Welcome to the Monkey House: A Collection of Short Works. New York, Delacorte Press, 1968; London, Cape, 1969.

Uncollected Short Stories

"2BR02B," in *If* (New York), January 1962.
"The Big Space Fuck," in *Again, Dangerous Visions,* edited by Harlan Ellison. New York, Doubleday, 1972; London, Millington, 1976.
"The Dream of the Future (Not Excluding Lobsters)," in *The Esquire Fiction Reader 2,* edited by Rust Hills and Tom Jenks. Green Harbor, Massachusetts, Wampeter Press, 1986.
"The Boy Who Hated Girls," in *Saturday Evening Post* (Indianapolis), September 1988.

Plays

Happy Birthday, Wanda June (as *Penelope,* produced Cape Cod, Massachusetts, 1960; revised version, as *Happy Birthday, Wanda June,* produced New York, 1970; London, 1977). New York, Delacorte Press, 1970; London, Cape, 1973.
The Very First Christmas Morning, in *Better Homes and Gardens* (Des Moines, Iowa), December 1962.
Between Time and Timbuktu; or, Prometheus-5: A Space Fantasy (televised 1972; produced New York, 1976). New York, Delacorte Press, 1972; London, Panther, 1975.
Fortitude, in *Wampeters, Foma, and Granfalloons,* 1974.
Timesteps (produced Edinburgh, 1979).
God Bless You, Mr. Rosewater, adaptation of his own novel (produced New York, 1979).

Television Plays: *Auf Wiedersehen,* with Valentine Davies, 1958; *Between Time and Timbuktu,* 1972.

Other

Wampeters, Foma, and Granfalloons: Opinions. New York, Delacorte Press, 1974; London Cape, 1975.
Sun Moon Star. New York, Harper, and London, Hutchinson, 1980.
Palm Sunday: An Autobiographical Collage. New York, Delacorte Press, and London, Cape, 1981.
Fates Worse Than Death. Nottingham, Spokesman, 1982(?).

Nothing Is Lost Save Honor: Two Essays. Jackson, Mississippi, Nouveau Press, 1984.

Conversations with Kurt Vonnegut, edited by William Rodney Allen. Jackson, University Press of Mississippi, 1988.

Fates Worth than Death: An Autobiographical Collage of the 1980s. New York, Putnam, 1991.

*

Bibliography: *Kurt Vonnegut: A Comprehensive Bibliography* by Asa B. Pieratt, Jr., Julie Huffman-Klinkowitz, and Jerome Klinkowitz, Hamden, Connecticut, Archon, 1987.

Critical Studies: *Kurt Vonnegut, Jr.,* by Peter J. Reed, New York, Warner, 1972; *Kurt Vonnegut: Fantasist of Fire and Ice* by David H. Goldsmith, Bowling Green, Ohio, Popular Press, 1972; *The Vonnegut Statement* edited by Jerome Klinkowitz and John Somer, New York, Delacorte Press, 1973, London, Panther, 1975, *Vonnegut in America: An Introduction to the Life and Work of Kurt Vonnegut* edited by Klinkowitz and Donald L. Lawler, New York, Delacorte Press, 1977; *Kurt Vonnegut,* London, Methuen, 1982 and *Slaughterhouse Five: Reforming the Novel and the World,* Boston, Twayne, 1990, both by Klinkowitz; *Kurt Vonnegut, Jr.* by Stanley Schatt, Boston, Twayne, 1976; *Kurt Vonnegut* by James Lundquist, New York, Ungar, 1977; *Vonnegut: A Preface to His Novels* by Richard Giannone, Port Washington, New York, Kennikat Press, 1977; *Kurt Vonnegut: The Gospel from Outer Space* by Clark Mayo, San Bernardino, California, Borgo Press, 1977; *Vonnegut's Duty-Dance with Death: Theme and Structure in Slaughterhouse-Five* by Monica Loeb, Umeå, Sweden, Umeå Studies in the Humanities, 1979; *Critical Essays on Kurt Vonnegut* edited by Robert Merrill, Boston, Hall, 1990; *Forever Pursuing Genesis: The Myth of Eden in the Novels of Kurt Vonnegut* by Leonard Mustazza, Lewisburg, Pennsylvania, Bucknell University Press, 1990; *Understanding Kurt Vonnegut* by William Rodney Allen, Columbia, University of South Carolina Press, 1991; *Kurt Vonnegut* by Donald E. Morse, San Bernardino, California, Borgo Press, 1992; *Critical Response to Kurt Vonnegut* edited by Leonard Mustazza, Westport, Connecticut, Greenwood Press, 1994.

* * *

Kurt Vonnegut achieved international fame and popular culture status with the success of his sixth novel, *Slaughterhouse-Five* (1969). Since then he has continued as a bestselling author and noteworthy public spokesman on social and cultural issues. But the roots of both his personal genius and his great popular appeal are found in his fiction of the 1950s and earlier 1960s, much of it appearing in such family magazines as *Collier's* and *The Saturday Evening Post* and eventually taking shape as paperback-original novels.

Raised in a formerly well-to-do family in Indianapolis, Indiana, and educated in that city's civic-minded public school system, Vonnegut (who did not drop the "Junior" from his name until 1976) wrote student journalism, but at his father's behest planned for a career in biochemistry. His studies at Cornell University were halted by WWII. After Army training as a mechanical engineer he was thrown into frontline duty as an advanced infantry scout and was captured by the German army during the Battle of the Bulge in December, 1944. Interned as a prisoner-of-war in the supposedly open city of Dresden, Vonnegut survived the Allied firebombing that destroyed that architectural treasure and killed between 70,000 and 180,000 civilians. It didn't end the war one day earlier, didn't save the life of one Allied soldier or free one concentration camp inmate more quickly. "Only one person benefitted," he recalls today. "And that was me. I got five dollars for every man, woman, and child killed."

Vonnegut's self-deprecatory cynicism at the great success of his novel about the Dresden firebombing, *Slaughterhouse-Five,* is an example of the gallows humor that permeates and to some extent motivates his earlier fiction. *Player Piano* (1952) is a sardonically dystopian novel in which a future of scientific improvement not only destroys human values but shows how humankind's loveable propensity to tinker and improve is the real culprit. *The Sirens of Titan* (1959), *Mother Night* (1962), *Cat's Cradle* (1963), and *God Bless You, Mr. Rosewater* (1965) explore more specific social, political, and historical issues, but in each case resolution means destruction or dissolution. Vonnegut's magazine fiction dating back to 1950 is collected in *Welcome to the Monkey House* (1968), where such short stories as "The Euphio Question" and "Unready to Wear" locate science-fiction themes within solidly American middle-class habits in order to show how comic ineptitude wreaks far greater havoc than any exotically alien threats.

With the arrival of his great public fame as the author of *Slaughterhouse-Five,* Vonnegut adopted a style of more overt spokesmanship. With his older markets for short fiction now closed, he turned increasingly to essays, writing about popular phenonema and international issues for such journals as *Esquire, McCall's,* and *Vogue*. His 1974 collection *Wampeters, Foma and Granfalloons* gathers the best of these. With *Palm Sunday* (1981) he adopts the sermon format for his spokesmanship, and in *Fates Worse Than Death* (1991) draws on commentaries and reflections to form what he calls "an autobiographical collage of the 1980s." From *Breakfast of Champions* (1973) through *Hocus Pocus* (1990), his novels change as well, drawing increasingly on the eminence of his protagonists as commentators on crucial issues ranging from Watergate (as the ultimate failure of New Deal politics) to the Vietnam War's legacy half a generation later.

—Jerome Klinkowitz

W-Z

WALKER, Alice (Malsenior)

Nationality: American. **Born:** Eatonton, Georgia, 9 February 1944. **Education:** Spelman College, Atlanta, 1961-63; Sarah Lawrence College, Bronxville, New York, 1963-65, B.A. 1965. **Family:** Married Melvyn R. Leventhal in 1967 (divorced 1976); one daughter. **Career:** Voter registration and Head Start program worker, Mississippi, and with New York City Department of Welfare, mid-1960s; teacher, Jackson State College, 1968-69, and Tougaloo College, 1970-71, both Mississippi; lecturer, Wellesley College, Cambridge, Massachusetts, 1972-73, and University of Massachusetts, Boston, 1972-73; associate professor of English, Yale University, New Haven, Connecticut, after 1977. Distinguished Writer, University of California, Berkeley, Spring 1982; Fannie Hurst Professor, Brandeis University, Waltham, Massachusetts, Fall 1982. Co-founder and publisher, Wild Trees Press, Navarro, California, 1984-88. **Awards:** Bread Loaf Writers Conference scholarship, 1966; *American Scholar* prize, for essay, 1967; Merrill fellowship, 1967; MacDowell fellowship, 1967, 1977; Radcliffe Institute fellowship, 1971; Lillian Smith award, for poetry, 1973; American Academy Rosenthal award, 1974; National Endowment for the Arts grant, 1977; Guggenheim grant, 1978; American Book award, 1983; Pulitzer prize, 1983; O. Henry award, 1986. Ph.D.: Russell Sage College, Troy, New York, 1972; D.H.L.: University of Massachusetts, Amherst, 1983. Lives in San Francisco. **Address:** c/o Harcourt Brace Jovanovich Inc., 1250 Sixth Avenue, San Diego, California 92101, U.S.A.

Publications

Novels

The Third Life of Grange Copeland. New York, Harcourt Brace, 1970; London, Women's Press, 1985.
Meridian. New York, Harcourt Brace, and London, Deutsch, 1976.
The Color Purple. New York, Harcourt Brace, 1982; London, Women's Press, 1983.
The Temple of My Familiar. San Diego, Harcourt Brace, and London, Women's Press, 1989.
Possessing the Secret of Joy. New York, Harcourt Brace, and London, Cape, 1992.

Short Stories

In Love and Trouble: Stories of Black Women. New York, Harcourt Brace, 1973; London, Women's Press, 1984.
You Can't Keep a Good Woman Down. New York, Harcourt Brace, 1981; London, Women's Press, 1982.
Complete Short Stories, London, Women's Press, n.d.
Everyday Use, edited by Barbara T. Christian. New Brunswick, Rutgers University Press, 1994.

Uncollected Short Stories

"Cuddling," in *Essence* (New York), July 1985.
"Kindred Spirits," in *Prize Stories 1986,* edited by William Abrahams. New York, Doubleday, 1986.

Poetry

Once. New York, Harcourt Brace, 1968; London, Women's Press, 1986.
Five Poems. Detroit, Broadside Press, 1972.
Revolutionary Petunias and Other Poems. New York, Harcourt Brace, 1973; London, Women's Press, 1988.
Good Night, Willie Lee, I'll See You in the Morning. New York, Dial Press, 1979; London, Women's Press, 1987.
Horses Make a Landscape Look More Beautiful. New York, Harcourt Brace, 1984; London, Women's Press, 1985.
Her Blue Body Everything We Know: Earthling Poems 1965-1990. San Diego, Harcourt Brace, and London, Women's Press, 1991.

Other (for children)

Langston Hughes, American Poet (biography). New York, Crowell, 1974.
To Hell with Dying. San Diego, Harcourt Brace, and London, Hodder and Stoughton, 1988.
Finding the Green Stone. San Diego, Harcourt Brace, and London, Hodder and Stoughton, 1991.

Other

In Search of Our Mothers' Gardens: Womanist Prose. New York, Harcourt Brace, 1983; London, Women's Press, 1984.
Living by the Word: Selected Writings 1973-1987. San Diego, Harcourt Brace, and London, Women's Press, 1988.
Warrior Marks: Female Genital Mutilation and the Sexual Blinding of Women, with Pratibha Parmar. New York, Harcourt Brace, 1993.
The Same River Twice. New York, Simon and Schuster, 1996.

Editor, *I Love Myself When I Am Laughing . . . and Then Again When I Am Looking Mean and Impressive: A Zora Neale Hurston Reader.* Old Westbury, New York, Feminist Press, 1979.

*

Bibliography: *Alice Malsenior Walker: An Annotated Bibliography 1968-1986* by Louis H. Pratt and Darnell D. Pratt, Westport, Connecticut, Meckler, 1988; *Alice Walker: An Annotated Bibliography 1968-1986* by Erma Davis Banks and Keith Byerman, London, Garland, 1989.

Critical Studies: *Brodie's Notes on Alice Walker's "The Color Purple"* by Marion Picton, London, Pan, 1991; *Alice Walker* by Conna Histy Winchell, New York, Twayne, 1992; *Alice Walker* by Tony Gentry, New York, Chelsea, 1993; *Alice Walker and Zora Neale Hurston: The Common Bond* edited by Lillie P. Howard, Westport, Connecticut, and London, Greedwood Press, 1993; *Alice Walker: Critical Perspectives Past and Present* edited by Henry Louis Gates and K.A. Appiah, New York, Amistad, 1993;

* * *

When Alice Walker's Pulitzer Prize winning novel *The Color Purple* (1982) became a movie, she gained her widest acclaim as an author. In the characters of Celie, Sophia, and Shug, Walker builds strong and assertive black women who survive abuse and racism. Celie, played by Whoopie Goldberg, bore several children and was raped and beaten by the abusive "Mister" Albert. Her outlet was writing letters to God until Shug Avery, "Mister's" mistress arrived and consumed the attention of all the occupants of Celie's household. When "Mister" brought the half-drunk Shug home with him, she declared to Celie that she "sho' was an ugly thang." However, it was Shug who pointed Celie toward her own self-love and actualization while revealing "Mister" as the miscreant who withheld letters from Celie's sister Nettie. When Shug finally decided to move on, Celie followed her and found strength to reach for all that was rightfully hers.

The scheming husband of *The Color Purple* was yet another stereotyped black male character who brought critical wrath upon Walker for her negative portrayal of black men. Even in her first novel, *The Third Life of Grange Copeland* (1970), Walker drew a negative portrait of the black male. Grange and Brownfield Copeland became the alcoholic, abusive, wife beating models of black men. The novel shows how Grange Copeland wrecks two lives—his own and that of his son Brownfield. His irresponsibility, a penchant for women other than his wife, and his indulging in alcohol, do nothing to endear him as a black male role model. The novel has its share of needless violence including the freezing death of Grange's wife's infant. Likewise, Brownfield beats Mem down in a drunken rage and finally murders her before their children. However, Grange ultimately returns and redeems himself by handing down his strengths and money to his granddaughter, Ruth. Ruth is the daughter of Mem, a character drawn from a woman whom Walker knew as a child. Like Mem, the woman was the victim of spousal violence.

Walker's first two books were collections of poetry, *Once* (1968) and *Revolutionary Petunias* (1973) that she wrote to work through her personal issues of pain, a contemplated suicide, and abortion. The central pain in Walker's life may have begun as some rift between Walker and her father Willie. But the pain just as likely came from an incident in which her brother partially blinded her with a BB shot in the eye. Walker's strength and focus came from her mother, Minnie Tallulah Grant Walker, who gave her a typewriter, a suitcase, and a sewing machine that got her out of Eatonton, Georgia and took her to college.

Walker titled her first collection of essays *In Search of Our Mothers' Gardens* (1983). This work established Walker as the spokesperson for black feminists. She coined the term "womanist" to distinguish between black and white feminists. Womanism focused on the experiences and historic connections of black women, whom the domain of white feminist critical thought neglected. Walker's book of essays asserts the need for black women to search for strength in the literal and metaphorical gardens and quilts of their biological and black ancestral mothers.

In another collection of essays, *Living By the Word* (1988), Walker examines social issues ranging from homosexuality to animal rights. Throughout her essays, short stories, poems, and novels, Walker is committed to political activism, especially the Civil Rights Movement.

The Temple of My Familiar (1989) reveals the influence of Gabriel Garcia Marquez and magic realism. Miss Lissie, the protagonist, enjoys at least twelve supernatural personas. One of these is the red-slippered lion that graces the cover of the book. Walker also leaves the reader to infer that the lion is Lissie's own "familiar." Suwelo, Rafe, and Arveyda are much more compassionate toward their women, and therefore are much more rounded than Brownfield and Grange. However, the most positive of Walker's male characters appears in *Possessing the Secret of Joy*.

From its arrival in bookstores and on to its documentation in the collaborative *Warrior Marks* (1993), the fictional *Possessing the Secret of Joy* (1992) brought Walker the most controversy. Many critics admonished Walker to mind her own business and cease her Western meddling in the sexuality of African women. One critic even asserts that Walker's interference with the ritual clitoridectomy deprived the African women of their inherent rights to motherhood, wifehood, and any claim to agency allowed a woman by African culture.

—Bennis Blue

WALLACE, Irving

Nationality: American. **Born:** Chicago, Illinois, 19 March 1916. **Education:** Attended Williams Institute, Berkeley, California, and Los Angeles City College. **Military Service:** U.S. Army Air Forces, writer in the First Motion Picture Unit and Signal Corps Photographic Center, 1942-46; became staff sergeant. **Family:** Married Sylvia Kahn in 1941; children: one son and one daughter. **Career:** Freelance magazine writer and interviewer, 1931-53; screenwriter, 1949-58, for Columbia, Warner Bros., Twentieth Century-Fox, Universal, RKO, Metro-Goldwyn-Mayer, and Paramount. Reporter for the Chicago Daily News/Sun Times Wire Service at the Democratic and Republican national conventions, 1972. **Awards:** Supreme Award of Merit and honorary fellowship from George Washington Carver Memorial Institute, 1964, for writing *The Man* and for contributing "to the betterment of race relations and human welfare"; Commonwealth Club silver medal, 1965; Bestsellers magazine award, 1965, for *The Man*; Paperback of the Year citation, National Bestsellers Institute, 1970, for *The Seven Minutes;* Popular Culture Association award of excellence, 1974; Venice Rosa d'Oro award, 1975, for contributions to American letters.

Publications

Novels

The Sins of Philip Flemming. Fell, 1959; reprinted, New American Library, 1985.
The Chapman Report. Simon & Schuster, 1960; reprinted, New American Library, 1985.
The Prize. Simon & Schuster, 1962; reprinted, New American Library, 1985.
The Three Sirens. Simon & Schuster, 1963.
The Man. Simon & Schuster, 1964.
The Plot. Simon & Schuster, 1967; reprinted, Pocket Books, 1984.
The Seven Minutes. Simon & Schuster, 1969; reprinted, Pocket Books, 1983.
The Word. Simon & Schuster, 1972.

The Fan Club. Simon & Schuster, 1974.
The R Document. Simon & Schuster, 1976.
The Pigeon Project. Simon & Schuster, 1979.
The Second Lady. New American Library, 1980.
The Almighty. Doubleday, 1982.
The Miracle. Dutton, 1984.
The Seventh Secret. Dutton, 1986.
The Celestial Bed. Delacorte, 1987.
The Guest of Honor. Delacorte, 1989.

Plays

Screenplays: *The West Point Story,* with John Monks, Jr. and Charles Hoffman, 1950; *Meet Me at the Fair,* 1953; *Desert Legion,* with Lewis Meltzer, *1953; Split Second,* with William Bowers, *1953; Gun Fury,* with Roy Huggins, *1953; Bad for Each Other,* with Horace McCoy, *1954; The Gambler from Natchez,* with Gerald Adams, 1954; *Jump into Hell,* 1955; *Sincerely Yours,* 1955; *The Burning Hills,* 1956; *Bombers B-52,* 1957; *The Big Circus,* with Irwin Allen and Charles Bennett, *1959.*

Nonfiction

The Fabulous Originals: Lives of Extraordinary People Who Inspired Memorable Characters in Fiction. Knopf, 1955; reprinted, Kraus, 1972.
The Square Pegs. Knopf, 1957.
The Fabulous Showman: The Life and Times of P. T. Barnum. Knopf, 1959.
The Twenty-Seventh Wife. Simon & Schuster, 1960; reprinted, New American Library, 1985.
The Sunday Gentleman. Simon & Schuster, 1965.
The Writing of One Novel. Simon & Schuster, 1968; reprinted, Dutton, 1986.
The Nympho and Other Maniacs. Simon & Schuster, 1971.
The Two: A Biography, with Amy Wallace. Simon & Schuster, 1978.

Editor, with David Wallechinsky, *The People's Almanac,* Doubleday, 1975.
Editor, with David Wallechinsky and Amy Wallace, *The People's Almanac Presents the Book of Lists.* Morrow, 1977.
Editor, with David Wallechinsky, *The People's Almanac #2.* Morrow, 1978.
Editor, with Sylvia Wallace, Amy Wallace, and David Wallechinsky, *The People's Almanac Presents the Books of Lists #2.* Morrow, 1980.
Editor, with Amy Wallace and David Wallechinsky, *The People's Almanac Presents the Book of Predictions.* Morrow, 1980.
Editor, with Amy Wallace, Sylvia Wallace, and David Wallechinsky, *The Intimate Sex Lives of Famous People.* Delacorte, 1981.
Editor, with David Wallechinsky, *The People's Almanac #3.* Morrow, 1981.
Editor, with Amy Wallace and David Wallechinsky, *The People's Almanac Presents the Book of Lists #3.* Morrow, 1983.
Editor, with Amy Wallace and David Wallechinsky, *Significa.* Dutton, 1983.

*

Media Adaptations: Films—*The Chapman Report,* 1962; *The Prize,* 1963; *The Man,* 1972; *The Seven Minutes,* 1971. Television miniseries—*The Word,* 1978.

* * *

Prolific writer Irving Wallace is often criticized but widely read. He started his career as a writer in the Army during WWII. Most of his early books were nonfiction works, such as *The Fabulous Showman: The Life and Times of P. T. Barnum* (1959). He published his first novel, *The Sins of Philip Fleming,* in 1959. His second novel, *The Chapman Report* (1960), brought notoriety to the author.

The Chapman Report delved into the consequences of a survey which explored the sexual conduct of a group of women in Los Angeles. The book was bought for movie production before it even hit the streets. The theme of his novel, that a survey cannot embody the true picture of the relationships between men and women, gets lost in a morass of outrageous coincidences and boring erotica.

Wallace fared much better with *The Prize* (1962), which inquired into the private lives of a group of Nobel Prize winners: a French husband-and-wife team of chemists, an American heart surgeon irritated at having to share the award with an Italian doctor, a German-born Atlanta physicist sought after by the Communists of East Germany, and an alcoholic American novelist. Wallace packs the novel facts uncovered in his research, and the result is a highly entertaining look behind the scenes ripe with gossip and dramatic action. "I doubt very much that *The Prize* is literature, but it is three or four evenings of pulsating entertainment," noted V.P. Hass.

The Man (1964) is the story of the first African-American president, Douglass Dilman. Thrown into the White House after the deaths of the president, vice president, and speaker of the house, he is resented by white southerners who are scandalized by a black president, and by blacks who feel he is becoming an Uncle Tom. Once again Wallace researched his topic assiduously and brought his considerable talent into play. The plot is carefully constructed, the setting is detailed, the pace is suspenseful, and he handles the huge cast of characters deftly. The main character, however, remains curiously one-dimensional, described by R.K. Burns as "a national cliché."

Wallace offered yet another huge tome with *The Word* (1972), in which a gospel ostensibly written by Jesus's brother "James the Just" has been discovered. The new gospel offers the most compelling evidence to date of Jesus's existence and the revelation that he survived the crucifixion and lived to be 50. Steve Randall is hired to promote the publication of a Bible with the new gospel, but he begins to doubt its authenticity even after he falls in love with the daughter of the archaeologist who found it. Again, Wallace offers the type of lengthy storytelling that his fans desire. "Wallace is one of the few practitioners around who can tell a story without stopping to refuel," wrote *Kirkus Reviews.*

The *Pigeon Project* (1979) showcases Wallace at his best. Professor Davis MacDonald is an American scientist studying the amazing longevity of Soviet Georgians. In the process he discovers a formula which will double human life by eliminating disease. Of course, when the Russians learn of his discovery, they must have it. He manages to reach Venice only to be taken hostage by Italian Communists. He escapes, and the city is shut down in the search for him. Wallace takes his great talent for storytelling and spreads it against an exciting, vivid background.

By combining painstaking research and inventive storytelling, Wallace has remained a commercially popular and entertaining novelist since the early 1960s.

—Jennifer G. Coman

WALLER, Robert James

Nationality: American. **Born:** 1939. **Education:** Indiana University, Ph.D. **Family:** Married; one daughter. **Career:** University of Northern Iowa, Cedar Falls, professor of economics, applied math, and management; contributor of essays to *Des Moines Register;* writer. **Awards:** American Booksellers Book of the Year (ABBY) award, 1993, for *The Bridges of Madison County.* **Agent:** Aaron M. Priest Literary Agency, 708 Third Ave., 23rd Floor, New York, New York 10017, U.S.A.

Publications

Novels

The Bridges of Madison County. New York, Warner Books, 1992.
Slow Waltz in Cedar Bend. New York, Warner Books, 1993.
Border Music. New York, Warner Books, 1995.
Puerto Vallarta Squeeze. New York, Warner Books, 1995.

Other

Just Beyond the Firelight: Stories and Essays. Iowa State University Press, 1988.
One Good Road Is Enough. Iowa State University Press, 1990.
Iowa: Perspectives on Today and Tomorrow. Iowa State University Press, 1991.
Images. New York, Warner Books, 1994.
Old Songs in a New Cafe: Selected Essays by Robert James Waller. New York, Warner Books, 1994.

*

Film Adaptation: *The Bridges of Madison County,* 1995.

* * *

With the unexpected success of *The Bridges of Madison County* (1992) Robert James Waller became, almost overnight, a focus for both popular adulation and critical hostility. Outselling *Gone With the Wind,* Waller's first work of fiction became the most widely purchased novel of all times. By offering middle-aged women the hope that one cherished memory of adultery could counterbalance a lifetime of boredom and disappointment, it had a major influence on how wives in the American 1990s perceived and reacted to their husbands. Yet by virtue of its amateurishly overwritten prose and uncritical acceptance of male-dominant attitudes, this novel occasioned some of the most viciously effective attacks in critical history. Author Waller welcomed identifications with his male protagonist, to the extent of dressing like him for an appearance on *Oprah* during which otherwise happily married women were invited to embrace true loves of their lives (to their surprised spouses' dismay). As a result, Waller has been a personal target for complaints by moralists and intellectuals.

A Professor of Management and later Dean of the School of Business at University of Norhtern Iowa, Waller worked until his fifties as a highly paid teacher, administrator, and consultant. During the last decade of his academic life he began writing travel and nature essays for *The Des Moines Register.* Collected as *Just Beyond the Firelight* (1988) and *One Road Is Good Enough* (1990), these ruminations targeted a Sunday readership intrigued by the figure of a college professor who could tramp soggy Iowa marshes in search of peregrine falcons and also fly off to Paris, on a moment's notice, for a romantic weekend with his wife. Eventually the author expressed disenchantment with his teaching duties and took leave, accepting a $200,000 grant from the State of Iowa's Department of Economic Development to study the region's future. Published as *Iowa: Perspectives on Today and Tomorrow* (1991), his report made such controversial suggestions as eliminating one-third of Iowa's small towns and recognizing that "our agricultural land really belongs to everyone, though farm owners may temporarily hold title." During this same period, reportedly over a single weekend, Waller wrote *The Bridges of Madison County.*

Beyond the astronomical sales figures for his first novel, Waller's economic success has been supported by business-style spinoffs. Gifted as both a song writer and performer, he was able to produce *The Ballads of Madison County* (1993) as sheet music and a compac disc. As sensitive a photographer as his novel's hero, Waller marketed a tear-out book of postcards titled *Images: Photographs by the Author of The Bridges of Madison County* (1994). In 1994 an agreement between Iowa State University Press and Waller's commercial publisher, Warner Books, allowed *Old Songs in a New Cafe* to achieve bestseller status while remaining copies of his first two essay collections were withdrawn from the market.

In the wake of this success, Robert James Waller has launched three subsequent novels—none of them as popular as *Bridges,* but each making *The New York Times* bestseller list for a week or more. *Slow Waltz in Cedar Bend* (1993) is set within a university world of adulteries and high-priced consultantships; as in Waller's first novel, the male protagonist wins over a middle-aged woman by offering her what her husband has forbidden: cigarettes. *Border Music* (1995) links a Vietnam war veteran with a honky-tonk dancer in a love story that draws on the travel tradition of Jack Kerouac's *On the Road,* while *Puerto Vallarta Squeeze* (1995) counterpoints the lust for writing with more ethereal fellings about Mexican women.

A capitve of his fame, Waller has become a self-described recluse on the Texas ranch he purchased to avoid Iowa's glare of publicity and its 9.98-percent state income tax rate. Now ridiculed by the newspaper that gave him his start as a writer, he is best appraised by *The Des Moines Register*'s less biased columnist, Donald Kaul, who has assessed his former colleague as "a writer of modest talent who has achieved a success undreamed of even by people who play the lottery"—a circumstance Waller's defenders believe has resulted in spite of the envy of the critics who demean his work.

—Jerome Klinkowitz

WAMBAUGH, Joseph (Aloysius, Jr.)

Nationality: American. **Born:** East Pittsburgh, Pennsylvania, 22 January 1937. **Education:** Chaffey College, A.A., 1958; California State College (now University), Los Angeles, B.A., 1960, M.A., 1968. **Military Service:** U.S. Marine Corps, 1954-57. **Family:** Married Dee Allsup in 1955; two sons (one deceased) and one daughter. **Career:** Los Angeles Police Department, Los Angeles, 1960-74, began as patrolman, became detective sergeant; writer, 1971—. Creator and consultant, *The Blue Knight,* Columbia Broadcasting Company (CBS-TV), and *Police Story,* National Broadcasting Company (NBC-TV), 1973-77. **Awards:** Edgar Allan Poe award, special award for nonfiction, Mystery Writers of America, 1974, for *The Onion Field;* Edgar Allan Poe award, best motion picture, 1981, for *The Black Marble;* Rodolfo Walsh prize for investigative journalism, International Association of Crime Writers, 1989, for *Lines and Shadows.* **Address:** 70-555 Thunderbird Mesa, Rancho Mirage, California 92270, U.S.A.

PUBLICATIONS

Novels

The New Centurions. Atlantic-Little Brown, 1971.
The Blue Knight. Atlantic-Little Brown, 1972.
The Choirboys. Delacorte, 1975.
The Black Marble. Delacorte, 1978.
The Glitter Dome. Morrow, 1981.
The Delta Star. Morrow, 1983.
The Secrets of Harry Bright. Morrow, 1985.
The Golden Orange. Morrow, 1990.
Fugitive Nights. Morrow, 1992.
Finnegan's Week. Morrow, 1993.
Floaters. Morrow, 1996.

Other

The Onion Field. Delacorte, 1973.
Lines and Shadows. Morrow, 1984.
Echoes in the Darkness. Morrow, 1987.
The Blooding. Morrow, 1989.

Plays

Screenplays: *The Onion Field,* 1979; *The Black Marble,* 1980.

Television Plays: *The Glitter Dome,* 1984; *Echoes in the Darkness,* 1987; *Fugitive Knights,* 1993.

*

Media Adaptations: Films—*The New Centurions,* 1972; *The Choirboys,* 1977. Television miniseries—*The Blue Knight,* 1973.

* * *

The fiction and nonfiction books of Joseph Wambaugh, Jr., decisively changed the public concept of police work. Wambaugh was still a member of the Los Angeles Police Department when he produced his first novel, *The New Centurions* (1971). His fictional account of the human beings under the uniforms reveals their flaws, vulnerability, and disillusionment. *The New Centurions* is the story of police officers at the beginning of their careers, idealistic young cadets entering the Policy Academy. As they progress through training, they grow callous and hard in response to the reality of police work.

Prior to Wambaugh's revelations, police were generally portrayed in written and visual media as cool, dispassionate types who always came out on top. They were untouched by the corruption and vice that surrounded them—superheroes who conquered evil. Wambaugh presents a different view. His police officers are fully human and as capable of wrongdoing as the criminals. *The Blue Knight* (1972) illustrates the life of an officer at the end of his career. He frequently bends the law because he believes the criminal justice system doesn't always serve justice. So he handles the law his own way. He perjures himself in court, for example, so that a conviction will occur. Wambaugh also examines the loneliness of police life.

These first two novels gathered considerable public attention and were made into a movie (*The New Centurions*) and a television miniseries (*The Blue Knight*) almost immediately. Wambaugh's superiors in the L.A.P.D. were not pleased with the publicity. They felt Wambaugh portrayed a negative image of the police, which ultimately forced Wambaugh to take an extended leave of absence. That gave him the time to research his most significant work, a nonfiction account of the murder of a Los Angeles policeman. The murder had taken place 11 years earlier, in 1963. Wambaugh based the story on interviews, case records, and thousands of pages of court transcripts. His effort resulted in *The Onion Field* (1974), which he described as the fulfillment of a personal mission.

In *The Onion Field,* two policemen pull over a suspicious-looking car and are overpowered by its occupants, two small-time criminals. The criminals drive them to a remote onion field where they kill Officer Ian Campbell. Officer Karl Hettinger escapes and the criminals are caught the next day. The case turned into one of the longest trials in history because of new laws (Escobedo and Miranda) that protect the rights of criminals. Wambaugh sought vindication for Hettinger, who suffered a nervous breakdown from the experience and the lengthy trial period. Hettinger's reaction can only be understood with knowledge of police psychology. There was an implicit assumption among Hettinger's peers that he failed his partner in some way, that no crime happened by chance. Somehow, Hettinger had not been alert enough, or brave enough, to prevent the murder. So in their minds, he was as guilty as the criminals.

The Onion Field was generally praised by critics. James Conaway, in the *New York Times Book Review,* compares it to Truman Capote's *In Cold Blood* and concludes that Wambaugh's book, "In terms of scope, revealed depth of character, and dramatic coherence, . . . is the more ambitious book." The success of *The Onion Field* caused Wambaugh to resign from the police force due to the constant barrage of phone calls and visits from interviewers and fans. While unfortunate in some ways, in another sense it freed him. No longer accountable to his superiors, he tackled his next project, *The Choirboys* (1975), with even greater honesty and intensity.

In *The Choirboys,* a group of police officers relieve stress by meeting frequently at night in a nearby park. They drink excessively, pursue off-color humor with a vengeance, and involve themselves in senseless violence. Wambaugh's use of black comedy to handle serious topics marks a change in his writing style. The humor provides needed balance to the coarse nature of his subjects. He gravitates again to this method in his next three novels; *The Black Marble* (1978), *The Glitter Dome* (1981) and *The Golden Orange* (1990.)

Wambaugh's literary contributions are two. First, he reveals the humanity of police men and women. While this may tarnish their image and remove some of the glory, it enlightens the public to the needs of individuals in the protective services. Second, his research and writing in the nonfiction arena demonstrate that suspense and drama are present in actual police work. Defending the public's safety is a real-life challenge and adventure, and not just the work of someone's imagination.

—Colin Maiorano with Carolyn Eckstein-Soule

WELCH, James

Nationality: American. **Born:** Browning, Montana, in 1940. **Education:** The University of Montana, Missoula, B.A.; Northern Montana College, Harve. **Awards:** National Endowment for the Arts grant, 1969; Los Angeles *Times* prize, for *Fools Crow,* 1987. **Address:** Roseacres Farm, Route 6, Missoula, Montana 59801, U.S.A.

Publications

Novels

Winter in the Blood. New York, Harper, 1974.
The Death of Jim Loney. New York, Harper, 1979; London, Gollancz, 1980.
Fools Crow. New York, Viking, 1986.
The Indian Lawyer. New York, Norton, 1990.

Poetry

Riding the Earthboy 40. Cleveland, World, 1971; revised edition, New York, Harper, 1975.

Nonfiction

Killing Custer: The Battle of the Little Bighorn and the Fate of the Plains Indians. New York, Viking, 1995.

Editor, with Ripley S. Hugg and Lois M. Welch, *The Real West Marginal Way: A Poet's Autobiography,* by Richard Hugo. New York, Norton, 1986.

*

Critical Studies: *Four American Indian Literary Masters* by Alan R. Velie, Norman, University of Oklahoma Press, 1982; *James Welch* by Peter Wild, Boise, Idaho, Boise State University 1983; "Beyond Myth: Welch's *Winter in the Blood*" by Jack Brenner, in *Under the Sun: Myth and Realism in Western American Literature* edited by Barbara Howard Meldrum, Troy, New York, Whitston, 1985; "Beyond Assimilation: James Welch and the Indian Dilemma" by David M. Craig, in *North Dakota Quarterly* (Grand Forks), Spring 1985; "Variations on a Theme: Traditions and Temporal Structure in the Novels of James Welch" by Roberta Orlandini, in *South Dakota Review* (Vermillion), Autumn 1988; *Place and Vision: The Function of Landscape in Native American Fiction* by Robert M. Nelson, New York, Lang, 1993.

* * *

James Welch, poet and novelist, is one of several notable Montana writers. The son of a Blackfeet father and Gros Ventres mother, Welch is concerned with place—cultural, regional, and historical—and how his Native American characters orient themselves to it.

His only collection of poetry, *Riding the Earthboy 40* (1971), is firmly rooted in the plains of Montana. Abbreviated yet lyrical, the poems enter moments of thought or experience that deal with seasons, animals, and the stories reservation Indians tell. The animals that populate his poems, as in "Magic Fox," have a near-mythical significance, touching on Welch's Indianness. But more often than not, Welch bitterly notes that the days of the Blackfeet are past. In "Spring for All Seasons," he wryly states "Our past is ritual/cattle marching one way to remembered mud."

Often noted is Welch's use of surrealism in these poems. At best, the surrealism works subtly to underscore the spiritual connection these poems establish with the land and the elements. At worst, however, Welch's surrealism is awkward and ungainly.

Welch brought his spare narrative style to the novel, prompting critics to compare his prose to Ernest Hemingway's. *Winter in the Blood* (1974) elegiacally tells the story of an unnamed narrator who lives on a Montana reservation. The protagonist's life is marred by loss; his father and brother are dead, and his mother dies during the course of the novel. He is aimless and wastes his time drinking at the bar, where he can lose himself in fist fights and sexual encounters with barflies.

Thus sadness permeates, but the novel is not flatly nihilistic. In the end, there is some hope for the narrator, who takes steps toward reclaiming his heritage. And technically, Welch's subtle irony and comic undercutting holds the novel off from utter despair. Even with the first person narrative, Welch is able to keep the story moving without falling into melodrama.

Welch's second novel, *The Death of Jim Loney* (1979) doesn't fare as well. Criticized for its melodrama, the novel offers no redemption for the main character, Jim Loney, whose very name calls to mind the word "loneliness." Like the narrator of *Winter in the Blood,* Loney is caught in a cultural abyss between his heritage and the white man's world; he too seeks to numb himself in hard drinking. But as the novel progresses, Loney remains caught in the abyss. The sheriff who hunts him down represents the white man's world; Loney, moving closer to death, experiences visions that may be from his ancestors' spirit world, but he can't interpret them. In the end, there is no real resolution for this character.

With *Fools Crow* (1986), Welch's approach to prose changed. A historical novel, *Fools Crow* depicts a small band of Blackfeet Indians who escape the Marias River massacre of 1870. As such, the world Welch depicts is vastly different from that of his first two novels. The protagonist—and the reader—journey through dreams and visions, guided by talking animals. It is a world with a firm sense of culture and history, as in Welch's *Killing Custer* (1995).

For the epic story of *Fools Crow,* Welch opened up his narrative style. As he describes in an interview with *Publisher's Weekly,* "I needed a much bigger canvas to write an historical novel so I loosened up my language and started emphasizing my story, telling more." Praised roundly by critics, the masterful work earned him a *Los Angeles Times* prize for best fiction of 1987.

Indian Lawyer (1990) returns to modern America, this time visiting a successful lawyer who is on a political fast track. In this novel of intrigue, the lawyer is blackmailed by a convict he had once denied parole. As a result, his dreams of winning a Congressional seat and helping less fortunate Indians are disrupted. The novel has more plot than his other novels, and thus appeals to a wider audience.

Critics often write about how to describe James Welch, as Indian storyteller or American author. The truth is that Welch's work transcends such categorization; he joins Native American traditions and concepts with the best of Western literary conventions to form unique and compelling narratives.

—Aimee M. Houser

WELDON, Fay

Nationality: British. **Born:** Fay Birkinshaw in Alvechurch, Worcestershire, 22 September 1931; grew up in New Zealand. **Education:** Girls' High School, Christchurch; Hampstead Girls' High School, London; University of St. Andrews, Fife, 1949-52, M.A. in economics and psychology 1952. D. Litt, University of Bath, 1988, University of St. Andrews, 1992. **Family:** Married Ron Weldon in 1960; four sons. **Career:** Writer for the Foreign Office and *Daily Mirror,* both London, late 1950s; later worked in advertising. **Awards:** Writers Guild award, for radio play, 1973; Giles Cooper award, for radio play, 1978; Society of Authors traveling scholarship, 1981; Los Angeles *Times* award, for fiction, 1989. Lives in London. **Agent:** Ed Victor, 6 Bayley St., London WC1B 3HB; Casarotto Company, National House, 62-66 Wardour Street, London W1V 3HP, England.

Publications

Novels

The Fat Woman's Joke. London, MacGibbon and Kee, 1967; as *And the Wife Ran Away,* New York, McKay, 1968.
Down among the Women. London, Heinemann, 1971; New York, St. Martin's Press, 1972.
Female Friends. London, Heinemann, and New York, St. Martin's Press, 1975.
Remember Me. London, Hodder and Stoughton, and New York, Random House, 1976.
Words of Advice. New York, Random House, 1977; as *Little Sisters,* London, Hodder and Stoughton, 1978.
Praxis. London, Hodder and Stoughton, and New York, Summit, 1978.
Puffball. London, Hodder and Stoughton, and New York, Summit, 1980.
The President's Child. London, Hodder and Stoughton, 1982; New York, Doubleday, 1983.
The Life and Loves of a She-Devil. London, Hodder and Stoughton, 1983; New York, Pantheon, 1984.
The Shrapnel Academy. London, Hodder and Stoughton, 1986; New York, Viking, 1987.
The Heart of the Country. London, Hutchinson, 1987; New York, Viking, 1988.
The Hearts and Lives of Men. London, Heinemann, 1987; New York, Viking, 1988.
Leader of the Band. London, Hodder and Stoughton, 1988; New York, Viking, 1989.
The Cloning of Joanna May. London, Collins, 1989; New York, Viking, 1990.
Darcy's Utopia. London, Collins, 1990; New York, Viking, 1991.
Life Force. London, Collins, and New York, Viking, 1992
Affliction. London, Collins, 1994; as *Trouble,* New York, Viking, 1994.
Splitting. London, Collins, and New York, Grove Atlantic, 1994.
Worst Fears. London, Collins, and New York, Grove Atlantic, 1996.

Short Stories

Watching Me, Watching You. London, Hodder and Stoughton, and New York, Summit, 1981.
Polaris and Other Stories. London, Hodder and Stoughton, 1985; New York, Penguin, 1989.
The Rules of Life (novella). London, Hutchinson, and New York, Harper, 1987.
Moon over Minneapolis. London, Harper Collins, 1991.

Uncollected Short Story

"Ind Aff; or, Out of Love in Sarajevo," in *Best Short Stories 1989,* edited by Giles Gordon and David Hughes. London, Heinemann, 1989; as *The Best English Short Stories 1989,* New York, Norton, 1989.

Plays

Permanence, in *We Who Are about to . . . ,* later called *Mixed Doubles* (produced London, 1969). London, Methuen, 1970.
Time Hurries On, in *Scene Scripts,* edited by Michael Marland. London, Longman, 1972.
Words of Advice (produced London, 1974). London, French, 1974.
Friends (produced Richmond, Surrey, 1975).
Moving House (produced Farnham, Surrey, 1976).
Mr. Director (produced Richmond, Surrey, 1978).
Polaris (broadcast 1978). Published in *Best Radio Plays of 1978,* London, Eyre Methuen, 1979.
Action Replay (produced Birmingham, 1978; as *Love among the Women,* produced Vancouver, 1982). London, French, 1980.
I Love My Love (broadcast 1981; produced Richmond, Surrey, 1982). London, French, 1984.
After the Prize (produced New York, 1981; as *Word Worm,* produced Newbury, Berkshire, 1984).
Jane Eyre, adaptation of the novel by Charlotte Brontë (produced Birmingham, 1986).
The Hole in the Top of the World (produced Richmond, Surrey, 1987).
Someone Like You, music by Petula Clark and Dee Shipman (produced London, 1990).

Radio Plays: *Spider,* 1973; *Housebreaker,* 1973; *Mr. Fox and Mr. First,* 1974; *The Doctor's Wife,* 1975; *Polaris,* 1978; *Weekend,* 1979; *All the Bells of Paradise,* 1979; *I Love My Love,* 1981; *The Hole in the Top of the World,* 1993.

Television Plays: *Wife in a Blonde Wig,* 1966; *A Catching Complaint,* 1966; *The Fat Woman's Tale,* 1966; *What about Me,* 1967; *Dr. De Waldon's Therapy,* 1967; *Goodnight Mrs. Dill,* 1967; *The 45th Unmarried Mother,* 1967; *Fall of the Goat,* 1967; *Ruined Houses,* 1968; *Venus Rising,* 1968; *The Three Wives of Felix Hull,* 1968; *Hippy Hippy Who Cares,* 1968; *£13083,* 1968; *The Loophole,* 1969; *Smokescreen,* 1969; *Poor Mother,* 1970; *Office Party,* 1970; *On Trial* (*Upstairs, Downstairs,* series), 1971; *Old Man's Hat,* 1972; *A Splinter of Ice,* 1972; *Hands,* 1972; *The Lament of an Unmarried Father,* 1972; *A Nice Rest,* 1972; *Comfortable Words,* 1973; *Desirous of Change,* 1973; *In Memoriam,* 1974; *Poor Baby,* 1975; *The Terrible Tale of Timothy Bagshott,* 1975; *Aunt Tatty,* from the story by Elizabeth Bowen, 1975; *Act of Rape,* 1977; *Married Love* (*Six Women* series), 1977; *Act of Hypocrisy* (*Jubilee* series), 1977; *Chickabiddy* (*Send in the Girls* series), 1978; *Pride and Prejudice,* from the novel by Jane Austen, 1980; *Honey Ann,* 1980; *Life for Christine,* 1980; *Watching Me, Watching You* (*Leap in the Dark* series), 1980; *Little Mrs. Perkins,* from a story by Penelope Mortimer, 1982; *Redundant! or, The Wife's Revenge,* 1983; *Out of the Undertow,* 1984; *Bright Smiles* (*Time for Murder* series), 1985; *Zoe's Fever* (*Ladies in Charge* series), 1986; *A Dangerous Kind of Love* (*Mountain Men* series), 1986; *Heart of the Country* serial, 1987.

Other

Simple Steps to Public Life, with Pamela Anderson and Mary Stott. London, Virago Press, 1980.
Letters to Alice: On First Reading Jane Austen. London, Joseph, 1984; New York, Taplinger, 1985.
Rebecca West. London and New York, Viking, 1985.
Wolf the Mechanical Dog (for children). London, Collins, 1988.
Sacred Cows. London, Chatto and Windus, 1989.
Party Puddle (for children). London, Collins, 1989.

Editor, with Elaine Feinstein, *New Stories 4.* London, Hutchinson, 1979.

* * *

Fay Weldon's novels convey a characteristic tone of satire coupled with insight. Weldon's parents divorced when she was six and she gave birth out of wedlock in 1955. Consequently, the hardships suffered by single mothers and the feelings of abandonment experienced by their children receive much attention in Weldon's books.

Weldon's wry sense of humor was apparent in her first novel, the seriocomic *Fat Woman's Joke* (1967), which was originally a television play (*The Fat Woman's Tale,* 1966). Hefty, middle-aged Esther leaves her equally obese husband, Alan, in the aftermath of their disastrous joint crash-diet. She escapes to a basement apartment and binges in self-pity until a younger friend discovers her. The novel is an excellent portrayal of women's desire to be young, thin, and beautiful, lest their husbands cheat on them (Alan unabashedly carries on an affair with his youthful, lithe secretary). For all of the suffering portrayed in *Fat Woman's Joke,* Weldon is not about to let her protagonist wallow in self-indulgence because she has been wronged. Instead, Weldon's characters gain a better sense of self while working toward understanding each other.

Female Friends (1974) features Chloe and her longtime friends Marjorie and Grace as they travel through life—sometimes loving, sometimes loathing each other. Connecting the three is not only the friendship itself but artist Patrick Bates, whom all three women have slept with. Instead of ruining the friendship, this commonality has strangely cemented relations between the three. Indeed, this complex relationship between the women and Patrick, as well as between each of the women and several other men, provides the centerpiece for the novel. Chloe is trapped in a marriage with a bullying, domineering man; Marjorie is a spinster (she is also the only one of the three who does not have a child with Patrick); and Grace is a wild divorcee. Whatever problems these women have where men are concerned, they ultimately count on each other.

Another of Weldon's memorable works is the psychological thriller *Puffball* (1980). The novel features a couple who move to a lonely cottage in Somerset; Liffey, who desperately desires to live in the country, compromises with her husband, Richard, by agreeing to a pregnancy she has long put off because of fear. They immediately attract the oddly doting attentions of their childless neighbors, Mabs and Tucker. In Mabs' pathologically obsessive quest to have a baby, she feeds Liffey concoctions that cause Liffey to allow Tucker to have sex with her. But the poisonous substance causes major complications with Mab's pregnancy that threaten her life and the life of her baby. Again, Weldon pits an older, less attractive woman against a younger, prettier one. But unlike *Fat Woman's Joke,* the action is hardly light-hearted, comic, or satirical, and this time the younger woman is the hero.

Another difference in perspective lies in *Life Force* (1992), which features Leslie, a male womanizer. Though the action is seen through the eyes of Nora, a woman whose friends have been the man's targets, he still takes center stage. Most of the man's aforementioned deeds took place 20 years before, but Weldon picks up the action when Leslie returns after the death of his second wife. The novel assumes the form of Nora's autobiography, in which she details Leslie's numerous exploits with her friends.

Although some critics fault Weldon for shallowness and negative characterization of men, most admire her for her astute observation, sarcastic wit, and originality, and she is popular in both England and the United States.

—Tracy Clark

WELLS, John J. *See* **BRADLEY, Marion Zimmer.**

WEST, Morris (Langlo)

Nationality: Australian. **Born:** Melbourne, Victoria, 26 April 1916. **Education:** St. Mary's College, St. Kilda, Victoria; University of Melbourne, B.A. 1937; University of Tasmania, Hobart. **Military Service:** Served in the Australian Imperial Forces Corps of Signals, in the South Pacific, 1939-43: Lieutenant. **Family:** Married Joyce Lawford in 1953; three sons and one daughter. **Career:** For several years member of the Christian Brothers Order, and taught in New South Wales and Tasmania, 1933 until he left the order before taking final vows, 1939; secretary to William Morris Hughes, former Prime Minister of Australia, 1943; publicity manager, Radio Station 3 DB, Melbourne, 1944-45; founder, later managing director, Australian Radio Productions Pty Ltd., Melbourne, 1945-54; after 1954, film and dramatic writer for the Shell Company and the Australian Broadcasting Network, and freelance commentator and feature writer. Lived in England, 1956-58. **Awards:** National Conference of Christians and Jews Brotherhood award, 1960; James Tait Black Memorial prize, 1960; Royal Society of Literature Heinemann award, 1960; Dag Hammarskjöld prize, 1978; *Universe* prize, 1981. D.Litt.: University of California, Santa Clara, 1969; Mercy College, New York, 1982; University of Western Sydney, Australia, 1993. Fellow, Royal Society of Literature, 1960, and World Academy of Arts and Sciences, 1964. **Member:** Order of Australia, 1985. **Address:** P.O. Box 102, Avalon, New South Wales 2107, Australia.

Publications

Novels

Moon in My Pocket (as Julian Morris). Sydney, Australasian Publishing Company, 1945.
Gallows on the Sand. Sydney, Angus and Robertson, 1956; London, Angus and Robertson, 1958.
Kundu. Sydney and London, Angus and Robertson, and New York, Dell, 1957.
The Big Story. London, Heinemann, 1957; as *The Crooked Road,* New York, Morrow, 1957.
The Second Victory. London, Heinemann, 1958; as *Backlash,* New York, Morrow, 1958.
McCreary Moves In (as Michael East). London, Heinemann, 1958; as *The Concubine,* as Morris West, London, New English Library, 1973; New York, New American Library, 1975.
The Devil's Advocate. London, Heinemann, and New York, Morrow, 1959.
The Naked Country (as Michael East). London, Heinemann, 1960; New York, Dell, 1961.
Daughter of Silence. London, Heinemann, and New York, Morrow, 1961.
The Shoes of the Fisherman. London, Heinemann, and New York, Morrow, 1963.
The Ambassador. London, Heinemann, and New York, Morrow, 1965.
The Tower of Babel. London, Heinemann, and New York, Morrow, 1968.
Summer of the Red Wolf. London, Heinemann, and New York, Morrow, 1971.
The Salamander. London, Heinemann, and New York, Morrow, 1973.
Harlequin. London, Collins, and New York, Morrow, 1974.
The Navigator. London, Collins, and New York, Morrow, 1976.
Proteus. London, Collins, and New York, Morrow, 1979.
The Clowns of God. London, Hodder and Stoughton, and New York, Morrow, 1981.
The World Is Made of Glass. London, Hodder and Stoughton, and New York, Morrow, 1983.
Cassidy. New York, Doubleday, 1986; London, Hodder and Stoughton, 1987.
Masterclass. London, Hutchinson, 1988; New York, St. Martin's Press, 1991.
Lazarus. London, Heinemann, and New York, St. Martin's Press, 1990.
The Ringmaster. London, Heinemann, 1991.
The Lovers. London, Heinemann, and New York, Fine, 1993.

Plays

Daughter of Silence (produced New York, 1961). New York, Morrow, 1962.
The Heretic (produced London, 1970). New York, Morrow, 1969; London, Heinemann, 1970.
The World Is Made of Glass (produced New York, 1982).

Screenplays: *The Devil's Advocate,* 1977; *The Second Victory,* 1984.

Television Plays: *Vendetta,* 1958 (UK).

Other

Children of the Sun. London, Heinemann, 1957; as *Children of the Shadows: The True Story of the Street Urchins of Naples,* New York, Doubleday, 1957.
Scandal in the Assembly: A Bill of Complaints and a Proposal for Reform on the Matrimonial Laws and Tribunals of the Roman Catholic Church, with Robert Francis. London, Heinemann, 1970.

* * *

Morris West was born in Melbourne in 1916 and studied to become a Christian Brother, a training he has compared to that of a terrorist, but he left before taking his final vows. He wrote a number of pot-boilers under a variety of pseudonyms before making his reputation with *Children of the Sun* (1957), a documentary account of the slum children of Naples. This was followed by the bestselling novel *The Devil's Advocate* (1959), an account of the Catholic Church's investigation by the "devil's advocate" (a tortured and complex English priest) into whether Giacomo Nerone, a deserter who finds himself again in God, should be canonized. This made the author an instant millionaire. There followed a long string of internationally bestselling novels based on either major political or religious themes, or both. West said before the release of the last of his 24 novels, *The Lovers* (1993), which was disappointingly reviewed, that he has now finished as a novelist.

West has been described as "Graham Greene meets Jeffrey Archer," but, moral and specifically Catholic dilemmas aside, one quality he shares with Greene is his uncanny prescience—or luck—in predicting future world shocks. The *Shoes of the Fisherman* (1963), for example, begins with the sentence "The Pope is dead." Almost immediately after the book was released Pope John XXIII died. It also foretold the election of a pope from behind the Iron Curtain fifteen years before it occurred, although West's pope is Ukrainian, not Polish. Slow, stilted, and overly respectful to Church rituals as the novel is, it is also almost uncanny in the way that it predicts the liberating changes that John Paul II brought to the

Church after his election as pope. Finally, in *The Ringmasters* (1991) West predicted the breakup of the Soviet Union.

When he is not prescient, West is nearly always carefully topical. *Proteus* (1979) concerns an underground organization dedicated to the release of prisoners of conscience all over the world. Similarly, *The Ambassadors* (1965) deals with the Vietnam War in terms that are sympathetic to Vietnamese leader Phung Van Cung, transparently based on the murdered Ngo Dinh Diem. The subject of *Tower of Babel* (1968) is the Arab-Israeli conflict. In a rare return to West's native Australia, the eponymous character of *Cassidy* is the Premier of New South Wales, a crook controlling a vast criminal empire with interests all over the world, including drug trafficking and smuggling.

Although in his later novels West often turned to secular issues of power and politics, his stance remains uncompromisingly Christian, but of an increasingly liberal persuasion. In the so-called Vatican trilogy—*The Shoes of the Fisherman, The Clowns of God* (1981), and *Lazarus* (1990)—he argues for a Church that will place forgiveness before punishment. Secular liberalism, as personified in the Jewish doctor Salviati, is viewed sympathetically, yet is portrayed as ultimately ineffective, failing as it failed with the similarly enlightened Jewish doctor Aldo Meyer in *The Devil's Advocate.* In the same novel, the Communist Il Lupo, who has Nerone executed, is a good man according to his lights, but his lights are rather dim. Thus, without God, man is helpless. Homosexuality, too, is a "maimed and incomplete manhood," and homosexuals and promiscuous women tend to feature fairly regularly in West's novels, largely as pathological figures deserving of sympathy and forgiveness rather than judgment. He displays a kind of benign homophobia.

West may have left the Christian Brothers, but his Catholic upbringing has stayed with him. It informs many of the novels and even his language when speaking about them. In describing how he creates a novel, he told an interviewer that "having tested the theme, I begin to clothe it with the vestments of drama." He has claimed that the world is stricken with a "plague of unreason" and speaks of the Islamic movement as taking God's name in vain.

The novels have been attacked by critics for mechanical plotting; humorless and cliched dialogue; and crude portraits of women and homosexuals. But West clearly knows his audience and continues to sell—at the last count, some 60 million copies in 27 different languages.

—Laurie Clancy

WEST, Owen. *See* **KOONTZ, Dean R(ay).**

WESTLAKE, Donald E(dwin)

Pseudonyms: John B. Allan, Curt Clark, Tucker Coe, Richard Stark. **Nationality:** American. **Born:** New York City, 12 July 1933. **Education:** Attended Champlain College and State University of New York at Binghamton. **Military Service:** U.S. Air Force, 1954-56. **Family:** Married Nedra Henderson, 1957 (divorced, 1966); married Sandra Foley, 1967 (divorced, 1975); married Abigail Adams, 1979; four sons, two stepsons, and one stepdaughter. **Career:** Worked at odd jobs prior to 1958; associate editor at literary agency, 1958-59; full-time writer since 1959. **Awards:** Edgar Allen Poe award from Mystery Writers of America, 1967, for *God Save the Mark*; Grand Master, Mystery Writers of America, 1993; Mystery Master award, Magna cum Murder, 1995. **Agent:** Knox Burger, 39 1/2 Washington Square South, New York, New York 10012. **Address:** 409 Bleecker St., New York, New York 10014, U.S.A.

Publications

Novels (series: Dortmunder)

The Mercenaries. Random House, 1960.
Killing Time. Random House, 1961.
361. Random House, 1962.
Killy. Random House, 1963.
Pity Him Afterwards. Random House, 1964.
The Fugitive Pigeon. Random House, 1965.
The Busy Body. Random House, 1966.
The Spy in the Ointment. Random House, 1966.
God Save the Mark. Random House, 1967.
Philip. Crowell, 1967.
The Curious Facts Preceding My Execution and Other Fictions. Random House, 1968.
Who Stole Sassi Manoon? Random House, 1968.
Somebody Owes Me Money. Random House, 1969.
Up Your Banners. Macmillan, 1969.
The Hot Rock (Dortmunder). Simon & Schuster, 1970.
Adios. Scheherezade, Simon & Schuster, 1970.
I Gave at the Office. Simon & Schuster, 1971.
Under an English Heaven. Simon & Schuster, 1971.
Bank Shot (Dortmunder). Simon & Schuster, 1972.
Cops and Robbers. M. Evans, 1972.
Gangway, with Brian Garfield. M. Evans, 1972.
Jimmy the Kid (Dortmunder). M. Evans, 1974.
Help I Am Being Held Prisoner. M. Evans, 1974.
Two Much. M. Evans, 1975.
A Travesty. M. Evans, 1975.
Brothers Keepers. M. Evans, 1975.
Dancing Aztecs. M. Evans, 1976; as *A New York Dance,* Hodder & Stoughton, 1979.
Enough! M. Evans, 1977.
Nobody's Perfect. M. Evans, 1977.
Castle in the Air. M. Evans, 1980.
Kahawa. Viking, 1982.
Why Me? (Dortmunder). Viking, 1983.
Levine. Mysterious Press, 1984.
A Likely Story. Penzler Books, 1984.
High Adventure. Mysterious Press, 1985.
Good Behavior (Dortmunder). Mysterious Press, 1986.
High Jinx, with Abby Westlake. McMillan, 1987.
Transylvania Station, with Abby Westlake. McMillan, 1987.
Trust Me on This. Mysterious Press, 1988.
Tomorrow's Crimes. Mysterious Press, 1989.
Sacred Monster. Mysterious Press, 1989.

Drowned Hopes (Dortmunder). Mysterious Press, 1990.
Humans. Mysterious Press, 1992.
Don't Ask (Dortmunder). Mysterious Press, 1993.
Baby, Why Would I Lie? A Romance of the Ozarks. Mysterious Press, 1994.
Smoke. Mysterious Press, 1995.

Novels as Tucker Coe

Kinds of Love, Kinds of Death. Random House, 1966.
Murder among Children. Random House, 1968.
Wax Apple. Random House, 1970.
A Jade in Aries. Random House, 1971.
Don't Lie to Me. Random House, 1972.

Novels as Richard Stark

The Hunter. Pocket Books, 1963; as *Point Blank*, Berkley, 1973; reprinted under original title with a new introduction by the author, Gregg Press, 1981.
The Man with the Getaway Face. Pocket Books, 1963; published as *The Steel Hit*, Coronet, 1971.
The Outfit. Pocket Books, 1963.
The Mourner. Pocket Books, 1963.
The Score. Pocket Books, 1964.
The Jugger. Pocket Books, 1965.
The Seventh. Pocket Books, 1966; as *The Split*, Allison & Busby, 1984.
The Handle. Pocket Books, 1966; published as *Run Lethal*, Berkley, 1966.
The Damsel. Macmillan, 1967.
The Dame. Macmillan, 1967.
The Rare Coin Score. Fawcett, 1967; reprinted, Schocken, 1984.
The Green Eagle Score. Fawcett, 1967.
The Black Ice Score. Fawcett, 1968.
The Sour Lemon Score. Fawcett, 1969.
The Blackbird. Macmillan, 1969.
Deadly Edge. Random House, 1971.
Slayground. Random House, 1971.
Lemons Never Lie. World Publishing Co., 1971.
Plunder Squad. Random House, 1972.
Butcher's Moon. Random House, 1974.

Plays

Screenplays: *Hot Stuff*, with Michael Kane, 1979; *The Stepfather*, 1986; *The Grifters*, 1990.

Other

Elizabeth Taylor: A Fascinating Story of America's Most Talented Actress and the World's Most Beautiful Woman, as John B. Allan. Monarch, 1961.

*

Film Adaptations: *Made in the USA*, 1966, adapted from his novel *The Jugger; The Busy Body*, 1967; *Point Blank*, 1967, adapted from his novel *The Hunter; Mise en Sac*, 1967, adapted from his novel *The Score; The Split*, 1968, adapted from his novel *The Seventh; The Hot Rock*, 1972; *Bank Shot*, 1974; *The Outfit*, 1974; *Jimmy the Kid*, 1982; *Slayground*, 1984; *Le Jumeau*, adapted from his novel *Two Much*.

* * *

Westlake wrote under the Richard Stark pseudonym from 1960 until 1974. "Richard" was from Richard Widmark, and "Stark" was how he wanted his writing to be. His first Stark book, *The Hunter*, centers on a crook named Parker. Parker is a tough, Dillenger-type character who avenges a betrayal, is caught by police, and subsequently escapes. Pocket Books picked it up and contracted for seven more Parker novels. Stark subsequently wrote four more Parker books for Gold Medal Books, and four additional hardcover Parker stories for Random House. He eventually wrote four other books about a friend of Parker's named Grofield. The Stark novels were extremely successful. "The last Richard Stark novel was published in 1974, and now, in 1990 I still cannot enter a bookstore for an autograph session without three or four people asking me when Parker will reappear," Westlake said in *Contemporary Authors*.

Six Parker books have been made into movies, including one major film, *Point Blank* (1967) starring Lee Marvin, and one strong minor film, *The Outfit* (1973) starring Robert Duvall.

While writing books under the Stark pseudonym, Westlake also wrote under his own name. Anthony Boucher wrote: "One can speak of his oeuvre in terms of periods. In his First Period (1960-1963), Westlake proved himself one of the ablest practitioners of the absolutely tough, hard-nosed novel of crime, with an acute insight into criminal thinking and an enviable ability to shock legitimately, without excess or bad taste. Then, after a one book interlude (a psychological whodunit in 1964; *Period 1-A*) he entered on his present and glorious Second Period of criminous farce-comedies, as warm and funny as his early books were cold and frightening. . . . I'm sure that his second period will go down as one of the most entertaining episodes in suspense novel history."

Westlake's first five books for Random House are traditional mystery-suspense novels. His sixth novel, *The Fugitive Pigeon* is a more humourous story which sold nearly twice as many copies as his preceding novels and was a hit in the foreign market. This began a new career direction for Westlake.

Westlake created a character named John Dortmunder five years later. He has since written seven novels and three short stories about Dortmunder and his partner Andy Kelp. They are two petty thieves from New York who are not always the cleverest of characters. Their persistent robbery attempts always get complicated, and they are not always successful. The characters do, however, endear themselves to the reader, who can't help but cheer them on. These books are heartwarming and funny, even if they aren't deep and psychological. This series of books is described by Westlake as "the corner of my empire which outshines the rest."

Westlake is an entertaining writer who enjoys what he does, and it shows.

—Amy Faulkenberry

WHITE, E(lwyn) B(rooks)

Nationality: American. **Born:** Mount Vernon, New York, 11 July 1899. **Education:** Mount Vernon High School, graduated 1917;

Cornell University, Ithaca, New York (editor, *Cornell Daily Sun*, 1920-21), 1917-21, A.B. 1921. **Military Service:** United States Army, 1918: Private. **Family:** Married Katharine Sergeant Angell in 1929 (died 1977); one son. **Career:** Worked for United Press and the American Legion News Service, 1921; reporter, Seattle *Times*, 1922-23; advertising copywriter and production assistant, Frank Seaman Inc. and Newmark Inc., New York, 1924-25; contributing editor, *New Yorker*, from 1926; columnist (*One Man's Meat*), *Harper's* magazine, New York, 1938-43. **Awards:** National Association of Independent Schools award, 1955; American Academy Gold Medal, for essays, 1960; Presidential Medal of Freedom, 1963; American Library Association Laura Ingalls Wilder award, 1970; George G. Stone Center for Children's Books award, 1970; National Medal for Literature, 1971; Pulitzer Special citation, 1978. Litt.D.: Dartmouth College, Hanover, New Hampshire, 1948; University of Maine, Orono, 1948; Yale University, New Haven, Connecticut, 1948; Bowdoin College, Brunswick, Maine, 1950; Hamilton College, Clinton, New York, 1952; Harvard University, Cambridge, Massachusetts, 1954; L.H.D.: Colby College, Waterville, Maine, 1954. Fellow, American Academy of Arts and Sciences, 1973; member, American Academy. **Died:** 1 October 1985.

PUBLICATIONS

Novels (for children)

Stuart Little, illustrated by Garth Williams. New York, Harper, 1945; London, Hamish Hamilton, 1946.
Charlotte's Web, illustrated by Garth Williams. New York, Harper, and London, Hamish Hamilton, 1952.
The Trumpet of the Swan, illustrated by Edward Frascino. New York, Harper, and London, Hamish Hamilton, 1970.

Poetry

The Lady Is Cold. New York, Harper, 1929.
The Fox of Peapack and Other Poems. New York, Harper, 1938.
Poems and Sketches. New York, Harper, 1981.

Other

Is Sex Necessary? or, Why You Feel the Way You Do, with James Thurber. New York, Harper, 1929; London, Heinemann, 1930.
Alice through the Cellophane. New York, Day, 1933.
Every Day Is Saturday. New York, Harper, 1934.
Farewell to Model T. New York, Putnam, 1936.
Quo Vadimus? or, The Case for the Bicycle. New York, Harper, 1939.
One Man's Meat. New York, Harper, 1942; London, Gollancz, 1943; augmented edition, Harper, 1944.
World Government and Peace: Selected Notes and Comment 1943-1945. New York, F. R. Publishing, 1945.
The Wild Flag: Editorials from the New Yorker on Federal World Government and Other Matters. Boston, Houghton Mifflin, 1946.
Here Is New York. New York, Harper, 1949.
The Second Tree from the Corner. New York, Harper, and London, Hamish Hamilton, 1954.
The Points of My Compass: Letters from the East, The West, The North, The South. New York, Harper, 1962; London, Hamish Hamilton, 1963.
An E. B. White Reader, edited by William W. Watt and Robert W. Bradford. New York, Harper, 1966.
Letters of E. B. White, edited by Dorothy Lobrano Guth. New York, Harper, 1976.
Essays of E. B. White. New York, Harper, 1977.

Editor, *Ho Hum: Newsbreaks from the New Yorker*. New York, Farrar and Rinehart, 1931.
Editor, *Another Ho Hum: More Newsbreaks from the New Yorker*. New York, Farrar and Rinehart, 1932.
Editor, with Katharine S. White, *A Subtreasury of American Humor*. New York, Coward McCann, 1941.
Editor, *Onward and Upward in the Garden*, by Katharine S. White. New York, Farrar Straus, 1979.

*

Film Adaptation: *Charlotte's Web*, 1973.

Bibliography: *E. B. White: A Bibliography* by A. J. Anderson, Metuchen, New Jersey, Scarecrow Press, 1978; *E. B. White: A Bibliographic Catalogue of Printed Materials in the Department of Rare Books, Cornell University Library* by Katherine R. Hall, New York, Garland, 1979.

Manuscript Collection: Olin Library, Cornell University, Ithaca, New York.

Critical Studies: *E. B. White* by Edward C. Sampson, New York, Twayne, 1974; *E. B. White: A Biography* by Scott Elledge, New York, Norton, 1984; *Katharine and E. B. White: An Affectionate Memoir* by Isabel Russell, New York, Norton, 1988.

* * *

Perhaps best known for his children's books *Charlotte's Web* (1952) and *Stuart Little* (1945), as well as his contribution to William Strunk's famous guide to effective writing, *The Elements of Style* (1959), E. B. White was in fact one of the leading practitioners of the modern American "familiar" essay and one of the formative figures behind the establishment of the preeminent American literary magazine, the *New Yorker*.

But White's earliest literary ambitions centered on poetry. The poems in his collections *The Lady Is Cold* (1929) and *The Fox of Peapack and Other Poems* (1938), reflected White's lifelong fascination with what he called "the small things of the day [and] the trivial matters of the heart," and focused on the quotidian frictions and compensations of 20th-century urban life. Although some critics have conceded that White's poetry is "clever," "respectable," and often amusing, his poems have largely been characterized as "undistinguished" and even "second-rate."

White gradually began to abandon poetry for prose. Beginning with his first published prose piece in the newly founded *New Yorker* in 1925, the natural grace and unpretentious humor of his contributions to the magazine's "Notes and Comment" section began to provide him with a forum to explore the themes that would typify his life's work: distrust of technological progress and the complexities of modern society; the pleasures of urban and rural life; a skepticism toward organized religion; the importance of personal freedom and the right to privacy; the urgency of global peace and world government; and a respect for nature, the cycles of life, and simple living. In his first booklength prose work, *Is Sex Necessary?* (1929), White and coauthor James Thurber parodied the growing popularity of psychoanalytic theories of human sexuality associated with Sigmund Freud and Carl Jung ("Kiss a girl," White complained, "and it reminds you of a footnote.")

With his reputation on the rise, White turned more and more to weightier themes, and in the pieces collected in *Every Day Is Saturday* (1934), *Quo Vadimus?* (1939), *One Man's Meat* (1942), and *The Wild Flag* (1946), White focused with increasing seriousness on the problems of progress, war, religion, internationalism, and politics. In the late 1930s White moved from the *New Yorker* and New York City to *Harper's* magazine and Maine, where he wrote many of the essays published in his last collections (*The Second Tree from the Corner* [1954] and *The Points of My Compass* [1962]). Critics have often cited such short stories as "The Door" and "The Second Tree from the Corner" and such essays as "Farewell, My Lovely" and "Once More to the Lake" as examples of White at his best and most enduring. Critic Joseph Epstein, in particular, has praised "Once More to the Lake" (an evocative recounting of White's trip with his son to a Maine lake he had visited as a youth) as "dazzling and devastating."

Although critics regard White's contribution to William Strunk's previously unpublished manual *Elements of Style* as a definitive exposition of the guidelines for clear and effective prose, White's permanent reputation may well rest on his three popular children's novels. The sheer charm of his style and his moving exploration of such themes as salvation, friendship, rural living, and the cycles of death and rebirth earned White some of his strongest praise and have made his juvenile fiction a staple of many young readers' first forays into fiction.

Stuart Little tells the story of a questing, mouselike hero—"he is a small guy," White wrote, "who *looks* like a mouse, but he obviously is not a mouse"—in search of adventure and romance in a threatening world dismayingly larger than himself. Although *Stuart Little* has been criticized for its disjointed structure and unlikely premise, critics now regard it as one of the classics of American juvenile literature. Even more widely acclaimed, however, is *Charlotte's Web,* in which a barnyard pig is saved from the slaughterhouse by the last-minute heroics of a linguistically adept spider. In part because of its implausibility (even for a children's story), White's third work for children, *The Trumpet of the Swan* (1970), received more muted critical praise, although John Updike has called it the "most spacious and serene" of White's juvenile fiction.

While some critics have argued that White is "vastly overrated," "not . . . sufficiently serious," and "a relatively minor figure," his reputation as one of the America's finest stylists and essayists now seems secure. "No one can write a sentence like White," James Thurber wrote. For his contribution to the development of a uniquely American prose style alone, White will likely remain an important figure in 20th-century popular literature.

—Paul Bodine

WHITE, Jude Gilliam

Pseudonym: Jude Deveraux. **Nationality:** American. **Born:** 20 September 1947, in Louisville, Kentucky. **Education:** Murray State University, B.S., 1970; College of Santa Fe, teaching certificate, 1973; University of New Mexico, remedial reading certificate, 1976. **Family:** Married 1) Richard G. Sides, 1967 (divorced 1969); 2) Claude B. White, 1970. **Career:** Writer. Worked as an elementary school teacher, Santa Fe, New Mexico, 1973-77. **Awards:** *Romantic Times* Reviewer's Choice award for most humourous romance, 1987, for *The Raider.* **Member:** Romance Writers of America, Costume Society of America. **Address:** Route 9, Box 53JW, Santa Fe, New Mexico 87505, U.S.A.

Publications

Novels; as Jude Devereaux (series: James River)

The Enchanted Land. Avon, 1978.
The Black Lyon. Avon, 1980.
The Velvet Promise. Pocket Books, 1981.
Casa Grande. Avon, 1982.
Highland Velvet. Pocket Books, 1982.
Velvet Song. Pocket Books, 1983.
Velvet Angel. Pocket Books, 1983.
Sweetbriar. Pocket Books, 1983.
Counterfeit Lady (James River). Pocket Books, 1984.
Lost Lady (James River). Pocket Books, 1985.
River Lady (James River). Pocket Books, 1985.
Twin of Ice. Pocket Books, 1985.
Twin of Fire. Pocket Books, 1985.
The Temptress. Pocket Books, 1986.
The Raider. Pocket Books, 1987.
The Princess. Pocket Books, 1987.
The Maiden. Pocket Books, 1988.
The Awakening. Pocket Books, 1988.
The Taming. Pocket Books, 1989.
A Knight in Shining Armor. Simon & Schuster, 1990.
Wishes. Pocket Books, 1990.
Mountain Laurel. Pocket Books, 1990.
The Conquest. Pocket Books, 1991.
The Duchess. Pocket Books, 1991.
Eternity. Pocket Books, 1992.
Sweet Liar. Pocket Books, 1992.
The Invitation. Pocket Books, 1993.
Remembrance. Pocket Books, 1994.
A Holiday of Love. Pocket Books, 1994.
The Heiress. Pocket Books, 1995.

* * *

Jude Gilliam White, whose pen name is Jude Deveraux, is known for her historical romances or, as they are more colloquially known, "bodice rippers." Although she early on tried her hand at the contemporary romance with *Casa Grande* (1982), she had little luck with that form and has since decided to stick with her proven success with historical romances. White has gained a wide audience for her many novels by incorporating a humor which reveals that, while she takes her craft very seriously, she also has fun exploring the possibilities of the genre.

White was a sixth-grade teacher when she started writing romance novels. The money she earned with the publication of her first book more than doubled her teacher's salary for the year, so she gradually decided to pursue writing as a career. But the field of romance writing has changed since she began, she explained in *Writer's Digest.* When she first published, it was easy: "All a writer needed then was an angry hero, a feisty, big-busted heroine and a lot of sex." But today, romance novels need a lot more than those surface elements to be successful. She wrote, "Today's romance readers want characters with complex personalities, not simply hormones that put a teenager's to shame. Readers want a plot that has meat." As a result, White has learned over the years to provide her readers with intricate plots with many twists and turns in addition to the staples of traditional romances. Her novels are replete with mistaken identities, forced marriages, abductions, rescues, disguises, and her trademark humor.

In addition, White provides her readers with powerful heroines who, despite their inferior position in past societies, manage to thwart villains on their own and often pursue goals of their own. White once said that she began writing romances to counter the "rape sagas" of victimized women she was reading. "I wanted to write about women who had some power, who could create things, could make things happen," she said. The heroines of her James River trilogy are such women. All are initially forced into marriage, but they are later estranged from their husbands, giving them the opportunity to "make things happen." One woman manages a grain mill, another becomes a weaver, and the last runs her own tavern. The twin heroines of *Twin of Ice* (1985) and *Twin of Fire* (1985) are also fairly powerful women, especially considering that they live in the 1890s. One is a doctor and the other is an undercover agent aiding the families of oppressed miners.

White advised aspiring romance writers in her *Writer's Digest* article to avoid cliches in the construction of plot. She said, "Sometimes as I write I come up with scenes just by thinking of what one would predict a character in a romance to do, and then writing something that is as close to the opposite as I can make it." Not all of her own novels have remained free of cliches, though, according to some reviewers. *Publisher's Weekly* wrote of her novel *Sweet Liar* (1992), "her cliche-laden dialogue makes it seem that her characters speak English as a second language. The highly improbably story line, overloaded with convoluted plots and subplots, will discourage even the most die-hard romance fans."

Her novel *Remembrance* (1994) received a more positive review from the same source. The novel provides an interesting twist on the historical romance and shows White's ability to explore the possibilities of the genre. It is about a popular romance writer who becomes obsessed with her fictional hero, a fixation which disrupts her marriage. When she undergoes past-life therapy, she discovers that her hero is modeled after a husband she had in a past life and with whom she has some unfinished business. *Publisher's Weekly* wrote, "The novel gets off to a shaky start as the author and her alter ego rattle on about the virtues of romance writers and the vices of reviewers who fail to praise them, but once Hayden discovers her past lives, this is standard Deveraux—that is, a smart and savvy swoon of a yarn."

—Anne Boyd

WHITNEY, Phyllis A(yame)

Nationality: American. **Born:** Yokahama, Japan, 9 September 1903. **Education:** Attended public schools in Chicago, Illinois. **Family:** Married George A. Garner, 1925 (divorced, 1945); one daughter; married Lovell F. Jahnke, 1950 (died, 1973). **Career:** Author, 1941—. Children's book editor with the Chicago Sun (now Chicago Sun Times), 1942-46, and Philadelphia Inquirer, 1946-48. Teacher of juvenile writing at Northwestern University, Evanston, Illinois, 1945-46, New York University, New York City, 1947-58, and at writers' conferences. **Awards:** Youth Today contest winner, and Book World's Spring Book Festival award, both 1947, both for *Willow Hill*; Edgar Allan Poe award for best juvenile mystery, Mystery Writers of America, 1961, for *Mystery of the Haunted Pool*, and 1964, for *Mystery of the Hidden*; Sequoyah Children's Book award, 1963, for *Mystery of the Haunted Pool;* "Today's Woman" citation, Council of Cerebral Palsy Auxiliaries of Nassau County, 1983; Grandmaster award, Mystery Writers of America, 1988, for lifetime achievement; Malice Domestic award, 1989, for lifetime achievement; Romance Writers of America award, 1990, for lifetime achievement; Agatha award, 1990, for lifetime achievement. **Member:** Authors League of America, Mystery Writers of America (member of board of directors, 1959-62; president, 1975), Malice Domestic, American Crime Writers League, Society of Children's Book Writers, Children's Reading Round Table, Midland Authors. **Agent:** McIntosh and Otis Inc., 310 Madison Ave., New York, New York 10017, U.S.A.

PUBLICATIONS

Novels

Red Is for Murder. Ziff-Davis, 1943; as *The Red Carnelian,* Paperback Library, 1965.
The Quicksilver Pool. Appleton, 1955.
The Trembling Hills. Appleton, 1956.
Skye Cameron. Appleton, 1957.
The Moonflower. Appleton, 1958.
Thunder Heights. Appleton, 1960.
Blue Fire. Appleton, 1961.
Window on the Square. Appleton, 1962.
Seven Tears for Apollo. Appleton, 1963.
Black Amber. Appleton, 1964.
Sea Jade. Appleton, 1965.
Columbella. Doubleday, 1966.
Silverhill. Doubleday, 1967.
Hunter's Green. Doubleday, 1968.
The Winter People. Doubleday, 1969.
Lost Island. Doubleday, 1970.
Listen for the Whisperer. Doubleday, 1972.
Snowfire. Doubleday, 1973.
The Turquoise Mask. Doubleday, 1974.
Spindrift. Doubleday, 1975.
The Golden Unicorn. Doubleday, 1976.
The Stone Bull. Doubleday, 1977.
The Glass Flame. Doubleday, 1978.
Domino. Doubleday, 1979.
Poinciana. Doubleday, 1980.
Vermilion. Doubleday, 1981.
Emerald. Doubleday, 1982.
Rainsong. Doubleday, 1984.
Dream of Orchids. Doubleday, 1985.
Flaming Tree. Doubleday, 1986.
Silversword. Doubleday, 1987.

Feather on the Moon. Doubleday, 1988.
Rainbow in the Mist. Doubleday, 1989.
The Singing Stones. Doubleday, 1990.
Woman without a Past. Doubleday, 1991.
The Ebony Swan. Doubleday, 1992.
Star Flight. Crown, 1993.
Daughter of the Stars. Crown, 1994.

Nonfiction

Writing Juvenile Fiction. Writer, Inc., 1947; revised edition, 1960.
Writing Juvenile Stories and Novels: How to Write and Sell Fiction for Young People. Writer, Inc., 1976.
Guide to Writing Fiction. Writer, Inc., 1982; 2nd edition, 1988.

Fiction for Children

A Place for Ann, illustrated by Helen Blair. Houghton, 1941.
A Star for Ginny, illustrated by Hilda Frommholz. Houghton, 1942.
A Window for Julie, illustrated by Jean Anderson. Houghton, 1943.
The Silver Inkwell, illustrated by Hilda Frommholz. Houghton, 1945.
Willow Hill. McKay, 1947.
Ever After. Houghton, 1948.
Mystery of the Gulls, illustrated by Janet Smalley. Westminster, 1949.
Linda's Homecoming. McKay, 1950.
The Island of Dark Woods, illustrated by Philip Wishnefsky. Westminster, 1951.
Love Me, Love Me Not. Houghton, 1952.
Step to the Music. Crowell, 1953.
A Long Time Coming. McKay, 1954.
Mystery of the Black Diamonds, illustrated by John Gretzer. Westminster, 1954.
Mystery on the Isle of Skye, illustrated by Ezra Jack Keats. Westminster, 1955.
The Fire and the Gold. Crowell, 1956.
The Highest Dream. McKay, 1956.
Mystery of the Green Cat, illustrated by Richard Horwitz. Westminster, 1957.
Secret of the Samurai Sword. Westminster, 1958.
Creole Holiday. Westminster, 1959.
Mystery of the Haunted Pool, illustrated by H. Tom Hall. Westminster, 1960.
Secret of the Tiger's Eye, illustrated by Richard Horwitz. Westminster, 1961.
Mystery of the Golden Horn, illustrated by Georgeann Helmes. Westminster, 1962.
Mystery of the Hidden Hand, illustrated by H. Tom Hall. Westminster, 1963.
Secret of the Emerald Star, illustrated by Alex Stein. Westminster, 1964.
Mystery of the Angry Idol, illustrated by Al Fiorentino. Westminster, 1965.
Secret of the Spotted Shell, illustrated by John Mecray. Westminster, 1967.
Secret of Goblin Glen, illustrated by Al Fiorentino. Westminster, 1968.
Mystery of the Crimson Ghost. Westminster, 1969.
Secret of the Missing Footprint, illustrated by Alex Stein. Westminster, 1970.
The Vanishing Scarecrow. Westminster, 1971.
Nobody Likes Trina. Westminster, 1972.
Mystery of the Scowling Boy, illustrated by John Gretzer. Westminster, 1973.
Secret of Haunted Mesa. Westminster, 1975.
Secret of the Stone Face. Westminster, 1977.

* * *

Born in Yokohama, Japan, and educated in Japan, China, the Philippines, California, Texas, and Illinois, Phyllis Ayame Whitney is a "rootless" romance/mystery writer whose beleaguered heroines ultimately find a welcoming home.

Her novels are in part travelogues, with Whitney bringing to life a region and a cultural history, lovingly portraying the local architecture (particularly of a special home), describing the local food and festivals, the traditional arts and crafts, and sometimes regional legends. Whitney rightly says that setting often becomes an important character in her writing. Each of her books explores a new location (Harper's Ferry, the Hamptons, the Catskills, the Poconos, the Hudson Valley, the Tennessee hills, a Colorado silver-mining town, a Florida mansion, a ranch near Santa Fe), usually out-of-the-way places particularized and made intriguing by loving descriptive detail. Her eye moves inward to details of complementing colors, design, and decoration in family rooms and bedrooms to create an ambience integral to the extended families at their core. This sense of home is vital to the psychology of her characters and to the twists of her plots.

Despite changed settings, a Whitney novel is somewhat predictable (though her endings surprise). Each book is a familiar friend in fresh attire, changed superficially by time. Her heroines usually grow up at some distance from any relatives, but death, curiosity, inheritance, or other motivators draw them as young adults back to a childhood home pushed out of memory. Their return acts as a catalyst, threatening a villain and bringing to the forefront the long forgotten. The heroines remember an intriguing blend of the pleasantly familiar (the scent of an old man's pipe, cookies baking, flowers on night air, the call of an owl, or the feel of turquoise) and the disturbingly sinister (frightening shadows, a disembodied voice, an idiosyncratic gesture, or blood on a walkway).

Those memories are sometimes accompanied by whispered threats, an irritating destruction of private property, and other signs of hostility. Clearly, something unpleasant or even murderous occurred in the past, precipitated the heroine's removal to distant parts, and now has resurfaced to threaten and haunt. The meeting between parent/grandparent and daughter/granddaughter is often strained, but with genetic parallels emerging. As past conflicts surface and old entanglements are reassessed, ancient hatreds surface and a new murder ensues. This second death leads eventually to an unexpected resolution that is all in the family, though finding out who and why necessitates facing the buried memories of the past.

Occasionally, it is a young bride (a daughter substitute), who enters a closed family circle and must act decisively to protect both herself and some innocent like a step-daughter or mother. Discovering her personal identity and inner strength is part of the process of saving those dependent on her and confirming love. The mystery may hinge on repressed childhood memories, father-daughter relationships, love, money, land, and/or inheritance. Somewhere in the process romance is born and a male who initially seems antagonistic proves enamored and protective. Quiet, unassuming, and highly competent, he is usually committed to a strong code of ethics. The movement of the heroine is from weakness and fear to understanding and strength, and from loneliness and isolation to commitment to family and full-standing in the group. With the past explained, the nightmares expunged, and the villain exposed, the heroine takes her rightful place in the family hierarchy, marries or renews her love with the man who has saved her, and rediscovers the beauty of her childhood home/village. Indeed, each book rejuvenates this time-tested formula.

Phyllis Whitney provides American readers the same satisfaction Georgette Heyer provides British readers: a suspenseful gothic romance in a wealthy, established family setting (usually a somewhat isolated family manor). Like Victoria Holt's, Whitney's romances are domestic. The pattern is that of eccentric relatives newly encountered, family secrets involving murder, a handsome, educated hero who is kind to the elderly, a vulnerable heroine touched by childhood trauma and trapped in a current, unpleasant domestic situation, and a resolution of present conflicts based on self-discovery and an understanding of the past. Whitney's three books on writing fiction (*Writing Juvenile Fiction* [1947]; *Writing Juvenile Stories and Novels* [1976]; *Guide to Writing Fiction* [1982]) examine her creative process.

—Gina Macdonald

WIGHT, James Alfred. *See* **HERRIOT, James.**

WILL, George F(rederick)

Nationality: American. **Born:** Champaign, Illinois, 4 May 1941. **Education:** Trinity College, B.A., 1962; attended Magdalen College, Oxford, 1962-64; Princeton University, Ph.D., 1967. **Career:** Michigan State University, East Lansing, professor of politics, 1967-68; University of Toronto, professor of politics, 1968-69; U.S. Senate, Washington, D.C., congressional aide to Senator Alcott of Colorado, 1970-72; *National Review,* New York City, Washington editor, 1972-76; writer. Author of a syndicated column for the *Washington Post,* 1974—, and for *Newsweek;* columnist for the *New York Daily News.* Contributor to *London Daily Telegraph* and other periodicals. Contributing editor, *Newsweek,* 1976—. Panelist, "Agronsky and Company," Post-Newsweek Stations, 1979-84; participant, "This Week with David Brinkley," American Broadcasting Co. (ABC-TV), 1981—; commentator, "World News Tonight," ABC-TV, 1984—. **Awards:** Named Young Leader of America, Time magazine, 1974; Pulitzer prize, 1977, for distinguished commentary. **Address:** ABC-TV Public Relations, 1330 Avenue of the Americas, New York, New York 10019, U.S.A.

Publications

Nonfiction

The Pursuit of Happiness, and Other Sobering Thoughts. Harper, 1978.
The Pursuit of Virtue, and Other Tory Notions. Simon & Schuster, 1982.
Statecraft as Soulcraft: What Government Does. Simon & Schuster, 1983.
The Morning After: American Successes and Excesses, 1981-1986. Free Press, 1986.
The New Season: A Spectator's Guide to the 1988 Election. Simon & Schuster, 1987.
Men at Work: The Craft of Baseball. Macmillan, 1990.
Suddenly: The American Idea Abroad and at Home, 1986-1990. Macmillan, 1990.
Restoration: Congress, Term Limits, and the Recovery of Deliberative Democracy. Viking, 1992.
The Leveling Wind: Politics, the Culture, and Other News, 1990-1994. Viking, 1994.

* * *

George F. Will began his journalistic career with the *Washington Post* and *National Review* in the early 1970s after brief stints as a professor and congressional aide. Within five years, his articulate and thoughtful columns on political and social issues had earned him a Pulitzer Prize for commentary and launched his celebrated tenure as a weekly essayist for *Newsweek* magazine. By 1990 his syndicated opinion column was appearing in over 450 American newspapers and he had become a regular commentator on ABC's "This Week with David Brinkley." *The New York Times* has called Will "one of our most influential contemporary political columnists," and the *Wall Street Journal* has described him as "perhaps the most powerful journalist in America."

The Pursuit of Happiness (1978) was the first of six anthologies collecting Will's newspaper and magazine columns. Will's political perspective draws heavily from the traditional conservative ideas of such figures as Edmund Burke, John Henry Newman, and Benjamin Disraeli, a body of thought that Will sees as delineating a "Tory" philosophy of individualism, republicanism, and a sort of aristocracy of intellect and taste, now threatened by the "vulgarization" and "trivialization" of social discourse. *The New York Times* praised *Pursuit*'s "wit and style," and the *New Republic* applauded Will's philosophical consistency an "aversion to cant." Will's second collection, *The Pursuit of Virtue* (1982) was also warmly received. *The New Republic,* for example, while arguing that Will's conservatism was outdated and arbitrary in its values, praised the collection as "pithy, epigrammatic, and often elegant."

With *The Morning After* (1986), Will's honeymoon with the "liberal" media appeared to have ended. The *Los Angeles Times* faulted Will for making "little effort to understand" those who disagreed with him, and *The New York Times* detected a deterioration of quality and a growing predictability in Will's columns. In perhaps the most scathing review of Will's career, the *New Republic* attacked the scholarly trappings of Will's essays, his intellectual "philistinism," and the absence of a recognizably authentic America in his writings.

In the essays collected in *The New Season* (1987), Will previewed the elections of 1988 in individual sections on Ronald Reagan and the Republican and Democratic parties. The collection reflected Will's gradual disenchantment with the Reagan "Revolution," which he saw largely as a diluted "New Deal" conservatism. In *Suddenly* (1990), Will celebrated the triumph of American values overseas in the late 1980s while lamenting their continuing decay at home. Will's more recent collection, *The Leveling Wind* (1994), contains essays on such subjects as America's "welfare culture," the sprawling federal government, and the rise of victim psychology as a tactic for wangling the redress of perceived wrongs.

In the first of Will's three original book-length works, *Statecraft as Soulcraft* (1983), Will presented his conception of the proper role and function of good government—namely, to instill civic virtue in its citizens. *National Review* complained that in his discussion of the principles of governing, Will "never really tells us 'what government does,'" while the *Los Angeles Times* worried that the "dark side" of Will's conservatism was the "uncritical acceptance of privilege for its own sake under the guise of 'tradition.'" Other reviewers, however, applauded the elegance of Will's style and defended the generality of his arguments by claiming that his purpose was not so much to advance specific programs as "to change the character and tone of the debate."

Will described *Men at Work* (1990), his best-selling book on the abstruse mysteries of baseball, as "an antiromantic look at a game that brings out the romantic in the best of its fans." Will employs the perspectives of four prominent practitioners of the "craft" to explore the nuances of the game's four disciplines: Tony LaRussa anchors the chapter on managing; Orel Hershiser explicates pitching; Tony Gwynn ruminates on hitting; and Cal Ripken illuminates the mechanics of fielding. *The New York Times* praised *Men at Work* as "an excellent book about excellence," and *New Yorker* writer Roger Angell called it a "classic."

In *Restoration* (1992), Will argues that the only way to eliminate the "legislative careerism" that thwarts effective congressional action is to limit House and Senate officeholders to twelve years of service. *The New York Times* praised Will for his "biting, humorous, and often perceptive" polemic but claimed his argument for term limits was "far from persuasive." The *New Republic* conceded that Will's arguments were "the strongest case for term limits yet" but argued that the term limits debate masks larger problems than Will's proposals address.

Will has half-jokingly ascribed his enormous success to his image as a "lovable, housebroken conservative," implicitly distancing himself from his more shrill, patrician, and humorless ideological contemporaries. His ability to practice what he calls "journalism with a human face," however, may be precisely what has enabled Will's resolutely antipopulist philosophy to attract so large an audience for as long as it has.

—Paul S. Bodine

WILLIAMS, Walter Jon

Also writes as Jon Williams. **Nationality:** American. **Born:** 1953.

Publications

Novels (series: Crown Jewels; Hardwired)

Ambassador of Progress. New York, Tor, 1984; London, Orbit, 1987.
Knight Moves. New York, Tor, 1985; London, Orbit, 1987.
Hardwired. New York, Tor, 1986; London, Macdonald, 1987.
Voice of the Whirlwind (Hardwired). New York, Tor, 1987; London, Orbit, 1989.
The Crown Jewels. New York, Tor, 1987.
The House of Shards (Crown Jewels). New York, Tor, 1988.
Angel Station. New York, Tor, 1989; London, Orbit, 1990.
Days of Atonement. New York, Tor, 1991; London, Grafton, 1992.
Aristoi. New York, Tor, 1992, London, Grafton, 1993.
Wall, Stone, Craft. Eugene, Oregon, Pulphouse, 1993.
Metropolitan. New York, HarperPrism, 1995.
Rock of Ages (Crown Jewels). New York, Tor, 1995.

Short Stories

Solip:System. Eugene, Oregon, Axolotl, 1989.
Facets. New York, Tor, 1990; London, Grafton, 1992.
Elegy for Angels and Dogs, bound with *The Graveyard Heart,* by Roger Zelazny. New York, Tor, 1990; London, Grafton, 1992.
Dinosaurs. Eugene, Oregon, Pulphouse, 1991.

Other

Hardwired: The Source Book. Berkeley, California, Talsorian Games, 1989.

* * *

Walter John Williams began his writing career with nautical historical tales under the name Jon Williams. But he has received much more attention and recognition as a writer of science fiction. Williams's first two science fiction novels were *Ambassador of Progress* (1984) and *Knight Moves* (1986). But *Hardwired* (1986), a novel that plugged into the cyberpunk movement, seems to have marked his critical success.

Hardwired features a male protagonist named Cowboy and a female protagonist named Sarah. They attempt to fight against the domination of the Orbitals, the economic overlords of this future. Cowboy drives an armored car, to which he is cybernetically connected, on smuggling runs. Sarah has the same cybernetic relationship to the Weasel, a weapon concealed in her throat. But it isn't Williams's use of technology as much as his rich characterization that brought the notice of many critics. Both Cowboy and Sarah are fully realized characters. The novel's greatest flaw may be the ending, which has been criticized as capitulating to book-marketing forces instead of the aesthetic conclusion to which it seems to be leading.

Williams gradually became known as a writer that could incorporate hard science with masterful characterization. Roz Kaveney, in an article in *Foundation,* calls the hero of *Days of Atonement* (1991) "an authentically tragic figure." *Reviewers also praised the characterization in Aristoi* (1992), a novel about a godlike race of beings who create a utopia yet are susceptible to the corruption that comes with absolute power. Kaveney, though, questioned the possible stereotypes of some of the secondary characters.

In *Metropolitan* (1995), Williams changes gears slightly and writes a fantasy novel. A vast, sprawling metropolis covers the earth, and a substance called plasm fuels this world. The main character, Aiah, discovers an unregistered supply of the substance that, uniquely, grants amazing powers. She joins forces with Constantine, a rebel, as they try to overthrow the government. Even though this is fantasy instead of the hard science-fiction for which he was known, reviewers still see characterization as a main strength of this novel. Williams admits that he enjoys writing female characters.

Williams's peers must agree with reviewers over the quality of the *Metropolitan,* as it was nominated for a Nebula Award. Award nominations are nothing new for Williams. He was nominated for the Philip K. Dick Award for *Knight Moves,* and received Nebula nominations for "Witness" in 1988, "Surfacing" in 1989, "Prayers on the Wind" in 1993, and "Wall, Stone, Craft" in 1994. He has also been nominated for the Hugo award four times, among other distinctions. His short fiction was collected in *Facets* (1990).

Williams has also written the Crown Jewel series consisting of *Crown Jewels* (1987), *House of Shards* (1988), and *Rock of Ages* (1995). These novels feature the adventures of a gentleman thief known as Drake Maijstral. Williams considers these works "divertimenti"—lighter entertainments that he writes in between his more serious novels.

Some of Williams novels have been compared to Roger Zelazny's work, particularly *Knight Moves* and *Aristoi.* Williams recognizes Zelazny as both a friend and an influence, a fact he draws attention to in the dedication to *Hardwired.* He also directly references Zelazny in that novel by having Cowboy drive along the Alley, an allusion to Zelazny's *Damnation Alley.*

Though Williams's novels continue to be in print in the United States and his new works continue to be nominated for awards, he has received little critical attention in the United States, his home country. Meanwhile, he has had many interviews and articles written about him in Japan, Germany, Finland, the Netherlands, and elsewhere.

—P. Andrew Miller

WILLIAMS, Patrick J. *See* **BUTTERWORTH, W. E.**

WINTERSON, Jeanette

Nationality: British. **Born:** Lancashire in 1959. **Education:** St. Catherine's College, Oxford. **Awards:** Whitbread award, 1985; John Llewellyn Rhys Memorial prize, 1987. **Address:** c/o Bloomsbury, 2 Soho Square, London W1V 5DE, England.

Publications

Novels

Oranges Are Not the Only Fruit. London, Pandora Press, 1985; New York, Atlantic Monthly Press, 1987.
Boating for Beginners. London, Methuen, 1985.
The Passion. London, Bloomsbury, 1987; New York, Atlantic Monthly Press, 1988.
Sexing the Cherry. London, Bloomsbury, and New York, Atlantic Monthly Press, 1989.
Written on the Body. London, Cape, 1992; New York, Knopf, 1993.
Art and Lies. London, Cape, 1994; New York, Knopf, 1995.

Uncollected Short Stories

"Orion," in *Winter's Tales 4* (new series), edited by Robin Baird-Smith. London, Constable, and New York, St. Martin's Press, 1988.
"The Green Man," in *The New Yorker,* 26 June-3 July 1995.

Play

Radio Play: *Static,* 1988.

Television Play: *Oranges Are Not the Only Fruit* (series), from her own novel, 1990.

Other

Fit for the Future: The Guide for Women Who Want to Live Well. London, Pandora Press, 1986.
Art Objects: Critical Essays. London, Cape, and New York, Knopf, 1995.

Editor, *Passion Fruit: Romantic Fiction with a Twist.* London, Pandora Press, 1986.

* * *

Jeanette Winterson's first novel, *Oranges Are Not the Only Fruit* (1985), won England's Whitbread Prize in 1985. The subject is the rejection by the main character (also named Jeanette) of the religious fanaticism which has structured her life since her adoption. She lives her young life fully expecting to become a missionary, but after her mother discovers she is a lesbian, Jeanette's position in the church becomes threatened. An opposition arises between the outside world and the world of the church. She is not concerned, though, with transcending opposites in the novel, but with maintaining a balance. Though some critics have chided Winterson for not exploring the issue of lesbian identity, the fact that Jeanette's lesbianism is simply one facet of her life and not the central issue in this novel is one of its most positive attributes.

The Passion (1987), alternating between two first-person narrators, takes the reader back to Napoleon's Europe and offers a surrealistic romance. Henri, a French soldier who works in Bonaparte's kitchen, becomes disillusioned after the fall of Napoleon. While in Russia he meets and falls in love with Villanelle, a mysterious Venetian who had been sold as a traveling whore by her husband to Napoleon's officer corps. A previous affair resulted in her heart being literally stolen and imprisoned by the

Venetian noblewoman she once loved. Henri is sent to steal back her heart. Can Henri keep himself sane after the wholesale rejection of his beliefs in the quest for his passion? This arresting tale of passion (whether it be religious, heroic, or sexual) is brewed up in a mix of fairy tale, myth, and fact. Winterson has refined her considerable power in the realm of language in this novel into beautiful prose and an engrossing tale of magic, lust, and love.

Sexing the Cherry (1989) is a journey through time, history, and the imagination. The novel is loosely set in 17th-century London before the execution of Charles I and continues into the time of the Great Plague and Fire. The two main characters are Dog Woman and Jordan. Dog Woman saves Jordan from the Thames as a small boy and raises him alongside the dogs she breeds. Dog Woman is a giantess, uninterested in sex, and a passionate Royalist to the point of violence. Both characters move back and forth through time throughout the novel. Jordan searches for his true love, who when found refuses to leave with him. Though praised for the interplay of character and imagination she created in this work, Winterson has been criticized for letting her feminist and ecological concerns turn the novel almost into a polemic. In addition, she portrays men as overwhelmingly stupid.

In her next novel, *Written on the Body* (1992), Winterson is again working at breaking down the conventions. Throughout the entire novel the reader is never directly told the protagonist's gender or name. The feeling from the work, though, is that the protagonist is female. The narrator has affairs with a number of women until the great love of her life, Louise, enters the picture. Louise is married to Elgin, an orthodox Jew who is a rich and famous cancer specialist. Louise and the narrator move in together, and Elgin, the only real male in the book, becomes a monstrous presence. He informs the narrator that his wife has leukemia and will die if she does not leave immediately for his clinic in Switzerland. Knowing Louise would never agree, the narrator runs off to Yorkshire and ends up working in a wine bar. She changes her mind later on, but Louise has disappeared. Critics have derided the narrator's sacrifice as contrived; they have also detected the same vein of hatred of men that appeared in her previous novel. The novel has been praised for its sardonic humor and sense of the absurd and for what it reveals about the phenomenon of love.

Her last novel, *Art and Lies* (1995), has been critically panned for attempting and failing to deal with all the issues of our time. The writing has been described as inflated, pedantic, and excessive. Interestingly, when asked to name her favorite current author writing in the English language, Winterson replied, "No one working in the English language now comes close to my exuberance, my passion, my fidelity to words."

—Jennifer G. Coman

WODEHOUSE, P(elham) G(renville)

Nationality: American. **Born:** Guildford, Surrey, 15 October 1881; naturalized U.S. citizen, 1955. **Education:** Attended Dulwich College, 1894-1900. **Family:** Married Ethel Rowley in 1914; one stepdaughter (deceased). **Career:** Novelist, short story writer, and playwright. Hong Kong & Shanghai Bank, London, England, clerk, 1901-03; *London Globe,* London, assistant on "By the Way" column, 1902-03, writer of column, 1903-09; writer, under various pseudonyms, and drama critic for *Vanity Fair,* 1915-19. **Awards:** Litt.D., Oxford University, 1939; named Knight Commander, Order of the British Empire, 1975. **Member:** Dramatists Guild, Authors League of America, Old Alleynian Association (New York; president), Coffee House (New York). **Died:** Southampton, New York, of a heart attack, 14 February 1975.

Publications

Novels

A Prefect's Uncle. A & C Black, 1903.
The Head of Kay's. A & C Black, 1905.
Love among the Chickens. George Newnes, 1906.
Not George Washington, with A. W. Westbrook. Cassell, 1907.
The White Feather. A & C Black, 1907.
Mike: A Public School Story, two parts. A & C Black, 1909; revised edition of second part published as *Enter Psmith,* Macmillan, 1935; entire book published in two volumes as *Mike at Wrykyn* and *Mike and Psmith,* both Jenkins, 1953.
The Swoop!; or, How Clarence Saved England: A Tale of the Great Invasion. Alston Rivers, 1909.
The Intrusion of Jimmy. W. J. Watt, 1910; as *A Gentleman of Leisure,* Alston Rivers, 1910.
Psmith in the City. A & C Black, 1910.
The Prince and Betty. W. J. Watt, 1912; as *Psmith, Journalist,* A & C Black, 1915.
The Little Nugget. Methuen, 1913.
Something New. Appleton, 1915; as *Something Fresh,* Methuen, 1915.
Uneasy Money. Appleton, 1916.
Piccadilly Jim. Dodd, 1917; revised edition, 1931.
A Damsel in Distress. Doran, 1919.
Their Mutual Child. Boni & Liveright, 1919; as *The Coming of Bill,* Jenkins, 1920.
The Little Warrior. Doran, 1920; as *Jill the Reckless,* Jenkins, 1921.
The Adventures of Sally. Jenkins, 1922; as *Mostly Sally,* Doran, 1923.
Three Men and a Maid. Doran, 1922; as *The Girl on the Boat,* Jenkins, 1922.
Leave It to Psmith. Jenkins, 1923.
Bill the Conqueror: His Invasion of England in the Springtime. Methuen, 1924.
Sam in the Suburbs. Doran, 1925; as *Sam the Sudden,* Methuen, 1925; reprinted with a new preface by the author, Barrie & Jenkins, 1972.
The Small Bachelor. Doran, 1927.
Money for Nothing. Doubleday, Doran, 1928.
Fish Preferred. Doubleday, Doran, 1929; as *Summer Lightning,* Jenkins, 1929.
Big Money. Doubleday, Doran, 1931.
If I Were You. Doubleday, Doran, 1931.
Doctor Sally. Methuen, 1932.
Hot Water. Doubleday, Doran, 1932.
Heavy Weather. Little, Brown, 1933.
Brinkley Manor. Little, Brown, 1934; as *Right Ho, Jeeves,* Jenkins, 1934.
Thank You, Jeeves. Little, Brown, 1934.
The Luck of the Bodkins. Jenkins, 1935.
Trouble Down at Tudsleigh. International Magazine Co., 1935.

Laughing Gas. Doubleday, Doran, 1936.
Summer Moonshine. Doubleday, Doran, 1937.
The Code of the Woosters. Doubleday, Doran, 1938.
Uncle Fred in the Springtime. Doubleday, Doran, 1939.
Quick Service. Doubleday, Doran, 1940.
Money in the Bank. Doubleday, Doran, 1942.
Joy in the Morning. Doubleday, 1946; reprinted with a new preface by the author, Jenkins, 1974; as *Jeeves in the Morning*, HarperCollins, 1983.
Full Moon. Doubleday, 1947.
Spring Fever. Doubleday, 1948.
Uncle Dynamite. Jenkins, 1948.
The Mating Season. Didier, 1949.
The Old Reliable. Doubleday, 1951.
Angel Cake. Doubleday, 1952; as *Barmy in Wonderland*, Jenkins, 1952.
Pigs Have Wings. Doubleday, 1952; reprinted with a new preface by the author, Barrie & Jenkins, 1974.
Ring for Jeeves. Jenkins, 1953; as *The Return of Jeeves*, Simon & Schuster, 1954.
Jeeves and the Feudal Spirit. Jenkins, 1954; as *Bertie Wooster Sees It Through*, Simon & Schuster, 1955.
French Leave. Jenkins, 1956; reprinted with a new preface by the author, Barrie & Jenkins, 1974.
The Butler Did It. Simon & Schuster, 1957; as *Something Fishy*, Jenkins, 1957.
Cocktail Time. Simon & Schuster, 1958.
How Right You Are, Jeeves. Simon & Schuster, 1960; as *Jeeves in the Offing*, Jenkins, 1960.
Ice in the Bedroom. Simon & Schuster, 1961.
Service with a Smile. Simon & Schuster, 1961.
Stiff Upper Lip, Jeeves. Simon & Schuster, 1963.
Biffen's Millions. Simon & Schuster, 1964; as *Frozen Assets*, Jenkins, 1964.
The Brinkmanship of Galahad Threepwood: A Blandings Castle Novel. Simon & Schuster, 1965; as *Galahad at Blandings*, Jenkins, 1965.
The Purloined Paperweight. Simon & Schuster, 1967; as *Company for Henry*, Jenkins, 1967.
Do Butlers Burgle Banks? Simon & Schuster, 1968.
A Pelican at Blandings. Jenkins, 1969; as *No Nudes Is Good Nudes*, Simon & Schuster, 1970.
The Girl in Blue. Barrie & Jenkins, 1970.
Jeeves and the Tie That Binds. Simon & Schuster, 1971; as *Much Obliged, Jeeves*, Barrie & Jenkins, 1971.
Pearls, Girls, and Monty Bodkins. Barrie & Jenkins, 1972; as *The Plot That Thickened*, Simon & Schuster, 1973.
Bachelors Anonymous. Barrie & Jenkins, 1973.
The Cat-Nappers: A Jeeves and Bertie Story. Simon & Schuster, 1974; as *Aunts Aren't Gentlemen: A Jeeves and Bertie Story*, Barrie & Jenkins, 1974.
Sunset at Blandings. Chatto & Windus, 1977.
Life with Jeeves. Viking, 1983.
The World of Jeeves. HarperCollins, 1988.

Short Stories

The Pothunters and Other School Stories. A & C Black, 1902.
Tales of St. Austin's. A & C Black, 1903.
The Gold Bat and Other School Stories. A & C Black, 1904.
The Man Upstairs and Other Stories. Methuen, 1914.
The Man with Two Left Feet and Other Stories. Methuen, 1917.
My Man Jeeves. George Newnes, 1919; as *Carry On, Jeeves*, Jenkins, 1925.
The Indiscretions of Archie. Doran, 1921.
The Clicking of Cuthbert. Jenkins, 1922; as *Golf without Tears*, Doran, 1924.
Jeeves. Doran, 1923; as *The Inimitable Jeeves*, Jenkins, 1923.
Ukridge. Jenkins, 1924; as *He Rather Enjoyed It*, Doran, 1926.
The Heart of a Goof. Jenkins, 1926; as *Divots*, Doran, 1927.
Meet Mr. Mulliner. Jenkins, 1927.
Mr. Mulliner Speaking. Jenkins, 1929.
Very Good, Jeeves. Doubleday, Doran, 1930.
Mulliner Nights. Doubleday, Doran, 1933.
Blandings Castle. Doubleday, Doran, 1935; as *Blandings Castle and Elsewhere*, Jenkins, 1935.
Young Men in Spats. Doubleday, Doran, 1936.
The Crime Wave at Blandings. Doubleday, Doran, 1937; as *Lord Emsworth and Others*, Jenkins, 1937.
Dudley Is Back to Normal. Doubleday, Doran, 1940.
Eggs, Beans and Crumpets. Doubleday, Doran, 1940.
Nothing Serious, Jenkins. 1950, Doubleday, 1951.
Selected Stories, introduction by John W. Aldridge. Modern Library, 1958.
A Few Quick Ones. Simon & Schuster, 1959.
Plum Pie. Jenkins, 1966.
Jeeves, Jeeves, Jeeves. Avon, 1976.
The Swoop and Other Stories, edited by David A. Jasen, foreword by Malcolm Muggeridge. Seabury, 1979.
The World of Mr. Mulliner. Taplinger, 1985.
The Golf Omnibus. Outlet Book, 1991.
Tales from the Drones Club. International Polygonics, 1991.
The Uncollected Wodehouse, edited by D. A. Jasen, foreword by M. Muggeridge. International Polygonics, 1992.

Plays

A Gentleman of Leisure, with John Stapleton, adaptation of Wodehouse's novel (produced New York, 1911).
A Thief for the Night, with Stapleton (produced New York, 1913).
Brother Alfred, with H. W. Westbrook (produced London, 1913).
Miss Springtime, with Guy Bolton and H. Reynolds, music by Emmerich Kalman and Jerome Kern (produced New York, 1916).
Have a Heart, with Bolton, music by Kern (produced New York, 1917).
Leave It to Jane, with Bolton, music by Kern, adaptation of *The College Widow* by George Ade (produced New York, 1917).
Miss 1917, with Bolton, music by Victor Herbert and Kern (produced New York, 1917).
Oh, Boy, with Bolton (produced New York 1917, produced in London as *Oh, Joy*, 1919).
Ringtime, with Bolton (produced New York, 1917).
The Riviera Girl, with Bolton, music by Kalman (produced New York, 1917).
The Second Century Show, with Bolton (produced New York, 1917).
The Girl behind the Gun, with Bolton, music by Ivan Caryll, adaptation of the play *Madame et son filleul* by Hennequin and Weber (produced New York, 1918; produced in London as *Kissing Time at Winter Garden Theatre*, 1918).

Oh! Lady, Lady!, with Bolton, music by Kern (produced New York, 1918).
Oh My Dear, with Bolton, music by Louis Hirsch (produced New York, 1918; produced in Toronto as *Ask Dad,* 1918).
The Rose of China, with Bolton, music by Armand Vecsey (produced New York, 1919).
Sally, with Clifford Grey, music by Kern (produced New York, 1920).
The Golden Moth, with Fred Thompson, music by Ivor Novello (produced London, 1921).
The Cabaret Girl, with George Grossmith, music by Kern (produced London, 1922).
The Beauty Prize, with Grossmith, music by Kern (produced London, 1923).
Sitting Pretty, with Bolton, music by Kern (produced New York, 1924).
Hearts and Diamonds, with Laura Wylie, adaptation of *The Orlov* by Biuno Granichstaedten and Ernest Marischka (produced London, 1926). Keith Prowse & Co., 1926.
Showboat, with others, music by Oscar Hammerstein (produced New York, 1927).
Oh Kay!, with Bolton, lyrics by Ira Gershwin, music by George Gershwin (produced New York, 1926).
The Play's the Thing, adaptation of *Spiel in Schloss* by Ferenc Molnar (produced New York, 1926). Brentano's, 1927.
Her Cardboard Lover, with Valerie Wyngate, adaptation of a play by Jacques Deval (produced New York, 1927).
The Nightingale, with Bolton, music by Vecsey (produced New York, 1927).
Good Morning, Bill, adaptation of a play by Ladislaus Fodor (produced London, 1927). Methuen, 1928.
A Damsel in Distress, with Ian Hay, adaptation of Wodehouse's novel of the same title (produced New York, 1928). Samuel French, 1930.
Rosalie, with Ira Gershwin, Bolton and Bill McGuire, music by George Gershwin and Sigmund Romberg (produced New York, 1928).
The Three Musketeers, with Grossmith and Grey, adaptation of the novel by Alexandre Dumas (produced New York, 1928).
Baa, Baa, Black Sheep, with Hay (produced New York, 1929). Samuel French, 1930.
Candlelight, adaptation of "Kleine Komodie" by Siegfried Geyer (produced New York, 1929). Samuel French, 1934.
Leave It to Psmith, with Hay, adaptation of Wodehouse's novel of the same title (produced London, 1930). Samuel French, 1932.
Who's Who, with Guy Bolton (produced London, 1934).
Anything Goes, with Bolton, Howard Lindsay, and Russel Crouse, music and lyrics by Cole Porter (produced New York, 1934). Samuel French, 1936.
The Inside Stand (produced London, 1935).
Don't Listen, Ladies, with Bolton, adaptation of the play *N'ecoutez pas, mesdames* by Sacha Guitry (produced New York, 1948).
Carry On, Jeeves, with Bolton, adaptation of Wodehouse's novel of the same title. Evans Brothers, 1956.

Screenplays: *A Damsel in Distress,* adapted from his novel of the same title, 1920; *Rosalie,* adapted from his play of the same title, 1930.

Other

William Tell Told Again. A & C Black, 1904.
The Globe "By the Way" Book: A Literary Quick-Lunch for People Who Have Only Got Five Minutes to Spare, with H. W. Westbrook. Globe, 1908; edited by W. K. Haselden, Heineman, 1985.
Louder and Funnier. Faber, 1932.
Performing Flea: A Self-Portrait in Letters, introduction by William Townsend. Jenkins, 1953; as *Author! Author!,* Simon & Schuster, 1962.
Bring on the Girls!: The Improbable Story of Our Life in Musical Comedy with Pictures to Prove It, with Guy Bolton. Simon & Schuster, 1953.
America, I Like You. Simon & Schuster, 1956; revised edition published as *Over Seventy: An Autobiography with Digressions,* Jenkins, 1957.
Most of P. G. Wodehouse. Simon & Schuster, 1969.
The Great Sermon Handicap, 8 volumes, photographs by William Hewison. James H. Heineman, 1983.
Fore! The Best of Wodehouse on Golf, edited by D. R. Bensen. Ticknor & Fields, 1985.
A Wodehouse Bestiary, edited by D. R. Bensen. Houghton, 1985.
Life at Blandings. Viking, 1988.
Yours, Plum. Heineman, 1990.

Editor, with Meredith, and author of introduction, *The Best of Modern Humour.* Metcalf, 1952.
Editor, with Scott Meredith, and author of introduction, *The Week-End Book of Humour,* Washburn, 1952; as *P. G. Wodehouse Selects the Best of Humor,* Grosset, 1965.

*

Bibliography: *A Bibliography and Reader's Guide to the First Editions of P. G. Wodehouse* by David A. Jasen, Archon, 1970.

Critical Studies: *Wodehouse at Work,* Jenkins, 1961, and *Wodehouse Nuggets,* Hutchinson, 1983, by Richard Usborne; *P. G. Wodehouse* by R. B. D. French, Oliver & Boyd, 1966; *P. G. Wodehouse* by Richard Voorhees, Twayne, 1966; *Wooster's World,* 1967, and *Blandings the Blest and the Blue Blood,* 1968, by Geoffrey W. Jaggard, Macdonald & Co.; *The World of P. G. Wodehouse* by H. W. Wind, Praeger, 1972; *Homage to P. G. Wodehouse,* edited by Thelma Cazalet-Keir, Barrie & Jenkins, 1973; *The Comic Style of P. G. Wodehouse* by Robert A. Hall, Jr., Archon, 1974; *P. G. Wodehouse: A Portrait of a Master* by David A. Jasen, Mason & Lipscomb, 1974; *P. G. Wodehouse: A Literary Biography* by Benny Green, Rutledge Press, 1981; *P. G. Wodehouse: A Centenary Celebration, 1881-1981,* edited by James H. Heinemen and Donald R. Benson, Pierpoint Morgan Library, 1981; *Wodehouse at War* by Iain Sproat, Ticknor & Fields, 1981.

* * *

P. G. Wodehouse wrote ninety-six novels in all, the best known of which involve the antics of Bertie Wooster, an idle man whose most important aspirations are being faithful to his chums and getting out of sticky marriage proposals. Bertie has a heart of gold but negligible intelligence. He is often performing chivalrous deeds of Old England, getting into a mess, and asking for the help of his valet, Jeeves.

Jeeves is a gentleman's gentleman. His intellect is superior to Bertie's and he quietly untangles some of the most improbable situations that baffle Bertie and his friends. The pairing of Bertie and Jeeves has been compared to the pairing of Sherlock Holmes and Dr. Watson; they work that well together, one as a foil to the other.

The Jeeves books, which appear under various titles that include the name Jeeves, rarely change much in time, setting, or personalities of the frequent characters. But Wodehouse fans like that, as well as the intricate plots and the mix of Shakespearean quotes (or calculated misquotes) with American slang. Wodehouse always keeps the reader on his toes.

Wodehouse is a master craftsman. He makes his work look effortless. In fact, Wodehouse has been called "the master" by the likes of Ogden Nash and Evelyn Waugh. Hilaire Belloc, an English essayist, said in a 1939 radio broadcast that Wodehouse was "the best writer in English now alive."

A Wodehouse story typically involves a country estate and a group of men who went to school together and who would do anything to defend a woman's honor. Yet these same chaps would pull a prank at the snap of a finger. The plots are unduly complicated. The language usage is a combination of famous quotes, famous sayings misquoted, several turns of phrase and a vast repertoire of wordplay. Some call Wodehouse's England Edwardian, others say it never existed at all, except in Wodehouse's fiction. Wodehouse himself claims he was writing about the period between the two World Wars, but doesn't specify dates.

In addition to ninety-six novels, Wodehouse penned lyrics to twenty-eight musicals while collaborating on their scripts. He also wrote sixteen plays and three hundred short stories. Four familiar collections of his work have appeared in various forms. Foremost is the Jeeves collection, probably the best loved and most widely read. Another collection is about golfing, where the "Oldest Member" tells golfing stories that relate to the predicaments that the younger players bring into him at the clubhouse. The "Oldest Member" stories can be found on either side of the Atlantic, and include *The Golf Omnibus* (1991).

Wodehouse is also famous for stories set at Blandings Castle, with Lord Emsworth, the Empress of Blandings, his prize pig and main obsession, and all the annoying people around him. Emsworth has domineering sisters, one who keeps insisting that he write the family history, and a much-too-efficient secretary, Baxter, who comes off as Jeeves wound a little too tight. The Blandings stories include: "How Clarence Saved England" (1909), "Blandings Castle" (1935), "Galahad at Blandings" (1965), "A Pelican at Blandings" (1969), and "Sunset at Blandings" (1977), which was an unfinished novel.

Finally, with "Meet Mr. Mulliner" (1927), "Mr. Mulliner Speaking" (1929), and "Mulliner Nights" (1933), the reader becomes acquainted with an old angler who tells fish stories about his numerous relatives.

When asked his favorite work, Wodehouse responded "Mike," referring to the two-part *Mike: A Public School Story* (1909). Critics point out that this book was a transition from his early Kipling-like stories to Wodehouse's now familiar broad humor.

Wodehouse's writing generally attracts admiration. One critic said when Oxford gave Wodehouse an honorary doctorate that they [Oxford administrators] were "dead from the chin up." Such detractors are isolated, however. Generally, readers from all over the world regard Wodehouse as a sort of genial genius.

—Liz Mulligan

WOLFE, Aaron. *See* **KOONTZ, Dean R(ay).**

WOLFE, Gene (Rodman)

Nationality: American. **Born:** Brooklyn, New York, 7 May 1931. **Education:** Texas A&M University, College Station, 1949, 1952; University of Houston, B.S. 1956; Miami University. **Military Service:** Served in the United States Army, 1952-54. **Family:** Married Rosemary Frances Dietsch in 1956; two sons and two daughters. **Career:** Project engineer, Procter and Gamble, 1956-72; senior editor, *Plant Engineering,* Barrington, Illinois, 1972-84. **Awards:** Nebula award, 1973, 1982; Rhysling award, for verse, 1978; *Locus* award, 1982, 1987; World Fantasy award, 1982; British Science Fiction Association award, 1982; British Fantasy award, 1983; John W. Campbell Memorial award, 1984. **Agent:** Virginia Kidd, Box 278, Milford, Pennsylvania 18337. **Address:** P.O. Box 69, Barrington, Illinois 60010, U.S.A.

Publications

Novels (series: Book of the Long Sun; Book of the New Sun; Latro)

Operation ARES. New York, Berkley, 1970; London, Dobson, 1977.
Peace. New York, Harper, 1975; London, Chatto and Windus, 1985.
The Devil in a Forest (for children). Chicago, Follett, 1976; London, Panther, 1985.
The Shadow of the Torturer (New Sun). New York, Simon and Schuster, 1980; London, Arrow, 1986.
The Claw of the Conciliator (New Sun). New York, Timescape, 1981; London, Legend, 1991.
The Sword of the Lictor (New Sun). New York, Timescape, and London, Sidgwick and Jackson, 1982.
The Citadel of the Autarch (New Sun). New York, Timescape, and London, Sidgwick and Jackson, 1983.
Free Live Free. Willimantic, Connecticut, Ziesing, 1984; London, Gollancz, 1985.
Soldier of the Mist (Latro). New York, Tor, and London, Gollancz, 1986.
The Urth of the New Sun. London, Gollancz, and New York, Tor, 1987.
There Are Doors. New York, Tor, 1988; London, Gollancz, 1989.
Soldier of Arete (Latro). New York, Tor, 1989; London, New English Library, 1990.
Castleview. New York, Tor, 1990; London, New English Library, 1991.
Pandora by Holly Hollander. New York, Tor, 1990.
Nightside the Long Sun. New York, Tor, and London, New English Library, 1993.
Lake of the Long Sun. New York, Tor, and London, New English Library, 1994.
Litany of the Long Sun (omnibus). New York, Guild America, 1994.
Caldé of the Long Sun. New York, Tor, and London, New English Library, 1994.

Exodus of the Long Sun. New York, Tor, and London, New English Library, 1995.

Short Stories

The Fifth Head of Cerberus. New York, Scribner, 1972.
The Island of Doctor Death and Other Stories and Other Stories. New York, Pocket Books, 1980.
Gene Wolfe's Book of Days. Garden City, New York, Doubleday, 1981; London, Arrow, 1985.
The Castle of the Otter. Willimantic, Connecticut, Ziesing, 1982.
The Wolfe Archipelago. Willimantic, Connecticut, Ziesing, 1983.
Bibliomen: Ten Characters Waiting for a Book. New Castle, Virginia, Cheap Street, 1984.
Plan[e]t Engineering. Cambridge, Massachusetts, NESFA Press, 1984.
The Boy Who Hooked the Sun (New Sun). New Castle, Virginia, Cheap Street, 1985.
Empires of Foliage and Flower (New Sun). New Castle, Virginia, Cheap Street, 1987.
The Arimaspian Legacy. New Castle, Virginia, Cheap Street, 1987.
Storeys from the Old Hotel. Worcester Park, Surrey, Kerosina, 1988; New York, Tor, 1992.
Endangered Species. Norwalk, Connecticut, Easton Press, 1989; London, Orbit, 1990.
Seven American Nights, bound with *Sailing to Byzantium,* by Robert Silverberg. New Yor, Tor, 1989.
Slow Children at Play. New Castle, Virginia, Cheap Street, 1989.
The Death of Doctor Island, bound with *Fugue State,* by John M. Ford. New York, Tor, 1990.
The Old Woman Whose Rolling Pin Is the Sun. New Castle, Virginia, Cheap Street, 1991.
The Hero as Werwolf. Eugene, Oregon, Pulphouse, 1991.
Young Wolfe: A Collection of Early Stories. Weston, Ontario, United Mythologies Press, 1992.
Castle of Days (includes *Gene Wolfe's Book of Days* and *The Castle of the Otter*). New York, Tor, 1992.

Poetry

For Rosemary. Worcester Park, Surrey, Kerosina, 1988.

Other

Letters Home. Weston, Ontario, United Mythologies Press, 1991.
Gene Wolfe's Orbital Thoughts (quotations), edited by Rosemary Wolfe. Weston, Ontario, United Mythologies Press, 1992.

*

Bibliography: in *The Castle of the Otter,* 1982.

Manuscript Collection: Merril Collection, Toronto Public Library, Canada.

* * *

Within the genre of science fiction, Gene R. Wolfe has earned acclaim for both his short stories and his novels. *The Encyclopedia of Science Fiction* notes that "though neither the most popular nor the most influential author in the science fiction field, [Wolfe] is today quite possibly the most important." Before launching his writing career, Wolfe, a mechanical engineer, acted as editor of the trade periodical *Plant Engineering.* Ironically (and fortunately) Wolfe's fiction reveals his creative and didactic thoughts, supported but not overwhelmed by his technical understanding. During the early years of Wolfe's career, Damon Knight's *Orbit* anthologies often published the best of his short stories, including *Trip, Trap* (1967) and *Forlesen* (1970).

Wolfe's second novel, *The Five Heads of Cerebrus* (1972), gained attention as a "stylistic breakthrough." This novel consisted of three tightly interwoven novellas addressing the challenges of individualism and identity, with these challenges being further confused by the cloning of characters and shapeshifting aliens. These stories read as a confession of the protagonist, although his true identity is often in question, providing the stage for Wolfe's fantastic identity crisis. *The Five Heads of Cerebrus* is an "unforgettable tale of culture shock."

Wolfe's introduction to and climax in the world of popular fiction came with his series *The New Sun Sequence.* This sequence consists of four novels: *The Shadow of the Torturer* (1980), *The Claw of the Conciliator* (1981), *The Sword of the Lictor* (1982), and *The Citadel of the Autarch* (1983). Critics celebrate this series as Wolfe's most ambitious and successful work, blending science fiction with fantasy on a futuristic planet Urth where technology has become sorcery, and where the future represents a distorted return to the past. At the center of the action stands Severian, a disconcerting mesh of innocence and guilt. As a young apprentice to the executioning trade, Severian offers a victim escape from torture by allowing her to commit suicide, and for this act of mercy Severian himself becomes condemned. *The New Sun Sequence* follows Severian's path of condemnation and eventual triumph within this morally decayed society. Most remarkable in this series is the expertly presented challenge to moral absolutes, proving the fallacy of pure right and wrong.

Repeating the success of *The New Sun Sequence* proved too difficult for Wolfe in subsequent novels. Indeed, *Castleview* (1990) fell short of critical expectations and was labeled "mildly diverting entertainment." Wolfe shares with the reader a mirage of a medieval castle hanging over a provincial Illinois town and the strange happenings that come as a result of this mirage. According to the *New York Times Book Review,* the "suspense slackens too soon" and the story is complicated and difficult to follow. Also lost in *The New Sun Sequence*'s shadow is a collection of Wolfe's short stories known as *Endangered Species* (1989), which was disappointing to critics only because of the Wolfe's past genius. Somewhat favorably received, this collection boasts a stunning dramatization of "memory's seductive yet life-threatening undertow" and a weaker tale, *The Cat,* confusing in content with "motives and actions so tightly interwoven" that the story is difficult to follow.

—Amy Eldridge

WOLFE, Tom

Nationality: American. **Born:** Thomas Kennerly Wolfe, Jr. in Richmond, Virginia, 2 March 1930. **Education:** Washington and Lee

University, Lexington, Virginia, A.B. (cum laude) 1951; Yale University, New Haven, Connecticut, Ph.D. 1957. **Family:** Married Sheila Berger in 1978; one daughter and one son. **Career:** Reporter, Springfield *Union,* Massachusetts, 1956-59, Washington *Post,* 1959-62, and New York, *Herald Tribune,* 1962-66; writer, New York *World Journal Tribune,* 1966-67. **Awards:** American Book award, 1980; Columbia award, for journalism, 1980. D.Litt.: Washington and Lee University, 1974. **Agent:** Lynn Nesbit, Janklow and Nesbit, 598 Madison Avenue, New York, New York 10022, U.S.A.

Publications

Novel

The Bonfire of the Vanities. New York, Farrar Straus, 1987; London, Cape, 1988.

Uncollected Short Stories

"The Commercial," in *Esquire* (New York), October 1975.
"2020 A.D.," in *Esquire* (New York), January 1985.

Other

The Kandy-Kolored Tangerine Flake Streamline Baby (essays). New York, Farrar Straus, 1965; London, Cape, 1966.
The Electric Kool-Aid Acid Test. New York, Farrar Straus, and London, Weidenfeld and Nicolson, 1968.
The Pump House Gang (essays). New York, Farrar Straus, 1968; as *The Mid-Atlantic Man and Other New Breeds in England and America,* London, Weidenfeld and Nicolson, 1969.
Radical Chic and Mau-Mauing the Flak Catchers. New York, Farrar Straus, 1970; London, Joseph, 1971.
The Painted Word. New York, Farrar Straus, 1975.
Mauve Gloves and Madmen, Clutter and Vine, and Other Stories (essays). New York, Farrar Straus, 1976.
The Right Stuff. New York, Farrar Straus, and London, Cape, 1979.
In Our Time (essays). New York, Farrar Straus, 1980.
From Bauhaus to Our House. New York, Farrar Straus, 1981; London, Cape, 1982.

Editor, with E.W. Johnson, *The New Journalism.* New York, Harper, 1973; London, Pan, 1975.

*

Critical Study: "Tom Wolfe's Vanities" by Joseph Epstein, in *New Criterion* (New York), February 1988.

* * *

More a comic moralist and literary nonconformist than the Balzacian grand realist he affects, Tom Wolfe landed early in his career on an understanding of the role of status in American society that has enabled him to gain perceptive and often wildly humorous insights into his subjects, from the racial pretensions of affluent New York liberals (*Radical Chic and Mau-Mauing the Flak Catchers,* 1970) and the provincialism of the American art industry (*The Painted Word,* 1975) to the narrow-mindedness of modern architecture (*From Bauhaus to Our House,* 1981). Combining a brilliantly attuned eye for what he calls the "status detail" with an original writing style that relies on hyperbole, verbal inventiveness, and the ability to convey the psychological universe of his subjects, Wolfe began gleefully skewering the "statuspheres" of such uniquely American subcultures as car customizing, topless waitressing, and stockcar racing in magazines like *Esquire, New York,* and *Harper's.* Through his advocacy of a "New Journalism," Wolfe called for (and practiced) a marriage of the novelist's creative techniques with the journalist's research methods and concern for accuracy.

In his first major work, *The Electric Kool-Aid Acid Test* (1968), Wolfe explored the adventures of author Ken Kesey and his Merry Pranksters as they attempted to convert the unsuspecting to the delights of LSD while traveling cross-country in a ramshackle bus painted in neon colors. Through a dazzling verbal barrage, Wolfe successfully recreated the "mental atmosphere or subjective reality" of his characters' minds and the hallucinatory experience of LSD itself. Although some critics derided the book's "bogus erudition and intellectuality," *The Electric Kool-Aid Acid Test* was immediately embraced as an entertaining and important exploration of the spirit of the 1960s counterculture.

In his next important work, *The Right Stuff* (1979), Wolfe traced the origins of the U.S. space program and early Mercury missions through the experiences of the first seven astronauts chosen for manned space flight. Only those with the personality traits ("the right stuff") that enabled them to continually push themselves and their machines to the limit could join the select club; an elite that originated, Wolfe argued, with famed U.S. Air Force test pilot Chuck Yeager. Wolfe again combined his exaggerated, jazzed-up style with a wicked sense of humor and penetrating social analysis to recreate the ambience and excitement of his subject. Although critics like Charles Ross in *The Journal of General Education* suggested that the absence of "precision and documentation" prevented *The Right Stuff* from being a "great book," it became a highly esteemed bestseller and quickly returned Wolfe to the center stage of American popular letters.

The Bonfire of the Vanities (1987) was Wolfe's first attempt at the novel of "highly detailed realism" he had long advocated. It tells the story of Sherman McCoy, superrich bond salesman and self-styled "Master of the Universe" who is unjustly arrested after his mistress runs over a black youth while they are lost in the bowels of the Bronx. The hit-and-run case turns into a full-blown, media-saturated class conflict as New York's various ethnic and social groups and the novel's major characters maneuver to exploit the case for their own ends.

Some critics have argued that far from being the "big novel of manners and society" to which Wolfe aspired, *Bonfire* was actually a "literary satire" in which the characters were allegorical caricatures of lust, pride, greed, and ambition rather than fully realized individuals. Others criticized the book's vague and contrived ending and even accused Wolfe of being "cynical, racist, and elitist." "That's nonsense," Wolfe countered, "[*Bonfire*] . . . was a book about vanity in New York in an age of money fever." Most reviewers were quick to praise *Bonfire* as a superior work of fiction and social analysis that demonstrated that the father of the New Journalism was capable of writing compelling novels.

Throughout his career, Wolfe has been dogged by the accusation that his nuanced analyses of the central role of status in American life are just so much flashy intellectual riffing, and that in reality he is the consummate literary conman who doesn't really expect or even care to be taken seriously. Other critics have assailed Wolfe's writing style as "overheated" and "over-fried," and spellbinding but often "gratuitous and cavalier." As Wolfe's popularity and reputation have grown over the years, however, a larger number of critics have described Wolfe as, for example, "the most astute and popular social observer and cultural chronicler of his generation," and "the best . . . of any American journalist since Mencken." Wolfe has described himself in humbler terms: "I am just the chronicler. My passion is to discover, and to write about it."

—Paul Bodine

WOODCOTT, Keith. *See* **BRUNNER, John.**

WOODS, Stuart

Nationality: American. **Born:** Stuart Lee, 9 January 1938, in Manchester, Georgia; legally changed to stepfather's surname in 1955. **Education:** University of Georgia, B.A., 1959. **Military Service:** Air National Guard, 1960-68, active duty, 1961; served in Germany. **Career:** Advertising writer and creative director with firms in New York City, 1960-69, including Batten, Barton, Durstine & Osborne; Paper, Koenig & Lois; Young & Rubicam; and J. Walter Thompson; creative director and consultant with firms in London, England, 1970-73, including Grey Advertising and Dorland; consultant to Irish International Advertising and Hunter Advertising, both in Dublin, both 1973-74; free-lance writer since 1973. Past member of board of directors of Denham's, Inc. **Awards:** Advertising awards from numerous organizations in New York, including Clio award for television writing and Gold Key award for print writing. **Address:** c/o HarperCollins, 10 E. Fifty-Third St., New York, New York, 10022, U.S.A.

PUBLICATIONS

Novels

Chiefs. Norton, 1980.
Run Before the Wind. Norton, 1983.
Deep Lie. Norton, 1986.
Under the Lake. Simon & Schuster, 1987.
White Cargo. Simon & Schuster, 1988.
Grass Roots. Simon & Schuster, 1989.
Palindrome. HarperCollins, 1991.
New York Dead. HarperCollins, 1991.
Santa Fe Rules. HarperCollins, 1992.
L.A. Times. HarperCollins, 1993.
Dead Eyes. HarperCollins, 1994.
Heat. HarperCollins, 1994.
Imperfect Strangers. HarperCollins, 1995.
Choke. HarperCollins, 1995.

Nonfiction

Blue Water, Green Skipper. Norton, 1977.
A Romantic's Guide to the Country Inns of Britain and Ireland. Norton, 1979.
A Romantic's Guide to London. Norton, 1980.
A Romantic's Guide to Paris. Norton, 1981.
A Romantic's Guide to the Country Inns of France. Norton, 1981.

* * *

Crime and thriller novelist Stuart Woods began as a nonfiction writer, publishing his memoirs of sailing as well as several guides to country inns in Great Britain, Ireland, and France. With the publication of *Chiefs* (1981), his first novel, Woods began a series of suspense narratives that includes over a dozen novels investigating crime, abuse, murder and revenge.

Chiefs drew much praise, not only for its narrative but also for what *Booklist*'s Julia M. Ehresmann called Woods's "fine sense of the Old and New South's ways and values." Spanning five decades, *Chiefs* opens in the 1920s with the murder of an adolescent boy. Various events keep the murder from being investigated as new police chiefs emerge and reveal the vices and virtues of small-town politics. Finally, the town's first black police chief takes office in the 1960s and begins investigating the case. *Kirkus Reviews* proclaimed, "Woods's first novel is strong, decent, and suspenseful—especially rich in its varied, appealing characterizations." Notable is Woods's insight into the life of southern blacks from the 1920s to the 1960s.

Woods's subsequent novels have received mixed criticism. *White Cargo* (1988) deals with the Colombian drug scene as investigated by Cat Catledge, a wealthy businessman whose family is murdered by drug runners in the Caribbean. Surviving the attack, Catledge discovers that his daughter is still alive and attempts to find her in Colombia. While Peter Robertson in *Booklist* proclaimed *White Cargo* "superior adventure fare," the *New York Times Book Review* found the plot unrealistic and unconvincing. *Palindrome* (1991), the story of a woman's escape from her abusive, drug-using husband and journey to a remote tropical island was received more favorably. Robertson said, "Woods is a capable writer with a good eye for detail; if he sometimes seems a mite soulless, he's also never less than a consummate professional."

Woods's more recent novels seem to have grown more concerned with violence and death. *New York Dead* (1991), a cop-thriller, relates the apparent suicide of TV news personality Sasha Nijinsky, who falls to her death from her 12th-story penthouse. The investigation is conducted by lawyer-turned-cop Stone Barrington. Witnessing Nijinsky's death, a horrified Barrington later learns that Nijinsky's body is missing, and the chase is on. *Kirkus Reviews* praised *New York Dead* as "stylish suspense among the gray-flannel/black velvet set, with a winsome hero and agreeable dollops of sex, gore, and demented mayhem."

L.A. Times (1993) investigates the world of the Mafia as shakedown artist Vincente Michaele Callabrese leaves New York for his dream of being a big-time movie producer in Los Angeles. When Callabrese produces a triumphant movie, the sparks and bullets fly. *Publisher's Weekly* praised Callabrese as a "dynamic protagonist" and claimed that readers would be "entertained by the abundant suspense Woods creates as he depicts this licentious, adulterous and violent milieu." *Imperfect Strangers* (1995) is the story of two strangers who meet on a flight from London to New York and agree to murder each other's bothersome wives. "Enjoyable for a time, the tony tinsel is overtaken by a blandness that ultimately undercuts the novel's would-be dramatic and psychological aspects," reported *Publisher's Weekly*.

Readers wanting to test Woods's nonfiction should read his *Blue Water, Green Skipper* (1977), in which Woods describes his experience sailing in the 1976 *Observer* Single-Handed Transatlantic Race only 18 months after learning to sail. As Holger Lundbergh of *Yachting* puts it, "The step-by-step account of how this green skipper in a remarkably short time became a seasoned blue-water sailor is beautifully told by a young American from Georgia, a brilliant stylist, a man of humor, courage, and patience . . . dramatic and inspiring reading of rare quality." Those readers with a taste for adventure should find Woods's writings satisfying.

—Christopher Swann

WOUK, Herman

Nationality: American. **Born:** New York City, 27 May 1915. **Education:** Townsend Harris Hall, New York, 1927-30; Columbia University, New York (Fox prize, 1934), 1930-34, A.B. 1934. **Military Service:** Served in the United States Naval Reserve, 1942-46: Lieutenant. **Family:** Married Betty Sarah Brown in 1945; three sons (one deceased). **Career:** Radio writer, 1935; scriptwriter for the comedian Fred Allen, 1936-41; consultant, United States Treasury Department, 1941. Since 1946 full-time writer. Visiting professor of English, Yeshiva University, New York, 1952-58; scholar-in-residence, Aspen Institute, Colorado, 1973-74. Trustee, College of the Virgin Islands, 1961-69; member of the Board of Directors, Washington National Symphony, 1969-71, and Kennedy Center Productions, 1974-75. Lives in Washington, D.C. **Awards:** Pulitzer prize, 1952; Columbia University Medal of Excellence, 1952, and Hamilton medal, 1980; *Washingtonian* award, 1986; American Academy of Achievement Golden Plate award, 1986; U.S. Navy Memorial Foundation award, 1987; Kazetnik award, 1990. L.H.D.: Yeshiva University, 1955; LL.D.: Clark University, Worcester, Massachusetts, 1960; D.Lit.: American International College, Springfield, Massachusetts, 1979; Honorary Ph.D.: Bar-Ilan University, Ramat-Gan, Israel, 1990. **Agent:** BSW Literary Agency, 3255 N Street N.W., Washington, D.C. 20007, U.S.A.

PUBLICATIONS

Novels

Aurora Dawn. New York, Simon and Schuster, and London, Barrie, 1947.
The City Boy. New York, Simon and Schuster, 1948; London, Cape, 1956.
The Caine Mutiny. New York, Doubleday, and London, Cape, 1951.
Marjorie Morningstar. New York, Doubleday, and London, Cape, 1955.
Slattery's Hurricane. New York, Permabooks, 1956; London, New English Library, 1965.
Youngblood Hawke. New York, Doubleday, and London, Collins, 1962.
Don't Stop the Carnival. New York, Doubleday, and London, Collins, 1965.
The Lomokome Papers. New York, Pocket Books, 1968.
The Winds of War. Boston, Little Brown, and London, Collins, 1971.
War and Remembrance. Boston, Little Brown, and London, Collins, 1978.
Inside, Outside. Boston, Little Brown, and London, Collins, 1985.
The Hope. Boston, Little Brown, and London, Hodder and Stoughton, 1993.
The Glory. Boston, Little Brown, and London, Hodder and Stoughton, 1994.

Uncollected Short Stories

"Herbie Solves a Mystery," in *Feast of Leviathan*, edited by L.W. Schwarz. New York, Rinehart, 1956.
"Old Flame," in *Good Housekeeping* (New York), May 1956.
"Irresistible Force," in *Fireside Treasury of Modern Humor*, edited by Scott Meredith. New York, Simon and Schuster, 1963.

Plays

The Traitor (produced New York, 1949). New York, French, 1949.
Modern Primitive (produced Hartford, Connecticut, 1951).
The Caine Mutiny Court-Martial (produced Santa Barbara, California, 1953; New York, 1954; London, 1956). New York, Doubleday, 1954; London, Cape, 1956.
Nature's Way (produced New York, 1957). New York, Doubleday, 1958.

Television Series: *The Winds of War*, 1983, and *War and Remembrance*, 1986, from his own novels.

Other

The Man in the Trench Coat. New York, National Jewish Welfare Board, 1941.
This Is My God: The Jewish Way of Life. New York, Doubleday, 1959; London, 1960; revised edition, London, Collins, 1973.

*

Manuscript Collection: Columbia University Library Special Collections, New York.

Bibliography: *A Checklist of the Works of Herman Wouk*, Brunswick Press, 1995.

Critical Studies: "You, Me and the Novel" by Wouk, in *Saturday Review-World* (New York), 29 June 1974; *Herman Wouk: The Novelist as Social Historian* by Arnold Beichman, New Brunswick, New Jersey, Transaction, 1984; *Herman Wouk* by Laurence W. Mazzeno, New York, Twayne, 1994.

* * *

Herman Wouk manages to remain on bestseller lists without sacrificing his moral integrity. Wouk perceives himself as a realist in the tradition of Cooper, Howells, and Dreiser, and like his predecessors he addresses his fiction to a popular, rather than critical, audience. Although a wave of post-WWII experimentation inspired his first novel, *Aurora Dawn* (1947), he quickly assumed a conventional narrative pattern and unpretentious use of language for his second novel *City Boy* (1948).

The Caine Mutiny (1951), considered to be his best book, highlights Wouk's concern with moral values. The story is about relationships between men trapped in the military. Wouk's novel is a study of how different personality types react to the hierarchical relationships found in military life. Willie Keith, the main character, comes of age as he witnesses the events which take place aboard the *Caine*. Wouk depicts Captain Queeg, the tragic figure of the novel, as a mentally unstable individual who despite his incompetence attempts to complete his job. Maryk, another officer, eventually takes responsibility for a mutiny and is forced to stand trial. His legal defender, Lieutenant Greenwald, does not support the mutiny, yet he still believes Maryk acted according to his best judgment. Tom Keefer, the villain of the novel, is a modern man who chooses to instigate the mutiny while denying having had any part in it. Although a jury acquits Maryk, Wouk's presentation of the verdict is deliberately ambiguous. The author moralizes through the character of Keith, who learns to judge matters by his own understanding. He also finds that despite great limitations one can aspire to excellence.

Wouk continued with *Marjorie Morningstar* (1955) and *Youngblood Hawke* (1962). Majorie Morningstar, a beautiful and talented actress, learns to cope with her failure to become an actress and grows truer to herself as she becomes concerned with understanding her Jewish identity. Similarly, *Youngblood Hawke* depicts the obsession of a writer, Thomas Wolfe, for his work. Yet unlike Morningstar, Hawke fails to achieve a deep understanding of events and eventually becomes a victim of secularized society.

Wouk's weakest novel, *Don't Stop the Carnival* (1965), is considered a feeble attempt at satire. Dennis McInerny wrote, "[the] humor, instead of carrying the moral import of the tale, more often than not obstructs it. The work's humor is hampered by obtrusive heavy-handed moralizing."

After a six-year absence, Wouk produced *The Winds of War* (1971), the first volume of what is considered his *magnum opus*. Critics described the novel as a large canvas of the relationship between the varying actions of individuals and the events leading up to the Japanese attack on Pearl Harbor. *War and Remembrance* (1978) concludes the story *Winds* begins, and attempts to elucidate the causes and implications of the war. Wouk's moral is that peace can be achieved only through memory of war.

With *Inside Out* (1985), *The Hope* (1993), and *Glory* (1994), Wouk turned towards the Jewish experience in his fiction. In *Inside Out*, the Jewish American experience is treated with humor and there is a believable placement of the characters next to historical figures such as Richard Nixon. Yet the ending of the novel has a home movie quality that tends to sentimentalize the fiction. Both *The Hope* and its sequel *Glory* are entertaining and optimistic accounts of the struggles of modern Israel.

Although Wouk won the Pulitzer Prize for *The Caine Mutiny*, has had both *The Winds of War* and *War and Remembrance* adapted for television, and has enjoyed immense popularity, critics generally don't pay serious attention to his work. His conservative prose style and his attempts to moralize are usually cited as weaknesses and generally limit his influence on aspiring writers.

—Chris Godat

ZAHN, Timothy

Nationality: American. **Born:** Chicago, Illinois, 1 September 1951. **Education:** Michigan State University, East Lansing, 1969-73, B.A. in physics 1973; University of Illinois, Urbana, 1973-79, M.S. in physics 1975. **Family:** Married Anna L. Zahn in 1979; one son. **Career:** Since 1980, full-time writer. **Awards:** Hugo award, 1984. **Agent:** Russell Galen, Scott Meredith Literary Agency, 845 Third Avenue, New York, New York 10022. **Address:** 2014 Vawter Street, Apt. 2, Urbana, Illinois 61801, U.S.A.

Publications

Novels (series: Blackcollar; Cobra; Star Wars)

The Blackcollar. New York, DAW, 1983; London, Arrow, 1986.
A Coming of Age. New York, Bluejay, 1985.
Spinneret. New York, Bluejay, 1985; London, Arrow, 1987.
The Backlash Mission (Blackcollar). New York, DAW, 1986; London, Legend, 1988.
Triplet. New York, Baen, 1987; London, Legend, 1988.
Cobra Bargain. New York, Baen, 1988; London, Legend, 1989.
Deadman Switch. New York, Baen, 1988.
Warhorse. New York, Baen, 1990.
Heir to the Empire (Star Wars). New York and London, Bantam, 1991.
Cobras Two. Riverdale, New York, Baen, 1992.
  Cobra. New York, Baen, 1985.
  Cobra Strike. New York, Baen, 1986.
Dark Force Rising (Star Wars). New York and London, Bantam, 1992.
The Last Command (Star Wars). New York and London, Bantam, 1993.
Conqueror's Pride. New York, Bantam, 1994.
Conqueror's Heritage. New York, Bantam, 1995.
Conqueror's Legacy. New York, Bantam, 1996.

Short Stories

Cascade Point and Other Stories. New York, Bluejay, 1986; as *Cascade Point,* New York, Baen, 1987; title story bound with *Hardfought* by Greg Bear, New York, Tor, 1988.
Time Bomb and Zahndry Others. New York, Baen, 1988.
Distant Friends and Others. New York, Baen, 1992.

* * *

Three-time Hugo Award winner Timothy Zahn began writing science fiction as a hobby in graduate school. Today he is one of the bestselling authors of the genre. Most recently known for his contributions to the new *Star Wars* series of novels, Zahn has proven to be an inventive and entertaining writer of both novels and short stories.

While working toward his Ph.D. in physics at the University of Illinois, Zahn sold his first story in December of 1978 and considered the possibilities of writing full time. In 1979 his thesis adviser died suddenly, and although the department offered him the chance to continue in his graduate studies, Zahn declined, as he revealed to *Contemporary Authors:* "I decided instead that my trial writing year had merely arrived earlier than I'd expected it to. In that first year I sold nine stories—enough to encourage me to continue."

Between 1979 and 1986 Zahn published more than 30 short stories in magazines such as *Space Gamer, Rigel,* and *Fantasy and Science Fiction.* His first novel, *The Blackcollar* (1983) is a blend of science-fiction and martial-arts adventure. It focuses on the conflict between the Ryqril, an alien race, and a group of their human subjects. The humans rebel against their tyrannical masters, developing highly-trained warriors known as Blackcollars whose lives are prolonged with drugs. The book's success led to the sequel, *Blackcollar: The Backlash Mission* (1986).

Many of Zahn's early works are concerned with the psychological growth of their characters. For example, *A Coming of Age* (1984), his second novel, depicts a society whose children develop psychic powers at age five but lose them at puberty. *Cobra* (1985) and *Cobra Strike* (1986) also deal with superhuman warriors, much as the *Blackcollar* novels, but focus on the warriors' purpose in society during peacetime; the weapon implants of the Cobra warriors terrify peaceful civilians, and the Cobras must eventually find their place by policing distant colonies. Tom Easton of *Analog Science Fiction/Science Fact* found *Cobra* to be "an admirable study of maturation" and said of Zahn's second *Cobra* novel, "*Cobra Strike*'s point is . . . the coming of a new generation to handle the parent's problems in a new way."

Spinneret (1985) earned Zahn much critical praise. According to David Mead in *Fantasy Review,* the novel "deals with a serious theme—the equitable distribution of wealth and power—and [Zahn] blends his theme, plot, and character well." When Earth's first interstellar colonists discover that alien races have already claimed everything of apparent worth, they find an ancient artifact that suddenly places them in conflict with Earth's United Nations, alien races, and themselves. Mead commented that the novel lacked imaginative detail but praised its "energetic plot" and found it a "sound, entertaining novel" that was superior to many of Zahn's earlier stories.

Zahn's writing tends toward the style of hard sci-fi authors, who base their works on technical information and scientific data. His collection *Cascade Point* (1986), however, drew criticism from some critics for its reliance on hard sci-fi. Gregory Frost of the *Washington Post Book World,* for example, was disappointed in the weakness in style and characterization in the book (a common criticism of hard sci-fi writers). However, Frost did say that "Every story of Zahn's contains a novel idea" and praised Zahn for the collection's concepts; he found the story "The Dreamsender," the portrayal of a man who can enter people's dreams at will, to be the most intriguing. *Cascade Point* also contains the Hugo Award-winning novella of the same name.

In 1992 Zahn published the first of a series of *Star Wars* novels, all based on George Lucas' characters and situations from his famous movie series. *Dark Force Rising* (1992) depicts the Rebel Alliance as it struggles to defeat the now-fragmented Empire, many of the forces of which have gathered around Grand Admiral Thrawn. Thrawn takes the place of the defeated Emperor and his servant, Darth Vader, as the Alliance's arch-nemesis. While preserving the movie characterizations of Han Solo, Princess Leia, Luke Skywalker, and others, Zahn takes creative liberties with the storyline and produced a very credible and entertaining version of what could have happened after the final *Star Wars* movie, *Return of the Jedi.* The success of Zahn's *Star Wars* novels, also including *The Last Command* (1993), has generated the publication of several other *Star Wars* novels from today's best science fiction writers. The following speaks to Zahn's creative vision and storytelling ability. While he insists that he has no "major pulpit-thumping 'message'" in his writing, Zahn does admit that a recurring theme is his "strong belief that there is no prison—whether physical, social, or emotional—that can permanently trap a person who truly wishes to break free of the bonds."

—Christopher Swann

NATIONALITY INDEX

Below is the list of entrants divided by nationality. The nationalities were chosen largely from information supplied by the entrants. It should be noted that "British" was used for all English entrants and for any other British entrant who chose that designation over a more specific one, such as "Scottish."

American

Cleveland Amory
V. C. Andrews
Maya Angelou
Piers Anthony
Isaac Asimov
Jean Auel
Richard Bach
Nicholson Baker
James Baldwin
Amiri Baraka
Dave Barry
Charles Baxter
Ann Beattie
Peter Benchley
Lawrence Block
Judy Blume
Erma Bombeck
T. Coraghessan Boyle
Ray Bradbury
Marion Zimmer Bradley
Terry Brooks
Dee Brown
Rita Mae Brown
Sandra Brown
William F. Buckley, Jr.
Jimmy Buffett
Charles Bukowski
William S. Burroughs
Leo Buscaglia
Octavia E. Butler
W. E. Butterworth
Truman Capote
Orson Scott Card
Raymond Carver
John Cheever
Deepak Chopra
Tom Clancy
Mary Higgins Clark
James Clavell
Pat Conroy
Robin Cook
Stephen Coonts
Patricia Cornwell
Michael Crichton
Amanda Cross
Clive Cussler
Janet Dailey
Don DeLillo
Nelson DeMille
Pete Dexter
Philip K.Dick
James Dickey
E. L. Doctorow
Stephen R. Donaldson
Dominick Dunne
David Eddings
Stanley Elkin
Bret Easton Ellis
Harlan Ellison
Louise Erdrich
Loren D. Estleman
Howard Fast
Harvey Fierstein
Carrie Fisher
Fannie Flagg
Shelby Foote
Alan Dean Foster
Marilyn French
Robert Fulghum
John C. Gardner, Jr.
Elizabeth George
William Gibson
Ellen Gilchrist
Gail Godwin
Eileen Goudge
Stephen Jay Gould
Sue Grafton
Spalding Gray
Andrew M. Greeley
Martha Grimes
John Grisham
Lewis M. Grizzard, Jr.
Allan Gurganus
Alex Haley
Thomas Harris
Robert A. Heinlein
Joseph Heller
Mark Helprin
Frank Herbert
John Hersey
Carl Hiaasen
Patricia Highsmith
Oscar Hijuelos
Tony Hillerman
S. E. Hinton
Shere Hite
Alice Hoffman
L. Ron Hubbard
John Irving
Susan Isaacs
John Jakes
Tama Janowitz
Erica Jong
Garrison Keillor
Jonathan Kellerman
Jack Kerouac
Ken Kesey

GENRE/SUBJECT INDEX

Below is the list of entrants categorized by the primary genres in which they wrote or broad subject areas covered in their works.

Adventure fiction
W. E. Butterworth
Tom Clancy
James Clavell
Stephen Coonts
Bernard Cornwell
Michael Crichton
Clive Cussler
Alistair MacLean
Patrick O'Brian
Wilbur Smith

Animals
Cleveland Amory
James Herriot

Autobiography
Maya Angelou
Laurie Lee

Biography
Irving Wallace
Margaret Truman

Children's/Young Adult Fiction
Judy Blume
Roald Dahl
S. E. Hinton
Madeleine L'Engle
R. L. Stine
J. R. R. Tolkien
Susan Elaine Townsend
Judith Viorst
E. B. White
Phyllis A. Whitney

Children's Nonfiction
Pierre Berton

Cultural and Ethnic Topics
Maya Angelou
James Baldwin
Amiri Baraka
Dee Brown
Alex Haley
Joseph Heller
Oscar Hijuelos
Tony Hillerman
Terry McMillan
Toni Morrison
Walter Mosley
Gloria Naylor
Philip Roth
Leslie Marmon Silko
Amy Tan
Alice Walker
James Welch

Fantasy Fiction
Piers Anthony
Ray Bradbury
Marion Zimmer Bradley
Terry Brooks
Octavia E. Butler
Stephen R. Donaldson
David Eddings
Alan Garner
Ursula K. Le Guin
Anne McCaffrey
Terry Pratchett
Dan Simmons
J. R. R. Tolkien
Timothy Zahn

Fiction
Jacqueline Briskin
Margaret Atwood
Jean M. Auel
Richard Bach
Nicholson Baker
James Baldwin
Charles Baxter
Ann Beattie
Maeve Binchy
T. Coraghessan Boyle
Anita Brookner
Dee Brown
Rita Mae Brown
Jimmy Buffett
Charles Bukowski
William S. Burroughs
A. S. Byatt
Truman Capote
Raymond Carver
Bruce Chatwin
John Cheever
Jon Cleary
Jackie Collins
Pat Conroy
Bernard Cornwell
Douglas Coupland
Bryce Courtenay
Roald Dahl
Robertson Davies
Don DeLillo
Pete Dexter
James Dickey
E. L. Doctorow

History

Horror Fiction

Humor

TITLE INDEX

The following index lists the titles of all major works included in the "Publications" sections of the entries. The name in parentheses is meant to direct the user to the appropriate entry, where full publication information is given. The term "series" indicates a recurring distinctive word, phrase, or name, in the titles of the entrant's books; series characters are also listed here, even if their names do not appear in specific titles of works.

Another Roadside Attraction (Robbins), 1971
Another You (Beattie), 1995
Answer Yes or No (Mortimer), 1950
Answered Prayers (Capote), 1986
Anthem (Rand), 1938
Anthonology (Anthony), 1985
Anthropologist on Mars (Sacks), 1995
Anti-Man (Koontz), 1970
Antonietta (Hersey), 1991
Anvil of Time (Silverberg), 1969
Any Man's Death (Estleman), 1986
Any Woman's Blues (Jong), 1990
Anything for Billy (McMurtry), 1988
Anything Goes (Bradley), 1964
Apocalypse Postponed (Eco), 1994
Apocalypse Watch (Ludlum), 1995
Apple Tree (du Maurier), 1952
Appointment with Death. Peril at End House (Christie), 1938
Apprentice Adept series (Anthony), from 1980
Approaching Oblivion (Ellison), 1974
April 13 (Baraka), 1959
April Evil (MacDonald), 1956
April Lady (Heyer), 1957
April Morning (Fast), 1961
April Robin Murders (McBain), 1958
April's Grave (Howatch), 1969
Aqueduct (Bradbury), 1979
Aquitaine Progression (Ludlum), 1984
Arabella (Heyer), 1949
Archer, Lew series (Macdonald), from 1949
Arctic Grail (Berton), 1988
Arctic Wings (Hubbard), 1991
Are You There God? It's Me, Margaret (Blume), 1970
Area of Suspicion (MacDonald), 1954
Arena (Jakes, as Scotland), 1963
Ariel (Block), 1980
Arimaspian Legacy (Wolfe, G.), 1987
Aristoi (Williams), 1992
Arm of the Starfish (L'Engle), 1965
Armageddon (Uris), 1964
Armored Cav (Clancy), 1994
Armour against Love (Cartland), 1945
Armourer's House (Sutcliff), 1951
Arms of Krupp, 1587-1968 (Manchester), 1968
Arrow of Love (Cartland), 1976
Art and Beauty in the Middle Ages (Eco), 1986
Art and Lies (Winterson), 1994
Art of Living, and Other Stories (Gardner, John [1933-1982]), 1981
Article 92: Murder-Rape (Butterworth, as Beech), 1965
Artists in Crime (Marsh), 1938
Arwen series (Bradley), from 1974
As Eagles Fly (Cartland), 1975
As I Walked Out One Midsummer Morning (Lee), 1969
As the Crow Flies (Archer), 1991
Ascension Factor (Herbert), 1988
Ascent into Hell (Greeley), 1983
Asimov's Mysteries (Asimov, as French), 1968
Asimov's Sherlockian Limericks (Asimov, as French), 1978
Aspects of the Presidency: Truman and Ford in Office (Hersey), 1980
Aspen Gold (Dailey), 1991
Aspire to the Heavens (Clark), 1969
Assassin (Butterworth, as Griffin), 1992
Assassin Who Gave Up His Gun (Fast, as Cunningham), 1969
Assassination File (Gardner, John [1926—]), 1974
Assassins: A Book of Hours (Oates), 1975
Assault on the Free Market (Buckley), 1974
Assembling California (McPhee), 1993
Assignation (Oates), 1988
Assignment in Brittany (MacInnes), 1942
Assignment in Eternity (Heinlein), 1953
Assistant (Malamud), 1957
Asta's Book (Rendell, as Vine), 1993
Astronauts Must Not Land (Brunner), 1963
Asylum World (Jakes), 1969
At Bertram's Hotel (Christie), 1965
At Home on St. Simons (Price), 1981
At Night the Salmon Move (Carver), 1976
At Paradise Gate (Smiley), 1981
At Risk (Hoffman), 1988
At Terror Street and Agony Way (Bukowski), 1968
At the Edge of the Body (Jong), 1979
At the Pillars of Hercules (James, C.), 1979
At Winter's End (Silverberg), 1988
At Wit's End (Bombeck), 1967
Athabasca (MacLean), 1980
Atlantean Chronicles series (Bradley), from 1983
Atlantic Abomination (Brunner), 1960
Atlantic High (Buckley), 1982
Atlas: People, Places, and Visions (Vollmann), 1996
Atlas Shrugged (Rand), 1957
Atmospheres of Mars and Venus (Sagan), 1961
Aton series (Anthony), from 1970
Attack of the Aqua Apes (Stine), 1995
Attack of the Mutant (Stine), 1994
Attack on the King (Stine), 1986
Attic Where the Meadow Greens (Bradbury), 1980
Aubrey-Maturin series (O'Brian), from 1969
Audacious Adventuress (Cartland), 1972
Aunt Erma's Cope Book: How to Get from Monday to Friday in Twelve Days (Bombeck), 1979
Aunts Aren't Gentlemen (Wodehouse), 1974
Aurora Dawn (Wouk), 1947
Author Considers His Resources (Bradbury), 1979
Authorized Murder (Asimov), 1976
Autobiographical Notes (Baldwin), 1953
Automatic Horse (Hubbard), 1994
Autumn Maze (Cleary), 1994
Autumn of the Patriarch (Garcia Marquez), 1976
Autumn People (Bradbury), 1965
Avengers of Carrig (Brunner), 1969
Aviators (Butterworth, as Griffin), 1989
Awakening (White, J., as Devereaux), 1988
Awakenings (Sacks), 1973
Ax (McBain), 1964
Axbrewder, Mick series (Donaldson, as Stephens), from 1984
Azazel (Asimov, as French), 1988

"B" Is for Burglar (Grafton), 1985
Babies and Other Hazards of Sex (Barry), 1984
Baby, Why Would I Lie? A Romance of the Ozarks (Westlake), 1994

Belinda (Rice, as Rampling), 1986
Bell for Adano (Hersey), 1944
Bellefleur (Oates), 1980
Beloved (Morrison), 1987
Beloved (Updike), 1982
Beloved Invader (Price), 1965
Beloved World (Price), 1961
Bendigo Shafter (L'Amour), 1978
Beneath an Opal Moon (Van Lustbader), 1980
Benefactor (Sontag), 1963
Benjamin's Bicentennial Blast (Asimov, as French), 1976
Benjamin's Dream (Asimov, as French), 1976
Beowulf's Children (Niven), 1995
Berets (Butterworth, as Griffin), 1985
Berlin Game (Deighton), 1983
Bertie Wooster Sees It Through (Wodehouse), 1955
Best Cat Ever (Amory), 1993
Best Friend (Stine), 1992
Best Kept Secrets (Brown, S.), 1989
Best Man to Die (Rendell), 1969
Best New Thing (Asimov), 1971
Best of Bombeck (Bombeck), 1987
Best of Friends (Trollope), 1995
Best of James Herriot (Herriot), 1983
Best of John Brunner (Brunner), 1988
Best of Robert Heinlein (Heinlein), 1973
Best of Travis McGee (MacDonald), 1985
Best Way to Lose (Dailey), 1983
Bethlehem Road (Perry), 1990
Betrayal (Stine), 1993
Better than Sex (Thompson, H.), 1993
Between Planets (Heinlein), 1951
Beware of the Purple Peanut Butter (Stine), 1996
Beware of the Stranger (Dailey), 1978
Bewildered in Berlin (Cartland), 1987
Bewitched (Cartland), 1975
Bewitching Women (Cartland), 1955
Beyond the Blue Mountains (Holt, as Burford), 1947
Beyond the Fall of Night (Clarke), 1990
Beyond the Safe Zone (Silverberg), 1986
Beyond the Stars (Cartland), 1995
Beyond This Horizon (Heinlein), 1948
BFG (Dahl), 1982
Bible and Sword (Tuchman), 1956
Bibliomen (Wolfe, G.), 1984
Bicentennial Man and Other Stories (Asimov, as French), 1976
Biffen's Millions (Wodehouse), 1964
Big Apple (Follett), 1975
Big as Life (Doctorow), 1966
Big Black (Follett, as Myles), 1974
Big Bounce (Leonard), 1969
Big Fix (McBain, as Hunter), 1952
Big Four (Christie), 1927
Big Hit (Follett, as Myles), 1975
Big Man (McBain, as Marsten), 1959
Big Money (Wodehouse), 1931
Big Needle (Follett, as Myles), 1974
Big Sell (Berton), 1963
Big Sky Country (Dailey), 1978
Big Story (West), 1957
Big Sun of Mercury (Asimov), 1974
Big Sur (Kerouac), 1962
Bike Repairman (Bradbury), 1978
Bilbo's Last Song (Tolkien), 1974
Bill the Conqueror: His Invasion of England in the Springtime (Wodehouse), 1924
Billion-Dollar Brain (Deighton), 1966
Billy Bathgate (Doctorow), 1989
Billy Gashade (Estleman), 1996
Binary (Crichton, as Lange), 1972
Bingo (Brown, R.), 1988
Bingo Palace (Erdrich), 1994
Bio of a Space Tyrant series (Anthony), from 1983
Birds, and Other Stories (du Maurier), 1977
Birth Control King of the Upper Volta (Rooke), 1982
Bitch (Collins), 1979
Bitter Medicine (Paretsky), 1987
Bitter Sweet (Spencer), 1990
Bitter Winds (Cartland), 1938
Bitter Winds of Love (Cartland), 1978
Bittersweet Rain (Brown, S.), 1984
Black Amber (Whitney), 1964
Black Anti-Semitism and Jewish Racism (Baldwin), 1969
Black Art (Baraka), 1966
Black as He's Painted (Marsh), 1974
Black Betty (Mosley), 1994
Black Blade (Van Lustbader), 1992
Black Candle (Cookson), 1989
Black Genesis (Hubbard), 1986
Black Gold (Butterworth), 1975
Black Heart (Van Lustbader), 1984
Black Hole (Foster), 1979
Black Holes and Baby Universes, and Other Essays (Hawking), 1993
Black House (Highsmith), 1981
Black House (Theroux), 1974
Black Ice Score (Westlake, as Stark), 1968
Black in Time (Jakes), 1970
Black Is the Color (Brunner), 1969
Black Joke (Mowat), 1962
Black Lightning (Saul), 1995
Black Lyon (White, J., as Devereaux), 1980
Black Magic (Baraka), 1970
Black Marble (Wambaugh), 1978
Black Money (Macdonald), 1966
Black Moth (Heyer), 1921
Black Opal (Holt, as Carr), 1993
Black Panther (Cartland), 1939
Black Rainbow (Mertz, as Michaels), 1982
Black Sheep (Heyer), 1966
Black Ships before Troy (Sutcliff), 1993
Black Shrike (MacLean), 1961
Black Sunday (Harris), 1975
Black Swan (Holt, as Carr), 1991
Black Tower (James, P.), 1975
Black Towers to Danger (Hubbard), 1991
Black Trillium (Bradley), 1990
Black Unicorn (Brooks), 1987
Black Velvet Gown (Cookson), 1984
Black Water (Oates), 1992
Black Widowers series (Asimov, as French), from 1974
Blackbird (Westlake, as Stark), 1969

Boy Who Hooked the Sun (Wolfe, G.), 1985
Boyfriend (Stine), 1990
Boys from Brazil (Levin), 1976
Bozos on Patrol (Stine), 1992
Brain (Cook), 1981
Brainchild (Saul), 1985
Brak series (Jakes), from 1968
Brak the Barbarian (Jakes), 1968
Branded Outlaw (Hubbard), 1994
Brass Cupcake (MacDonald), 1950
Brass Dragon (Bradley), 1969
Brass Keys to Murder (Hubbard), 1993
Brave & Startling Truth (Angelou), 1995
Brave the Wild Wind (Lindsey), 1984
Brazil (Updike), 1994
Bread (McBain), 1974
Bread upon the Waters (Shaw), 1981
Breadhorse (Garner), 1975
Breakfast at Tiffany's (Capote), 1958
Breakfast in Bed (Brown, S.), 1983
Breakfast of Champions (Vonnegut), 1973
Breakheart Pass (MacLean), 1974
Breaking Point (du Maurier), 1959
Breast (Roth), 1972
Breath of Scandal (Brown, S.), 1991
Breathing Lessons (Tyler), 1988
Bride of Death (Marsh), 1955
Bride of Pendorric (Holt), 1963
Bride of the Delta Queen (Dailey), 1979
Bride to a Brigand (Cartland), 1984
Bride to the King (Cartland), 1979
Bridesmaid (Rendell), 1989
Bridge Across Forever (Bach), 1984
Bridge at Andau (Michener), 1957
Bridge Builder's Story (Fast), 1995
Bridge of Corvie (Pilcher, as Fraser), 1963
Bridge-Builders (Sutcliff), 1959
Bridges at Toko-Ri (Michener), 1953
Bridges of Madison County (Waller), 1992
Bridging the Galaxies (Niven), 1993
Brief History of Time (Hawking), 1988
Brief Lives (Brookner), 1990
Brigadier and the Golf Widow (Cheever), 1964
Bright Captivity (Price), 1991
Bright Lights, Big City (McInerney), 1984
Bright Orange for the Shroud (MacDonald), 1965
Bright Tomorrow (Holt, as Burford), 1952
Brightness Falls (McInerney), 1992
Brilliant Creatures (James, C.), 1983
Brimstone Wedding (Rendell), 1995
Bring Larks and Heroes (Keneally), 1967
Bring Me Your Love (Bukowski), 1983
Brink (Brunner), 1959
Brinkley Manor (Wodehouse), 1934
Brinkmanship of Galahad Threepwood (Wodehouse), 1965
Brionne (L'Amour), 1971
Britannia Bright's Bewilderment in the Wilderness of Westminster (James, C.), 1976
British Museum Is Falling Down (Lodge), 1965
Broad Back of the Angel (Rooke), 1977
Broca's Brain (Sagan), 1979
Broken Barriers (Cartland), 1938
Broken Bubble (Dick), 1988
Broken Date (Stine), 1988
Broken Gun (L'Amour), 1966
Broken Hearts (Stine), 1993
Brokenclaw (Gardner, John [1926—]), 1990
Bronwen, The Traw, and the Shape-Shifter (Dickey), 1986
Brother Dusty-Feet (Sutcliff), 1952
Brotherhood of War series (Butterworth, as Griffin), from 1983
Brotherly Love (Dexter, P.), 1993
Brothers Keepers (Westlake), 1975
Brothers No More (Buckley), 1995
Brought in Dead (Higgins, as Patterson), 1967
Brown Fields (Pilcher, as Fraser), 1951
Brrm! Brrm! (James, C.), 1991
Bryan's Dog (Butterworth, as Scholefield), 1967
Buckdancer's Choice (Dickey), 1965
Buckskin Brigades (Hubbard), 1937
Buckskin Run (L'Amour), 1981
Budding Prospects (Boyle), 1984
Buddwing (McBain, as Hunter), 1964
Buffalo Gals (Le Guin), 1990
Buffalo Gals and Other Animal Presences (Le Guin), 1987
Buffalo Gals, Won't You Come Out Tonight (Le Guin), 1994
Buffalo Girls (McMurtry), 1990
Bugman Lives (Stine), 1996
Bullet for Cinderella (MacDonald), 1955
Bullet Park (Cheever), 1969
Bully for Brontosaurus (Gould), 1991
Burden (Christie), 1956
Burden Is Light (Price), 1955
Burden of Proof (Turow), 1990
Burglar in the Closet (Block), 1978
Burglar Who Liked to Quote Kipling (Block), 1979
Burglar Who Painted Like Mondrian (Block), 1983
Burglar Who Studied Spinoza (Block), 1981
Burglar Who Thought He Was Bogart (Block), 1995
Burglar Who Traded Ted Williams (Block), 1994
Burglars Can't Be Choosers (Block), 1977
Burn Marks (Paretsky), 1990
Burning (Stine), 1993
Burning Chrome (Gibson), 1986
Burning Hills (L'Amour), 1956
Burning House (Beattie), 1982
Burning in Water, Drowning in Flame (Bukowski), 1974
Burning Shore (Smith, W.), 1985
Burr (Vidal), 1973
Bury My Heart at Wounded Knee (Brown, D.), 1970
Bus 9 to Paradise: A Loving Voyage (Buscaglia), 1986
Busy Body (Westlake), 1966
But Never Free (Cartland), 1937
But What of Earth? (Anthony), 1976
Butcher's Moon (Westlake, as Stark), 1974
Butcher's Theatre (Kellerman), 1988
Butler Did It (Wodehouse), 1957
Butterfly Stories (Vollmann), 1993
Buy Jupiter and Other Stories (Asimov, as French), 1975
By Royal Appointment (Archer), 1980
By the Line (Keneally), 1989
By the North Gate (Oates), 1963
By the Pricking of My Thumbs (Christie), 1968

By the Rivers of Babylon (DeMille), 1978
Bygones (Spencer), 1993

"C" Is for Corpse (Grafton), 1986
C's Songs (Palmer), 1973
Cabal (Barker), 1988
Cachalot (Foster), 1980
Cadillac Jack (McMurtry), 1982
Cain and His Brother (Perry), 1995
Caine Mutiny (Wouk), 1951
Cal (Asimov, as French), 1991
Caldé of the Long Sun (Wolfe, G.), 1994
Calder Born, Calder Bred (Dailey), 1983
Calibrated Alligator (Silverberg), 1969
California Generation (Briskin), 1970
California Gold (Jakes), 1989
California Voodoo Game (Niven), 1992
Californios (L'Amour), 1974
Call: An American Missionary in China (Hersey), 1985
Call for the Dead (le Carré), 1961
Call in the Night (Howatch), 1967
Call of Earth (Card), 1993
Call of Fife and Drum (Fast), 1987
Call of the Blood (Holt, as Kellow), 1956
Call of the Heart (Cartland), 1975
Call of the Highlands (Cartland), 1982
Call to Arms (Butterworth, as Griffin), 1987
Call to Arms (Foster), 1991
Call Waiting (Stine), 1994
Callaghen (L'Amour), 1972
Callander Square (Perry), 1980
Calypso (McBain), 1979
Camelot Caper (Mertz, as Peters), 1969
Camilla (L'Engle), 1965
Camilla Dickinson (L'Engle), 1951
Campion series (Cornwell, as Kells), from 1983
Canada North (Mowat), 1967
Canada North Now (Mowat), 1976
Canada Under Seige (Berton), 1991
Canary in a Cat House (Vonnegut), 1961
Cancel All Our Vows (MacDonald), 1953
Cancelled Czech (Block), 1967
Candle for the Dead (Higgins, as Marlowe), 1966
Cannibal (DeMille), 1975
Cannibal Galaxy (Ozick), 1983
Cannibal in Manhattan (Janowitz), 1987
Cannibal Queen (Coonts), 1992
Canto for a Gypsy (Smith, M.), 1972
Cape Fear (MacDonald), 1962
Caper (Sanders, as Andress), 1980
Capital Crimes (Sanders), 1989
Capitol (Card), 1979
Capricorn Bracelet (Sutcliff), 1973
Capricorn Games (Silverberg), 1976
Capricorn One (Follett, as Ross), 1976
Captains (Butterworth, as Griffin), 1983
Captive (Holt), 1989
Captive Bride (Lindsey), 1977
Captive Heart (Cartland), 1956
Captive of Kensington Palace (Holt, as Burford), 1972
Captive Queen of Scots (Holt, as Burford), 1963
Capture of Detroit (Berton), 1991
Cara (Trollope, as Harvey), 1983
Caravan to Vaccares (MacLean), 1970
Caravans (Michener), 1963
Cardinal of the Kremlin (Clancy), 1988
Cardinal Sins (Greeley), 1981
Cardinal Virtues (Greeley), 1990
Cardington Crescent (Perry), 1987
Cards on the Table (Christie), 1936
Careers in the Services (Butterworth), 1976
Caribbean (Michener), 1989
Caribbean Mystery (Christie), 1964
Carnival of Death (Hubbard), 1991
Carol (Highsmith, as Highsmith), 1990
Caroline, The Queen (Holt, as Burford), 1968
Carousel (Pilcher), 1982
Carousel (Plain), 1995
Carpentered Hen and Other Tame Creatures (Updike), 1958
Carpet People (Pratchett), 1971
Carradyne Touch (McCaffrey), 1988
Carrie (King), 1974
Carrion Comfort (Simmons), 1990
Carry On, Jeeves (Wodehouse), 1925
Carstairs, "Apples" series (Follett), from 1974
Carter, Nick series (Smith, M., as Carter), from 1972
Casa Grande (White, J., as Devereaux), 1982
Cascade Point and Other Stories (Zahn), 1986
Case of Lucy Bending (Sanders), 1982
Case of Need (Crichton, as Hudson), 1968
Case of Painter's Ear (Brunner), 1991
Case of the Angry Actress (Fast, as Cunningham), 1984
Case of the Friendly Corpse (Hubbard), 1991
Case of the Kidnapped Angel (Fast, as Cunningham), 1982
Case of the Murdered Mackenzie (Fast, as Cunningham), 1984
Case of the One-Penny Orange (Fast, as Cunningham), 1977
Case of the Poisoned Eclairs (Fast, as Cunningham), 1979
Case of the Russian Diplomat (Fast, as Cunningham), 1978
Case of the Sliding Pool (Fast, as Cunningham), 1981
Cashelmara (Howatch), 1974
Casino Royale (Fleming), 1954
Cassidy (West), 1986
Castaways' World (Brunner), 1963
Castile for Isabella (Holt, as Burford), 1960
Castle d'Or (du Maurier), 1962
Castle in Italy (Trollope), 1992
Castle in the Air (Westlake), 1980
Castle Made for Love (Cartland), 1977
Castle of Days (Wolfe, G.), 1992
Castle of Fear (Cartland), 1974
Castle of the Otter (Wolfe, G.), 1982
Castle of Wizardry (Eddings), 1984
Castle Roogna (Anthony), 1979
Castle Terror (Bradley), 1965
Castles in Spain (Holt, as Burford), 1954
Castleview (Wolfe, G.), 1990
Cat Among the Pigeons (Christie), 1959
Cat and the Curmudgeon (Amory), 1990
Cat Chaser (Leonard), 1982
Cat Who Came for Christmas (Amory), 1987
Cat Who Walks through Walls (Heinlein), 1985
Cat, You Better Come Home (Keillor), 1995

Conglomeroid Cocktail Party (Silverberg), 1984
Congo (Crichton), 1980
Conquered by Love (Cartland), 1976
Conqueror (Heyer), 1931
Conquerors from the Darkness (Silverberg), 1965
Conqueror's series (Zahn), from 1994
Conquest (White, J., as Devereaux), 1991
Conquest of the Planet of the Apes (Jakes), 1974
Conquest of the Time Master (Stine), 1985
Conspiracy (Hersey), 1972
Conspiracy of Knaves (Brown, D.), 1986
Consul's File (Theroux), 1977
Contact (Sagan), 1985
Contagion (Cook), 1995
Contrary Pleasure (MacDonald), 1954
Control of Nature (McPhee), 1989
Controversy and Other Essays in Journalism (Manchester), 1976
Convenient Marriage (Heyer), 1934
Convergent Series (Niven), 1979
Cool, Crazy, Committed World of the Sixties (Berton), 1966
Cool Kids' Guide to Summer Camp (Stine), 1981
Cop Hater (McBain), 1956
Copenhagen Connection (Mertz, as Peters), 1982
Copper Beach (Binchy), 1992
Copper Peacock and Other Stories (Rendell), 1991
Copperhead (Cornwell), 1993
Cops and Robbers (Westlake), 1972
Corinthian (Heyer), 1940
Corner Men (Gardner, John [1926—]), 1974
Cornish Trilogy (Davies), 1991
Corps series (Butterworth, as Griffin), from 1986
Cosmic Connection (Sagan), 1973
Cosmic Puppets (Dick), 1957
Cosmos (Sagan), 1980
Cotillion (Heyer), 1953
Count the Stars (Cartland), 1981
Count Zero (Gibson), 1986
Counter-Clock World (Dick), 1967
Counterattack (Butterworth, as Griffin), 1990
Counterfeit Lady (White, J., as Devereaux), 1984
Counterlife (Roth), 1987
Country Habit (Trollope), 1993
Country of Marriage (Cleary), 1962
Coup (Updike), 1978
Couples (Updike), 1968
Court-Martial (Butterworth), 1962
Courtneys (Smith, W.), 1988
Courts of Love (Holt, as Plaidy), 1987
Cousin Kate (Heyer), 1968
Covenant (Michener), 1980
Covenant, Thomas the Unbeliever series (Donaldson), from 1993
Cover Her Face (James, P.), 1962
Coward's Kiss (Block), 1987
Coyote Waits (Hillerman), 1990
Crack in Space (Dick), 1966
Crackdown (Cornwell), 1990
Cradle (Clarke), 1988
Cradle Will Fall (Clark), 1980
Crashlander (Niven), 1995
Crazy to Race (Butterworth), 1971
Creating Affluence (Chopra), 1993
Creating Community Anywhere (Peck), 1993
Creating Health (Chopra), 1987
Creation (Vidal), 1981
Creature (Saul), 1989
Creatures of the Kingdom (Michener), 1993
Creed for the Third Millennium (McCullough), 1985
Creek Mary's Blood (Brown, D.), 1980
Creole Holiday (Whitney), 1959
Crescent City (Plain), 1984
Crewel Lye (Anthony), 1985
Criers and Kibitzers, Kibitzers and Criers (Elkin), 1966
Crime in Cabin 66 (Christie), 1944
Crime Wave at Blandings (Wodehouse), 1937
Criminal (Thompson, J.), 1953
Criminal Conversation (McBain, as Hunter), 1994
Crimson Joy (Parker), 1988
Crimson Witch (Koontz), 1971
Crisis on Doona (McCaffrey), 1992
Crocodile Bird (Rendell), 1993
Crocodile on the Sandbank (Mertz, as Peters), 1975
Crofter and the Laird (McPhee), 1969
Crooked House (Christie), 1949
Crooked Road (West), 1957
Crooked Way (Estleman), 1993
Cropper's Cabin (Thompson, J.), 1952
Crossfire Trail (L'Amour), 1954
Crossing (Fast), 1971
Crossing (McCarthy), 1994
Crossing the Border (Oates), 1976
Crossings (Steel), 1982
Crossroads (MacDonald), 1959
Crowd Pleasers (Rogers), 1978
Crown Jewels series (Williams), from 1987
Crown of Columbus (Erdrich), 1991
Crowned Heads (Tryon), 1976
Crowned with Love (Cartland), 1986
Crowning Mercy (Cornwell, as Kells), 1983
Crucible of Time (Brunner), 1983
Crucifix in a Deathhand (Bukowski), 1965
Cruel & Unusual (Cornwell), 1993
Cruel Count (Cartland), 1974
Cruel Doubt (McGinniss), 1991
Cruising Speed (Buckley), 1971
Crutch of Memory (Brunner), 1964
Cry Evil (Rooke), 1980
Cry for the Strangers (Saul), 1979
Cry Hard, Cry Fast (MacDonald), 1955
Cry in the Night (Clark), 1982
Cry Like a Bell (L'Engle), 1987
Cry of the Halidon (Ludlum, as Ryder), 1974
Cry of the Hunter (Higgins, as Patterson), 1960
Cry of the Owl (Highsmith), 1962
Cry to Heaven (Rice), 1982
Cry Wolf (Smith, W.), 1975
Crying Child (Mertz, as Michaels), 1973
Crying of Lot 49 (Pynchon), 1966
Crystal Bucket (James, C.), 1981
Crystal Cave (Stewart), 1970
Crystal Line (McCaffrey), 1992
Crystal Singer (McCaffrey), 1982
Cube Root of Uncertainty (Silverberg), 1970

Dreams Do Come True (Cartland), 1981
Dreams with Sharp Teeth (Ellison), 1991
Drena and the Duke (Cartland), 1992
Dress Her in Indigo (MacDonald), 1969
Drifters (Michener), 1971
Drifting Home (Berton), 1973
Drink with the Devil (Higgins), 1996
Drop of the Dice (Holt, as Carr), 1981
Drowned Hopes (Westlake), 1990
Drowner (MacDonald), 1963
Drowning Pool (Macdonald), 1950
Drowning Season (Hoffman), 1979
Drowning with Others (Dickey), 1962
Drug of Choice (Crichton, as Lange), 1970
Druid of Shannara (Brooks), 1991
Drums of Darkness (Bradley), 1976
Drums of Love (Cartland), 1979
Drunk with Love (Gilchrist), 1986
du Mauriers (du Maurier), 1937
Dubin's Lives (Malamud), 1979
Dublin 4 (Binchy), 1982
Dublin People (Binchy), 1993
Duchess (White, J., as Devereaux), 1991
Duchess Disappeared (Cartland), 1979
Dudley Is Back to Normal (Wodehouse), 1940
Duel of Hearts (Cartland), 1949
Duel with Destiny (Cartland), 1977
Duke and the Preacher's Daughter (Cartland), 1979
Duke Finds Love (Cartland), 1994
Duke in Danger (Cartland), 1983
Duluth (Vidal), 1983
Dumb Witness (Christie), 1937
Dune series (Herbert), from 1965
Dunster (Mortimer), 1992
Duplicate Death (Heyer), 1951
Duplicate Keys (Smiley), 1984
Dust in the Sun (Cleary), 1957
Dutchman's Flat (L'Amour), 1986
Dutiful Daughter (Keneally), 1971
Dwelling Place (Cookson), 1971
Dying Inside (Silverberg), 1972
Dynamite Do-It-Yourself Pen Pal Kit (Stine), 1980
Dynamite's Funny Book of the Sad Facts of Life (Stine), 1980

"E" Is for Evidence (Grafton), 1988
E.S.P. Worm (Anthony), 1970
Eagle and the Raven (Michener), 1990
Eagle Has Flown (Higgins), 1991
Eagle Has Landed (Higgins), 1975
Eagle in the Sky (Smith, W.), 1974
Eagle of the Ninth (Sutcliff), 1954
Eagle's Egg (Sutcliff), 1981
Eagle's Mile (Dickey), 1990
Earl Escapes (Cartland), 1987
Earl Rings a Belle (Cartland), 1990
Earl Warren (Stone), 1948
Early Autumn (Parker), 1981
Early Ayn Rand (Rand), 1984
Early Elkin (Elkin), 1985
Early Motion (Dickey), 1981
Early Routines (Burroughs), 1981
Early Stories (du Maurier), 1959
Early Will I Seek Thee (Price), 1957
Earth Is Room Enough (Asimov, as French), 1957
Earthborn (Card), 1995
Earthfall (Card), 1995
Earthlight (Clarke), 1955
Earthly Possessions (Tyler), 1977
Earthman, Go Home (Ellison), 1964
Earth's Children series (Auel), from 1980
Earth's Other Shadow (Silverberg), 1973
Earthsea (Le Guin), 1977
Earthsea Trilogy (Le Guin), 1979
East Is East (Boyle), 1991
East of Desolation (Higgins), 1968
East, West (Rushdie), 1994
Easter Man (a Play) and Six Stories (McBain, as Hunter), 1972
Easy Go (Crichton, as Lange), 1968
Easy Steps to Successful Decorating (Bradford), 1971
Easy to Kill (Christie), 1939
Eaters of the Dead (Crichton), 1976
Ebony Swan (Whitney), 1992
Echo in the Skull (Brunner), 1959
Echoes (Binchy), 1985
Echoes from the Macabre (du Maurier), 1976
Echoes of Thunder (Ellison), 1991
Eco-Spasm Report (Toffler), 1975
Eden Burning (Plain), 1982
Edge of Day (Lee), 1960
Edge of Tomorrow (Asimov, as French), 1985
Edible Woman (Atwood), 1969
Edith's Diary (Highsmith), 1977
Edsel (Estleman), 1996
Education of a Wandering Man (L'Amour), 1989
Edward Longshanks (Holt, as Burford), 1979
Egg Monster from Mars (Stine), 1996
Eggs, Beans and Crumpets (Wodehouse), 1940
Eight Black Horses (McBain), 1985
Eight Little Piggies (Gould), 1993
Eight Million Ways to Die (Block), 1982
Eighth Commandment (Sanders), 1986
Eighty Million Eyes (McBain), 1966
Elegy for Angels and Dogs (Williams), 1990
Elenium series (Eddings), from 1989
Elephant, and Other Stories (Carver), 1988
Elephant Song (Smith, W.), 1991
Elephants Can Remember (Christie), 1972
Eleven (Highsmith), 1970
Eleven Declarations of War (Deighton), 1975
Elf-Queen of Shannara (Brooks), 1992
Elfstones of Shannara (Brooks), 1982
Elidor (Garner), 1965
Eliza Stanhope (Trollope), 1978
Elizabethan Lover (Cartland), 1953
Ellis Island and Other Stories (Helprin), 1981
Ellison Wonderland (Ellison), 1962
Eloquent Silence (Brown, S., as Ryan), 1982
Elusive Earl (Cartland), 1976
Elvis Is Dead and I Don't Feel So Good Myself (Grizzard), 1984
Emerald (Whitney), 1982
Emerson, Amelia Peabody series (Mertz, as Peters), from 1975
Empire (Vidal), 1987

Glass-Blowers (du Maurier), 1963
Glide Path (Clarke), 1963
Glitter Dome (Wambaugh), 1981
Glittering Images (Howatch), 1987
Glittering Lights (Cartland), 1974
Glitz (Leonard), 1985
Glorious Angel (Lindsey), 1982
Glory (Wouk), 1994
Glory and the Dream (Manchester), 1974
Glory Game (Dailey), 1985
Glory! Glory! Georgia's 1980 Championship Season (Grizzard), 1981
Glory Lane (Foster), 1987
Glory Road (Heinlein), 1963
Glued to the Box (James, C.), 1983
Gnasty Gnomes (Stine), 1981
Go Eat Worms! (Stine), 1994
Go Straight on Peachtree (Siddons), 1978
Go Tell It on the Mountain (Baldwin), 1953
Go Tell It to Mrs. Golightly (Cookson), 1977
Go the Distance (Kinsella), 1995
God and Man at Yale (Buckley), 1951
God Bless You, Mr. Rosewater (Vonnegut), 1965
God Emperor of Dune (Herbert), 1981
God Game (Greeley), 1986
God Knows (Heller), 1984
God Makers (Herbert), 1972
God of Tarot (Anthony), 1979
God Project (Saul), 1982
God Save the Child (Parker), 1974
God Save the Mark (Westlake), 1967
God Speaks to Women Today (Price), 1964
God Was Here, But He Left Early (Shaw), 1973
Goddess and Other Women (Oates), 1974
Goddess and the Gaiety Girl (Cartland), 1980
Goddess of Love (Cartland), 1988
Goddess of the Green Room (Holt, as Burford), 1971
Godfather (Puzo), 1969
Godling, Go Home! (Silverberg), 1964
Godplayer (Cook), 1983
Gods Forget (Cartland), 1939
God's Grace (Malamud), 1982
God's Pocket (Dexter, P.), 1984
Gods Themselves (Asimov), 1972
Godwulf Manuscript (Parker), 1973
Going Abroad (Updike), 1987
Going after Cacciato (O'Brien), 1978
Going Home (Steel), 1973
Going Out! Going Steady! Going Bananas! (Stine), 1980
Going Out with Peacocks and Other Poems (Le Guin), 1994
Going Solo (Dahl), 1986
Going to Extremes (McGinniss), 1980
Going to Meet the Man (Baldwin), 1965
Going Wrong (Rendell), 1990
Gold (Asimov, as French), 1995
Gold Bat and Other School Stories (Wodehouse), 1904
Gold Cell (Olds), 1987
Gold Coast (DeMille), 1990
Gold Coast (Leonard), 1980
Gold Mine (Smith, W.), 1970
Golden Apples of the Sun (Bradbury), 1953
Golden Ball, and Other Stories (Christie), 1971
Golden Cage (Cartland), 1986
Golden Cup (Plain), 1987
Golden Fox (Smith, W.), 1990
Golden Gate (MacLean), 1976
Golden Gizmo (Thompson, J.), 1954
Golden Gondola (Cartland), 1958
Golden Illusion (Cartland), 1976
Golden Lads (du Maurier), 1975
Golden Man (Dick), 1980
Golden Ocean (O'Brian), 1956
Golden Orange (Wambaugh), 1990
Golden Rendezvous (MacLean), 1962
Golden River (Fast), 1960
Golden Sabre (Cleary), 1981
Golden Straw (Cookson), 1993
Golden Sword of Dragonwalk (Stine), 1983
Golden Trail (Berton), 1954
Golden Unicorn (Whitney), 1976
Goldeneye (Gardner, John [1926—]), 1995
Goldfinger (Fleming), 1959
Goldilocks (McBain), 1977
Goldsmith's Wife (Holt, as Burford), 1950
Golf Omnibus (Wodehouse), 1991
Golf without Tears (Wodehouse), 1924
Golgotha (Gardner, John [1926—]), 1980
Good as Gold (Heller), 1979
Good Baby (Rooke), 1990
Good Behavior (Westlake), 1986
Good Bones (Atwood), 1992
Good Guys, Bad Guys (Hite), 1991
Good Help (Gurganus), 1988
Good Husband (Godwin), 1994
Good Men Do Nothing (Brunner), 1970
Good Night, Willie Lee, I'll See You in the Morning (Walker), 1979
Good Old Stuff (MacDonald), 1982
Good Omens (Pratchett), 1990
Good Taste (Asimov, as French), 1976
Goodbye, California (MacLean), 1977
Goodbye, Columbus, and Five Short Stories (Roth), 1959
Goodbye, Darkness (Manchester), 1980
Goodbye Hamilton (Cookson), 1984
Goodbye Look (Macdonald), 1969
Goodbye Mickey Mouse (Deighton), 1982
Goodnight Kiss (Stine), 1992
Goosebumps series (Stine), from 1992
Gordon, Chet series (Macdonald, as Millar), from 1944
Gorky Park (Smith, M.), 1981
Gossamer Card (Holt, as Carr), 1992
Gossip from the Forest (Keneally), 1975
Gourd Dancer (Momaday), 1976
Governor Listeth (Buckley), 1970
Grand Man (Cookson), 1954
Grand Prix Driver (Butterworth), 1969
Grand Prix Racing (Butterworth, as Williams), 1968
Grand Sophy (Heyer), 1950
Granny Reardun (Garner), 1977
Grass Crown (McCullough), 1991
Grass Harp (Capote), 1951
Grass Is Always Greener over the Septic Tank (Bombeck), 1976
Grass Roots (Woods), 1989

Gratitude (Buckley), 1990
Grave Descend (Crichton, as Lange), 1970
Grave Mistake (Marsh), 1978
Graveyard for Lunatics (Bradbury), 1990
Graveyard Heart (Williams), 1990
Graveyard Shift (Higgins, as Patterson), 1965
Gravity's Rainbow (Pynchon), 1973
Greasy Lake and Other Stories (Boyle), 1985
Great Alone (Dailey), 1986
Great American Novel (Roth), 1973
Great and Secret Show (Barker), 1989
Great Betrayal (Mowat), 1976
Great Deliverance (George), 1988
Great Depression (Berton), 1990
Great Jones Street (DeLillo), 1973
Great Roxhythe (Heyer), 1922
Great Santini (Conroy), 1976
Great Shark Hunt (Thompson, H.), 1979
Great Steamboat Race (Brunner), 1983
Great Train Robbery (Crichton), 1975
Greek Treasure (Stone), 1975
Green Brain (Herbert), 1966
Green Eagle Score (Westlake, as Stark), 1967
Green Ghost (Butterworth, as Williams), 1969
Green Helmet (Cleary), 1957
Green Hills of Earth (Heinlein), 1951
Green Mountain Man (Dailey), 1979
Green Ripper (MacDonald), 1979
Green Shadows, White Whale (Bradbury), 1992
Greenlanders (Smiley), 1988
Greenthieves (Foster), 1994
Gremlins (Dahl), 1943
Grendel (Gardner, John [1933-1982]), 1971
Grey Beginning (Mertz, as Michaels), 1984
Grey Havens (Tolkien), 1990
Grey, Roman series (Smith, M.), from 1971
Grey Seas Under (Mowat), 1958
Greygallows (Mertz, as Michaels), 1972
Grierson's Raid (Brown, D.), 1954
Grifters (Thompson, J.), 1963
Grimus (Rushdie), 1975
Grip the Walls (Bukowski), 1964
Gripping Hand (Niven), 1993
Grossery of Limericks (Asimov, as French), 1981
Growing Pains (du Maurier), 1977
Growing Pains of Adrian Mole (Townsend), 1984
Guardian (Saul), 1994
Guardian Angel (Paretsky), 1992
Guardians of the West (Eddings), 1987
Guards! Guards! (Pratchett), 1989
Gudgekin the Thistle Girl and Other Tales (Gardner, John [1933-1982]), 1976
Guest of Honor (Wallace), 1989
Guide to Contemporary Politics (Dexter, C.), 1966
Guide to Writing Fiction (Whitney), 1982
Guilty Thing Surprised (Rendell), 1970
Gun Man (Estleman), 1985
Guns (McBain), 1976
Guns of August (Tuchman), 1962
Guns of Mark Jardine (Hubbard), 1991
Guns of Navarone (MacLean), 1957
Guns of the Timberlands (L'Amour), 1955
Gunsights (Leonard), 1979
Gunslinger (King), 1988
Gwilan's Harp (Le Guin), 1981
Gypsy in Amber (Smith, M.), 1971
Gypsy Magic (Cartland), 1983

"H" Is for Homicide (Grafton), 1991
H.M.S. Surprise (O'Brian), 1973
H.M.S. Ulysses (MacLean), 1955
Habit Is an Old Horse (McCaffrey), 1986
Hail, Hail, The Gang's All Here! (McBain), 1971
Hail to the Chief (McBain), 1973
Haj (Uris), 1984
Half Asleep in Frog Pajamas (Robbins), 1994
Half-Lives (Jong), 1973
Half Moon Street (Theroux), 1984
Halfway to the Moon (Pilcher, as Fraser), 1949
Halloween Night (Stine), 1993
Halloween Night II (Stine), 1994
Hallowe'en Party (Christie), 1969
Halloween Party (Stine), 1990
Halo for the Devil (Cartland), 1972
Ham on Rye (Bukowski), 1982
Hamilton (Cookson), 1983
Hamlet's Mother and Other Women (Cross, as Heilbrun), 1990
Hammer of God (Clarke), 1993
Hammer of God (DeMille), 1974
Hammer of the Scots (Holt, as Burford), 1981
Hand in Glove (Marsh), 1962
Hand That Cradles the Rock (Brown, R.), 1971
Handful of Darkness (Dick), 1955
Handle (Westlake, as Stark), 1966
Handmaid's Tale (Atwood), 1985
Hands Off, He's Mine (Goudge), 1985
Hanging On (Koontz), 1973
Hanging Woman Creek (L'Amour), 1964
Hannah Massey (Cookson), 1964
Happenstance (Shields), 1980
Happiness of Others (Rooke), 1992
Happy Are the Clean of Heart (Greeley), 1986
Happy Are the Meek (Greeley), 1985
Happy Are the Merciful (Greeley), 1992
Happy Are the Peacemakers (Greeley), 1993
Happy Are the Poor in Spirit (Greeley), 1994
Happy Are Those Who Mourn (Greeley), 1995
Happy Are Those Who Thirst for Justice (Greeley), 1987
Happy Christmas (du Maurier), 1940
Happy Days Were Here Again (Buckley), 1993
Happy New Year, Herbie, and Other Stories (McBain, as Hunter), 1963
Happy to Be Here (Keillor), 1982
Hard Core (Thompson, J.), 1986
Hard Facts (Baraka), 1976
Hard Sell (Anthony), 1990
Hard Words and Other Poems (Le Guin), 1981
Hardfought (Zahn), 1988
Hardwired series (Williams), from 1986
Harlan Ellison's Dream Corridor Special (Ellison), 1995
Harlem Quartet (Baldwin), 1987
Harlequin (West), 1974

Harlot's Ghost (Mailer), 1991
Harmful Intent (Cook), 1990
Harmony of the World (Baxter), 1984
Harold (Cookson), 1985
Haroun and the Sea of Stories (Rushdie), 1990
Harper (Macdonald), 1966
Harper Hall of Pern (McCaffrey), 1984
Harper Hall series (McCaffrey), from 1979
Harpy Thyme (Anthony), 1993
Harrogate Secret (Cookson), 1988
Hart's Hope (Card), 1983
Harvest (Plain), 1990
Harvest Home (Tryon), 1973
Hasan (Anthony), 1979
Hassan's Tower (Drabble), 1980
Hastily Thrown-Together Bit of Zork (Brunner), 1974
Hatrack River (Card), 1987
Haunted (Cartland), 1986
Haunted (Oates), 1994
Haunted (Stine), 1991
Haunted Computer and the Android Pope (Bradbury), 1981
Haunted Earth (Koontz), 1973
Haunted Heart (Cartland), 1990
Haunted Mask (Stine), 1993
Haunted Mask II (Stine), 1995
Haunted Mesa (L'Amour), 1987
Haunted Sisters (Holt, as Burford), 1966
Have Space Suit—Will Travel (Heinlein), 1958
Have You Seen These? (Asimov, as French), 1974
Havoc, Johnny series (Jakes), from 1960
Hawaii (Michener), 1959
Hawaiian Christmas (Goudge), 1986
Hawk O'Toole's Hostage (Brown, S.), 1988
Hawkmistress! (Bradley), 1982
Hawksbill Station (Silverberg), 1968
Hazard of Hearts (Cartland), 1949
He Rather Enjoyed It (Wodehouse), 1926
He Who Hesitates (McBain), 1965
Head of Kay's (Wodehouse), 1905
Head-Deep in Strange Sounds (Dickey), 1979
Headless Ghost (Stine), 1995
Headmaster (McPhee), 1966
Healing Touch (Dailey), 1994
Health unto His Majesty (Holt, as Burford), 1956
Heapin' Helping of True Grizzard (Grizzard), 1991
Hear That Lonesome Whistle Blow (Brown, D.), 1977
Heart for Sale (Goudge), 1986
Heart Is Broken (Cartland), 1974
Heart Is Stolen (Cartland), 1980
Heart of a Goof (Wodehouse), 1926
Heart of Stone (Dailey), 1980
Heart of the Clan (Cartland), 1981
Heart of the Country (Weldon), 1987
Heart of the Lion (Holt, as Burford), 1977
Heart of Thunder (Lindsey), 1983
Heart So Wild (Lindsey), 1986
Heart Songs, and Other Stories (Proulx), 1988
Heart Speaks (Spencer), 1986
Heart Triumphant (Cartland), 1976
Heartbeat (Steel), 1991
Heartbeeps (Koontz, as Hill), 1981
Heartbreak Hotel (Siddons), 1976
Heartbreak Ridge (Butterworth, as Blake), 1962
Heart's Afire (Holt, as Burford), 1954
Hearts Aflame (Lindsey), 1987
Hearts and Lives of Men (Weldon), 1987
Heartstones (Rendell), 1987
Heat (McBain), 1981
Heat (Woods), 1994
Heat and Other Stories (Oates), 1991
Heather, Oak, and Olive (Sutcliff), 1972
Heaven (Andrews), 1985
Heaven and Hell (Jakes), 1987
Heaven and Other Poems (Kerouac), 1977
Heaven Makers (Herbert), 1968
Heavenly Host (Asimov, as French), 1975
Heaven's Price (Brown, S.), 1983
Heavy Weather (Wodehouse), 1933
Heckler (McBain), 1960
Heed the Thunder (Thompson, J.), 1946
Heir to the Empire (Zahn), 1991
Heiress (Dailey), 1987
Heiress (White, J., as Devereaux), 1995
Heirs of Hammerfell (Bradley), 1989
Helen (Fast, as Cunningham), 1966
Helen (Heyer), 1928
Helga in Hiding (Cartland), 1986
Helga's Web (Cleary), 1970
Helicopter Pilot (Butterworth), 1967
Hell Is Always Today (Higgins, as Patterson), 1968
Hell Is Too Crowded (Higgins, as Patterson), 1962
Hell of a Woman (Thompson, J.), 1954
Hell on Wheels (Butterworth), 1962
Hell-cat and the King (Cartland), 1977
Hellbound Heart (Barker), 1988
Heller with a Gun (L'Amour), 1954
Hellfire (Saul), 1986
Hellfire Club (Straub), 1996
Hellion (Spencer), 1984
Hell's Angels (Thompson, H.), 1966
Hell's Gate (Koontz), 1970
Hell's Legionnaire, The Conroy Diary, Buckley Pays a Hunch (Hubbard), 1991
Hellstrom's Hive (Herbert), 1973
Helmets (Dickey), 1964
Help from the Heart (Cartland), 1984
Help I Am Being Held Prisoner (Westlake), 1974
Help the Poor Struggler (Grimes), 1985
Hen's Teeth and Horse's Toes (Gould), 1983
Her Blue Body Everything We Know (Walker), 1991
Her Mother's Daughter (French), 1987
Her Own Rules (Bradford), 1996
Herb of Happiness (Cartland), 1988
Here Comes a Hero (Block), 1968
Here Comes and Other Poems (Jong), 1975
Here I Stay (Mertz, as Michaels), 1983
Here Lies Our Sovereign Lord (Holt, as Burford), 1957
Here to Stay: Studies on Human Tenacity (Hersey), 1962
Here's to You, Rachel Robinson (Blume), 1993
Heretics of Dune (Herbert), 1984
Heritage of Folly (Cookson, as Marchant), 1963
Heritage of Hastur (Bradley), 1975

Lost Road and Other Writings (Tolkien), 1987
Lost World (Crichton), 1995
Lottery Winner (Clark), 1994
Louis, The Well-Beloved (Holt, as Burford), 1959
Love (Buscaglia), 1972
Love Affair (Bradbury), 1983
Love Ain't Nothing But Sex Misspelled (Ellison), 1968
Love Always (Beattie), 1985
Love among the Chickens (Wodehouse), 1906
Love and Glory (Parker), 1983
Love and Its Derangements (Oates), 1970
Love and Kisses (Cartland), 1987
Love and Linda (Cartland), 1976
Love and Lucia (Cartland), 1983
Love and Marriage (Cartland), 1971
Love and Mary Ann (Cookson), 1961
Love and Other Demons (Garcia Marquez), 1995
Love and the Loathsome Leopard (Cartland), 1977
Love and the Marquis (Cartland), 1982
Love and War (Jakes), 1984
Love at First Sight (Cartland), 1990
Love at Forty (Cartland), 1977
Love at the Helm (Cartland), 1977
Love at the Ritz (Cartland), 1993
Love beyond Reason (Brown, S., as Ryan), 1981
Love Casts Out Fear (Cartland), 1986
Love Child (Cookson), 1990
Love Child (Holt, as Burford), 1950
Love Child (Holt, as Carr), 1978
Love Climbs In (Cartland), 1979
Love Comes West (Cartland), 1984
Love Cookbook (Buscaglia), 1994
Love, Dad (McBain, as Hunter), 1981
Love for Sale (Cartland), 1980
Love Forbidden (Cartland), 1957
Love Has His Way (Cartland), 1979
Love Holds the Cards (Cartland), 1965
Love in a Dry Season (Foote), 1951
Love in Another Town (Bradford), 1995
Love in Hiding (Cartland), 1959
Love in Pity (Cartland), 1976
Love in the Clouds (Cartland), 1979
Love in the Dark (Cartland), 1979
Love in the Moon (Cartland), 1981
Love in the Ruins (Cartland), 1995
Love in the Ruins (Percy), 1971
Love in the Time of Cholera (Garcia Marquez), 1988
Love Is a Dog from Hell (Bukowski), 1977
Love Is a Gamble (Cartland), 1985
Love Is a Maze (Cartland), 1989
Love Is an Eagle (Cartland), 1951
Love Is Contraband (Cartland), 1968
Love Is Dangerous (Cartland), 1963
Love Is Eternal (Stone), 1954
Love Is Heaven (Cartland), 1985
Love Is Innocent (Cartland), 1975
Love Is Invincible (Cartland), 1988
Love Is Mine (Cartland), 1952
Love Is the Enemy (Cartland), 1952
Love Is the Key (Cartland), 1990
Love Joins the Clans (Cartland), 1986
Love Killers (Collins), 1975
Love Leaves at Midnight (Cartland), 1978
Love Letters (L'Engle), 1966
Love, Life and Sex (Cartland), 1957
Love Lifts the Curse (Cartland), 1991
Love Locked In (Cartland), 1977
Love, Lords, and Lady-Birds (Cartland), 1978
Love Me for Ever (Cartland), 1954
Love Me Forever (Lindsey), 1995
Love Me, Love Me Not (Whitney), 1952
Love Medicine (Erdrich), 1984
Love on a Dark Street and Other Stories (Shaw), 1965
Love on the Run (Cartland), 1965
Love on the Wind (Cartland), 1983
Love Only Once (Lindsey), 1985
Love Parlour (Rooke), 1977
Love Pirate (Cartland), 1977
Love Play (Rogers), 1981
Love Poem (Bukowski), 1979
Love Poems to Marina (Bukowski), 1973
Love Puzzle (Cartland), 1987
Love Rules (Cartland), 1982
Love Song (Greeley), 1989
Love Songs (Sanders), 1972
Love Stories (Pilcher), 1996
Love Story (Segal), 1970
Love Talker (Mertz, as Peters), 1980
Love to the Rescue (Cartland), 1967
Love Trap (Cartland), 1986
Love under Fire (Cartland), 1960
Love Wins (Cartland), 1982
Loved and the Lost (Butterworth, as Blake), 1962
Lovedeath (Simmons), 1993
Love-Go-Round (Butterworth), 1962
Lovehead (Collins), 1974
Loveless Marriage (Cartland), 1995
Lovelock (Card), 1994
Lovely Liar (Cartland), 1989
Loveroot (Jong), 1975
Lovers (West), 1993
Lovers and Gamblers (Collins), 1977
Lovers in Lisbon (Cartland), 1988
Lovers in Paradise (Cartland), 1978
Love's Encore (Brown, S., as Ryan), 1981
Loves Music, Loves to Dance (Clark), 1991
Loves of Harry D (Sanders), 1986
Loves of Harry Dancer (Sanders), 1986
Lovesounds (Sheehy), 1970
Loving (Steel), 1980
Loving Each Other: The Challenge of Human Relationships (Buscaglia), 1984
Loving Spirit (du Maurier), 1931
Low Country Liar (Dailey), 1979
Low-lands (Pynchon), 1978
Luana (Foster), 1974
Luciano's Luck (Higgins), 1981
Lucifer and the Angel (Cartland), 1980
Lucifer's Hammer (Niven), 1977
Luck Logan Finds Love (Cartland), 1993
Luck of the Bodkins (Wodehouse), 1935
Lucky (Collins), 1985

Lucky in Love (Cartland), 1982
Lucky Starr series (Asimov, as French), from 1985
Lucrezia Borgia (Holt, as Burford), 1976
Lucy Crown (Shaw), 1956
Lullaby (McBain), 1989
Luna series (Heinlein), from 1966
Lust for Life (Stone), 1934
Lust Killer (Rule), 1983
Luxury Designs for Apartment Living (Bradford), 1981
Luxury of Sin (Oates), 1984
Lydia (Fast, as Cunningham), 1964
Lying in the Sun and Other Stories (O'Brian), 1956
Lynley, Inspector Thomas Lynley and Sergeant Barbara Havers series (George), from 1988
Lyon's Pride (McCaffrey), 1994
Lyon's Share (Dailey), 1977
Lyre of Orpheus (Davies), 1988
Lythande (Bradley), 1986

M*A*S*H series (Butterworth), from 1974
Macguffin (Elkin), 1991
Machineries of Joy (Bradbury), 1964
Macklin, Peter series (Estleman), from 1984
Macroscope (Anthony), 1969
Mad Amos (Foster), 1996
Madam, Will You Talk? (Stewart), 1955
Madame du Barry (Holt, as Tate), 1959
Madame Serpent (Holt, as Burford), 1951
Madonna of the Seven Hills (Holt, as Burford), 1958
Madrigal (Gardner, John [1926—]), 1967
Maestro (Gardner, John [1926—]), 1993
Maggie Cassidy (Kerouac), 1959
Maggie Rowan (Cookson), 1954
Magic Barrel (Malamud), 1958
Magic Finger (Dahl), 1966
Magic Goes Away (Niven), 1978
Magic Hour (Isaacs), 1991
Magic Kingdom (Elkin), 1985
Magic Kingdom For Sale/Sold! (Brooks), 1986
Magic of Honey (Cartland), 1970
Magic of Honey Cookbook (Cartland), 1976
Magic of Love (Cartland), 1977
Magic of Xanth (Anthony), 1981
Magic of You (Lindsey), 1993
Magic or Mirage? (Cartland), 1978
Magic series (Niven), from 1978
Magical Moment (Cartland), 1995
Magician in Love (Rooke), 1981
Magician's Gambit (Eddings), 1983
Magician's Spell (Stine), 1996
Magnificent Marriage (Cartland), 1975
Maiden (White, J., as Devereaux), 1988
Majipoor Chronicles (Silverberg), 1982
Majipoor series (Silverberg), from 1980
Majors (Butterworth, as Griffin), 1984
Make Death Love Me (Rendell), 1979
Make Love Your Aim (Price), 1967
Make Mine Mavis (Jakes, as Ard), 1961
Make Out with Murder (Block), 1974
Make War in Madness (Butterworth, as Beech), 1966
Maker, Alvin series (Card), from 1987
Making It Big (Jakes), 1968
Making of Ashenden (Elkin), 1972
Making Space Grow (Bradford), 1979
Malafrena (Le Guin), 1979
Male Cross-Dresser Support Group (Janowitz), 1992
Malice (Steel), 1996
Mallen series (Cookson), from 1973
Mallorean series (Eddings), from 1987
Maltese Angel (Cookson), 1992
Mama (McMillan), 1987
Mama Day (Naylor), 1988
Mambo Kings Play Songs of Love (Hijuelos), 1989
MAMista (Deighton), 1991
Mammoth Hunters (Auel), 1985
Man (Wallace), 1964
Man Called Noon (L'Amour), 1970
Man from Barbarossa (Gardner, John [1926—]), 1991
Man from Cannae (Jakes, as Scotland), 1977
Man from Japan (James, C.), 1993
Man from Mundania (Anthony), 1989
Man from Skibbereen (L'Amour), 1973
Man from St. Petersburg (Follett), 1982
Man from the Broken Hills (L'Amour), 1975
Man in the Brown Suit (Christie), 1924
Man in the High Castle (Dick), 1962
Man in the Maze (Silverberg), 1969
Man Kind? (Amory), 1974
Man Lay Dead (Marsh), 1934
Man of Affairs (MacDonald), 1957
Man of My Dreams (Lindsey), 1992
Man of Two Worlds (Herbert), 1986
Man Rides Through (Donaldson), 1987, and London, Collins, 1988
Man Upstairs and Other Stories (Wodehouse), 1914
Man Who Changed the World: The Lives of Mikhail Gorbachev (Sheehy), 1990
Man Who Cried (Cookson), 1979
Man Who Japed (Dick), 1956
Man Who Killed His Brother (Donaldson, as Stephens), 1986
Man Who Mistook His Wife for a Hat, and Other Clinical Tales (Sacks), 1985
Man Who Risked His Partner (Donaldson, as Stephens), 1984
Man Who Sold the Moon (Heinlein), 1952
Man Who Tried to Get Away (Donaldson, as Stephens), 1990
Man Who Upset the Universe (Asimov), 1955
Man Who Used the Universe (Foster), 1983
Man Whose Teeth Were All Exactly Alike (Dick), 1984
Man with a Load of Mischief (Grimes), 1981
Man with Nine Lives (Ellison), 1960
Man with the Getaway Face (Westlake, as Stark), 1963
Man with the Golden Gun (Fleming), 1965
Man with Two Left Feet and Other Stories (Wodehouse), 1917
Man, Woman and Child (Segal), 1980
Man-Kzin Wars series (Niven), from 1988
Man's Estate (Cleary), 1972
Manshape (Brunner), 1982
Mansions of Limbo (Dunne), 1991
Manticore (Davies), 1972
Man-Trap (MacDonald), 1961
Many Facets of Love (Cartland), 1963
Many Waters (L'Engle), 1986
Mao II (DeLillo), 1991

Men to Match My Mountains (Stone), 1956
Menace from Earth (Heinlein), 1959
Menagerie (Cookson), 1958
Menfreya (Holt), 1966
Menfreya in the Morning (Holt), 1966
Mention My Name in Atlantis (Jakes), 1972
Mer-Cycle (Anthony), 1991
Mercenaries (Westlake), 1960
Mercenary (Anthony), 1984
Mercycle (Anthony), 1992
Merely Murder (Heyer), 1935
Meridian (Walker), 1976
Merlin series (Stewart), from 1970
Mermaids on the Golf Course and Other Stories (Highsmith), 1985
Message from Màlaga (MacInnes), 1972
Message from Nam (Steel), 1990
Message in the Bottle (Percy), 1975
Messenger of Love (Cartland), 1961
Messiah (Vidal), 1954
Messiah of Stockholm (Ozick), 1987
Methuselah's Children (Heinlein), 1958
Metrognome and Other Stories (Foster), 1990
Metropolitan (Williams), 1995
Metropolitan Critic (James, C.), 1974
Metternich: The Passionate Diplomat (Cartland), 1964
Mexico (Michener), 1992
Mexico City Blues (Kerouac), 1959
Mexico Set (Deighton), 1984
Mezzanine (Baker), 1988
Miami Mice (Stine), 1986
Mickelsson's Ghosts (Gardner, John [1933-1982]), 1982
Microserfs (Coupland), 1995
Midas Coffin (Smith, M., as Quinn), 1975
Middle-Class Education (Oates), 1980
Middle Ground (Drabble), 1980
Midnight (Koontz), 1989
Midnight Man (Estleman), 1982
Midnight Never Comes (Higgins, as Fallon), 1966
Midnight's Children (Rushdie), 1981
Midpoint and Other Poems (Updike), 1969
Midsummer's Eve (Holt, as Carr), 1986
Midworld (Foster), 1975
Mighty Minicycles (Butterworth), 1976
Migraine: Evolution of a Common Disorder (Sacks), 1970
Migraine: Understanding a Common Disorder (Sacks), 1985
Mike (Wodehouse), 1909
Mike and Psmith (Wodehouse), 1953
Mike at Wrykyn (Wodehouse), 1953
Miko (Van Lustbader), 1984
Mila 18 (Uris), 1961
Milady Charlotte (Holt, as Kellow), 1959
Miller, Nick series (Higgins, as Patterson), from 1965
Millie (Fast, as Cunningham), 1973
Millroy the Magician (Theroux), 1993
Millstone (Drabble), 1965
Milo Talon (L'Amour), 1981
Mind Fields (Ellison), 1994
Mind of My Mind (Butler), 1977
Mind Reader (Stine), 1994
Mind to Murder (James, P.), 1963
Mindbend (Cook), 1985
Minotaur (Coonts), 1989
Minpins (Dahl), 1991
Minstrel and the Dragon Pup (Sutcliff), 1993
Miracle (Wallace), 1984
Miracle at St. Bruno's (Holt, as Carr), 1972
Miracle for a Madonna (Cartland), 1984
Miracle in Mexico (Cartland), 1991
Miracle in Music (Cartland), 1983
Miracle in Seville (Michener), 1995
Mirage (Fast), 1965
Mirror Crack'd (Christie), 1963
Mirror Crack'd from Side to Side (Christie), 1962
Mirror Image (Brown, S.), 1991
Mirror of Her Dreams (Donaldson), 1987, and London, Collins, 1988
Misalliance (Brookner), 1986
Mischief (McBain), 1993
Misery (King), 1987
Mismeasure of Man (Gould), 1981
Misreadings (Eco), 1993
Miss Hobbema Pageant (Kinsella), 1989
Miss Martha Mary Crawford (Cookson, as Marchant), 1975
Missing (Stine), 1990
Missing Joseph (George), 1993
Mission Earth series (Hubbard), from 1985
Mission to Monte Carlo (Cartland), 1983
Mission to Moulokin (Foster), 1979
Mistaken Virtues (Trollope), 1980
Mister St. John (Estleman), 1983
Mistletoe and Holly (Dailey), 1982
Mistral's Daughter (Krantz), 1982
Mistress of Death (Anthony), 1974
Mistress of Mellyn (Holt), 1960
Mists of Avalon (Bradley), 1982
Mitla Pass (Uris), 1988
Mixed Blessings (Steel), 1992
Mixed Company (Shaw), 1950
Mixture of Frailties (Davies), 1958
Moat around Murcheson's Eye (Niven), 1993
Moat series (Niven), from 1993
Moccasin Telegraph and Other Indian Tales (Kinsella), 1983
Mockingbird, Wish Me Luck (Bukowski), 1972
Mode series (Anthony), from 1991
Modern Manners: An Etiquette Book for Rude People (O'Rourke), 1983
Modigliani Scandal (Follett), 1976
Mojave Crossing (L'Amour), 1964
Moment of the Magician (Foster), 1984
Moment of War (Lee), 1991
Moments of Love (Cartland), 1982
Mona (Block), 1961
Mona Lisa Overdrive (Gibson), 1988
Money for Nothing (Wodehouse), 1928
Money in the Bank (Wodehouse), 1942
Moneychangers (Hailey), 1975
Mongoose, R.I.P (Buckley), 1988
Monster Blood (Stine), 1992
Monster Blood II (Stine), 1994
Monster Blood III (Stine), 1995
Monte Cristo #99 (Jakes), 1970
Montezuma Strip (Foster), 1995

Never Cry Wolf (Mowat), 1963
Never Forget Love (Cartland), 1985
Never Laugh at Love (Cartland), 1976
Never Lose Love (Cartland), 1994
Never Send Flowers (Gardner, John [1926—]), 1993
Never to Forget the Battle of the Warsaw Ghetto (Fast), 1946
New and Collected Poems (Paley), 1991
New Boy (Stine), 1994
New Breed (Butterworth, as Griffin), 1988
New Centurions (Wambaugh), 1971
New City (Berton), 1961
New Evil (Stine), 1994
New Fear (Stine), 1996
New Founde Land (Mowat), 1989
New Girl (Stine), 1989
New Girl Friend (Rendell), 1985
New Lease of Death (Rendell), 1967
New Life (Malamud), 1961
New Moon Rising (Price), 1969
New Passages (Sheehy), 1995
New Path to the Waterfall (Carver), 1989
New Season: A Spectator's Guide to the 1988 Election (Will), 1987
New Springtime (Silverberg), 1990
New Sun series (Wolfe, G.), from 1980
New Year's Party (Stine), 1995
New York Dance (Westlake), 1979
New York Dead (Woods), 1991
Next Stop Earth (Butterworth), 1978
Next Stop the Stars (Silverberg), 1962
Niagara: A History of the Falls (Berton), 1992
Nice Bloke (Cookson), 1969
Nice Work (Lodge), 1988
Nick and the Glimmung (Dick), 1988
Nickel Mountain (Gardner, John [1933-1982]), 1973
Nidor series (Silverberg), from 1957
Night after Night (Goudge), 1986
Night and the Enemy (Ellison), 1987
Night at the Vulcan (Marsh), 1951
Night Chills (Koontz), 1976
Night for Treason (Jakes), 1956
Night in Terror Tower (Stine), 1995
Night in Werewolf Woods (Stine), 1996
Night Judgment at Sinos (Higgins), 1970
Night Manager (le Carré), 1993
Night Mare (Anthony), 1983
Night of Four Hundred Rabbits (Mertz, as Peters), 1971
Night of Gaiety (Cartland), 1981
Night of Stars (Holt, as Burford), 1960
Night of the Cotillion (Dailey), 1977
Night of the Fox (Higgins), 1986
Night of the Living Dummy (Stine), 1993
Night of the Living Dummy III (Stine), 1996
Night of the Moonbow (Tryon), 1988
Night of the Phoenix (DeMille), 1975
Night over the Solomons (L'Amour), 1986
Night over Water (Follett), 1991
Night Probe (Cussler), 1981
Night Shift (King), 1978
Night Side (Oates), 1977
Night Train (Macdonald, as Millar), 1955
Night Way (Dailey), 1981
Night without End (MacLean), 1960
Nightfall (Asimov, Silverberg), 1990
Nightfall and Other Stories (Asimov, as French), 1969
Nightingale Sang (Cartland), 1979
Nightless Nights (Oates), 1981
Nightmare in Pink (MacDonald), 1964
Nightmare Journey (Koontz), 1975
Nightmares and Dreamscapes (King), 1993
Nightmares in the Sky (King), 1988
Night's Daughter (Bradley), 1985
Night's Work (Bukowski), 1966
Nightside the Long Sun (Wolfe, G.), 1993
Nightwing (Smith, M.), 1977
Nightwings (Silverberg), 1969
Nightwork (Shaw), 1975
Nine Billion Names of God (Clarke), 1967
Nine Coaches Waiting (Stewart), 1958
Nine Stories (Salinger), 1953
Nine Tomorrows (Asimov, as French), 1959
Ninja (Van Lustbader), 1980
Ninja's Revenge (Anthony), 1975
Ninth Marquess (Cleary), 1972
Nipper (Cookson), 1970
Niven's Laws (Niven), 1984
No Adam for Eve (Bradley, as Dexter), 1966
No Comebacks (Forsyth), 1982
No Darkness for Love (Cartland), 1974
No Deals, Mr. Bond (Gardner, John [1926—]), 1987
No Disguise for Love (Cartland), 1991
No Doors, No Windows (Ellison), 1975
No Escape from Love (Cartland), 1977
No French Leave (Butterworth, as Beech), 1960
No Future in It and Other Science Fiction Stories (Brunner), 1962
No Greater Love (Steel), 1991
No Heart Is Free (Cartland), 1948
No More Dying Then (Rendell), 1971
No Name in the Street (Baldwin), 1972
No Night Is Too Long (Rendell, as Vine), 1994
No Nudes Is Good Nudes (Wodehouse), 1970
No One Writes to the Colonel and Other Stories (Garcia Marquez), 1968
No Other Gods but Me (Brunner), 1966
No Pat Answers (Price), 1972
No Quarter Asked (Dailey), 1976
No Score (Block), 1970
No Time for Love (Cartland), 1976
No Wind of Blame (Heyer), 1939
No Word from Winifred (Cross), 1986
Noble House (Clavell), 1981
Nobody Knew They Were There (McBain, as Hunter), 1971
Nobody Knows My Name (Baldwin), 1961
Nobody Likes Trina (Whitney), 1972
Nobody Lives Forever (Gardner, John [1926—]), 1986
Nobody's Perfect (Westlake), 1977
Nonesuch (Heyer), 1962
Nor Crystal Tears (Foster), 1982
Norby series (Asimov), from 1983
Norman Trilogy (Holt, as Plaidy), from 1974
North and South trilogy (Jakes), from 1982
North from Rome (MacInnes), 1958

North from Thursday (Cleary), 1960
North to Dakota (Smith, M., as Logan), 1976
North to the Rails (L'Amour), 1971
Northern Lights (O'Brien), 1975
Northern Magic (Dailey), 1982
Nostradamus Traitor (Gardner, John [1926—]), 1979
Not a Penny More, Not a Penny Less (Archer), 1976
Not after Midnight (du Maurier), 1971
Not Before Time (Brunner), 1968
Not Comin' Home to You (Block), 1974
Not Even for Love (Brown, S., as St. Claire), 1982
Not George Washington (Wodehouse), 1907
Not in Our Stars (Holt, as Burford), 1945
Not Love Alone (Cartland), 1933
Notes for Echo Lake (Palmer), 1981
Notes from China (Tuchman), 1972
Notes of a Dirty Old Man (Bukowski), 1969
Notes of a Native Son (Baldwin), 1955
Notes Towards a Poem That Can Never Be Written (Atwood), 1981
Nothing but a Man (Thompson, J.), 1970
Nothing Lasts Forever (Sheldon), 1994
Nothing Man (Thompson, J.), 1954
Nothing More Than Murder (Thompson, J.), 1949
Nothing Serious, Jenkins (Wodehouse), 1950
Notorious (Dailey), 1996
Nova Express (Burroughs), 1964
Novel (Michener), 1991
Novel-Writing in an Apocalyptic Time (Percy), 1986
November of the Heart (Spencer), 1992
Novotny's Pain (Roth), 1980
Now and Forever (Steel), 1978
Now and On Earth (Thompson, J.), 1942
Now and Then, Amen (Cleary), 1988
Now Rough, Now Smooth (Cartland), 1941
Now Sheba Sings the Song (Angelou), 1987
Now That April's Gone (Holt, as Burford), 1961
Now Then (Brunner), 1965
Now Wait for Last Year (Dick), 1966
N-Space (Niven), 1990
Nuclear Age (O'Brien), 1981
Number of the Beast (Heinlein), 1980
Nuplex Red (Smith, M., as Quinn), 1974
Nursing-Home Murder (Marsh), 1935
Nutmeg of Consolation (O'Brian), 1991

Oakes, Boysie series (Gardner, John [1926—]), from 1964
Oath of Fealty (Niven), 1981
Oath of the Renuciates (Bradley), 1984
Oblivion (Hart), 1995
Obsession (Cookson), 1994
Occasion of Sin (Greeley), 1992
Ocean Planet (Benchley), 1995
Oceans of Venus (Asimov), 1974
October Country (Bradbury), 1955
October Light (Gardner, John [1933-1982]), 1976
Octopussy (Fleming), 1966
Odd Woman (Godwin), 1974
Oddkins (Koontz), 1988
Oddly Lovely Day Alone (Updike), 1979
Odds On (Crichton, as Lange), 1966
Odessa File (Forsyth), 1972
Odious Duke (Cartland), 1973
Of Man and Mantra (Anthony), 1968
Of the Farm (Updike), 1965
Of Time and Stars (Clarke), 1972
Off with His Head (Marsh), 1957
Ogre, Ogre (Anthony), 1982
Oh Pray My Wings Are Gonna Fit Me Well (Angelou), 1975
Oh, What a Paradise It Seems (Cheever), 1982
Oklahoma Punk (Estleman), 1976
Ola and the Sea Wolf (Cartland), 1980
Old Ahab's Friend, and Friend to Noah, Speaks His Piece (Bradbury), 1971
Old Contemptibles (Grimes), 1991
Old Enough (Goudge), 1986
Old Fox Deceiv'd (Grimes), 1982
Old Man of Mow (Garner), 1967
Old Man Who Loved Cheese (Keillor), 1996
Old Reliable (Wodehouse), 1951
Old Silent (Grimes), 1990
Old Woman Whose Rolling Pin Is the Sun (Wolfe, G.), 1991
Oldest Living Confederate Widow Tells All (Gurganus), 1989
Ole Doc Methuselah (Hubbard), 1970
Olinger Stories (Updike), 1964
Oliver's Story (Segal), 1977
Omnivore (Anthony), 1968
On a Pale Horse (Anthony), 1983
On Dangerous Ground (Higgins), 1994
On Going out to Get the Mail (Bukowski), 1966
On Her Majesty's Secret Service (Fleming), 1963
On the Black Hill (Chatwin), 1982
On the Firing Line (Buckley), 1989
On the Make (MacDonald), 1960
On the Night of the Seventh Moon (Holt), 1972
On the Road (Kerouac), 1957
On the Run (MacDonald), 1963
On Wheels (Jakes), 1973
On Wings of Eagles (Follett), 1983
Once (Walker), 1968
Once a Princess (Lindsey), 1991
Once in a Lifetime (Steel), 1982
Once More with Passion (Butterworth, as Blake), 1964
One (Bach), 1988
One Across, Two Down (Rendell), 1971
One Brief Shining Moment (Manchester), 1983
One Christmas (Capote), 1983
One Evil Summer (Stine), 1994
One Fearful Yellow Eye (MacDonald), 1966
One Flew over the Cuckoo's Nest (Kesey), 1962
One Hundred and One Silly Monster Jokes (Stine), 1986
One Hundred and One Vacation Jokes (Stine), 1990
One Hundred Years of Solitude (Garcia Marquez), 1970
One in the Middle Is the Green Kangaroo (Blume), 1969
One L (Turow), 1977
One Monday We Killed Them All (MacDonald), 1961
One More Sunday (MacDonald), 1984
One of Our Asteroids Is Missing (Silverberg, as Knox), 1964
One of the Boys (Dailey), 1980
One Tree (Donaldson), 1982
One, Two, Buckle My Shoe (Christie), 1940
Only a Dream (Cartland), 1988

Only Girl in the Game (MacDonald), 1960
Only Love (Cartland), 1979
Only One Woof (Herriot), 1985
Only When I Larf (Deighton), 1968
Only When I Laugh (Deighton), 1987
Only You Can Save Mankind (Pratchett), 1992
Ontogeny and Phylogeny (Gould), 1977
Onyx (Briskin), 1982
Open Air (Straub), 1972
Open All Night (Vollmann), 1995
Open Wings (Cartland), 1942
Open Work (Eco), 1989
Opening Night (Marsh), 1951
Operation ARES (Wolfe, G.), 1970
Operation: Deadly Decoy (Stine), 1986
Operation Shylock (Roth), 1993
Orange Fish (Shields), 1989
Oranges (McPhee), 1967
Oranges Are Not the Only Fruit (Winterson), 1985
Oratorio for Sasquatch, Man and Two Androids (Atwood), 1970
Orc's Opal (Anthony), 1990
Orchard Keeper (McCarthy), 1965
Ordeal by Innocence (Christie), 1958
Order Out of Chaos (Toffler), 1984
Orders to Vietnam (Butterworth), 1968
Ordinary Love and Good Will (Smiley), 1989
Ordinary Miracles (Jong), 1983
Origin (Stone), 1980
Original Sin (James, P.), 1994
Orn (Anthony), 1971
Orphan Star (Foster), 1977
Orphans of the Sky (Heinlein), 1963
Orsinian Tales (Le Guin), 1976
Oscar, Cat-about-Town (Herriot), 1990
Osterman Weekend (Ludlum), 1972
Other (Tryon), 1971
Other Passports (James, C.), 1986
Other Side of Love (Briskin), 1992
Other Side of Midnight (Sheldon), 1974
Other Side of the Sky (Clarke), 1958
Other Side of the Sun (L'Engle), 1971
Other Times, Other Worlds (MacDonald), 1978
Other Voices, Other Rooms (Capote), 1948
Other Worlds (Sagan), 1975
Others (Shields), 1972
Otherwise Known as Sheila the Great (Blume), 1972
Our Father (French), 1994
Our Friend the Vowel (O'Rourke), 1975
Our Friends from Frolix 8 (Dick), 1970
Our Game (le Carré), 1995
Our Gang (Starring Tricky and His Friends) (Roth), 1971
Our House in the Last World (Hijuelos), 1983
Our John Willie (Cookson), 1974
Our Kate (Cookson), 1969
Out of My Mind (Brunner), 1967
Out of Reach (Cartland), 1945
Out of Sight (Leonard), 1996
Out of the Shelter (Lodge), 1970
Out on the Cutting Edge (Block), 1989
Outbreak (Cook), 1987
Outcast (Sutcliff), 1955
Outcroppings (McPhee), 1988
Outer Banks (Siddons), 1991
Outer Dark (McCarthy), 1968
Outfit (Westlake, as Stark), 1963
Outland (Foster), 1981
Outlaws of Mesquite (L'Amour), 1991
Outrageous Lady (Cartland), 1977
Outrageous Queen (Cartland), 1956
Outsider (Fast), 1984
Outsiders (Hinton), 1967
Over on the Dry Side (L'Amour), 1975
Over the Edge (Ellison), 1970
Over the Edge (Kellerman), 1987
Over to You (Dahl), 1946
Overdose of Death (Christie), 1953
Overdrive (Buckley), 1983
Overkill (Crichton, as Lange), 1970
Overload (Hailey), 1979
Overnight (Stine), 1991
Overture to Death (Marsh), 1939
Owl King (Dickey), 1977
Owl Service (Garner), 1967
Owls in the Family (Mowat), 1961
Ox (Anthony), 1976
O-Zone (Theroux), 1986

P. J.'s Very Own Public Enemies List (O'Rourke), 1996
Pacific Vortex! (Cussler), 1983
Pagan Rabbi and Other Stories (Ozick), 1971
Pageant of Youth (Stone), 1933
Pain and the Great One (Blume), 1984
Paingod and Other Delusions (Ellison), 1965
Pair from Space (Silverberg), 1965
Pale Blue Dot (Sagan), 1994
Pale Gray for Guilt (MacDonald), 1968
Pale Horse (Christie), 1961
Pale Kings and Princes (Parker), 1987
Pale Rider (Foster), 1985
Palindrome (Woods), 1991
Palomino (Steel), 1981
Paloverde (Briskin), 1978
Pan Book of Charm (Cartland), 1965
Panda's Thumb (Gould), 1980
Pandora by Holly Hollander (Wolfe, G.), 1990
Pandora series (Herbert), from 1966
Panthermania (Sheehy), 1971
Papa, My Father (Buscaglia), 1989
Paper Doll (Parker), 1993
Paper Dragon (McBain, as Hunter), 1966
Paper Money (Follett), 1977
Paperboy (Dexter, P.), 1995
Parable of the Sower (Butler), 1993
Parachutes and Kisses (Jong), 1984
Paradise Found (Cartland), 1985
Paradise in Penang (Cartland), 1989
Paradise News (Lodge), 1991
Paradise Party (McBain, as Hunter), 1968
Paradise Postponed (Mortimer), 1985
Paradise Wild (Lindsey), 1981
Paragon Walk (Perry), 1981
Parasites (du Maurier), 1949

Pure and Untouched (Cartland), 1981
Pure as the Lily (Cookson), 1972
Purloined Paperweight (Wodehouse), 1967
Purple Place for Dying (MacDonald), 1964
Pursuit of Happiness, and Other Sobering Thoughts (Will), 1978
Pursuit of Virtue, and Other Tory Notions (Will), 1982
Pusher (McBain), 1956
Pushing Fifty Is Exercise Enough (Grizzard), 1993
Puss in Boots (McBain), 1987
Put On by Cunning (Rendell), 1981
Put Yourself in My Shoes (Carver), 1974
Puttering about in a Small Land (Dick), 1985
Puzzles of the Black Widowers (Asimov, as French), 1990
Pyramids (Pratchett), 1989

Q Clearance (Benchley), 1986
Q.B. VII (Uris), 1970
Quantum Healing (Chopra), 1989
Quartet in H (McBain, as Hunter), 1957
Queen (Haley), 1993
Queen and I (Townsend), 1992
Queen and Lord M (Holt, as Burford), 1973
Queen Elizabeth Story (Sutcliff), 1950
Queen from Provence (Holt, as Burford), 1979
Queen in Waiting (Holt, as Burford), 1967
Queen Jezebel (Holt, as Burford), 1953
Queen of Diamonds (Holt, as Tate), 1958
Queen of Hearts (Cartland), 1993
Queen of Sorcery (Eddings), 1982
Queen of Springtime (Silverberg), 1989
Queen of the Damned (Rice), 1988
Queen of This Realm (Holt, as Plaidy), 1984
Queen Saves the King (Cartland), 1991
Queenie (Korda), 1985
Queen's Confession (Holt), 1968
Queen's Favourites (Holt, as Burford), 1966
Queen's Husband (Holt, as Burford), 1973
Queen's Messenger (Cartland), 1971
Queens of England series (Holt, as Plaidy), from 1983
Queen's Secret (Holt, as Plaidy), 1989
Queer (Burroughs), 1985
Query (Updike), 1974
Quest (DeMille), 1975
Quest for Karla (le Carré), 1982
Question of Max (Cross), 1976
Question Quest (Anthony), 1991
Quick and the Dead (L'Amour), 1973
Quick Red Fox (MacDonald), 1964
Quick Service (Wodehouse), 1940
Quicksand (Brunner), 1967
Quicksilver Pool (Whitney), 1955
Quiet Dogs (Gardner, John [1926—]), 1982
Quiet Gentleman (Heyer), 1951
Quiver Full of Arrows (Archer), 1982
Quotations from Chairman Bill (Buckley), 1970
Quozl (Foster), 1989

R Document (Wallace), 1976
R. L.'s Dream (Mosley), 1995
Rabbi of Lud (Elkin), 1987
Rabbit at Rest (Updike), 1990
Rabbit Is Rich (Updike), 1981
Rabbit Redux (Updike), 1971
Rabbit, Run (Updike), 1960
Race Against Time (Anthony), 1973
Race Car Team (Butterworth), 1973
Race Driver (Butterworth), 1972
Race for Love (Cartland), 1978
Racing Mechanic (Butterworth, as Williams), 1969
Racing through Paradise: A Pacific Passage (Buckley), 1987
Racing to Glory (Butterworth, as Douglas), 1969
Radiant Way (Drabble), 1987
Radigan (L'Amour), 1958
Radio Free Albemuth (Dick), 1985
Rag Nymph (Cookson), 1991
Rage (King, as Bachman), 1977
Rage (Smith, W.), 1987
Rage of Angels (Sheldon), 1980
Ragtime (Doctorow), 1975
Raider (White, J., as Devereaux), 1987
Railway Pathfinders (Berton), 1992
Rainbow in the Mist (Whitney), 1989
Rainbow Stories (Vollmann), 1989
Rainbow to Heaven (Cartland), 1976
Rainbow Warehouse (Kinsella), 1989
Rainbow's End (Grimes), 1995
Rainmaker (Grisham), 1995
Rainsong (Whitney), 1984
Raise High the Roof Beam, Carpenters, and Seymour (Salinger), 1963
Raise the Titanic (Cussler), 1976
Rama II (Clarke), 1989
Rama Revealed (Clarke), 1993
Rana Look (Brown, S.), 1986
Random Walk (Block), 1988
Random Winds (Plain), 1980
Ransom (Cleary), 1973
Ransom (McInerney), 1985
Ransom of Russian Art (McPhee), 1994
Rap on Race (Baldwin), 1971
Rare Coin Score (Westlake, as Stark), 1967
Ratner's Star (DeLillo), 1976
Raven's Wing (Oates), 1986
Reach for Tomorrow (Clarke), 1956
Real Food Places (Block), 1981
Real Love or Fake (Cartland), 1990
Reality Check (Clancy), 1995
Reality Trip and Other Implausibilities (Silverberg), 1972
Realms of Gold (Drabble), 1975
Reaper Man (Pratchett), 1991
Rebecca (du Maurier), 1938
"Rebecca" Notebook, and Other Memories (du Maurier), 1980
Rebel (Cornwell), 1993
Rebel Angels (Davies), 1981
Rebel Princess (Cartland), 1985
Rebels (Jakes), 1975
Rebuilding Coventry (Townsend), 1988
Recalled to Life (Silverberg), 1962
Recessional (Michener), 1994
Recipes for Lovers (Cartland), 1977
Recoil (Thompson, J.), 1953
Rector's Wife (Trollope), 1991

Silent Treatment (Palmer), 1996
Silent World of Nicholas Quinn (Dexter, C.), 1977
Silhouette in Scarlet (Mertz, as Peters), 1983
Silk Road (Thompson, H.), 1990
Silk Vendetta (Holt), 1987
Silken Web (Brown, S., as Jordan), 1982
Silmarillion (Tolkien), 1977
Silver Angel (Lindsey), 1988
Silver Branch (Sutcliff), 1957
Silver Canyon (L'Amour), 1956
Silver Hook (Mortimer), 1950
Silver Inkwell (Whitney), 1945
Silver Locusts (Bradbury), 1951
Silver Wedding (Binchy), 1988
Silver Wings, Santiago Blue (Dailey), 1984
Silverhill (Whitney), 1967
Silversword (Whitney), 1987
Simisola (Rendell), 1994
Simon (Sutcliff), 1953
Simon the Coldheart (Heyer), 1925
Simulacra (Dick), 1964
Sin (Hart), 1992
Sing Me No Love Songs, I'll Say You No Prayers (Rooke), 1984
Singing in the Shrouds (Marsh), 1958
Singing Stones (Whitney), 1990
Single Pebble (Hersey), 1956
Sinners (Collins), 1984
Sinning with Annie and Other Stories (Theroux), 1972
Sins of Philip Flemming (Wallace), 1959
Sins of the Fathers (Block), 1976
Sins of the Fathers (Howatch), 1980
Sins of the Fathers (Rendell), 1970
Sins of the Wolf (Perry), 1994
Sir Scoundrel (Jakes, as Scotland), 1962
Sirens (Van Lustbader), 1981
Sirens of Titan (Vonnegut), 1959
Sitka (L'Amour), 1957
Sittaford Mystery (Christie), 1931
Six of One (Brown, R.), 1978
Six Poems (Palmer), 1973
Six Walks in the Fictional Woods (Eco), 1994
Six White Horses (Dailey), 1979
Six-Gun Caballero (Hubbard), 1991
Six-Gun Planet (Jakes), 1970
Sixth Column (Heinlein), 1949
Sixth Commandment (Sanders), 1979
Sixth Wife (Holt, as Burford), 1953
Skeleton Crew (King), 1985
Ski Weekend (Stine), 1991
Skin Tight (Hiaasen), 1989
Skinny Legs and All (Robbins), 1990
Skinwalkers (Hillerman), 1987
Skull Beneath the Skin (James, P.), 1982
Sky-Crasher (Hubbard), 1993
Sky-Liners (L'Amour), 1967
Skye Cameron (Whitney), 1957
Skyjacked! (Butterworth), 1972
Skynappers (Brunner), 1960
Slam the Big Door (MacDonald), 1960
Slapstick (Vonnegut), 1976
Slats Grobnik and Some Other Friends (Royko), 1973
Slattery's Hurricane (Wouk), 1956
Slaughterhouse-Five (Vonnegut), 1969
Slavers of Space (Brunner), 1960
Slaves of Love (Cartland), 1976
Slaves of New York (Janowitz), 1986
Slaves of Sleep (Hubbard), 1948
Slayground (Westlake, as Stark), 1971
Sleeping Beauty (Macdonald), 1973
Sleeping Beauty (Michael), 1991
Sleeping Beauty Novels (Rice, as Roquelaure), 1991
Sleeping Life (Rendell), 1978
Sleeping Murder (Christie), 1976
Sleeping Swords (Cartland), 1942
Sleepwalk (Saul), 1990
Sleepwalker (Stine), 1991
Slinky Jane (Cookson), 1959
Slippage (Ellison), 1995
Slipping-Down Life (Tyler), 1970
Slipt (Foster), 1984
Sliver (Levin), 1991
Slow Awakening (Cookson, as Marchant), 1976
Slow Children at Play (Wolfe, G.), 1989
Slow Heat in Heaven (Brown, S.), 1988
Slow Learner (Pynchon), 1984
Slow Waltz in Cedar Bend (Waller), 1993
Slowly, Slowly in the Wind (Highsmith), 1979
Smack Man (DeMille), 1975
Small Assassin (Bradbury), 1962
Small Bachelor (Wodehouse), 1927
Small Ceremonies (Shields), 1976
Small g (Highsmith), 1995
Small Gods (Pratchett), 1992
Small Rain (L'Engle), 1945
Small Rain (Pynchon), 1980(?)
Small Sacrifices (Rule), 1987
Small Town in Germany (le Carré), 1968
Small World (Lodge), 1984
Smart Enough to Know (Goudge), 1984
Smart Women (Blume), 1984
Smile (Bradbury), 1991
Smiley's People (le Carré), 1980
Smith of Wootton Major (Tolkien), 1967
Smoke (Westlake), 1995
Smoke and Mirrors (Mertz, as Michaels), 1989
Smoke from this Altar (L'Amour), 1939
Smoke Ring (Niven), 1987
Smudge, the Little Lost Lamb (Herriot), 1991
Smug Minority (Berton), 1968
Smuggled Heart (Cartland), 1959
Snail-Watcher and Other Stories (Highsmith), 1970
Snake Eyes (Oates, as Smith), 1992
Snake Poems (Atwood), 1983
Snakecharmers in Texas (James, C.), 1988
Snare of Serpents (Holt), 1990
Snare of the Hunter (MacInnes), 1974
Sniper (DeMille), 1974
Snow in April (Pilcher), 1972
Snow Walker (Mowat), 1975
Snow White and Rose Red (McBain), 1985
Snowfall (Oates), 1978
Snowfire (Whitney), 1973

Snowman (Stine), 1991
So Long, and Thanks for All the Fish (Adams), 1984
So Long as You Both Shall Live (McBain), 1976
So Many Steps to Death (Christie), 1955
So Nude, So Dead (McBain, as Marsten), 1956
So Speaks the Heart (Lindsey), 1983
So the Dreams Depart (Holt, as Burford), 1944
Soft Come the Dragons (Koontz), 1970
Soft Machine (Burroughs), 1961
Soft Touch (MacDonald), 1958
Solar Lottery (Dick), 1955
Soldier of Arete (Wolfe, G.), 1989
Soldier of the Great War (Helprin), 1991
Soldier of the Mist (Wolfe, G.), 1986
Soldier Spies (Butterworth, as Baldwin), 1987
Soldiers on Horseback (Butterworth), 1966
Solip:System (Williams), 1989
Solita and the Spies (Cartland), 1989
Solo (Higgins), 1980
Solomon Leviathan's Nine Hundred and Thirty-First Trip Around the World (Le Guin), 1983
Solstice (Oates), 1985
Some Can Whistle (McMurtry), 1989
Some Days You Get the Bear (Block), 1993
Some Lie and Some Die (Rendell), 1973
Some People, Places and Things That Will Not Appear in My Next Novel (Cheever), 1961
Somebody Owes Me Money (Westlake), 1969
Somebody's Darling (McMurtry), 1978
Someday You'll Be Lying (Kerouac), 1968
Someone in the House (Mertz, as Michaels), 1981
Someone Like You (Dahl), 1953
Someone to Love (Cartland), 1995
Something Borrowed, Something Blue (Goudge), 1988
Something Extra (Dailey), 1978
Something Fishy (Wodehouse), 1957
Something Fresh (Wodehouse), 1915
Something Happened (Heller), 1974
Something New (Wodehouse), 1915
Something Wicked This Way Comes (Bradbury), 1962
Sometime Never (Dahl), 1948
Sometimes a Great Notion (Kesey), 1964
Sometimes They Bite (Block), 1983
Son of a Wanted Man (L'Amour), 1984
Son of Man (Silverberg), 1971
Son of Spellsinger (Foster), 1993
Son of the Circus (Irving), 1994
Son of the Morning (Oates), 1978
Song for a Dark Queen (Sutcliff), 1978
Song of Kali (Simmons), 1985
Song of Love (Cartland), 1980
Song of Solomon (Morrison), 1977
Song of the Siren (Holt, as Carr), 1980
Songmaster (Card), 1980
Songs for the Philologists (Tolkien), 1936
Songs of Distant Earth (Clarke), 1986
Songs of Muad'Dib (Herbert), 1992
Songs of Summer and Other Stories (Silverberg), 1979
Songs of the Doomed (Thompson, H.), 1990
Songs to a Handsome Woman (Brown, R.), 1973
Sonora Sundown (Dailey), 1978
Sons (McBain, as Hunter), 1969
Sons of the Wolf (Mertz, as Michaels), 1967
Sophie's Choice (Styron), 1979
Sorceress of Darshiva (Eddings), 1989
Sos, the Rope (Anthony), 1968
Soul Catcher (Herbert), 1972
Soul Music (Pratchett), 1994
Soul-Mate (Oates, as Smith), 1989
Souls and Bodies (Lodge), 1982
Sound of Lightning (Cleary), 1976
Sound of Thunder (Smith, W.), 1991
Sounds of Love (Buscaglia), 1989
Sour Lemon Score (Westlake, as Stark), 1969
Source (Michener), 1965
Source of Magic (Anthony), 1979
Sourcery (Pratchett), 1988
South by Java Head (MacLean), 1958
South Dakota Guidebook (Baxter), 1974
South of Heaven (Thompson, J.), 1967
South of No North (Bukowski), 1973
Southern Discomfort (Brown, R.), 1982
Southern Family (Godwin), 1987
Southern Nights (Dailey), 1980
Souvenir of Monique (Bradley), 1967
Space (Michener), 1982
Space Cadet (Heinlein), 1948
Space Cadets series (Stine), from 1991
Space Dreamers (Clarke), 1969
Space Family Stone (Heinlein), 1969
Space Ranger (Asimov), 1973
Space-Time Juggler (Brunner), 1963
Spain for the Sovereigns (Holt, as Burford), 1960
Spanish Bride (Heyer), 1940
Spanish Bridegroom (Holt, as Burford), 1954
Spanish Lover (Trollope), 1993
Spare Her Heaven (Bradley, as Ives), 1963
Sparkling Cyanide (Christie), 1945
Sparks (Bukowski), 1983
Sparrow Falls (Smith, W.), 1976
Spartacus (Fast), 1951
Speaker for the Dead (Card), 1986
Speaker of Mandarin (Rendell), 1983
Spearfield's Daughter (Cleary), 1982
Special Operations (Butterworth, as Griffin), 1989
Specialists (Block), 1969
Speeches for Doctor Frankenstein (Atwood), 1966
Speed Is of the Essence (Sheehy), 1971
Spell for Chameleon (Anthony), 1977
Spell Sword (Bradley), 1974
Spellsinger (Foster), 1983
Spellsinger at the Gate (Foster), 1983
Spellsinger Scherzo (Foster), 1987
Spellsinger series (Foster), from 1983
Spencerville (DeMille), 1994
Spenser series (Parker), from 1973
Sphere (Crichton), 1987
Sphinx (Cook), 1979
Sphinx at Dawn (L'Engle), 1982
Spider Kiss (Ellison), 1975
Spider, Spin Me a Web (Block), 1988
Spiked Heel (McBain, as Marsten), 1956

Story of Henri Tod (Buckley), 1984
Story of Lola Gregg (Fast), 1956
Story of Michelangelo's Pieta (Stone), 1964
Story of My Life (McInerney), 1988
Story-Teller (Highsmith), 1965
Storyteller (Silko), 1981
Strange Bedfellow (Dailey), 1979
Strange Highways (Koontz), 1995
Strange Pilgrims (Garcia Marquez), 1993
Strange Wine (Ellison), 1978
Strange Women (Bradley, as Gardner), 1962
Strange Yesterday (Fast), 1934
Stranger beside Me (Rule), 1980
Stranger in a Strange Land (Heinlein), 1961
Stranger in Savannah (Price), 1989
Stranger in the Mirror (Sheldon), 1976
Stranger Is Watching (Clark), 1978
Strangers (Estleman), 1984
Strangers (Koontz), 1986
Strangers on a Train (Highsmith), 1950
Strangers When We Meet (McBain, as Hunter), 1958
Strata (Pratchett), 1981
Strawberry Tree (Rendell), 1990
Street of the Five Moons (Mertz, as Peters), 1978
Streets of Chance (Burroughs), 1981
Streets of Gold (McBain, as Hunter), 1974
Strength of Fields (Dickey), 1977
Stress (Estleman), 1996
Strictly Personal (Price), 1960
Strike Deep (Koontz, as North), 1974
Strike the Black Flag (Jakes, as Scotland), 1961
Striker, Jason series (Anthony), from 1974
Strip Tease (Hiaasen), 1993
Strong Medicine (Hailey), 1984
Strong Shall Live (L'Amour), 1980
Stuart Little (White, E.), 1945
Stud (Collins), 1969
Submarine (Clancy), 1993
Subterraneans (Kerouac), 1958
Such Bitter Business (Holt, as Ford), 1953
Such Devoted Sisters (Goudge), 1992
Such Men Are Dangerous (Block), 1969
Sudden Country (Estleman), 1992
Sudden Death (Brown, R.), 1983
Sudden, Fearful Death (Perry), 1993
Suddenly: The American Idea Abroad and at Home, 1986-1990 (Will), 1990
Suffer the Children (Saul), 1977
Sugar and Other Stories (Byatt), 1987
Sugartown (Estleman), 1984
Suitable Vengeance (George), 1992
Sula (Morrison), 1974
Sullivan's Sting (Sanders), 1990
Sum of All Fears (Clancy), 1991
Summer at the Lake (Greeley), 1996
Summer Bird-Cage (Drabble), 1962
Summer Lightning (Wodehouse), 1929
Summer Mahogany (Dailey), 1979
Summer Moonshine (Wodehouse), 1937
Summer of Night (Simmons), 1991
Summer of the Dragon (Mertz, as Peters), 1979
Summer of the Red Wolf (West), 1971
Summer's End (Steel), 1979
Summer's Lease (Mortimer), 1988
Sun (Palmer), 1988
Sun Horse, Moon Horse (Sutcliff), 1977
Sun in Splendour (Holt, as Burford), 1982
Sun My Monument (Lee), 1944
Sunbird (Smith, W.), 1972
Sunburn (Stine), 1993
Sundance and Other Science Fiction Stories (Silverberg), 1974
Sunday Simmons and Charlie Brick (Collins), 1971
Sundowners (Cleary), 1952
Sunlight Dialogues (Gardner, John [1933-1982]), 1971
Sunningdale Mystery (Christie), 1933
Sunny Chandler's Return (Brown, S.), 1987
Sunrise on Mercury (Silverberg), 1975
Sunset at Blandings (Wodehouse), 1977
Sunset Embrace (Brown, S.), 1984
Sunset Warrior series (Van Lustbader), from 1977
Super Barbarians (Brunner), 1962
Superfudge (Blume), 1980
Superstitious (Stine), 1995
Sure of You (Maupin), 1989
Surfacing (Atwood), 1972
Surfeit of Lampreys (Marsh), 1941
Surgeon's Mate (O'Brian), 1980
Surprise Party (Stine), 1990
Surprise! Surprise! (Christie), 1965
Surrender, My Love (Lindsey), 1994
Surrender the Pink (Fisher), 1990
Surrender to Love (Rogers), 1982
Surrogate (Parker), 1982
Surrounded (Koontz, as Coffey), 1974
Survey Ship (Bradley), 1980
Survival of the Bark Canoe (McPhee), 1975
Survivor (Butler), 1978
Survivor (Keneally), 1969
Survivors (Bradley), 1979
Susan and Her Classic Convertible (Butterworth), 1970
Susan Howatch Treasury (Howatch), 1978
Suspension of Mercy (Highsmith), 1965
Suttree (McCarthy), 1979
Swag (Leonard), 1976
Swan Lake (Helprin), 1989
Swann (Shields), 1987
Sweet Adventure (Cartland), 1957
Sweet Anger (Brown, S., as St. Claire), 1985
Sweet Death, Kind Death (Cross), 1984
Sweet Enchantress (Cartland), 1958
Sweet Lass of Richmond Hill (Holt, as Burford), 1970
Sweet Liar (White, J., as Devereaux), 1992
Sweet Memories (Spencer), 1984
Sweet Promise (Dailey), 1979
Sweet Punishment (Cartland), 1931
Sweet Savage Love (Rogers), 1974
Sweet Slow Death (Block), 1986
Sweet Talk (Goudge), 1986
Sweet Women Lie (Estleman), 1990
Sweetbriar (White, J., as Devereaux), 1983
Swell-Looking Babe (Thompson, J.), 1954
Swept Away Number One (Goudge), 1986

Thanksgiving Visitor (Capote), 1968
That Boston Man (Dailey), 1980
That Camden Summer (Spencer), 1996
That Carolina Summer (Dailey), 1982
That Son of Richard III (Bradbury), 1974
That Was Then, This Is Now (Hinton), 1971
Thawing of Mara (Dailey), 1980
Theban Mysteries (Cross), 1971
Thebes of the Hundred Gates (Silverberg), 1993
Theft of a Heart (Cartland), 1966
Their Mutual Child (Wodehouse), 1919
Them (Oates), 1969
Then Again, Maybe I Won't (Blume), 1971
Thendara House (Bradley), 1983
Theory of Semiotics (Eco), 1976
Therapy (Lodge), 1995
There Are Doors (Wolfe, G.), 1988
There Is a Tide . . . (Christie), 1948
There Was a Little Girl (McBain), 1994
There's No Business (Bukowski), 1984
There's No Such Place as Far Away (Bach), 1979
Theresa and a Tiger (Cartland), 1984
These Old Shades (Heyer), 1926
These Small Glories (Cleary), 1946
They Also Ran (Stone), 1945
They Came to Baghdad (Christie), 1951
They Do It with Mirrors (Christie), 1952
They Found Him Dead (Heyer), 1937
They Tore out My Heart and Stomped That Sucker Flat (Grizzard), 1982
They Went Thataway (Brown, D.), 1960
Thief of Always (Barker), 1993
Thief of Love (Cartland), 1957
Thief of Time (Hillerman), 1988
Thief Who Couldn't Sleep (Block), 1966
Thin Air (Parker), 1995
Thing (Foster), 1982
Things They Carried (O'Brien), 1990
Thinner (King, as Bachman), 1984
Third Deadly Sin (Sanders), 1981
Third Evil (Stine), 1992
Third George (Holt, as Burford), 1969
Third Girl (Christie), 1966
Third Horror (Stine), 1994
Third Life of Grange Copeland (Walker), 1970
Third Twin (Follett), 1996
Third Wave (Toffler), 1980
Thirsty Evil (Vidal), 1956
Thirteen at Dinner (Christie), 1933
Thirteen Problems (Christie), 1932
Thirteen Stories and Thirteen Epitaphs (Vollmann), 1991
Thirteen-Gun Salute (O'Brian), 1989
This Calder Range (Dailey), 1982
This Calder Sky (Dailey), 1981
This Is Love (Cartland), 1994
This Old Bill (Estleman), 1984
This Perfect Day (Levin), 1970
This Rock within the Sea (Mowat), 1969
This Rough Magic (Stewart), 1964
This Sweet Sickness (Highsmith), 1960
This Time It's Love (Cartland), 1977
This Was a Man (Holt, as Tate), 1961
This Water (Carver), 1985
This'll Slay You (Jakes, as Payne), 1958
Thistle and the Rose (Holt, as Burford), 1963
Thorman Inheritance (Cookson), 1989
Thorn Birds (McCullough), 1977
Thorns (Silverberg), 1967
Thornyhold (Stewart), 1988
Those Who Love (Stone), 1965
Those Who Walk Away (Highsmith), 1967
Those Who Watch (Silverberg), 1967
Thoughts for You! (Baraka), 1984
Thousand Acres (Smiley), 1991
Thousand Faces of Night (Higgins, as Patterson), 1961
Thousandstar (Anthony), 1980
Three Act Tragedy (Christie), 1935
Three Astronauts (Eco), 1989
Three Bear Witness (O'Brian), 1952
Three Blind Mice (McBain), 1990
Three Blind Mice, and Other Stories (Christie), 1950
Three Cheers for the Paraclete (Keneally), 1968
Three Crowns (Holt, as Burford), 1965
Three Days to Love (Cartland), 1996
Three for McGee (MacDonald), 1967
Three Illuminations in the Life of an American Author (Updike), 1979
Three Legions (Sutcliff), 1980
Three Men and a Maid (Wodehouse), 1922
Three Roads (Macdonald, as Millar), 1948
Three Sirens (Wallace), 1963
Three Stigmata of Palmer Eldritch (Dick), 1965
Three Survived (Silverberg), 1969
Three Winters (Mortimer), 1956
Three Women (McCaffrey), 1992
Threshold (Le Guin), 1980
Threshold of Eternity (Brunner), 1959
Thrill Club (Stine), 1994
Thrill of the Grass (Kinsella), 1984
Thrill of Victory (Brown, S., as St. Claire), 1989
Throat (Straub), 1993
Through a Glass, Clearly (Asimov, as French), 1967
Through the Forest of Twisted Dreams (Stine), 1984
Through the Ice (Anthony), 1989
Through the Safety Net (Baxter), 1985
Thrump-o-moto (Clavell), 1986
Thunder at Noon (Higgins, as Patterson), 1964
Thunder Heights (Whitney), 1960
Thunder on the Right (Stewart), 1957
Thunder Point (Higgins), 1993
Thunderball (Fleming), 1961
Thursday's Child (Brown, S.), 1985
Thurston House (Steel), 1983
Thy Brother's Wife (Greeley), 1982
Tick Tock, You're Dead (Stine), 1995
Tick-Tock (Koontz), 1995
Ticket That Exploded (Burroughs), 1962
Ticket to the Boneyard (Block), 1990
Tide of Life (Cookson), 1976
Tides of Time (Brunner), 1984
Tidewater Lover (Dailey), 1979
Tidings of Great Joy (Brown, S.), 1988

Towards Androgyny (Cross, as Heilbrun), 1973
Towards Asmara (Keneally), 1989
Towards the Stars (Cartland), 1975
Towards Zero (Christie), 1944
Tower of Babel (West), 1968
Tower of Glass (Silverberg), 1970
Town and the City (Kerouac), 1950
Toxic Shock (Paretsky), 1988
Toynbee Convector (Bradbury), 1988
Tracks (Erdrich), 1988
Tradition of Pride (Dailey), 1981
Trail Driving Days (Brown, D.), 1952
Trail of Secrets (Goudge), 1996
Trail to Crazy Man (L'Amour), 1986
Trail to the West (L'Amour), 1986
Train from Katanga (Smith, W.), 1965
Traitor's Exit (Gardner, John [1926—]), 1970
Traitor's Gate (Perry), 1995
Traitors' Legion (Jakes, as Scotland), 1963
Tramp (Hubbard), 1992
Transbluesency (Baraka), 1995
Transformation of Philip Jettan (Heyer), 1923
Transgressors (Thompson, J.), 1961
Transit to Narcissus (Mailer), 1978
Transmigration of Timothy Archer (Dick), 1982
Transylvania Station (Westlake), 1987
Trantorian Empire series (Asimov), from 1961
Trap for Fools (Cross), 1989
Trap Line (Hiaasen), 1982
Trapped in Batwing Hall (Stine), 1995
Trapped in the Arctic (Berton), 1993
Traveler in Black (Brunner), 1971
Traveling Kind (Dailey), 1981
Travels in Hyperreality (Eco), 1986
Travesty (Westlake), 1975
Treason (Card), 1988
Treason of Isengard (Tolkien), 1989
Treason's Harbour (O'Brian), 1983
Treasure (Cussler), 1988
Treasure Is Love (Cartland), 1979
Treasure Mountain (L'Amour), 1972
Treasure Worth Seeking (Brown, S., as Ryan), 1982
Treasures (Plain), 1992
Treasury of du Maurier Short Stories (du Maurier), 1960
Treat Me Right (Goudge), 1986
Treaty at Doona (McCaffrey), 1994
Treaty Planet (McCaffrey), 1994
Tree of Hands (Rendell), 1984
Tree of Night, and Other Stories (Capote), 1949
Trembling Hills (Whitney), 1956
Tremor of Forgery (Highsmith), 1969
Trevayne (Ludlum, as Ryder), 1973
Trial of Abigail Goodman (Fast), 1993
Triangle series (Asimov), from 1961
Tricks (McBain), 1987
Trillium series (Bradley), from 1990
Trinity (Uris), 1976
Trip (Brunner), 1966
Trip Trap (Kerouac), 1973
Triple (Follett), 1979
Triple Détente (Anthony), 1974
Triplet (Zahn), 1987
Tristan and Iseult (Sutcliff), 1971
Tristessa (Kerouac), 1960
Triton, and Battle of Wizards (Hubbard), 1949
Triumph of Evil (Block), 1971
Triumph of the Spider Monkey (Oates), 1976
Trojan Gold (Mertz, as Peters), 1987
Trouble (Weldon), 1994
Trouble Dolls (Buffett), 1991
Trouble Down at Tudsleigh (Wodehouse), 1935
Trouble Follows Me (Macdonald, as Millar), 1946
Trouble on His Wings (Hubbard), 1994
Trouble With Nowadays (Amory), 1979
Troubled Air (Shaw), 1950
Troubling a Star (L'Engle), 1995
Truce of the Games (Sutcliff), 1971
Truckers/Bromeliad series (Pratchett), from 1989
True Stories (Atwood), 1981
True Story (Bukowski), 1966
Truelove (O'Brian), 1992
Trumpet of the Swan (White, E.), 1970
Trust (Ozick), 1966
Trust Me (Updike), 1987
Trust Me on This (Westlake), 1988
Truth or Dare (Stine), 1995
Trying to Save Piggy Snead (Irving), 1993
Tucker (L'Amour), 1971
Tucker's Last Stand (Buckley), 1990
Tuesday Club Murders (Christie), 1933
Tunnel in the Sky (Heinlein), 1955
Tunnel Vision (Paretsky), 1994
Turning Hearts (Card), 1994
Turning Wheel and Other Stories (Dick), 1977
Turquoise Lament (MacDonald), 1973
Turquoise Mask (Whitney), 1974
Turtle Moon (Hoffman), 1992
Twelve Red Herrings (Archer), 1994
Twelve-Cylinder Screamer (Butterworth, as Douglas), 1970
Twenty-Nine Kisses from Roald Dahl (Dahl), 1969
Twice Loved (Spencer), 1984
Twice Twenty Two (Bradbury), 1966
Twilight (Koontz), 1984
Twilight Eyes (Koontz), 1985
Twilight Lovers (Bradley, as Gardner), 1964
Twin Hieroglyphs That Swim the River Dust (Bradbury), 1978
Twin of Fire (White, J., as Devereaux), 1985
Twin of Ice (White, J., as Devereaux), 1985
Twinkle, Twinkle, Little Spy (Deighton), 1976
Twist in the Tale (Archer), 1989
Twisted (Stine), 1987
Twists and Turns of Love (Cartland), 1978
Twits (Dahl), 1980
Two Against the North (Mowat), 1977
Two Alone (Brown, S., as St. Claire), 1987
Two Fables (Dahl), 1986
Two Faces of January (Highsmith), 1964
Two for Tanner (Block), 1967
Two Loves in Her Life (Holt, as Burford), 1955
Two Mrs. Grenvilles (Dunne), 1985
Two Much (Westlake), 1975
Two Poems (Carver), 1982

NOTES ON ADVISERS AND CONTRIBUTORS

ANDERSON, Kristine J. English and theater bibliographer at Purdue University, Lafayette, Indiana. Formerly a librarian at the mid-Manhattan branch of the New York Public Library. Holds a Ph.D. in comparative literature from the State University of New York at Binghamton. Special interests include feminist detective novels and science fiction.

BALL, John C. Assistant professor of English at the University of New Brunswick, Fredericton. Has published numerous articles, reviews, and interviews relating to post-colonial and Canadian literature. Former host of *Title Waves,* a Toronto radio show on which he interviewed Salman Rushdie in 1988. **Essay:** Salman Rushdie.

BARBER, Samantha. Research student at the University of Sheffield, United Kingdom. Co-editor of a book of critical essays on the fantastic in literature, in press. **Essays:** Colin Dexter; Martha Grimes; Susan Isaacs.

BEELER, Karin. Assistant professor of English at the University of Northern British Columbia in Prince George, Canada. Has taught and published in the areas of Canadian literature, women's writing, and comparative literature (including British, French, and German literature). Her Ph.D. dissertation, *"Stranger in a Strange Land": Images of Canada in European Literature, 1800-1990* focuses on popular fiction and travel literature about Canada. Interests encompass literature and other media such as hypertext computer technology. **Essays:** Margaret Atwood; Amy Tan.

BEELER, Stan. Assistant professor of English at the University of Northern British Columbia, Canada. Author of *The Invisible College: A Study of the Three Original Rosicrucian Texts,* dealing with the influence of alchemical literature on popular writing. Specializes in the application of computer technology to the teaching of literature and has taught courses on fantasy literature. **Essay:** Anne Rice.

BELL, Christopher Michael. Graduate student at the University of Missouri, Columbia, working toward M.A. in English. Awarded the Thurgood Marshall Academic Fellowship for Graduate Study (January 1996 to May 1997), among other honors. **Essay:** Edmund White.

BELL, Ian A. Professor of English, University of Wales, Swansea. Author of *Defoe's Fiction* (1985) and *Literature and Crime in Augustan England* (1991). Editor, with Graham Daldry, of *Watching the Detectives: Essays in Crime Fiction* (1990) and *Henry Fielding* (1994). **Essay:** Elmore Leonard, Jr.

BELLMAN, Samuel I. Professor of English at California State Polytechnic University, Pomona. Has taught literature and composition in the California State University system since 1955. Visiting professor at Portsmouth Polytechnic in Portsmouth, Hampshire, England, 1975-1976. Author of biographies on Marjorie Rawlings and Constance Rourke; has also published poetry and fiction. **Essay:** Stephen Jay Gould.

BLUE, Bennis. Ph.D. candidate in English, with a specialization in African-American women writers, American literature to 1900, and composition, Ohio State University, Columbus. **Essays:** Toni Morrison; R. L. Stine; Alice Walker.

BODINE, Paul. Freelance editor and writer. Reviews and features have appeared in the Baltimore *Sun,* the *Milwaukee Journal-Sentinel,* and the *Sheperd Express* (Milwaukee). Contributor to *Encyclopedia of American Industries, DISCovering Authors,* and *Encyclopedia of Global Industries.* **Essays:** Cleveland Amory; William F. Buckley; John Cheever; Deepak Chopra; Dominick Dunne; Shelby Foote; John Hersey; Rush Limbaugh; Norman Maclean; Joe McGinnis; Jay McInerney; P. J. O'Rourke; William Manchester; Faith Popcorn; Ayn Rand; Mike Royko; Tom Wolfe; E. B. White.

BOYD, Anne. Doctoral candidate in American studies at Purdue University; dissertation covers popular American women writers of the 19th century. **Essays:** Leo Buscaglia; Mary Higgins Clark; Janet Dailey; Erica Jong; Tom Robbins; Jude Gilliam White.

BRONSON, Tammy J. Graduate assistant at SUNY Potsdam, New York, working toward M.A. in English. Published the poem "To Mary" in the *American Poetry Annual.* **Essays:** Jeffrey Archer; Barbara Taylor Bradford; Jacqueline Briskin; Victoria Holt; Terry McMillan; N. Scott Momaday; Eugenia Price.

BUXTON, Jackie. Doctoral candidate, York University, Toronto. Author of an article about postmodernism in *English Studies in Canada.* **Essays:** William F. Gibson; Thomas Harris.

CARCHIDI, Victoria. Lecturer in English, Massey University, Palmerston North, New Zealand. Author of articles on cultural studies, film, T. E. Lawrence, and post-colonialism. **Essays:** Barbara Kingsolver; Ursula LeGuin; Ellis Peters.

CARNEY, Sean. Doctoral candidate in English literature at York University, Toronto, Canada. **Essays:** Amiri Baraka; William S. Burroughs; Harlan Ellison; Dan Simmons.

CHABOT, Bruce Guy. Doctoral candidate, Department of English, Texas A&M University, College Station. **Essays:** Dave Barry; Jimmy Buffet; Clive Cussler; Stephen R. Donaldson; Garrison Keillor.

CLANCY, Laurie. Reader of English at La Trobe University, Bundoora, Victoria, Australia. Author of *A Reader's Guide to Australian Fiction* (1992), as well as three novels, two collections of short stories, and various critical works. Reviews and writes widely in Australian journals on a variety of literary topics, including popular writing. **Essays:** Jon Cleary; Bryce Courtenay; Thomas Keneally; Morris West.

CLARK, Daniel A. Instructor in composition at the University of Cincinnati; technical writer and document designer for a management service organization in Cincinnati. Co-edited *Drinking Water Quality Management* (1995) and has been published in the *Journal of General Education.* **Essays:** Carl Hiassen; Madeleine L'Engle.

CLARK, Tracy. Doctoral candidate, Department of English, Indiana State University, specializing in 20th-century British literature and postcolonial literature and theory. Has presented papers at the Popular Culture Association/American Culture Association meeting and at the Midwest PCA/ACA meeting. **Essays:** A. S. Byatt; Clive Barker; Ray Bradbury; Harvey Fierstein; Armistead Maupin; Gloria Naylor; Cynthia Ozick; Camille Paglia; Fay Weldon.

COALE, Samuel. Instructor of American literature at Wheaton College. Author of *William Styron Revisited* (1991), *In Hawthorne's Shadow: American Romance from Melville to Mailer* (1985), *Mesmerism and Hawthorne: Mediums of American Romance* (in press), as well as books on John Cheever, Anthony Burgess, and Paul Theroux. Fulbright scholar, 1995; has lectured in Pakistan, India, the former Yugoslavia, and the Czech Republic, among other places. **Essays:** Walter Mosley; John W. Saul; Paul Theroux.

COMAN, Jennifer. Pursuing M.A. in English at Texas A&M University; focus on creative writing. Assistant editor for Creative Publishing Company, College Station, Texas. **Essays:** V. C. Andrews; Isaac Asimov; J. G. Ballard; Ann Beattie; John Brunner; W. E. Butterworth; Stephen Coonts; Catherine Cookson; Douglas D. Coupland; Philip K. Dick; Carrie Fisher; Ellen Gilchrist; Eileen Goudge; Robert A. Heinlen; W. P. Kinsella; David Leavitt; Judith Michael; Larry Niven; Robert Parker; Robert Pirsig; Mary Stewart; Irving Wallace; Jeanette Winterson.

CONKRIGHT, Jane. Freelance writer in Frankfort, Indiana. **Essays:** Ann Rule; LaVyrle Spencer.

DOYLE, Paul A. Professor of English at Nassau College, State University of New York. Author or editor of 18 books; specialist on 20th-century literature. Has published books on Sean O'Faolain and Pearl Buck, among others. Recent works include *A Reader's Companion to the Novels and Short Stories of Evelyn Waugh*. **Essay:** Anita Brookner.

DUPLER, Doug. Freelance writer in Columbus, Ohio. Teaches college-level writing. Engineer by training; novelist. **Essays:** M. Scott Peck; Erich Segal; Irwin Shaw; Josephine Hart.

ECKSTEIN-SOULE, Carolyn. Freelance writer, Indianapolis, Indiana. **Essays:** (co-authored with Colin Maiorano) Barbara Cartland; Alice Hoffman; Rosemary Rogers; Joseph Wambaugh, Jr.

ELDRIDGE, Amy. Freelance writer in Frankfort, Indiana. **Essays:** Alan Dean Foster; William C. Knott; Gene Wolfe.

EVANS, Melissa L. M.A. in English, with a specialization in British and American Literature, from Indiana State University, Terre Haute; thesis on the short stories of Flannery O'Connor. **Essays:** Oscar Hijuelos; Leslie Marmon Silko.

FAULKENBERRY, Amy. Freelance writer, Panama City, Florida. **Essays:** Jackie Collins; Lewis Grizzard; Dean Koontz; Fern Michaels; Danielle Steel; Donald Westlake.

FRANCIS, Diana Pharaoh. Doctoral candidate, Ball State University, Muncie, Indiana. Special interest in science fiction. **Essays:** Piers Anthony; Marian Zimmer Bradley; Terry Brooks; Octavia E. Butler; David Eddings.

FRANKS, Jill. Writing instructor at Whatcom Community College, Bellingham, Washington. Holds a Ph.D. in English literature from Rutgers University. Has taught at various universities, including University of British Columbia, University of Massachusetts, and Rutgers University. Recently published books include *Revisionist Resurrection Mythologies: A Study of D. H. Lawrence's Italian Works*. Areas of special interest include African-American women writers. **Essays:** Maya Angelou; Marilyn French; Walker Percy; Susan Sontag.

FRENCH, Anne. Managing editor, *Museum of New Zealand*, Wellington, New Zealand. Author of four books on poetry and contributor to *The Oxford Companion to Contemporary Poetry*, *The Oxford Companion to New Zealand Literature*, and *The Routledge Encyclopaedia of Commonwealth Literature*.

GODAT, Chris. Pursuing M.A. in English literature at the University of Missouri, Columbia. **Essays:** Richard Bach; Robin Cook; James Dickey; Fannie Flagg; John Edmund Gardner; Stephen Hawking; James A. Michener; Patrick O'Brien; Mario Puzo; Philip Roth; Irving Stone; Barbara W. Tuchman; Gore Vidal; Herman Wouk.

GRELLA, George. Professor of English and film studies, University of Rochester, New York. Special interests related to popular literature include baseball, crime and mystery fiction, and film. **Essay:** Jim Thompson.

HARRIS, June. Associate professor of literature and language at East Texas State University. Holds a Ph.D. from the University of Arizona. Contributor to *Contemporary Novelists*, *Cyclopedia of World Authors*, *Masterplots II*, and the *Encyclopedia of Fantasy and Science Fiction*. Has also published articles in the *ALAN Review*. **Essays:** S. E. Hinton; Susan Howatch; Daphne DuMaurier; Judith Krantz; Sidney Sheldon; Tom Tryon.

HOUSER, Aimee. Received M.A. in English, with a creative writing emphasis, from Iowa State University. Author of a book of poetry titled *The Strangely Beautiful Interior: Monologues and other Poems*. Also publishes on the World Wide Web. **Essays:** Charles Bukowski; James Welch.

KING, Nicola. Lecturer in English at LSU College of Higher Education, Southampton, England. Was educated at Cambridge, Sussex, and Southampton Universities. Doctoral work on the representation of memory in recent fiction. Has researched and published on writers such as Toni Morrison and Margaret Atwood, and on recent fictional representatives of the Holocaust. **Essays:** Ruth Rendell; Carol Shields.

KLINKOWITZ, Jerome. Professor of English and University Distinguished Scholar at the University of Northern Iowa. Author of thirty books on literature, art, philosophy, music, and popular culture. Is also a working musician and the former owner/operator of a minor league baseball team. Fiction has been collected as *Short Season* (1988) and *Basepaths* (1995). Latest critical book is *Yanks Over Europe: American Flyers in World War II* (1996). **Essays:** William Least Heat Moon; John Irving; David Lodge; Grace Paley; Kurt Vonnegut; Robert James Waller.

KOHL, Judith C. Professor emeritus of English and humanities, Dutchess Community College, and visiting professor, Vassar College. Has taught contemporary drama, recent American literature, contemporary international literature, and autobiographies of marginalized Americans. Reviewer for library journals and contributor to many biographical encyclopedias. **Essays:** Gail Godwin; Jack Kerouac; Joyce Carol Oates; Anne Rivers Siddons; Anne Tyler.

LITTLE, Michael R. Doctoral candidate at Texas A&M University, studying metafictional novels. **Essay:** E. L. Doctorow.

MACDONALD, Andrew. Holds a Ph.D. in English from University of Texas. Co-author of a text for bilingual writing students,

Mastering Writing Essentials, and has published widely on popular culture concerns. Author of the book *Howard Fast* (1996). **Essays** (with Gina Macdonald): James Clavell; Patricia Cornwell; Michael Crichton; Nelson DeMille; Howard Fast; Ken Follett; Frederick Forsyth; Elizabeth George; Andrew M. Greeley; Frank Herbert; Patricia Highsmith; Jonathan Kellerman; Ken Kesey; Louis L'Amour; Robert Ludlum; John D. MacDonald; Ross MacDonald; Helen MacInnes; Ed McBain; Barbara Michaels; Anne Perry; Scott Turow; Phyllis Whitney.

MACDONALD, Gina. Holds a Ph.D. in English from the University of Texas, Austin. Co-author of a text for bilingual writing students, *Mastering Writing Essentials;* has published numerous articles and dictionary/encyclopedia entries about detective fiction, popular fiction, and popular culture for Bruccoli Press, Salem Press, and St. James Press. Has written two books, *James Clavell* (1996) and *Robert Ludlum* (1996), for Greenwood Press. **Essays** (with Andrew Macdonald): James Clavell; Patricia Cornwell; Michael Crichton; Nelson DeMille; Howard Fast; Ken Follett; Frederick Forsyth; Elizabeth George; Andrew M. Greeley; Frank Herbert; Patricia Highsmith; Jonathan Kellerman; Ken Kesey; Louis L'Amour; Robert Ludlum; John D. MacDonald; Ross MacDonald; Helen MacInnes; Ed McBain; Barbara Michaels; Anne Perry; Scott Turow; Phyllis Whitney.

MAIORANO, Colin. Public speaker and freelance writer based in Indianapolis, Indiana. **Essays** (with Carolyn Eckstein-Soule): Barbara Cartland; Alice Hoffman; Rosemary Rogers; Joseph Wambaugh, Jr.

MAJUSKY, Fran. Head of Adult Services Department, General Library, Boston Public Library. Publishes bibliographies to highlight portions of an open-shelf collection of over 700,000 books. Holds a B.A. in history from Albertus Magnus College and an M.L.S. from the University of Rhode Island.

MCLEOD, John. Lecturer in English at LSU University College, Southampton, England. Ph.D. thesis was on contemporary fiction. Has published articles on various contemporary authors. Reviews popular Japanese fiction for *Insight: Japan.* **Essays:** Nicholson Baker; Bret Easton Ellis.

MILLER, D. Quentin. Freelance writer and writing instructor. Holds a Ph.D. in English from the University of Connecticut; dissertation investigated the effects of the Cold War on the writings of John Updike. Has published a number of critical articles on modern and contemporary writers such as Edith Wharton, Ernest Hemingway, James Joyce, John Updike, Cormac McCarthy, and Tim O'Brien. Has reviewed fiction by contemporary writers such as Joanna Scott and Luisa Valenzuela. **Essays:** James Baldwin; Tim O'Brien; Thomas Pynchon.

MILLER, P. Andrew. Teaches writing and literature at colleges in the Cincinnati area. Member of the Popular Culture Association in the South and the International Association of the Fantastic in the Arts. Author of fantasy and science fiction stories and member of Science-fiction and Fantasy Writers of America. **Essays:** Terry Pratchett; Walter Jon Williams.

MILLS, Kirby. Reference librarian at Eugene Public Library, Eugene, Oregon. Formerly worked in various branches of the Free Library of Philadelphia. Holds a B.A. from the University of Oregon and M.L.S. from University of Washington.

MORACE, Robert A. Instructor at Daemen college in Amherst, New York. Author of *The Dialogic Novels of Malcolm Bradbury and David Lodge* and *John Gardner: An Annotated Secondary Bibliography,* as well as numerous essays on contemporary fiction. Co-editor of *John Gardner: Critical Perspectives.* **Essays:** Don DeLillo; Umberto Eco; Stanley Elkin; Louise Erdrich; John C. Gardner, Jr.

MULLIGAN, Elizabeth. Freelance writer. M.A. in teaching from Oakland University. Has held several positions in education, and was formerly the assistant editor of *Metro Parent Magazine.* **Essays:** Erma Bombeck; Sue Grafton; Jerome David Salinger; P. G. Wodehouse.

NOWAK, Maril. Writer and teacher in the Finger Lakes Region of Central New York. **Essays:** T. C. Boyle; Judith Viorst.

PAGE, Malcom. Professor of English at Simon Fraser University, Burnaby, British Columbia, Canada. Has served as president of the Association for Canadian Theatre History. Published books include *John Arden, Richard II,* and *Howards End* ("The Critics Debate" series) and nine compilations on contemporary British dramatists for Methuen's "Writers on File" series. Was educated at Cambridge, McMaster University, and the University of California. **Essay:** John Mortimer.

PATTERSON, Eric. Freelance writer in Boulder, Colorado. Work has appeared in over a dozen magazines, including *Vegetarian Times* and *Flatirons: The Boulder Magazine,* as well as in the *Dictionary of Hispanic Biography.* **Essays:** Truman Capote; Roald Dahl; Larry McMurtry; Farley Mowat; Jane Smiley.

PEPPER, Sheila. Assistant university librarian and head of reader services, McMaster University Library, Hamilton, Ontario, Canada. Holds M.A. in English literature; has worked for 25 years in various public service roles, and has taught advanced reference courses. Co-editor of *Women in Canada: A Bibliography, 1965-1982* (1984).

ROWLAND, Susan. Researches Jungian ideas in contemporary literature at the University of Liverpool, England. Has published articles on Doris Lessing, Michele Roberts, Saul Bellow, Jong and feminism, and Jung and postmodernism. Was educated at Oxford and London Universities. **Essays:** Robertson Davies; Margaret Drabble; Georgette Heyer; Ngaio Marsh; Sara Paretsky.

SADLER, Geoff. Assistant librarian, local studies department, Chesterfield, Derbyshire, United Kingdom. Author of western fiction as "Jeff Sadler," "Wes Calhoun," and local history books under own name. Editor and contributor, *Twentieth Century Western Writers,* and contributor to *Contemporary Novelists, Contemporary Dramatists, Contemporary Poets, Twentieth Century Romance & Historical Writers.* **Essays:** Bernard Cornwell; Len Deighton; Alan Garner; Alex Haley; Tony Hillerman; Bernard Malamud; Norman Mailer; Rosemary Sutcliff; Joanna Trollope.

SHREVE, Jack. Teaches English and Spanish at Allegany Community College in Cumberland, Maryland. Holds a Ph.D. in Spanish linguistics from the University of Pittsburgh. Author of hundreds of book reviews in more than a dozen journals and newspapers, including *Choice, Library Journal, Maryland Historical Magazine,* and the *James White Review.* Book review editor of

Delos and an associate editor of the *Maryland English Journal*. **Essay:** Gabriel Garcia Marquez.

SULLIVAN, Maggi. Adjunct instructor of English at Finger Lakes Community College in Canandaigua, New York. **Essay:** Allan Gurganus.

SUTHERLAND, Fraser. Freelance writer. Managing editor of *Books in Canada* magazine. Author of several books, including *The Style of Innocence: A Study of Hemingway and Callaghan* (1972), *Madwomen* (a collection of poetry published in 1978), and *The History oƒ Canadian Magazines* (1988). **Essays:** Pierre Berton; James Herriot.

SWANN, Christopher C. Candidate for M.A. in English, with an emphasis in creative writing, at the University of Missouri, Columbia. Awarded the Jean Amory Wornom Award for Distinguished Critical Writing and the George A. Mahan Award for Creative Writing. Taught high school English for three years in the Atlanta public school system. Short fiction has appeared in the *Crescent Review*. **Essays:** Douglas Adams; Jean Auel; Peter Benchley; Lawrence Block; Judy Blume; Orson Scott Card; Pat Conroy; Thomas L. Clancy; Ian Fleming; Robert L. Fulghum; Jack Higgins; John Jakes; Eric Van Lustbader; Alistair Maclean; Anne McCaffrey; Cormac McCarthy; Michael Palmer; Rosamunde Pilcher; Belva Plain; Annie Proulx; Martin Cruz Smith; Peter Straub; J. R. R. Tolkien; John Updike; Stuart Woods; Timothy Zahn.

SYLKA, Christina. Reference librarian in the David Lam Management Research Library at the University of British Columbia. Holds a M.A. in English from Queen's University at Kingston and a M.L.I.S. from the University of Western Ontario. **Essays:** Maeve Binchy; Johanna Lindsey; Sue Townsend.

TRUESDALE, C. W. Poet, short story writer, and essayist. Founding editor and publisher of *New Rivers Press*. **Essays:** Charles Baxter; Bruce Chatwin; Amanda Cross; John LeCarre; John McPhee; Oliver Sacks.

VARTY, Jean. Librarian, Central Library, Liverpool, United Kingdom; head of Central Lending department.

WIGGINTON, Christopher. Engaged in postgraduate research in the diversity of contemporary literature at the University of Wales, Swansea. **Essays:** Agatha Christie; P. D. James.

WITHERUP, Bill. Working-class writer and self-taught poet. Grew up in Richmond, Washington, a nuclear-industry manufacturing town. Published book of poetry titled *Men at Work* (1990). **Essay:** Raymond Carver.

WOODS, Tim. Lectures in modern and contemporary English and American literature at the University of Wales, Aberystwyth, United Kingdom. Special interest in postmodernism and literary theory. Has written on English poetry, American poetry, and poststructuralist theories; essay on Paul Alister appeared in *Beyond the Red Notebook* (1995); co-author of a book on history in post-war literature for Edward Arnold (in press). **Essays:** Spalding Gray; Shere Hite; Tama Janowitz; Laurie Lee; Sharon Olds; William T. Vollman.